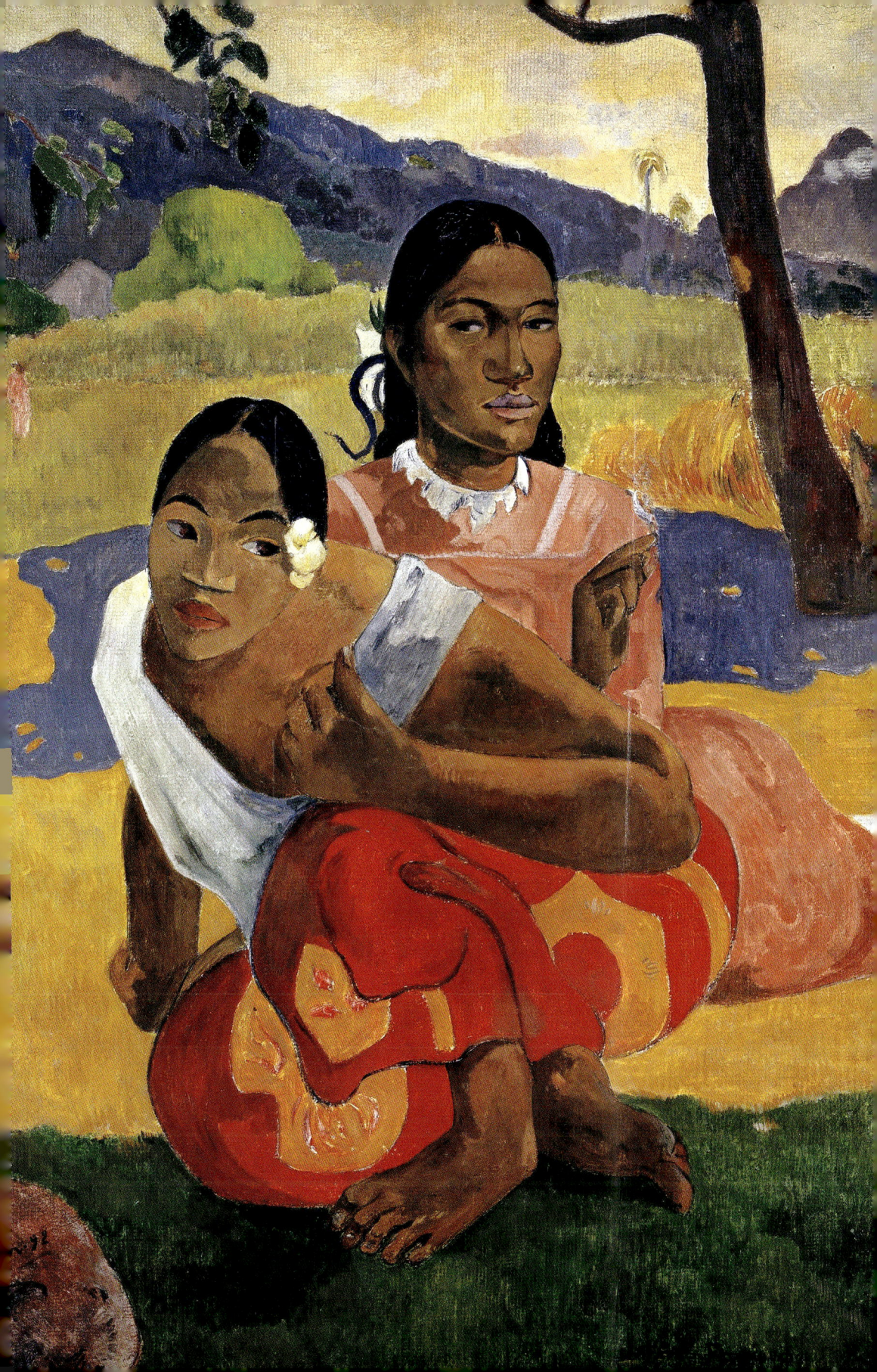

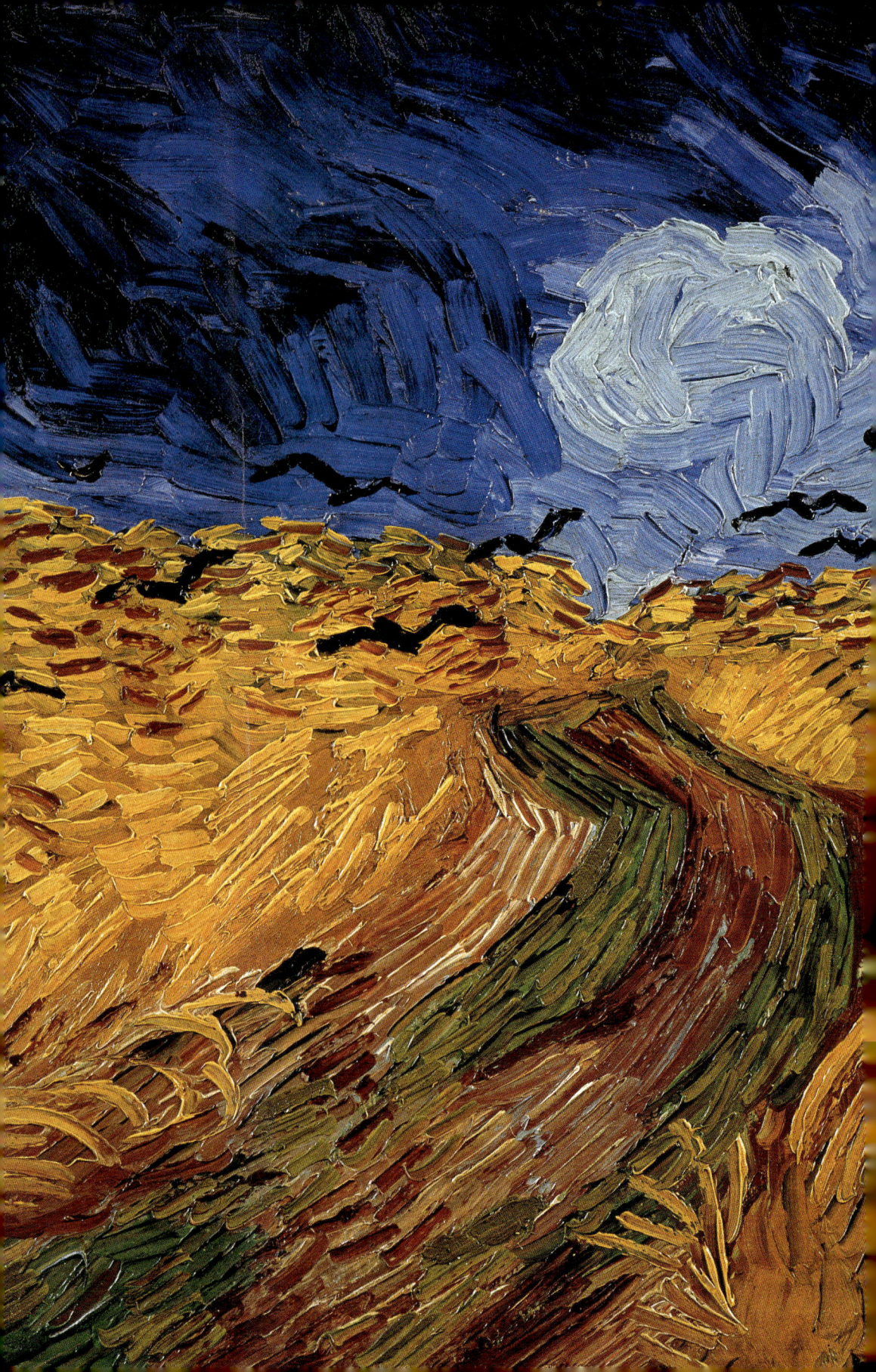

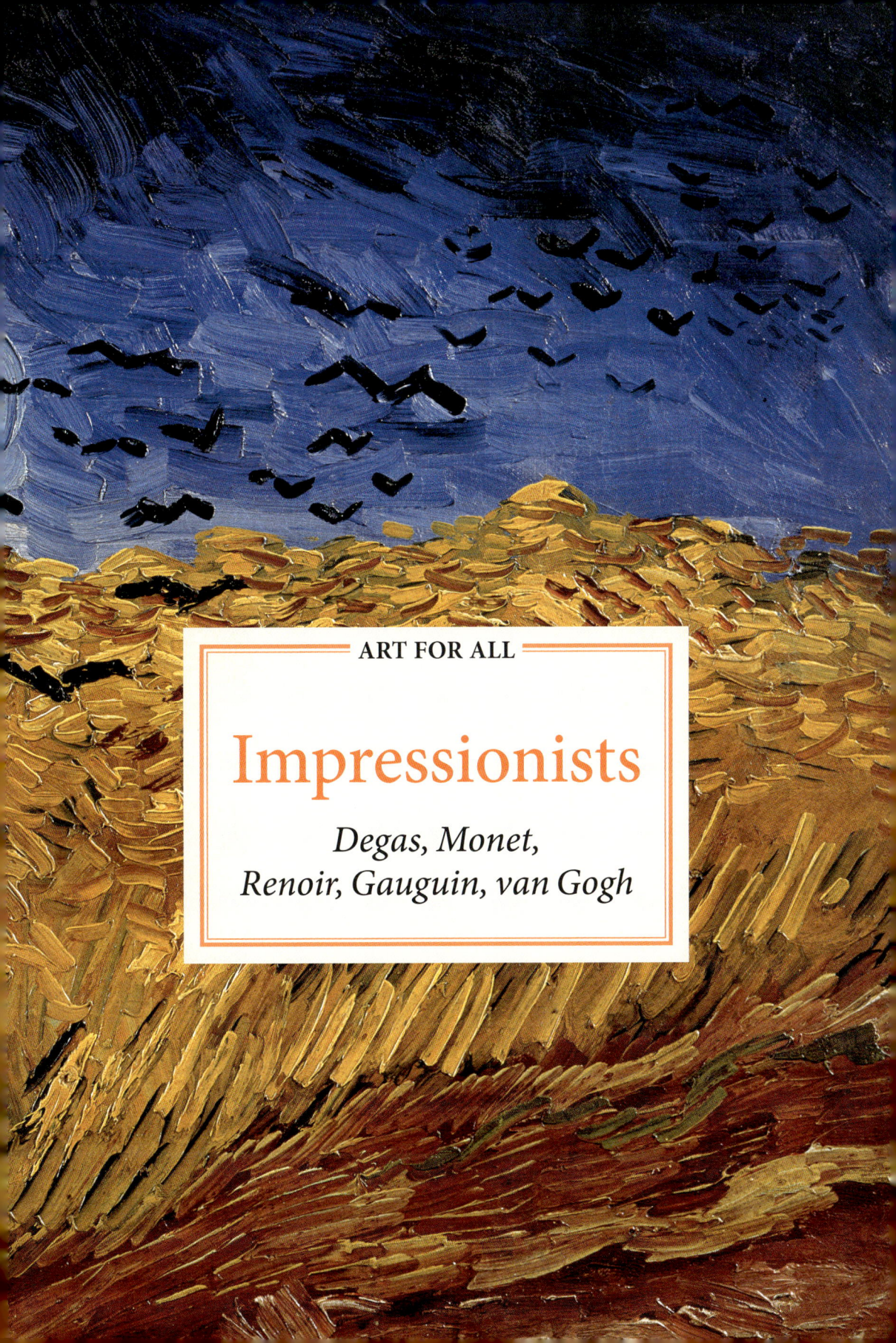

ART FOR ALL

Impressionists

Degas, Monet,
Renoir, Gauguin, van Gogh

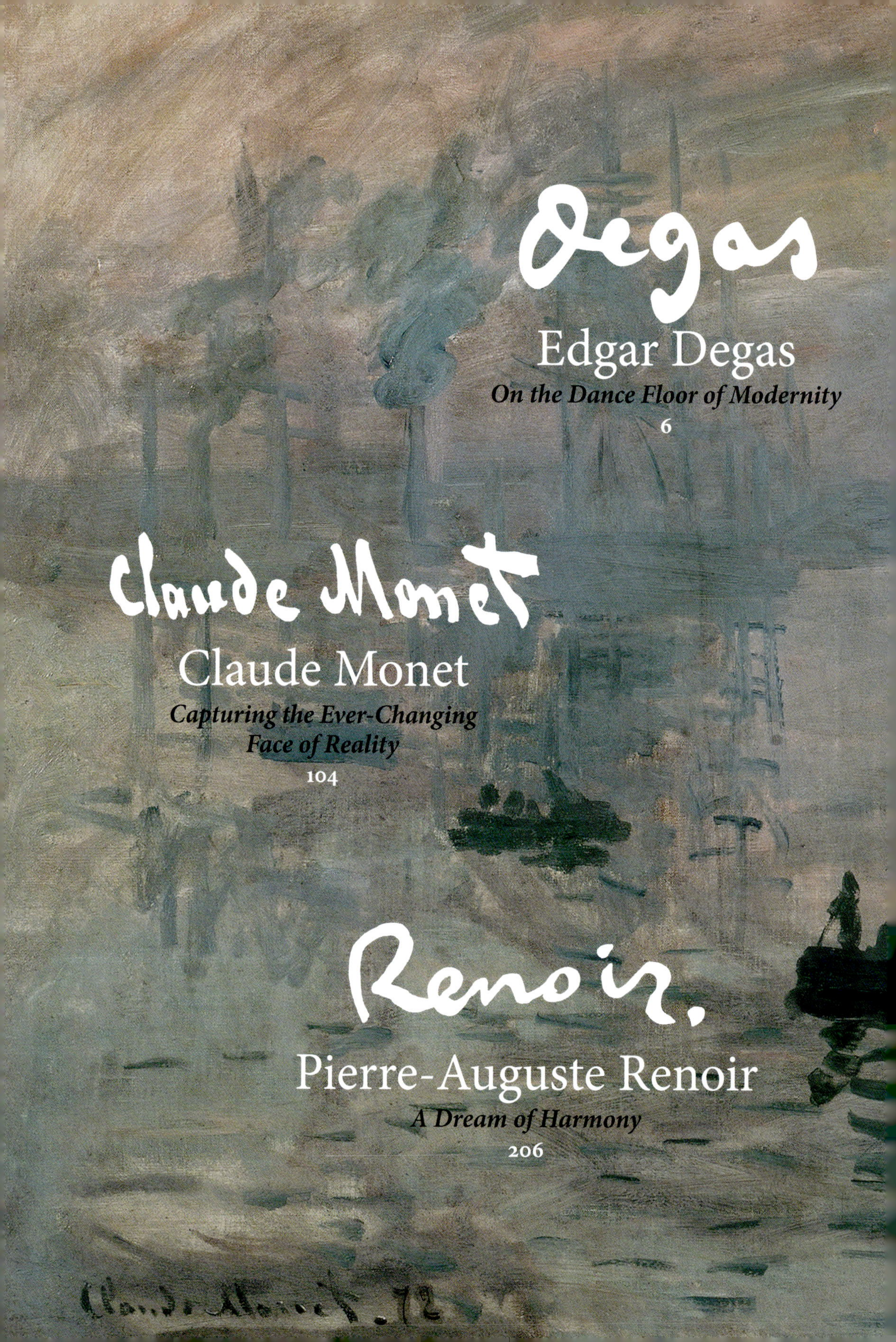

P Gauguin.

Paul Gauguin
The Primitive Sophisticate

Vincent

Vincent van Gogh
Vision and Reality

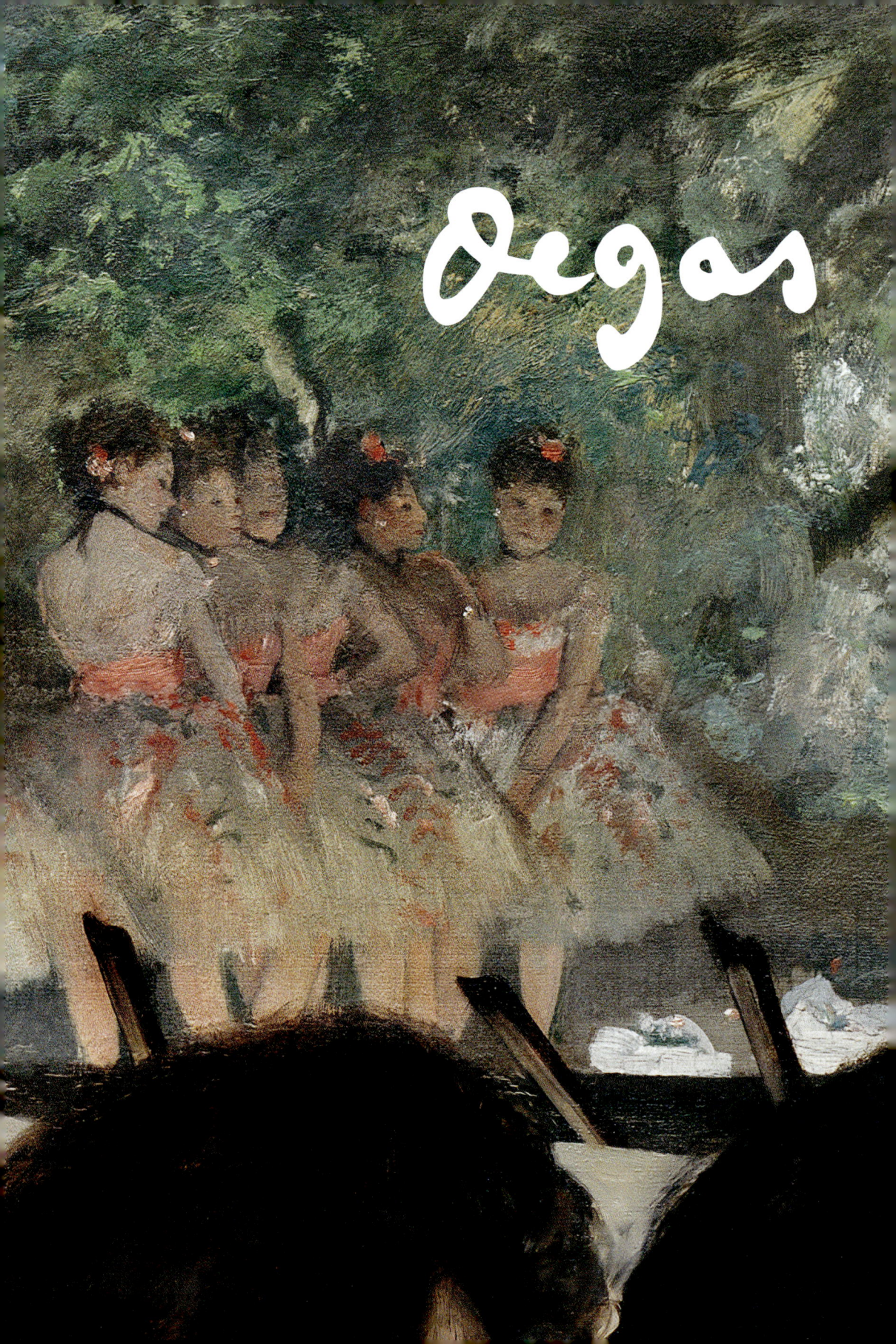

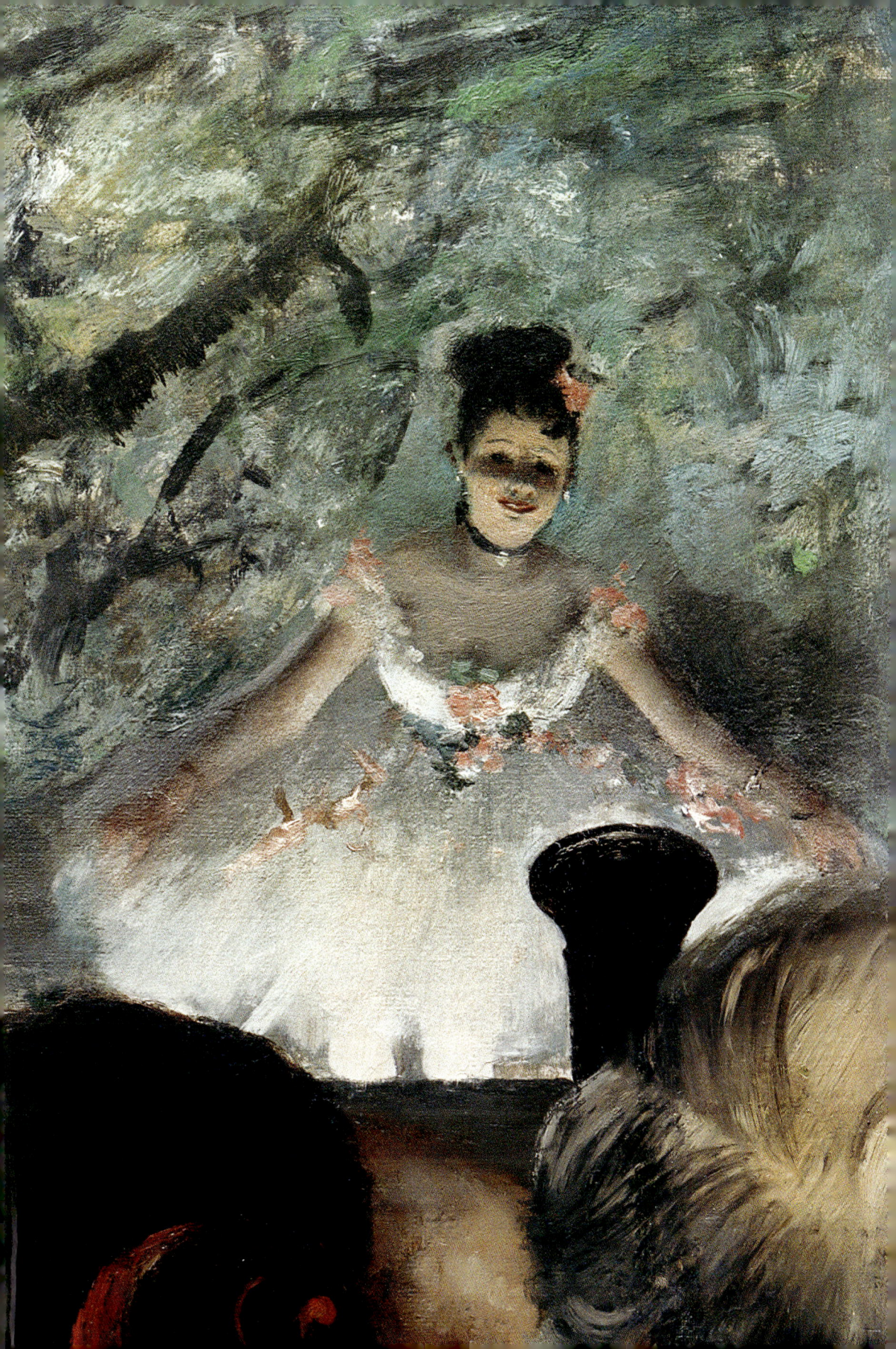

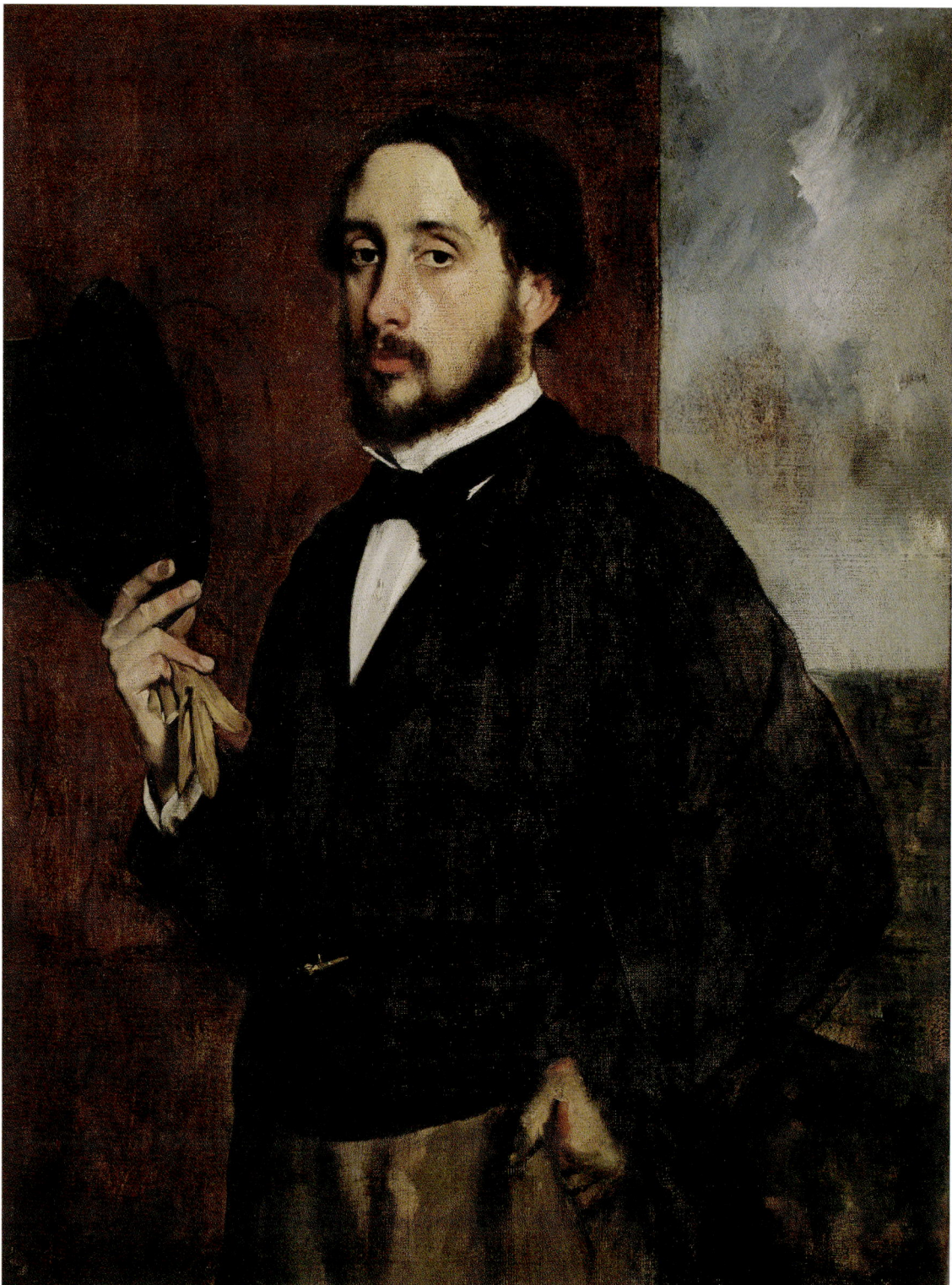

Bernd Growe

Edgar Degas

On the Dance Floor of Modernity

"In art, nothing should look like chance,
not even movement."

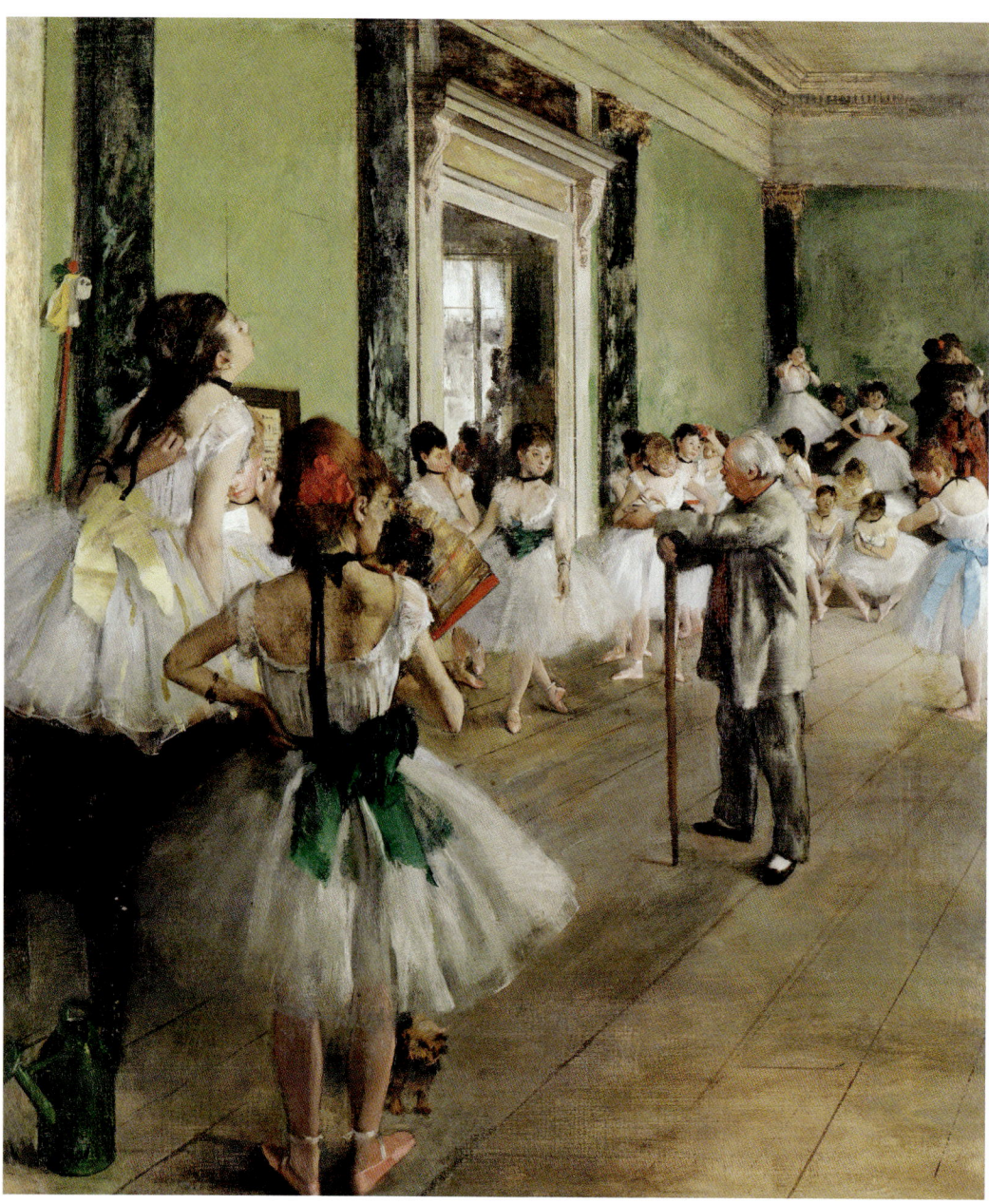

Contents

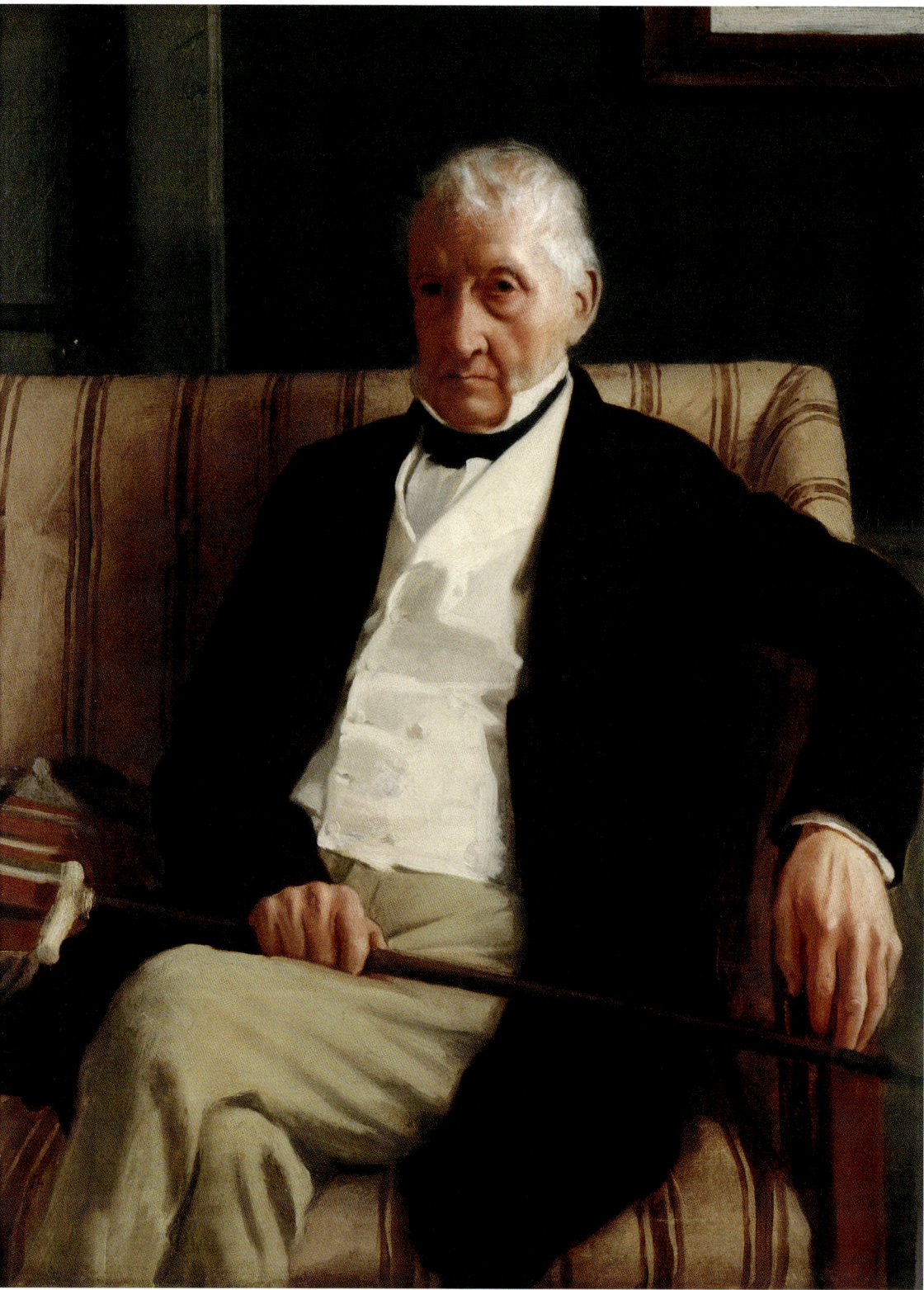

Wonderful Years

Degas's background and beginnings would scarcely suggest he was predestined to be the revolutionary he became, who so comprehensively reconceived our visual perceptions. He was born in the Rue Saint-Georges, Paris, on 19 July 1834. His father, Auguste de Gas, was a banker, and ran a branch of a Neapolitan bank owned by the family. A temperamental man, Degas was always to be Mediterranean in nature. His mother died in 1847, so the boy's father and grandfather were the most influential figures in his early life. Even in hard times, Degas's social position assured him freedom from the material worries which all too often plagued his fellow artists.

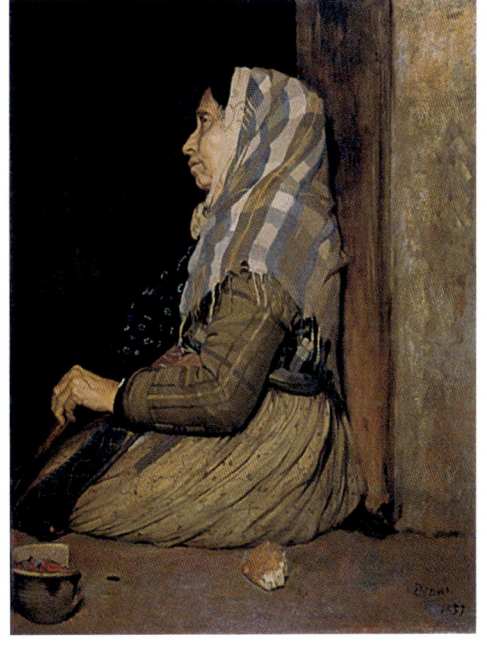

The present study is not a biography of Edgar Degas, a history of his art, or an attempt to explain the one by means of the other. I shall be trying to describe the phenomenon or entity we mean when we say "Degas"; the identification of biographical or historical roots will not be my concern. The style of art monograph evolved by Vasari in the 16th century has largely remained the norm down to the present day: an account of the artist's background and youth is followed by a descriptive list of the works and then an overall appraisal of the artist's personality and achievement. In an age which no longer views the interrelations of creator and creation in terms of a single, unified self, we cannot altogether subscribe to this norm. Thumbnail biography and close analysis of particular works will therefore alternate in what follows.

The present study aims to convey the expressive richness, the scope, and the experimental diversity of Degas's art. Those who approach his art via specific avenues of enquiry – his preference for particular subjects, his artistic methods – will soon realize that his range is far broader than a handful of popular works might suggest. No single approach can do justice to an artist of such

OPPOSITE
Hilaire de Gas, 1857
Oil on canvas, 53 x 41 cm (21 x 16¼ in.)
Paris, Musée d'Orsay

ABOVE RIGHT
Roman Beggar Woman, 1857
Oil on canvas, 100.3 x 75.2 cm
(39½ x 29½ in.)
Birmingham, Museum and Art Gallery

"In order to travel alone, one must go through countries where life is vibrantly alive or there are a great many works of art…"
EDGAR DEGAS

diversity, affected by Realism and Impressionism alike, familiar with the major aesthetic movements of his time, yet still independent, pursuing his own ideas. Both in his art and as a private person, Degas was an uncompromising man, and this too confirmed him in his independence and made him something of an outsider.

From 1845 to 1853 Degas attended the Lycée Louis-le-Grand, a well-thought-of school where he rapidly acquired a name for his skill at drawing. There he made friendships that were to last a lifetime with Paul Valpinçon, Henri Rouart and Ludovic Halévy. Despite his own wish to paint, he began to study law, but broke off his studies in 1853. He frequented Félix Joseph Barrias's studio and spent his time copying Renaissance works; all those Sunday visits to the Louvre with his father, and his familiarity with the art collections of family friends, were paying dividends now. One of these collectors, Prince Grégoire Soutzo, played an important part in Degas's choice of vocation, as did his father's remarkably understanding attitude and advice: the atmosphere in which Degas's decisions were taken was a favourable one. Barrias soon referred Degas to Louis Lamothe, whose studio Degas joined a year later, to receive proper technical training.

In 1855 he met Ingres and warily admitted that he wanted to be an artist. Ingres advised: "Draw lines … a lot of lines, whether they're from memory or from Nature." His words became the young Degas's gospel. At the Paris World Fair in the same year he had ample opportunity to study the work of Delacroix and Ingres in major retrospective shows.

At that time Degas began to keep a journal. Along with records of theatre visits, and analysis of his own character, it contained his first attempts to formulate artistic principles. His choice of early heroes betrays Degas's characteristic reconciliation of tradition and the new. It was a tension that informed his response to Impressionism and deeply affected his adoption of modern subjects. "Ah, Giotto!" he wrote, "let me see Paris. And, Paris, let me see Giotto!"

In 1856 Degas travelled to Italy, where he had the chance to see Giotto. First he stayed in Naples, at the Palazzo Pignatelli di Monte Leone, with grandfather René Hilaire de Gas, uncles Henri Édouard and Achille, and aunts Rosa Adelaide Morbilli and Stefanina. It was not so much for its picturesqueness that Naples impressed Degas, but rather as a city where the arts throve. He went to the opera and studied the old masters, including landscape drawings by Claude Lorrain. He drew portraits, bearing in mind his father's urgent advice to concentrate on portraiture. Later, in painting grandfather Hilaire (ill. p. 12), this preparatory work assisted him greatly. The eighty-seven-year-old is seen sitting on a sofa, relaxed, his ivory-handled cane in his lap. Degas has been frank about the stern presence of the old man: that cane is a discreet but definite reminder of the calm authority of the head of the family.

The following year he moved on to Rome, where he met a number of acquaintances, among them Léon Bonnat, another former student of Lamothe's. He made new friends such as Georges Bizet and (a close friendship) Gustave Moreau, who were to be found in the Académie Française circles at the Villa Medici, run by Victor Schnetz. (Those such as Degas who did not have an academy stipend were allowed to work there too.) *Roman Beggar Woman* (ill. p. 13), which Degas was much later to date to the year 1857, was a type of picture Victor Schnetz had long been advocating. Schnetz felt that scenes of everyday life in Italy offered a way of avoiding the dangers of too crude a realism. Degas's picture shows the old woman in profile in a doorway, with her meagre rations; the artist draws our attention via the folds in her clothing and her checked headscarf to the woman's facial features, set off against the darkness of the doorway.

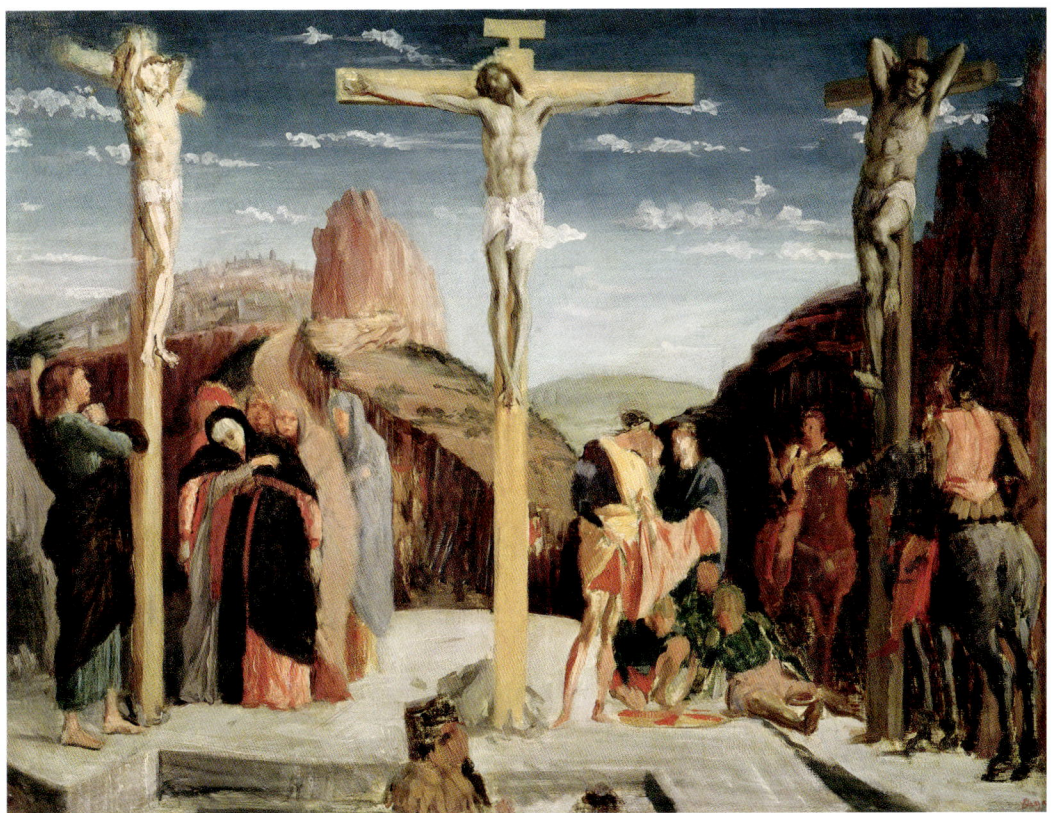

In Rome, together with his new friend Moreau, Degas visited the art galleries. The formidable cornucopia of art afforded him a bountiful harvest, and he filled no fewer than twenty-eight sketchbooks.

Copy of Mantegna's Crucifixion, c. 1861
Oil on canvas, 69 x 92.5 cm (27¼ x 36½ in.)
Tours, Musée des Beaux-Arts

In summer 1858 he travelled via Viterbo, Orvieto, Perugia, Assisi and Arezzo to Florence. The Italian landscape and light fascinated him; nonetheless, Degas was already quite clearly wary of taking the natural world as a subject for his art. This early mistrust, or lack of interest, was later to become a regular aversion. Giotto's frescoes at Assisi, however, excited him greatly – and he even refused to draw them on the grounds that he wanted to retain the first impression for ever.

By 1860 Degas had drawn over seven hundred copies of other works, mainly early Italian Renaissance and French classical art. What interested Degas was movement, and arabesques, so he tended to view individual figures in isolation from their visual contexts, for reasons of his own rather than in obedience to the principles of art history. This exploration of physical shapes and gestures provided him with a repertoire which he could always fall back on whenever the need arose.

Degas was registered as a copyist at the Louvre in Paris as early as 1853. There, he pressed ahead with his artistic training in a spirit idiosyncratically his own: "One must copy the masters again and again …" The paintings he copied were more than objects of research to him: "The air we see in the pictures of the old masters is not an air that can be breathed!" Degas claimed to have copied all the old masters in the Louvre. Among the works was Mantegna's *Crucifixion,* the centre predella panel of the 1458 altarpiece done for San Zeno in Verona, which Napoleon had carried off to Paris in the course of his Italian campaign. Quite probably the copy (ill. p. 15) was not done till 1861. It is not an exact reproduction of the original; rather, it is a rare attempt on Degas's part to capture the special atmosphere of the work in silhouettes and strong colours, in a mood beyond the dry linearity of Mantegna. Mantegna became a touchstone to Degas. "The frame of a painting by Mantegna contains the world, whereas the moderns are only capable of rendering a tiny corner of it, a mere moment, a fragment."

It was at the invitation of Baron Gennaro Bellelli and his wife Laura (an Italian aunt) that Degas went to Florence in August 1858. There he did numerous drawings of the family. It was not till March 1859 that he returned to Paris – where, in his Rue Madame studio, he finally painted his group portrait *The Bellelli Family* (ill. p. 17), which he had planned in Florence and had indeed already rethought repeatedly. It originated in a planned double portrait of his cousins Laura and Giulia (in November 1857); later, the mother and then the baron were also included in the composition.

The Bellelli Family is an extraordinarily ambitious work. It records psychological tensions with immense precision, tensions which undermine the social poise and pose of the sitters. Degas combines imposing presence with domesticity. The painting has been interpreted as rendering the different ages of humankind by showing us various generations and indeed including the unborn and the dead: the baroness was pregnant at the time, while on the wall behind her we see a red chalk drawing of her father, René Hilaire de Gas, who had died in 1858. But social standing and domesticity are not the real subject of the painting, as we will realize if we take a closer look. What looks like unruffled family life turns out to reveal a psychological contrast through Degas's inclusion of the baron.

The baron is seated with his back to us at the right-hand edge of the composition, and has no real

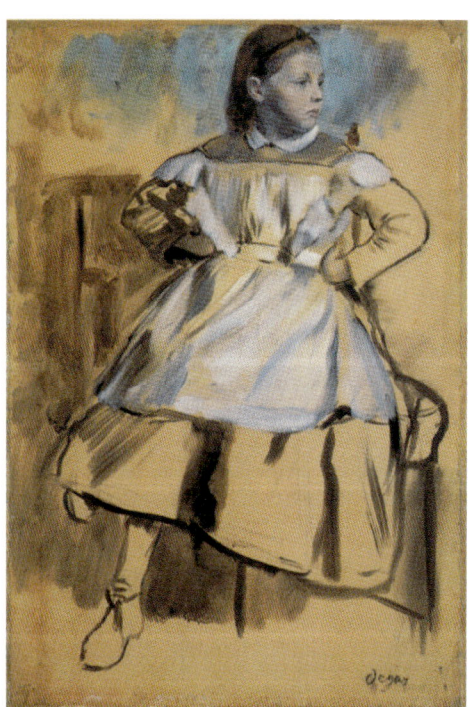

presence to counterbalance the group of mother and daughters. As a sketch shows, Degas originally positioned the father in a frontal posture at the end of the table; but in the final version he has been marginalized, removed from the family centre. The mother and wife is the focus of attention. She was twenty-eight when she married Gennaro Bellelli, a lawyer and liberal journalist; the marriage was probably an arranged one. The picture lays bare the frustrations of that marriage by highlighting the distance between the father and the female members of the family.

Degas has given special attention to Giulia. Though her bodily posture allies her with her mother, she is looking sideways towards her father. Her left leg under her, hands nonchalantly on her hips, she constitutes an untroubled midway point between the tensed poles of her parents. Capturing the moment in this way enables Degas to convey a sense of immediate presence; the sheer relaxation of Giulia's pose (which Degas

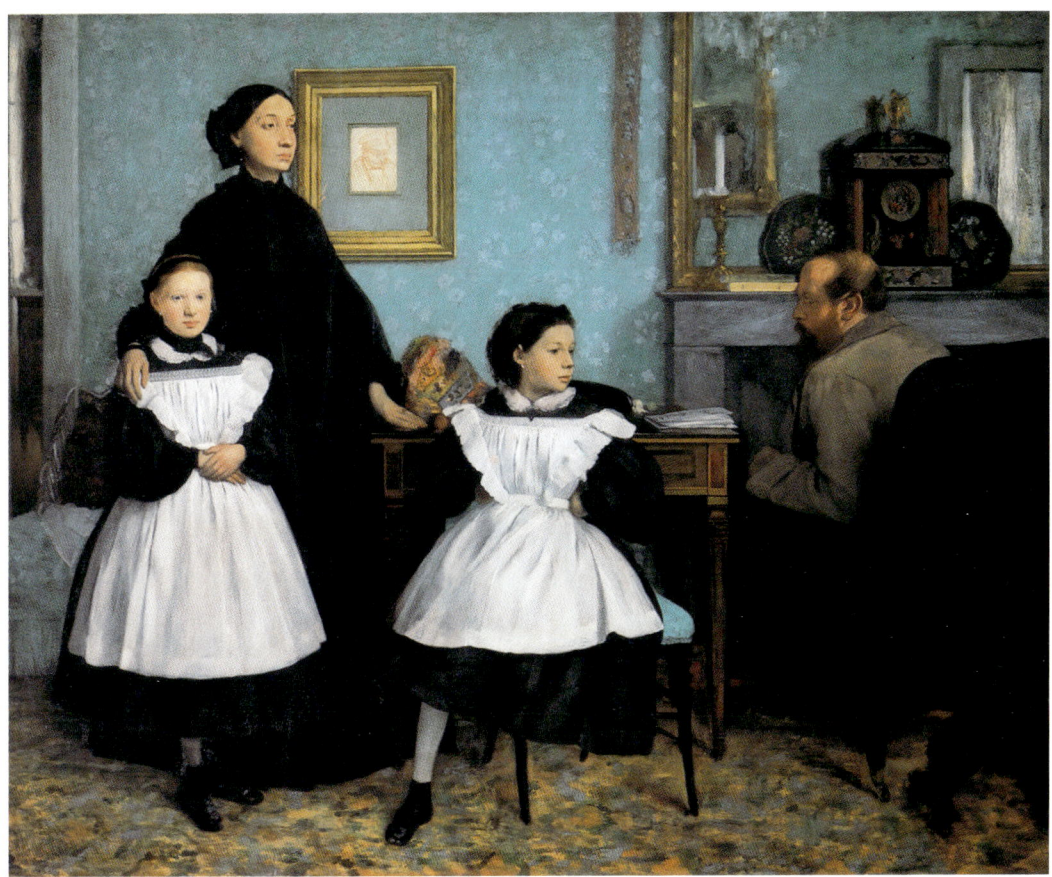

attained through a series of studies) marks off this family portrait from the prevailing conventions of the time. (Degas was later to do further portrait work involving the point at which a pose can be defined as a temporary posture.) Without caricaturing, but equally without covering anything up, *The Bellelli Family* uses the unmet and unanswered gaze of the marital partners to analyze irreconcilable differences in their inner lives. It also contrasts the generations, now unbound by formal, conventional ideals. But, more than this, in the evasion of contact there is also an implied confrontation with us, looking on, to whom the onus of evaluation and commentary is left. In a sense, the painting was Degas's manifesto. It not only documented his aim "to create a family portrait … in the undaunted spirit of the *ronde de nuit*; it also indicated the ways his work would evolve. For the first time we see the artist exploring the isolation of the individual, a subject which Degas was to examine in every walk of society.

The visit to Italy had roused his ambition. Degas returned to Paris with great plans and strengthened self-confidence. To his friend Valernes he later remarked that that period was the most wonderful in his entire life. The unfinished self-portrait of 1863 (ill. p. 8) shows a man not quite thirty, a stylish man of the middle classes, with gloves and top hat, facing whatever the future may have in store with calm self-assurance.

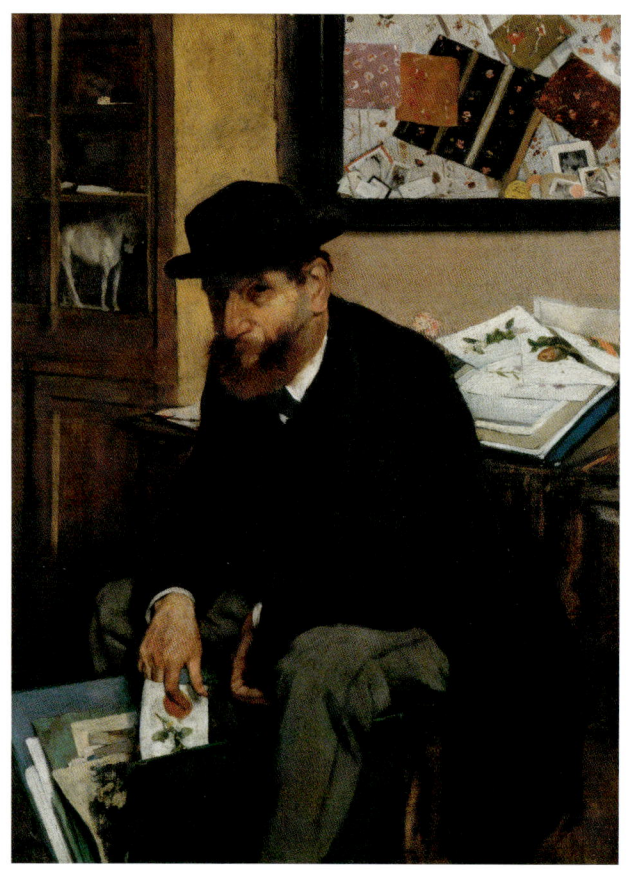

"Art is not what you see,
but what you make others see."

EDGAR DEGAS

The Collector, 1866
Oil on canvas, 53 x 40 cm (21 x 15¾ in.)
New York, The Metropolitan Museum of Art,
H. O. Havemeyer Collection,
Bequest of Mrs H. O. Havemeyer, 1929

OPPOSITE
Monsieur and Madame Edmondo Morbilli, c. 1865
Oil on canvas, 116.5 x 88.3 cm (46 x 34¾ in.)
Boston, Museum of Fine Arts,
Gift of Robert Treat Paine II, 1931

PAGES 20/21
Hortense Valpinçon, 1871
Oil on canvas, 75.6 x 113.7 cm (29¾ x 44¾ in.)
The Minneapolis Institute of Arts,
John R. Van Derlip Fund

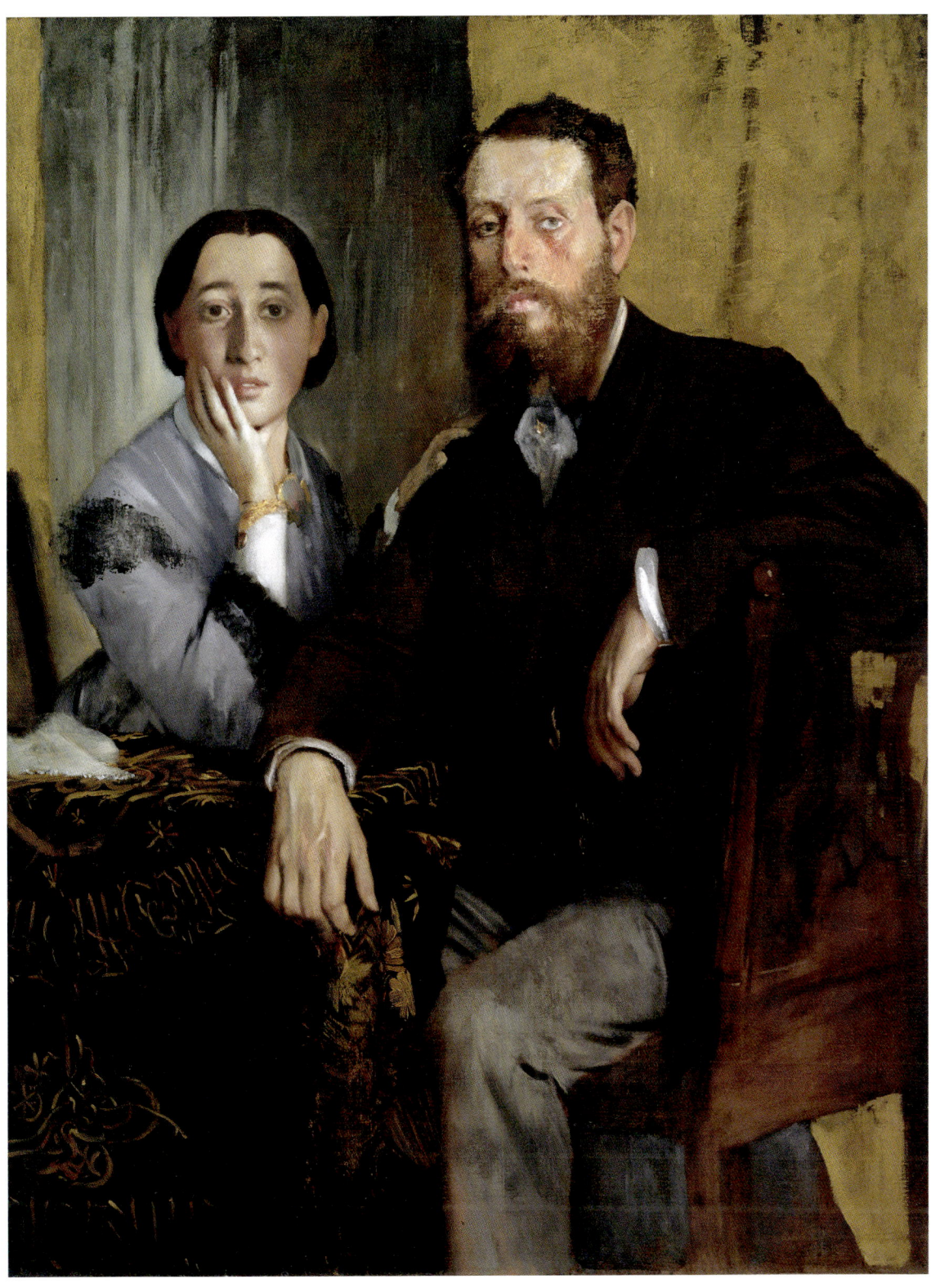

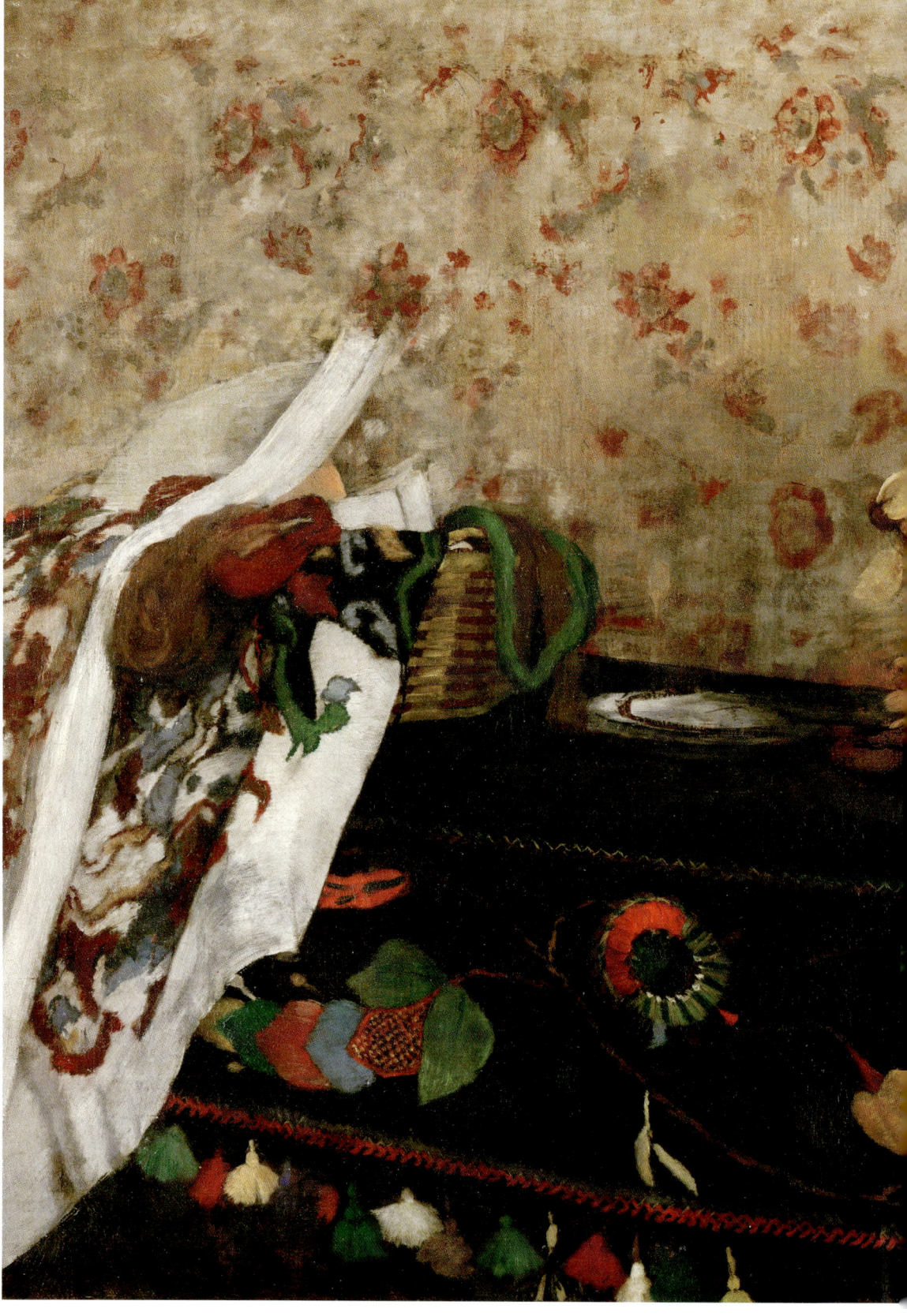

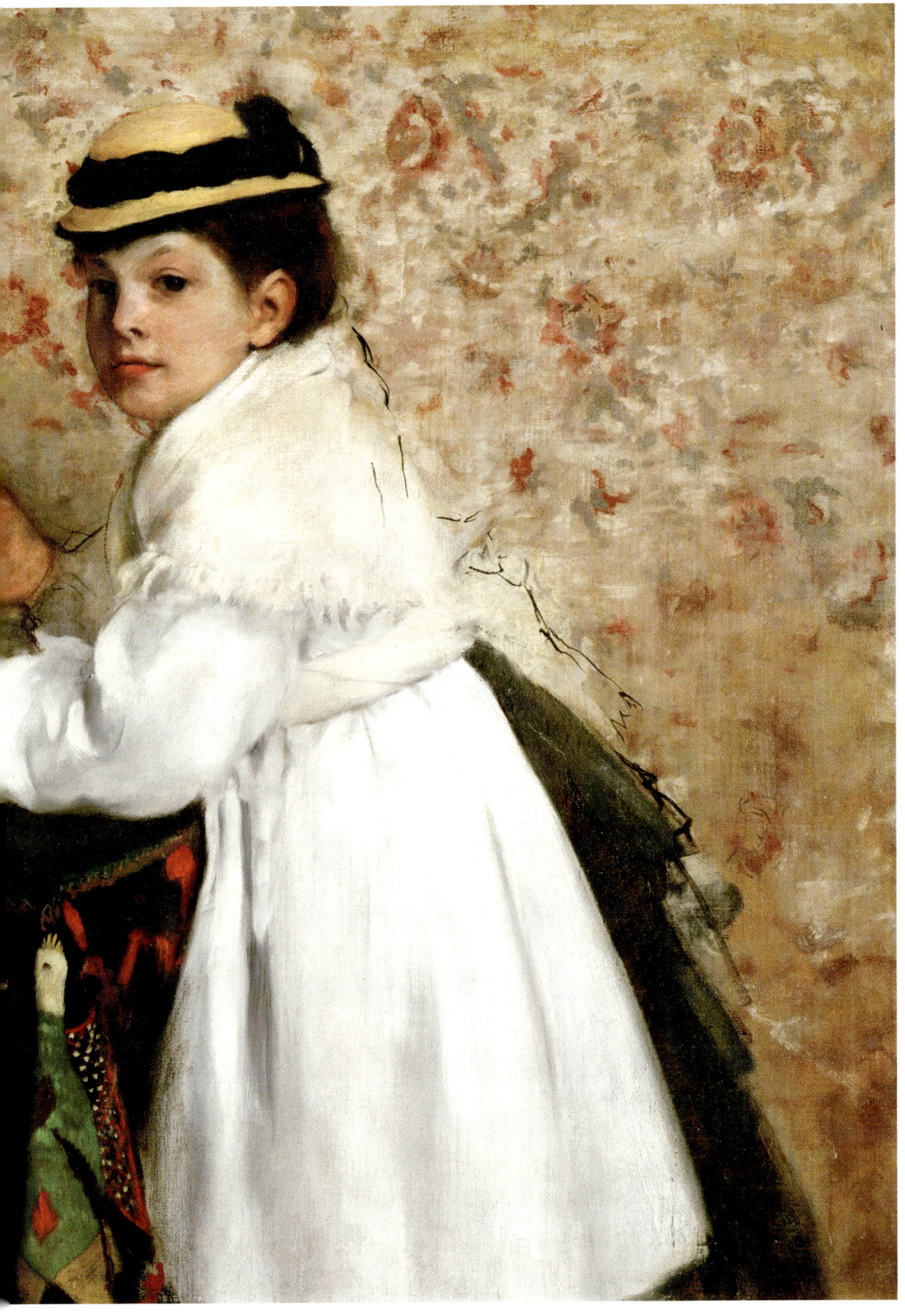

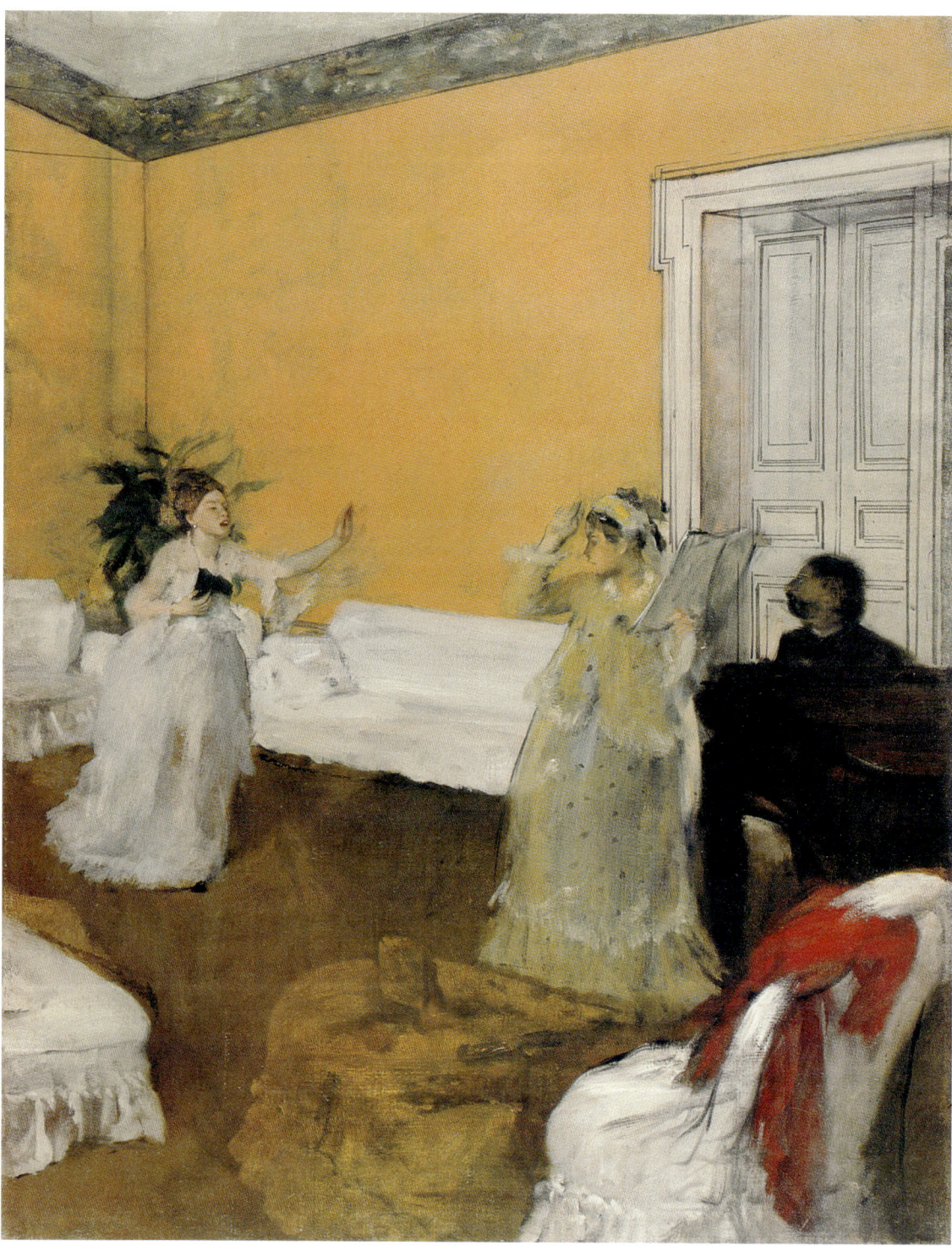

Historical and Portrait Paintings

Now that French 19th-century art is no longer viewed in the simplistic terms of salon art versus avant-garde art, historical painting has been evaluated afresh. This process has also affected our interpretation of early Degas. For Degas, despite the waning importance of grand historical art in the post-classical period, was not without his aspirations to satisfy aesthetic doctrines and the prevailing taste of the time by producing historical paintings.

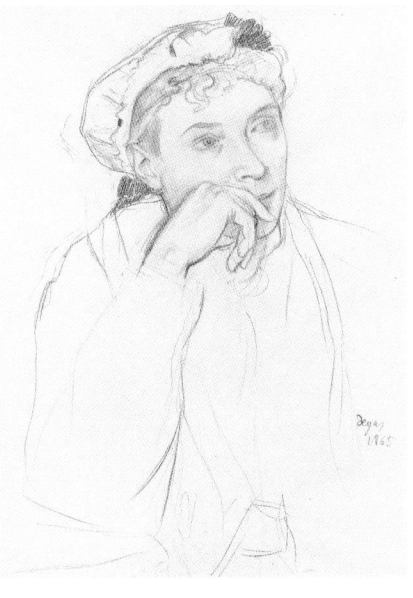

From 1855 to 1865, Degas was occupied with a number of such works, some of them large-format. His models were Jean-Auguste-Dominique Ingres, who had emphasized the significance of history, and Eugène Delacroix; among his contemporaries, Degas also valued Puvis de Chavannes. Many of his projects never left the planning stage, or remained unfinished. It was an early indication of Degas's aversion to the completed artefact. His historical works all betray a hint of doubt as to the relevance of what he was doing. In his treatment, they became a place to approach the conflict between genre requirements and the artist's current interests. It is a conflict which we might describe as the polarity of history and authenticity.

The most important work of this period was *Spartan Girls Challenging Boys,* painted in 1860–62 (ill. p. 28). Degas did no fewer than sixteen drawings and two oil sketches by way of preparation. For him, thinking of the subject and presenting it in a particular way were in themselves acts of history. It is typical of his history paintings, indeed of his procedure in general, that the work was not done spontaneously but as a careful process of construction, even of assemblage. The painting's source may have been a passage in Plutarch concerning competitive rituals in ancient Sparta. Degas's presentation of the boys and girls, their strutting and their reactions, may perhaps be seen as a projection of the artist's own longings and fears – which might make it easier to understand why he exhibited it as late as the fifth Impressionist show in 1879, and kept it in his studio throughout his life.

The rivalling youngsters strike us as Parisian rather than Spartan. The girls are aggressive and provocative; the boys are seen responding to the challenge. The closed group of girls are dominant; the boys are grouped more loosely, and behave as individuals. Just as the recoil of the boys responds to the forward movement of the girls, the entire choreography of move and counter-move produces a complex interaction of gestural to and fro, polarities and couplings indicative of choice and consent. The scene records the moment when a game begins to be meant seriously.

Degas's staggering composition (the first girl's outstretched hand is precisely in the centre of the painting) links the jerky and spontaneous movements of the moment into a well-conceived spatial entity.

This picture of young Spartans strikes us as true to life. And yet, it remains an attempt to render the historical painting relevant by the use of inappropriate means. The ancient subject and the up-to-date naturalism are strictly at odds – and contemporary critics were not slow to ridicule the resulting conceptual fracture: in place of the idealized figures expected in a historical painting, they said, Degas had offered the unattractive reality of "skinny suburban brats".

It was with a historical painting that Degas made his Salon debut in 1865. *The Sufferings of the City of New Orleans* (ill. p. 29), to the artist's disappointment, was given scant attention. The reason was perhaps that Manet's *Olympia,* also selected by a liberal-minded jury, was monopolizing

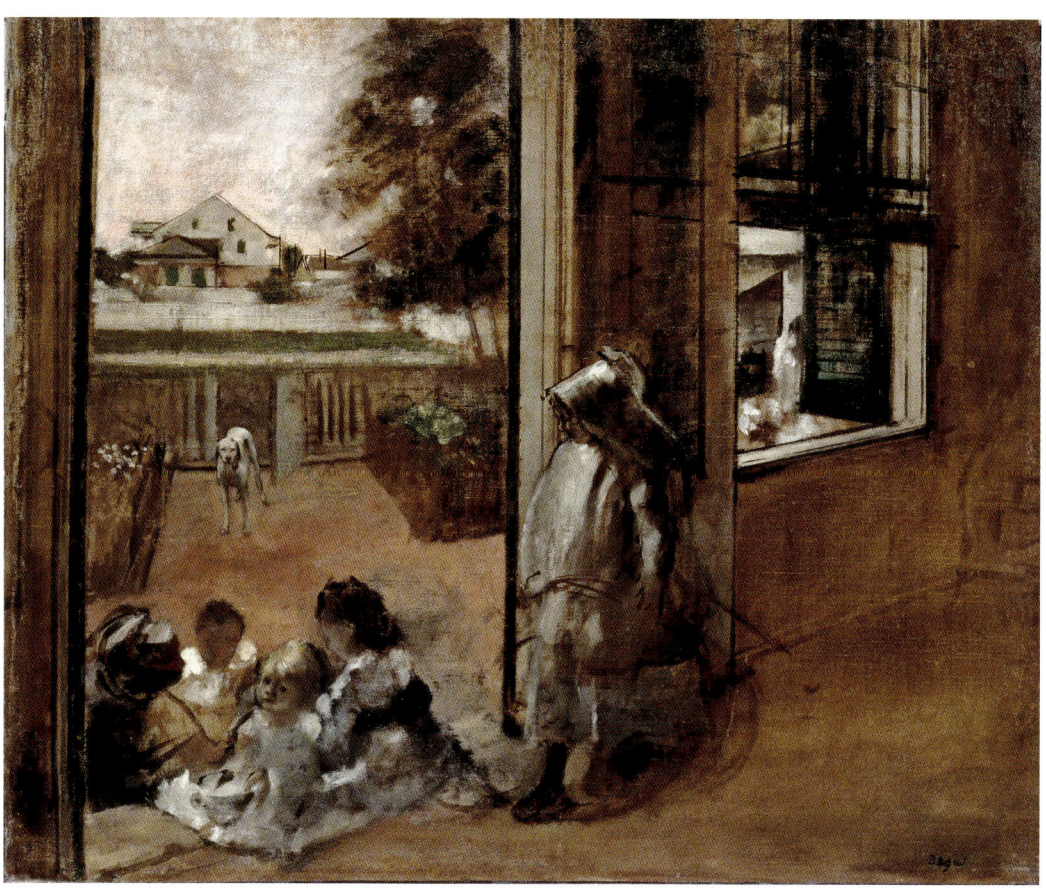

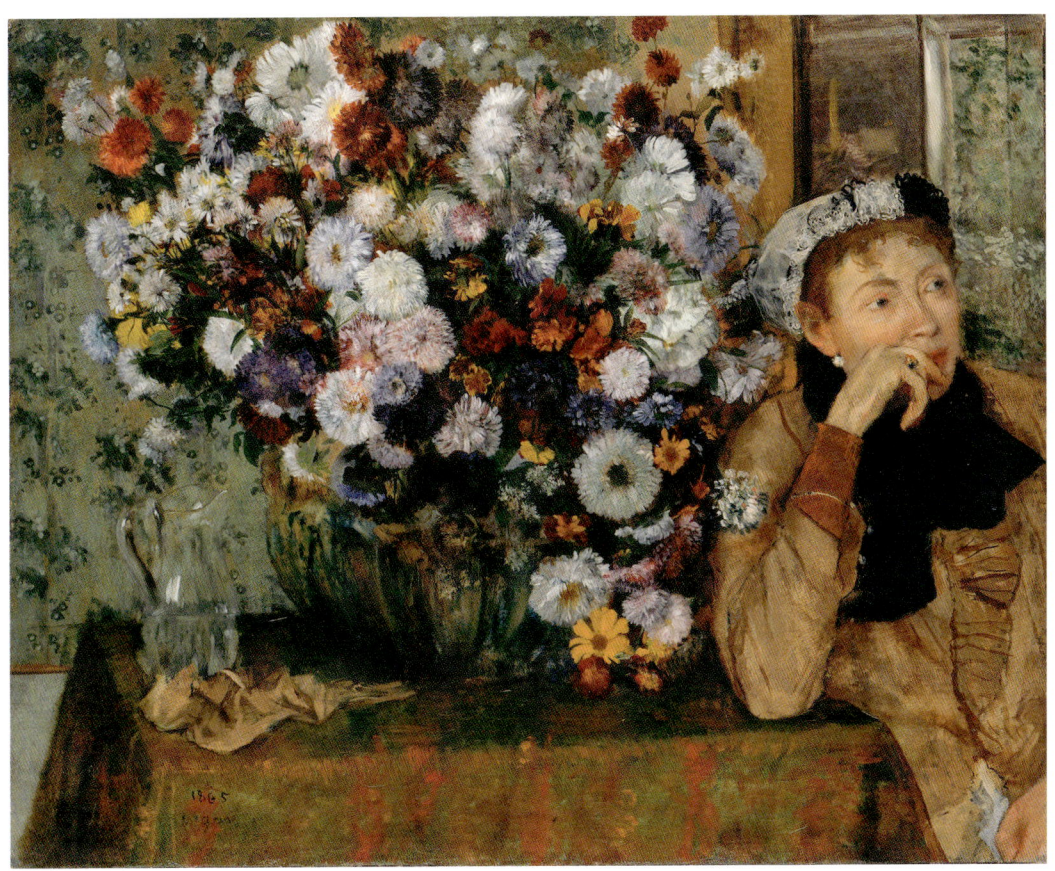

*"I assure you no art was ever
less spontaneous than mine."*

EDGAR DEGAS

Woman with Chrysanthemums, 1865
Oil on canvas, 73.7 x 92.7 cm (29 x 36½ in.)
New York, The Metropolitan Museum of Art,
H. O. Havemeyer Collection,
Bequest of Mrs H. O. Havemeyer, 1929

OPPOSITE
Courtyard of a House in New Orleans, 1872
Oil on canvas, 60 x 75 cm (22½ x 29½ in.)
Copenhagen, Designmuseum Danmark

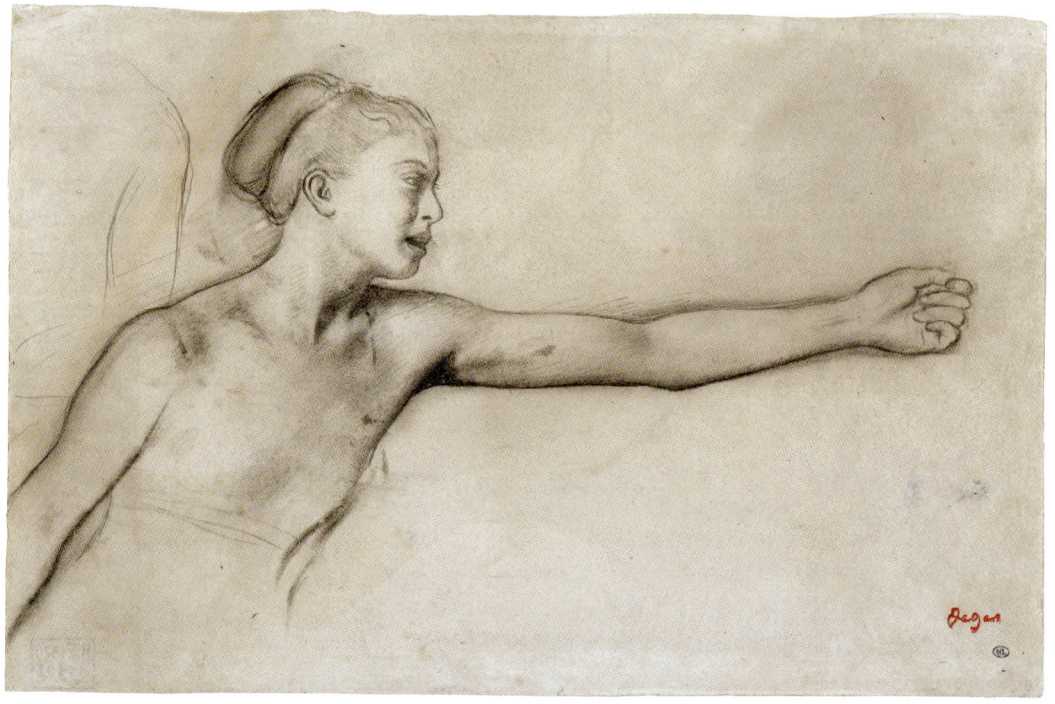

Spartan Girl, *c.* 1860
Pencil on paper, 28 x 38 cm (11 x 15 in.)
Paris, Musée d'Orsay

critical controversy. Degas's work must have seemed anachronistic and artificial; a mediaeval landscape setting, of all things, was being used to symbolize the sufferings of the American city of New Orleans, which was occupied by Union troops in 1862 in the course of the Civil War. Despite the burning city in the background, and the contrast of soldiers and helpless victims, there is no real dramatic tension in the painting. The figures make a scattered impression – particularly the prostrate female nudes, to whom Degas (as his preliminary drawings show) had devoted careful attention. He has put them in poses that emphasize the torment they are undergoing; but the more expressive their bodies are, the more they seem nudes independent of the action of the picture. Degas has also squeezed the action out to the margins of the scene, leaving an empty central section and a badly cropped figure (the rider at right, carrying off a nude figure). For the sake of these visual effects, Degas has dispensed with a coherent narrative statement. *The Sufferings of the City of New Orleans* turned out to be his last historical painting.

The years from 1852 to 1865 were crucial to the subsequent evolution of Degas's work. After 1862 Degas gradually took his bearings anew, via history and portrait painting. He had to decide whether to go on applying traditional approaches to new subjects or to locate his own alternatives. Ways of seeing that were schooled on the conventions of historical art could only confront the issue of authentic experience in a spirit of opposition. And so Degas's history paintings attest the emptiness and theatricality of the genre: history as a spectacle that has little to do with what may really have happened.

Spartan Girls Challenging Boys was an attempt to locate contemporary affairs in history. But the great tradition of history, which Baudelaire had identified as lost in 1846, could no longer be re-established by *grande peinture.* The dividing line between history and genre had vanished.

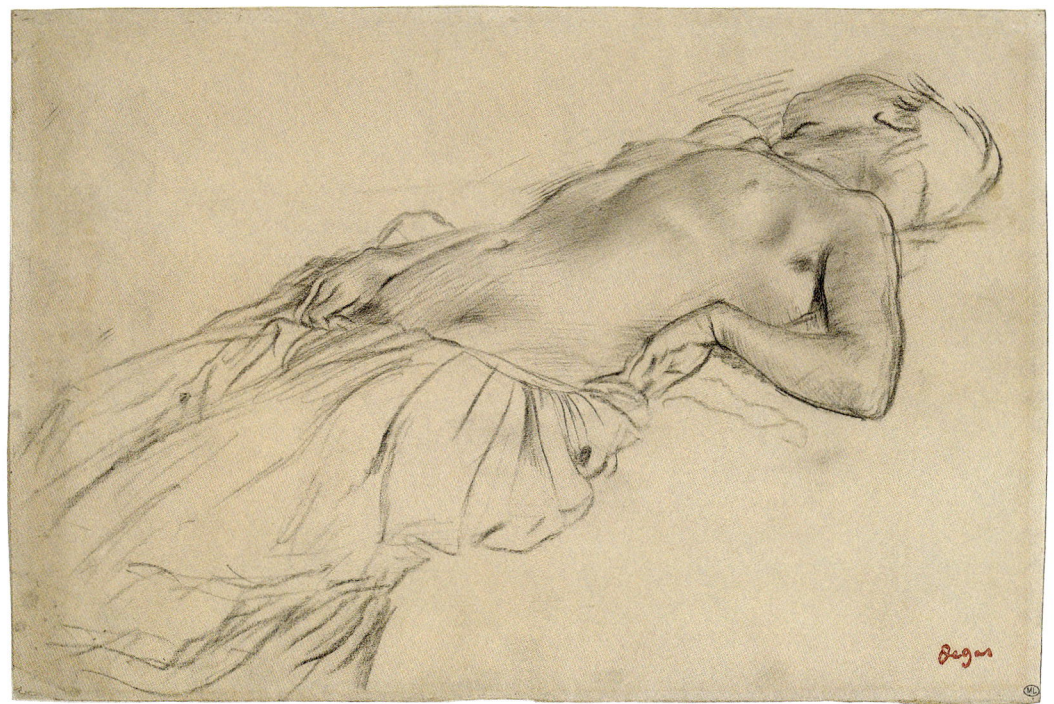

Reclining Woman, 1865
Pencil, 22.8 x 35.6 cm (9 x 14 in.)
Paris, Musée d'Orsay

In mid-century, interest in historical art began to flag noticeably, because private collectors who commissioned works had quite different preferences. One critic, Castagnary, observed: "Little by little, religious and historical or heroic art has been relegated to the same level as theocracy and monarchy. The social structures that supported it have become extinct." If history is increasingly seen as a reconstructable process, historical content can no longer be imposed upon the present as a norm. The irreconcilability of contemporary experience and history leads to a shift in perception, too: what now became of greatest importance was not scrutiny of heroes and their deeds but the situation of the onlooker.

Degas redoubled his efforts in portrait painting. In 1865 he painted *Monsieur and Madame Edmondo Morbilli* (ill. p. 19), one of a number of double portraits for which Degas may have been inspired by daguerrotypes. It was in portraits that seemed most obviously to abide by handed-down conventions that Degas was best able to establish his own distance from the genre.

Seated before a neutral background, the Morbillis are presented with all the characteristic psychological verve of our artist. The duke, though the dominant partner, is slightly displaced from the centre, which creates spatial tension between the two sitters. Their characters begin to seem as different as the colours of the backgrounds they are seen against. Relaxed as his posture may be, the duke is clearly a man of aristocratic reserve; and the duchess's gently melancholy air provides a contrast. The character difference between the two emerges not through any action or compositional dichotomy in the painting but through our own perception as we look at it. The gentleness of Thérèse's body language serves as a kind of commentary on the passivity visible in Edmondo's hands. Her own left hand is resting on her husband's shoulder while the fingers of her right lie thoughtfully against her cheek, as if she were momentarily turning from her husband

and towards us. The shadow of the man falls across her earnest features.

In *Woman with Chrysanthemums* (ill. p. 25), painted in the same year, Degas takes a different approach: the chrysanthemums and the woman (squeezed almost out of the picture by the flowers) rival each other in their claims on our attention. The woman may be Madame Valpinçon. We are inclined, by the force of convention, to see the human figure as the centre of the composition; but the position Degas has put her in is at odds with this. He has indeed further teased our sense of the true subject by showing her with face partly hidden by her hand. The asymmetrical, excentric composition serves purposes of immediacy and impact; but it does so at the expense of the sitter. The egalitarian treatment of the woman and the flowers also gives Degas an opportunity to compare the chrysanthemums' physical presence and the mental absence of the woman, lost in a daydream.

The scene is a simple glimpse of everyday life; in this respect, Theodore Duret (in his commentary on the 1870 Salon) put his finger on the heart of the matter when he observed that Degas was always primarily interested in a "distinctive type" and that the Parisian type (say) counted for more with him than individual qualities. Degas – as Duranty foretold at the time – was well on his way to becoming a "painter of the upper ten thousand". His portraits were documents recording the impossibility of capturing any authentic individuality in the changed circumstances of modern life.

During the Franco-Prussian War of 1870, Degas volunteered for the infantry. In marksmanship training his eye trouble became apparent for the first time. Degas was under the command of

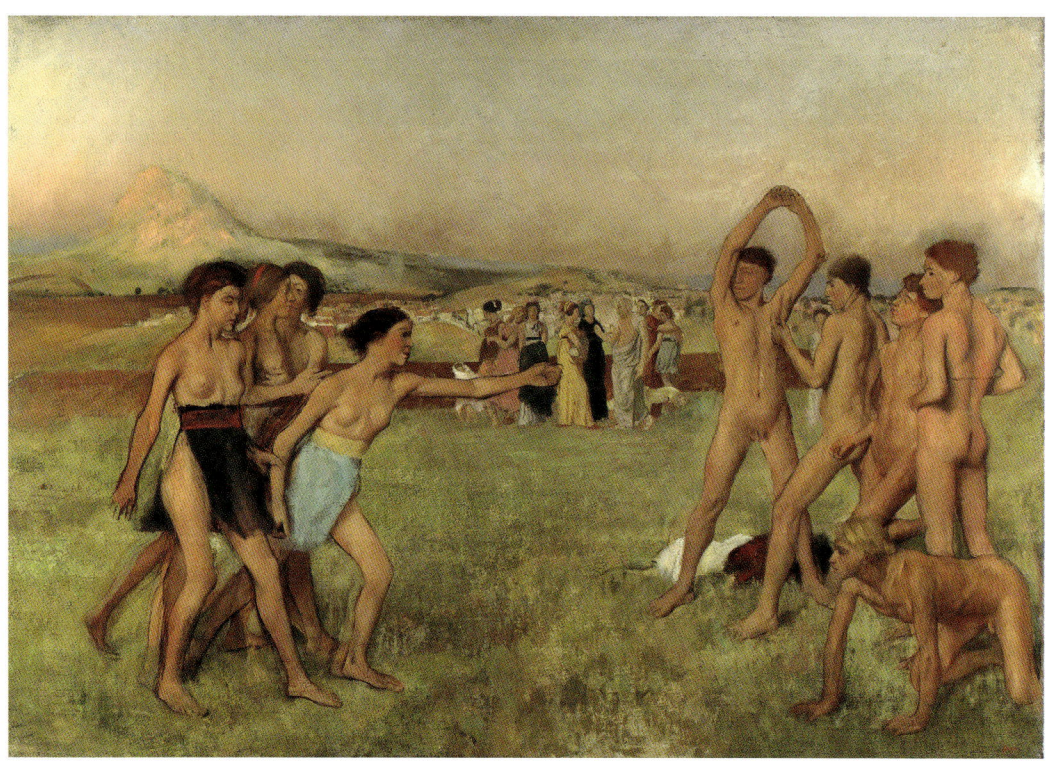

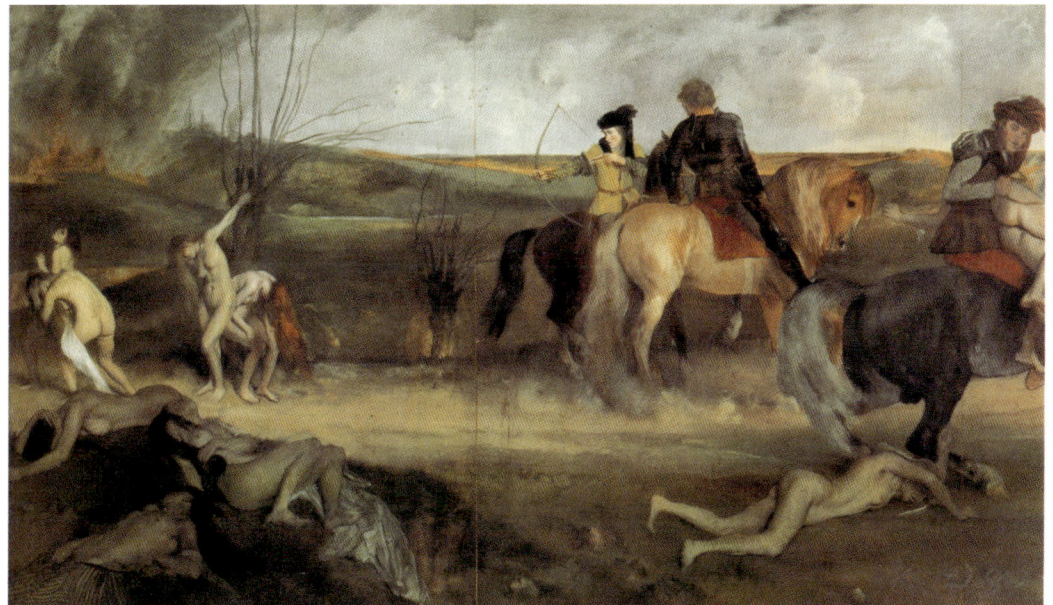

his old fellow-student Henri Rouart, who was still a good
friend. For the duration of the Commune he left Paris and
joined the Valpinçons at Ménil-Hubert. There he painted
the almost impressionist portrait of the nine-year-old Hortense Valpinçon (ill. pp. 20/21), with whom he was to remain
in touch in later years. The asymmetry of the composition
is comparable with that of *Woman with Chrsyanthemums.*

The Sufferings of the City of New Orleans, 1865
Oil on paper, mounted on canvas,
83.5 x 148.5 cm (33 x 58½ in.)
Paris, Musée d'Orsay

OPPOSITE
Spartan Girls Challenging Boys, c. 1860–62
Oil on canvas, 109 x 155 cm (43 x 61 in.)
London, The National Gallery

The table and embroidery are seen at an angle, and the girl is well to the right of centre, looking up
from the piece of apple in her hand across to the painter. All of this, together with the unconstrained
style in which the wallpaper has been painted, gives the work a vividly dynamic quality which we
may well interpret as expressing the child's natural restlessness.

It was in the troubled post-war years that Degas undertook his longest journey. In 1872, with
his younger brother René, he travelled via London to New York and New Orleans, where his uncle
Michel Musson ran a cotton business. Degas stayed in Louisiana for five months and did not return
to Paris till February 1873. He was excited by America's technological progress – such as the railway
sleeping cars – but he sorely missed the cultural and social life of Paris: "The lack of the opera is a
real torment to me." Performances in private homes such as the one that prompted the 1872/73 *Song
Rehearsal* (ill. p. 22) could not afford any substitute. The picture's subject is not the music on offer
but the activity of rehearsal. The perspective and gestures highlight the duet relation of the two
singers. Even the pianist is depicted in the act of turning, and Degas goes so far as to emphasize the
movement of his head through the contrast with the hard-line precision of the door.

Courtyard of a House in New Orleans (ill. p. 24) shows part of the Musson home in Esplanade
Avenue and possibly the room that served Degas as a studio during his stay. Little Carrie Bell is in
the doorway with her hoop, and other children are on the step with the nanny. Of all the paintings
Degas did in America, this one best conveys a sense of the distinctive New Orleans atmosphere
and light.

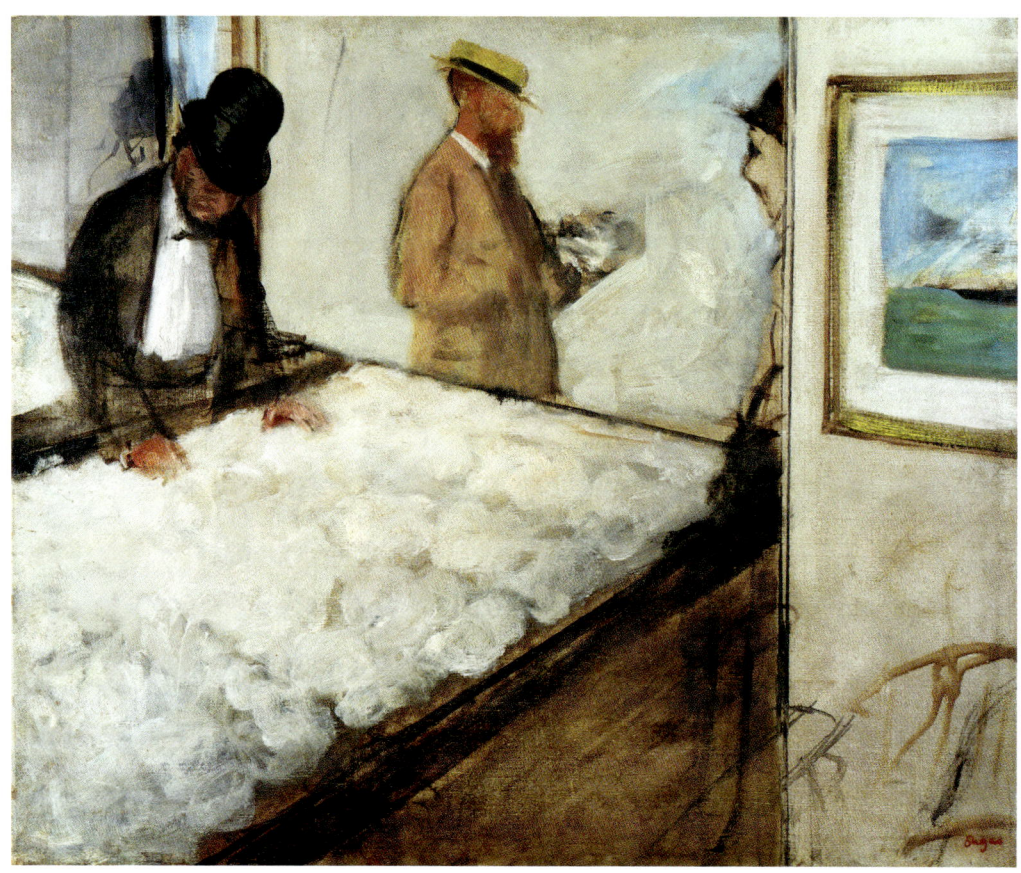

Cotton Dealers in New Orleans, 1873
Oil on canvas, 58.7 x 71.8 cm (23 x 28¼ in.)
Cambridge, Massachusetts,
Harvard Art Museums/Fogg Museum,
Gift of Herbert N. Straus

The Pedicurist (ill. p. 33) is another of Degas's tireless studies of everyday situations. Plainly the artist relishes showing the play of light on the bath towels and the pedicurist's bald patch; the translucence of the towel draped over the chair is particularly well achieved.

Degas's portrait of *Estelle Musson* (ill. p. 32), done in 1872/73, is one of the daintiest in touch that Degas ever did. It is a flood of delicate whites, greys and pinks (in the gown) and background, with only the belt and her hairdo offering the eye an arresting purchase. Estelle looks lost on her canapé, hands resignedly folded in her lap. Not long after marrying René de Gas, Estelle had gone blind; and Degas shows her gaze by-passing us, a vacant gaze bent upon vacancy. It is a discreet and simple portrait of one woman's solitude and isolation – of one woman among his American relatives to whom he felt especially drawn.

The most important work resulting from his visit to the USA, however, was *The Cotton Exchange at New Orleans* (1873; ill. p. 31). Unfortunately none of the preliminary drawings have survived. The small picture shows fourteen men at work in his uncle's cotton office. Michel Musson is sitting in the foreground, checking the cotton; René de Gas is reading the paper; Achille de Gas is leaning by the window. Musson's partner James Prestridge is on a stool, discussing a deal with a client. The accountant is checking the books. Musson's son-in-law William Bell is offering the wares to a client, to inspect the quality.

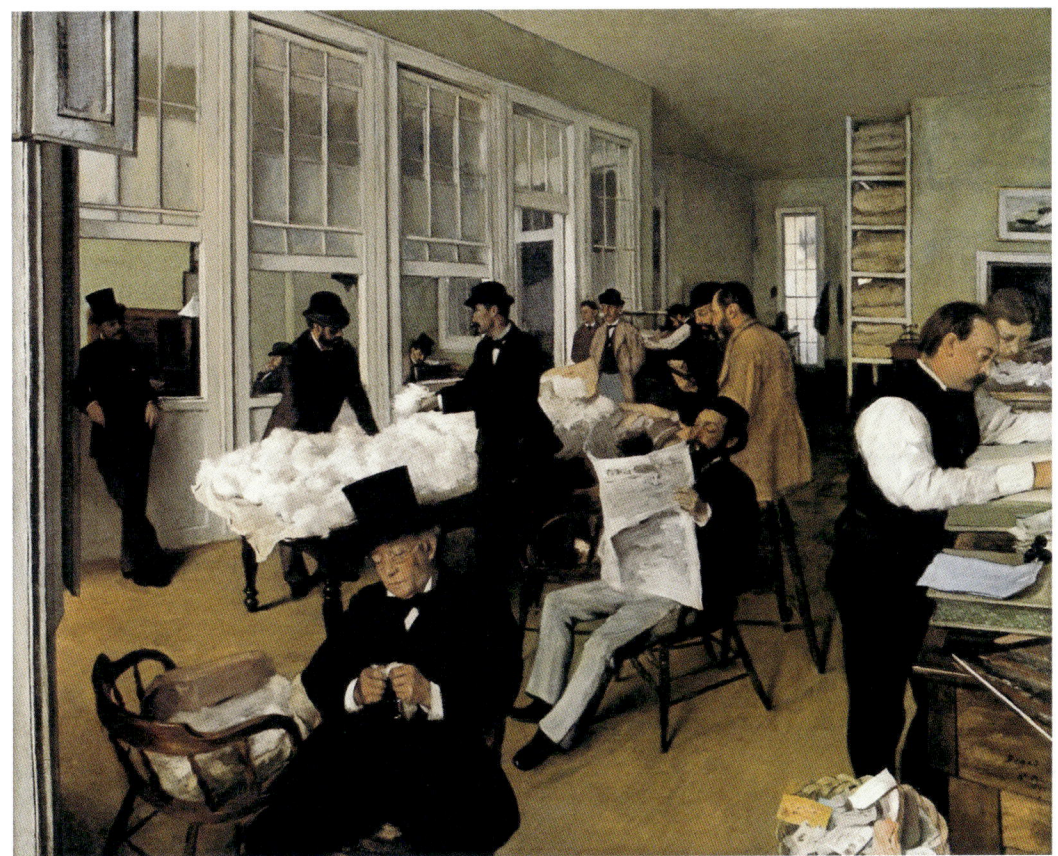

Everyone in the picture is quite absorbed in his own particular activity, which prompts an impression of quite remarkable lack of contact or interaction. The office is not an especially big one; yet these people seem to have nothing to do with each other. They

The Cotton Exchange at New Orleans (Portraits in an Office), 1873
Oil on canvas, 73 x 92 cm (28¾ x 36¼ in.)
Pau, Musée des Beaux-Arts

just happen all to be in the same place – which perfectly expresses a truth of the business world. Degas was planning a second, less complex version; his oil sketch *Cotton Dealers in New Orleans* (ill. p. 30) indicates what it might have been like. With fewer people in the scene, but a far more radical visual fragmentation, it achieves a similar effect.

The cotton office painting is no mere memento of an occasion, to record all Degas's hosts in one picture; it also had a commercial purpose. Degas was hoping that an English art dealer by the name of Agnews could interest a Manchester cotton mill owner in it. The self-assured Degas wrote to Tissot: "If ever a cotton manufacturer wanted a painter, I would be his man." But the deal fell through; and so it was that in 1876 the painting, with all its old master tonalities, was seen at the second Impressionist exhibition, and in 1878 became Degas's first work to be bought by a museum. His American relatives were evidently less enamoured of the works, for Degas ended up taking every one of them home with him to Paris.

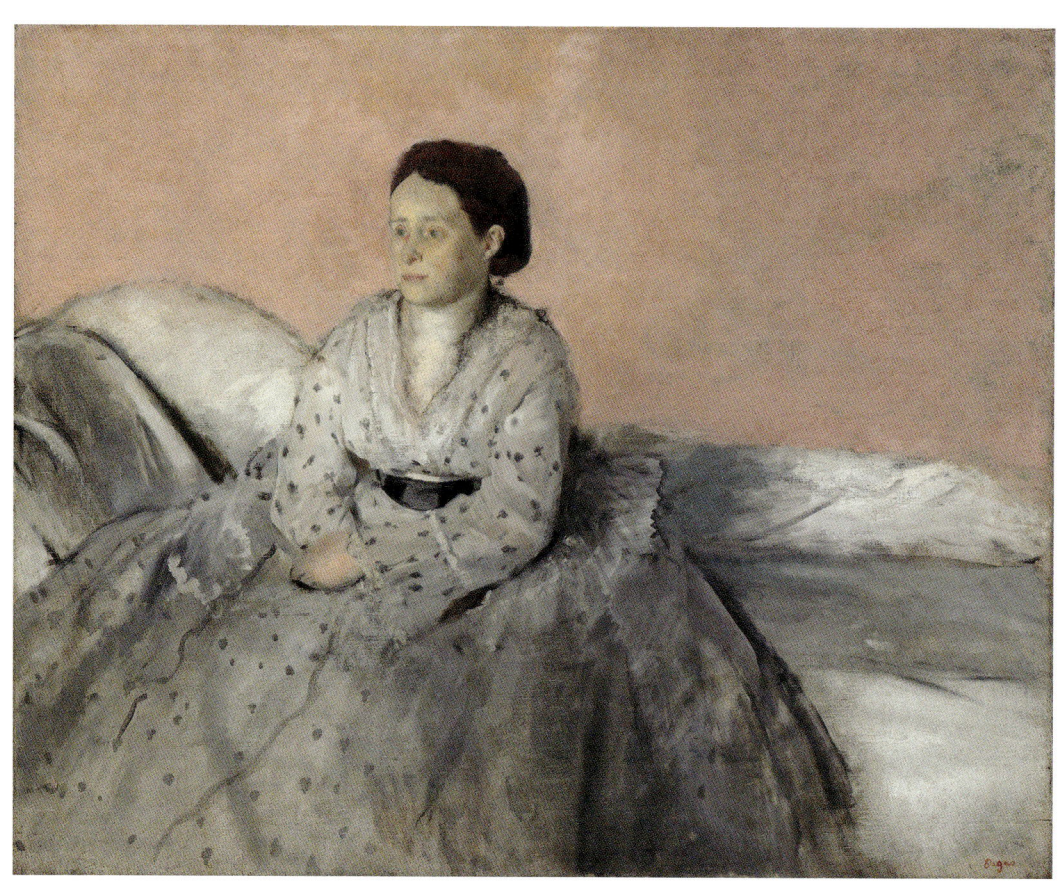

Estelle Musson, 1872/73
Oil on canvas, 72.9 x 92 cm (28¾ x 36¼ in.)
Washington, D.C., National Gallery of Art,
Chester Dale Collection

OPPOSITE
The Pedicurist, 1873
Oil on paper, mounted on canvas,
61 x 46 cm (24 x 18 in.)
Paris, Musée d'Orsay

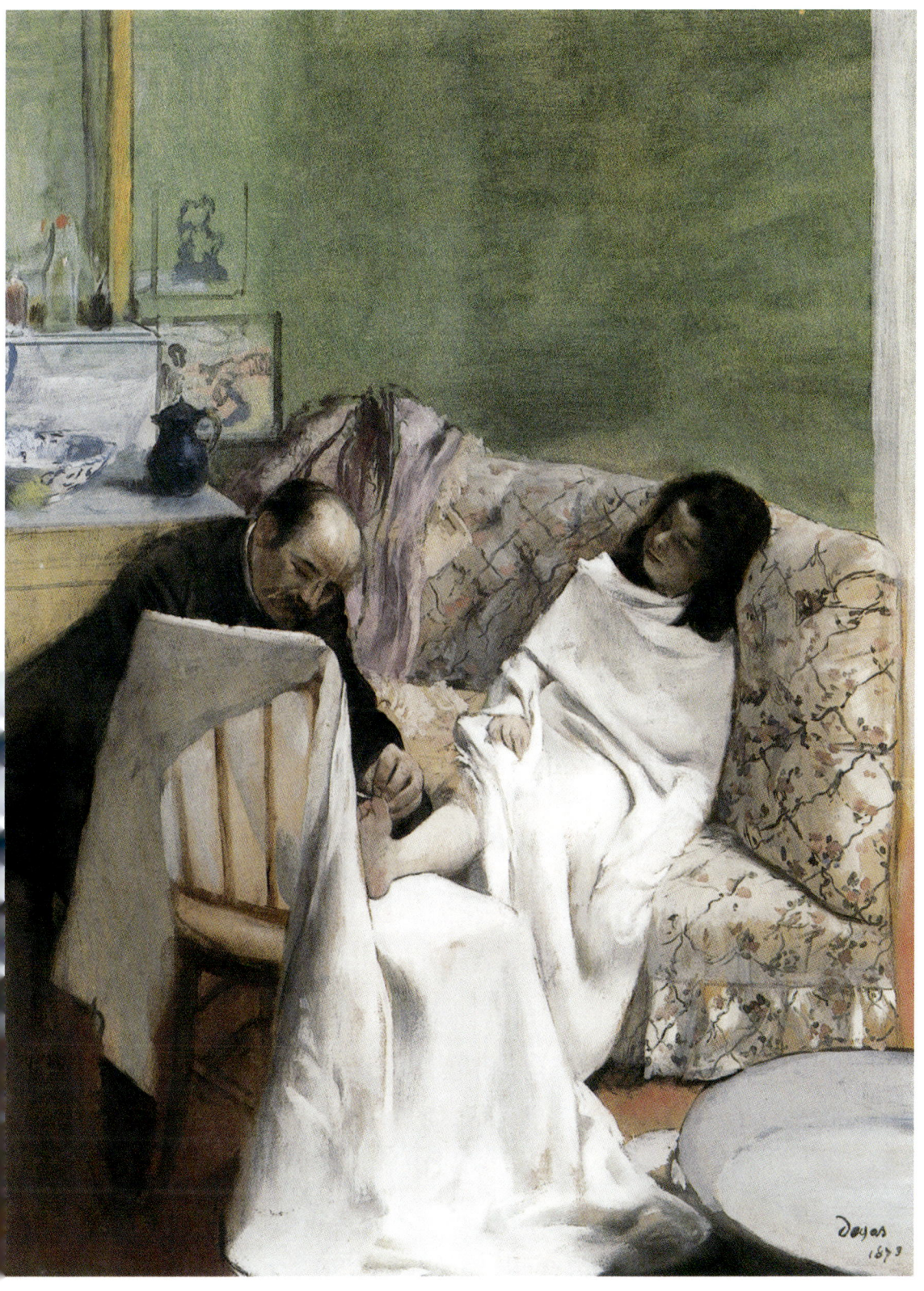

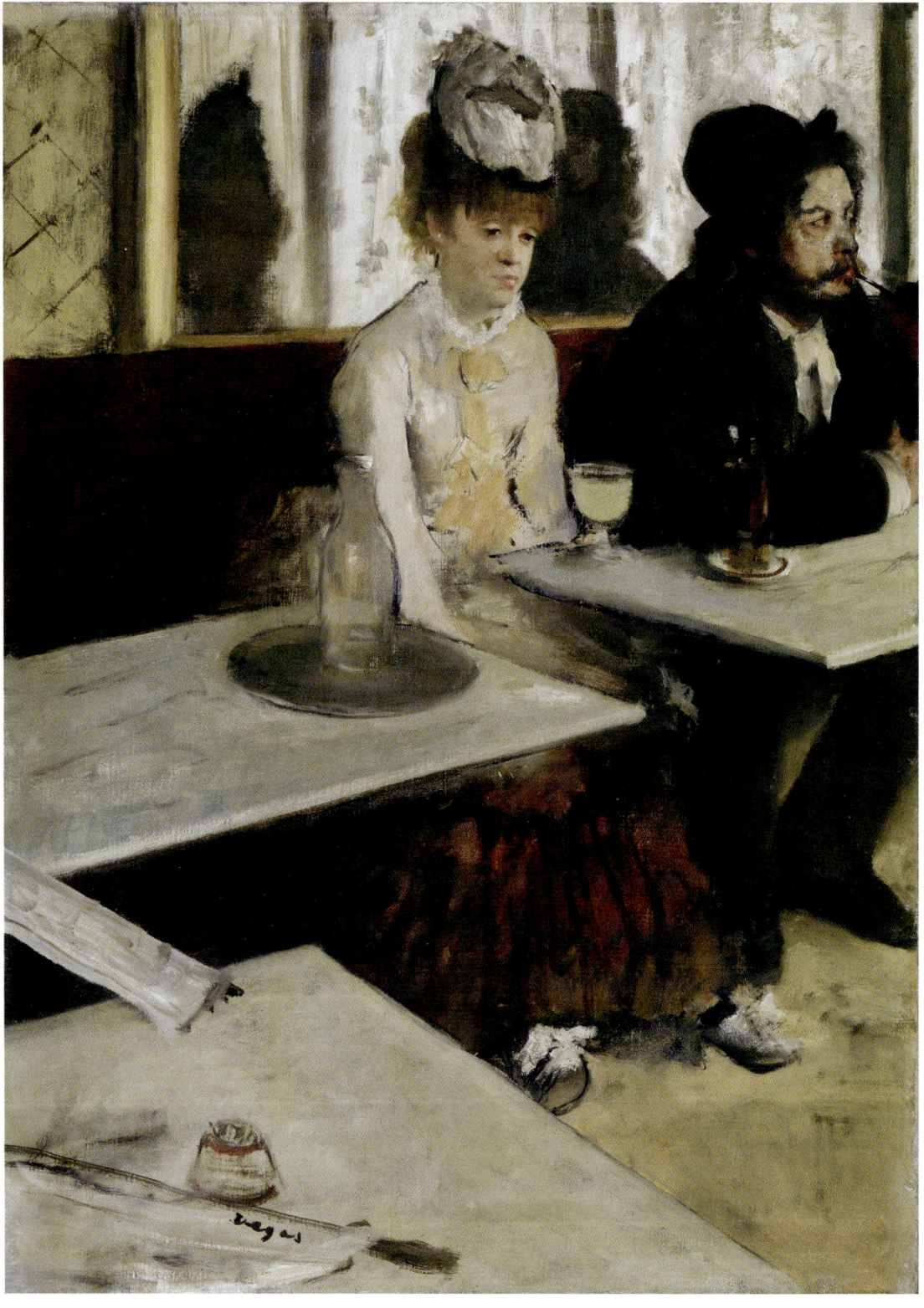

The Discovery of the Present Moment

After his return from America, Degas had closer contact with dealers such as Durand-Ruel, in an attempt
to bring his work to public attention independently of
the Salon. The attempt also produced a greater interest in contemporary subject matter. Not that the path
he took to modernity was a direct one; one of Degas's
cardinal tenets was that tradition and the present were
reconcilable. This was something that Manet and
Degas had in common; and by a curious coincidence
it was in the Louvre in 1862, when Degas was copying a Velázquez, that the two artists met. In the 1860s
Manet was at the centre of a group of artists who met
at the Café Guerbois, and during that period he played
the important role of a catalyst in Degas's development,
helping him take his bearings anew. He introduced him
to the young artists in his group, and Degas's sharp
tongue soon earned him a reputation. Degas did several portraits of his new friend, showing him as a cool,
stylish man.

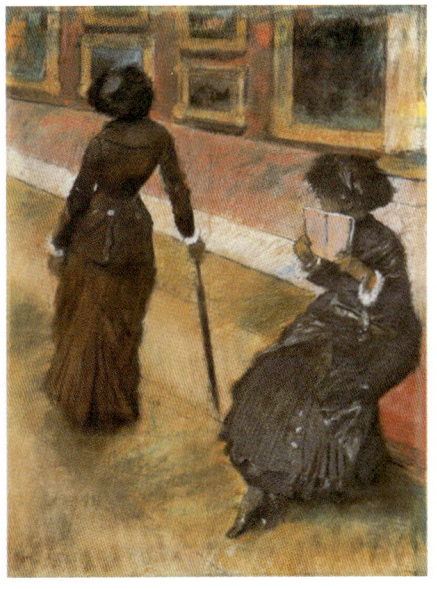

The Café Guerbois group included writer Zacharie Astruc, painters Antoine Guillemet and
Philippe Burty, and occasionally Alphonse Legros, J. M. Whistler, Camille Pissarro and Edmond
Duranty. Their vigorous debates, a continuous conflict of aesthetic polarities, provided Degas with
an entirely new mental environment. "Nothing could have been more gripping than those verbal
duels," Monet reminisced many years later. "They sharpened the wits and filled us all with an enthusiasm that lasted for weeks, till at last an idea would acquire final form." Degas was particularly close
to Duranty, a man about his own age, an art critic on the *Gazette
des Beaux Arts*. In 1856 Duranty had edited the shortlived magazine of aesthetics *Le Réalisme*; and in 1876, for the second Impressionist exhibition at the Galerie Durand-Ruel, he published "La
Nouvelle Peinture", a theory of Impressionism from a naturalist
point of view. Duranty declared that art had to confront the present and "catch the appearance of modernity as it is on the wing".

OPPOSITE
The Absinthe Drinker, 1875/76
Oil on canvas, 92 x 68 cm (36¼ x 26¾ in.)
Paris, Musée d'Orsay

ABOVE RIGHT
In the Louvre, c. 1879
Pastel, 71 x 54 cm (28 x 21¼ in.)
Private collection

In his 1879 portrait of Duranty (ill. p. 37), Degas seems to have been keeping faithfully to the letter of his sitter's law. We see the writer in his study, seated at a desk piled with papers, hemmed in by bookshelves. As Duranty's precept required, the subject's environment provides the key to his character. Still, Degas's contrast of the sitter's calm expression and eloquent gestures with a free and colourful style of painting for the setting goes far beyond mere definition of a social ambience.

In Duranty's eyes, though, he nonetheless remained "the inventor of social chiaroscuro". The expression seems apter to Degas's *Intérieur* of 1868/69, later titled *The Rape* (ill. p. 39). Degas himself never accepted this title, always referring to his "tableau de genre". To his way of thinking, as his notebooks reveal, the picture was primarily a study in nocturnal light effects. He was especially interested in "showing the feel of evening, lamplight, a candle, and so on".

By the pale light shed by an oil lamp we see two people in a room. To the left, a woman in her undergarments has collapsed on a chair; to the right, a man is leaning against the door, feet apart. Their positions suggest conflict: "hands can still be eloquent even in pockets," commented Duranty. The contrasting light and dark of the woman's gleaming shoulder and the man's huge shadow add to the effect. We are witnesses of a scene not intended for outsiders to see; compared with *The Pedicurist* (ill. p. 33), it is distinctly more delicate in character. Quite deliberately, Degas shows us a number of things that discharge their meaning only gradually: the still-made bed, the corset on the floor, the open scissors beside the jewellery on the table, and the small case with its salmon-red lining glowing in the soft light.

The painting contains quite a number of intensified details of this kind, such as the man's glinting eye in the dark. The scene, which anticipates one by Edvard Munch, not only records the woman's abuse and humiliation but also, in the contrast between aggression and defencelessness, suggests that neither will find any escape from the fraught tension between the sexes. Degas's painting effects a startling reversal of a teasing erotic theme of the 18th century, such as we see in Fragonard's

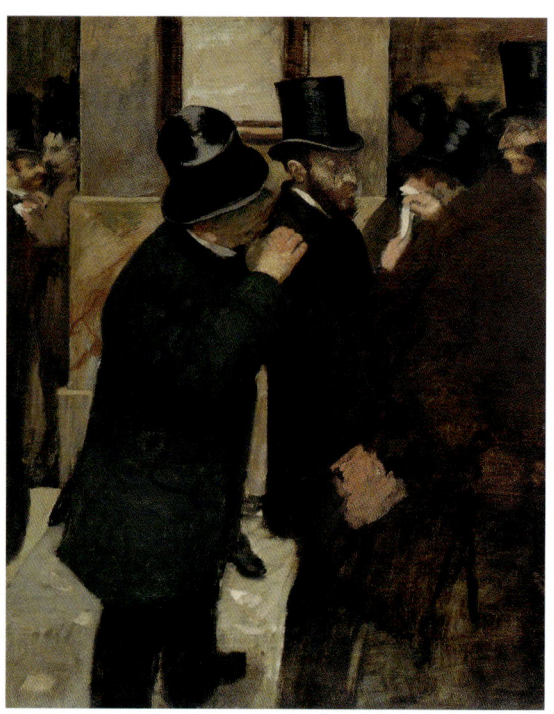

Portraits at the Stock Exchange,
c. 1878/79
Oil on canvas, 100 x 82 cm
(39¼ x 32¼ in.)
Paris, Musée d'Orsay

OPPOSITE
Edmond Duranty, 1879
Pastel and tempera, 100.9 x 100.3 cm
(39¾ x 39½ in.)
Glasgow Museums & Art Galleries,
The Burrell Collection

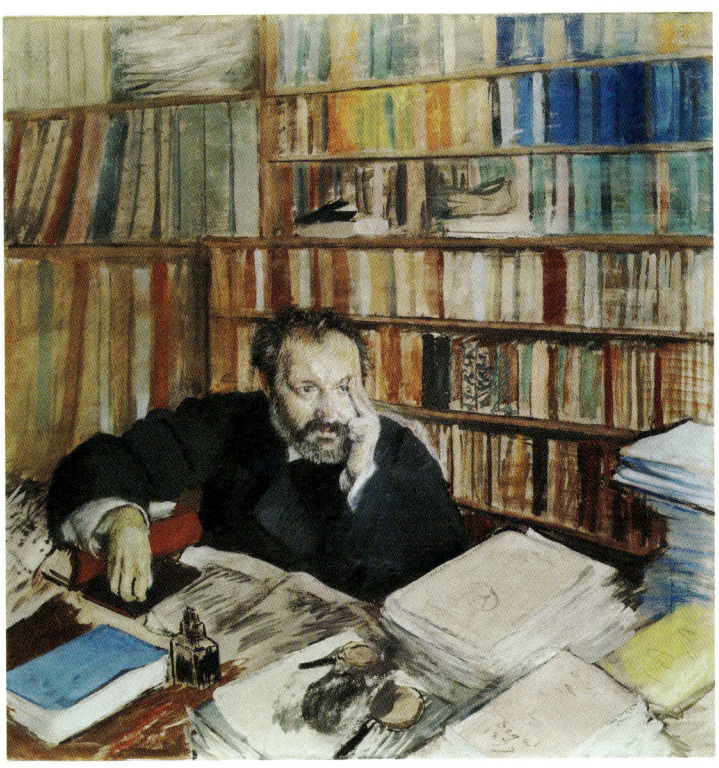

The Bolt (1785), where a playful preliminary tussle over the door-bolt serves to herald pastoral pleasures. In Degas's painting, both players are locked in – in the room and in their definitive isolation from each other.

In *Bad Mood* (ill. p. 38) Degas is less interested in his narrative content than in an aesthetic quality. The painting, done in 1869–71, shows a woman looking across at us; a piece of paper in her hand, she has just joined her husband where he is working. It looks as if talk between them has just been broken off; the tension is palpable. The two are moodily taking no notice of each other; their mutual alienation is of a subtler order than that in *The Rape*. Psychological distance is present in these people's physical proximity. Degas highlights his insight by framing both heads in the picture on the wall; the sheer movement in that picture provides a curious link between the two and a commentary on them.

Degas may have been thinking of paintings such as this one when he told Paul Poujaud that he too had taken "the Dutch road". He had a high opinion of Vermeer, and, unlike his Café Guerbois friends, valued Dutch art. He also liked the everyday scenes of the Le Nain brothers, about whom the advocate of realism Jules Champfleury had just published a book in 1862. To Degas, however, the discovery of the present moment was not merely a matter of contemporary genre work.

The Absinthe Drinker (ill. p. 34) is the best known of Degas's coffee house pictures, and indeed one of his most famous of all. It was painted in 1876 and the title was added later; Degas simply referred to it as *In the Café*. When he exhibited it at Brighton in 1876 it was bought despite savage criticism; in 1892 it was derided so loudly at another show that the collector decided to sell it.

Two friends, copper engraver Marcellin Desboutin and actress Ellen Andrée, sat as Degas's models for this café couple. At the time absinthe was a controversial drink; the high alcoholism rate

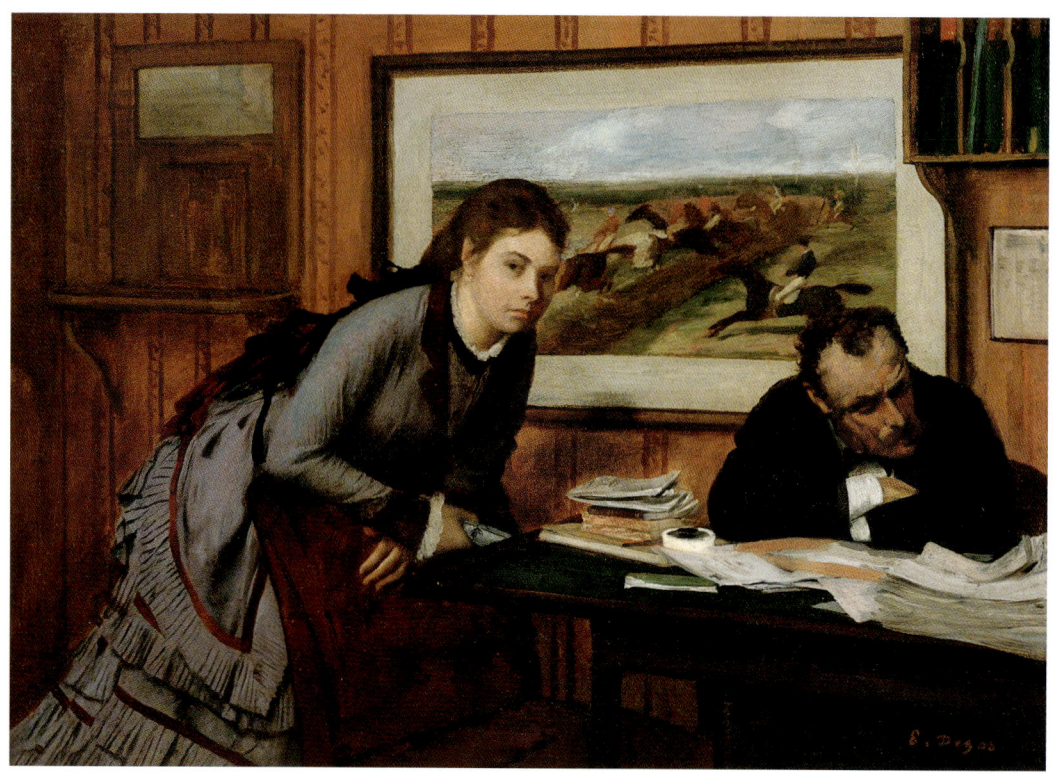

Bad Mood, c. 1869–71
Oil on canvas, 32.4 x 46.4 cm (12¾ x 18¼ in.)
New York, The Metropolitan Museum of Art,
H. O. Havemeyer Collection,
Bequest of Mrs H. O. Havemeyer, 1929

among the working classes was blamed on it, as Zola's novel *L'Assomoir* (also 1876) makes clear. The angle of vision, the positioning of the couple, and the arrangement of the tables, establish the picture as a section of a larger view. This sectionality emphasizes the isolation and dislocation of the two. It is not hard to see what Degas meant when he said that he wanted to "portray people in their customary, typical attitudes, above all with facial expressions that match their bodily postures". The sad weariness of their faces is made the more striking by the lack of clarity in the background. The shadowy reflections express alienation; they render the two even more isolated from each other. From our slant perspective on these figures, spaces and reflections it is quite impossible to keep a grip on any clarity of relationship or any defined perception.

When Manet destroyed a double portrait Degas painted (ill. p. 41) the friendship was temporarily at an end. Degas had painted his fellow-artist listening to his wife playing the piano; Madame Manet was considered a particularly gifted player of German music. Degas gave the painting to Manet; but the latter was dissatisfied with Suzanne's face and cut the canvas accordingly. In his outrage at this wilful damage, Degas returned a still life with plums to Manet (though he soon regretted it).

The two artists shared an affinity for certain subjects which now one and then the other would discover. Horse races were one such; so was boulevard life; so was the loneliness of city people in Paris, that great capital of the 19th century. But Manet's approach to these subjects was different from Degas's. Where Degas's eye tended to accelerate time, in Manet it seemed to stand still. Both recorded alienation as a problem of city life. They did not invent their stories, but attempted to find ways of rendering experience in visual terms.

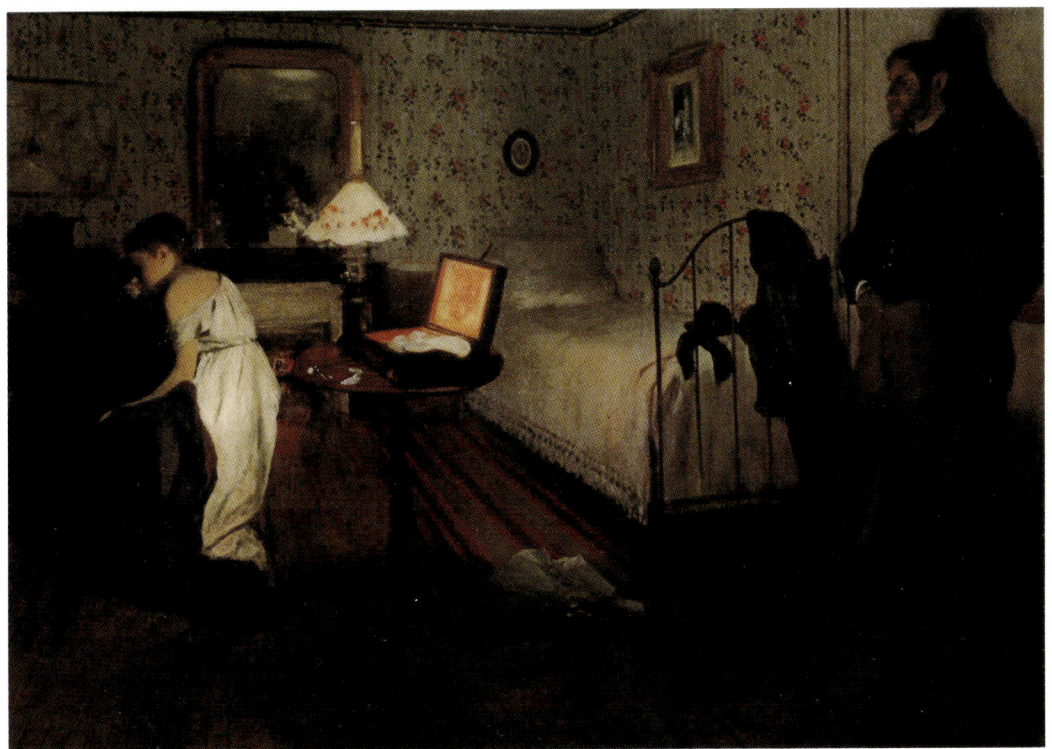

The Rape, c. 1868/69
Oil on canvas, 81.3 x 114.3 cm (32 x 45 in.)
Philadelphia Museum of Art,
The Henry P. McIlhenny Collection
in memory of Frances P. McIlhenny

Both Degas and Manet subscribed to Baudelaire's idea that the "heroism of modern life" was the true subject of modern art. For Baudelaire, modernity constituted an entirely new historical quality; in art, modern times were fundamentally different from all that had gone before. "The painter, the true painter, will be the one who can reveal the epic side of present-day life, who can use paint or draw lines to make us see and grasp how great we are and how poetic in our neckerchiefs and patent leather boots." Degas not only read Baudelaire's occasional newspaper articles; he studied him closely. In July 1869 Manet was begging Degas finally to return a volume of the complete works which he had borrowed. It is not impossible that Degas personally met Baudelaire at one of Manet's mother's soirées.

The Opera Orchestra (ill. p. 42) confirms Baudelaire's claim that "Parisian life is rich in poetic, wonderful subjects. Wonder is all about us, it soaks into us like air, but we do not see it." Starting with a portrait of his friend Désiré Dihau, who played bassoon in the opera house orchestra, Degas painted a group portrait of a number of friends, some of whom were not in fact musicians at all. Degas was not after absolute fidelity to fact; he wanted what seemed typical of a particular social group. The body language of figures was not meant to present them so much as be an integral part of them. The musicians are in the orchestra pit, with brightly-lit dancers' skirts and legs providing a contrast above them and the dark auditorium. This orchestra picture, with its three-part horizontal division, established a new kind of picture, and Toulouse-Lautrec was among those who were to follow Degas's example.

Degas's antecedents were to be found in the drawings of Daumier. But Degas was not using the sectional approach to unmask his subjects; rather, he wanted to stress the authenticity of his presentation. One disembodied head in the box at top left highlights this aim. A second treatment of

"Why I never married? Well, I was always afraid that my wife might look at one of my paintings and say: 'Mmm, very nice, dear ...' There's love and there's painting. And we only have one heart."
EDGAR DEGAS

the subject, the 1872 *Orchestra Musicians* (ill. p. 43), opposes stage and pit as two halves of the pictorial space. We are closer than ever, with the result that our spatial perception is almost changed to a perception of planes.

In turning to the contemporary Paris of coffee houses, racetracks, theatres and boulevards, Degas – unlike Manet – was out to capture the sense of present tempo: "One only paints what has gripped and affected one, that is to say, what is necessary." The sense of recorded fleeting moments matches the isolation of Degas's individuals. By driving his wedge into perception itself, fragmenting the stream of events, Degas was determining not only a way of seeing but the very content of the pictures.

When the Café Guerbois group regathered after the Franco-Prussian War, prospects at the Salon and with the critics looked bleaker than ever. As a result, Claude Monet's proposal of a group show financed by the members was readily adopted. It opened on the Boulevard des Capucines in April 1874. Degas had ten works in the exhibition. The group rather dryly called themselves the Anonymous Association of Artists, Painters, Sculptors and Engravers – which sounds more like a business co-operative than a group of avant-garde artists. One critic, Louis Leroy, writing in the satirical magazine *Le Charivari*, used the show to dismiss Monet as "impressionist", and the tag was rapidly adopted as the group's semi-official name. Supposedly Manet had said as early as 1867 that his art aimed solely to "convey his impressions". Degas always found the term unacceptable – mainly, perhaps, because he did not share the Impressionists' overriding interest in landscape and colour. He did not care to be tied down to one method of painting. Nonetheless, Degas was to participate in all the group exhibitions except that of 1882, and even organized one himself. His financial independence made him impatient with the others, and thus difficult to get on with; he made protégés of Italian painters such as de Nittis or Raffaelli and made no bones about including them in the show, to the annoyance of his friends. Gustave Caillebotte felt compelled to voice his criticism: "He is quite intolerable. But we have to concede that he is extremely talented."

Doubtless there is truth to the criticism. Degas used the group and the exhibitions high-handedly to promote himself. Within the group he insisted on his own independence; yet he made no demur when art critics lauded him as the leader of the new school of painters. His strategy seems to have been to show off his own diversity at the exhibitions, for he always entered works that were thematically and technically very varied. In 1874, for example, along with the colourful *At the Races in the Countryside* (ill. p. 47) he also exhibited *Rehearsal of a Ballet on Stage* (ill. p. 56), in a style resembling grisaille work. In 1876 the meticulous *The Cotton Exchange at New Orleans* (ill. p. 31) hung alongside the eccentric *The Absinthe Drinker* (ill. p. 34). In 1879, as well as the dazzling *Mlle La La at the Circus Fernando* (ill. p. 72) he had painted fans in the show. He also regularly submitted pastels and drawings – which had been one of his reform proposals for the Salon in 1870. Degas's technical and thematic versatility would have struck visitors to the exhibitions all the more powerfully when the hanging policy was changed: instead of mixing works throughout, the artists hung in separate rooms of their own. And so, with his Impressionist role to support him, with Paris and London successes to notch up and the active help of Durand-Ruel, and with a steadily-growing number of collectors such as Jean-Baptiste Faure, Henri Rouart and Captain Henry Hill buying his work, Degas soon became one of the pre-eminent figures on the art scene of his day.

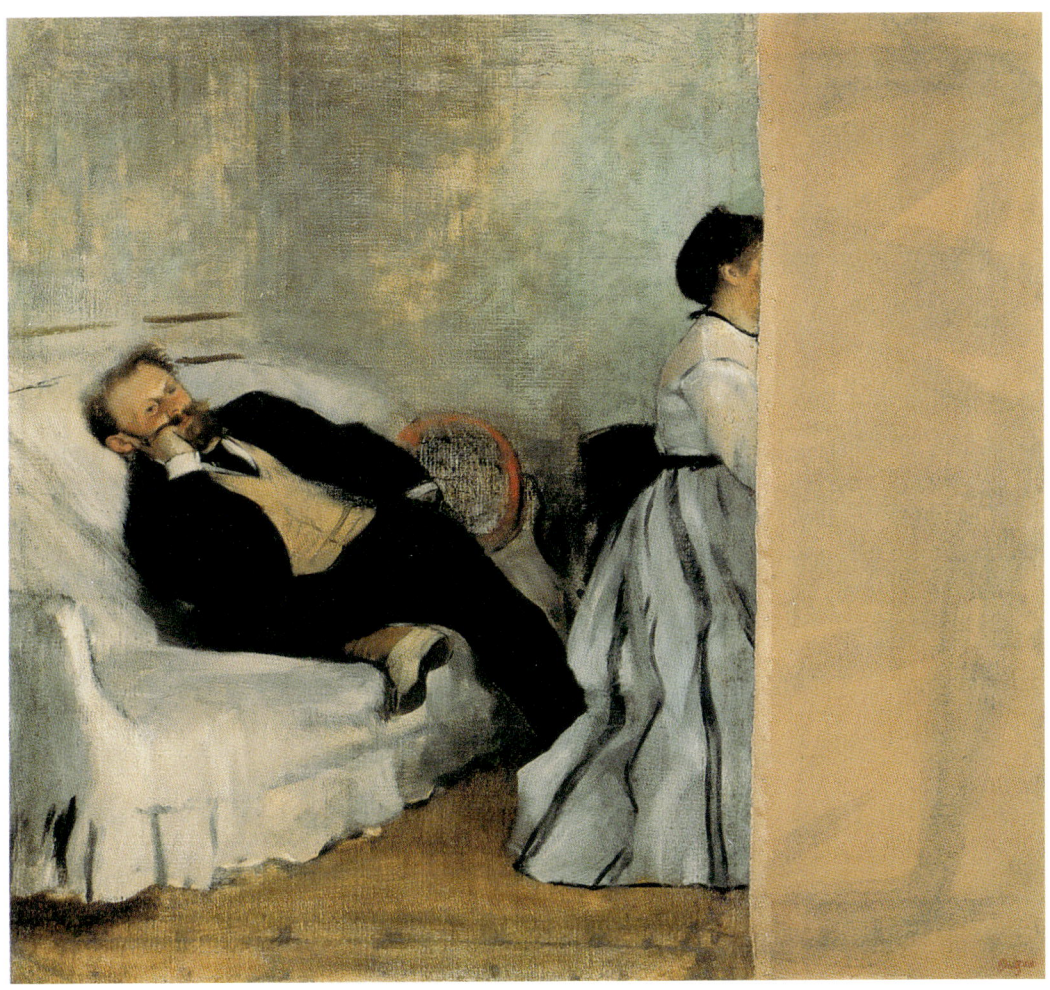

"A painting requires a little mystery, some vagueness, and some fantasy."

EDGAR DEGAS

Monsieur and Madame Édouard Manet, c. 1868/69
Oil on canvas, 65.2 x 71.1 cm (25¾ x 28 in.)
Kitakyushu, Japan, Municipal Museum of Art

PAGE 42
The Opera Orchestra, c. 1870
Oil on canvas, 56.5 x 46.2 cm (22¼ x 17¾ in.)
Paris, Musée d'Orsay

PAGE 43
Orchestra Musicians, 1872
Oil on canvas, 63.6 x 49 cm (25 x 19⅜ in.)
Frankfurt am Main, Städel Museum

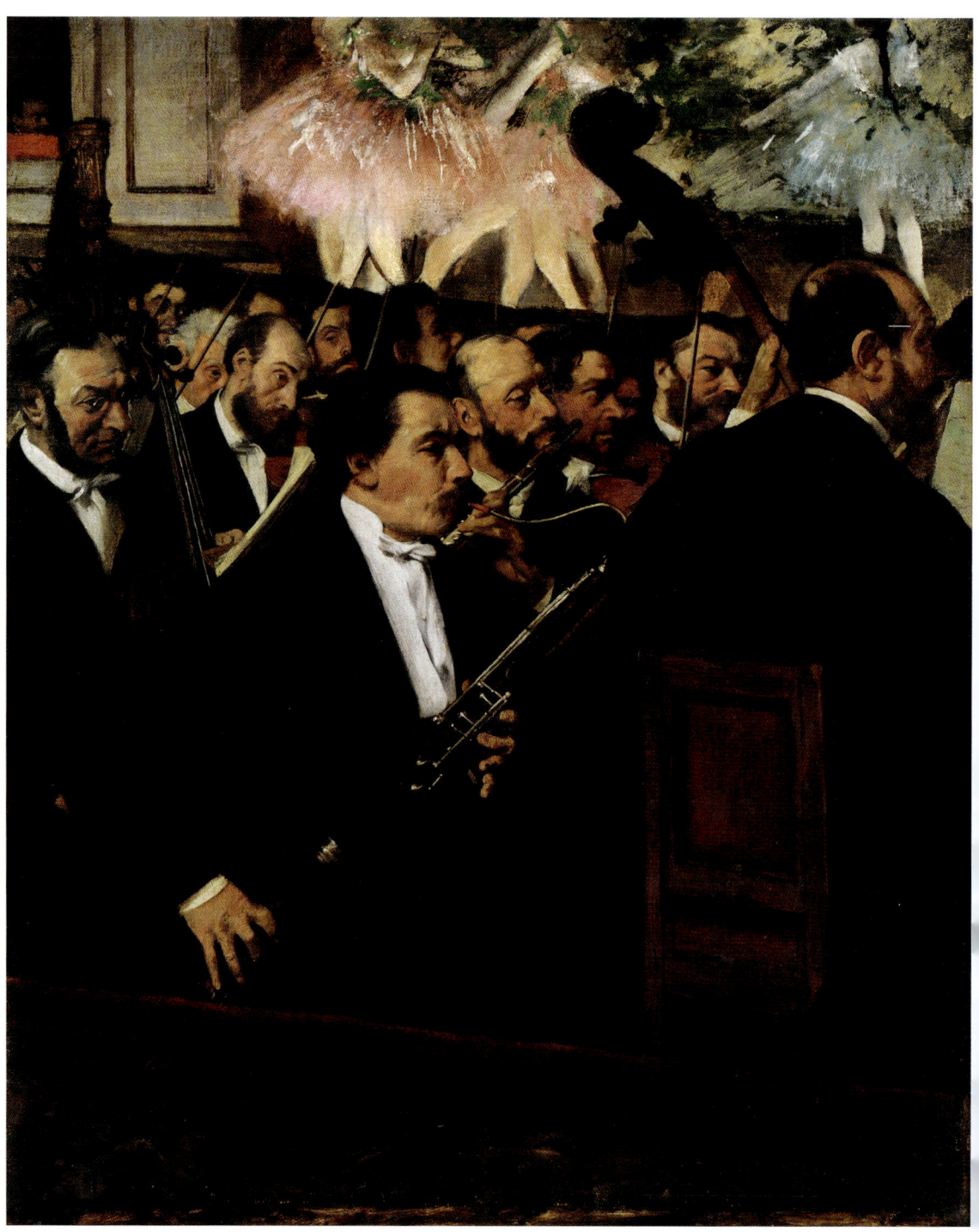

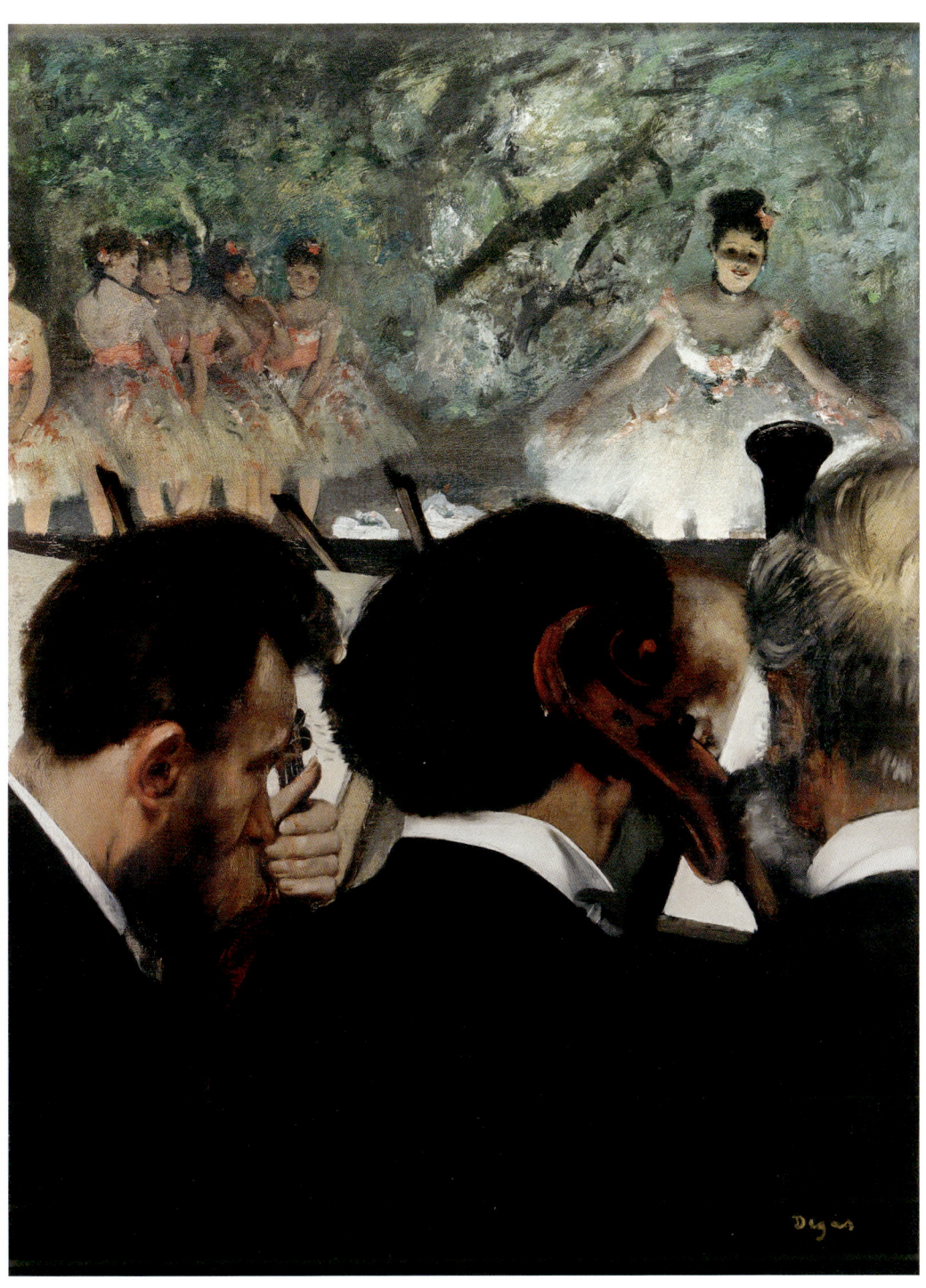

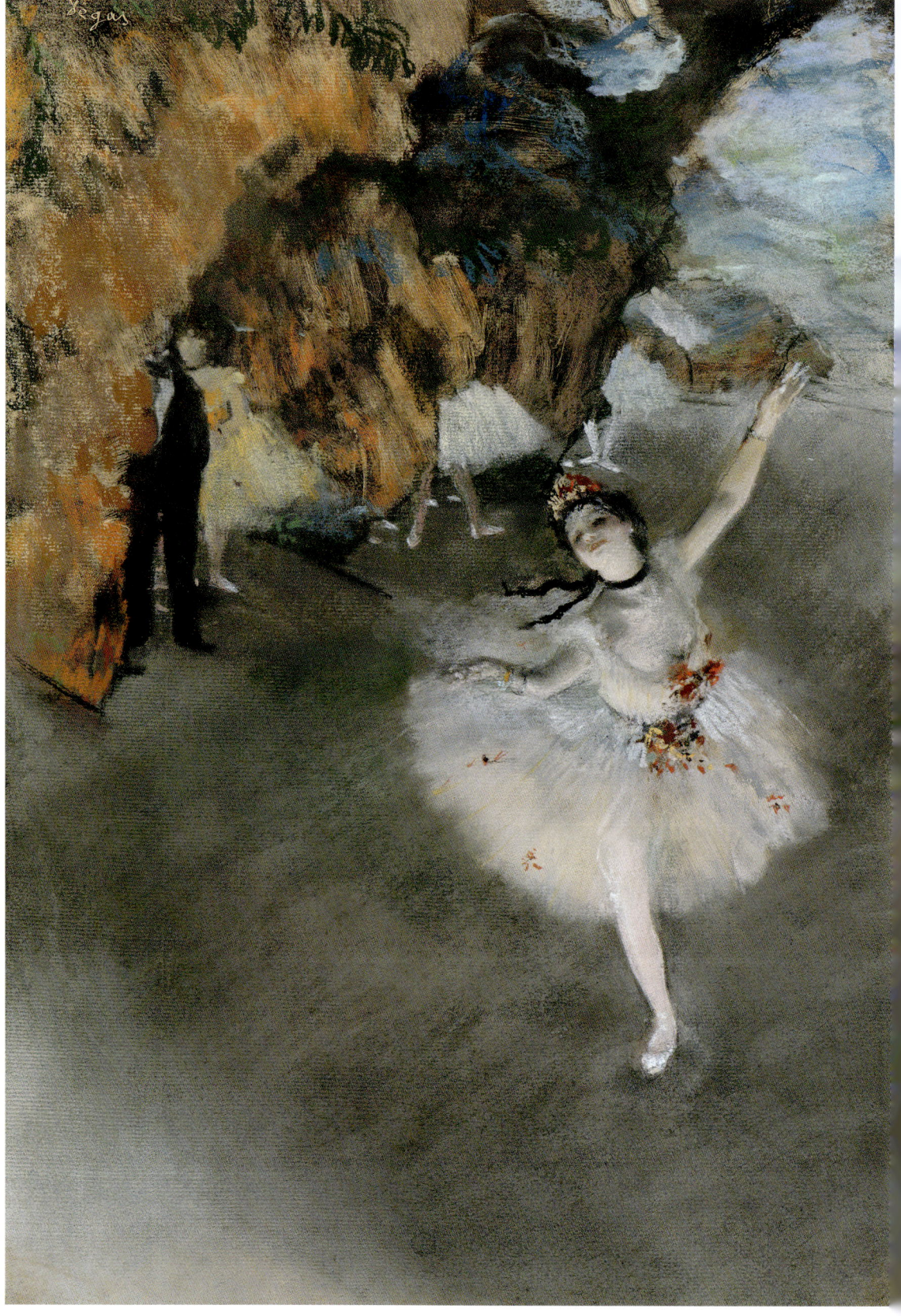

Jockeys and Ballerinas

The name of Degas is chiefly associated with certain subjects. Racetrack and ballet scenes are as closely identified with him as water lilies are with Monet or Mt Sainte-Victoire with Cézanne. Degas discovered racetracks as a subject for art in the early 1860s; his interest had already been expressed in other pictorial contexts, though, and merely entered a new phase.

Horse racing, a sport imported from England, was a novelty in Paris at that time. The Longchamp course was opened at Napoleon III's initiative, with new grandstands in a redesigned Bois de Boulogne, in 1857. The emperor was himself an active patron of horse racing and was even involved in drawing up the rules. French horses won important races in England in 1865, and soon the races were pulling crowds of thousands and had become one of the growing metropolis's major attractions. The Jockey Club, with its blend of money, sport and politics, called the shots. Zola, in his novel *Nana*, left a splendid description of the Longchamp Grand Prix.

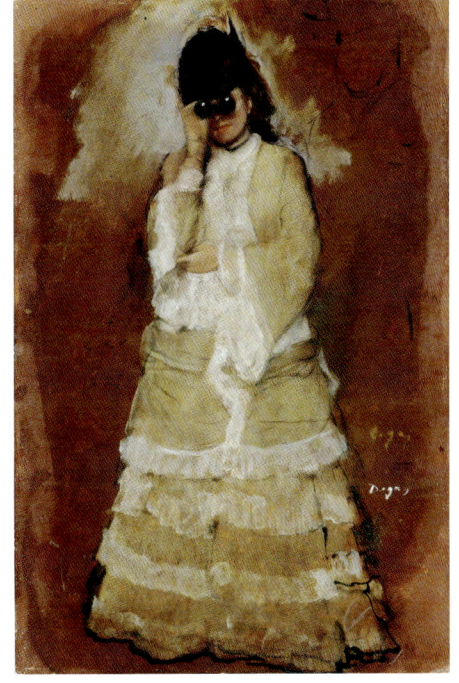

Degas rarely painted the course itself. Paintings such as *Race Horses in Front of the Stands* (1866–68; ill. p. 46) or *False Start* (1869–71) are exceptions. In general, the location is not entirely clear; the factory chimneys visible in *Race Horses,* for instance, could not in fact be seen from Longchamp. In that painting, Degas recorded a fleeting interplay of light and movement. A sense of restlessness builds through the depth to the nervous horse in the background. From the left, our gaze follows changes of light, from the shady grandstand across the parasols held by some of the ladies to the brightness of the paddock. Against the shades of ochre, the light and shadow set up a complex interplay. In *Horses at the Longchamp Race Track* (1871) the sheer poetry of horses' movements is not dissimilar to the mood of *Race Horses in*

OPPOSITE
The Star or ***Dancer on the Stage***, 1876/77
Pastel on monotype, 58 x 42 cm (23 x 16½ in.)
Paris, Musée d'Orsay

ABOVE RIGHT
Lady with Eyeglasses, c. 1877
Oil on canvas, 48 x 32 cm (19 x 12½ in.)
Dresden, Galerie Neue Meister,
Staatliche Kunstsammlungen

Front of the Stands, but now the spectators are far off and what is important is the colour qualities of the landscape and the jockeys' tops.

At the Races in the Countryside (ill. p. 47), painted in 1869, is a moderately colourful work using delicate silvery greys; Degas showed it at the first Impressionist exhibition. The race itself is in the background; the foreground is occupied by a family scene centred on a baby, with the nurse, mother, father and (Degas's irony!) even the dog atop the box all giving the infant their undivided attention. The family is the Valpinçon family. The picture's point lies in the contrast between the action in the background and the foreground self-absorption of the family; and Degas highlights the contrast by emphasizing a random quality in the cropping of visual subjects. The barouche at left has been sliced in half by the edge of the painting. The race spectators are all isolated, wrapped up in themselves. And yet, the composition is the product of exact consideration: the horses' ears, for instance, are precisely in the vertical centre, while the tip of the mother's parasol is squarely in the middle (in terms of width). By allowing the principle of random selection into his compositional organization, Degas has not only intensified the contrast of near and far, empty space and populated areas, but has also established a new visual vitality. It has to be added, though, that by far the majority of his race course scenes focus on jockeys and not spectators, even if the broad social spectrum at the races is plainly very closely observed. The *Lady with Eyeglasses* (c. 1877; ill. p. 45) is gazing straight towards us, in a parodic reflection of the brief racing season's code of seeing and (most importantly for the city sophisticate) being seen.

Race Horses in Front of the Stands, *c.* 1866–68
Oil on canvas, 46 x 61 cm (18 x 24 in.)
Paris, Musée d'Orsay

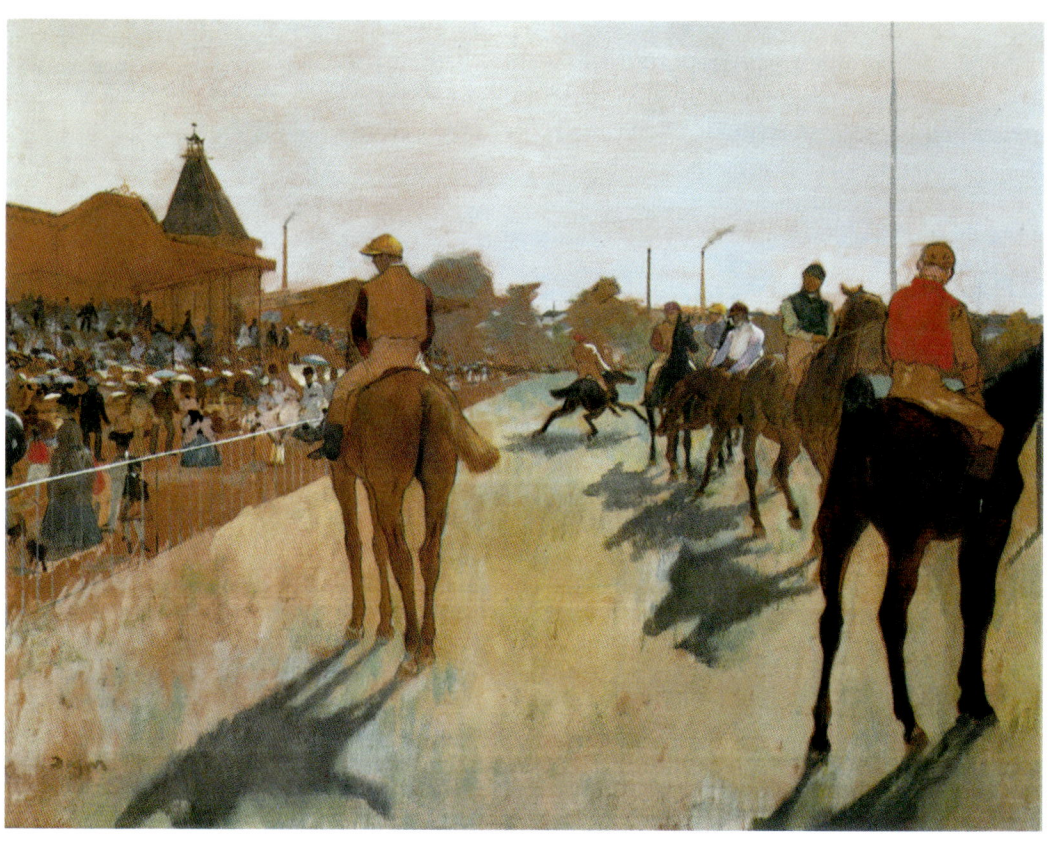

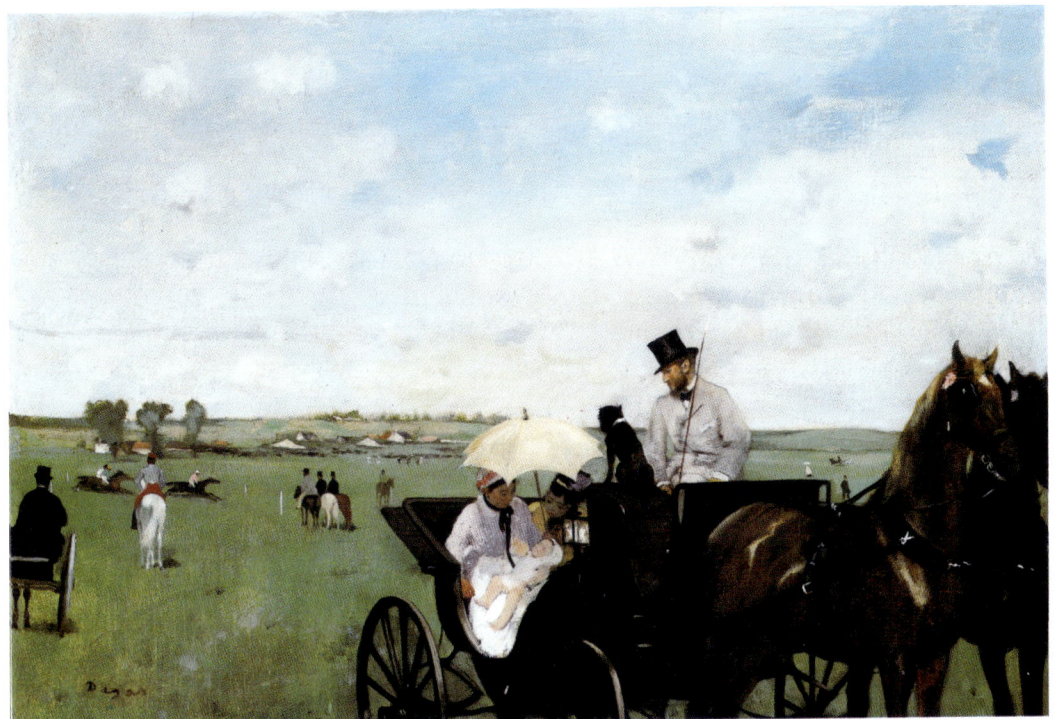

From time to time Degas went to the races together with Manet, and on one occasion drew him there. Manet too did a series of racing pictures, though they are distinctly different from his friend's. His *Horse Racing at Longchamp* (1867) shows

At the Races in the Countryside, 1869
Oil on canvas, 36.5 x 55.9 cm (14¼ x 22 in.)
Boston, Museum of Fine Arts,
1931 Purchase Fund

the finish, with the horses hurtling frontally towards us. A perspective *tour de force,* the work arrestingly captures the sheer speed of the race. Though Degas's *Race Horses in Front of the Stands* is not dissimilar in its approach to perspective, the painting is not out to record speed. Movement in the Degas picture is seen frozen, and the style in which it is painted is correspondingly meticulous. Rather than being an undifferentiated crowd, Degas's spectators are a host of individual figures.

At the Races, Amateur Jockeys (ill. p. 49) brings us closer to the action, and the spatial values have been compressed. It is difficult to see how the figures relate; they seem to be there at the dictates of chance. The bunching of figures at the right displaces attention from the centre of the picture and, together with the overlapping and cropping of horses and carriage, creates a strong impression of a chance momentary glimpse. This dimension of chance is no mere display of adroitness or compositional ingenuity, as the parallel of the cantering horse and the train in the background shows. The two movements, horse and train, echo each other: Is Degas, we wonder, commenting on the rivalry of the two, or is he merely indulging in an ironic game?

In the mid-1870s his interest in the subject slackened. Colours and purely visual effects began to interest him more than the races as such. *Jockeys* (ill. p. 51), painted in 1882/83, is a jostling canvas that gives us a sense of being in the thick of it. Degas merely suggests his visual effects, and we are there, in the midst of a bustling scene. These hints are enough; we can easily reconstruct the agitated mood from the fragments we are offered. The sense of movement is not a spatial one here; rather,

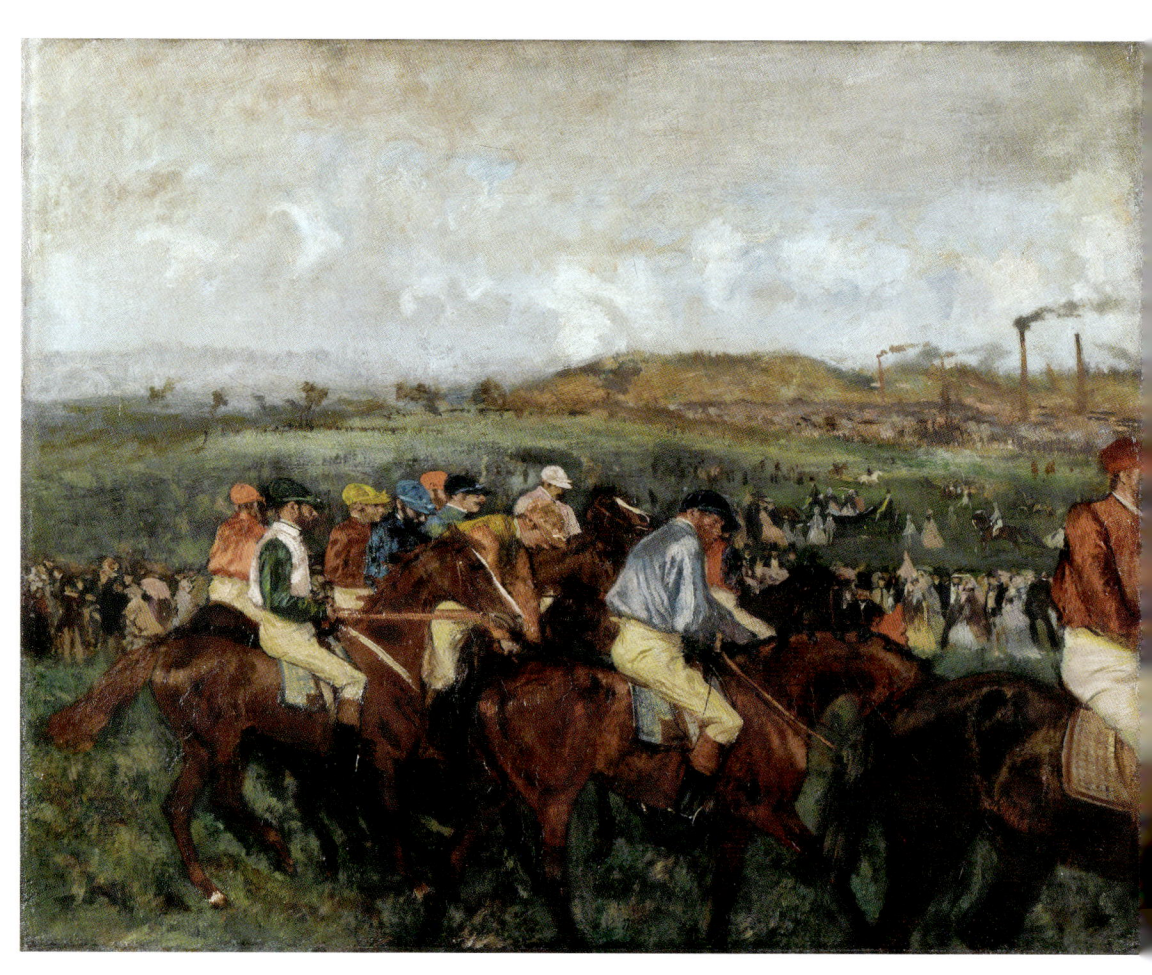

Gentleman's Race. Before the Start, 1862
Oil on canvas, 48.5 x 61.5 cm (19 x 24¼ in.)
Paris, Musée d'Orsay

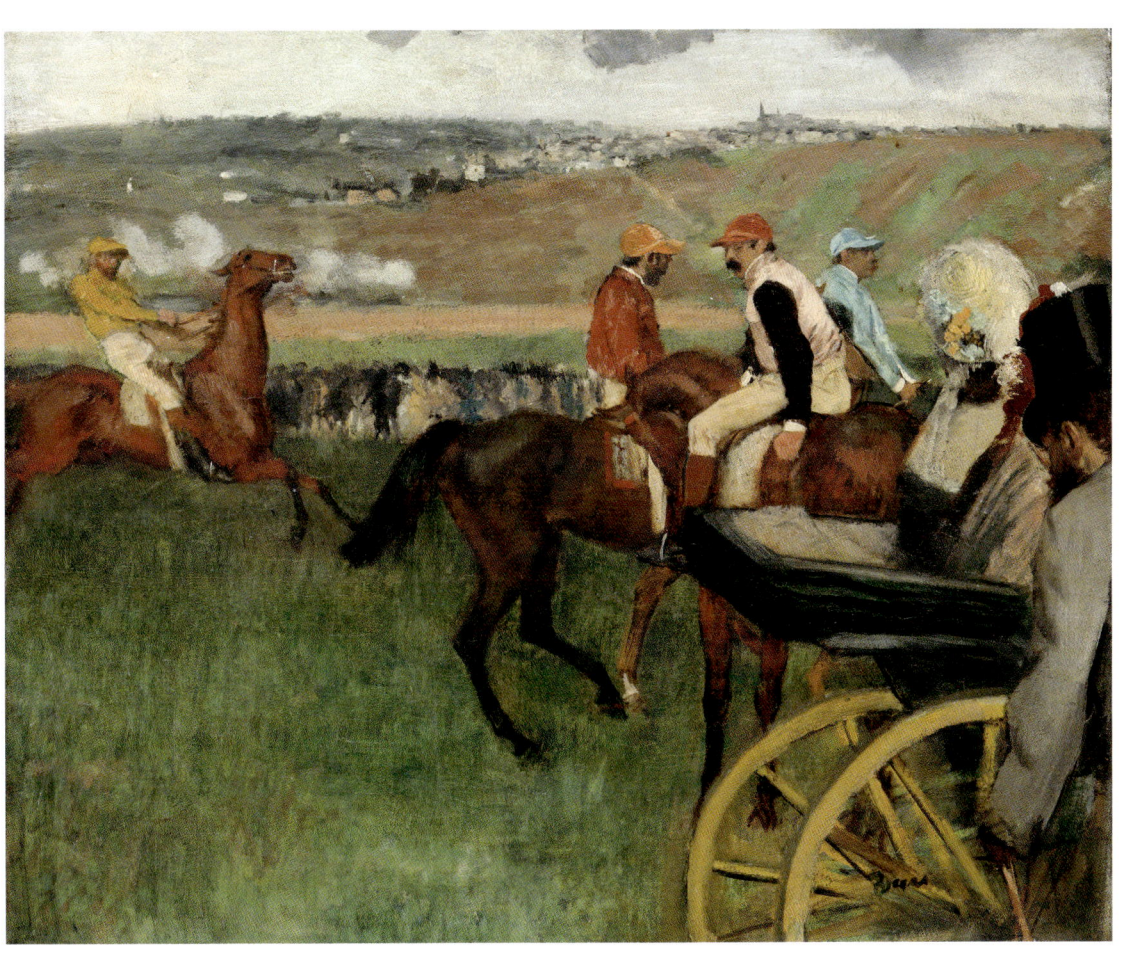

At the Races, Amateur Jockeys, 1876–87
Oil on canvas, 65.2 x 81.2 cm (25¾ x 32 in.)
Paris, Musée d'Orsay

it derives from the compositional pressure generated by proximity and by the brightly contrasting colours of the jockeys' tops.

Degas rarely painted the actual races. He preferred to look elsewhere. He was fascinated by preparations for a race, by false starts and the wait before the start, by the tension and the release of tension – all of them moments hardly laden with action. This is one good reason why the *art* in Degas's work need not be sought in his subjects. For Degas, racetracks were primarily stages on which movement could be observed. Photographs had recently opened up ways of watching that movement more closely; in 1862 Nadar had published photos of horse racing, and it is possible that in 1878 Degas was present at Meissonier's studio to witness Edward Muybridge's experiments that revolutionized the photography of movement. Using horizontal sequentiality or diagonal lines of horses, most of them either entering or leaving the visual area of the picture, Degas was capturing entire sequences of movement. Even the most fleeting of movements was recorded by means of hard, precision work; it was Degas's conviction that "one conveys a sense of the truth by means of untruth". His racetracks merely afforded backdrops for movement, and his jockeys were no more than conceptual figures going through imaginary motions calculated by the artist.

Even more than his jockeys, it is Degas's ballerinas who have determined his popular image to this day. From 1870 he increasingly painted ballet subjects; among other reasons, they were easier to sell, and the family bankruptcy left Degas needing money. Durand-Ruel the dealer later reported that even in those early years the collectors "were forever only wanting dancing girls". Half in jest, Degas referred to them as "my merchandise". First he painted a series of ballet rehearsal pictures. *Dance Studio of the Opera, Rue Le Peletier* (1872; ill. pp. 60/61) shows ten ballerinas being examined in the great hall. The white-clad Louis François Mérante, instructor and subsequently *maître de ballet* at the opera house, is giving orders which the dancers have to follow. Those who are not busy exercising are watching the ballerina currently being examined with close attention. The work is organized around the polarity of group and single figure; ochres and greys are prevalent, with occasional coloured bows to add highlights. The scene, remarkable for the rigour of its composition, has a distinctive energy centre in the vacant chair at the fore.

In the 1874 *Rehearsal of a Ballet on Stage* (ill. p. 56), by contrast, Degas is out for atmosphere. The glare of the limelight contrasts with the rich shadows in the deep, dark stage. Degas maintained that "the attraction lies not in showing the source of light but in showing its effects". Arguably the non-colourful chiaroscuro of this work is some kind of allusion to the new visual technique of photography. The man straddling the chair functions as an observer within the scene we observe; and we notice that not only the lighting but also the unaccustomed emptiness of the theatre makes an eerie impression.

As in the orchestra pictures of the late 1860s, Degas in his ballet scenes explored the subject's potential through variations on the theme· In the 1873–76 *The Dance Class* (ill. p. 10) he has grouped some twenty girls and one or two mothers too, watching or comforting their daughters. Dominating the scene (and painted in as an afterthought) is instructor Jules Perrot, with the huge stick he used to beat out a rhythm. This trial session under the famed teacher is taking place in the rehearsal rooms of the old opera house in Rue Peletier, which has long since burned down. Despite the working of the scene as an overall harmony, the girls are individuals. One is adjusting her neckband or bow, another is sitting on the grand piano scratching her back. These individual gestures have become part of an overall impression, though; in creating this, Degas can still use the smallest scrap of individual detail, such as one girl hastily reaching up to her earring.

In 1874 Degas painted *Dancing Examination* (ill. p. 58), at first glance a very similar picture, but in fact harder and less unified than the first. Degas has dispensed with the marble pilasters; this time,

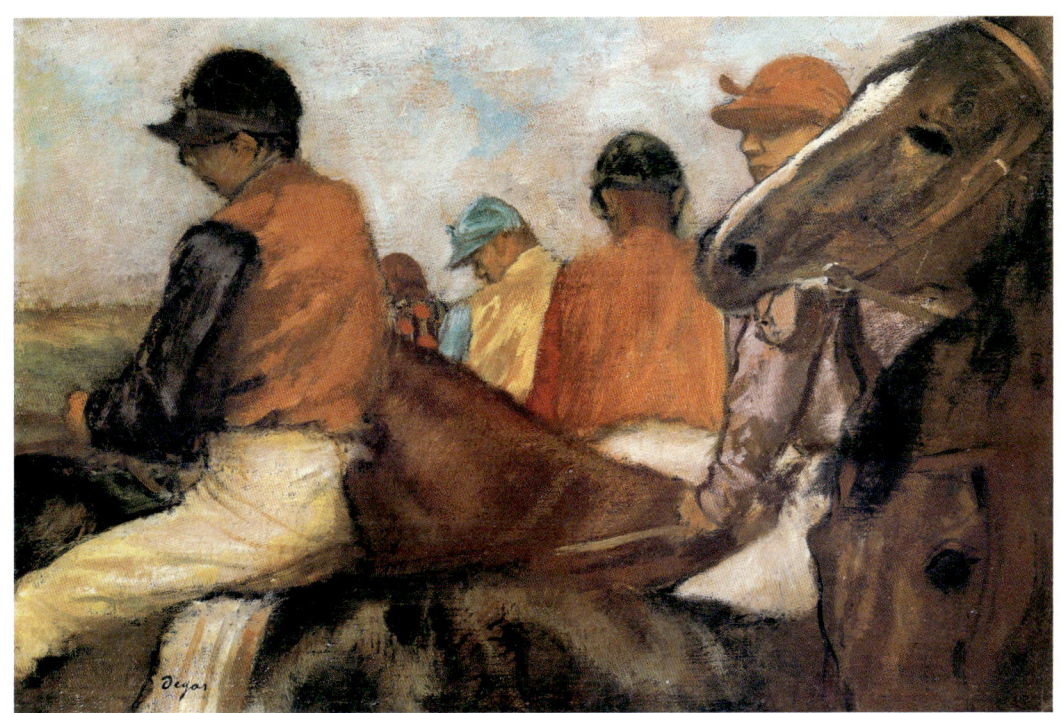

"*You must aim high, not in what you are going to do at some future date, but in what you are going to make yourself do today. Otherwise working is just a waste of time.*"

EDGAR DEGAS

Jockeys, 1882/83
Oil on canvas, 26.4 x 39.9 cm (10½ x 15¾ in.)
New Haven, Connecticut, Yale University
Art Gallery, Gift of J. Watson Webb B. A.,
and Electra Havemeyer Webb

PAGES 52/53
The Dancing Class, *c.* 1870
Oil on wood, 19.7 x 27 cm (7¾ x 10¾ in.)
New York, The Metropolitan Museum of Art,
H. O. Havemeyer Collection,
Bequest of Mrs H. O. Havemeyer, 1929

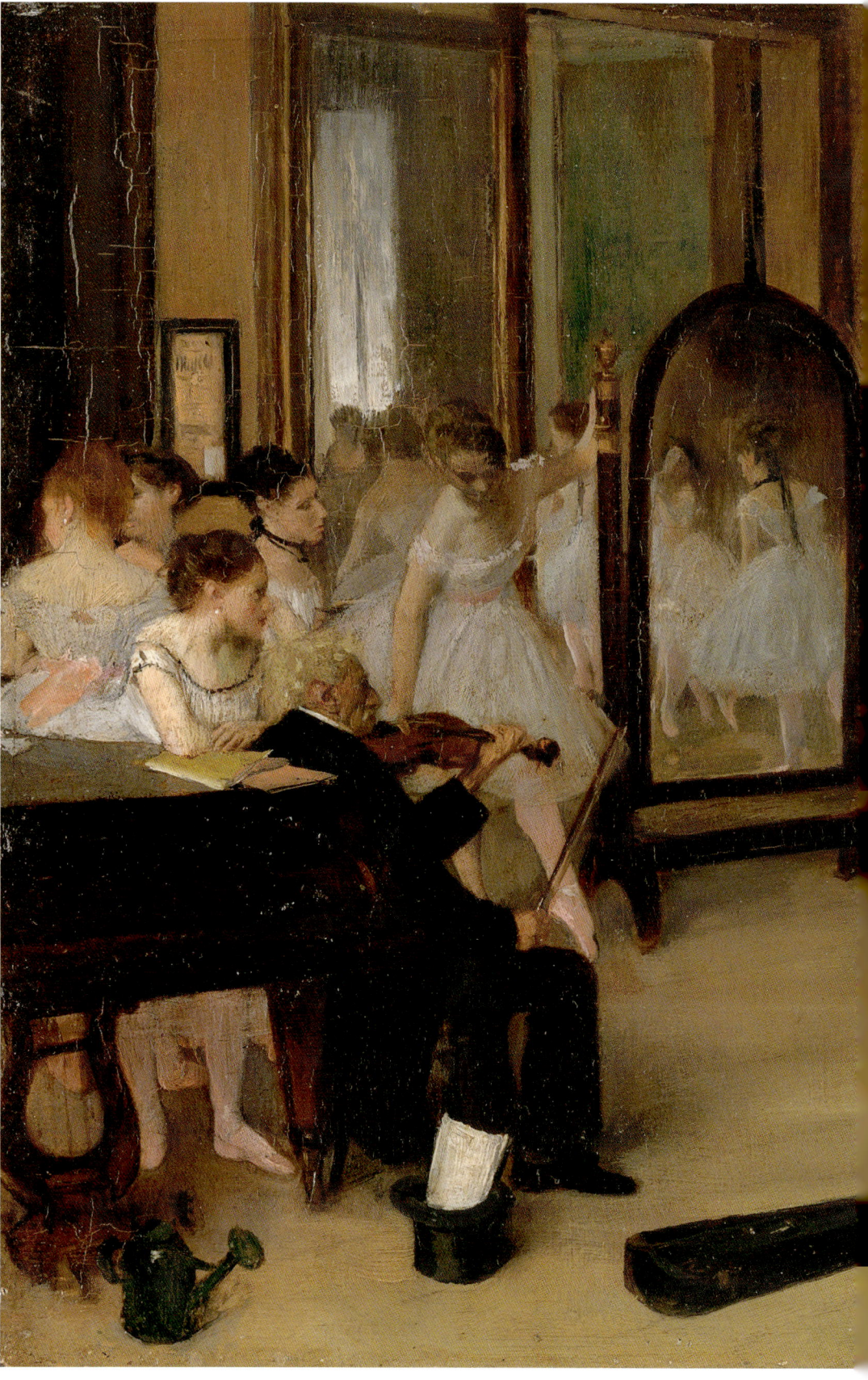

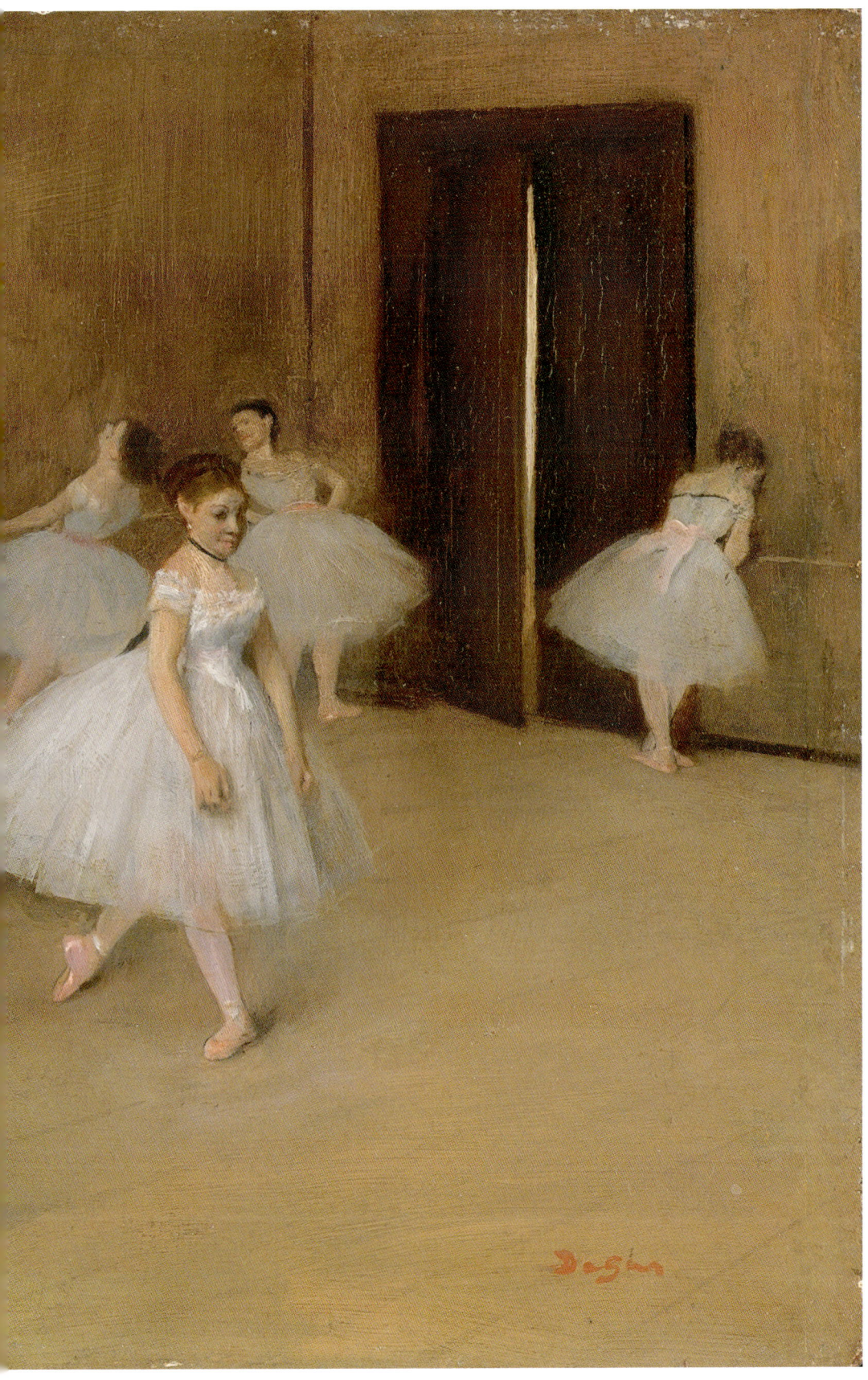

To Mademoiselle Salanville

Everything that the fine word mime implies,
Everything that is said of the ballet,
The body's silent eloquence – all they say
Of physical mystery in their witty lies,

Those who would pin down Woman as she flies,
Forever on the wing, severely gay,
A butterfly soul, immortal for a day,
Alive, unlike a book where pleasure dies –

All that, and the grace of an Atalanta,
The artful artless graces, you have, dancer.
The dance of tradition, the being and seeming,

The secret of the forest: at every dawn,
At every step I take, you are in my dreaming –
But you, you pause only to tease an elderly faun.
EDGAR DEGAS

with its black-framed mirror, the room is an altogether more austere place. The background seems close to us, but the floor, no longer marked out in perspective-enhancing diagonals, is divided by horizontals that seem to swallow space. The details have all been very slightly altered; the painting that results is quite different.

Since the latter 1870s, Degas had increasingly been using studies of ballerinas' movements as a means to unusual perspective effects. His interest in showing particular individuals and situations waned; the point of his art lay less in what was seen than in how it was rendered. The same figures (such as the ballerina scratching her back) reappeared in new configurations. At the same time, the pictures became more colourful and the chosen sections more fragmentary. As in the jockey pictures, observation of forms *of* movement led to the construction of forms *in* movement.

The Star (1876–78; ill. p. 44) shows the star of the show dancing a solo turn on an empty stage. Other dancers can partly be seen waiting in the wings. The ballerina is on her toes, completing an arabesque which Degas renders very precisely through the positions of arms and the one visible leg and the slight inclination of the head too. The sense that we have glimpsed a real passing moment is enhanced by the wispy lightness of the flower-speckled tutu and the trailing tapes of her black velvet neckband. We are seeing the stage from the angle of vision we would have from a box; the front of the stage is not in our line of vision, the ballerina is out on the right, and the empty stage takes up most of the field. The asymmetry of the composition reinforces the impression of a glimpse of the fleeting moment. And yet the movement has a strangely frozen quality, as if the sheer emphasis of the prima donna's movement suspended our sense of action. Like the figures on Keats's urn, the ballerina cannot move on through time; and she even looks as if she might fall over, since the slant-angled perspective of the stage has something of the abyss about it. Degas is not recording the continuity of movement, but rather the "forever" of arrested movement. The solo dancer is the only figure we can see uncropped; even so, she makes a fragmented impression – one leg is invisible because of our angle of vision, so that she is balanced on the other like a flower on its stem. Movement is paradoxically both signally present and conspicuously absent in the work, and Degas, in recording a simple ballet scene with such verisimilitude, has afforded us a curiously disturbing view of the abyss.

Degas certainly had an eye for the hard work dancing requires. His pictures tell an unvarnished tale of tough examinations. (Would-be dancers from the lower classes saw ballet as a means of social and economic improvement, since they were paid according to the training they had undergone.) Degas tells of the rigours that go into producing such seeming effortlessness; he tells of the boredom and weariness of routine training. Holders of season tickets to the ballet could meet dancers behind the scenes, and it is this informal view that Degas offers. Hippolyte Taine described dancing classes

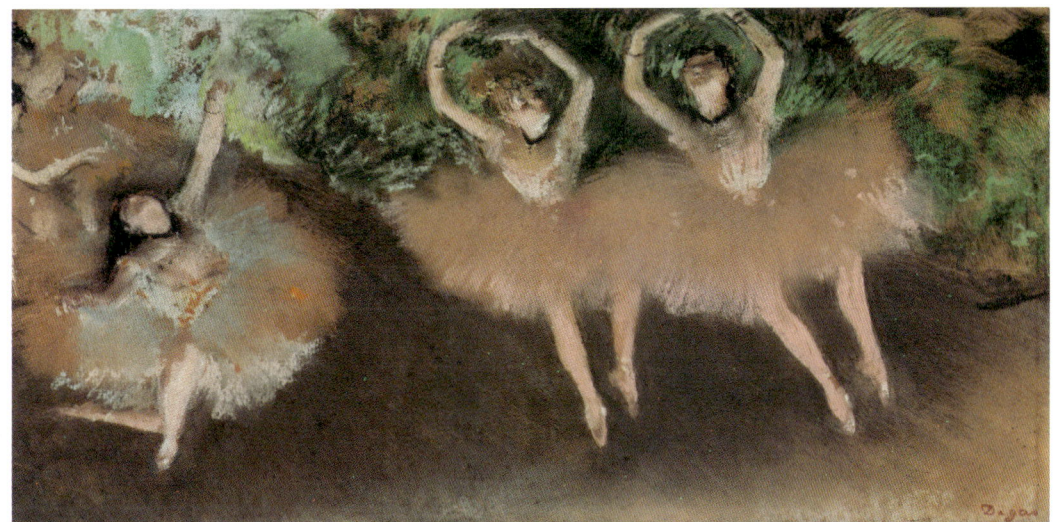

as a "market of female flesh", and Degas also recorded this aspect of backstage life. He certainly knew of the sexual charge of ballet, as his eye for the girls' legs shows.

Ballet Scene, c. 1878–80
Pastel on monotype,
40.8 x 200.4 cm (16 x 79 in.)
Whereabouts unknown

The final curtain, in an 1880 painting of that title, threatens to remove the girls from our vision altogether. The horizontals of pit and curtain cleave across the picture so violently

Dancers Climbing the Stairs, c. 1886–90
Oil on canvas, 39 x 89.5 cm (15¼ x 35¼ in.)
Paris, Musée d'Orsay

that there is a risk of entirely dislocating our understanding of context. People no longer establish a painting's norm – a perfectly logical consequence of Degas's sectional approach to the passing moment. Yet the artist is still out to invest the moment with value; for Degas, ballet represented "everything that remains of the harmonic, unified movement of the Greeks". The structure of time in Degas's moments is deeply ambiguous, containing "dynamic movement" and sheer paralysis at once, both motion and rigidity.

His dancers became parts of pictorial constructs which were none of their making. As in the racetrack pictures, Degas evolved from exact records of scenes to studies in movement, and so, ultimately, to compositions that were wholly invented. The vividness of his paintings results from his

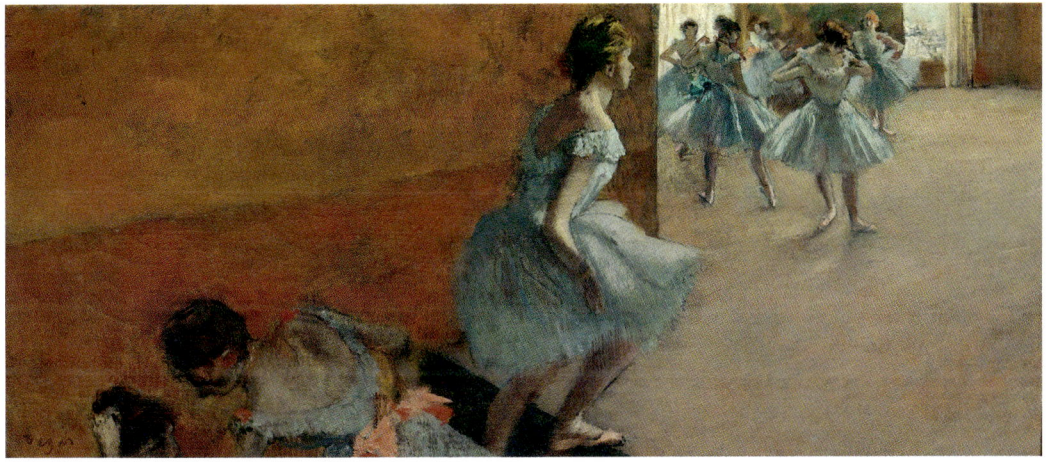

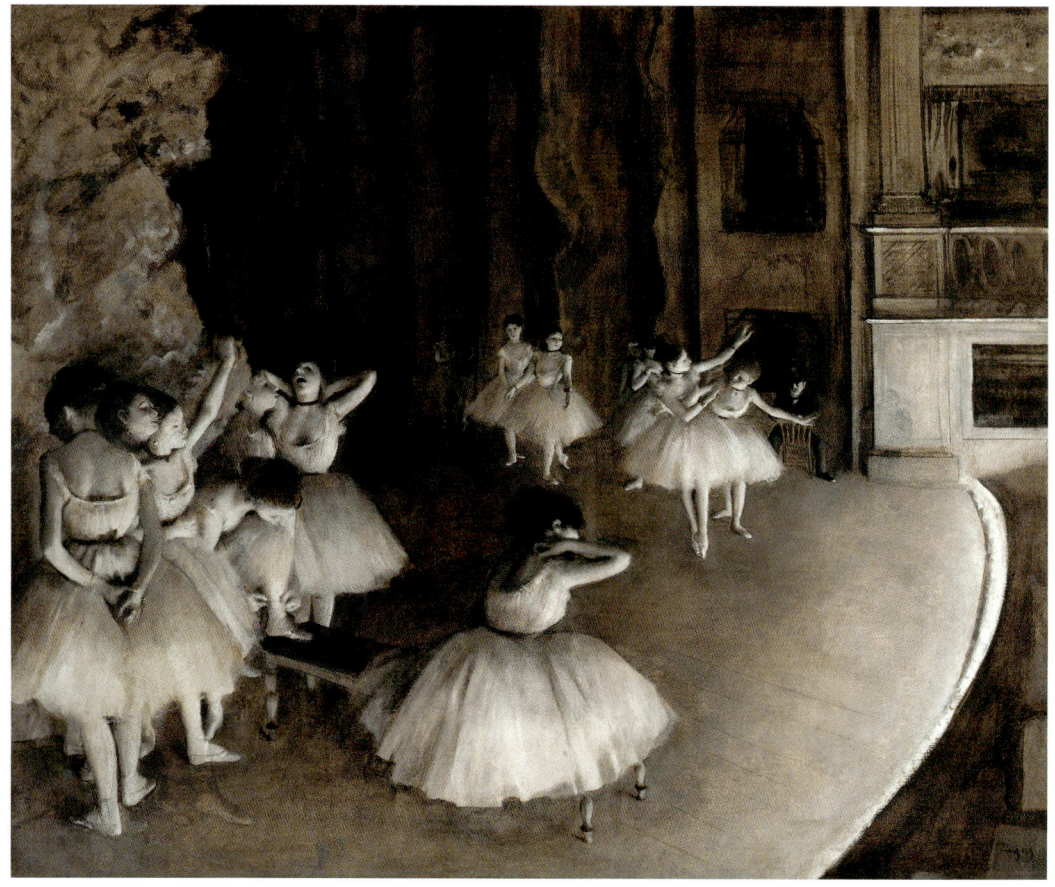

Rehearsal of a Ballet on Stage, 1874
Oil on canvas, 65 x 81 cm (25½ x 32 in.)
Paris, Musée d'Orsay

tireless quest for new arrangements. "The dancer is merely a pretext for a picture," said Degas. His art reveals a world where the passing and the solidly structured, appearance and truth, fiction and unfooled sobriety, can no longer be distinguished.

An extraordinary picture done *c.* 1880, *Ballet Class* (ill. p. 59), recapitulates these hallmarks. There is movement and the uncanny redoubling of movement. There is emptiness, and figures overlapping and cropped. And the composition is one of thorough calculation. Down the centre runs a diagonal demarcation separating Jules Perrot, two resting dancers and a mother from the three dancers currently exercising. The mother in her flowery dress and straw hat is reading *Le Petit Journal* and taking no interest in the class.

But the painting does not merely juxtapose the everyday and dance worlds. Degas has played a subtle trick with our perceptions: the glimpse we have of Paris beyond the room is not seen through a window on the rear wall – it is in fact the dancers' mirror, and the view of houses it affords us is in fact a reflection of a window view visible to the people in the room at some point behind where we ourselves must be imagined to be standing. It is a subtle interplay of spatial values, of seeing and not seeing. And it is a characteristic Degas irony that in a painting about the limits of vision and the very boundaries of a picture he depicts a figure (the reading mother) who is voluntarily accepting self-imposed limits on what is seen.

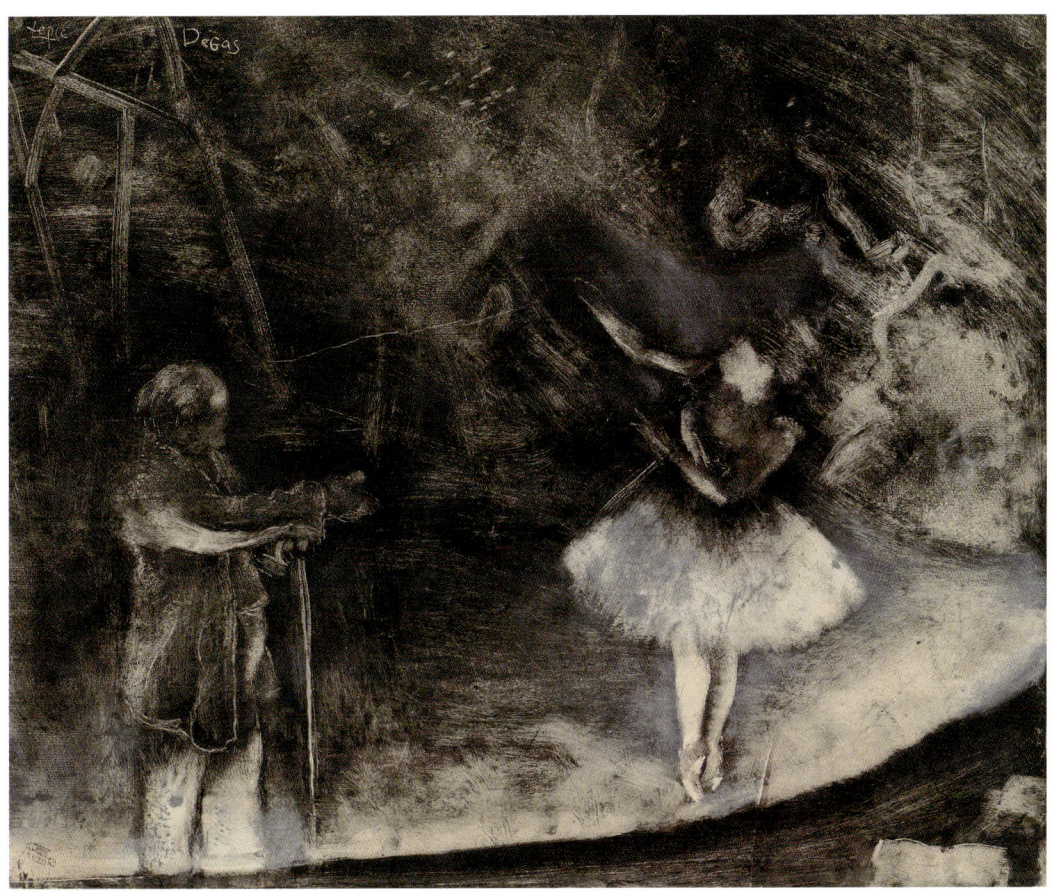

The Ballet Instructor, *c.* 1874
Charcoal, 56.5 x 70 cm (22¼ x 27½ in.)
Washington, D.C., National Gallery of Art,
Rosenwald Collection, 1964

*"People call me the painter of dancing girls.
It has never occurred to them that my chief
interest in dancers lies in rendering movement
and painting pretty clothes."*

EDGAR DEGAS

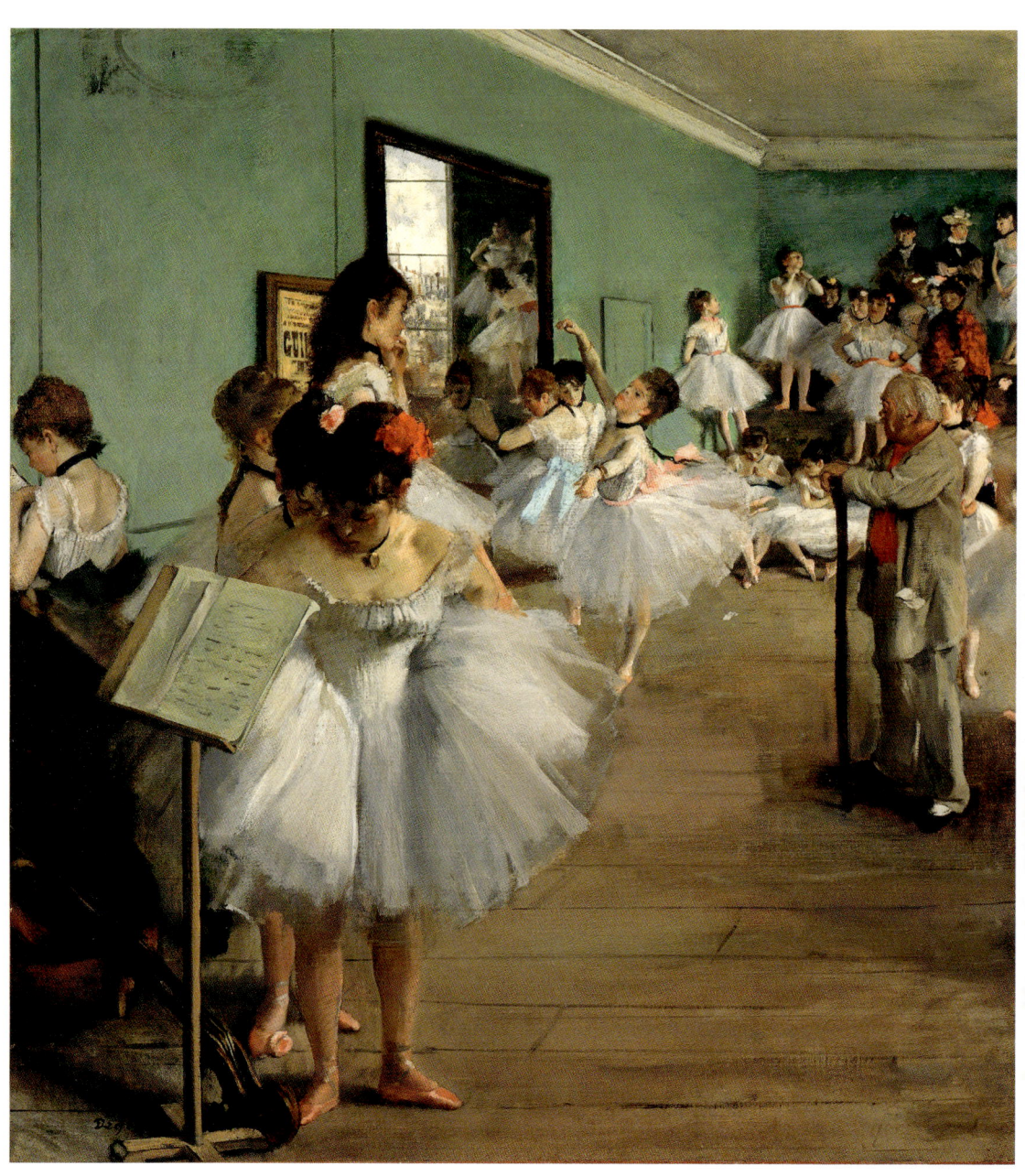

Dancing Examination, 1874
Oil on canvas, 83.5 x 77.2 cm (33 x 30½ in.)
New York, The Metropolitan Museum of Art,
Bequest of Mrs Harry Payne Bingham

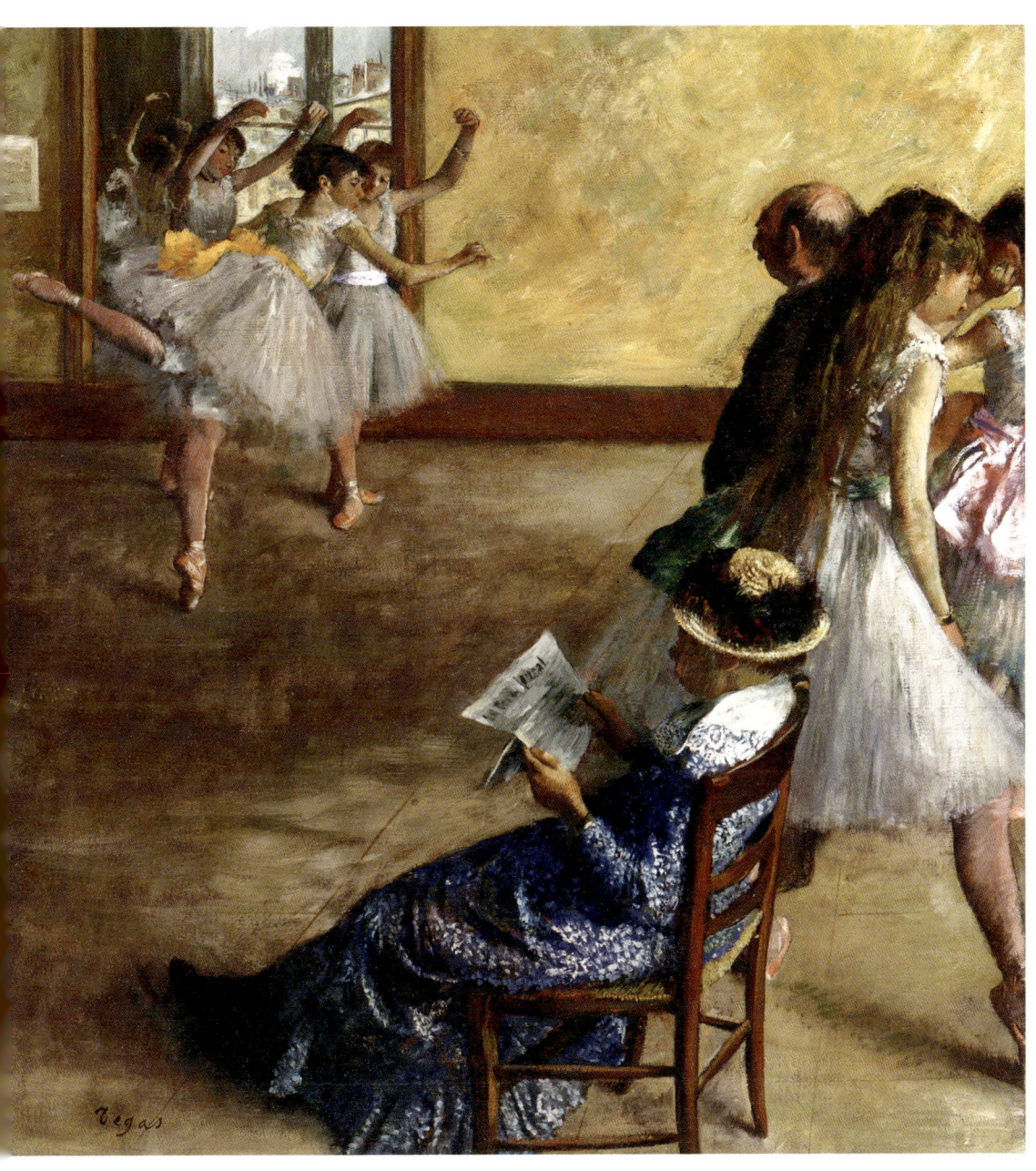

Ballet Class, *c.* 1880
Oil on canvas, 82.2 x 76.8 cm (32¼ x 30¼ in.)
Philadelphia Museum of Art,
Purchased with the W. P. Wilstach Fund, 1937

PAGES 60/61
Dance Studio of the Opera,
Rue Le Peletier, 1872
Oil on canvas, 32.7 x 46.3 cm (13 x 18¼ in.)
Paris, Musée d'Orsay

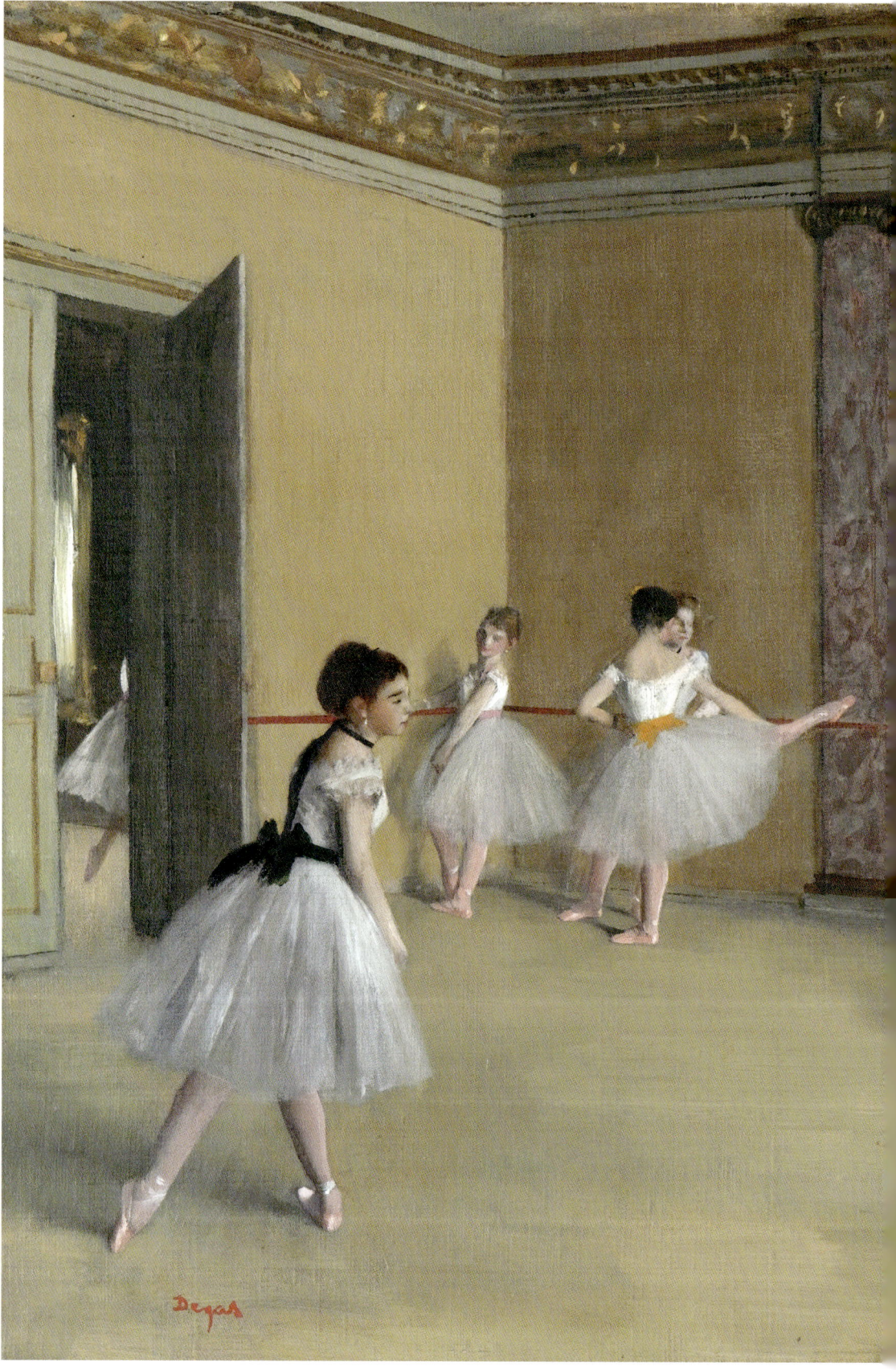

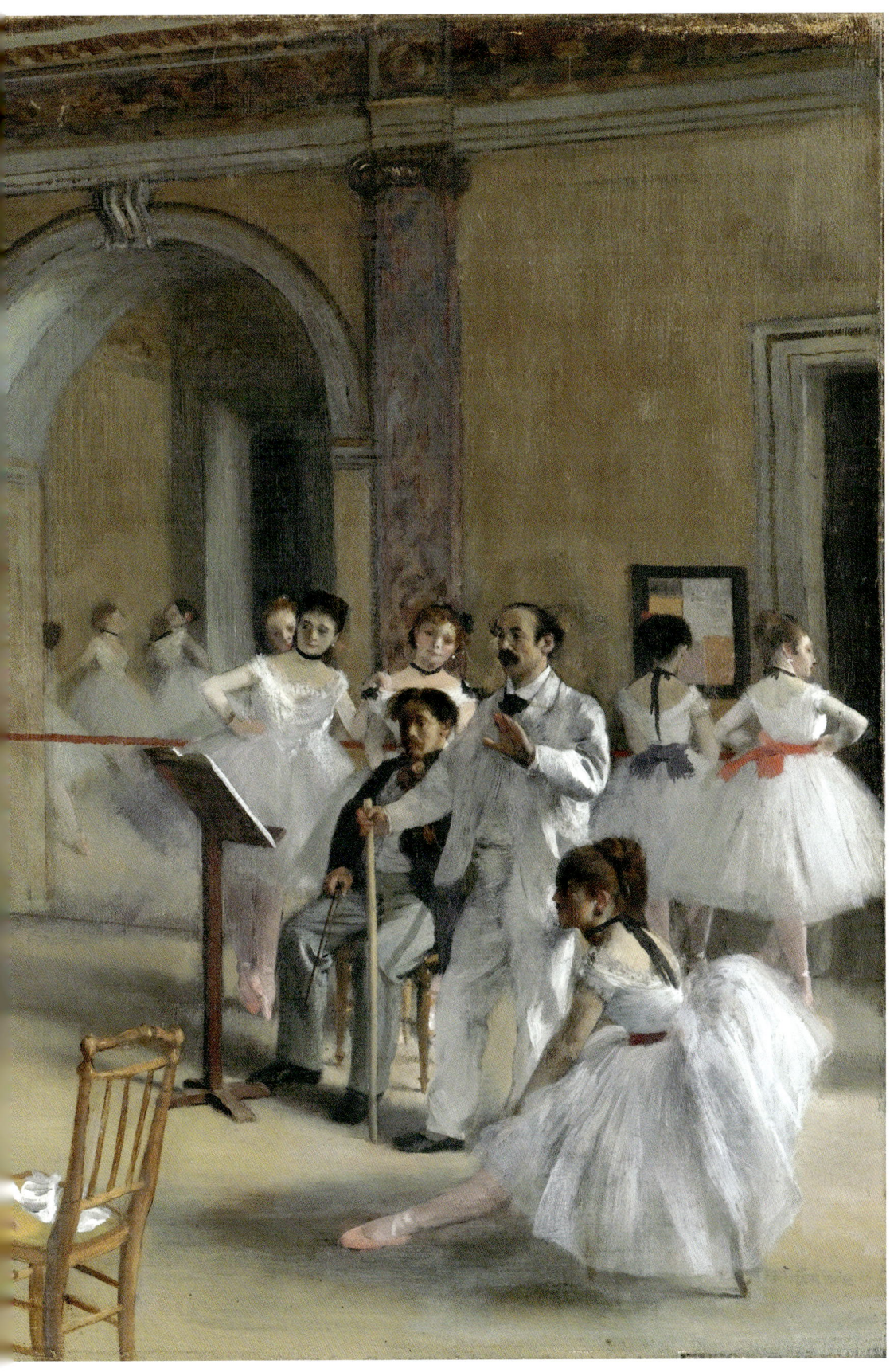

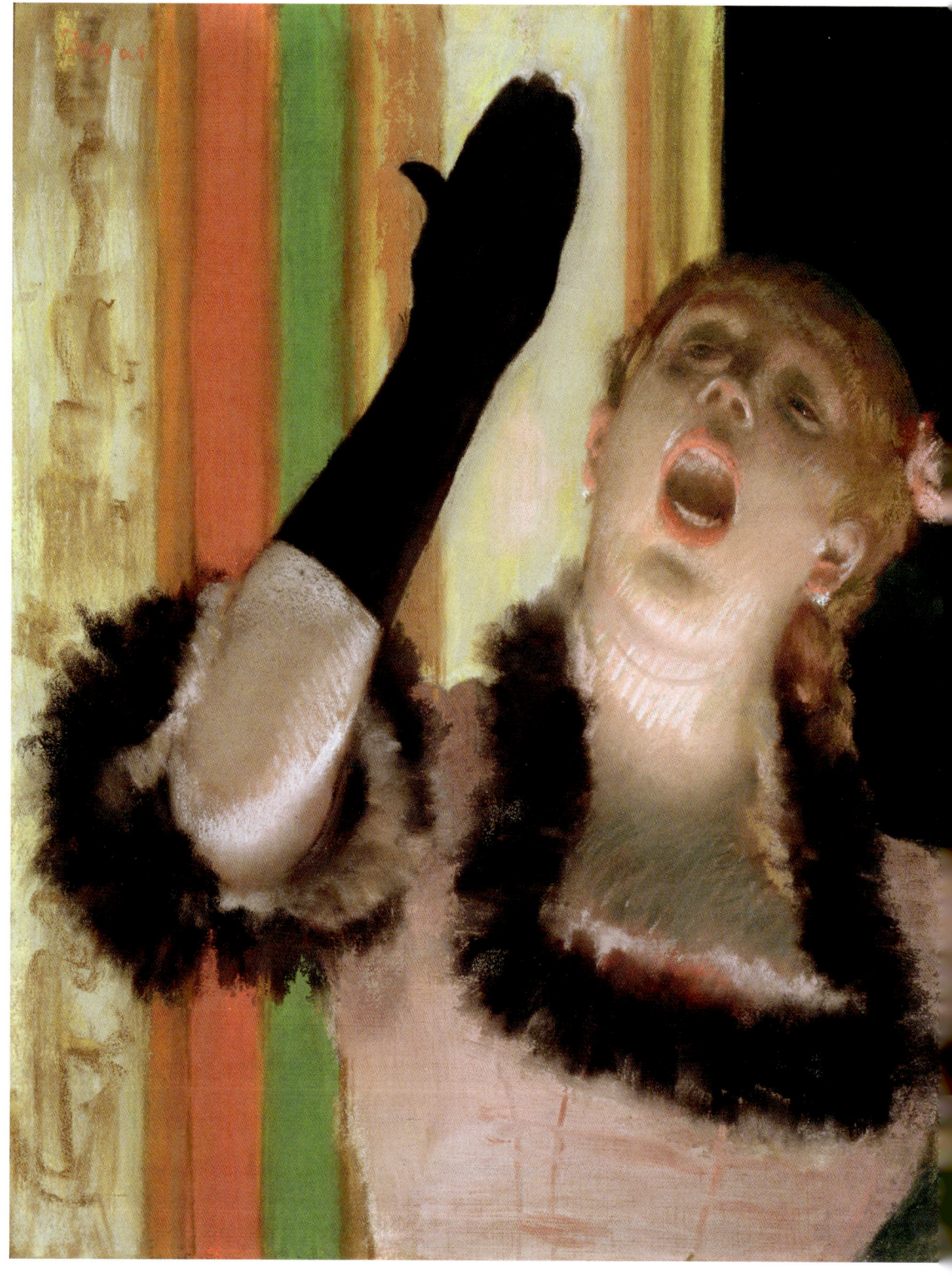

The Parisian Flaneur

*"I have painted portraits viewed from above,
now I shall do some seen from below –
seated close to a woman, looking up to her
from somewhere right down below."*
EDGAR DEGAS

In the mid-19th century the flaneur – as portrayed by the Goncourt brothers, Edmond Duranty or Baudelaire – came to be regarded as the very archetype of Parisian life. Not only did he affect particular kinds of dress and manners. He also saw everything. Bazin described the flaneur as the only true sovereign in Paris.

Degas identified with the urbane, city confidence of the flaneur, with the ease and sophistication the flaneur paraded in clubs and streets alike. The fact is that Degas was much of a flaneur himself. Paris at the time of the Second Empire and Third Republic was a rapidly expanding metropolis, with a population of 2.5 million by the end of the century. Baron Haussmann's radical restructuring of the city had swept away old quarters and changed the face of Paris for good. Sauntering about the city, Degas was constantly witnessing new scenes of a transformed urban life, and being inspired to paint new subjects. And Degas was not the only one. In 1862, in *Concert at the Tuileries,* Manet left an account of the city's public places as backdrop for the flaneur. Degas felt that his own approach must be a similar one if he was to make full use of the chance bounty the city put his way: "To bear good fruit, one must be an espaliered tree. And stand there a whole life long, arms outstretched and mouth open, to catch what comes one's way or is all about one and be nourished by it."

His pictures recorded images of life in a modern city. And, as Degas was quick to note, this entailed fundamental changes in ways of seeing: "No one has ever painted houses or monuments from down below, as close-up as one sees them when out walking in the street." The flaneur happened upon his subjects by chance whilst strolling along a boulevard – as we can see in the 1875 portrait of Baron Lepic and his daughters, *Place de la Concorde* (ill. pp. 66/67).

Lepic, art connoisseur and dog breeder, is immaculately turned out. Cigar in mouth, one hand behind his back, an umbrella under his arm, he is walking across the Place de la Concorde with his daughters and dog. He makes a blasé impression; certainly another passer-by seems to think so. Degas emphasizes the emptiness of the square as if to highlight the vacancy through which this flaneur is passing, in more senses than one. Max Imdahl justly observed that this painting sets down the conceivable maximum of contingency. It proves how acutely Degas's eye was forever on the alert for the "unanticipated moment" (Baudelaire), the moment the flaneur is really out to experience. In this composition, the fleeting moment coincides with artful construction.

Since the 1830s, the opera houses, theatres and vaudeville shows had grown in number and importance in the new Paris. Walter Benjamin observed that the flaneur's true

Singer with a Glove, 1878
Pastel on canvas, 53.2 x 41 cm (21 x 16¼ in.)
Cambridge, Massachusetts, Harvard Art Museums/Fogg Museum, Bequest from the Collection of Maurice Wertheim, Class of 1906

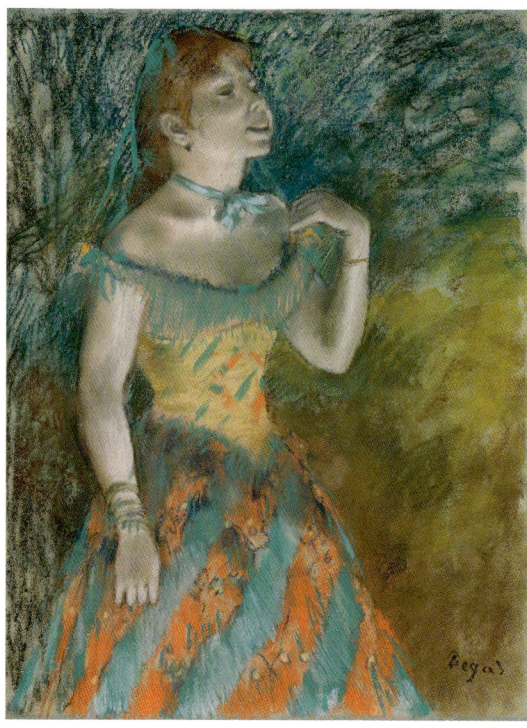

The Green Singer, c. 1884
Pastel on blue paper, 60.3 x 46.4 cm
(23¾ x 18¼ in.)
New York, The Metropolitan Museum of Art,
Bequest of Stephen C. Clark, 1960

OPPOSITE
Two Studies of Café Concert Singers, 1878–80
Pastel and charcoal on grey paper,
45.5 x 58.1 cm (18 x 23 in.)
Private collection

PAGES 66/67
Place de la Concorde
(Compte Lepic and His Daughters), 1875
Oil on canvas, 78.4 x 117.5 cm (30⅞ x 46⅜ in.)
St Petersburg, Hermitage Museum

dwelling place was the street; the flaneur "is as much at home between two rows of housefronts as others are in their own four walls"; similarly, for the flaneur, "the terraces of cafés are windowed bays from which he can look down on his own household domain after work". Artists were fascinated by famous cafés such as the Ambassadeurs or L'Alcazar. In 1872, René de Gas left a rather indignant account of being induced by his brother to endure "dull-witted songs such as the one about the builder's apprentice and other stuff and nonsense". The café was not only a place to exchange news; it was a very microcosm of society, and in the latter half of the 1870s Degas gave it his devoted attention.

The Café des Ambassadeurs was one of the oldest that offered musical entertainment. It had now had a pavilion built on, and there were gas lamps in the garden to light up the night. In *At the Café-Concert: the Song of the Dog* (1875; ill. p. 71), a monotype overpainted with gouache and pastel, our gaze is drawn past the singer to the auditorium and the lighted garden. The singer is Emma Valadon. Degas was fascinated: "She opens her large mouth and out comes the most sensuous voice, the finest, the most unphysically tender, that can possibly be." Ironically concentrating on the singer's mimicry and gestures, Degas highlights the attentiveness with which the audience are following her performance. The sheer visual wit of portraying the singer as she mimics the dog in her song is doubtless meant to underline the vulgarity of the song.

But Degas did not merely observe her pose. He recorded it as pure theatre, from her lamp-lit rouged cheeks (with a stark background of black and green) to the affectation of her finger-tipping. A pillar divides the stage from the auditorium and helps place the singer (Degas extended the monotype on three sides to establish the spatial proportions he needed); and Degas has used the compositional intersection of pillar, gas lamp and nose to mark Valadon's open mouth as the real centre of the scene, as it were. Of course, the irony already present in Valadon's animal mimicry is further intensified by the gaslit globes, which are like soap bubbles rising above the evening crowd and making an empty comment of sheer nothingness on the performance. In pictures such as this, Degas was evolving a new way of seeing, a way that came straight from the cafés themselves.

The 1877 *Women on a Café Terrace in the Evening* offers a similar view from a café interior out onto the street. The pillars divide the view into segments, so that the picture affords a number of sectional fragments such as the silhouette of a man out walking or a brief gesture of fingers at a mouth. Taken together, these fragments add up to a typical coffee house scene.

An 1878–80 charcoal drawing highlighted with pastel, *Two Studies of Café Concert Singers*, shows the same singer in the same pose from two different angles. Her pose is an attitude interpreting what she is singing; her head is nestling into her shoulder, her hands are in an imploring gesture, and she is the very image of despair. Degas has plainly been trying to find the best way to capture that image.

In *Singer with a Glove* (1878; ill. p. 62) the gesture is seen as important in itself. This juxtaposition of face and glove was later borrowed by Toulouse-Lautrec for his portrait of Yvette Guilbert. In Degas's picture, the woman was not a singer at all; she was a well-known pianist, Alice Desgranges. Degas was not out to convey singing as performance; rather, he was exploring various shock effects produced by so extreme a close-up. Though the woman's face is doubtless correctly rendered, given the angle of vision, her features nonetheless look oddly disproportioned. The lamplight

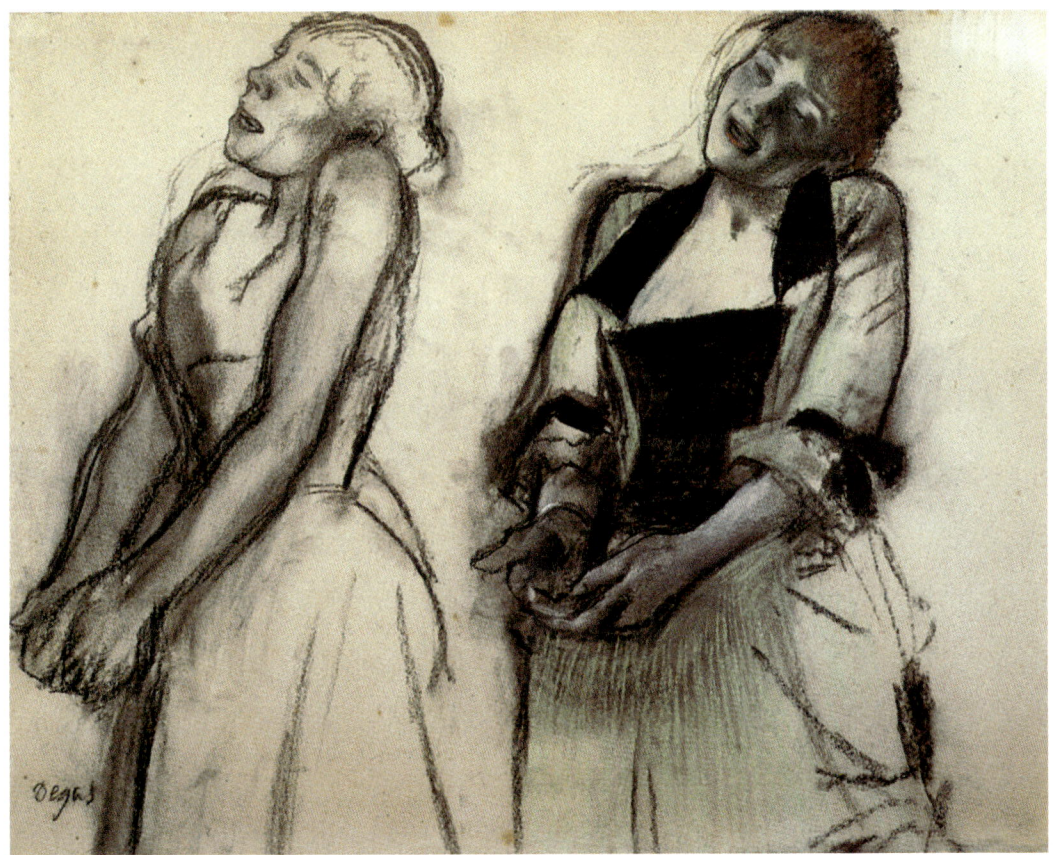

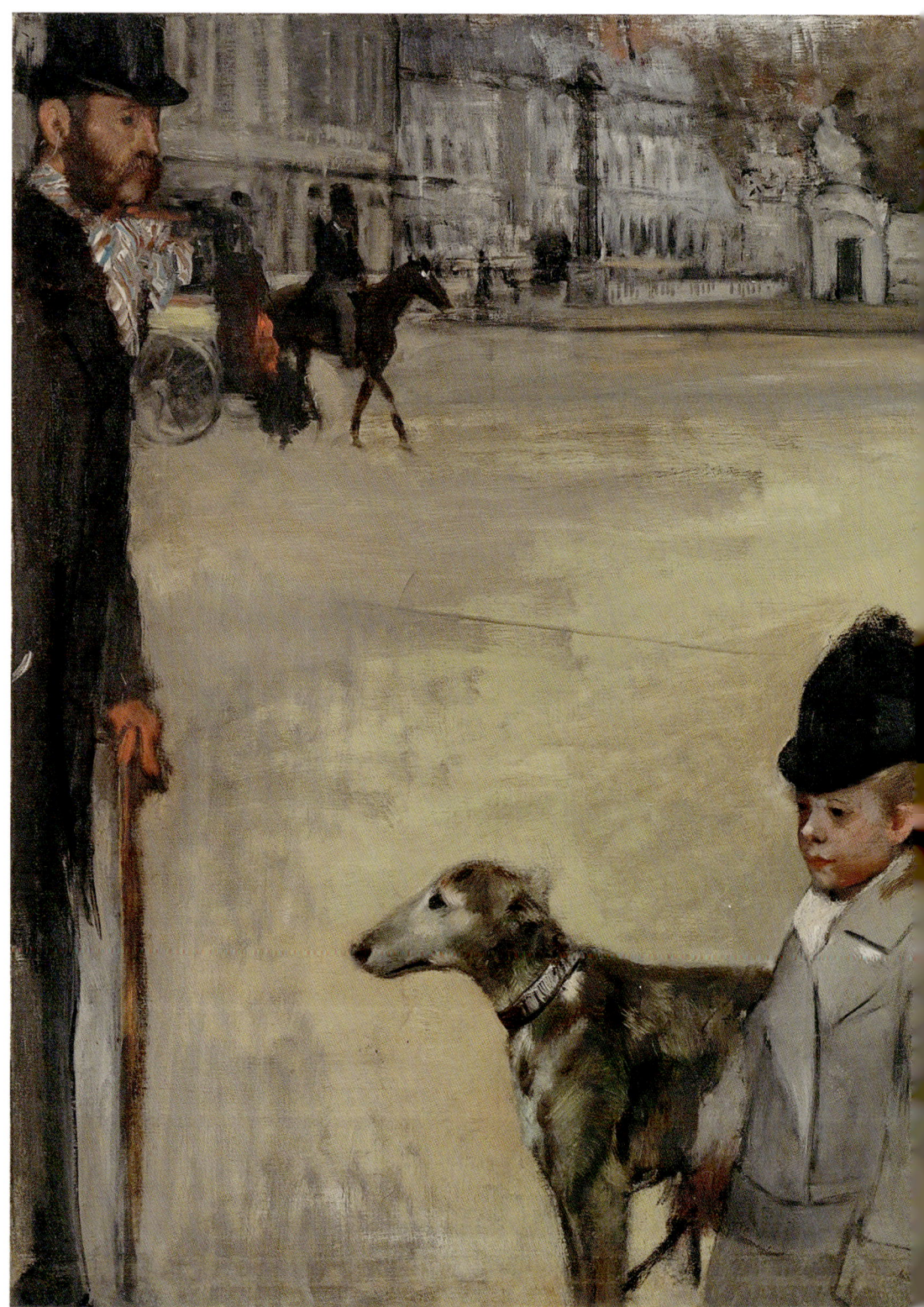

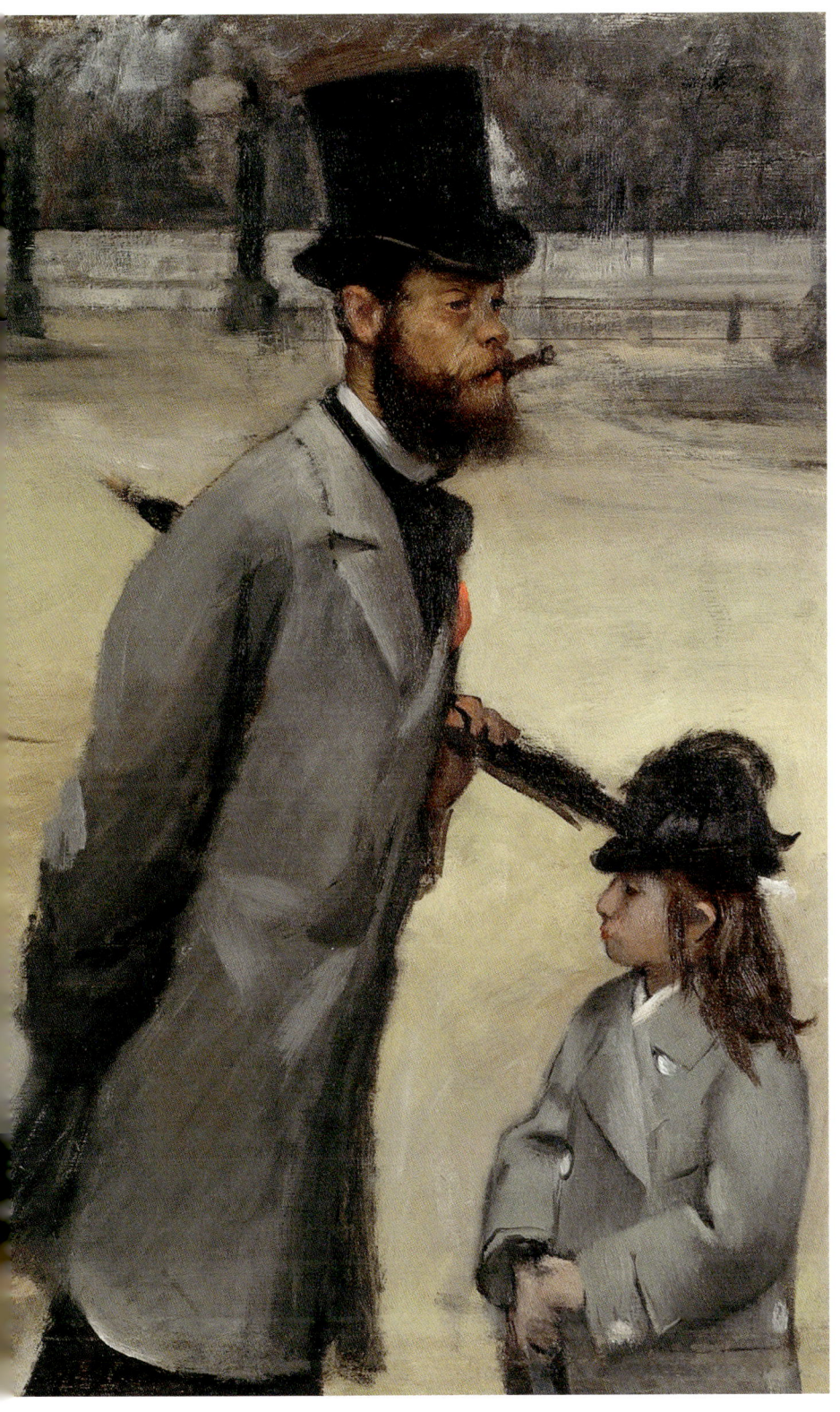

from below produces a caricature effect. In his ballet scenes, too, Degas was always interested in the curious insubstantiality of things when seen in artificial lighting, and fascinated by the way colours became acidic or pale and shadows acquired a phosphorescent gleam. A picture such as this demonstrates clearly that brighter lighting implies the loss of subtle auras and atmospheres (as critic Wolfgang Schivelbusch has pointed out). Gaslight and an evening sky, for Degas as for Baudelaire, stood for an unusual beauty, using artificial brightness to highlight both the dreamy and nightmarish aspects of people and objects. Limelight on a singer does more than illuminate a scene: it creates it.

The singer is startlingly close to us. In fact, we are looking right into her open mouth. Degas's sketchbooks show that he drew studies of grimacing mouths and exaggerated gestures, with the caricature grotesqueness of the expressions very much in mind. But here the effect is primarily achieved by the closely-focussed sectionality. The picture has lost none of its power to startle, even as it insists on its authenticity. The black glove, looking as if it were stencilled, bears a full charge of expressive movement. The gesture does not express the person's mood; rather, her character is perceived by us as an extension of that one isolated and conspicuous gesture.

"An artist has to be able to cut a great deal away."

EDGAR DEGAS

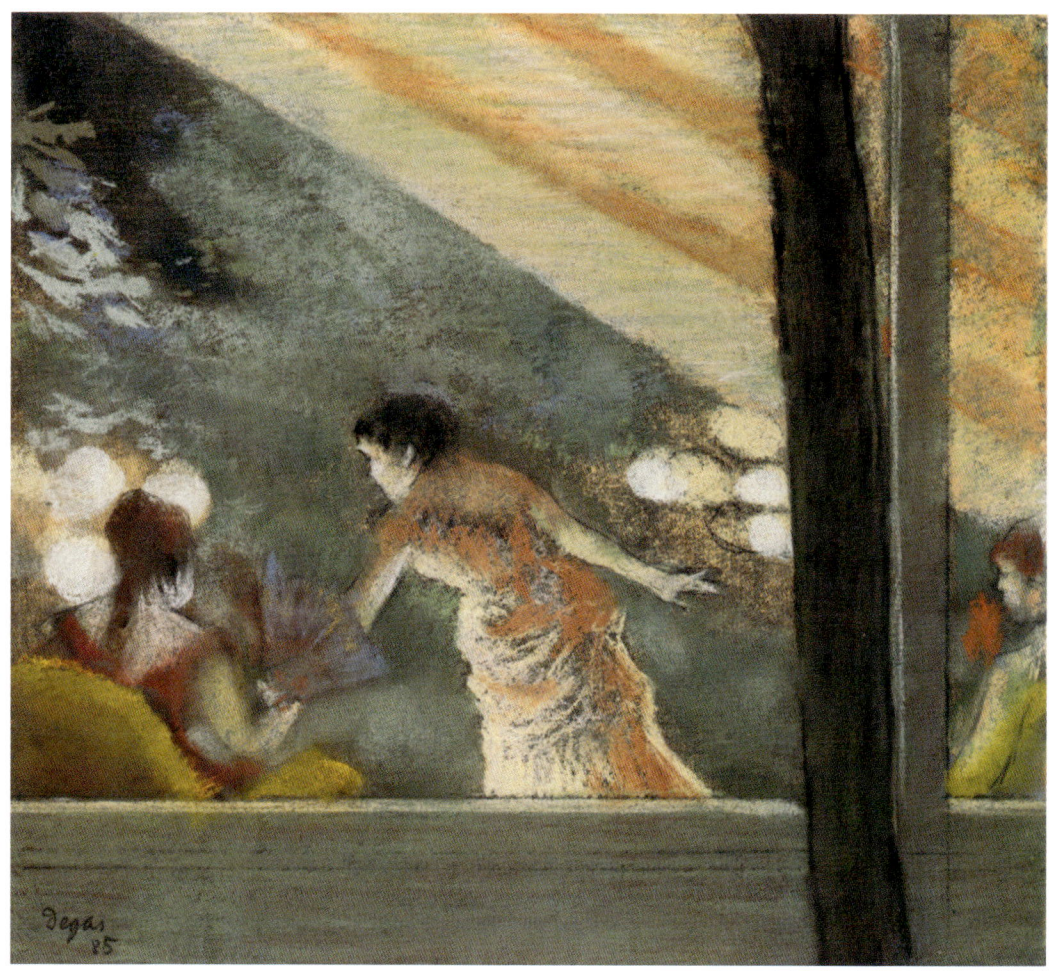

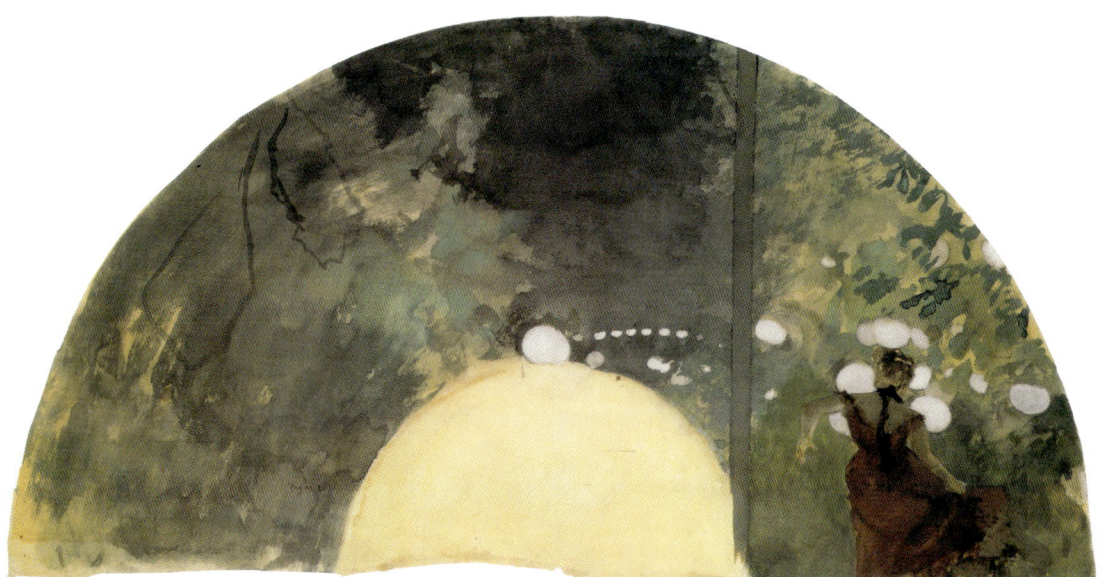

Singer with a Glove represents Degas's interest in singers at its peak; his interest passed from love of song to the interaction of singer and audience and so, finally, to the singer giving herself entirely to the spirit of performance before an audience.

Café Concert Singer, 1880
Watercolour and gouache on silk, mounted on cardboard, 30.7 x 60.7 cm (12 x 24 in.)
Karlsruhe, Staatliche Kunsthalle

OPPOSITE
At the Café des Ambassadeurs, 1885
Pastel on etching, 26.5 x 29.5 cm (10½ x 11½ in.)
Paris, Musée d'Orsay

Degas was self-evidently using a dynamic, point-of-view approach to composition in order to break with convention. His shifts in point of view, often extreme, owed something to photography and also something to the defamiliarization of vision effected in Japanese woodcuts, which had recently been discovered in Europe. For some time younger artists had felt imitation of Japanese art to be a useful way of avoiding the pitfalls of photographic naturalism and of Salon art alike. Interest peaked at the time of the 1878 World Fair, when crafts, interior design and fashion were all under the sign of *Japonaiserie*. Samuel Bing even published an arts magazine titled *Japon Artistique*, which was devoted to Japanese art and its influence on recent European art. As late as 1890 Bing organized a notable *ukiyo-e* exhibition including over 700 sheets.

Degas liked *ukiyo-e* work and himself owned a number of graphic works by Utamaro and Hokusai. The word *ukiyo-e* signifies a particular style of folk art and means "scenes of the transient, flowing world". Frequent *ukiyo-e* subjects included the lives of actors, courtesans, musicians and geisha girls, in every conceivable situation: the bath or toilet, walking, or at the tea ceremony. Degas used similar subjects, of course; but his debt to the Japanese really lay in other areas. He schooled his eye on unusual Japanese perspectives and positions, and studied asymmetrical composition, which was the most striking hallmark of Japanese art. All of this stimulated his own interest in unusual compositional techniques, such as the semicircular fan format of the 1880 *Café Concert Singer* (ill. p. 69).

Most of the fan vault is occupied by dark sky and the coffee house garden. The singer is at the right, making a lavish gesture as she sings. She is seen from the rear, coquettishly gathering up her dress. Degas may have been thinking of Mlle Bécat, whose style of delivery was known

*"I do not like carriages. One sees no one.
That is why I love the omnibus.
One can observe the people. We were
created to observe one another..."*

EDGAR DEGAS

as "epileptic"! Degas painted some twenty unmounted fans, using various techniques, in his quest for new compositional approaches to his subjects. In *Singer with a Glove* the fanning and the singer's gesture seem to converge, so that the format reinforces and extends the gesture. And the fact that the picture was painted on a fan meant that the action could quite literally be *unfolded*.

Essentially, what Degas adopted and adapted from the art of *ukiyo-e* was sectionality, the angle of vision, close-up technique, and greater autonomy for the vertical and horizontal values of a composition. Japanese ways of interrelating levels rather than using a central perspective prompted Degas increasingly to compose in zones and areas rather than in spatial relations. It was not only that what lay beyond or behind was now simply above. Spatial values in a picture were suddenly all in flux.

This applies, for instance, to *The Green Singer* (*c.* 1884; ill. p. 64). Seen from a vantage point diagonally above her, the singer is focussing attention on herself through her gesture. Degas had meticulously tried out the gesture and lighting effect in a preliminary drawing. The limelight from below makes the turquoise and red of her clothing and hair flare out. Degas is emphasizing the fact that the singer is being seen; he does so by stressing the circumstances in which she is seen. Quite often, Degas's use of gaze and gesture is further stressed by perspective means, so that we are forced more and more into the role of cool, distanced observers of city life. Huysmans was surely right when in 1880 he named Degas together with Baudelaire and Flaubert as one of the "painters of modern life".

*At the Café-Concert:
the Song of the Dog*, *c.* 1876/77
Gouache and pastel on monotype,
57.5 x 45.4 cm (22¾ x 18 in.)
Los Angeles County Museum of Art

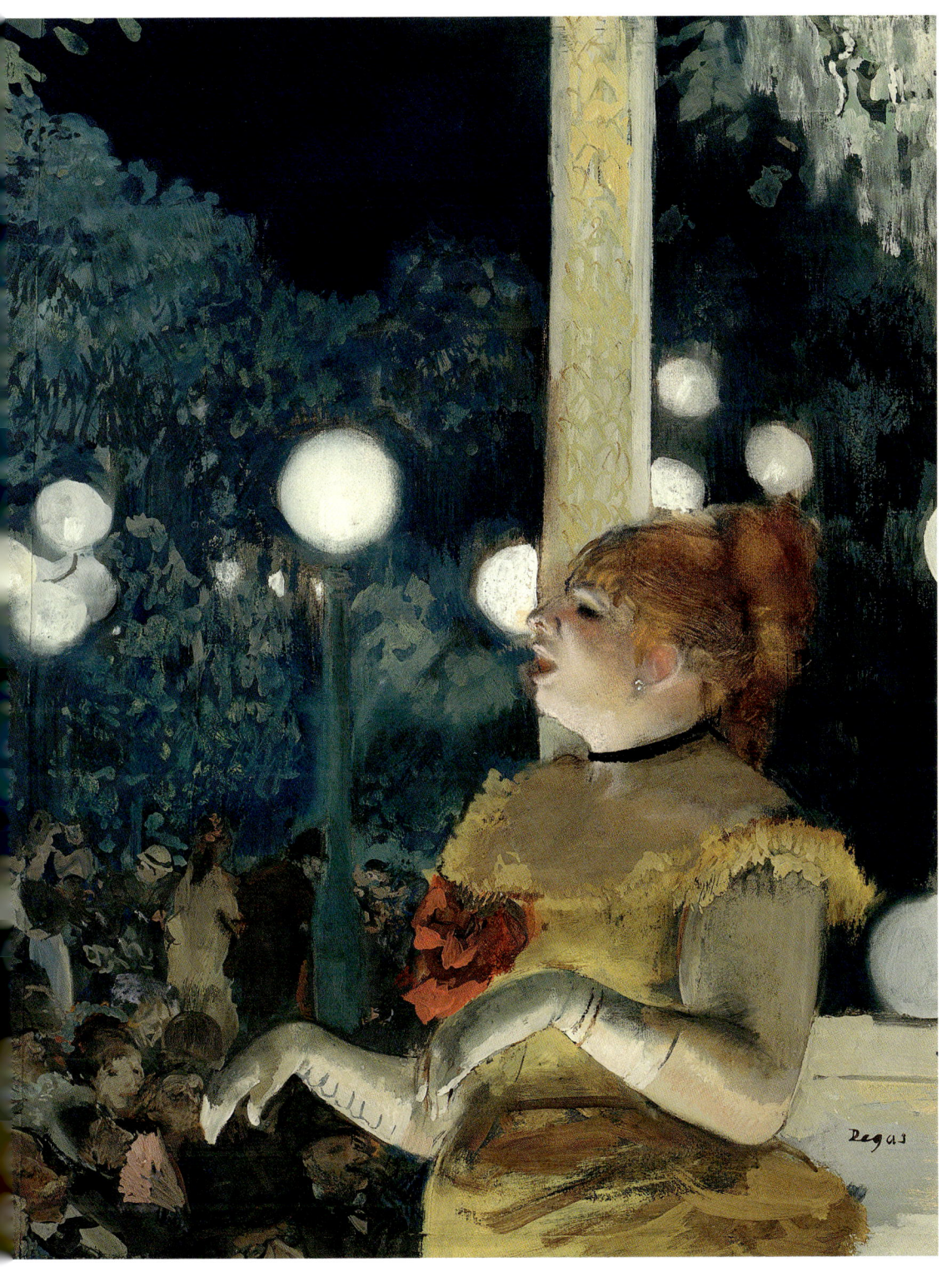

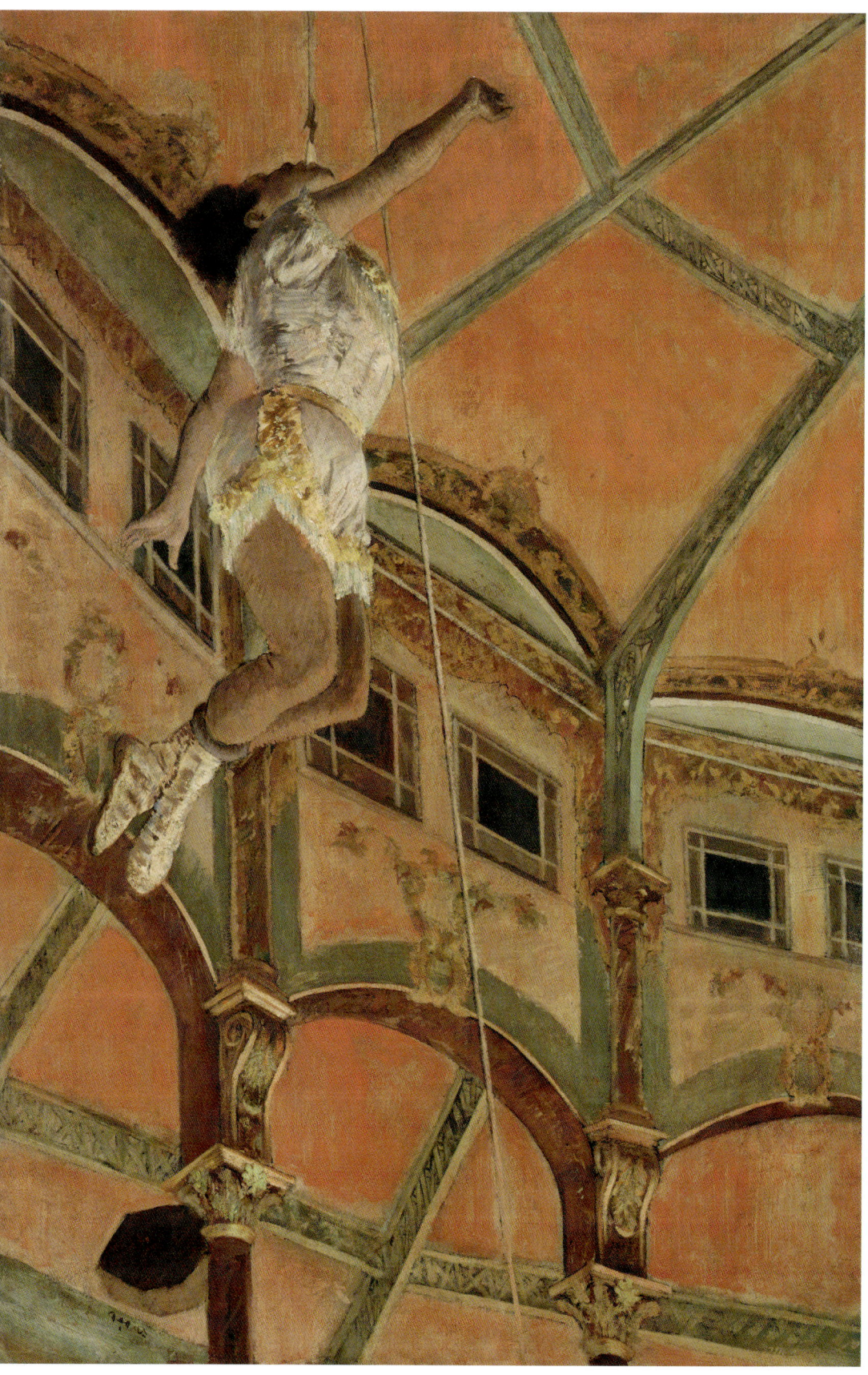

Art and Calculation

"A picture is an original combination of lines and tones that have an intensifying effect on each other."
EDGAR DEGAS

People have always been curiously affected by Degas's ability to fix the fleeting and ephemeral in the unmoving medium of a picture. The German painter Max Liebermann, who published one of the very first studies of Degas's work in 1899, observed: "At first sight, Degas's pictures give the impression of snapshots." And there can be no doubt that Degas did owe a debt to the new technology and art of photography. And yet, the impression Liebermann spoke of was born of artful, meticulous calculation – as Liebermann well knew, for he continued, "Degas is a master of creating compositions that do not look composed." Once our attention has been drawn to this, we realize that everything that appears so random in Degas's art is in fact carefully organized. One fine example is *Mlle La La at the Circus Fernando* (1879; ill. p. 72): if it is metaphorically true to say that Degas's figures often seem to hang by a thread, then in this work it is also literally and symbolically true.

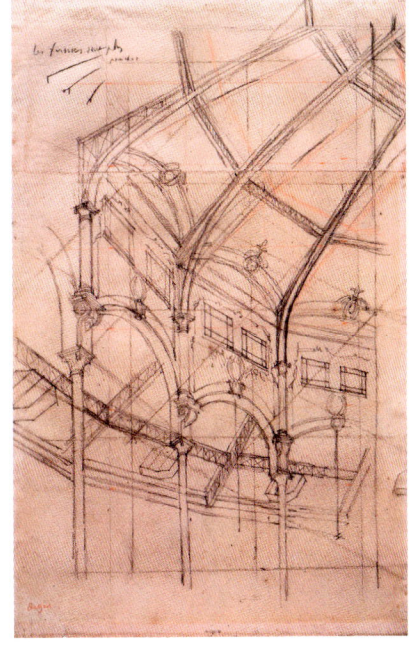

The Cirque Fernando, which had recently been established in 1875, was at Place Frodot; in 1890 it was renamed Cirque Medrano. It was a major attraction for Montmartre artists. From 19 to 25 January 1879 Degas went there at least four times, to see a mulatto trapeze artiste who called herself Mlle La La. She was also known as *la femme canon* because her most sensational trick was to fire a canon suspended on chains which she held in her teeth while she herself was hanging from the trapeze, hooked at the knee-joints. In Degas's painting, however, she is performing a different part of her act, and is being hauled up into the circus cupola. There could be no subject with greater fleeting spontaneity. Rotating as she goes, Mlle La La seems to be free in mid-air; the rope is only unobtrusively visible.

Degas was not out to portray the bravado of the trapeze artiste. His concern was not colourful authenticity or circus atmospherics. Instead, his attention is on the visual interplay

OPPOSITE
Mlle La La at the Circus Fernando, 1879
Oil on canvas, 117 x 77 cm (46 x 30¼ in.)
London, The National Gallery

ABOVE RIGHT
**The Cirque Fernando,
Architectural Study**, c. 1879
Pencil, black and red chalk on pink paper,
48 x 31.3 cm (19 x 12¼ in.)
University of Birmingham, The Barber
Institute of Fine Arts, The Henry Barber Trust

"No art could be less spontaneous than mine. Inspiration, spontaneity, temperament are unknown to me. One has to do the same subject ten times, even a hundred times over. In art, nothing should look like chance, not even movement."

EDGAR DEGAS

of artiste and architecture. Everything else (the trapeze, the ring, the audience) has been left out. He did a great many sketches and studies of both the artiste and the cupola building. It may well look like a snapshot; but of course a great deal of careful calculation went into the composition, so that a real harmony of chance and calculation should result.

The sheer, angular viewpoint from below is a modern variation on baroque *sotto-su* perspective; because of it, the picture of *Mlle La La at the Circus Fernando* was dubbed "Ascension at the Circus". What mattered to Degas was not any past religious association of his viewpoint, but enhancement of perspective efficacy and greater authenticity. As she hangs there, we realize that the artist has stripped his picture of anything that might provide her with a safe guarantee: both the anchor and pulley of the rope are out of sight, and the only counterbalance to Mlle La La's body-weight in the picture is the slender diagonal of the rope. Though the rope naturally intersects the lines of the background architecture at random points, certain patterns do emerge: for instance, the short vertical length by which the artiste is dangling, if extended to the bottom of the picture, would meet the slant cupola timber exactly.

There is an analogous balance in the upward-pulling and downward hanging momentums involved in La La's position on the rope: she is a centrepoint of tensions and forces. Of course her position in the picture, which appears randomly chosen, has its reasons. There is strict necessity in these spatial relations: the circus architecture requires that the grid of iron girders arch over to the top right, with the result that the artiste's revolving body seems caught in a web of taut linear interaction.

At first glance it looks as if Mlle La La's feet are resting on the archway at left and the fingers of her left hand are touching the upper sill. In fact, of course, the spatial proportions of this work are huge. Degas has succeeded in creating impressions of zoned unity out of compositional components that have nothing to do with each other. In the whole of this picture so strikingly made of diagonals and verticals there is not a single horizontal: everything strives upward, leaving La La literally in the air. It would not be going too far to say that Degas has rendered the circus artiste in metaphoric style as standing for the lost human condition.

Mlle La La at the Circus Fernando shows once again how distinctive Degas's iconographic world was in the Impressionist group; only Manet shared his interests in part. Both artists had a more complex sense of the new painting than the other Impressionists, who were mainly working on landscapes. From the early days, for example, Degas was interested in women who did the ironing at laundries; realist artists and writers such as Daumier, Pissarro and Zola had shared this interest. His first picture on this subject was done in 1869. The young woman looking up from her ironing did not in fact do the work for a living but was a professional model, Emma Dobigny. That notwithstanding, Degas has succeeded in recording a vacant, remote gaze and the weary attitude of a woman in this tedious line.

By the turn of the century Degas had painted fourteen pictures on the subject, showing women ironing from various angles, singly or in twos, silhouetted or behind laundry. There are four versions of the *c.* 1884 picture of two women alone (ill. p. 76). We see an unprosperous laundry, complete with stove and washing hung up to dry. It is not clear

Woman Ironing, *c.* 1869
Oil on canvas, 92.5 x 73.5 cm (36½ x 29 in.)
Munich, Bayerische Staatsgemälde-sammlungen, Neue Pinakothek

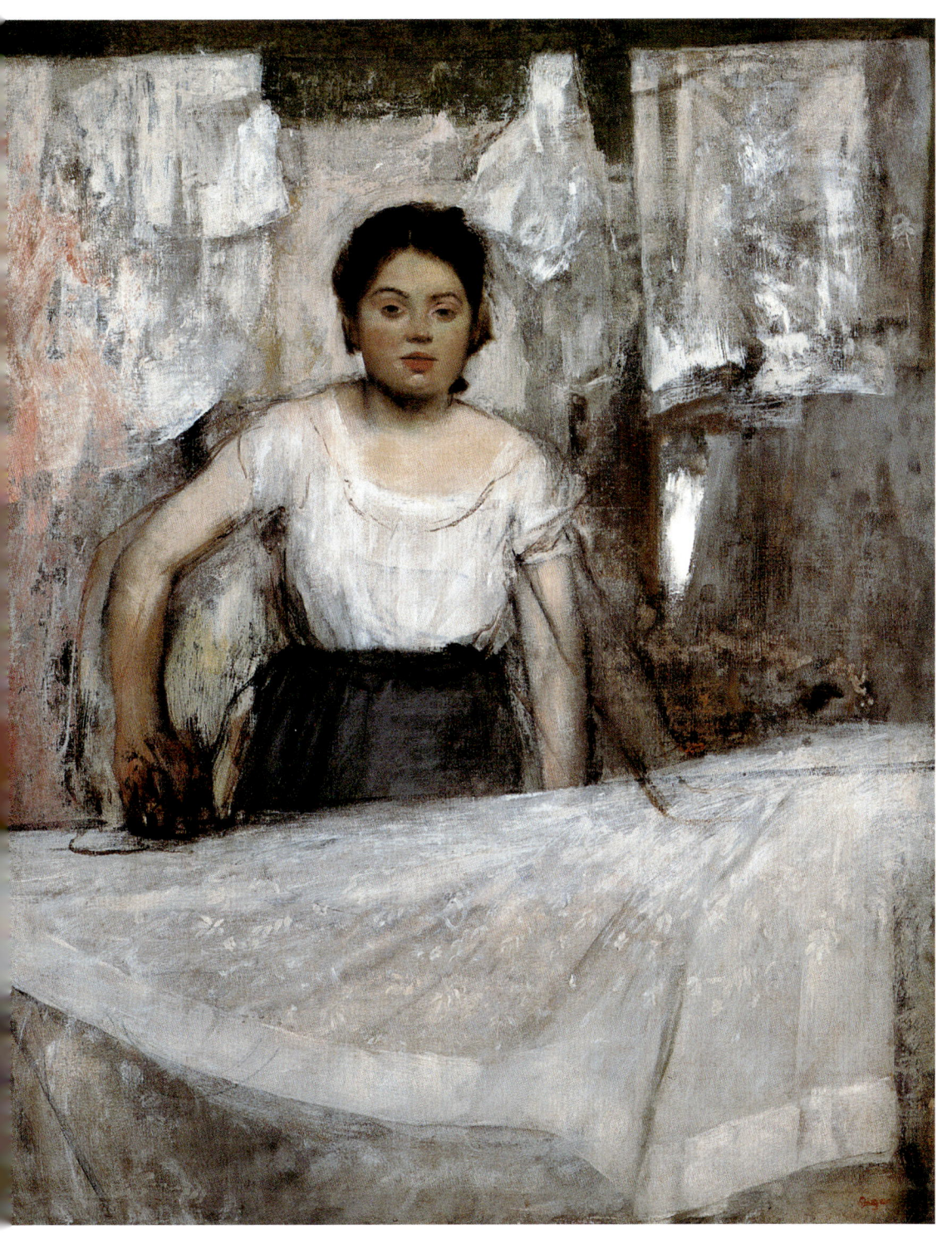

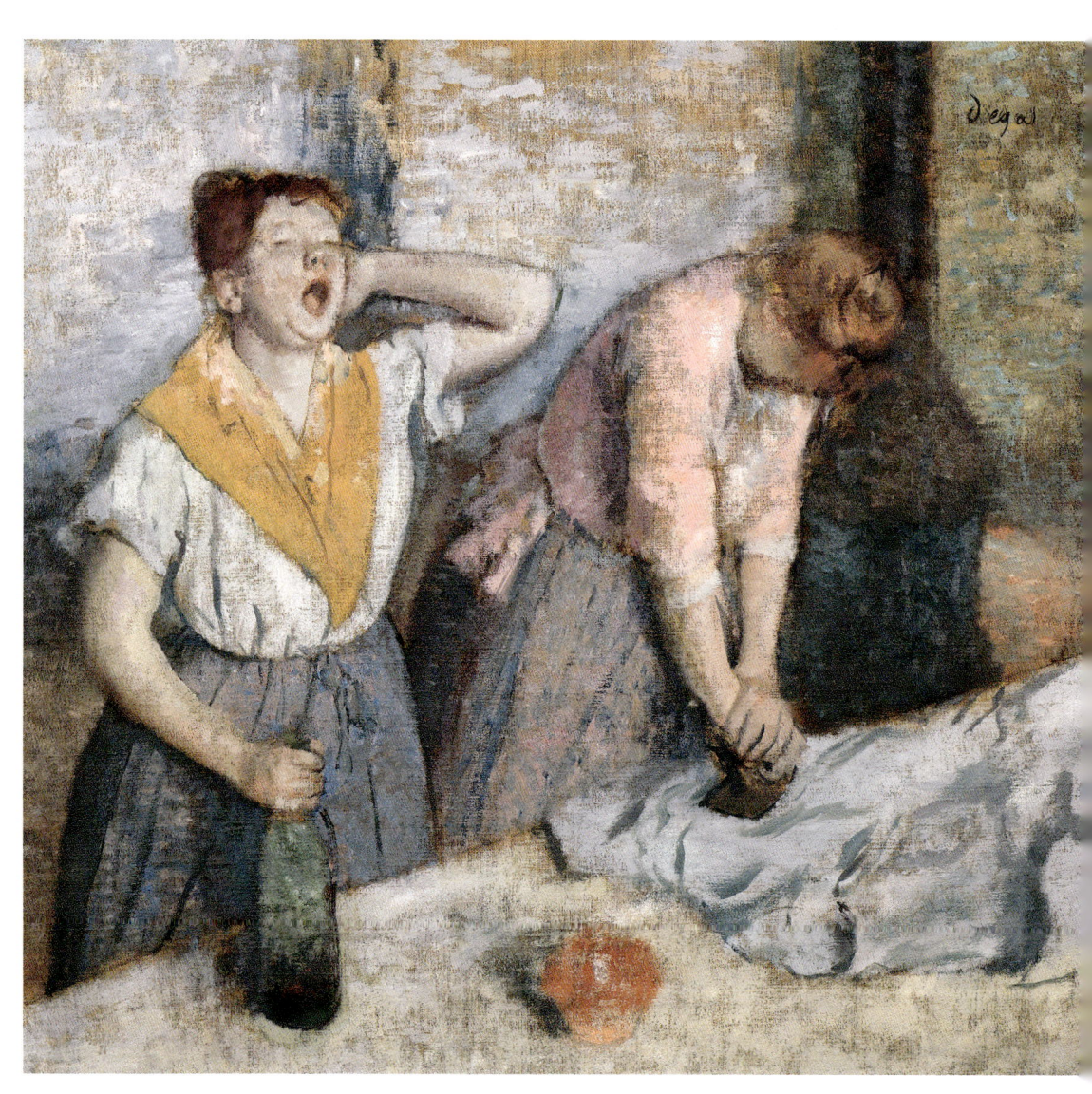

Women Ironing, *c.* 1884–86
Oil on canvas, 76 x 81.4 cm (30 x 32 in.)
Paris, Musée d'Orsay

whether these women were regulars or models. Behind the ironing table with its bowl of water stand two women; the left one is stretching and yawning, with one hand to her head and the other on the neck of a bottle, the right one is putting her whole strength into her ironing. The contrast of

"The painter tends increasingly to paint what he dreams rather than what he sees."

CHARLES BAUDELAIRE

a relaxed and a tensed body makes more of the picture than a mere milieu study. In such pictures, Degas was exploring the darker side of city life, and the everyday alienation experienced by many. It was in this respect that they still served as a model for Picasso some time later.

Degas did over twenty pictures of milliners, too. It was a subject that Eva Gonzalez had already painted before him. Paris, of course, was a great metropolis of fashion, and Degas was glad to accompany Mary Cassatt to milliners' and seamstresses' studios. What resulted was not psychological studies but searching scrutiny of an unfamiliar way of life.

In his pastel on paper, *At the Milliner's* (ill. p. 80), which he executed in 1882, Degas shows a customer examining herself in a new hat. The mirror not only divides up the composition; it also runs right down the milliner, so that, from our point of view, the hat she is holding out seems to be suspended in mid-air. Her face is hidden, her whole figure semi-concealed. Whatever situational contact might exist between these two women has been rendered null and void by this compositional approach.

That same year Degas painted two stylish young women in front of a mirror we cannot see; the light reflected from it falls on one woman's face as she tries on a hat (ill. p. 81). The asymmetrical view and close-up position allow us a sense of chance presence in mid-scene, so to speak. Half of the diagonally-divided space is occupied by the hats on the table, where we are impressed not only by Degas's ability to imply a whole situation but also by his occasionally disputed gifts as a colourist. The colour tones sounded by the hats harmonize with one another; the circles and ovals blend with the upright stands and cane and the angled arms to establish a delightful visual rhythm. In another pastel that dates from *c.* 1882, *Lady in Town Clothes* (ill. p. 79), Degas's interest is once again not so much in the fashionably dressed woman herself as in a certain tension of figure and space.

Degas likes to present the milliners and their clients as if they were in display windows. The people convey situations, and the situations act functionally as vehicles for compositions; in one picture, Degas goes so far as to hide the milliner completely behind hats.

In a note on other everyday Parisian scenes he was planning to record, Degas's habit of transferring his interest from the empirical facts to ways of seeing, colouring and composing becomes clear: "Series showing bakers' apprentices, in the bakeroom or even glimpsed from the street through the cellar windows; rosy flour, fine pastries, a still-life of various kinds of loaf. Big ones, oval, long, round, etc. Colour studies of yellow, rosy, grey and white loaves. Loaves in a row, foreshortened …" This is a far cry from the glamour of the opera and ballet; and, if we pause to reflect, our sense of the ballerinas in Degas's oeuvre undergoes a subtle change. What looks like elegance and grace is after all the product of toil too. The opera and theatre, even if their work is of an artistic nature, nonetheless do involve work.

But it is the artist's inventiveness that transforms what is merely seen into a cognitive mode. To one acquaintance who practised *plein air* painting (which Degas had no patience with), he said: "You need natural life and I need artificial." Degas's comments on his own work attest the pride he took in this: "My pictures are the product of a number of calculations and an infinite series of studies." Degas described his artistic method as a translation process in which the impressions of the moment were subordinate to a deliberate aesthetic aim and imagination: "To draw what sticks in the memory: it is a process in which fancy collaborates with memory. Only what really impressed one, only what is essential, is set down. Memory and fancy liberate one from the constraints imposed by Nature." Degas liked to prove that a crumpled handkerchief was all the model he needed in order to paint clouds! A flaneur, of course, only endows the things he sees with life once they have passed into his imagination. Degas must have derived great satisfaction from the fact that Baudelaire too advocated Art over Nature, the artificial over the natural.

The Impressionists (and chiefly Monet) liked to record fleeting effects of light in autonomous systems of painted colour. Degas, for his part, translated contingent situations involving movement into autonomous systems of forms. It is wise neither to overlook this nor to misunderstand it. Degas did not subscribe to ideas of *l'art pour l'art,* nor was he a prophet of abstract art. Rather, what he saw and chose to record was always semantically charged with the principle of the random and with laws of composition.

At a time when Salon art evaded present-day realities, at a time when historical art was still thriving, Degas devoted his unrestricted attention to the facts of his own present moment. The circus artiste and the women about their ironing were alike in that they both conveyed experiences of isolation in the everyday world.

Degas's art offers us artificial conditions of life and declares them to be normal; and it this this very declaration which draws attention to the cracks and fissures in our perceptions of everyday life. Degas's art, in short, is a devastating analysis of modern times. The flaneur, with his expertise in the quotidian, turned out to have observed the alienation of real lives far more acutely than most of the sociologists of the day.

Lady in Town Clothes, c. 1882
Pastel on grey paper, 48.5 x 42 cm (19 x 16½ in.)
Zurich, Walter Feilchenfeldt Collection

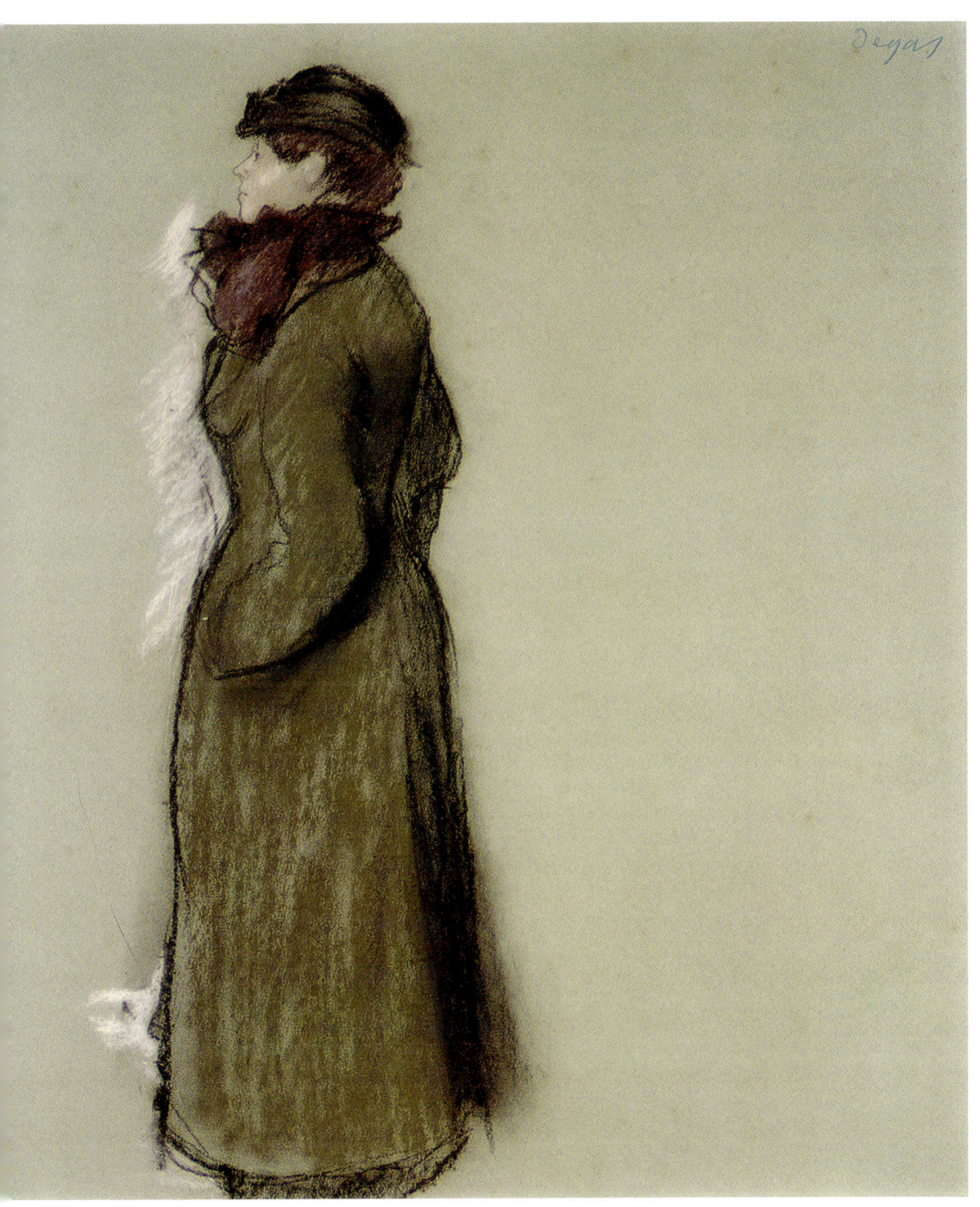

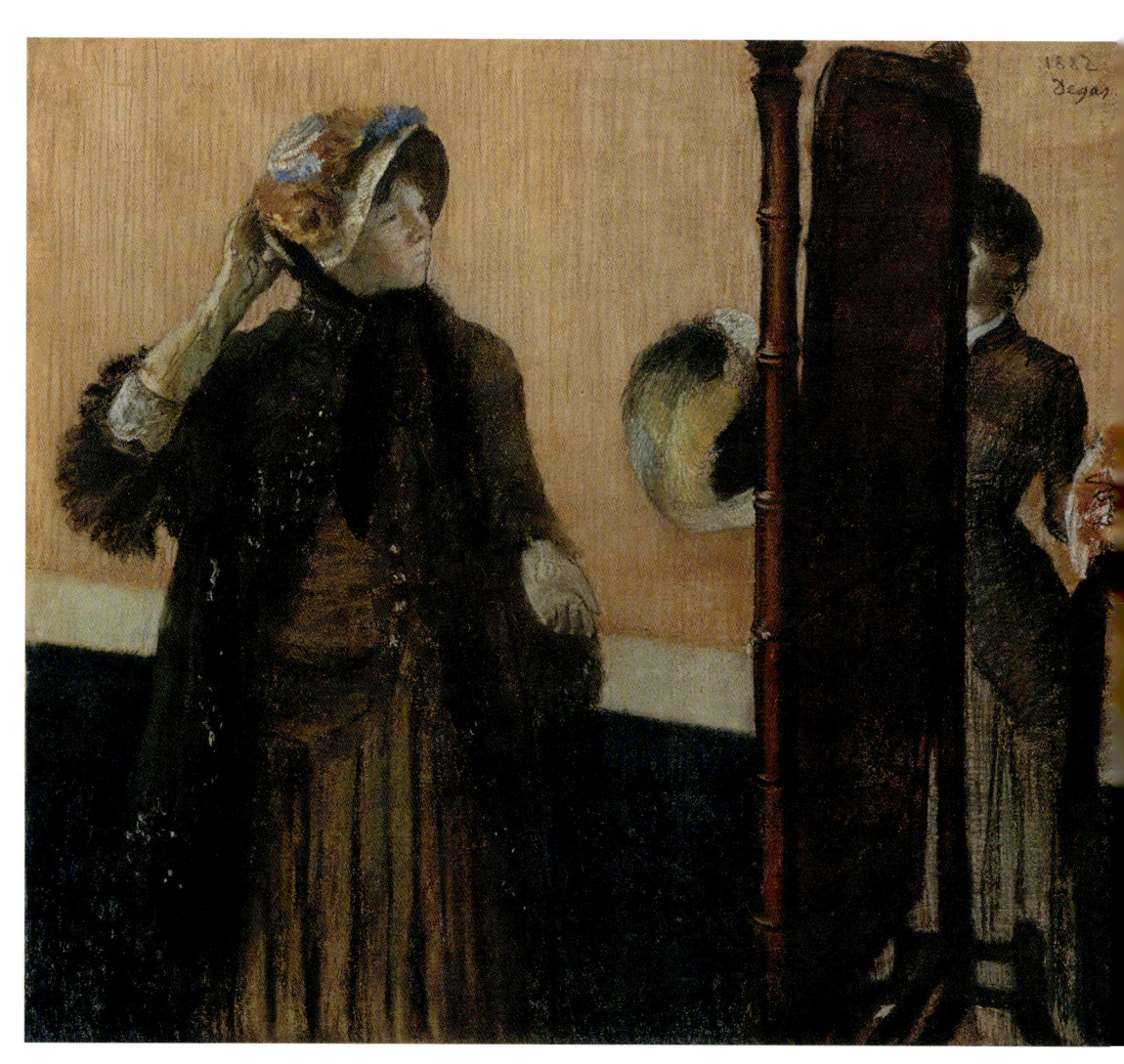

At the Milliner's, 1882
Pastel on grey paper, 76.2 x 86.4 cm (30 x 34 in.)
New York, The Metropolitan Museum of Art,
H. O. Havemeyer Collection,
Bequest of Mrs H. O. Havemeyer, 1929

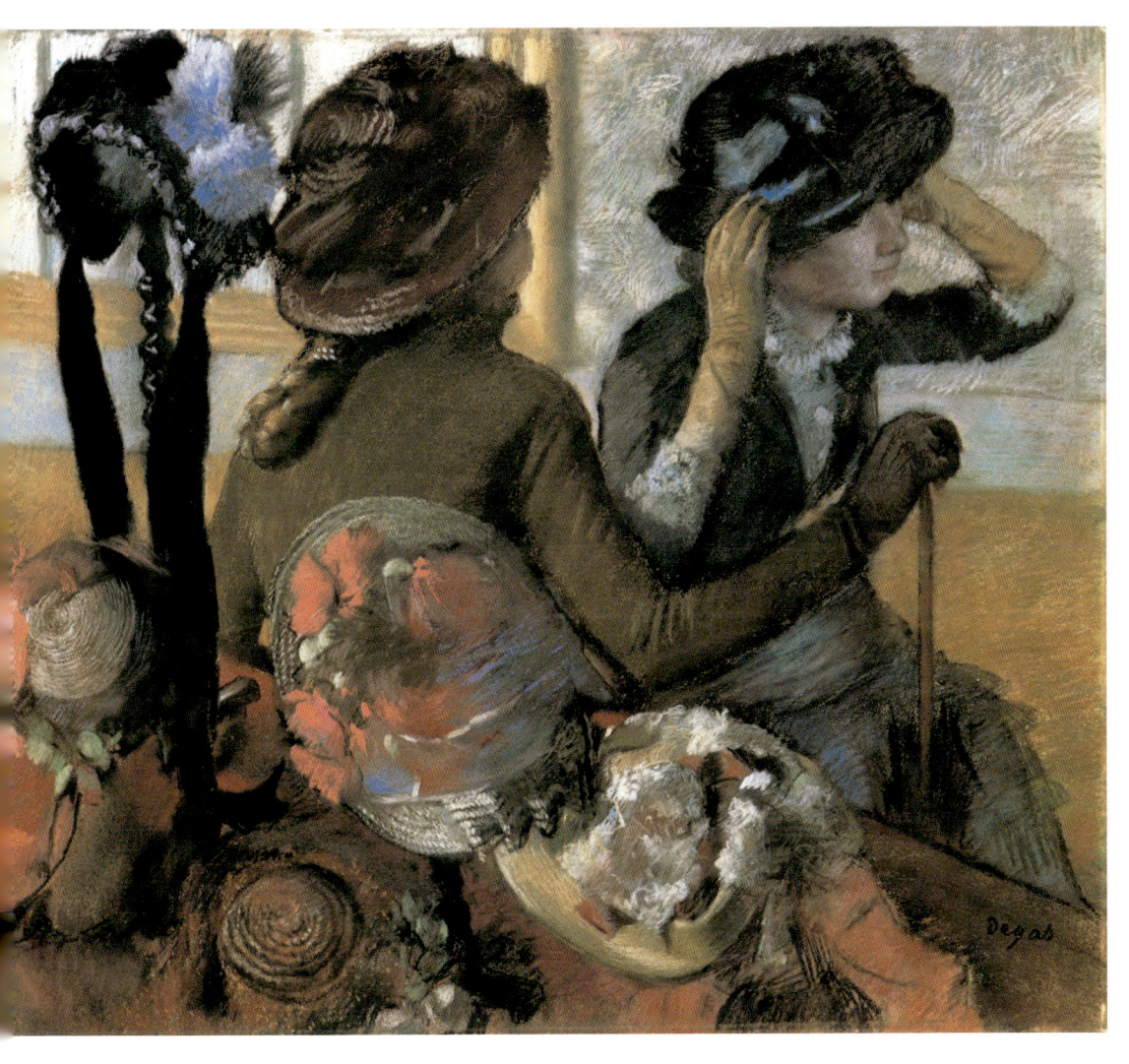

At the Milliner's, 1882
Pastel, 75.5 x 85.5 cm (29¾ x 33¾ in.)
Madrid, Museo Thyssen-Bornemisza

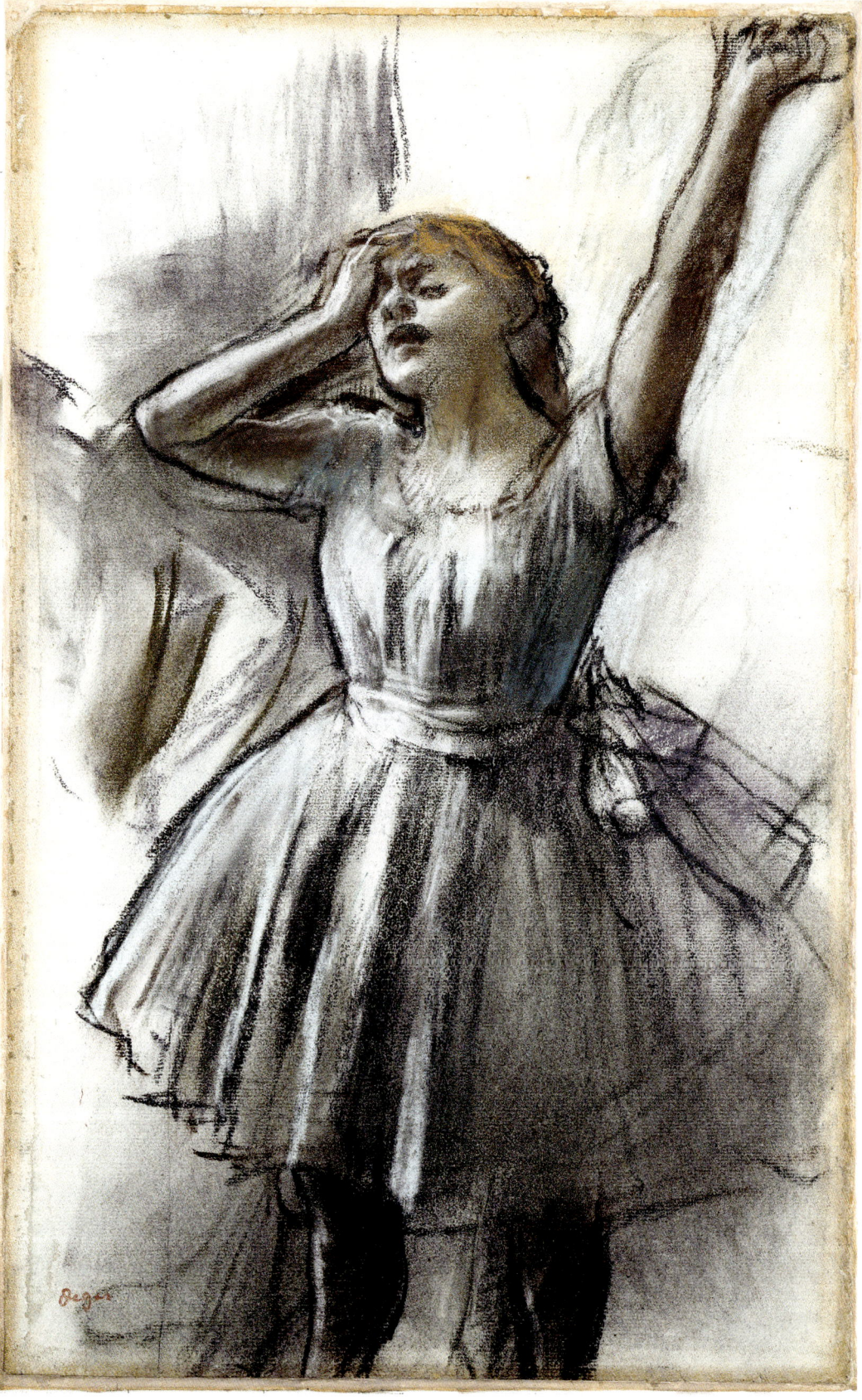

An Eye Condition

When exactly Degas began to work in clay and wax remains unclear, though it was probably in the mid-1860s. After his death, about 150 small sculptural works were found in his studio. Only half of them were in a state to allow of bronze casts being taken, and even then often after considerable repair work had to be done. Degas sculpted in clay, wax and putty, and unsurprisingly his subjects tended to be race horses or dancers. His first sculptural work involved horses: over a dozen movement studies constituted his first venture, and doubtless he partly had Renaissance sculptures by Donatello or Andrea del Verrocchio in mind.

At the sixth Impressionist exhibition (1881) he showed his sculptures publicly for the first and only time. They had been announced well in advance; and reactions to the *Little Fourteen-Year-Old Dancer* (1880; right) were very different. Some spoke of an "ideal of ugliness" while Huysmans discerned a "sculptural revolution". Critics were especially provoked by Degas's having clad his wax figure in a gauze tutu, satin shoes and pale yellow silk bow. Degas prepared the figure through a number of drawings and a red wax maquette, and the final result is so true to life that (in Huysman's words) "the dancer seems alive and on the point of quitting her plinth". Doubtless it was largely because Degas shelved public ambitions for his sculpture that he succeeded in creating works that now strike us as unique in the sculpture of the 19th century. Uninhibited by academy norms or the requirements of wealthy people offering commissions, Degas blithely flouted the rules, creating "sculptural snapshots" that deliberately stripped the art of its pomp and ceremony and need not be thought inferior to the achievement of Rodin.

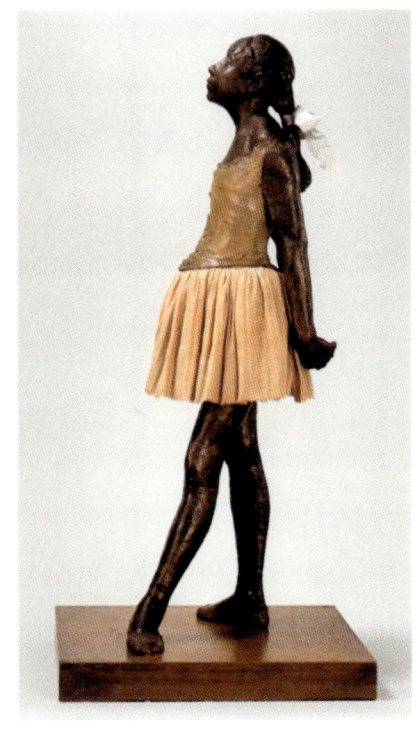

OPPOSITE
Tired Dancer, c. 1882–85
Pastel on pale blue gray paper,
46.7 x 29.7 cm (18½ x 11¾ in.)
Fort Worth, Texas, Kimbell Art Museum

ABOVE RIGHT
Little Fourteen-Year-Old Dancer, 1880
Bronze, painted in part, tulle skirt, satin bow,
wooden stand, height: 104.8 cm (41¼ in.)
New York, The Metropolitan Museum of Art,
H. O. Havemeyer Collection,
Bequest of Mrs H. O. Havemeyer, 1929

"The fumes of pipes, cigarettes and cigarette smokers, the smoke of locomotives, tall factory chimneys, steamer smokestacks etc., the way smoke is flattened under bridges."

EDGAR DEGAS

For Degas, a dancer was no more than a creature of movement, and he conceived his work as a record of that movement. The 1892–96 *Great Arabesque* (ill. p. 84) shows an essential classical ballet position, and neatly demonstrates the significance of equilibrium in dance. In sculptural terms, Degas has translated that equilibrium into a tension between taut stretching and a likelihood of collapse. To Georges Jeanniot he complained: "You would not credit the research and vexation that contraption has cost me. It is particularly hard to get the balance right." Seen in these extreme positions, Degas's figures have a quality of immediacy and presence in which the actual and the potential balance each other out.

Thus his dancers reach out into the space around them, and seem indeed to be growing into it. Compared with the postures approved by academic circles, these poses must have seemed wilfully unreal. Degas's lack of training in sculpture, a lack which meant his figures (supported on improvised frames) were always in great danger, was also an advantage. He was frequently helped by his sculptor friend Bartholomé, who in fact organized the first show of Degas's sculptures at the Petit Palais in 1918. Degas did not construct his sculptures from bottom to top. Rather, his figures seem centred upon a notional spatial midpoint, with axes and spatial volumes spreading out till some kind of balance, however precarious, has been established. That balance is the true subject of Degas's sculptural work: fleeting movement and construction are inseparable.

What Degas was looking for was motion that had not come to rest. In his paintings he had used sectional views in order to question the sense of a whole, and in his work as sculptor the very

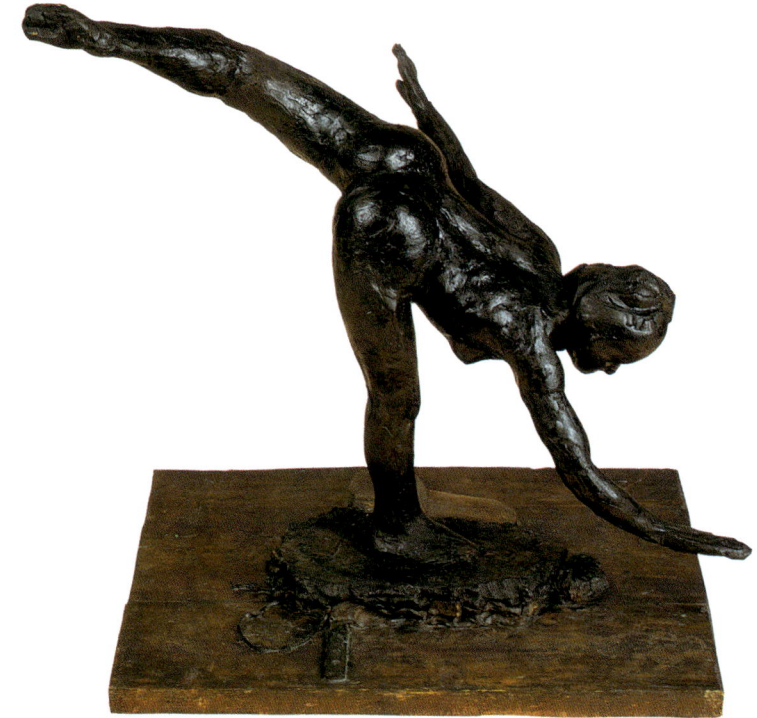

Great Arabesque, 1892–96
Bronze, height 40.5 cm (16 in.)
Paris, Musée d'Orsay

OPPOSITE
**Dancer Looking at
Her Right Foot**, 1895–1910
Bronze, height 48.2 cm (19 in.)
Paris, Musée d'Orsay

instability of his creations kept a similar insight accessible. For this reason, it seems as if sculpture were already somehow present in Degas's painting. Degas pulls and extends the human body in his sculptures: lacking a frame that he can crop, he has to establish a balanced sense of volume in other ways.

This is clearly visible in *Dancer Looking at Her Right Foot* (1895–1910; ill. p. 85). In a sense, the figure is no longer a woman but a jointed construct – Degas himself spoke of the "pretext" afforded by a subject. The dancer balancing on one foot to examine her other is a successful exercise in balancing movement and stasis, contingent flux and sculptural rigidity. The structure and material are in harmony, and the dancer's movement has become an equipoised construct of opposed forces and masses.

Degas moved from verisimilitude to a looser expression of volume. In relaxing his work's dependence on the body he allowed options for a free development of spatial qualities, and it is in this that his importance as a sculptor resides. The English sculptor Paul Tucker has even rated Degas higher than Rodin. Degas himself called

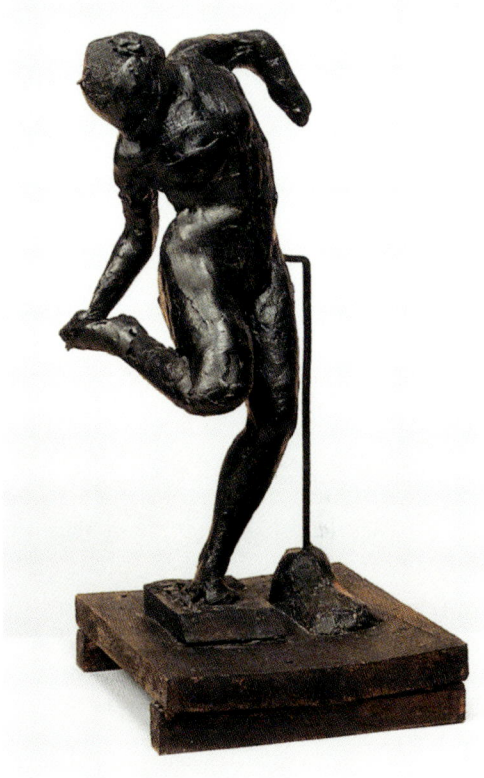

his modelled horses and dancers "craftwork for the blind" – a comment which should not be taken too literally, since many of his sculptural works were done between 1870 and 1880, in other words before he lost his sight.

Sculptural work was not so much Degas's response to his failing eyesight as one more strand of his continuing endeavour to locate expressive potential in various media. Wherever the possibility seemed available, he explored ways of linking graphic art and oil painting, drawing and pastel, sculpture and photography. Degas assigned the same significance to sculpture as to drawing: "Drawing is a way of thinking, modelling another." Degas was a master of both. Indeed, his sculptural work might not unfairly be seen as a peak in his exploration of artistic method.

Still, there can be no doubt that drawing lay at the heart of that exploration. Ever since Ingres gave the young Degas his advice to draw lines, he had remained true to that preference, as everything in his vast range and output attests. In 1877 Georges Rivière wrote in the periodical *L'Impressioniste*: "with a single stroke he can show everything that can be said of him, and show it more rapidly, than words can" – and it was indisputably true that Degas had an immense repertoire of drawing techniques and idioms. Unusual precision and finesse were as much his as fast, sure-touch charcoal sketching. From preparatory drawings of details (such as for *Mlle La La*) to drawings done in their own right (such as the portrait of Hortense Valpinçon), from charcoal drawings that used coloured pastel (such as *Tired Dancer*) to loosely done gouaches, drawings for Degas were not a tiresome convention, as they were for the Impressionists, but represented a challenge to experiment.

In his paintings, Degas increasingly abandoned a sense of precise contour, and in his drawings too he began to lose interest in strict linearity. His contours broke up, as they were later to do in Cézanne's work too; the line no longer denoted the exact boundary of a thing or body. In his sculptures this lack of definition is replicated in the restless unfinality of surface; the cursory quality of his late paintings and drawings appears as an unstable silhouette. The stroboscopic effect of many of his contour lines matched Degas's view of movement: every additional line stood for a change in the process of perception. Degas left an axiom that put his changed ideas well: "The line is not the shape; it is the way one sees the shape." Setting aside debates on colour and line in art, this comment alone highlights the importance the line had in Degas's conception of art. It also makes clear the ambiguous relations between the firm precision of a drawing and the continuously changing flux of perception itself.

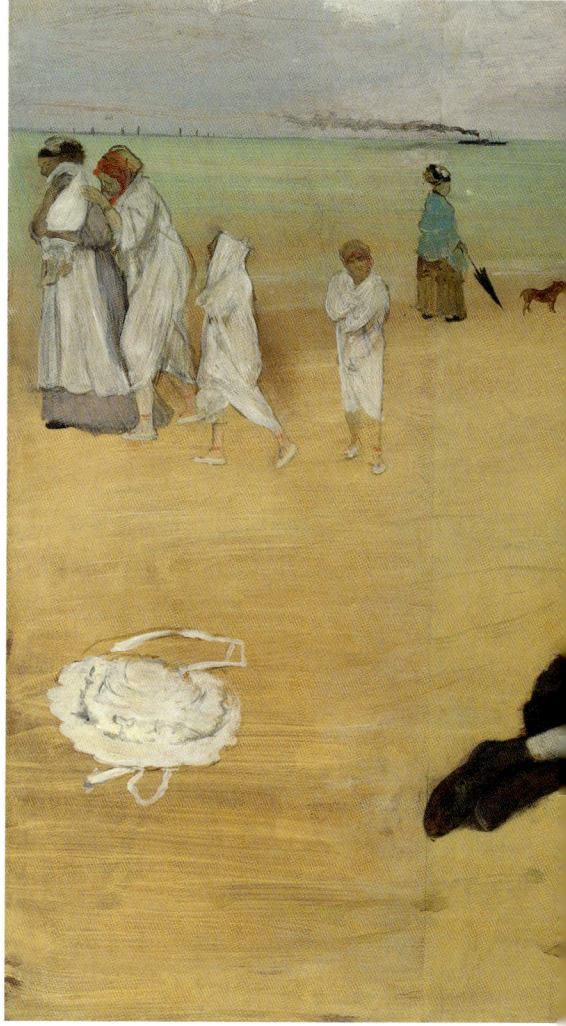

Experimental by nature, Degas naturally loved the monotype. He did well over 300, the earliest in the mid-1870s but most of them in the period from 1878 to 1885. Because the process required rapid work, it appealed to Degas's needs and wishes; he liked to use the chance effects and surprises that resulted. Usually he made single prints from copper or glass plates on which he had drawn the image in lithographic ink or oil. The sheets were printed in black or brown; later, poor-quality prints served him as a basis for new work – he would colour them with pastel crayon or otherwise rework them. A quarter of his pastels are reworkings of second or third monotype printings in this way. He called them "drawings done in lithographic ink and printed".

In the early 1880s, Degas did a series of forty monotypes to illustrate Ludovic Halévy's novel *Monsieur et Madame Cardinal,* which was set in the ballet world. Or rather, Degas's sheets with hastily sketched figures and a Japanese-style spatial approach did not so much illustrate Halévy as make a parallel visual narrative. Halévy's descriptions of backstage scenes, with young beaux waiting for ballerinas, or the girls themselves hurrying down spiral staircases, in fact read as if they were descriptions of Degas's pictures. Halévy, though, apparently did not care much for the artist's work, and the collaboration was never published.

Being a mixed medium of drawing and printing, monotypes afforded Degas a means of experimenting that also gave him unusual graphic freedom. He used all the positive and negative procedures to secure a full range of nuanced tones. Lines were drawn onto the plates with a brush,

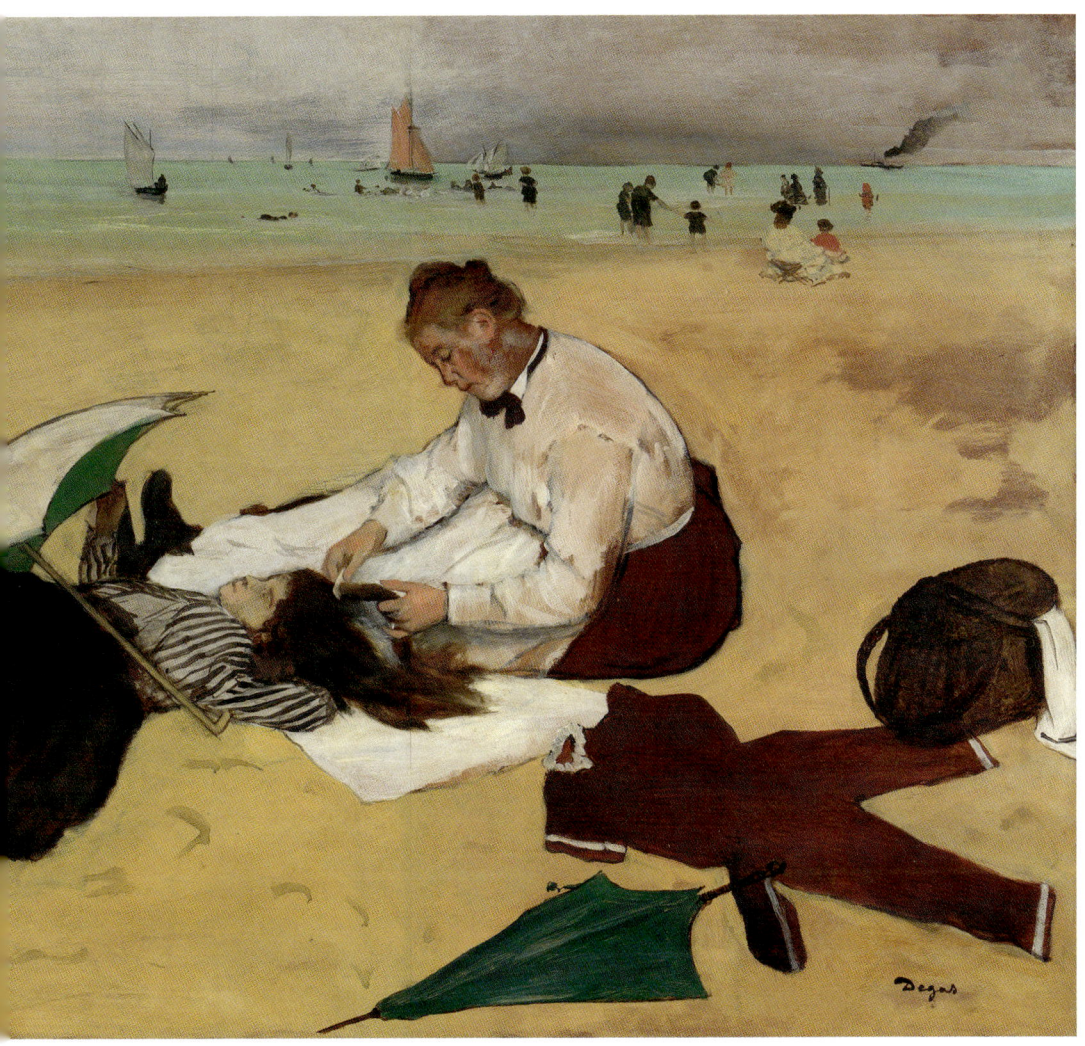

At the Beach, 1869/70
Oil on paper, 47.5 x 82.9 cm (18¾ x 32¾ in.)
London, The National Gallery

dark areas of colour dabbed in with a rag. A single well-placed smudge could place an entire face. Or, in a sheet such as *Sleep* (1879–85), the light areas of the canapé and the reclining woman are brought out against a blackened plate by means of brushes, brush handles or even fingertips.

And again Degas devised methods which are difficult to imagine in other types of art. *Smoking Chimneys,* done in 1878/79, is such a picture – a tiny monotype, barely there at all. And yet Degas tackled his subject in ambitious mood, and his meticulous notebooks recorded it as one of his important projects of the late 1870s. To submit to the element of chance in any process while at the same time remaining in control: that was the risky rule of thumb that governed Degas's work.

This technique led Degas to an area of work that he normally avoided and which the other Impressionists loved: landscape. The painting *At The Beach* (1869/70; ill. p. 87) is among Degas's few genuinely Impressionist landscapes, and it may even have been prompted by a similar work that

Manet did in 1869. But this is no Manet or Monet beach scene; rather, it gathers a number of characteristic Degas motifs, such as the nanny combing the girl's hair, or the family wrapped in towels. Nor does Degas do without his little ironies, such as the steamers' smoke drifting in two different directions, or the girl's bathing costume carefully laid out to dry, both of which underline the artifice in a supposedly natural scene. He proudly told one visitor that a flannel jacket spread on the studio floor and a model had been all he needed to paint the work.

Landscapes of quite a different kind resulted from a trip to Burgundy with Bartholomé in October 1890. He worked from memory; and the ill-defined products recall Victor Hugo's complaint in 1837 to the effect that rail travel made it impossible to perceive landscape. And yet it was these works, in November 1892, that were shown at Durand-Ruel's gallery in Degas's only solo exhibition in his lifetime.

Degas's method of working in pastel over a monotype permitted free colour improvisation over a light and dark prestructured fundament. In these works, Degas created phantasmagoric effects of colour. There are no people in these landscapes; the scenes are colourful impressions – of unusual sensuous power – caught in passing.

Degas was less interested in recording Nature than in relations between particular tones of colour that could be used, without any linear structure, to establish dream qualities. But he was not enamoured of hasty gabble about "conditions of the soul" and dryly retorted that it was "an eye condition". This is one more reason why these coloured monotypes seem more the work of a Rothko or a Graubner than of a 19th-century artist. They are colour sensations pure and simple, diaphanous, with minimal contrast and laden with light. The exactness of line that rules most of Degas's work has for once been displaced by colour.

What makes these works different from those of Degas's fellow Impressionists is not only the approach to colour but also his insight into the artificiality of Nature once it appears in a picture. Degas refused categorically to follow Nature: "A picture is first and foremost a product of the artist's imagination…!" And he had no good words for *plein air* painting: "Painting is not a sport!"

Degas insisted that the studio was the place for the creative, inventive faculty. All he needed, he said, was "vegetable soup and three old brushes dipped in it to paint all the landscapes in the world". What Degas had in mind was not so much the rule-book school of landscape art that Alexander Cozens had propagated in the 18th century, which attempted a clear-cut codification of all the

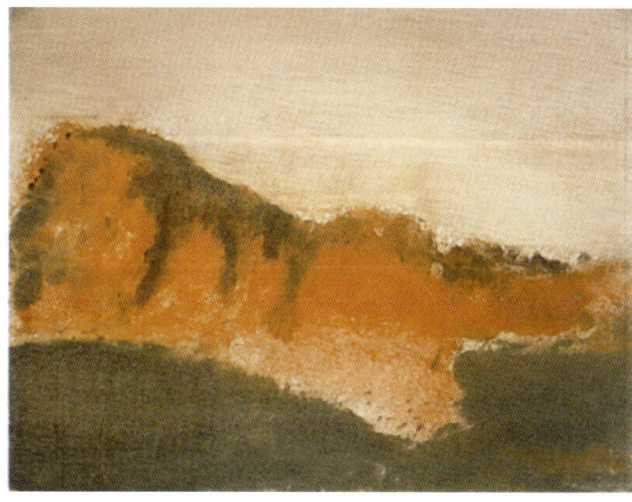

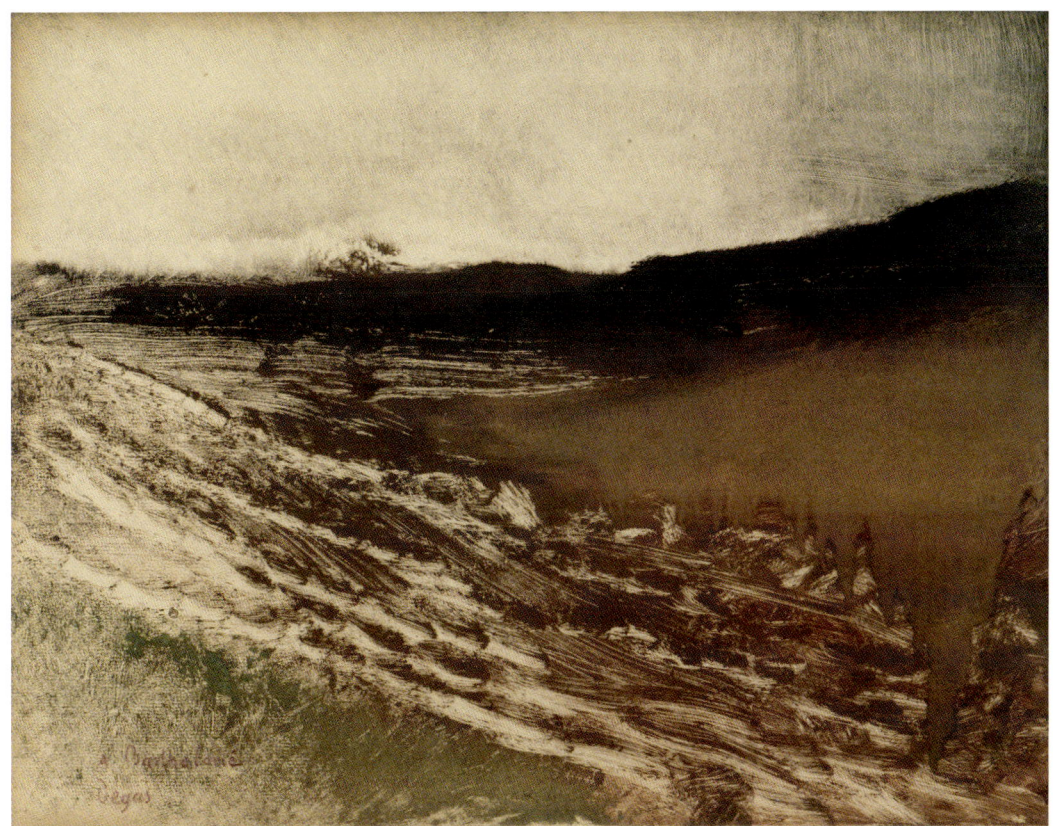

elements of landscape composition. Rather, he was himself practising a free adaptation (suited to his own synthetic
procedures) of the "de-forming" principle Valéry spoke of,
according to which humans could become landscapes and
rocks people. Thus he said of a block of granite: "What a
line, beautiful as a shoulder! I shall make a steep coast of it,
seen from the open sea…" It is in this sense that a reclining
nude, perhaps a reversed print of *Sleep,* becomes an anthro-

Landscape, 1890–92
Coloured monotype on paper,
30 x 40 cm (11¾ x 15¾ in.)
Paris, Musée d'Orsay

OPPOSITE
*Landscape (Le Cap Hornu près de
Saint-Valery-sur-Somme),* 1890–92
Coloured monotype, 30 x 40 cm (11¾ x 15¾ in.)
London, The British Museum

pomorphic coastal scene in *Coastal Landscape* (1890–92; ill. p. 91). Landscape, as for Proust, is "a
mysterious person with the broad, undefined physiognomy of a cliff, the gaze of sunset in the rain,
and even the deep waters of the sea." Degas's innate sarcasm could not resist developing the human
features of his landscape, though; the "male" companion piece (cf. ill. p. 90) shows how bluntly he
could choose to make his visual point. Rejecting landscape as a condition of the soul, and insisting
on "an eye condition", implies (as these pictures show) a reflexive way of seeing: what is experienced
and what is invented become one and the same.

Degas even appropriated and adapted, in like manner, the entirely new medium of photography,
which was first exhibited at the Salon in 1859. His attention was caught by the visual shifts which the
photographic way of seeing made possible for painters. He scrutinized subjects from all round, and
used visual contexts that implied things far beyond what was in the picture, as snapshots do. And at
times his photographic eye was turned to photography itself, with productive results.

Late in 1895 he took a photograph of Renoir and Mallarmé in Julie Manet's apartment. Paul Valéry has described how both sitters had to keep their poses for a quarter of an hour in the light of nine oil lamps. The photo is a portrait of two friends; Degas has posed them in such a way as to convey their personalities. Renoir, looking as relaxed as Manet in the 1868/69 double portrait, is staring straight at us. Mallarmé is leaning against the wall, looking sideways at the painter. Degas spent a good deal of time in Mallarmé's company and read the poet some of his own twenty sonnets.

In the photo, the mirror half is the Impressionist painter's, the empty white wall the symbolist poet's. But the blind patch of brightness in the mirror, right beside the camera, is where Degas should be visible. His photo juxtaposes image and mirror image. The space on this side of the scene, where the photographer and his camera (and we ourselves, looking on) are to be found, is integrated in as complex a manner as in the 1881 *The Dance Class.* The photo makes clear how little Degas felt his own attitude to pictures had in common with the making of illusions. Valéry nicely described Degas as "the phantom in the mirror": that is, as impalpable a presence as one could possibly imagine. This expresses more than the intended parallel to Mallarmé; it touches upon the very essence of Degas's method as an artist. In a photograph, of all places, Degas proved that in his eyes invention and imagination ranked higher than mere exposure and recording: "A snapshot of the moment is a photograph and no more!"

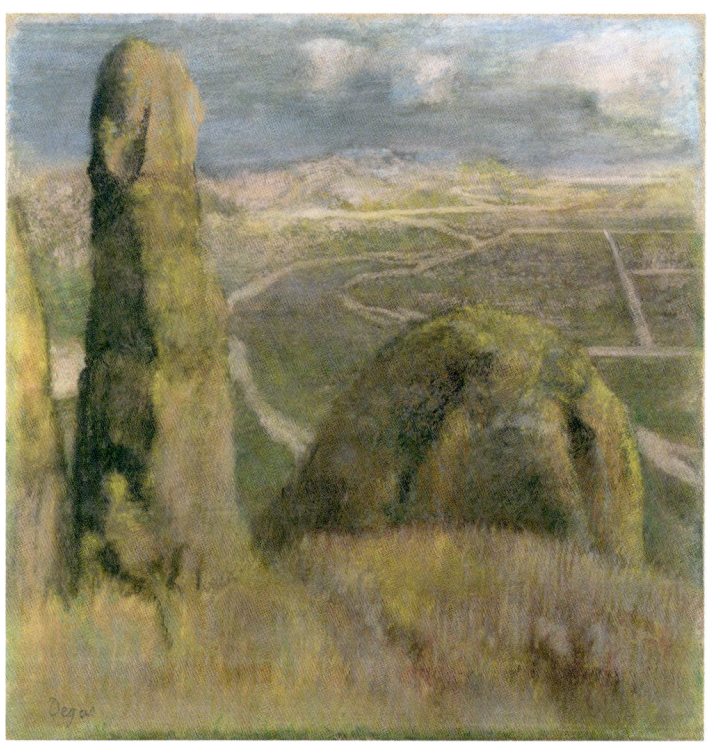

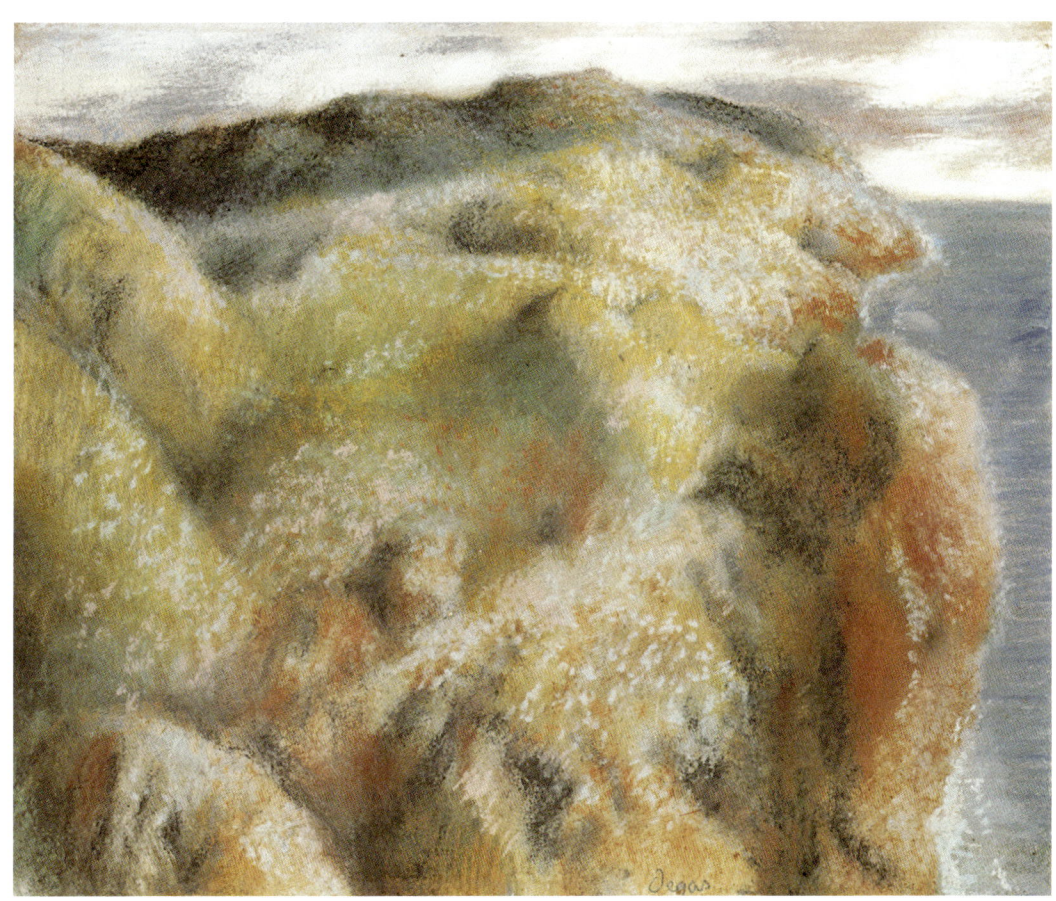

*"Only when he no longer knows what he
is doing does the painter do good things."*

EDGAR DEGAS

Coastal Landscape, 1890–92
Pastel on monotype on coloured
paper, 42 x 55 cm (16¼ x 21¾ in.)
Private collection

OPPOSITE
Landscape, *c.* 1892
Pastel on paperboard,
51.1 x 50.5 cm (20⅛ x 20 in.)
Houston, The Museum of Fine Arts,
Museum purchase funded by the
Brown Foundation Accessions
Endowment Fund

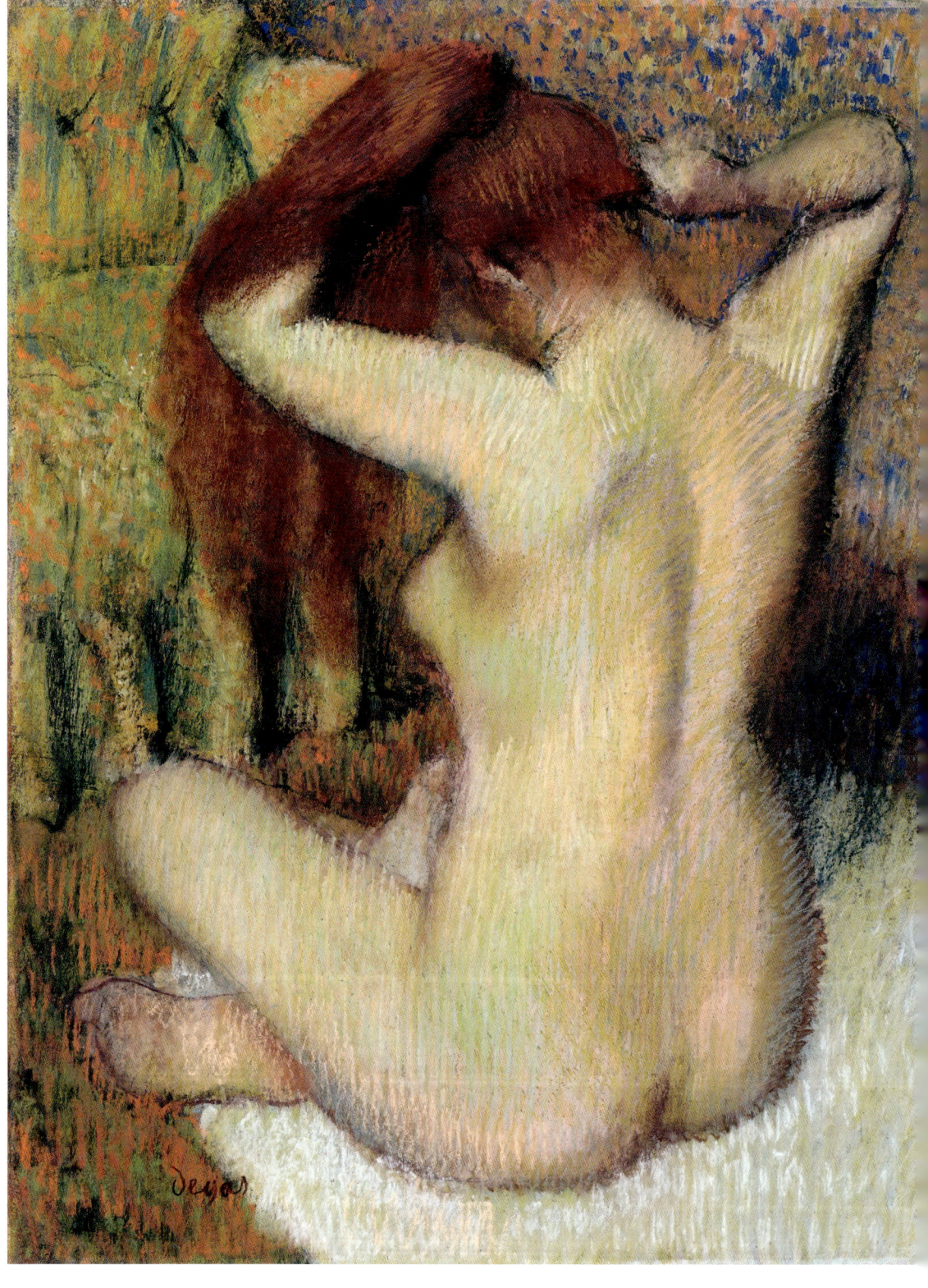

The Never-Ending Picture

In the late 19th century, pastels were largely the province of private collectors. Degas's habit of exhibiting paintings, pastels and drawings on an equal footing was the exception, not the rule. Even in the 18th century heyday of the pastel portrait, the technique was considered a sign of dilettantism. Initially Degas used pastel for sketch drawings, but in the 1880s it became his preferred medium. Soon it became impossible to draw clear distinctions between his media: just as Degas liked to overwork monotypes in pastel, so too he combined pastel with oil or with gouache. His increasing use of pastel had financial reasons too, since pastels were easier to produce and easier to sell. But Degas rapidly came to value the potential

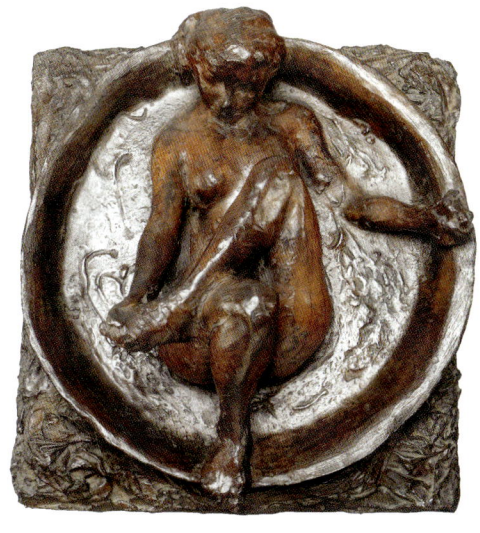

of coloured chalks; and, in his series of bathing women, pastel quite displaced paint and monotype from his technical interests. In these pictures, Degas's ability to develop a subject through a variety of visual strategies was arguably more in its element even than with the jockeys or ballerinas. *The Tub* (1885/86; ill. p. 97) shows a woman bending in the bath tub to moisten her sponge. Another (ill. p. 96) done in 1887 emphasizes the compositional zoning. Again we are looking down at a naked woman in a tub; she is supporting herself with one hand, the better to wash her neck with the other. On the chest at right are a number of toilet articles. The angle of vision has been so chosen as to run the edge of the chest down the picture; if it were not for the handles of a pot and a brush, we might think there were two distinct pictures. The different parts of the picture match in colour, of course, with the glowing chestnut of the woman's hair and sponge picked up in the copper pot and the strands of false hair.

Degas was forever inventing new ways of seeing and devising new approaches to his models. He did so without considering the possible consequences. In the late 1880s he did a sculpture of a woman reclining in a tub (ill. p. 93). It was one of his largest sculptures; and it forces us to look at the woman from above. The sculptural norm, by which a

OPPOSITE
Woman Combing Her Hair, *c.* 1888–90
Pastel on paper, 61.3 x 46 cm (24¼ x 18 in.)
New York, The Metropolitan Museum of Art,
Gift of Mr and Mrs Nate B. Spingold, 1956

ABOVE RIGHT
The Tub, 1886–89
Bronze, 45.8 x 43.8 x 22.5 cm (18 x 17¼ x 8⅞ in.)
Paris, Musée d'Orsay

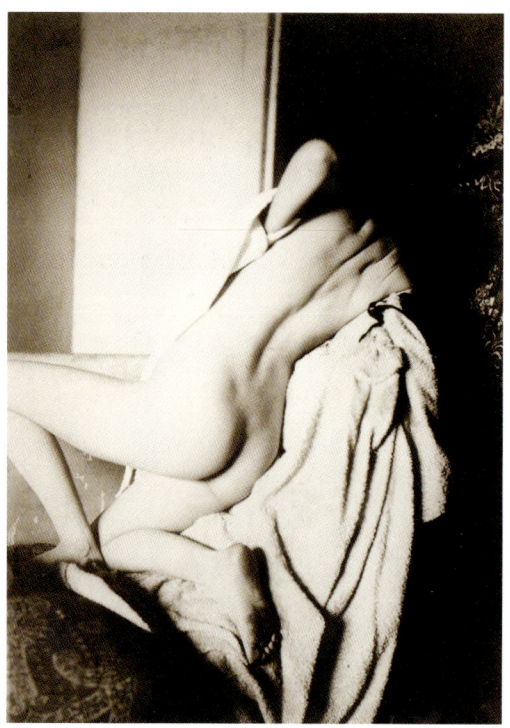

figure can be seen three-dimensionally, is gone. The position in which the woman appears in a work such as *Woman Drying Her Feet* (1885/86) prompted Valéry's sharp-witted insight: "In the naked figure, which he has been scrutinizing a whole life long in every conceivable manner and position, and even in vigorous motion, Degas has been seeking the unique linear system that might articulate a particular physical gesture as precisely and arrestingly as possible."

Degas was out to free the nude of poses. He refused to idealize his nudes in the style then thought obligatory. His women getting out of the tub, washing or drying themselves, were at odds with the literary or mythological approaches preferred by his contemporaries. These women are indifferent to the kind of imagined viewer envisaged by the makers of Salon Venuses. Perhaps for that very reason, unlike the Salon painters, he attracted the charge of voyeurism, even from friends such as George Moore, when he exhibited a group of these works in 1886. As long ago as the nude drawings for *The Sufferings of the City of New Orleans* (ill. p. 29) Degas had achieved the kind of directness that threw viewers who interpreted it as shamelessness or indiscretion. But Degas's gaze was a steady one: "My women are simple human beings, but honest; they are merely looking after their bodies. This one is washing her feet. It is as if one were watching her through a keyhole."

Because it was the physical presence and movements of his nudes that interested Degas, he was able to break the rules of the genre. The flaky textures of pastel chalk are subtly used to suggest a dry glow of almost symbolic quality in the women's bodies. Employing a blatantly colourful hatching technique, Degas no longer uses the line to define form or indeed volume but rather amasses lines to lend colourful vitality to entire visual zones. "I am a colourist with lines," asserted Degas; and the dictum has a precise meaning if we consider the shimmer of hatched zones in these works. Skin gleams as pure colour, embedded in a radiant surround. Degas was open to technical experiments of any kind to achieve his ends. He cursed the "diabolical work of taking the brightness out of pastel colours, I wash them time after time". He changed the technique radically and fundamentally, making it an invention all his own.

He had long been in the habit of thinking in series of pictures which could implicitly never be completed. To an extent, serial work meant that Degas could pursue a gesture or movement through a sequence of pictures, or indeed through a single picture. Nowadays, these sequences remind us of film frames. It was only in such sequences that a subject's changes through time could be recorded in terms of light and movement. Degas decreed: "One must do the same motif ten times, even a hundred times over."

Degas was one of the first artists to work deliberately with the concept of the series in order to emphasize the conceptual dimension of his art. Serial work, together with fragmented sectionalization and a curt, abbreviated style of painting, afforded a way of dismissing the idea of completeness or perfection as an integral necessity in art. For Degas, pictures increasingly implied states of transition, both in terms of subject and of medium. Monotypes became pastels; photographs such as *After the Bath, Woman Drying Her Back* (1896; ill. p. 95) prompted whole series of drawings and paintings. Finally it is moot to establish which was the starting point and which the development, since the images feed off and continue each other. Seen like this, every picture is potentially never-ending. The pity is that today's museums and exhibitions scarcely allow us to follow the ramifications in the way they deserve.

His self-absorbed nudes, waiting for no one, prompted all manner of speculation about the artist (who lived alone). Even Édouard Manet, Émile Bernard, van Gogh and Raffaelli liked to swap jokes and *doubles entendres* about Degas's sex life. Confirmed bachelor though he was, he was even reported to have had an affair with Mary Cassatt. His whole life long, though, ever since his early notebooks lamented his isolation, his longing to be alone and his weariness of solitude went hand in hand.

That said, Degas by no means spent his closing decades in utter isolation. He had a large circle of acquaintances and was a sociable man. Every Thursday he was at Edmond Manet's, where Mallarmé and Renoir were often to be found too. They would do things together – going to the Cézanne exhibition at the Galerie Vollard, for instance. On Fridays he dined with building engineer Henri Rouart, who also fancied himself as a painter. In Rouart's collection, which extended from Chardin and Goya to the present, Degas occupied a prominent position. He painted some further portraits, among them the unusual

OPPOSITE
After the Bath, Woman Drying Her Back, 1896
Gelatin silver print, 16.5 x 12 cm (6½ x 4¾ in.)
Los Angeles, J. Paul Getty Museum

Woman by the Tub, *c.* 1884–86
Oil on canvas, 150.8 x 213.7 cm (59¼ x 84¼ in.)
New York, Brooklyn Museum,
Carl H. De Silver Fund

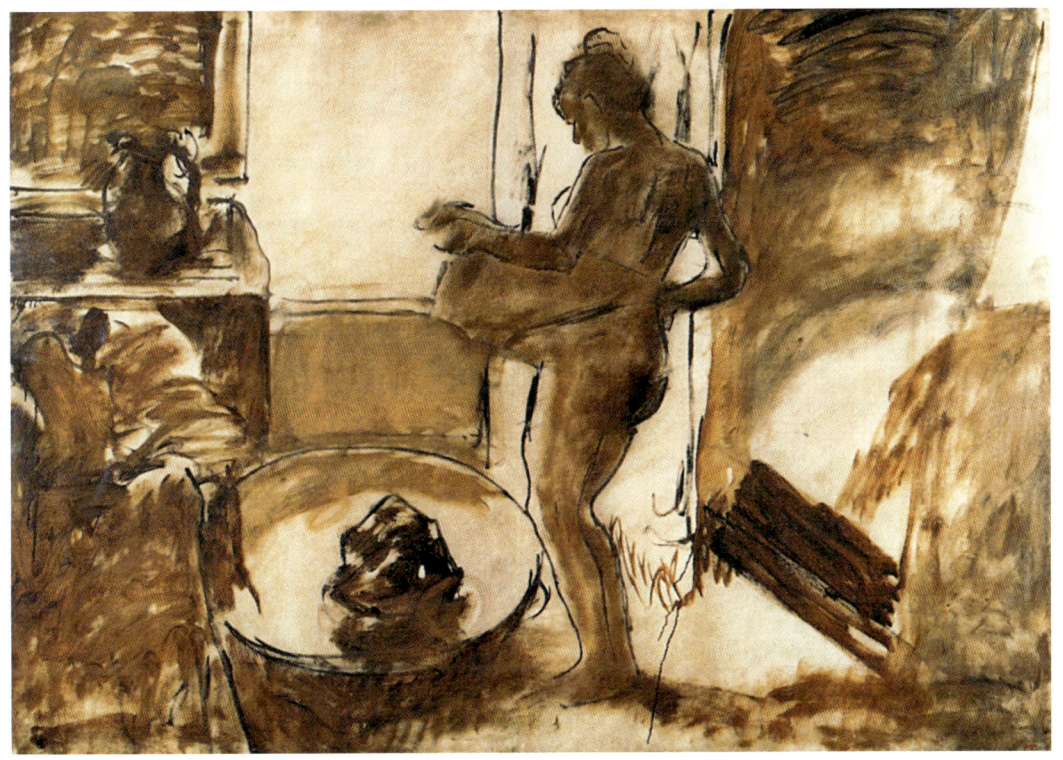

group portrait *Six Friends in Dieppe* (1885). His old friends such as the Valpinçons and Halévys were joined by new such as Suzanne Valadon, whose drawings he valued highly. Surely, as he grew older, there was more to Edgar Degas than the crotchety sharpness he was reported capable of.

It has to be said that any attempt to describe Degas the man or his work comes down to contradictions. He was mocking, arrogant and infatuated with himself; but he was also vulnerable, and a true friend. Affection for his extensive family, and a sense of duty, were dominant in his life. Yet he had little social tolerance, as his anti-Semitic stance in the Dreyfus affair (which lost him some of his closest friends) sadly proved. He was a man of contraries, and uncompromising; Mallarmé thought him "rigorous". Cool yet irascible, timorous yet razor-tongued, he made both friends and enemies all around. At fifty he felt he had wasted his life, and as he grew older he did not forbear to lash himself: "All in all I have had less courage than I hoped."

He was hardly at all the typical avant-garde 19th-century artist of post-Romantic cliché. A cultivated and methodical man, of encyclopaedic breadth in art, music and literature, he abruptly switched from an early leaning towards Salon art, and became the pre-eminent painter of modern life. He was well-to-do, had enjoyed a classical education, knew his art history, and yet was well able to breach tradition and familiarize himself with the dark sides of society. The few constants in his life include his formidable powers of observation, his ability to focus vision, an old-fashioned male ideology, and a rebarbative pride. One of his duties, as he saw it, was not to expose his inner self: "Art is the

OPPOSITE
The Tub, 1885/86
Pastel on paper, 70 x 70 cm (27½ x 27½ in.)
Farmington, Connecticut, Hill-Stead Museum,
Alfred Atmore Pope Collection

The Tub, 1886
Pastel on cardboard, 60 x 83 cm (23½ x 32¾ in.)
Paris, Musée d'Orsay

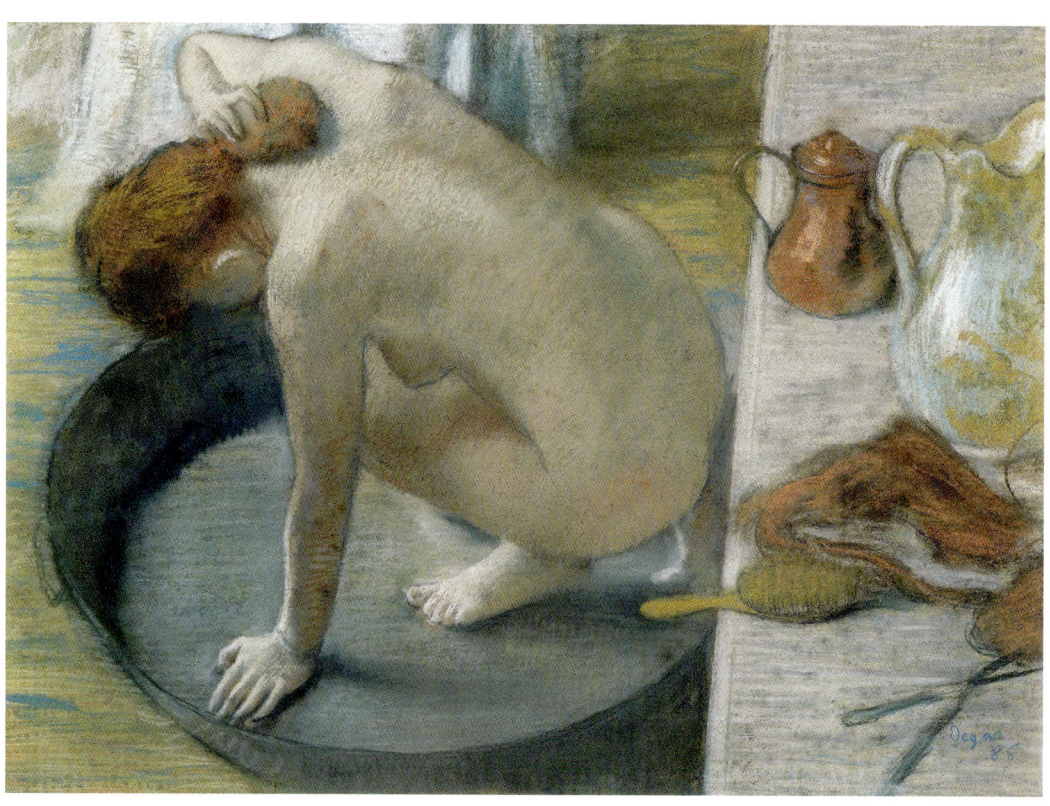

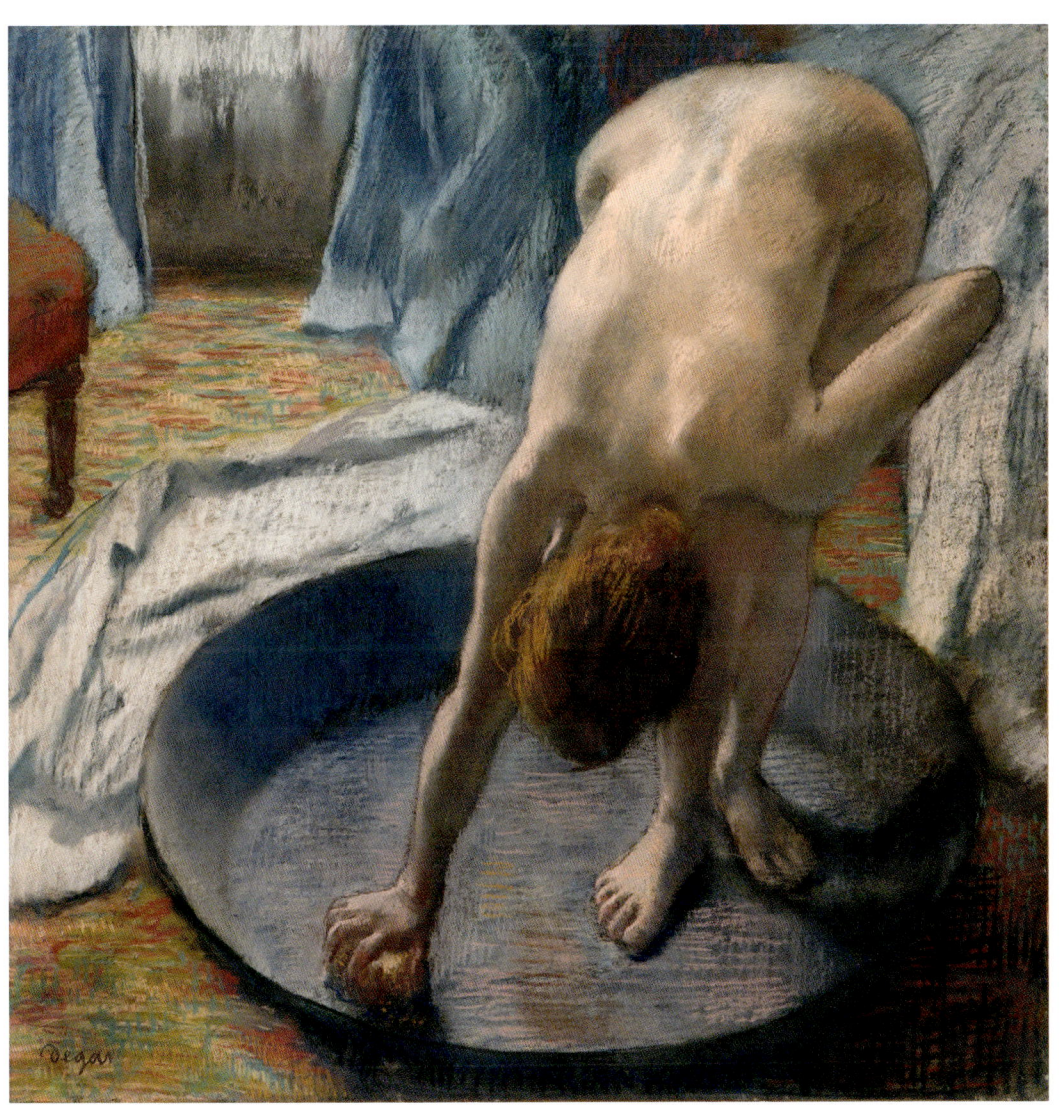

governance of pain by beauty." By 1908 he was so blind that he could no longer even draw. All attempt at artistic work had to be abandoned. He was condemned to inactivity. His housekeeper reported that he was afraid of dying. And still, even into old age, he would take his customary constitutional along the boulevards. On the morning of 27 September 1917 Degas died; he was buried in the family grave in Montmartre cemetery. He had requested that only a single statement should be uttered at his grave: "He very much loved drawing."

Of the artists of his time, Degas was the one who analyzed isolation, alienation, and the abyss of public pleasure. Coolly he assembled ways of seeing; his pictures constructed the very way they were seen. His rejection of official perceptions was his avowal of art. His own way of seeing, forced though it sometimes was, mattered as much to him as his subjects: "The idea of truth is conveyed by falsity."

This brings us back to Baudelaire, and unconditional preference of memory and its constructs over immediate perception. It was a preference Degas shared, and the sharing proved his modernity. "Modernity," Baudelaire famously wrote in his essay on modern painters, "is all things temporary, evanescent, random, and is one half of art, the other half of which is the eternal and immutable." Baudelaire saw modern art's task as prising out of modern reality the "fleeting eternity" it might contain. It is a good description of Degas's art.

Degas transformed fragmentary, random perception into images. For him, as for Mallarmé and Valéry in literature, this was a way of articulating what could not be said or shown. He rendered negative images in positive, and so made an issue of the alienation that went unseen. If his subjects were trivial and everyday, they went with a compositional perfection without compare. He has been called the most sophisticated compositional artist of the 19th century. And yet, at the very moment when we think Degas's visual world has become a mere function of compositional and painterly transactions, he demands that we see the reality in his work: "One has only to look – I have invented nothing!"

Woman Drying Her Neck, 1900–05
Charcoal and pastel on paper,
76.7 x 76.1 cm (30¼ x 30 in.)
Lausanne, Musée cantonal des Beaux-Arts

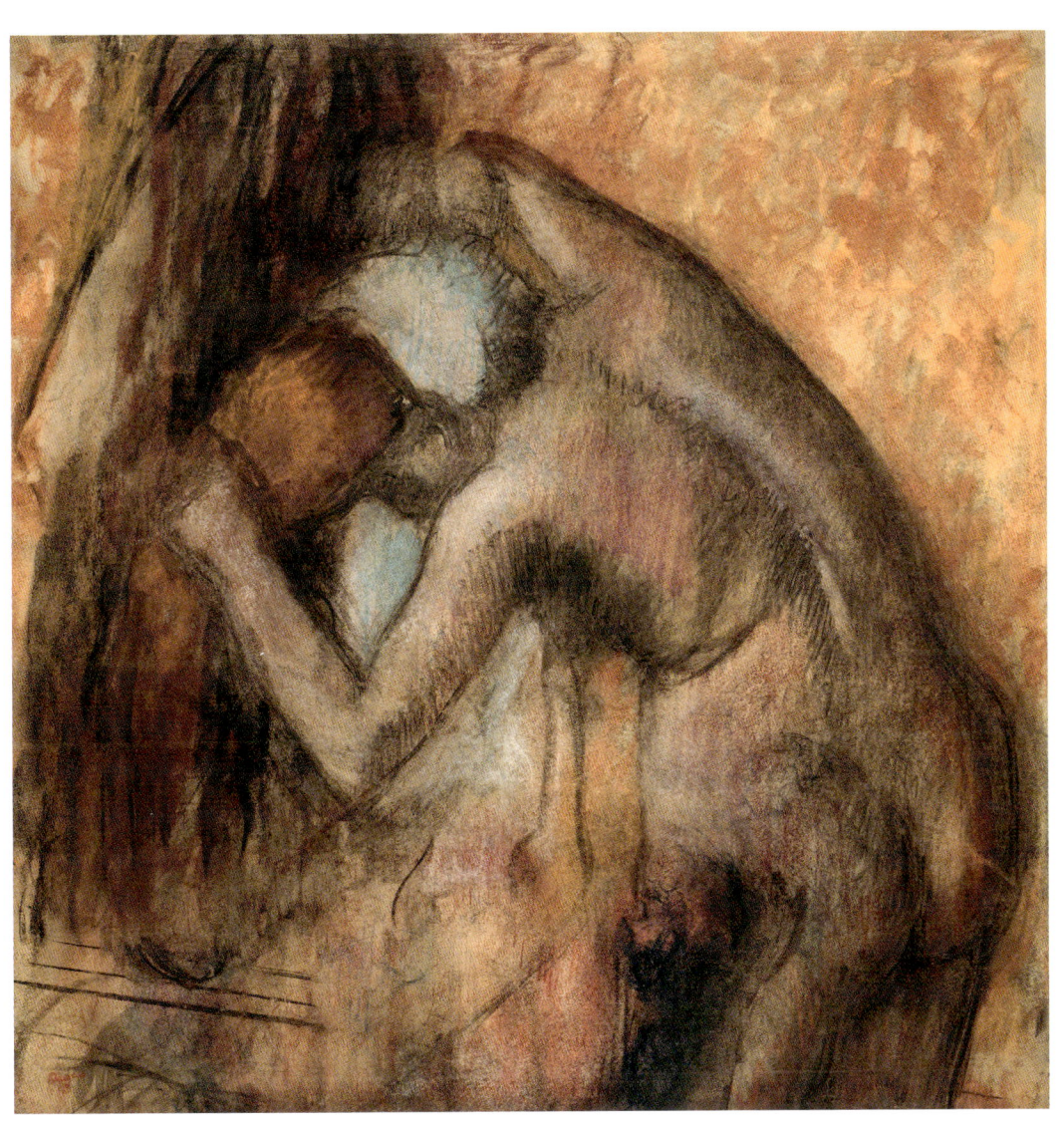

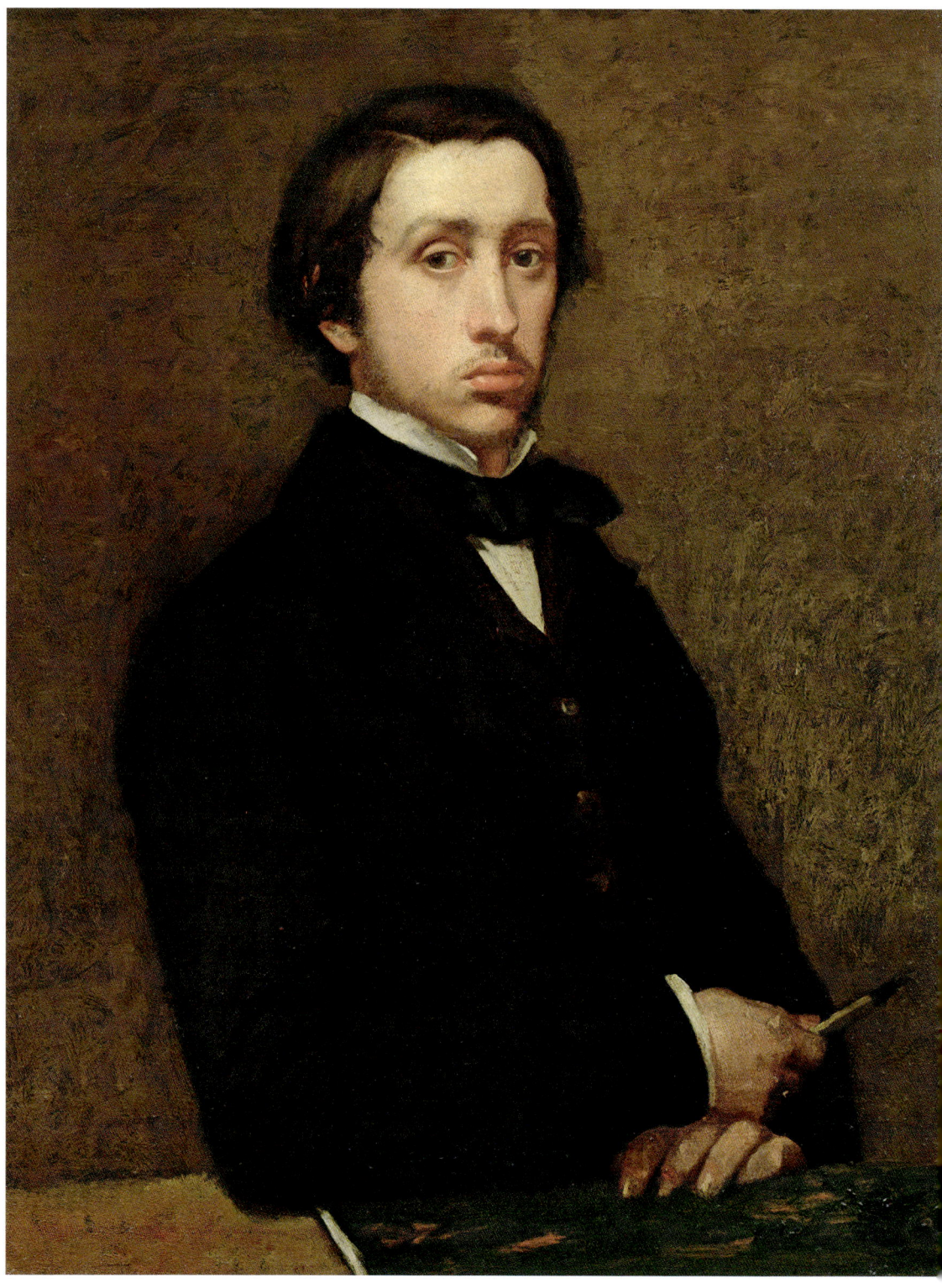

Edgar Degas 1834–1917
Life and Work

1834 Hilaire-Germain-Edgar de Gas is born on 19 July at 8, Rue Saint Georges in Paris, the first of five children. His father, Pierre-Auguste-Hyacinthe de Gas, is the manager of a branch of a private bank belonging to Edgar's grandfather in Naples. His mother, Célestine Musson, is of Creole descent and comes from New Orleans.

1845 Degas goes to the Lycée Louis-le-Grand.

1853 Passes his Baccalauréat and matriculates in the university faculty of law. Visits Félix Barrias's studio. Copies Mantegna's *Crucifixion.*

1855 In April enrols at École des Beaux-Arts in the painting and sculpture faculty.

1856 July: travels to Naples to visit relatives, and later continues to Rome.

1859 Returns to Paris. Works on portrait of the Bellelli family.

OPPOSITE
Self-portrait, 1855
Oil on canvas, 81 x 64.5 cm (32 x 25½ in.)
Paris, Musée d'Orsay

The Apotheosis of Degas, 1885, parody of Ingres's *The Apotheosis of Homer* (1827)
Photo: Walter Barnes

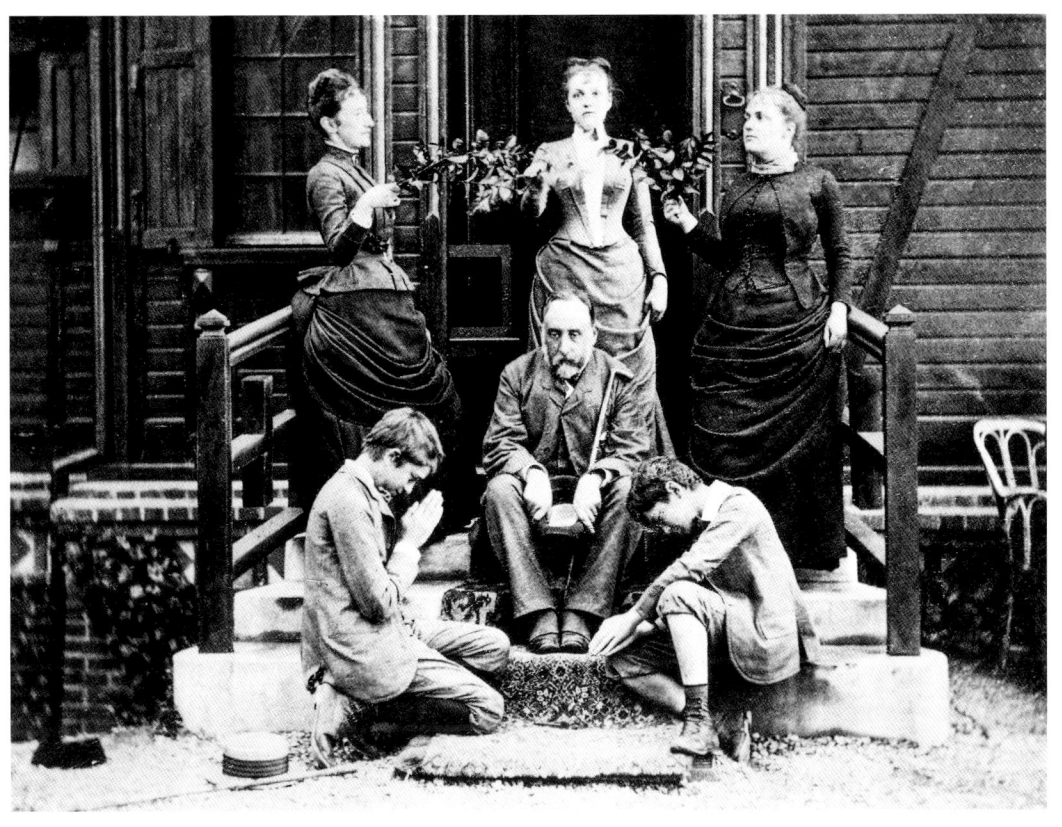

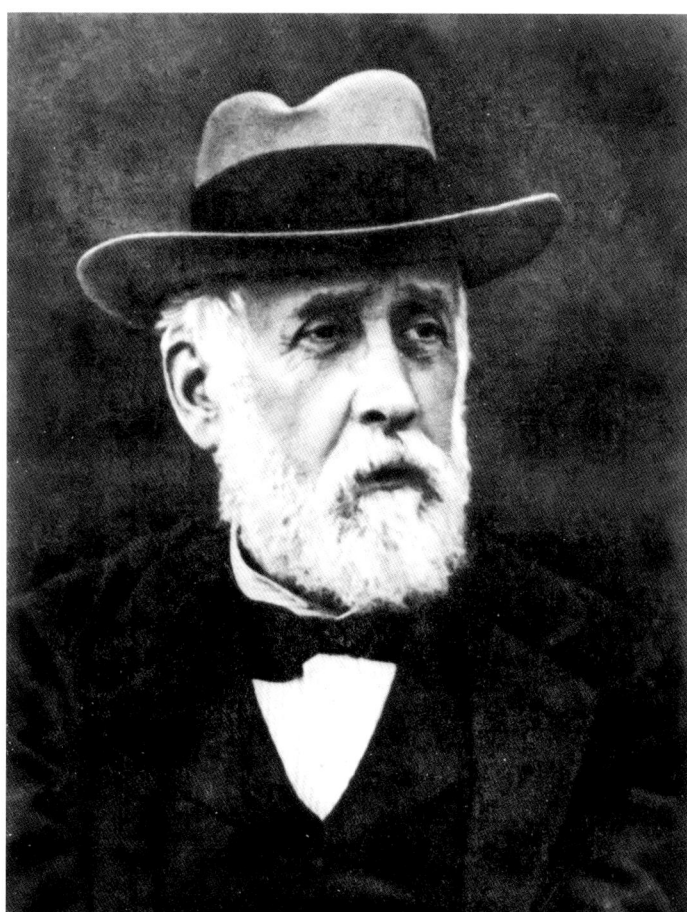

Edgar Degas at the Rouart's
in Paris, 1900
Photo: Ernest Rouart

1860 Stays with the Valpinçons at Ménil-Hubert in Normandy. Degas is particularly interested in historical art.

1865 Exhibits *The Sufferings of the City of New Orleans* at the Salon.

1869 Paints portraits. Stays with Manet at Boulogne-sur-Mer and Saint-Valery-en-Caux. Does landscapes from memory and close studies of horses and jockeys.

1870 Ordered to the Garde Nationale artillery in the Franco-Prussian War, under the command of

his old school friend Henri Rouart. Contracts an eye condition.

1871 During the Paris Commune he stays at Ménil-Hubert.

1872 Travels to London and on to New Orleans, where his relatives are in the cotton trade. Does a number of portraits, among them *The Cotton Exchange at New Orleans*.

1873 With others, Degas founds the Société anonyme to organize independent, unjuried exhibitions.

1874 February: his father dies in Naples. Degas exhibits ten works at

the first Impressionist exhibition, which opens on 15 April.

1876 30 March: The second Société anonyme exhibition opens, including 24 pictures by Degas. Edmond Duranty publishes "La Nouvelle Peinture", which contains a lengthy assessment of Degas. He works on monotypes and etchings.

1877 Degas shows 25 works in the third group exhibition.

1878 The *Cotton Office* is bought by the Musée des Beaux-Arts at Pau for 2,000 francs, the first of his works to be hung in a museum. His pictures are exhibited in America for the first time.

1879 Fourth Impressionist exhibition. Along with oil and pastel work, Degas exhibits painted fans.

1880 The fifth independent show opens on 1 April. Durand-Ruel buys work by Degas.

1881 Exhibits the sculpture of the little dancer at the sixth independent exhibition.

1882 First pictures of milliners and women ironing. Degas does not exhibit at the seventh independent show.

1883 Durand-Ruel exhibits Degas and other artists in London.

1886 At the eighth independent exhibition, Degas shows a series of nudes. With Georges Seurat's *Grande Jatte* they are the sensation of the show.

1888 Writes sonnets that deal with subjects treated in his art: dance, horses, singers.

1892 Almost entirely abandons painting in oils. September: exhibition of landscapes at Durand-Ruel, the first of only two solo exhibitions in his lifetime.

1900 Shows two paintings and five pastels in the century exhibition in Paris.

1901 Almost totally blind, Degas can no longer work except in large formats and with broad strokes of chalk; he sometimes retouches earlier work.

1911 Second solo exhibition at the Fogg Art Museum.

1914 The Cammondo collection, containing numerous works by Degas, is given to the Louvre.

1917 27 September: Degas dies. He is buried in the family grave in Montmartre cemetery.

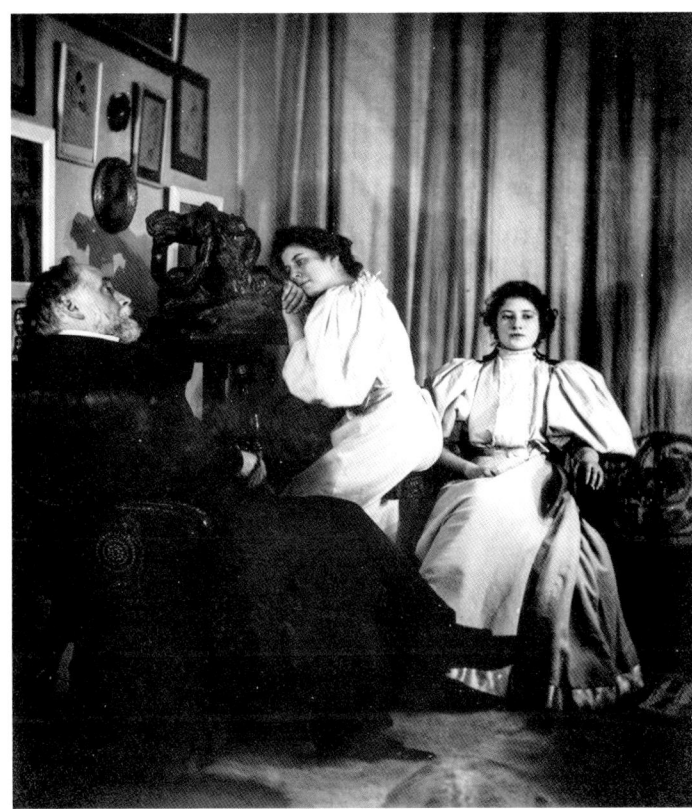

Self-portrait by Edgar Degas
with Christine and Yvonne Lerolle,
c. 1895/96

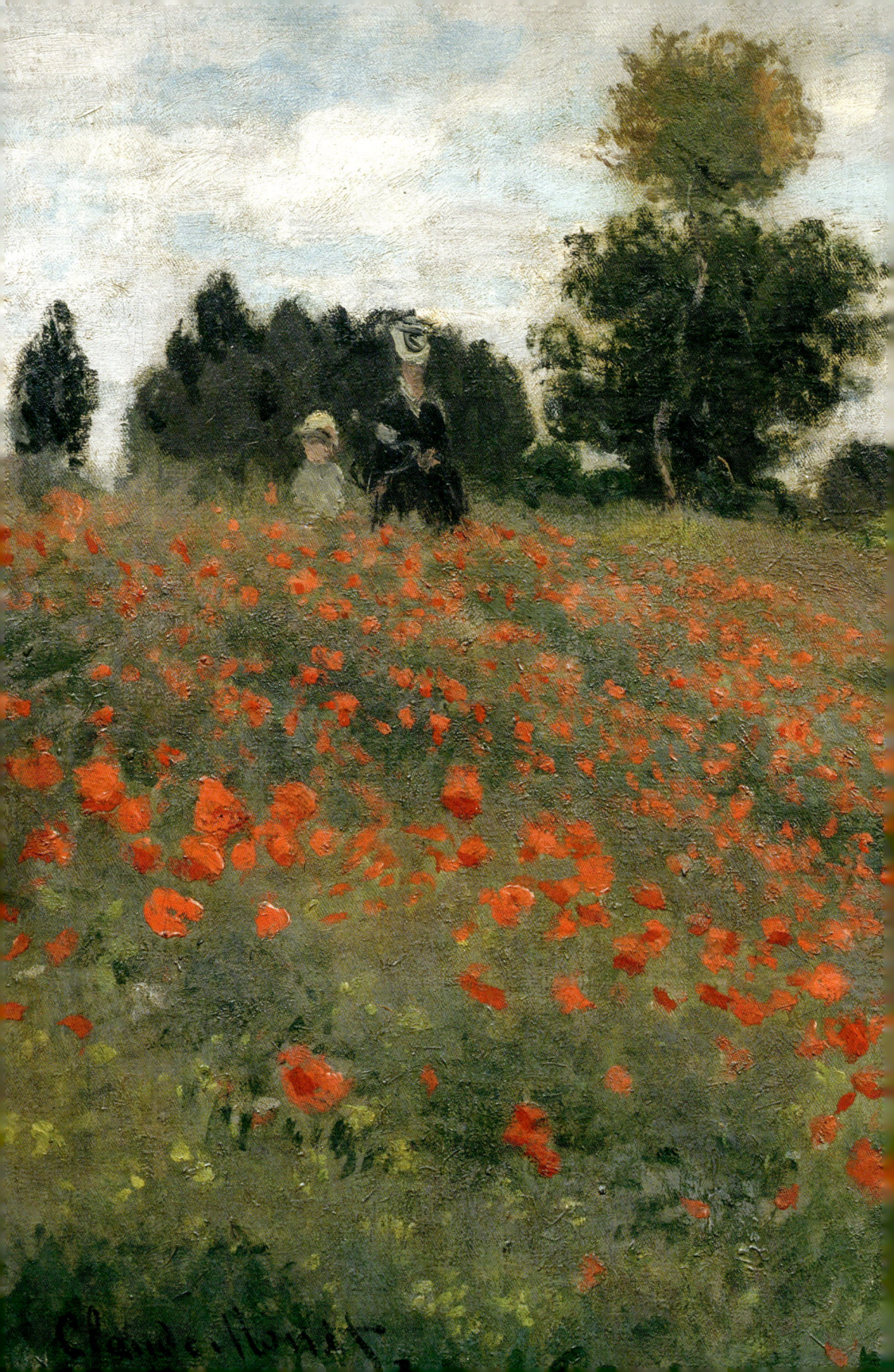

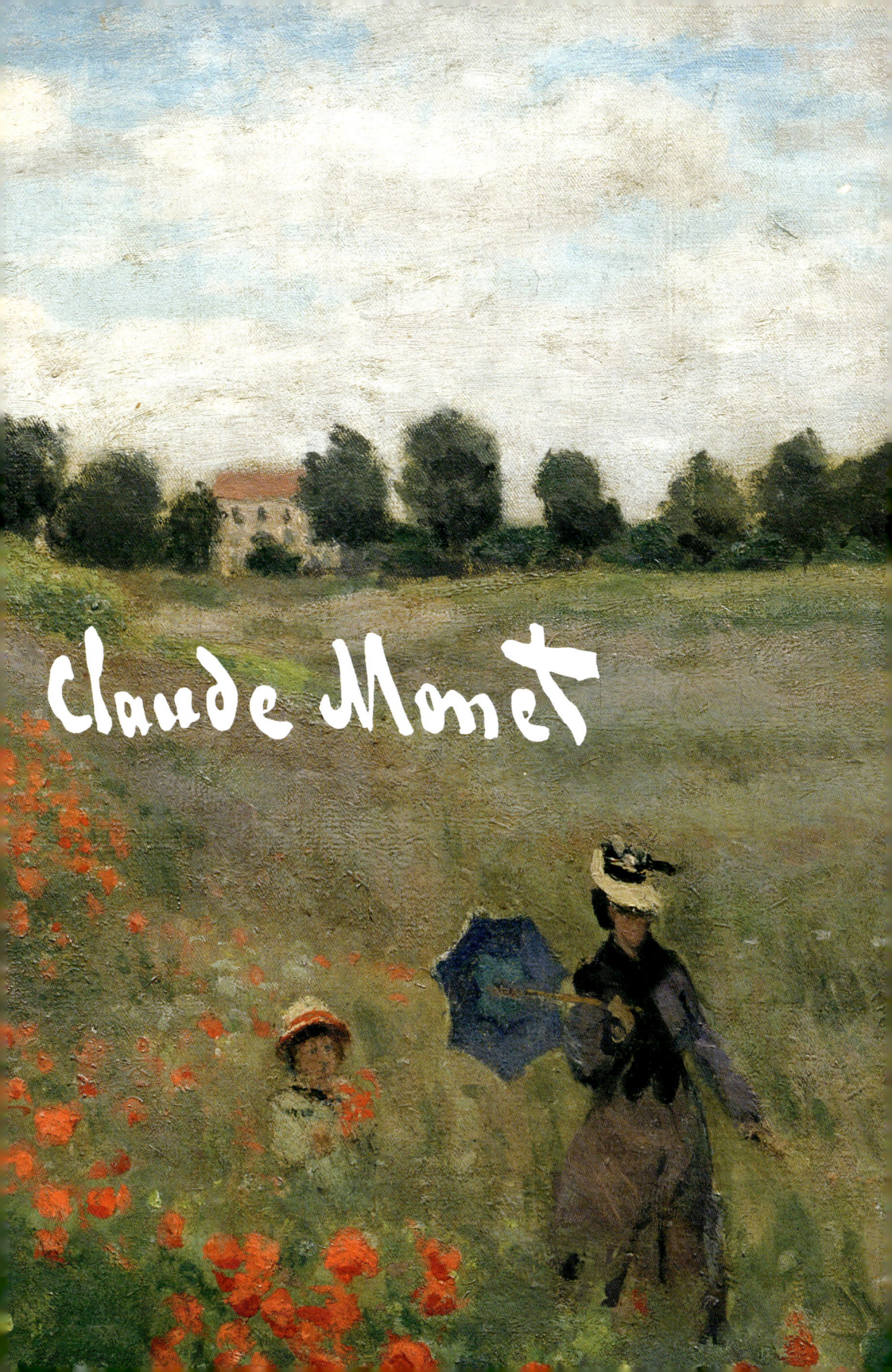

Claude Monet

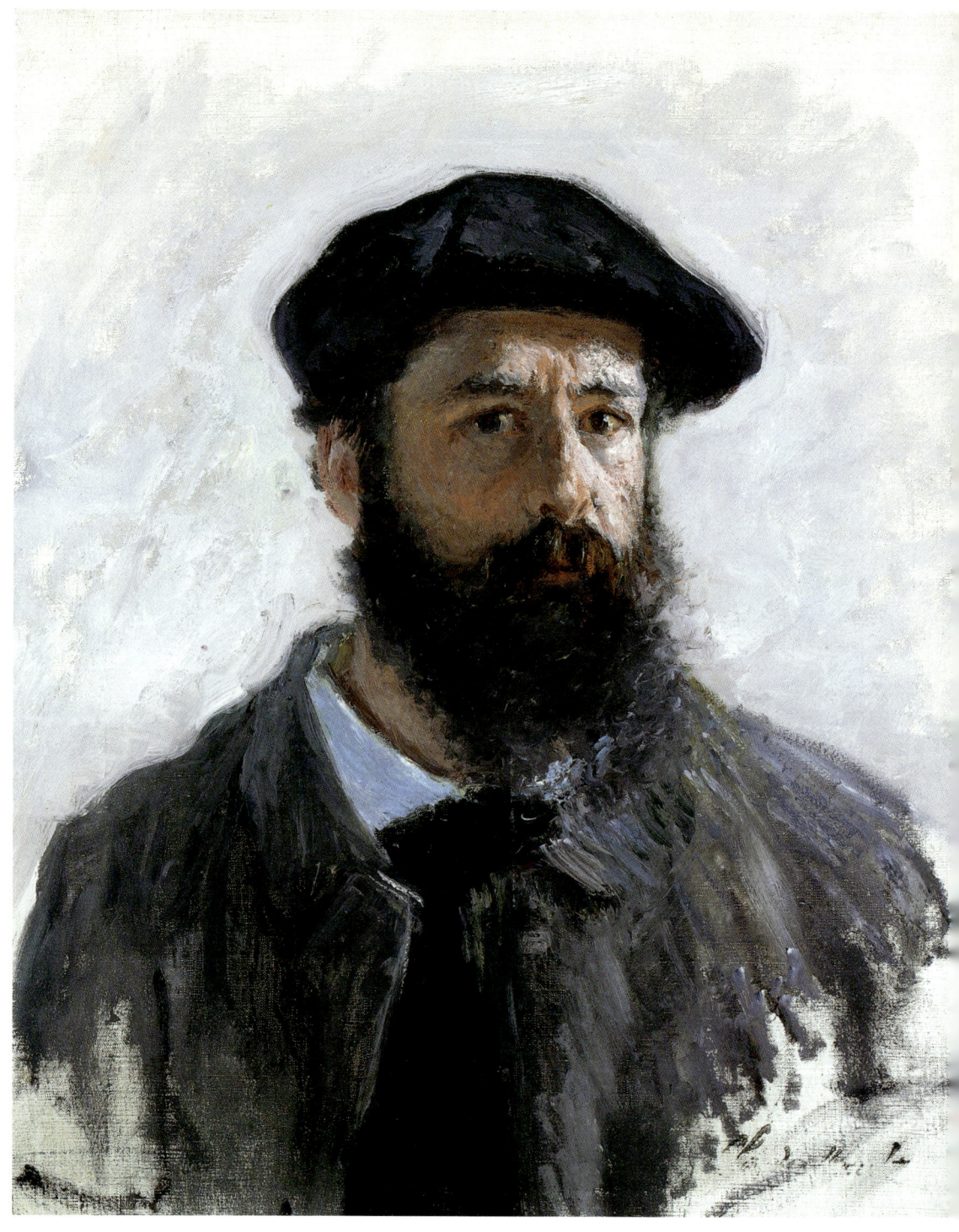

Christoph Heinrich

Claude Monet

*Capturing the Ever-Changing
Face of Reality*

*"For me, the subject is
of secondary importance:
I want to convey what is alive
between me and the subject."*

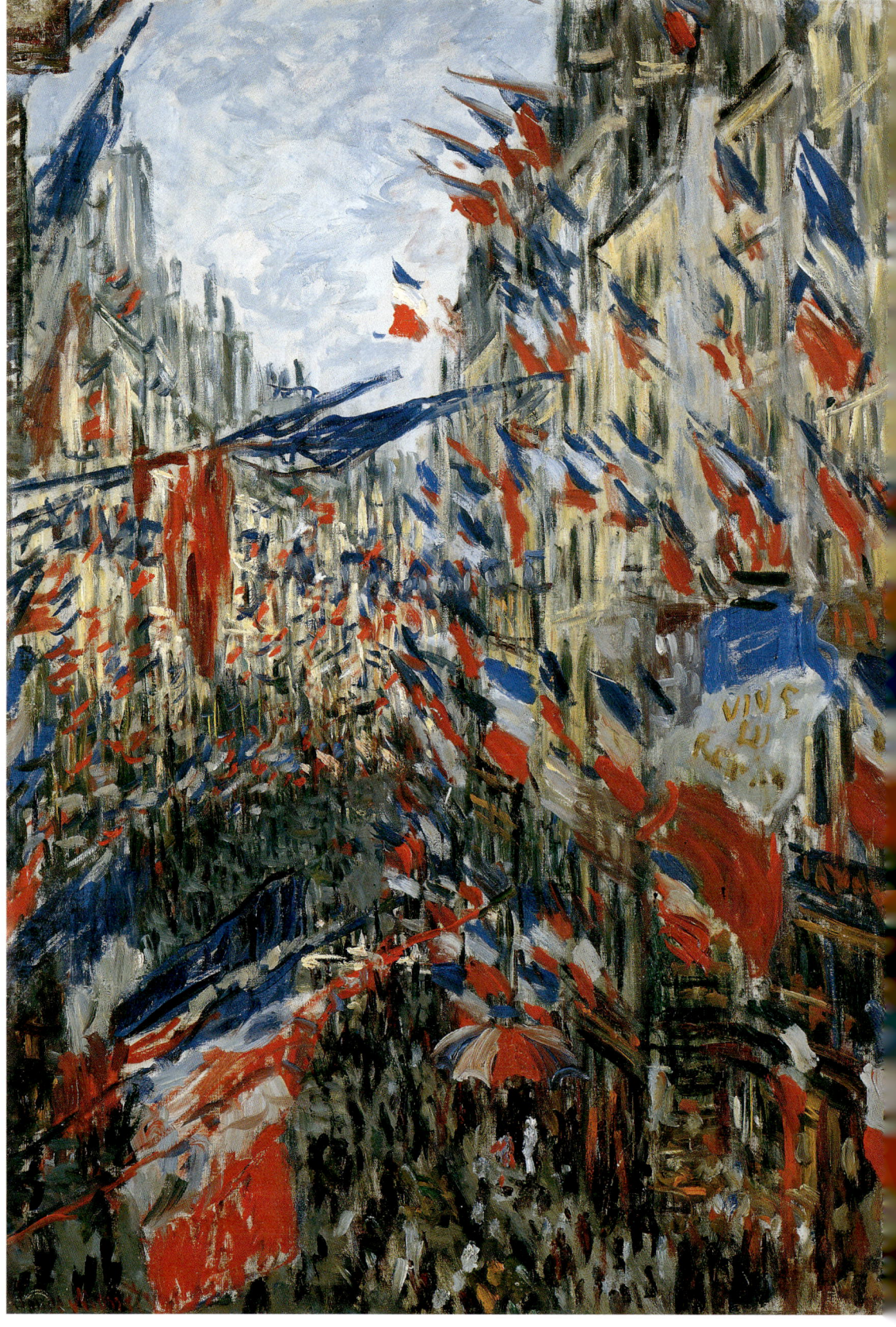

Contents

PAGES 104/105
Poppies at Argenteuil (detail), 1873
Oil on canvas, 50 x 65 cm (19¾ x 25¾ in.)
Paris, Musée d'Orsay

PAGE 106
Self-portrait with a Beret (detail), 1886
Oil on canvas, 56 x 46 cm (22 x 18 in.)
Private collection

OPPOSITE
The Rue Saint Denis,
30th of June 1878, 1878
Oil on canvas, 76 x 52 cm (30 x 20½ in.)
Rouen, Musée des Beaux-Arts

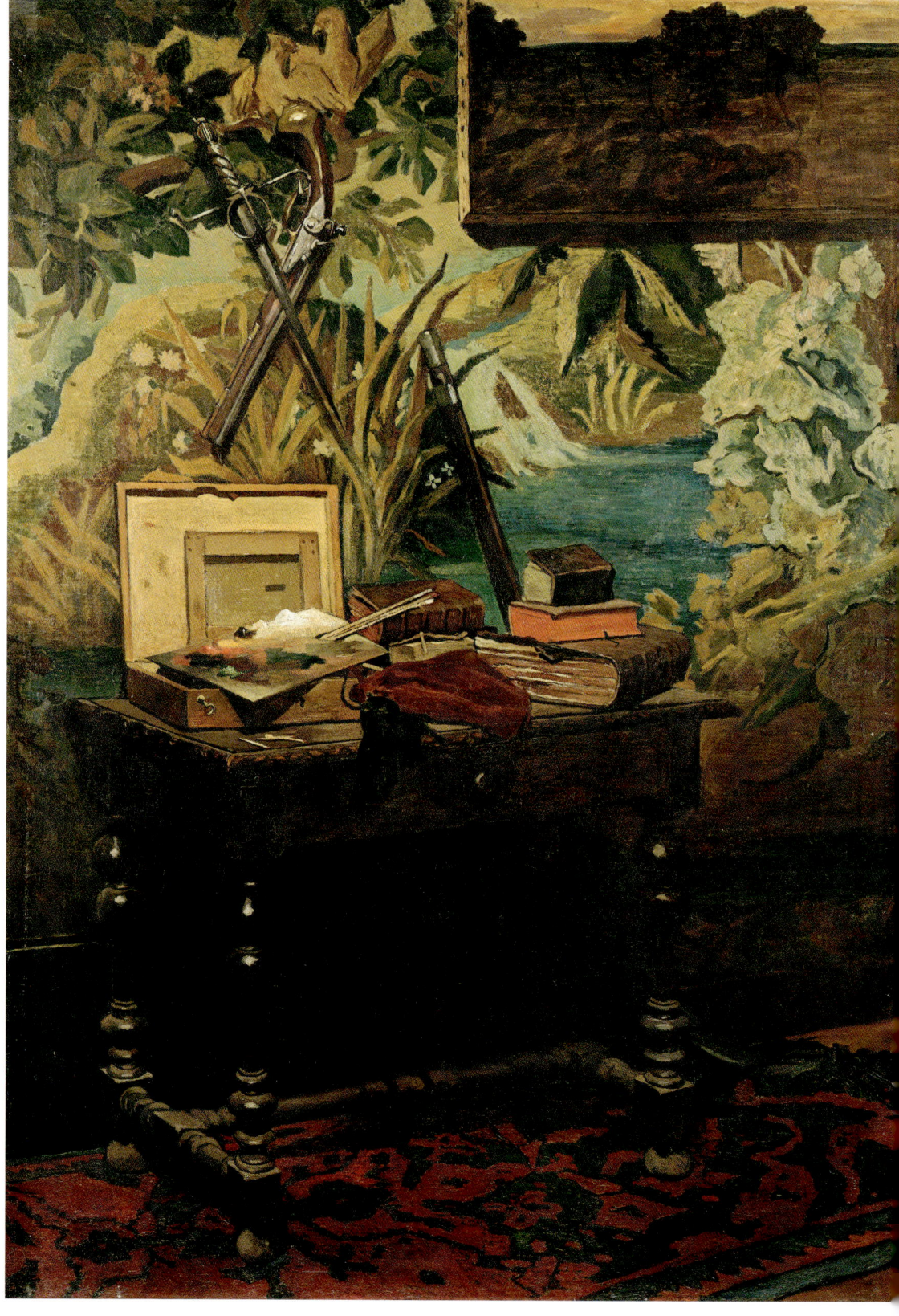

Making the Salon

With hindsight we can see *Corner of a Studio,* a still life Claude Monet painted at the outset of his long and prolific career (ill. p. 110), as a programmatic statement. Painter's brushes, paintbox and palette, as well as books, are on a table, with weapons against and above it, and as a backdrop is wallpaper featuring vegetation, water and exotic birds, in the manner of an old tapestry. The youthful artist is meticulous in his attempt to convey the moist gleam of the paint, the matt velvet of the cap, the dry bookbinding, and the metal on the guns and dagger. It is the work of an artist out to show what he can do. And it is a picture unusual in its contrasts – between the somewhat drab utilitarian objects and the opulent tropical river scene in the background, and between the earthy tonalities of the interior and the cool moist verdure of the lush scene behind.

What is also unusual in this early Monet is its captivating brightness. On the palette, alongside green, red and black, there is a mass of moist paint: white lead. That white lead is the source and crux of the painting's light. Its fresh whiteness fills the entire space, shedding its light upon a painter's entire life. And that light is the manifesto.

Claude Monet was *the* incomparable painter of bright daylight – the painter of the sky, the snow, clouds reflected in water, the first painter ever to paint pictures almost entirely monochrome white. Till his old age, till his majestic late paintings of water-lilies, Monet continued to mix this white into his pure colours, thus banishing the muted shades of somnolent interiors (still visible in this early work) from the art. Monet was the painter of light.

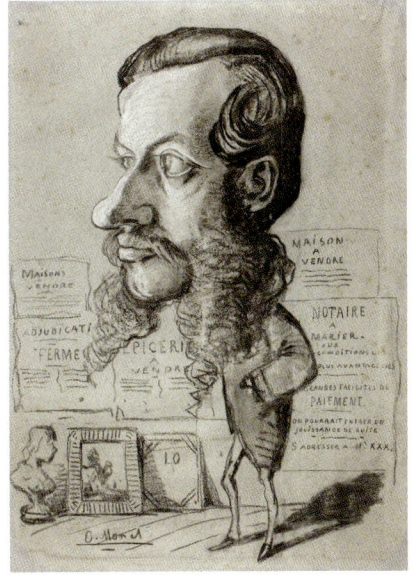

Léon Marchon Wearing a Jacket, c. 1858
Black crayon on brown paper
61.2 x 45.2 cm (24 x 17¾ in.)
The Art Institute of Chicago

In his hometown of Le Havre, Monet acquired the reputation of an *enfant terrible* and gifted cartoonist with his caricatures of local public figures.

OPPOSITE
Corner of a Studio, c. 1861
Oil on canvas, 182 x 127 cm (71¾ x 50 in.)
Paris, Musée d'Orsay

At a time when solo exhibitions were not yet customary, the biannual Paris Salon constituted the major showcase and market for French painters. For six weeks, the most recent work of establishment artists, diligent pupils, ambitious imitators, and every so

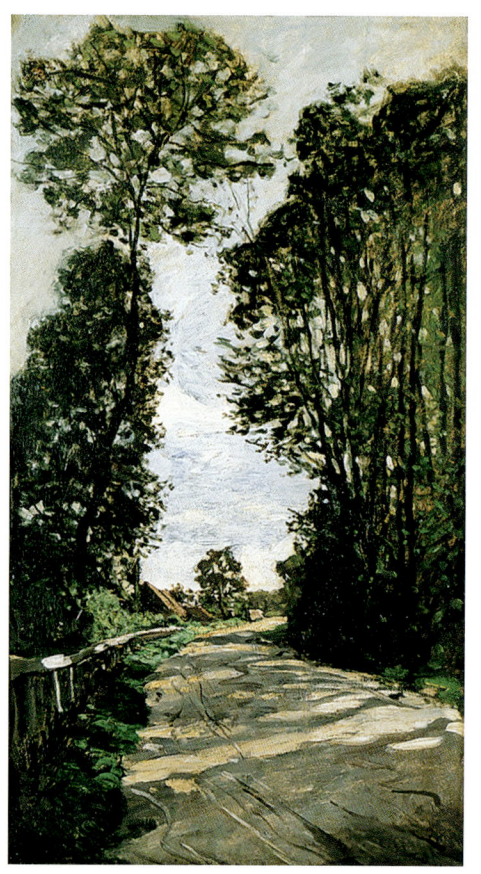

often a painter of genuine talent was on display to a public that stinted neither its praise nor its criticism. In the 18th century it had been possible to presuppose a certain expertise among aristocratic patrons of art; a century later, the Salon was a Sunday pastime open to all. In the Palais de l'Industrie (where the Salon had been held since the 1855 World's Fair) the middle classes, now enthroned as the socially dominant class, strolled by with hat and cane or in rustling gowns, holding relaxed conversation and eagerly aped by all who aspired to similar prosperity. The pleasure principle ruled. The critics would devote pages to the Salon in popular journals such as the *Journal du Rire* or *Charivari,* and their reviews served that principle, supplying euphoric paeans or malicious caricatures to create and shape public taste. Even before they had seen the paintings in the original, people would be going into raptures or fits of laughter. The opportunity to exhibit at the Salon, and the verdict of the critics, were decisive in gaining an artist recognition – or leaving him in obscurity, to drain his family's purses further and perhaps to end in penury.

It is true that the Salon was a thing of sensationalism and attention-getting. The painters ransacked mythology and folk tales in quest of murders, triumphant heroes, and a pretty excuse to paint a little naked flesh. Nevertheless, it would be wrong to imagine it the exclusive reserve of bad taste. At the Salon, after all, following a lengthy struggle, Eugène Delacroix and Gustave Courbet, Jean-François Millet, Jean-Baptiste-Camille Corot and Édouard Manet exhibited their paintings. At the Salon they attracted attention, scoring modest successes or sparking off scandals. A good Salon year would feature the entire spectrum of art, from skilful old-master styles to the Barbizon School's unconventional approach to the picturesque. To a young artist, much of the work on display could come as a revelation.

One of the youthful artists who walked the Salon wide-eyed in wonder was Claude Oscar Monet. Born in Paris in 1840, he grew up in modest lower-middle-class circumstances. His father's grocery was failing so the family moved to the port of Le Havre; there, Monet's father entered his brother-in-law Jacques Lecadre's wholesale business. Oscar (as he was initially called) was then six years old. He was to spend his boyhood on the rough coast of northern France, with its bright light, restless sea, and ever-changing wind and weather, but with its fashionable resorts of Deauville, Trouville and Honfleur too, it was a magnet for city folk. The family summered at Aunt Sophie's pretty country house at Sainte-Adresse, while in winter they remained at Le Havre. Monet roamed the beach, dunes and cliffs above the sea all day long, and often played truant from school to do so.

At the age of fifteen he achieved a certain notoriety with his barbed pencil caricatures of teachers and other persons of public note in Le Havre (ill. p. 111). Blessed with his family's business sense, Monet sold the drawings and managed to up his pocket money not insignificantly.

But of greater importance than such five-finger exercises (which were often closely based on magazine illustrations) was the young Monet's friendship with the painter Eugène Boudin. Boudin specialized in airy coastal pastels. He would take Monet along when he painted at beach resorts, and introduced the youth to the new technique of *plein-airisme.* "If I became a painter," Monet recalled in 1900, "it was thanks to Boudin. He was a man of infinite kindness and took it upon himself to teach me. Gradually my eyes were opened, I really understood nature, and at the same time I began to love it."

Monet left school shortly before the leaving exams to become a painter. His mother, who might have supported him in his wish, had died in 1857; his father, who saw the lad as his own successor in the now prosperous family business, was unenthusiastic and refused him an allowance, but let him go his way, doubtless hoping the fad would blow over. Taking his earnings from caricatures, Monet headed for Paris and enrolled at the Académie Suisse, a small private art school. He visited the Salon, and wrote to Eugène Boudin (on 20 February 1860): "I am surrounded by a small group of landscape artists here, who would be very happy to meet you. They are real painters."

While convalescing at Le Havre following his brief military service in Algeria, from which he returned with a bout of typhoid fever, Monet met the Dutch painter Johan Barthold Jongkind, whose landscapes the Frenchman had already admired at the Salon. Jongkind painted sunny landscapes, his brushwork light and relaxed, and was an immediate precursor of Impressionism. From their first meeting, he became Monet's "true master", as Monet recalled in 1900: "It was he who completed the education of my eye." In the opinion of the Monet-Lecadre family, though, this crazy Dutchman with

OPPOSITE
The Road to Saint-Siméon's Farm near Honfleur, 1864
Oil on canvas, 81.6 x 46.4 cm (32¼ x 18¼ in.)
Tokyo, The National Museum of Western Art, The Matsukata Collection

La Pointe de la Hève at Low Tide, 1865
Oil on canvas, 90.2 x 150.5 cm (35½ x 59¼ in.)
Fort Worth, Texas, Kimbell Art Museum

In his early paintings, Monet captured the sea and sky of his home parts in Normandy, watching the sun as it broke through clouds or lit a lane near Honfleur. His whole life long he remained true to the landscape of northern France.

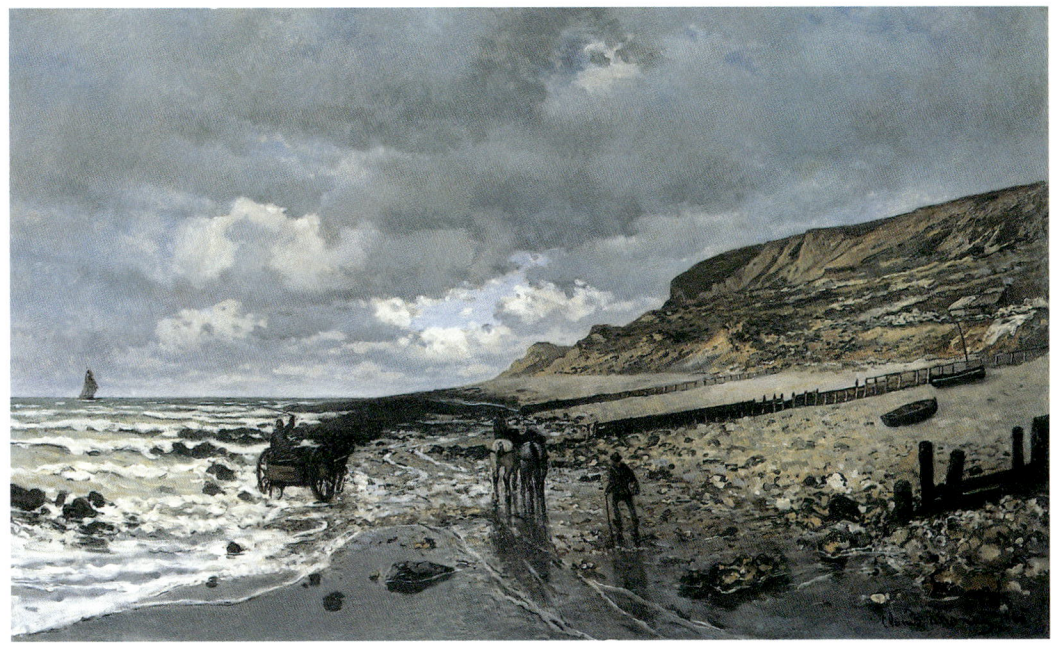

a penchant for the bottle was unsuitable company for young Claude – so in 1862 he was sent back to Paris, on condition that if he really insisted on becoming a painter he take the accepted course, via the École des Beaux-Arts.

Monet, however, had no interest in the prevailing tone of the academy. He joined Charles Gleyre's independent tuition studio. Gleyre's own style was idealistic, and well in line with Salon taste, but he granted his students their freedom and encouraged them to evolve an independent style of their own. The encouragement and instruction of this good-natured teacher, who seems to have been led a merry dance by his pupils, Monet largely rejected. For him, classes provided an opportunity to study nudes, and above all a way of meeting like-minded contemporaries.

At Gleyre's, Monet met three young artists named Frédéric Bazille, Alfred Sisley and Auguste Renoir; he had already made the acquaintance of Camille Pissarro before military service. These four were to be the core of the Impressionist movement. Monet himself was anything but bohemian, and indeed behaved in a distinctly bourgeois way. Renoir was later to tell his son that the other students called Monet "the Dandy": "He didn't have a sou, but he wore shirts with lace cuffs. [...] To one student who was making up to him, a pretty but vulgar girl, he replied: I'm sorry, but I only sleep with duchesses or maids. Anything in between I find revolting. The ideal would be a duchess's maid."

Still, the actual circumstances in which the two artists lived and worked (at times together) could fairly be called bohemian. They earned paltry sums from portrait work and occasional commissions, and Monet even tried to make his way as a cartoonist; but the money went on rent, fuel, and the girls who sat as models. They ate meagrely, accepted payment in groceries from one man who commissioned work, and at one point lived for a month on a sack of beans – which could be cooked on the stove, since it had to be lit anyway if a model was to pose in the nude. Once the beans ran out, they changed to lentils. In later years, when his son asked if a diet of pulses was not rather indigestible, Renoir merely laughed: "I was never so happy in my entire life. And Monet did contrive an invitation to dinner from time to time, whereupon we'd stuff ourselves with turkey washed down with Chambertin."

Despite this balanced diet and his resolute refusal to put himself in the hands of an academic teacher, Monet was presently scoring his first Salon successes. "A new name must be mentioned,"

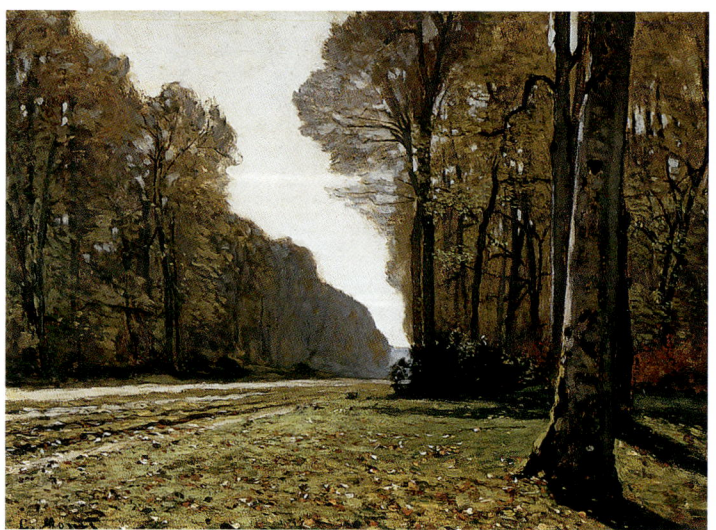

a critic wrote in the *Gazette des Beaux-Arts* in July, 1865. "Monsieur Monet, the painter of *La Pointe de la Hève at Low Tide* (ill. p. 113) and *The Mouth of the Seine at Honfleur,* was hitherto unknown. These works constitute his debut – and they still lack that finesse which comes with long study. But his feel for colour harmonies in an interplay of related tones, and indeed his sense of colour values as a whole, as well as the notable overall character,

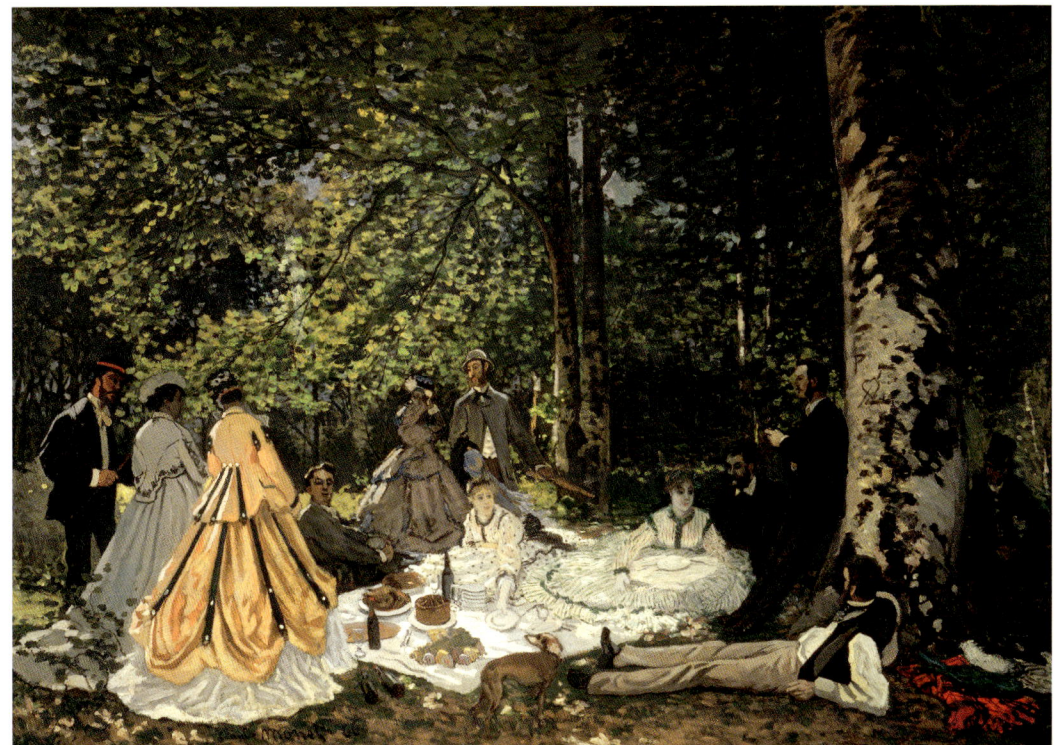

his daring way of seeing and of enforcing our attention – all these are advantages which Monsieur Monet already possesses in a high degree. Henceforth we shall be following the work of this upright painter of the sea with great interest."

The *Gazette* critic of the 1865 Salon was happy to hail a new young artist from whom much could be expected in future; and indeed it was to the critic's credit that, amid the countless paintings hung as many as five rows high, he was alert to the qualities of Monet's two landscapes, so reticent in colour tonalities, so simple in their choice of everyday subject matter. But of course it was also to the credit of the youthful painter, making a quiet Salon debut in marked contrast to the noise of some arrivals.

Perhaps it was the work of the Barbizon School that opened this critic's eyes to the immediacy in the handling of the natural scene. In his early years, Monet was in fact very close to that particular line of realist art. The Barbizon painters worked on the fringes of the Forest of Fontainebleau and included Corot, Charles François Daubigny and Constant Troyon. They took their subjects from ordinary life, spurning the lofty historical and anecdotal themes then so popular with the public. Their work was notable for its careful scrutiny of nature – though in point of fact their paintings were generally done in the studio. Monet too painted in the Forest of Fontainebleau at times (ill. p. 114), meeting the Barbizon artists; but his ambition went beyond painting landscapes in the manner of the Barbizon masters.

Luncheon on the Grass (study), 1865
Oil on canvas, 130 x 181 cm (51¼ x 71¼ in.)
Moscow, Pushkin Museum

This version, now in Moscow, is a smaller study for the painting Monet hoped to conquer the Salon with, and gives an idea of what the finished work was to have looked like. This is probably a preliminary study done in the Fontainebleau woods and later used for the painting proper in the studio.

OPPOSITE
Avenue at Chailly, c. 1865
Oil on canvas, 43.5 x 59.3 cm (17¼ x 23¼ in.)
Paris, Musée d'Orsay

During the Paris years, Monet and his newfound friends Renoir, Sisley and Bazille frequently painted in the Forest of Fontainebleau.

Figure painting, preferably in large formats, struck Monet as a guarantee of success: if works were not to be assigned remote, unworthy positions under the ceiling by the hanging commission, where Salon-goers would need binoculars to see them, they had to make an unmissable impact, and painters were therefore turning to immense, outsize formats – *grandes machines*, as the Parisians dubbed them. And Monet, young rebel though he was, unconventional though he was in his draughtsmanship and use of colour, was definitely out for success in the official arena of the Salon.

A few years before, Édouard Manet – whose work was controversial in the extreme, and repeatedly turned down by the Salon – had caused a sensation with *Luncheon on the Grass*. This scene, showing two city gentlemen in a clearing, lunching on bread, wine and fruit and accompanied by a naked lady, while in the background a second woman washes her feet, was a *succès de scandale*. The self-same public that lauded the nude Venus of Salon painter Alexandre Cabanel, a work that could scarcely be outdone in its saccharine lasciviousness, could barely be restrained from spitting upon Manet's *Luncheon*. Their outrage was presumably prompted by the fact that Manet did not hide behind a mythological fig-leaf; but the ease of his painting style also struck contemporaries as coarse.

Monet, for his part, was enthusiastic about Manet's skills. He had seen works by the other artist for the first time in 1863, and promptly began to lighten his palette. He himself then tried to outdo Manet in a *tour de force* of his own, a *Luncheon* measuring no less than 4.20 by 6.50 metres and including a full dozen life-size figures gathered in a birch forest to luncheon on stuffed fowl, pie and wine (ills. pp. 115 and 117).

Claude Monet at his Giverny home with the Duc de Trévise, 1920

Even as an old man, Monet kept the centre portion of the *Luncheon on the Grass* in his studio and liked to tell visitors how it came to remain unfinished.

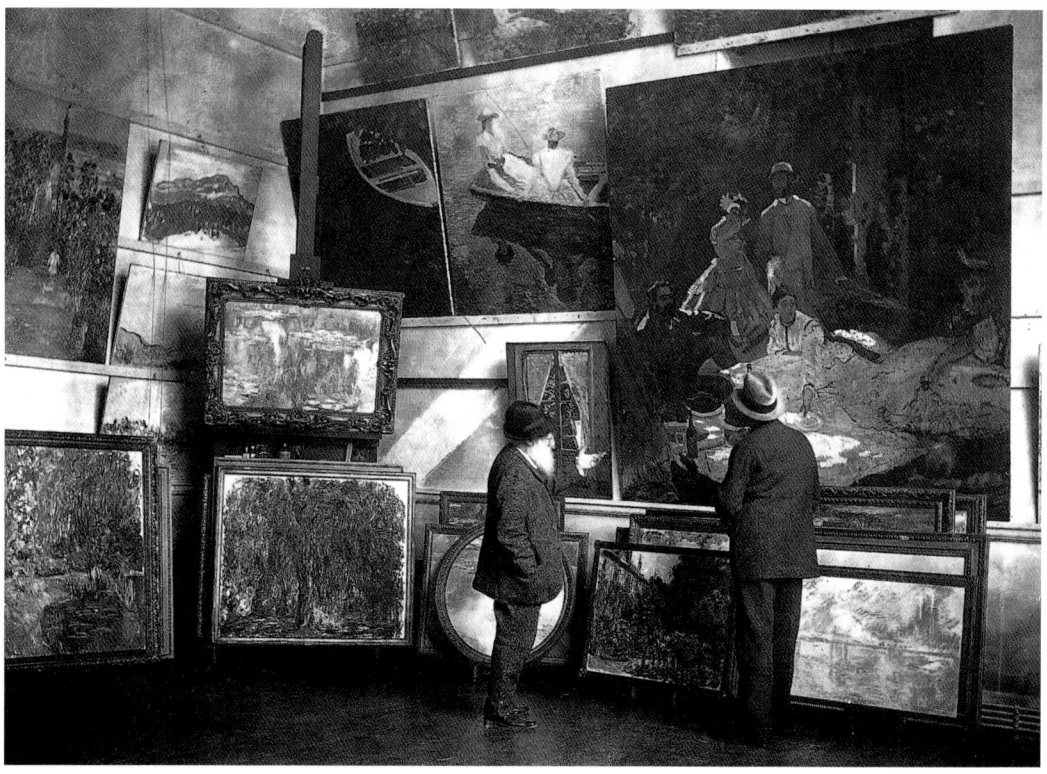

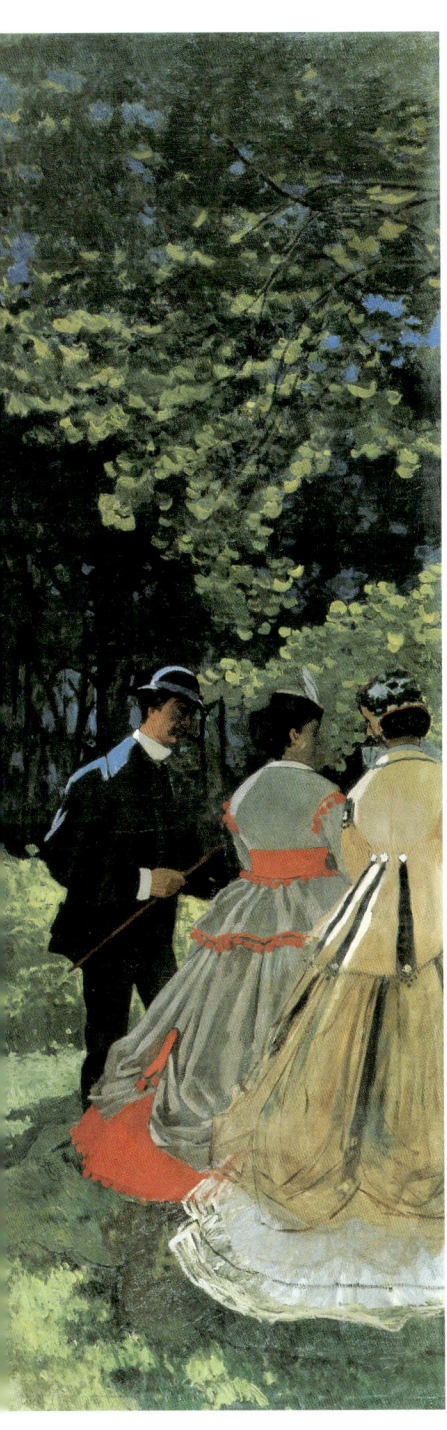

Luncheon on the Grass (left panel), 1865
Oil on canvas, 418 x 150 cm (164½ x 59 in.)
Paris, Musée d'Orsay

Luncheon on the Grass (central panel), 1865
Oil on canvas, 248 x 217 cm (97¾ x 85½ in.)
Paris, Musée d'Orsay

Several months behind on the rent, Monet gave
the painting to his landlord in lieu. Years later,
when he went to reclaim it, it was moulded over
and badly damaged by damp. Only two sections
of the huge work could be saved.

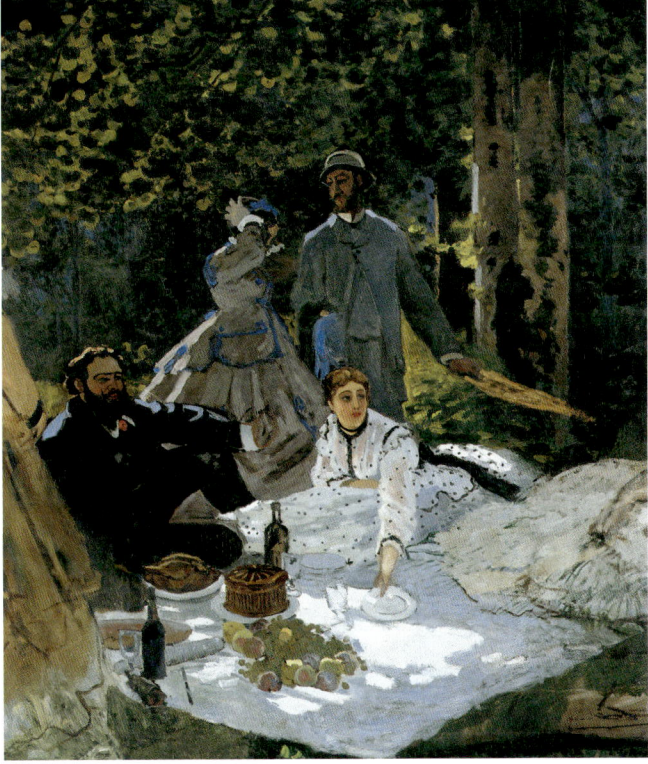

Manet's painting was a studio work, and used every trick of the trade; but Monet painted in the open, questing for immediacy of effect. Manet shocked his public by presenting a naked woman (gazing challengingly into our eyes) without any allegorical pretext, beside gentlemen dressed in the clothes of the day; Monet, in his painting, turned the occasion into a Paris society picnic. It was as if he had taken the criticism of his elder fellow-artist's work to heart and was on his best behaviour to curry favour with the Salon.

He painted it in 1865. That summer, together with his nineteen-year-old lover Camille Doncieux and his friend Bazille (with whom he was sharing a studio), he went out to the Forest of Fontainebleau, and there the two of them patiently sat, stood and lay – modelling for all of the figures in the painting. That autumn, in the Paris studio, Monet set about transposing the study to large format. He worked like one possessed that winter, only to realize – shortly before the Salon opened – that he would not have it finished. He put it aside, and in just four days, as legend insists, painted a full-length portrait of *Camille,* or *The Woman with a Green Dress* (ill. p. 119).

If the landscapes Monet exhibited at the previous Salon had attracted generous comment, the portrait of Camille scored a huge success. Critics never tired of praising his handling of the silken fabric of the dress, comparing it with the old masters and even with the famous materials of the Venetian artist, Veronese. "Just consider that dress," wrote Émile Zola. "It is both supple and firm. Softly it drags, it is alive, it tells us quite clearly something about this woman. It is not a doll's dress, the muslin dreams are wrapped in: this is fine, real silk, really being worn." Critics admired the lifelike figure, turning to go. The fleeting quality of the moment seemed to have been captured both in the pose and in the very painting. Zola was very interested in the realist painters, and exulted: "Truly – this is a temperament, this is a real man in this pack of eunuchs!"

In his *Luncheon,* Monet had hoped to outdo Manet; but *Camille,* or, *The Woman with a Green Dress* brought him acclaim, and he was named in the same breath as Manet. "Monet or Manet?" demanded the critic of *La Lune.* "Monet. But we have Manet to thank for Monet. Bravo, Monet! Thank you, Manet!" Success put wings on Monet's motivation, and he pressed on with figure painting. He did not abandon his plan to do a major figure painting, but now he turned to a somewhat smaller picture showing four women in the open, and determined to paint it completely out of doors.

Camille, or *The Woman with a Green Dress,* 1866
Oil on canvas, 231 x 151 cm (91 x 59½ in.)
Kunsthalle Bremen

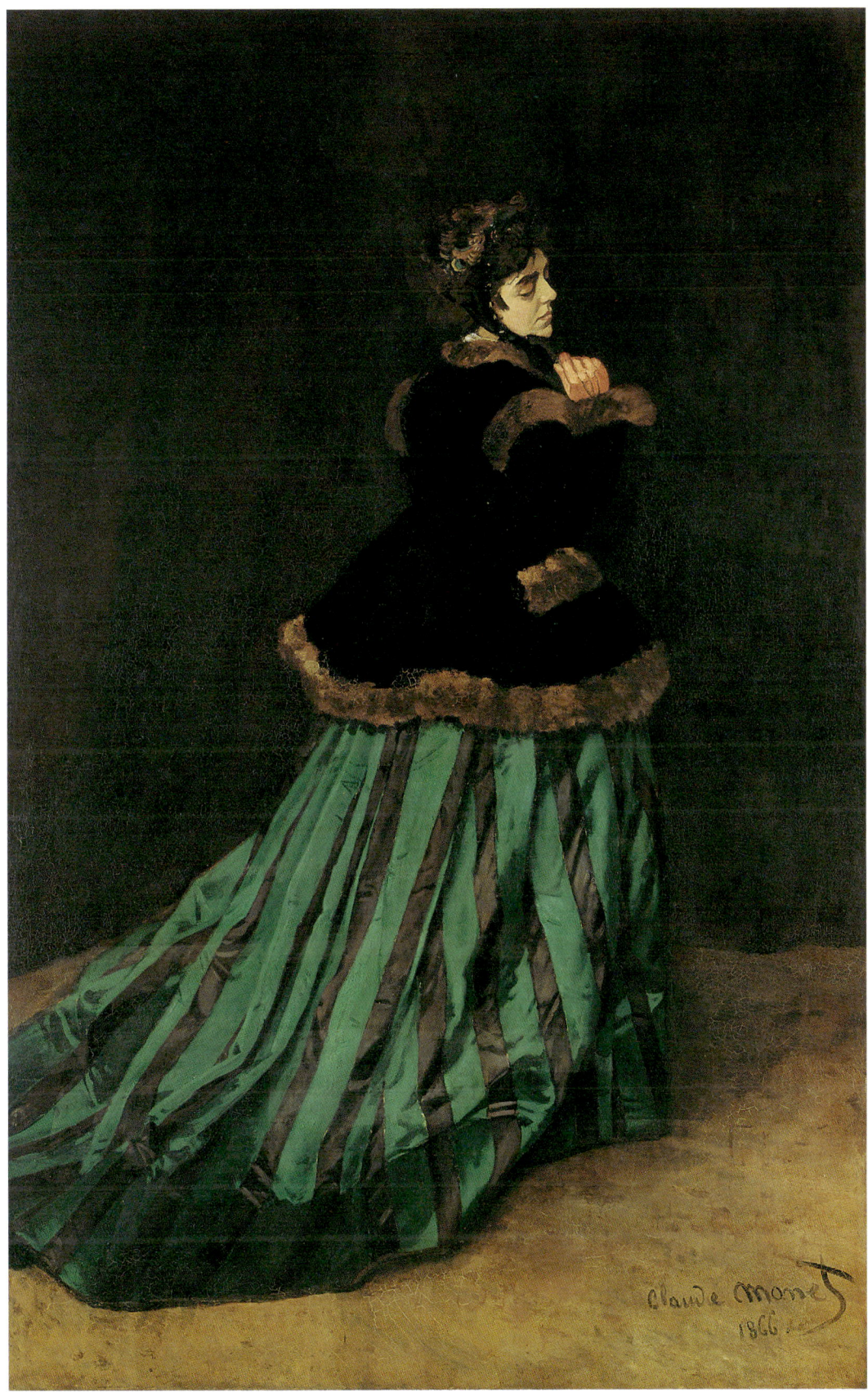

Claude Monet
1866

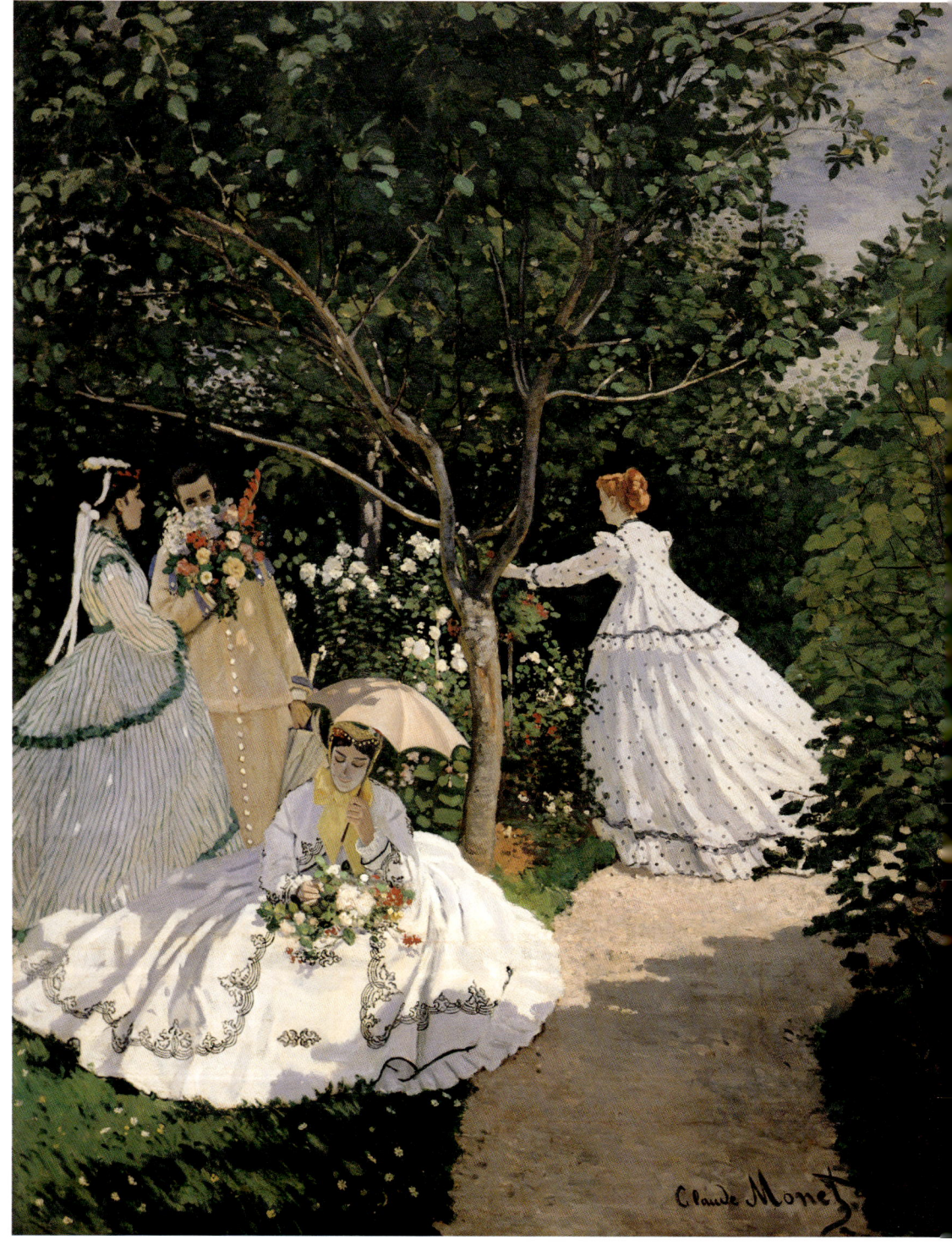

Claude Monet

Monet Finds His Subject Matter

Monet was unstoppable. Spurred on by his first Salon successes, he continued his work on figure painting – small wonder, given the belief among jury, critics and public that the human figure was everything and landscapes little better than nothing at all. Émile Zola wrote in the *Revue du XIXᵉ siècle* that it was every artist's dream to paint life-size figures in a landscape; and certainly it was a dream Monet dreamt.

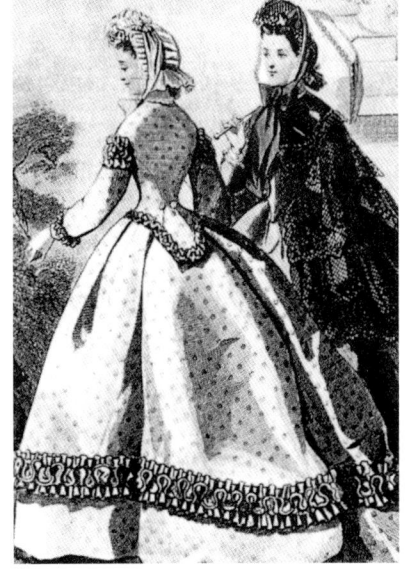

He felt the *Luncheon* debacle had taught him a lesson, and for *Women in the Garden* (ill. p. 120) he took a more manageably sized canvas out into the open rather than transferring sketches to a large format in the studio. Even with a canvas measuring 2.5 by 2 metres, though, it was no easy undertaking, and fellow artists such as Courbet poked fun at him when they stopped by – small wonder, given that Monet had dug a trench to accommodate the lower part of the painting while he worked on the upper.

Again Monet failed. He finished the picture, true; but the Salon jury turned it down, and posterity too has agreed that (unlike somewhat later works that were also rejected at first) *Women in the Garden* is not altogether successful. The figures do not seem a part of the natural scene; they are like dummies in a garden. Camille, with palpable patience, sat and stood for all the figures. She seems frozen in her poses, and the woman on the right is gliding across the ground as if she had a trolley concealed beneath her dress. The presence of the women in the garden seems curiously unmotivated, Monet's interest in their individual psychology nil. This painting is a far cry from the charismatic *Woman in a Green Dress*.

OPPOSITE
Women in the Garden, 1866
Oil on canvas, 256 x 208 cm (100⅞ x 82 in.)
Paris, Musée d'Orsay

ABOVE RIGHT
Illustration from the fashion magazine
Petit Courrier des Dames, 1864

Monet studied the Paris fashions carefully in order to record contemporary life accurately. As with *Luncheon on the Grass*, he used magazine illustrations to help him with *Women in the Garden*.

Nonetheless, the painting has a fascination that makes it unique in its time, and that is its use of sunlight, spread like a great towel on the path. Monet emphasizes the whiteness of the flowers, the shadows falling boldly across the gown of the woman in front, the silky glow of her face where sunlight

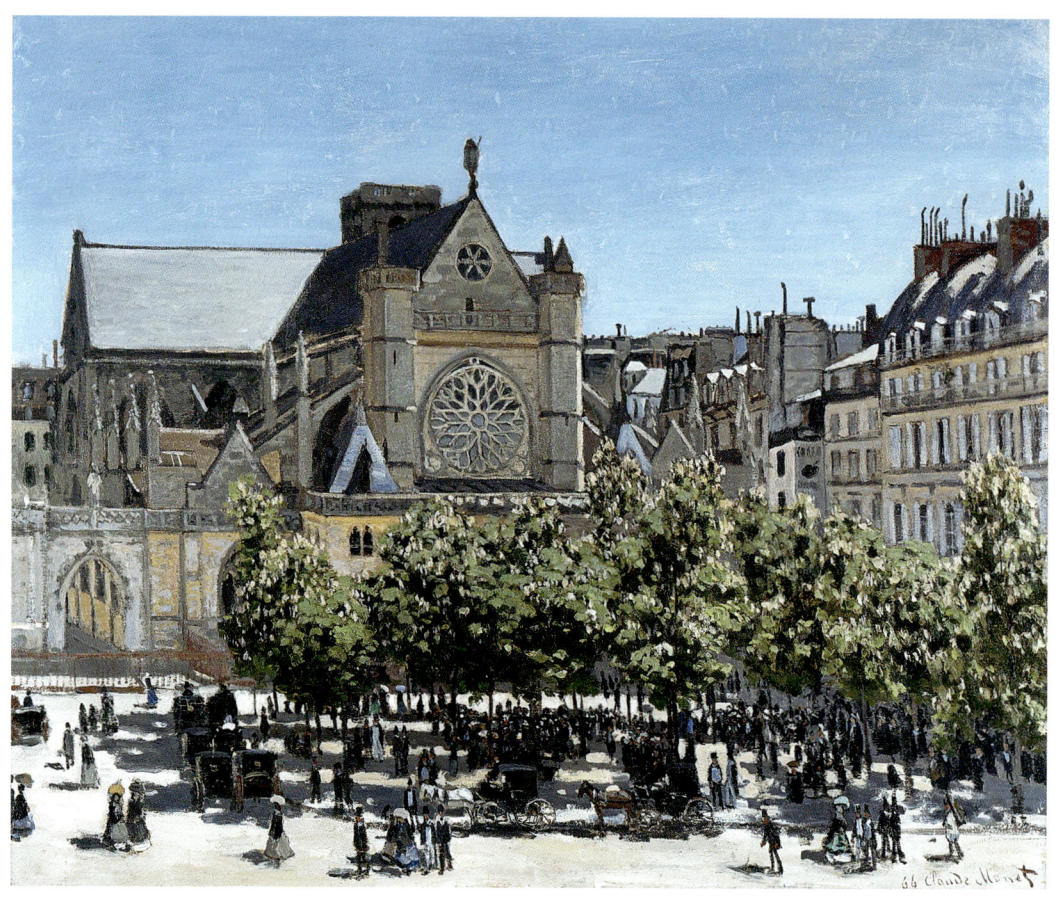

falling through her parasol meets light reflected from the sheeny dress. He has endowed his picture with life – not the life of people but the life of shadow and light. The freshness of his treatment was new, and the contrastive force with which he presented his figures in the open had an unconstrained power. In Manet's *Luncheon on the Grass*, by comparison, the people might as well be posing in a photographer's studio. It may be that *Women in the Garden* revealed Monet's subject to him for the first time: light.

The following year, 1867, he painted in Paris with Renoir. His view of the Gothic *Saint-Germain-l'Auxerrois* (ill. p. 122) was done from the second floor of the Louvre in glaring morning sunshine. *Garden of the Princess* (ill. p. 123) was likewise painted from the Louvre, but this time in overcast conditions. Details and modish accessories no longer interested Monet: the figures he now peopled his scenes with were mere dabs and strokes, not intended to tell any story or present the latest fashions but merely there to articulate spatiality and receive the light.

Both paintings show the new, modern Paris. The square in front of the Gothic church, with its young chestnut trees, had but recently been laid out; and the buildings in both pictures remind us

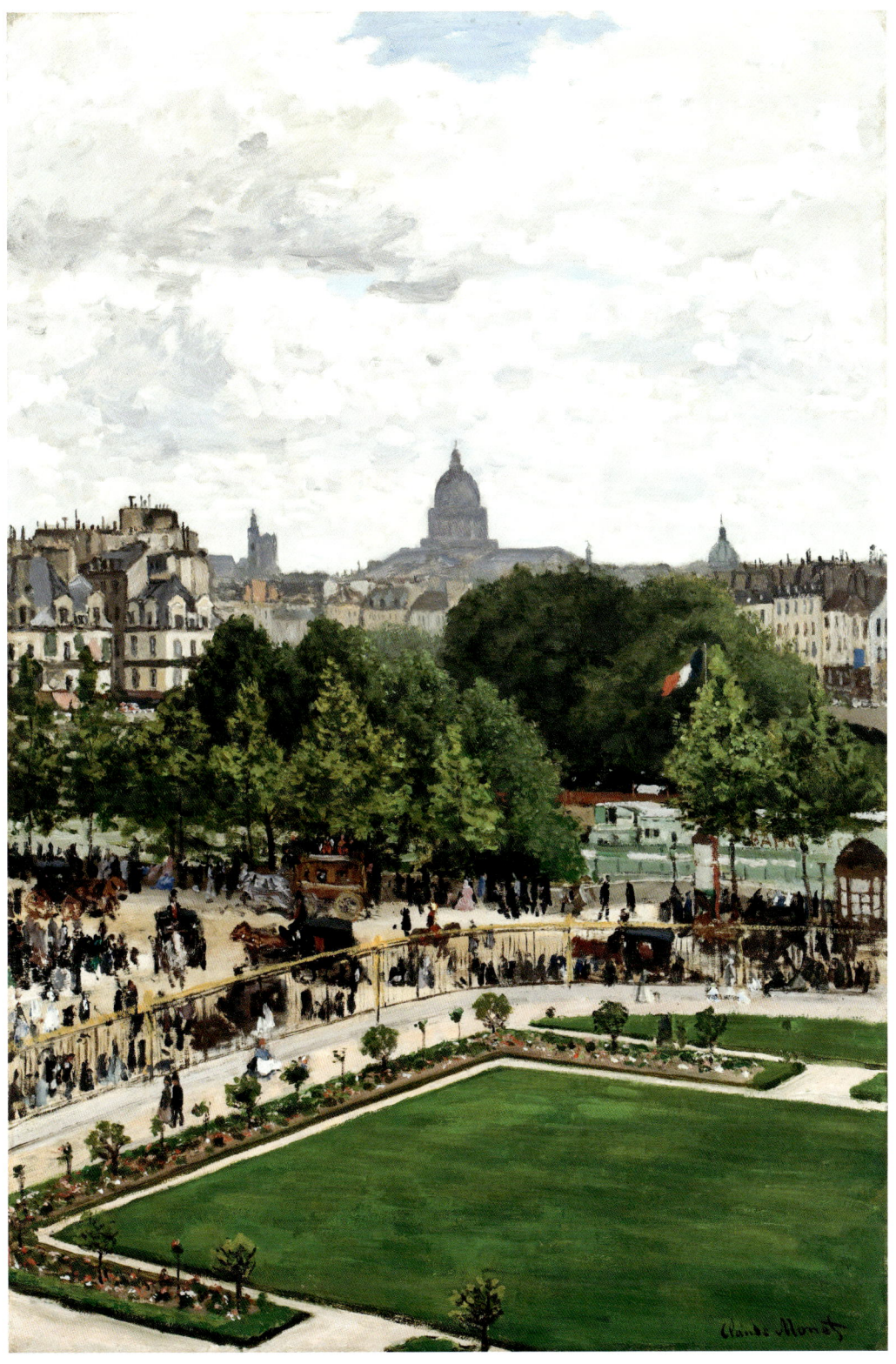

that radical urban reforms lay only a few years in the past. In those Second Empire years, Paris was creating the cosmopolitan urban profile it retains to this day. The crooked lanes and mediaeval alleys of the old quarters had been demolished to make way for the majestic neo-baroque of the avenues and monumental buildings created by Napoleon III's urban planner, Baron Haussmann, engineer of an ambitious new order in Paris. The city became lighter, more spacious and stylish than it had been. The changes admittedly had startling social consequences, making a handful of property speculators rich and banishing much of the poorer, traditional population of Paris to the suburbs; but they also prompted a prosperity and splendour that the young artists evidently found attractive. Thus Monet too painted the new metropolis with its carriages and its promenading citizens.

He himself, it is true, had little share in the prosperity of the time. Repeatedly rebuffed by the Salon, without any dependable patron, he struggled to get by on occasional commissions and the support of friends. His family refused him an allowance, disapproving of the fact that he was living with Camille, a woman of humble origins. Bazille, who was better off financially, frequently took Monet under his wing, sharing his own studio with him and even buying *Women in the Garden*. He paid 2,500 francs for it – a high price for a work by an unknown – and doled the money out in monthly instalments of fifty francs. This well-meant patronage was still not sufficient for Monet's rent, food and painting materials, though – so he pretended to his family that he and Camille had separated. They promptly reinstated him, and he spent the summer of 1867 at his aunt's country

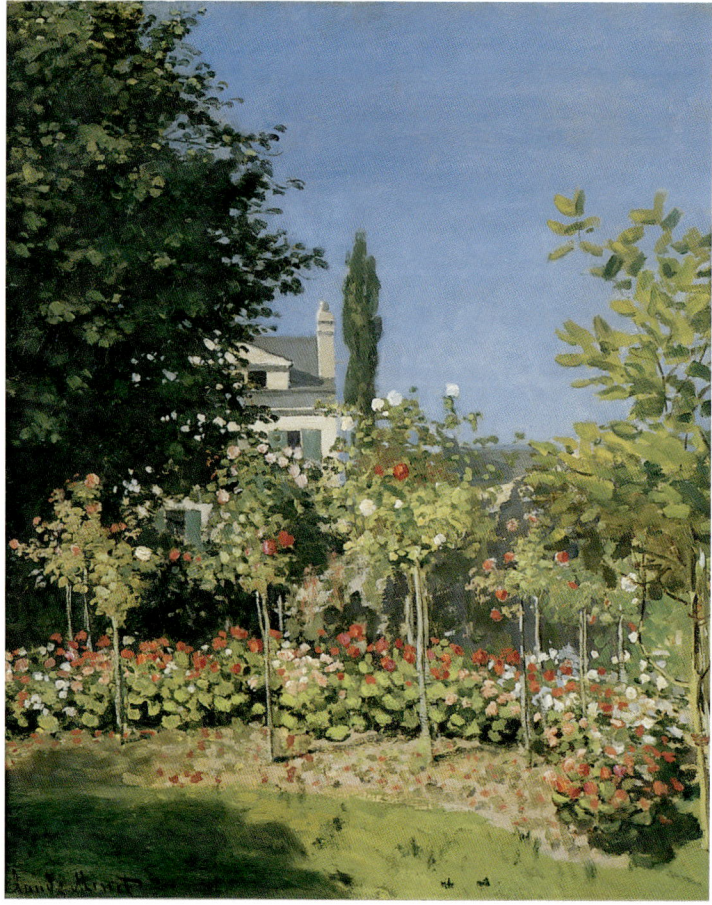

Flowering Garden, 1866
Oil on canvas, 65 x 54 cm
(25⅝ x 21⅜ in.)
Paris, Musée d'Orsay

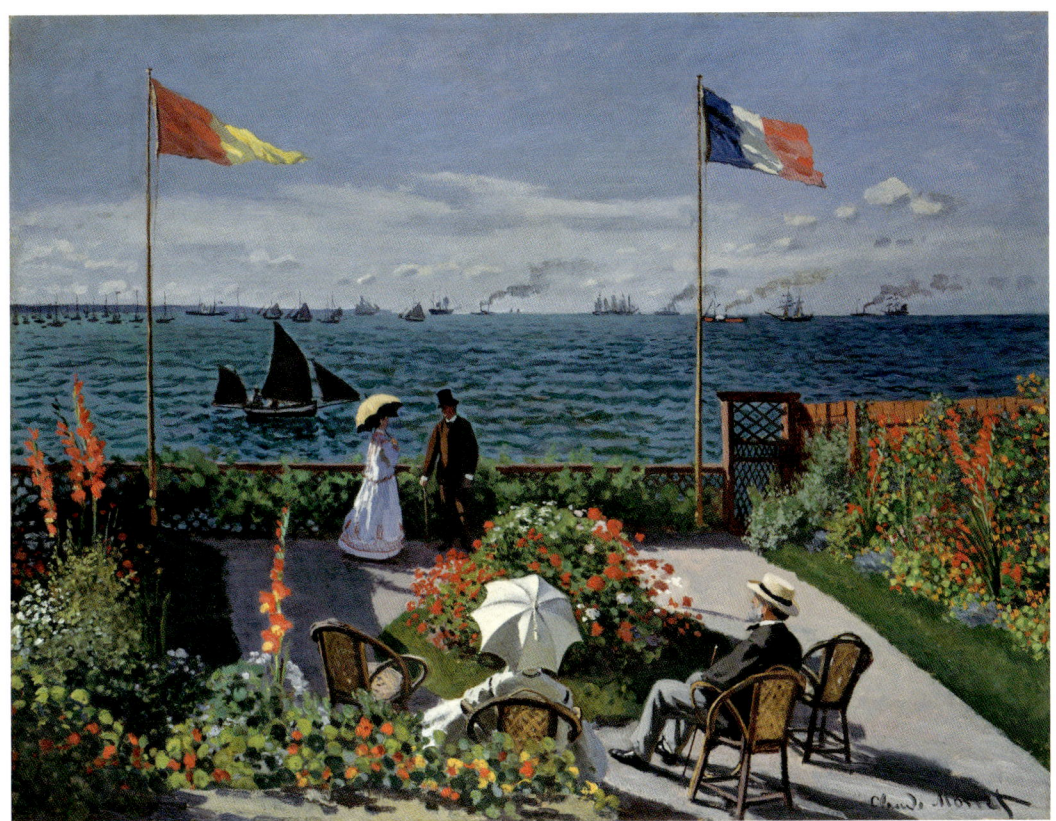

house at Sainte-Adresse, writing to Bazille of his concern and asking him to look after Camille, who had stayed in Paris. Camille was pregnant, and on 8 August gave birth to their first son, Jean. Monet remained in Normandy, playing the family part expected of him in the hope of ensuring the support of his relatives. "For two weeks," he wrote to Bazille on 26 June, "I have been in the bosom of my family, and am as happy as is possible. They are all nice to me, and go into raptures at every brushstroke. I have a good deal to do, about twenty seascapes, figures and gardens."

Garden at Sainte-Adresse, 1867
Oil on canvas, 98 x 130 cm (38⅝ x 51¼ in.)
New York, The Metropolitan Museum of Art

Monet binds the sunlight, sea, figures and flowers into a composition that must have seemed daring at the time. His use of colour and his brushwork, though, were still closer to his earlier realist mode than to Impressionism.

Gardens were to engage Monet his whole life long. He had hit upon this theme the year before at Sainte-Adresse, and was gripped by the colourfulness and opulence of flower gardens. The gleam and luxuriance of gardens allowed him a pretext to pursue the power and effects of light and colour to the full. The sunlight in *Flowering Garden* (ill. p. 124) awakens colour from the earthen sleep it had been kept in by realist art, with luminous red heightened by white and especially by the lush, rich complementary green. In *Garden at Sainte-Adresse* (ill. p. 125) the flowers and light have been combined with Monet's first subject, water. This picture was probably painted in the same year after *Flowering Garden,* and the figure in the foreground, as Monet later reported, is his father. The brush-work is not as relaxed as in the Paris paintings, and the figures, as well as the terrace and the sea, are oddly stiff and schematic; but still, in its use of sunlight the painting goes beyond *Women in the Garden.* For the first time, Monet was painting colourful shadows; and his flowers, with a greater

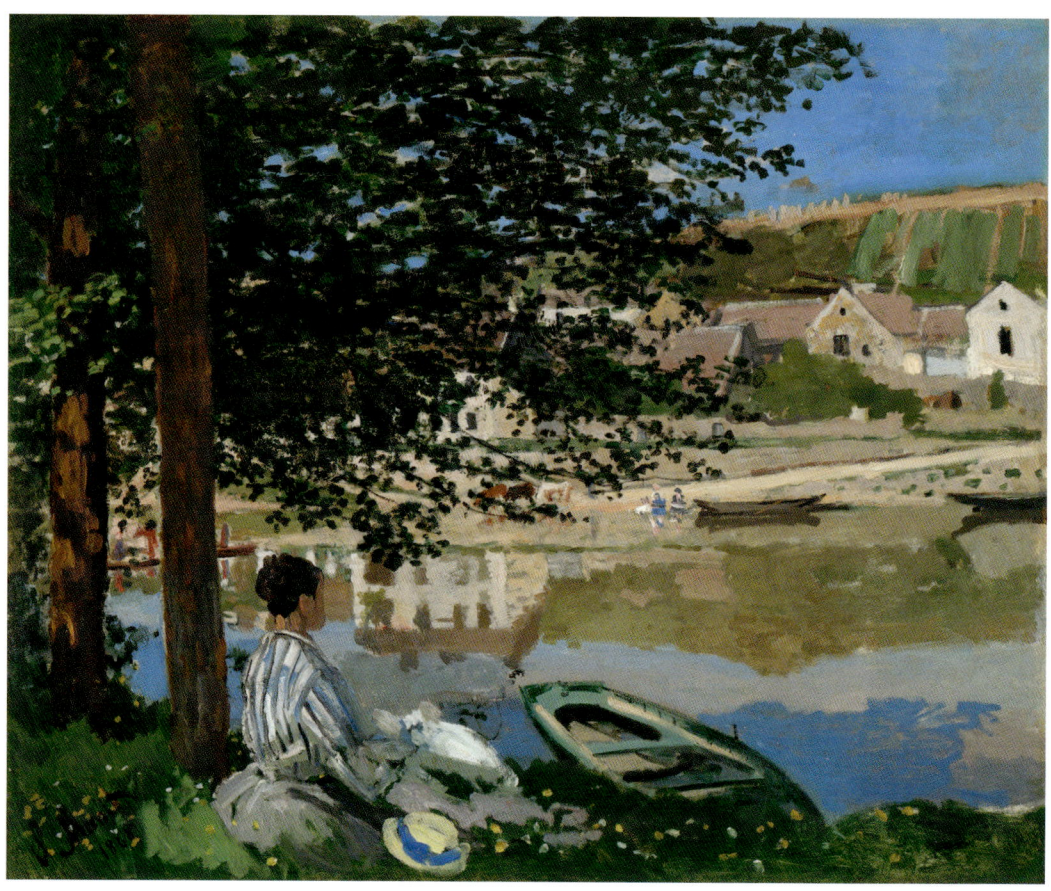

On the Bank of the Seine, Bennecourt, 1868
Oil on canvas, 81 x 100 cm (32 x 39⅜ in.)
The Art Institute of Chicago

Monet has used the reflections in the water
to move in an abstract direction. Nature and
its mirrored double become a single unity
patterned across the canvas in a spirit
detached from spatial illusion.

freedom than before, are rendered with loose dabs of luminous unmixed colour.

Monet's Salon debut had been as a painter of the sea, and he remained fascinated by it throughout his life – not only by stylish resorts and regattas, but above all by the waters, tranquil on sunny windless days, wild and stormy at other times, or broodily overcast. He also loved to paint lakes and ponds, and, time and again, his river, the Seine. In all of this he studied not only the shifting weather moods and shapes of water (ill. p. 127) but also its properties as a reflective surface that split and reassembled landscape features. On the water's mirror surface, the sky and clouds, houses and trees, people and boats became a two-dimensional image free of corporeal, spatial substance. A painting such as *On the Bank of the Seine, Bennecourt* (ill. p. 126) demonstrates that, for Monet, water was a means of abstraction. Areas of colour – scarcely distinguished by representational function – give the picture a rhythmic structure. The mirror of the water surface blurs the spatial dimensions of landscape art, thus taking a significant step toward non-representational, abstract art. Monet was to take this principle, apparent in early works such as this, much further in his late water landscapes, his paintings of cliffs, and above all his famous water-lilies.

But there were many years to go before that radical stage was reached. They were to be years in which Monet tried time after time to create compositions filled with traditional kinds of tension, and to locate picturesque views. And they were also years of poverty, even of despair. Needless to say, he could not keep up his charade indefinitely, and could not neglect his lover and son any longer. He returned to Paris, to face renewed official rejection of his paintings, and the struggle for mere subsistence. Bazille was often his only source of support. Countless letters in which Monet approached his loyal and generous friend for money have survived to document his predicament. The following autumn, the situation eased for a while when he met a Le Havre shipping magnate named Gaudibert. Monet painted a number of portraits, including one of Madame Gaudibert, and for a time his mood was calmer. In December 1868 he wrote to Bazille in Paris: "Here I am surrounded by the things I love. I spend my time in the open, on the beach in stormy weather or when the fishing boats put out [...] In the evenings, my dear friend, there is a warm fire in my cottage, and the cosiness of a small family. If only you could see how cute your godson is now! Thanks to the help of the gentleman in Le Havre, I am now enjoying a spell of quiet, free of chores. Ideally I should like to stay in a peaceful nook like this for ever." But the idyll was to end abruptly that very year. Monet had to flee his creditors, and returned to Paris, leaving a great many paintings behind in Le Havre. His concentration on gardens, water and light was diminishing his prospects of sales, and indeed of official recognition. Light, flowers and water were taking the young artist further and further from the Salon.

Rough Sea at Étretat, 1868/69
Oil on canvas, 66.2 x 130.5 cm
(26 x 51½ in.)
Paris, Musée d'Orsay

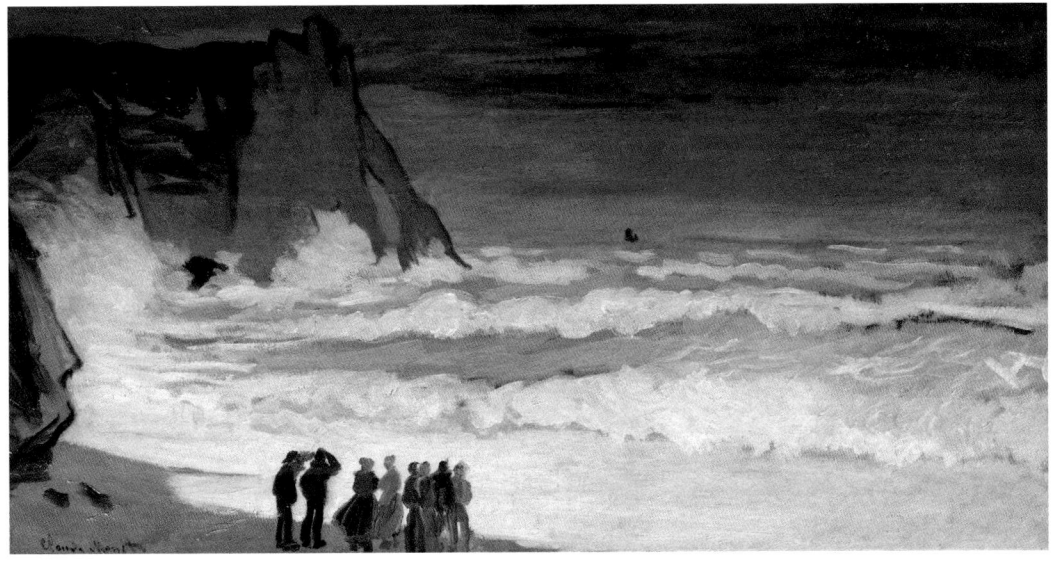

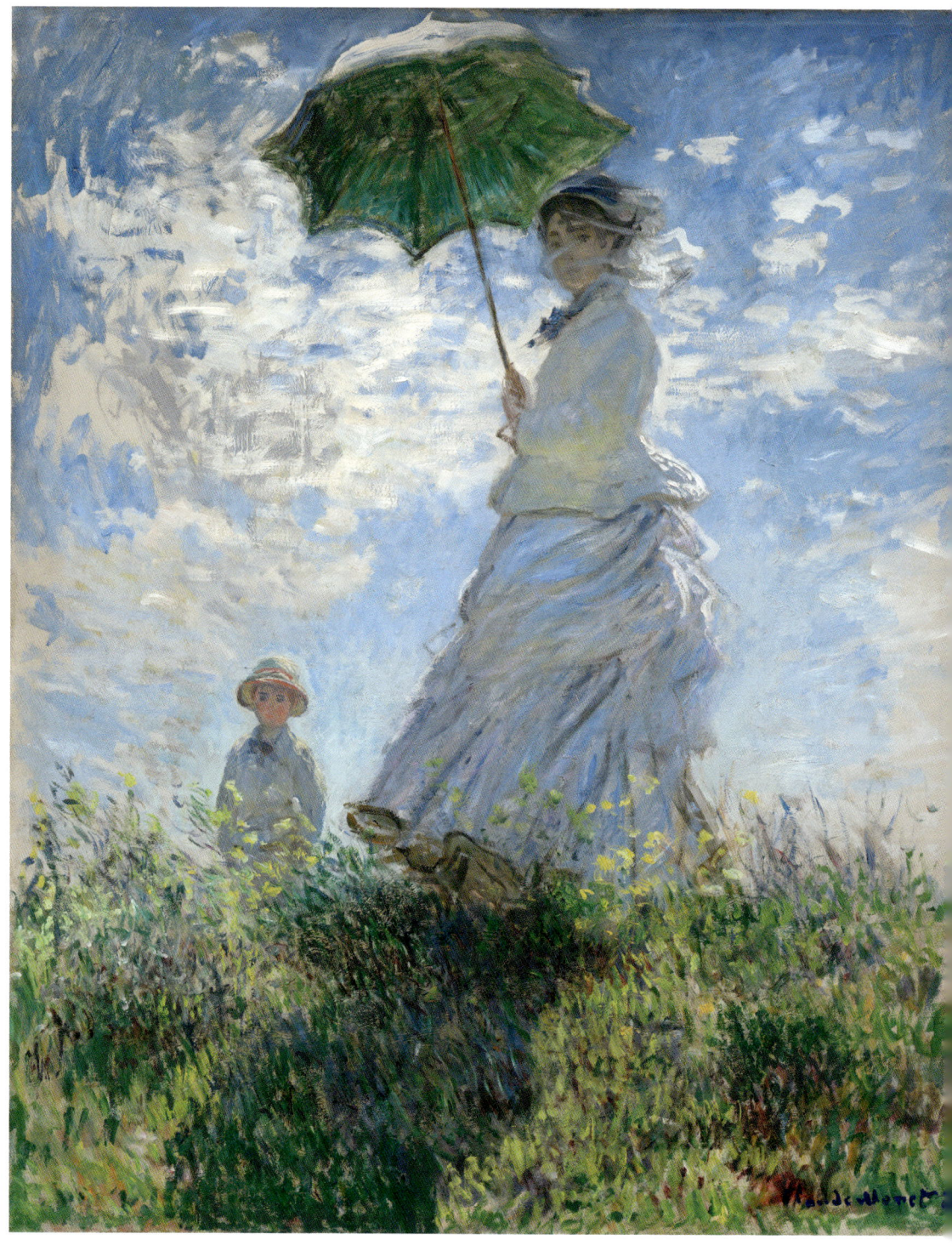

The World as a Month of Sundays

From Boudin, who encouraged him to paint out of doors, Monet had learnt that whatever was painted on the spot, in the open, possessed an energy and vitality in the brushwork that were unattainable in the studio. An artist working in a studio could fall back on academic conventions and his own repertoire of mannerisms, but painting *en plein air* compelled continual response to the changing atmosphere and light. Painters of every period had of course done sketches in the open, recording the phenomena of nature in pencil, chalk or watercolour, and since the late 18th century even in oils; but these were merely sketches destined for transfer to canvas in the studio, where academic rules would govern the creation of a traditional composition. What was new in art now, indeed revolutionary, was the principle of going out in the open with easel and canvas, palette and oils, to draft and work on paintings out of doors and perhaps even to finish them there.

Monet was one of the first to move his studio outdoors in this way. The recent invention of tubes for oil paints was a significant contributory factor, since mixing paint powders and oil in the open (certainly in the blustery winds of Normandy) would have been a tall order. Painting out of doors remained a complicated, uncomfortable business at all times, in any case. Monet would set off on summer days laden with his painting paraphernalia and a large parasol to keep direct sunlight off his canvas. At colder times of the year he could be seen in boots and woollens and several layers of coats and blankets, busy *sur le motif.* When a wind was blowing he would tie his easel and canvas fast with cord, but even so nature played its pranks on him, and on one occasion, when he had mistaken the times of the tides, a freak wave washed him into the sea, together with all his utensils and canvases. "Art demands bravery in its soldiers," mocked one contemporary critic.

To get out of the city centre, further than the park, with all one's oils and canvases, would have been a complex affair in itself just a few years earlier, requiring the use of a carriage or cab, and thus presupposing a certain level of prosperity in the artist. But the rail connections that had been established since the 1850s meant that villages close to Paris were now even closer, and even poor artists could afford to go out into the country. Trains left the Gare de l'Est hourly for Argenteuil, Bougival, Asnières and other villages along the Seine; and the capital was only a few hours from the stylish seaside resorts of Deauville, Honfleur and Trouville. Painters travelling out to work would share their compartments with trippers from every walk of life. For the first time in history, urban working populations and the lower middle classes were in a position to take trips, shaking the city dust from their feet – at least for a day.

"When I set off I said to myself: And there I shall have some air, some sun and greenery! […] Oh, yes, greenery! Instead of

The Walk, Woman with a Parasol, 1875
Oil on canvas, 100 x 81 cm (39¼ x 32 in.)
Washington, D.C., National Gallery of Art,
Collection of Mr and Mrs Paul Mellon

cornflowers and poppies, great prairies covered with old clothes and detachable collars […] laundresses everywhere and not a single shepherdess. […] Coach drivers who jeer at you, restaurateurs who take you for all they can get […] forests where you lose your daughter […] hotels where you mislay your son-in-law! […] And that, my dear Joseph […] that is the faithful description of what are customarily called […] the Environs of Paris! […]" Thus the good Monsieur Bartaval, the hero of an *opéra bouffe* in 1875, describing a weekend in the country. The satire and cartoons of the day described the denaturing and industrialization of the small towns along the Seine, and their transformation into day-trip resorts for the urban population, during the Impressionist period. "Wherever there was a wretched square of grass with half a dozen rachitic trees, there the proprietor made haste to establish a ball or a café-restaurant."

In summer 1869, Monet and Renoir painted one such day-trip resort at Bougival, *La Grenouillère* ("the Frog Pond"; ill. p. 133). The two artists adopted almost the same line of vision, Renoir probably standing a little to Monet's right and perhaps somewhat closer to the water. Both took as their subject the pleasure-seekers on the Flowerpot (as the tiny bathing island with its one tree was known). Both were plainly at pains to be topographically exact; but this very similarity also serves to focus the differences in the two artists' styles. Monet constructs his picture using clear, horizontal brushstrokes, using his highlights sparingly but forcefully. His brushwork is energetic, whereas Renoir's paint has an airily hazed look to it. Monet's colours are few, muted and cool, but Renoir's palette is a more tender thing, warmer through its inclusion of reddish hues. Monet is not interested in fashions, so his figures are no more than brushstrokes, whereas Renoir, for his part, is engaged by the material qualities of clothing in sunlight, and has an eye for modish details. Renoir's composition, with its central focus, conveys a cosy sense of intimate confinement, while Monet, evenly distributing his shadows and placing his white light emphatically at the margins, dissolves the central focus and instead establishes a broad, dynamic feel across the entire visual field, creating a harmony between the surface patterning and the spatial depth. This transfer of tensions towards the margins is characteristic of Monet's compositional approach. If we compare *On the Bank of the Seine, Bennecourt* (ill. p. 126) or *Garden at Sainte-Adresse* (ill. p. 125), we see that in *La Grenouillère* Monet has succeeded in capturing the material properties of the water surface while still allowing it functions of a patterning kind. It is a work in which we see his art losing the last of the stiffness which had given *Women in the Garden* (ill. p. 120) or *Garden at Sainte-Adresse* something of the appearance of opera backdrops.

Sunny scenes like that at *La Grenouillère* had a long tradition that had peaked in the *fêtes galantes* of Antoine Watteau. The Impressionists, and Renoir even more than Monet, were continuing that Arcadian tradition, but instead of a secluded idyll the scenes they painted were full of the kind of bustle Monsieur Bartaval described. Monet's bathing and regatta scenes present an early stage of the leisure industry which enables city dwellers to consume what nature makes available. These pictures of Sundays in the country, like paintings of modern life in Paris, were more than merely contemporary: they constituted a deliberate attempt to record what was definingly modern about everyday life in Monet's day.

From our own point of view, it is hard to understand why these paintings of recreation and Sunday pastimes should have met with such harsh criticism, and been so unbendingly rejected by the academy and the public alike. Three factors must have influenced this response: the painting technique, the handling of colour, and the approach to the human figure. In trying to set down their immediate impressions of light and colour, the Impressionists evolved a brushwork technique all their own. They used relaxed strokes and comma-like dabs, juxtaposing brighter

Hôtel des Roches Noires, Trouville, 1870
Oil on canvas, 80 x 55 cm
(31½ x 21¾ in.)
Paris, Musée d'Orsay

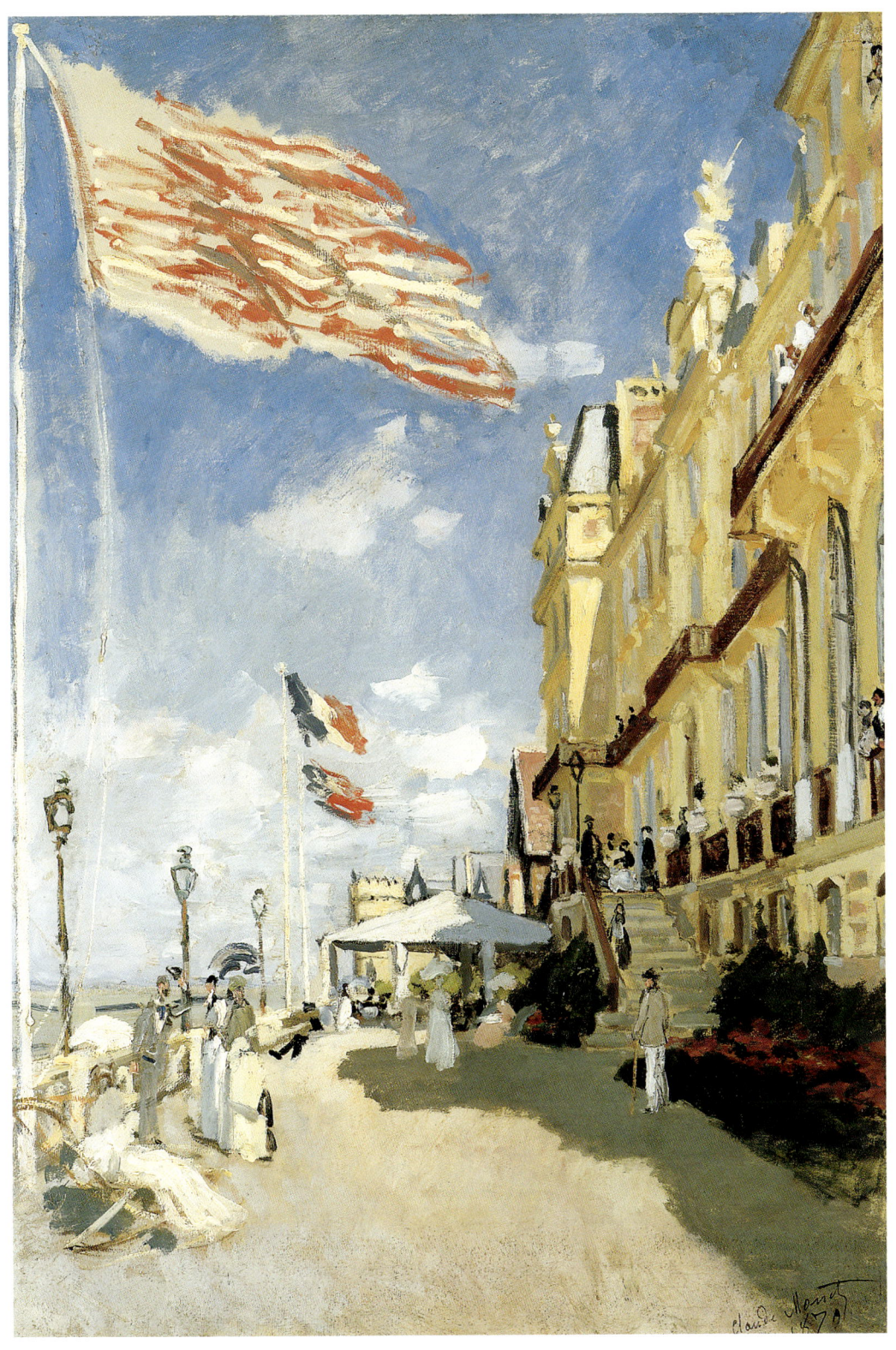

tones with contrasting, darker yet still colourful shades without any modulation of intermediate colours in between. This technique would have been widely accepted in an *ébauche,* or sketch, but quite different accomplishments were expected of a *tableau,* or finished painting; and the Impressionists were felt to be failing the tests of skill that artists were expected to pass. The fact that the size of their compositions suggested they were to be considered finished was felt to be particularly presumptuous. Furthermore, the public were used to the earthy tonalities of the Naturalists, or the cool metallic values of Ingres and his disciples, so that the gleaming splendour of Monet's art appeared a glaring, loud provocation.

Ingres's influence on academic art at that time was decisive, and he had made draughtsmanship the fundamental requisite of painting. A pupil of the classicist Jacques-Louis David and an ardent admirer of Raphael, Ingres had stressed clarity of outline, tender subtlety of colour, and amply weighted contouring, and the delighted bourgeoisie rewarded him with endless portrait commissions. The criterion for quality in a painting was the clarity of outline, schooled on antiquity, and its elegant grace. "Draw lines, lots of lines," was the imperative that Ingres used to din into his pupils. Colour was no more than an extra in his eyes. Jean-Auguste-Dominique Ingres, and a majority of academic artists, fought a lifelong war against Delacroix, who rated colour above all and (like Gustave Courbet and Manet later) had a long struggle to gain admission to the Salon at all. But even the dramatic chiaroscuro of a Delacroix – its lines and colours plunging from nowhere into the centre in order to establish a figure there as if by chance – had an almost old-masterly air when compared to the comma-like brushwork and luminous, spectral colours of the Impressionists.

If we consider the high valuation which was commonly placed on figure painting, the manner in which Monet and his fellows tackled the human figure must have been particularly vexing to their contemporaries. Academic painters would portray a bourgeois gentleman as Leonidas or Odysseus, and his madame as the beautiful Helen or virtuous Diana. They were cloaked in the ennobling robes of antiquity. The good citizens who appeared out for strolls in Monet's paintings, however, were mere ragged flaps of stuff, like pennants when the breeze dies. Like clumps of grass or clouds of smoke, Monet's people served simply as surfaces on which light could play. "Are you telling me that that is what I look like when I stroll along the Boulevard des Capucines?" demanded the critic and genre painter Louis Leroy in the satirical magazine *Le Charivari* when *Boulevard des Capucines* (ill. p. 137) was exhibited at the first joint Impressionist show in April 1874. "The devil take it! Are you taking the mickey?"

For ten years, the younger artists had been continually barred by the official world. Now they decided to take matters into their own hands. Monet, Renoir, Pissarro, Sisley, Degas, Cézanne, and a number of others, founded the Société anonyme des artistes, peintres, sculpteurs et graveurs in order to display their work independently of the Salon. Their first exhibition was far from a success with the public, though. Eight to ten thousand visitors crowded to the Salon every day; the Impressionist show drew a mere 175 on its first day, and on the last just 54, most of whom were in fact there to poke fun at the art exhibited. It was that show, though, that got the new movement its name. Louis Leroy's article in the magazine *Le Charivari* was headed "Exhibition of the Impressionists", and in it, borrowing a word from the title of Monet's sea piece *Impression, Sunrise* (ill. pp. 134/135), he damned the new art roundly: "Impression – too right! And I was just saying to myself that if an impression has been made on me, something must be making it. What freedom and ease in the brushwork! Wallpaper in its raw state is more finished than this marine picture!"

In this famous picture, Monet used delicate strokes of thinned paint to record his impression of morning at the harbour of Le Havre. With a few succinct, audacious strokes he juxtaposed the

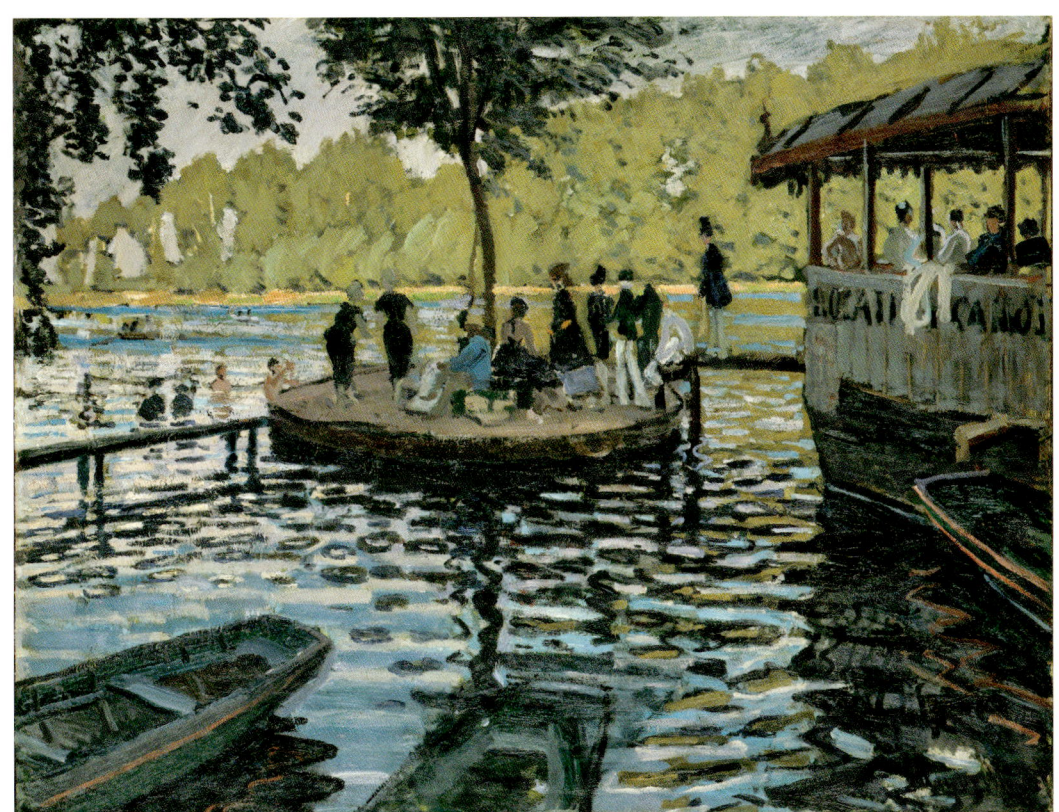

*"I'm never finished with my paintings;
the further I get, the more I seek the impossible
and the more powerless I feel."*

CLAUDE MONET

La Grenouillère, 1869
Oil on canvas, 75 x 100 cm (29⅝ x 39⅜ in.)
New York, The Metropolitan Museum of Art

The small circular island with its single
tree was nicknamed the "Flowerpot"
(or the "Camembert"), and for Monet and
Renoir it provided an attractive subject for
early "Impressionist" work. Easel by easel
they worked on the same subject – and their
paintings, similar though they naturally
are, reveal the fundamental differences
between the two artists.

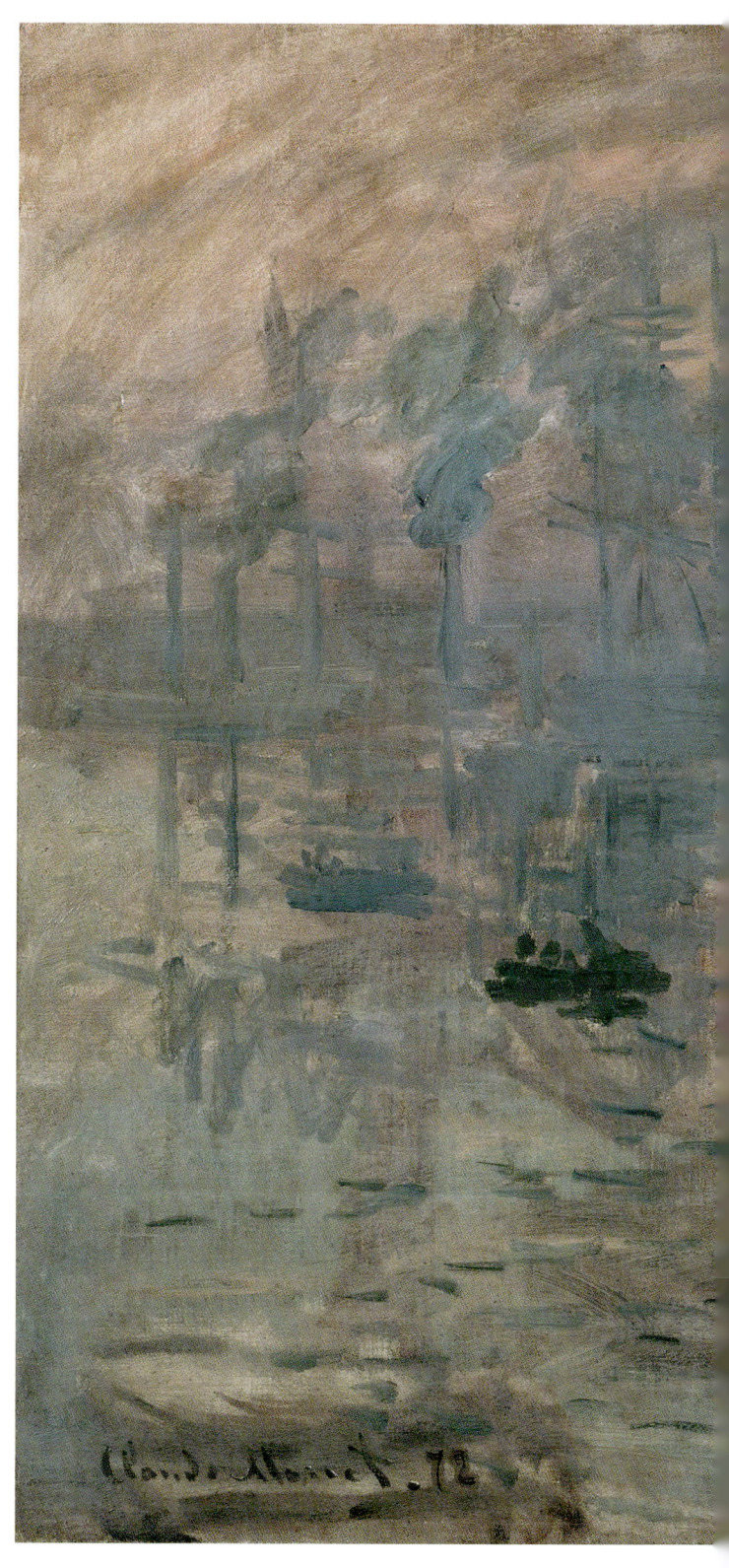

Impression, Sunrise, 1873
Oil on canvas, 48 x 63 cm (19 x 24¾ in.)
Paris, Musée Marmottan Monet

This atmospheric morning scene in the
port of Le Havre gave the new movement
its name. Critic Louis Leroy derisively
dubbed the new artists Impressionists,
adding: "Wallpaper in its raw state is
more finished than this marine picture."

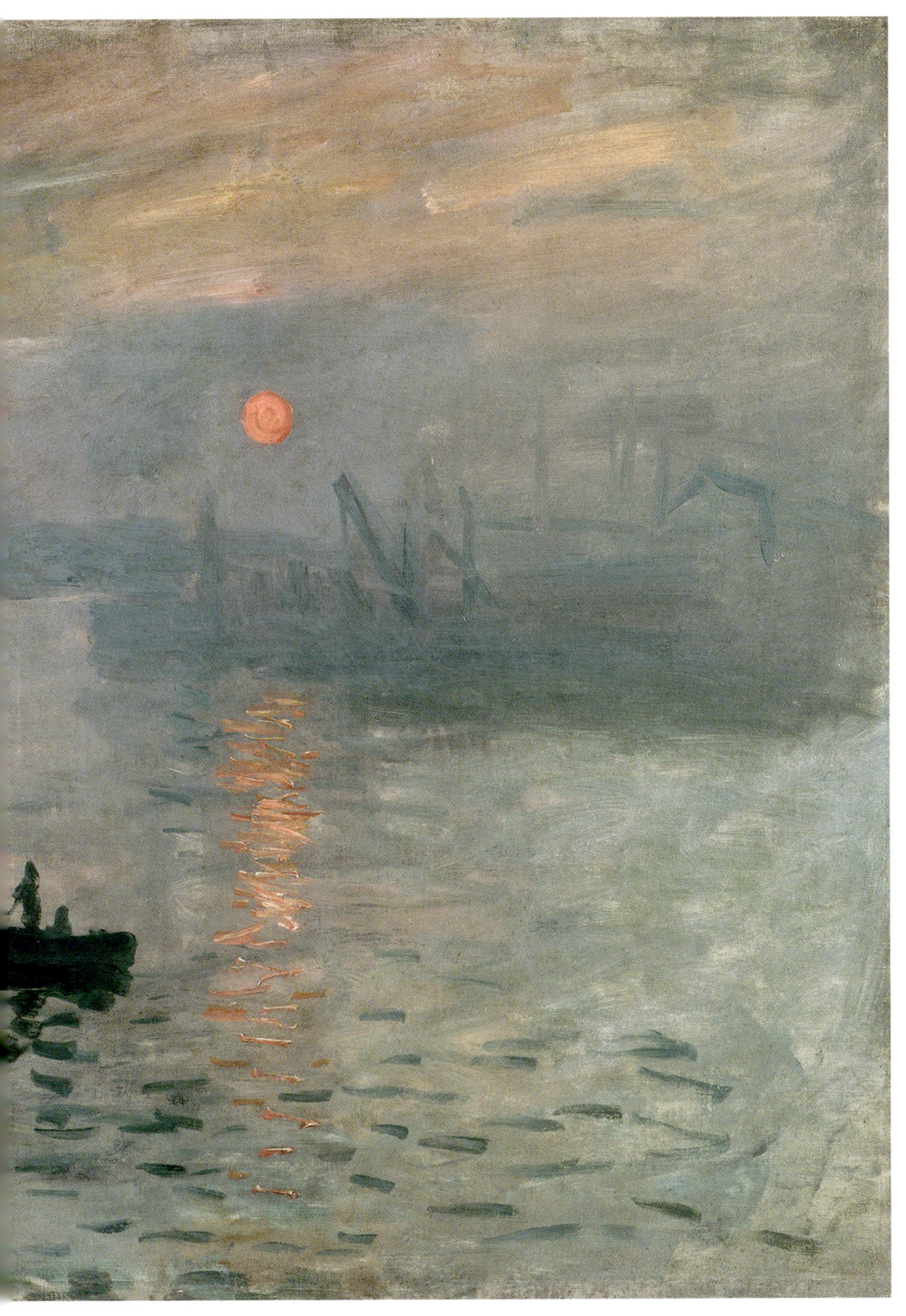

orange reflections of sunlight with a variety of greys. The ships' masts and chimneys, though hazed by mist, nonetheless constitute a graphic compositional fabric of verticals and diagonals that lends structure and vitality to the field. His loose brushwork, the sketchiness and immediacy with which he recorded the perception of a single moment, struck the public as a scandal, and were felt to be brutally coarse.

The Impressionists were initially so called in a spirit of ridicule, but the label stuck, and within days of Leroy's barbed article in *Le Charivari* a well-disposed critic was writing: "If their aims were to be described in a single word, we should need to coin the word Impressionists. They are Impressionists in that they do not reproduce a landscape but convey the impression it makes on the beholder."

Nowadays we do not perceive Impressionism as constituting a revolutionary new departure, or the achievement of a single artist; rather, we view it as a further development of ideas, techniques and observations that recurred throughout the first half of the 19th century, even if it was left to Monet and his fellows to apply them with full radical rigour. An impression was the visual impact made by a landscape or other motif in a single moment. The eye does not consciously register all the available detail in a moment; it is only by gazing at buildings, passers-by or other things for longer that we see individual windows, decorative features on façades, a fashionable hat or a dignified face, and in the course of this longer scrutiny the brain catches up with the eye, erasing the first impression and substituting the sum of experience, conventional perception, or imaginative projection. What the Impressionists in general, and Monet in particular, aimed to preserve was the visual freshness of that first fleeting moment, free of categories of perception or traditional precept. When Monet opened his eyes he saw blocks of colour, surface patterns, the very air, as defined by light; and the impressions he received were his subject matter on canvas.

"He was only an eye – but what an eye!" Paul Cézanne famously remarked of Monet; and his words aptly pinpoint his fellow artist's central concern. What Monet was to call *l'instantanéité* became his life's work, and time and again reduced him to despair, for there is an intrinsic and irresolvable contradiction in the aim to preserve in permanent form the passing moment.

The Boulevard des Capucines, 1873
Oil on canvas, 80 x 60 cm (31½ x 23⅝ in.)
Kansas City, The Nelson-Atkins
Museum of Art

Monet rendered the constant flow of passers-by along the boulevard as a flickering impression of haze and light, done in vibrant dabs of paint. As we look at the painting we receive an overall impression without registering individual figures or details.

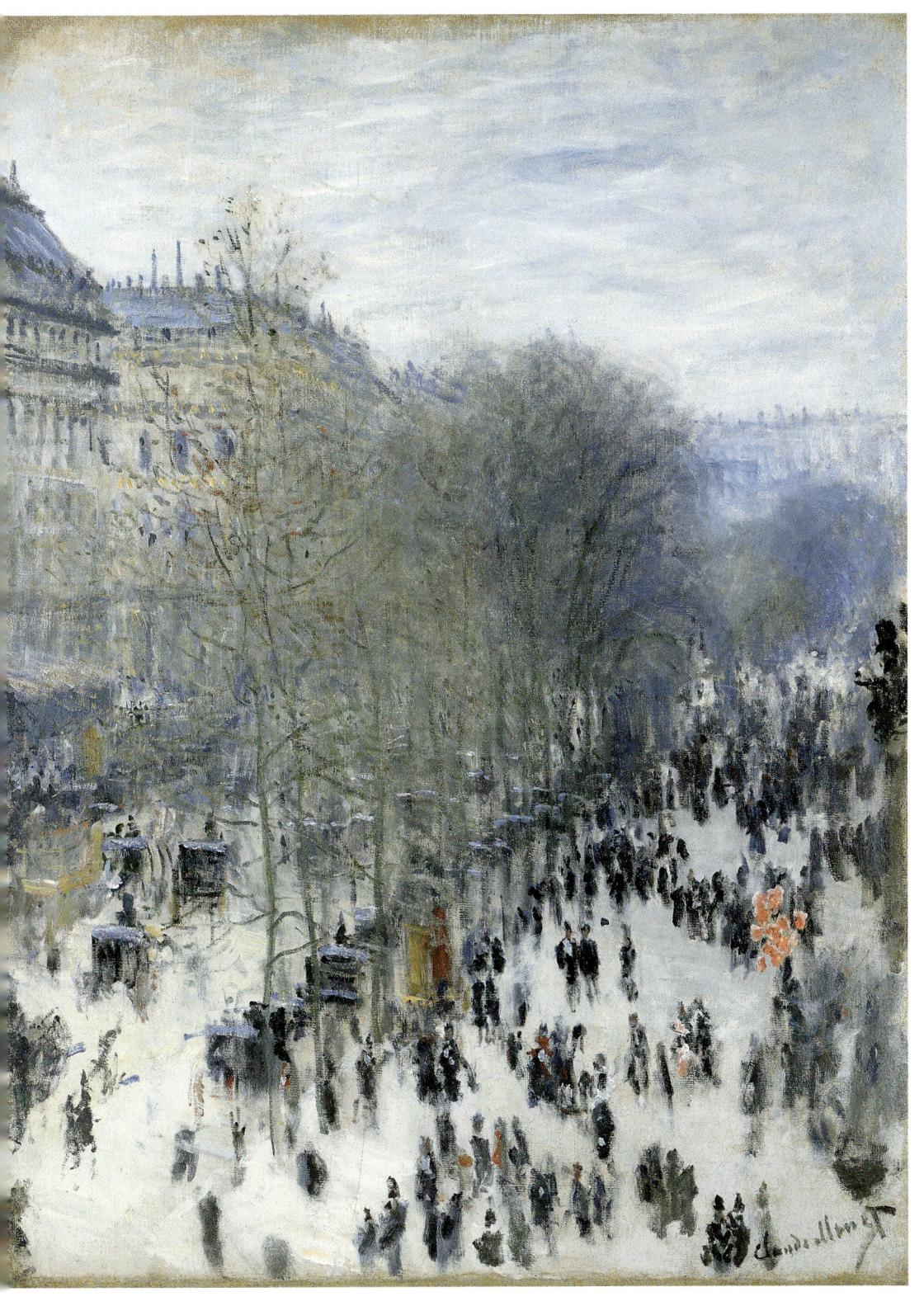

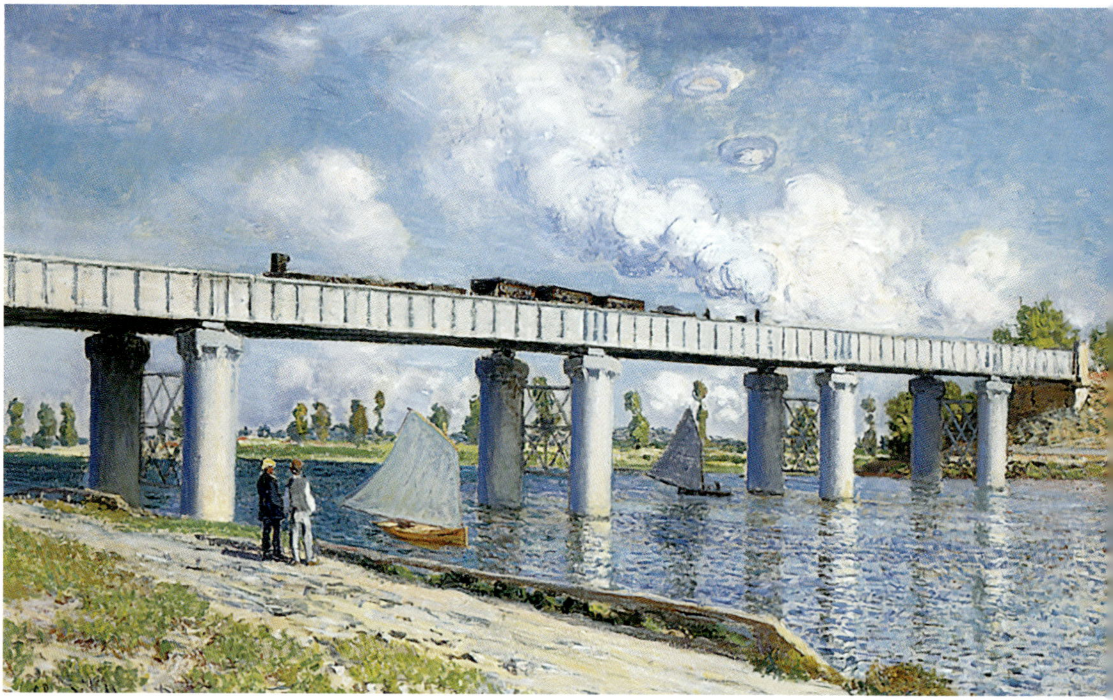

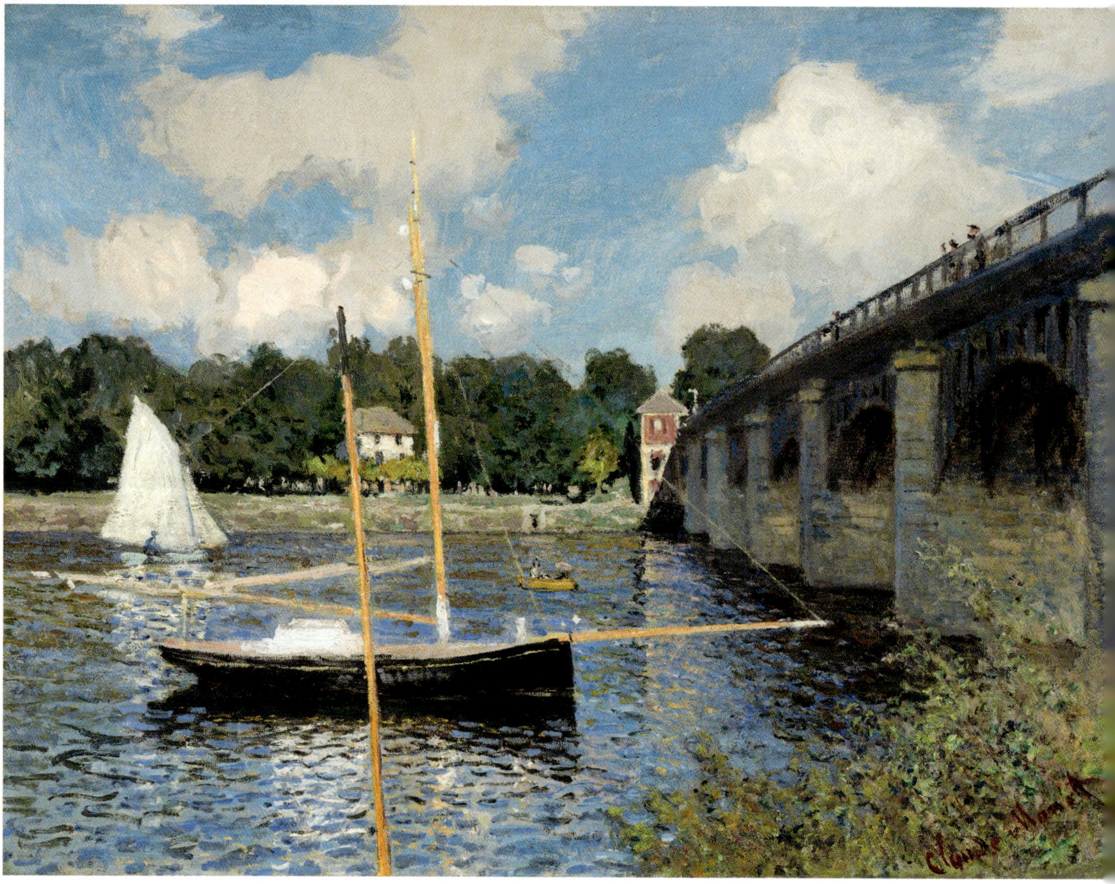

The Bridges at Argenteuil

Ladies in rustling dresses carrying dainty parasols, society people enjoying picnic lunches in the woods, or bathing pools at Bougival, generally appear to us now as if through the prettifying spectacles of nostalgia. To Monet's contemporaries, though, this subject matter was the height of modernity. The new generation of artists set out expressly to be of their time, an aim that put them at odds with academic predilections for the heroes of antiquity or mediaeval romance. Few of them were as consistent in their wish to record the spirit of the age as Monet. We can gauge his consistency by the startling amount of common ground between his early figure paintings, for instance, and the illustrations in contemporary fashion magazines. We can see it in his homage to the modern profile of Paris, in his smoking chimneys at Le Havre, or in his portrayals of modern leisure activities.

In autumn 1871, after the Franco-Prussian War (during which he had lived in London to avoid conscription), Monet moved to Argenteuil. The year before he had married Camille, and now the couple, with their little son Jean, rented a house and garden outside the city. Argenteuil, about ten kilometres north-east of Paris, was described at the time as "a very pretty town, pleasantly situated on a low hill where the vineyards slope down to the right bank of the Seine". Like Bougival and Asnières, it was a popular spot for Parisian weekend excursionists. It offered sailing regattas with stylish city crowds, restaurants, cafés and bathing spots, as well as unspoilt poppy fields or rowing boats idling in the sun – in a word, a cornucopia of motifs to tempt artists. In the years ahead, Argenteuil was to be the favourite patch of the Impressionists.

Apart from brief visits to Holland and Normandy, and of course Paris, Monet lived and painted at Argenteuil till he moved to Vétheuil in 1878. Camille's dowry, and the money Monet inherited on the death of his father, enabled them to lead a more comfortable, prosperous life for the first time. Moreover, Monet was now receiving support from the art dealer Paul Durand-Ruel, whom he had met in London. Durand-Ruel regularly bought Monet's paintings, despite the initial difficulties in reselling them.

From letters and meticulously kept account books we have a fairly clear picture of the Monet family's life. Till mid-decade, at least, they were well off, even affording two servants and a gardener. The circumstances and lifestyle of the *bonne bourgeoisie* were apparent in intimate paintings such as *The Luncheon* (ill. p. 141), which shows Camille and little Jean in a well-tended summer garden. On the table with its white cloth

OPPOSITE TOP
The Railway Bridge at Argenteuil, 1873
Oil on canvas, 60 x 98.4 cm (23½ x 38¾ in.)
Private collection

The bridge is a utopian monument to the new, modern age in Monet's painting. It carried city leisure-seekers out to the country but also encouraged the settlement of new industries out in the suburbs.

OPPOSITE BOTTOM
The Road Bridge at Argenteuil, 1874
Oil on canvas, 60 x 80 cm (23⅝ x 31½ in.)
Washington, D.C., National Gallery of Art

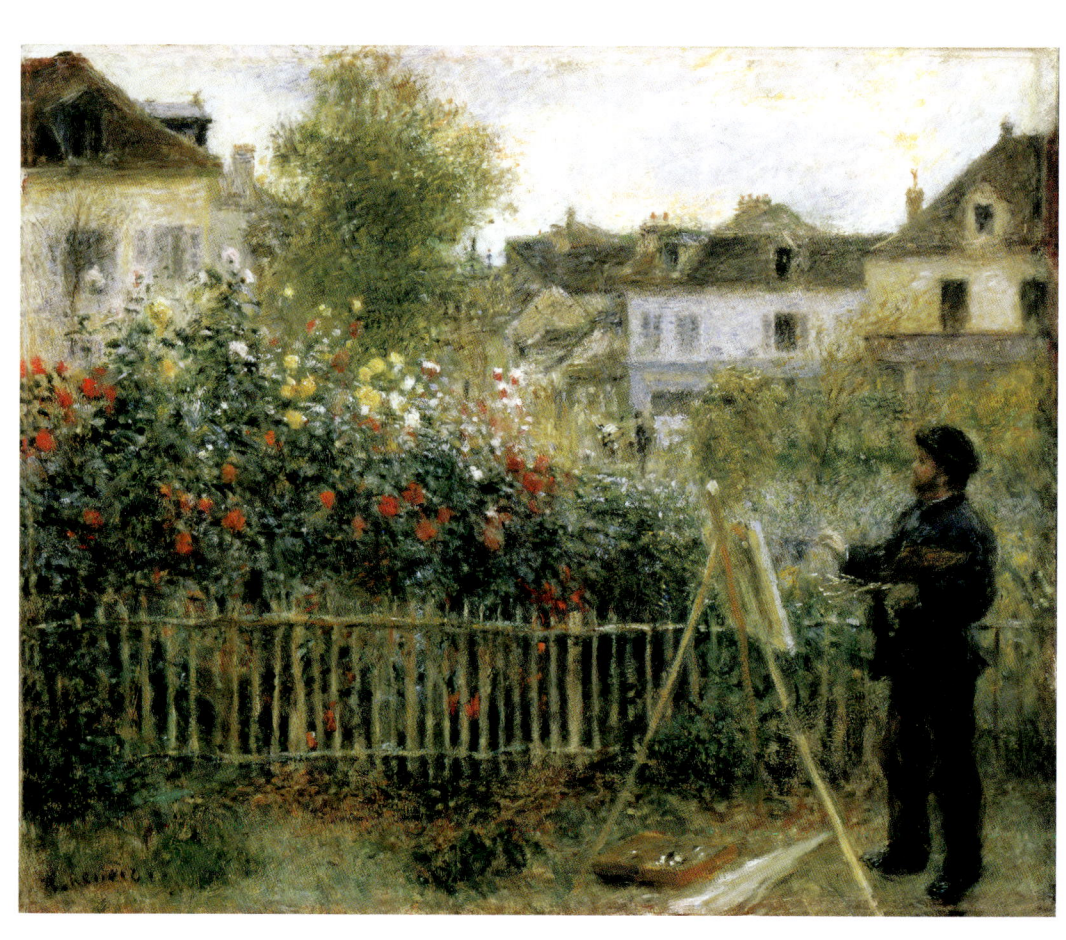

Pierre-Auguste Renoir
Monet Painting in His Garden, 1873
Oil on canvas, 46 x 60 cm (18⅛ x 23⅝ in.)
Hartford, Connecticut, Wadsworth Atheneum

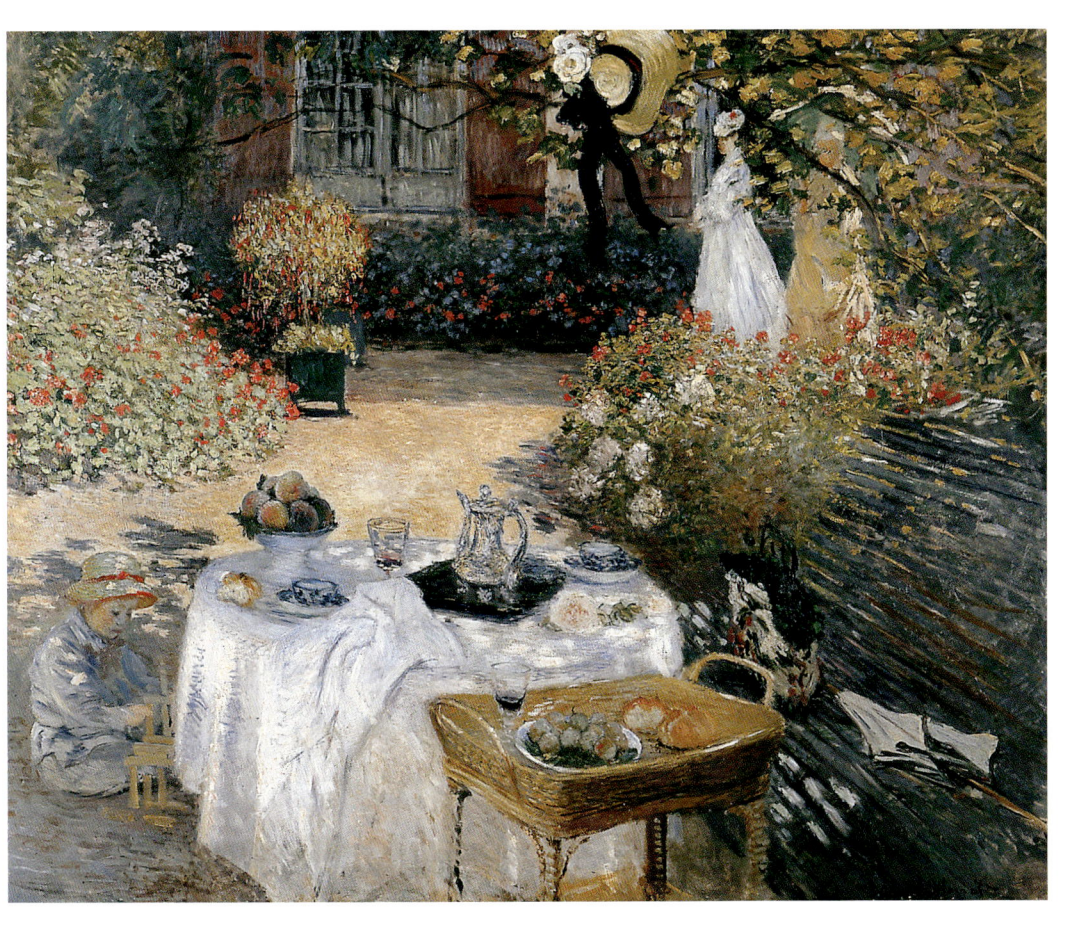

The Luncheon, c. 1873
Oil on canvas, 160 x 201 cm (63 x 79¼ in.)
Paris, Musée d'Orsay

are costly Chinese teacups and a silver pot, while the summer gowns of the ladies, and the straw hat hung on a branch, suggest the kind of leisure which in turn presupposes a certain affluence. *Apartment Interior* (ill. p. 143) affords us a glimpse of the shady interior of the house, and here too the chandelier, waxed parquet floor, and little Jean's sailor costume, all serve as reminders of the Monets' prosperity at that time.

Monet cultivated dealers and collectors, and also liked inviting friends to stay. Renoir and Pissarro were visitors, and Manet, who had jeered at *plein air* painting for years, became a convert at Argenteuil. It was there too that Monet met Gustave Caillebotte, a painter who was financially independent, thanks to a legacy, and who, over the next few years, was to become one of the first important collectors of Impressionist art. Caillebotte helped out Monet and his fellow Impressionists time and again, and paid for their exhibitions. When he died in 1894, his collection – which included sixteen works by Monet alone, among them major paintings such as *The Gare Saint-Lazare* (ill. p. 149), *The Luncheon* (ill. p. 141) and *Regatta at Argenteuil* – passed to the French state; but it was a long time before official quarters could bring themselves to exhibit at least a part of the collection. The Caillebotte bequest was the cornerstone of the Louvre's Impressionist collection, now on show at the Musée d'Orsay.

At Argenteuil, Monet took to the water. He added a cabin to a broad rowing boat, and an awning to keep off the sun, and used it as a floating studio. This had originally been an idea of Daubigny, the landscape artist, who had painted on the Seine and the Oise in his "botin" fifteen years before. Monet's studio boat can be seen in a number of his paintings, and was also painted by Manet in 1874 (ills. pp. 144 and 145), who showed Monet painting a river scene on the water, literally on his motif. Monet was capable of conveying the wind in the reeds, or the tranquil flow of water, with an immediacy that is altogether absorbing. *The Bridge at Argenteuil* (ill. p. 146 top) and *Poppies at Argenteuil* (ill. p. 147) demonstrate that painting *sur le motif* presented the artist with landscapes that were open-ended in every direction.

Argenteuil was not only a leisure resort. Since the mid-19th century it had been increasingly industrialized; and, for the Impressionists, this constituted an additional attraction, since industry betokened modernity. Argenteuil was linked to the city by two bridges, and Monet painted both. The older of the two (ill. p. 146 top), originally built of wood and stone, had been destroyed in the Franco-Prussian War but rebuilt afterwards, largely in its original state. The wooden beams were now replaced by cast-iron girders, but in the reconstruction considerable emphasis was placed on giving these a decorative air, as if wrought by the craftsman's hand. The other bridge (ills. pp. 138 top and 146 bottom) was a railway bridge, and both its function and the concrete and precast iron parts of which it was built made it highly modern. Among the local people it was controversial, some seeing it as a stylish sign of things to come, others dismissing it as an "ugly roofless tunnel".

Monet's paintings vividly and instantly convey the quite distinct characters of the two bridges. His pictures of the rail bridge, seen in sharp perspective or bathed in cool, almost metallic light, are eloquent of his unfeigned fascination with modern engineering, technology, industrial development – and speed, symbolized by the train. In one of the pictures (ill. p. 138 top) the rail bridge is a resplendent monument to a dawning era.

The old bridge (ill. p. 146 top) is more peaceful in mood. In appearance it is a memento of the July Monarchy, that golden age of the affluent middle classes; and in function it is still of a traditional order, crossed by pedestrians and horse-drawn vehicles, perhaps on their way to a restaurant or bathing spot.

Apartment Interior, 1875
Oil on canvas, 80 x 60 cm (31½ x 23⅝ in.)
Paris, Musée d'Orsay

The first few years at Argenteuil were a magical time for Monet and his small family. Financially secure for the time being, he settled into a relaxed life in a pleasant house and garden, painting some of his brightest pictures.

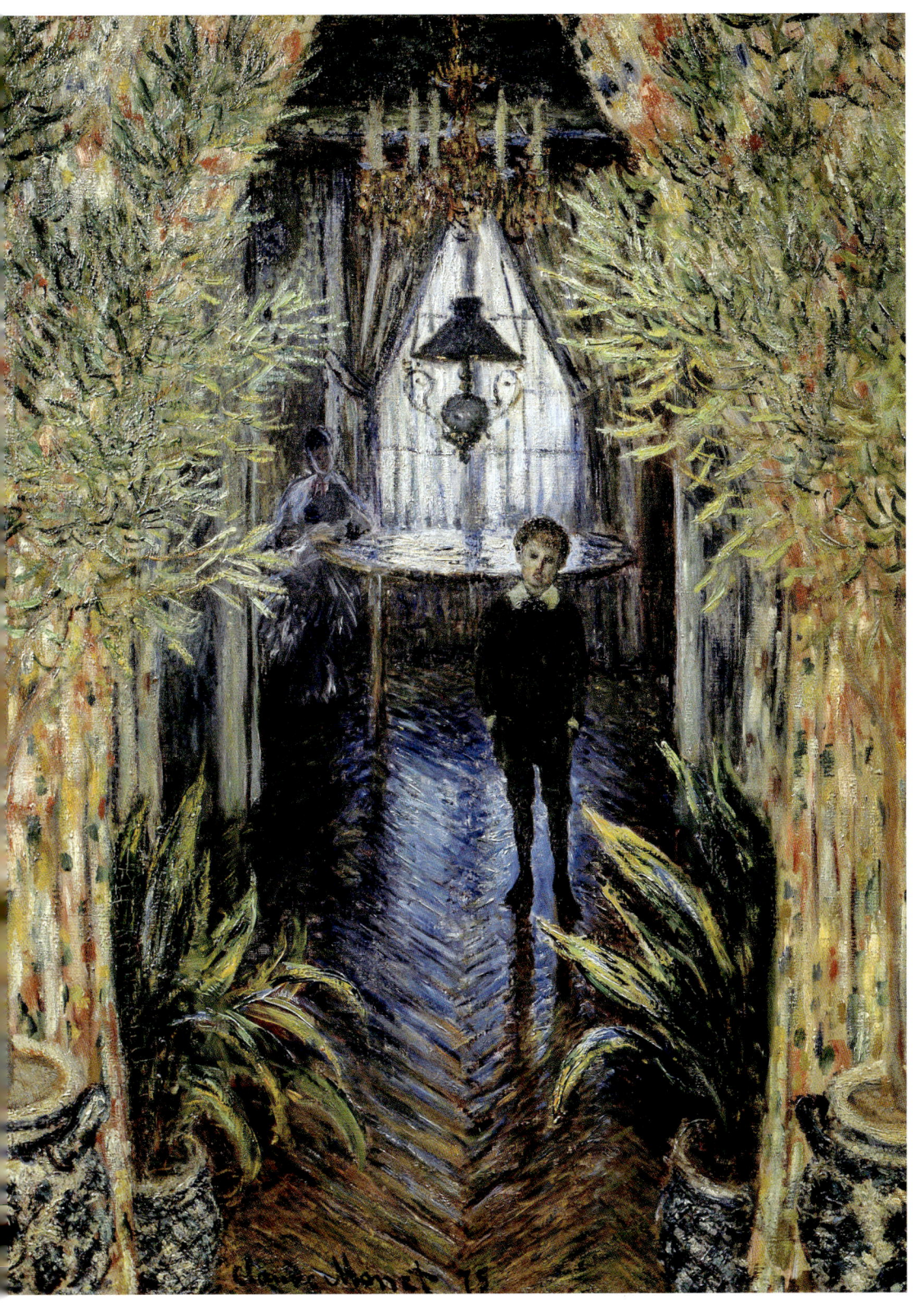

Painted in afternoon light, it is a thing of mellow majesty, four-square and solid. Like any bridge, though, it naturally represents a conquest of nature; it is a sign of civilization's relentless domestication of the wild. There is nothing remotely savage in the Argenteuil scenes, in fact; nor are there Arcadian idylls. Monet's Argenteuil landscapes are sunny and serene, peaceful and harmonious – without omitting the signs of the age. They are civilized. It is tempting, given the immediacy of Monet's paintings, to think of them as snapshots of a kind. But this would be to miss the structural attention that generally went into their composition. It is striking that Monet frequently used an axis to establish symmetries, an approach academic artists were careful to avoid because it tends to rob a composition of the illusion of spatial depth and draw attention to surface pattern. But it was this very property that made the principle attractive to Monet. Patterning was precisely what he was after. The Munich *Bridge at Argenteuil* (ill. p. 146 top) makes this clear: Monet lays out an exact grid of horizontals and verticals, thus creating a firm surface structure for the composition. His use of colour within that structure, though, serves to reintroduce a sense of spatial depth: the pale, bright ochre of the pillars where they catch the sun is in marked contrast to the grey-green of the shaded sides, and much the same applies to the ironwork. In the water, too, there are two distinct blues: the darker serves as a ground against which the lighter is highlighted. In such ways, within a surface-patterned linear structure, the painter uses colour to create three-dimensionality and spatiality in his subject.

A similar principle is at work in the pictures Monet painted of Saint-Lazare railway station in 1877 (ill. p. 149). The station had long fascinated Monet, and, if we can believe Renoir's account, he veritably took possession of it, pursuing his desire to paint it with a determination little short of insolence: "He put on his best clothes, pulled his lace cuffs to rights, and, idly swinging his gold-headed cane, handed the director of the western railways his card. The official froze, and ushered him in forthwith. The exalted personage asked his visitor to take a seat, and the latter introduced himself simply with the words: 'I am the painter Claude Monet'. The director knew nothing of art but did not dare admit as much. For a moment Monet left him twitching on the line, and then he announced the great news: 'I have decided to paint your station. For a long time I was undecided whether to take the Gare du Nord or yours, but I now feel yours has more character'. Monet got his way in everything. Trains were stopped, platforms closed off, the locomotives fired full of coal so they belched out steam in that way Monet loved. Tyrannically he set himself up in the station and for days, amidst universal

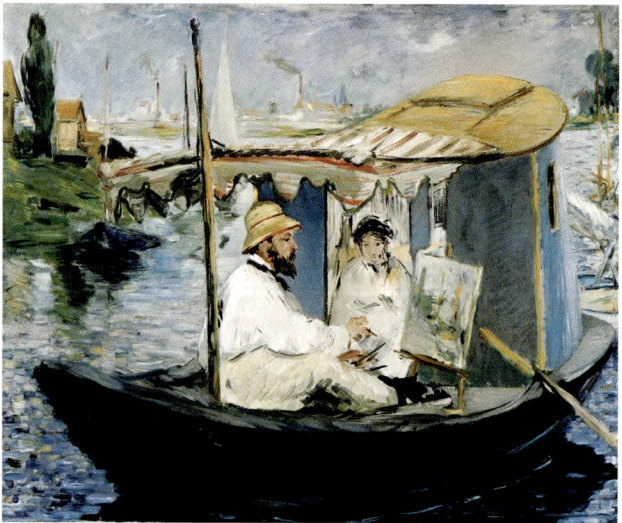

awe, he painted, then left again with half a dozen pictures done."

As in the pictures of bridges, in his paintings of the Gare Saint-Lazare Monet was excited by the linear structures modern engineering created. Again he used smoke, steam and sunlight to heighten the spatial atmospherics. Doubtless he was inspired in his compositional technique by Japanese prints, which he had been collecting since his visit to Holland in 1871, and perhaps longer (ill. p. 150). Time and again, Monet turned to Japanese compositions for ideas. The Japanese used surfaces in

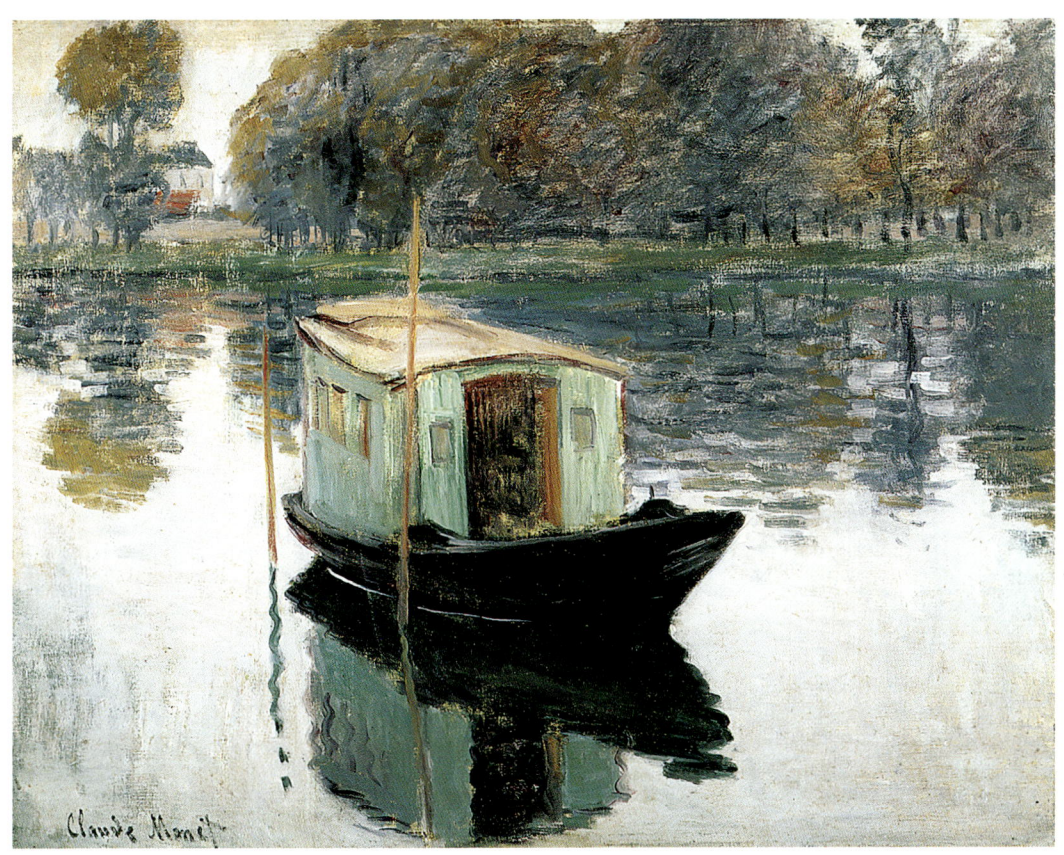

"For me, the subject is of secondary importance: I want to convey what is alive between me and the subject."

CLAUDE MONET

The Studio Boat, 1874
Oil on canvas, 50 x 64 cm (19¾ x 25¼ in.)
Otterlo, Kröller-Müller Museum

OPPOSITE
Édouard Manet
Monet Painting in His Studio Boat, 1874
Oil on canvas, 82.7 x 105 cm (32⅝ x 41⅜ in.)
Munich, Bayerische Staatsgemäldesammlungen,
Neue Pinakothek

Visiting Monet at Argenteuil, Manet painted
his friend working on riverbank landscapes
from his studio boat. Camille is quietly
keeping Monet company by the cabin door.

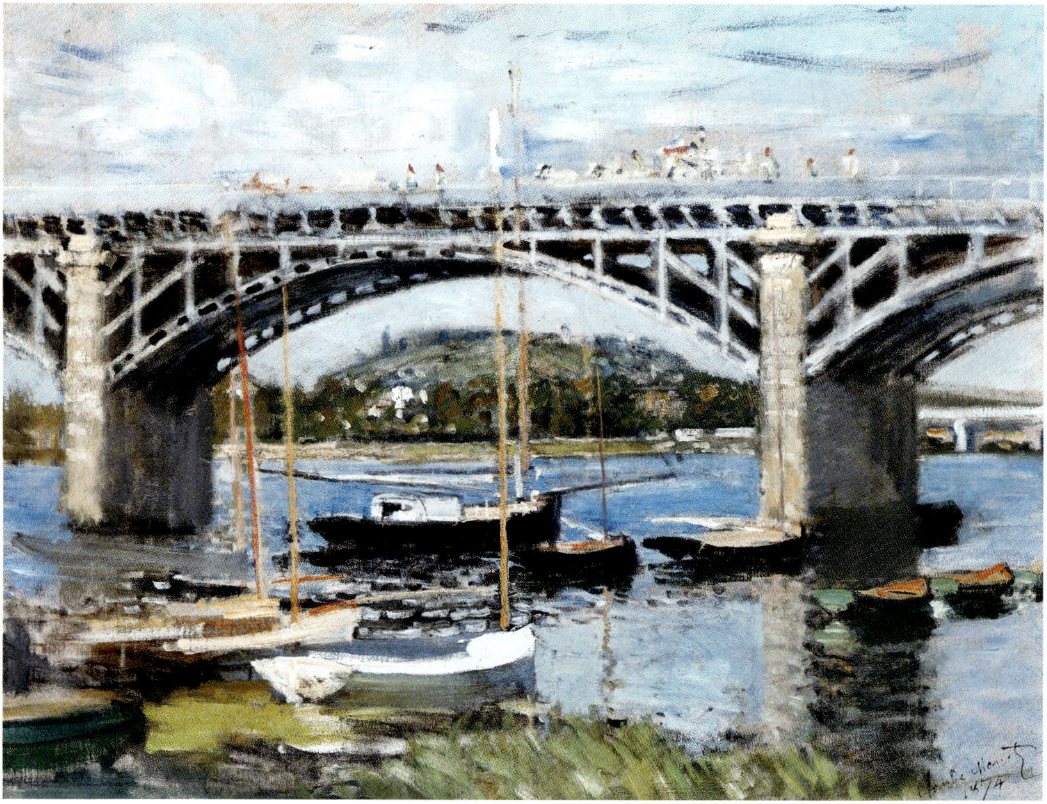

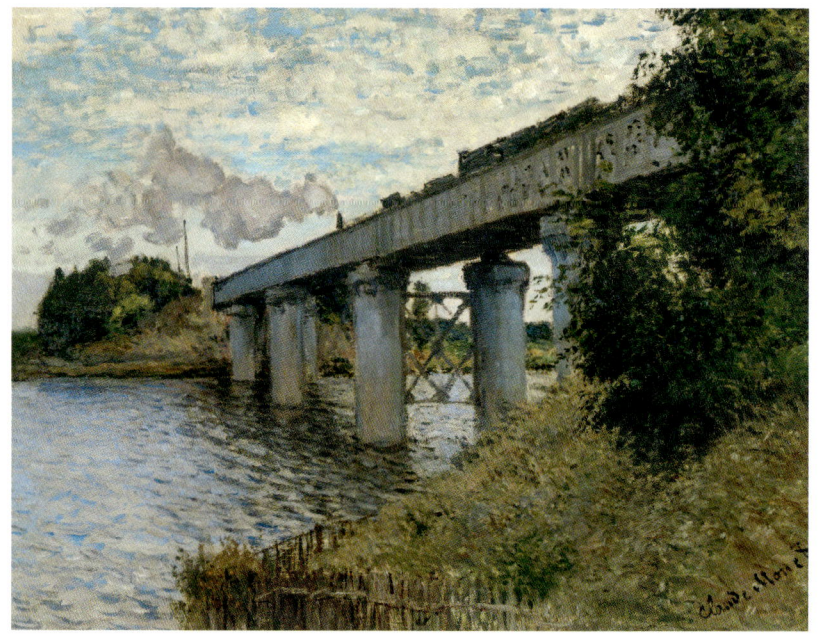

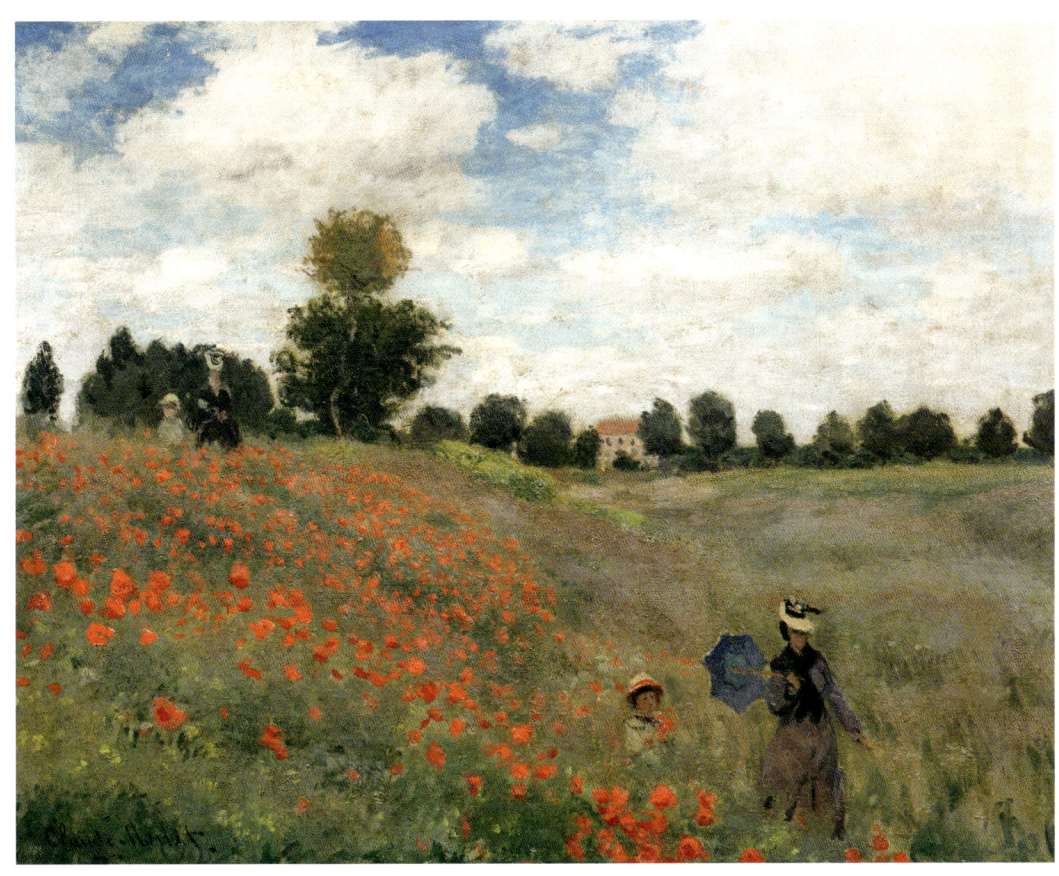

OPPOSITE TOP
The Bridge at Argenteuil, 1874
Oil on canvas, 60 x 81.3 cm (23½ x 32 in.)
Munich, Bayerische Staatsgemäldesammlungen,
Neue Pinakothek

It is a summer afternoon, and the road bridge is
broad and mighty in the warm light. Through
the centre arch we see the fertile hills of the Seine
valley, and through the arch at right the new
railway bridge.

OPPOSITE BOTTOM
The Railway Bridge at Argenteuil, 1873/74
Oil on canvas, 54 x 71 cm (21¼ x 28 in.)
Paris, Musée d'Orsay

Monet painted the new railway bridge, built in
the 1860s, with the light of a new day behind it.

Poppies at Argenteuil, 1873
Oil on canvas, 50 x 65 cm (19¾ x 25¾ in.)
Paris, Musée d'Orsay

"As a true Parisian, he takes Paris with him
to the country," Émile Zola wrote of the
early Monet. "He cannot paint a landscape
without adding ladies and gentlemen in
their finery. Nature seems not to interest
him if it does not bear the imprint of our
way of life." But over the years the figures
disappeared from Monet's landscapes, and
civilization was displaced by the direct
impression of nature.

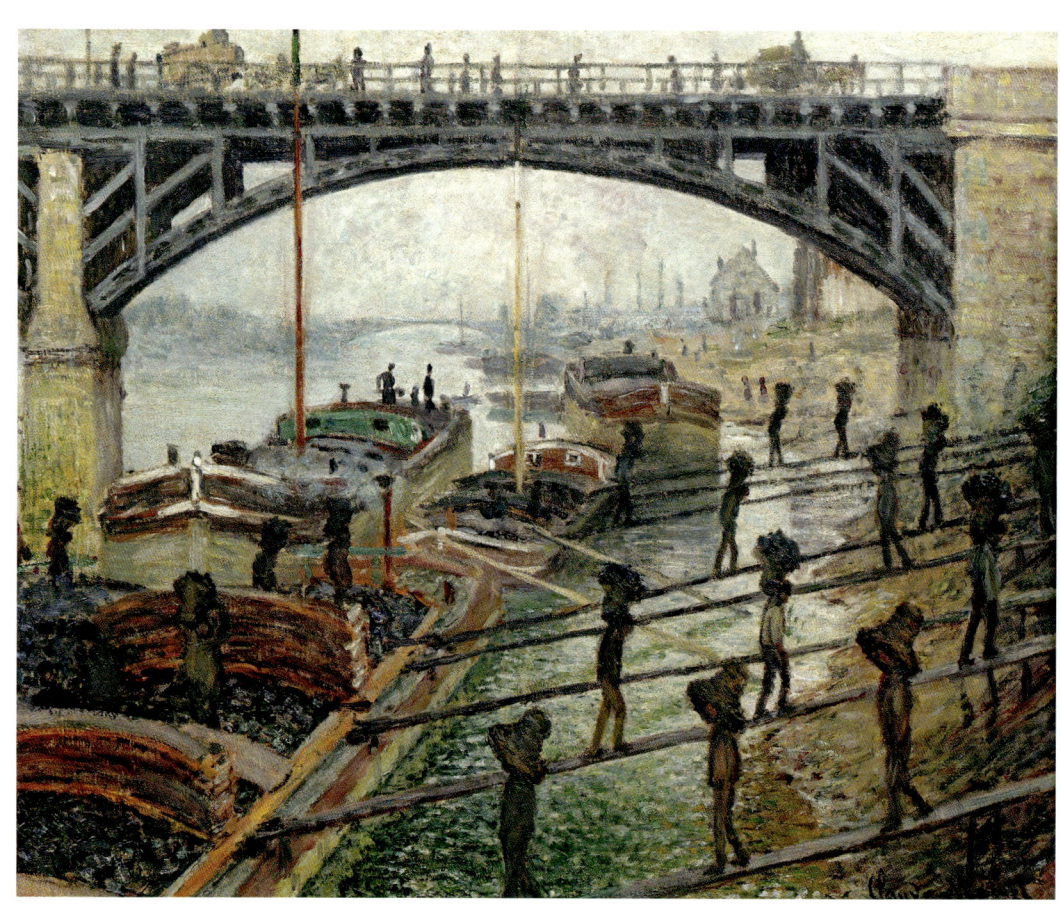

The Coal-Dockers, *c.* 1875
Oil on canvas, 54 x 65.5 cm (21¼ x 25¾ in.)
Paris, Musée d'Orsay

This painting, influenced compositionally by
Japanese woodblock prints, shows the figures,
walkways and coal barges as a grid-like
visual pattern, establishing its rhythm across
the entire canvas.

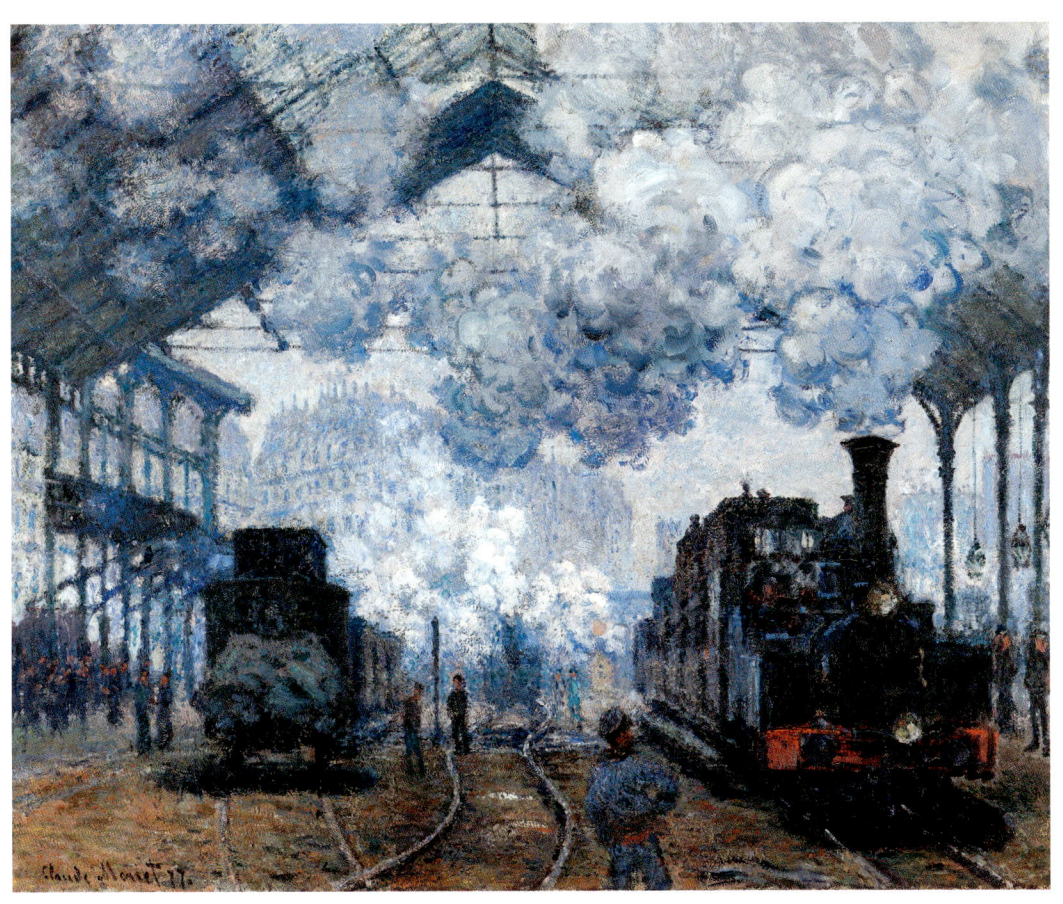

The Gare Saint-Lazare: Arrival of a Train, 1877
Oil on canvas, 83 x 101.3 cm (32¾ x 40 in.)
Cambridge, Massachusetts, Harvard Art
Museums/Fogg Museum, Bequest from the
Collection of Maurice Wertheim, Class of 1906

As in the paintings of bridges, Monet was
arrested by the linear structures created by
the engineers. The station, full of smoke
and steam and sunlight, is a cathedral of the
technological era.

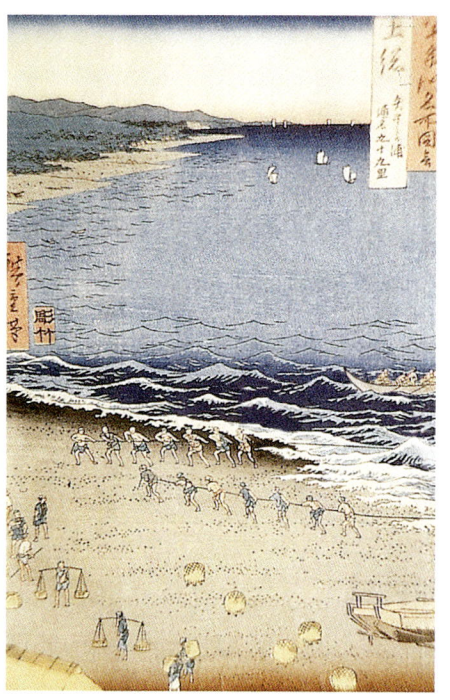

ways Western eyes found unfamiliar, cropping subjects audaciously and displacing major subjects from the centre, and it was these departures that engaged Monet's interest. In *The Coal-Dockers* (ill. p. 148) we can see clearly how he modulated individual subjects into a grid-like compositional structure. The motif establishes its distinctive and complex rhythm across the entire canvas.

It was not till the mid-19th century that Japan had opened up to the West. Quickly, the cities of the West were swept by Japanese fads and fashions, and Monet revelled in them, as his portrait of *Camille Monet in Japanese Costume* (ill. p. 151) suggests. Clad in a stunning gown, its embroidered warrior looking almost alive, she is turning towards the painter. Her pose is like that in *Woman in a Green Dress* (ill. p. 119), but now, rather than turning away, she is taking the time to banter coquettishly and fan herself. The Japanese fans scattered on the wall and floor seem frankly to be overdoing it. The picture can readily be seen as a concession to public taste and the Japanese mode of the day, and Monet did in fact sell it, at the second Impressionist exhibition, for a respectable 2,000 francs; assuredly its airy yet tight technique makes it a more conventional work than other paintings done at about the same time, such as *Woman with a Parasol* (ill. p. 128). It is worth pointing out, though, that Monet has put a blonde wig on the utterly un-Japanese Camille, and in her hand she holds a fan in the colours of the French tricolour. The picture, which Monet himself later dismissed as rubbish, is not only a break with the technique he was developing – it is also, surely, a shrill travesty of the Parisian fad for all things *à la japonaise*.

TOP
Utagawa Hiroshige
The Kujukuri Coast in Kaeusa Province
from: *Famous Views of the 60-Odd Provinces*,
1853–56
Woodblock print, 66.6 x 22.4 cm (26¼ x 8¾ in.)
Giverny, Académie des Beaux-Arts,
Fondation Claude Monet

OPPOSITE
Camille Monet in Japanese Costume, 1875
Oil on canvas, 231.5 x 142 cm (91¼ x 56 in.)
Boston, Museum of Fine Arts

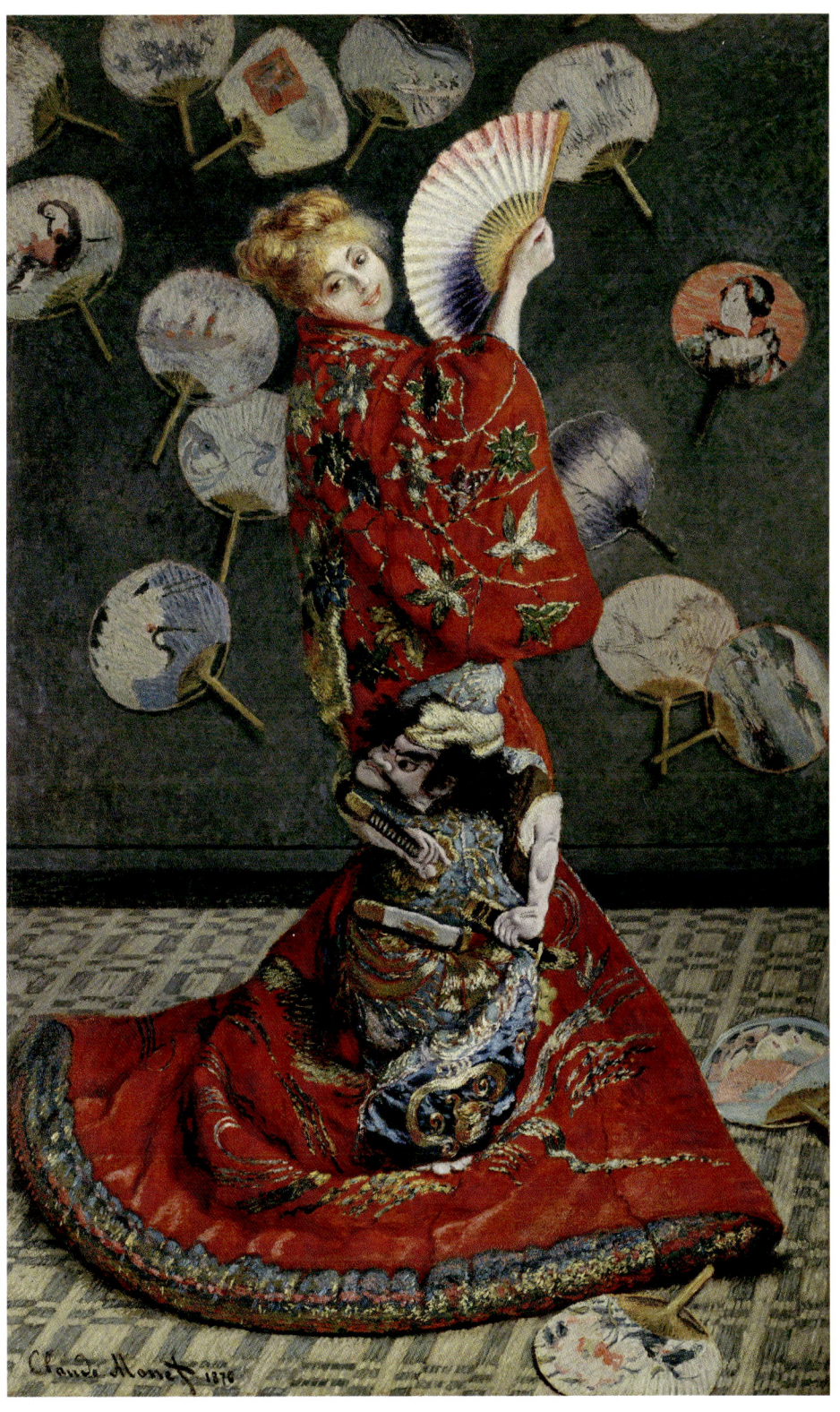

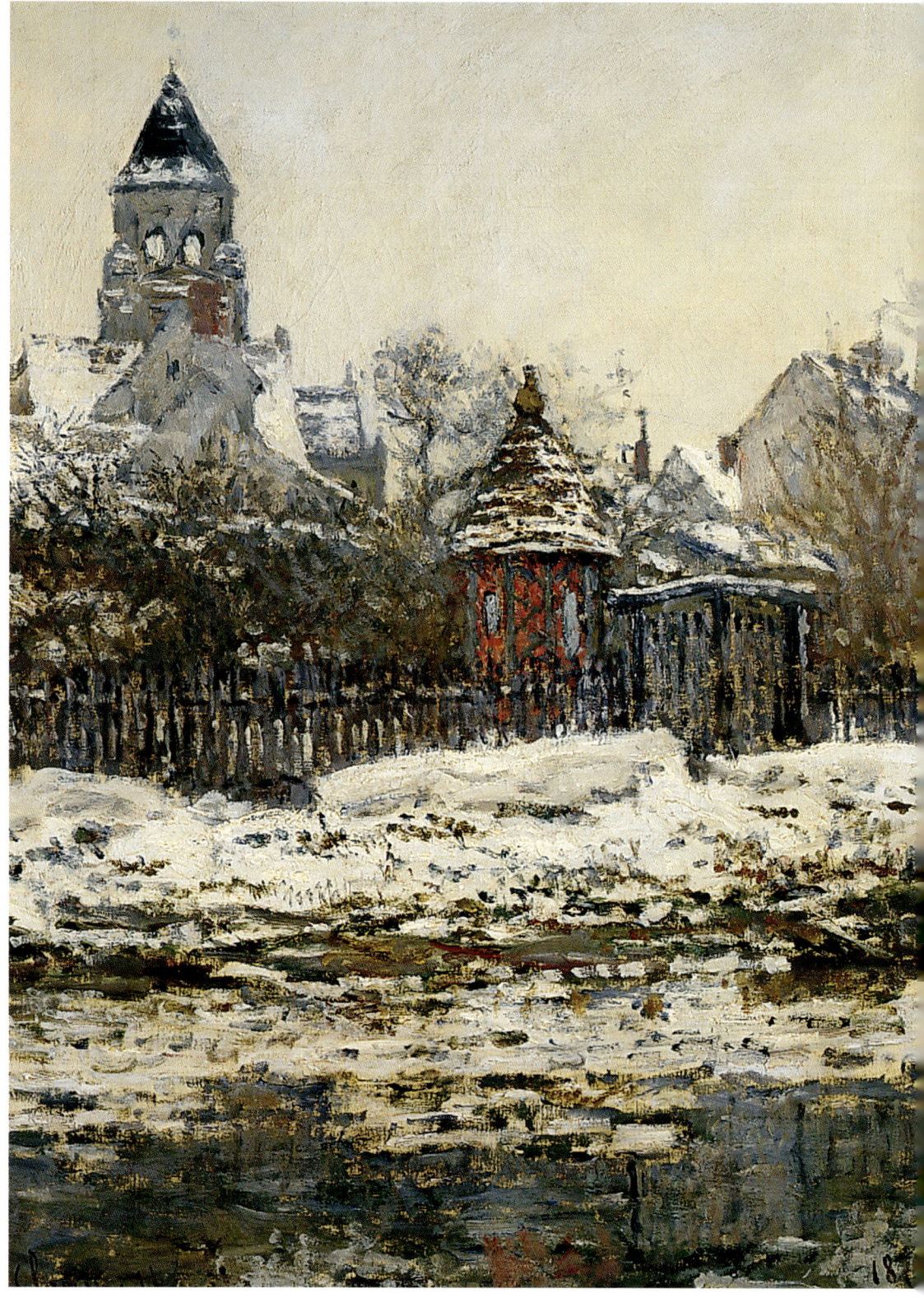

Winter at Vétheuil

The last years at Argenteuil had been a time of great financial difficulty, and this had a growing impact on Monet's motivation. Durand-Ruel's storerooms were full of pictures, and few people were buying; so he was obliged to keep new purchases to a minimum. The overall economic situation was deteriorating: there had been a brief boom, but by the mid-1870s the effects of a lost war were making themselves felt. The Impressionist group shows, held almost every year, continued to attract disappointing numbers and to be derided by critics in the academic camp. "Rue Le Peletier is having a run of bad luck," wrote Albert Wolff in *Le Figaro* on 3 April 1876. "First there was the fire at the opera house, and now Fate has struck again. An exhibition of so-called art has just opened at Durand-Ruel's [...] Five or six lunatics blinded by ambition, one of them a woman, have put their work on show. These self-appointed artists call themselves rebels, Impressionists;

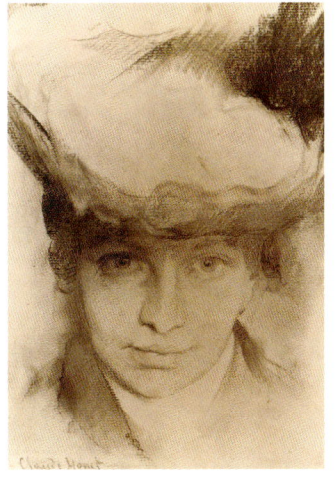

they take a canvas, brush and paint, fling on the colours indiscriminately, and then sign the thing."

Criticism such as this is not only of anecdotal interest; it is also revealing of the cult of the hatchet job that was prevalent in the arts pages at the time. Critics dipped their pens in acid, and were popular with the educated public if they were sarcastic and superior in passing their judgements. They affected to be defending the values of academic art, and of French art in particular; and in the process, often for the sake of a witty turn of phrase, they might ruin a painter's life. Their verdicts influenced not only the reputations of artists but also sales. Patrons and collectors might well be considered feeble-minded, or at least unable to see what was before their eyes, if the critics' opinion went against them – and this was the case with the market in Impressionist art for over twenty years.

One who chose to ignore the critics was Ernest Hoschedé. A department-store director and château owner, he began fairly early (and not without a speculator's ulterior motives) to collect the Impressionists on a large scale. In summer 1876 he commissioned Monet to paint decorative panels for a salon at his

OPPOSITE
The Church at Vétheuil, 1879
Oil on canvas, 65.5 x 50.5 cm (25¾ x 20 in.)
Paris, Musée d'Orsay

ABOVE RIGHT
Head of a Woman (Camille Monet?),
1866/67
Sketch in red chalk
Private collection

This red chalk drawing, one of the few drawings by Monet that have survived, is probably of Camille Doncieux – Monet's lover, wife, and mother of his two sons. But the sitter and date have not yet been definitely identified.

Montgeron residence. A brief year later, he was bankrupt, and when his collection was auctioned off a number of paintings were sold for extremely low prices. One was *Impression, Sunrise* (ill. pp. 134/135), for which Hoschedé had paid 800 francs at the first Impressionist exhibition the year before; it now changed hands for a quarter of the price. For the Impressionists, the auction was a disaster. The prices their paintings fetched, which had been inching their way up, now hit rock bottom in a glare of publicity; and Monet, for one, felt he was having to start all over again. Nearing forty, he was no further than he had been ten years earlier. On 28 June 1875 he had written to Manet: "Things are going worse and worse. Since the day before yesterday I have had not a sou, and no credit anywhere either – not at the butcher's, not at the baker's. Even if I have confidence in the future, the present remains very difficult […] Could you possibly send me 20 francs by return? It would tide me over for the moment."

He was to write countless begging letters in the second half of the 1870s; as well as this one, there were others to Durand-Ruel and other patrons and friends. Usually so proud and dynamic, Monet whined, abased himself and cursed his own work. Compelled by circumstances, he perfected the rhetoric of the begging letter, imploring the few collectors of his work to take whole batches of paintings at give-away prices. In summer 1878, after an intermezzo in Paris, Monet and his family (now including a second son,

Camille Monet on Her Deathbed, 1879
Oil on canvas, 90 x 68 cm (35½ x 26¾ in.)
Paris, Musée d'Orsay

Monet painted his dead wife as the first sunlight of the new day was entering the room. This is no conventional deathbed picture done to record the features of the dearly loved, but the highly personal record of a dark hour.

Ice Melting near Vétheuil, 1880
Oil on canvas, 65 x 93 cm (25½ x 36½ in.)
Paris, Musée du Louvre

After the hard winter of 1879/80, a sudden thaw transformed the river, sending ice floes crashing down the waters. The willows and bushes along the banks are reaching like weary fingers into a sky that looks as if it will never brighten again.

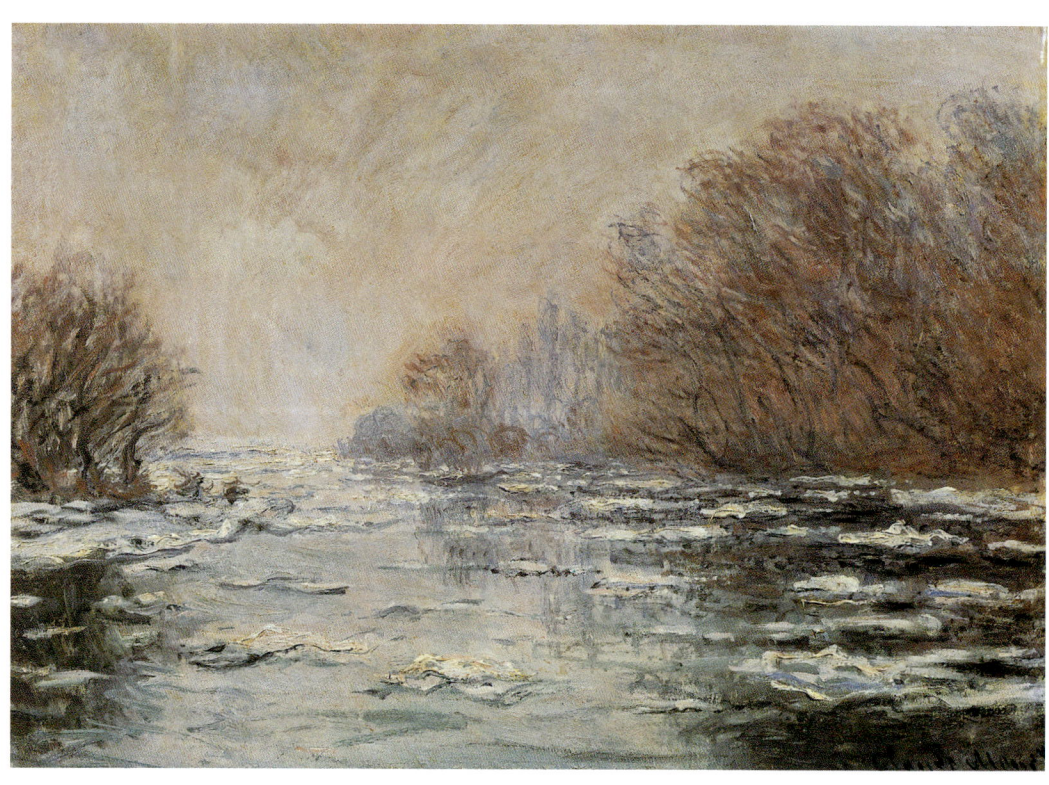

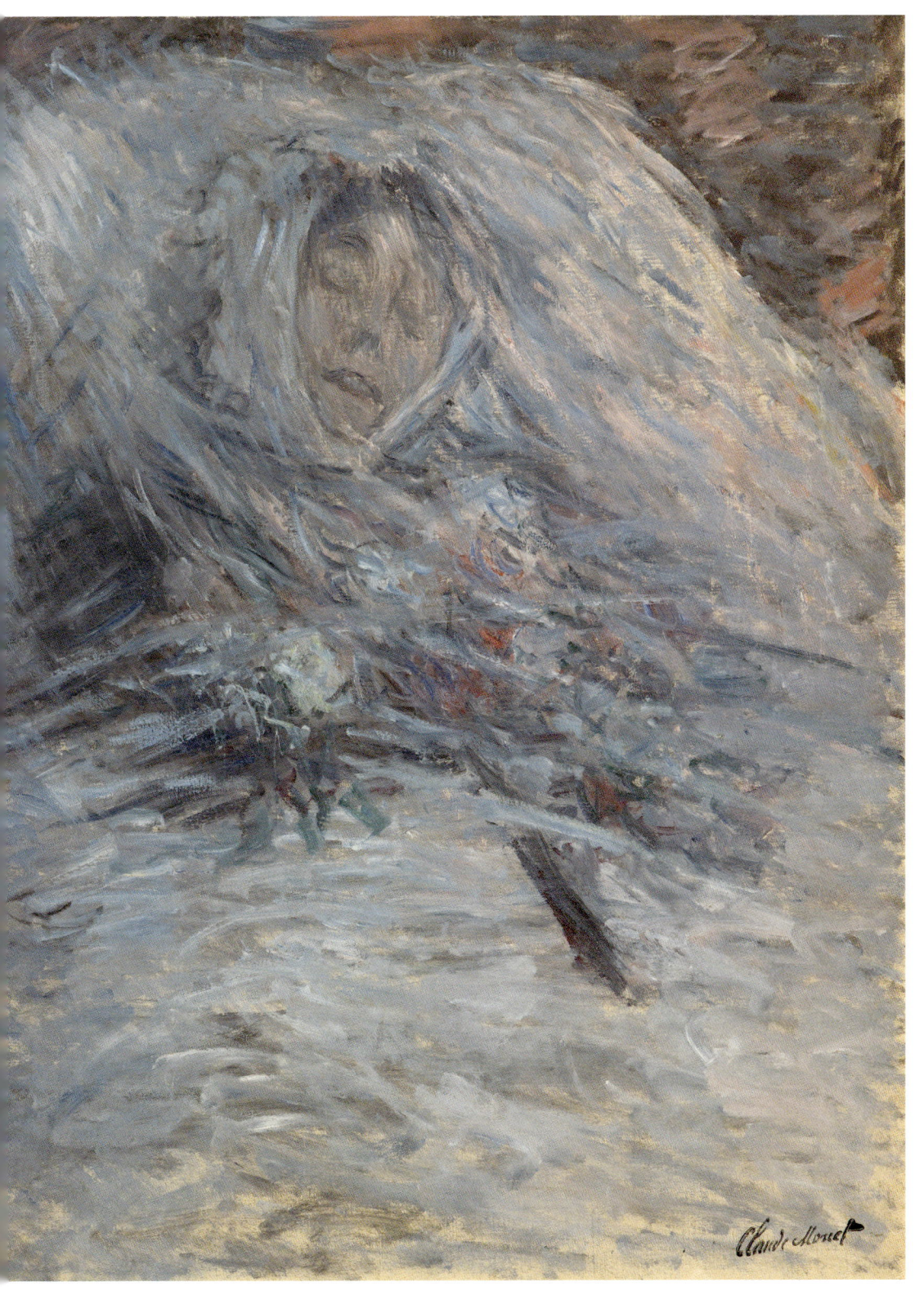

Michel, born in March) moved to a modest house at Vétheuil. The Hoschedés, now bankrupt, joined them with their six children.

The autumn sunshine revived Monet's spirits. "I have pitched my tent by the Seine at Vétheuil," he wrote to Murer on 1 September 1878, "in an enchanting area." From his studio boat he painted the banks of the river, and the little village with its Romanesque church. Money, though, remained in short supply, and Monet was in despair, writing to de Bellio on 30 December that year: "I am not a beginner any more, and it is dreadful to be in such a position at my age, forever begging and pestering buyers. As the year ends I am doubly aware of my misfortune, for '79 is beginning as this year has ended, in utter despondency, especially with regard to my dear ones, to whom I have not been able to give even the smallest present."

Monet's wife, apparently as a result of an unsuccessful abortion, had been weak for some time, and was in fact not to recover. Camille Doncieux, his only model, The *Woman with a Green Dress* (ill. p. 119), the lady who walked the poppy fields and meadows, her summer dress billowing and parasol held high (ill. p. 128), his sunny muse and the very personification of all Impressionism stood for, died on 5 September 1879, aged only thirty-two. She left two young sons and a despairing husband at odds with himself and the world. "One day," Clemenceau recalled his friend Monet confiding, "I found myself at daybreak at the bedside of a dead woman who had been and always will be dear to me. My gaze was fixed on her tragic temples, and I caught myself observing the shades and nuances of

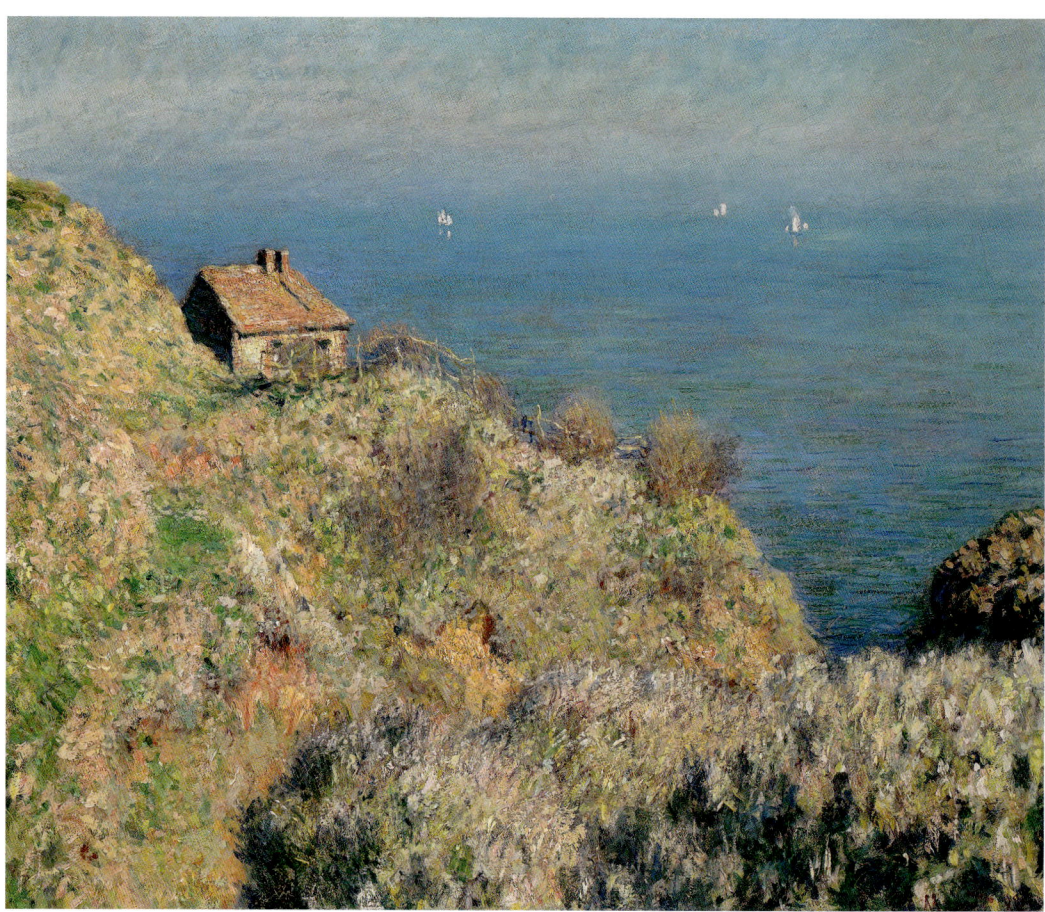

colour death brought to her countenance. Blues, yellows, greys, I
don't know what. That is the state
I was in. The wish came upon me,
quite naturally, to record the image
of her who was departing from us
for ever. But before it occurred to
me to draw those features I knew
and loved so well, I was first and
foremost devastated, organically,
automatically, by the colours.
Against my will, my reflexes took
possession of me in an unconscious process, as the everyday
course of my life took over. Like
a draught animal working at the
millstone. Pity me, my friend."

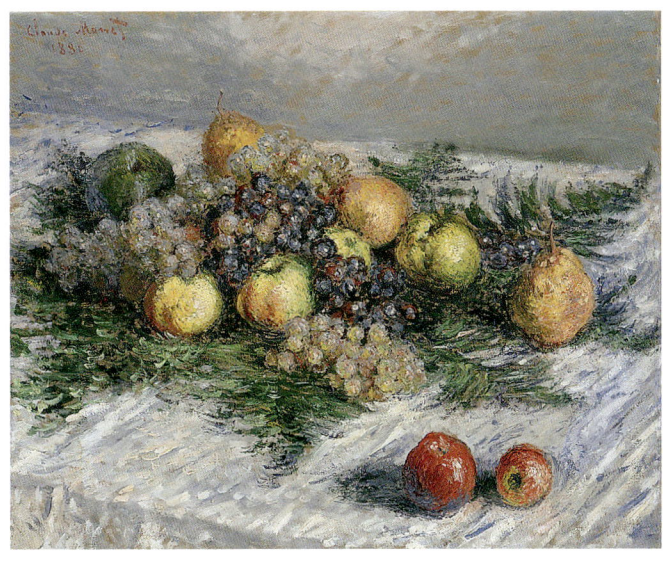

But Monet's picture of his wife on her deathbed (ill. p. 155) is more than a study in light. He had
recorded Camille's features in one of his rare drawings (ill. p. 153). Her alert, serious eyes and her soft,
expressive mouth suggest a person both tolerant and warm of heart. In the deathbed painting, though,
there is no eloquence in her features: the dead woman's face is merely sketched in as she lies on the pil-
lows, seeming to sink into depths of night and icy cold. Warm sunlight is lighting the bed from the side,
and it is as if the artist hoped those first beams of morning sunlight might warm the cold and frozen
face once more. But the sole answering glow comes from the handful of blossoms at her breast. Monet's
brushwork in this painting is disturbed, angry, immoderate, torn, and at points movingly tender. The
dichotomy between the coldness of death, on the one hand, and the warm sunlight of a day dawning
for the living on the other, makes this so very personal painting a document of utter, devastating loss.

Monet's paintings from the harsh winter that followed seem echoes of that experience. He had
already painted snow, gleaming and lit by clear winter sunlight, casting luminous blue shadows, but
also the dull, slushy browns of February, with farm folk stomping along muffled to the eyeballs, so
vivid that we can almost feel how cold and wet their feet are. But the winter Monet went through
in Vétheuil was different. Icy and grey, it was above all a deserted, solitary season. No birds are in
these pictures, nor people either: only ice floes logjammed in the frozen river (ill. p. 154). The very
sun seems cold. It is as if the landscape were pervaded by Monet's grief and desolation. It was during
this period that Monet began gradually to relax his ties with the other Impressionists. They accused

him of no longer supporting the group and its activities, for
his own ends. Monet was trying once again to exhibit at the
Salon; and in fact the jury did accept one of his paintings,
though it was hung in the topmost row. In the winter of 1881,
Monet moved again, to the small town of Poissy, some twenty
kilometres from Paris. It was not a particularly attractive area,
and at first left Monet dissatisfied. He wrote to his dealer:
"Poissy has yet to inspire me even remotely".

Nevertheless, 1882 turned out to be a productive year.
He visited the coast of Normandy a number of times, and

painted *The Fisherman's House at Varengeville* (ill. p. 156) and *The Customs House at Varengeville* (ill. p. 158) from a number of angles and at various times of day. He also painted a little chapel high above the sea, and repeatedly took the sheer cliffs as his subject. The cliffs served him not only as a subject in themselves but also as a means of trying out unusual visual angles. These coastal paintings show Monet venturing towards series work for the first time. "It is a real Monet," Auguste Rodin is said to have exclaimed when he saw the sea for the first time. Over the next few years, the river painter became a marine painter. Monet entered into lonely communion with his subject. Out in the icy cold, wrapped up in blankets and coats, the foam spraying about him, Monet studied the sea, moving closer and closer to his mighty subject. The high cliff faces became surfaces on which light was projected, where light reflected from the water warred with direct sunlight. *The Manneporte near Étretat* (ill. p. 161), a huge rock arch near Étretat, was seen powerfully confronting the vast waters of the ocean. Monet defied all kinds of weather in his pursuit of his subjects, and never gave up. As in his early days, struggling with his father or blasé critics or the prejudiced public, Monet throve on adversity. At Étretat and Belle-Île he took bare cliffs, choppy seas, and the constantly changing brightness and colours of the sky as his subjects, and tirelessly went in quest of the shifts in the light; people had well-nigh disappeared from his art.

Strictly speaking, Monet (unlike Manet or Degas) was never a figure painter anyway. In early works, the light that fell upon a woman through a parasol interested him more than the woman herself, and when later he placed figures in his paintings it was because they created a sense of spatial scope in his landscapes. He valued people for the rhythm and dynamics they introduced into his pictures, but disregarded their personal histories. When he painted two full-lengths of

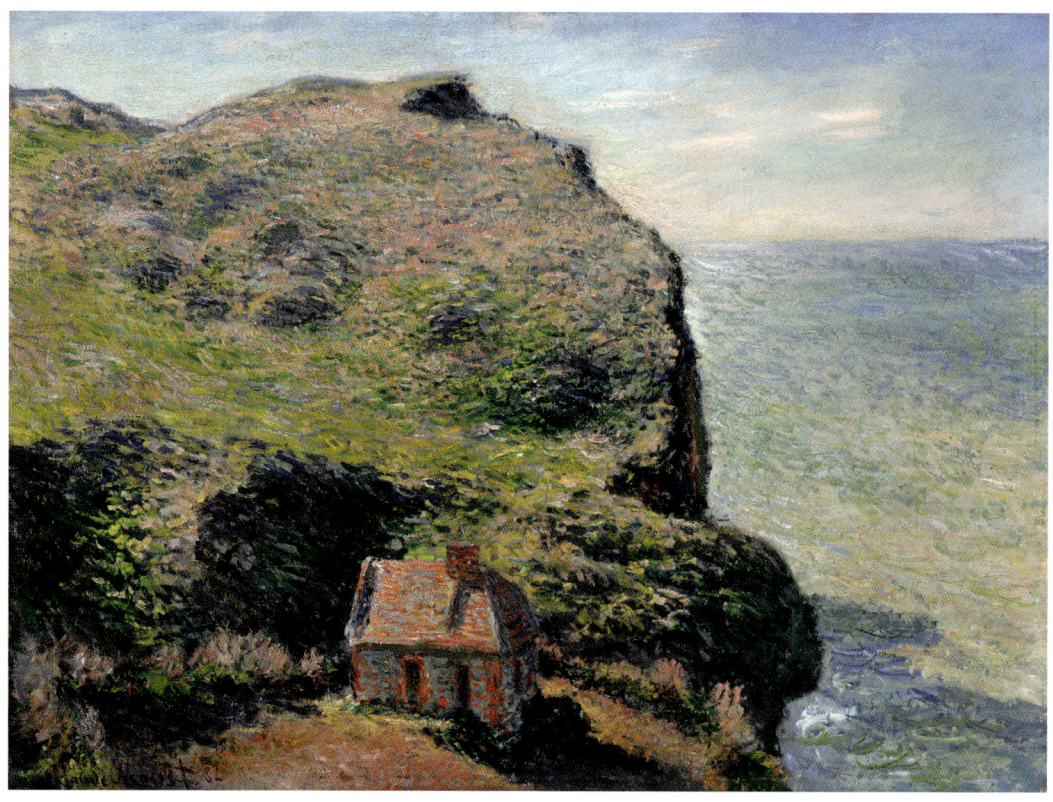

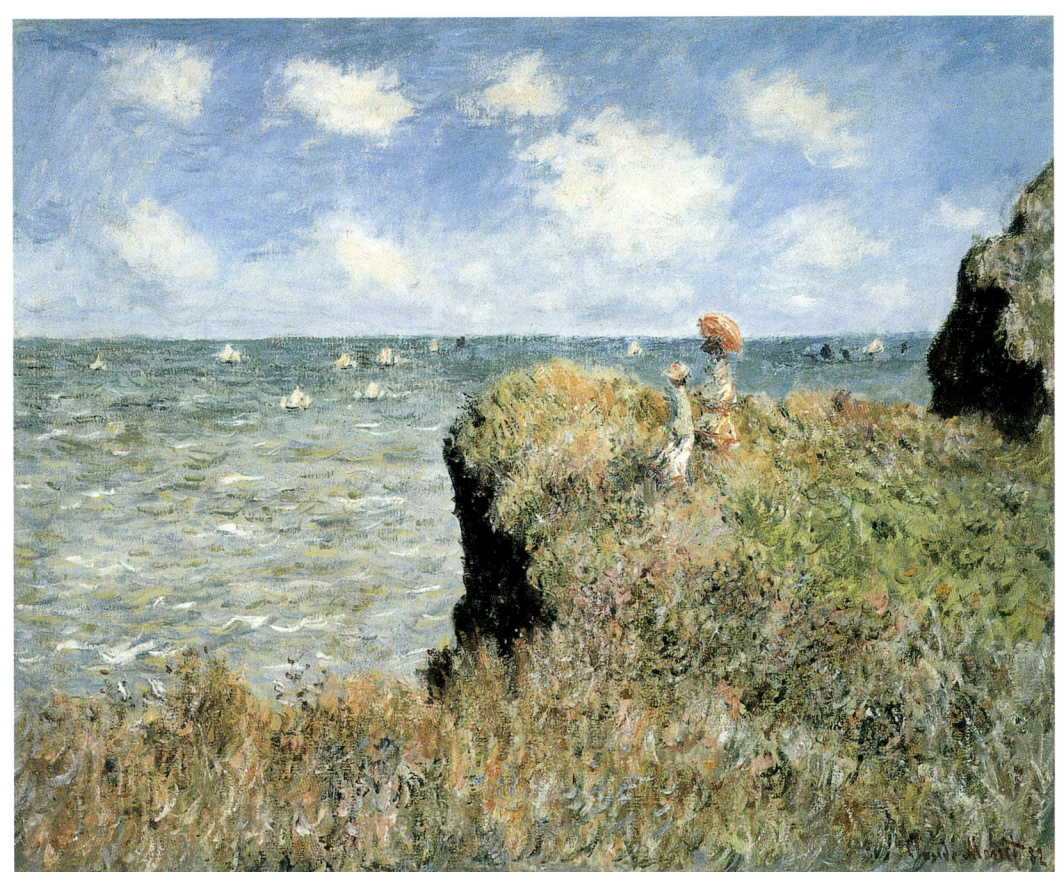

Suzanne Hoschedé in the 1880s, turning to a human figure in the open as he had done at the outset of his career,
the results were not so much freshly-conceived artworks
as dreamy reminiscences of old, happy days at Argenteuil
(ill. p. 164).

Monet had fled from Vétheuil, and had never really settled
in Poissy; and in 1883 he rented a house at Giverny and
moved there with a large family that included his two sons,
Alice Hoschedé (Ernest's wife), and her six children. Moving their possessions across the Seine by boat was quickly
accomplished and a more peaceful, happy time began in their spacious and simple country home. It
was the last time Monet moved. The second half of his life was spent at Giverny, and there he found
the calm and strength to complete his work.

In the early 1880s, the market in Impressionist art revived. Durand-Ruel was energetically representing their interests once again, and Monet's solo exhibition in his gallery in spring 1883, though
disappointingly few sales resulted, earned favourable reviews. A few years later, Durand-Ruel was to
open a gallery in New York and score great success with Monet's views of Belle-Île and the paintings
that resulted from his sojourns on the Riviera and the Côte d'Azur.

Walk on the Cliff at Pourville, 1882
Oil on canvas, 65 x 81 cm (25⅝ x 32 in.)
The Art Institute of Chicago

The cliffs of Normandy fascinated Monet, not
only for the light and shadow, the flowers and
grasses, but also because they made unusual
lines of vision possible.

OPPOSITE
The Customs House at Varengeville, 1882
Oil on canvas, 60.3 x 81.4 cm (23¾ x 32 in.)
Philadelphia Museum of Art,
The William L. Elkins Collection, 1924

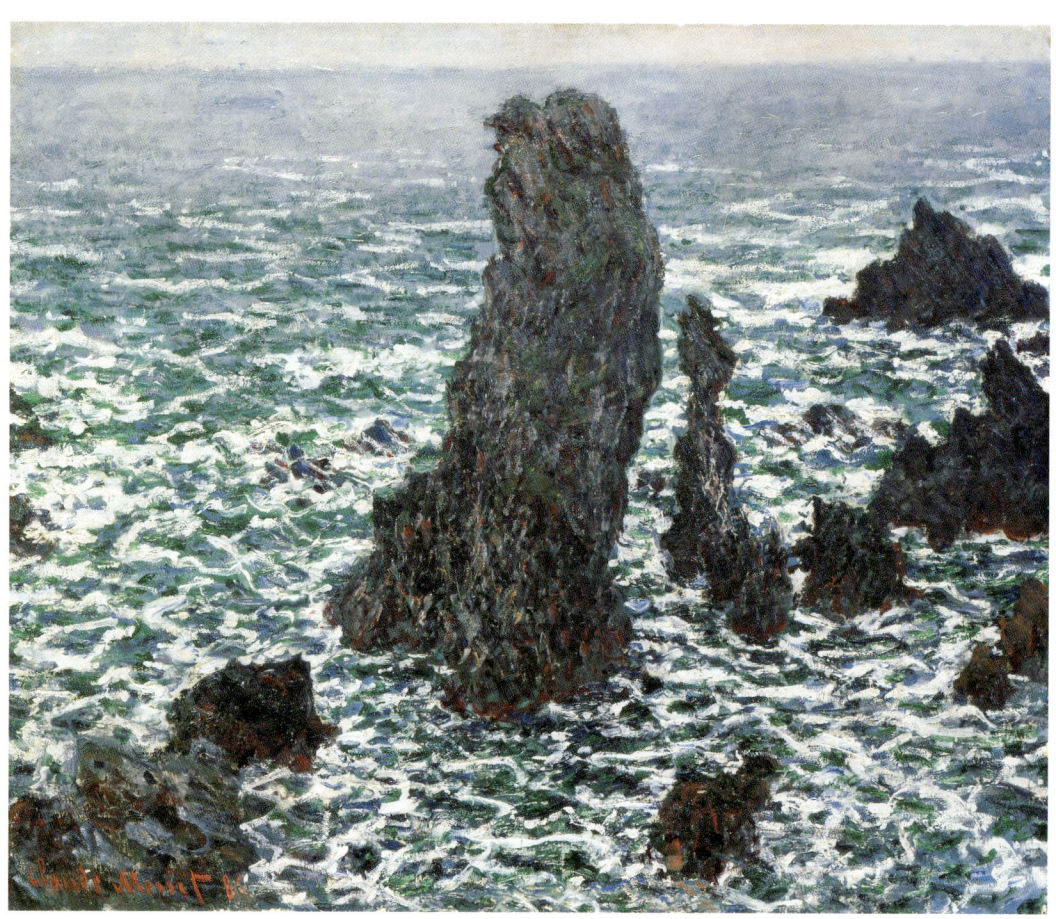

Rocks at Belle-Île, 1886
Oil on canvas, 60 x 73 cm (23⅝ x 28¾ in.)
Copenhagen, Ny Carlsberg Glyptotek

OPPOSITE
The Manneporte near Étretat, 1885/86
Oil on canvas, 81.3 x 65.4 cm (32 x 25¾ in.)
New York, The Metropolitan Museum of Art

"The sea is unbelievably beautiful and there are the most outlandish
rocks [...] I am filled with enthusiasm for this eerie area, because it
forces me to go beyond what I usually do. I have to admit I find it very
difficult to convey the foreboding, terrifying aspect of it."

CLAUDE MONET TO DURAND-RUEL, 1886

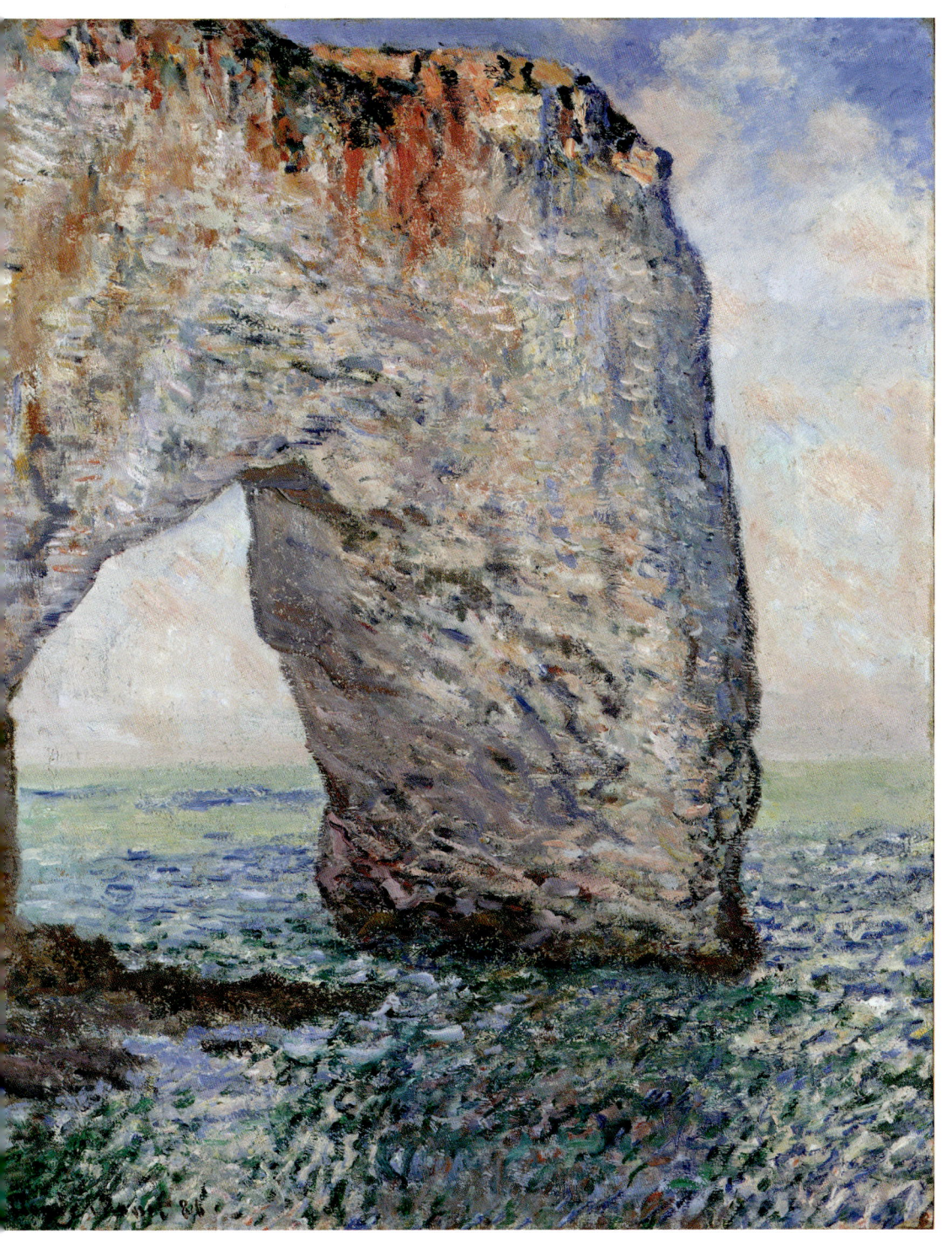

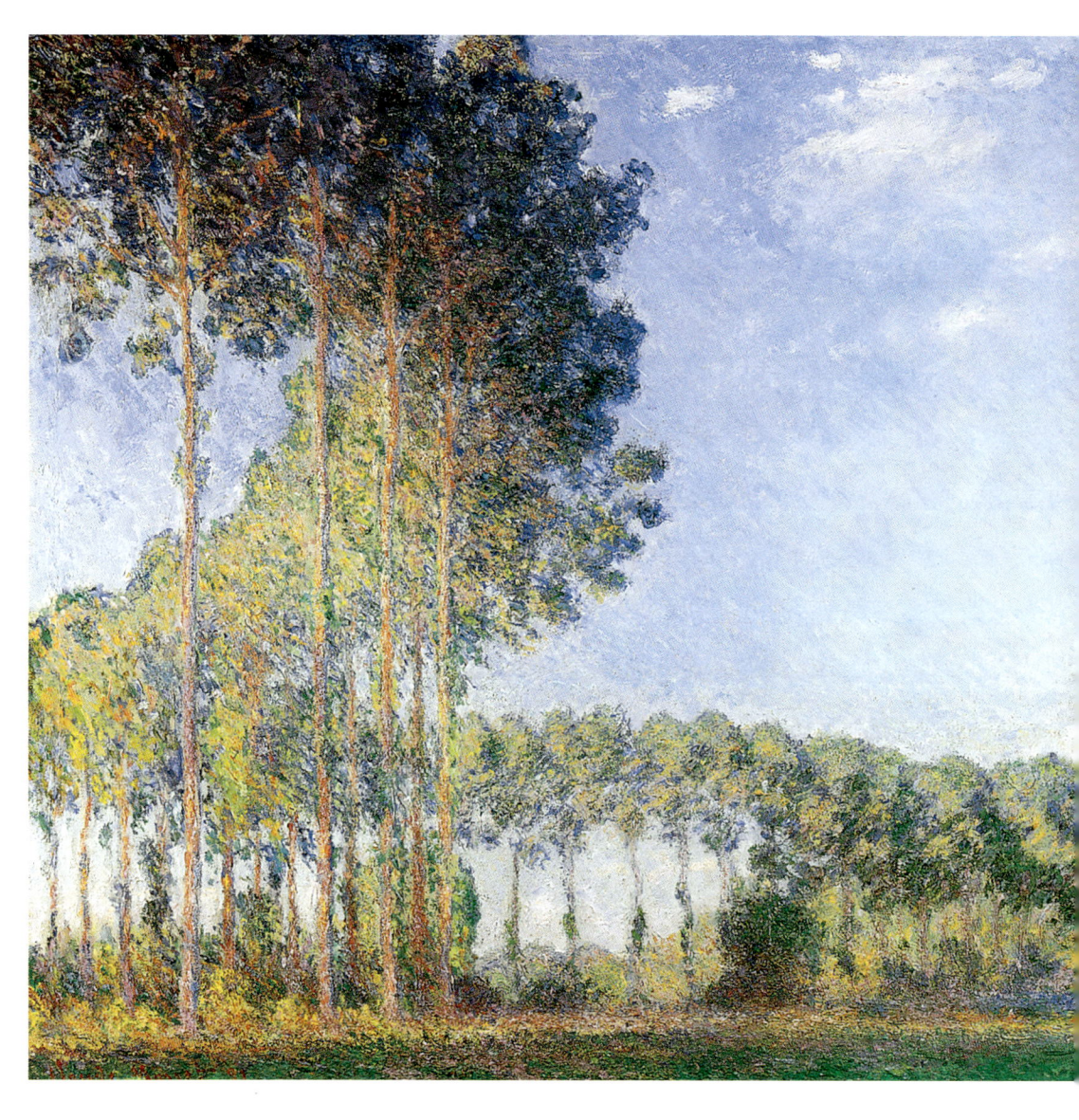

Concentration and Repetition:
Working in Series

At times Monet imagined what it would have been like to be born blind and then suddenly be able to see, and to paint, without knowing what the thing one saw actually was. He felt that one's first clear look at a subject was the most honest, because it was least sullied by preconceptions and prejudices. His interest in this thoroughly genuine way of seeing led Monet to an in-depth study of atmospheric effects. To him, a subject was not what it was but what the light made of it. It was in this spirit that he had already, at an earlier point in his life as an artist, painted various views of one and the same subject, in various moods. Thus, for instance, he had painted the bridges at Argenteuil in bright sunlight or in rain, in broad inclusive views or in detailed close-up. He painted Vétheuil, with its little Romanesque church, from the same position in fog and beneath the blue skies of summer. As the years went by, his studies in atmosphere became more and more systematic, his investigations veritably scientific in their thoroughness. From Impressionist studies he evolved whole series showing grainstacks, poplars, and finally the west front of Rouen Cathedral. And ultimately, in the *Nymphéas* (or water-lilies), he was to apply his principle to the very end.

In 1890 and 1891, Monet worked on a series of paintings of grainstacks (ills. pp. 166 and 167), a subject that would have struck contemporary taste as not merely simple but downright unimaginative. In some he painted them close to; in others he painted two stacks instead of one; but always the compact, snug shape of the grainstacks remained central. His treatment presented them in very different ways, vibrant in the ruddy glow of the setting sun, mutely massive in the snow.

At about the same time, Monet painted poplar trees along the banks of the Epte (ills. pp. 162 and 165), again working on his subject at various times of day and seasons of the year. Where the grainstacks had offered compact, solid shapes, though, the poplars tended to produce linear compositions. In a manner comparable to his work on bridges and railway stations, Monet wrought the skyward verticals of the trees, the horizontal of the riverbank, and the further verticals of the tree reflections in the water, into a grid-like pattern of lines. Upon this grid are superimposed the atmospherics of (say) autumn sunlight breaking through morning mist. In some of the series, the glaring light of a hot summer day, shining off the leaves, transforms the whole into a fabric of shimmering impressions.

Poplars on the Banks of the River Epte, as Seen from the Marsh, 1891
Oil on canvas, 88 x 93 cm (34¾ x 36½ in.)
Private collection

It was not the first time that artists had painted variations on the same theme. What made Monet's work more specifically a series, though, was the attempt to follow the selfsame visual motif through the most various of states. His most consistent experiment in this line was the series of views of Rouen

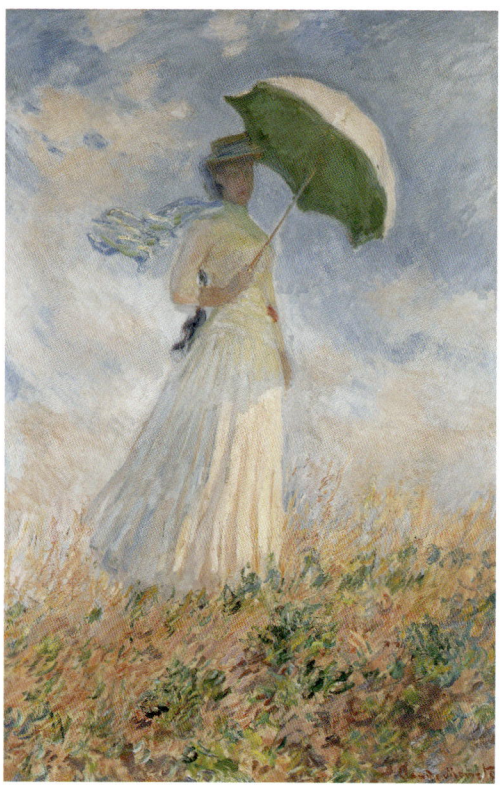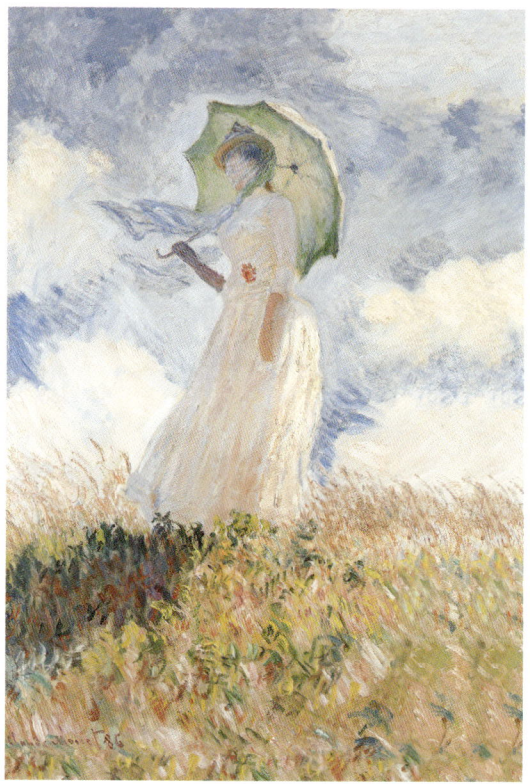

Study of a Figure Outdoors
(Facing Right), 1886
Oil on canvas, 131 x 88 cm (51⅝ x 34¾ in.)
Paris, Musée d'Orsay

TOP RIGHT
Study of a Figure Outdoors
(Facing Left), 1886
Oil on canvas, 131 x 88 cm (51⅝ x 34¾ in.)
Paris, Musée d'Orsay

Not Camille, but Suzanne Hoschedé now,
Monet's stepdaughter, modelling for him out
of doors. This pair of pictures (not a series)
were Monet's last venture into life-size
full-figure portrayal in the open.

Cathedral (ills. pp. 168 and 169), painted from 1892 to 1894. The mighty late-Gothic edifice, its history dating back to the 12th century, its west front richly adorned with tracery and opulent figure work, was one of the great achievements of the Middle Ages in France. In February 1892 Monet rented a small room opposite the west front for the first time, and that year and the next, as winter faded into spring, he painted the cathedral from three only minimally varying positions. Probably all thirty paintings of the façade would have been identical in their angle if Monet had been able to keep the room he first rented.

Never before had a painter viewed his subject so close to. The canvas space is not merely filled by the sectional view of the west door and towers; the picture is the façade. Monet observed the passing effects of light on the façade, from an early hour when the morning mist had yet to lift till the last rays of the setting sun. In some of the paintings, the cathedral is mysteriously shrouded. In others it is warm with morning light. And in yet others the last of the evening sun is setting gleams and highlights across the filigree of the majestic front.

Two years running, from early February to late April, Monet painted *sur le motif*, recording the cathedral in varying conditions of light; and he reported that some of the lights and atmospheres he observed lasted for only a few minutes. On 30 March 1893 he wrote to Durand-Ruel: "I am working as hard as I possibly can, and do not even dream of doing anything except the cathedral. It is an immense task." In the third year, Monet reworked the cathedral views in his studio, working on the different moods simultaneously and refusing to let any one of the pictures out of his hands until all of them were finished. The continual reworking resulted in impasto paintwork so richly textured that some who saw it compared it to mortar. Though fleeting shifts of light doubtless prompted each one of the pictures, the studio reworking played as germane a part in creating the finished images as the impressions gained on the spot. Harmonies are established by the contrasts between individual paintings often conceived in terms of a very few, complementary colours. The filigree façade became a pretext for patterned composition of a rhythmic type.

In his earlier studies of light at Argenteuil and Vétheuil, Monet had tried to make his eye a neutral monitor of the visual world, recording impressions in quasi-photographic manner. Much the same has been claimed where his series of the 1890s are concerned; but here, in fact, the artist is quite deliberately introducing into the pictures his own subjective response to what he has seen. The effects of colour he presents are analogous to what he has seen, rather than an exact record. And Monet's free technique matches his imaginative approach to colour. Even though his subjective experience of a fleeting moment provides the basis for each of Monet's canvases, the final reworked versions go beyond a record of passing phenomena. The motif is shorn not only of all detail but also of its material, textural qualities. Stripped of anecdotal elaboration or contextual placing, the paintings seem to stand monumentally above and beyond time.

Monet's dogged pursuit of the serial principle coincided with a growing demand for his work; in consequence, he was inevitably reproached by artist friends with painting series simply in order to satisfy that demand. And it was certainly true that the series paintings were well received. When

BOTTOM LEFT
Three Poplar Trees in Autumn, 1891
Oil on canvas, 93 x 74.1 cm (36½ x 29¼ in.)
Philadelphia Museum of Art,
The Chester Dale Collection

BOTTOM RIGHT
Three Poplars in Summer, 1891
Oil on canvas, 93 x 73.5 cm (36½ x 29 in.)
Tokyo, The National Museum of Western Art,
The Matsukata Collection

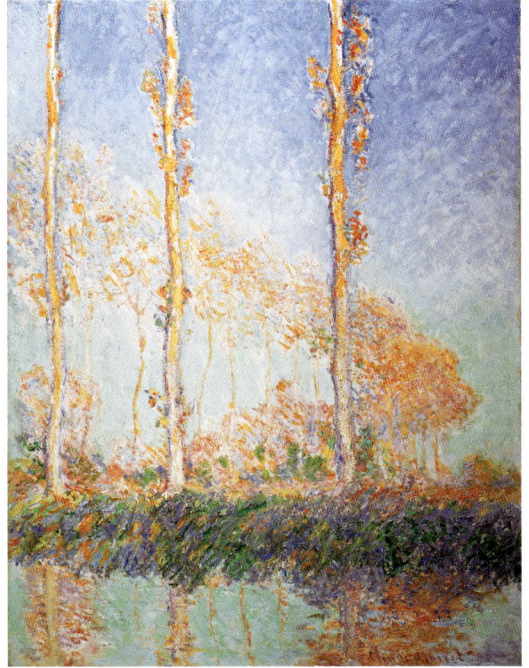

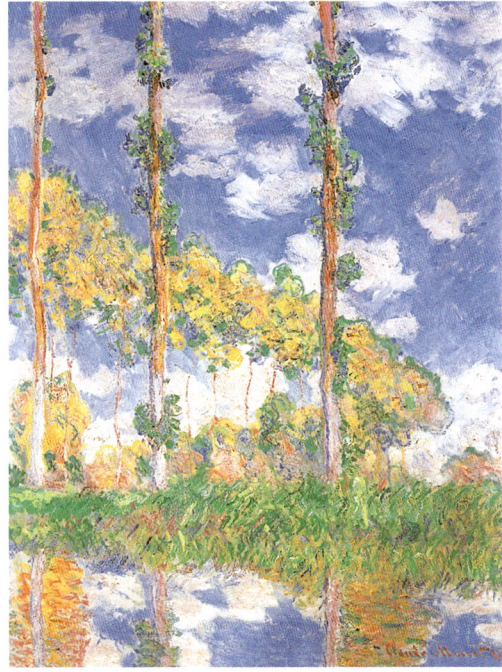

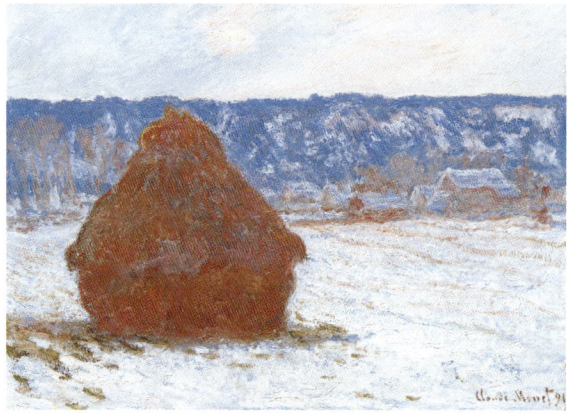

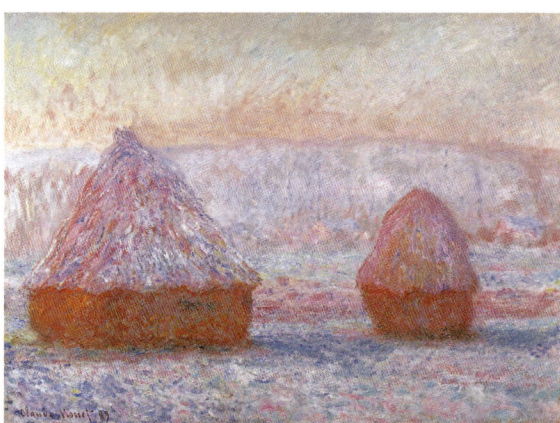

the *Grainstacks* were exhibited in 1891, for instance, every one of the paintings was sold within days. Monet, however, was highly critical of himself and his work, and more than once destroyed entire series of paintings. Furthermore, the various paintings within a series are so palpably the product of an intense study of conditions and changes that accusations of opportunist series production are clearly beside the point.

At long last, after years in reduced circumstances, after the endless humiliation of begging for paltry sums to cover the necessities of life, Monet was enjoying success. He was now recognized, and soon regarded as one of the most important painters of the times. The cathedral series was not only a major achievement in the creative work of a mature painter, but also clinched Monet's breakthrough. An exhibition of twenty of the approximately thirty Rouen Cathedral pictures, at Durand-Ruel's in May 1895, was a great success. Monet's friend, the politician and future prime minister Georges Clemenceau, pressed for the state to purchase the paintings; official, institutional distrust of the erstwhile rebel Monet was too great, though, for the purchase to come off. The series – conceived, painted and exhibited by the artist as a single set – was dispersed.

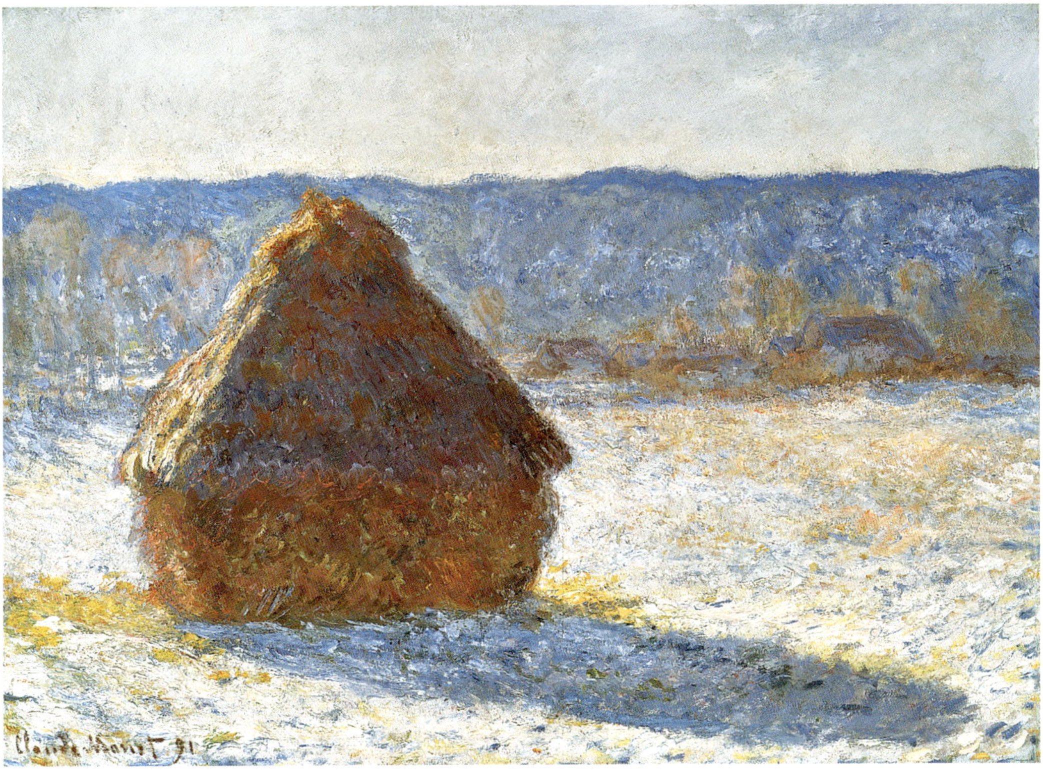

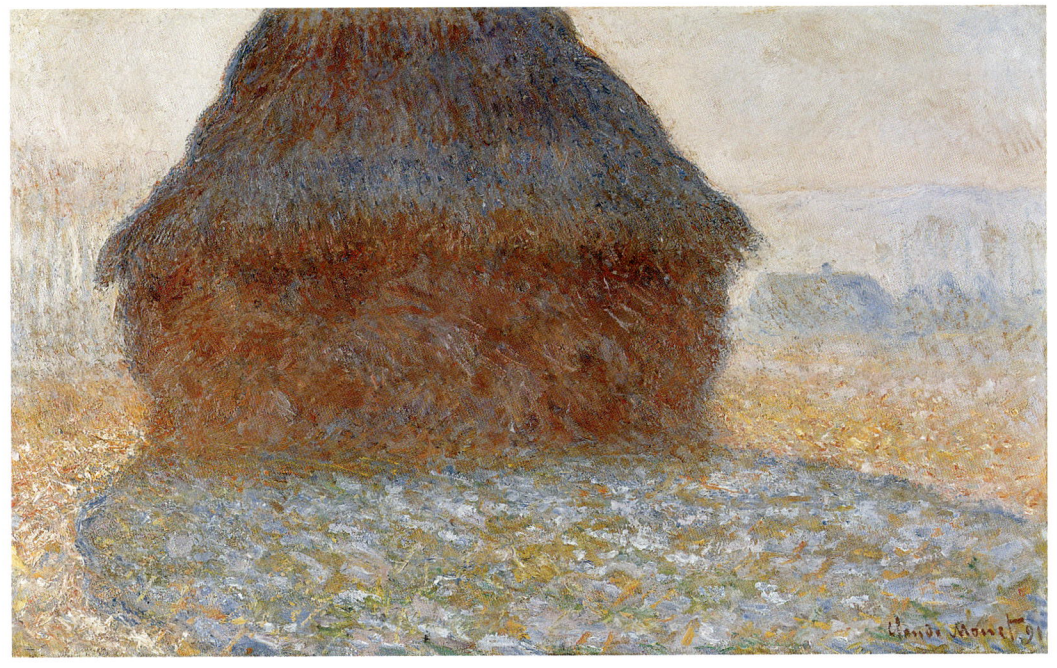

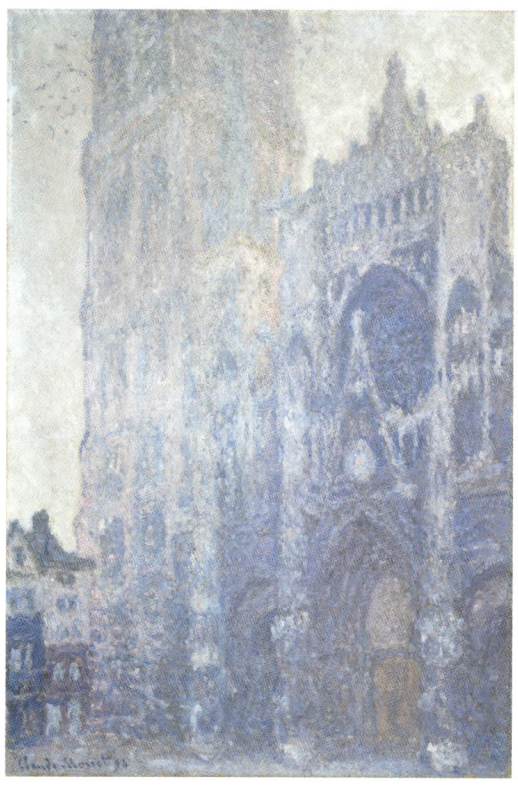

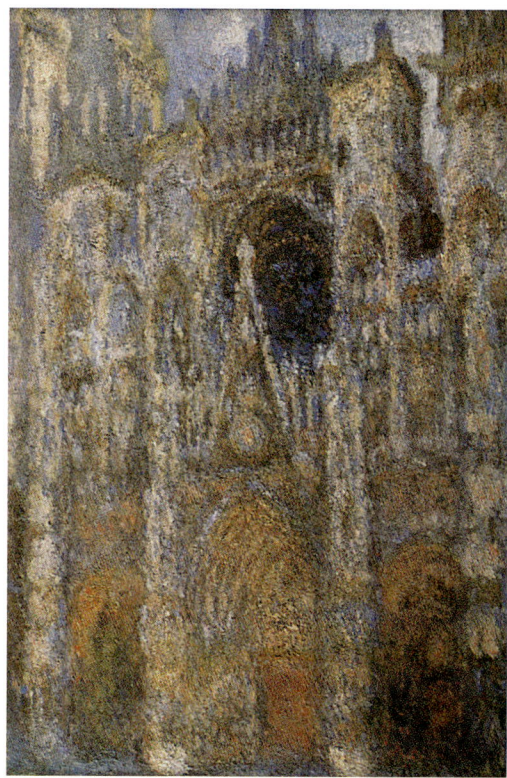

ABOVE LEFT
*The Portal and the Tour d'Albane
(Morning Effect)*, 1894
Oil on canvas, 106 x 73 cm
(41¾ x 28¾ in.)
Paris, Musée d'Orsay

ABOVE RIGHT
*Rouen Cathedral, the Portal at
Midday, Harmony in Blue*, 1893
Oil on canvas, 92.2 x 63 cm
(36¼ x 24¾ in.)
Paris, Musée d'Orsay

OPPOSITE
*The Portal and the Tour d'Albane
at Dawn*, 1894
Oil on canvas, 106 x 74 cm
(41¾ x 29¼ in.)
Boston, Museum of Fine Arts,
Tompkins Collection –
Arthur Gordon Tompkins Fund

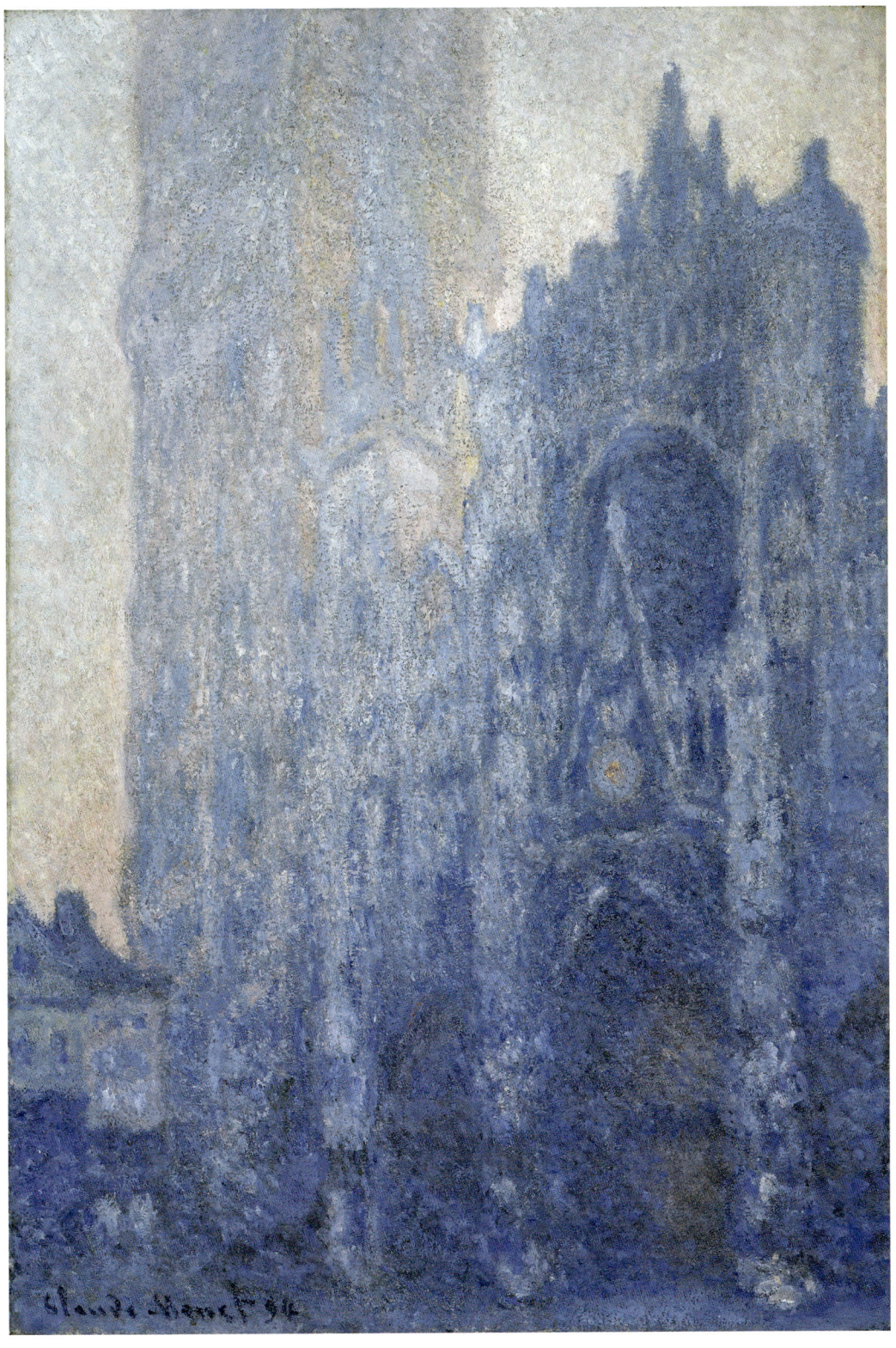

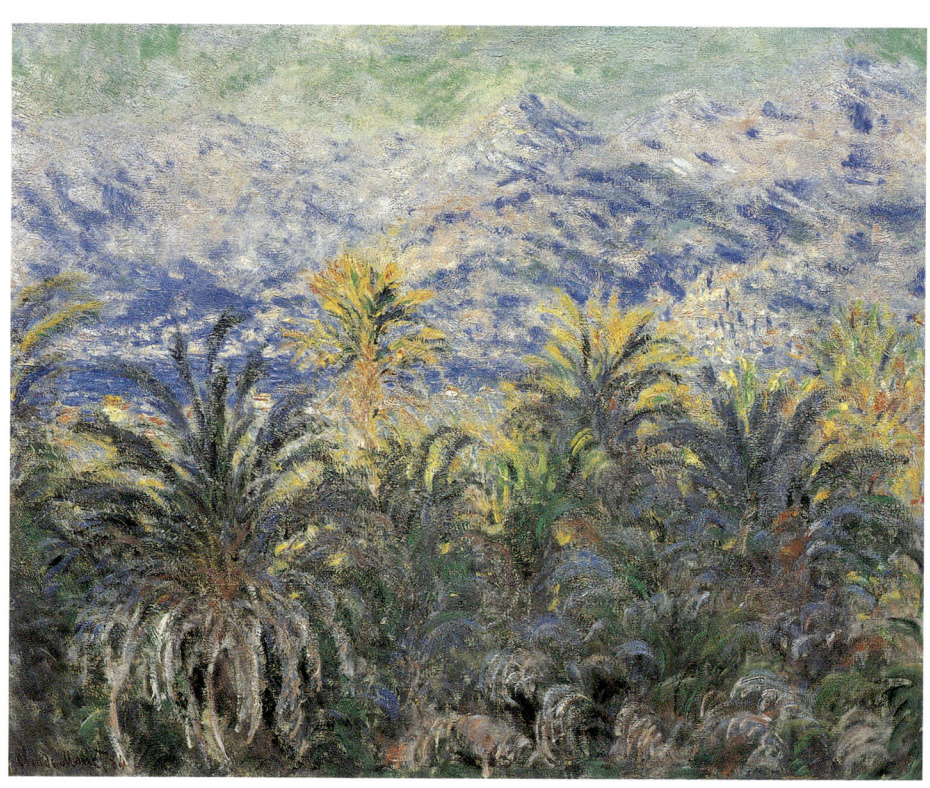

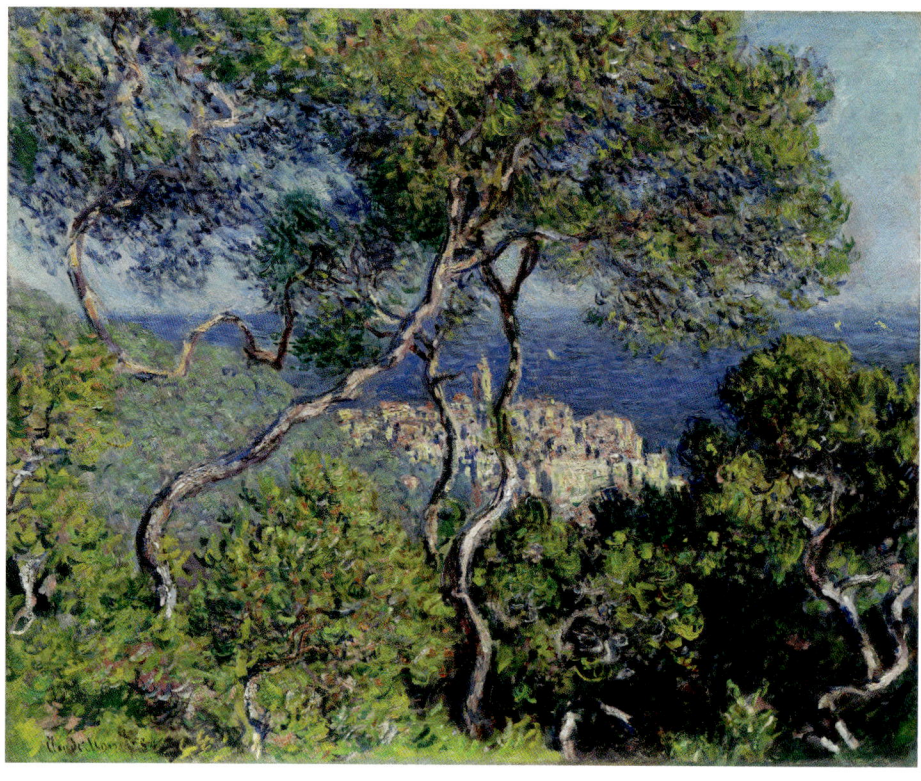

Different Countries and Different Light

Northern France, with the craggy cliffs and green pastures of Normandy and the coast of Brittany, was Monet's original home, and he revisited the region countless times with his palette and easel. But he was also drawn to unfamiliar parts where the landscape and vegetation were new to him. In quest of a different light, he travelled to other countries. The pines and palms of the Riviera and the winter gleam of the Côte Fleurie; the tranquil calm of snowy days in Norway; the resplendent tulip fields of Holland; London in the fog; and the iridescence of Venice – all of them captivated him. Even more alert and responsive (if that were possible) than on his home ground, Monet absorbed new moods and subjects, pouring his enthusiasm into letters home.

Soon after moving to Giverny, Monet travelled to the south of France with Renoir, in December 1883. He did not take his sketch pad, lead pencil and watercolours with him, as so many artists before and after did as they embarked on their apprentice and journeyman years. Rather, he took his easel, palette and a few dozen canvases, and a hefty suitcase full of warm woollens. The journey must have been a laborious business in consequence, and Monet will have attracted a fair amount of comment from fellow travellers. Renoir later described one such trip to his son. First-class passengers did their best to look bored or preoccupied, and a painter taking his seat among them with his umbrella and paintbox must have seemed "like a coalman who has accidentally wandered into a fashion show"; but in second class it was even more unpleasant, "for the affectation of the passengers was all the worse because they could not afford to travel first class".

The only passengers Renoir described as pleasant and even generous company were those in third class, which the two artists at first used of necessity and then because they felt uncomfortable in the other two classes. Some passengers were provisioned as if for a trip around the world, and, as the kilometres sped by, so their meals were produced – and shared with the lean and hungry painters, who fed on "Burgundy cheesecake or provençale pot roast [...], young Côte d'Or wines or fruity rosés from the banks of the Rhône". As the artists travelled they would be regaled with observations on the crops or taxes, tales of family troubles – or the ordeals of corset-wearing. "After a mouthful or so, one ample farm woman could not stand it any longer, and, begging our pardon, undid her underthings and asked the woman beside her to unlace the back of her corset. Her liberated flesh could now spread as it wished, and the pâté of hare finally tasted as good as it ought."

OPPOSITE TOP
Palm Trees at Bordighera, 1884
Oil on canvas, 64.8 x 81.3 cm (25½ x 32 in.)
New York, The Metropolitan Museum of Art,
Bequest of Miss Adelaide Milton de Groot
(1876–1967), 1967

Exotic plant life with snow-covered mountains in the background, the clear air and the blue water, all intoxicated Monet on his first winter visit to the Mediterranean.

OPPOSITE BOTTOM
Bordighera, 1884
Oil on canvas, 65 x 81 cm (25⅝ x 32 in.)
The Art Institute of Chicago

*"The palms will
make me despair [...]
So much blue in
the sea and the sky –
it is impossible!"*

CLAUDE MONET
TO ALICE HOSCHEDÉ, 1884

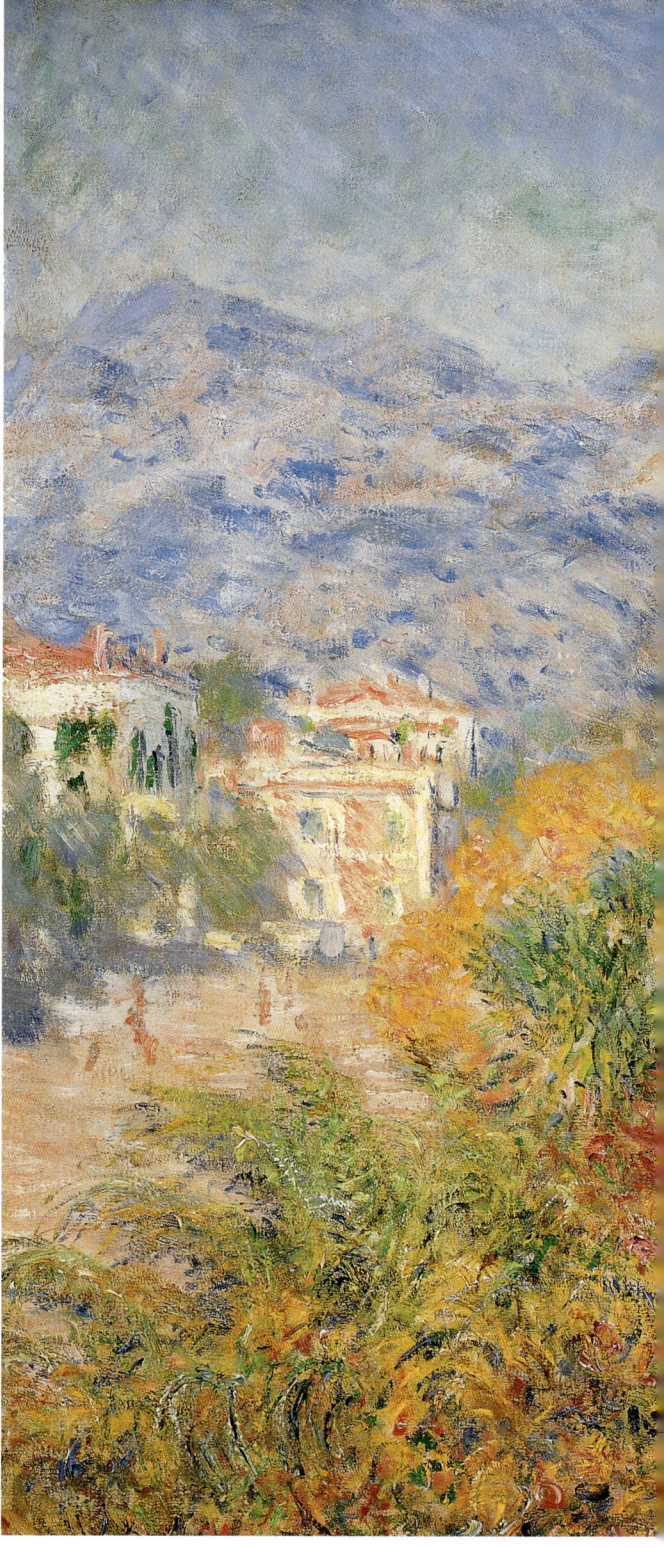

Villas at Bordighera, 1884
Oil on canvas, 73 x 92 cm
California, Santa Barbara Museum of Art

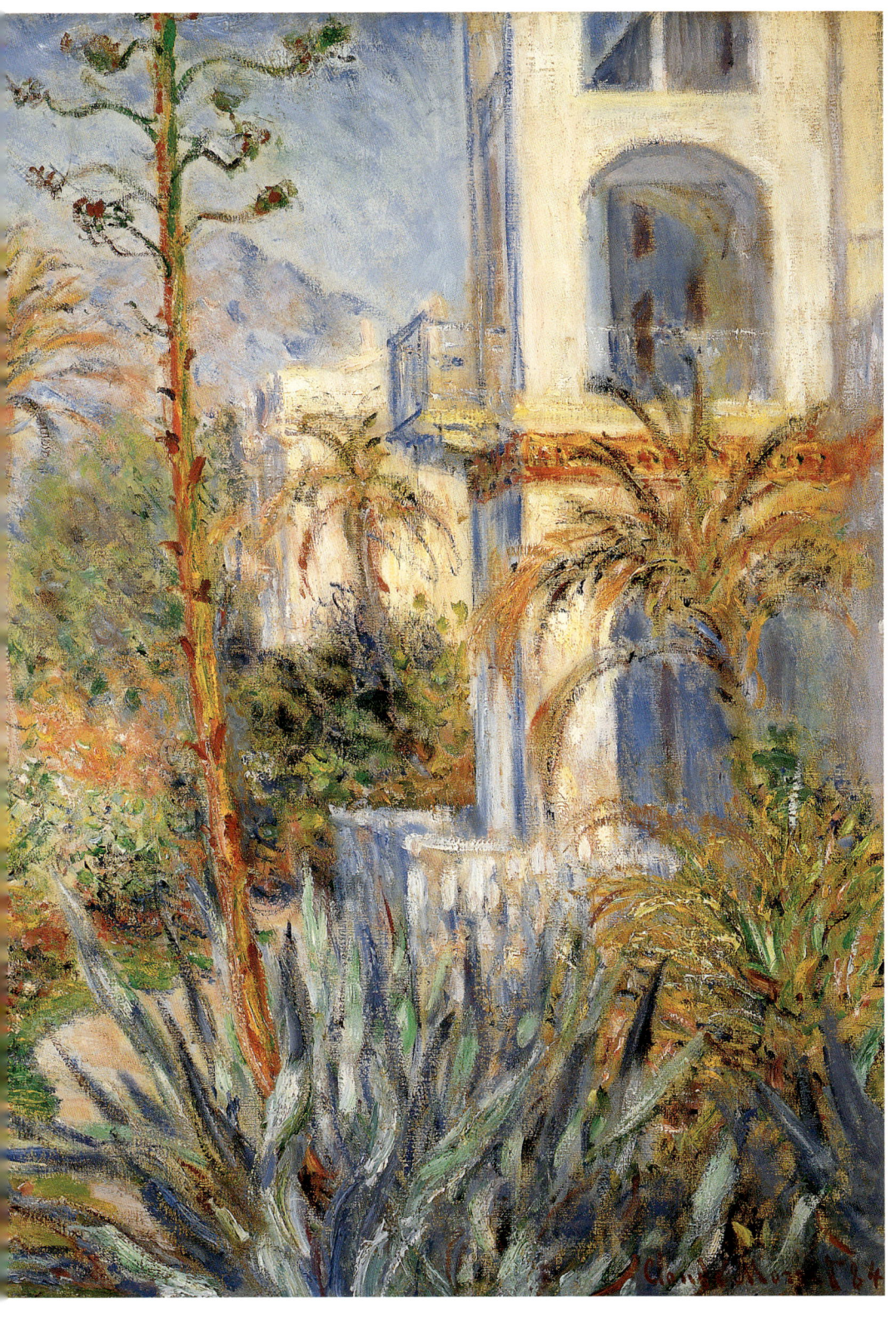

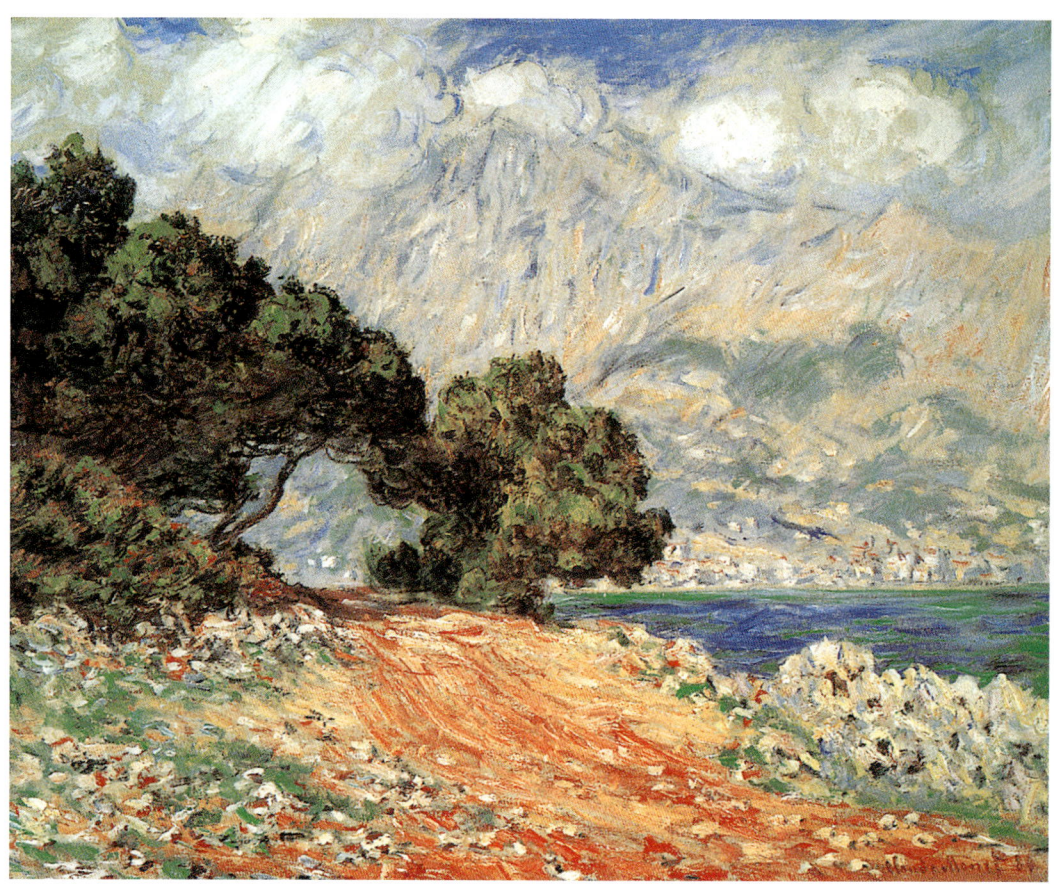

Menton Seen from Cap Martin, 1884
Oil on canvas, 67.2 x 81.6 cm (26½ x 32¼ in.)
Boston, Museum of Fine Arts,
Juliana Cheney Edwards Collection

Back home, it was only a few weeks till Monet departed for the south again, though this time without Renoir: "I have always worked best on my own, following my own impressions," he wrote to Durand-Ruel on 12 January 1884. He returned to Bordighera, a coastal village between Monte Carlo and San Remo that he had discovered on his first trip, and painted the sea, sky and pine trees contorted into arabesques, like mysterious living creatures dancing in the bright sun. For his pictures of lemon groves, olive trees and palms, Monet increasingly used colours almost new to his palette, such as turquoise and ultramarine, pink and a mandarin shade of orange. The palms grew in the walled garden of a Monsieur Moreno, and were considered the finest on the coast.

"This is fairytale country," Monet wrote to Théodore Duret on 2 February. "I do not know where to look first. It is all extraordinarily beautiful and I want to paint everything [...] This landscape is entirely new to me, something to be studied, and I am only just beginning to be familiar with it; and to know where I should go and what I can do is terribly difficult – one would need diamonds and precious stones in one's palette." Monet returned home having started on fifty canvases – though hardly one of the paintings was completed.

Five years later he again visited the Mediterranean. In January 1888 he stayed on the Côte d'Azur, painting the sea against the backdrop of the snow-covered Esterel Mountains (ill. p. 174). A pine marks a bold diagonal across the landscape horizontals, lending a scene almost non-spatial in

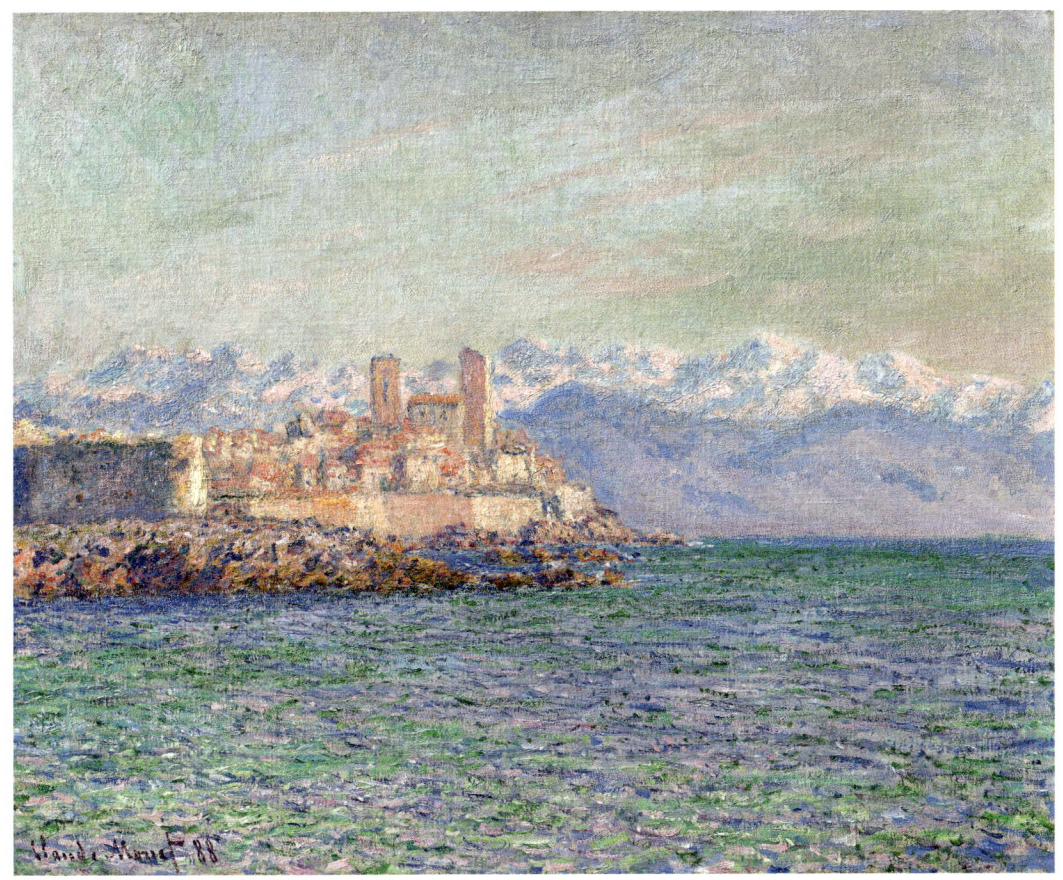

Antibes, Afternoon Effect, 1888
Oil on canvas, 66 x 82.5 cm (26 x 32½ in.)
Private collection

its muted winter colours a striking foreground that not only defines distance and size but also introduces tension into a placid composition based on horizontals. Unusually composed, the picture was again inspired by Japanese woodblock prints.

From the promontory of Cap d'Antibes, Monet painted the fortified town of Antibes (ill. p. 175), trying to capture on canvas the intensity of winter light by the Mediterranean. The bright radiance is conveyed by strong contrasts of cold and warm, an entire range of glowing creams, pinks and vermilions being juxtaposed with cold blues and greens on a ground of pale blue, and especially large quantities of white being admixed. "It is so beautiful here, so bright, so full of light!" Monet wrote to Gustave Geffroy on 12 February 1888. "One is afloat in blue air. It is awe-inspiring."

The south coast pictures were tremendously successful. "I have just left the exhibition, delighted by the work you did last winter," the poet Stéphane Mallarmé wrote to Monet on seeing the Antibes paintings. "For a long time I have ranked what you do above all else, but I believe you are now at the height of your powers." Monet, though, was dissatisfied. He was afire for a world of gold and precious stones – and in despair to see that what his brush recorded on the canvas was merely pink and sky blue. Time and again he wrote of his vain attempts to convey the Mediterranean atmosphere, only to be disappointed by the picture he in fact painted. The continuing cultivation of his paradise garden at Giverny notwithstanding, he was restless. Perhaps what he sought away from home was not only new impressions but also creative solitude and a respite from his ever-growing family, which included increasing numbers of sons- and daughters-in-law and was soon to include his first grandchildren too.

Monet took to travel. He visited his stepson in Norway, went to the south of France on several occasions, and, after the turn of the century, even undertook motoring tours, to Madrid and to Venice. London too – where the iridescent atmosphere and the countless, constantly changing shades of grey had fascinated him back in 1870 – attracted the artist on several occasions. Around 1900, from the balcony of his room at the Savoy Hotel and a window of St Thomas's Hospital, he painted his Thames series, including works such as the *Houses of Parliament* (ill. p. 177) and *Waterloo Bridge in the Mist*. Again Monet worked with a multitude of canvases, turning to the one or the other at various times according to whether his subject was shrouded in fog or the sun was breaking through. To Durand-Ruel he wrote on 23 March 1903: "I cannot let you have a single London picture, since it is essential that I have them all before me, and, to be honest, not one of them is finished. I am working on them all together." Nor were the paintings completed by the time he returned to Giverny, and over the next few years he continued to work on them in his studio.

Comparison of the *Houses of Parliament in London* with *Impression, Sunrise* (ill. pp. 134/135), painted thirty years earlier, shows clearly how Monet's art had changed. In both paintings there is a similarity of subject matter; indeed, there are several London canvases in which Monet has placed small vessels in the foreground water, like those in *Impression*. But the way in which the subject is seen is fundamentally different. The Thames scenes no longer have the sketchiness of *Impression*; instead, they have a meticulously achieved, monumental sense of completion. The atmospherics and light at particular moments may well have provided points of departure for the individual pictures, but Monet worked his

Mount Kolsaas (Rose Reflects), 1895
Oil on canvas, 65.5 x 100.5 cm (25¾ x 39½ in.)
Paris, Musée d'Orsay

Monet returned from an 1895 visit to his stepson in Norway with only a handful of paintings. Mount Kolsaas, heavily snow-clad, became an object of mystery and meditation in Monet's picture.

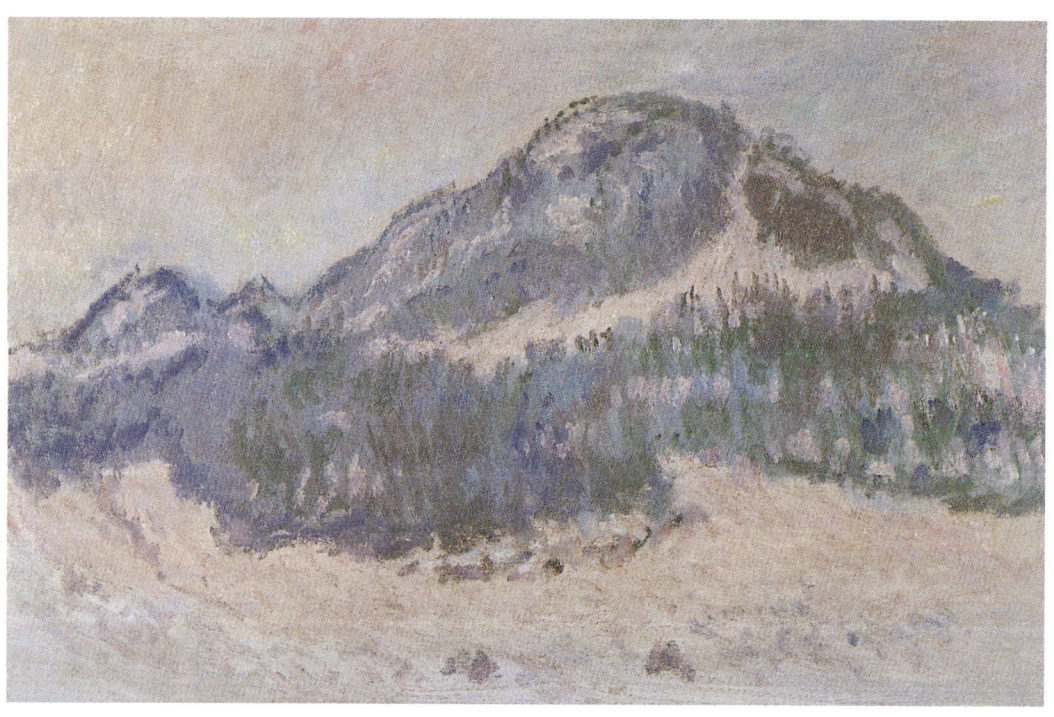

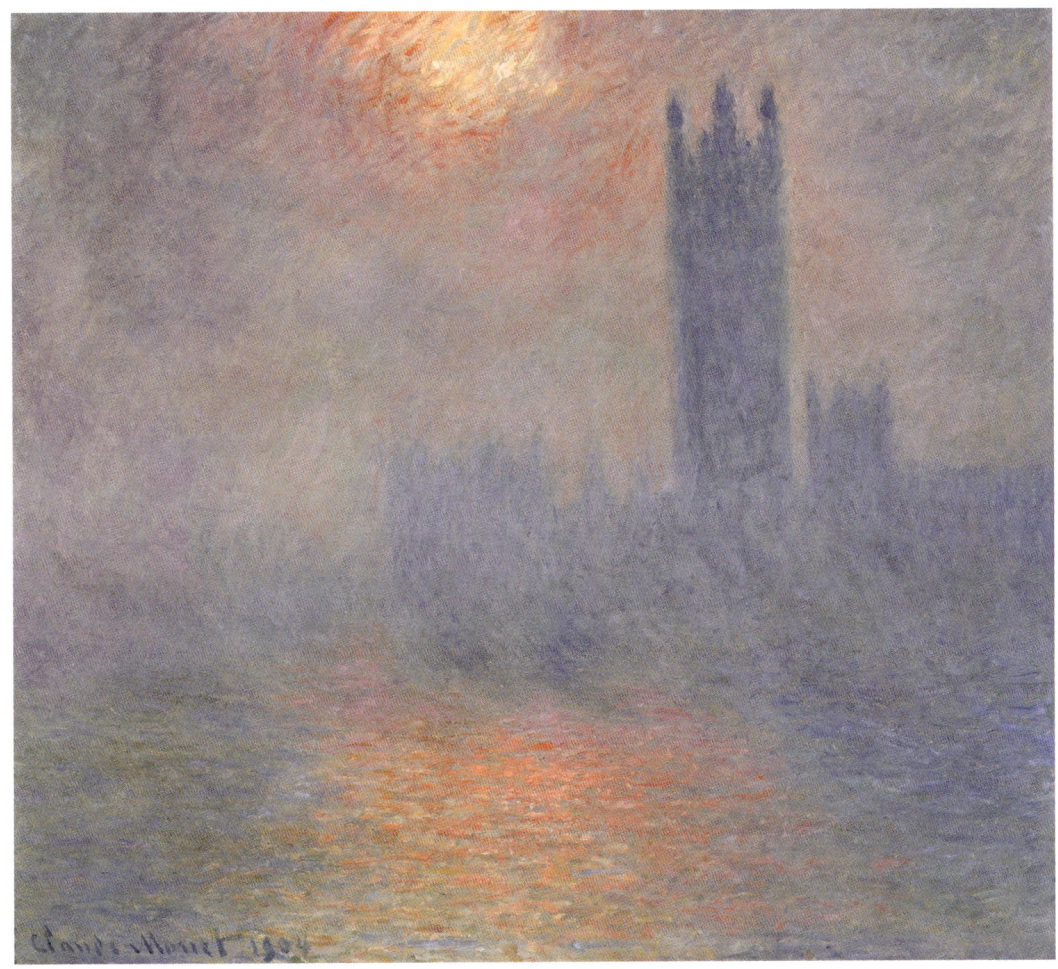

impressions into abstract complexes of colour. His architectural subjects no longer established graphic spatial structures like ships and bridges in earlier paintings, but demarcated a handful of larger zones in which to explore colour. Monet's water, sky and buildings became areas on which to project shimmers of colour, no more tangible than the hazy air itself. The Victorian Gothic of the new Houses of Parliament is eerily insubstantial in the mist. Both the subject and the overall scene are painted in abbreviated brushstrokes, and he has used every colour of the spectrum.

Houses of Parliament,
Effect of Sunlight in the Fog, 1904
Oil on canvas, 81 x 92 cm (32 x 36¼ in.)
Paris, Musée d'Orsay

For years, Monet continued to work on Thames scenes, with the Houses of Parliament or Waterloo Bridge, in his studio. The buildings rise enigmatically from their shrouds of shimmering fog, pierced by only a little sunlight.

When Monet visited Venice in 1908 he again created sublime tapestries of colour of this order, of an abstraction that no longer much resembled the instantaneous art of *Impression*. At the invitation of the Anglo-American artist John Singer Sargent, Monet and Alice Hoschedé (now married) spent two weeks in the Renaissance Palazzo Barbaro beside the Grand Canal. The first few days sped by, and Monet was so busy exploring the lanes and alleys and canals, absorbing the atmosphere, that he deferred his work. In the churches and museums he studied works by the great Venetian artists

Titian, Giorgione and Veronese, to whose paintings his own had frequently been compared. The city's unique atmosphere, he felt, was beyond the power of art to capture. Yet presently there he was, with his palette and easel, beside the Grand Canal or the Doge's Palace, painting like one possessed and observing a strict schedule, rising at six and giving himself two hours on each motif. Not till the sun went down did he permit himself a break. His wife, somewhat concerned, wrote to Germaine Salerou (3 December 1908): "It is high time he relaxed. He is working very hard, especially for a man of his age."

Critics of the Venice paintings tend to speak of a faerie realm of colour; and it is true that the views of San Giorgio Maggiore or the Palazzo Contarini (ills. pp. 178 and 179) share the mood of a Romantic fairytale or a Symbolist poem. As in the case of London's misty winter, the light of Venice need not necessarily have been as luminous, intense and glittering as it appears on Monet's canvases. When he was on his travels he would begin a great many paintings and subsequently complete them over the years in his studio or even begin afresh. The process of reworking would superimpose a multi-layered mantle of shimmering colours on the entire surface, and would also, inevitably, strip the pictures of their immediacy and sketch quality, transforming them into finely tuned fantasias in paint. Monet's Venice works are compositions of veiled blue haze and mother-of-pearl reflections.

OPPOSITE
The Palazzo Contarini, 1908
Oil on canvas, 92 x 81 cm (36¼ x 32 in.)
Kunstmuseum St Gallen,
purchased by the Ernst Schürpf
Stiftung in 1950

Venice at Dusk, c. 1908
Oil on canvas, 73 x 92.5 cm (28¾ x 36½ in.)
Tokyo, Bridgestone Museum of Art,
Ishibashi Foundation

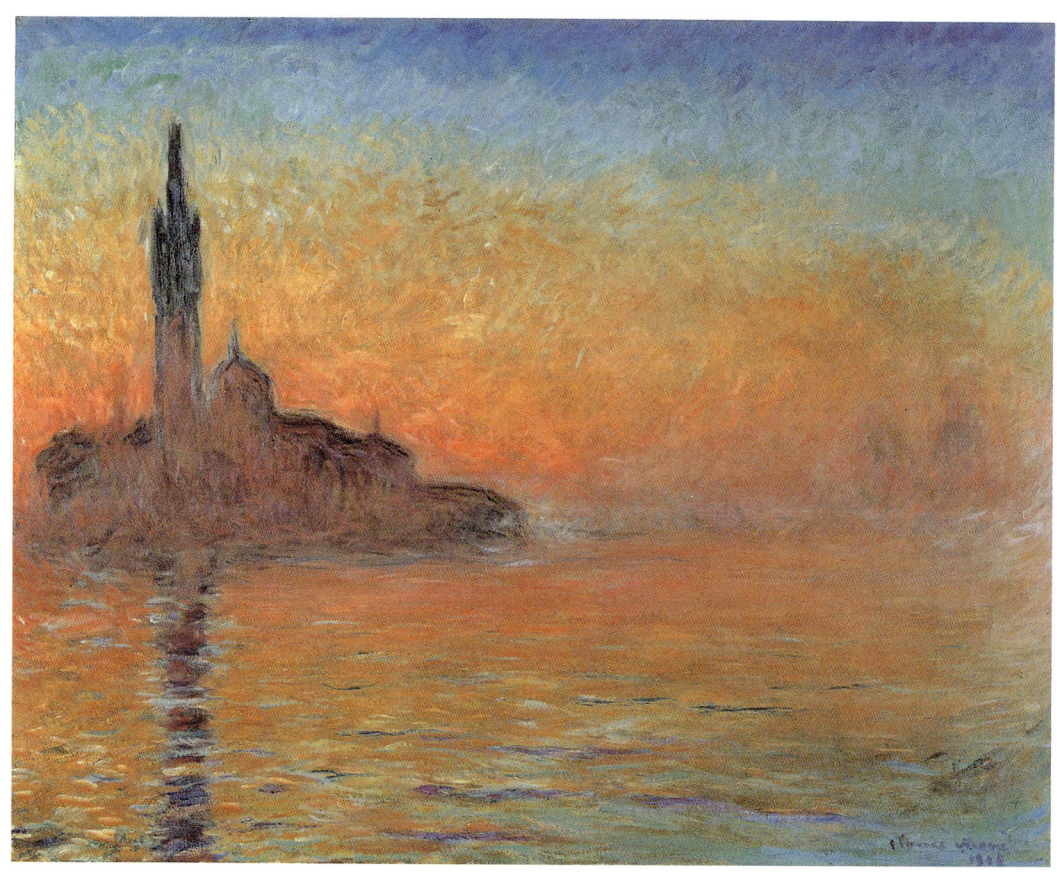

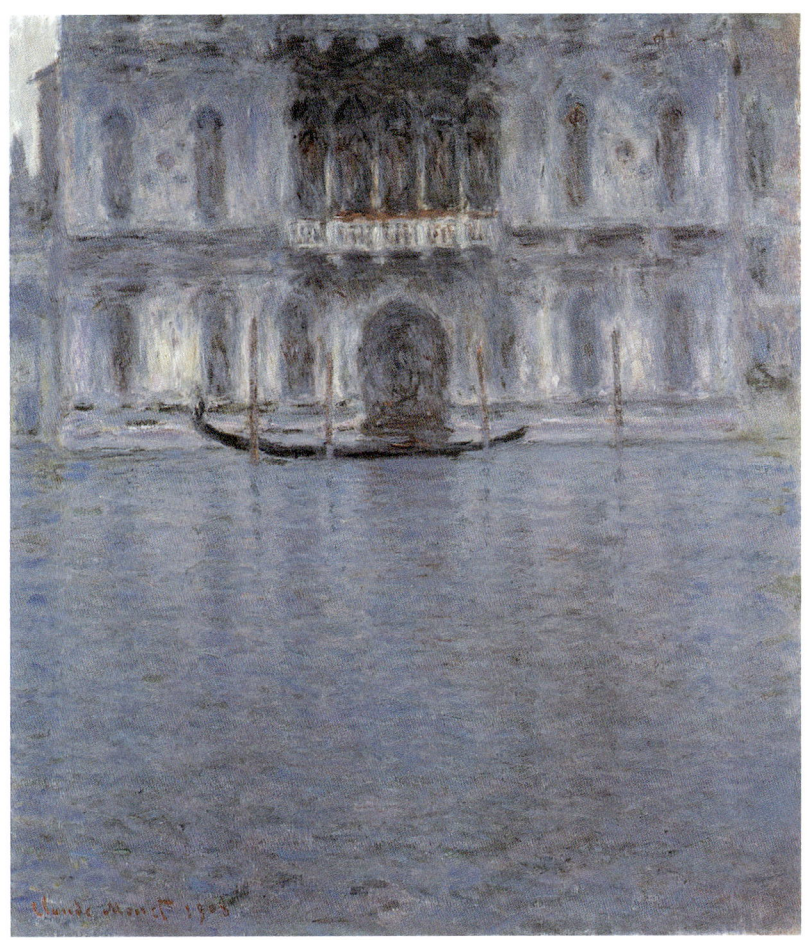

They consist of recollections and visions rather than of visual experience registered *sur le motif*. A tendency already apparent in the grainstacks, poplars and Rouen Cathedral series was confirmed in the pictures Monet painted from these travels in later life: the Impressionist had become a Symbolist, celebrating the mystical union of mist and architecture, of the material and the atmospheric, of stone and light.

"It is so beautiful [Church of San Giorgio Maggiore] ...
I console myself with the thought that I shall return
next year, for I have only been able to make a start.
But what a pity that I did not come here when I was
younger and more adventurous!"
CLAUDE MONET TO GUSTAVE GEFFROY, 1908

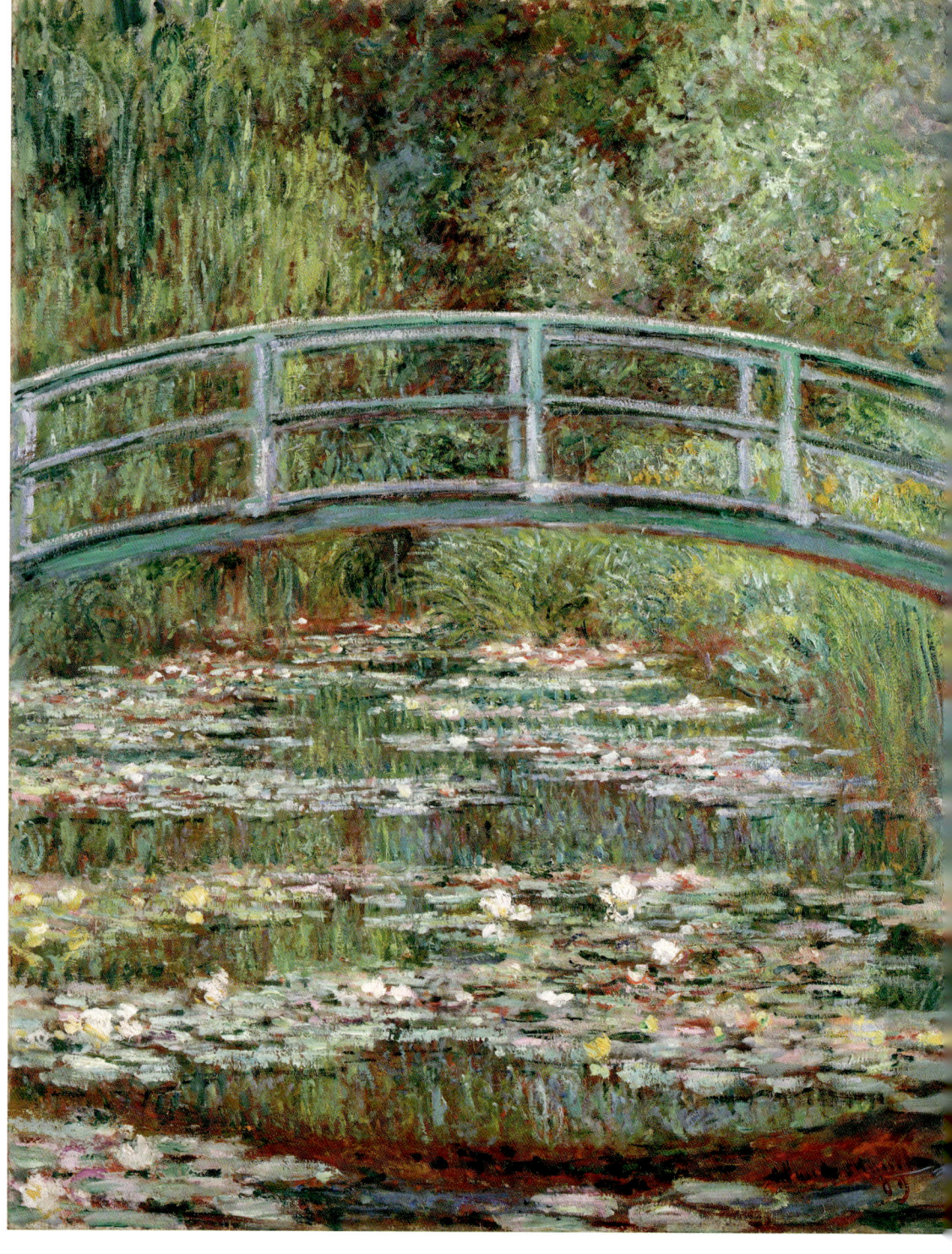

The Garden at Giverny

In August 1901, *Le Figaro*'s art critic Arsène Alexandre recorded his first impression of Giverny, where Monet spent the second half of his life. "And then at last, Giverny appears at the end of the road," wrote Alexandre. "It is a pretty village, albeit somewhat lacking in character: half rural, half a small town. But suddenly, just as one comes to the end of the village and is continuing towards Vernon, without having felt any strong urge to stop, a new and extraordinary sight greets one, as unexpected as any big surprise. Imagine all the colours of a palette, all the notes of a fanfare: that is Monet's garden!"

Monet's regular sales since the mid-1880s had secured his financial status, so that in 1890 he was even in a position to buy the house. He now turned to the plot of land (which he extended over the years through

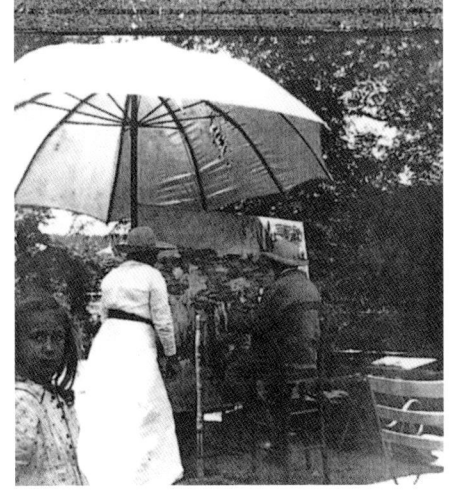

a number of purchases) and, with great energy and devotion, succeeded not only in creating a home for his family but also in establishing his own earthly paradise – the garden at Giverny.

Not that the beginning was straightforward. The couple, still unmarried when they moved there with their eight children, no doubt challenged the conventional views of a farming community. This fellow Monet, who was supposed to be a modern painter, would stride off across the meadows at dawn, followed by an entourage of children carting his paint and canvases on a wheelbarrow, and set up in front of trees and grainstacks, which he then set down in higgledy-piggledy brushwork on canvases he was forever exchanging. The locals soon found a way of turning this oddball to their own advantage, and charged him a toll whenever he crossed their fields on his way to paint. They would also dismantle grainstacks or fell poplars once he was busy painting them, and Monet had many a struggle to keep his motifs as he wanted them. At a later date, when he was planning to create a pond with exotic plants in his garden, the villagers protested that the plants might damage their laundry (which they washed in the river) or poison livestock grazing below the garden.

OPPOSITE
Water-Lily Pond, 1899
Oil on canvas, 93 x 74 cm (36⅝ x 29¼ in.)
New York, The Metropolitan Museum of Art

ABOVE RIGHT
Monet painting the water-lily pond with his stepdaughter Blanche Hoschedé-Monet and Nitia Saleron, 1915

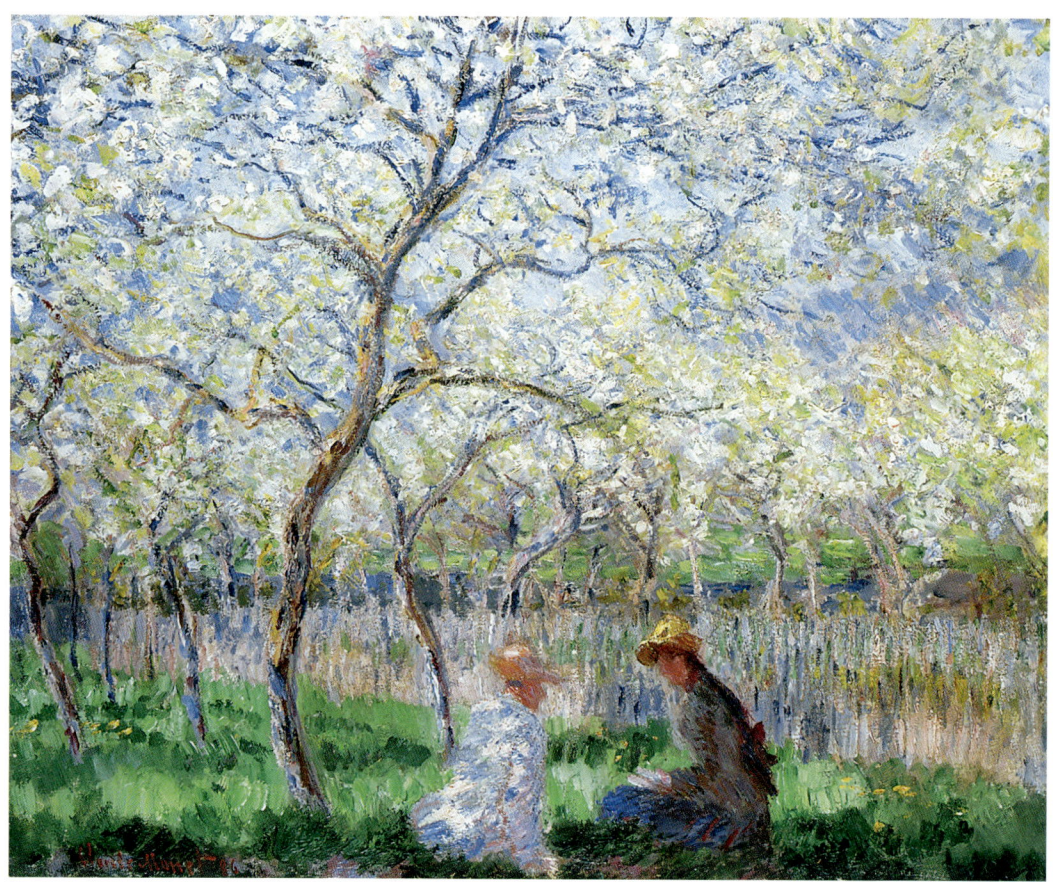

Springtime, 1886
Oil on canvas, 64.8 x 80.6 cm (25½ x 31¾ in.)
Cambridge, The Fitzwilliam Museum

Despite the difficulties, Monet and his family succeeded in transforming a Norman apple orchard into a garden that made history. Monet later said that he had simply leafed through a gardening catalogue and placed his orders, but this was doubtless one of his many understatements. In fact he put immense knowledge and patient toil into the creation of the garden, which became a veritable Eden of bloom and fertility. Arsène Alexandre described it thus: "Wherever one turns, at one's feet or head or at chest height there are pools, chains of flowers, blossoming hedges at once wild and cultivated, changing with the seasons, ever becoming new."

Quite clearly a power governed and shaped the garden, a power such as Monet displayed in his paintings, too. He assigned every plant its place, planning and ordering, laying out parallel borders according to varieties and colours. He was establishing his sovereignty over nature. With subjects for paintings already in mind, he chose his plants, composing his works not only by choosing a position but also, from the very outset, by determining the appearance of the natural world. Early one year, when a mighty oak he was painting began to bud, Monet, rather than alter his painting, recruited village youngsters to climb up and see to it that when he resumed work the next day there was not a trace of green to be seen. "One admires the painter, and feels sorry for the unhappy tree", observed the English painter Wynford Dewhurst, from whom we have the anecdote.

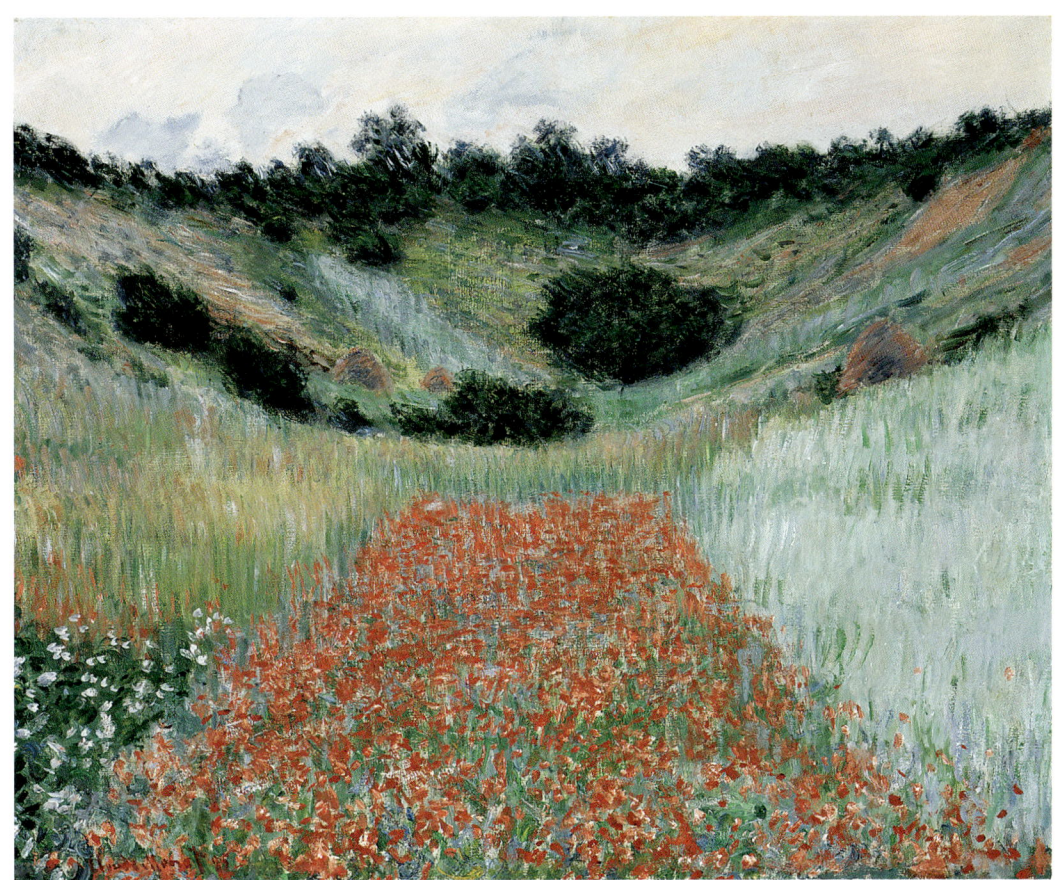

Quite unlike Emil Nolde, who created a down-to-earth farm garden at Seebüll, Monet had an unmistakable taste for the unusual and exotic in his Giverny garden. Of course he planted dahlias and nasturtiums too; but as the years went by the garden became more and more a place of pale blue wistaria and purple irises, tuberoses from Mexico, water-lilies gleaming like mother-of-pearl, tufty clumps of bamboo. Many of these plants, some of them imported from overseas, had only been grown in France for a short time; the local farming people's suspicion of the artist's unknown vegetation is therefore scarcely surprising. But it was not long before sophisticated circles in Paris and abroad began to take a keen interest in the garden. The first articles about it were published, and long after Monet's death (indeed, to this day) magazines and books gladly devoted their pages to the beauties of the Giverny garden, which still delights the many who visit it.

The garden became a part of Monet, and he of it; it entered into his soul and (most important for him) his eye. Wherever he travelled, he always asked after his flowers in letters home. The garden on sunny days was very life to him, and when it rained he withdrew to bed, depressed.

Not that Monet was a painter of flowers. In the early *Flowering Garden* at Sainte-Adresse (ill. p. 124), it is clear that he was unconcerned to identify individual species or varieties, and later – though tea

Poppy Field in a Hollow near Giverny, 1885
Oil on canvas, 65 x 81 cm (25⅝ x 32 in.)
Boston, Museum of Fine Arts

At Giverny, Monet returned to the motif of the poppy field in flower (cf. ill. p. 147). But in contrast to the bright, cheerful landscape that seemed casually noticed, the later picture is a symmetrical and almost austere composition based on the complementary colours of green and red.

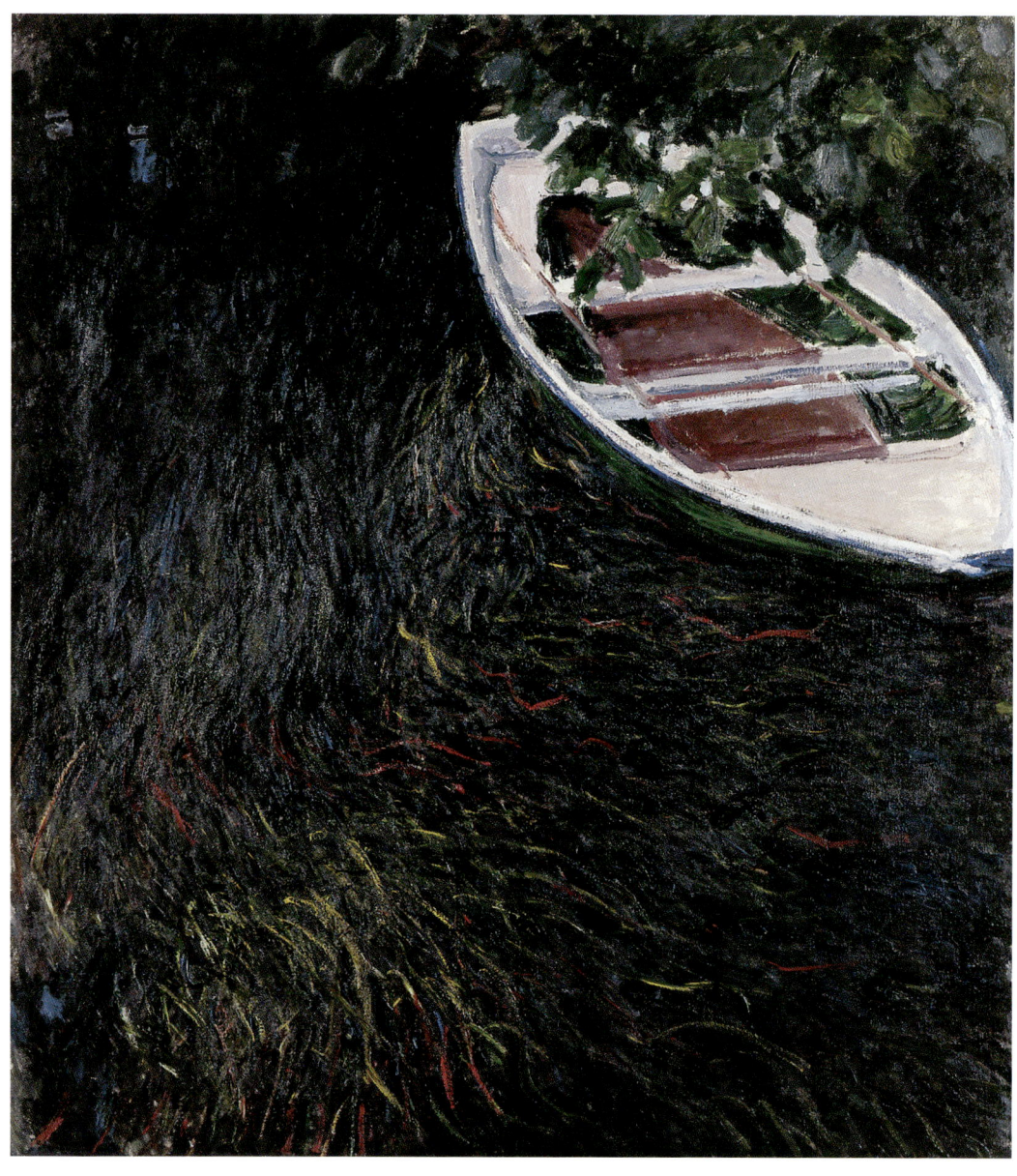

The Rowing Boat, 1887
Oil on canvas, 146 x 133 cm (57½ x 52¼ in.)
Paris, Musée Marmottan Monet

The whole family enjoyed boating trips
to the Île aux Orties (Nettle Island). It lay
near the bank of the Seine and could be
reached down a channel that ran to Monet's
property. Later he bought the island.

OPPOSITE TOP
Young Girls in the Rowing Boat, 1887
Oil on canvas, 145 x 134 cm (57 x 52⅞ in.)
Tokyo, The National Museum of
Western Art

OPPOSITE BOTTOM
The Pink Skiff, 1890
Oil on canvas, 135 x 175 cm (53¼ x 69 in.)
Hakone, Japan, Pola Museum of Art

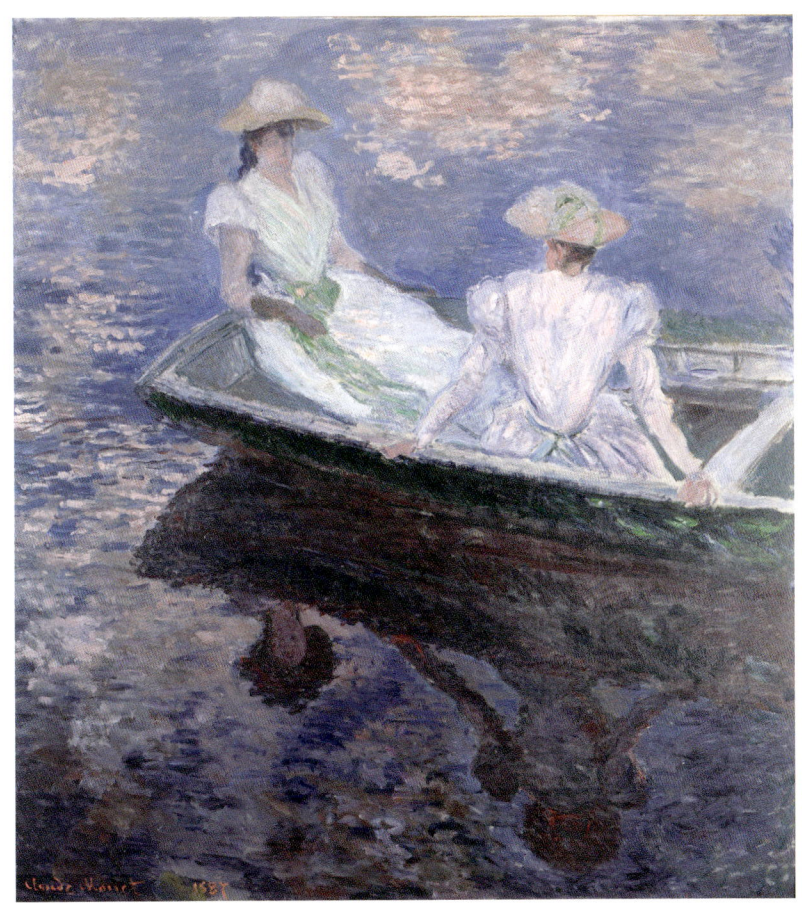

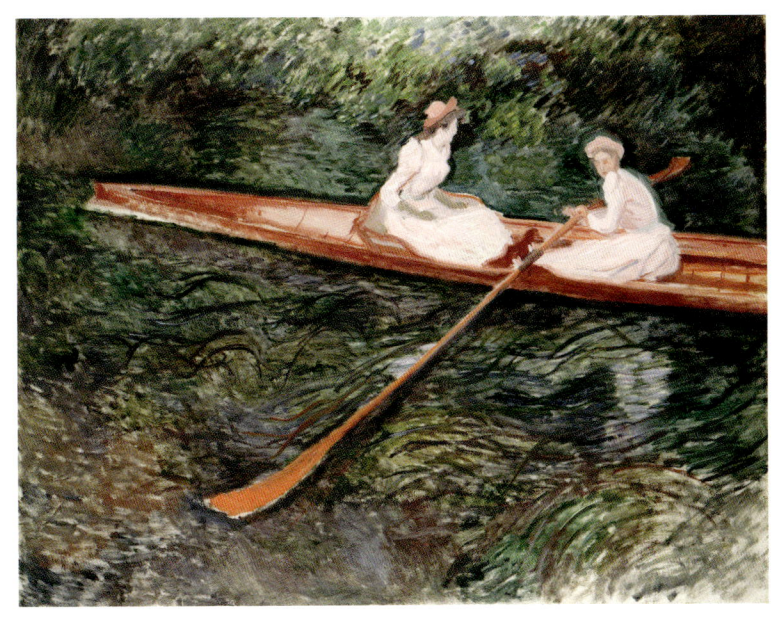

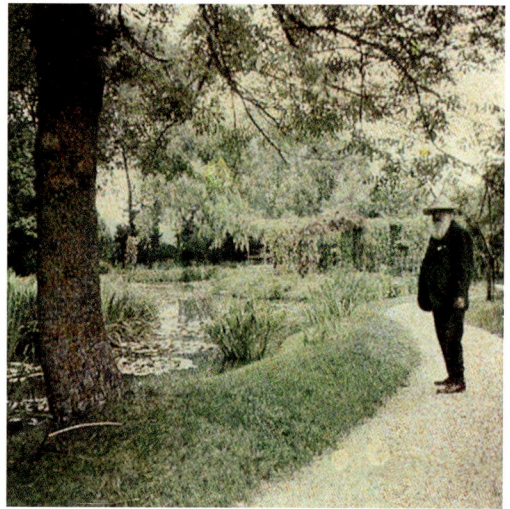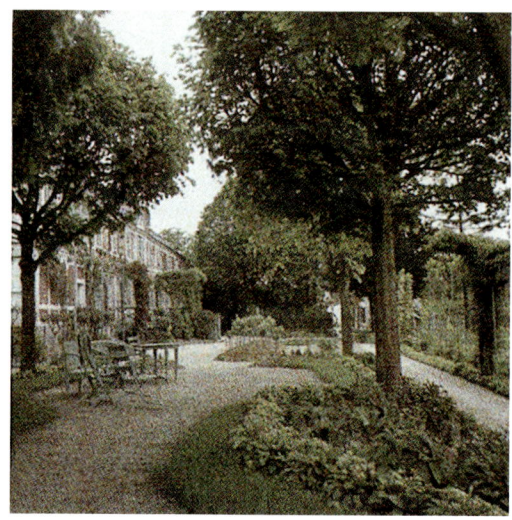

TOP LEFT
Monet in his garden at Giverny, *c.* 1917
Colour photograph by Étienne Clémentel

TOP RIGHT
Monet's house and garden at Giverny, *c.* 1917
Colour photograph by Étienne Clémentel

roses, poppies, and then water-lilies and wistaria, are all iden-
tifiable – Monet was never an artist meticulous in his botan-
ical detail. What he was after was the harmony of the whole,
the overall impression. For Monet, flowers were bearers of light,
and a feast for the eyes.

The house at Giverny was spacious, though compared with
the ornate opulence common at the turn of the century it was simple in style. The building itself,
essentially of a functional kind, was soon mantled in ivy and climbing roses. After the death of
Ernest Hoschedé, who had never recovered following his bankruptcy, Monet and Alice Hoschedé
had married in 1892, placing the seal of legitimacy on a long-lasting relationship which may well
have dated from old days at Montgeron, when Camille was indeed still alive. The fact that Alice had
never been merely a housekeeper and nanny must presumably have been apparent to their friends
and neighbours anyway.

Politicians and diplomats paid calls at Giverny, arriving by rail, crossing the Seine by boat, travelling in horse-drawn carriages, or, presently, driving up in rattling newfangled stinking automobiles.
American collectors and Japanese aristocrats visited Monet, and so too, of course, did his old friends
Renoir, Cézanne, Pissarro, his first biographer Gustave Geffroy, and above all Georges Clemenceau,
who served as prime minister from 1906 to 1909 and again from 1917 to 1920. Despite this high political friendship, though, Monet kept his distance from honours conferred by the state, declining the
Cross of the Legion of Honour in 1888 and in 1920 refusing to enter the Institut de France.

Hard on the heels of his friends and collectors came the admirers of Monet. As early as the late
1880s, a colony of American artists, known as the "Givernists", was established. Monet chose never
to teach, and contented himself with urging the young artists to use their eyes and study nature;
he soon felt that fame was making too many and too noisy demands of him, and among the young
Americans who came calling every day he acquired a reputation for being "extremely ill-tempered".
If he himself preferred to withdraw, though, his stepdaughter Suzanne married one of the ambitious
American artists, Theodore Butler, in 1892.

Over the years, the house, which was already a bustling place, opened its doors to further sons-
and daughters-in-law and grandchildren, till family celebrations (as photographs show) began to

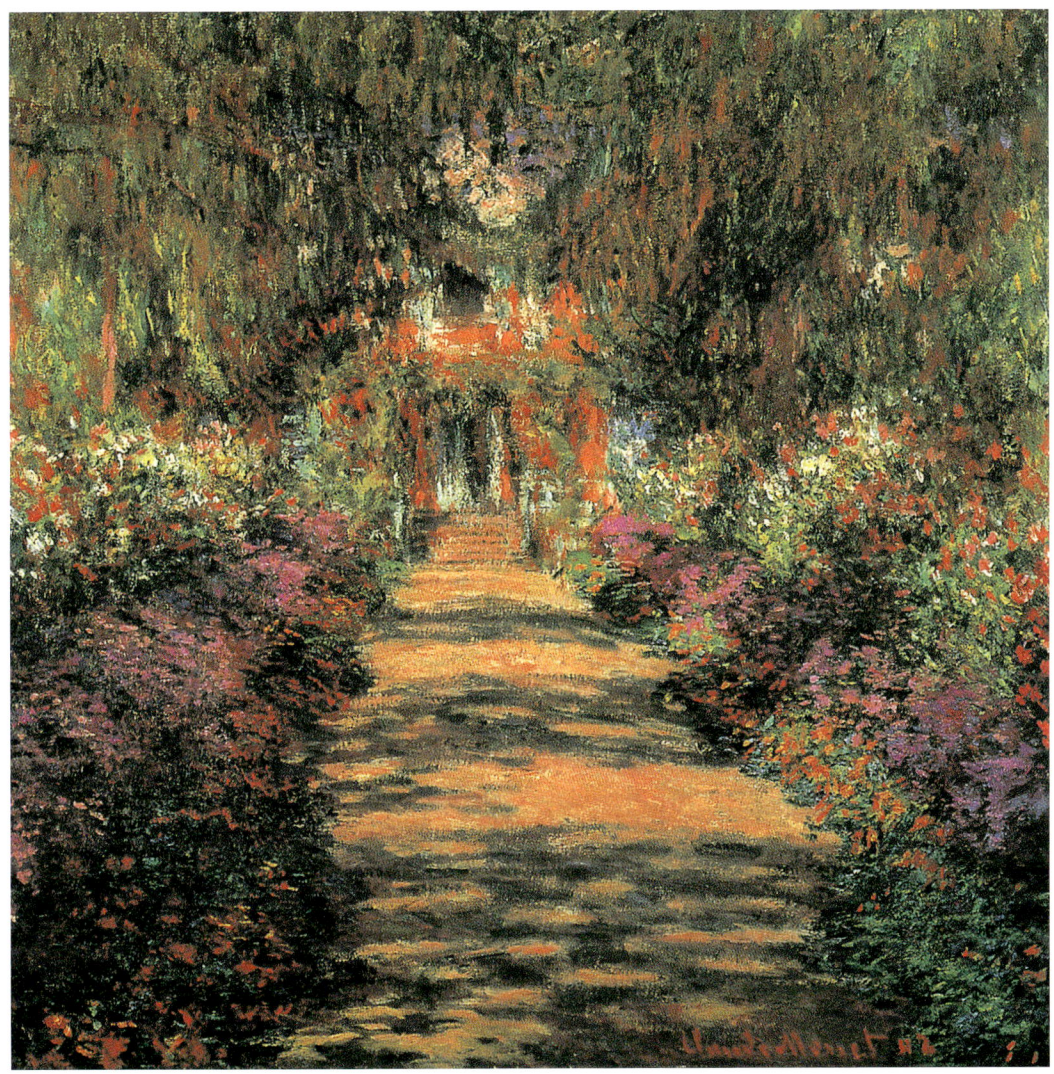

Main Path through the Garden at Giverny, 1902
Oil on canvas, 89.5 x 92.3 cm (35¼ x 36⅜ in.)
Vienna, Österreichische Galerie Belvedere

In the shade of old yew trees, a path with rambling roses trained over it ran down to the south garden gate. The flower beds to right and left were arranged symmetrically.

look like village carnivals. Monet, already the *bon bourgeois* in his Argenteuil days, became a great gourmet, and had the choicest delicacies served in his famous yellow dining room hung with a collection of his Japanese prints. Six closely-written books of recipes have survived, including tempting dishes such as *Truffes à la serviette, entrecôte marchand de vin* and the mysterious *vert-vert*. Making banana ice cream at Christmas was a complicated business involving cranking an ice machine, then a state-of-the-art gadget, for a full half-hour. Monet was a collector of recipes, and liked to plan menus and give orders; but he himself never did any of the cooking.

Meals played an important part in Monet's life, and provided the framework for daily life. Early in the morning, often before dawn in summer, he would rise and eat a hearty breakfast of the kind he had grown fond of in Holland. At half past eleven the family and any visitors would lunch;

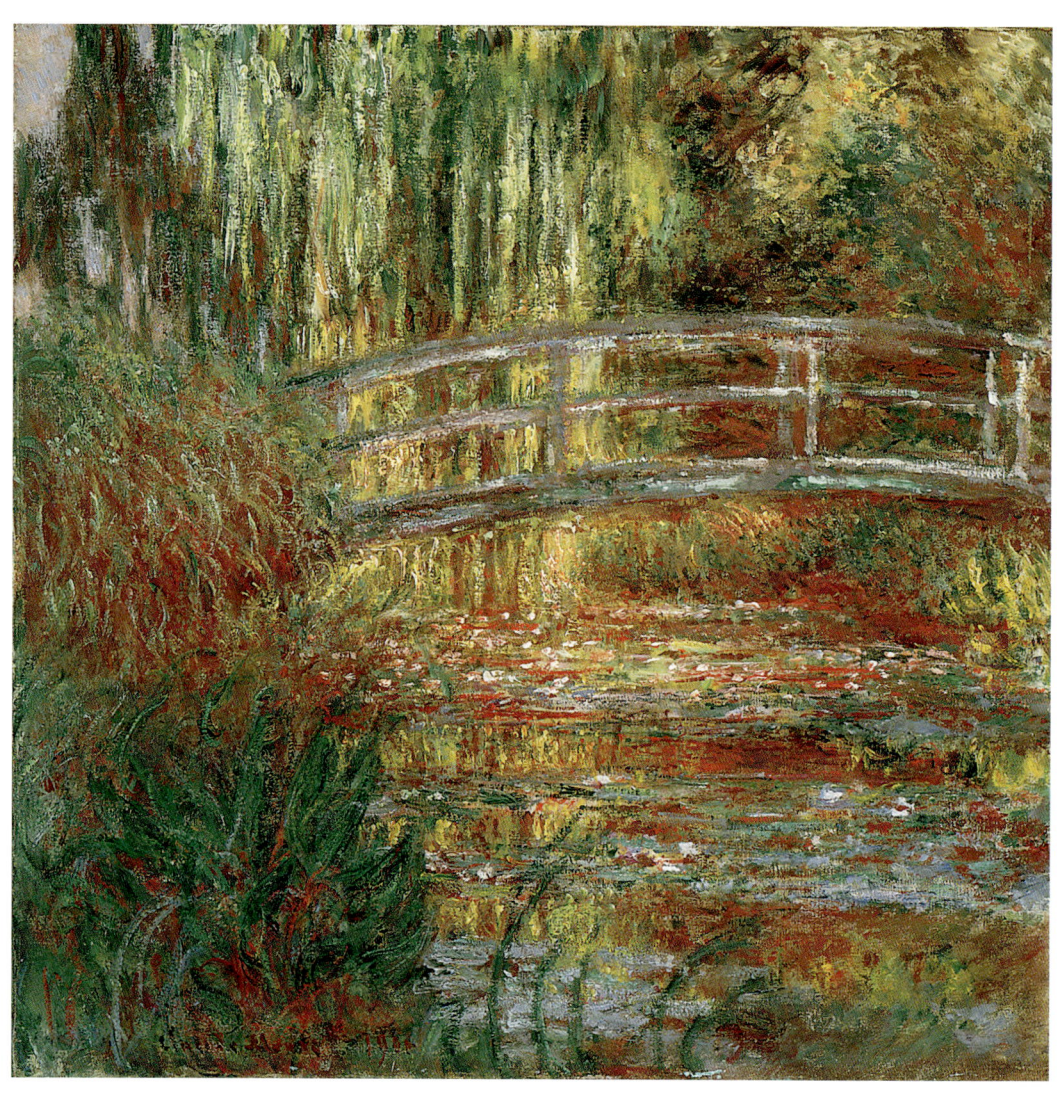

The Water-Lily Pond, 1900
Oil on canvas, 90.2 x 92.7 cm (35½ x 36½ in.)
Boston, Museum of Fine Arts,
Given in memory of Governor Alvan T. Fuller
by the Fuller Foundation

OPPOSITE
Irises, 1914–17
Oil on canvas, 199.4 x 150.5 cm (78½ x 59¼ in.)
Richmond, Virginia Museum of Fine Arts,
The Adolph D. and Wilkins C. Williams Fund

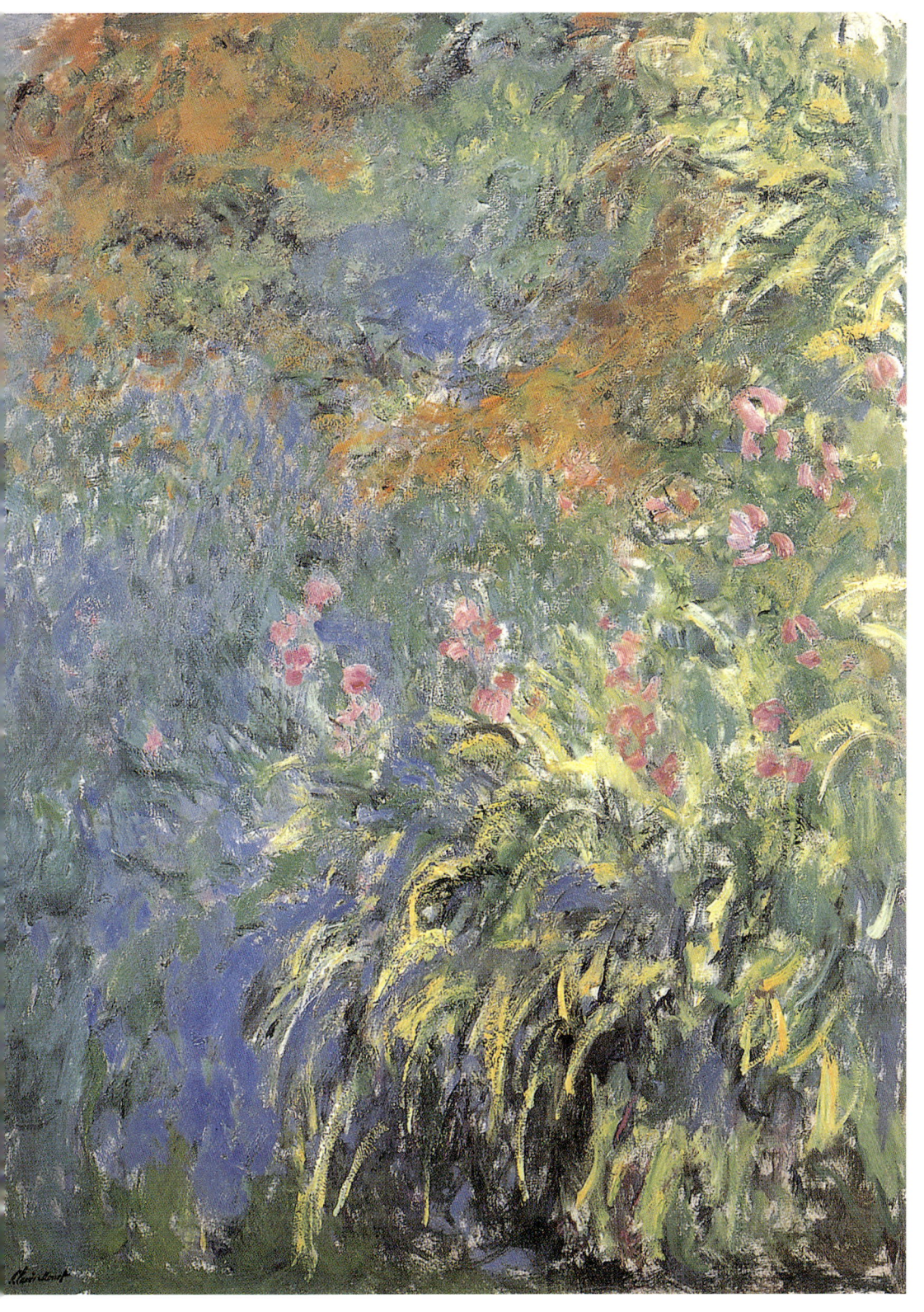

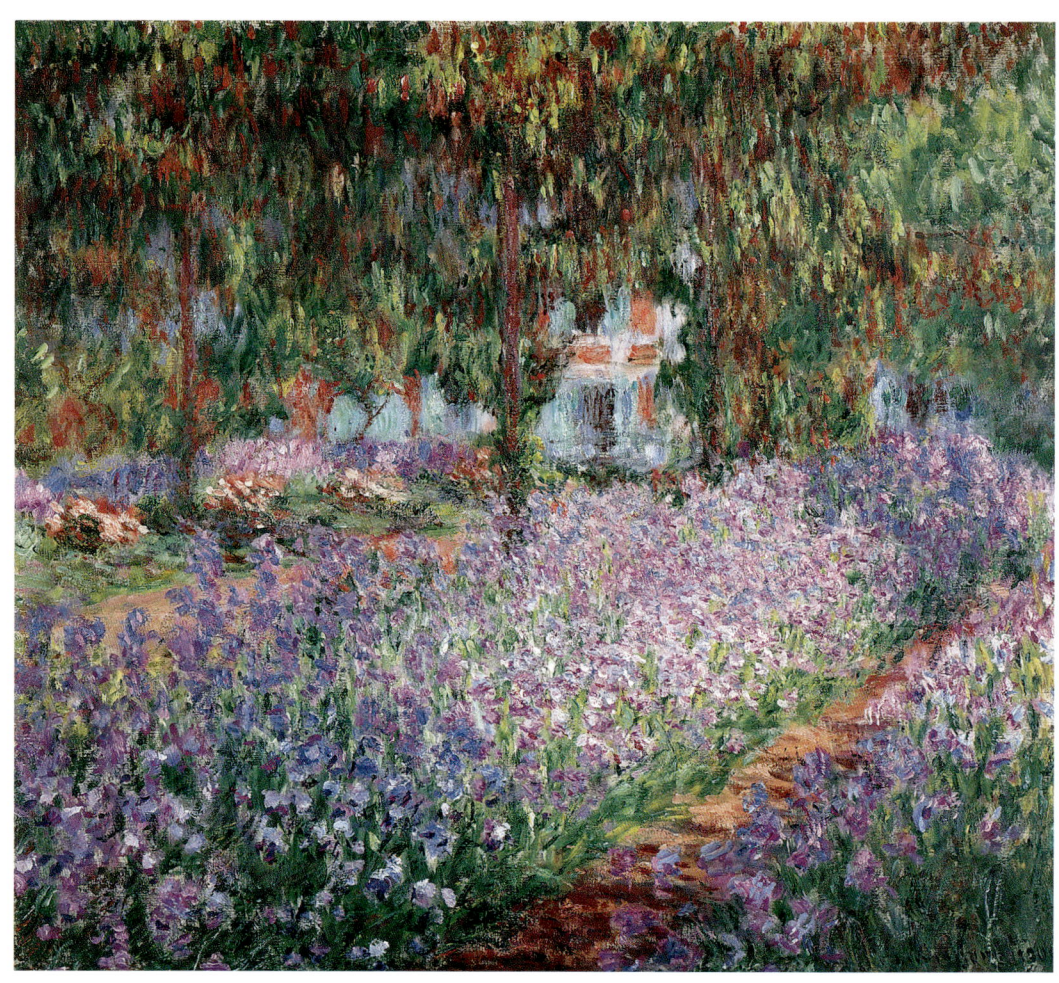

" *[...] Say, my dream, what shall I do?*
With a look to embrace the chaste absence of this vast solitude and, as one plucks
an enchantingly closed waterlily to remind one of a place, one of the waterlilies
that are suddenly there and whose deep whiteness includes the nothingness of an
untouched dream, a happiness that will never be, only to go on, holding one's
breath in awe of the apparition: to row on, very slowly, in silence, not breaking the
spell by dipping the oars, nor with the sound of splashing washing the shimmering
semblance of my theft of an ideal flower, visible in the rising bubbles as I flee,
before footfalls approaching unexpectedly [...]"

STÉPHANE MALLARMÉ, "LE NÉNUPHAR BLANC", 1885

Irises in Monet's Garden, 1900
Oil on canvas, 81.6 x 92.6 cm (32¼ x 36½ in.)
Paris, Musée d'Orsay

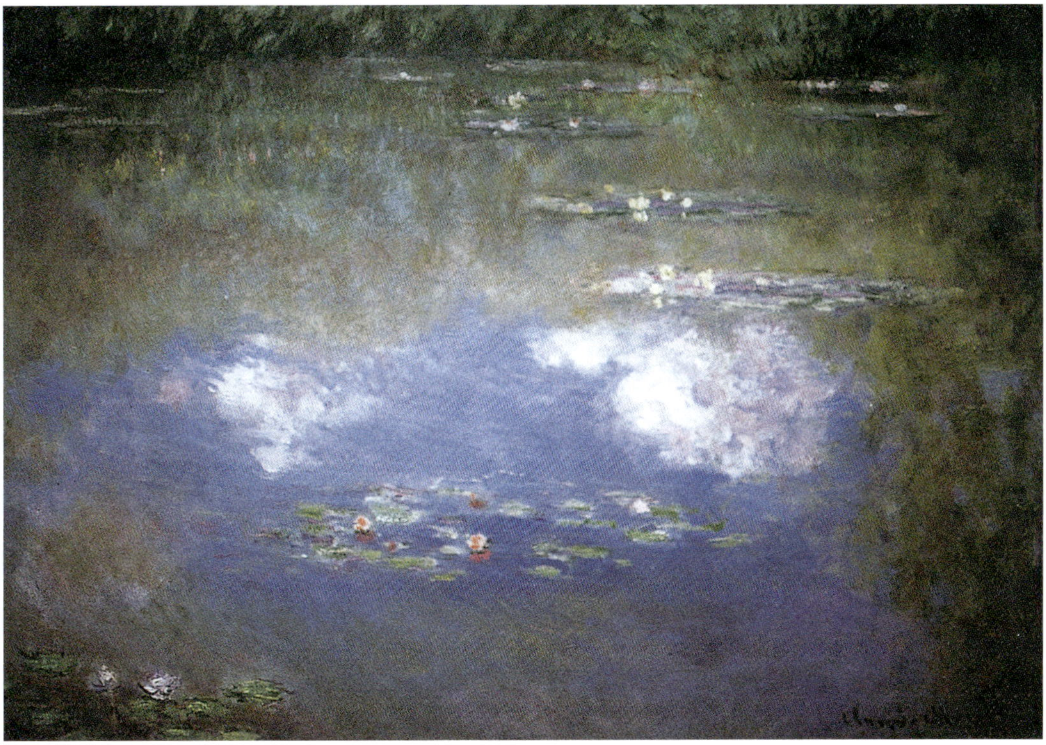

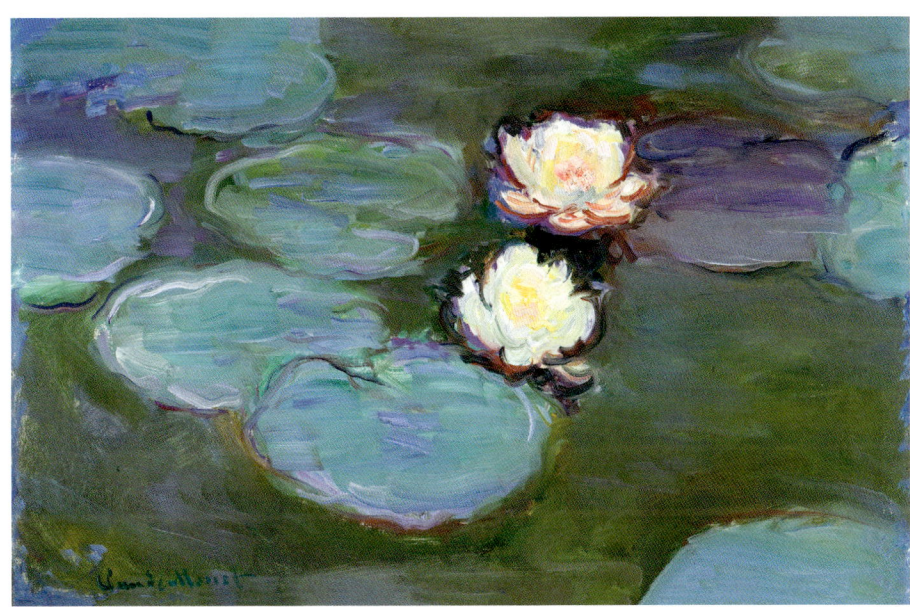

Water-Lily Pond (The Clouds), 1903
Oil on canvas, 74 x 106.5 cm (29¼ x 42 in.)
Private collection

Water-Lilies, 1897–99
Oil on canvas, 65 x 100 cm (25⅝ x 39⅜ in.)
Los Angeles County Museum of Art

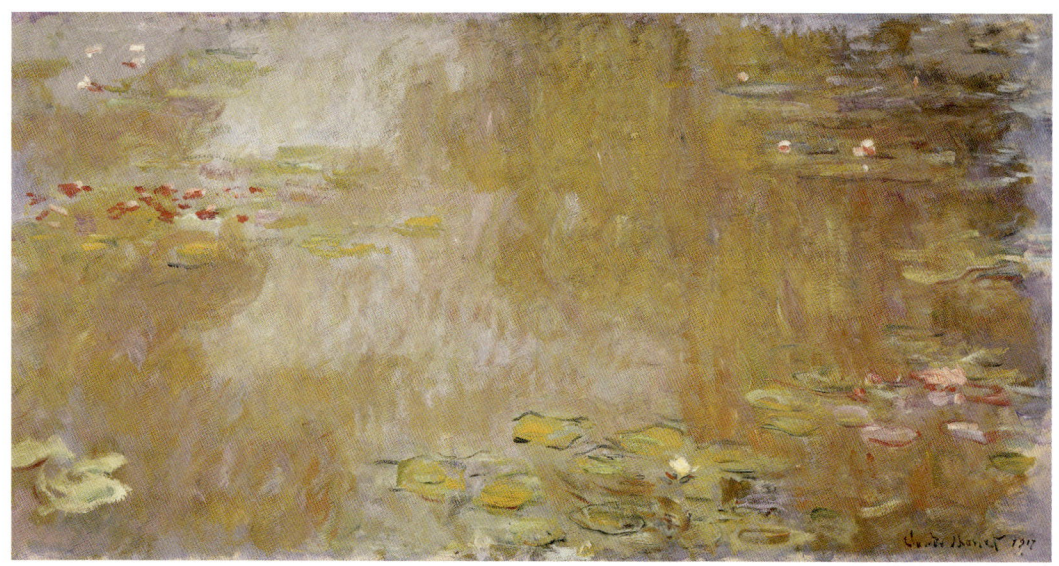

The Water-Lily Pond, 1917
Oil on canvas, 100 x 200 cm (39⅜ x 78¾ in.)
Musée des Beaux-Arts de Nantes

Monet expressly wanted an early lunch in order not to miss any of the afternoon sunlight. Tea would then be taken in the garden, and in the evening a dinner hardly to be described as frugal. The Monets rarely gave dinner parties, though, since the artist liked to turn in early, in order to be up at dawn the next day. The redoubtable Alice saw to it that Monet's work did not suffer under the bustle of the household.

Monet would sit out under his immense white umbrella (ill. p. 181), surrounded by as many as twelve canvases begun at different times of day and in various conditions of weather and light. His stepdaughter Blanche painted at his side from an early date, and after the death of Alice she became his constant companion. Silent and often grumpy, concentrating on his work, Monet would sit at his canvases, periods of great productivity alternating with times of deep depression.

Unlike the villages where Monet had previously lived, Giverny was not on the Seine, but it did have a small river, the Epte, and a number of streams; so Monet's beloved water was flowing all about him. Following his afternoons on the river at Argenteuil and his days facing the sea spray at Étretat, Monet was now in thrall to water in a different form: the pool. In the early 1890s he bought a field below the house, some 7,500 square metres in size and separated from his property by the railway tracks, and this he converted into a water garden with the aid of a little watercourse that ran through it. He was later to employ a gardener solely to look after the pool and the water-lilies that grew on it, while five more gardeners tended the rest of the grounds. In 1895 he had an arched wooden bridge built, of the kind seen on Japanese prints (ills. pp. 180 and 188). It was his peaceful realm, a place of meditation, hot in the sun, with dragonflies flitting about and frogs plopping into the water if they were disturbed where they rested amid the reeds.

The pool – with eelgrass and algae growing in it, irises, reeds and weeping willows along the margins, and on the surface the floating pads of water-lilies glimmering like mother-of-pearl in the sun – was to provide Monet's main subject matter for his last thirty years. Yet again he was palpably concerned to approach his subject closer and closer, till in the huge water-lily pictures of his final years he seemed to be immersed in it. From large-scale landscape composition, Monet moved on via views of the pool and the Japanese bridge to close-up sectional views of the surface of the water.

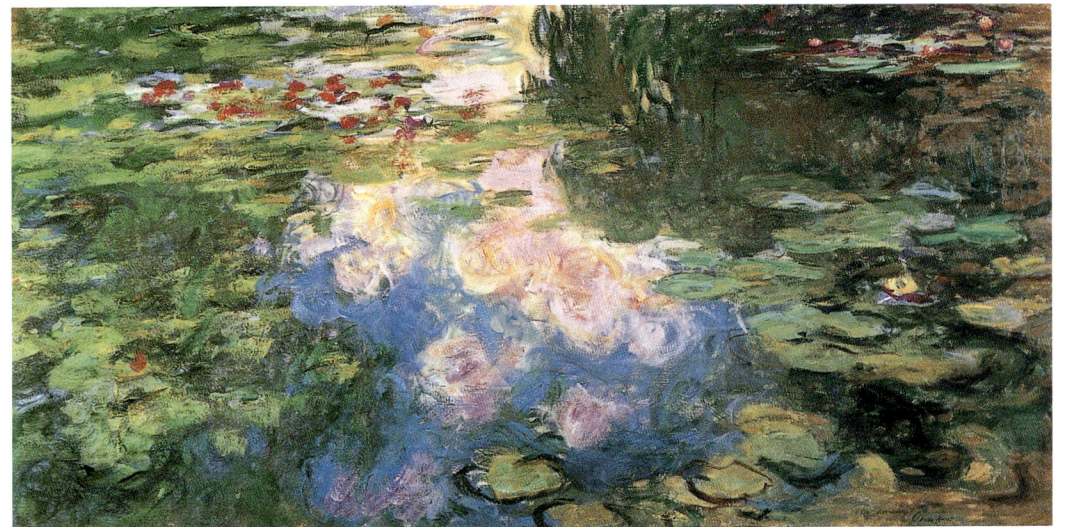

The Water-Lily Pond, 1919
Oil on canvas, 100 x 200 cm (39⅜ x 78¾ in.)
Private collection

The sky was only a reflection now (ill. p. 191 top), and no longer appeared at the top of Monet's paintings. His water pictures were landscapes shorn of horizons. However small the section viewed, it might still include the countryside, trees, the sky, or clouds – but of course these were not landscape paintings in the usual sense; Monet himself called them reflected landscapes.

Monet frequently insisted that his studio was the open air, but the fact was nevertheless that most of his paintings were completed or reworked in the studio. There were indeed times when he maintained three studios at Giverny, where he would receive visitors and talk about his work. His pool pictures too were not painted exclusively outdoors under his umbrella; but the difference between these and his paintings of the Thames or St Mark's Square, on which he worked for years in the studio only, was that he could easily refresh his impression of his subject and the light by strolling down to the pool and taking it in anew.

In his water-lily pool paintings, Monet went further than anywhere else in his art towards replacing representation with surface pattern or abstraction. The broad water-lily pads afforded Monet a means of establishing horizontals in his paintings, while the reflections of willows and reeds in particular provided vertical structuring. If these essentially geometrical and balanced patterns are neither monotonous nor lifeless, it is because the decorative lily pads and flowers are irregular in shape, and also, once again, because of Monet's use of colour. With unparalleled skill and subtlety he catches a thousand vibrant nuances of colour, assembling them into a mosaic of light. His dabs and strokes break and disassemble colours to infinity, juxtaposing and overlaying them. The first layers are extremely thin, almost transparent; yet they gleam through the superimposed, more forceful brushwork and impasto layers.

Monet's brushwork underwent constant change. The vibrant, abbreviated strokes and dabs and flickering light of the earliest series (ill. p. 191 bottom), transparent yet still with the quality of a tapestry, was steadily replaced by a more fluid style. It was as if Monet's broad, chalky stroke were itself becoming an alga or waterplant. His brushstrokes no longer ran horizontally or vertically, but coiled like mysterious tendrils, and began to dance. It was this freedom and daring in Monet's technique, together with the distance his colours moved from faithful representation, and his audacious use of outsize formats, that made his water-lily paintings so very important for future artists. The Abstract Expressionists of the 1950s – such as Sam Francis, Jackson Pollock or Mark Rothko – were fascinated by Monet's use of colour. The format of his water-lily decorative panels seems to have anticipated that of Pollock's *All-overs*. But whereas the Abstract Expressionists were after an autonomous art of pure form and colour, even the most visionary of Monet's pictures originated in a visual impression of something actually seen – in a word, in nature.

Immersion in an unending picture seen not only in front of the beholder but all around, as with Monet's water-lily decorative panels, was a particular aim of these painters. Monet himself had been pondering the use of several large-scale water-lily paintings to create a spatial environment ever since the closing years of the 19th century. In accordance with contemporary taste, and surely also with his own, he thought first of decorative panels for a dining room. Later, when Monet had fallen into a profound lethargy following the deaths of his wife Alice and his son Jean, Clemenceau tried to help his friend by proposing he paint a water-lily series for the French nation. A new studio was even built for the project, 24 metres by 12, to accommodate work on a vast scale. Building it was no easy undertaking during the First World War, and Monet only managed to obtain the materials and manpower thanks to his friends in high places.

Water-Lily Pond, Evening
(diptych), 1914/22
Oil on canvas, 200 x 600 cm
(78¾ x 236¼ in.) each
Zurich, Kunsthaus Zürich

To describe these paintings as decorative may seem now, as it did then, to partake of the dismissive. The adjective was used of Monet's work at a relatively early date, to account for a type of art that was neither narrative, historical nor topographical in character. The late water-lily series are the most radical expression of Monet's decorative art. Pure observations of

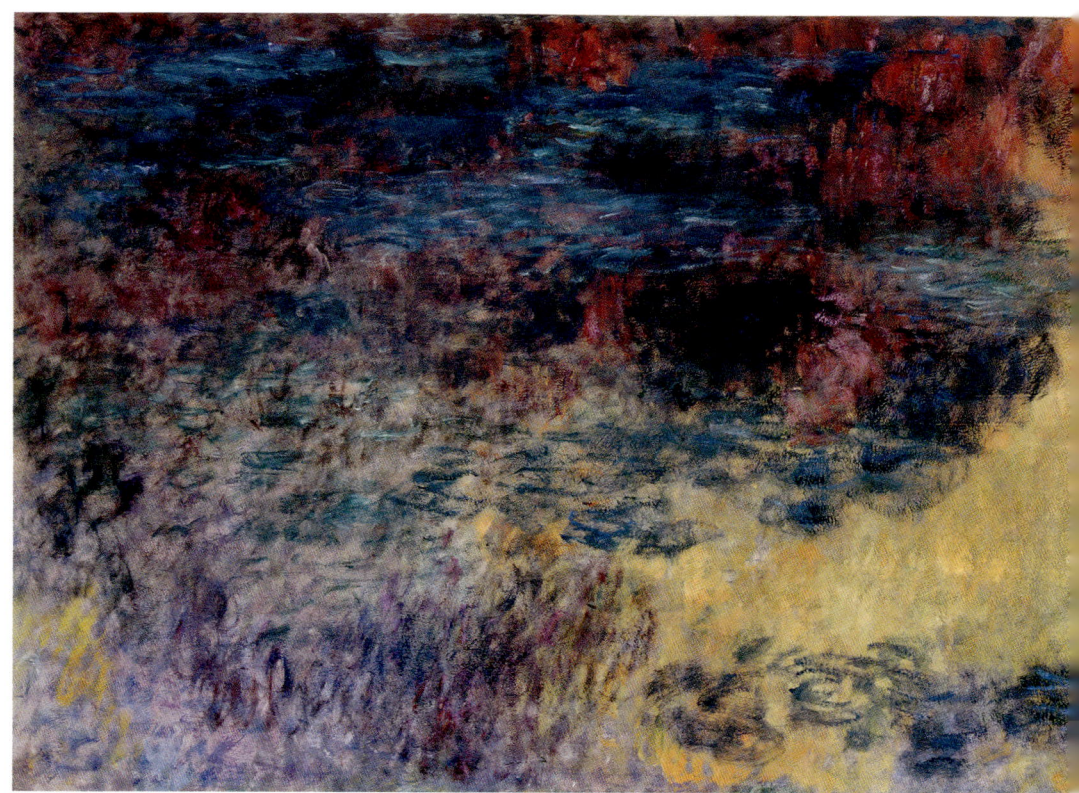

light and colour, they cannot be taken as symbolic either, even though they may constantly invite us to interpret them symbolically. The fact is that Monet's water-lily decorative paintings are indeed self-referential, but they still represent a given reality, and in so doing cannot be termed abstract.

When Monet's series of grainstacks or of Rouen Cathedral were exhibited, friends and critics pointed out time and again that they were conceived as unities, and regretted that trade imperatives would disperse the series throughout the world. For this very reason, Clemenceau had tried in the closing years of the 19th century to secure the cathedral series in its entirety for the French state, only to be thwarted by the official buying commission. In 1918, when Monet proposed giving two large water-lily paintings to the nation to mark the Armistice, Clemenceau and Geffroy succeeded in persuading him that the moment had now come to realize the project of a large-scale ensemble of decorative water-lily paintings.

Monet had long been thinking of presenting the water-lilies in such a way as to create the illusion of an infinite in a room where the beholder could relax and meditate. He agreed to give the nation a number of paintings on condition that they were hung in a new purpose-built space designed to his own specifications. A suitable location was chosen in the grounds of the Hôtel Biron, where a museum devoted to the sculptor Rodin had recently been established. An architect drew up plans for a pavilion on the edge of the grounds, a circular building by no means gigantic that could hold a dozen panels; but the department of public buildings rejected the proposal, plainly feeling that if Monet had a specially built pavilion for his own paintings it would be bestowing too great an honour on him.

Monet threatened to retract his offer, and prospective buyers began to flock in from Japan and the USA, hoping to acquire the entire series for museums in their own countries. It was owing solely

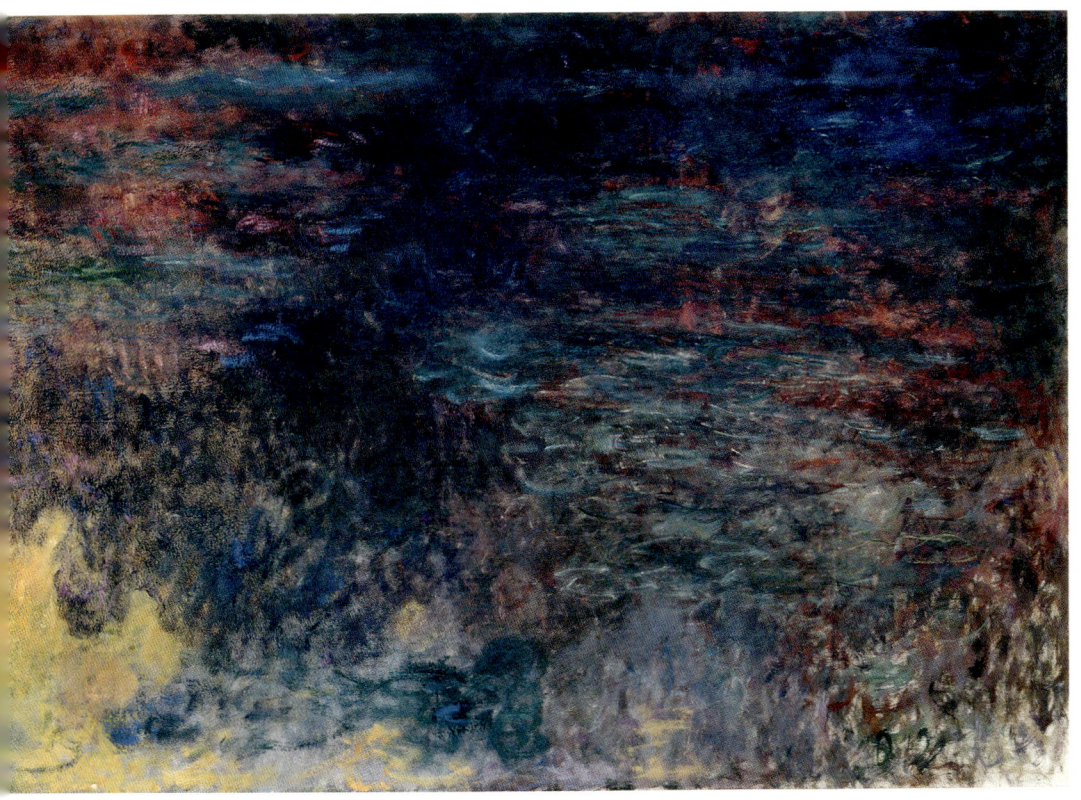

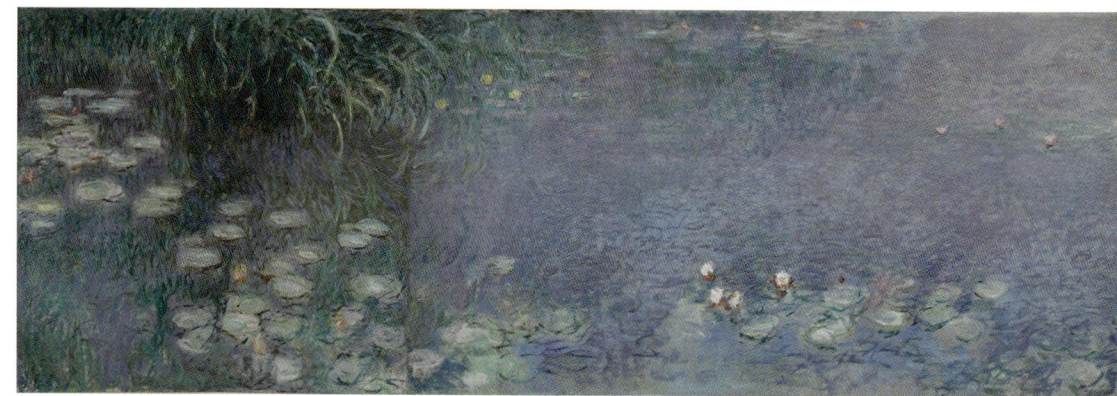

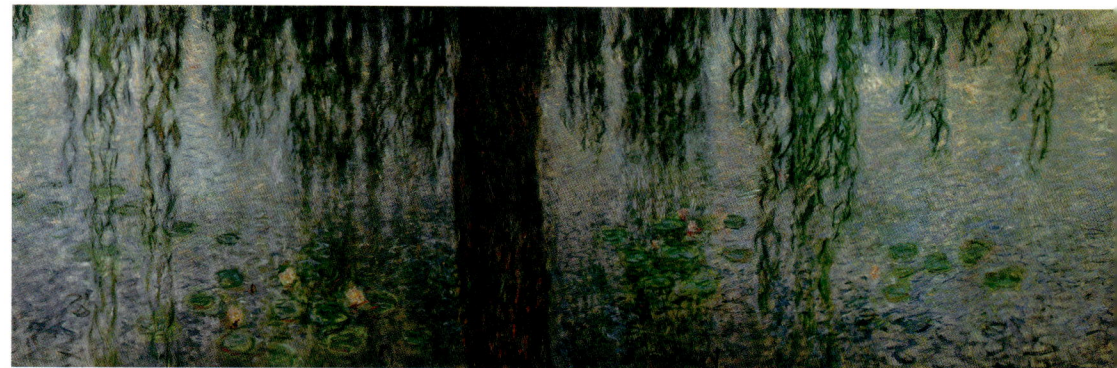

TOP
Water-Lilies, Morning (quadriptych), 1914–26
First of the Decorations Rooms in the Orangerie
Oil on canvas, 200 x 1275 cm (78¾ x 502 in.)
Paris, Musée de l'Orangerie

ABOVE
Water-Lily Pond, Morning with Willows (triptych), 1916–26
Oil on canvas, 200 x 425 cm (78¾ x 167¼ in.) each
Paris, Musée de l'Orangerie

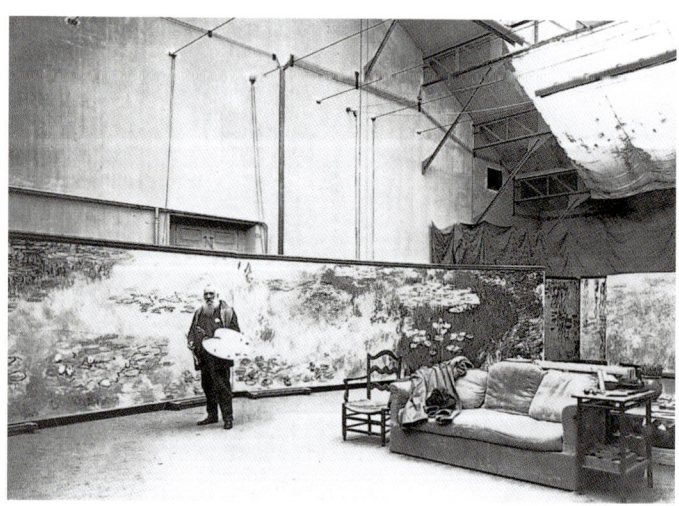

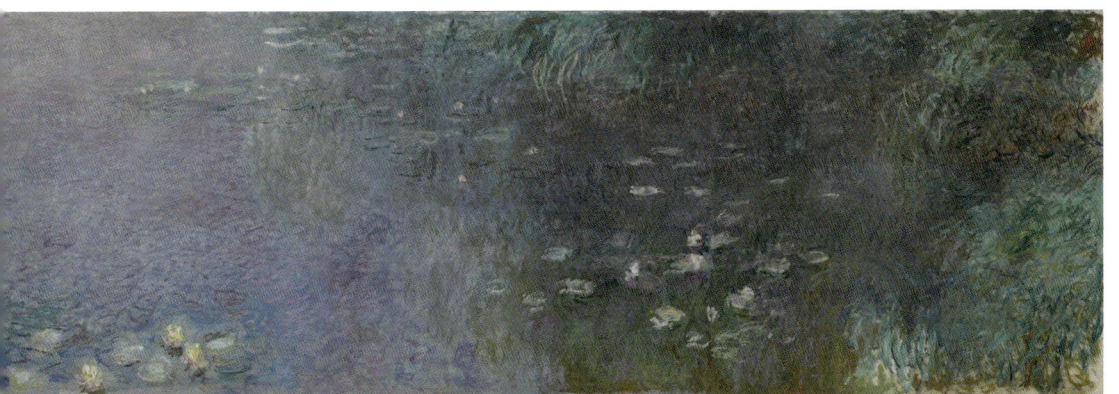

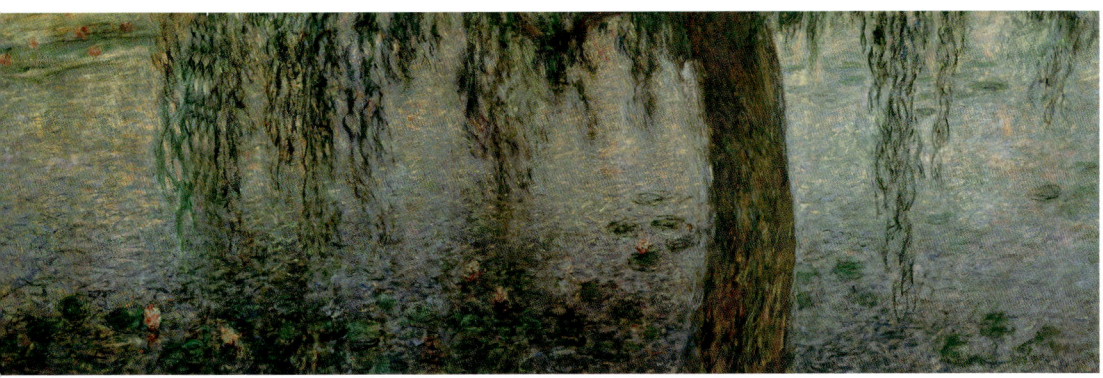

Monet in the Atelier des Grandes Décorations,
c. 1923

Room II of the Musée de l'Orangerie

The artist André Masson called the Orangerie
in Paris "the Sistine Chapel of Impressionism".
After Monet's death, the water-lily panels
he had gifted to the nation were put on public
display there.

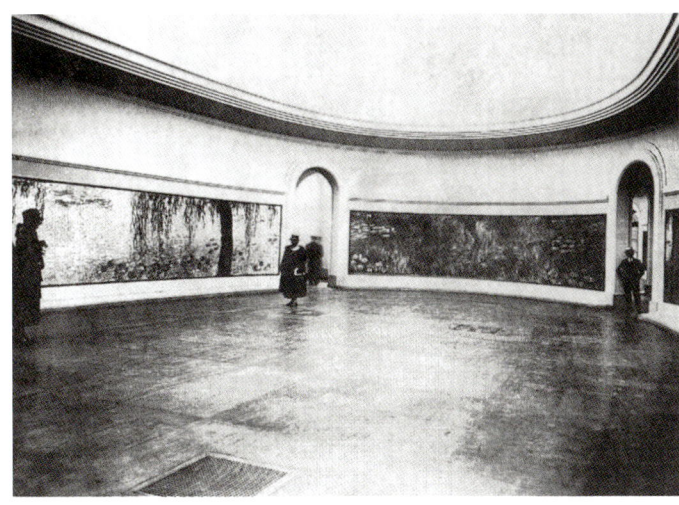

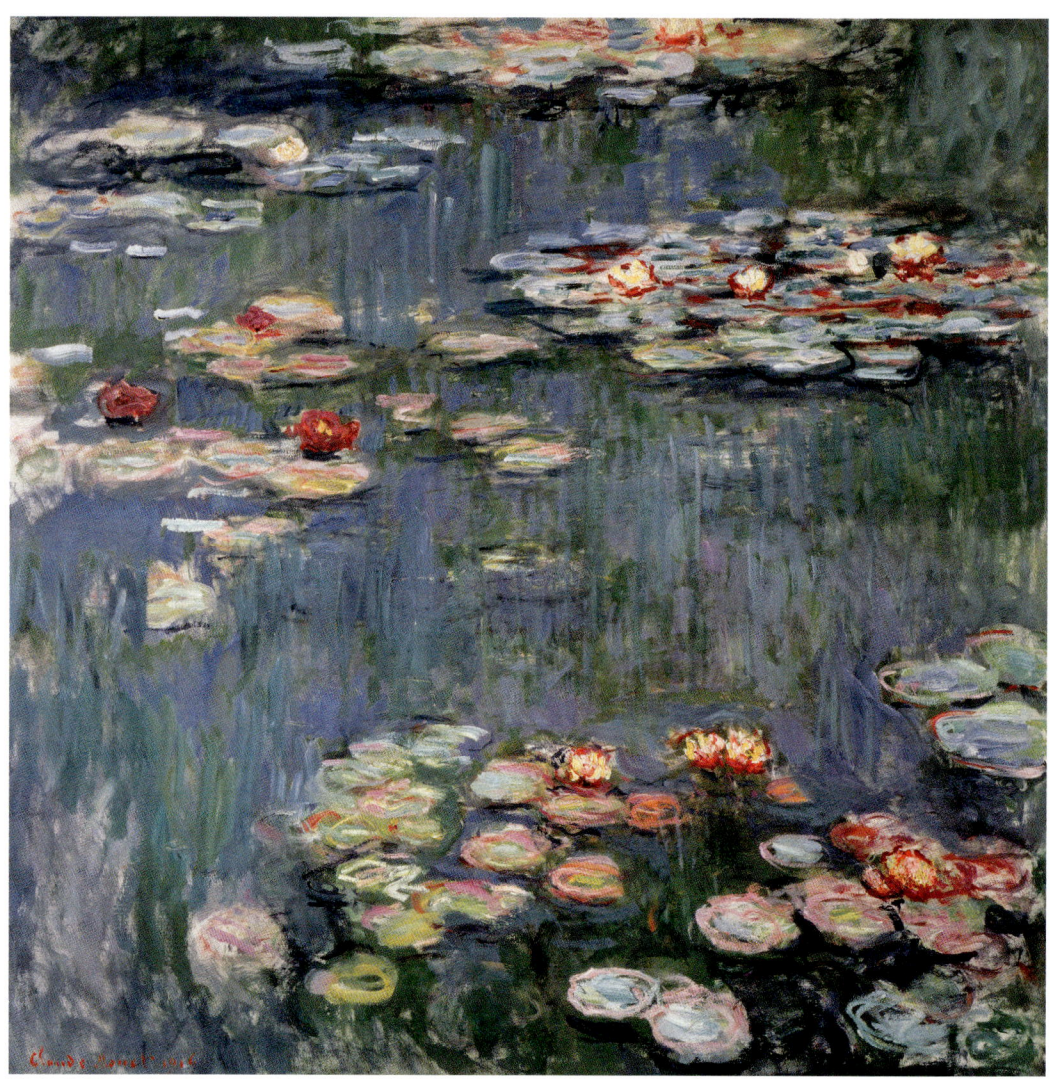

Water-Lilies, 1916
Oil on canvas, 200.5 x 201 cm (79 x 79¼ in.)
Tokyo, The National Museum of Western Art,
The Matsukata Collection

to Clemenceau, who felt the decorative project was "his", that Monet did finally agree to have the water-lily paintings hung in the Louvre's Orangerie. They were installed there in two oval rooms – though not, in the event, till after the artist's death. The Orangerie now attracts large numbers of visitors; but for many years Monet's paintings there were largely ignored, and it was not until the 1950s that the decorative water-lilies were discovered by painters such as Sam Francis. Only in the aftermath of Abstract Expressionism was the late Monet properly understood and valued.

Monet's last years were a time of prolific industry, and far from taking it easy in his old age, or working quietly on the artistic fruits of a long life, he made greater demands of himself than ever. Fear of producing mediocre work led him to burn and destroy many a picture. He had seen the dealers removing everything of Manet's after his fellow artist's death, and was determined to prevent sketches and unfinished work of dubious value from reaching the market.

From 1908 there were increasing indications that Monet's sight was failing, and in due course an ophthalmologist diagnosed cataracts. After lengthy hesitation, Monet underwent two operations, which restored his sight. In 1919 Renoir died, the last of Monet's old fellow-Impressionists, leaving the old man alone by the poolside.

Monet was not a religious man; his views were thoroughly positivist. He was a materialist of light. If it had been otherwise, the critics of his final paintings would doubtless long since have been quoting Dante's *Purgatorio,* claiming the Japanese bridge led to purgatory, and so forth. For it was not Monet's lifelong love of water (in which he wanted his mortal remains disposed of) that dominated his last works, but fire: his pool was in flames. Monet's long life as an artist closed with pictures of powerful energy, pictures that bespoke an unbroken and tenacious vitality in the painter.

Monet had helped break the stranglehold that academic eclecticism had had on art in his youth; Monet had taught fellow artists and the general public alike to use their eyes again; Monet was the Prometheus who set modern art ablaze from the sparks of *plein air* painting; and now it was as if Monet were determined to press Modernism to the ultimate in his own final works. The bright burning strength that was Monet's in all his art and life was extinguished abruptly. On 5 December 1926, he died at the age of eighty-six.

The Japanese Bridge, 1923–25
Oil on canvas, 89 x 116 cm (35 x 45¾ in.)
The Minneapolis Institute of Arts

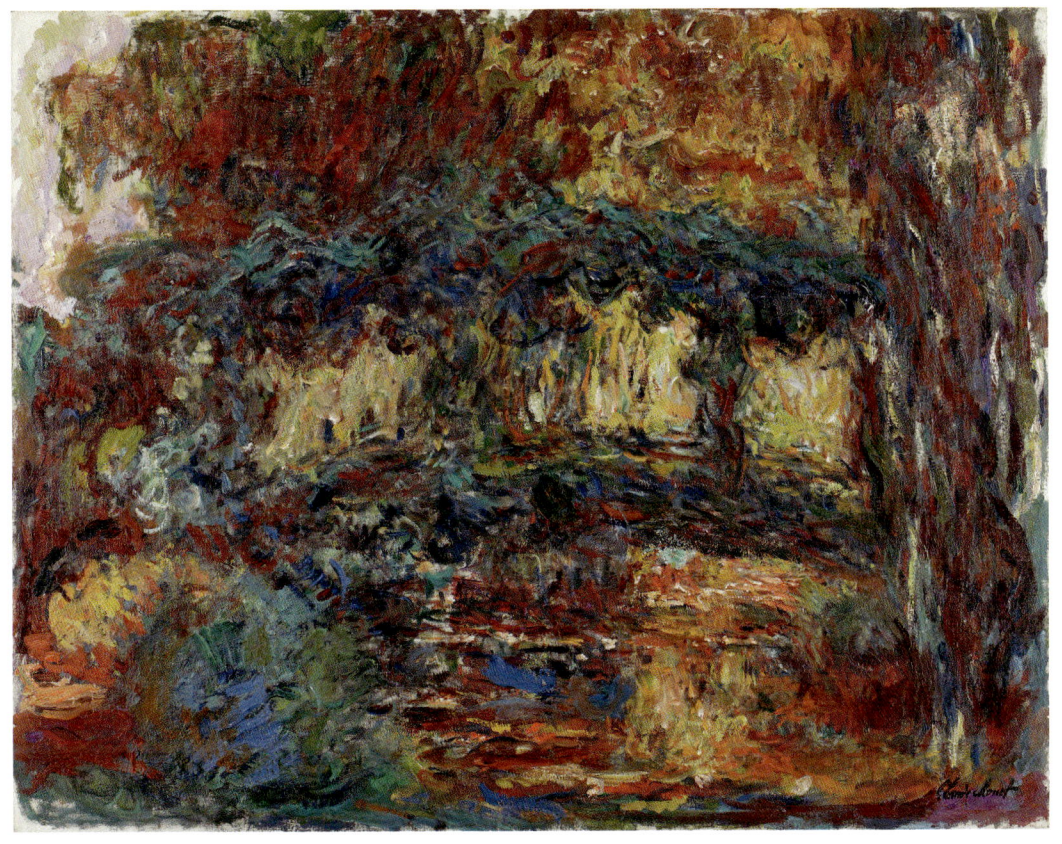

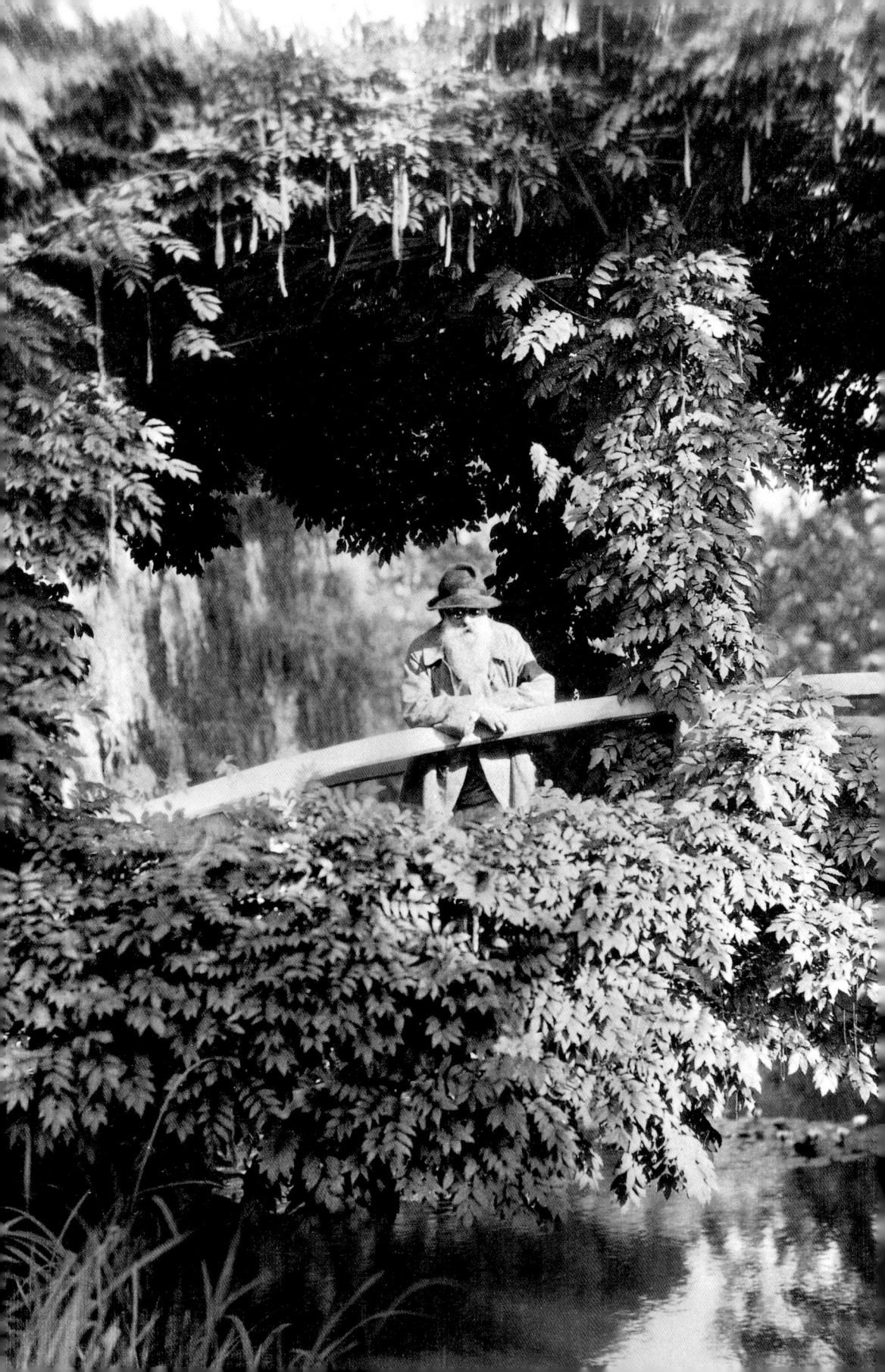

Claude Monet 1840–1926
Life and Work

1840 Claude Oscar Monet is born at 45, Rue Lafitte, Paris, on 14 November, the second son of a shopkeeper.

1845 Business is poor, and the family move to Le Havre, where Monet's father enters his brother-in-law Lecadre's business.

c. **1855** Monet's talent for drawing is apparent in caricatures of teachers and others.

1858 Meets the landscape artist Eugène Boudin (1824–1898) and paints in the open air with him.

1859 Monet goes to Paris to study art. He visits the Salon, and works at the Académie Suisse, where he meets Camille Pissarro (1830–1903).

1860 Monet is called up, and elects to serve with the Chasseurs d'Afrique in Algeria, but is discharged on grounds of ill health the following year.

OPPOSITE
Claude Monet on the Japanese bridge, 1925
Paris, Archives Musée Clemenceau

ABOVE RIGHT
Claude Monet at the age of twenty

1862 On holiday in Normandy he meets Johan Barthold Jongkind (1819–1891). Once Monet's health is restored, his family buys him out of the army, and in November he returns to Paris and enters the studio of artist Charles Gleyre (1806–1874). There he meets Pierre-Auguste Renoir (1841–1919), Alfred Sisley (1839–1899) and Frédéric Bazille (1841–1870).

1863 Monet and his new friends paint in the Forest of Fontaine-bleau. At the end of the year, all four leave Gleyre's studio.

1865 The Salon accepts two Monet marine paintings. He plans an immense *Luncheon on the Grass* (ill. p. 115) for the next Salon and starts work on it in the Forest of Fontainebleau immediately.

1866 *Woman in a Green Dress* (ill. p. 119) is exhibited at the Salon and well received. Monet spends summer and autumn with his family at Sainte-Adresse and Honfleur.

1867 Again he summers with his parents, while Camille gives birth to their first son Jean in Paris. Back in Paris, Bazille shares his studio with Monet and buys *Women in the Garden,* (ill. p. 120) which the Salon has turned down, by instalments.

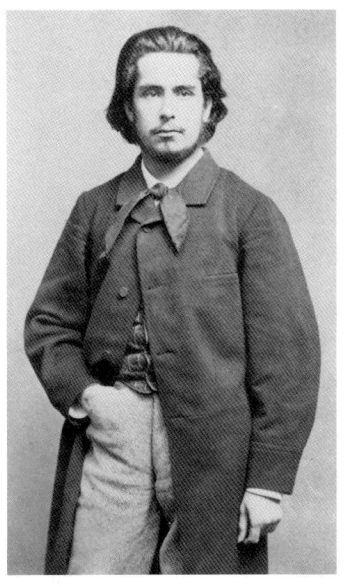

1868 Works at Étretat and Fécamp. Gaudibert, a ship owner, helps Monet through financial difficulties from 1864 on, and now gives him commissions and redeems pawned pictures.

1870 Again rejected by the Salon. 26 June: marries Camille Doncieux. On the outbreak of the Franco-Prussian War a month later, Monet moves to London, where the news of Bazille's death reaches him in November. He meets art dealer Paul Durand-Ruel (1831–1922).

1871 17 January: Monet's father dies, leaving a modest legacy. In the autumn, Monet returns to France via Holland, and rents a house and garden at Argenteuil.

1872 Durand-Ruel buys a large selection of paintings. Monet creates his studio boat and paints the banks of the Seine. At Le Havre he paints *Impression, Sunrise* (ill. pp. 134/135). Second visit to Holland.

1873 Works quietly at Argenteuil, where he meets Gustave Caillebotte (1848–1894). The Société anonyme des artistes peintres, sculpteurs et graveurs is founded to put on group shows. The members include the core Impressionists.

1874 The first group exhibition is held in the rooms of Nadar, the photographer, in Boulevard des Capucines, Paris. Leroy takes the title of *Impression, Sunrise* as a platform in an article deriding artists who merely presented impressions rather than finished artworks. The show is a fiasco, and the Société anonyme is dissolved at the end of the year.

1875 In financial difficulty again, Monet moves to a smaller house.

1876 At the second Impressionist show in Durand-Ruel's gallery, Monet exhibits 18 paintings. He meets department-store director Ernest Hoschedé, who commissions panels for a room in his château, Rottembourg, near Montgeron. This year and the next, Monet paints the Gare Saint-Lazare (ill. p. 149).

1878 Birth of the Monets' second son, Michel, in Paris. In the summer, the family move to a small house at Vétheuil, where Alice Hoschedé and her six children join them. The money problems continue.

1879 Caillebotte funds the fourth group exhibition. Monet paints at Vétheuil and Lavacourt. 5 September: Camille dies at the age of 32.

1881 Durand-Ruel buys more paintings and assists Monet in his travels. In December Monet, Alice Hoschedé and their children move to Poissy.

1883 Monet's solo exhibition at Durand-Ruel's is well received but does not result in many sales. Durand-Ruel commissions decorative work for his Paris home. Monet rents the house at Giverny, and in December goes to the south of France with Renoir.

1884 January to April: Monet paints on the Riviera.

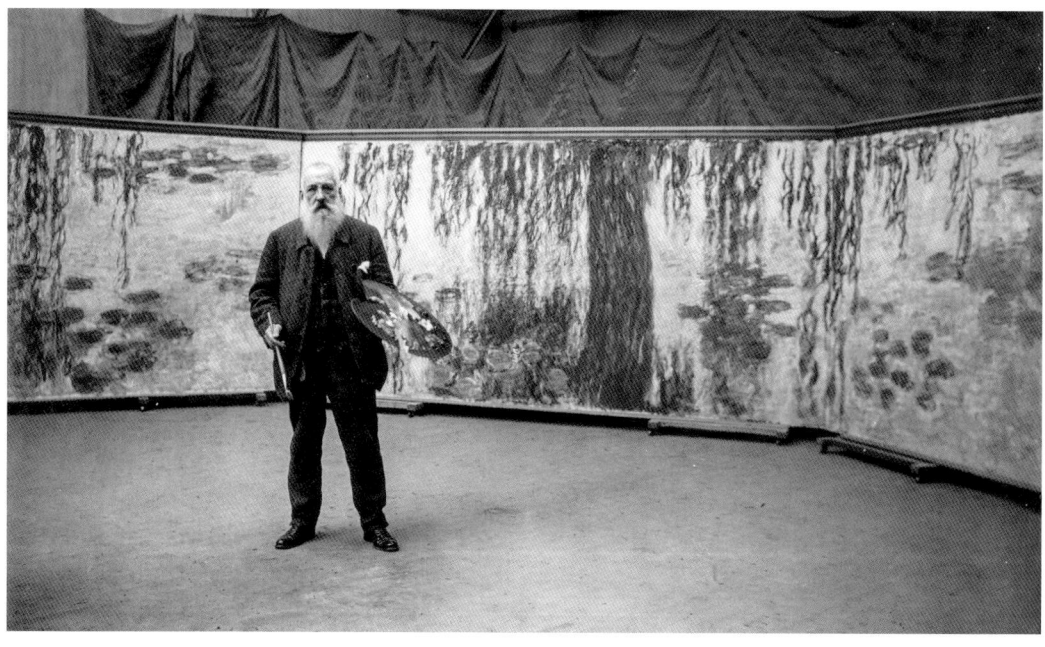

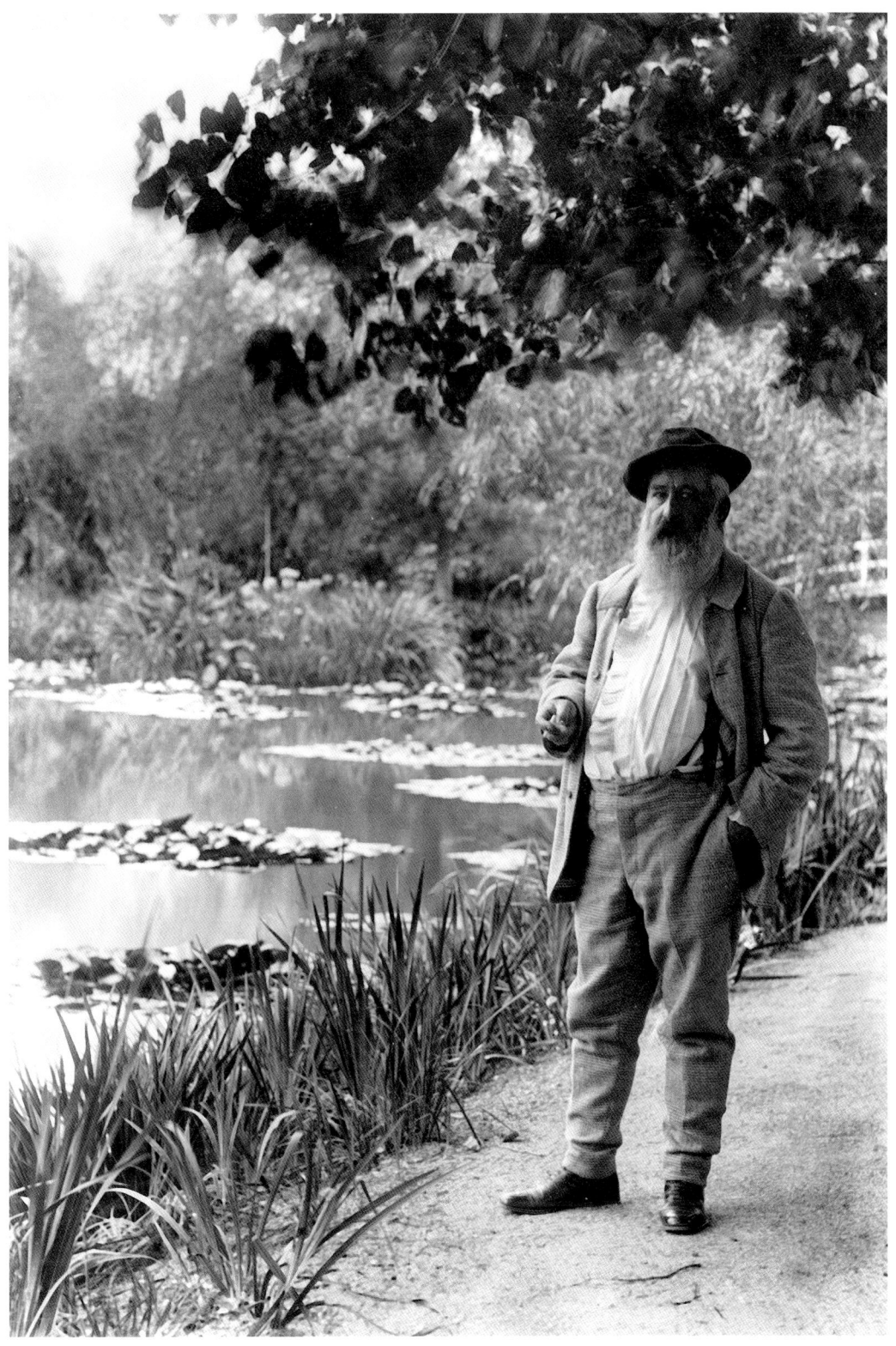

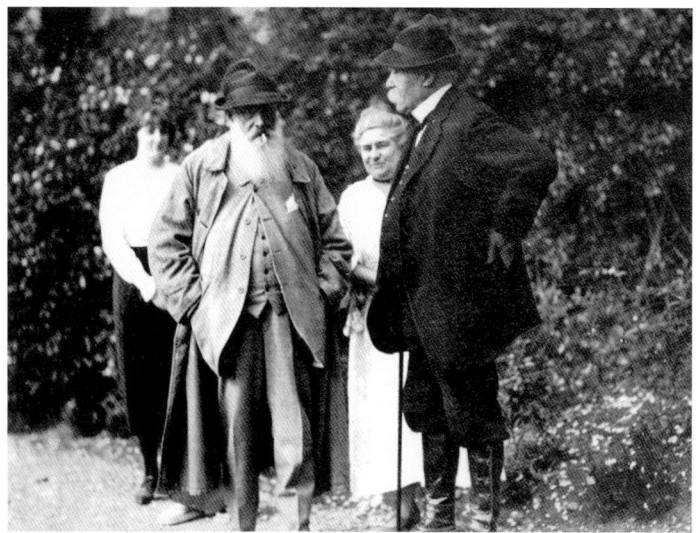

1886 Revisits Holland. In the autumn he paints at Étretat and in Brittany, where he meets his biographer-to-be, Gustave Geffroy (1855–1926).

1887 Durand-Ruel opens a New York gallery and exhibits Monet's works there. A Monet show at Georges Petit's in Paris, where he already exhibited in 1885, is a great success.

1888 From January to April: works on the Côte d'Azur and in summer revisits London. Back in France, he refuses the Cross of the Legion of Honour. Begins the *Grainstacks* series (ills. pp. 166 and 167).

1889 Georges Petit mounts a highly successful joint show of Monet and Auguste Rodin (1840–1917). Monet organizes a collection to buy Manet's *Olympia* from his widow, for the Louvre.

1890 Works on the *Grainstacks* and begins the *Poplars* series (ills. pp. 162 and 165). Buys the Giverny house where he has been living since 1883.

1891 The *Grainstacks* exhibition at Durand-Ruel's is a great success. December: painting in London.

1892 Spring: works on the Rouen Cathedral series. Ernest Hoschedé having died the previous year, Monet and Alice Hoschedé marry in July.

1895 Monet visits his stepson in Norway. In March, Durand-Ruel exhibits the Rouen Cathedral series (ills. pp. 168 and 169).

1896 Working in Normandy again, at Varengeville, Dieppe and Pourville. Begins his series *Morning by the Seine.*

1897 January to March: at Pourville. Builds a second studio at Giverny. In the summer, his son Jean marries stepsister Blanche Hoschedé. The second Venice Biennale includes 20 of Monet's paintings.

1899 Monet begins his water-lily series in the water gardens at Giverny. In the autumn he revisits London and paints views of the Thames again.

1900 Several visits to London. In the spring he works at Giverny, in the summer at Vétheuil.

1903 Studio work on the London pictures (till 1905). Death of Pissarro on 12 November.

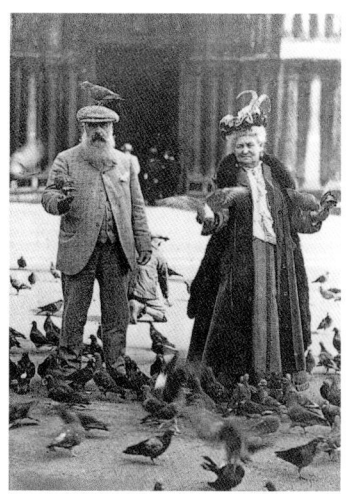

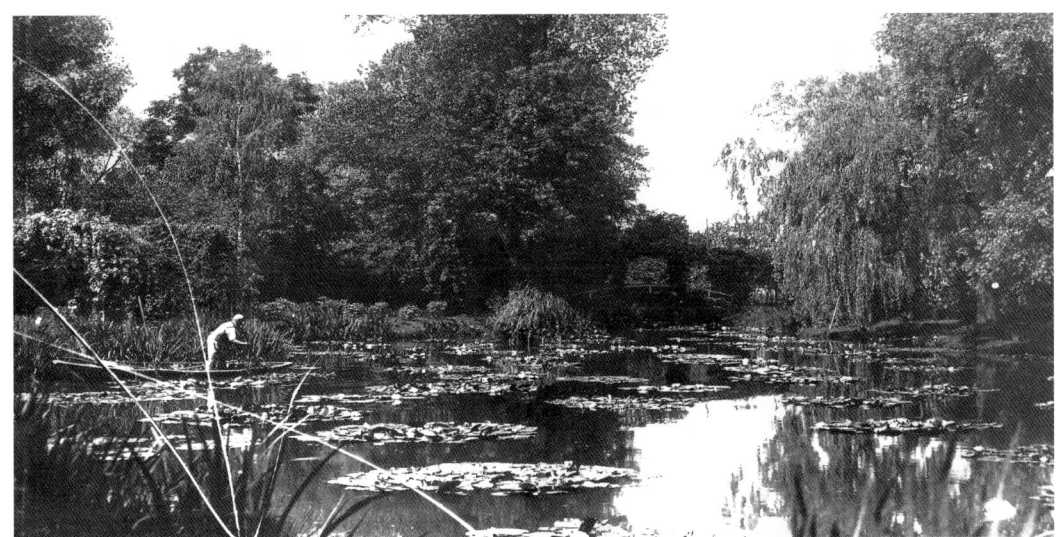

1904 In the autumn he drives to Madrid with Alice by automobile to study the Spanish masters such as Diego Velázquez.

1906 Monet continues work on his water-lily series but is dissatisfied and repeatedly postpones the exhibition due at Durand-Ruel's. Death of Cézanne on 22 October.

1908 First signs that his sight is failing. September to December in Venice with Alice.

1911 Alice Monet dies on 19 May.

1912 Gallery Bernheim-Jeune mounts a highly successful show of Monet's Venice work. His eyesight deteriorates, and an ophthalmologist diagnoses cataracts.

1914 Georges Clemenceau (1841–1929) and other friends suggest Monet give a water-lily series to the nation. Following his son Jean's death, Blanche, Jean's widow, takes over the running of the

Giverny household. 3 August: France declares war.

1915 Monet has a third studio built in order to work on the decorative water-lily project.

1918 On the occasion of the Armistice (11 November), Monet gives eight water-lily paintings to the nation.

1919 Death of Pierre-Auguste Renoir on 17 December, the last of Monet's old Paris friends.

1921 Major retrospective at Durand-Ruel's. Depressed and in despair at his failing sight, Monet plans to withdraw his gift.

1922 At the urging of Clemenceau, who has promoted the project from the outset, Monet signs the deed of gift.

1923 Monet undergoes two operations, which restore his sight, and returns to painting. Frequently depressed and downhearted, he

continues work on the great decorative water-lilies.

1926 5 December: Claude Monet dies at Giverny.

OPPOSITE TOP
Claude Monet and his daughter Blanche Hoschedé-Monet with Georges Clemenceau in Giverny, *c.* 1921

OPPOSITE BOTTOM
Monet and his wife Alice in St Mark's Square, Venice, 1908

TOP
The water-lily pool was the heart of Monet's life and work. Over the years it was enlarged, and more water-lilies added. A gardener was employed specially for the pool and the water-lilies. Inspired by Japanese prints, Monet had a small Japanese-style wooden bridge built in 1895, overhung with wistaria, and took it as a subject in numerous later paintings.

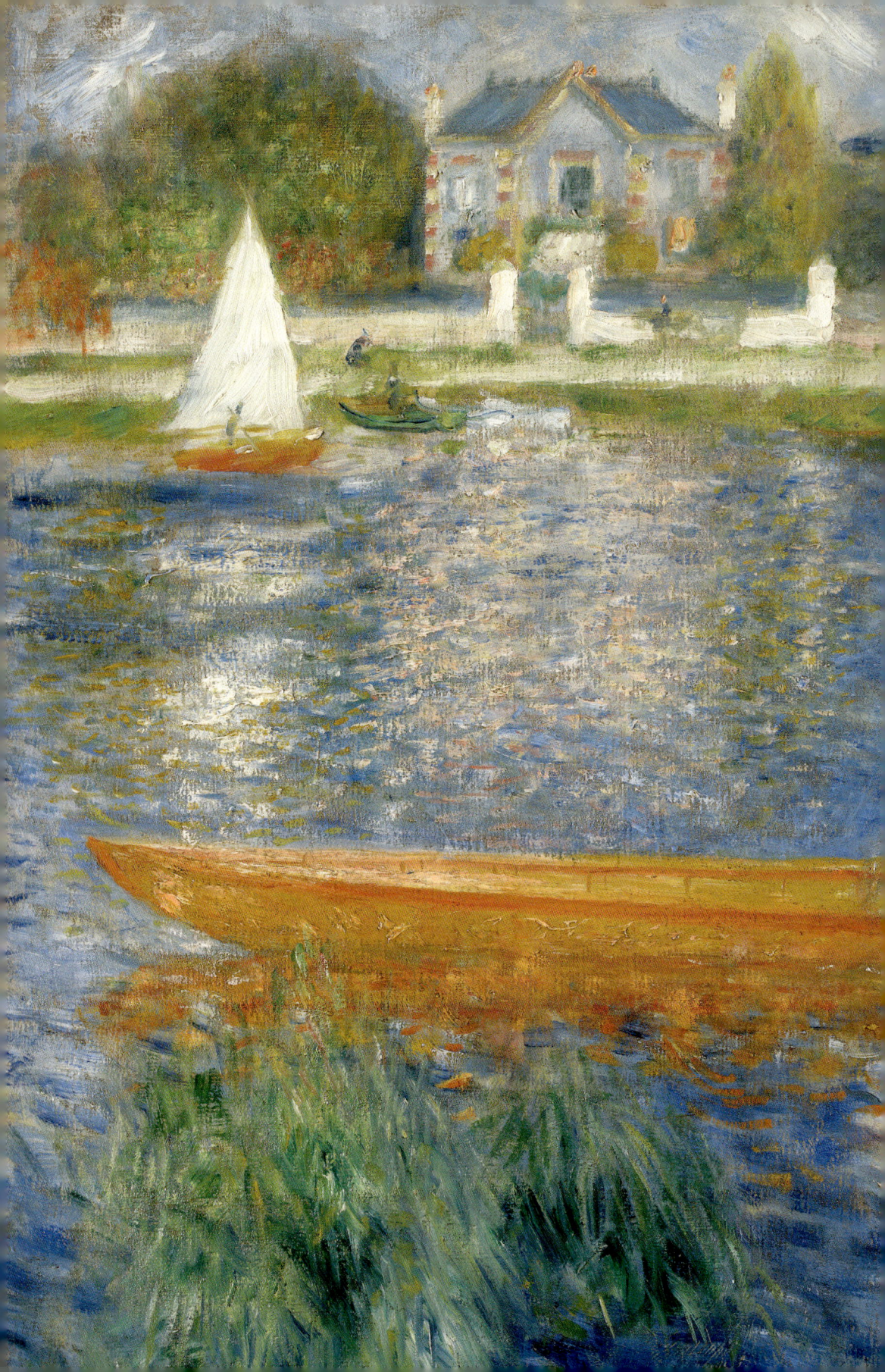

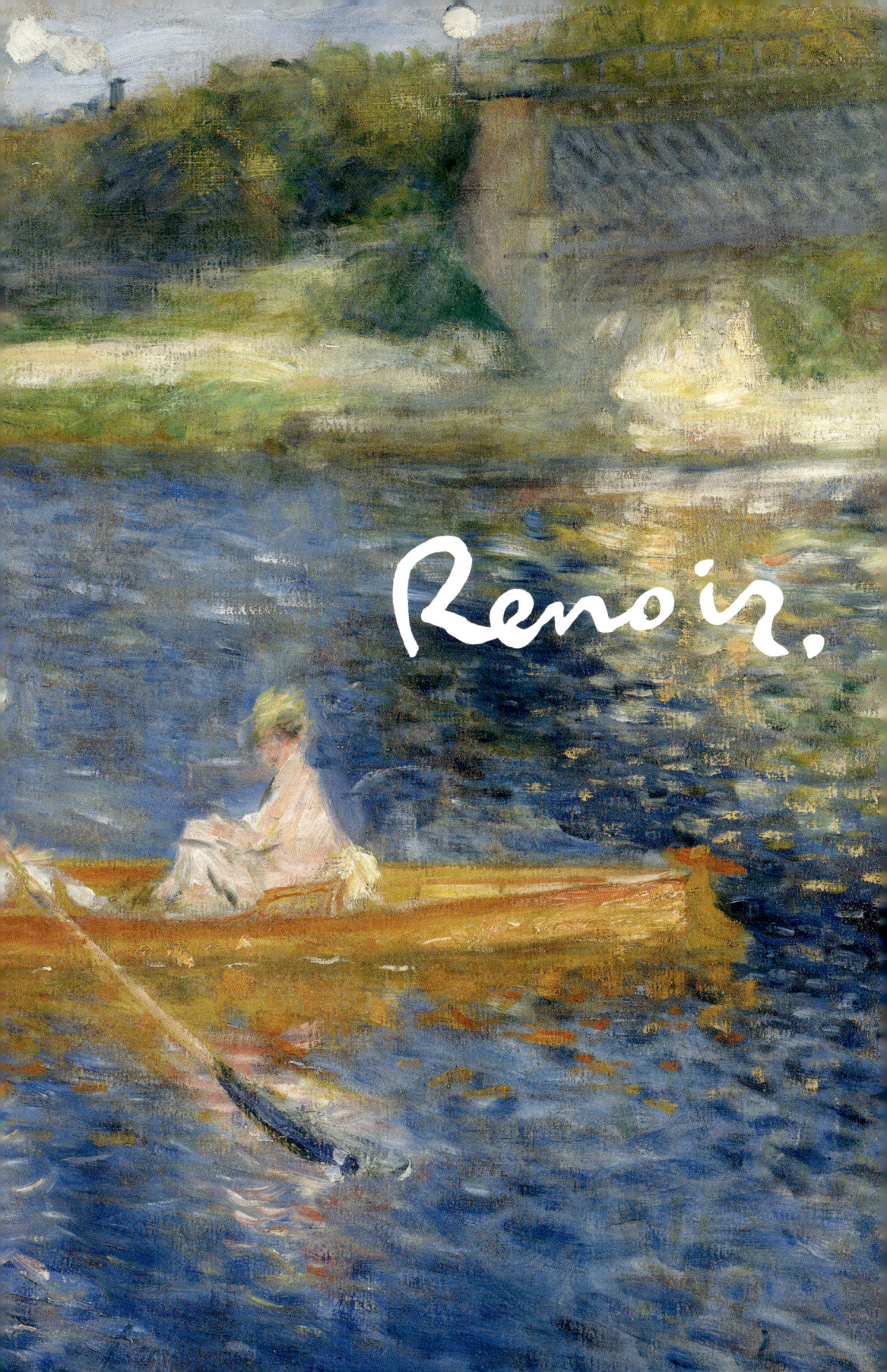

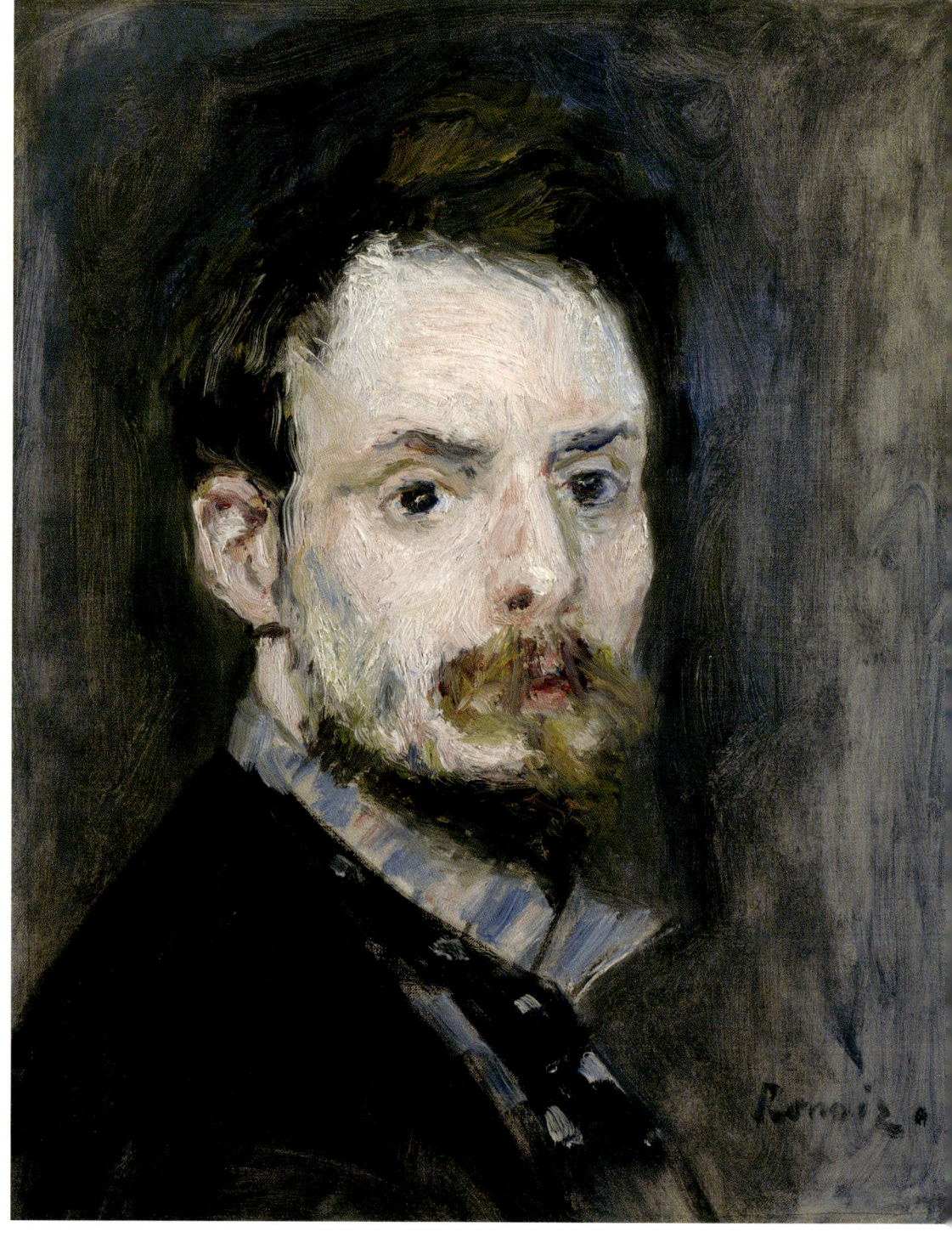

Peter H. Feist

Pierre-Auguste Renoir

A Dream of Harmony

"Why shouldn't art be pretty?
There are enough unpleasant things in the world."

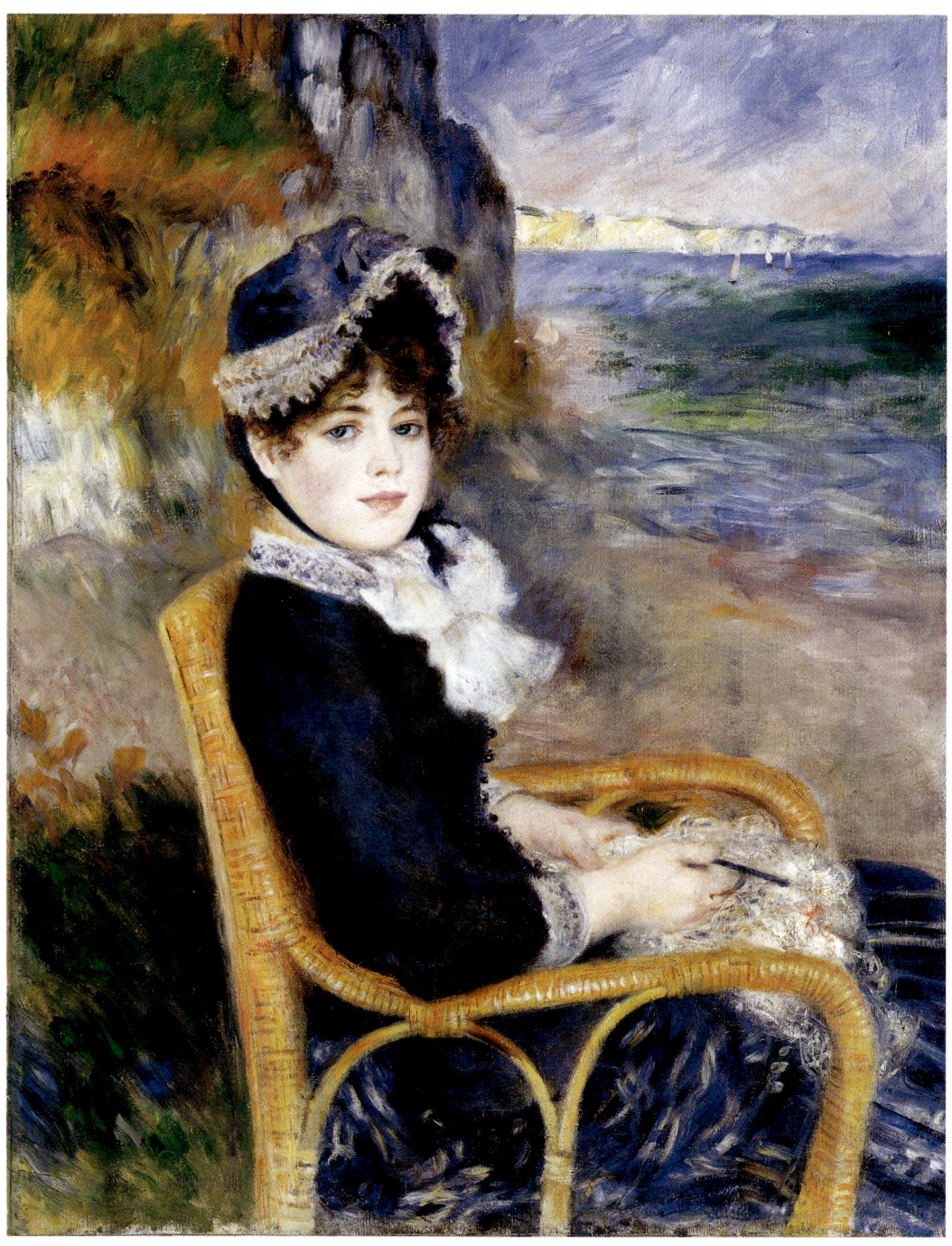

Contents

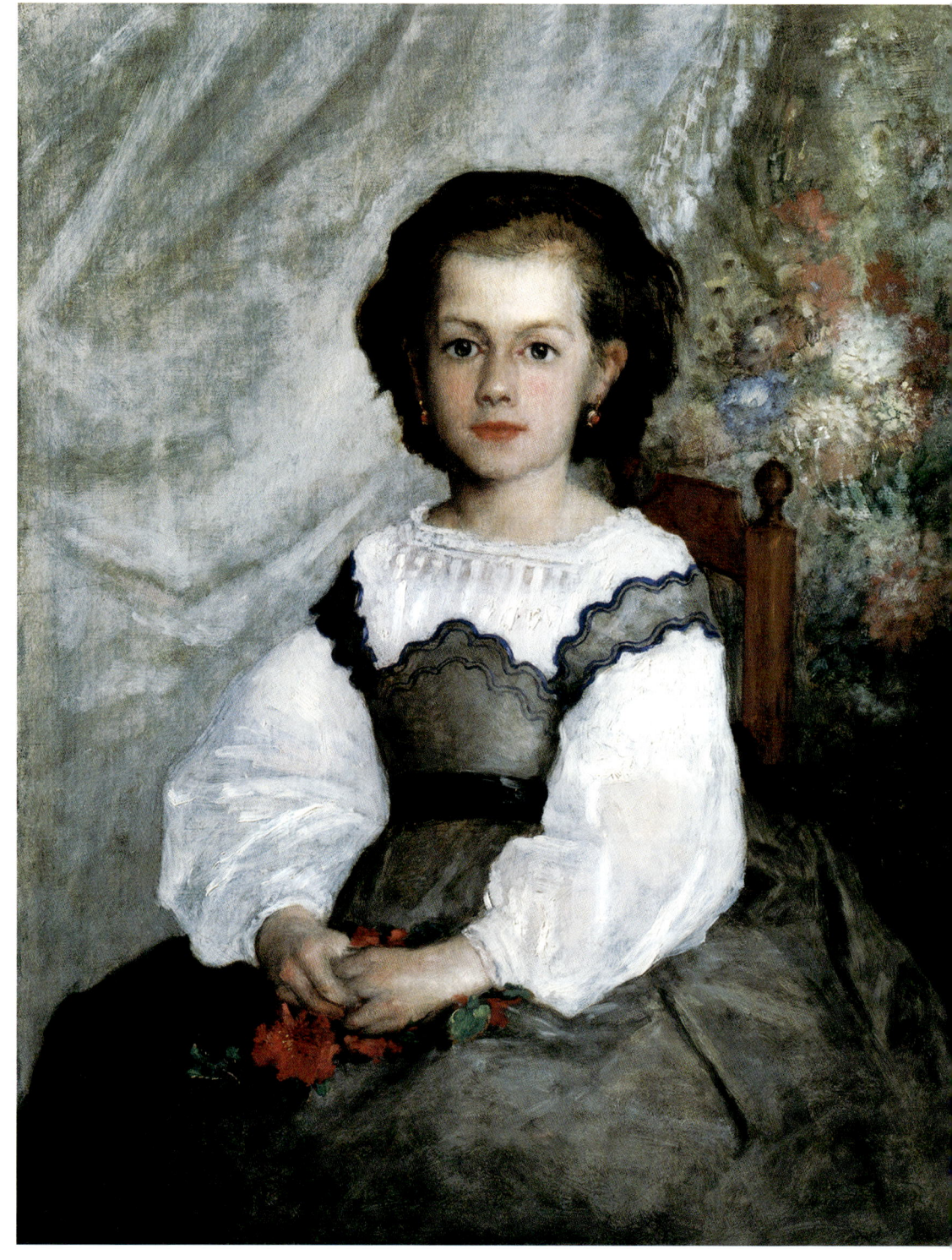

Renoir's Family, Friends and Teachers
1841–1867

"If I imagine I might have been born among intellectuals! It would have taken me years to get rid of the prejudices and to see things as they really are. And I might have got clumsy hands."

PIERRE-AUGUSTE RENOIR

When we look at one of the great collections of 19th-century French paintings and finally reach Pierre-Auguste Renoir, we may feel touched by a certain festive cheerfulness which surpasses that of any of his predecessors. Art as something uplifting, a feast for the eye – this is how we can describe both the greatness and also the limitations of his art. Renoir had almost sixty years of active life as an artist, during which he is said to have painted about 6,000 pictures. With the exception of Picasso, this was undoubtedly the most prolific achievement of any painter, and his best pictures now sell for millions of pounds. Born in Limoges on 25 February 1841, Renoir came from a rather narrow middle-class background. His father was a tailor. And when he decided to embark upon the dubious career of an artist, he had no idea how famous he would become.

Renoir's father Léonard was by no means a rich man, and his craft did not bring in a lot of wealth, either in Limoges or in Paris, where his family moved in 1845, hoping for better prospects. At that time Paris was the capital of one of the leading world powers. Unlike the surrounding nations, France had been able to prepare her unification as early as the Middle Ages. The whole country was completely centralized, both economically and politically, with Paris as its heart and crowning glory. People were able to look back on several centuries of glorious history. The bourgeoisie had achieved control of political affairs in a series of great revolutionary power struggles. It had borne on its shoulders that little Corsican officer Napoleon Bonaparte, who had ruled over the whole of Europe. The glamour of those times could still be felt, long after the success of his conquests had been blown to bits and broken by the other European nations' desire for freedom. When, as a result of the third bourgeois revolution of 1848, Louis Bonaparte acquired the title of French Emperor and took his place as Napoleon III among the European potentates, he was able to do so on the strength of his uncle's fame.

Art played an extremely important part during the Second Empire. A rich body of literature had developed, which included works by authors of more popular appeal as well as a number of sensitive poets. There were sharp-witted realists who wrote descriptions of contemporary life, and there were more critical writers like Gustave Flaubert and the young Émile Zola. The theatres were full of audiences who really appreciated the plays of Victorien Sardou and Alexandre Dumas Jr. Operettas by Jacques Offenbach, concerts, operas and ballets provided a rich harvest of artistic delight for the eyes and ears of the rich middle classes. The type of architecture that had become fashionable in Paris was of a very sumptuous kind, richly decorated in the Baroque style. A thorough rebuilding programme, which affected the entire city

Mademoiselle Romaine Lacaux, 1864
Oil on canvas, 81.3 x 65 cm (32 x 25⅝ in.)
The Cleveland Museum of Art,
Gift of the Hanna Fund 1942

of Paris, was initiated by its prefect, Baron Georges Eugène Haussmann. Magnificent avenues were created, as well as large expensive buildings, both private and public, such as the Grand Opera and the gigantic glass and steel construction of the Market Halls, the "Belly of Paris". Sculptors such as Jean Baptiste Carpeaux created the kind of sculptures that were appropriate to this Neo-Baroque pomp. There were a vast number of painters who produced oil paintings. Some did this extremely accurately, to the point of pedantry, while others were seductively daring in their endeavours. All of them attempted to arouse pleasant feelings with their art, which was displayed in salons and boudoirs, theatre foyers and restaurants – places where the better circles of society used to meet. Every year the Salon, a panel which consisted mainly of professors from the Academy chose about two and a half thousand or more products of artistic endeavour, and the public were keen enough to rely on their judgement.

When Renoir first showed signs of being talented at painting and drawing, he could only make use of his gifts as an apprentice in a factory: thus, at the age of thirteen, he became a porcelain painter, decorating coffee cups with pictures of little flowers, idyllic pastoral scenes, and – for eight sous – the profile of Marie Antoinette. It may well be due to these early habits and impressions that, later on in his life, he developed a feeling for the shining luminosity of paint, for its delicate shades, and sometimes also its porcelain-like smoothness. During his lunch breaks, instead of having lunch, he would often go straight to the Louvre to paint antique sculptures. On one occasion, while he was looking for a cheap restaurant, he suddenly saw the *Fontaine des Innocents,* richly decorated with reliefs by the Renaissance sculptor Jean Goujon. "I immediately decided not to go to the pub, bought myself some sausage and spent my free hour walking round the fountain," he would recount later, and there are quite a number of paintings in which we can discern a faint echo of his early discovery of Goujon's nymphs.

Renoir only spent four years as a porcelain painter. The industrial revolution made an immediate and irreversible impact on his life: a machine for printing pictures on china had been invented, which made him and many other porcelain painters redundant. He now turned to painting ladies' fans and then church banners which were used by missionaries overseas. Thus he acquired a certain skilfulness and swiftness in using the paintbrush. Later, in his old age, he would look back with gratitude to the time when he had to copy Rococo masters again and again.

Renoir's industriousness soon began to bear fruit. By the time he was twenty-one, he had earned enough money to study art academically. In April 1862 he joined the École des Beaux-Arts (the College of Fine Art) in Paris. It was run by the Imperial Director of Fine Art, Count Alfred de Nieuwekerke, who rejected realism in art as "democratic and objectionable". The students had to copy paintings, make accurate drawings of plaster casts and were encouraged to regard history paintings more highly than any others. Renoir was taught by a number of professors, but his real teacher was Charles Gleyre who, twenty years before, had become famous for a rather frosty allegorical picture. Above all, Renoir used to go to private classes which Gleyre taught outside the École and in which thirty or forty students had to draw or paint nude models. Thanks to his previous experience he had a confident hand, and he was always full of keen enthusiasm to perform each task to the best of his ability. Whether it was by nature or because of the Rococo paintings he had copied previously, he used to love strong, glowing colours. These, however, were not particularly popular at the college. During the very first week there was a clash between Renoir and Gleyre. Years later, Renoir commented, "I had really done my utmost to paint the model. Gleyre looked at my picture and said, with an icy expression on his face: 'You obviously paint for your

Arum and Conservatory Plants, 1864
Oil on canvas, 130 x 96 cm (51¼ x 37¾ in.)
Winterthur, Oskar Reinhart Collection
"Am Römerholz"

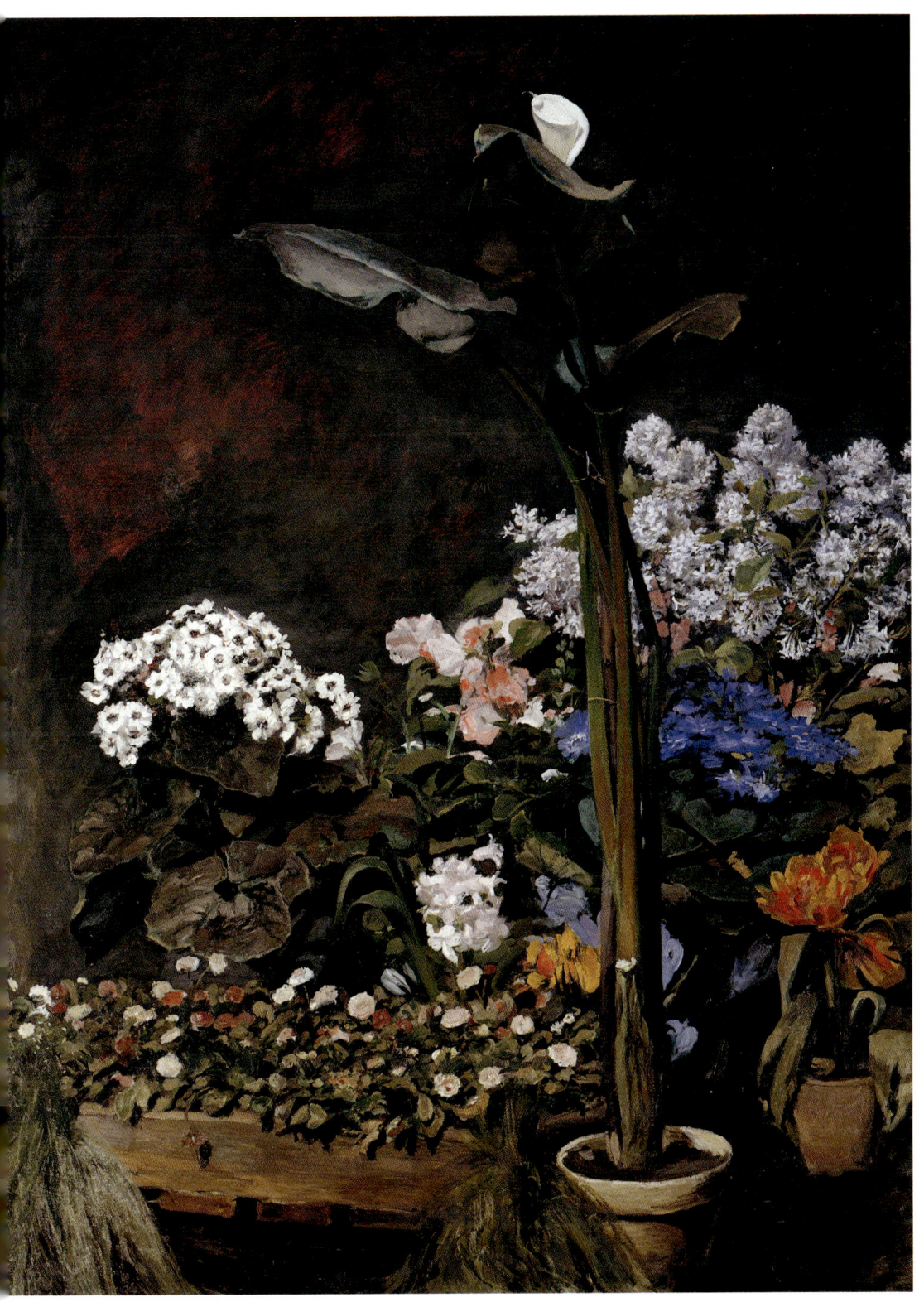

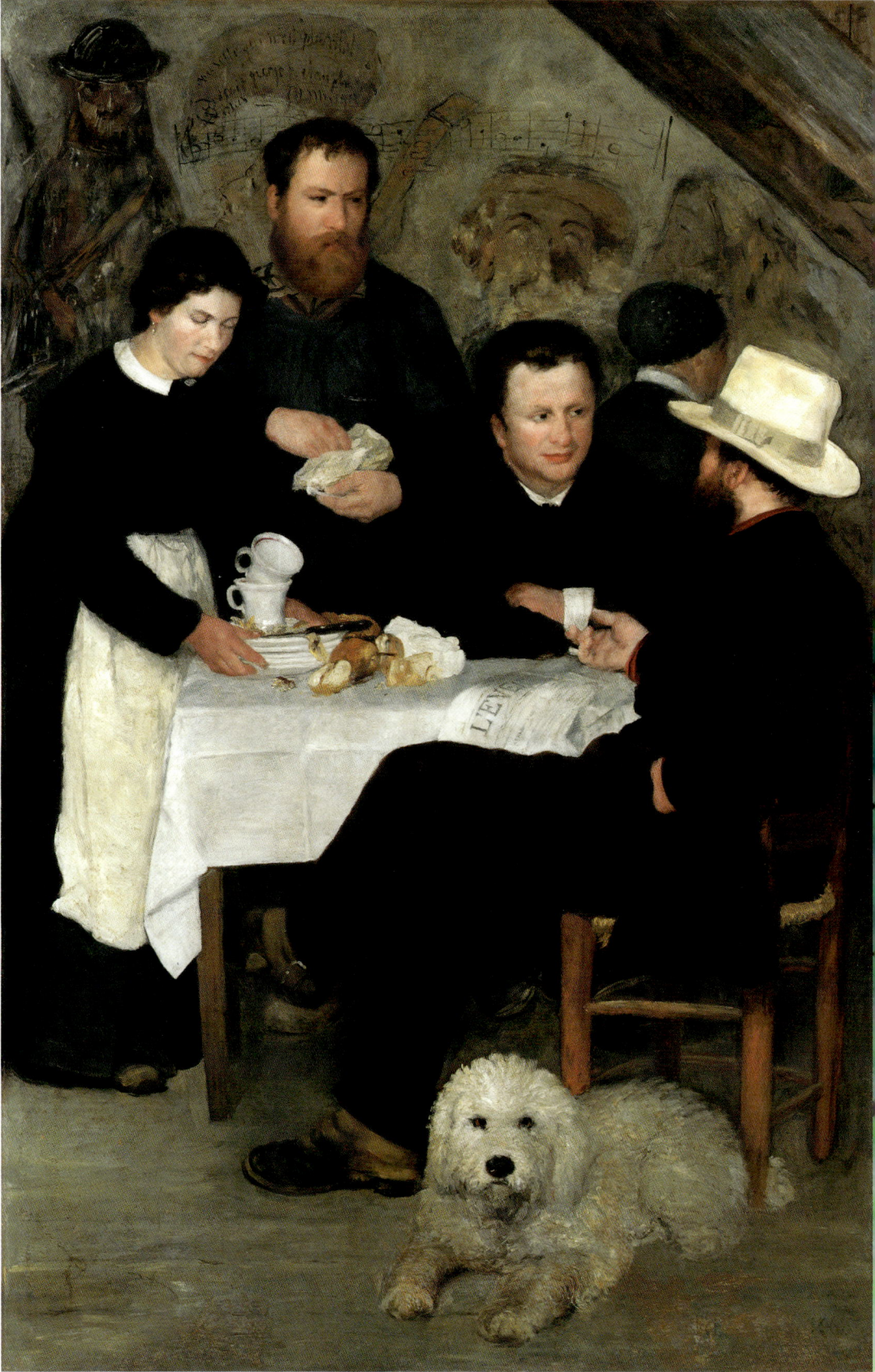

own enjoyment, don't you?' – 'But of course,' I replied, 'you can be sure that I wouldn't do it if I didn't enjoy painting.' I'm not sure if he understood me correctly," Renoir added. His answer was probably not meant as provocatively as it sounded, but it nevertheless summed up very nicely a totally new attitude to art: less solemn and dutiful towards "the noble goddess of art", but more sensuous, alive and personal.

"When we look at the works of the ancients, we really don't have any reason for thinking that we are clever. Above all, what wonderful craftsmen these people were! They really knew their craft. And that is indeed everything. Painting is not a matter of sloppy sentimentalism. It is first of all the work of your hand, and you have to be a hard worker."
PIERRE-AUGUSTE RENOIR

There was one student who was even less inclined to bow to the doctrines of the teachers: Claude Monet. Renoir made friends with him, and also with Alfred Sisley and Frédéric Bazille (ills. pp. 216 and 218). Monet was the most energetic among them. He had learned from Eugène Boudin how to see and paint a landscape under natural lighting conditions, and disliked the cold light of the studio more than anything else. In May 1863, at the Salon des refusés ("Salon of the Rejected"), these friends first saw Manet's *Luncheon on the Grass* (now in the Musée d'Orsay, Paris) – a picture which had met with ridicule and indignation among the general public. It had a somewhat perplexing theme and was painted in rather bright colours, which was quite unusual at the time. They immediately recognized how much they had in common with Manet. When, at the beginning of 1864, Gleyre retired from teaching, Renoir and his friends continued to work without a tutor. In spring Monet took his fellow painters to Chailly-en-Bière, a village in the Fontainebleau woods, to study nature. This was thirty years after another group of young painters had first thought it worth their while to paint the unobtrusively beautiful nooks and crannies of the woods and rivers near Paris. They were called the Painters of Barbizon, after their home on the edge of the Fontainebleau woods. Some of them, Charles François Daubigny, Narcisso Virgilio Díaz de la Peña and Camille Corot, were still working in the area. The realistic way in which they depicted their native countryside was still rather controversial.

It was in 1864 that Renoir first submitted a picture to the Salon, and it was in fact accepted: *Esmeralda Dancing with a Goat,* which drew its theme from Victor Hugo's novel *The Hunchback of Notre-Dame.* It must have had that darkness about it which was considered to be suitable for galleries at the time and which was achieved by means of an admixture of asphalt. We can conclude this because Renoir, rather self-critically, destroyed it when Díaz, one of the Barbizon Painters, advised him not to use asphalt. The two of them became close friends, and the fifty-seven-year-old Díaz, who was earning quite a decent amount of money at the time, gave his twenty-three-year-old fellow-painter not only good advice, but also some financial assistance, which was very welcome.

The other painters whom Renoir admired at that time were Gustave Courbet and Eugène Delacroix. In 1848 Courbet had caused a great deal of excitement and indignation with his realistic paintings. These were pictures of stone breakers making roads, very simple landscapes, portraits and female nudes whose strong, peasant-like bodies were in fact true to life. He used to prefer very dark shades of colour, and the general appearance of his pictures was one of compact solidity. Most of them violated practically all academic rules of composition but had a certain beauty about them that appeared to be wrenched away from nature itself. Courbet's realism was closely related to his democratic and materialistic world view; as an admirer of the middle-class socialist Pierre Joseph Proudhon, he believed that a work of art should not just be appreciated in itself, but should be judged according to its function within society. This view had its origin in the Romantic

At the Inn of Mother Anthony, 1866
Oil on canvas, 194 x 131 cm (76½ x 51⅝ in.)
Stockholm, Nationalmuseum

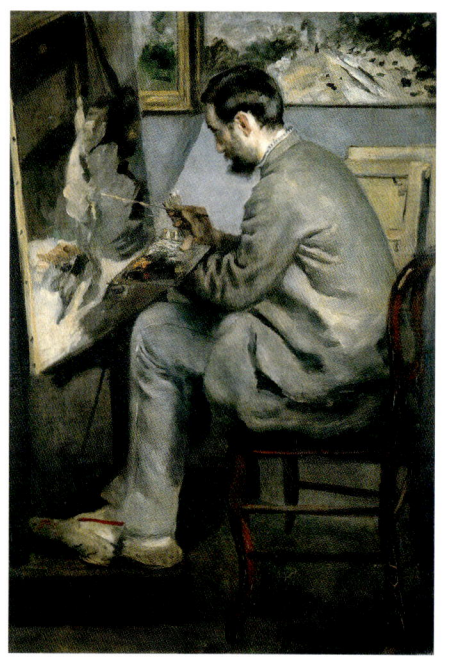

movement, of which Delacroix, the other artist whom Renoir admired, was an adherent. Among his early pictures there were quite a number of paintings with social relevance, thus contributing to the general trend of artists trying to break away from the rigid framework of the rules of Classicism.

Although Classicism had been very progressive in its day, it turned out to be rather a hindrance for further development after a while. Classicists showed very little sensitivity for the colourful elements of this world. Delacroix, on the other hand, helped colour to come into its own again, and he also allowed more scope for a reflection of reality in a work of art that was personal, passionate and imaginative. It was in fact the magnificence of the glowing colours in his pictures that Renoir felt attracted to. He would no doubt have agreed wholeheartedly if he had known of Delacroix's last entry in his diary: "The first obligation of a painting is to be a feast for the eyes."

In summer 1865 Renoir and his friend Sisley went down the Seine in a sailing boat as far as Le Havre, where they wanted to see the regattas. These were to become one of their favourite themes in later pictures. From their boat they painted the river and its banks, just as Daubigny had done. The Salon in fact accepted Renoir's works again. However, a year later, the panel decided to take a much harder line in their decisions, thus marking the real beginning of Renoir's tough struggle for the recognition of a new artistic style.

Renoir now spent most of his time with his friends in the village of Marlotte near Fontainebleau, where he painted them in his picture *At the Inn of Mother Anthony:* a group of people, cheerfully gathered round a table and discussing articles from the paper *L'Événement.* This was the periodical in which young Zola had published his critique of the 1866 Salon and defined a work of art as "a piece of nature seen through a person's temperament". The individual people in the painting cannot be identified unambiguously, but his colleagues Sisley and Jules Le Coeur are sure to be among them. Some music and cartoons had been scribbled on the wall, among them a sketch drawing of Henri Murger who had written *La Bohème* in 1851. All these young painters saw themselves as Bohemians, i.e. poor artists who felt passionately inspired by missionary zeal but who were misunderstood by the world. The 1867 panel of the Salon were particularly harsh with them and rejected Renoir's *Diana* (ill. p. 219). Renoir had painted a beautifully accurate nude, without the coarseness of Courbet's *Bather* fourteen years before, which had been scornfully rejected as a "Hottentot Venus". In fact, his *Diana* looked far more healthy and realistic than – as Zola put it – the pampered, lustful nudes, powdered with rice flour, of the fashionable painters of that time.

So he draped a loincloth of fur round his nude and also added a bow and a freshly killed deer, changing her into the ancient goddess of hunting. This concession to the Salon's academic partiality towards mythological themes, however, did not save his picture from being rejected. There was going to

TOP
Frédéric Bazille, 1867
Oil on canvas, 105 x 73.5 cm (41¼ x 29 in.)
Paris, Musée d'Orsay

OPPOSITE
Diana, 1867
Oil on canvas, 199.5 x 129.5 cm (78½ x 51 in.)
Washington, D.C., National Gallery of Art,
Chester Dale Collection

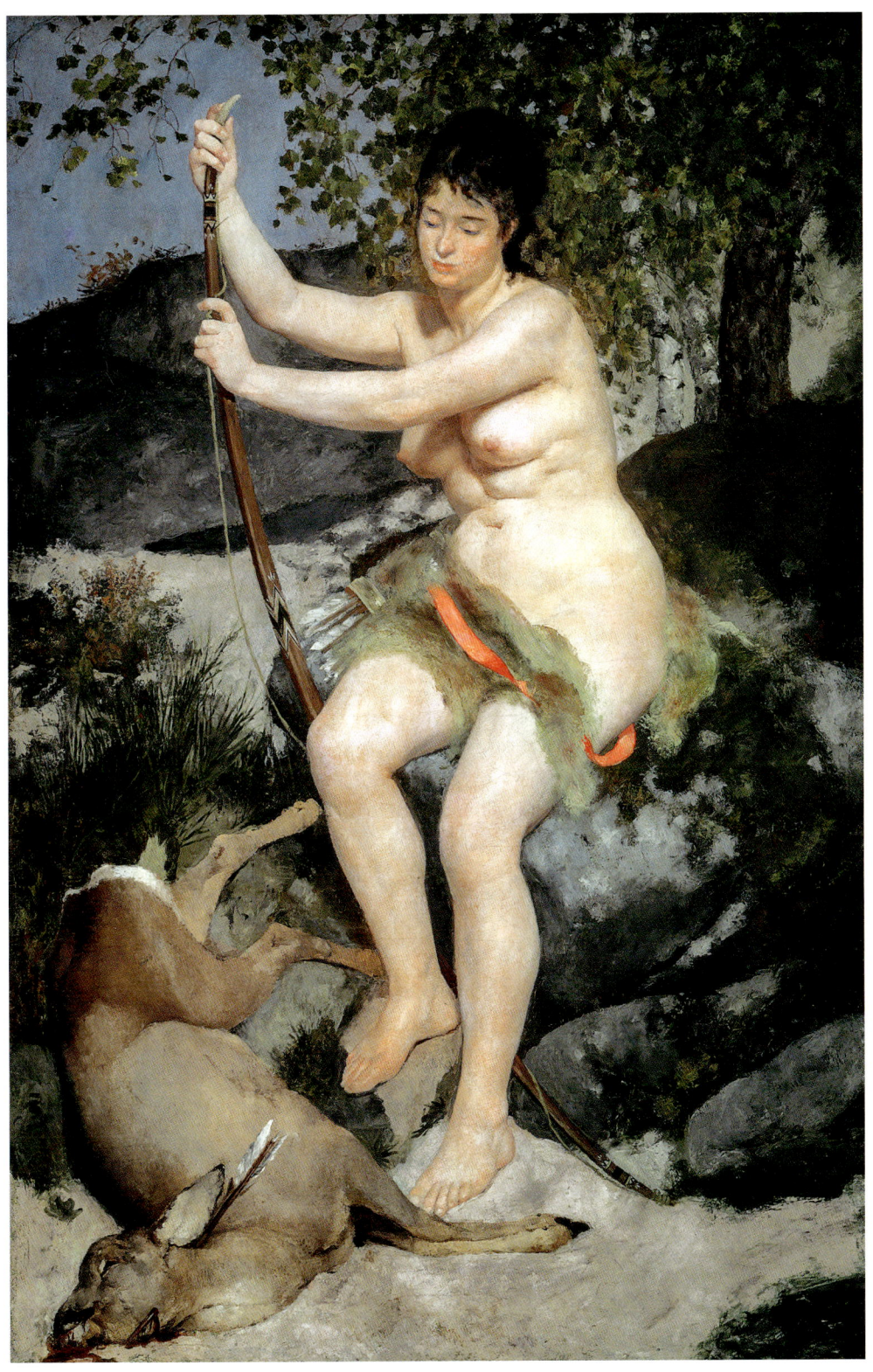

"From time to time Monet used to get us an invitation for a dinner party. And then we stuffed ourselves with larded turkey, served with Chambertin."
PIERRE-AUGUSTE RENOIR

be a World Exhibition in Paris that year, and the panel wanted to present an image of French art that was "without a blemish".

During the subsequent three years, though, Renoir succeeded in gaining recognition for his paintings at the Salon, even though they were even more modern in style. The panel had become considerably more liberal in their attitudes, mainly under the influence of Daubigny who had begun to speak up for the young Realists. The imperial government (now in its last years) could not afford any unnecessary feelings of discontent among the middle classes.

These minor successes, however, did not save Renoir from material hardship. His savings had long come to an end. His wealthy friend Bazille allowed him to share his studio and to live there. Together they made a living by painting postcards. In summer 1867 Renoir put up his easel in the woods of Fontainebleau again, with the nineteen-year-old Lise Tréhot as his model (ill. p. 221). In summer 1869 Renoir lived with her and her parents in Ville-d'Avray just outside Paris. Occasionally he would take some food to Monet, who was living in abject poverty in Bougival. Renoir was not really any better off: "Although we don't eat every day, I'm still quite cheerful," he wrote to Bazille. It seemed to Renoir and Monet that the worst hardship was not being able to buy paint. During those months they would often go to *La Grenouillère* (The Frog Pond), a public swimming pool in Bougival, by the river Seine, and paint the same themes again and again. It must have been very touching to see how these two young artists together began to paint brighter and brighter pictures, in spite of their pressing material need. Like their fellow painters Sisley and Camille Pissarro, they really had to fight hard simply to stay alive, but neither now nor in the hard years to come did they ever paint a picture that expressed any kind of weariness, anxiety, depression or pessimism.

OPPOSITE
Lise, 1867
Oil on canvas, 184 x 115.5 cm (72½ x 45½ in.)
Essen, Museum Folkwang

The Pont des Arts, Paris, 1867/68
Oil on canvas, 60.9 x 100.3 cm (24 x 39½ in.)
Pasadena, The Norton Simon Foundation

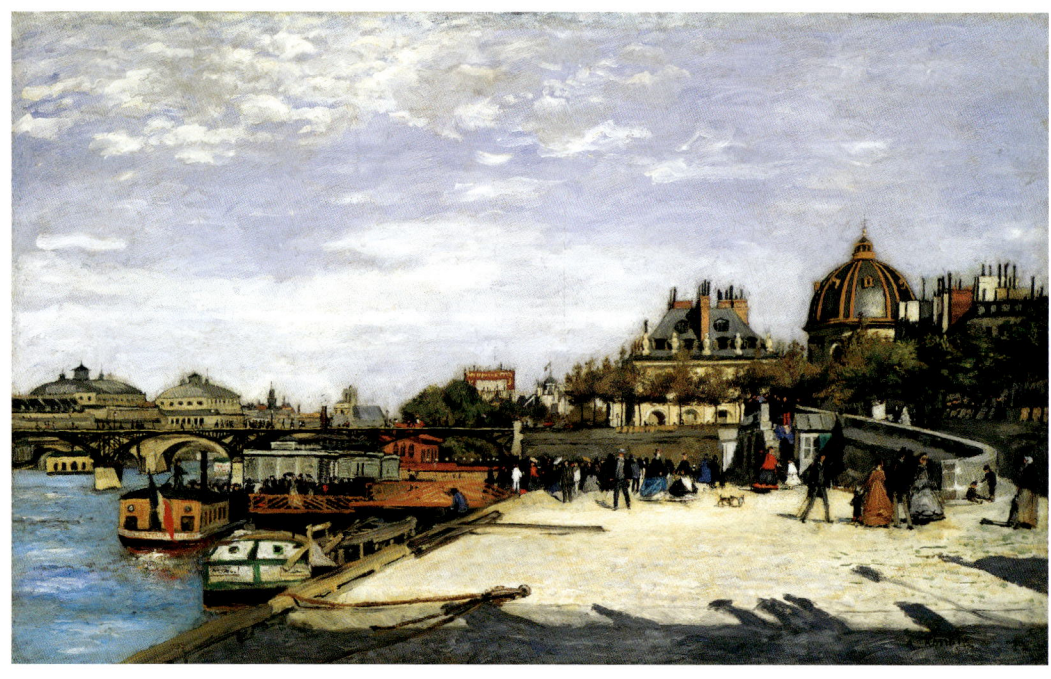

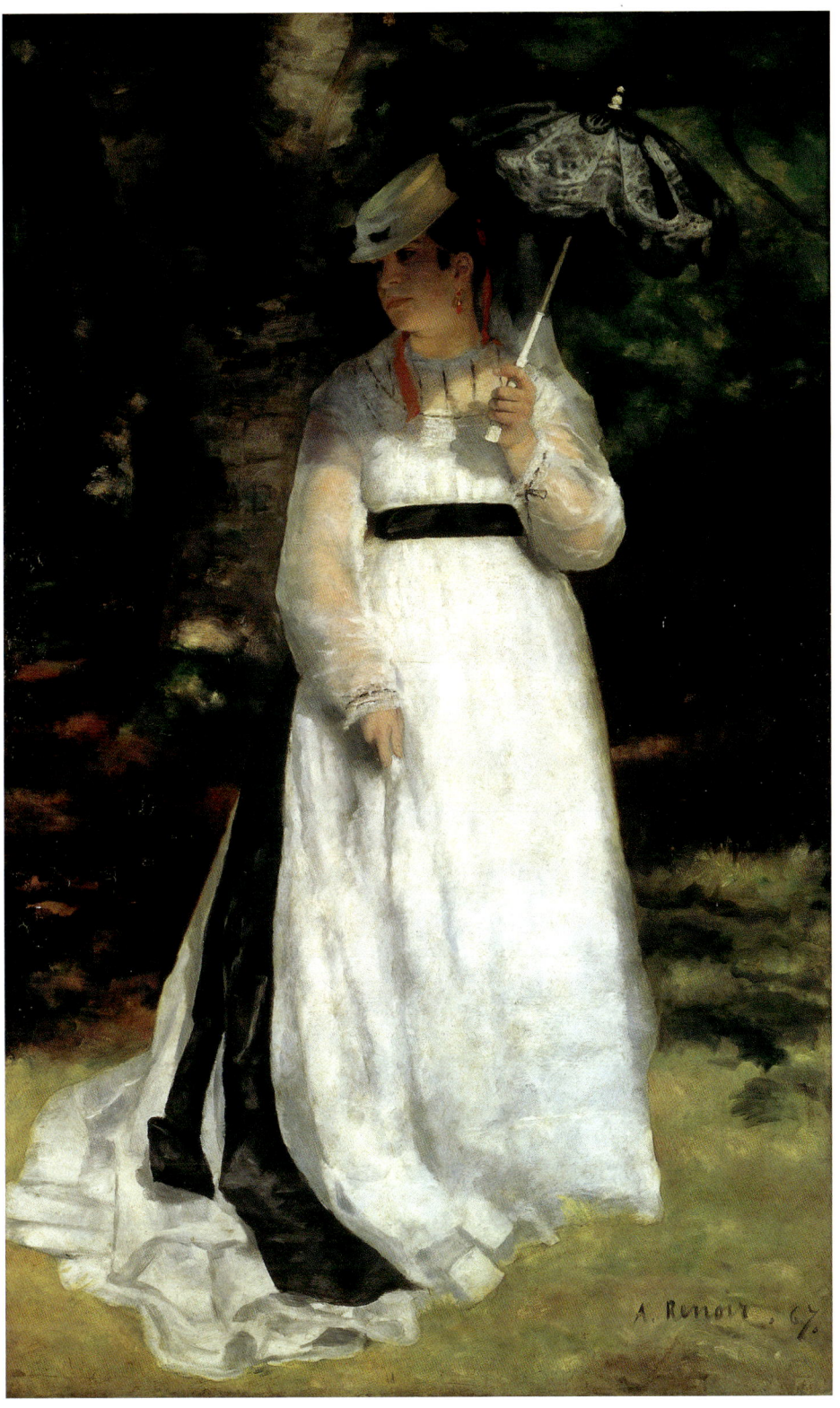

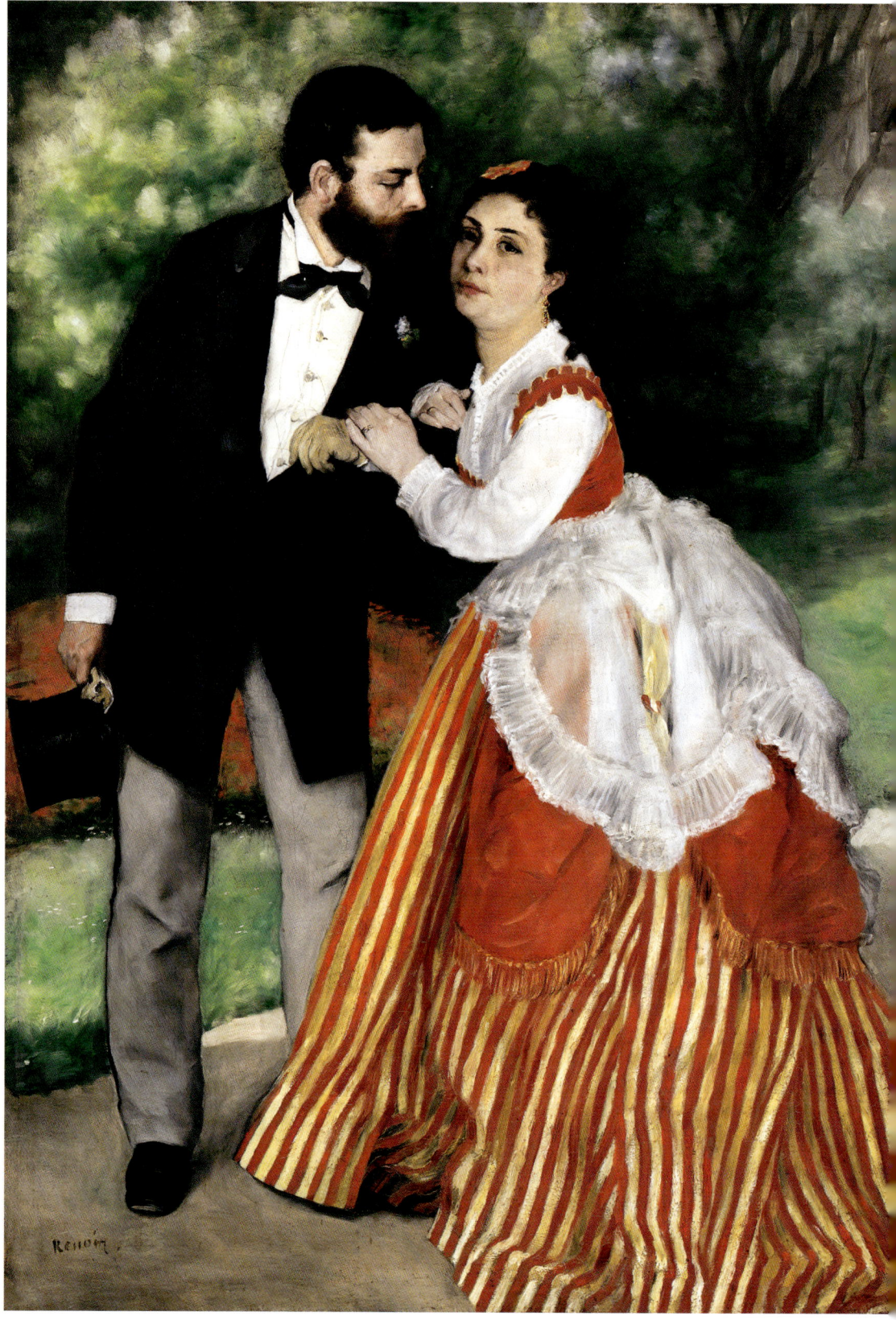

A New Style of Art
1867–1871

The young painters were struggling hard to find their new artistic principles. Whenever they were in Paris, they would go to the Café Guerbois in the Grande rue de Batignolles in the evenings, where they often had quite heated discussions. They were soon known as the Painters of Batignolles. Manet was at the centre of this group, which also included writers and art critics such as Zola, Théodore Duret, Zacharie Astruc and Edmond Duranty. Renoir, who was thin and rather nervous, never contributed much to the discussions. He was lively and intelligent with a sense of humour, but he did not believe in fighting or theorizing. For him painting was not so much a matter of strict programmes, but a beautiful craft which was to be practised humbly and joyfully. His paintings, on the other hand, turned out to be the most daring and progressive of all. The underlying principle was to paint only what could be seen with one's

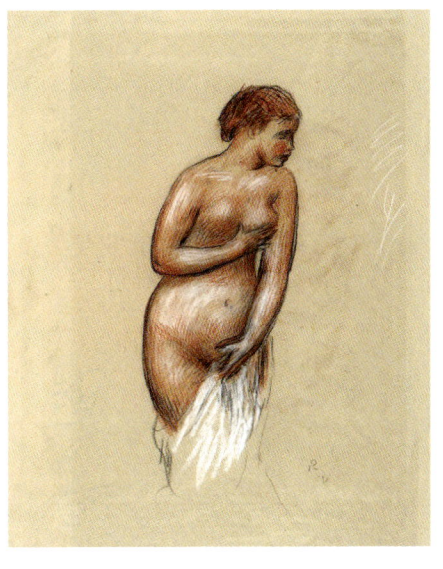

eyes and to render this as faithfully as possible. The Barbizon school, including Jean François Millet, and Courbet had started this. But most of their pictures had been painted in studios and lacked that brightness which made objects so beautiful outside, in the sunlight. In their endeavour to depict nature more and more truthfully the painters came up against the problem of coloured shadows. On closer inspection they discovered that there was in fact a great variety of different shades even in shadows, with blue as the predominant colour. This was something that could only be studied accurately outside, i.e. when faced with the subject itself, and for this reason Renoir and Monet used to work outside, in the open air. They could see how various objects changed their colours, depending on the lighting conditions and the colours reflected from other things around them. They noticed how the flickering of the air dissolved the sharpness of the contours and that not everything could be discerned equally clearly.

Certain objects lent themselves more than others to this way of seeing: the foliage of trees, flowers, water, clouds, smoke,

OPPOSITE
A Couple (Lise and Sisley), c. 1868
Oil on canvas, 105 x 75 cm (41¼ x 29½ in.)
Cologne, Wallraf-Richartz-Museum &
Fondation Corboud

ABOVE RIGHT
Standing Nude, 1919
Red and black chalk, heightened with
white chalk, on buff wove paper,
37.3 x 29.8 cm (14¾ x 11¾ in.)
Ottawa, National Gallery of Canada

"What delights me about Velázquez is the joy that pours forth from his art, the joy he felt when he painted his pictures… If I can feel the painter's passion with which he created, then I enjoy his own enjoyment with him."

PIERRE-AUGUSTE RENOIR

boats, women's filmy dresses, delicate parasols, and people moving about casually and at ease. They loathed anything that smacked of tradition and strict rules. What they were looking for was beauty in the life of the people around them, life where it poured forth in all its freshness, i.e. in the intimate circle of the family, on a walk, during their leisure time, and wherever something new could be experienced: at sporting events or in the rapidly changing conditions of the big city.

Renoir's first masterpiece was his *Lise* of 1867 (ill. p. 221), which was exhibited at the Salon the following spring. It depicted his young girlfriend full-length and life-size – as though it were a state portrait of a royal personage. "The whole thing is so natural and has been observed so accurately that it will seem wrong because we are used to imagining nature in terms of conventional colours," wrote W. Bürger-Thoré, and Astruc called Lise "the daughter of the people, with all her typical Parisian features." Three years later Renoir used Lise as a model for his *Odalisque* (ill. p. 225), a rather spectacular painting in that oriental style which was fashionable at the time, having been started by Delacroix's *Women of Algiers*.

Renoir's picture *A Couple* (ill. p. 222) was only half as large. The woman's eyes and her skirt make it quite obvious that she is meant to be the more important of the two. His use of line and colour

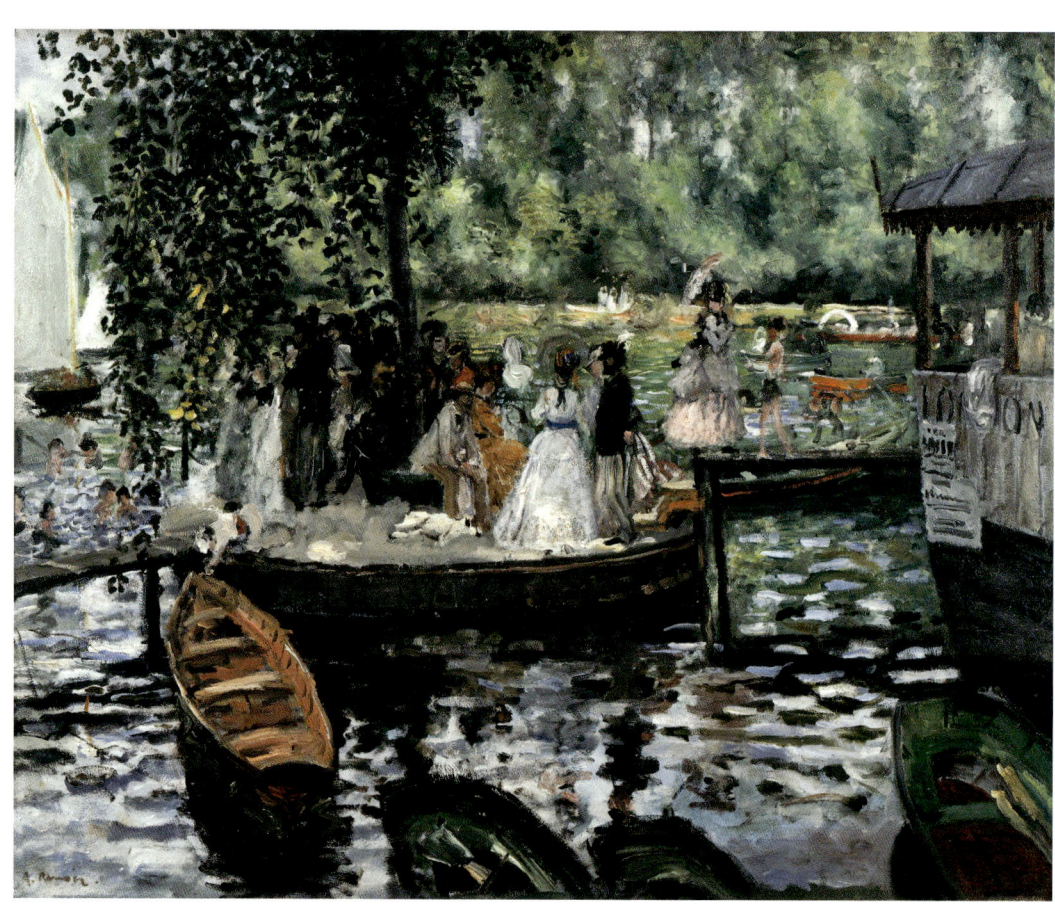

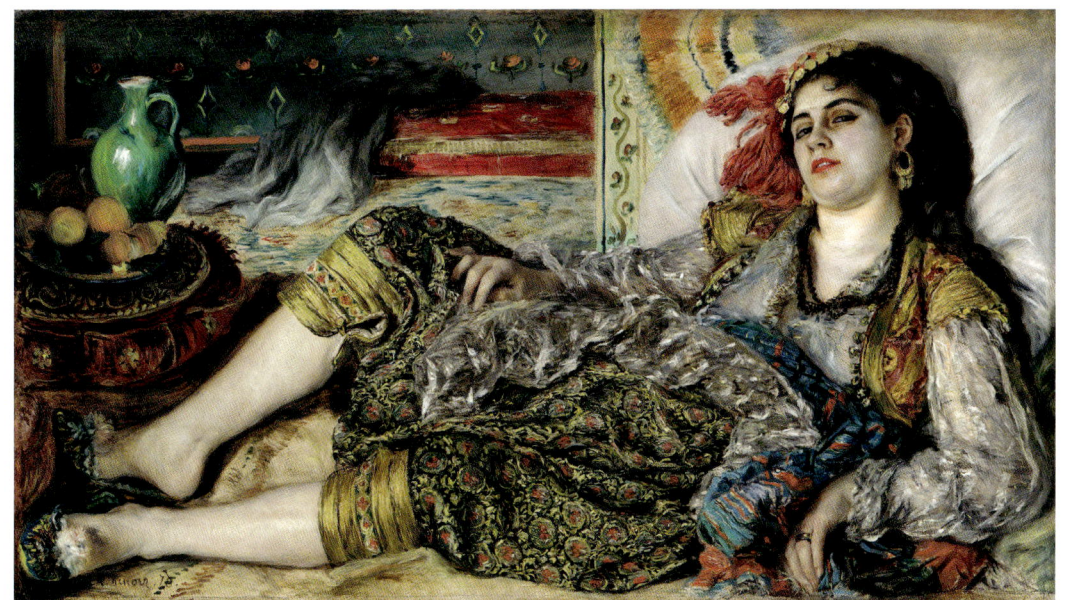

is well balanced and shows that he paid very careful attention to the laws of composition, which he had learned from
many masterpieces in the Louvre. The interplay of light and
reflected colour, on the other hand, is weaker here than in his
Lise, and the figures do not merge with their natural environment as much. This used to be a typical feature of his large-
scale landscapes. There is a certain lightness about Renoir's

Odalisque, 1870
Oil on canvas, 69.2 x 122.6 cm (27¼ x 48¼ in.)
Washington, D.C., National Gallery of Art,
Chester Dale Collection

OPPOSITE
La Grenouillère, 1869
Oil on canvas, 66.5 x 81 cm (26¼ x 32 in.)
Stockholm, Nationalmuseum

Pont des Arts (ill. p. 220), but at the same time its composition is firm and geometrically accurate,
affording a glimpse of the very heart of Paris: the Academy of Art, the steam boat pier and the modern iron bridge.

Monet and Renoir's joint efforts found their most beautiful expression in the pictures of the
Grenouillère. Three paintings by Monet and three by Renoir can still be traced back to that time, and
their style is almost indistinguishable. The crowd of people on the bank of the river and on the pier,
the changing cabins, the bathers, the rowing boats and above all the glistening surface of the water
with its many colourful reflections – all these elements had been captured with broad, sketch-like
strokes of the brush. These pictures lack all composition in the conventional sense of the word; they
are as turbulent as the cheerful crowds described in the stories of Guy de Maupassant.

"The impression of nature" was the most popular phrase in the discussions at the Café Guerbois,
and now it had been put into practice in real pictures. Once the decision had been taken that scenes
like this should be painted rather than a bathing Diana, it became obvious that the new subject had
to be matched by new stylistic devices, and in the process of trying them out new subjects were discovered. The chance encounter of a random but attractive moment had to be captured as quickly as it
occurred. Everything was in motion, and the light was forever changing. It was this continuous state
of flux that had to be caught, with its luminous colours that brought something of a bright summer
day into the room. These were the kind of pictures that gave birth to something that was not given a
name until five years later: Impressionism.

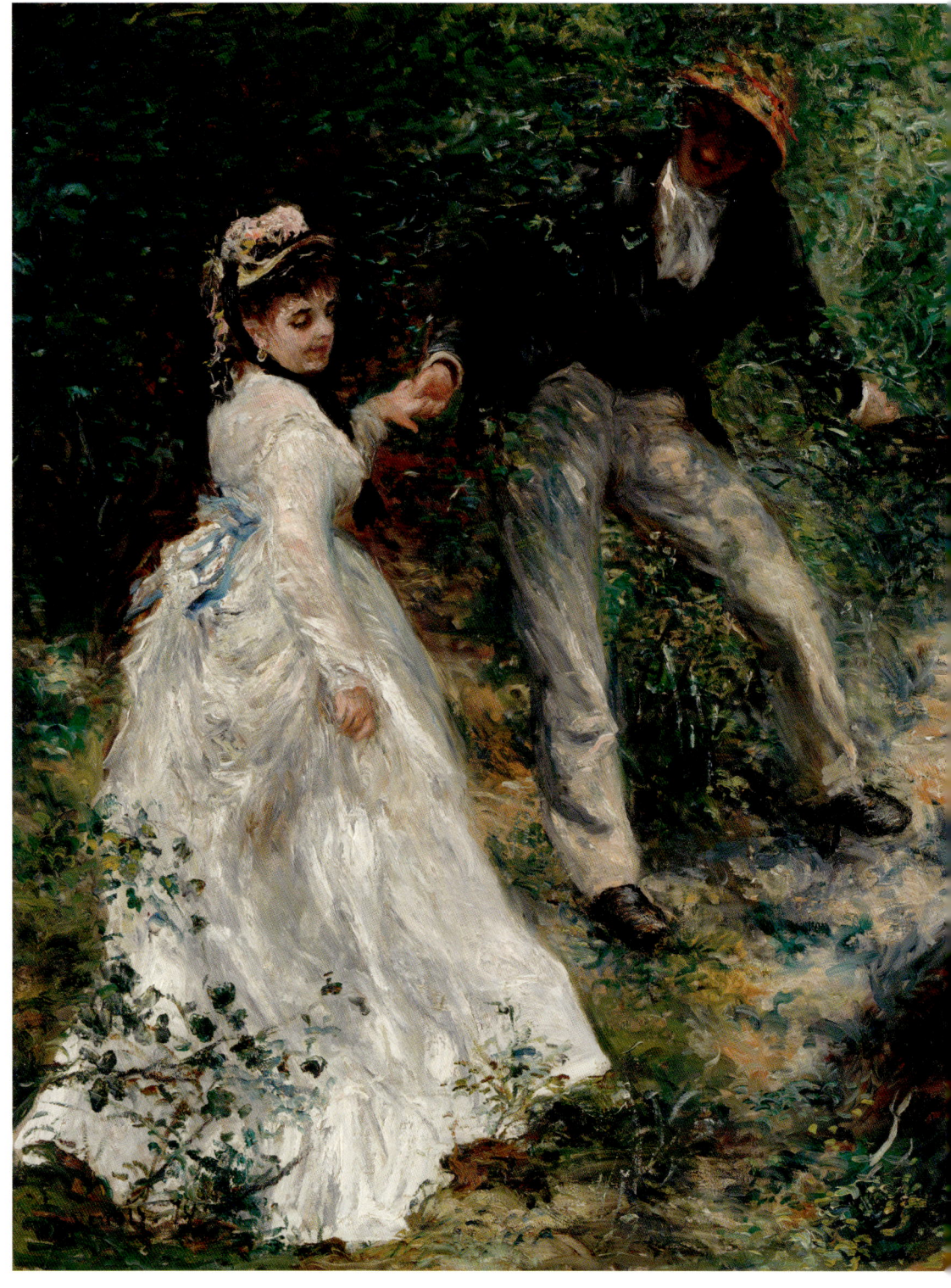

The Great Decade of Impressionism
1872–1883

In spring 1870 Renoir and almost all his friends were represented at the Salon. But in July war broke out with Prussia and her allies, and Renoir had to join the cavalry. Napoleon III and his armed forces were beaten, and France became a republic. In spring 1871 Parisian workers, craftsmen and many intellectuals and artists, too, rebelled and proclaimed the Commune as the revolutionary government. This first attempt to found a new state came to a bloody end. Renoir took very little notice of the dramatic events that were happening. But the sharp differences between the middle classes and the working classes, which had come to the surface, were to change forever the climate of the country, and both directly and indirectly, the situation influenced Renoir himself and the new art in general.

"My concern has always been to paint human beings like fruits. The greatest of modern painters, Corot – his women aren't 'thinkers', are they?"
PIERRE-AUGUSTE RENOIR

When Renoir submitted pictures to the Salon again in 1872, his *Parisian Women in Algerian Costumes* (National Museum of Western Art, Tokyo) was rejected. He had paid tribute to Delacroix with this painting. After the revolution the upper middle classes had become doubly suspicious of innovations of any kind. Nor did this attitude change in the years to come. They were now being fought by official critics and had to suffer scorn and ridicule. People like Renoir, who were not gentlemen of independent means, had to go though times of bitter hardship. But at this time of official rejection, ridicule and insult, a number of impoverished artists, many of them approaching forty, were finally forming themselves, as it were, into an artistic combat unit, fully developing their own new style and in fact unfolding it in all its splendour. These were the years when the most mature works of French Impressionism were created and Renoir especially developed the full magic of his art and the prolific sumptuousness of his imagination and his stamina. Between 1872 and 1883 Renoir was at the height of his skill as an artist. Before then, in the 1860s, he had still been feeling his way and had been dependent on older masters, and later, in the 1880s, he was to limit himself considerably in his choice of subjects and fell into a certain monotony of never-ending variations on the same themes. But now almost every single one of his pictures could be enjoyed in its own right as a distinct masterpiece which was different from any other.

Surprisingly, the time shortly after the lost war and the Commune was one of great economic prosperity in France. The economy was blossoming, and even paintings were sold for unexpectedly large sums of money. A lot of this money passed through the hands of Paul Durand-Ruel, who had been instrumental in helping the Batignolles painters towards their success. Ever since he had

The Walk, 1870
Oil on canvas, 81.3 x 64.8 cm (32 x 25⅝ in.)
Los Angeles, J. Paul Getty Museum

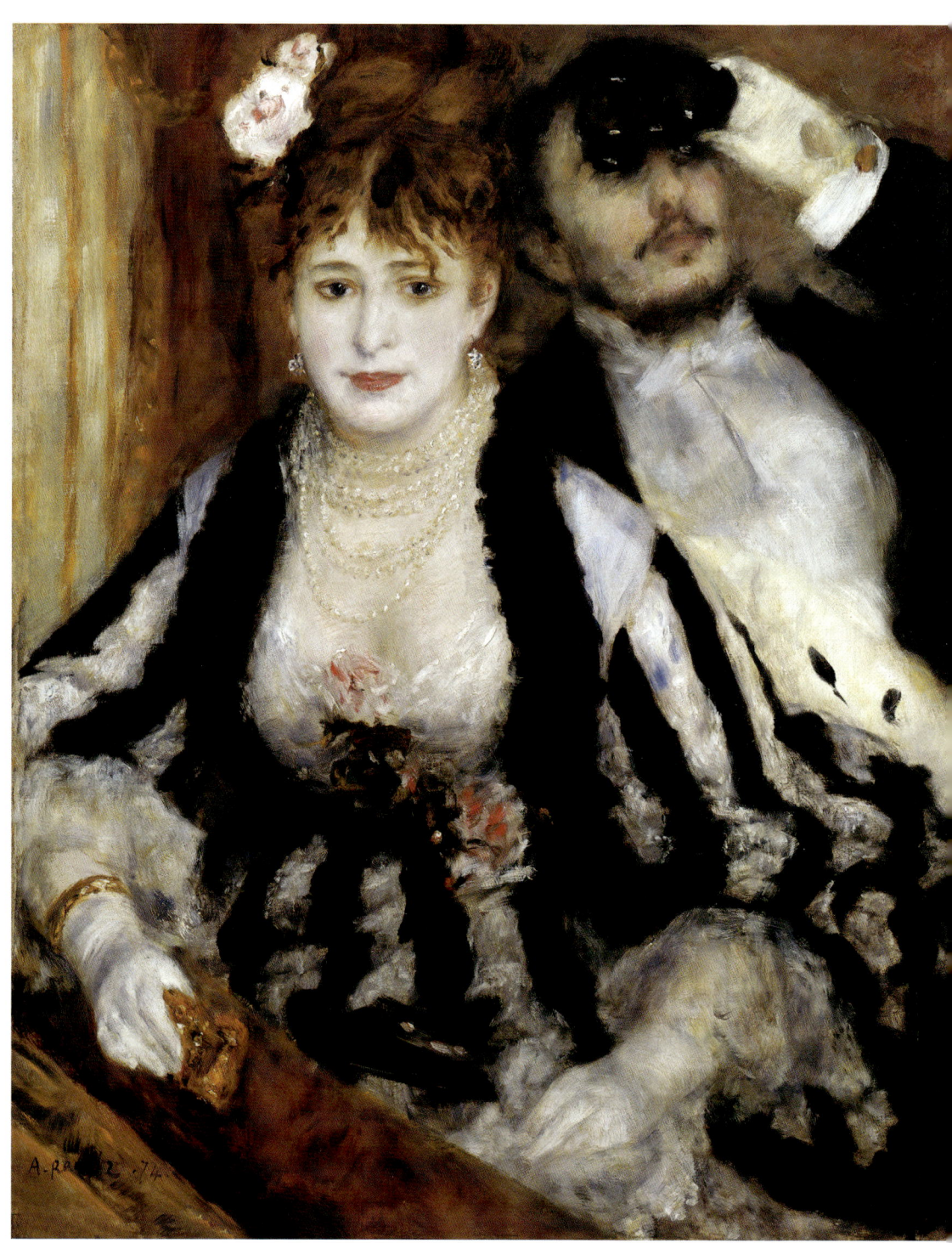

taken over his father's art business in 1862, he had been using his intuition and his skill to fight for the recognition of the Barbizon painters. And in fact he soon began to make good business out of their paintings. This was because he immediately recognized quality when he saw it, and he was not lacking in courage. For years he would patiently take those artists under his wing who had been rejected by the official critics, and buy their pictures even when he knew that there was no certainty as to whether he would be able to sell them. In 1870 he met Pissarro and Monet in London, where they had fled from the Franco-Prussian war, and in 1873 he discovered Renoir. As their pictures were almost unsaleable he did not pay them very much, but for a man in Renoir's position even a small amount of money was most welcome.

Nevertheless, in 1873, Durand-Ruel found himself forced to reduce the assistance he had been giving Renoir and his friends. France was going through a bad industrial crisis, which also affected his art business. It was now up to the painters themselves to display their pictures and to offer them for sale. So they founded a so-called Société anonyme coopérative, and on 15 April 1874 they opened their own exhibition on the premises of the photographer Nadar (Boulevard des Capucines), which had just become vacant. Renoir was represented by six paintings and one pastel drawing. On 25 April a critical article by Louis Leroy was published in the satirical magazine *Charivari,* a paper which had been printing Daumier's lithographs for the last forty years. The "impressionists' exhibition" was severely and sarcastically criticized for the dull lifelessness of the drawings, the shoddiness of the paintings, the lack

OPPOSITE
The Theatre Box, 1874
Oil on canvas, 80 x 63.5 cm (31½ x 25 in.)
London, The Courtauld Institute of Art

Madame Monet Reading
"Le Figaro", 1872–74
Oil on canvas, 53 x 71.7 cm (20⅞ x 28¼ in.)
Lisbon, Museu Calouste Gulbenkian

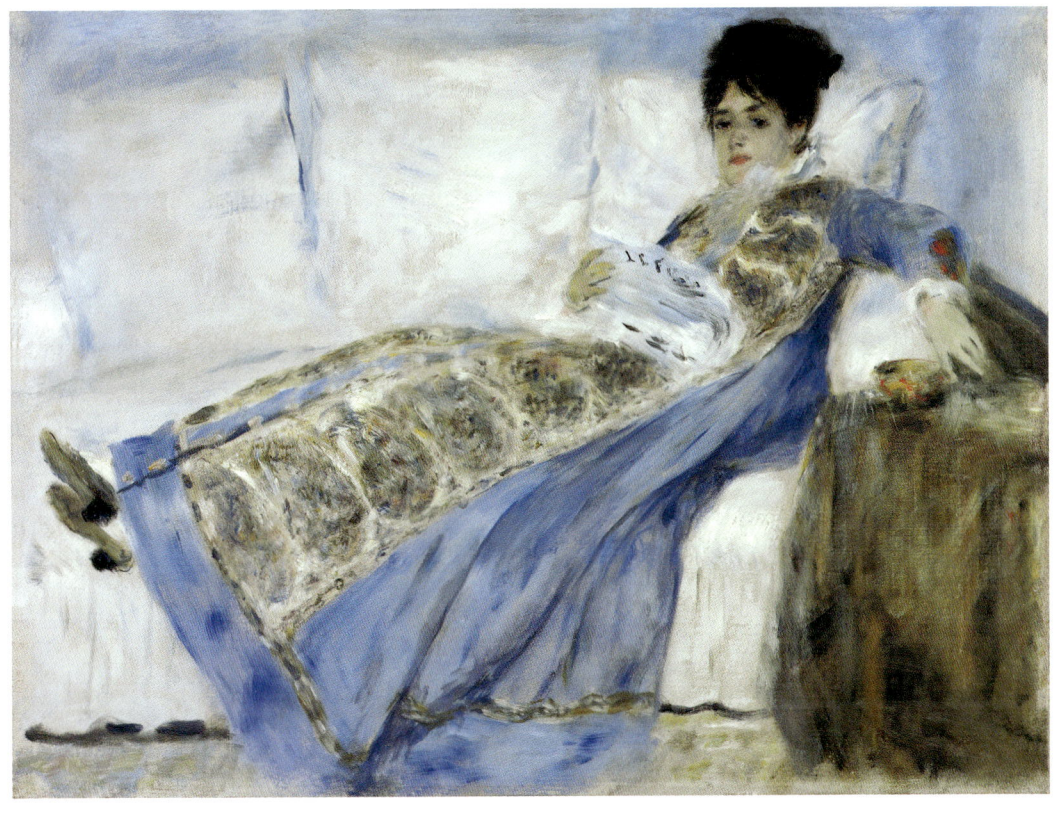

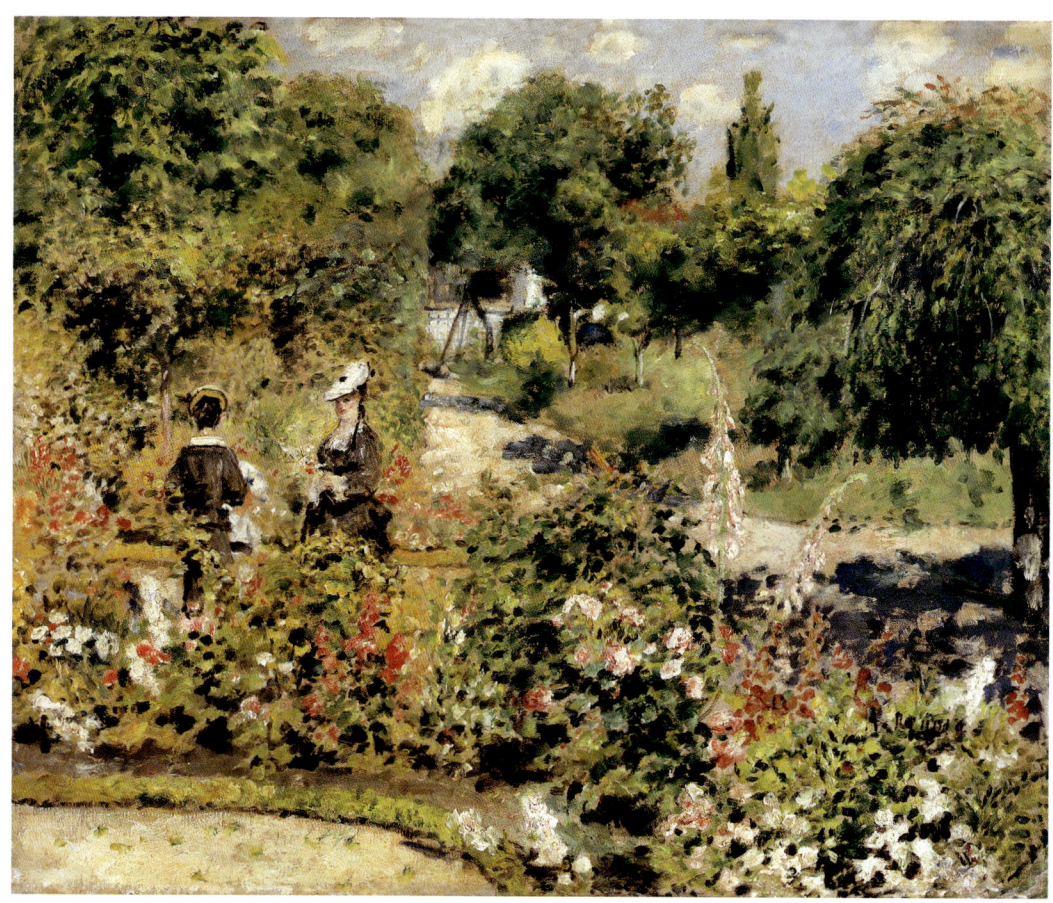

Garden at Fontenay, c. 1873/74
Oil on canvas, 51 x 62 cm (20 x 24½ in.)
Winterthur, Oskar Reinhart Collection
"Am Römerholz"

of attention to detail, and the general slipshod nonchalance that was displayed in this "hair-raising show". The writer said that the highest ideal of these new painters seemed to be that of their own impressions.

The "new school" had found its nickname, and other critics soon began to use the term "impressionists". For years now there had been a tendency among young artists to try and render vital impressions, and they had been discussing the best way of achieving this. The exhibition, though, did nothing to improve the image of the artists. They were called demented and comical, their pictures were regarded as pointless daubs and declarations of war on the very concept of beauty. But this did not deter them. Once Monet had found a flat in Argenteuil on the river Seine, both he and Renoir were joined by Manet, and together the three artists painted quite a few of their sunniest open-air pictures. One of their neighbours, a naval engineer, owned several sailing yachts and also enjoyed painting. He often used to go sailing with Renoir and Monet, and as he was unmarried and wealthy, he also bought quite a few of their works. His name was Gustave Caillebotte, and when he died in 1894, he left all his collection to the French state. These also included six major works by Renoir, which he had painted in 1875/76, such as his *Nude in the Sunlight* and *Le Moulin de la Galette.*

By now Renoir had already met the writer Théodore Duret, who, in 1878, wrote the first more detailed and theoretical account of the aims and the successes of the Impressionists. He, too,

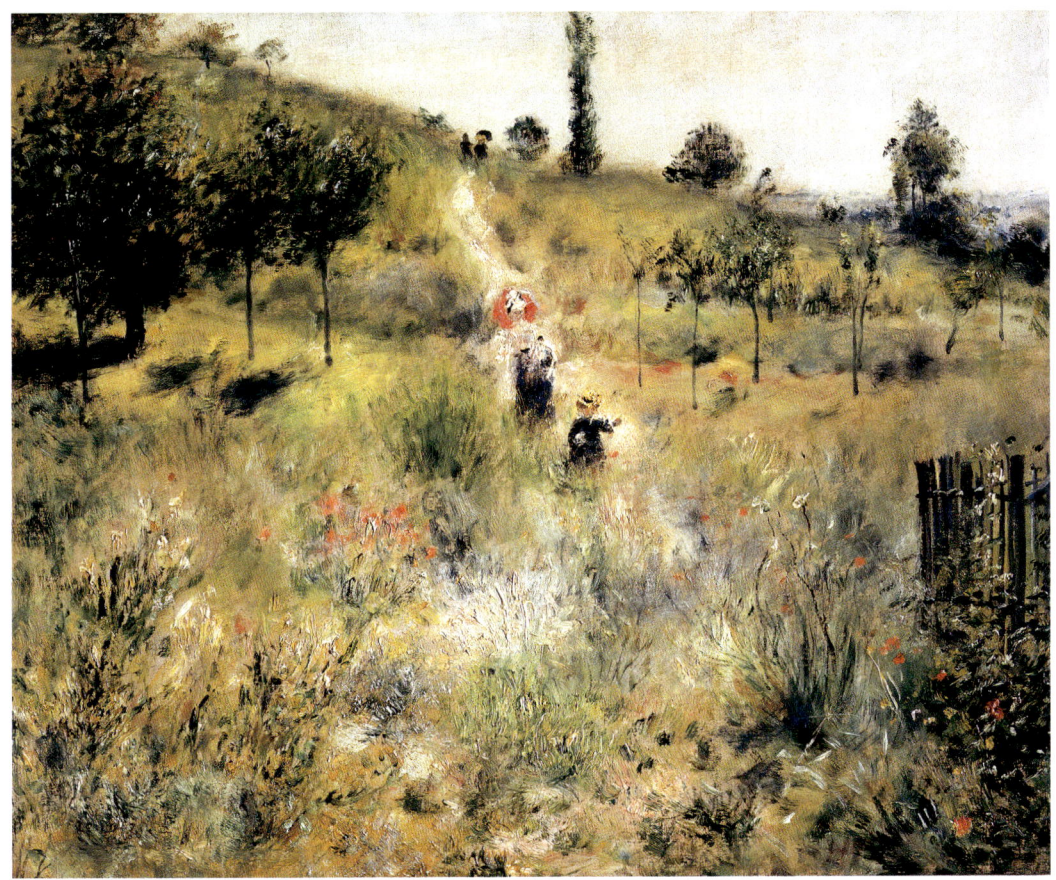

started off by buying pictures, including Renoir's *Lise* for 1,200 francs. This meant that the painter could afford to move into a better studio. But such moments of joy were very short-lived. The artists' society was running at a loss and had to be dissolved.

Country Footpath in the Summer, *c.* 1875
Oil on canvas, 60 x 74 cm (23½ x 29¼ in.)
Paris, Musée d'Orsay

In April 1876 the Impressionists gave their second exhibition, this time at Durand-Ruel's gallery in the Rue Le Peletier. Renoir was represented by fifteen pictures, six of which had already been bought by Victor Chocquet, a new admirer of his art. Albert Wolff, an influential art critic, wrote in the newspaper *Le Figaro:* "Five or six madmen, … blinded by their own ambition, have gathered together in that place to exhibit their works. Many people just kill themselves laughing when they see these shoddy pieces of work …." Some people, however, made quite positive comments on the Impressionists. Edmond Duranty, a Realist writer, published a brochure called *The New Painting,* in which he defended the depiction of contemporary everyday life, open-air painting and the attempt to capture brief moments. Renoir met Zola's publisher Georges Charpentier, who commissioned him for a portrait of his wife and children as well as several paintings to decorate his walls. This enabled Renoir to rent a house in Montmartre and to use its neglected garden as an open-air studio.

In April 1877 the Impressionists organized their third exhibition and, for the first time, described themselves as such, thus using their nickname. Caillebotte rented a few rooms for them in the Rue Le Peletier, and the preliminary work was done mainly by him and Renoir, who contributed over twenty paintings, including *The Swing* (ill. p. 243) and *Le Moulin de la Galette* (ill. pp. 240/241). Chocquet discussed with the people who visited the exhibition, and Renoir's new friend Georges Rivière published a small magazine called *Impressionnisme, journal d'art*, in which the new style was defended. But, as before, the critiques printed in the big newspapers were full of derogatory remarks, and so nobody bought anything.

The following year Renoir gave in and submitted a more moderate picture to the Salon. His *Cup of Hot Chocolate,* a charming portrait of a woman, was accepted. He himself admitted that he had painted it for purely commercial reasons. Nearly all art enthusiasts were only willing to buy pictures by an artist whose works had been exhibited at the Salon. Nevertheless, even in this painting Renoir did not abandon his ideals entirely. Nor did he betray them in 1879, when he exhibited his picture of *Madame Charpentier and Her Children* (ill. pp. 248/249) and finally achieved a genuine break-through and public success. Charpentier gave him an opportunity to show pastel drawings in an exhibition of his own, and he managed to find several other patrons, notably the diplomat Paul Bérard. During the next few years he spent quite a lot of time living and working on Bérard's Wargemont estate near Berneval in Normandy. He did not contribute to the Impressionists' exhibitions in 1879, 1880 or 1881. The relationship

OPPOSITE
Young Girl Reading, 1880
Oil on canvas, 57 x 47.5 cm (22½ x 18¾ in.)
Frankfurt am Main, Städel Museum

Picking Flowers, 1875
Oil on canvas, 54.3 x 65.2 cm (21½ x 25¾ in.)
Washington, D.C., National Gallery of Art,
Ailsa Mellon Bruce Collection

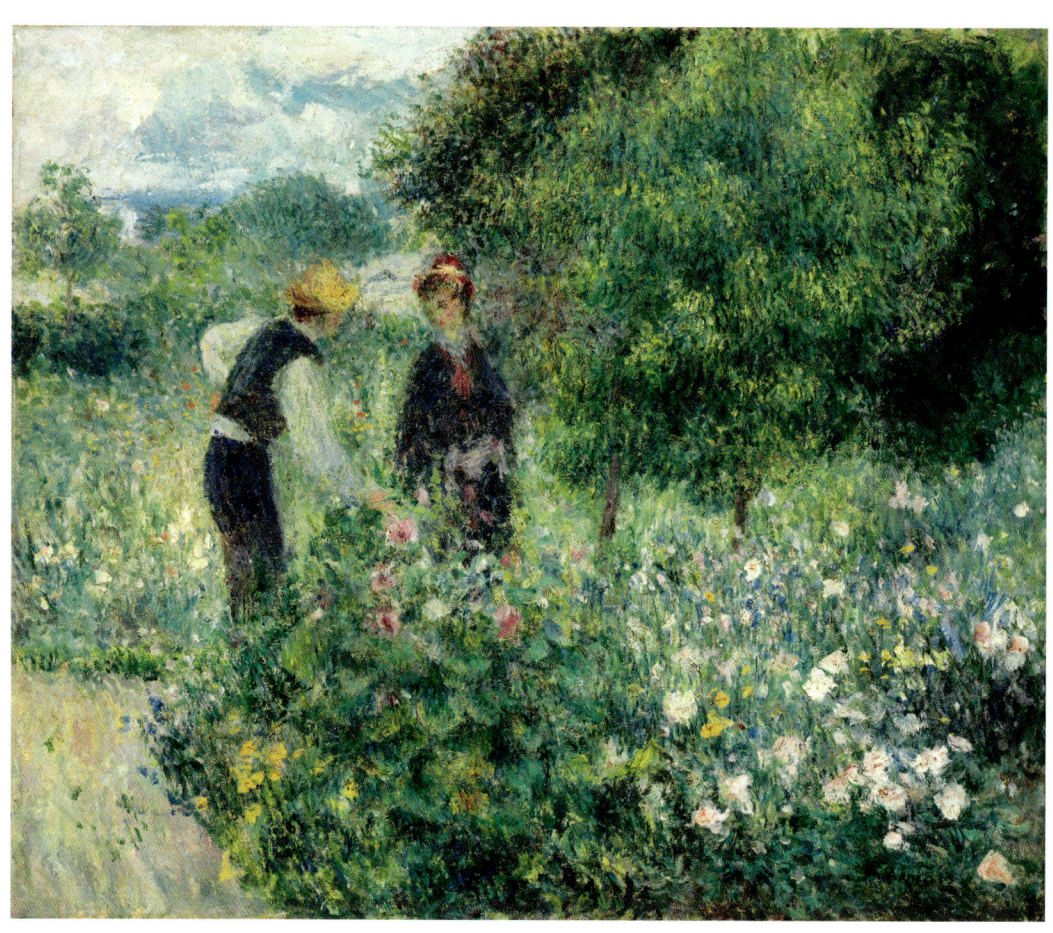

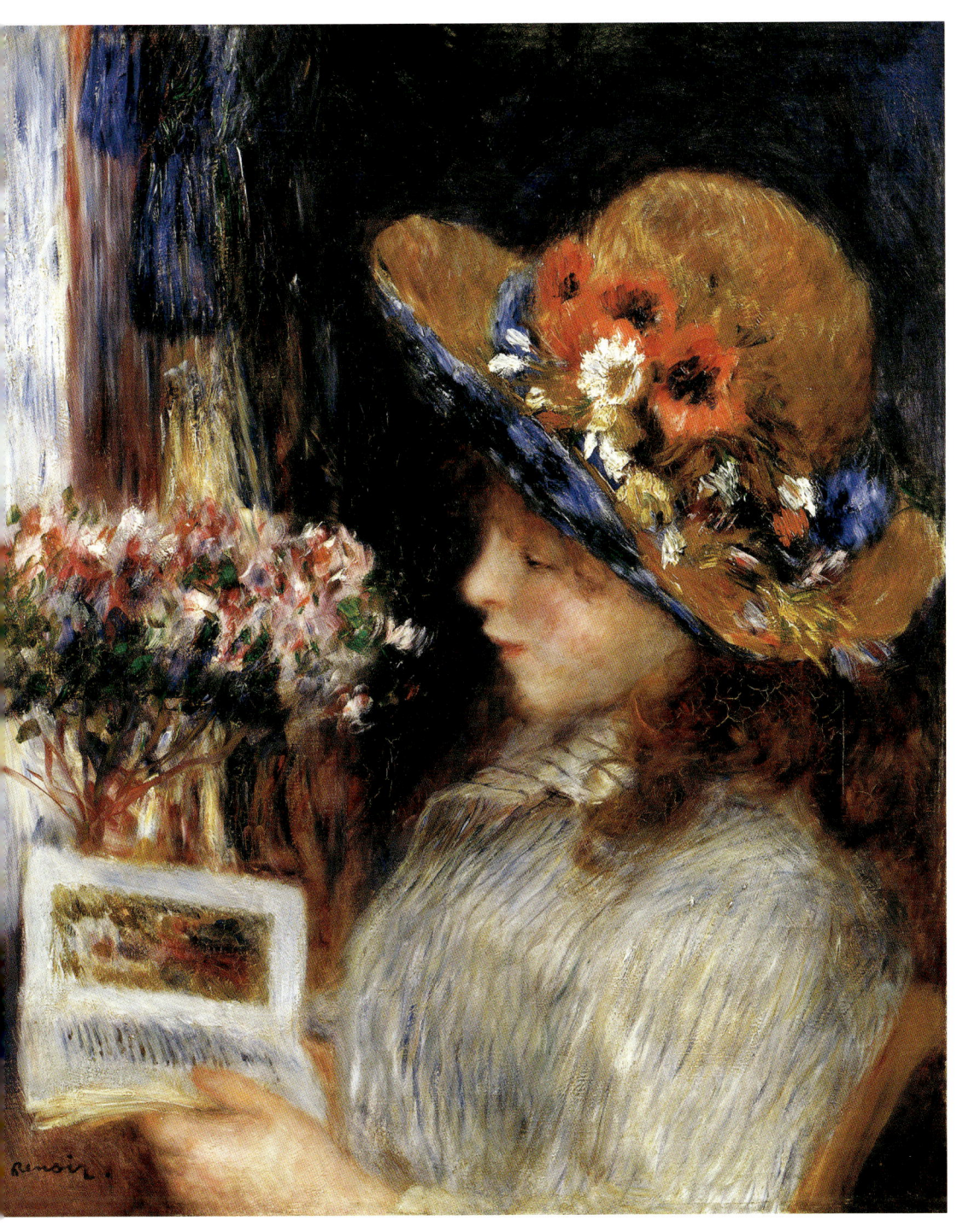

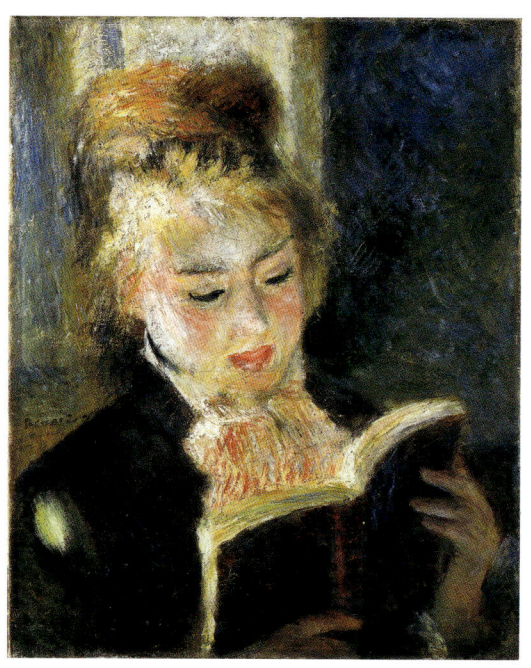

between him and his old friends had become somewhat strained, and this may have been due partly to political differences of opinion. He detested the "anarchism" of some painters, such as François Raffaëlli and Armand Guillaumin, nor did he share Pissarro's socialist ideas. And he did not feel at ease with Edgar Degas's attitude of aggressive contempt towards the public for letting him down.

In 1881 the sale of some of his pictures enabled him for the first time to travel. In March he went to Algiers where the scorching sun and the wealth of different colours attracted him in the same way that they had fascinated the painter whom Renoir admired so much, Delacroix, on his visit half a century earlier. In autumn and spring he visited Venice (cf. ills. pp. 262 and 263), where he felt enchanted by its lights and water; in Rome he was impressed by Raphael's austere fresco style, and near Naples the delicate but energetic mural paintings on the ancient houses of Pompeii reminded him of Corot's pictures. In Palermo, Sicily, he painted a portrait of his hero Richard Wagner, who nevertheless treated him quite impatiently. And when he caught pneumonia on a holiday with his friend Paul Cézanne in Provence, he went straight to Algiers again, where the hot climate soon helped to restore his health.

In April 1882 the seventh exhibition of the Group of Independent Realist and Impressionist Artists took place, where twenty-five of his paintings were shown, including *The Luncheon of the Boating Party* and views of Venice. However, he still had his reservations about the "independent artists", and so he insisted that his pictures should be marked as submitted by his agent Durand-Ruel and not by himself. Durand-Ruel, who had been going through quite a hard time as a result of another economic crisis, really needed this exhibition, and in fact the new understanding of art was now beginning to gain ground in wider circles. Renoir was quite welcome to display his works at the Salon as well, which he did regularly between 1878 and 1883. This gave him an opportunity to "get rid of that revolutionary image", which rather frightened him, as he put it. In 1883 Durand-Ruel organized a special Renoir exhibition at his new gallery on the Boulevard de la Madeleine. Towards the end of summer that year Renoir did some painting on the island of Guernsey; in the winter he and Monet went to Genoa together and then visited Cézanne in L'Estaque in Provence. From then on he would spend part of each summer and winter outside Paris. He often went to stay on the coast in Normandy and Brittany, and also the Côte d'Azur as well as Essoyes in Burgundy, the home of Aline Charigot, the charming little model whom he married in 1890.

From 1884/85 onwards a number of new elements entered into his art, thus marking a definite turning point. But before we discuss this in detail we shall focus on the works he produced during that rich and joyful period of his life. This was the triumph of Impressionism, and it can be clearly defined in terms of Renoir's art and his life at that time.

TOP
Woman Reading, 1874–76
Oil on canvas, 46.5 x 38.5 cm (18¼ x 15¼ in.)
Paris, Musée d'Orsay

OPPOSITE
The First Outing, 1876/77
Oil on canvas, 65 x 49.5 cm (25½ x 19½ in.)
London, The National Gallery

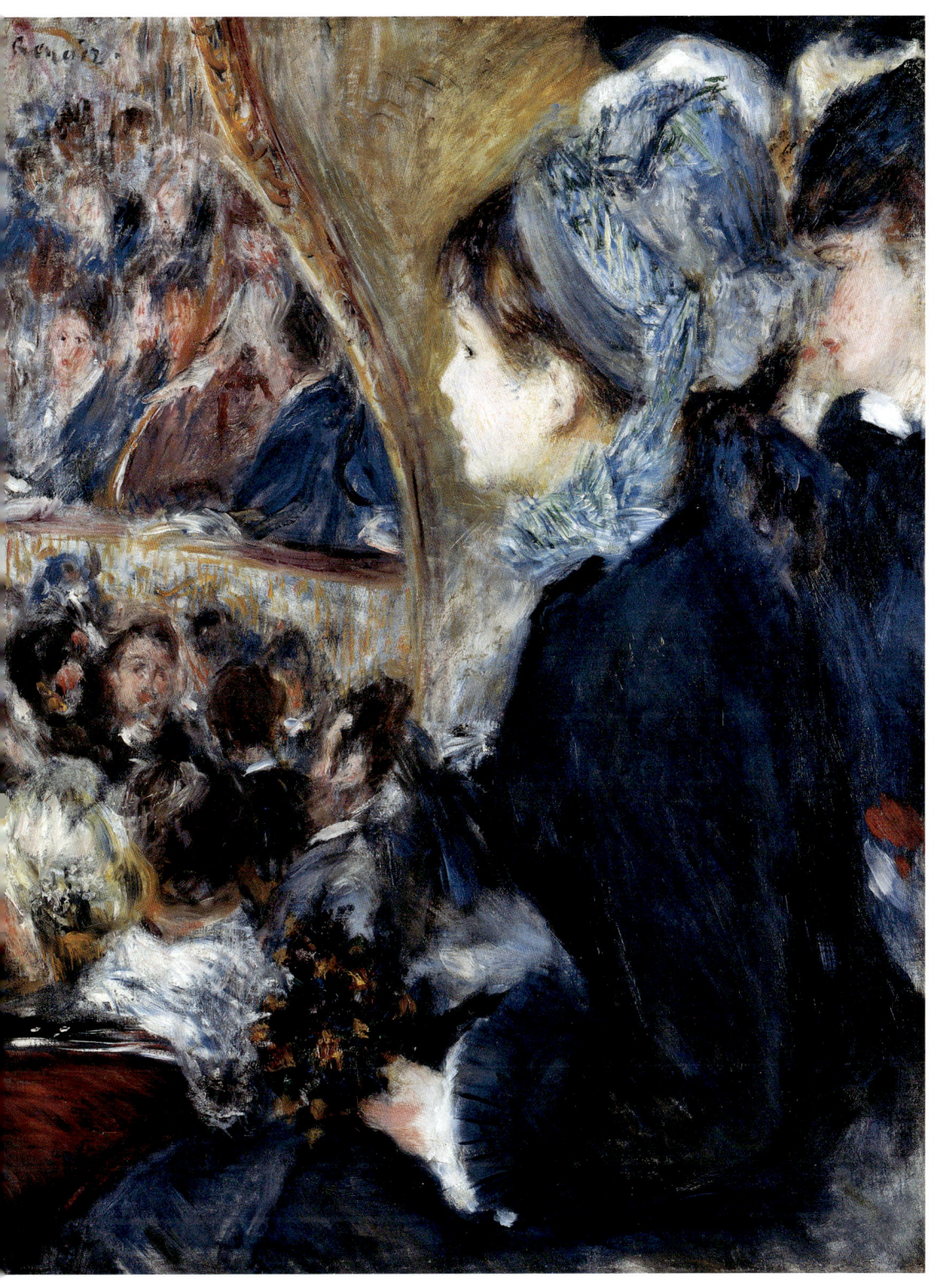

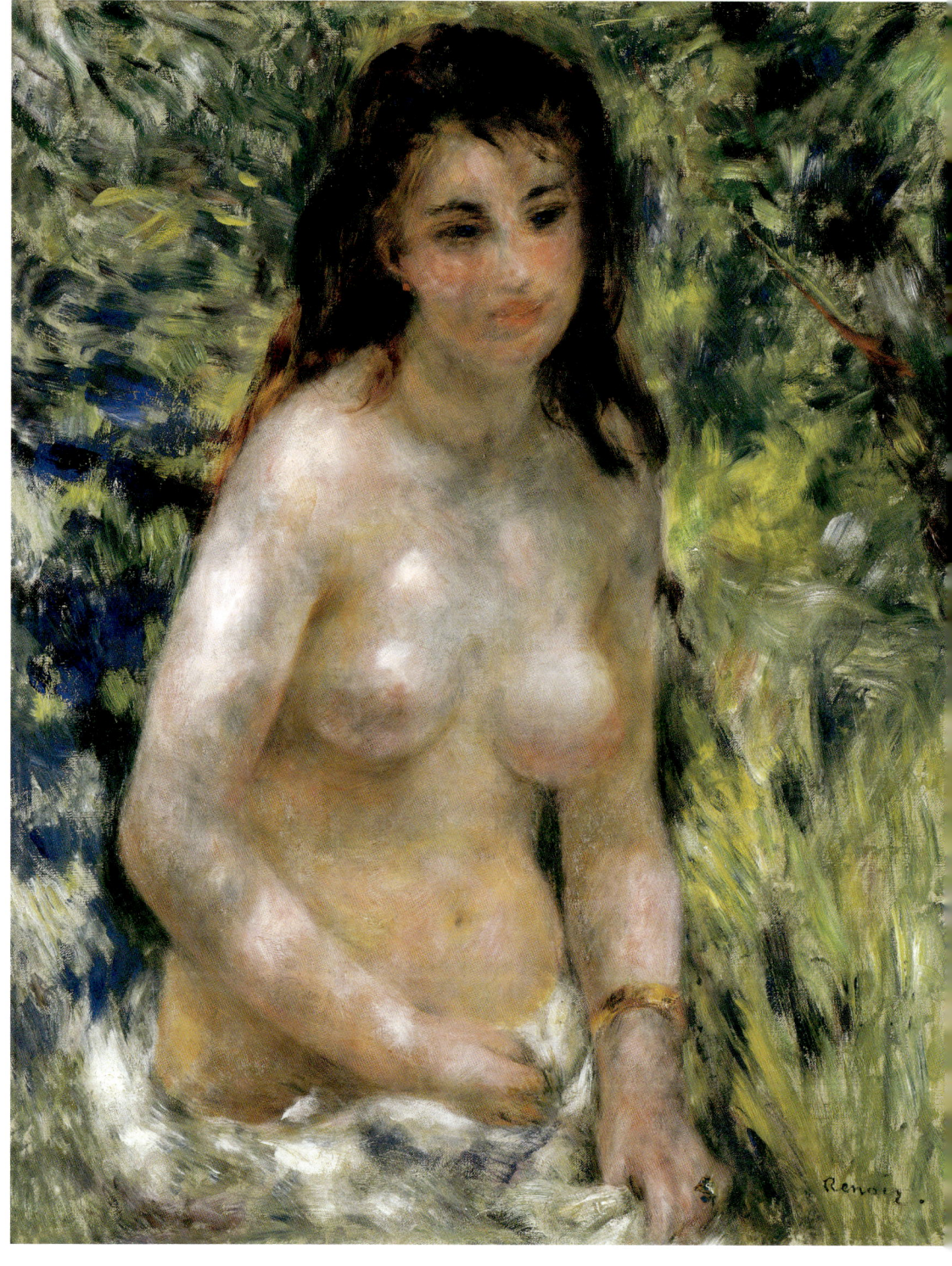

Masterpieces of Realist Impressionism

Renoir painted all those elements of real life that he saw and approved of: the life of the rich, on whose benevolence he depended in order to make a living as a painter, and also the little pleasures of the lower-middle-class bohemians, the class to which he himself belonged and which looked very respectable and had nothing rebellious or tragic about it. But although his art did not encompass everything that could be said about society, we can still call it realistic because it shed some light on facets of life which did indeed exist. Also, it helped people to experience and accept themselves in a new way, both in their normal, humdrum existence and in their sensuality. For the first time they were able to look at important features of their lives from an aesthetic point of view.

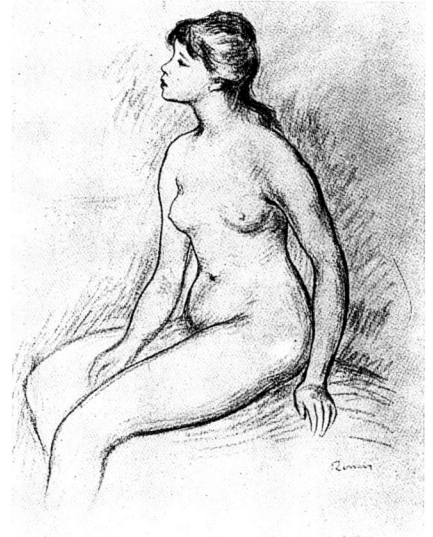

There were a number of subjects which Renoir particularly concentrated on: portraits and portrait-like individual figures, dances, the theatre, the company of good friends, country walks, the hustle and bustle of the big city, and landscapes. Both his portraits and his pictures of people in general showed his special gift for expressing feminine charm; what is more, he knew how to express the whole range of that enticing attractiveness which could emanate from a woman. Again and again he managed to express very skilfully the enchantment of feminine beauty and to convey a feeling of deep joy. Renoir may have painted only a rather narrow area of human existence; indeed, there are no sad, angry, ugly or old women in his pictures, no profound or problematic characters, and even his male figures have a certain soft femininity about them. But hardly anybody has ever been able to capture that smile of blissful joy, the tantalizing sweetness of being in love, and a luxurious, easy-going enjoyment of life. Having learnt his craft from the noble masters of the Rococo, he succeeded in reflecting all these feelings in the features and postures of his figures.

OPPOSITE
Nude in the Sunlight, *c.* 1876
Oil on canvas, 81 x 65 cm (32 x 25⅝ in.)
Paris, Musée d'Orsay

ABOVE RIGHT
Female Nude Seated
Black crayon
Private collection

There were many "ladies' painters" in those days: skilled craftsmen of the art of painting and willing flatterers of the tastes of the upper-middle classes. They knew how to turn every banker's wife

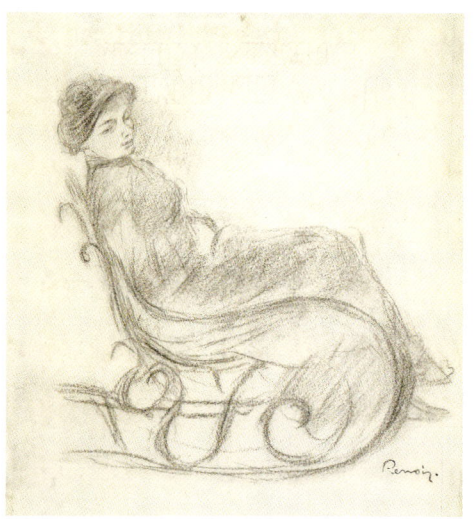

into a Renaissance duchess or a ravishing seductress. They painted costly clothes and furniture, and the faces of their figures had a certain soulless, stylized complacency and morbidity about them. Renoir, who had to live by his art, did not always manage to escape the danger of superficiality in his portraits. He was quite capable of painting a brilliant picture of gleaming silk and velvet, but he never did so unless his heart was in it, and so his natural naivety protected him from the false glitter of the fashionable. He would observe real life rather than studied poses, and his paintings were a celebration of the freshness and beauty of simple, unspoilt people.

His best pictures are of people with whom he had a personal relationship. He frequently used to paint his friend Monet and his wife Camille. Painted with broad strokes of the brush, Madame Monet can be seen recumbent on the sofa, reading *Le Figaro* (ill. p. 229). She is wearing a delicate, light-blue morning dress, and the sofa has been draped with white gauze. Her dark hair and eyes are in sharp contrast with the general summer-like brightness of this colourful painting. The Impressionists loved showing their subjects in the intimate privacy of their own homes, with a casual nonchalance that these people would not normally have displayed in front of complete strangers. And in order to preserve a natural and lifelike impact, the painters had to abandon the classical tradition of balance and symmetry. Instead they tried to capture individual moments and used asymmetrical and spontaneous elements to emphasize the fleeting impression of chance.

In fact this approach was noticeable even where Renoir had to do justice to people's demands, i.e. when they expected to be portrayed in a certain way to present a definite image. The picture of the publisher's wife, Madame Charpentier, and her children is a good example (ill. pp. 248/249). This intelligent and distinguished lady is shown as displaying a good deal of studied nonchalance. And although her little darlings have obviously been smartened up specially for the occasion, like dolls, there is nevertheless still something in their faces and their postures that looks attractively childlike and uncomplicated. The pyramid of figures, which includes a St Bernard dog, has been moved diagonally into the middle of the room, thus changing the classical scheme of composition into something rather extravagant. The surprisingly empty area in the bottom right-hand corner introduces a certain asymmetrical tension into the structure of the picture, and, together with the large gold-lacquer screen and its pheasants, shows the aesthetic pleasure which people at that time used to derive from Japanese art and its highly original decorative effect.

Renoir refused to jump on this "Japoniste" bandwagon, but in this picture, where he had to render the way in which Madame Charpentier's room was decorated, he could not really avoid it. So he combined the glowing colours of the screen with the flowers, curtains, sofa cover and children's dresses and achieved an overall impression of a still life that was both clever and in good taste, with the black-and-white contrasts of the lady's dress and of the dog as the

TOP
Woman Seated in a Chair, 1883
Pencil and crayon, 36.2 x 31 cm (14¼ x 12¼ in.)
The Art Institute of Chicago,
Samuel P. Avery Fund

OPPOSITE
A Girl with a Watering Can, 1876
Oil on canvas, 100 x 73 cm (39¼ x 28¾ in.)
Washington, D.C., National Gallery of Art,
Chester Dale Collection

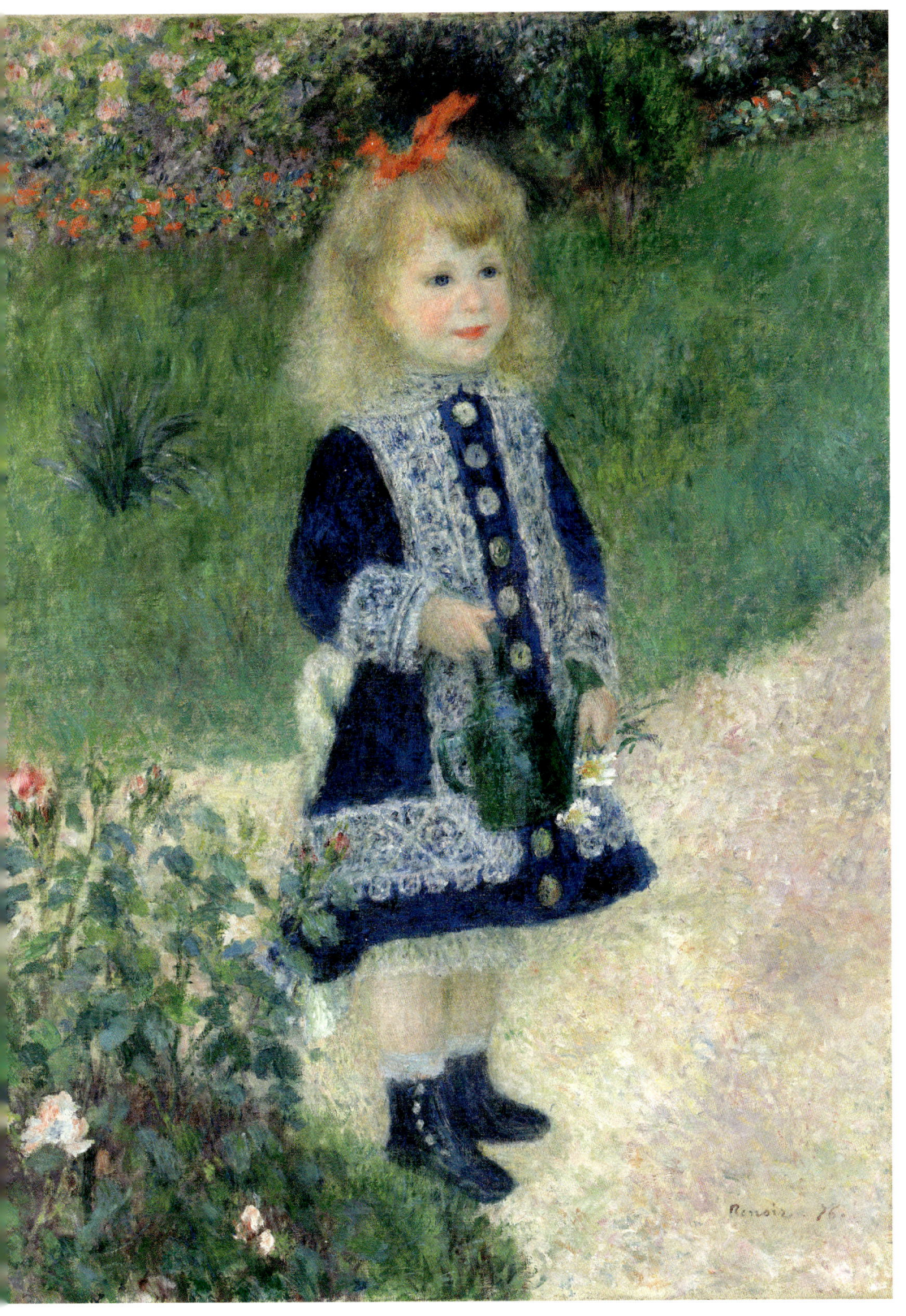

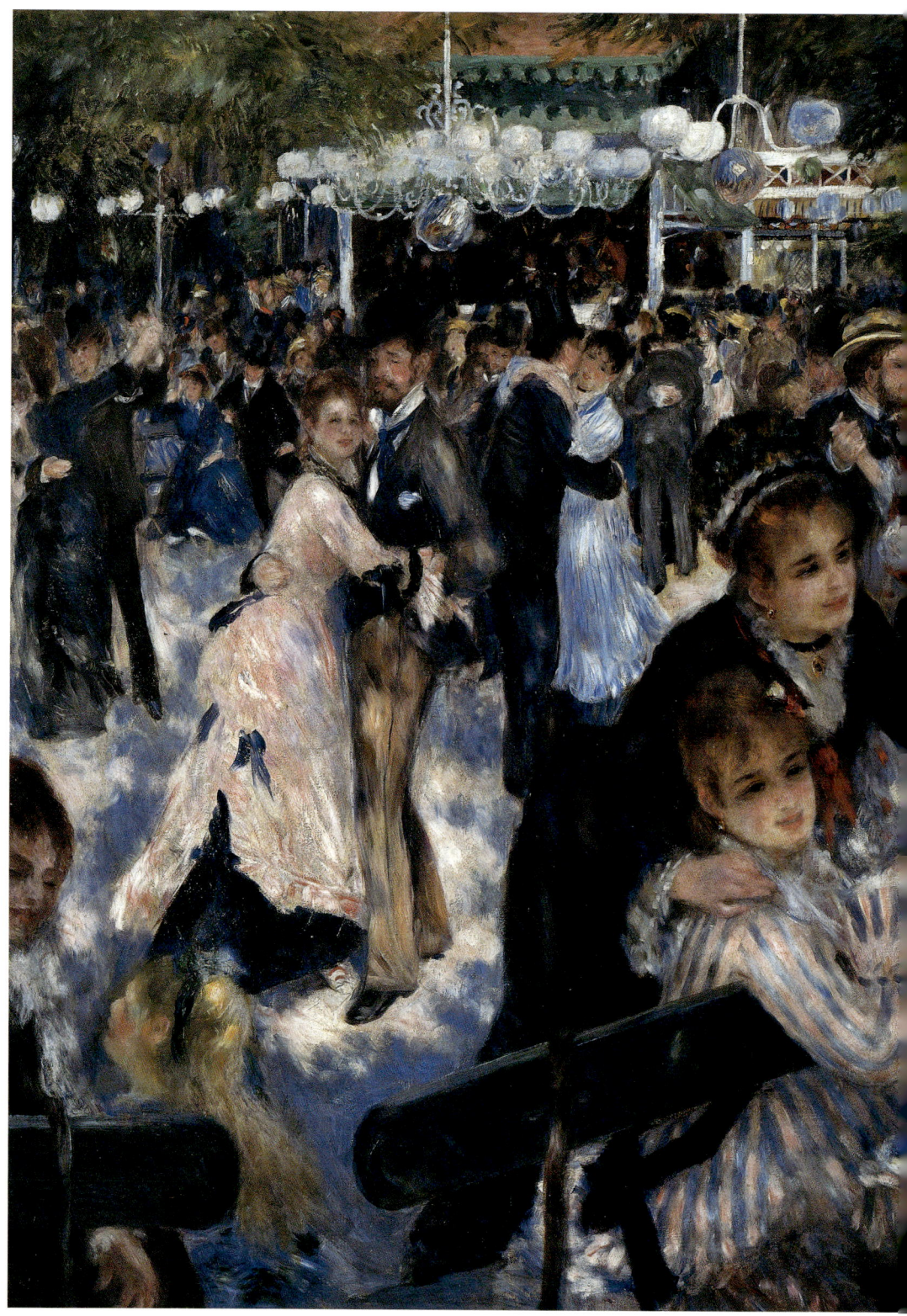

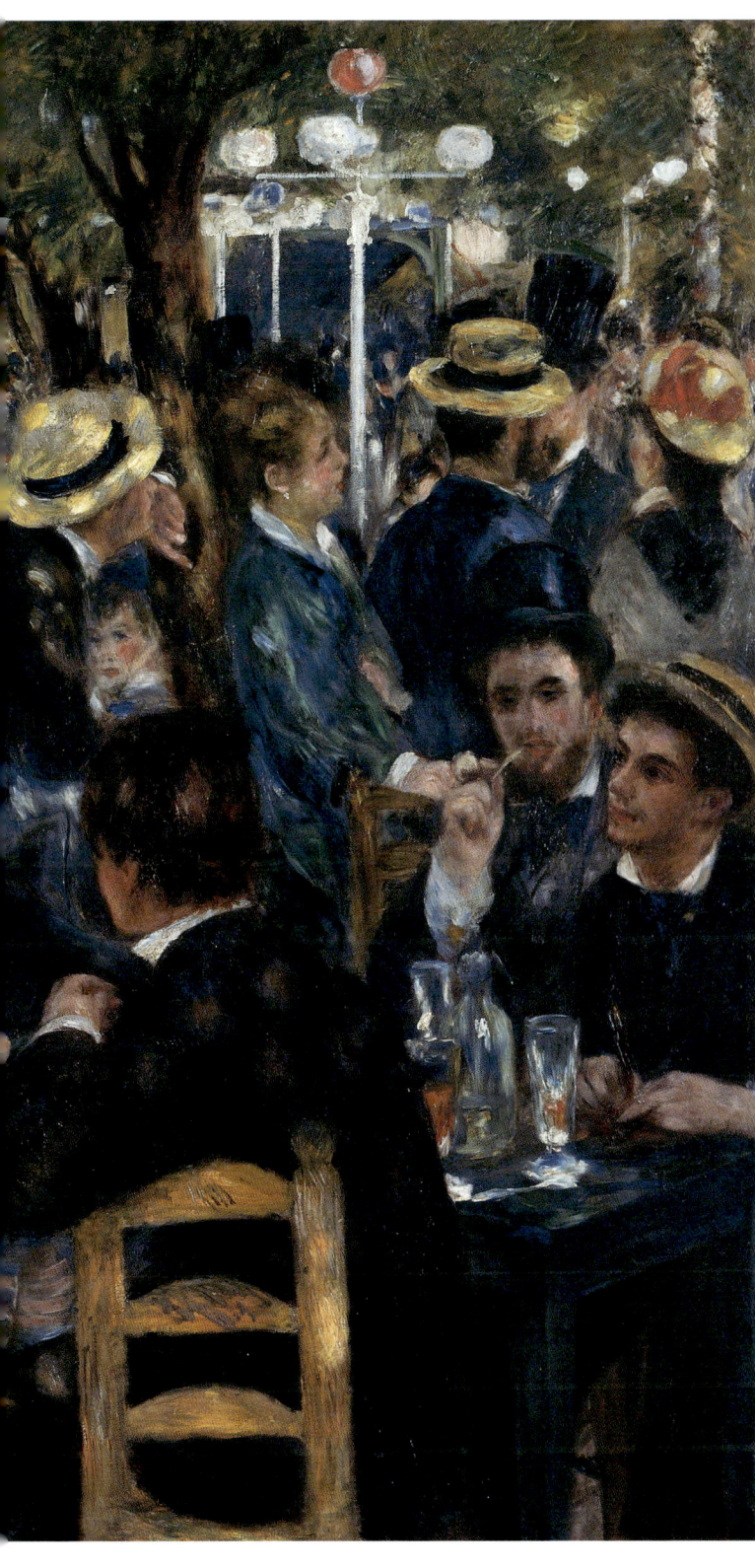

Le Moulin de la Galette, 1876
Oil on canvas, 131.5 x 176.5 cm
(51⅞ x 69½ in.)
Paris, Musée d'Orsay

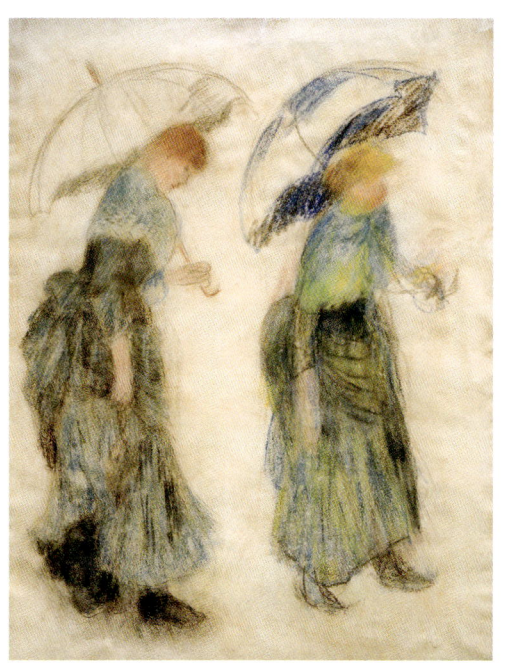

most emphatic elements. For Renoir neither black nor white were dead colours that always stayed the same. On the contrary, he knew how to make black come to life. Black was very common in people's dresses at the time, and Renoir often managed to create it by mixing red with blue. Quoting Tintoretto as his authority, he even called black the queen of colours.

The children form the most natural part of this portrait of the Charpentiers. Renoir painted many children's portraits that year. He had a finely developed feeling for the rosy complexion of a child's skin, for the dreamlike purity and gentleness of their eyes, but also for that capricious self-confidence which was typical of some little lady, not just among the daughters of the Parisian middle classes.

Apart from the portraits of friends and the ones that had been commissioned by customers, there are also a large number of pictures and studies which Renoir used to paint of professional models; these are so-called genre pictures, i.e. portraits of people who were somehow typical of the time and whose names we do not know. Artistically, they do not differ greatly from Renoir's real portraits. Nearly all of them are of women; Renoir liked them, and their pictures were easier to sell. His *Woman Reading* (ill. p. 234) is one such work: a blonde woman sitting by the window and reading a paperback novel. The bright paper of the book reflects the yellow sunlight onto her face, so that her face and her hair are filled with a brightness that comes from several different sources. In contrast to prevalent pre-Impressionist methods, light and shade do not serve to enhance the plasticity of the outlines, but the light, as it were, swallows up all contours and details, leaving no more than a ripple of yellow and red, accompanied by some colourful black.

People in the sunlight – this was one of the most widely discussed problems among the Impressionists, and Renoir picked up this theme in a number of female nude pictures, the most magnificent being that of his model Anna, a semi-nude painting which he began in the garden of his studio in the Rue Cortot in 1875 and showed at the second Impressionist exhibition in 1876. It is the figure of an extremely shapely girl, bending over slightly, and is like some of the Greek sculptures of Aphrodite rising from the waves (ill. p. 236). Her long chestnut-brown hair runs down the length of her body, as do the patches of light and the subtle shades of purple and green that are reflections of the foliage that surrounds and protects her. Rising out of the blossoming shrubs, it seems as if she were a flower herself. The shrubs themselves consist of no more than a few yellow, blue and green strokes of the brush woven together by the artist. Never before had any painter achieved such a subtle merging of a naked human being with light and nature. Indeed, it would have been impossible to paint like that without a new awareness of life, of the sun, of the open air. At the same time, however, the picture affects us as if it were an ancient myth of nature. The girl, whose fingers and wrists are adorned in costly splendour, is both a child of nature

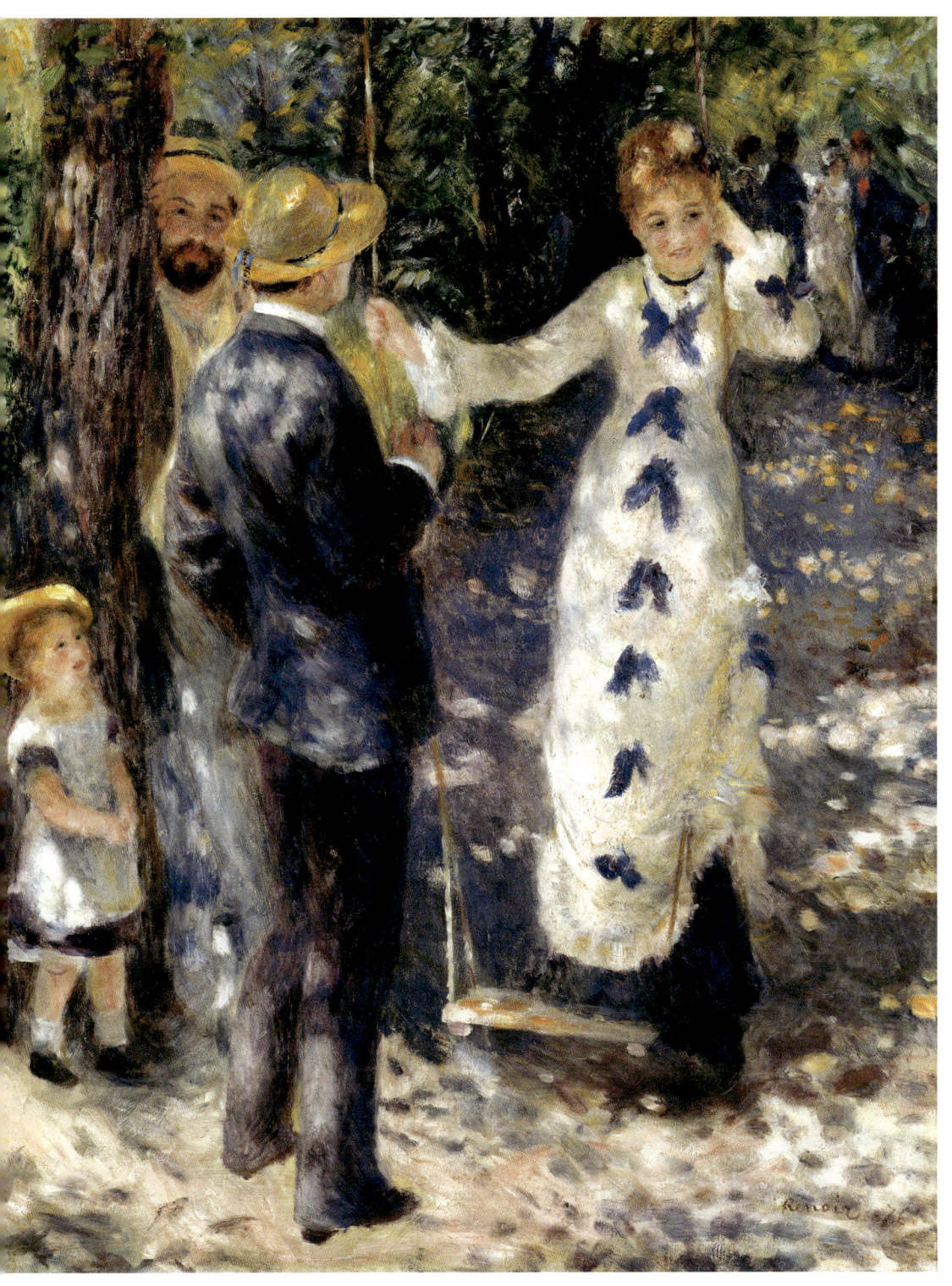

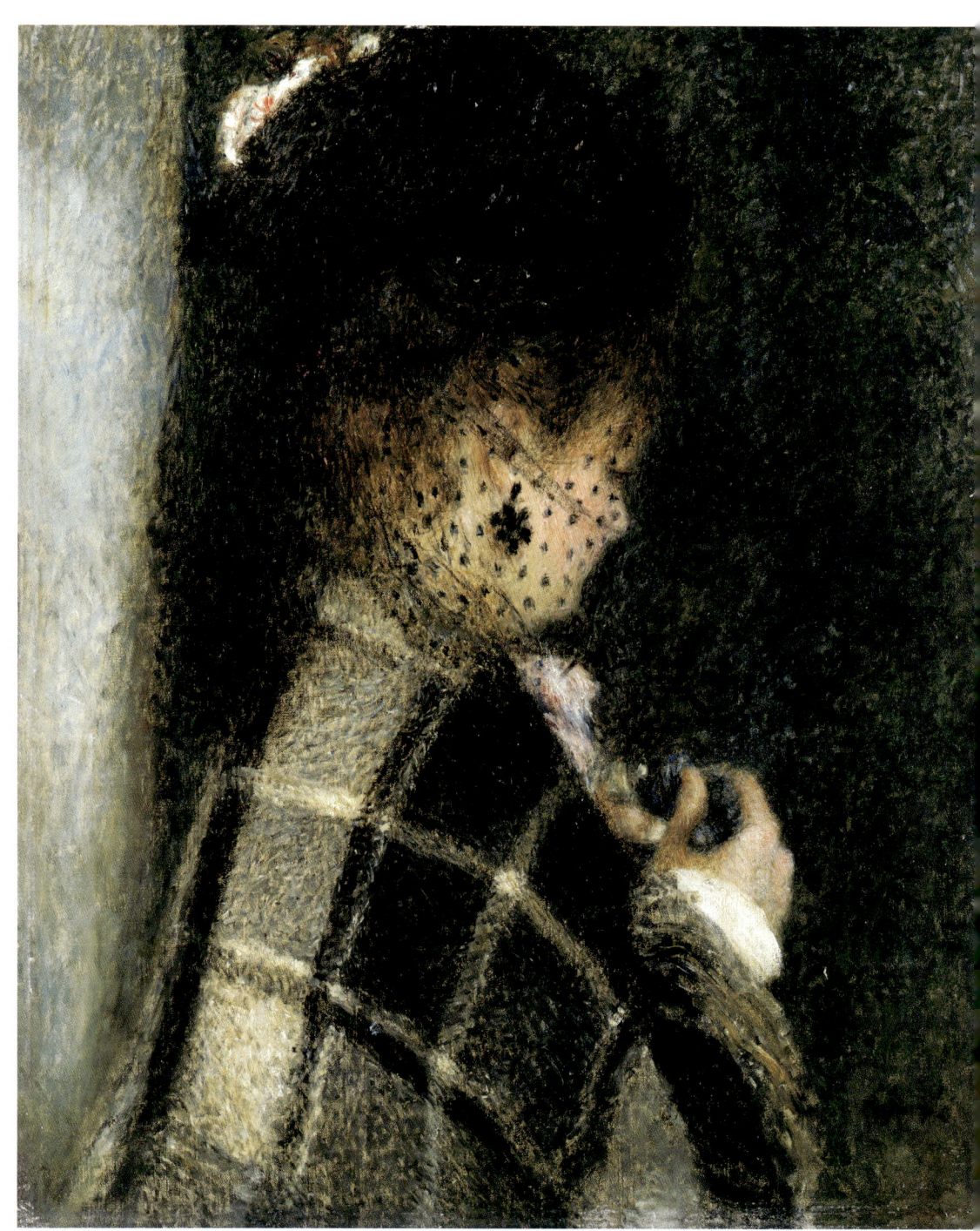

and a goddess of nature – a painted poem in which an ancient truth is expressed in a completely novel manner. No wonder it left the critics baffled. Nevertheless, Caillebotte bought the picture.

In his portraits, Renoir always aimed at painting his subjects in a posture that was both natural and characteristic, but at the same time captured a chance impression of a brief, fleeting moment. He continually tried to achieve impressions that were true to life, a tendency which also prevailed in his genre paintings of the life of the middle classes. Paintings of this kind were not highly regarded at the time. Those who set the tone in the art world believed that the most worthy objects of artistic endeavour were, first and foremost, themes from mythology and history as well as religious and allegorical depictions. As for those other pictures that merely showed the life of ordinary people, they preferred scenes which they regarded as "picturesque", i.e. scenes from Italy or the Orient. Members of the Salon panel as well as visitors to the exhibitions and prospective buyers used to demand that each painting should include either an element of suspense or a clever, amusing event, something that was somehow unusual, a story which the artist succeeded in telling by means of the skilful arrangement of the figures and the expressions on their faces. In Realism, on the other hand, as represented by Courbet, Millet and their first followers, it was maintained that there was beauty in simple, ordinary, everyday life, and that this could be portrayed in art. As a result, Realism was looked down upon as the "cult of ugliness".

Like other Impressionists, Renoir concentrated on the things which he regarded as the beauty of middle-class life in the big city of Paris. In fact, his pictures tell us little stories, too, but they are all taken from contemporary everyday life in Paris, or rather from a typical Parisian Sunday. His stories are always short. They are glimpses of people passing by, captured in brief moments, snatched from the ever quickening flow of modern life and scribbled down in the shorthand of the artist's own experience. They are deliberately void of climactic effects or indeed of anything unusual. Renoir never used to paint anything that could not have been repeated a thousand times in exactly the same way – and would still have remained something totally different and unique. It was the Impressionists who discovered the individual value of every single chance occurrence, and their conclusion that everything was in perpetual motion was forcefully expressed in their art. They recorded the attractive features of the ephemeral and the momentary.

Like his colleague Degas, Renoir also made his observations at the theatre and the circus. And when he painted a graceful ballet dancer and two little artistes at the Fernando Circus (ill. p. 251), he did so far more gently and lovingly than Degas with his sarcasm. Above all, however, he observed the spectators. *The Theatre Box* (ill. p. 228) shows a couple waiting for the beginning of the show. The gentleman, Renoir's brother Edmond, remains in the background, and half of his face is covered by a pair of opera glasses, while the lady shows herself in all her beauty at the balustrade. She is portrayed in a posture that is almost classical in its simplicity. The stripes on her dress guide our gaze to the tranquil features of her gentle countenance. The pale pink of the camellia blossom in her hair and on her neck matches the shades of her powdered complexion which, in turn, has a greenish yellow sheen that reflects the cold light from the gas lamp. The entire picture, which features Nini Lopez, a local model, is an ode to the young woman's charm, and although Renoir faithfully recorded her self-conscious tension, it is completely fresh and without affectation.

We no longer understand nowadays how such an inspired and refined painting could possibly have met with scornful contempt, but when Renoir showed this picture at the first Impressionist exhibition, the only person who was prepared to buy it was a rather insignificant art dealer called Père Martin. Renoir sold it for a mere 425 francs, which he desperately needed to pay the

Young Woman with a Veil, c. 1875
Oil on canvas, 61.3 x 50.8 cm (24¼ x 20 in.)
Paris, Musée d'Orsay

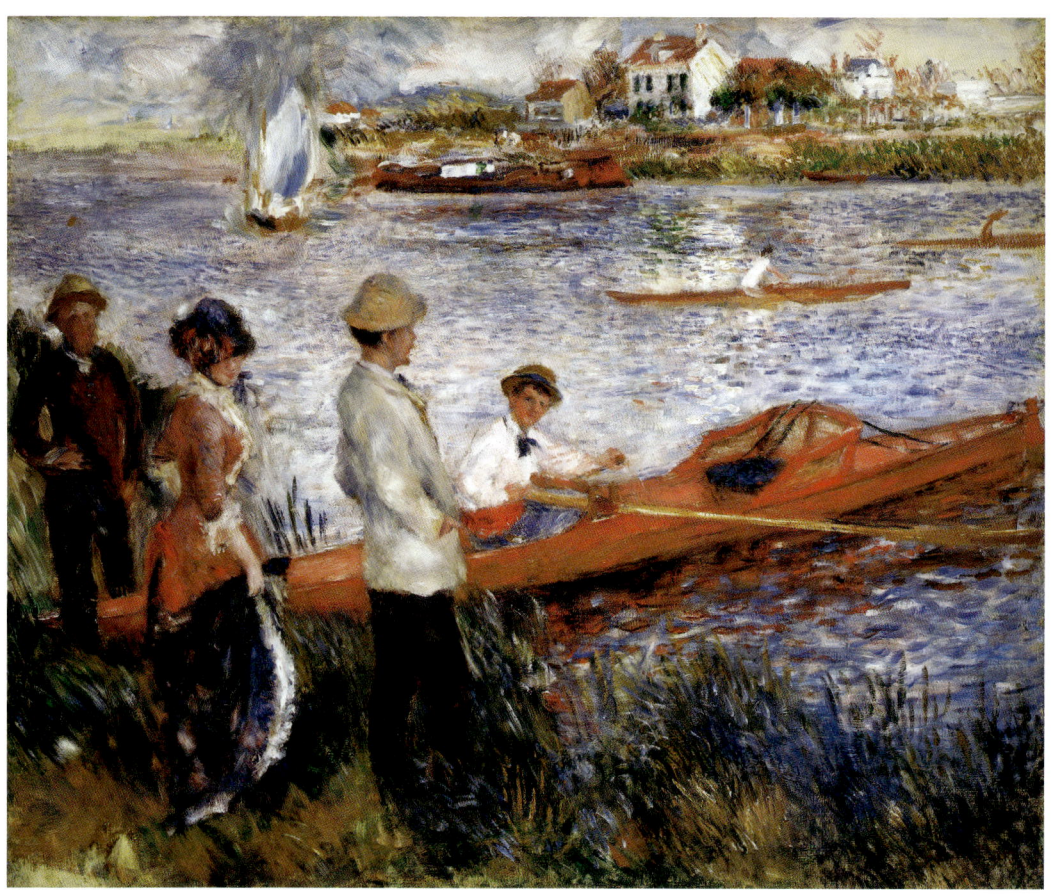

Oarsmen at Chatou, 1879
Oil on canvas, 81.2 x 100.2 cm (32 x 39½ in.)
Washington, D.C., National Gallery of Art

rent. Two years later he painted a similar theatre scene called *The First Outing* (ill. p. 235), showing a young girl's first visit to the opera. Her stunned expectation is captured beautifully in her posture and her expression, even though we can only see her delicate little face in the form of a very hazy profile. Before her eyes there is the scuttling movement of the crowds whose impatient hustle and bustle fills the neighbouring boxes. A certain type of atmosphere had been perfectly expressed, an atmosphere that tingled with excitement and that was an important element in the lives of people who simply loved going to the theatre.

During the summer months, when the theatres were closed, there was another pleasure which Parisians used to enjoy: outings into the country. This was popular both among the respectable and the bohemians.

At the Grenouillère swimming pool Renoir had paid more attention to the overall colour scheme and the changing light. Now his open-air paintings were composed of individual figures, grouped together informally, smiling, flirting, chatting and generally enjoying the fresh air all around them, which is reflected in delicate yellow, blue and pink spots of colour. Renoir broke all academic rules of composition and arrangement. Shedding the straitjacket of rigid formality, he portrayed life as it really was, emphasizing everything that was cheerful and innocent. Unlike any other painter, he knew how to express the soft gracefulness of a woman's head turned tenderly to one side, the magic

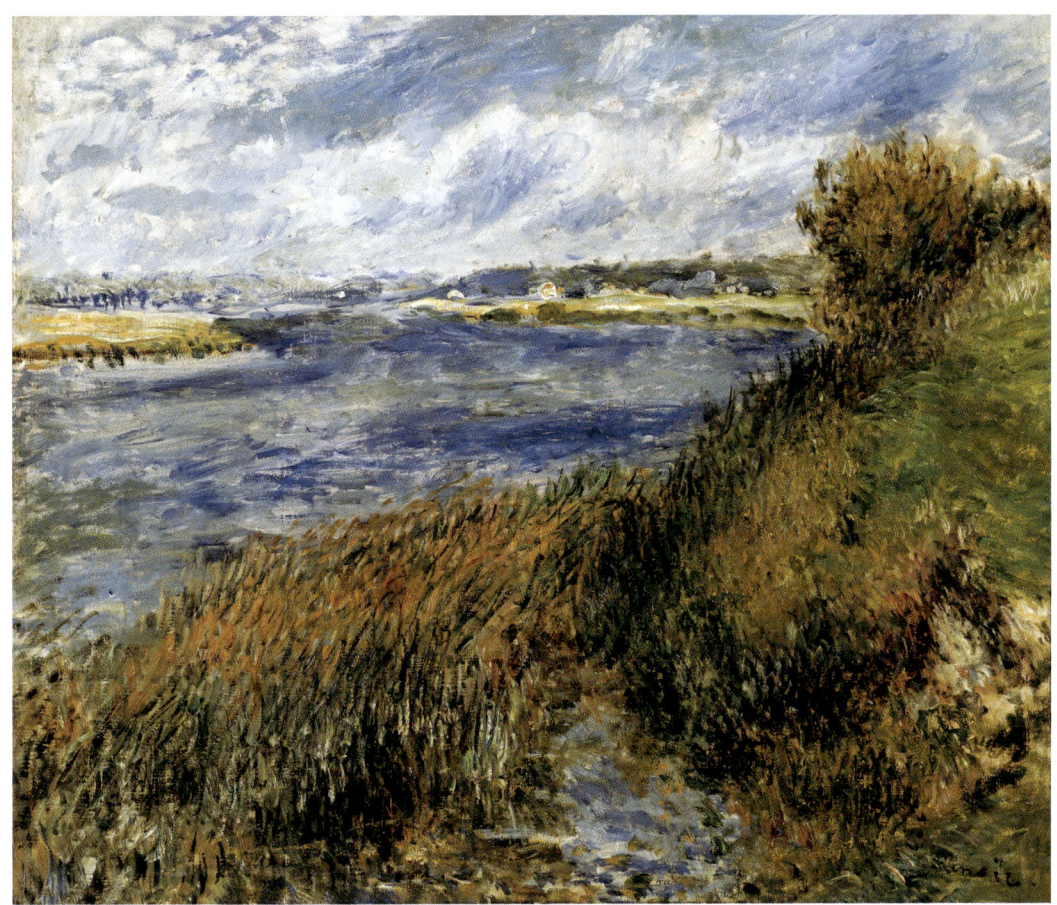

Banks of the Seine at Champrosay, 1876
Oil on canvas, 54.6 x 66 cm (21½ x 26 in.)
Paris, Musée d'Orsay

of a loving gesture, the warm radiance of dark, fawn-like eyes and the happy atmosphere of good friends or lovers gathered together. *The Walk* (ill. p. 226) and *The Swing* (ill. p. 243) both seem to be telling little tales, which puts them in the tradition of the gallant masters of the 18th century; at the same time, however, they emphasize the vibrant quality of various spots of colour and the subtle play of light and shade.

The most significant painting during this fruitful period in Renoir's life is *Le Moulin de la Galette* of 1879 (ill. pp. 240/241). It has even been referred to as the most beautiful picture of the 19th century. The Butte Montmartre is a hill in the north-east of Paris, affording a magnificent view of the entire city. At the beginning of the 19th century the landscape painter Georges Michel, who was later rediscovered as one of the forerunners of the Barbizon Painters, had painted Montmartre as a hill with a thin growth of vegetation and towered over by windmills with turning sails.

By now the village had become a suburb, but it still had a certain rural simplicity about it and was therefore a popular place for excursions. Open-air restaurants and night bars soon opened their doors and provided merriment, until it gradually became the world-famous artists' and nightclub district. In the 1870s the Moulin de la Galette was a converted mill which served as a dance hall for the unpretentious lower-middle classes and the bohemians among them. One of the two former windmills was still occasionally used for pressing orris root for the perfume industry, but both

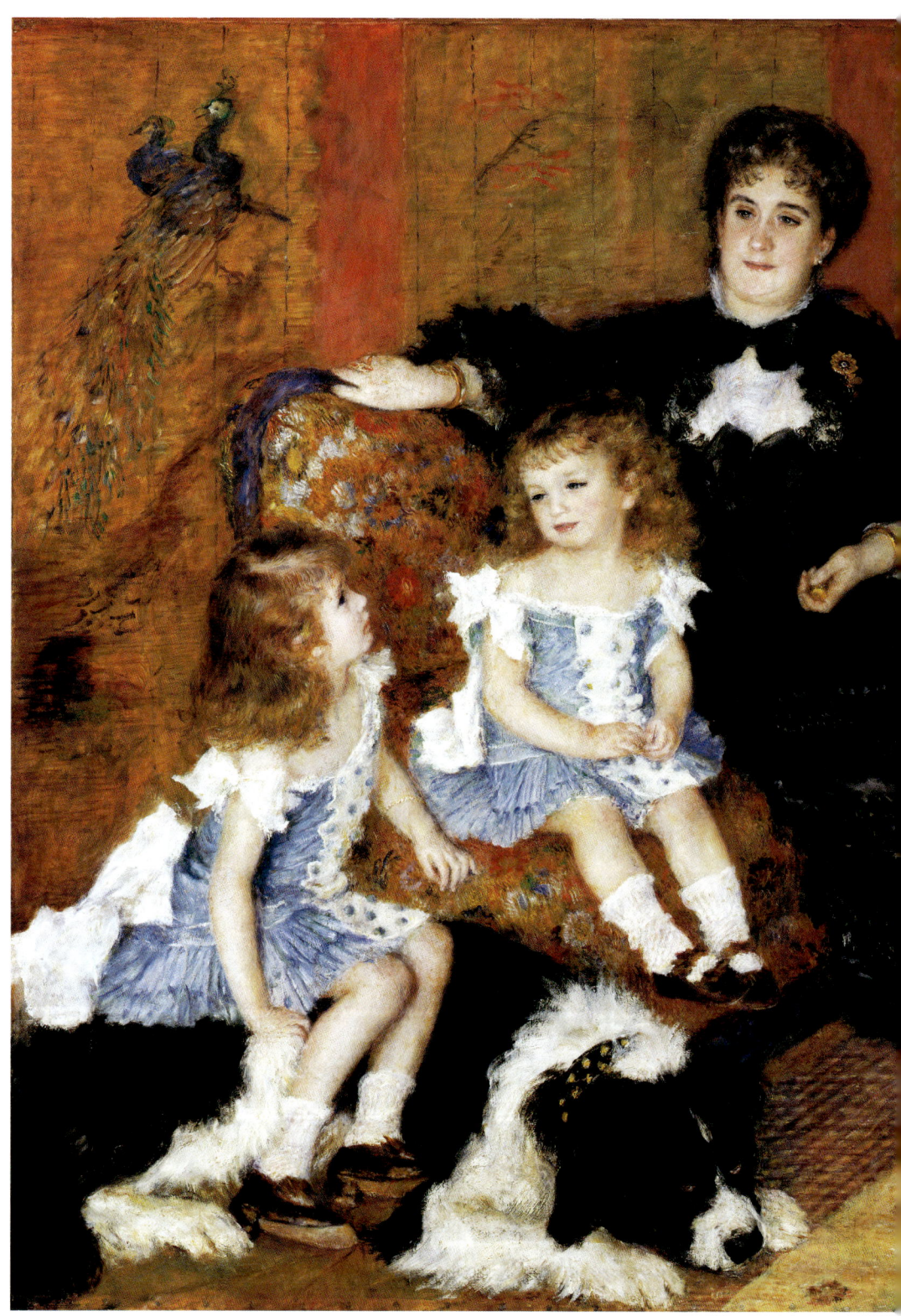

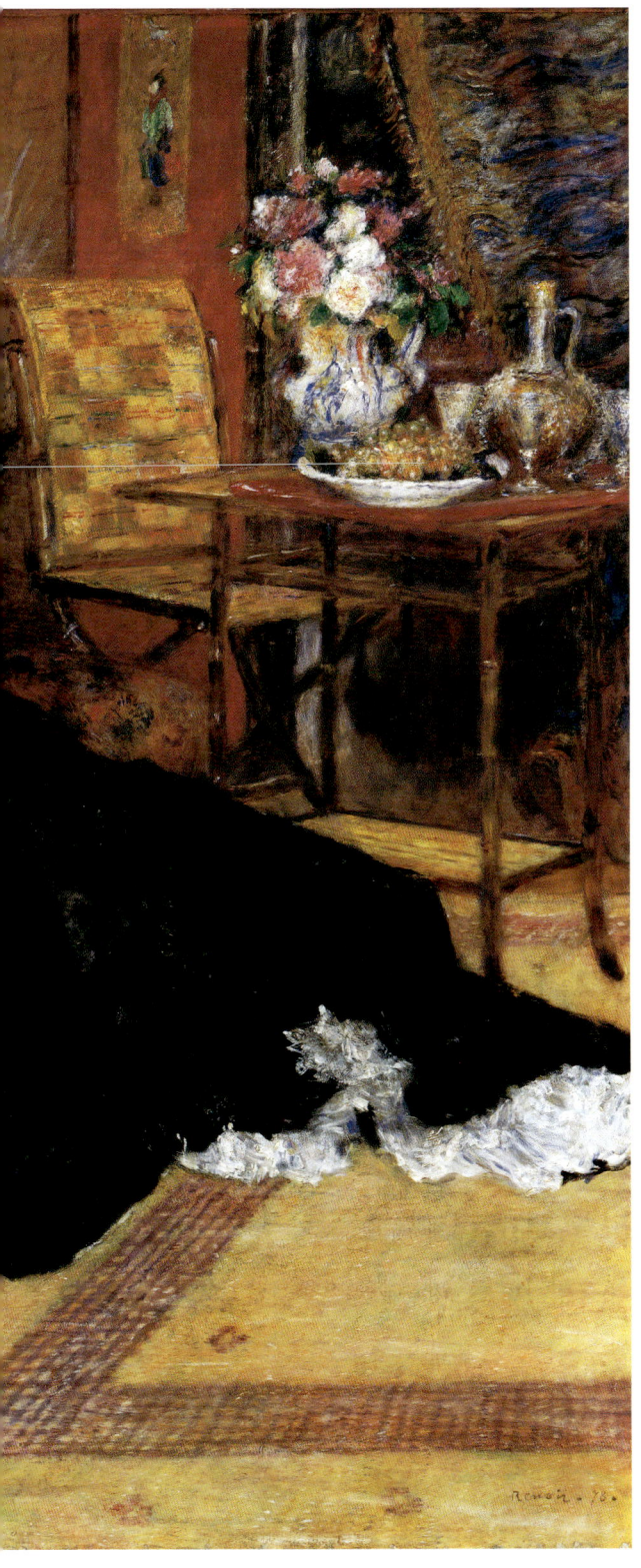

"*Madame Charpentier reminds me of the sweethearts of my youth, the models of Fragonard. The two daughters had lovely dimples. I was congratulated. I forgot the attacks of the newspapers. I had models who were willing to sit for free and who were full of goodwill.*"

PIERRE-AUGUSTE RENOIR

Madame Charpentier and Her Children, 1878
Oil on canvas, 153.7 x 190.2 cm (60½ x 75 in.)
New York, The Metropolitan Museum of Art,
Catharine Lorillard Wolfe Collection,
Wolfe Fund

of them had been redecorated to accommodate bar rooms with low ceilings, and there were gas lanterns and tables in the gardens.

Renoir used to put up his painting equipment in the garden, between the tables, where people came on summer afternoons to drink, dance and flirt. His friends would help him carry his easel from his studio flat nearby, and they also served as models for the main figures in his pictures. Seated at the table, there are the painters Lamy, Goeneutte and Georges Rivière, who left us an account of that time, with the sisters Estelle and Jeanne and other Montmartre girls. At the centre of the picture is the somewhat dandyish Cuban painter Don Pedro Vidal dancing with his girlfriend Margot, who was also a popular model, and in the background there are the painters Gervex, Cordey, Lestringuez and Lhote. When we look at this picture we have the feeling that Renoir enjoyed an intimate friendship with every single person in the crowd and also with each of the objects that fill this glimpse of life.

The picture is rather large, and our first impression is one of disorderliness and chaos. Such was in fact the judgement of the leading art critics when the picture was shown to the public at the third Impressionist exhibition in 1877. This effect is due to the random way in which the characters appear to be arranged, and also the consistent casualness with which both the foreground and the background have been painted. Above all, however, Renoir has dissolved and broken down the original colours of the place by means of the foliage, which casts a diffused sunlight onto the entire scene, permeating it with its light-blue shadow, and combining in a variety of ways with the green leaves, bright yellow straw hats and chairs, the blond hair of the people and the black suits of the men. The ground as well as people's faces and clothes are strewn with yellowish-pink spots – squiggles of sunshine that come through the foliage. The figures in this picture are surrounded by a somewhat dusty, flickering and uncommonly genuine atmosphere, which deprives their contours and details of that definiteness to which people's eyes were used to at the time. The impression of turbulence, which is inherent in the subject, was undoubtedly intended by Renoir. How could the joyful abandon of these cheerful people possibly have been pressed into the narrowly defined postures that were regarded as classical? Another impression that was intended is the generally random appearance of this section of reality: some figures are cut off at the edge of the picture, and the scene is speckled with motley spots of light. After all, did not this scene look almost exactly the same to the left and the right of this section, as well as before and after?

However, none of this means that such a picture is less intelligently composed than any of the paintings which were approved by the academic critics. Renoir arranged his figures in two circles: a more compact, closed group around the table in the bottom right-hand area, and a wider and more open circle around the dancing couple, who appear to have a special emphasis to the left of the centre. This composition is further reinforced by a group of three figures at the centre, forming an almost classically shaped pyramid. Also, the picture includes a whole system of verticals and horizontals. The vertical dimension is marked by the people, both dancing and standing, the trees, the backs of the yellow chairs as well as the standard lamps and those which are suspended from above. A clearly horizontal impression is created by the cluster of figures in the background, who all appear to be equally tall, as well as another group at the centre, the bright line of round lanterns and the white wooden buildings. These latter elements all form the upper third of the pictures, i.e. the background. They do not interfere directly with the less stringent composition of the foreground, which is dominated by the curved vertical lines of people's arms and backs, but they nevertheless lend stability to the entire painting, which depends, as it were, on

Acrobats at the Cirque Fernando
(Francisca and Angelina Wartenberg), 1879
Oil on canvas, 131.2 x 99.2 cm (51¾ x 39 in.)
The Art Institute of Chicago,
Potter Palmer Collection

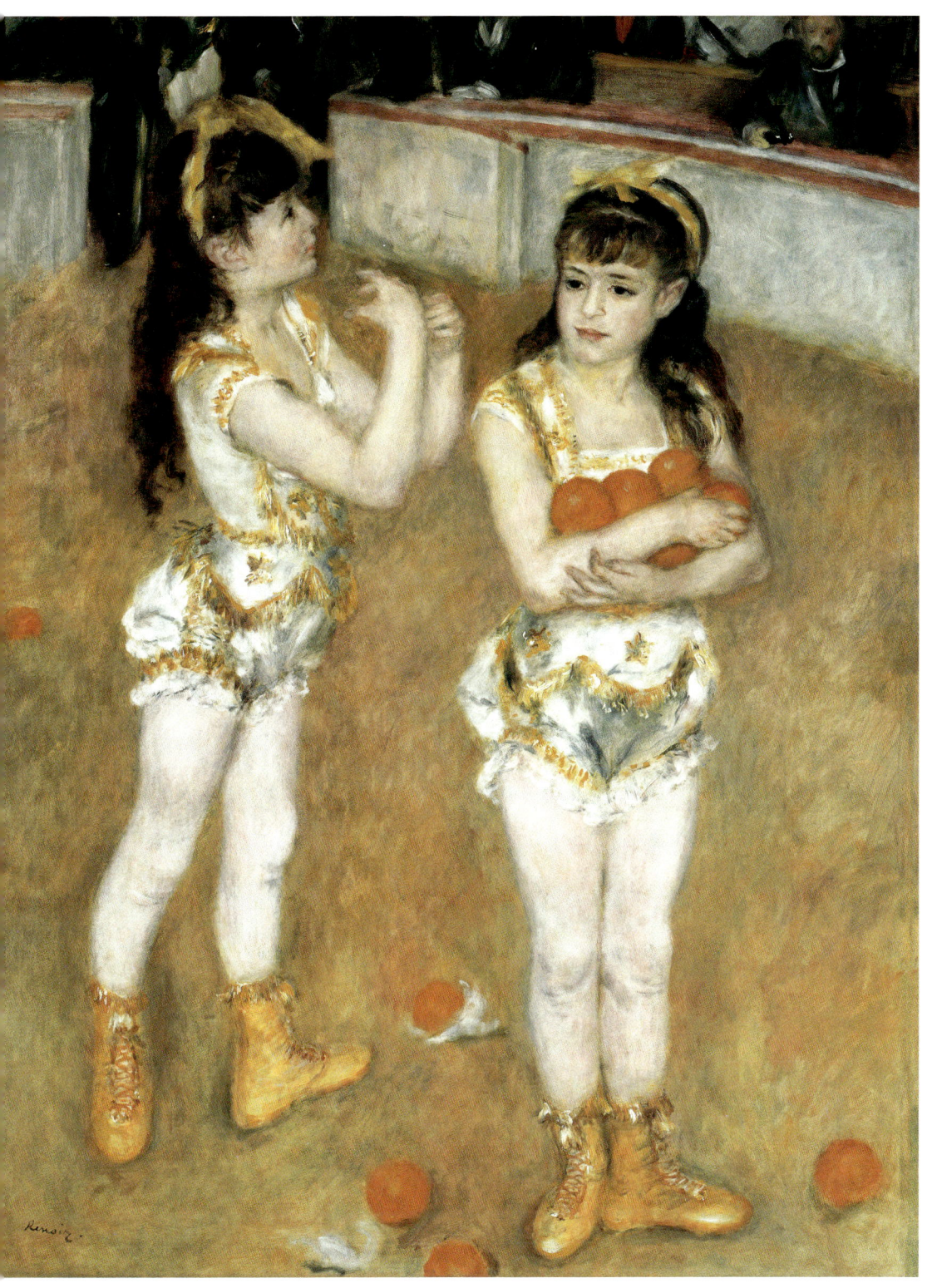

these horizontal lines. This basic grid structure enabled the painter to introduce an element of apparent casualness.

Another principle of composition was Renoir's use of colour, which appears to result entirely from the play of the sunlight but was in fact quite intentional. There is a strong base of black submerged in blue and forming, as it were, a repeated theme in the bassline of this harmony of colours. This is accompanied by a powerful lemon-like yellow; the hair of the child and the back of the chair, both of them at the front of the painting, are thus emphasized very strongly and guide our glance to the top right-hand corner; our attention is attracted by two colours, pink and forget-me-not blue. Both colours combine in the striped dress of the figure at the centre, from where they separate again in the monochrome dresses of the two dancing girls further left until they are scattered about as patches of shade and sunshine, especially in the left half of the picture. A beautiful glowing vermilion is distributed very sparingly over the entire painting in spots that add fire to the overall effect.

However, any formal analysis would be rather incomplete if it did not also include the psychological arrangement of the figures. Again and again we become aware of the glances that are exchanged between the blonde beauty in black at the centre of the picture and the young man on the yellow chair. This line is emphasized by the postures of the two sisters, whose heads are exactly parallel. If we were to draw this line into the painting and then extended it, we would almost have one of the two diagonals of the blue dancing girl. Also, it has a surprising number of parallels in the general composition of the painting. The dominating eye contact between the two people is vividly counterbalanced by the loving glance of the handsome young man on the right who is looking towards Jeanne in the middle of the picture, while the girl is directing all her attention towards the other man. Thus they form a triangle which is so intense that they are almost detached from the rest

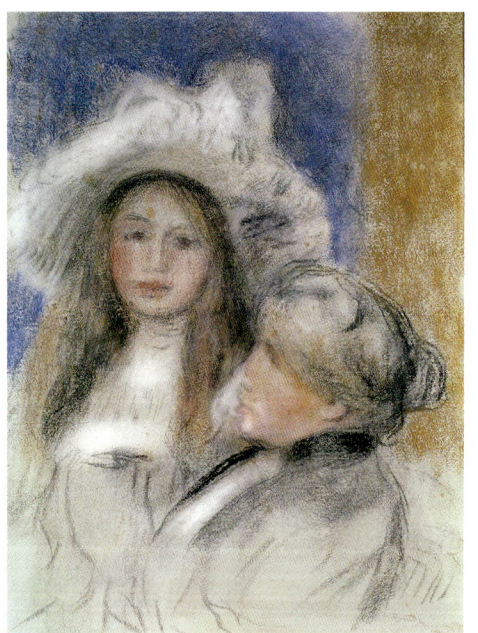

of the people. There are several figures who seem to be looking straight at the observer, especially the three dancing girls. Two figures at the table, the pipe-smoker and Estelle, dressed in blue and pink, are lost in thought and are looking past the observer. And maybe this blissful, dreamy look in the face of a smiling young girl at the centre of the picture is its most important element, its pivotal point. The easy-going, tender cheerfulness of her glance, her face, her figure seem to provide a focal point which sums up the whole atmosphere and everything that the picture is trying to convey.

The joy of being young and in love, the pleasure of a free-and-easy party where everyone can relax and enjoy themselves together with other young people, the conscious affirmation of life in the form of sunshine, music and the babble of voices, the capricious naivety of a tender flirt – these are the feelings which Renoir expressed with every stroke of his paintbrush.

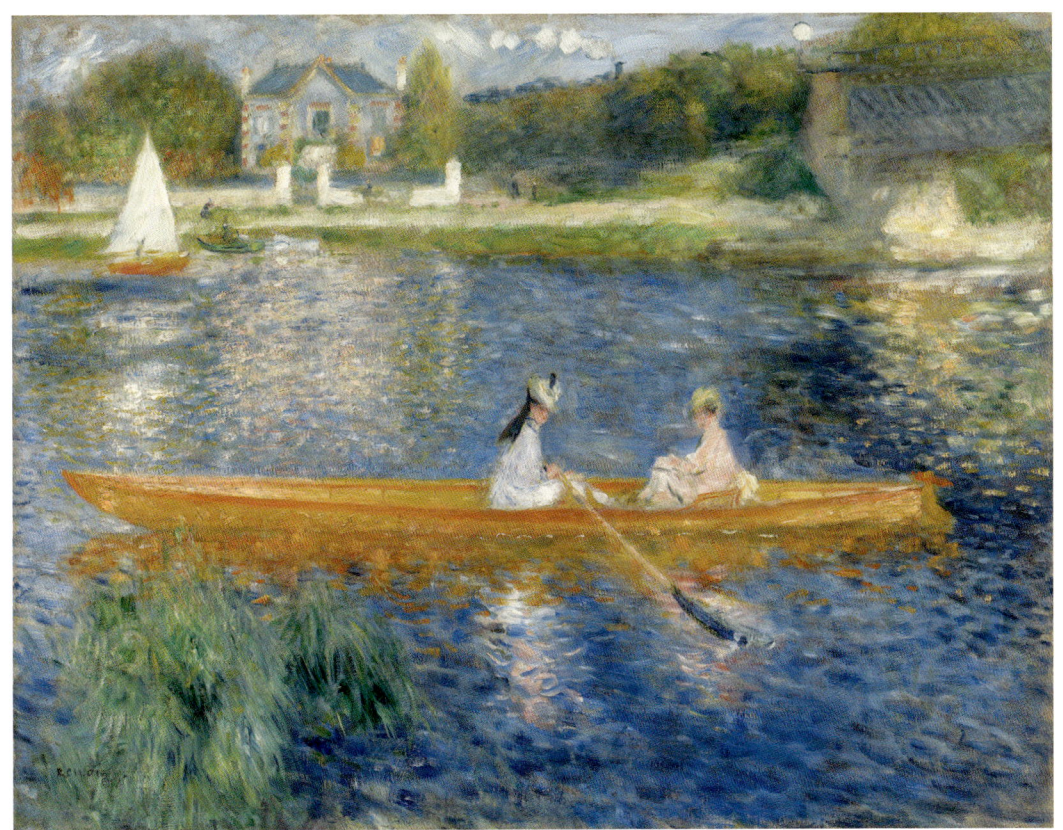

In doing so he was firmly rooted in two traditions which he both preserved and surpassed, thus abolishing them in his own perfect synthesis. With a picture like this he was paying tribute to the masters of the French Rococo period, i.e. Jean-Antoine Watteau, Nicolas Lancret and their *fêtes galantes*. There were the same yearning, courting glances, the same lightness and intimacy of postures and floating movement, the same blue and pink striped dresses, a similar loosening up of constellations of figures who seem to relate to one another freely. After all, Renoir did belong to the age of Neo-Baroque and Neo-Rococo, and ever since the time when he had had to paint Rococo scenes on china cups, he had admired the ingenious masters of the *Ancien Régime*. But rather than repeating their themes and methods in their precise historical settings, he translated them into the language of his own art and of his own period.

The second tradition which Renoir used was that of contemporary French graphic art: with its depiction of the pleasures of the middle classes in the big cities, it already had quite a long history. For several decades artists such as Honoré Daumier, Paul Gavarni, Constantin Guys and a number of others had been illustrating books and magazines with pictures of the merry life of Parisian *bons viveurs, grisettes,* bohemians and the middle classes. These small-format drawings were made to suit particular occasions on certain days and were therefore quickly out of date. They were produced and duplicated by means of the simple method of lithography, and they covered all areas of Parisian life, both people's day-to-day routines and their leisure. Outdoor pleasures, however, were a relatively

The Seine at Asnières, 1875
Oil on canvas, 71 x 92 cm (28 x 36¼ in.)
London, The National Gallery

OPPOSITE
Berthe Morisot and Her Daughter, 1894
Pastel, 59 x 44.5 cm (23¼ x 17½ in.)
Petit Palais, Musée des Beaux-Arts de la Ville de Paris

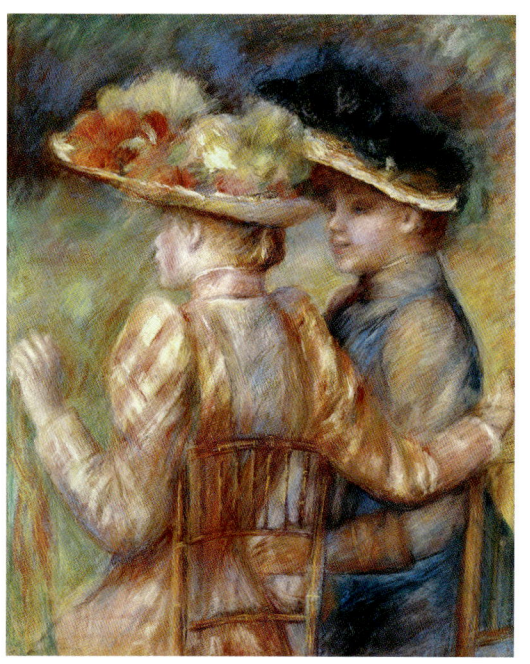

rare subject compared with the theatre. The Impressionists took up these themes and topics, depicting them in the form of large paintings. In 1862 Manet had made the first step with his *Music in the Tuileries Gardens* (The National Gallery, London), and Renoir's *Le Moulin de la Galette* was a further development. Manet had not really painted an open-air picture, whereas Renoir had achieved a merging of fully individualized human beings with an open space that was filled with sunshine and liveliness. What is more, he had managed to do so on the basis of a standard theme from the life of Paris, using a format that was unusually large and therefore quite an artistic challenge for him.

At the end of this period Renoir painted another gathering of young friends – this time at Alphonse Fournaise's inn at Chatou on the river Seine, near the Grenouillère, where they used to meet with their girlfriends for lunch after a boating party (*The Luncheon of the Boating Party,* ill. pp. 256/257). This large painting had been prepared very thoroughly, summing up all his endeavours to render this topic adequately. It was preceded by more sketchy pictures such as his *Oarsmen at Chatou* (ill. p. 246) and a different *Lunch at the Restaurant Fournaise* (ill. p. 259). The overall composition is firmly defined by both sides and held together by a number of lines. And yet the entire scene is even more broken up into individual figures and small groups than *Le Moulin de la Galette*. A scatter of relaxed people – this is how his art has often been summed up. The life-size figures are more individualized, and the colours are more glowing, though less regular. This is particularly true of the figure of a man – a portrait of Caillebotte – sitting astride a chair in the bottom right-hand corner: here Renoir anticipated the firmer, more solid style of the following years. On the other hand, the bottles, glasses and fruit on the table come alive, as it were, because of the sparkling casualness with which they are depicted. And it was with loving tenderness that Renoir painted the charmingly attractive young girl with her flowery hat and a little dog. Her name was Aline Charigot, and she was to become his wife.

Before Impressionism hardly anybody had taken any interest in the inherent beauty of life in the big city, let alone in the hustle and bustle of the crowds in the streets and market squares. Although it cannot be said that this was his major theme, he nevertheless created a number of beautiful examples of the two prototypes of street scenes, i.e. both general impressions of streets and crowds of people randomly hurrying past one another and the same people observed at close quarters. It was the latter type that Renoir sought to capture in the life-size figures of *The Umbrellas* (ill. p. 267). He used subtle shades of blue, grey and brown and then added emphasis by means of some brightly glowing colours. The main characters are some children with enormous hats, a *grisette*, and a milliner who is carrying a

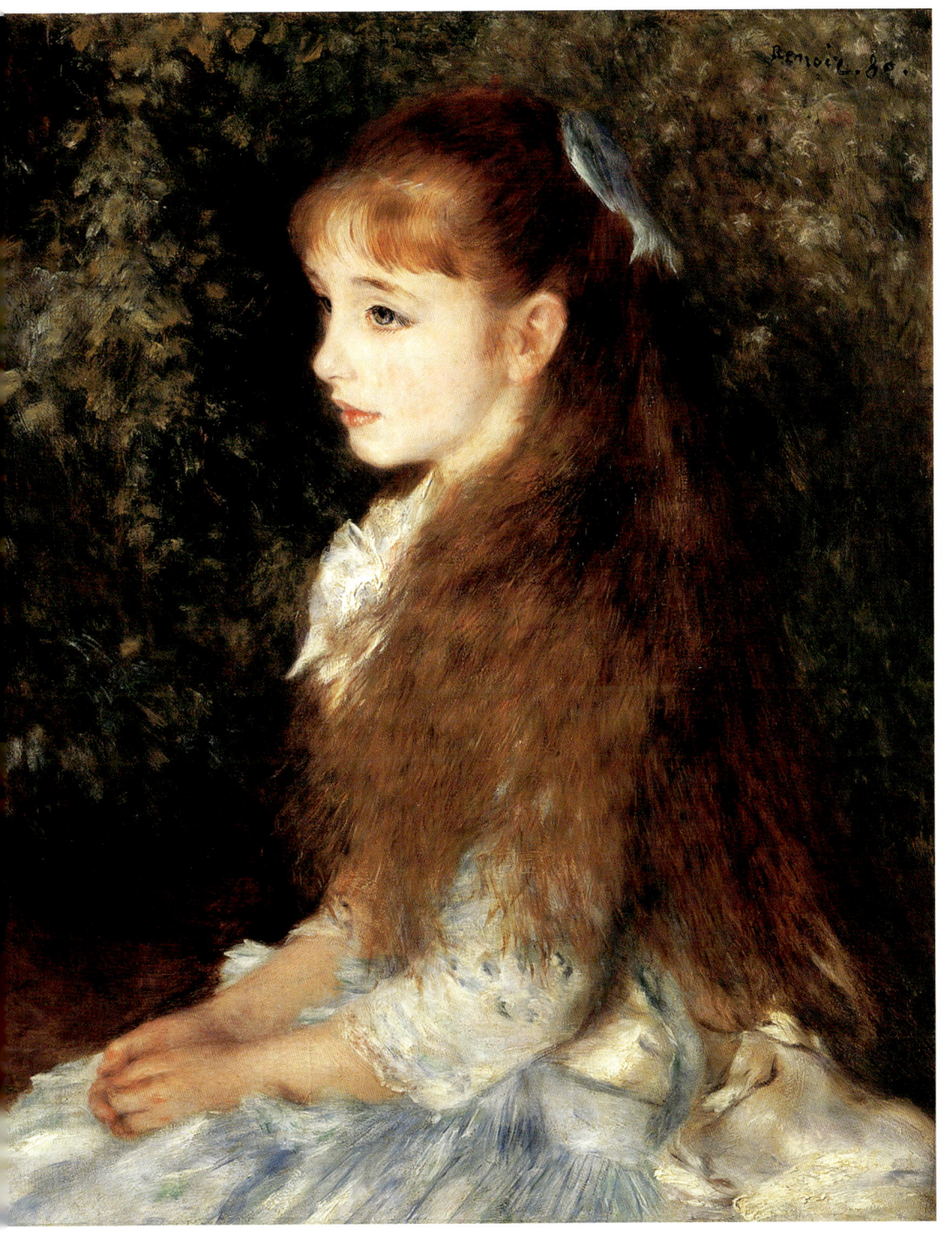

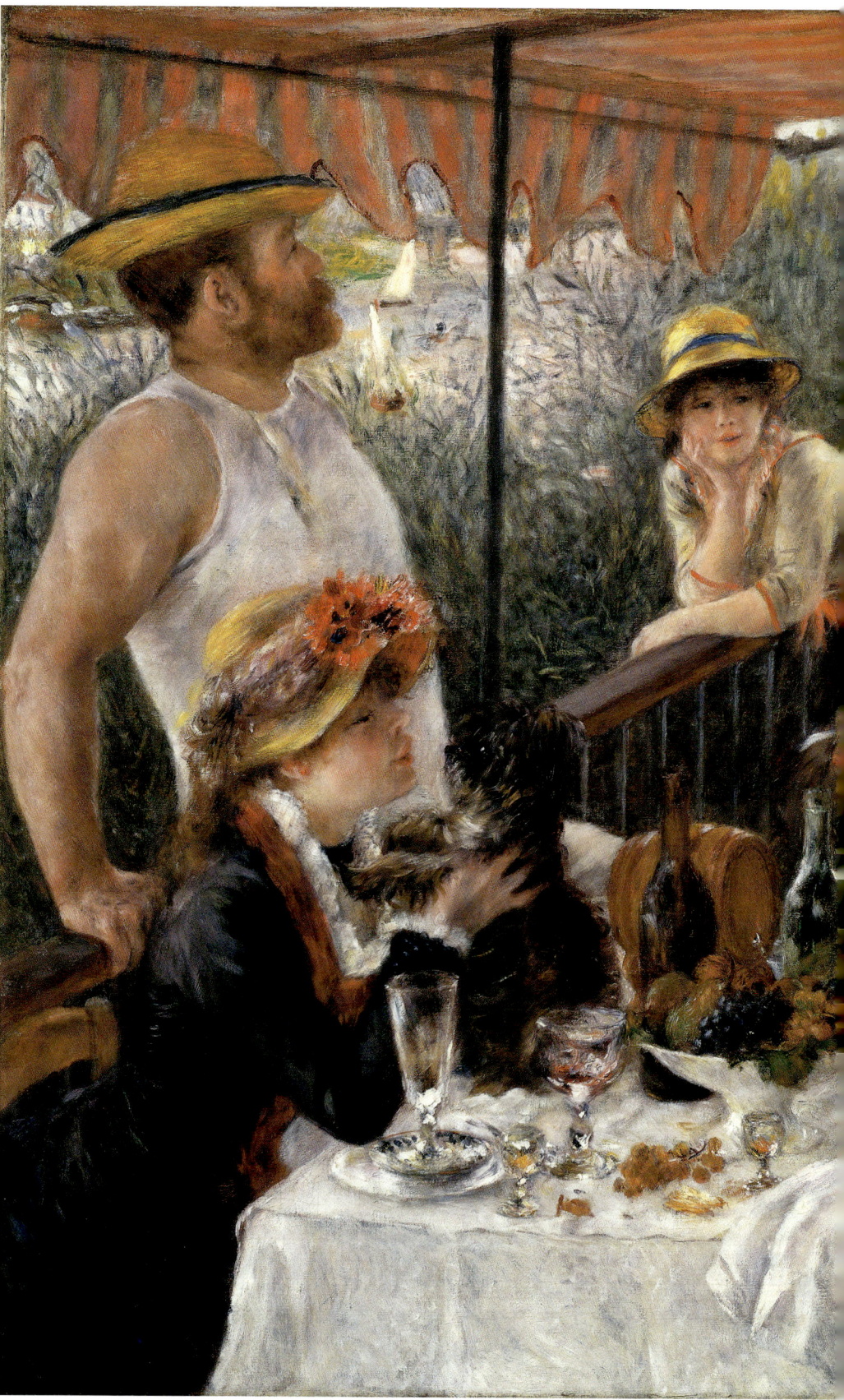

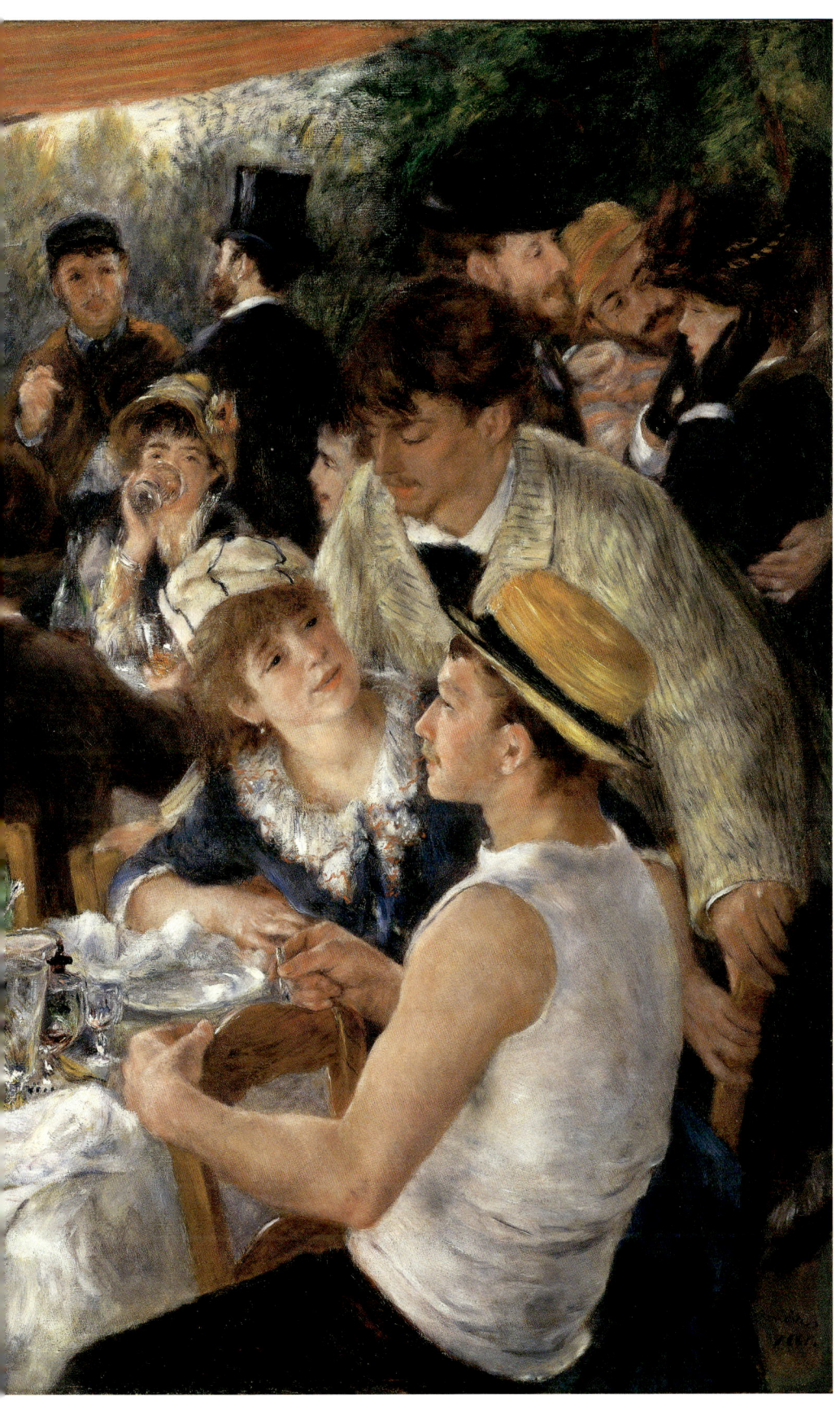

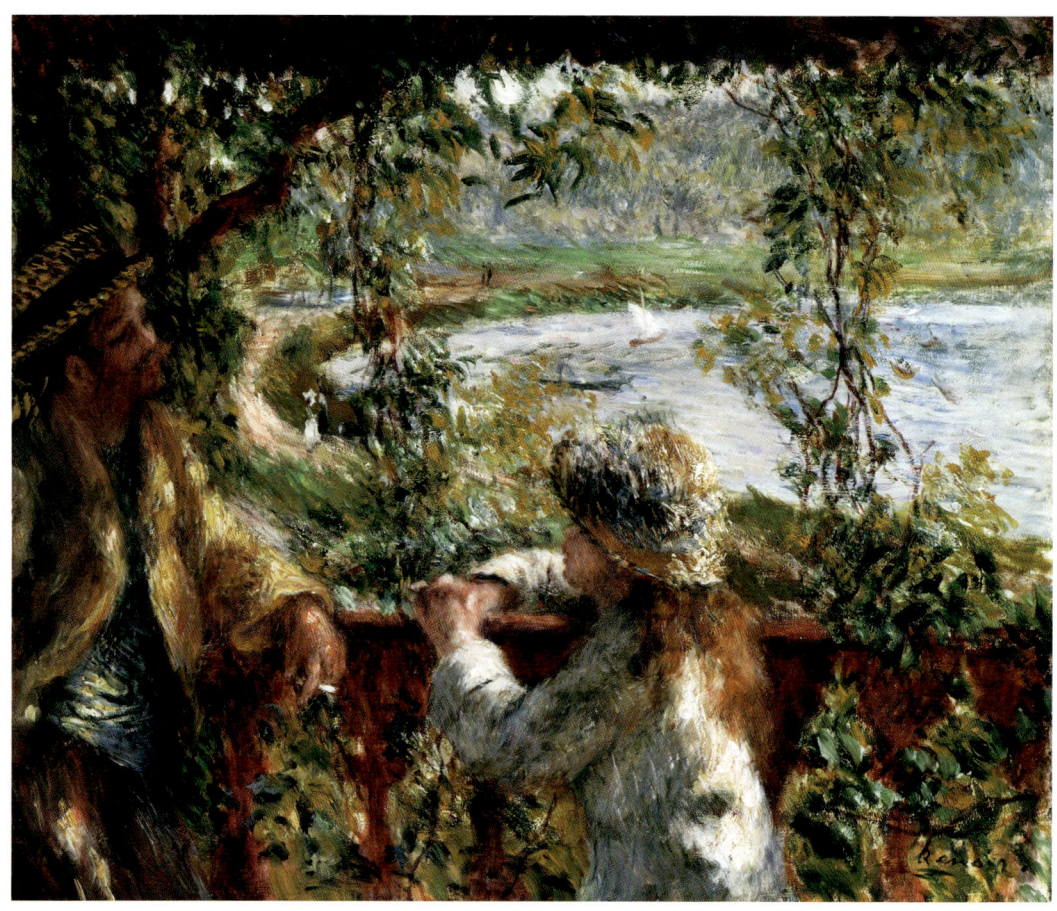

Near the Lake, 1879/80
Oil on canvas, 47.5 x 56.4 cm (18¾ x 22¼ in.)
The Art Institute of Chicago,
Potter Palmer Collection

hatbox and is on her way to a customer, while a gentleman is very bravely offering to accompany her and carry her umbrella for her. The charm of the picture lies in the variations on the shape of the umbrella and in the beauty of the people's postures and faces, particularly that of the milliner. She is looking straight into the eyes of the spectator and seems to have the stature and dignity of an ancient goddess. But the picture rather lacks the convincing impact of the moment when the rain has just started: the sudden rush of people, the sparkle of moistness in the atmosphere. A somewhat artificial calm pervades the scene, a certain formal and emphatic self-consciousness, which is further enhanced by the fact that the spectator is looked at by two pairs of eyes. And yet, what is reflected even more clearly than in *Le Moulin de la Galette* or *The Luncheon of the Boating Party* is the isolation of man. Even the two main groups of people are totally unrelated, the parallel positions of their heads and the directions of their glances equally reflect a complete absence of responsiveness towards one another: the grisette is ignoring the gentleman, and the little girl with the hoop is paying no attention to her playmate.

The use of such themes unconsciously reflects a structural principle that was quite typical of society at that time, i.e. the dissolution of all continuity. Renoir was trying to move from the depiction of turbulence to a firmer order within his picture. Both objectives clash with each other, and Renoir's method of applying paint changed over the years which he must have spent working on the painting.

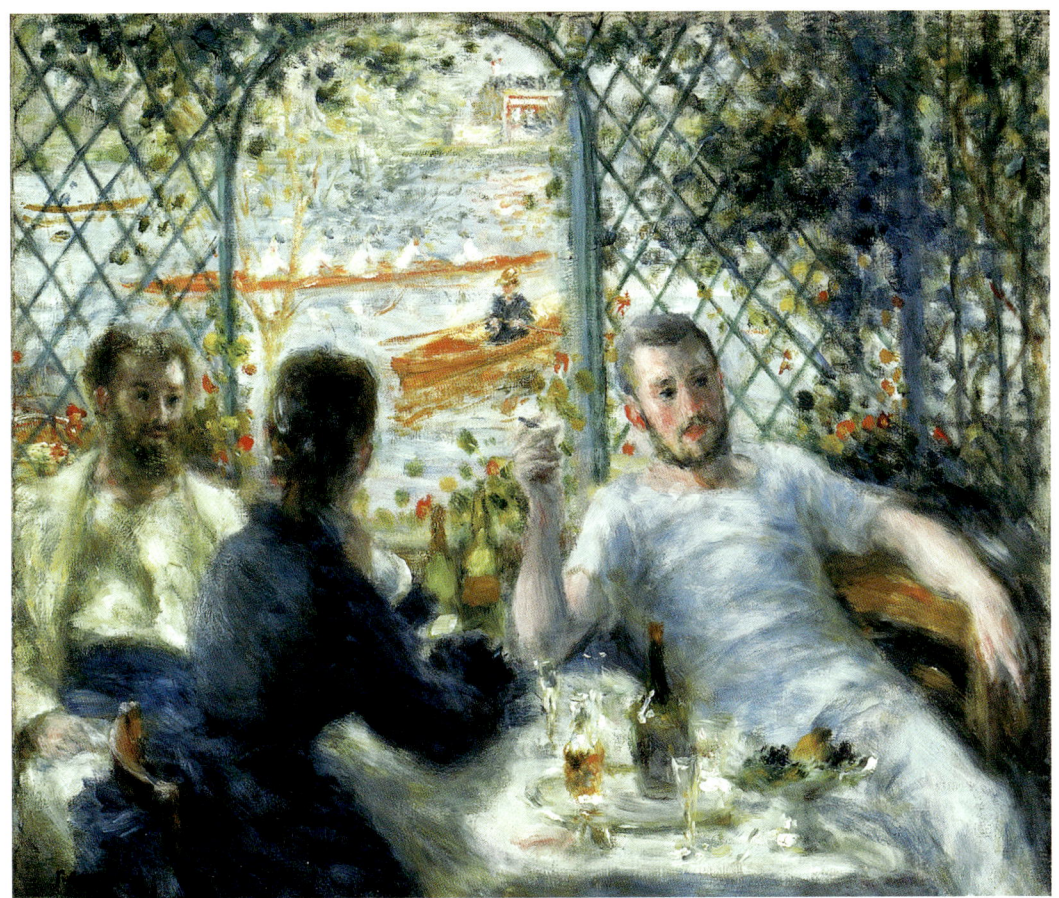

During the 70s, which were such a fruitful period in Renoir's life, he also painted a number of landscapes, among which his *Country Footpath in the Summer* (ill. p. 231) is particularly beautiful and quite typical. These compositions are nearly always dominated by flowers or other colour effects, and one might almost be inclined to say that the simple, graphically linear structures of these paintings have a certain dullness about them. Compared with the other Impressionist landscape painters, Renoir was even less concerned with clear, unambiguous and forceful structures, but preferred to weave colourful tapestries with his pictures, something which he began to do with landscapes long before he did it with people. He was just as capable as his contemporaries of rendering the flickering of the sun-soaked air above the grass and the shrubs, the warmth and the cheerful atmosphere of the summer, the exuberant sumptuousness of the different colours which, as an Impressionist, he was inclined to see in nature. He would paint lovingly and skilfully, but he was not really a landscapist. He always preferred to paint human beings or female bodies. He even voiced his reservations about open-air painting, the technique which was inextricably linked with landscapes: "Nature leads the artist into loneliness; I want to remain among people."

Lunch at the Restaurant Fournaise (The Rowers' Lunch), 1875
Oil on canvas, 55.1 x 65.9 cm (21¾ x 26 in.)
The Art Institute of Chicago,
Potter Palmer Collection

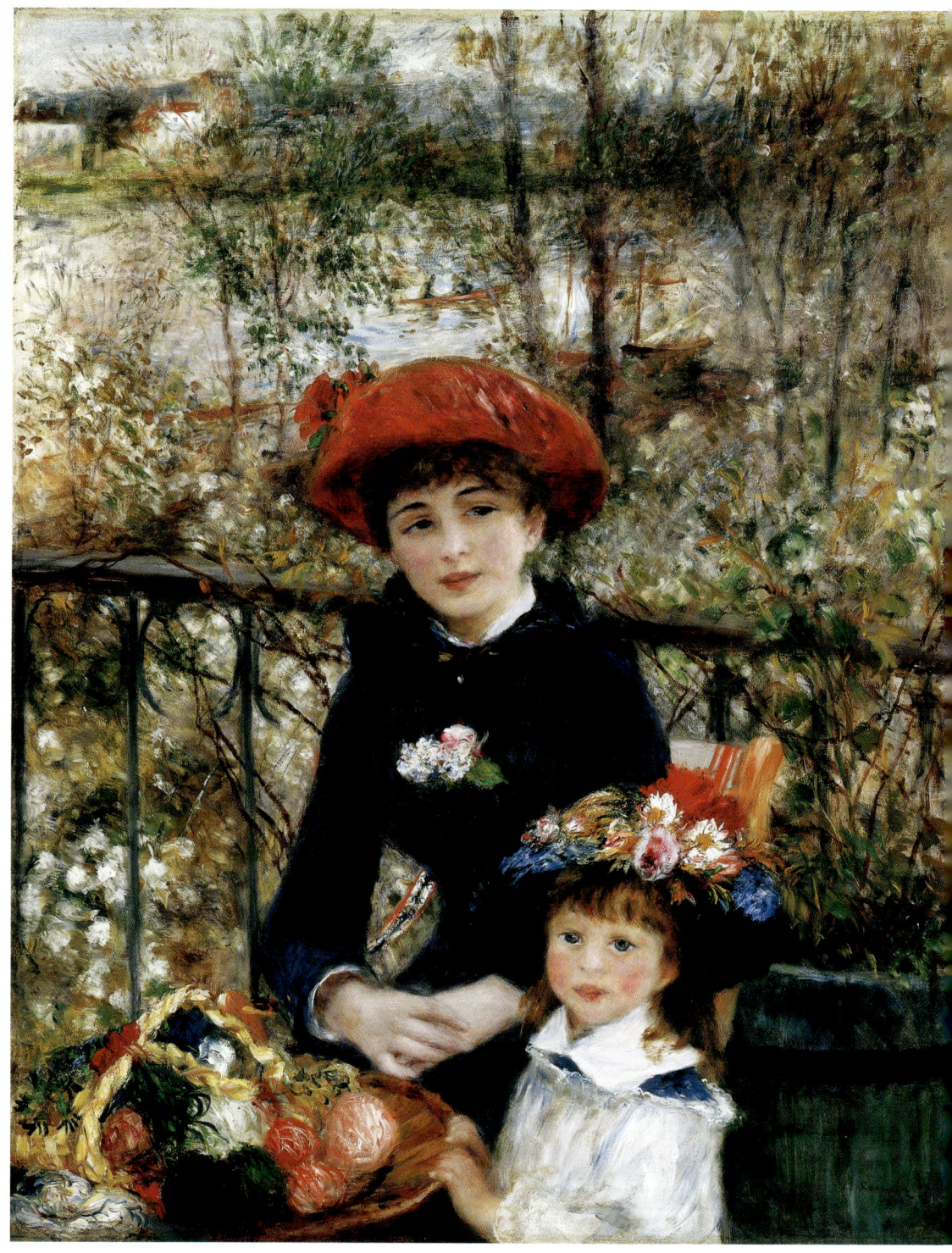

The Crisis of Impressionism
and the "Dry Period"
1883–1887

During his visit to Italy in 1881, Renoir was deeply impressed by the works of Raphael. "They are full of knowledge and wisdom. Unlike myself, he never tried to achieve the impossible. But they are wonderful. I prefer Ingres' oil paintings. The frescos, on the other hand, are magnificent in their greatness and simplicity," he wrote to Durand-Ruel, and, in a letter to Madame Charpentier, "although Raphael never worked in the open air, he still used to observe the sun, because all his frescos are filled by it." The full significance of such words does not really strike home until we consider that in the mid-19th century, Ingres was regarded as the epitome of fossilized Neo-Classicism. This was because, as a member of the Academy, he had bitterly opposed any expression of personal temperament, Realism and especially the colourful style of his contemporary Delacroix. Like all other Classicist painters, Ingres had regarded Raphael as the highest ideal since the 16th century. And now such words from Renoir who had only just followed in the footsteps of his much-admired Delacroix and returned from a trip to Algiers, that blaze of brilliant colours! But in fact Renoir had never been narrow-minded. Even during the days when there were heated discussions about art at the Café Guerbois, he did not entirely agree with his friends. "They did not want to know about Ingres. I just let them talk … and secretly enjoyed the beautiful belly in Ingres' *Spring* and the neck and arms of *Mme Rivière* (a portrait by Ingres)," he later told his fellow-painter André. Renoir still saw himself as a searcher and was not content with himself. "Around the year 1883 I had exhausted Impressionism and came to the conclusion that I could neither paint nor draw," he said. The Impressionist style and the view that went with it were beginning to seem inadequate to him.

Renoir now began to work more carefully and meticulously, and his colours became cooler and smoother. He shaped his figures more precisely and paid more attention to their arrangement within the picture. The years between 1884 and 1887 are known as the "Dry Period" in the artist's life, and most critics at the time thought that he had gone astray. George Moore, an Irish contemporary of his, wrote that within a matter of two years Renoir had completely destroyed his own charmingly delightful art, after he had spent twenty years building it up. Everybody – including Renoir himself – saw this break with Impressionism as a profound crisis. This crisis, however, was not just an individual matter. It affected not only Renoir, but also Monet, Pissarro and Degas and finally led to a complete collapse of this group of Impressionists. The eighth and last joint exhibition took place in 1886 – this time without Renoir. It was indeed the final and absolute crisis of Impressionism, inasmuch as Impressionism was the final phase of middle-class Realism. The areas of middle-class life which had been painted by the Impressionists turned out to

On the Terrace, 1881
Oil on canvas, 100.4 x 80.9 cm (39½ x 32 in.)
The Art Institute of Chicago, Mr and Mrs Lewis
Larned Coburn Memorial Collection

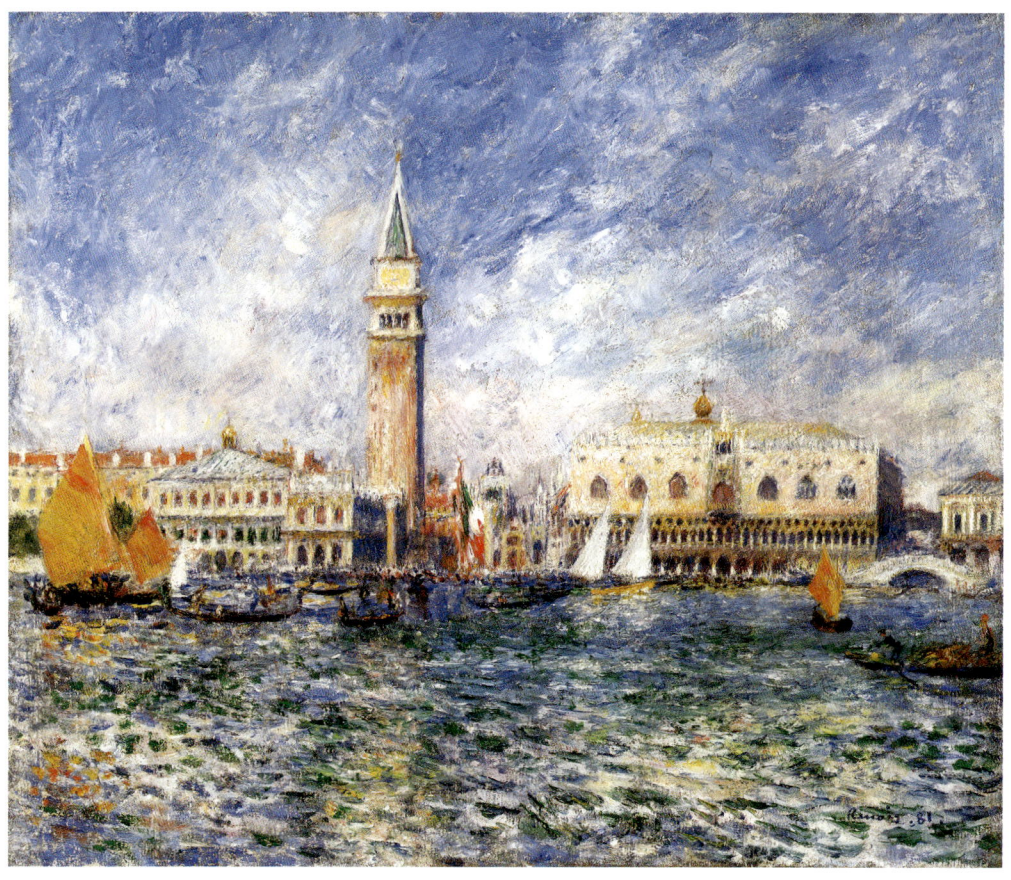

Venice, The Doge's Palace, 1881
Oil on canvas, 54.5 x 65.7 cm (21½ x 26 in.)
Williamstown, Massachusetts, The Clark

have been exhausted artistically, and they came to the conclusion that honest seekers of the truth would not find it satisfying in the long term. In limiting itself to merry parties and the beauty of intimate relationships, the world which was depicted in Impressionist paintings drifted further and further away from real life and society in general. The Impressionists had been concentrating on observing external phenomena, and this is where they had made a lot of progress. To see accurately and to paint what one could see, to be no more than eye and hand – that was their aim. "Corot said, 'When I paint, I want to be a stupid fellow,' I'm a little bit from Corot's school," admitted Renoir. He did not want to think or use his mind while painting – just as was demanded by the contemporary British art critic John Ruskin, who was very influential at the time. But any mindless copying of what was there, and that only if it was "beautiful", became a rapid exercise. Most of the things and people around them were not "beautiful". The painters knew that. And if they pushed their knowledge aside while they were painting, they ceased to be Realists. But if they wanted to remain Realists, they had to move from telling of the beautiful side of middle-class life to criticizing it. None of the Impressionists wanted to take such a revolutionary step. Renoir avoided it. He did not have to give in where people had been fighting against him: in the glowing luminosity of colours, in their subtle play with light and colourful shadows, or in the open arrangement of shapes or the general sketch-like character of his paintings. Probably without being aware of it, he gave in whenever he felt that there was a basic contradiction between a certain topic or message on the one hand, and reality on the other.

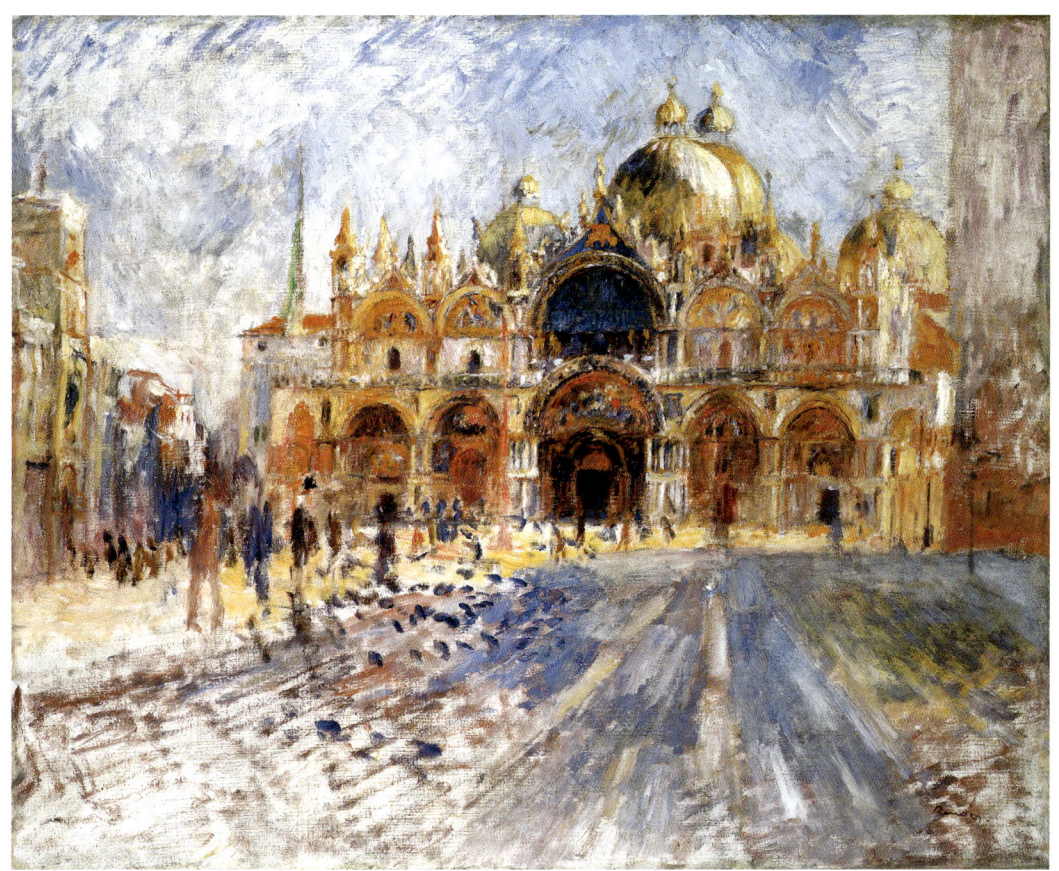

Renoir's "Dry Period" marked the turning point in his art: with the exception of a small number of family portraits, he virtually ceased to paint scenes from everyday life in Paris. There was still the odd picture of a girl resting in the grass, a woman

The Piazza San Marco, Venice, 1881
Oil on canvas, 65.4 x 81.3 cm (25¾ x 32 in.)
The Minneapolis Institute of Arts,
John R. Van Derlip Fund

selling apples, or a washerwoman, but such paintings had now lost much of their specificness with regard to time and space. And the mass of work which he produced during this period was in fact quite different. Renoir and his fellow Impressionists were beginning to shift their emphasis onto something that had already been present in their art in the form of a tendency, i.e. the expression of purely subjective feelings and the subjective use of their artistic methods. Having selected these methods as carefully as possible, they then proceeded to apply them to subjects that were neutral as regards the social conditions of the times. As soon as Impressionism had achieved general recognition, it became socially harmless by no longer concentrating on painting the world as it really was. Or, to put it the other way round, it began to be tolerated because of its change of topics. Nevertheless, many contemporaries had formed the mistaken idea that Impressionism was "the embodiment of communism" and that it "boldly advocated the use of unrestrained violence."

In 1885 and 1886 Renoir worked in La Roche-Guyon and Wargemont on several different occasions. In the following years he displayed his pictures together with those of a modern artists' group called *Les XX* in Brussels and also at the art exhibitions organized by Georges Petit, one of Durand-Ruel's rivals in the art trade of Paris. However, this did not mean that Renoir broke off

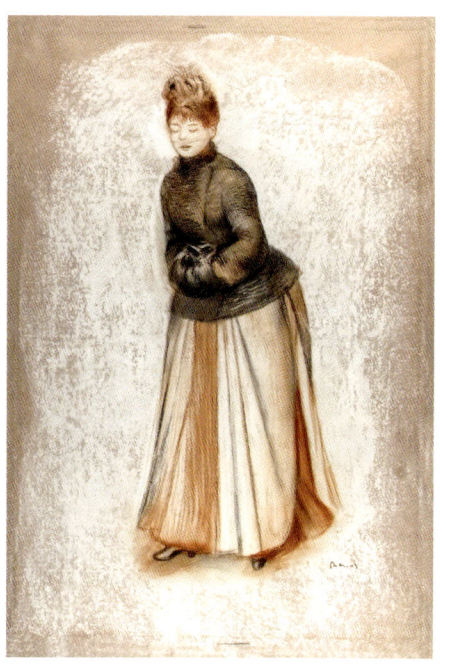

his contact with his old benefactor. In 1886 Durand-Ruel exhibited thirty-two of Renoir's paintings in New York, thus opening the American market for French Impressionism. His success can still be seen in the enormous number of Renoir's pictures and those of other Impressionists which can now be viewed in several museums in Washington, New York, Chicago and other American cities.

Renoir's transition to a new style was very gradual, but could be seen quite clearly in his three large upright paintings which were to serve as decorative panels in one of Durand-Ruel's rooms (ills. pp. 270 and 271). They are three pictures of waltzing couples. The picture in the centre, which is set in the open-air restaurant in Bougival, shows a man with a straw hat and without a shirt collar somewhat crudely swinging around his beloved. The picture on the left, also outside, is a little more refined and graceful and shows the painter Paul Lhote dancing with Aline Charigot, the young girl who was to become Renoir's wife and whose radiant smile dominates the picture even more than the rich intensiveness of her colourful dress. The third painting shows the young model Suzanne Valadon dancing in the arms of the painter Eugène-Pierre Lestringuez at a function organized by the city of Paris. The movement of the last couple is least convincing, whereas in the other two we feel swept along by the swirling and swaying of the young women who are happy and in love and whose beauty and gracefulness forms the most important message of these paintings.

Later, in 1886, Renoir painted several pictures of his wife Aline breastfeeding their oldest son Pierre (ill. p. 273). He showed a certain amount of restraint in his use of colour, which reflects his tendency to be more concerned with accurate modelling and graphic precision. He felt that objects had been falling apart under his paintbrush, and so he wanted to make them solid and tangible again – very much like his contemporary Cézanne, who set himself the aim of turning Impressionism into an art that was as "durable" as that of the old masters. To achieve this, Cézanne tried to analyse everything into the basic stereometric forms of cones, spheres and cylinders. Renoir emphasized everything that was round. The young woman and the sprightly little baby have a plump rotundity about them, so that they appear to be composed of spherical segments. It may of course be that Aline's face gave rise to that sort of style, but it is nevertheless noticeable that there was an increase in graphicness from Renoir's *Boating Party* via his dancing couple to this picture of Aline and Pierre. Later, however, Renoir turned to a softer style again.

Although, as we saw, Renoir painted a number of significant nude pictures before 1885, it was not a subject that occupied a major position in his art. This changed in the second half of the 1880s. Nudes in the open air, frequently called *Bathers,* began to take a dominant role in the artist's repertoire. More and more, his pictures were filled with a uniform degree of brightness. Unlike in his *Nude in the Sunlight*

TOP
Young Woman with a Muff, 1860–1919
Pastel, 52.7 x 36.2 cm (20¾ x 14¼ in.)
New York, The Metropolitan Museum of Art,
H. O. Havemeyer Collection,
Bequest of Mrs H. O. Havemeyer, 1929

OPPOSITE
Two Girls, 1881/82
Oil on canvas, 81.3 x 65.2 cm (32 x 25¾ in.)
Moscow, Pushkin Museum

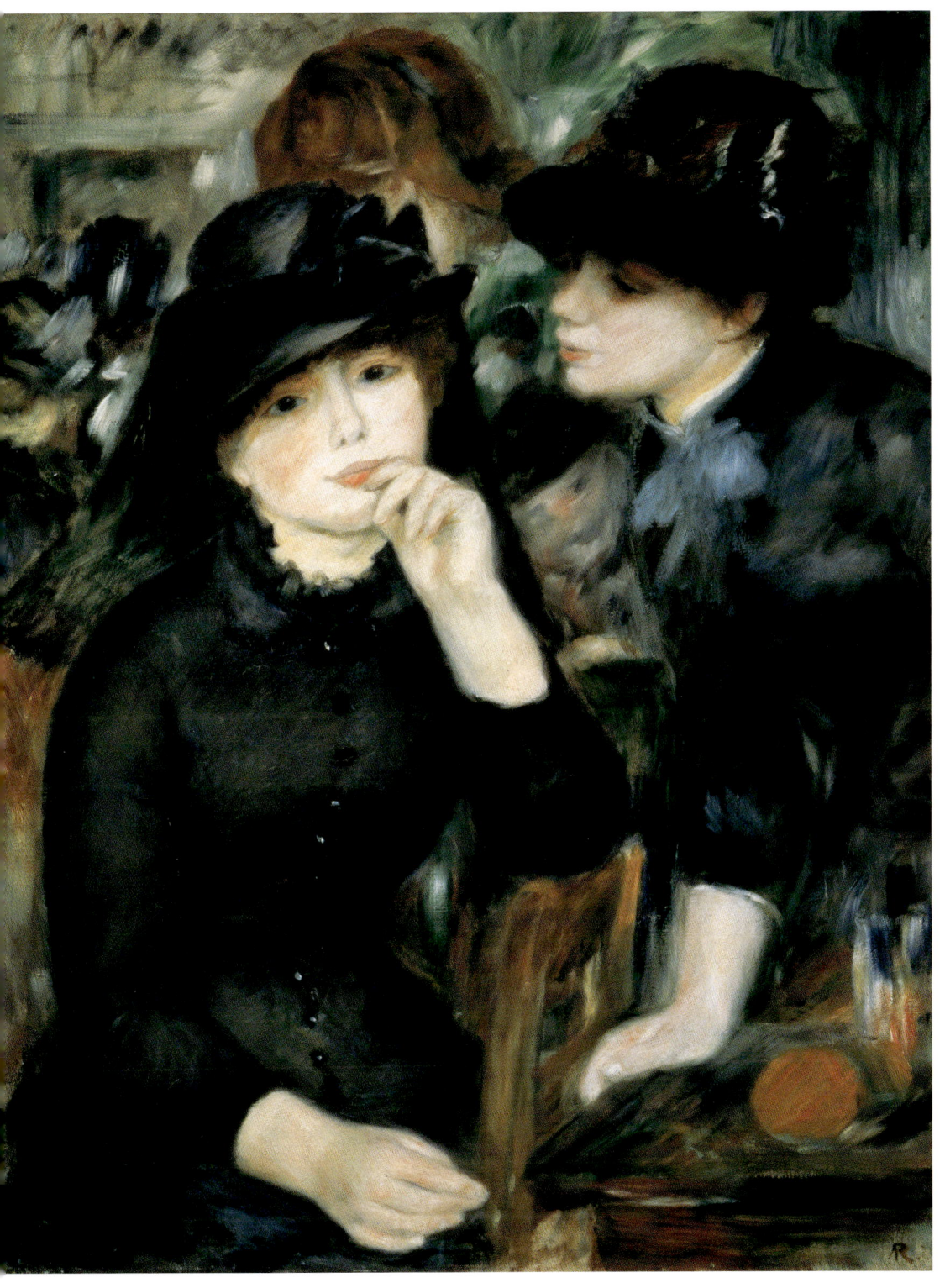

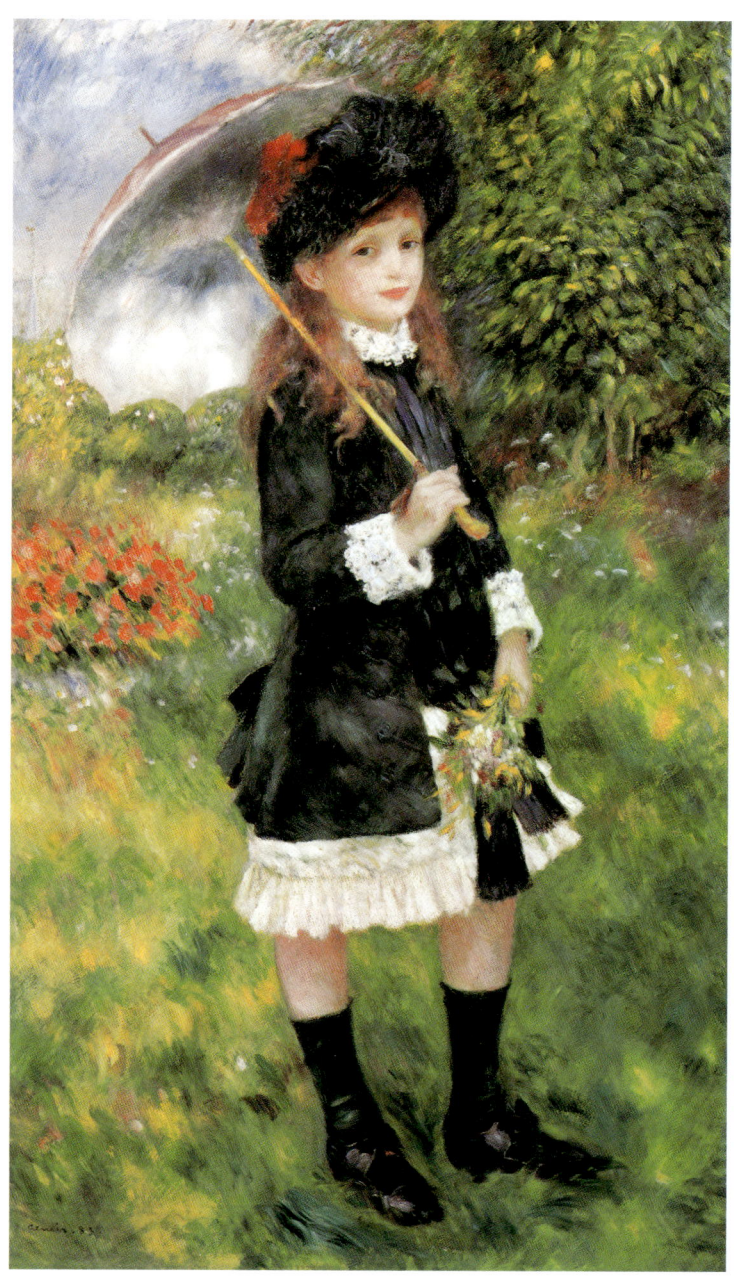

Young Girl with a Parasol (Aline Nunès), 1883
Oil on canvas, 130 x 79 cm (51¼ x 31 in.)
Private collection

The Umbrellas, *c.* 1881–86
Oil on canvas, 180.3 x 114.9 cm (71 x 45¼ in.)
London, The National Gallery,
Sir Hugh Lane Bequest

266 THE CRISIS OF IMPRESSIONISM AND THE "DRY PERIOD"

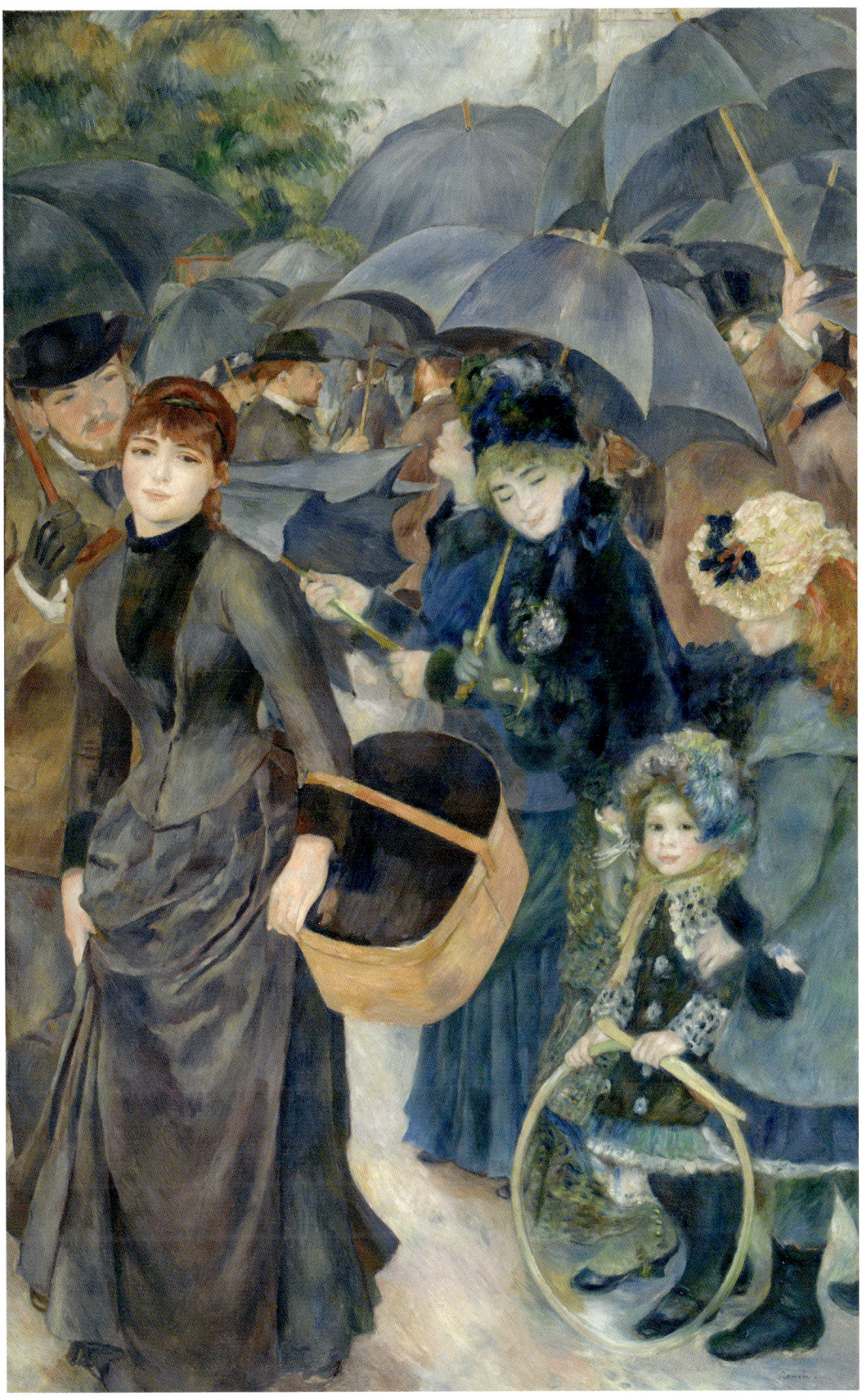

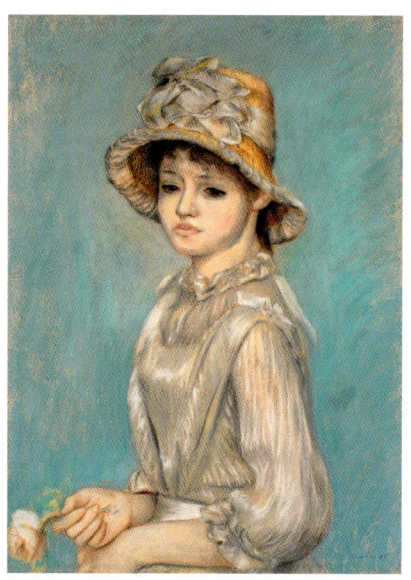

Young Girl with a Rose, 1886
Pastel, 59.7 x 44.2 cm (23½ x 17½ in.)
Private collection

of 1875/76 (ill. p. 236), Renoir no longer tried to achieve an accurate rendering of the squiggly patches of sunlight and purple spots of shadow moving about on a person's skin, which itself was breathing and constantly in motion. Rather, he aimed at an evenly distributed glow of peaceful lines which he drew clearly and accurately. The nonchalance of people's movements and the casualness of their postures still provided a link with the convictions that Renoir had expressed in his Impressionist paintings half a decade earlier. Generally, his style of painting and drawing showed that Renoir had been studying the Classicist Ingres.

Renoir was indeed struggling to change his whole concept of art, in fact he was constantly searching and experimenting. This can be seen in the fact that the pictures which he painted at that time still somehow reflected his previous views, even though their colours were cooler, and he applied the paint more loosely and sketchily. It can be observed in several portraits of children (cf. ills. pp. 276 and 280) as well as still lifes with flowers (cf. ills. pp. 274 and 285) and his little study of young women and children playing in the Jardin du Luxembourg (ill. p. 269).

Unlike with any other painting, Renoir spent three years on his major work of this period before having it displayed by Georges Petit in 1887. *The Great Bathers* (ill. pp. 278/279) is a picture of girls with firm, cool bodies enjoying themselves at a pond in the woods. The atmosphere is one of joyful abandonment, and the girls are in fact very close to life and quite typical of that particular time, especially the boisterous, tomboy-like teenager who is about to splash her friends with water. But the sewing-girls have become nymphs, and their play has become secondary to a composition of graphic shapes and lines, which includes some amazing details but does not add up to a convincing whole. The girls' gestures have become affected, and the kicking mass of entangled legs at the centre of the picture seems confused. The faces of the playing girls lack expressiveness. Renoir was first inspired to paint this picture when he saw one of François Girardon's lead reliefs of 1672 on a fountain in the park of Versailles. His subsequent sketches clearly show his inability to come to grips with the classical orderliness he was aiming at; it is only in his very careful studies of the girls' movements that we can detect any vigour and liveliness (cf. his drawing of 1884/85, p. 277, now in the Art Institute of Chicago).

The Realist element of the Impressionist masterpieces had been the way in which they rendered aspects of contemporary life that were momentary but nevertheless characteristic. Renoir wanted to move away from this style. He wanted to give his pictures a greater universal appeal while at the same time retaining the freshness of a personal impression. Neither did he want to go back on the artistic achievements of Impressionism, i.e. the use of brightness, of colourful shadows and

OPPOSITE
Le Jardin du Luxembourg, c. 1883
Oil on canvas, 64 x 53 cm (25¼ x 21 in.)
Private collection

PAGE 270 LEFT
*Dance in the Country
(Aline Charigot and Paul Lhote)*, 1883
Oil on canvas, 180.3 x 90 cm (71 x 35½ in.)
Paris, Musée d'Orsay

PAGES 270/271 CENTER
*Dance at Bougival
(Suzanne Valadon and Paul Lhote)*, 1883
Oil on canvas, 182 x 98 cm (71¾ x 38½ in.)
Boston, Museum of Fine Arts

PAGE 271 RIGHT
*Dance in the City (Suzanne Valadon and
Eugène-Pierre Lestringuez)*, 1883
Oil on canvas, 179.7 x 89.1 cm (70¾ x 35 in.)
Paris, Musée d'Orsay

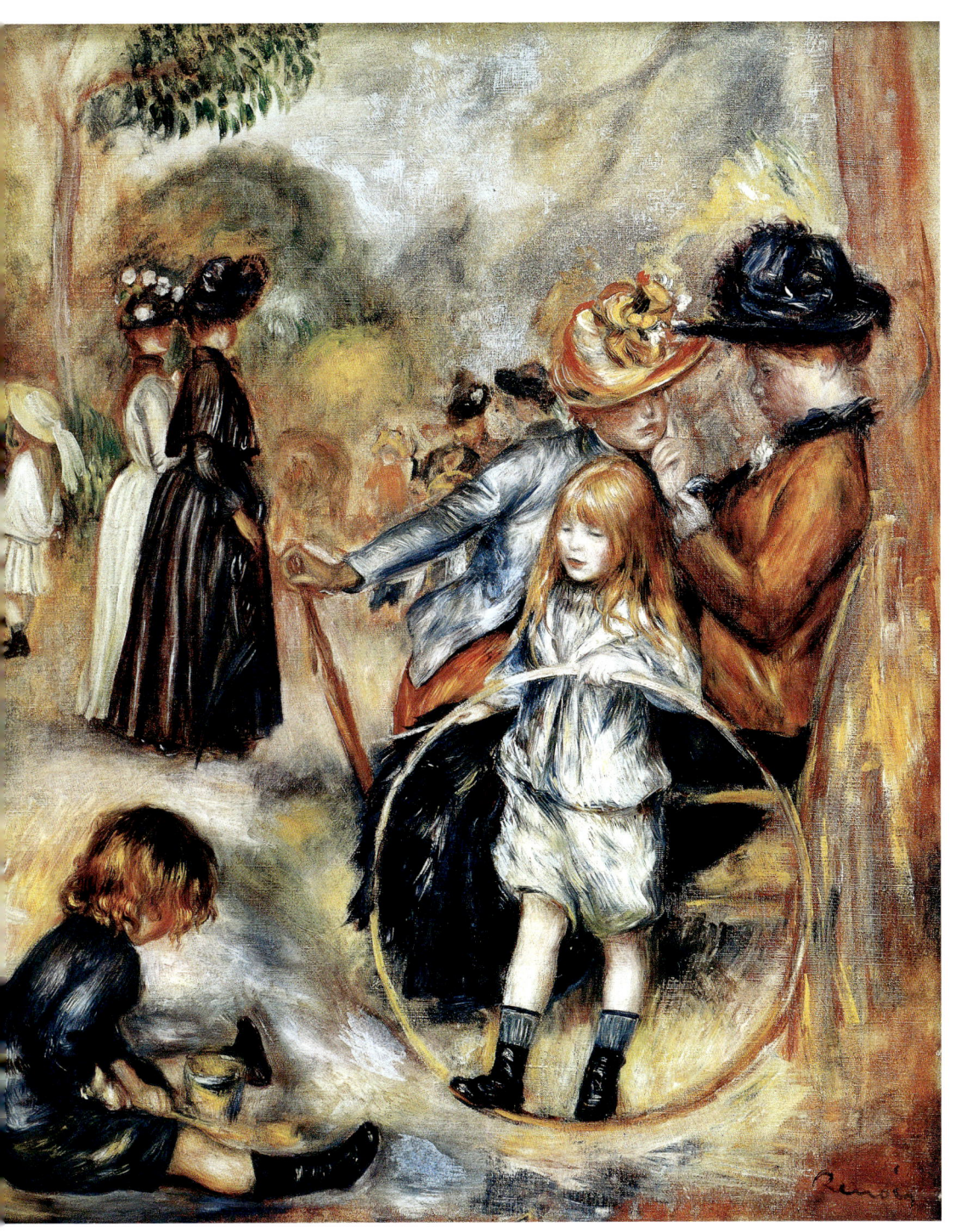

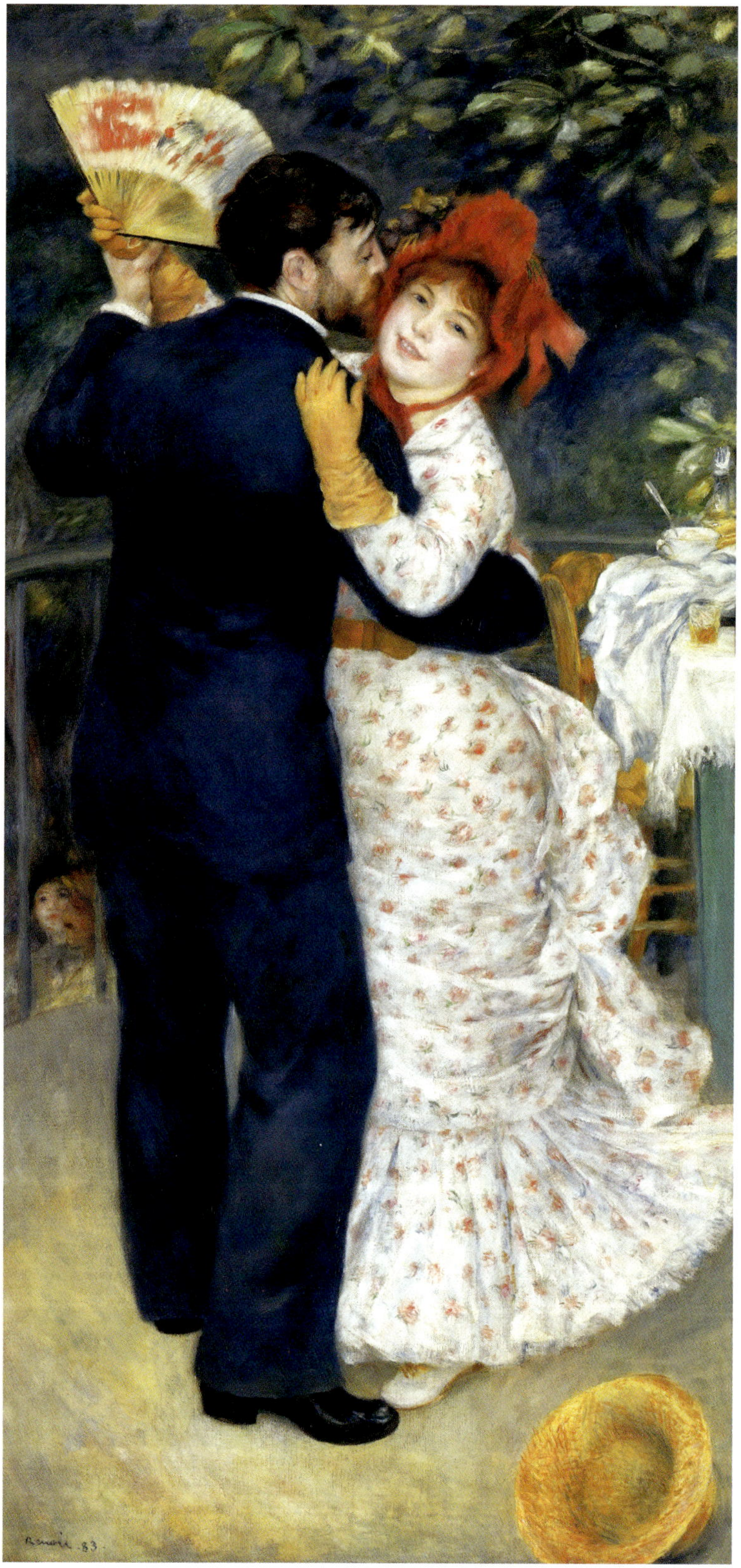

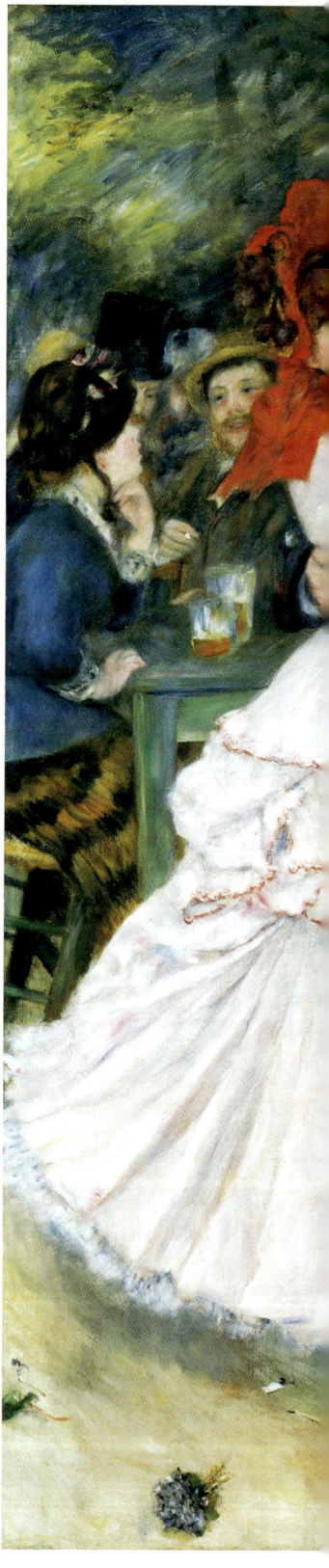

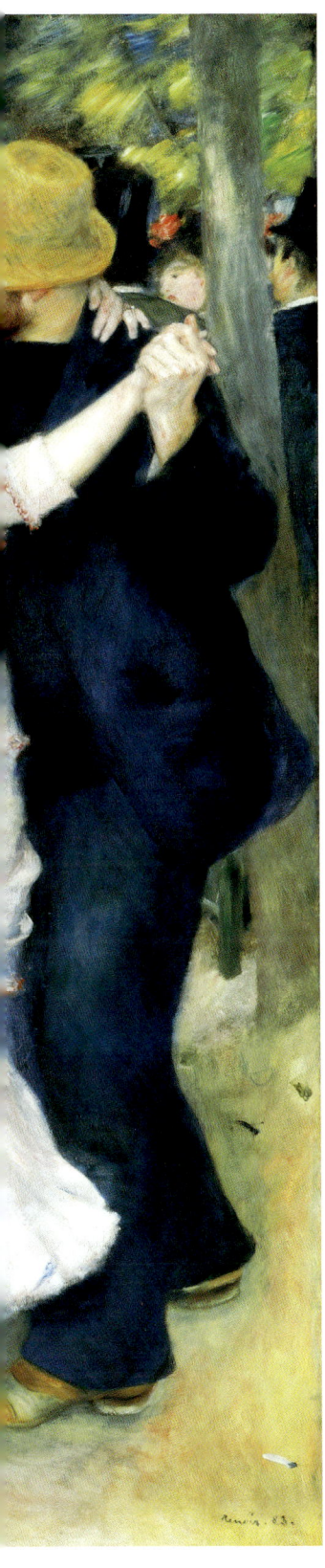

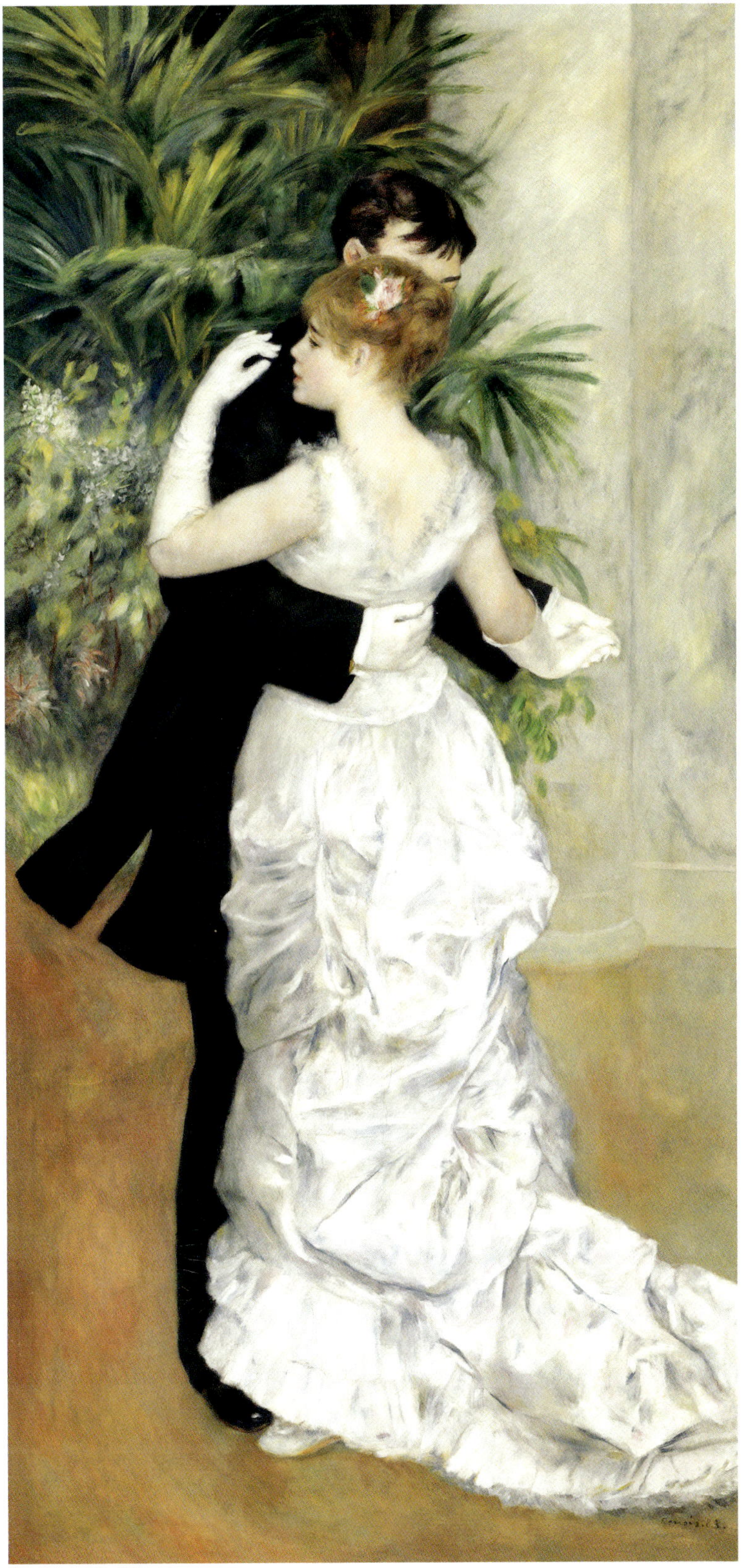

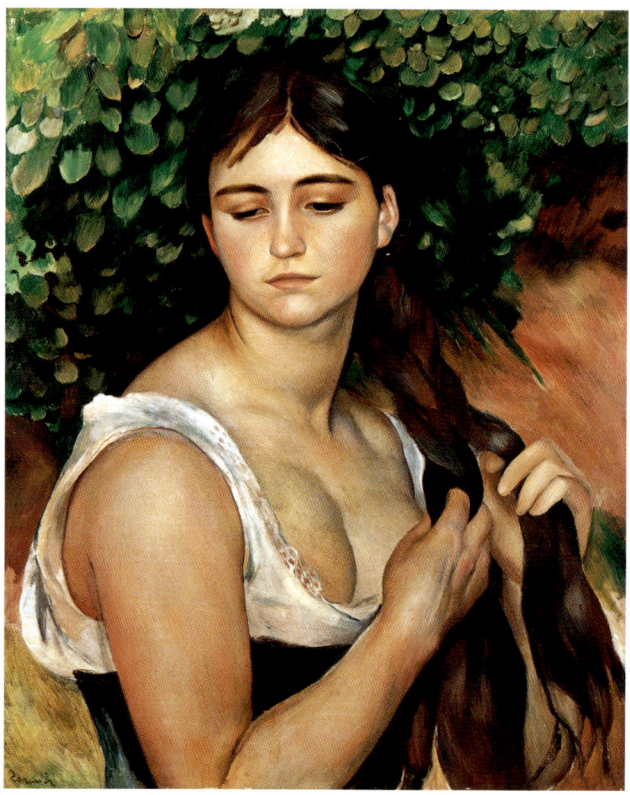

the capturing of people in motion. What he was looking for was more firmness as well as a unified, self-contained whole within the organic structure of the picture. He tried to achieve this by superimposing Neo-Classical structural principles on the seemingly coincidental turbulence of his subjects. This, however, gave rise to contradictions which remained largely unsolved.

Renoir was no more able to reach his goal in a convincing and productive way than any other Neo-Classical painter in Europe at that time. Faced with a reality that was complicated and full of contradictions, it had become necessary to aim at a more profound and varied way of capturing the truth, one that would solve these contradictions. However, there would have been no need to idealize reality by turning towards Classical principles. What was called for was a vigorous depiction of tangible scenes and figures, and they had to be historically and socially truthful. Renoir did not take this path. Instead, he concentrated on inventing a charmingly beautiful refuge that was full of harmony and bliss and that consisted of creatures who dwelt somewhere between fantasy and reality.

This so-called "Dry Period" in Renoir's life added a firmness of line to his artistic signature. Soon, however, he combined this with a new surge of sumptuously blossoming colourfulness that was even richer than the previous one. Whole torrents of colour began to pulsate rhythmically in the pictures he created and gave them a festively decorative effect. It was in the course of 1888 that Renoir began to develop this late style.

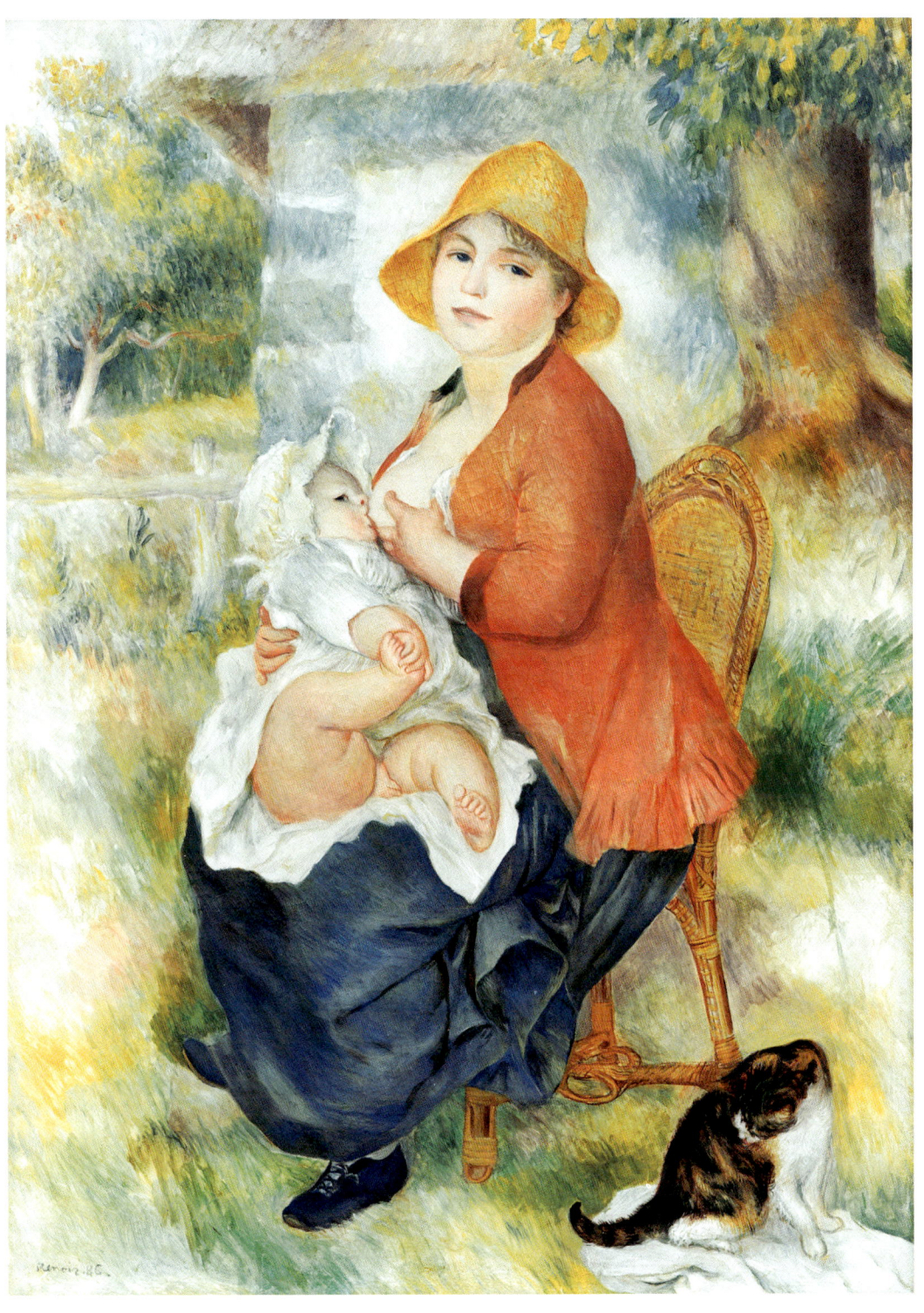

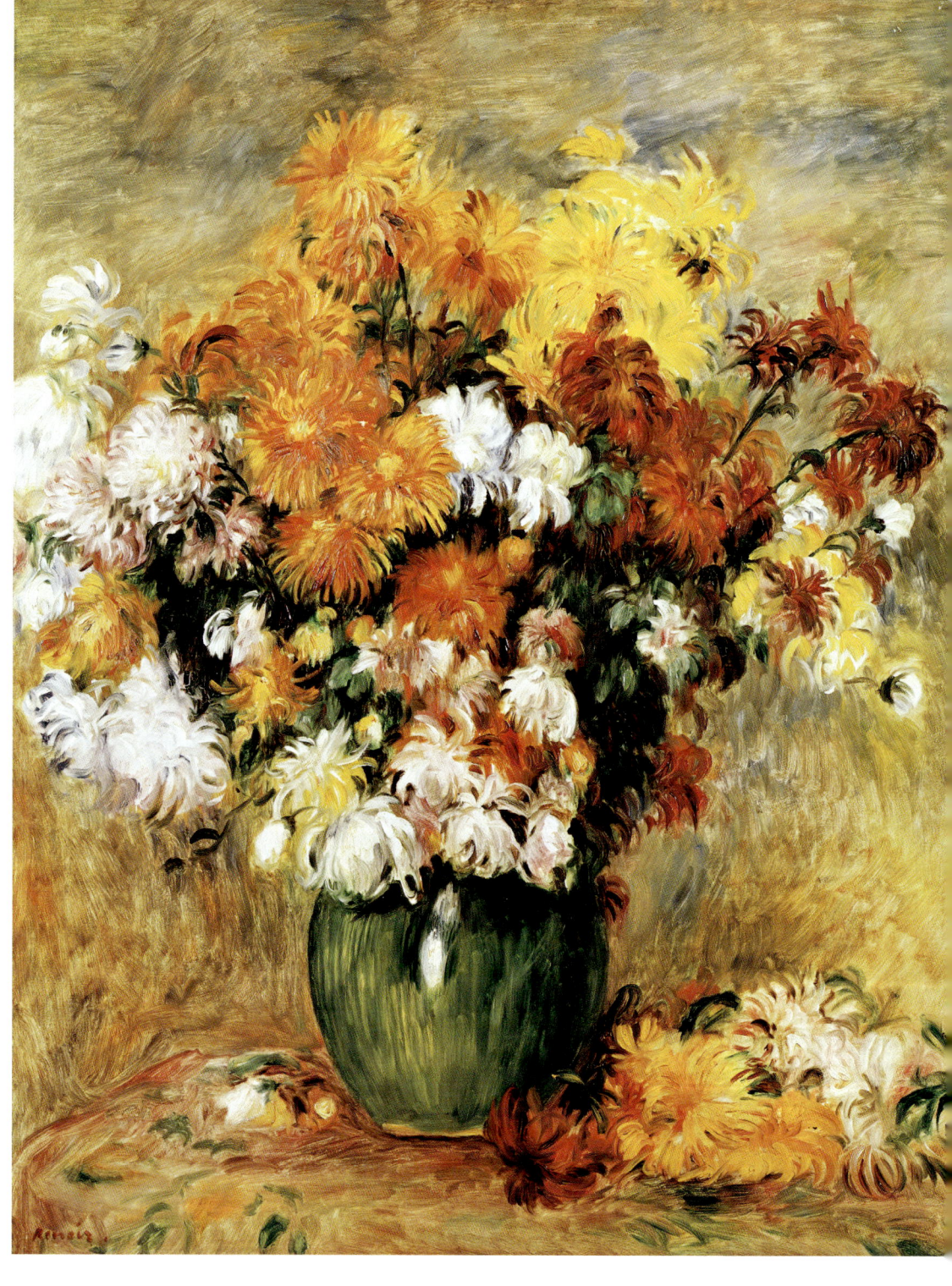

Sickness and Old Age
1888–1919

Although the last three decades in Renoir's life do not appear to have been very dramatic, they were overshadowed by personal tragedy. On the one hand, they were filled with the quiet triumph of his art, its general recognition and also financial success, so that these external worries were taken off his shoulders. On the other hand, however, they were darkened by the bitter fate of serious illness, against which he had to fight very hard. Also he was to suffer the same destiny as all ageing artists, i.e. that of seeing their art being overtaken and reduced to nothing by the subsequent generation.

At the end of the 1880s he worked together with Cézanne several times, and then with Berthe Morisot, who was the most gifted woman among the Impressionist painters and whom Renoir admired very much indeed. She died in 1895. The year 1890 was the first and last time for seven years that he exhibited paintings at the Salon again. In 1892 he travelled to Spain with his friend Gallimard and was very impressed by the treasures in the museums there. But whereas in the early phase of Impressionism Spanish paintings by Diego Velázquez and Francisco de Goya had had quite an impact, especially on Manet, it had now become too late for Renoir to change. 1890 was also the year when Renoir finally achieved public recognition. Durand-Ruel exhibited 110 of his works at a special exhibition, and for the first time the French government bought a picture for the Musée du Luxembourg: *Yvonne and Christine Lerolle Playing the Piano* (ill. p. 288). But when, two years later, Caillebotte's legacy became the property of the state and Renoir was appointed executor, he had to struggle hard to persuade the authorities to accept at least the larger part of the collection. The old gentlemen on the relevant committees were extremely sceptical toward an art that had been rejected and ridiculed for such

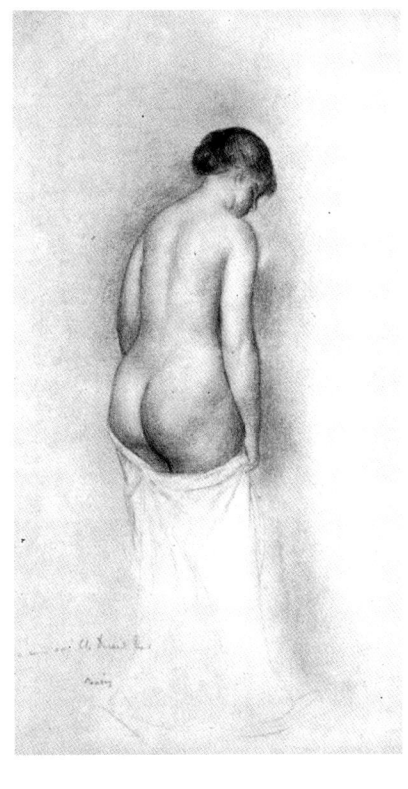

OPPOSITE
Bouquet of Chrysanthemums, *c.* 1884
Oil on canvas, 82 x 66 cm (32¼ x 26 in.)
Rouen, Musée des Beaux-Arts

ABOVE RIGHT
After the Bath, 1884
Red crayon, 44.5 x 24.5 cm (17½ x 9¾ in.)
Private collection

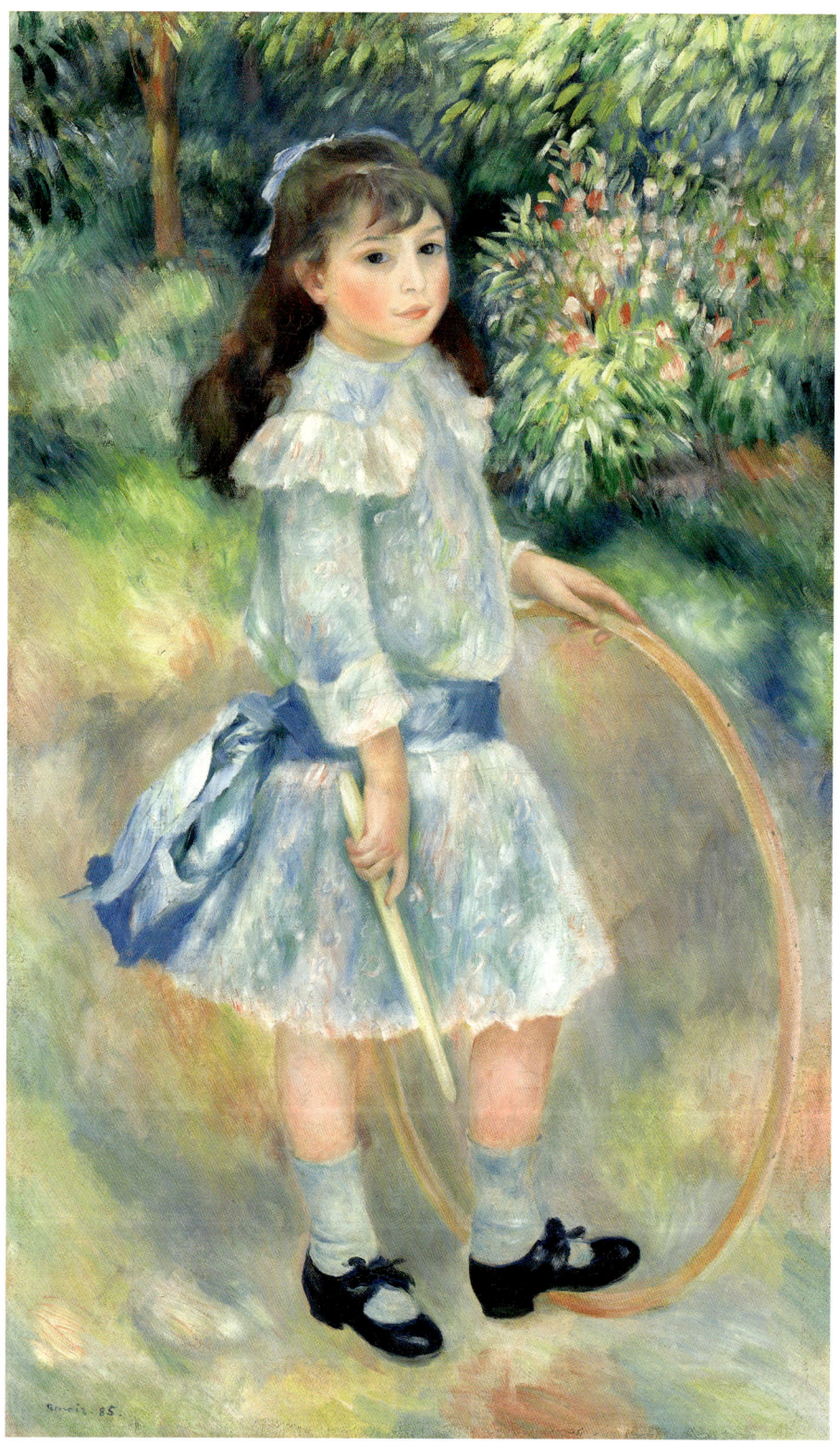

a long time, and they were reluctant to put them into state-owned, public museums. What is more, the Parisian middle classes at that time were trembling with fear after a wave of anarchist assassinations, and some of the anti-academic painters were known to have anarchist leanings. Professor Gérôme of the École des Beaux-Arts publicly referred to Impressionist paintings as filth, saying that accepting them would be a sign of moral cowardice on the part of the state. And so only thirty-eight of the sixty-five paintings bequeathed by Caillebotte were hung at the Luxembourg, including just six of the eight Renoirs.

Renoir now spent several summers (1892, 1893, 1895) in the coastal town of Pont-Aven, a spot which was very popular among painters. In particular, it attracted adherents of Symbolism, which was the latest dominant trend in the world of art. Among them, Paul Gauguin had played an important part until he left for the South Seas in 1891, where he was hoping to find that paradise which Europe was unable to offer him. "What for?" said Renoir when he heard about it, "one can paint ever such lovely pictures in Batignolles." However, Renoir himself

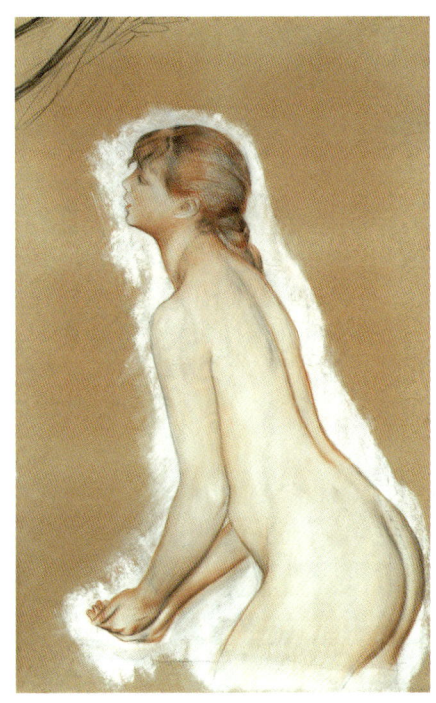

had been looking for a paradise outside his real environment – in the idyllic landscapes which he populated with the bathing and dreaming figures of his voluptuously free-and-easy girls. One of the people who served as a model for their plump bodies was Gabrielle Renard, a cousin of Aline's, who, at the age of fourteen, was employed as a maid shortly before the birth of Renoir's second son, Jean. She stayed with the family until about 1914 when she married the American painter Conrad Slade. Other models were the nurses and nannies of his two sons, and the cook. He now often spent the summer at Essoyes, his wife's hometown, where he bought a house in 1898. In the same years, if not before, he probably suffered his first severe attack of rheumatoid arthritis, which forced him to spend the winter months in the south of France, in Provence, and to seek medical treatment in the summer.

But before his illness he went abroad again. In 1896 he visited Bayreuth. He was still fascinated by Wagner's music, but felt rather disappointed by the Wagner cult in the festival town. Later, during a brief period when his health improved, he went to Germany for a second time. Following an invitation from the Thurneyssens in Munich, he went to stay with them in 1910, painted portraits and enjoyed the Rubens paintings at the Pinakothek museum. His fame had gone beyond the borders of France. Not only did he exhibit his pictures with Durand-Ruel in 1896 and 1899, then again at the autumn Salon in 1904 and the Galerie Bernheim in Paris in 1913, but also at the Centennale, the new-century art show at the 1900 Paris World Fair, where he received the Cross of the Legion of Honour. At the beginning of the new century his pictures could also be seen in London and Budapest, Vienna and Stockholm, Dresden and Berlin, and the Moscow wholesale merchant Sergei Shchukin

OPPOSITE
Girl with a Hoop (Marie Goujon), 1885
Oil on canvas, 125.7 x 75.6 cm (49½ x 29¾ in.)
Washington, D.C., National Gallery of Art,
Chester Dale Collection

TOP
Splashing Figure
(Study for *The Great Bathers*), 1884/85
Red crayon, 98.9 x 63.5 cm (39 x 25 in.)
The Art Institute of Chicago,
Bequest of Kate L. Brewster

PAGES 278/279
The Great Bathers, 1884–87
Oil on canvas, 117.8 x 170.8 cm (46½ x 67¼ in.)
Philadelphia Museum of Art,
Mr and Mrs Carroll S. Tyson, Jr, Collection

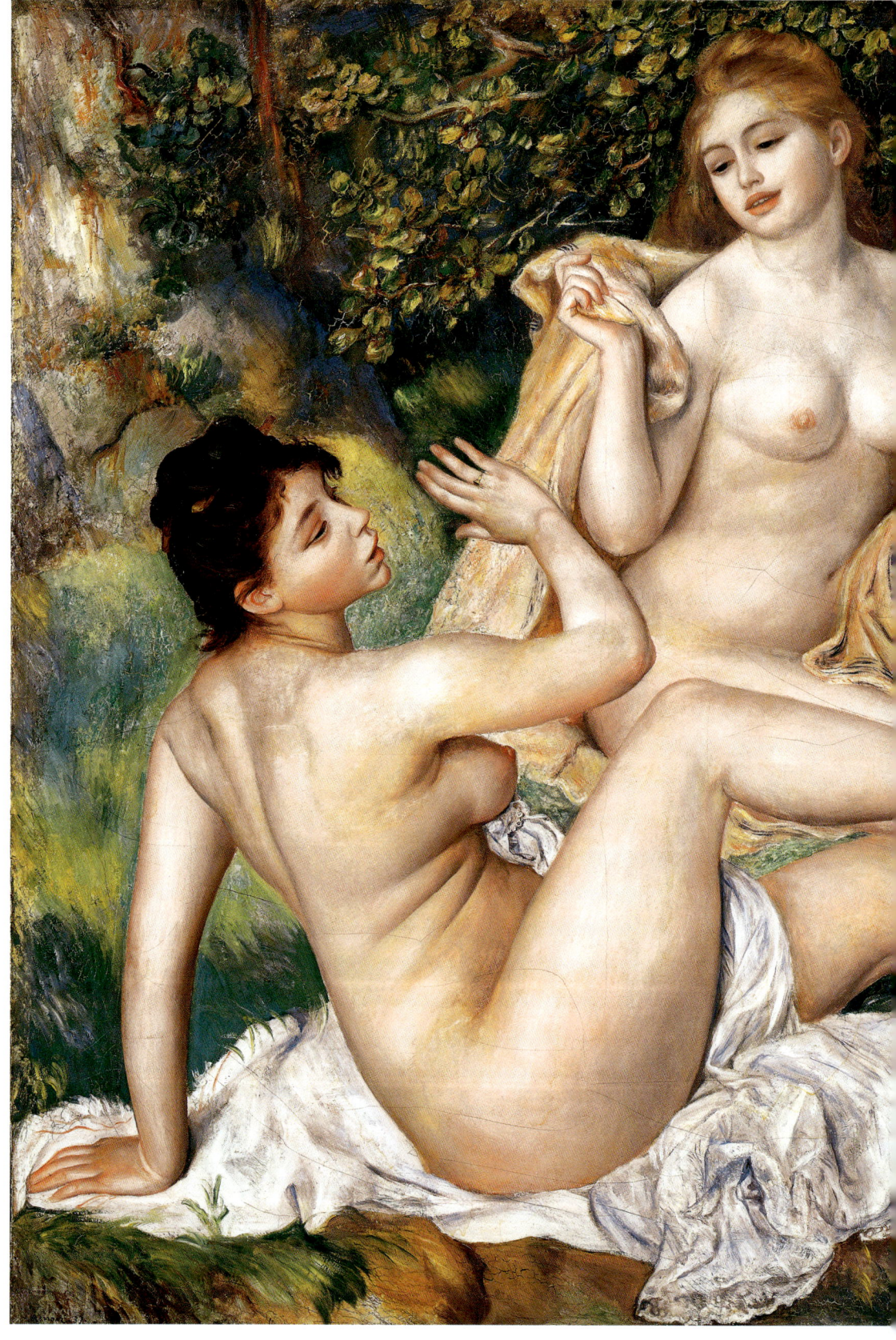

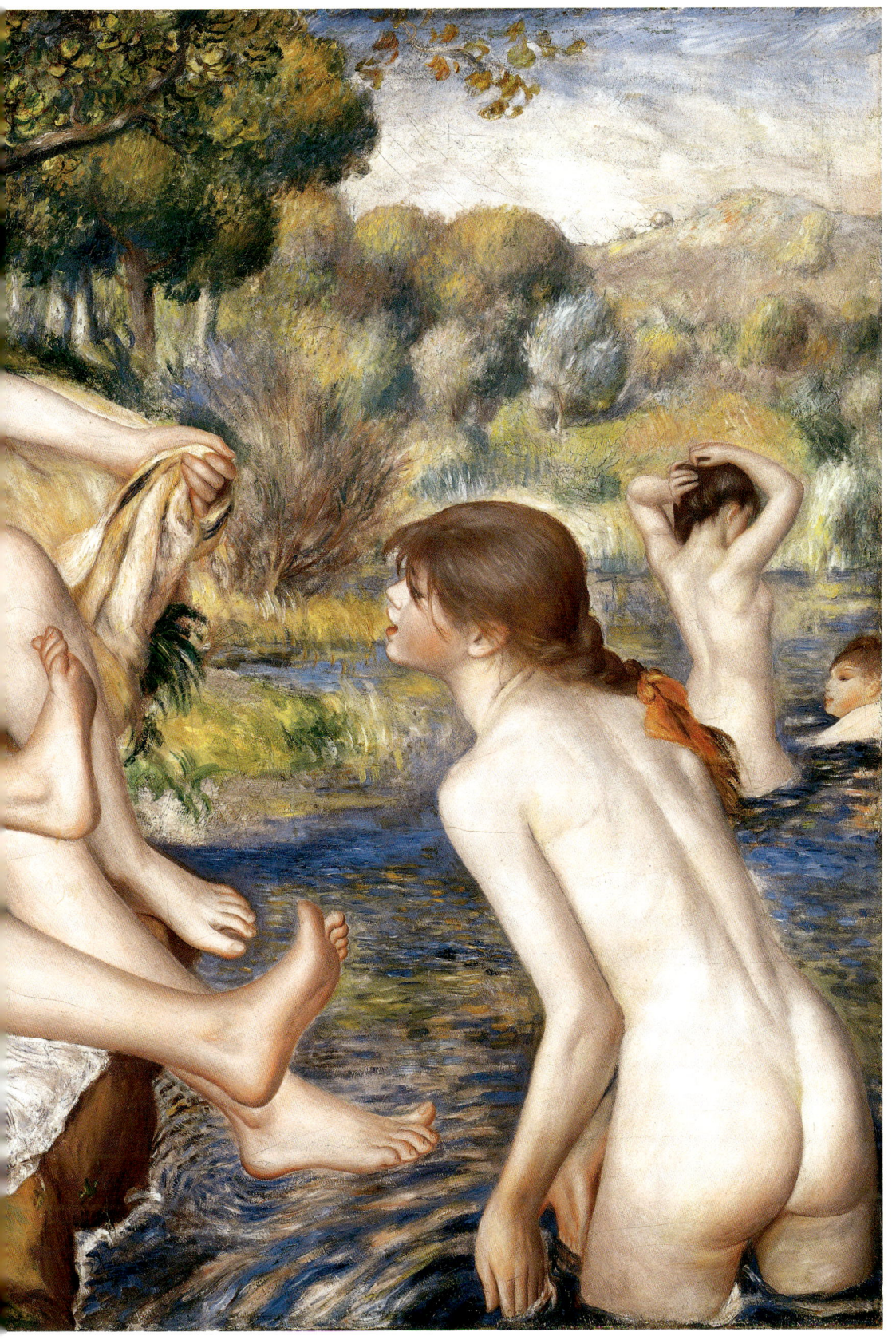

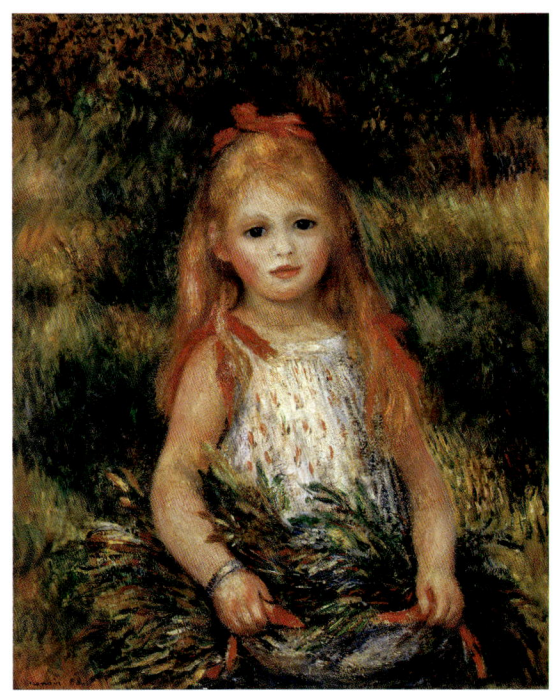

enjoyed showing his beautiful Renoirs to his customers. These paintings are now among the prize possessions of the Pushkin Museum in Moscow. Renoir himself settled down in Magagnosc near Grasse in 1899, and then in Le Cannet near Cannes in 1902. In 1901 his third son Claude, called Coco, was born – a delightful model for many pictures (ill. p. 295).

Finally, in 1905, he and his family moved to Cagnes, near Antibes, an area with the same warm climate and countryside on the Côte d'Azur. At first they lived in the post office building until Renoir had "Les Colettes" built, a house in a thick grove of olive trees that was to become the open-air studio of his later years. Tourists travelling through the area used to disturb him when he was painting, because their hotel porter had suggested to them that they should include the famous painter in their "sightseeing". Good-natured man that he was, he could not say no when businessmen kept flattering him until he agreed to paint the portraits of their wives and children – sometimes in order to sell these pictures at a profit shortly afterwards, as if they were shares that had risen in value. But there were also visitors who were very welcome: the sculptors Auguste Rodin and Aristide Maillol, the painters Albert André and Walter Pach, as well as the art dealer Ambroise Vollard. All of these have handed down to us some valuable notes of their talks with the old master (who hated this term). He always expressed himself in simple words and without any clever philosophical ideas. A large number of pretentious theories of art were being discussed at the time, and it was probably because of these that Renoir was suspicious of any theory whatsoever. Above all, however, he felt profound respect for the tradition of the great masters and that craftsman-like skilfulness which had been destroyed completely by the increasing division of labour. He was neither a critic nor a rebel, and, in a way, he was living outside his own time, but this enabled him to maintain a purity and kind-heartedness that was rare in those days.

His rheumatoid arthritis soon became excruciatingly painful and gave him a lot of trouble. His bones became deformed, and his skin dried up. In 1904 he only weighed about seven and a half stone and was scarely able to sit. From 1910 onwards he could not even move about with crutches and became a prisoner in his wheelchair. His hands were completely deformed, like the claws of a bird, and a gauze bandage had to prevent his fingernails from growing into the flesh. He was not able to pick up his paintbrush, it had to be wedged between his rigid fingers. And so, day after day, he painted undaunted, unless an attack forced him to lie on his bed where a wire construction protected his body from being touched by the bedclothes. There were occasions when he was completely paralysed. Visitors were getting used to interruptions in a conversation, when Renoir

TOP
Little Girl Gleaning, 1888
Oil on canvas, 61.8 x 54 cm (24¼ x 21¼ in.)
Museo de Arte de São Paulo

OPPOSITE
In the Meadow, 1888–92
Oil on canvas, 81.3 x 65.4 cm (32 x 25¾ in.)
New York, The Metropolitan Museum of Art, Bequest of Sam A. Lewisohn

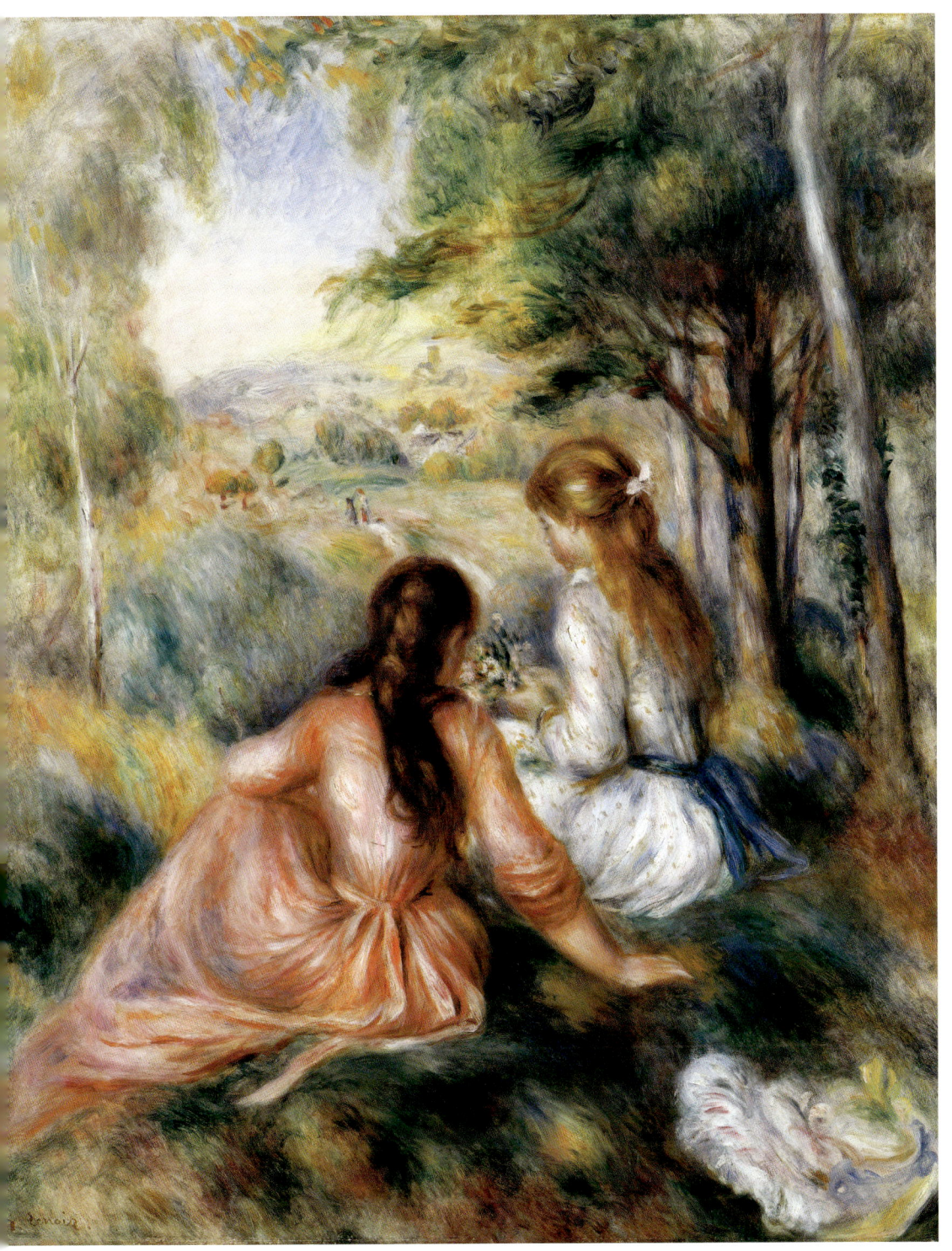

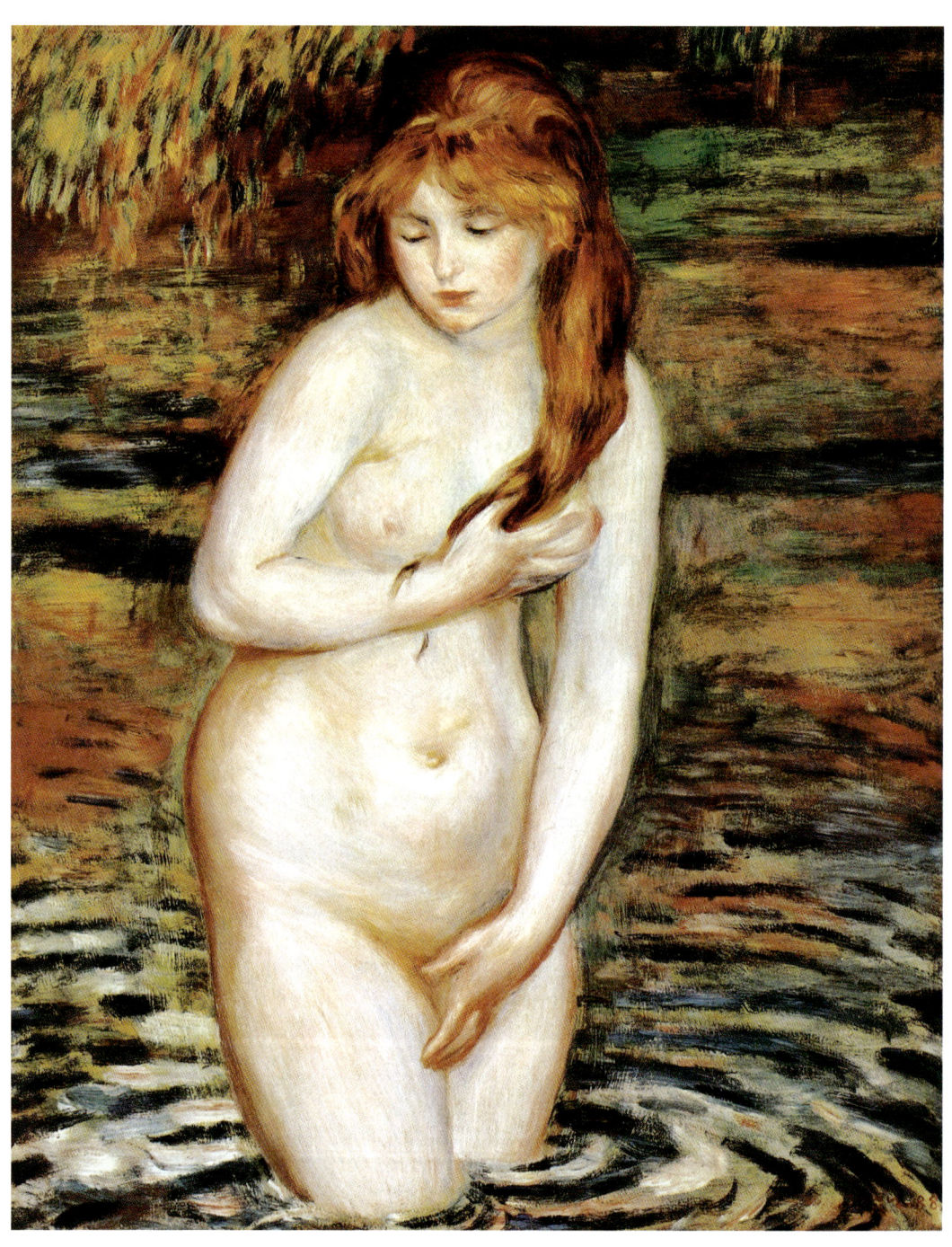

The Bather (After the Bath), 1888
Oil on canvas, 81 x 66 cm (32 x 26 in.)
Private collection

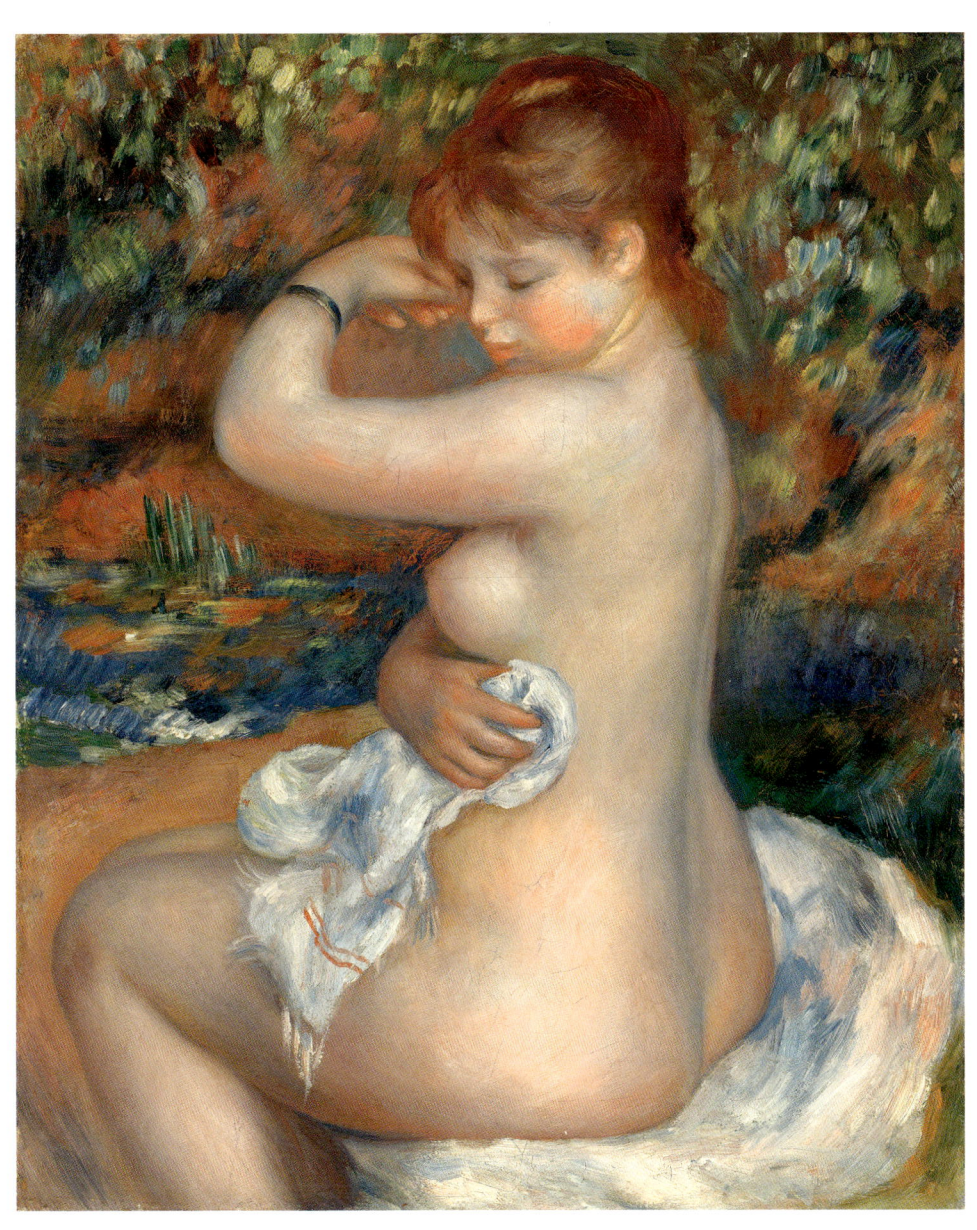

After the Bath, 1888
Oil on canvas, 65 x 54 cm (25½ x 21¼ in.)
Private collection

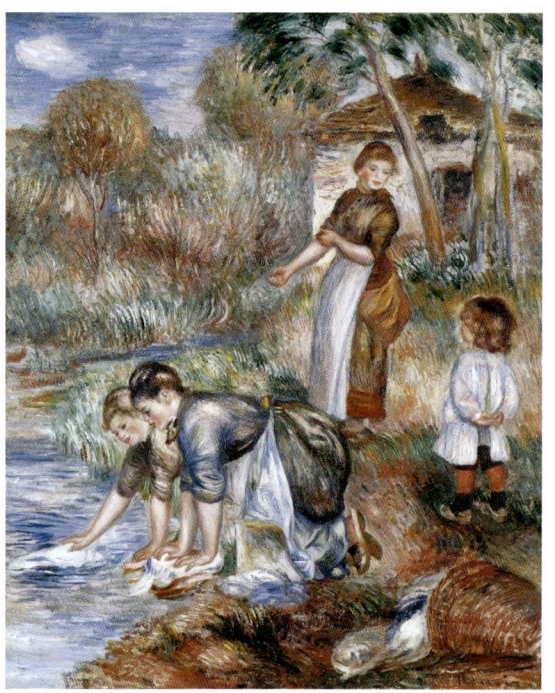

would suddenly stop and then have a painful attack that lasted for a quarter of an hour, after which he usually continued at exactly the same point where he had left off. He had an easel where each canvas could be rolled up like a woven product on a loom. Thus he was able to cope with larger formats, even though he had to sit in a wheelchair and could only move his arm to thrust the paintbrush forward in short, sudden jerks. "You see," he said to the art dealer Vollard who was watching him paint with his deformed claw, "you don't even need a hand for painting!"

It was at this time that Renoir took up sculpture: he used somebody else's hands to form the clay according to his instructions. The young Spaniard Richard Guino turned out to be a very thoughtful and diligent assistant, though the person who took over from him was less suited for this task. He used sketches by Renoir as his starting point and then carried them out in detail. Moving close to him with his wheelchair, Renoir would then give instructions with a pointer: "Take a bit off there … a little more … that's right! This should be rounder, fuller …!" The two were so well coordinated that in the end they communicated with each other by means of short noises and exclamations, and a critical or pleased grunt from Renoir was sufficient. In this way sculptures were created which had never been touched by Renoir's hands but which are nevertheless works that come from his own mind, made according to Renoir's ideas of what is beautiful in human being.

One thing is indeed incredible, unique and wonderful about these late works: even though Renoir was old, sick and decrepit, there was never so much as a shadow of despair or weariness in his art. Nor did he ever allow it to be invaded by feelings of envy or anger towards those who were in good health. In fact, all the hundreds of works which he produced during the last few years of his life were a single ode to happiness and joy, a single Arcadian smile.

At the beginning of the First World War, which Renoir abhorred, his sons Jean and Pierre were badly wounded. They were nursed by their mother until she died in 1915, overwhelmed by sorrow. Renoir visited her grave in Essoyes during the first summer after the war, and then went on to Paris for the last time. The seventy-eight-year-old was taken in his wheelchair to see his favourite paintings by François Boucher, Delacroix and Corot, as well as to Paolo Veronese's large and colourful *Wedding in Cana*. At Renoir's request it had been displayed side by side with a small portrait of Madame Charpentier of 1877, which was now given a special place of honour. "I'm still making progress," he said a few days before his death, and his last reported words on 3 December 1919 were about the arrangement of a still life that he was going to paint, called: "Flowers …"

TOP
Washerwomen, *c.* 1888
Oil on canvas, 56.5 x 47.5 cm (22¼ x 18¾ in.)
Baltimore Museum of Art,
The Cone Collection

OPPOSITE
Moss Roses, *c.* 1890
Oil on canvas, 35.5 x 27 cm (14 x 10¾ in.)
Paris, Musée d'Orsay

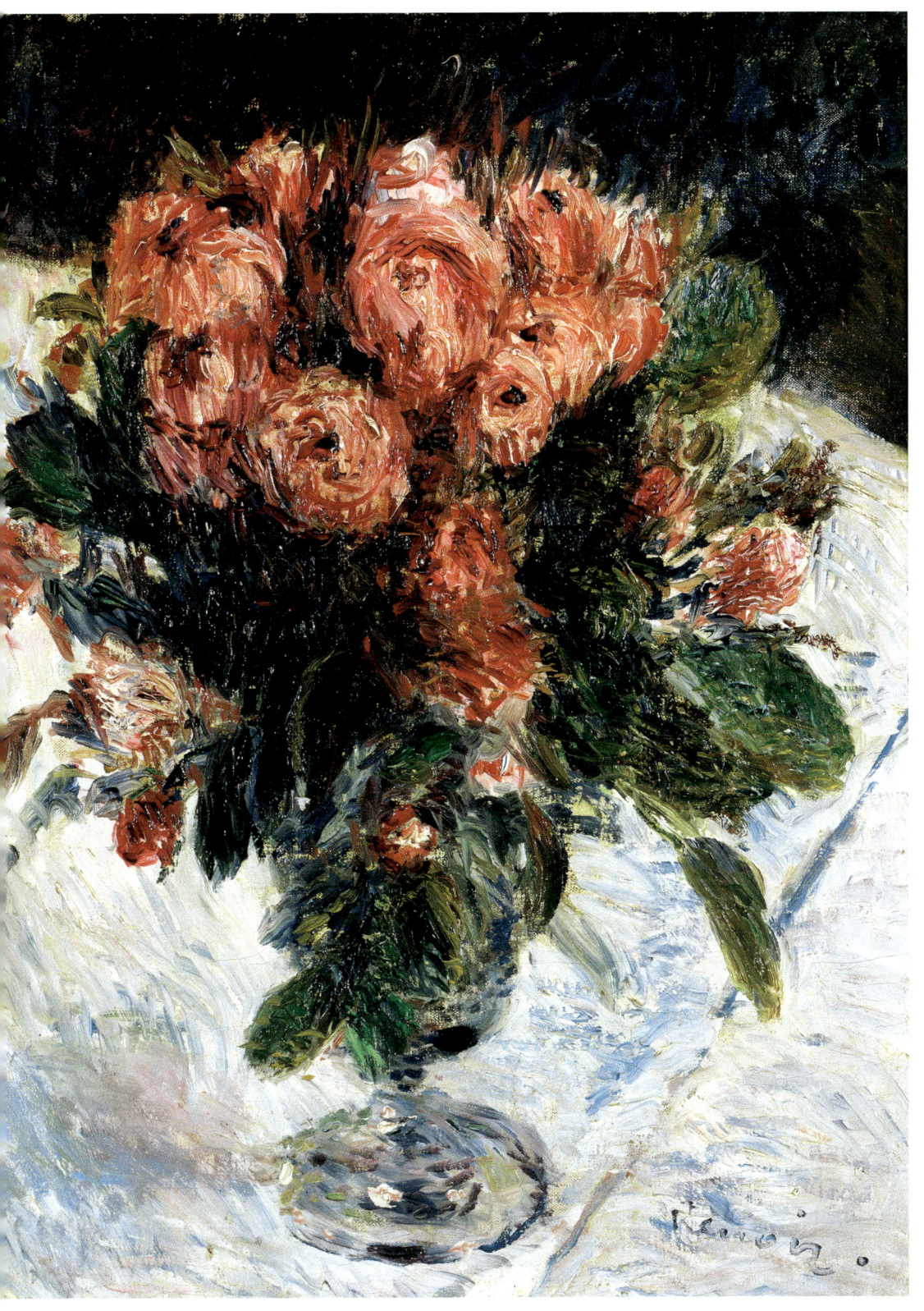

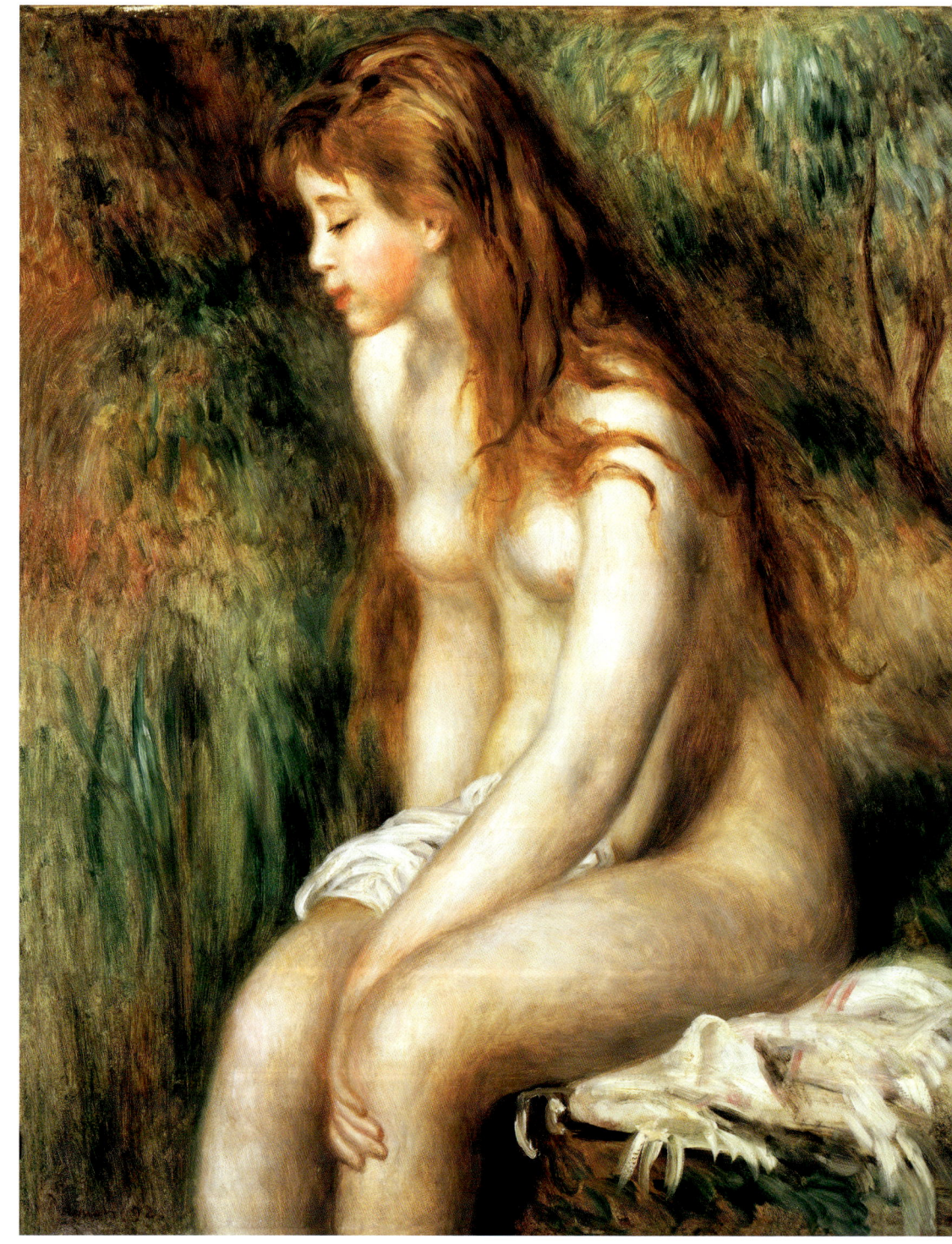

Renoir's Late Works

Once Renoir had got over his "Dry Period" in 1888, there was a flower-like quality in practically everything he painted. His pictures vibrate with strong, sparkling colours, evenly distributed. But even a picture as early as his *Young Girl Reading* (ill. p. 233, now in Frankfurt) calls to mind the way in which Renoir treated the same subject some years earlier (ill. p. 234). The magic of the colours has become even more sumptuous and powerful. In his previous pictures, Renoir used to show people in new situations and immersed in light, whereas now the person in the painting is virtually engulfed by a whole sea of colourful flowers and is no longer interesting as an individual, but rather as someone who serves as a vehicle for colours – colours which almost transcend the material world.

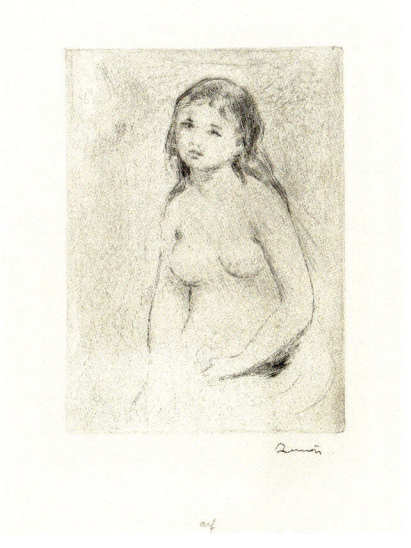

The beauty of his late works is due to their intoxicating blaze of colour and the lightness of Renoir's brushwork. The lines in these compositions move in broad curves, and the paint is often dotted across the canvas like the fine dust on the wings of a butterfly. Whether it is the white cubes of houses, seen quite differently by Cézanne, or the gnarled shapes of olive trees, dramatized so expressively by Vincent van Gogh, the bright light of Provence always flows through his landscapes and lets the colours blossom in all their fantastic splendour. Renoir painted everything as a veiled fairy-tale garden with cheerful harmonies of red, yellow, green and blue, or a woven fabric of confusing, decorative splendour.

OPPOSITE
Young Girl Bathing, 1892
Oil on canvas, 81.3 x 64.8 cm (32 x 25½ in.)
New York, The Metropolitan
Museum of Art,
Robert Lehman Collection

ABOVE RIGHT
Bather, 1906
Etching, 23.7 x 17.5 cm (9¼ x 7 in.)
Paris, Bibliothèque Nationale

Whenever Renoir painted people in their natural environment, he linked them to their surroundings by using the same texture of colours. He still had the sensitivity of an Impressionist when it came to detecting various nuances and the charm of an uninhibited, impulsive movement, especially that of a lithe young girl. Take, for example, his picture of two girls at the piano, which he painted in several different versions (ills. pp. 288 and 289). There is a delightful naturalness about the postures of the Lerolle sisters, and also their facial expressions

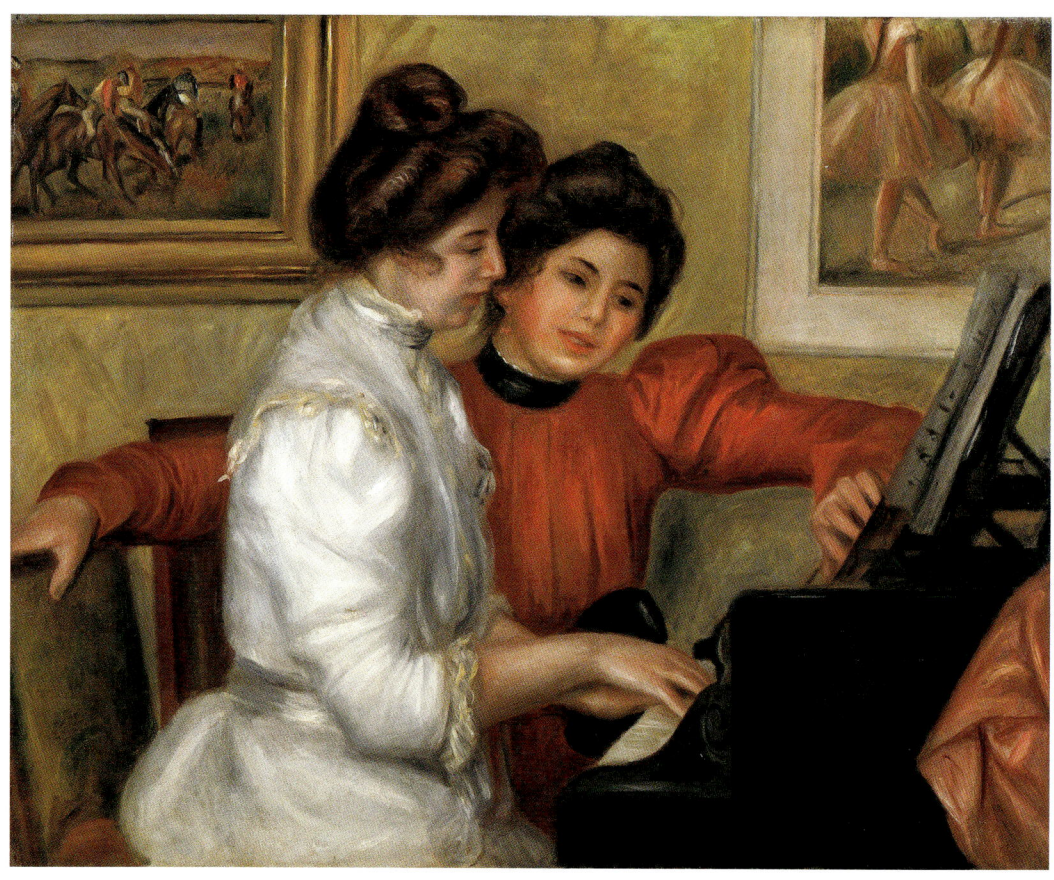

Yvonne and Christine Lerolle
Playing the Piano, 1897
Oil on canvas, 73 x 92 cm (28¾ x 36¼ in.)
Paris, Musée de l'Orangerie

OPPOSITE
Girls at the Piano, 1892
Oil on canvas, 116 x 90 cm (45¾ x 35½ in.)
Paris, Musée d'Orsay

as they are trying out a new tune. Their faces, however, are the least important element.

The girls who are sitting and making garlands of flowers on a meadow under a tree are images of a romantic pantheism that flows in torrential waves and effortlessly merges man and nature into one another. The girls are no longer tangible people at a given point in time, people with distinct actions and feelings placed in the surroundings of sun-soaked nature, as they might have been had they appeared in the scenes which Renoir depicted in the 1870s and early 80s.

Not only was the painter's relationship towards "simple people" without pretence, it was also full of sympathy. This can be seen in a series of pictures showing servant girls doing their washing by the side of a river (ill. p. 284). Renoir focused on the beauty of their figures and movements. He was not interested in the seriousness of their hard work, as painted by Daumier decades before.

As a rule, his pictures no longer show signs of psychological composition, and there is less tension in the constellation of the figures. This is because the rhythmic pattern of the colours has detached itself from the objects and has spread across the entire area of each picture in the form of a pattern that springs from the artist's imagination. Spots of light on the grass or on the objects are still the result of accurate observation of colours in real life, but they no longer serve to render objective reality as authentically as possible. Rather, they have become playthings of the artist's dream colours.

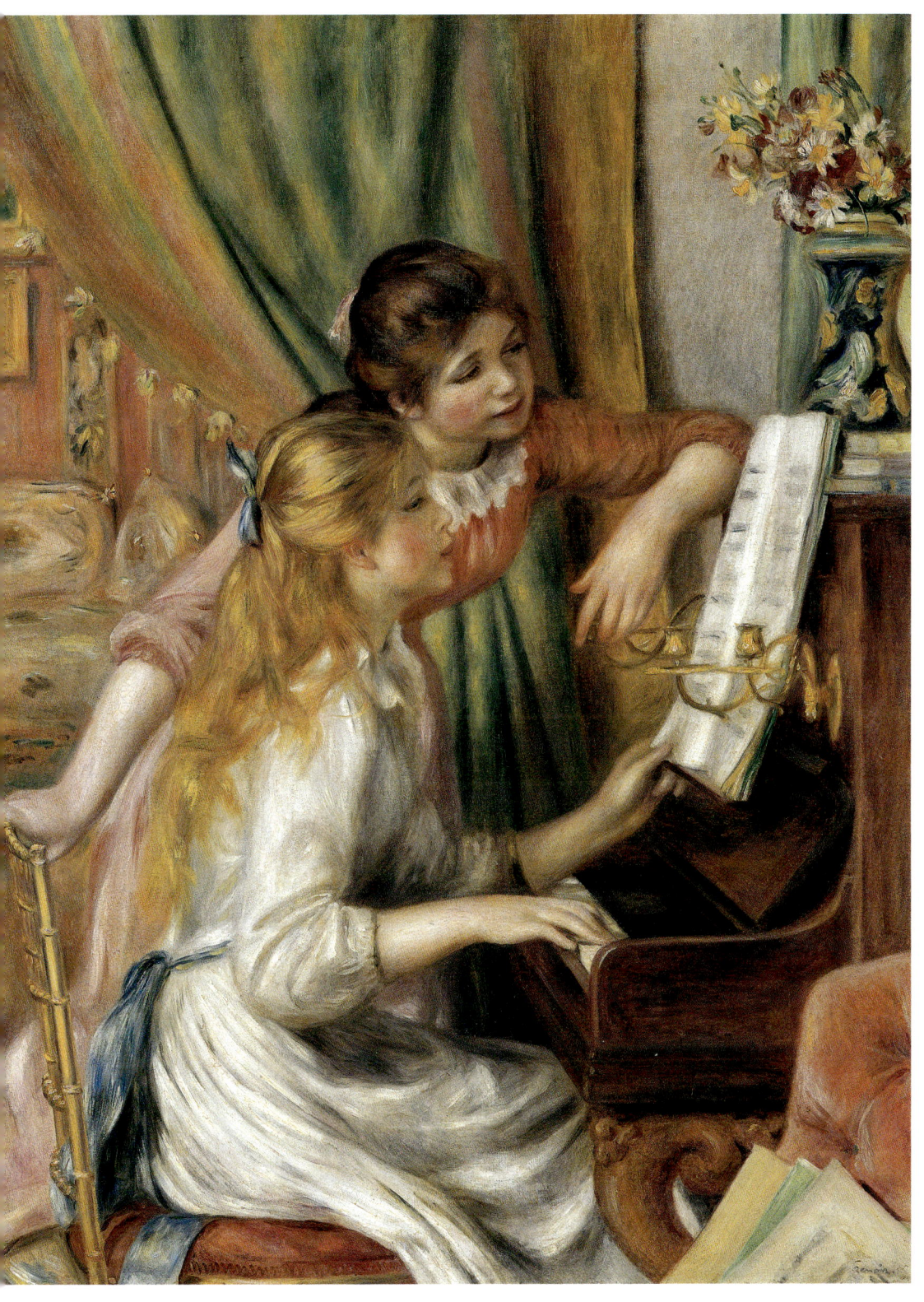

We must bear in mind that the works Renoir produced during the last fifteen years of his life were already contemporaneous with the expressive pictures of the so-called Fauves group of artists around Henri Matisse (who visited Renoir shortly before he died), as well as the birth of Cubism, as represented by Picasso and Georges Braque, and also the abstract or "absolute" art of Wassily Kandinsky.

Most of Renoir's later paintings of people are devoid of any psychological appeal. Many of the faces are disappointingly empty, while others still show signs of an attempt to achieve an appropriate individualization of each character. The most beautiful ones are the pictures he painted as the delighted father of his little son Coco (ill. p. 295), a relatively late addition to the family. They tell the tale of how Coco grew up with the help of Gabrielle, how he was fed by the girl, how he developed the bewitching charm of a spoilt little Goldilocks. In fact, when Renoir concentrated on the flower-like quality of little children in his pictures, he was always at his best.

Then there are a number of beautiful portraits and studies of Gabrielle (ill. p. 294). Some of them show her with simple, grave industriousness which must have been painted by Renoir with a feeling of calm and sincere gratitude. Most of the time, however, Renoir painted her in a state of transfiguration, with flowers and ornaments and with movements that were probably far more graceful than in real life. Rather than creating a completely accurate image of his model, he used her as a source of inspiration. Intimate scenes, such as that of a girl putting on make-up or combing her hair, have become far more simple than they used to be, without complicated lighting effects or capricious movements.

The gestures which he built into his pictures were of a more general nature, they were calm and timeless and did not display any of the clashes and tensions that he used to love in the 1870s. On the other hand, they were far from commonplace or banal, due to the magical formulas of Renoir's colour fantasies. We no longer see them as mere everyday routines, but as the free rhythmic patterns of lyrical songs. What helped him was a mild tendency towards music and dance, which enabled him to appreciate the harmonious movements of his models. In summer 1909 he asked Gabrielle and another favourite model to pose as dancers with tambourines and castanets in

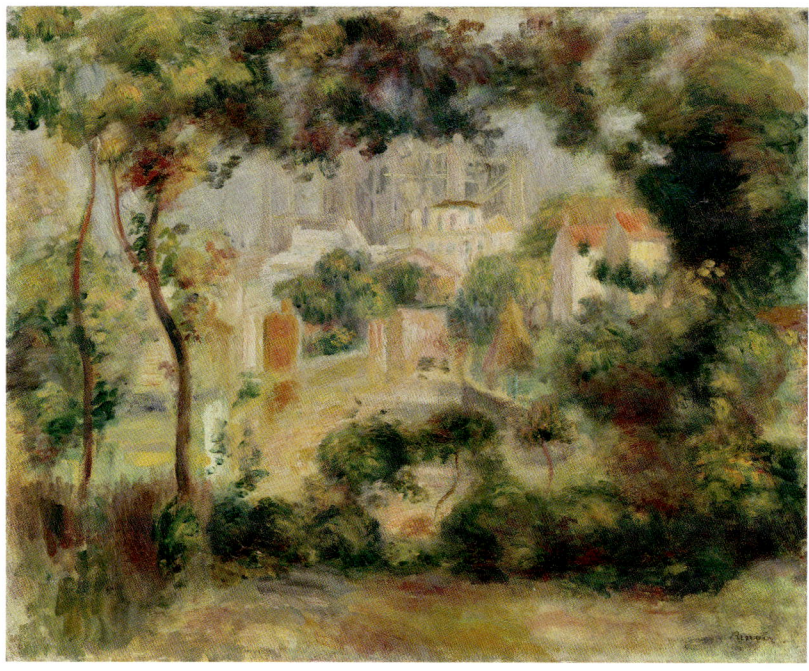

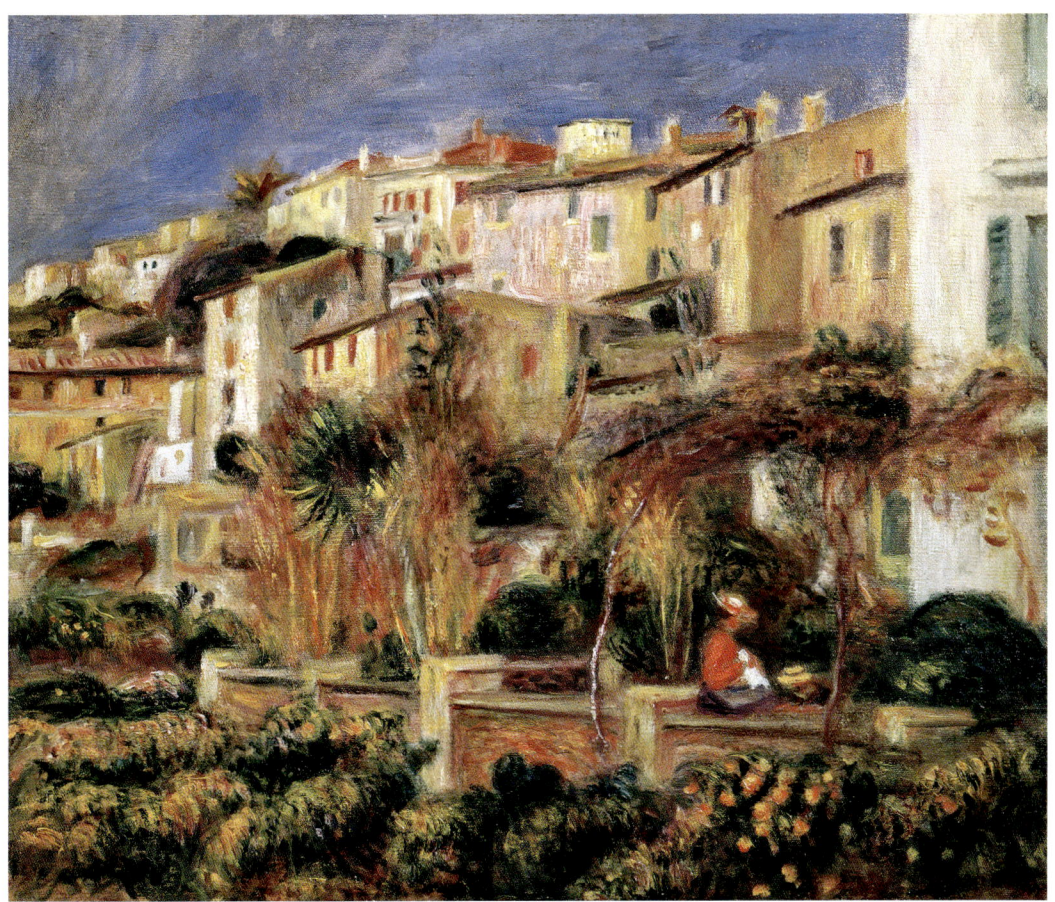

oriental costumes that were reminiscent of Delacroix's Algerian women. This painting was to decorate the dining room of the Parisian art collector Maurice Gagnat (ills. p. 293).

From Renoir's "Dry Period" onwards his favourite theme was nude girls. Once people had got used to the vivid porcelain-like colours of the early 90s and the strawberry pink of his later works, these were the pictures which had the greatest impact on subsequent generations and which they came to associate most closely with the artist. This is somewhat misleading, because during the time when Impressionism was at its height, the 1870s, there were relatively few nude pictures compared with scenes from the life of the middle classes. The Realism of this genre of pictures, however, had been given up by Renoir and the majority of contemporary French painters. Instead, they wanted to create a realm for their art that was pure and detached from the life of society with all its contradictions.

Renoir's blissfully innocent nude girls were nearly always painted in the open air (cf. ills. pp. 282, 283, and 286), and it is obvious from their bodies and faces that all his models must have been of a certain type which he preferred. He was not trying to revive classical rules of proportion or to construct slim, pseudo-antique and idealized figures in line with the academic tradition. His ideal of beauty was that of a well-rounded woman with broad hips. Unlike many other contemporary

Terrace at Cagnes, 1905
Oil on canvas, 45.3 x 54.3 cm (17⅞ x 21½ in.)
Tokyo, Bridgestone Museum of Art

OPPOSITE
View of the New Building of the Sacré-Coeur, 1896
Oil on canvas, 32.6 x 41.2 cm (13 x 16¼ in.)
Munich, Bayerische Staatsgemälde-sammlungen, Neue Pinakothek

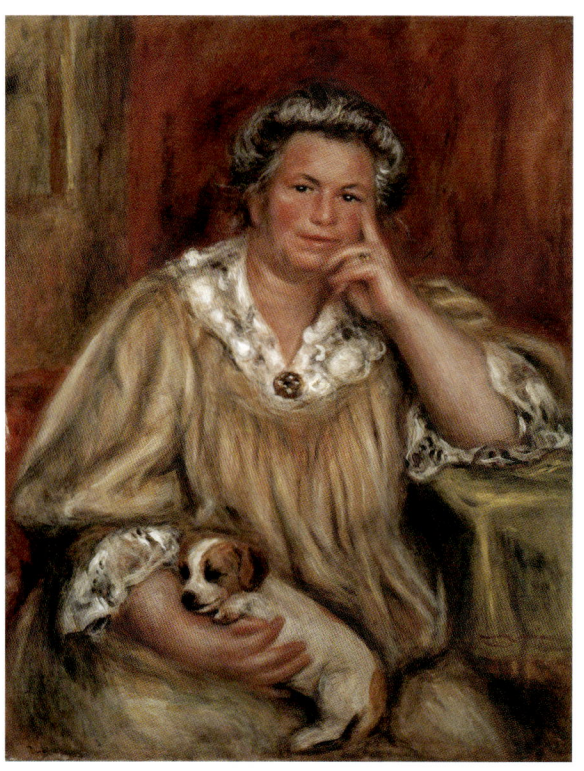

painters, Renoir always remained closely in touch with nature and had his feet firmly on the ground of reality. This, however, was a reality which was confined to individual people whom he could perceive with his own eyes; or, to be more precise, it was confined to their bodies. He only ever painted the bodies of girls.

He saw girls and women as exclusively animal-like creatures that were mainly guided by their instincts. It was a dominant view in contemporary society that women were generally less intelligent and more instinctive creatures. There was a certain way of looking at human beings entirely in terms of science and biology, and this view had persisted among positivist philosophers and naturalist authors since the time of Impressionism. But it was not until his later works that Renoir gave so much emphasis to the animal-like nature of human beings. His girls are endowed with no more "soul" than their bodies are able to express. They are without spirit or intellect or even the awareness that they form part of society at large. In their abundant sumptuousness, they were like beautiful animals for him, or like fruits or flowers. Whenever he employed a servant girl, he always took her on as a model at the same time, and all he demanded was that "their skins should respond well to the light". Renoir himself admitted without embarrassment that, for him, the most beautiful part of a woman's body was her buttocks, although on another occasion he said that if God had not created women's breasts, he might never have become a painter. The main artistic aim of his late works was to praise and glorify the fascination of the female body. He did so without the slightest hint of lust and – paradoxical as it may seem – with a chaste sensuousness that was in itself animal-like, natural and naive. In his pictures he displayed a certain aesthetic relationship towards nudity that could be called classical because it does indeed come closest to the works of the ancient Greeks. But this was as far as his classicism went, i.e. the yearning and striving for beauty in human beings who dwelt in a timeless, sun-soaked Arcadian paradise.

Sometimes he even quoted, as it were, the well-known postures of Greek Venuses, whereas on other occasions he painted his models in a totally unself-conscious, and usually somewhat dream-like, mood –with their heavy bodies, small, firm breasts, round shoulders, small, spherical heads, beaming eyes and broad lips. At the beginning of the 1890s he painted their complexion with shades of silvery grey – a colour known as "mother-of-pearl", though later he preferred warmer, more glowing colours.

TOP
Madame Renoir, c. 1910
Oil on canvas, 81.2 x 65 cm (32 x 25½ in.)
Hartford, Connecticut, Wadsworth Atheneum, The Ella Gallup Sumner and Mary Catlin Sumner Collection Fund

OPPOSITE LEFT
Dancing Girl with Tambourine, 1909
Oil on canvas, 155 x 64.8 cm (61 x 25½ in.)
London, The National Gallery

OPPOSITE RIGHT
Dancing Girl with Castanets, 1909
Oil on canvas, 155 x 64.8 cm (61 x 25½ in.)
London, The National Gallery

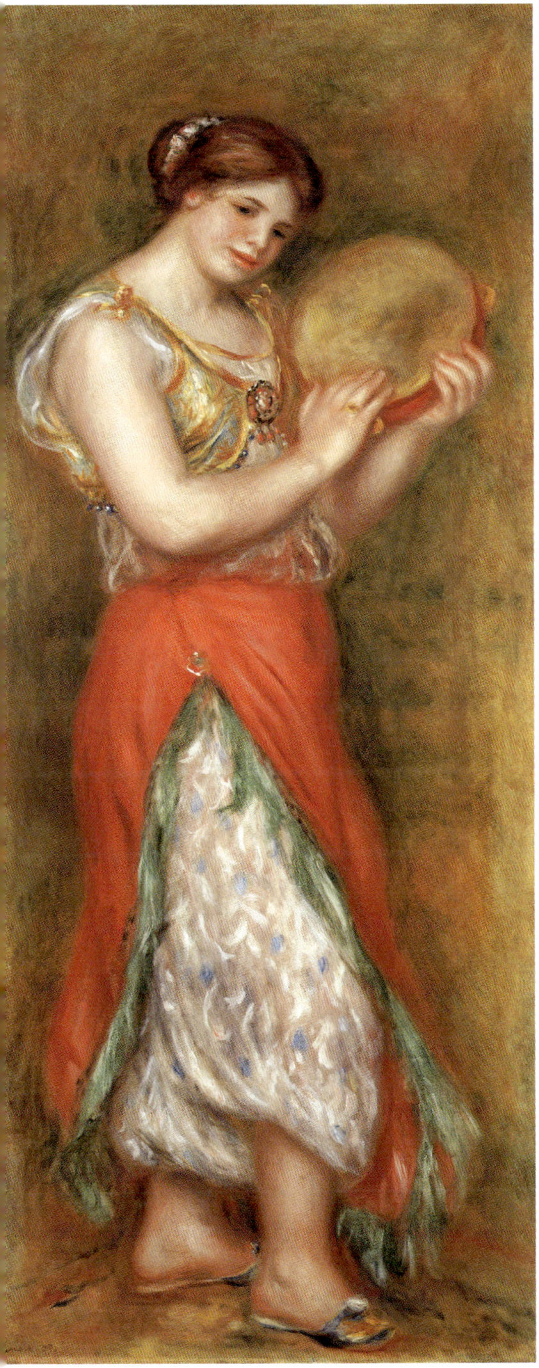
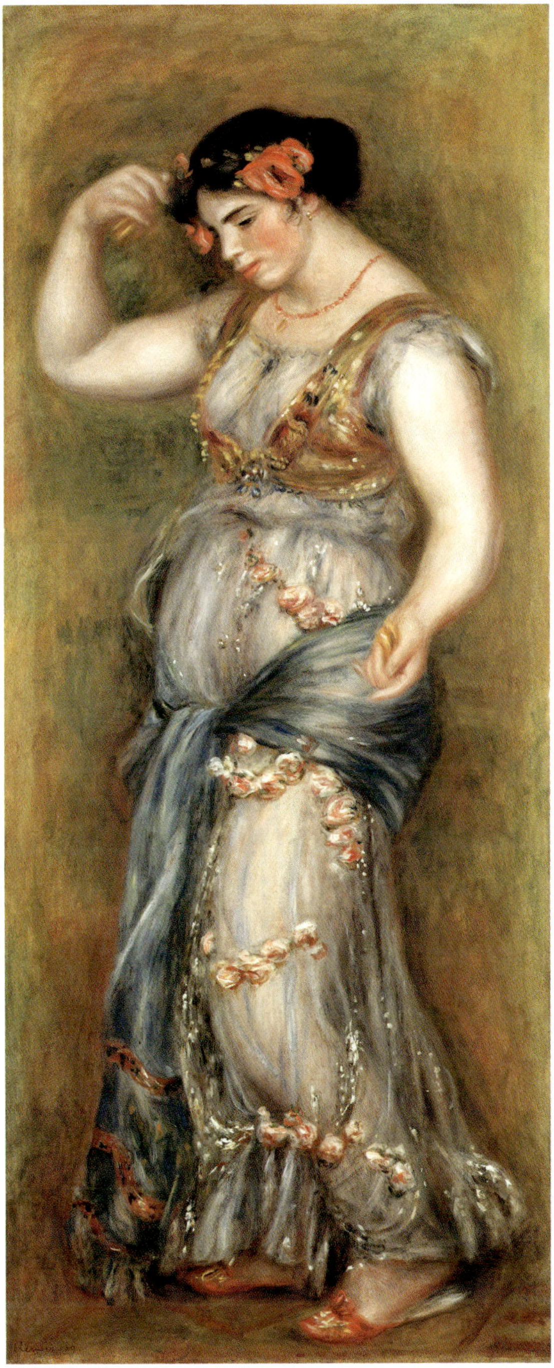

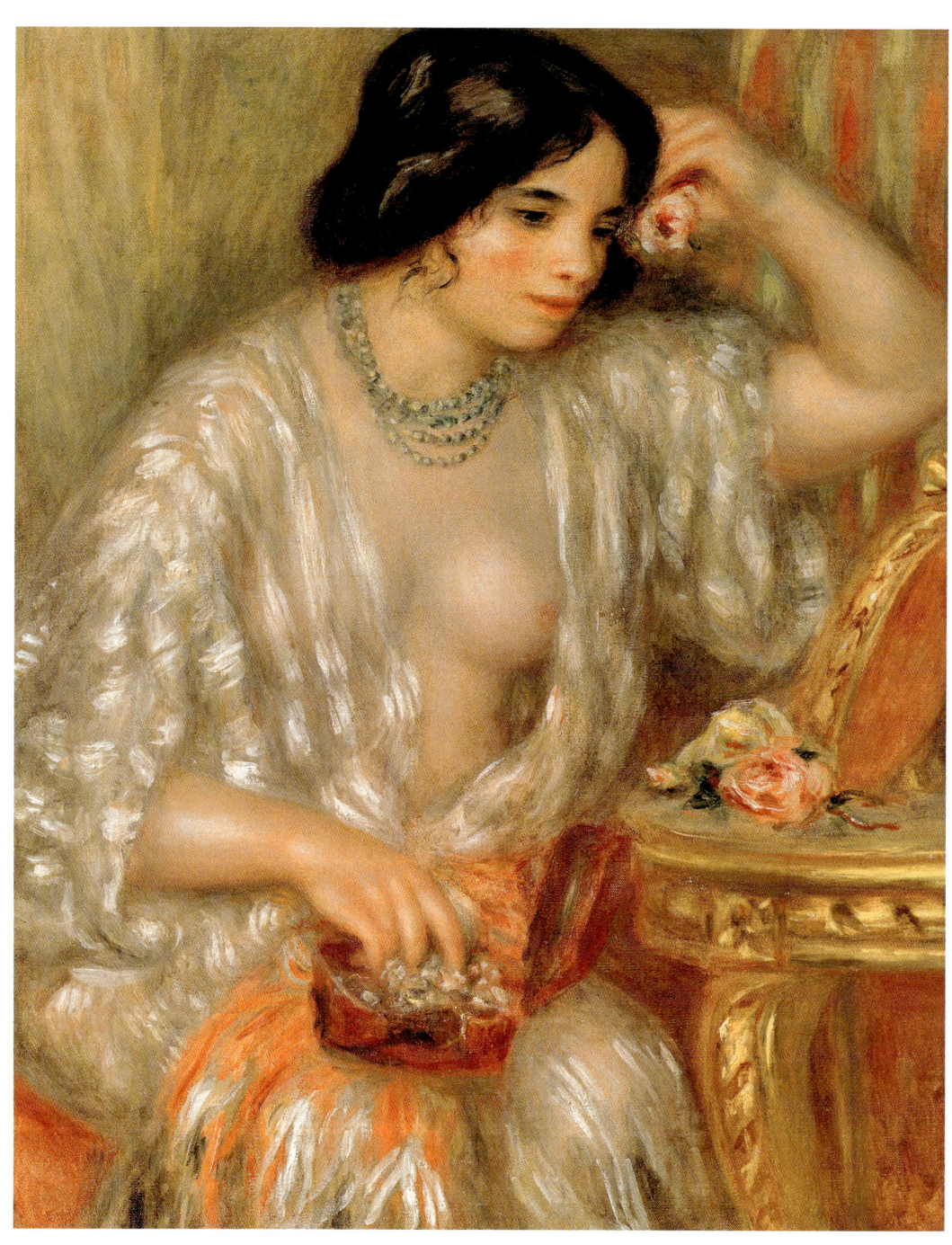

Gabrielle with Jewels, c. 1910
Oil on canvas, 82 x 65.5 cm (32¼ x 25¾ in.)
Private collection

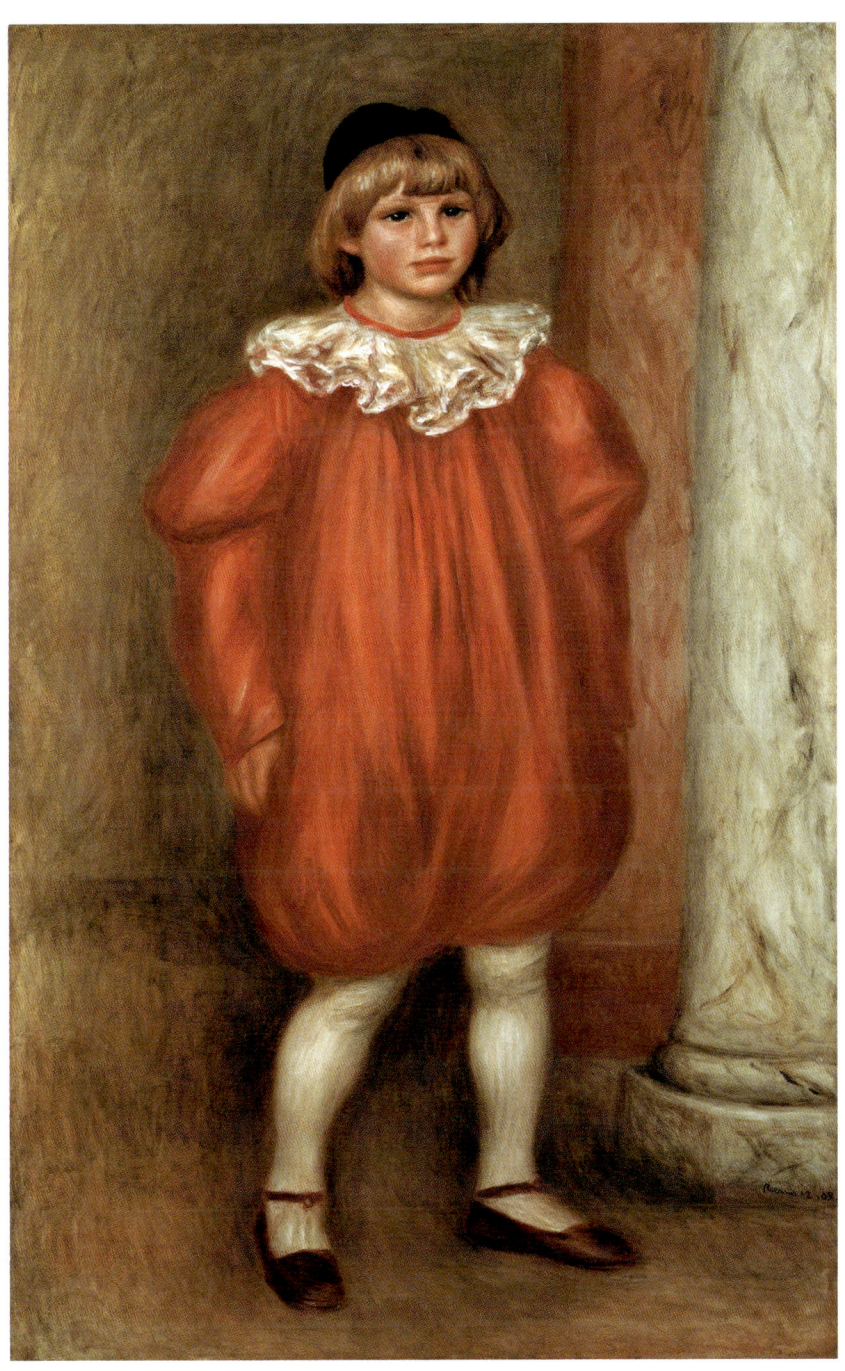

Claude Renoir in Clown Costume, 1909
Oil on canvas, 120 x 77 cm (47¼ x 30¼ in.)
Paris, Musée de l'Orangerie

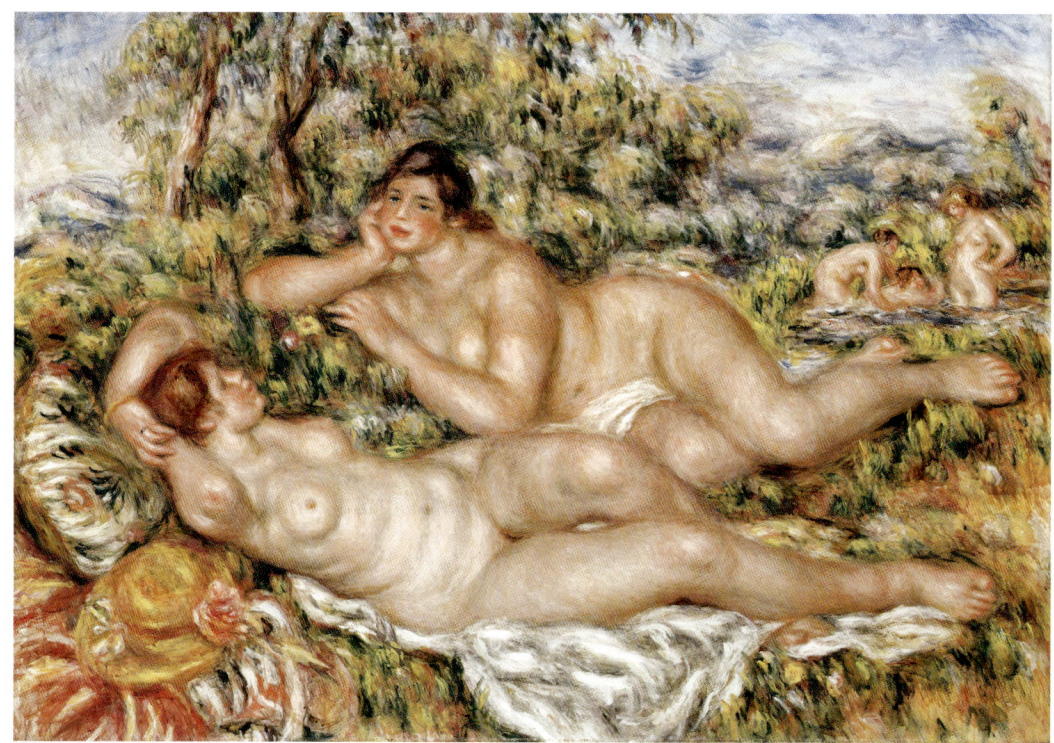

Rest after a Bath, 1918/19
Oil on canvas, 110 x 160 cm (43¼ x 63 in.)
Paris, Musée d'Orsay

Right at the end of Renoir's life his nudes acquired a certain dignity and grandeur that was indeed truly classical. His *Seated Bather* of 1914 (ill. p. 297) shows this quite clearly. With their strawberry red, which is overshadowed by a flamboyant purple, embedded in orgies of green, yellow and blue, they often seem rather obtrusive; their flesh sometimes seems unbearably supple and ample, like the feverish dream of a painter who had become a haggard, emaciated cripple. Not only do some of them recall the postures of ancient Greek sculptures again, but their rare movements have a natural forcefulness and a detached timelessness that makes them earthly goddesses. There is a magnificent bronze figure, which Guino modelled for Renoir, of a woman with a smile, strutting about fully conscious of her own power, and she was very appropriately called *Venus Victrix*: the goddess of love has won her victory.

This is a name which, in a deeper sense, can serve to summarize the whole of Renoir's works. He was a good and unsophisticated man. In his pictures he unfolded a world that was pure and beautiful, and he could not relate to people who wanted to see that world as being founded on a firmer and more rational basis than the cult of beauty as perceived by our senses. Such people were questioning the whole of his familiar world. Renoir did not want to be a revolutionary. In his continuous search for new and eternal expressions of beauty he was only ever able to see and shape a part of the truth. But he never lied, and he never inflated his own ego to the extent that the proportions of reality around him became distorted. His art never humiliated or offended people. He loved humanity, light and eternal nature. At a time when all around him there was an increasing feeling of existential fear, uneasiness with the bourgeois world, and despair, Renoir never ceased to show the possibility of a life of happiness and harmony in his pictures.

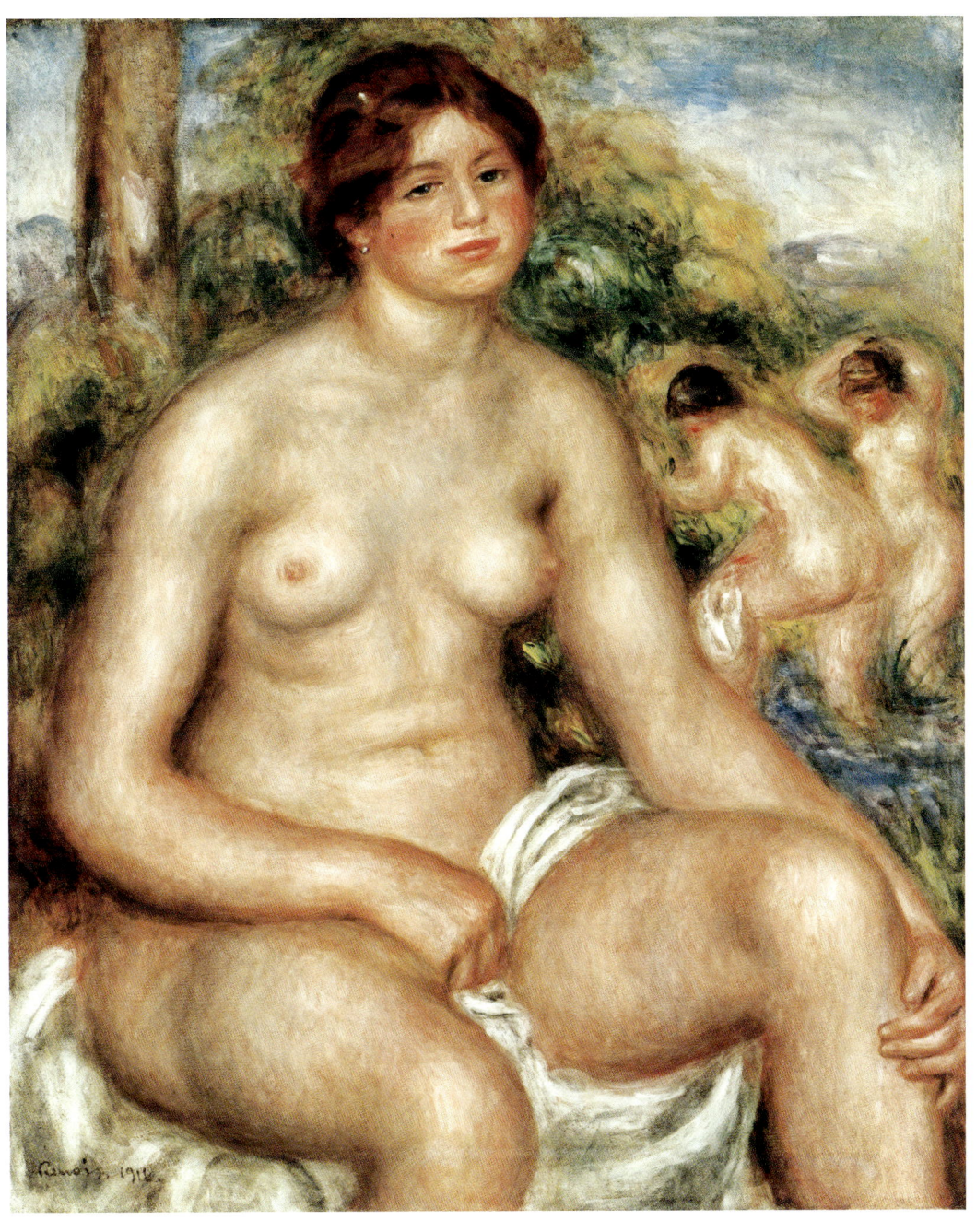

Seated Bather, 1914
Oil on canvas, 81.1 x 67.2 cm (32 x 26½ in.)
The Art Institute of Chicago,
Mr and Mrs Lewis Larned
Coburn Endowment

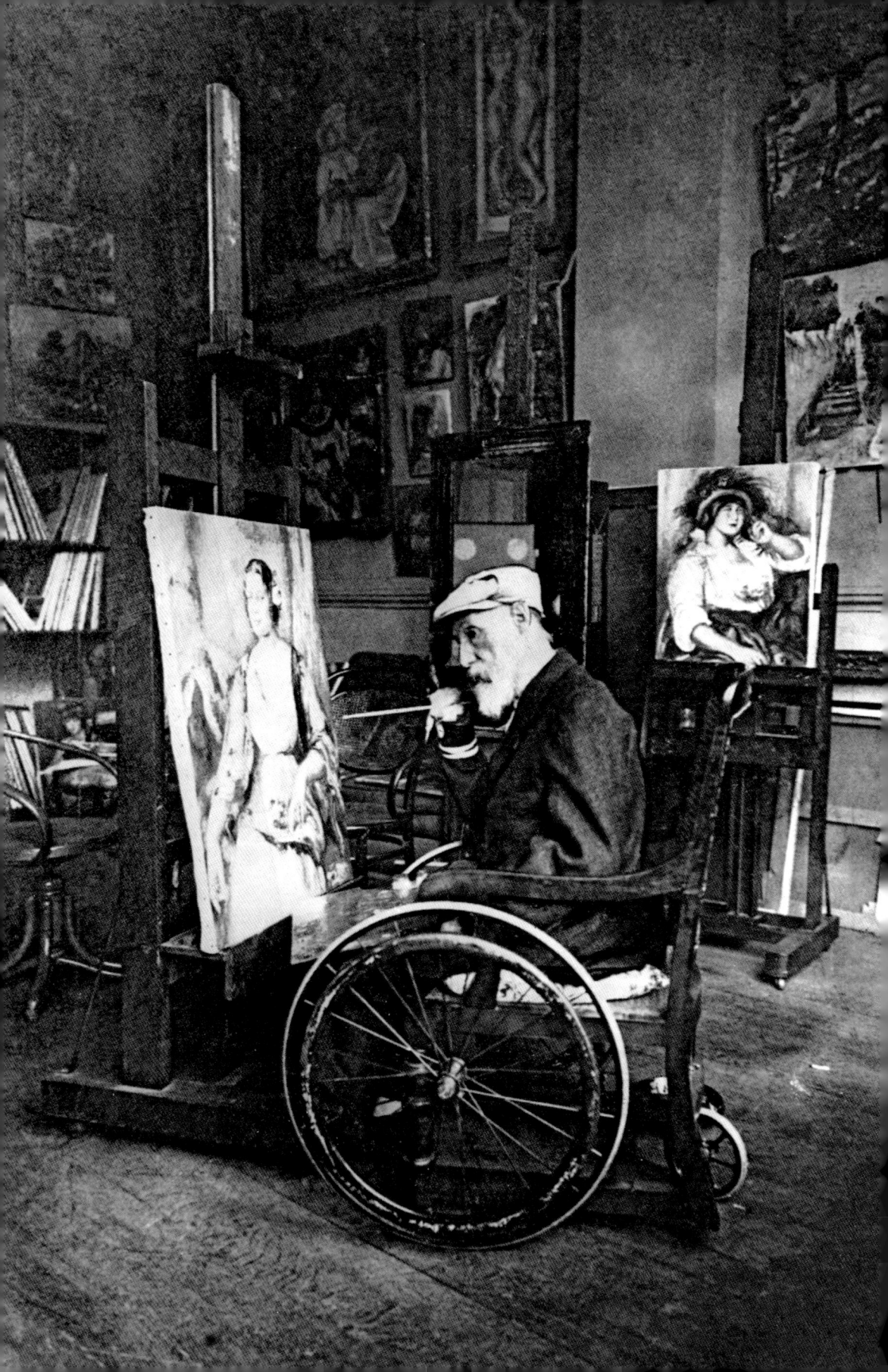

Pierre-Auguste Renoir 1841–1919
Life and Work

1841 Pierre August Renoir born 25 February in Limoges, sixth of the seven children of Léonard Renoir (1799–1874) and his wife, Marguerite Merlet (1807–1896). His father was a tailor.

1844 His family moves to Paris.

1848–54 Goes to a Catholic primary school.

1849 Birth of his brother Edmond Victoire.

1854–58 Apprenticeship as a porcelain painter. Paints flowers, and later also portraits, onto vases and plates. Also takes evening classes in drawing.

1858 The invention of a technique for printing pictures onto porcelain makes him redundant. Spends some time painting ladies' fans and colouring in coats of arms for his brother Henri, an engraver, later also transparent curtains for a decorator. Earns a lot because he works ten times as fast as others.

1860 He is admitted to the Louvre as a copyist. Studies Rubens, Fragonard and Boucher.

1862–64 Studies at the École des Beaux-Arts and Gleyre's studio, where he meets Monet, Sisley and Bazille.

1863 Takes up open-air painting in the woods of Fontainebleau together with Sisley, Monet and Bazille. Meets Pissarro and Cézanne.

1864 Decides to work as a painter independently and rents studio, while his family moves to Ville-d'Avray. His painting *Esmeralda Dancing with a Goat* is accepted by the Salon, but he destroys it after the exhibition.

1865 Paints in the woods of Fontainebleau together with Sisley, Monet and Pissarro. Moves into Sisley's studio. Goes sailing on the river Seine as far as Le Havre. Meets Courbet, whom he admires. In Marlotte he meets Lise Tréhot who becomes his model.

1866 Commutes between Marlotte and Paris. Moves in with Bazille when Sisley gets married. Is rejected by the Salon despite recommendation by Corot and Daubigny. Paints *At the Inn of Mother Anthony* in Marlotte.

1867 Monet joints Renoir and Bazille. *Diana* is not accepted by the Salon. Protests together with Bazille, Pissarro and Sisley, demanding a Salon des Réfusés. Paints *Lise*.

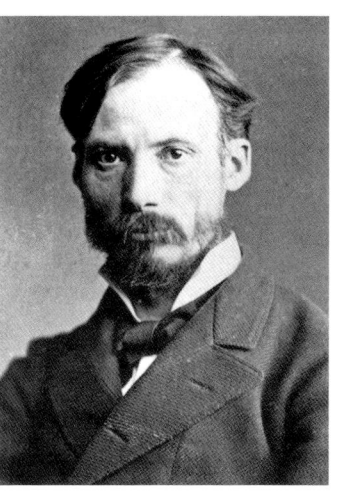

1868 Commissioned to paint two pictures for Count Bibesco. Portraits of Sisley and his wife. *Lise* is shown at the Salon and given recognition. Spends summer with Lise and parents. Frequently at the Café Guerbois, where he meets Manet and Degas.

1869 Exhibits at the Salon together with Degas, Pissarro and Bazille. Parents move to Voisins-Louveciennes, where he spends summer with Lise. Pays almost daily visits to Monet in Saint-Michel near Bougival. Paints with him and supports him. First "Impressionist" landscapes: *La Grenouillère*.

1870 Military service with cavalry regiment in Bordeaux July 1870 to March 1871. Bazille is killed in the war.

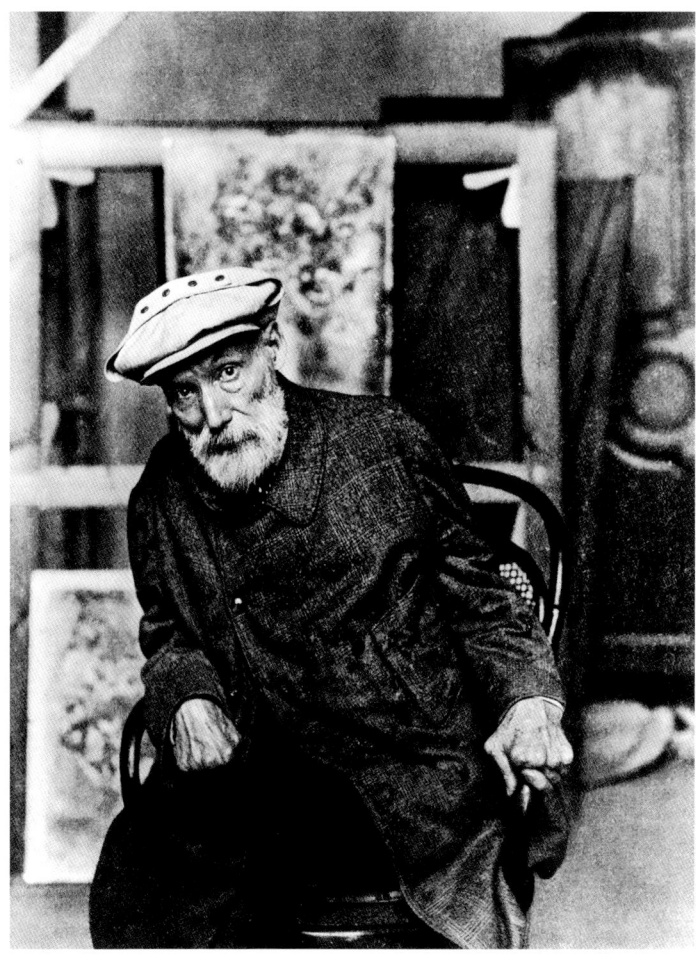

Renoir in his studio, 1912

1875 Organizes an auction of paintings together with Morisot, Sisley and Monet at the Hotel Drouot, where there are some scandalous scenes and fights. Sells 20 pictures for no more than 2,254 francs. Meets the collector Chocquet and several wealthy merchants and bankers who buy or commission pictures. Summer in Chatou. Paints *Nude in the Sunlight*.

1876 Shows 15 pictures at the second Impressionists' exhibition. Meets Charpentier, the publisher, and his family, who order pictures. Visits the poet Daudet in Champrosay. Paints *Le Moulin de la Galette* and *The Swing*.

1877 Shows 22 pictures together with other Impressionists. Organizes a second auction at the Hotel Drouot together with Caillebotte, Pissarro and Sisley. Sells 16 pictures for 2,005 francs.

1878 Represented at the Salon again after a long gap. Sells three pictures for 157 francs at the Hoschedé auction. Paints *Madame Charpentier and Her Children*.

1879 Like Cézanne and Sisley, he does not take part in the fourth Impressionists' exhibition. Success at the Salon for *Madame Charpentier*. First individual exhibition on the premises of the magazine *La Vie moderne*. Summer in Wargemont (Normandy). Paints women and children on the beach.

1880 Breaks his right arm and paints with his left. Together with Monet, he protests against unfavourable positions at the Salon. First doubts about his own art. Spends some time in Chatou with

1871 Returns to Paris during the time of the Commune. Paints views of Paris, then stays with his parents and in Bougival.

1872 Two pictures bought by art dealer Durand-Ruel. Lise gets married. Joins Manet, Pissarro and Cézanne in signing a petition to the Minister of Culture for a Salon des Réfusés. Spends summer painting with Monet in Argenteuil.

1873 Meets the writer Duret at Degas's studio. Duret buys Renoir's *Lise*. Moves into larger studio at Montmartre. Spends summer and autumn painting with Monet in Argenteuil. Joins a newly founded group of independent artists which also includes Cézanne, Degas, Manet, Pissarro and Sisley.

1874 First "Impressionists' exhibition" (a term of abuse, coined by the art critic Leroy in the magazine *Charivari*) at Nadar's photographic studio. Sells three pictures, including *The Theatre Box*. Visits Monet in Argenteuil, where he also meets Manet and Sisley.

Aline Charigot, his future wife. Cahen d'Anvers, a banker, commissions him to paint portraits of his daughters.

1881 Travels to Algeria with friends (spring). April in Chatou, where he is visited by Whistler. Paints *Breakfast of the Boating Party* with portraits of his friends. Visits Italy in autumn and winter, including Venice, Florence, Rome and Naples.

1882 After he returns, joins Cézanne in L'Estaque. Paints landscapes. Ill with pneumonia. Durand-Ruel shows 25 of his pictures at the seventh Impressionists' exhibition. Holiday in Algeria in March/April. Summer in Wargemont and Dieppe.

1883 Beginning of his so-called "Dry Period". Important individual exhibition of seventy pictures at Durand-Ruel's in April. Exhibitions in London, Boston and Berlin. Summer in Étretat, Dieppe, Le Havre, Wargemont, Trepart. Spends some time on the Channel Islands with Aline. Finishes series of three "Dance" pictures. In search of subjects together with Monet on the Mediterranean, between Marseille and Genoa. Visits Cézanne.

1884 Commutes between Paris and Louvecienne because his mother is ill. Plans new painters' circle. Spends some time with Aline in Chatou. Travels to La Rochelle to study Corot's landscapes.

1885 Birth of his son Pierre on 23 March. Longer holiday with Aline in La Roche-Guyon. Visited by Cézanne. Autumn in Essoyes, Aline's home. Frequently paints bathers. Attacks of depression.

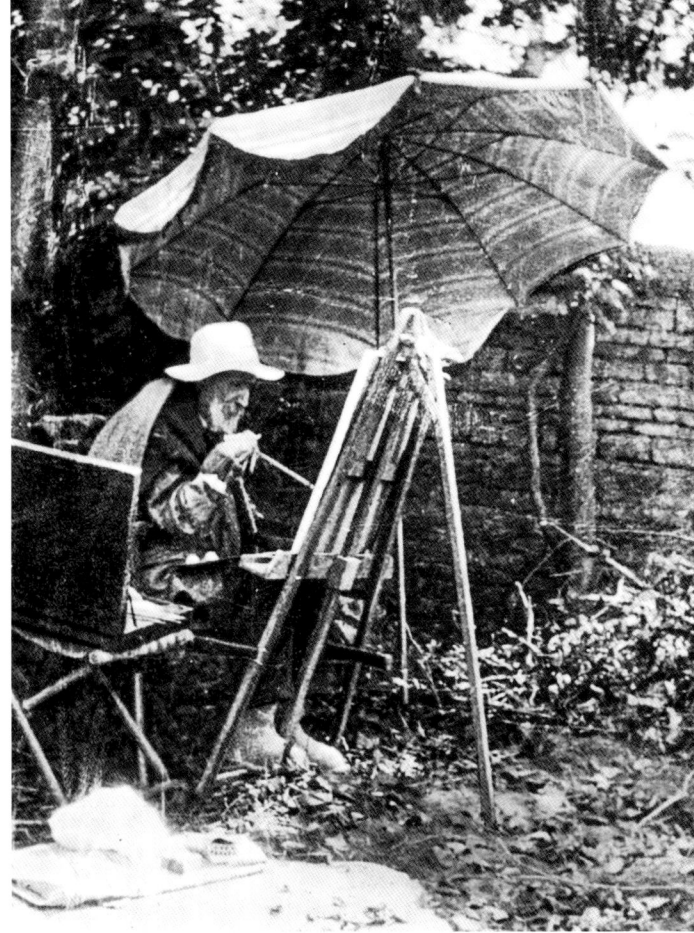

Pierre Auguste Renoir painting with two hands, *c*. 1916/17

1886 Shows eight pictures with *Les XX* in Brussels, then 32 in New York. Paintings sell well. Summer with Aline and Pierre in Roche-Guyon, then in Dinard (Brittany). In October he destroys all the pictures painted during the last two months. Durand-Ruel dislikes his new style. Spends December with Aline's family in Essoyes.

1887 Finishes *The Great Bathers*. Makes friends with Morisot.

1888 Visits Cézanne in Aix, but leaves for Martigues earlier than planned. Spends summer working in Argenteuil and Bougival. In Essoyes from autumn onwards. Attack of rheumatoid arthritis and facial paralysis in December.

1889 Has to avoid the cold and works in Essoyes most of the time. Spends summer with family in Montbriant. Visits Cézanne in Aix. Refuses to participate in world exhibition in Paris. Depressions, doubt about his own work.

1890 Exhibits pictures with *Les XX* again. First etching. Marries Aline, Pierre's mother, on 14 April. Moves into the Rue Girardon on the Montmartre. Spends July in Essoyes. Visits Morisot in Mézy.

1891 Travels to Toulon, Tamaris-sur-Mer, Lavandou and Nîmes. Spends summer in Mézy. Durand-Ruel buys the three "Dance" pictures for 7,500 francs each.

1892 Durand-Ruel organizes largest retrospective exhibition with 110 pictures. First purchase by French state and end of financial worries. Visits Spain together with the collector Gallimard, and admires Titian, Velázquez and Goya at the Prado. With his family in Brittany. Visits artists' colony in Pont-Aven.

1893 Seeks the warmth of the Mediterranean sun. Spends June with Gallimard near Deauville, and August with his family in Pont-Aven.

1894 Death of Caillebotte. Renoir is appointed executor. Museums are not interested in important Impressionist collection left by Caillebotte. Gabrielle Renard, Aline's cousin, is employed as a nanny, stays until 1914 and becomes Renoir's favourite model. 15 September: birth of his son Jean, who is to become an important film director. First contacts with the art dealer Vollard. His rheumatoid arthritis forces him to walk on crutches. Seeks healing in thermal baths.

1895 Seeks refuge from the Parisian cold in Provence. Returns to attend Morisot's funeral. Spends summer with family and Gabrielle in Brittany. Breaks with Cézanne in winter.

1896 Goes to Wagner Festival in Bayreuth, Germany. Finds music boring. 11 November: death of his 89-year-old mother.

1897 Caillebotte's collection is accepted by museums. Summer in Essoyes. Falls from his bicycle and breaks his right arm.

1898 Spends summer in Berneval. Buys house in Essoyes. Travels to Holland, where he is more impressed by Vermeer than by Rembrandt. Serious attack of rheumatoid arthritis in December. Right arm paralysed.

1899 Winter in Cagnes and Nice. Paints in the open air again. Spends summer in Cloud and Essoyes, followed by health holiday in the thermal baths at Aix-les-Bains. Falls out with Degas.

1900 Spends January in Grasse. Has special health holiday for his rheumatoid arthritis in Aix-les-Bains. Changes his mind and takes part in Paris world exhibition with 11 pictures. He is made Knight of the Legion of Honour. Rheumatic pains increase. Hands and arms are deformed.

1901 Another health holiday in Aix. Summer in Essoyes, where his third son Claude, called "Coco", is born on 4 August.

1902 Moves into a villa near Cannes with Aline, Jean and Claude. Has house in Essoyes extended. His health deteriorates. Weakness in his left eye, bronchitis.

1903 Because of his illness, he now spends every winter on the Mediterranean, and the summers in Paris and Essoyes. Some trouble because of forgeries of his pictures.

1904 Paints at his easel despite great pain. Has a health holiday in Bourbonne-les-Bains together with his family. Triumphant success at the autumn Salon (35 pictures), which gives him new courage.

1905 Finally settles in Cagnes because of climate. Shows 59 pictures at an exhibition in London. The number of his admirers is steadily increasing. Exhibits at the autumn Salon and is made honorary president.

1906 Paints models, especially Gabrielle. Meets Monet in Paris.

1907 *Madame Charpentier and Her Children* is bought for 84,000 francs by the Metropolitan Museum, New York, at an auction. Renoir buys "Les Colettes", an estate in Cagnes, and has a house built on it.

1908 Moves into his new house. Following suggestions by Maillol and Vollard, he makes two wax sculptures. A visit from Monet.

1909 Continues to paint despite painful illness. Spends summer in Essoyes, where he finishes the two *Dancing Girls*. Claude poses as a clown.

1910 Has a mobile easel made for himself in Cagnes, to enable him to work more easily. After some improvement in his health, he and his family travel to Wessling near Munich, where he paints the

Thurneyssen family. Sees pictures by Rubens at the Pinakothek. After his return, both legs are paralysed.

1911 He is now confined to a wheelchair. Has the paintbrush tied to his crippled hand with pieces of string so that he can paint. He is made Officer of the Legion of Honour. Renoir monograph by Meier-Graefe is printed.

1912 Rents studio in Nice. A new attack leaves his arms paralysed, too. Deep depression because he cannot paint any longer. Short-term reprieve after he is operated on by a Viennese doctor. High prices at auctions.

1913 Works on sculptures together with Guino, a pupil of Maillol's. Renoir "dictates" the shapes which are then moulded by the healthy hands of Guino.

1914 Renoir is visited by Rodin. Pierre and Jean have to serve in the army and are wounded in the war. Hard times for Aline and Renoir. Gabrielle Renard marries and leaves Cagnes.

1915 Jean is badly wounded again. Aline dies in Nice on 27 June at the age of 56 and is buried in Essoyes. Renoir is carried to his easel every morning and continues to work. Has a garden studio built in Cagnes, to enable him to work in the open air again.

1916 Although he can hardly sleep at night, he feels revived again by his work. Takes Guino with him to Essoyes.

1917 A picture by Renoir is displayed at the National Gallery

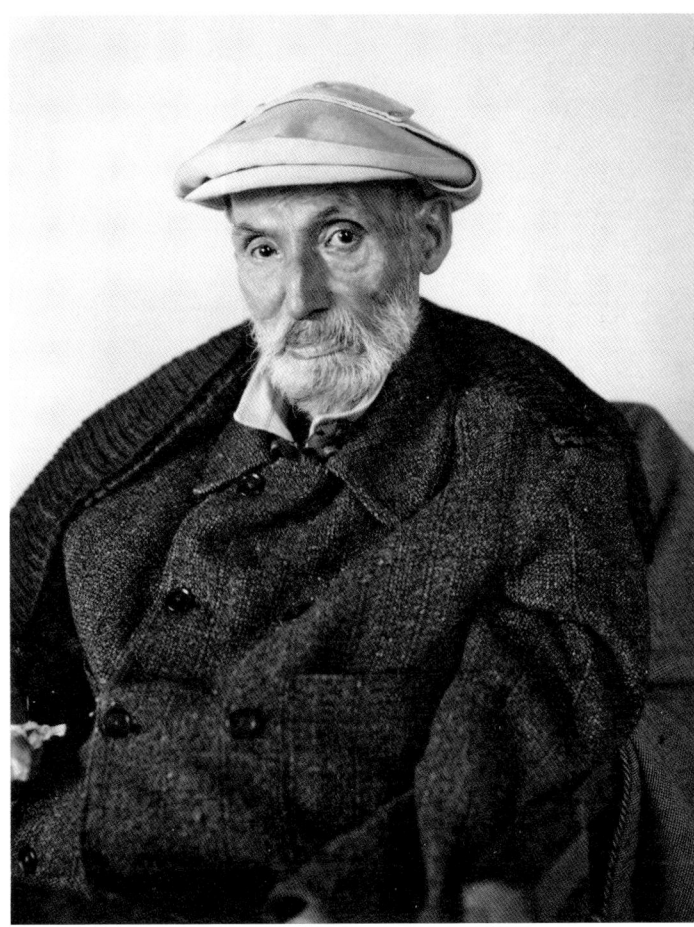

in London. He is visited by Vollard in Essoyes. Exhibits 60 paintings in Zurich. The end of his work with Guino. A visit from Matisse.

1919 Finishes his large-scale composition *Rest after a Bath* in great pain. He is made Commander of the Legion of Honour. Spends July with his sons in Essoyes. Visits the Louvre where one of his pictures is displayed next to Veronese. In his wheelchair he is wheeled through the various rooms like a "Pope of Painting". November: pneumonia, which results in congestion of the lungs. Paints one more still life with apples.

Renoir, 1914
Paris, Musée Marmottan Monet

Dies in Cagnes on 3 December and is buried in Essoyes, next to Aline, on 6 December.

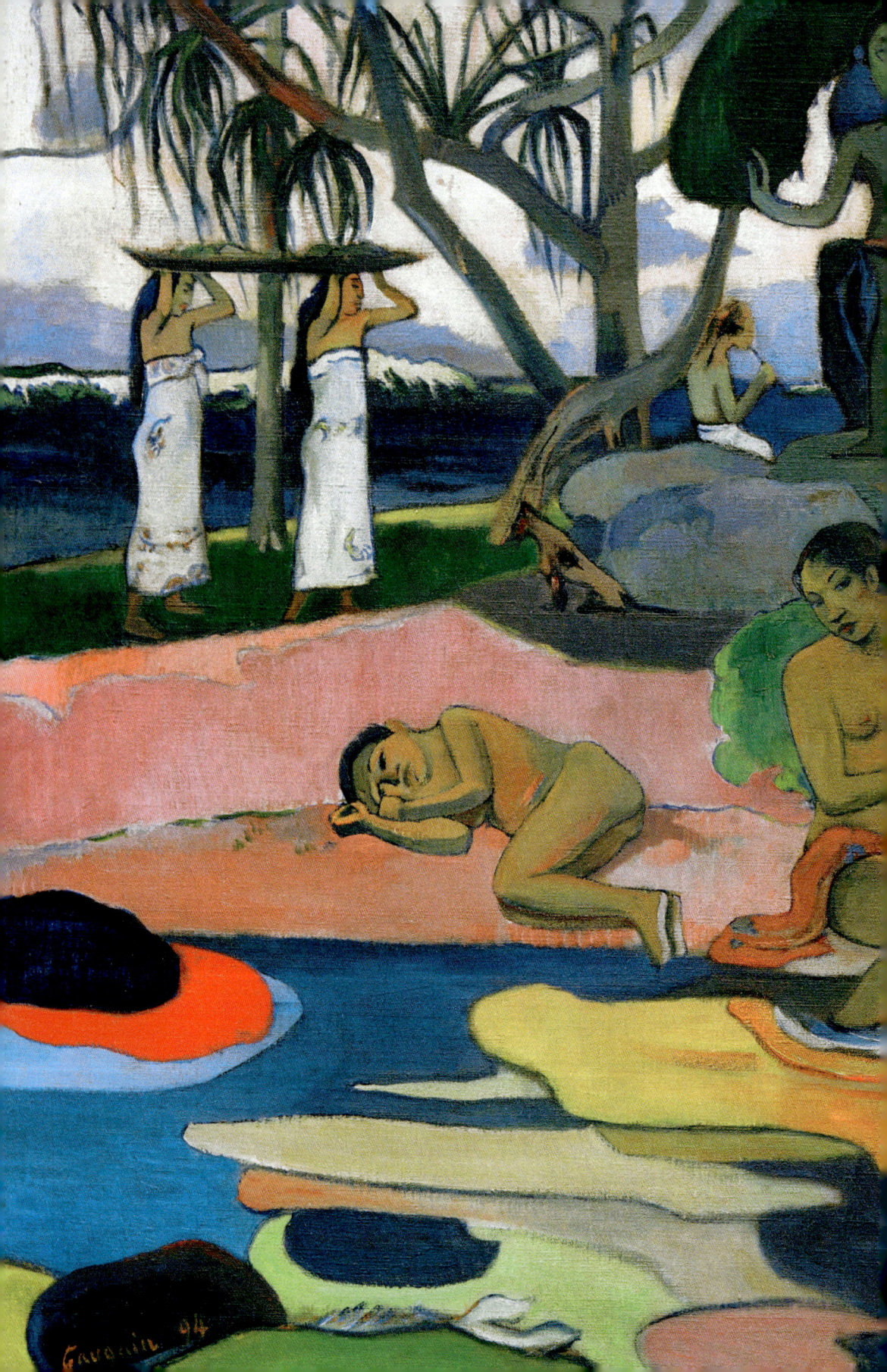

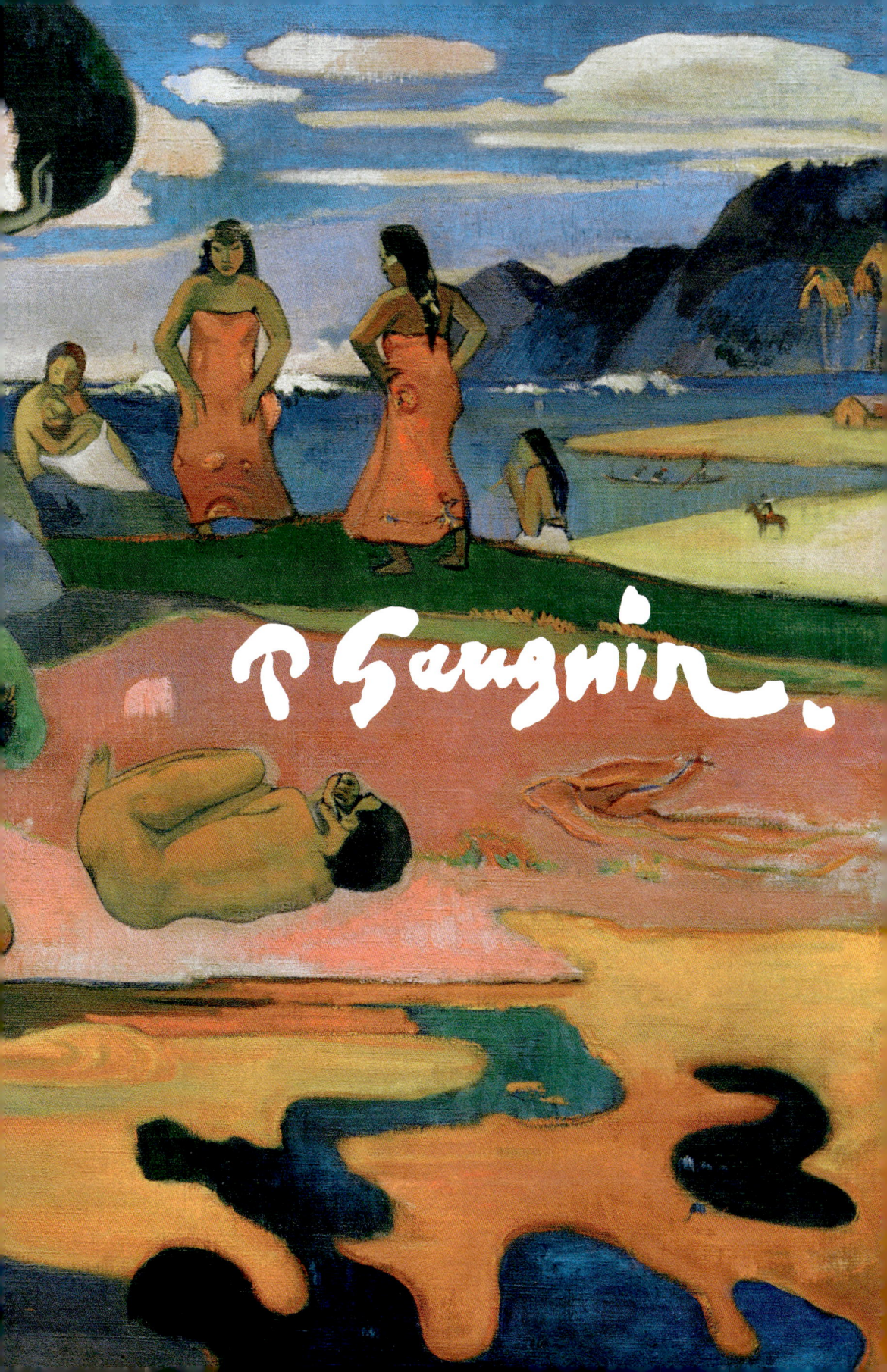

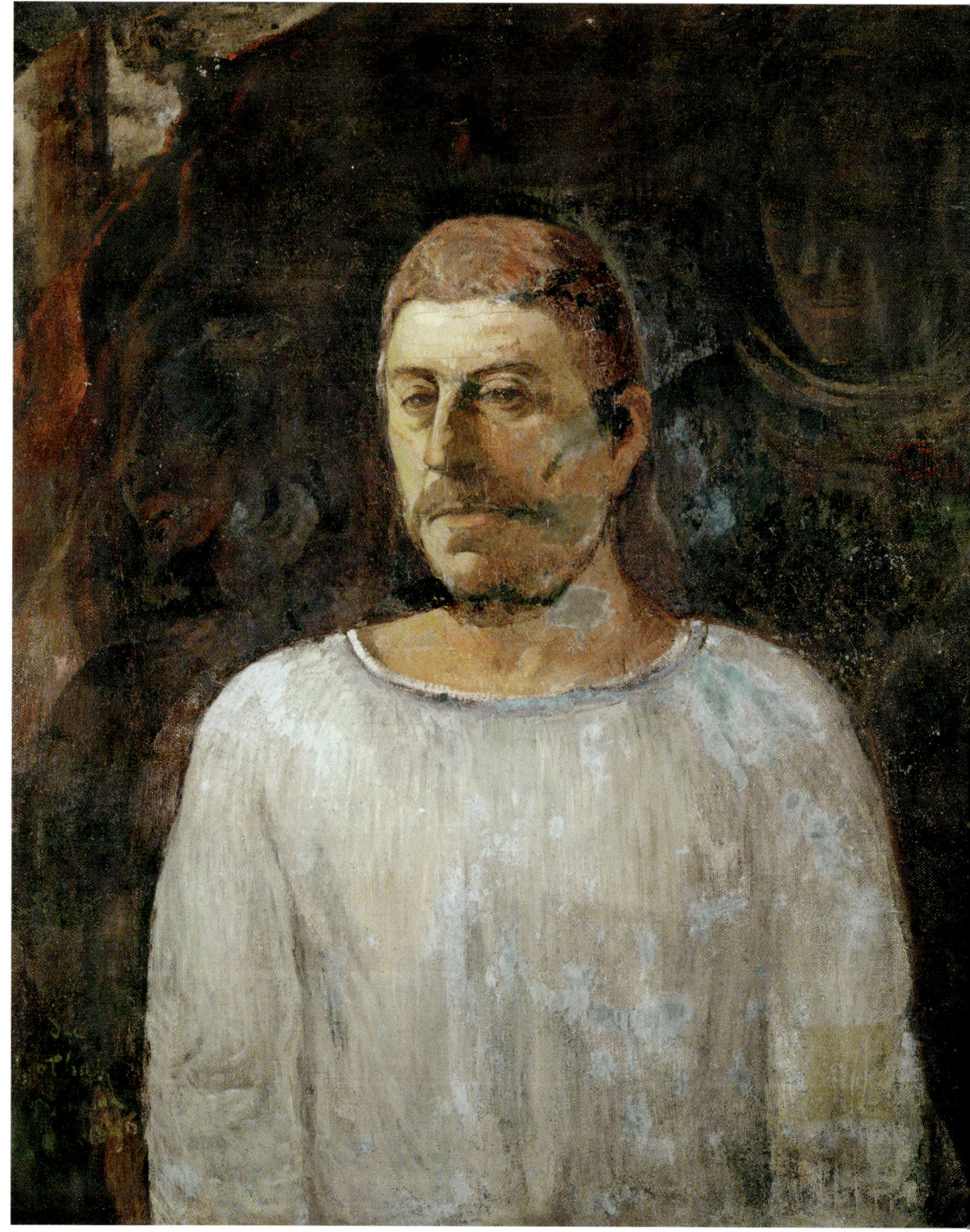

Ingo F. Walther

Paul Gauguin

The Primitive Sophisticate

"Art is either plagiarism or revolution."

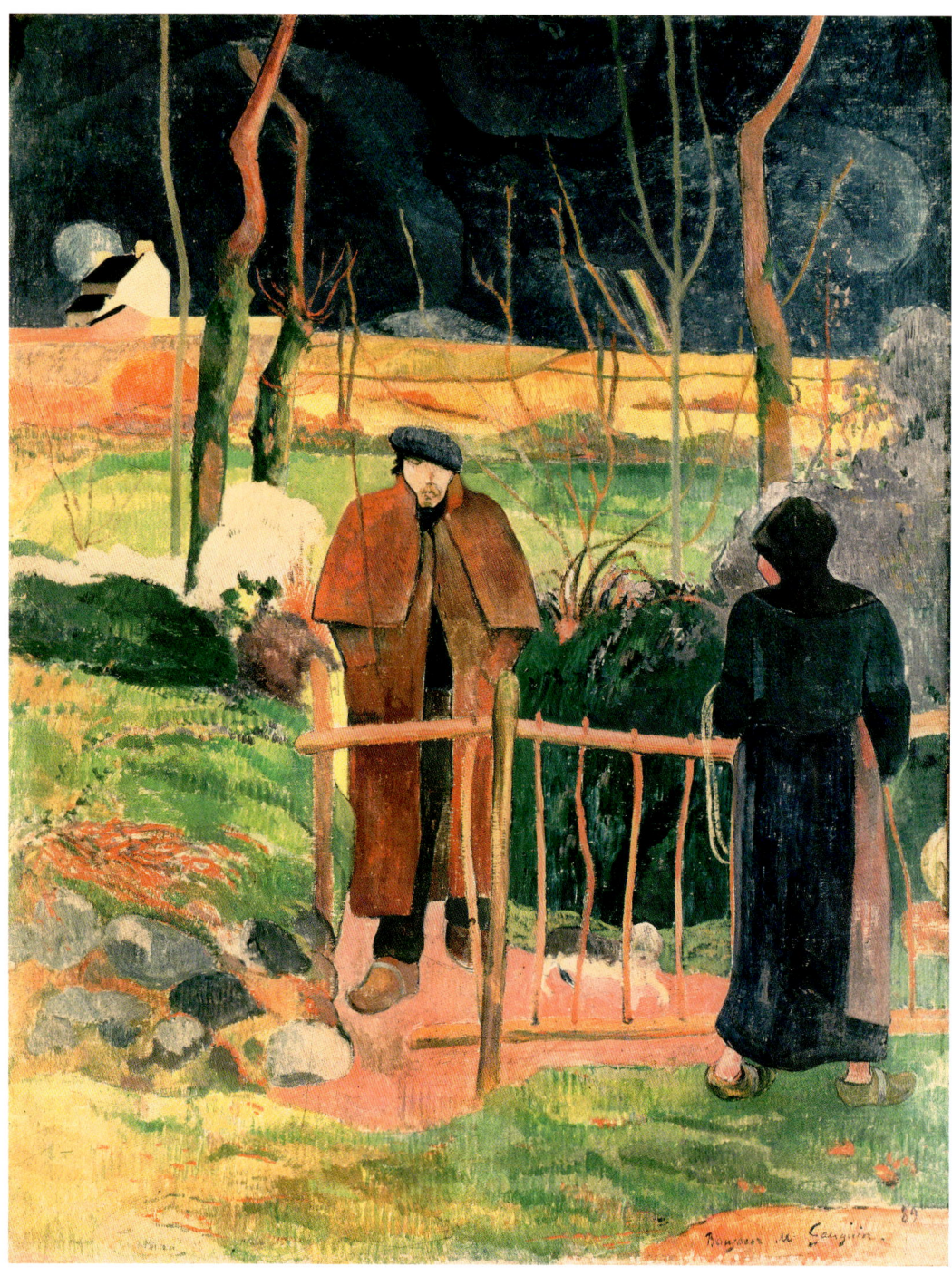

PAGES 304/305
Day of God (detail), 1894
Oil on canvas, 68.3 x 91.5 cm (27 x 36 in.)
The Art Institute of Chicago,
Helen Birch Bartlett Memorial Collection

PAGE 306
Self-portrait, 1896
Oil on canvas, 76 x 64 cm (30 x 25¼ in.)
Museo de Arte de São Paulo

ABOVE
Bonjour, Monsieur Gauguin, 1889
Oil on canvas, 113 x 92 cm (44½ x 36¼ in.)
Prague, Národní Galerie

Contents

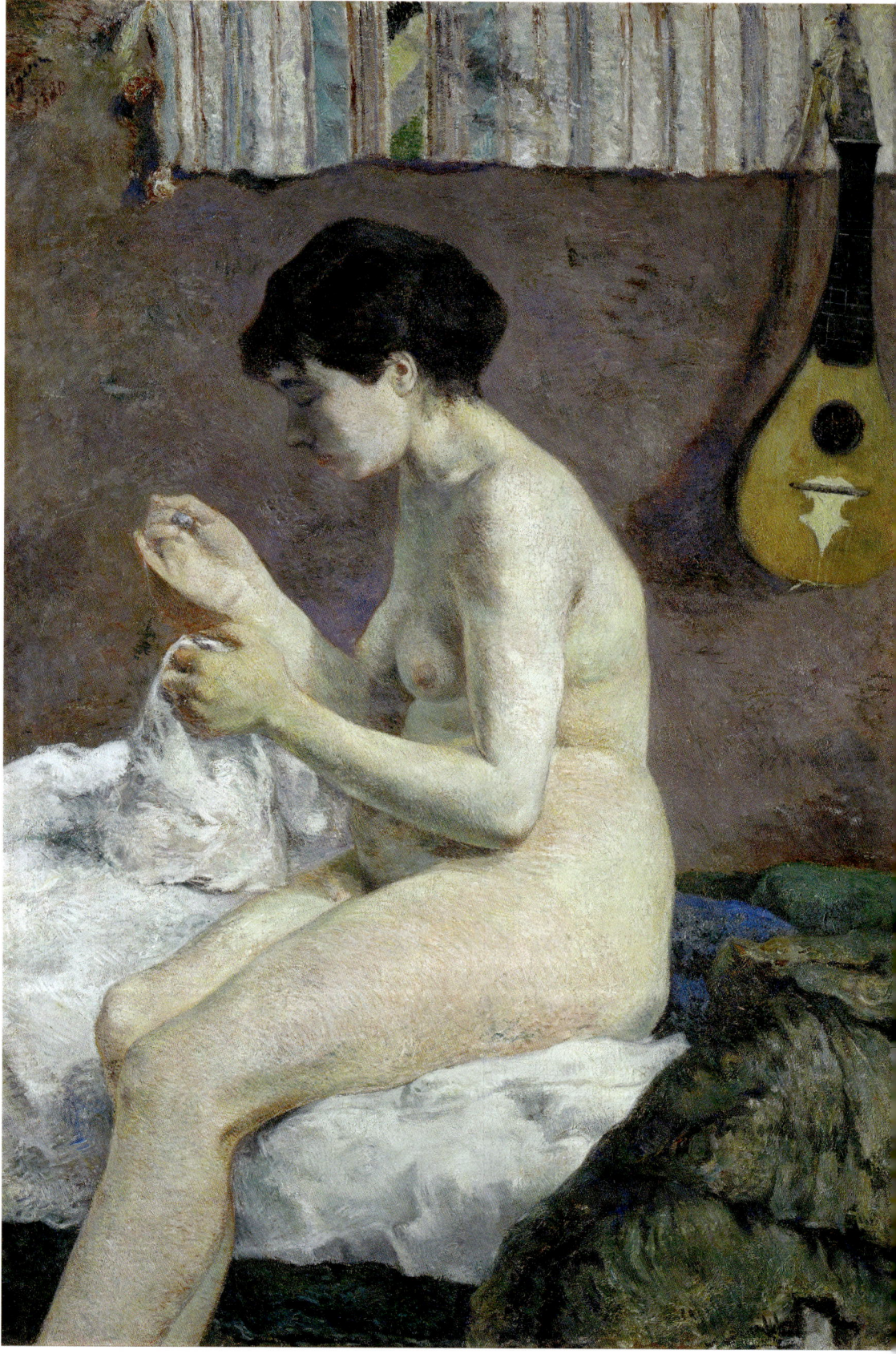

The Age of Impressionism
1848–1887

There cannot have been many other artists who set out as wholeheartedly to live the life they envisioned in their art as Paul Gauguin did. He lived between two worlds. In this art he held up a mirror to his own civilization, which he despised, and showed an alternative, primitive life in all its simple, naive harmony. But painting was not enough for Gauguin. He wanted to experience it himself. He wanted to prove that South Seas exoticism was not merely a forced and illusory escapism, of the kind that was fascinating his European contemporaries in an age of world fairs and newspaper reports. Gauguin personified a new union of art and life, imagination and order, and in anticipating this predominant 20th-century characteristic he became one of the true pioneers of modernism.

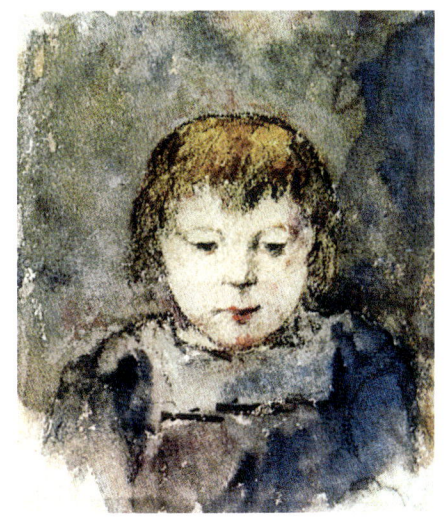

Gauguin discovered his artistic bent relatively late. When he made his break with comfortable middle-class life, he already had a wife, a family and a small fortune. In making the break he liked to see himself as an unconventional anti-hero, forging ahead on his own, indifferent to the recognition of his fellow men. But much as he would have liked to despise the bourgeois world, Gauguin the outsider still hankered after the success that Gauguin the stock-market speculator had formerly achieved. As his failure in his new life grew ever deeper, he became a wrathful critic of the European civilization that ignored him, and in the end even actively took to resisting the colonial administration in Tahiti.

Gauguin's artistic models were Giotto, Raphael and Jean-Auguste-Dominique Ingres, and the literary tradition he valued was that of Montaigne and Rousseau, who had considered the circumstances of the colonial peoples and gone on to accuse their own civilization of thinking too highly of itself and indeed of being megalomaniac. The "noble savage" was the better human being because he was more contented and dwelt at peace with Nature. And that automatically meant he led a happier life. It was that happiness that Gauguin was seeking.

OPPOSITE
Study of a Nude (Suzanne Sewing), 1880
Oil on canvas, 115 x 80 cm (45¼ x 31½ in.)
Copenhagen, Ny Carlsberg Glyptotek

ABOVE RIGHT
Portrait of Gauguin's Daughter Aline,
c. 1879/80
Watercolour on paper,
18.6 x 16.2 cm (7¼ x 6½ in.)
Private collection

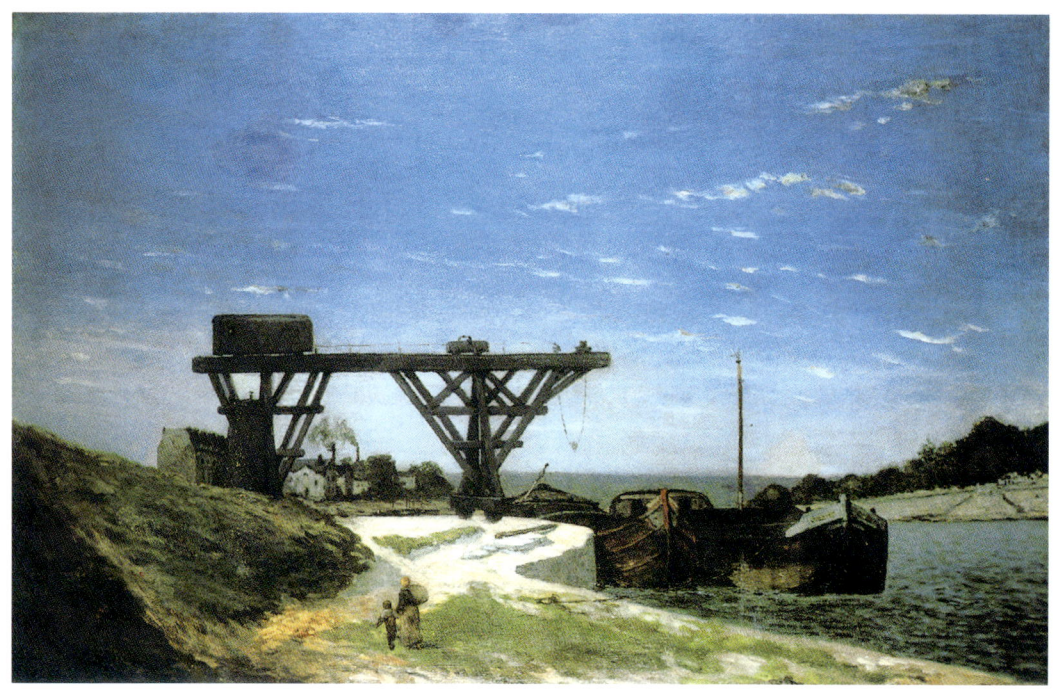

The Seine in Paris between the Pont d'Iéna and the Pont de Grenelle, 1875
Oil on canvas, 81 x 116 cm (32 x 45¾ in.)
Private collection

OPPOSITE
Aubé the Sculptor and His Son, 1882
Pastel on paper, 53 x 72 cm (21 x 28¼ in.)
Petit Palais, Musée des Beaux-Arts de la Ville de Paris

Gauguin's dreams of escape, though resigned and melancholy, were not without an element of shrewd calculation. He shared his longing for a distant paradise with the whole of high society. When he sprang his exotic pictures on an unsuspecting public, he was not only revealing the source of his inspiration but the source of his income as well. Rolling up his canvases and sending them in secure packages from Tahiti to France, to adorn the walls of European salons, he was no less the bourgeois than when he urged his son to take to a useful career, such as that of engineer, rather than the penury of an artist's life. "He is a tremendous businessman, or at least he thinks like one," Camille Pissarro once said. And at heart Gauguin remained a businessman his whole life long. Whatever his intentions, he had been subjected to the same education as his contemporaries, conditioned to compete and to uphold the norms and orderly values that were believed to be best, and that damned him to failure the moment he began. Just as nations sought out peoples they could subjugate and colonize, so Gauguin needed conquests, for his own sake and for his art.

In November 1873, aged twenty-five, Gauguin married a young Danish woman called Mette Sophie Gad in Paris. He had travelled far and wide as a sailor. She was a children's nanny. A longing for security (on his side) and a fascination with travellers' tales (on hers) had brought them together, but the marriage was flimsy and did not survive Gauguin's discovery of his artistic talent. Although he and Mette did not divorce, they duly went their separate ways. At first, however, their household flourished. The young wife could afford major purchases because Gauguin was earning good money at the stock exchange. They had five children – Émile, Aline, Clovis, Jean René and Pola – and doted on them all. The doors of Parisian high society were presently opened to them, and Gauguin – behaving as his social standing required – began to collect Impressionist paintings. It was not very long before he took up painting himself, as a hobby. With another painter, Claude Émile Schuffenecker, he studied the Old Masters in the Louvre. In his own unambitious works he chose to depict scenes of family life.

The Seine in Paris between the Pont d'Iéna and the Pont de Grenelle (ill. p. 312) is one of the earliest paintings in which Gauguin abandons the subject of idyllic family life. It is a tranquil and atmospheric Sunday scene. No one is working, and the crane that dominates the picture seems forlorn. The sky is peaceful and blue, the two figures in the foreground are doing nothing to disturb the sense of quiet, and the very barges and houses look sleepy. In this painting we see Gauguin toying with Impressionism, albeit tentatively. Impressionism was the major art movement of his time, and its hallmark was unemotional scrutiny of a busy, lively world. Gauguin appears to be fixing his attention on lack of emotion itself. Impressionism liked to set its images adrift in a shimmering sea of light. Gauguin, by contrast, highlights a personal love of static detail. The mood of the painting remains cool, and the painter himself distant.

Consistently enough, when Gauguin came to exhibit one of his paintings for the first time it was not alongside the Impressionists but at the official Salon. The Salon was notorious for its conservatism amongst the group of young artists led by Édouard Manet and Claude Monet. Only three years later, however, at Pissarro's lively encouragement, Gauguin did exhibit with the Impressionists. There he encountered the rejection of traditional middle-class notions of art that he was to espouse time and again in the years ahead. Gauguin continued to work at the stock exchange. But the provocative

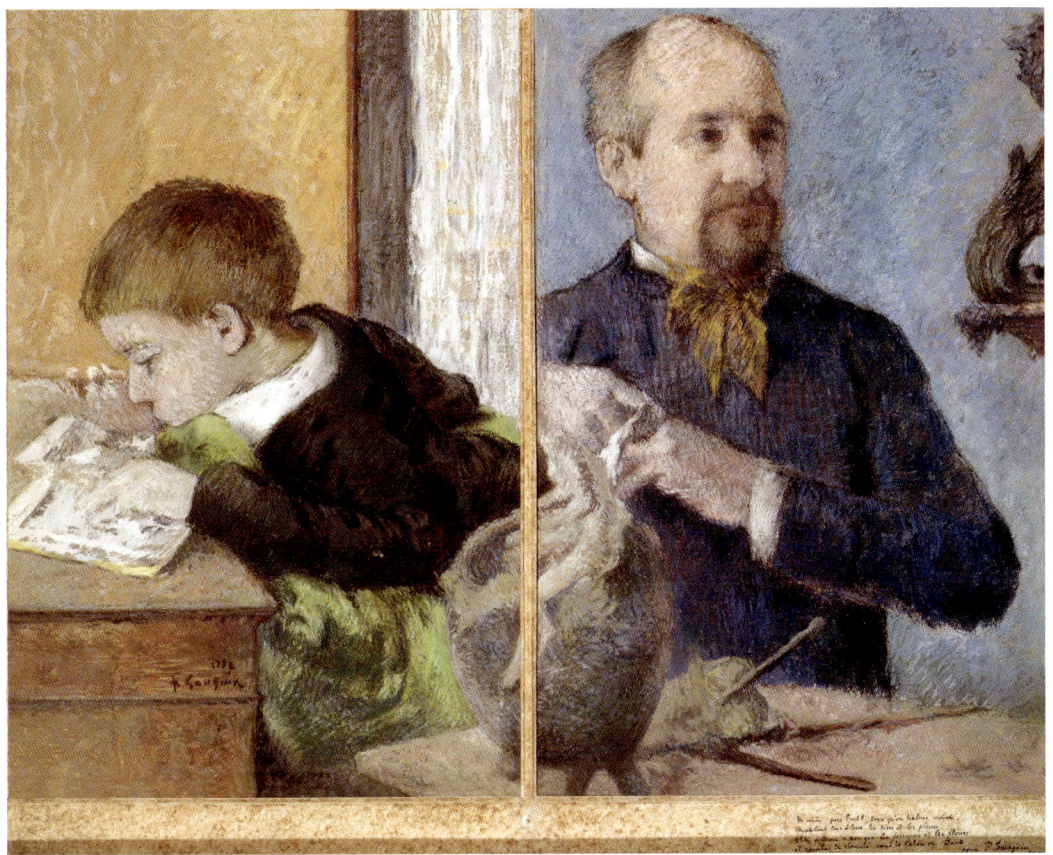

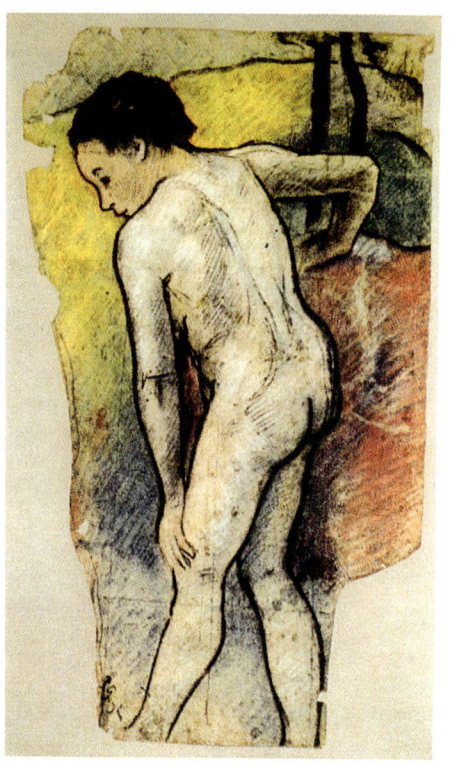

and novel stance adopted by the Impressionists sharpened his own critical faculty. And he became a success, showing seven canvases at the annual Impressionist exhibition in 1880.

Study of a Nude (Suzanne Sewing) (ill. p. 310) is a thoroughly Impressionist work in its use of dynamic light effects produced by innumerable thin brushstrokes. The writer and art critic Joris-Karl Huysmans, a contemporary of Gauguin, spoke of the "little creases below the bosom, which is highlighted by dark patches and seems to be doing some wild dance". It is as if a nervous, colourful element had been introduced into a wholly static subject, a subject that hardly seems Impressionist in character at all. The naked woman seated at her work possesses a quiet dignity that awakens no shameful responses, and the way in which Gauguin has perceived her anticipates his later attempts to capture the calm but powerful presence of the South Sea peoples. It is true that Gauguin made use of Impressionist methods. But he did not share their view of the world, or their emphasis on dynamic flux.

In November 1882 a stock market crash put an abrupt stop to Gauguin's double life as broker and artist. The crash cost him and his friend Émile Schuffenecker their jobs. And it left Gauguin free to indulge in the wayward life of a dandy to his heart's content. He had always longed for the bohemian existence that suddenly became available to him; but the snag was that now he had a family to care for, five children to feed, and a house. None of this fitted in with the romantic image of a dropout adrift in the big city. As if to prove that artists could be responsible family men, he painted his double portrait, *Aubé the Sculptor and His Son* (ill. p. 313), the same year. The boy, who is naturally destined to follow in his father's footsteps and is drawing on a sketchpad, and the artist, wholly absorbed in this work, together show that a cosy family idyll and independent creative labour are compatible. But Gauguin was no sculptor. Nor was he an Aubé.

At any rate, Mette, unable to share her husband's euphoric view of art, went to stay with her parents in Denmark. Gauguin felt obliged to look for another remunerative job, but his quest was half-hearted, the economic climate poor, and he was unsuccessful. For a while he worked as a sales representative for a French textiles firm in his wife's hometown, Copenhagen. But all he got out of his northern venture was an exhibition of his paintings, and it was a disaster. "I deeply loathe Denmark, and the Danish people, and the Danish climate," he wrote, and soon returned to Paris. All the family, which saw him as a ne'er-do-well, stayed behind, apart from Clovis. Gauguin then had to provide for him out of his income as an artist.

"When the lad had his attack of smallpox I had just twenty centimes in my pocket," Gauguin wrote to his wife from the depths of the Parisian winter. His tone was resigned, but also betrayed the spiteful condescension of the misunderstood genius

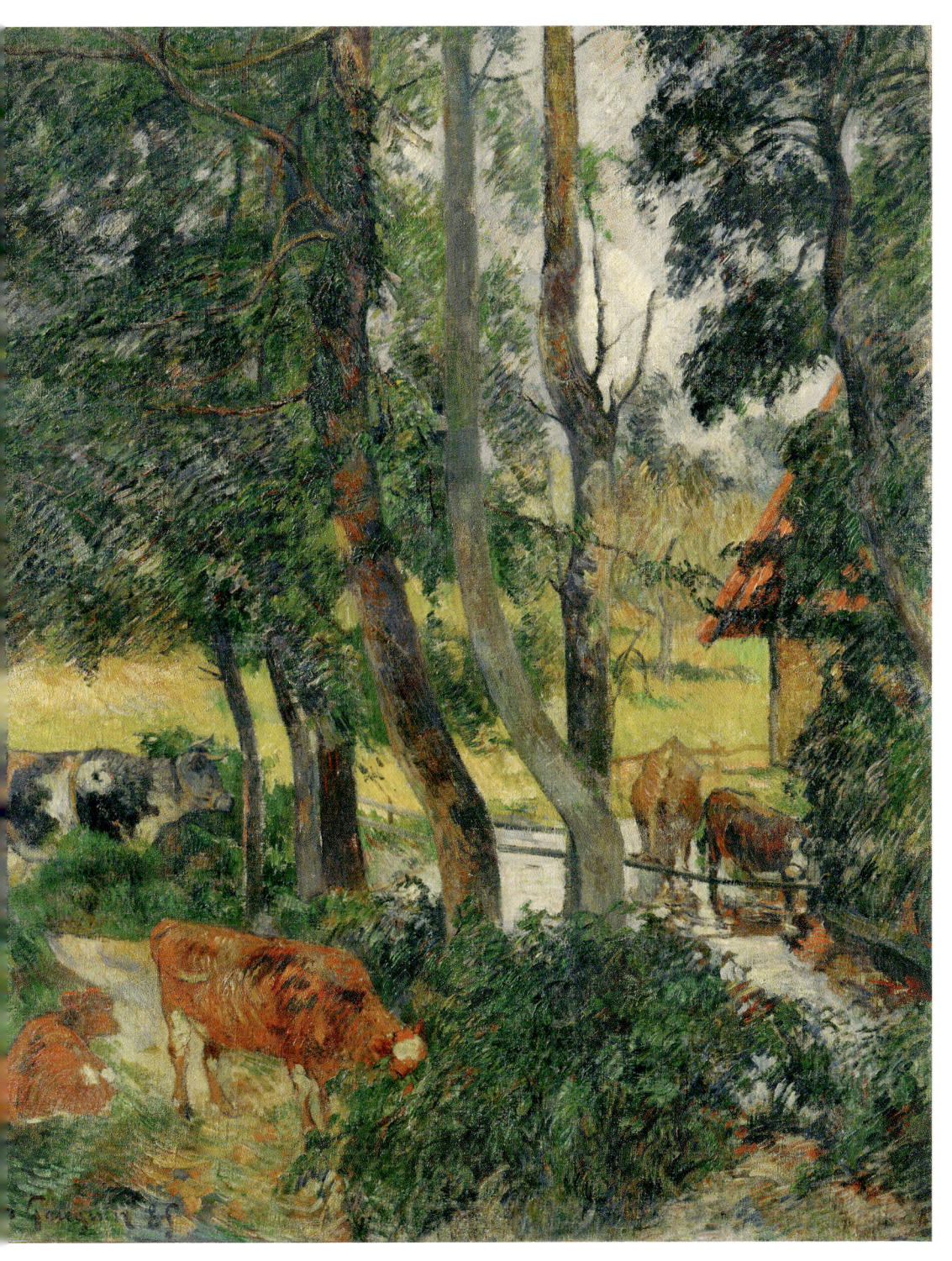

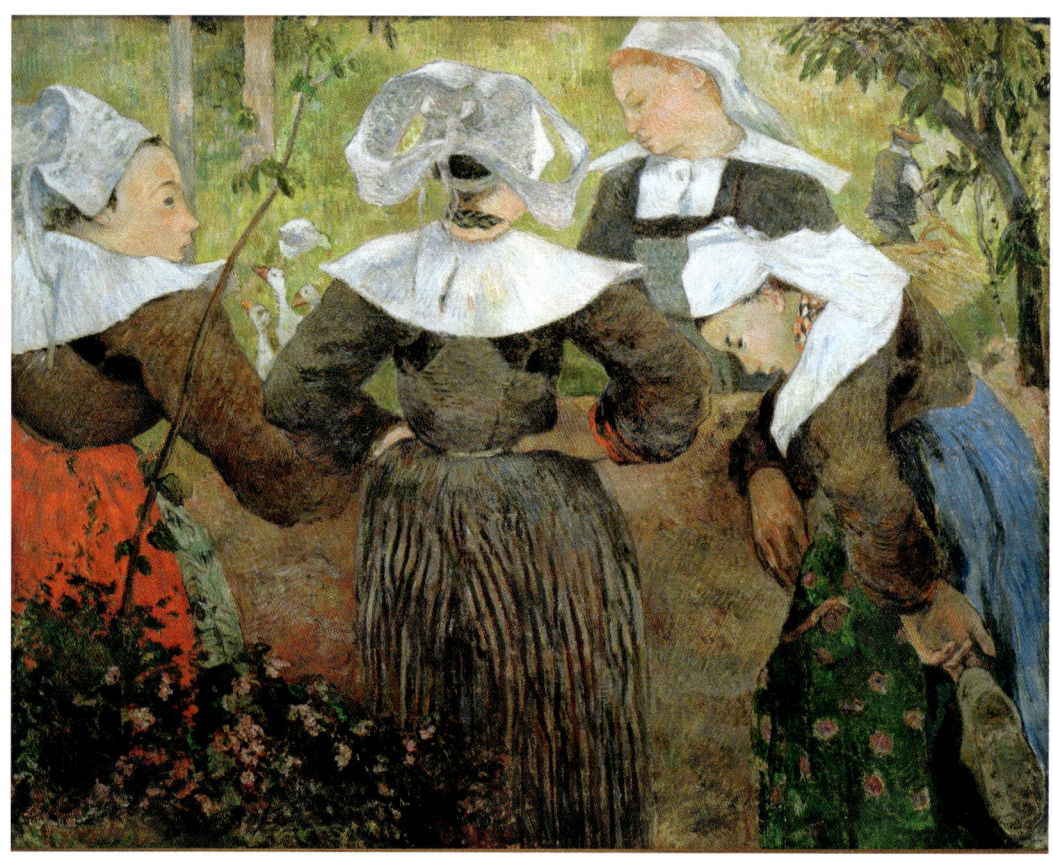

The Four Breton Girls, 1886
Oil on canvas, 71.8 x 91.4 cm (28¼ x 36 in.)
Munich, Bayerische Staatsgemälde-
sammlungen, Neue Pinakothek

who blamed others for his own misfortunes. He had not sold a single painting, and was earning a miserable five francs a day pasting up posters. He had longed to drop out of his bourgeois career, but when the time came the move was unplanned and proved unsuccessful. Escape into the bohemia of dandies, pleasure-seekers and self-proclaimed artists had cost him dearly. When his flight into the city's subculture had turned out to be a failure, Gauguin contemplated retreat to the country.

In the summer of 1886 Gauguin moved to the little village of Pont-Aven on the Atlantic coast of Brittany, "where you can live on next to nothing". He had sent Clovis back to Denmark, to his mother – indeed, to put it baldly, he had got rid of the boy. By now it was not only a middle-class career that seemed beyond his powers; he even felt unequal to being a father. He compensated by plunging all the more energetically into his artistic labours. At Madame Gloanec's boarding house he attracted like-minded young artists who were tempted by the region's spartan beauty and an inexpensive life. Now he could at least write to Mette to tell her he enjoyed recognition as a painter: "I am working well here and successfully. They respect me as the best painter in Pont-Aven. Respect won't earn me a single centime, true. But my reputation is excellent, at any rate, and everyone wants my advice." Gauguin was still very poor, but at least he was increasingly confident.

In *The Four Breton Girls* (ill. p. 316) we see him relying wholly on a quality of monumental simplicity in his subject. Folk costumes and traditions show his interest in the uncomplicated rustic life

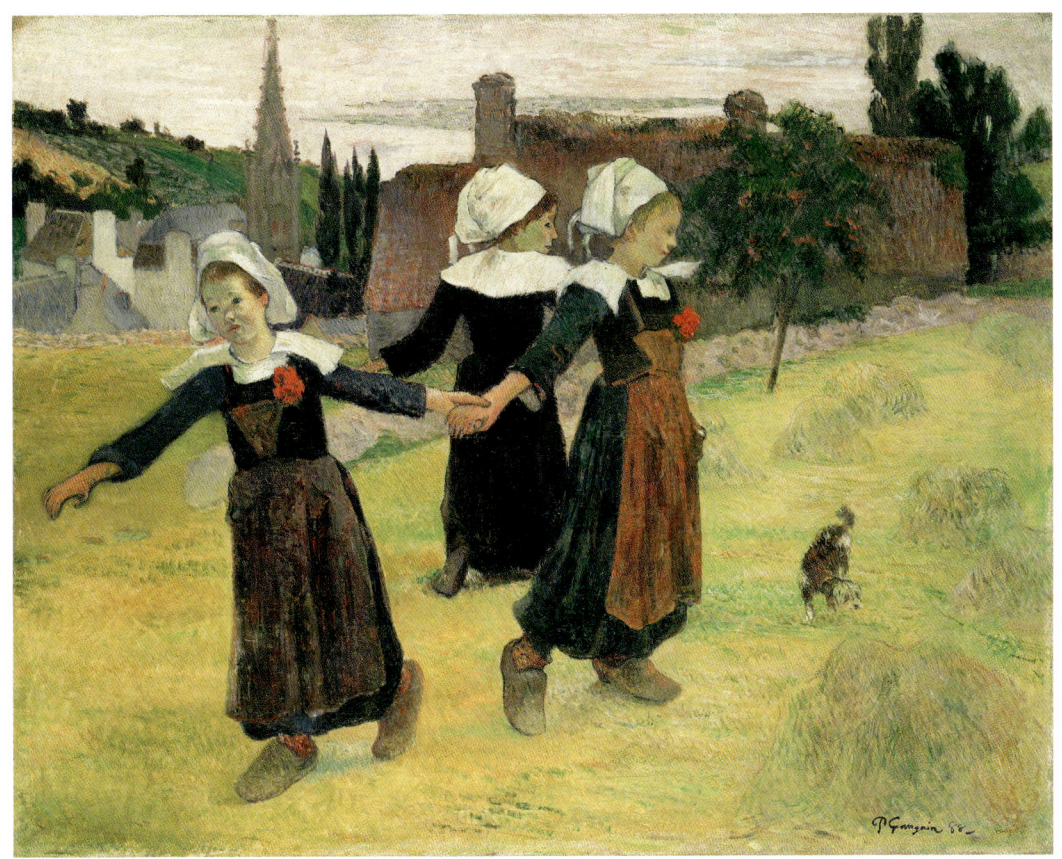

Breton Girls Dancing, Pont-Aven, 1888
Oil on canvas, 73 x 92.7 cm (28¾ x 36½ in.)
Washington, D.C., National Gallery of Art,
Collection of Mr and Mrs Paul Mellon

of Brittany, while the painting's colourfulness still owes a good deal to the shimmering effects of Impressionism. What is newly important in this work is a sense of static equilibrium, quiescent introversion – as here conveyed by the women engrossed in conversation. In his future work, Gauguin was to emphasize major form, and firm, upright lines that define shape and contour were to be its characteristic hallmark. The silhouetted faces of three of the women already bear traces of this.

In 1886, Gauguin exhibited no fewer than nineteen paintings at the Impressionists' salon. This was ironical. While Claude Monet was painting the glittering diversity of city life, Gauguin had gone in the opposite direction, in search of tranquillity. Furthermore, Gauguin was upstaged at the salon by Georges Seurat, who exhibited his massive *Sunday Afternoon at the Île de la Grande Jatte* (1884–86). In this work, Seurat underpinned Impressionist approaches with theoretical principles of perception. Both Seurat and Gauguin were questing for major, inviolable form, in their different ways, but Seurat was using the refined means of civilization in his attempt, while Gauguin was impelled to look elsewhere, hoping to find what he sought in Primitivism.

After Brittany, Gauguin intended to escape for good by making for the unspoilt simplicity of the tropics. None too sure of his plans, he decided to start in Panama, where the building of the Canal promised a livelihood. Charles Laval, a friend and one of the Pont-Aven painters, accompanied him. Yet again, however, Gauguin's artistic skills proved unwanted, and the two men, somewhat rudely

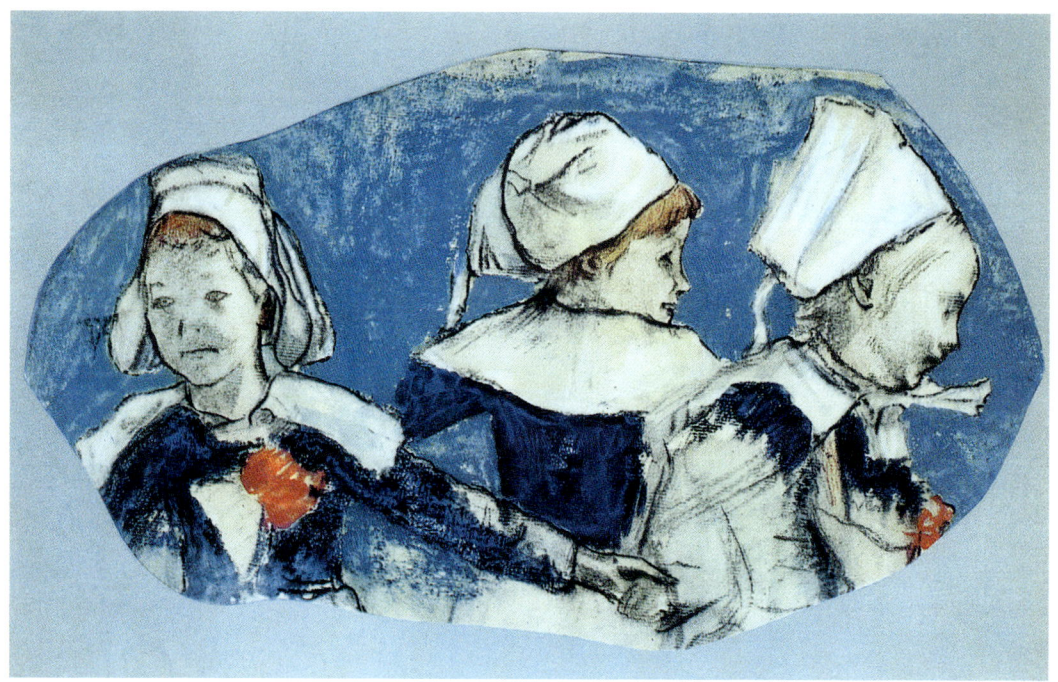

Breton Girls Dancing, 1888
Pastel on paper, 24.2 x 41 cm (9½ x 16¼ in.)
Amsterdam, Van Gogh Museum,
Vincent van Gogh Foundation

awakened, moved on to the French island colony of Martinique in the Caribbean.

On the Banks of the River at Martinique (ill. p. 319) was painted there. Gauguin's feel for the brightness of colours had a new sensitivity, and the picture finds him continuing his efforts to use Impressionist methods of applying paint when tackling motifs of some dignity. Here once more the most important elements in the composition – the trees on the centre axis, and the animals – were highlighted, marked out against the colourful confusion of bright lines that remains predominant. And at last Gauguin had discovered an instinct for colour. The intense sun of Martinique gave him a sense of resplendent brightness that Brittany could never have offered him.

Gauguin's love of the tropics may have been an escapist flight from Western civilization, but it was also an attempt to rediscover the happiness of his South American childhood. Born in Paris, Paul Gauguin had gone to Peru with his family at the tender age of one. His parents had strong republican convictions and when Louis-Napoléon returned to France they left the country. Peru was the home of Gauguin's grandfather, then one hundred years old, with the evocative name Don Pio Tristan Orosco; doubtless the old man made an unforgettable impression on the infant Paul. At all events, Paul Gauguin was fascinated by everything exotic from his childhood on. Although his family returned to France in 1855, Gauguin betrayed a hankering for foreign parts in his youth, and went to sea as a sailor. In a sense, his settled years of bourgeois life from 1872 to 1882 were merely an interval of quiet along his restless way.

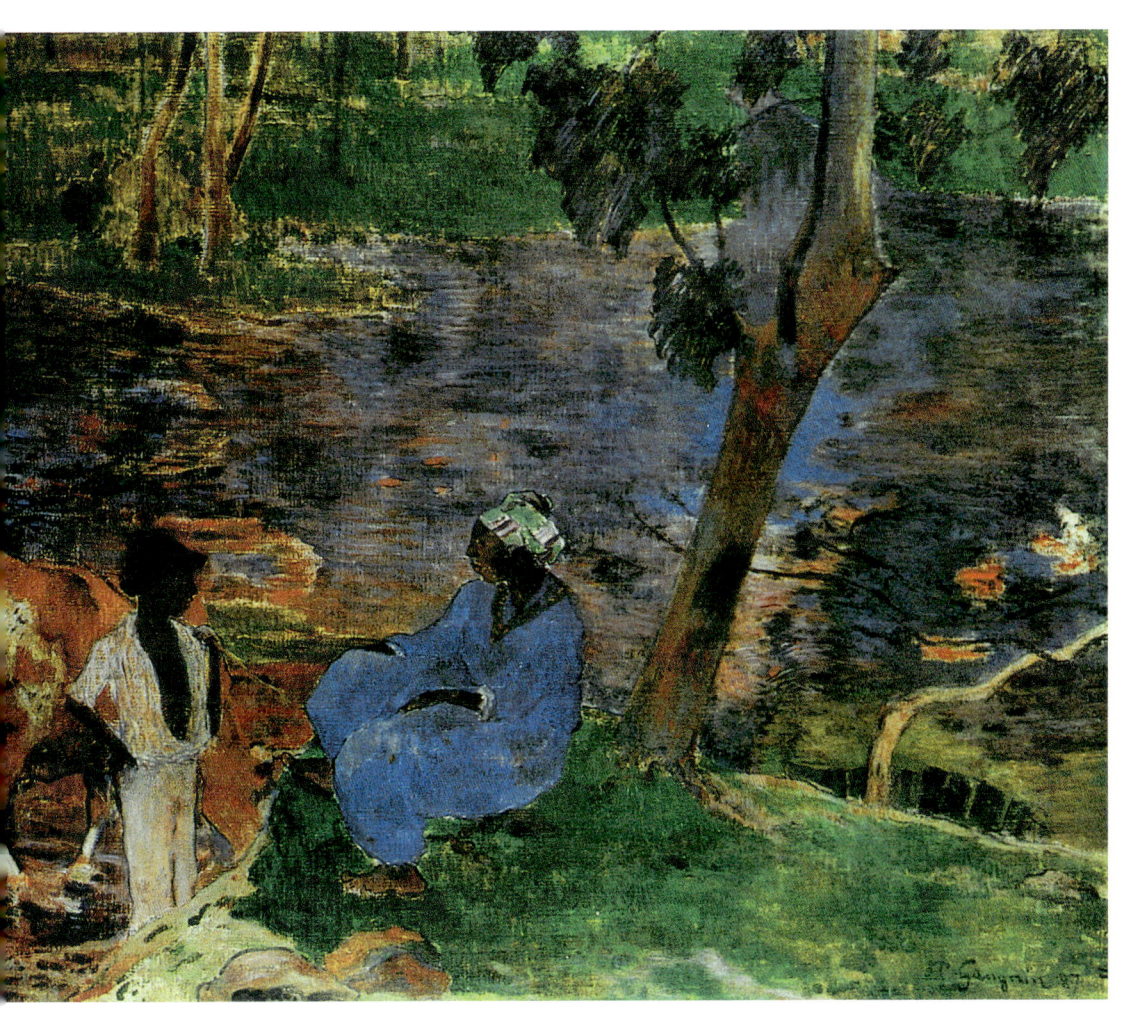

On the Banks of the River at Martinique, 1887
Oil on canvas, 54.5 x 65.5 cm (21½ x 25¾ in.)
Amsterdam, Van Gogh Museum,
Vincent van Gogh Foundation

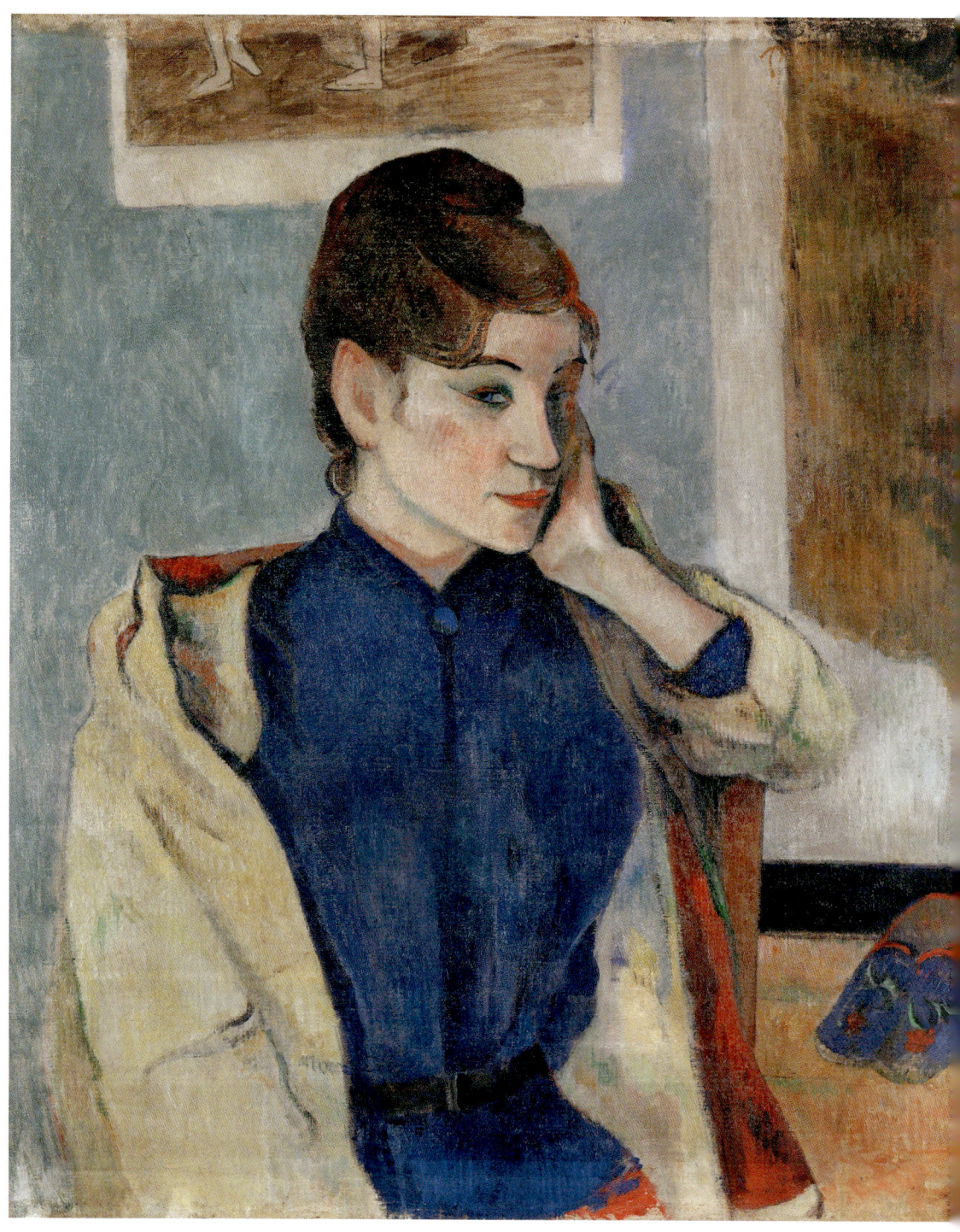

Suggestion and Expression
1888–1891

The year 1888, when he returned to France, was to see Gauguin's most decisive artistic progress. As he himself attested: "This year I have sacrificed everything, all my technique, all my colour, to style." Finally he broke free of the urbane world of Impressionism. In the peasant simplicity of provincial life he not only discovered an inexhaustible source of subjects but also began to take his own artistic bearings from the unaffected originality of folk art.

In the age of the great world fairs, the promise of progress and a future of technological well-being were beguiling. But there was also an awareness of an alternative world of peace and harmony that industrialization threatened with extinction. That other world was elsewhere; not in the urban sophistication of the modern cities but in provincial backwaters and, above all, in the unspoilt reaches of faraway continents. Bourgeois society was tirelessly hardworking and had grown rich through its efforts. But it was intoxicated by visions of remote and magical worlds – as long as they stayed remote. Art was just the place for such visions. Paintings took on an exoticism, showing mysterious and colourful things that excited the public's longings. The world of these paintings was artificial; it was a sensational world as far from the reality of the tropics as the tropics were from Paris.

Gauguin too had fallen under the spell. In his art, however, he aimed to portray a primitive world on its own terms, stripped of exotic props and without the cottage romanticism of peasant idylls. He was out to show the genuine, unposed, original character of subjects drawn from an unfamiliar, simple world. If the impression they made was also one of rudimentary crudeness, so be it; their very lack of refined sophistication was the guarantee of their authenticity.

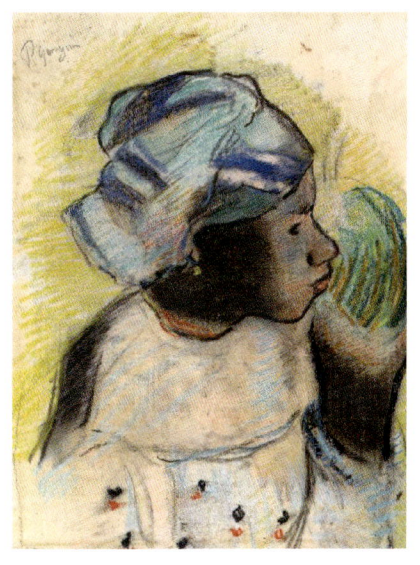

During his quest for a Primitivist method in Brittany, Gauguin had hit upon a new style: Cloisonnism. He developed this style at Pont-Aven together with one of his fellow painters, Émile Bernard. The name came from a mediaeval enamelling technique in which the individual surfaces were compartmented off

OPPOSITE
Madeleine Bernard, 1888
Oil on canvas, 72 x 58 cm (28¼ x 23 in.)
Musée de Grenoble

ABOVE RIGHT
Study of a Martinican Woman, 1887
Pastel on paper, 36 x 27 cm (14¼ x 10¾ in.)
Amsterdam, Van Gogh Museum,
Vincent van Gogh Foundation

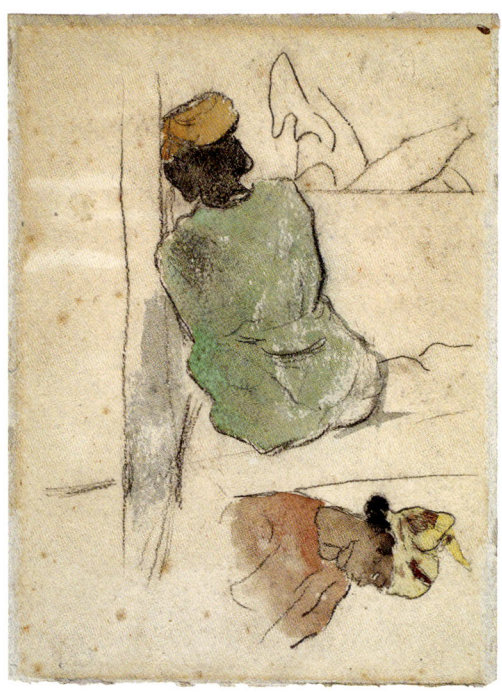

Page from the *Martinique sketchbook*, 1884–89
Chalk and watercolour on mottled wove paper,
20.3 x 26.1 cm (8 x 10⅜ in.)
Private collection

OPPOSITE
Still Life with Three Puppies, 1888
Oil on wood, 91.8 x 62.6 cm (36¼ x 24¾ in.)
New York, The Museum of Modern Art,
Mrs Simon Guggenheim Fund

in fillets of metal. Similarly, the two painters took to contouring all their colour surfaces with thick lines of colour, with a rigour that verged on the dogmatic. The graphic line acquired as distinct a visual value as the area it encompassed. Naturally it was still representational art, and the lines and surfaces still clearly depicted recognizable figures and objects; but at the same time a kind of abstract pattern was superimposed on the canvas, and the lines and surfaces took on an independent existence of their own. Quite apart from its representation of reality, a painting's union of fabric and paint, lines and surfaces, figures and decorative content had to suggest a world beyond what was immediately apparent, just as the Bretons' Celtic ancestors had represented their gods in abstract, ornamental form as entangled strands. The deeper and more harmonious world must remain hidden and invisible. It could only be felt, or sensed associatively.

"I should like to keep as much distance as possible from the creation of illusions," said Gauguin, in explanation of the coolly analytic gaze he directed to what lay beneath the surface of things. The strategy he adopted to avoid creating illusions is apparent in his *Still Life with Three Puppies* (ill. p. 323). The still life consists of fruit, glasses, and puppies drinking from a bowl. The objects in the painting are familiar enough; yet within the new context they are subverted and destabilized. The tabletop on which they are placed looks unequal to the business of maintaining balance, and is seemingly being pulled down by some mysterious force. This has the effect of making the juxtaposition of objects look like a mere heap. It does not detract from the spatial solidity of the glasses, apples and pears, however, and they have a firm and even palpable quality. Yet, if the individual elements are thoroughly ordinary, the composition of the picture is distinctly unusual; and it is only in reference to the top edge of the canvas, which robs us of any logical sense of spatial dimension, that we can see the point in this composition. The visual motifs become components in a decorative whole: the three glasses provide a rhythmic counterpoint against the white of the tablecloth, and the three puppies pick up the rounded shape of the bowl. The decorative embroidery on the

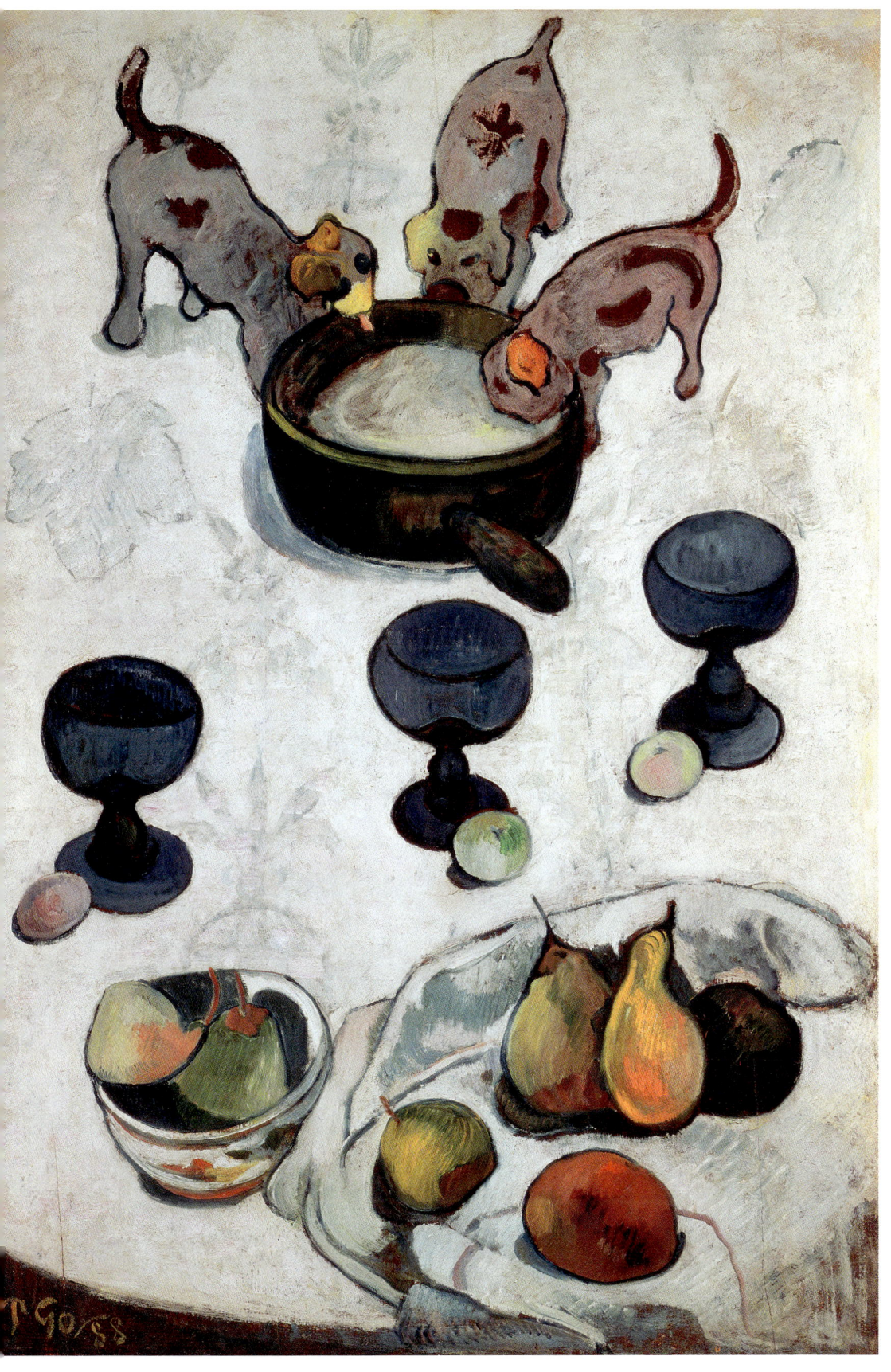

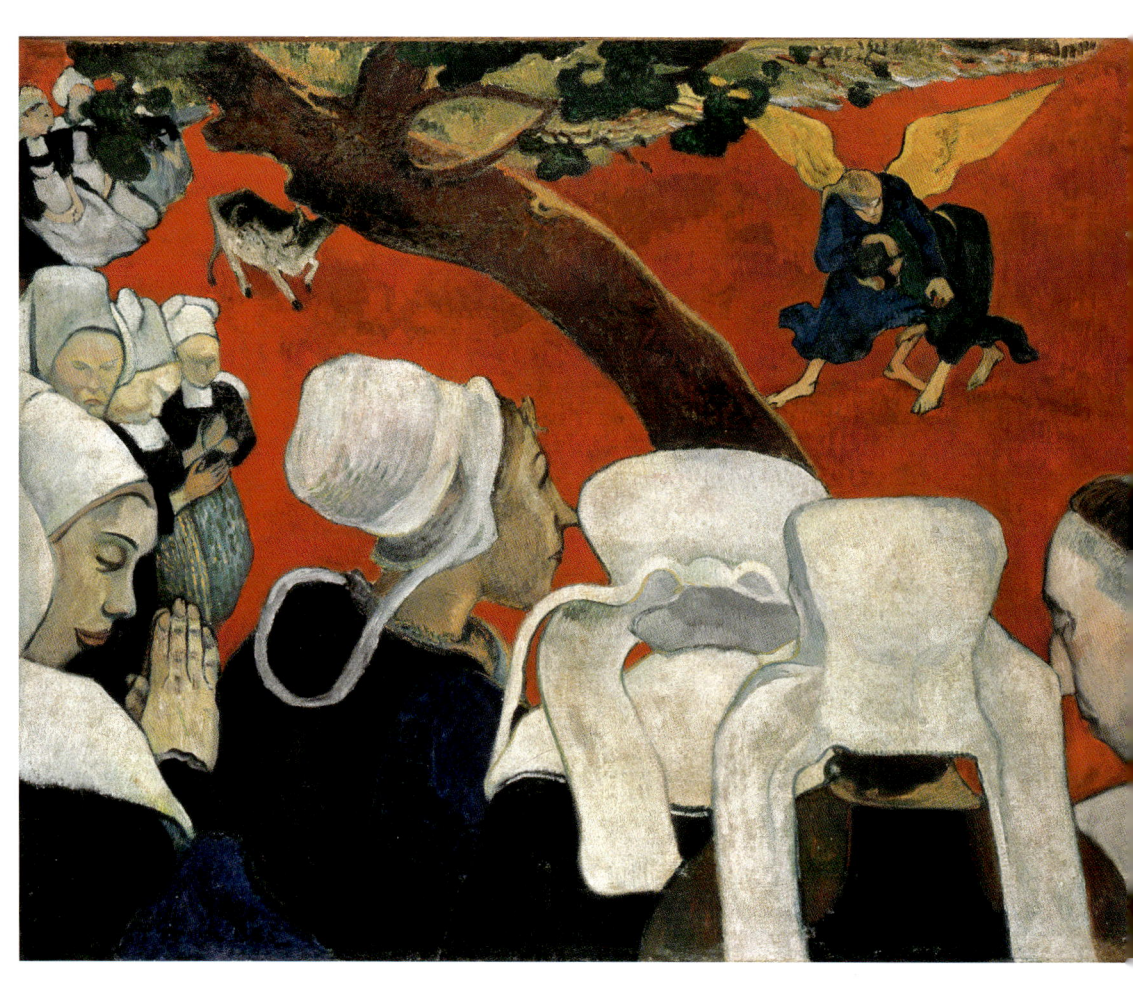

Vision after the Sermon
(Jacob Wrestling with the Angel), 1888
Oil on canvas, 72.2 x 91 cm (28½ x 36 in.)
Edinburgh, Scottish National Gallery

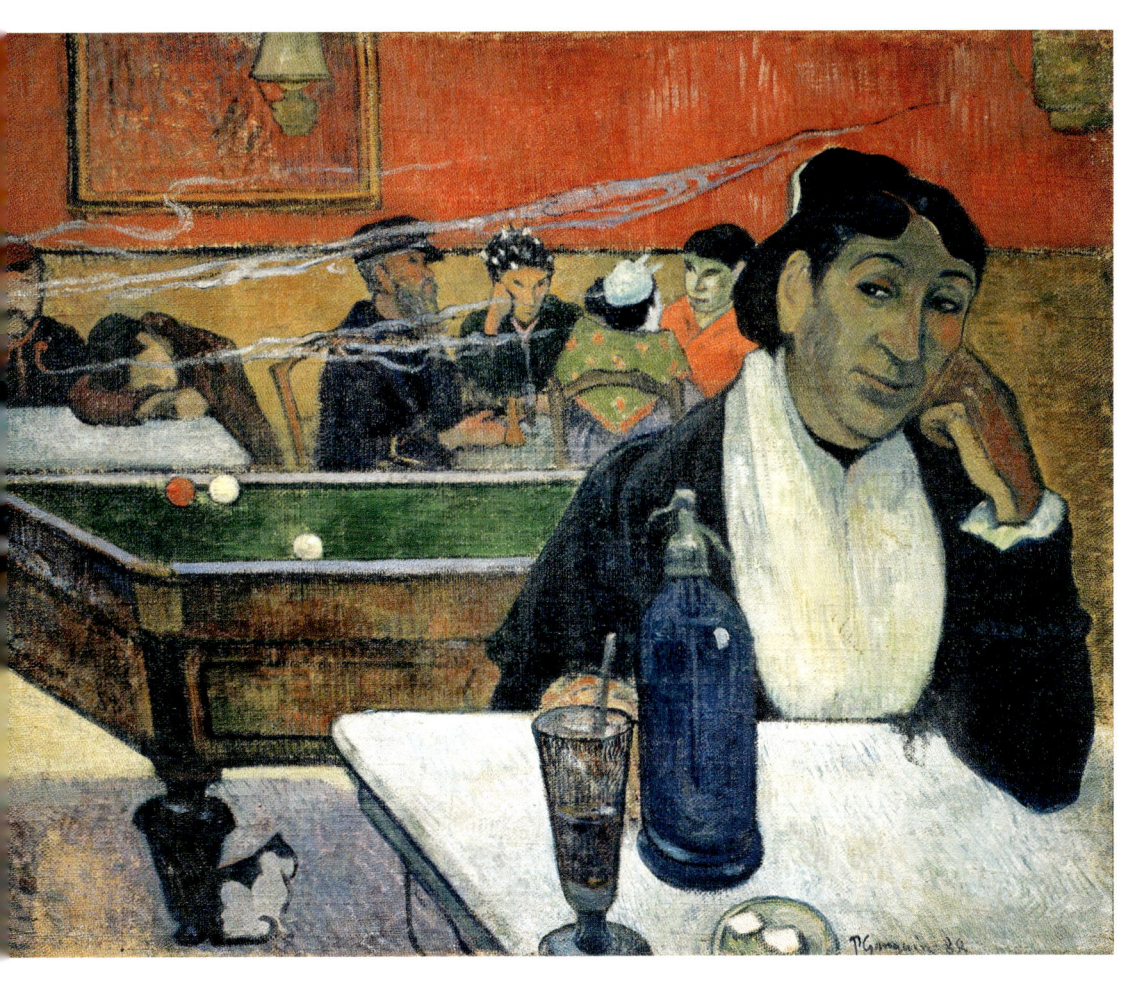

Night Café at Arles, 1888
Oil on canvas, 73 x 92 cm (28¾ x 36¼ in.)
Moscow, Pushkin Museum

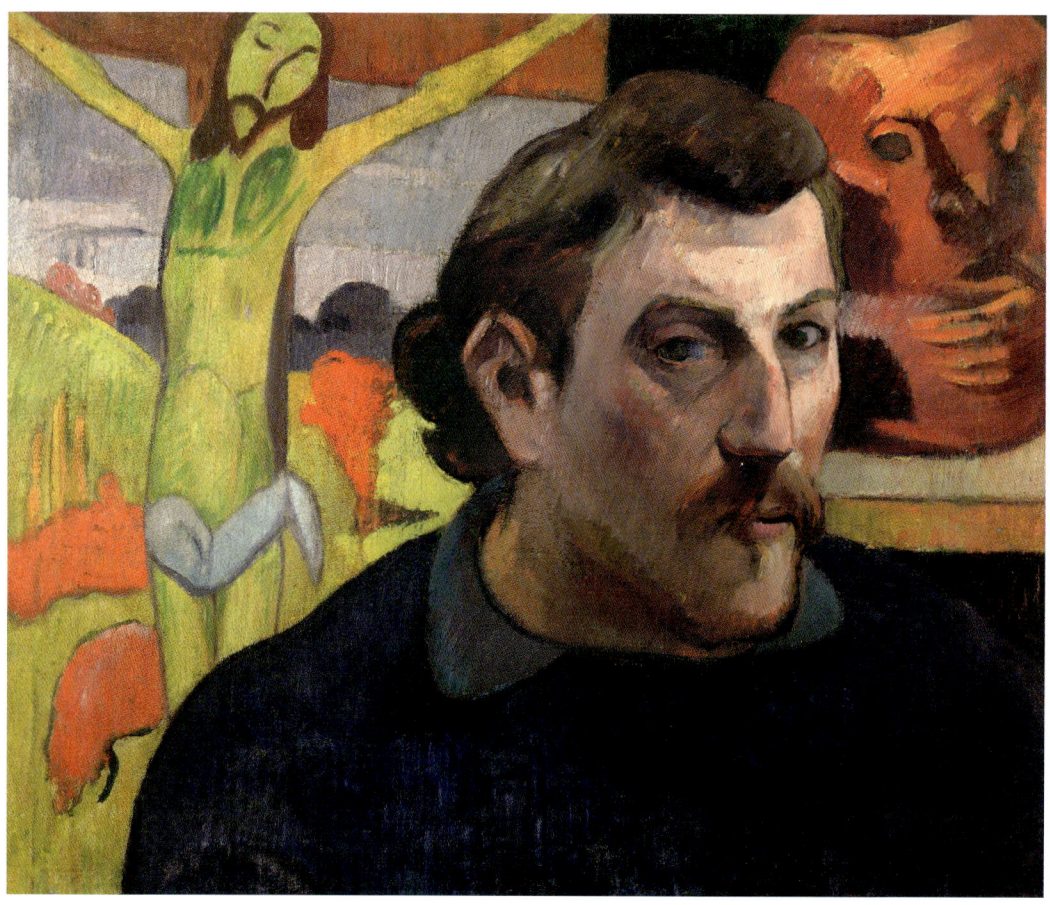

Self-portrait with Yellow Christ, 1890/91
Oil on canvas, 38 x 46 cm (15 x 18 in.)
Paris, Musée d'Orsay

OPPOSITE
Van Gogh Painting Sunflowers, 1888
Oil on canvas, 73 x 91 cm (28¾ x 36 in.)
Amsterdam, Van Gogh Museum,
Vincent van Gogh Foundation

linen cloth can be seen as a basic pattern for the whole painting, which constitutes a single decorative piece. Its forms are taken from visible reality, but they have undergone a creative process that has fitted them into an abstract scheme.

Gauguin had borrowed this tendency toward ornamental arrangement from Japanese woodcuts. The vogue for the exotic extended to Oriental art, and Japanese clothing and accessories were particularly fashionable. In European art, this trend was known as *Japonaiserie*. True, the sophisticated sensitivity of Oriental art was a total contrast to the rough-and-ready robustness that was valued in the West for its supposed primitiveness. Both visual worlds were novel, however, and their freshness could be enlisted to revitalize European artistic expression. Gauguin was not alone in thinking along these lines.

The programmatic painting *Vision after the Sermon (Jacob Wrestling with the Angel*; ill. p. 324) is an excellent example of his ability to accommodate Oriental and Primitivist visual modes within a single work. Undoubtedly the most ambitious of all Gauguin's paintings, it is in part symbolic of his struggle for recognition, and of his failure to achieve it. We see two groups of figures, separated diagonally down the middle (in the manner of Japanese woodcuts) by a huge tree trunk. Dominating the foreground, and almost obstructing our view of the rest, is a group of women in traditional Breton costume, reverently meditating on the sermon they have been listening to. In the background, however, we see an angel with wings outstretched locked in combat with the biblical figure of Jacob.

Gauguin combines an everyday scene of women leaving church with a scene that exists only in the realm of religion, and in doing so he is also combining two different pictorial traditions. The tranquil and rough-hewn style of folk art has influenced the large figures in the foreground, while the dramatic struggle in the background draws on traditions in Christian art. A third element is provided by the tree, with its axis function reminiscent of Oriental art.

The painting makes a direct appeal to a world beyond the senses, and in doing so has recourse to singularly apt artistic means: hard and contrasting colours, a perspective that draws us deeply into the background, together with a powerful emphasis on the foreground, and large, compact areas of colour that only suggest the figures. These artistic means do not represent things as they are so much as evoke a particular mood. Gauguin was trying to show a vision, but at the same time his painting aims quite simply to be a vision.

This painting (at the very latest) established Gauguin as the presiding spirit of the Pont-Aven painters' colony. The group included Laval, Paul Sérusier, Louis Anquetin, Armand Séguin, Jacob Meijer de Haan and of course Émile Bernard. The muse who inspired them was Émile's sister Madeleine, Charles Laval's fiancée. Gauguin kept up a lively correspondence with her, which must have become rather too intense, since Madeleine's parents finally persuaded her to break it off. Gauguin still had a portrait to remember her by (ill. p. 320), painted in 1888.

Another painter had quit Paris at the same time as Gauguin: Vincent van Gogh. He had headed south, to Arles in Provence, where the shimmering light and the sunlit natural world provided him with inspiration for his work. Van Gogh had already had quite enough of the bare simplicity Gauguin sought in Brittany, in his own Dutch childhood. The two artists shared not only their escape into the provinces but also their plans to found an artists' colony. Gauguin's work alongside

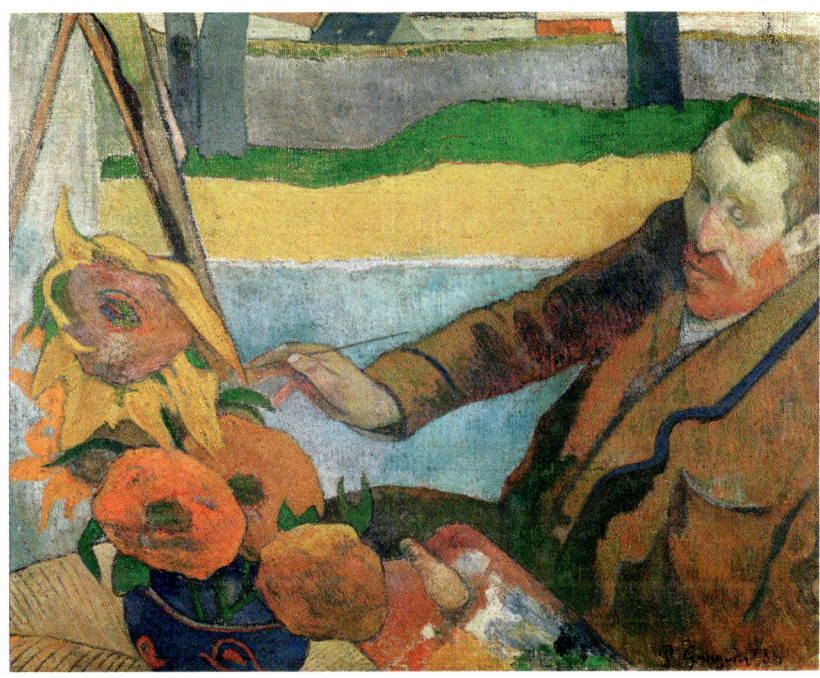

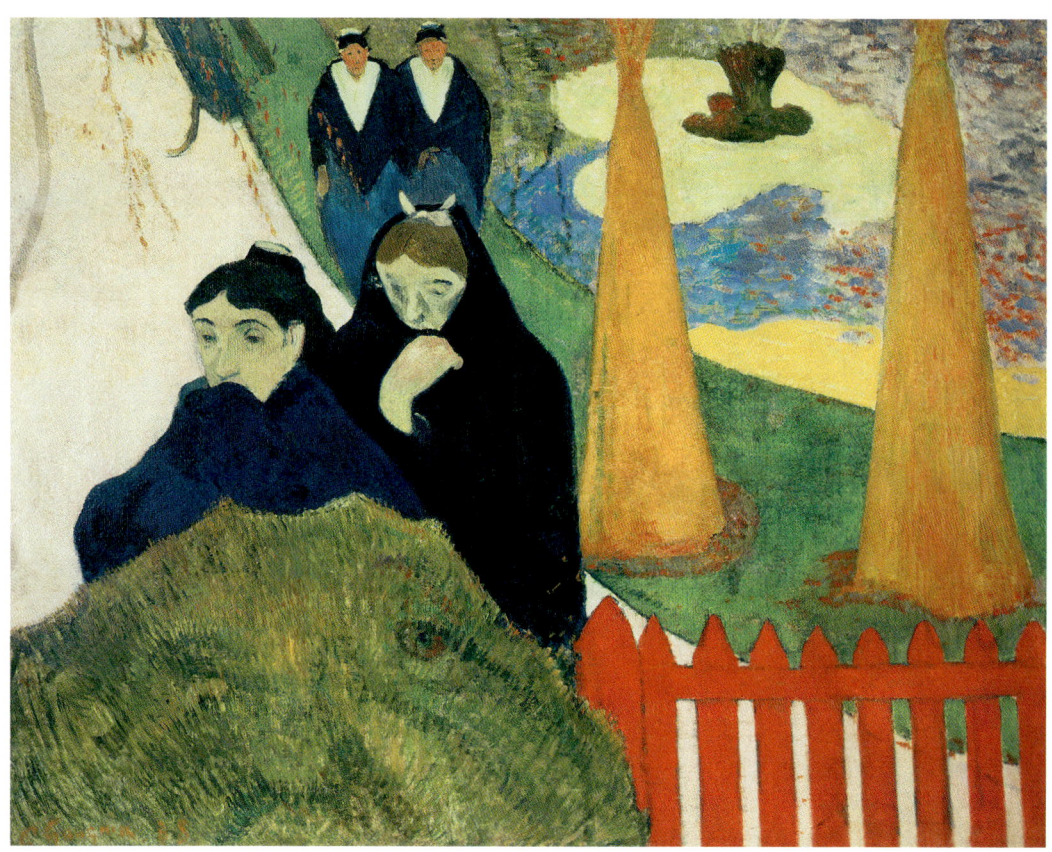

Arlésiennes (Mistral), 1888
Oil on canvas, 73 x 92 cm (28¾ x 36¼ in.)
The Art Institute of Chicago,
Mr and Mrs Lewis Coburn Collection

his fellow artists had given him a new self-confidence; van Gogh, on the other hand, had hitherto remained alone, and now had plans for the two loners to work together for a few months. His brother Theo, who represented both van Gogh and Gauguin in his capacity as a Montmartre art dealer in Paris, was to see to the arrangements. Weeks in advance, Vincent was already overwhelmed with excitement. He renovated and prettified the "Yellow House", where he then lived, so that Gauguin would have everything he required. Gauguin, however, repeatedly delayed his arrival in Provence, apparently suspecting his dealer of a business ruse: "Theo likes me, but still he wouldn't agree to support me in the Midi just because I have a pretty face. He is a cool Dutchman, he has worked out what's what, and he is out to get the best, exclusive deal out of it."

As always, however, Gauguin was in debt. Theo came to the financial rescue once more, and then there was nothing for it: on 23 October 1888 Gauguin joined van Gogh at Arles. Two months of fighting and quarrelling ensued, during which each painter jealously tried to establish the superiority of his own work. Van Gogh had had a high opinion of his fellow artist: "Everything he does is tender, moving, astonishing. People do not understand him yet, and he is suffering from his inability to sell – like other true poetic spirits." Their differences, however, grew increasingly obvious. "He is a Romantic," noted Gauguin irritably, "whereas my preferences lie with primitive art. When he applies paint he loves the chance effects of impasto, but I for my part detest disorderly workmanship."

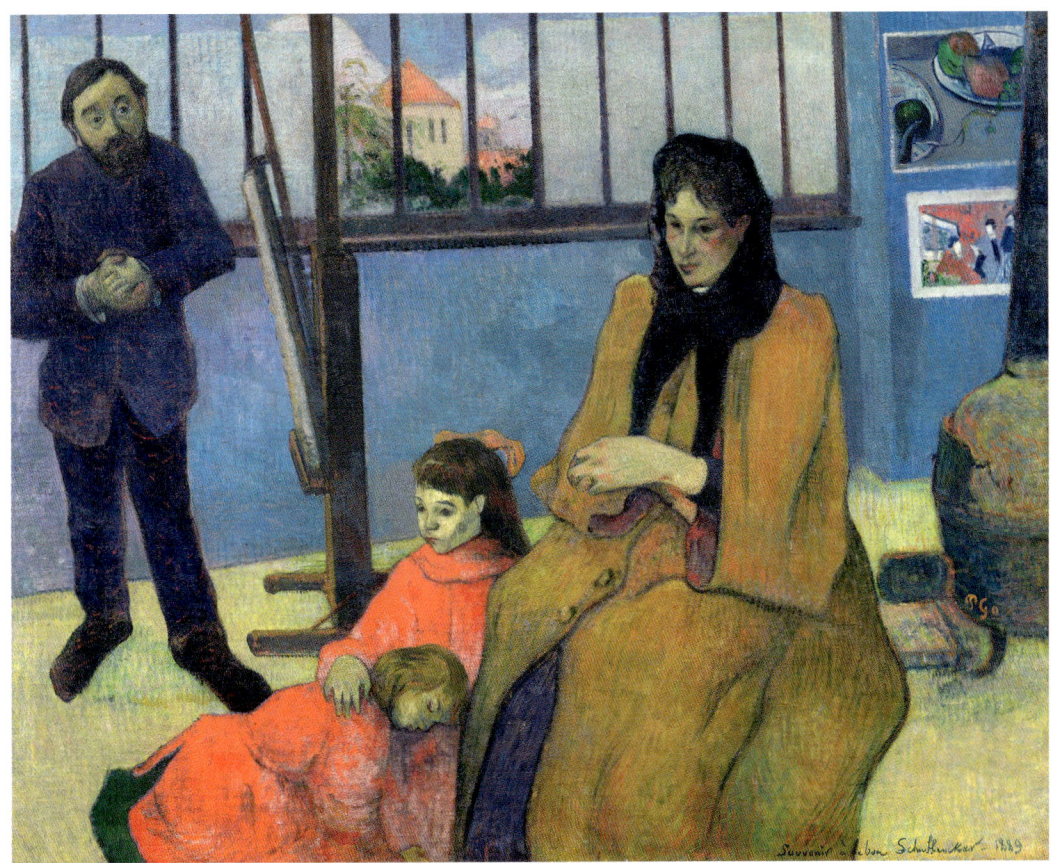

Gauguin had hoped to find a keen pupil to boss around. In fact, both had travelled too far along their respective ways as painters to achieve any deeper mutual understanding.

Schuffenecker's Studio, 1889
Oil on canvas, 72.7 x 92 cm
(28½ x 36¼ in.)
Paris, Musée d'Orsay

During their period together, van Gogh and Gauguin worked on the same subjects in a spirit of competition. Each would try his hand at the other's works, as a kind of test. *Night Café at Arles* (ill. p. 325) shows Gauguin interpreting one of van Gogh's paintings – or, to be exact, two: *The Night Café* (1888, New Haven, Yale University Art Gallery) and two portraits of its owner, Madame Ginoux (1888/89, New York, The Metropolitan Museum of Art; 1888, Paris, Musée d'Orsay). The combination highlights Gauguin's knack of juxtaposing different motifs. The impression of desolate and overwhelming loneliness that made van Gogh's version of the café inimitably his own has disappeared from Gauguin's treatment. Van Gogh had seen the isolated and nameless customers huddled in the corners as his true subject, but Gauguin banishes them to the background, behind the proprietress. She is presented gazing out of the picture, in a manner that eases contact and relieves that oppressive sense of isolation with which van Gogh had invested the café. Gauguin's attention was not on the darker aspects of life, and he preferred to pursue the lighter sides of the imagination.

He had seen van Gogh as a Romantic and himself as a Primitivist, and it was certainly true that Vincent's art was as impetuous and vehement as the man himself. Van Gogh was in all things a man of feeling, passionately devoted to an art of expressive intensity. His impulsive will refused to pause before the fearful abysses in the soul of man. Gauguin's involvement with the human condition,

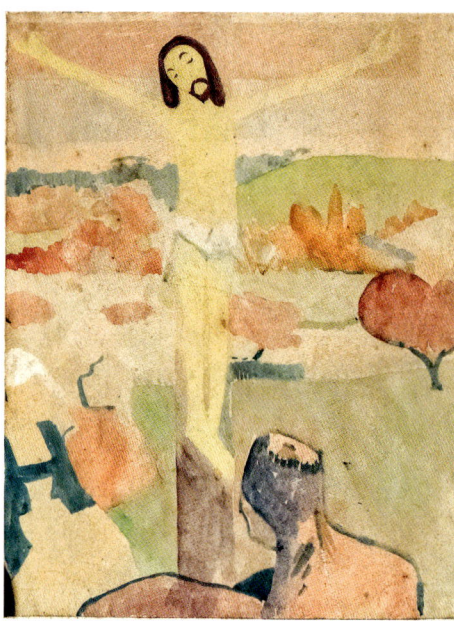

comparatively speaking, was marked by distance. His watchwords were happiness and harmony, and he arrived at them not through any struggle within himself but by yielding to the alien promises of Edenic worlds. Gauguin's art was an art of suggestion, vividly conjuring up realms of alternative realities that lay beyond his ken. Van Gogh's was a more introspective art, an art of expression that was centred on his own personality and problems.

The break was not long in coming. "Ever since I had decided I wanted to leave Arles," wrote Gauguin, "he had been behaving so oddly that I scarcely dared breathe. 'You want to go,' he said, and when I replied 'Yes' he tore off a strip of newspaper bearing the following words and handed it to me: 'The murderer has fled.'" For van Gogh, it meant the collapse of his hopes for relaxed work with fellow artists in the southern sun. At night he would often get up and creep into Gauguin's room to reassure himself that the other was still there. It was only Vincent's illness that still kept Gauguin in Arles: "Though we are at odds on some things, I cannot be angry at a good fellow who is sick and suffering and needs me."

On 23 December, exactly two months after Gauguin's arrival, the situation grew dramatically worse. Gauguin went out for an evening stroll, and Vincent, forever suspicious, followed him. Gauguin heard his familiar footfall, turned, gazed into van Gogh's distraught face, and supposedly saw an open razor in his hand. Vincent instantly turned and ran home, and Gauguin spent the night in a hotel. Next morning, as he was about to return to the "Yellow House", he found the whole of Arles in an uproar: once he was at home, Vincent, tormented by hallucinations and pain, had cut off his left earlobe, with the very razor Gauguin claimed to have seen him carrying. After he had stanched the flow of blood, van Gogh had wrapped the severed lobe in a handkerchief and hurried to the town brothel, where he gave it to one of the prostitutes. He had then walked home and went to bed as if nothing had happened. And there the police found him when they were alerted early in the morning. He was taken to hospital.

At the time, Gauguin had just completed *Van Gogh Painting Sunflowers* (ill. p. 327). In his fellow painter's portrayal, van Gogh has a wild look and his brush arm is stretched out awkwardly. Gauguin

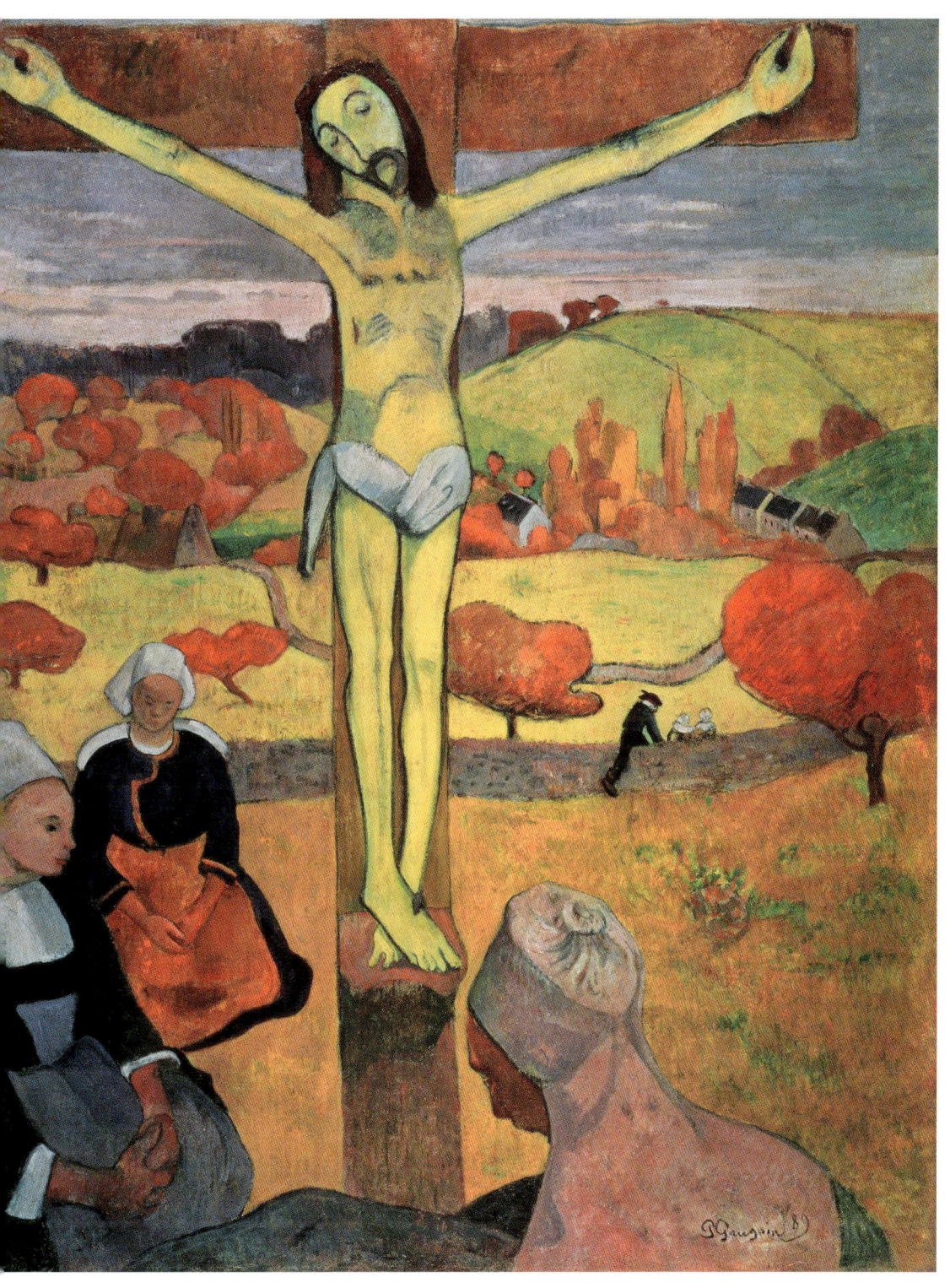

was trying to capture the manic compulsion that drove van Gogh to paint, and the way his paintings seemed almost to make themselves. "It really is me," van Gogh commented, "although it looks as if I had gone mad." And in fact the Gauguin affair was what broke van Gogh: he became profoundly ill, and his time with Gauguin was his last at total liberty. The brief spell that remained to van Gogh in his short life was mostly to be spent in confinement.

Gauguin, meanwhile, left Arles the same morning, without seeing the other artist again. His prompt retreat looked distinctly shamefaced; later, however, in his book *Avant et après* (1903), Gauguin justified his conduct by claiming Vincent had threatened him with the razor. At all events, the episode was not inconveniently timed from Gauguin's point of view: now no one stood between him and the wide world any more. The van Gogh adventure nicely exemplifies a certain man-of-the-world wiliness that constantly accompanied Gauguin's artistic endeavours. He was always capable of keeping his distance. Gauguin too saw the unison of art and life as his goal; but van Gogh's attempt to reach that goal was the more earnest of the two. Gauguin wrote off the time he had spent in Arles as a bad experience and as a strategic concession to his dealer, Theo van Gogh.

Gauguin began 1889 in Paris. He had fled to his old friend Schuffenecker – "le bon Schuff", as he affectionately called him – who had taken a job as a drawing teacher after the stock exchange crash. Schuffenecker had abandoned his artistic ambitions for a steady income, and now seemed to be a happy family man. Aptly enough, Gauguin therefore painted the friend in the studio with his family: indeed, in *Schuffenecker's Studio* (ill. p. 329) Émile's wife and children are the central figures. Typically for Gauguin, they are positioned emphatically up front, even cropped by the edge of the picture. Gauguin's friend, on the other hand, is standing discreetly aside, by the easel, as if he too intended to paint the mother and children. He is looking at his family with a curious, almost fearful gaze. Schuffenecker's fears may not have been altogether unfounded: Gauguin is said to have had intimate talks with Schuffenecker's wife. The composition, with its massively dominant female figure and the timid man in the background, is certainly unusual: the artist has used his knowledge of the family's life for a quite merciless exposure of the couple's relations.

Schuffenecker's flat remained Gauguin's base for a few months. He exhibited with a group of twenty Brussels artists known as Les XX, and had high hopes for *Vision after the Sermon* (ill. p. 324), but he was doomed to disappointment. If one critic, Octave Maus, felt Gauguin's work occasioned "great hilarity", the painter could put it down to the ignorance of the public. It was different, however, when an eminent authority whose own art played an important role in Gauguin's development expressed his contempt. Pissarro wrote: "What I find reprehensible in him is that his synthesis is unrelated to our modern philosophy, which is a social, anti-authoritarian and anti-mystical philosophy. For this reason, the problem is serious. He is taking a step backwards. Gauguin is not a seer. He is simply crafty."

The Yellow Christ (ill. p. 331) makes clear what Pissarro meant. Once again we find Gauguin attempting a vision: a crucifix appearing to women deep in prayer. The starkness of the colours used for the crucified figure and the tops of the trees creates a supernatural mood. The yellow Christ is appearing both to the women (within the painting) and to us (the whole painting is a vision). Pissarro's criticism was apt – Gauguin's art must indeed have been seen as antisocial, authoritarian and mystical.

It is true that Gauguin paid no attention to considerations of societal progress; quite the contrary, conditions in France were among his reasons for leaving the country. In his art, Gauguin sought refuge and security in a familiar realm of faith and

Self-portrait, 1889
Oil on wood, 79.2 x 51.3 cm (31¼ x 20¼ in.)
Washington, D.C., National Gallery of Art, Chester Dale Collection

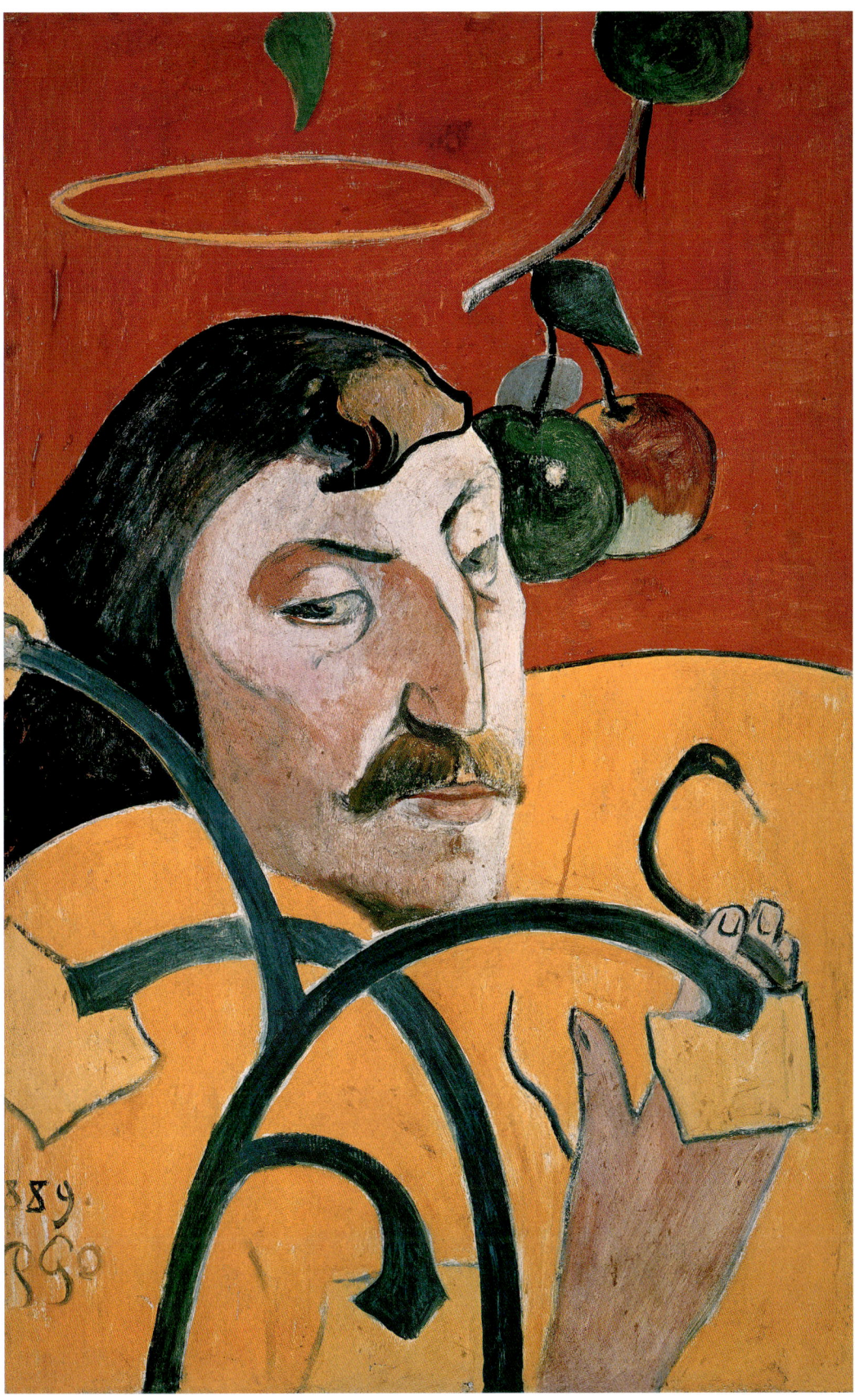

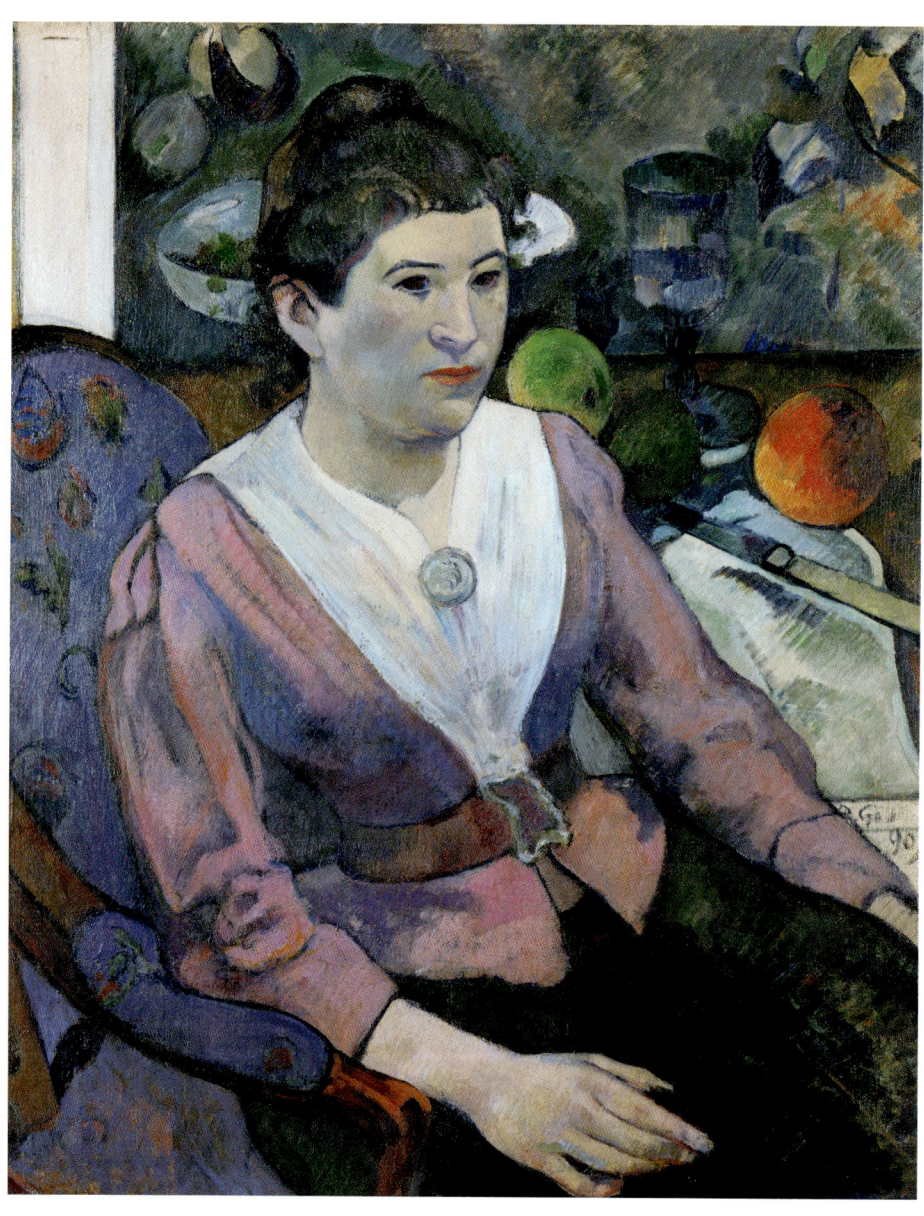

Woman in Front of a Still Life
by Cézanne, 1890
Oil on canvas, 65.3 x 54.9 cm (25¾ x 21½ in.)
The Art Institute of Chicago,
Joseph Winterbotham Collection

Ondine, 1889
Oil on canvas, 92.5 x 72.4 cm
(36½ x 28½ in.)
The Cleveland Museum of Art,
Gift of Mr and Mrs William Powell Jones

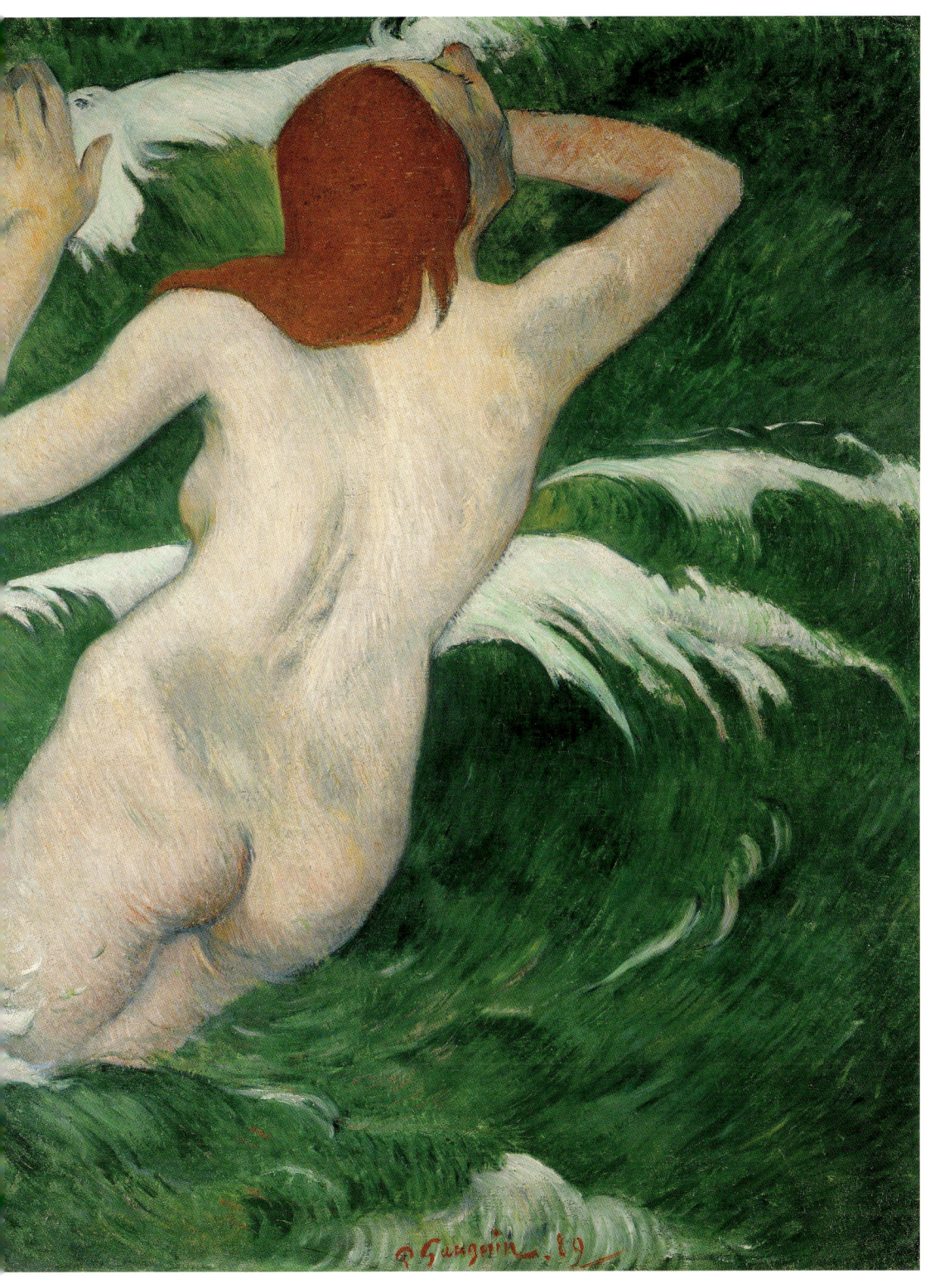

tradition, personal sympathy and individual freedom. The slogans of Impressionism resembled the period's middle-class ideals in stressing dynamic change and progress. Such notions had no place in Gauguin's pursuit of the supernatural.

The monumental crucifix had already figured in the background of *Self-portrait with Yellow Christ* (ill. p. 326). It was a cross Gauguin had seen in the village church at Trémalo, near Pont-Aven. As an image of simple belief, and as a folk artefact, it fitted into Gauguin's visual world very well. And as an element in his self-portrait it implies parallels between artistic creativity and the Creation. Furthermore, the image of God dying in human form suggests in turn that the artist suffers. Gauguin's expression in the picture is one of acute self-centredness that hardly seems to accord with thoughts of suffering and piety. For Gauguin, however, the role of the artist always remained just that: a role. And best of all he liked to put on the mask of the solitary, suffering seer whose creative powers were ignorantly despised.

We see him in that mood in his *Self-portrait* (ill. p. 333). His arrogant air has been replaced by one of despondency and dejection, so that the artist appears before us as a melancholic. Ever since the Renaissance, melancholy had been considered a hallmark of creative people, who were seen as suffering not for any particular reason but because of the general condition of the world, which obliged the artist to practise renunciation.

Fair Harvest, 1889
Oil on canvas, 73 x 92.5 cm
(28¾ x 36½ in.)
Paris, Musée d'Orsay

Gauguin looks so infatuated with himself in this work that we might interpret it as an unintentional caricature, if it were not for the wavy ornamentation that threatens to engulf the artist's head at the centre. There is

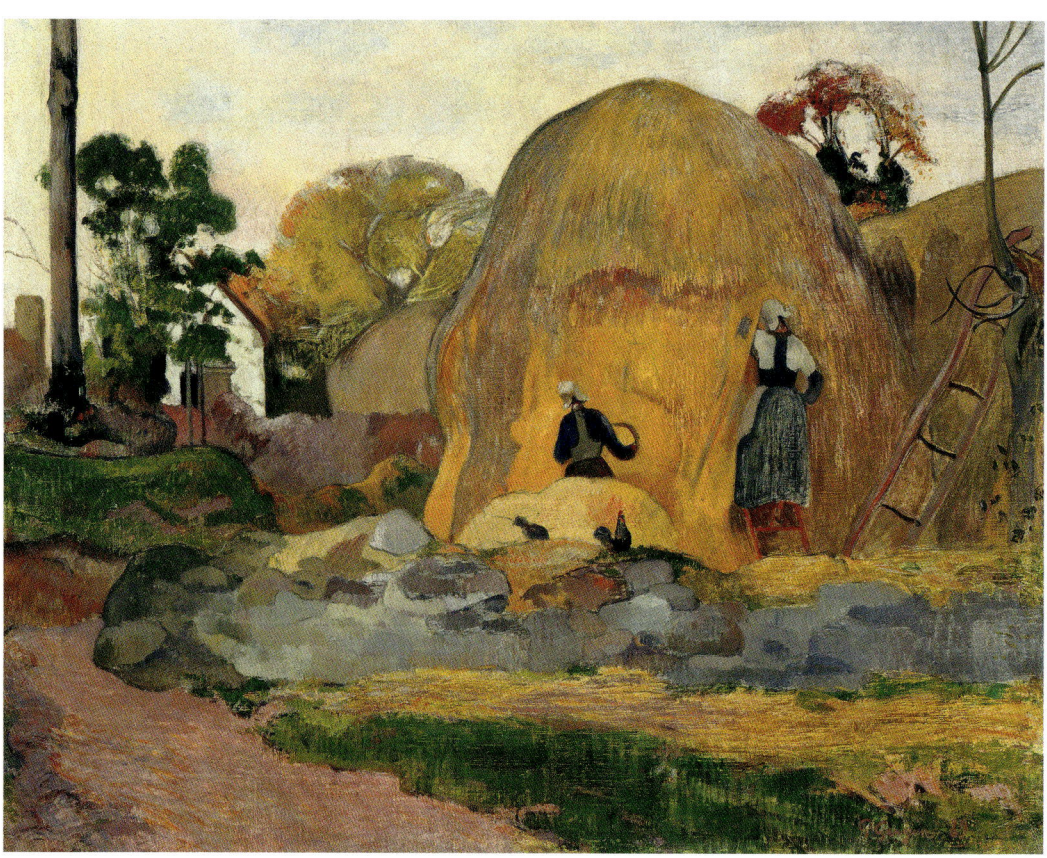

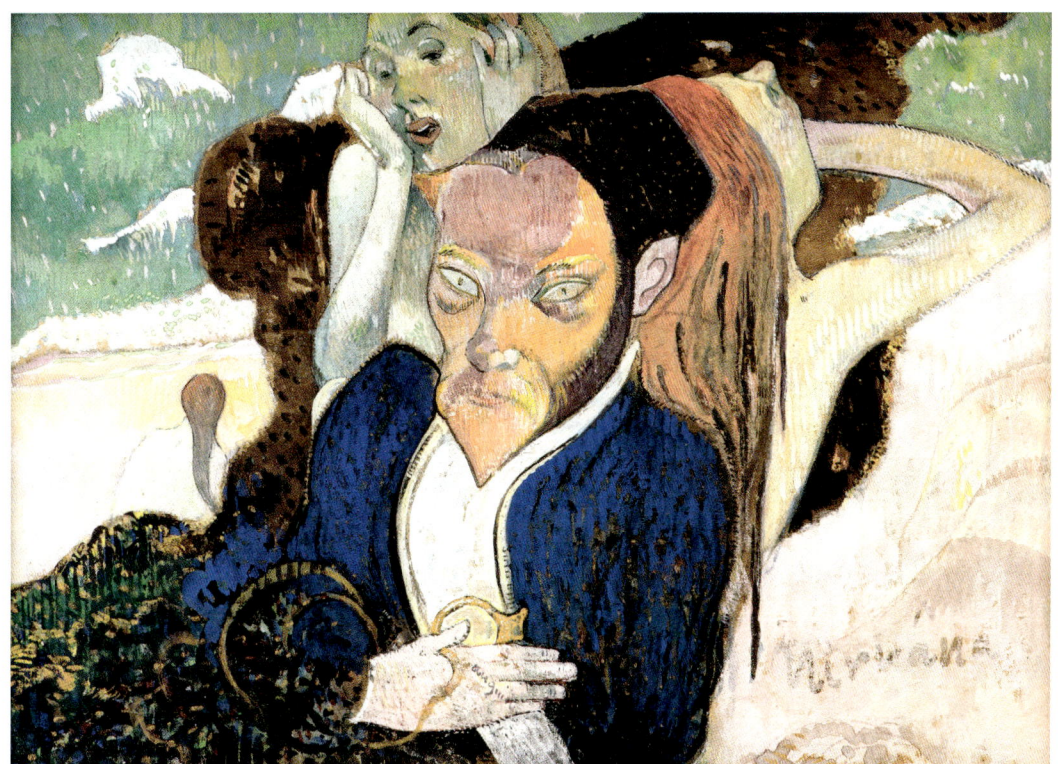

Nirvana: Portrait of Jacob Meijer de Haan, c. 1889/90
Gouache on cotton, 20 x 29 cm (8 x 11½ in.)
Hartford, Connecticut,
Wadsworth Atheneum

no sense of spatial dimensions in the free flow of colours in the background. Three Christian symbols – the apple, the halo and the snake – bridge the gap between representation and abstraction; and it is their association with sin and redemption that makes us see Gauguin's painting with greater sympathy. What emerges from the combination of a seemingly unambiguous expression of woe and decorative elements apparently devoid of meaning is an evocative portrayal of the enigmatic character of the artist.

In the years 1888 to 1891, Gauguin was wholly under the influence of an artistic circle whose avowed aims were to be more inventive, more individual, and quite simply more different, than anyone else. They were dandies who liked to stroll about the streets of Paris eccentrically and strikingly dressed, revelling in the feeling of being outsiders. Writers such as Stéphane Mallarmé and Paul Verlaine were the heart of this circle. Every Tuesday evening there was a soirée at Mallarmé's, where the latest fashions were discussed and plans were made to capture the public limelight with further sensations.

Jean Moréas had published the *Symbolist Manifesto* in 1886, and that had given the clique its name: the Symbolists. They aired their views in the *Mercure de France*, which published Albert Aurier, the only critic to have taken notice of van Gogh during his lifetime. What linked these individualists was their somewhat forced pose of being ahead of their time; affinities united them, however they might disagree on current affairs. In due course, protesting against the movement's obsession with grandeur, Gauguin observed that Symbolism was "no more than another name for a deficient response to life". Still, his paintings of the period demand the same sensitive empathy as Symbolism, irrespective of theoretical notions. And his visionary works require the public to be in tune with him, and

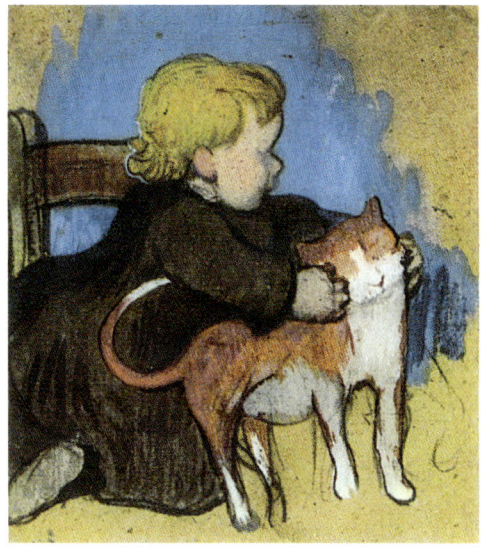

Mimi and Her Cat, 1890
Gouache on cardboard, 17.6 x 16 cm (7 x 6¼ in.)
Private collection

OPPOSITE
La Belle Angèle, 1889
Oil on canvas, 92 x 73.2 cm (36¼ x 28¾ in.)
Paris, Musée d'Orsay

prepared to accept the suggestiveness of different and profounder worlds. If we do not grasp his art instantly, we never shall.

Aurier's essay "Gauguin, or The Symbolist Movement in Painting" was the circle's farewell present when Gauguin departed for the tropics for the second time. It appeared in the March 1891 issue of *Mercure de France* and – ironically enough – used Gauguin's work in order to illustrate the programmatic tenets of Symbolism. Aurier declared that a work of art must possess five characteristics in order to be defined as Symbolist – characteristics that Gauguin's paintings naturally had: (1) "A work of art must be ideative, because its sole ideal must be the expression of an idea." (2) "A work of art must be symbolic, because it gives formal expression to an idea." (3) "A work of art must be synthetic, because it records its forms and signs within a general system of meaning." (4) "A work of art must be subjective, because the object is never viewed qua object but as a sign perceived by the subject." (5) "A work of art must be decorative, because – in the true sense of the word – decorative art as understood by the Egyptians and in all probability by the Greeks and primitive peoples too was nothing other than an artistic revelation which was at once subjective, synthetic, symbolic and ideative." This timely statement gave Gauguin the theoretical support he needed: his art, it seemed, was primitive in the best of senses. Confirmed in his position, he presently felt able to set off in quest of immediate primitive experience in the South Seas.

In a work such as *Ondine* (ill. p. 335) we see Gauguin getting his own back. This woman, who belongs so entirely to the element she personifies, and thus programmatically foregrounds the essential naturalness that the Symbolists insisted is innate to women, could only have been painted by the Gauguin of about 1890. The human figure and the waves merge in a highly artificial, contrived manner that draws upon literary models and stands in direct contradiction to Gauguin's avowed aim of simplicity. The image is no more than an illustration of a story the artist had read. And reading a book, after all, is a quite different business from contemplating the tranquillity of rural life.

But Gauguin still had not a centime for the travels he felt were so urgent. Friends and fellow artists organized a wholesale auction at the Hôtel Drouot in Paris. One reason they were so eager to help may have been that they were feeling pangs of conscience: at one time or another they had all agreed to accompany Gauguin to Tahiti, only to decide they preferred life in the big city to

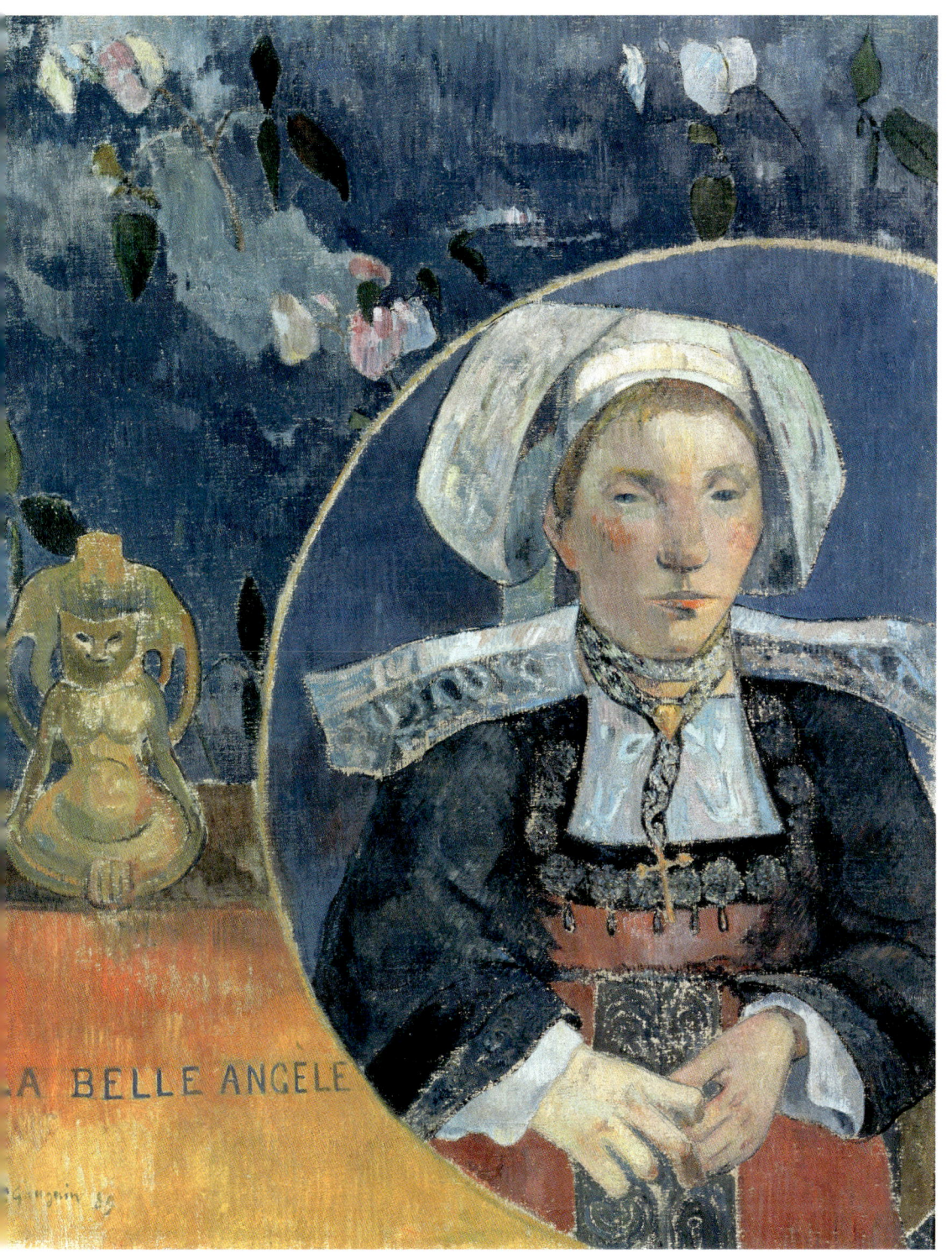

LA BELLE ANGÈLE

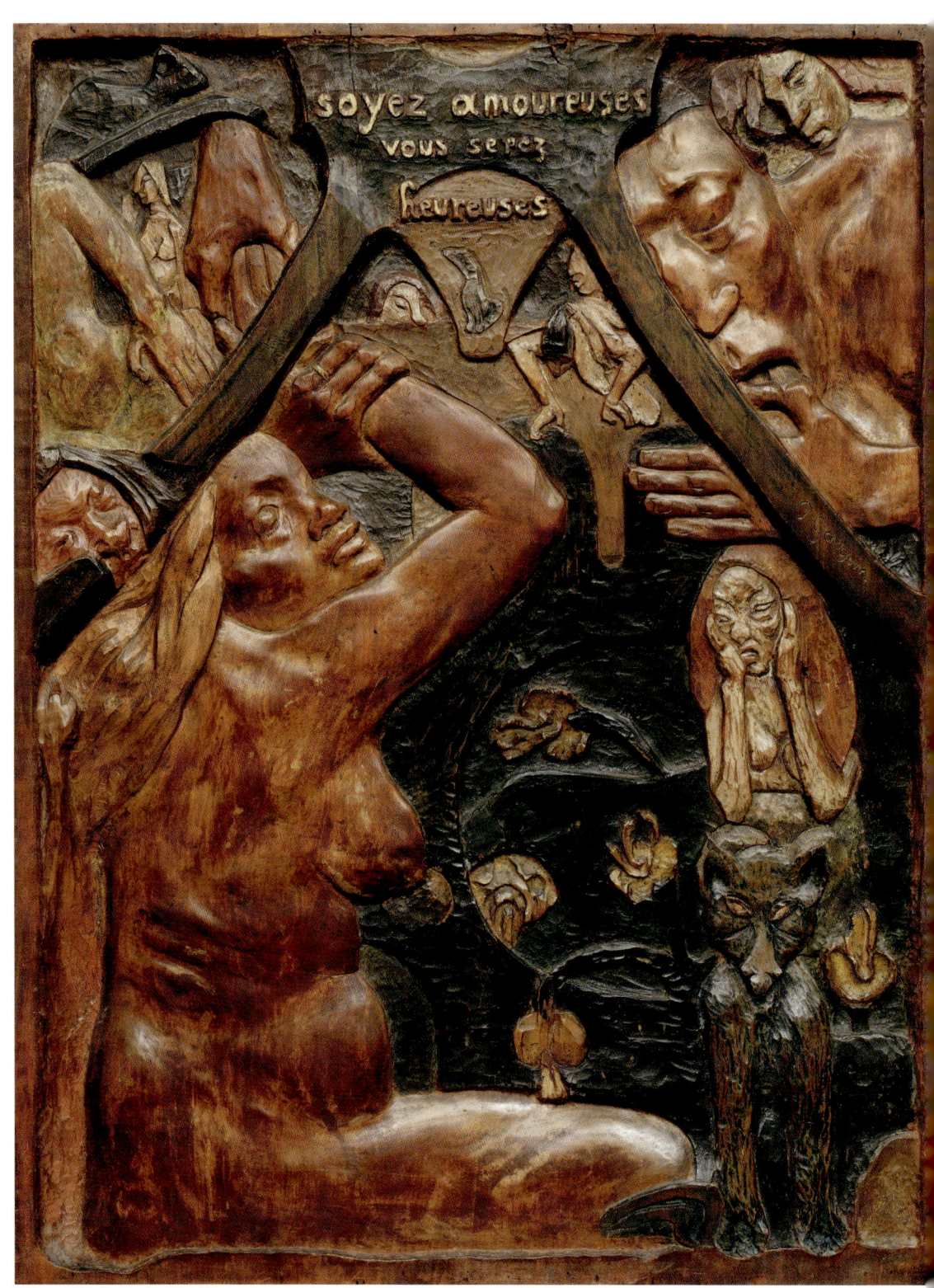

soyez amoureuses
vous serez
heureuses

peaceful boredom in thatched huts beneath a tropical sun. Thirty canvases were offered for sale at the auction. Eighteen months before, at the great Impressionist and Symbolist exhibition in the Café Volpini, Gauguin had failed to sell a single one of the seventeen works he put on show. This time he found purchasers for no fewer than twenty-nine.

Among them was Edgar Degas. He bought *La Belle Angèle* (ill. p. 339) for 450 francs. Doubtless it was not mere chance that led him to choose this picture, combining as it does all Gauguin's principal and characteristic motifs of the past three years: the rustic features of the girl in her Breton costume, with the primitive cult figure posed beside her like an accessory. Both motifs are related to a background of decorative detail; spatial considerations are replaced by a juxtaposition of areas that can be seen to mark out each motif's territory.

The financial success of the auction boosted Gauguin's self-confidence, and in March 1891 he journeyed to Copenhagen. He was hoping, as he wrote to his wife, "to embrace my children without being told by you or your family that I am a worthless individual". The reunion reawakened hopes of family happiness in him, and after his return he wrote in emphatic tones to Mette: "I assure you that in the next three years I shall win my battle, so that we – you and I – will be able to live safe from troubles and cares … Farewell, dear Mette, dear children. Keep me in your hearts. And when I come back we shall marry anew."

Plainly Gauguin saw his art as a mission, a task that he had to perform and for the sake of which he had to forgo domestic happiness. Viewed in this way, his move to the South Seas appears to have been made less in hope of a life of bliss than with a sense of needing purification. Gauguin's conception of art had always included a reverent feeling that piety and faith were essentials in life; now, as he wrote his letter of parting, art itself acquired a religious dimension.

A grand farewell buffet was organized at the Café Voltaire, a favourite rendezvous. Mallarmé, as master of ceremonies, drank a toast to Gauguin's future return. People drank, acted and read out poems. Gauguin is reported to have been very depressed; he was seen weeping, and staring blankly into nowhere. Nevertheless, on 4 April 1891 he left Paris by the night train. He was bound for faraway Tahiti.

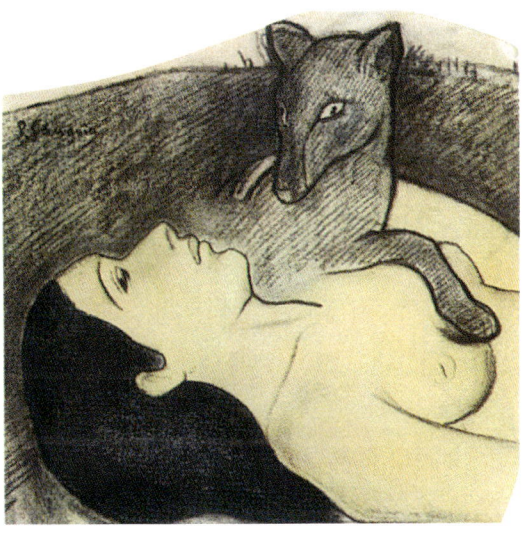

OPPOSITE
Be in Love and You Will Be Happy", 1889
"Soyez amoureuses vous serez heureuses"
Carved and painted linden wood,
95 x 72 cm (37½ x 28¼ in.)
Boston, Museum of Fine Arts

Girl with Fox, *c.* 1890/91
Study for the painting *The Loss of Virginity*, 1890/91
(Norfolk, Virginia, Chrysler Museum of Art)
Chalk on paper, 31.3 x 32.5 cm (12¼ x 12¾ in.)
Chicago, Block Museum

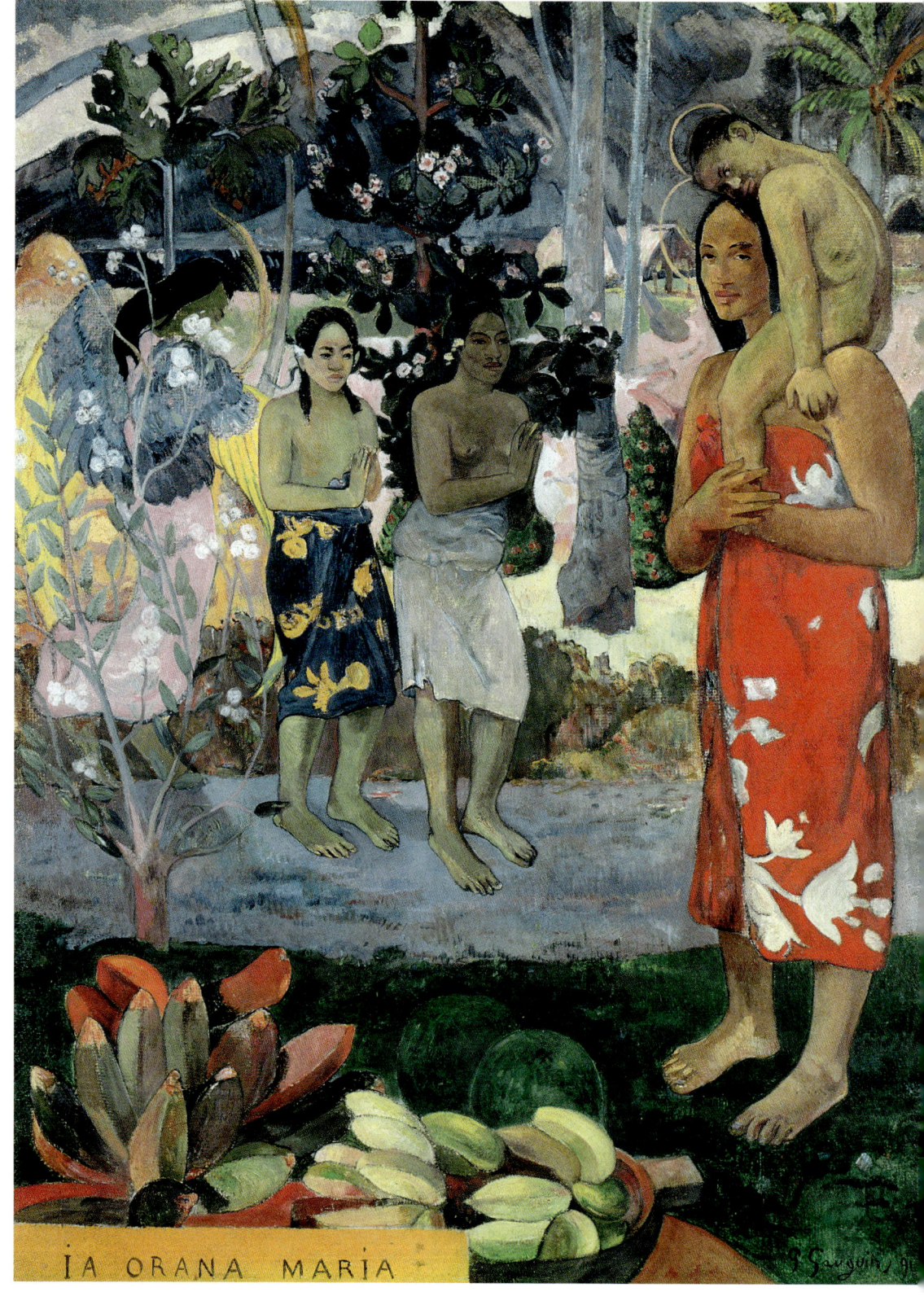

IA ORANA MARIA

Tahiti: A Studio in the Tropics
1891–1893

Tahiti was no longer quite the paradise that the stage-set magic of the world fair had promised. Discovered in 1767, the Pacific island was now a mere colony, where French officials and soldiers strutted about as self-importantly as they did back home. And Gauguin's repeated and enthusiastic insistence on Primitivism paled a little once he was on the spot. The painter, seen as a kind of ambassador from the homeland, was given an official reception at the harbour; and in his pocket he had a letter of recommendation, doubtless intended to make his alien environment more bearable. The governor himself attended, and ceremonially welcomed the rebel – who affected to be enduring society's contempt with heroic patience. The nature of his arrival exposes the character of Gauguin's South Seas adventure: he went as a colonist. Not, it is true, as a colonist bent on political subjugation, but as one who wanted to take from the local culture whatever he felt could be of use in the Old World.

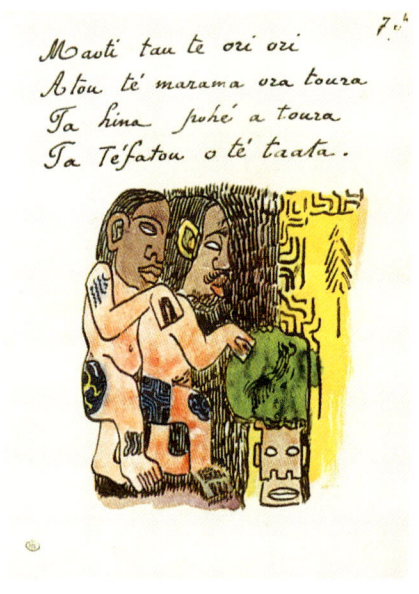

"We're wasting our time here," the critic Charles Morice complained, shivering in a wintry Paris and daydreaming of the adventurous Gauguin. Paul Signac, who doubted the artistic value of the journey from the outset, was more sceptical: "A man who paints black in the North and blue in the South is a buffoon." Of course the Symbolist belief in the all-powerful supremacy of the imagination was certain to provoke questions concerning Gauguin's aims; after all, anyone with the necessary imagination hardly needed to travel halfway round the world to instil new verve into his art.

Gauguin was aware of the dangers. But his wish to find out about the Polynesian peoples and their culture, and to get to know them as wholly and informally as his European background and education permitted, was genuine – and he leapt in at the deep end. His letters home show how good his intentions were: "It was like decay and blossoming, law and fidelity,

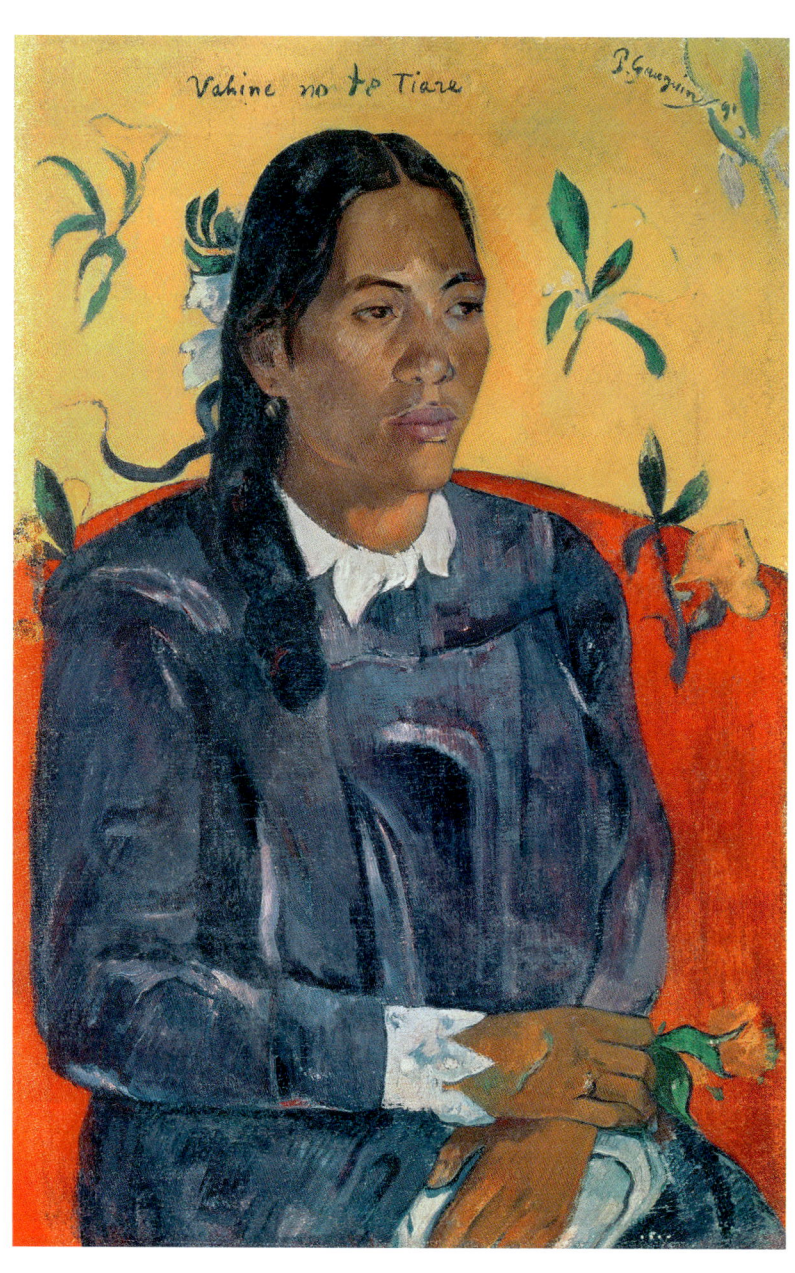

Woman with a Flower, 1891
"Vahine no te Tiare"
Oil on canvas, 70 x 46 cm (27½ x 18 in.)
Copenhagen, Ny Carlsberg Glyptotek

Brooding Woman, 1891
"Te Faaturuma"
Oil on canvas, 91.1 x 68.7 cm (36 x 27 in.)
Worcester Art Museum

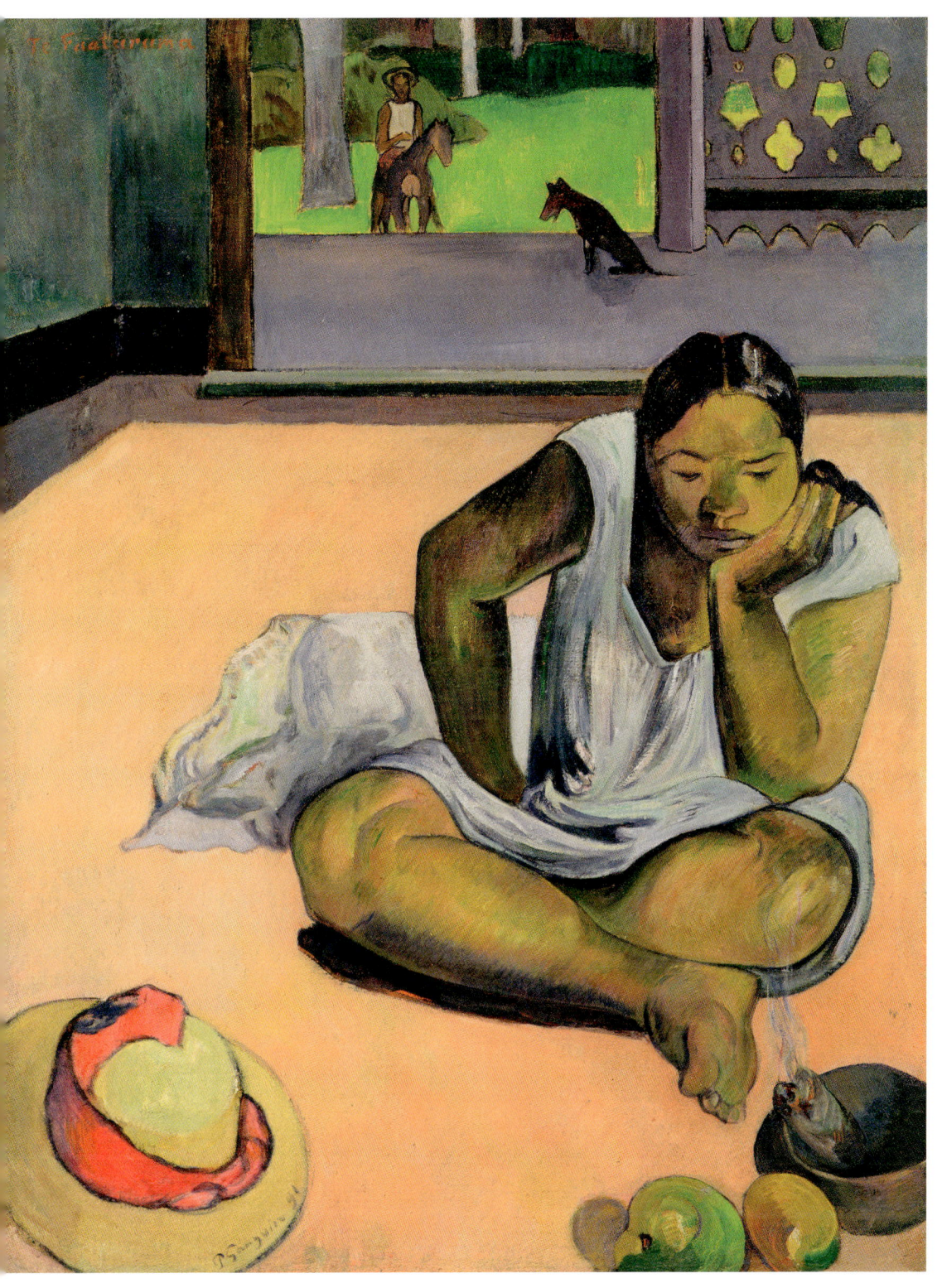

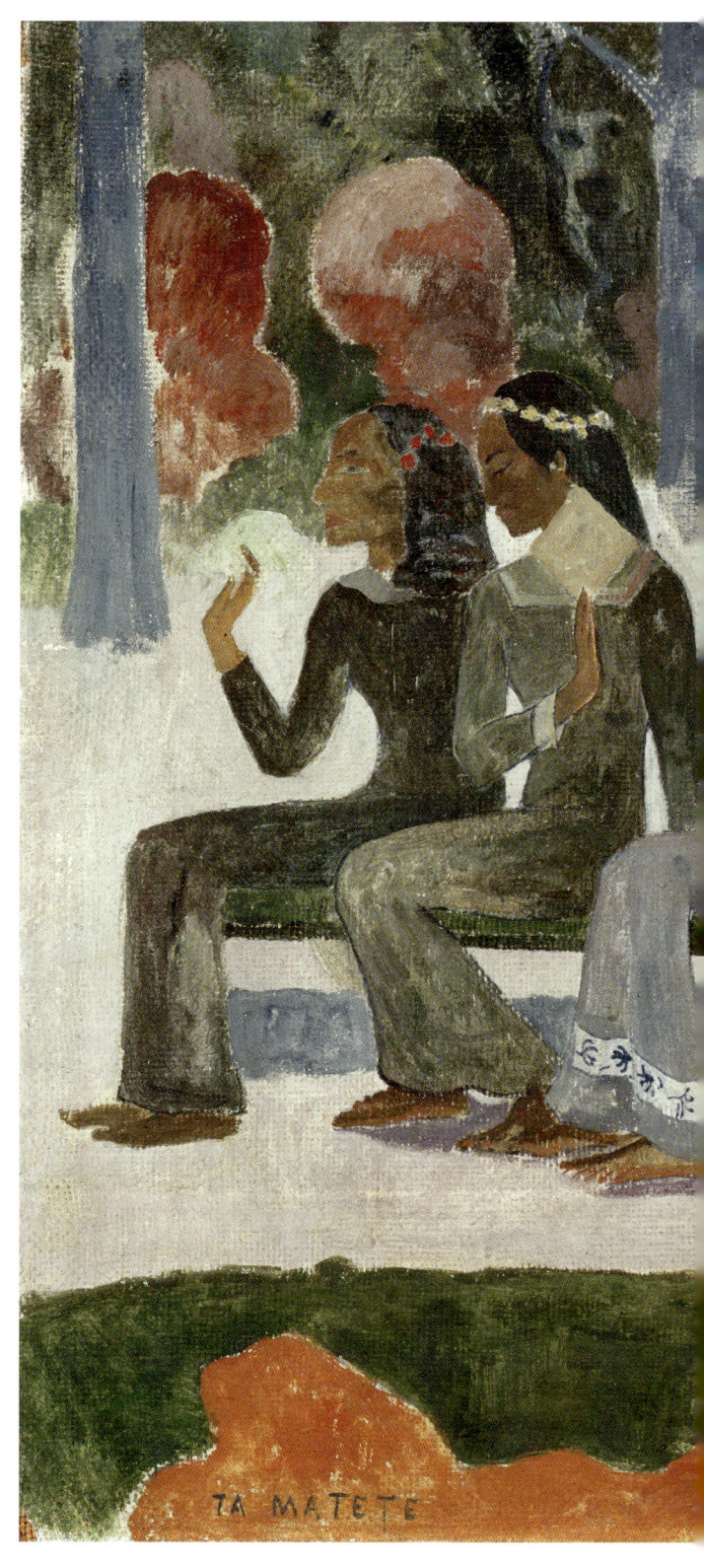

We Shall Not Go to Market Today, 1892
"Ta Matete"
Oil on jute, 73.2 x 91.5 cm (28¾ x 36 in.)
Kunstmuseum Basel

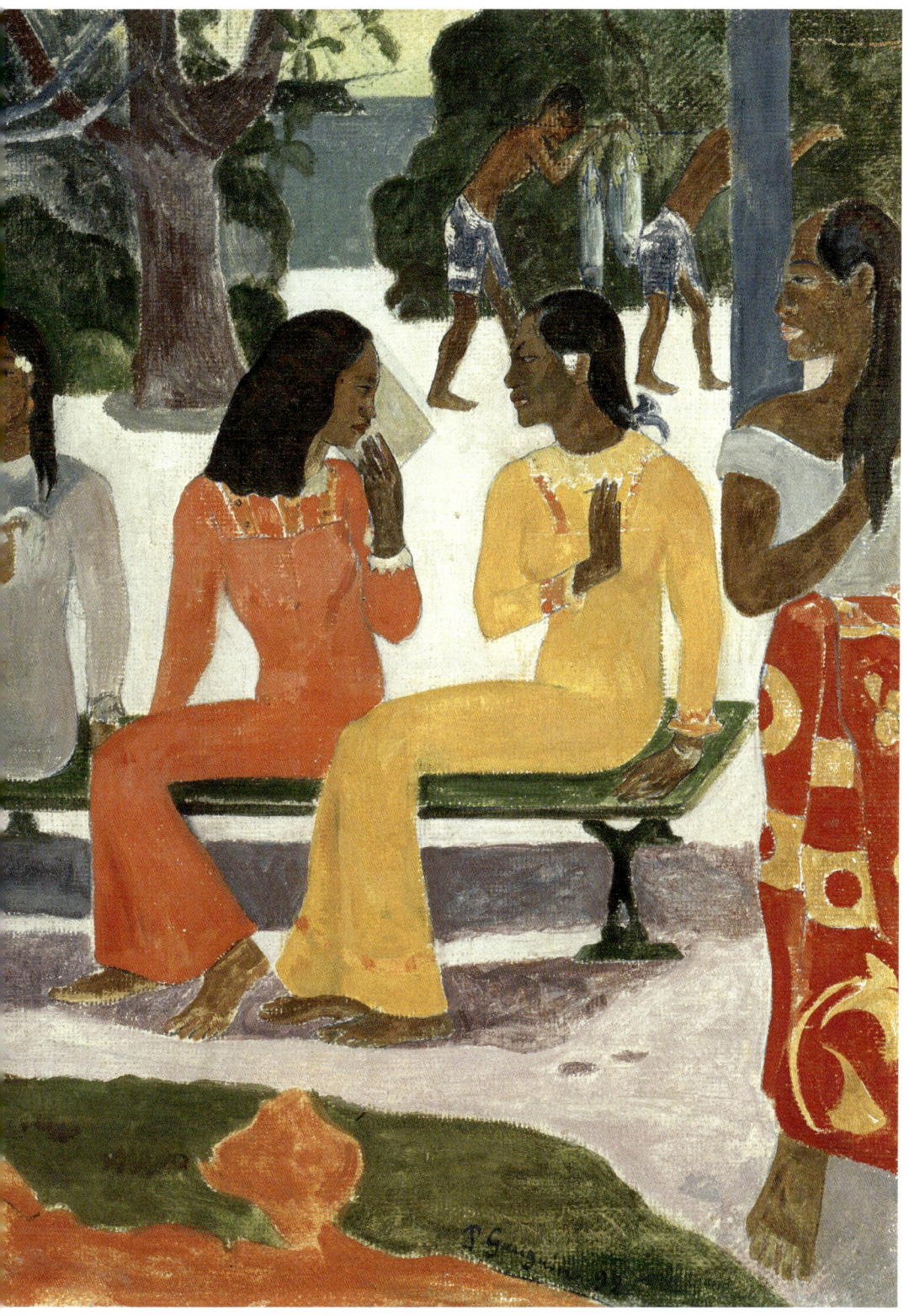

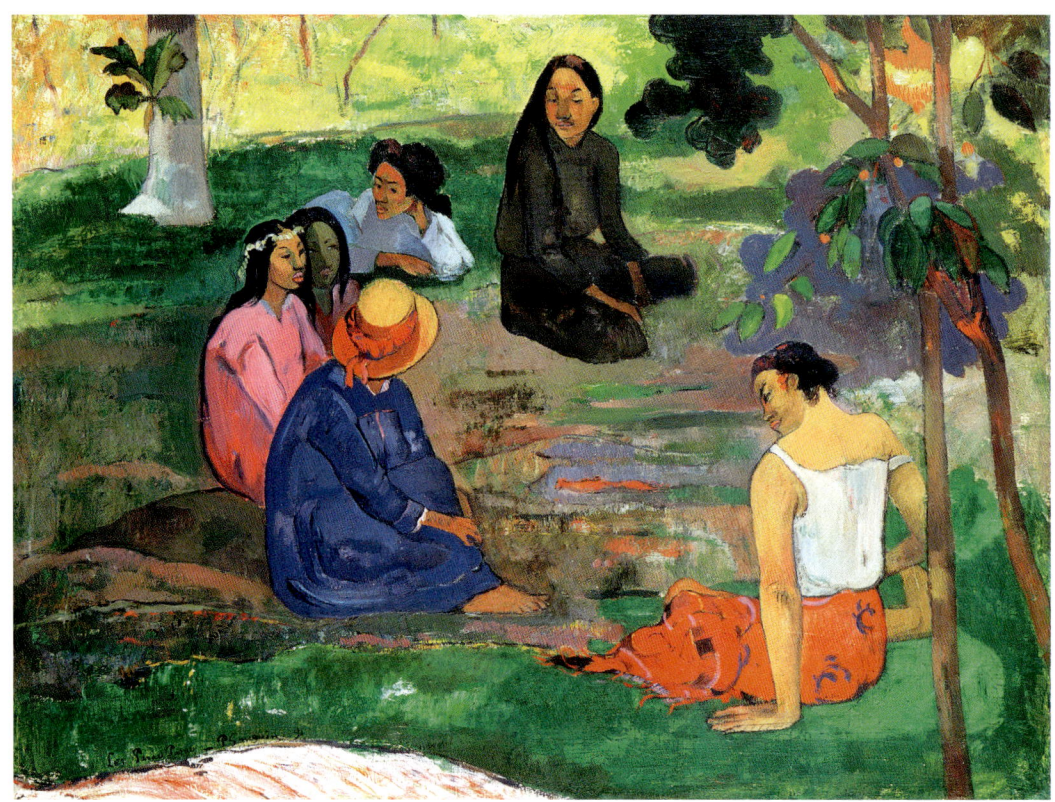

Conversation, 1891
"Les Parau Parau"
Oil on canvas, 70.5 x 90.3 cm (27¾ x 35½ in.)
St Petersburg, Hermitage Museum

artificiality and naturalness – there was the evil one, breathing her impurity and lies and wickedness over the good woman," he wrote, contrasting the wife of a French gendarme with a local beauty. He hadn't a positive thing to say about Europe any more; and by the same token his rosy view of the tropics was coloured by his dreams and preconceptions. We see the words "Ia Orana Maria" in Roman characters at the bottom-left corner of the painting of that name (ill. p. 342). The words mean "Hail Mary" and, like the lettering, the subject of the picture returns us to Europe.

Gauguin transposes the Christian story of the Son of God to a South Seas setting; and, like Christian missionaries who took for granted that foreign peoples would give them an enthusiastic welcome, the painter places his own religion in the foreground. Everyone in this Nativity, the mother and child and the women approaching to worship, is Polynesian. Part-concealed in the greenery, however, there is also an angel, as if in wait, with the same golden wings as the angel in *Vision after the Sermon*. The setting may be more colourful, decorative and varied, but the principle of mixing the everyday and the supernatural has survived from Gauguin's Brittany days.

The folk piety of the Pont-Aven pictures stands revealed as implicitly political in the new work. The local people had not been spared the colonizers' Christian evangelizing, and their own gods were now at odds with the Christian diety. Gauguin described the beliefs of a young woman named Tehura, a Polynesian beauty, in these terms: "I do not really know how she reconciles Jesus and Taaroa in her belief. I suspect she worships both." He saw this as one of the islanders' many miraculous talents, an intuitive ability to reconcile opposites. It was an ability he was himself questing for, and which he therefore assumed the local people possessed; but he missed the yawning gap that had opened up between traditional and imposed beliefs. He had wanted to hold a mirror up to his own world, and that meant that his paintings had to testify to that better world he was convinced he would find in the South Seas. Almost everything he wrote about daily life on Tahiti smacked of the utopian. The negative elements, without which life is in fact lifeless, were largely eliminated from his paintings.

Gauguin later recorded his memories of the first Tahiti stay in his book *Noa Noa*. The title is the native name for the island and means "scented land". Gauguin writes of fantastic beauty and tranquillity; but *Noa Noa*, of course, was written for a European audience. It was published in instalments beginning in 1897, and was calculated to excite middle-class readers' longing for exotic places. It is thus difficult to tell how Gauguin genuinely felt at the time. He presented the island as a paradise, and his paintings and letters from Tahiti conjured up a dream landscape – yet always in contrast with civilized France, of course, which Gauguin affected to despise. His very wish to create art was a product of that civilization. And it certainly did not occur to Gauguin to abandon that wish.

Some thirty miles from Papeete, the Tahitian capital, Gauguin set up house in a bamboo hut in the jungle district of Mataiea. Tehura became his live-in lover, and he told her mischievous tales of his wife, saying he had a photograph of her. The "photograph" was a reproduction of Édouard Manet's scandalous nude *Olympia* (1863, Musée d'Orsay, Paris) which Gauguin had pinned up and which doubled as Mette when he told his stories. With the choice between the innocent nakedness of the native people on

"What's New?", 1892
"Parau Api"
Oil on canvas, 67 x 92 cm (26½ x 36¼ in.)
Dresden, Galerie Neue Meister,
Staatliche Kunstsammlungen

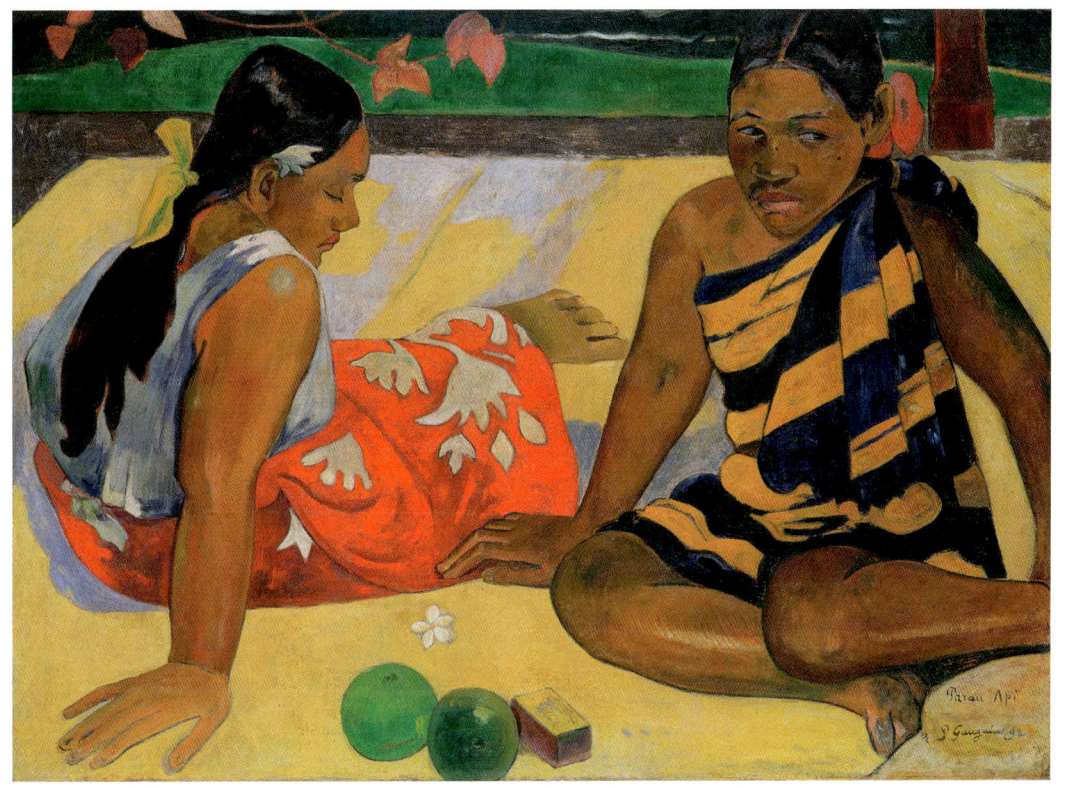

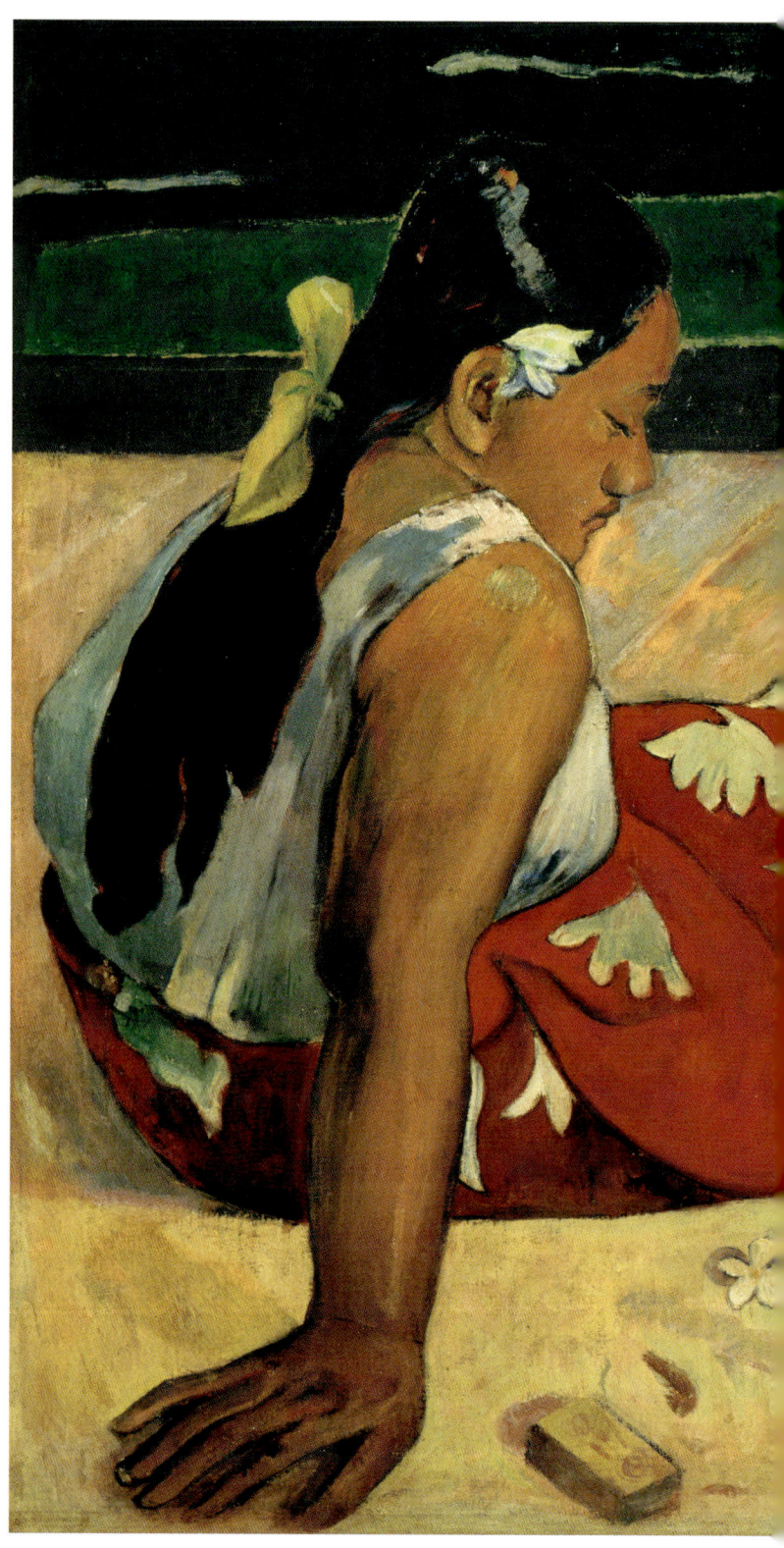

*Two Women
on the Beach*, 1891
Oil on canvas,
69 x 91.5 cm (27¼ x 36 in.)
Paris, Musée d'Orsay

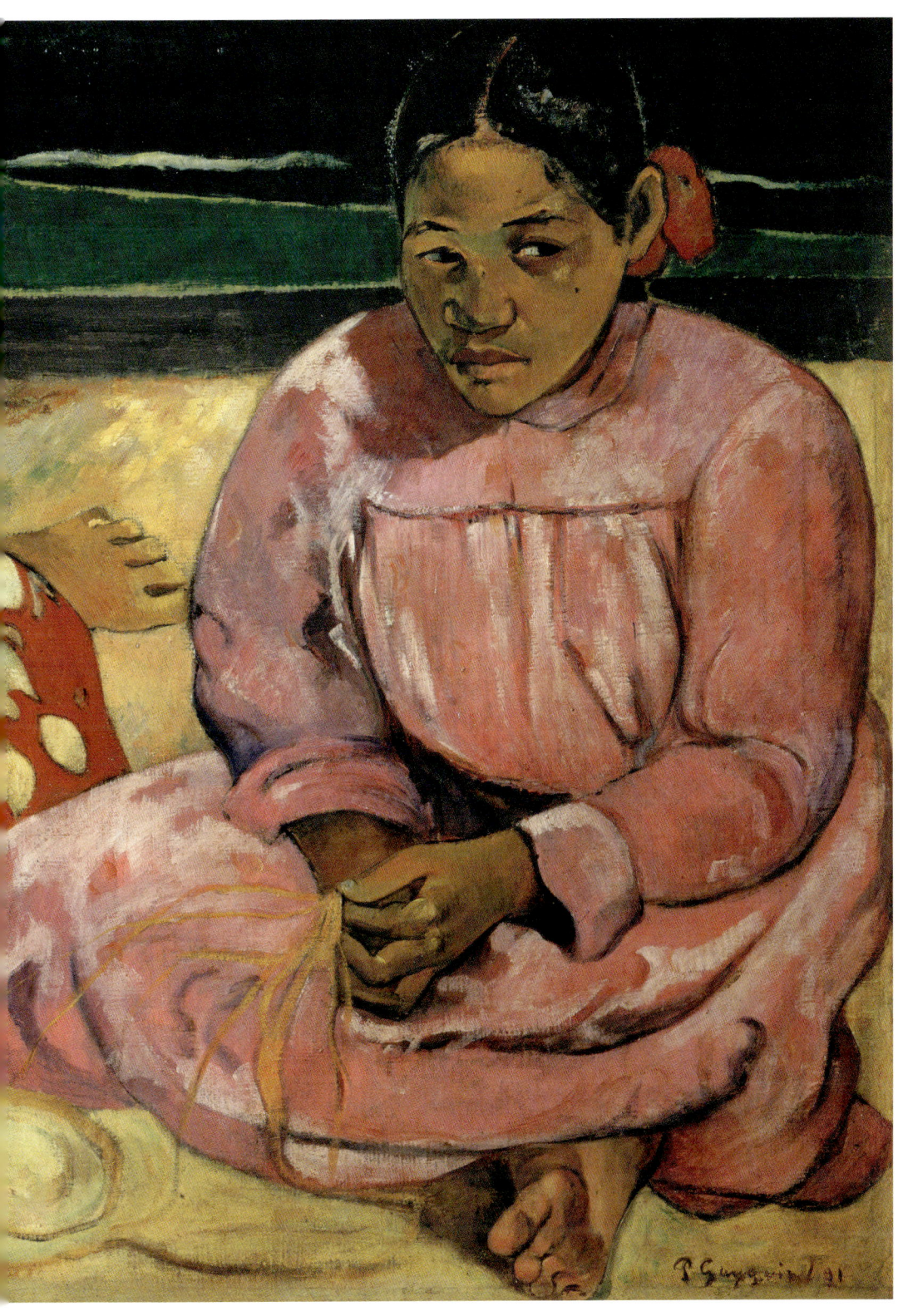

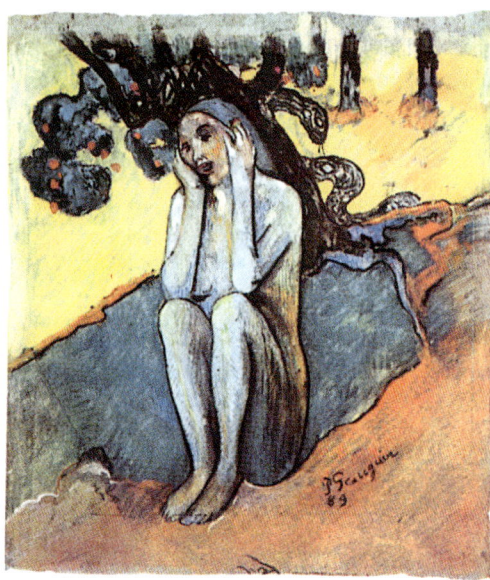

Eve, 1889
Watercolour and pastel on paper,
33.7 x 31.1 cm (13¼ x 12¼ in.)
San Antonio, McNay Art Museum

OPPOSITE
Woman with a Mango, 1892
"Vahine no te Vi"
Oil on canvas, 73 x 45.1 cm (28¾ x 17¾ in.)
Baltimore Museum of Art,
The Cone Collection

the one hand, and civilization's notoriously ambiguous double standards on the other, Gauguin was apparently more likely to find his ideal woman in Manet's nude than in the simple, graceful women of the village.

"Out in the open yet intimate, beneath the shady trees, with women whispering in a mighty palace designed by nature itself," wrote Gauguin in *Noa Noa*, describing the ambience of *Conversation* (ill. p. 348). We see a group of the local people sitting in a circle, relaxed and talking. Gauguin's approach is still that of the remote outsider; there is nothing contrived in the handling of the foreground, and the people merge into the restrained colourfulness of the setting.

The approach is the same in *Brooding Woman* (ill. p. 345). The Tahitian girl is seen with a new closeness and directness, although we still sense a discrepancy between the model and the picture's format. It is as if Gauguin were painting as an anthropologist, and the details of the hut are included as though for study purposes. The naturalness of the hut, the carvings that adorn the rear wall, and the objects the girl has collected, are all essential components in the portrait – which (as usual) does not tell us the model's name. During his time on Tahiti, Gauguin was not interested in the individuality of his subjects. Still, in the first pictures he painted he was plainly trying to capture the environment that was to become his artistic home.

"In any country I first need a gestation period," wrote Gauguin, describing the problems he encountered in coming to terms artistically with his new life. "I first have to grasp the essence of the plants and trees, of the vast variety of nature, which is so capricious and so copious and refuses to be defined or taken hold of." During his first years on Tahiti he painted relatively few pictures; the new lease of artistic life he had anticipated was proving slow to materialize. Indeed, even on the island, which seemed so easy-going and delightful, he was plagued by bad moods. "For some time I had been surly and dejected. And my work was suffering. I lacked certain essentials, and it was depressing to find myself powerless to tackle the artistic tasks confronting me. But above all I simply wasn't in the mood."

It was this frame of mind that produced paintings such as *Brooding Woman*. The melancholy that supposedly afflicts the creative had him in its power again – and he projected his own moods onto

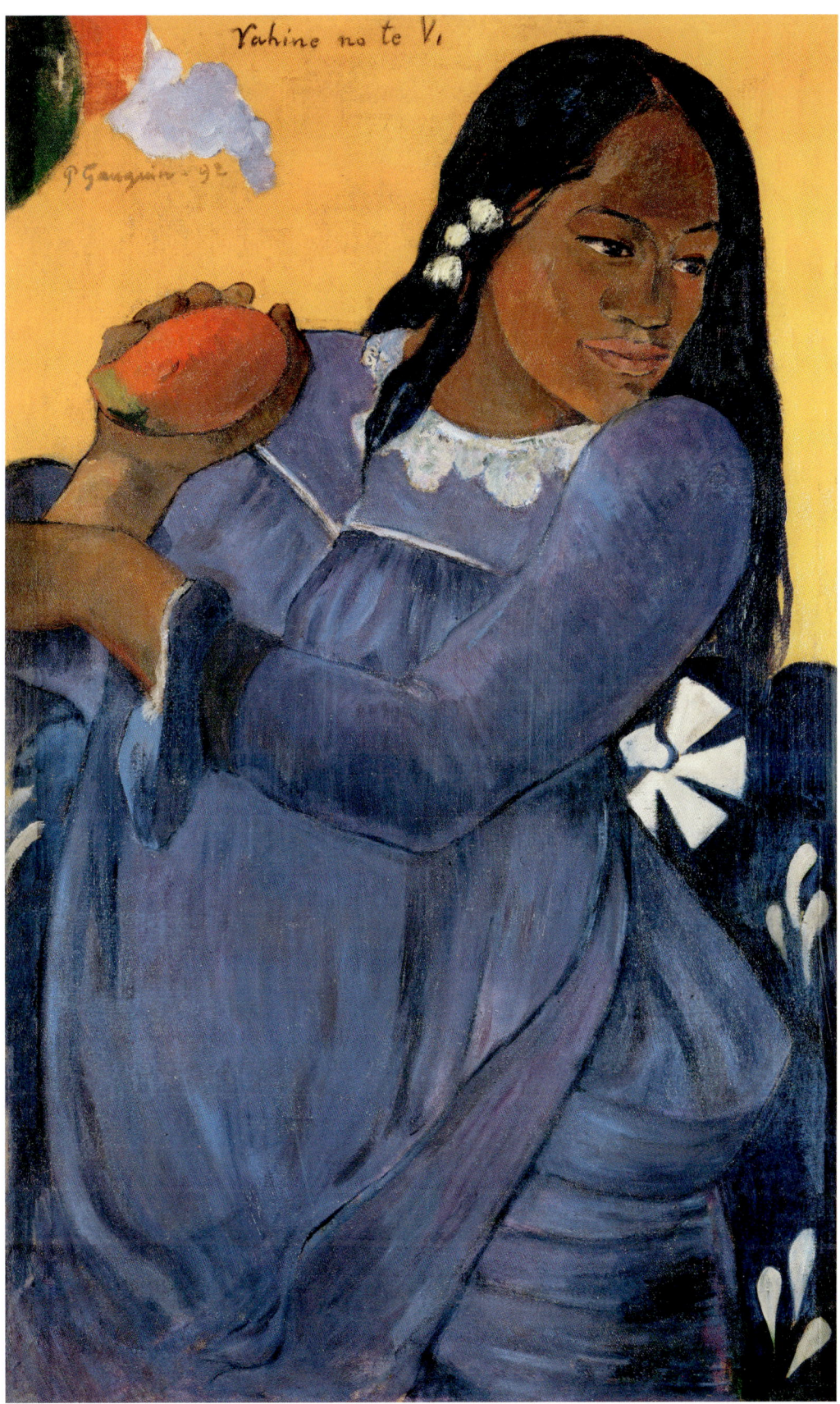

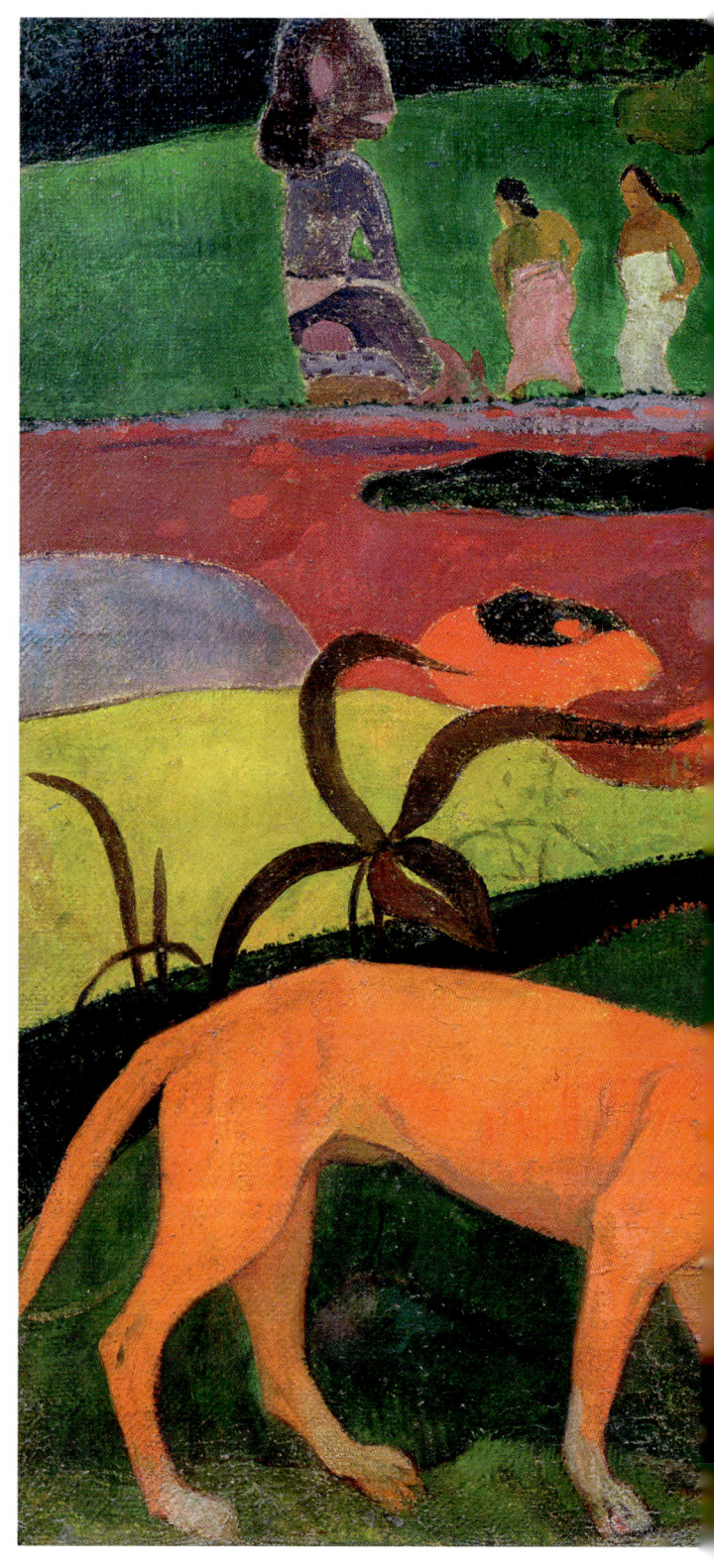

Joyeuseté, 1892
"Arearea"
Oil on canvas,
74.5 x 93.5 cm (29¼ x 36¾ in.)
Paris, Musée d'Orsay

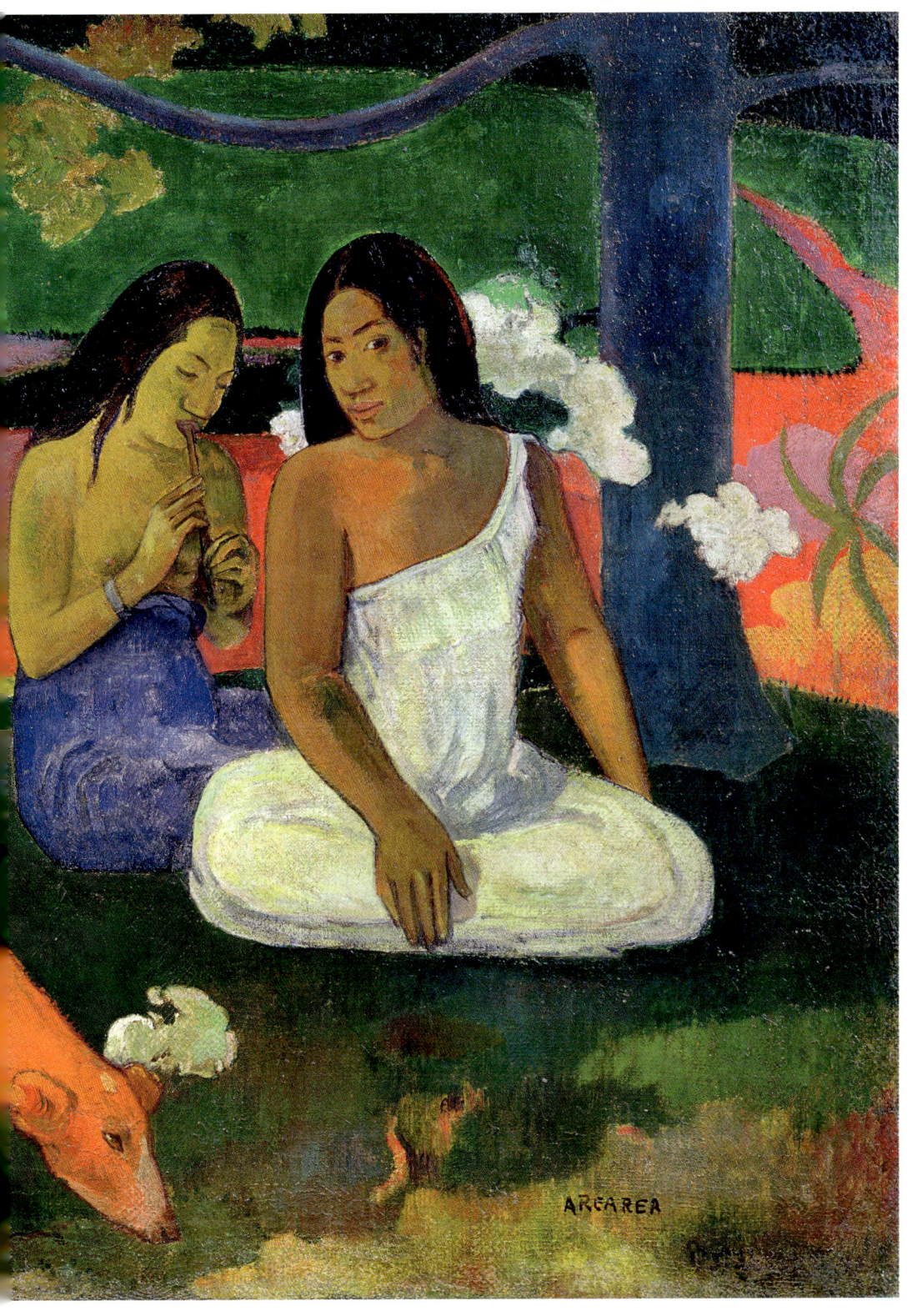

ARÉAREA

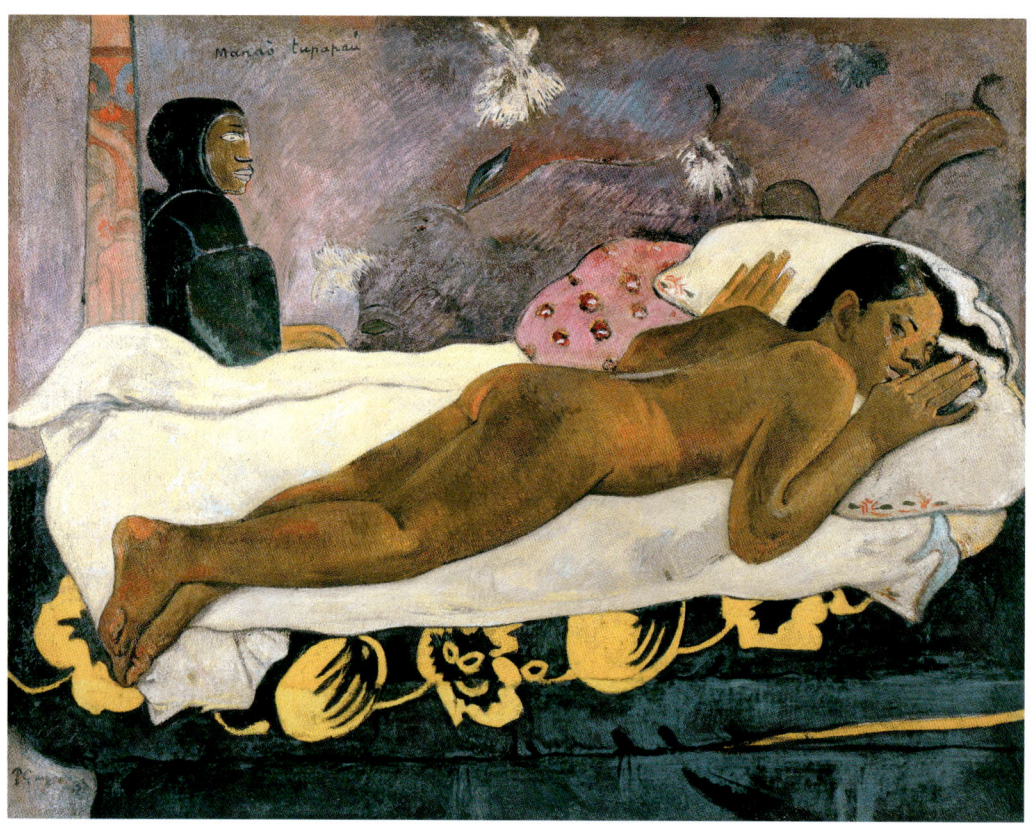

Spirit of the Dead Watching, 1892
"Manao tupapaú"
Oil on burlap mounted on canvas,
73 x 92 cm (28¾ x 36¼ in.)
Buffalo, New York, Albright-Knox Art Gallery,
A. Conger Goodyear Collection

the Tahitian people, without troubling to ask if it were right to do so. They too (he claimed) had creative powers. Their indolence was part of their view of life, and they did not see work as the most important thing. They lolled drowsily in the sun, immersed in peaceful talk, taking the day as it came.

In his portraits of Tahitian beauties, Gauguin was trying to reconcile the graceful idleness of the island people with his own sorrowfulness. But the two outlooks on life were radically different.

The best example of his attempt at this is *Woman with a Flower* (ill. p. 344). The painting uses the same background as the *Self-portrait* (ill. p. 333), but this time the abstract pattern in fact does no more than provide the rearward limit of the picture. The woman portrayed is not hopelessly at the mercy of ornamental colours and lines, but instead sits with a monumental presence. In her right hand she holds a flower, symbolic of growth and fertility. In the self-portrait, the passion flowers echoed Gauguin's own wretchedness and misery; but in the new painting their significance pales before the tranquil charisma of the woman. In the self-portrait, Gauguin's compulsive efforts to establish several levels of meaning had resulted in a bold but tawdry exhibitionism; but in the new painting his respect for the woman's ingenuous dignity is dominant. It is an honest attempt to represent the clash of different cultures, where civilized sophistication meets natural simplicity.

In *Woman with a Mango* (ill. p. 353), Gauguin's sensitivity towards that polarity takes on the form of European classical iconography. Evidently Gauguin had abandoned his wish to appropriate a primitive language to his own use. The physical presence of this woman, carrying her fertility symbol

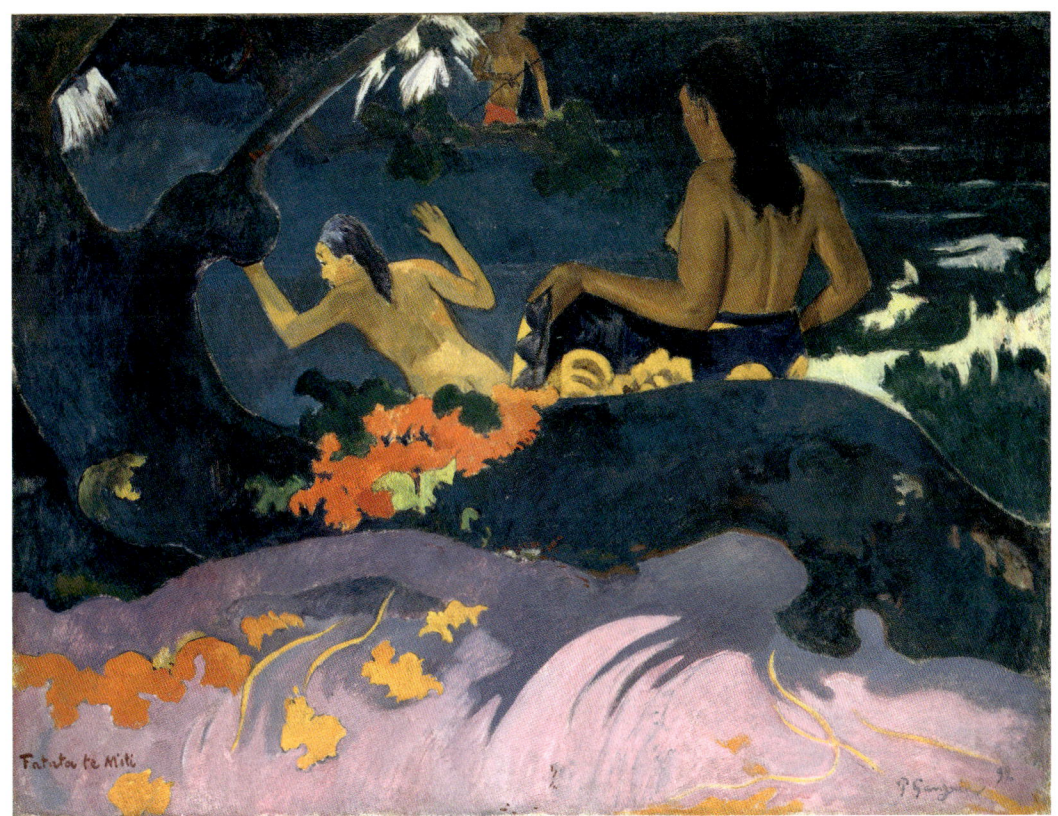

Near the Sea, 1892
"Fatata te Miti"
Oil on canvas, 67.9 x 91.5 cm (26¾ x 36 in.)
Washington, D.C., National Gallery of Art,
Chester Dale Collection

as a saint might carry her attribute, was conceived in the visual terms of a Giotto or a Leonardo. The decorative detail was kept to a minimum, and the massive figure of the woman filled the canvas without any need for the painter to indulge his talent. It is rare for Gauguin to acknowledge roots in Western art so unambiguously; but we see that when he does avail himself of traditional modes his work no longer appears in any way contrived and indeed acquires a dimension of natural inevitability that remains impressive, irrespective of fashions in art.

Gauguin preferred not to name his models; and not only their identities but even their very sex is often unclear. He saw them with a European eye, to which people of a different race often looked alike. It was the colonist's typical way of seeing; but in Gauguin there was also that love of reconciling opposites that led him to stylize the Tahitian people as if they were mythical creatures. Hermaphroditism is an ancient notion: even the account of Eve's creation from Adam's rib given in Genesis reflects the idea. In Gauguin's day, the Symbolists had revived the notion. And Paul Gauguin, in his island paradise, had all the time in the world to experience the merging of the sexes, or at least to effect that merging in his dreams and paintings. "With the sensuous animal grace of the androgyne," wrote Gauguin in *Noa Noa*, "he walked before me. It seemed as if the profusion of plant life all around were embodied in him, vital and alive. Was it a man that walked before me? Was it a childhood friend who attracted by virtue of his simplicity and his complexity? Or was it not rather the forest itself, living, sexless and seductive?"

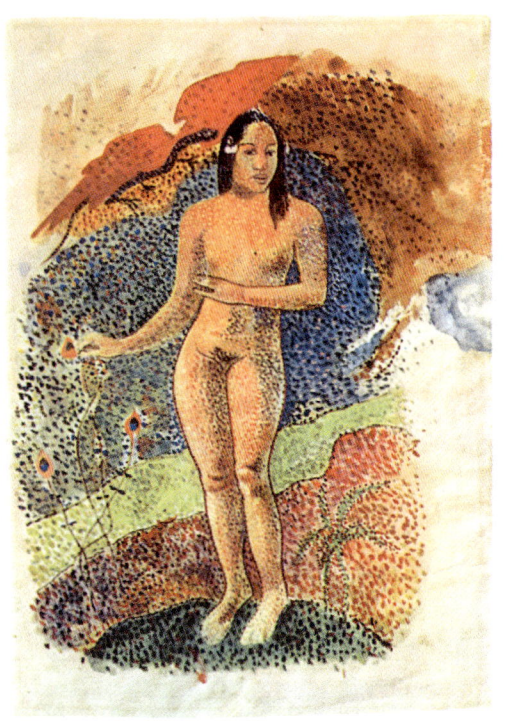

In these words, everything is unsettled and in flux. Man and woman, child and adult, man and nature merge. The duality of body and soul, always a torment to Westerners, and at the root of the new psychoanalysis of Gauguin's day, is conspicuous by its absence. Gauguin felt as if he had penetrated to the core of human nature, and tirelessly he extolled the unspoilt harmony of that imaginary world – which he perceived only from a distance.

Near the Sea (ill. p. 357) is one of his attempts to capture that imaginary world in appropriate imagery. The harmony of mankind and the elements is symbolized most clearly in the positions of the women: the figure in the foreground is slowly stripping, offering herself to the sea, while the second woman is bent over with her arms raised, as if in worship. These attitudes of offering and worship represent a process of unification with nature that has ritual and cultic qualities and indeed seems religious. A quest for that same unification can be seen on Gauguin's part, in his use of elaborate formal decoration and colouring: through his artistic technique, through the sensual colourfulness of abstract patterns, the painter attempted to create a harmony of Man and Nature.

One of the means of creating such a harmony is known as synaesthesia. In painting, synaesthesia relates to the art's proximity to music, dance or drama: an appeal is made not only to the eye but also to all the senses, and the rhythms of form and colour are equivalent to the rhythms of sound and movement. The Symbolists had revived this concept of synaesthesia, which had been largely neglected since the Classicist separation of the various artistic genres. A "complete" work of art should be intoxicatingly staged so as to grip the beholder; Edgar Allan Poe's statement that "the greatest praise we can bestow on a poet is that he seems to be seeing with his ear" might have served as a motto for this kind of aesthetic.

One of Gauguin's most ambitious attempts at putting the principle of synaesthesia into practice was *Joyeuseté* (ill. pp. 354/355). We see two Tahitians of scarcely distinguishable sex, and a dog. Both the human forms and the animal are handled in glowing colours, in such a way as to establish them on the same level of natural, animal existence. The woman playing the flute, and the background figures performing a ritual dance before an idol, call forth associations with music. Gauguin's painting aims to produce a sense of peaceful elation in us, so that we ourselves can imagine we feel the grace of nature and of music that the picture's colourful play of patterns and forms presents. Here too, Gauguin presupposes that we are in sympathy with his views and responses. And only if we are will we be able to feel the nature of the artist's intuitions.

During the Tahiti years, Gauguin expanded his artistic repertoire only slightly. In Brittany he had learnt how to alternate the figurative and the abstract, how to use colour without reference to its representational function, and how to balance foreground close-ups with the compelling pull of visual depth; and in the South Seas he employed the same approach. But if his work did not develop in formal respects, he certainly acquired new subjects. The change of environment, with its unfamiliar greenery and myths, gave Gauguin a new artistic line to follow. He repeatedly described the idyllic way of life he claimed to have found. Call the brave new world an Elysium, arcadia, utopia or what you will, Gauguin discovered it all on Tahiti.

God's covenant with mankind applied in the South Seas too: indeed, in that unspoilt, simple world the deity could even take a human wife, and father a new and happier race of people. That, at least, was what Gauguin's lover Tehura told him. The myth suited his notions of Polynesia, and furthermore contained elements that were familiar to a European. Zeus, after all, had occasionally had his pleasure of mere mortals. And the God of the Old Testament had singled out His chosen people. According to Tehura, the supreme god Oro had fallen in love with Vairaumati and had chosen her to be the progenitress of a people to whom paradise would be open wide. Gauguin related the myth himself in *Noa Noa*: "To receive him, Vairaumati had prepared a spread of the most wonderful fruits and a bed of the finest and rarest materials. Filled with divine grace and strength, they abandoned themselves to love in the groves and meadows. Every morning the god would return to the peak of Paia, and every evening he descended to sleep with her."

Her Name Is Vairaumati (ill. p. 363) illustrates the story. The exotic beauty is seen waiting for her lover, smoking. At present he can only be seen in the form given him by man, as a stone

OPPOSITE
Tahitian Eve, c. 1892
Watercolour and pastel on paper,
40 x 32 cm (15¾ x 12½ in.)
Musée de Grenoble

Tahitian Landscape, 1891
Oil on canvas, 68 x 92.3 cm (26¾ x 36¼ in.)
The Minneapolis Institute of Arts,
Julius C. Eliel Memorial Fund

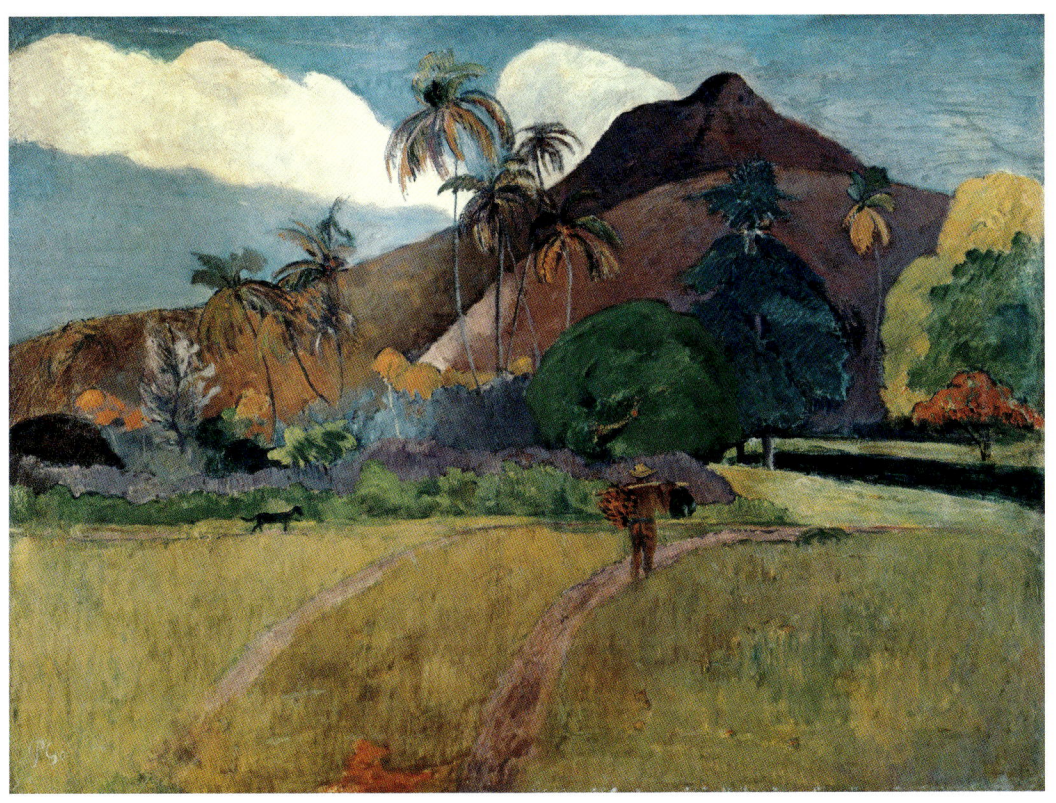

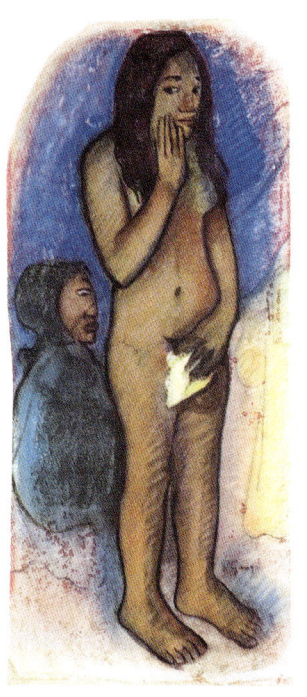

idol dominating the background. Choice fruits and costly fabrics are there, and all is in readiness for homage to be paid to the god. In this work, Gauguin takes a different approach to that favourite theme of his, the intrusion of the supernatural into day-to-day life. Instead of contrasting both areas, he presents the figure of Vairaumati (so reminiscent of Ancient Egyptian tomb reliefs) as containing the extraordinary character of the event within her, as it were. The sense of something alien that we have when we look at Egyptian images stood Gauguin in good stead in this picture: to the artist, the Polynesian myths are as extraordinary as the hieroglyphs of the ancient people of the Nile.

In *We Shall Not Go to Market Today* (ill. p. 346/347) Gauguin once again avails himself of Ancient Egypt's schematic visual language. Here, however, the rigid row of five figures looks like a quotation, and seems unmotivated. There is no real connection between the formal arrangement of the figures, alternating between frontal and profile views, and the simple scene that is the painting's subject. Gauguin learnt the lesson and made no further attempts to adapt the style of Ancient Egyptian art.

Gauguin had to rethink. The emotional universe of the people among whom he was living was not the mixture of instinct and superstition that he would have liked to suppose. Little by little he gained better access to it, mainly through the daily presence of his lover, Tehura. Then one night the gap between the two cultures was strikingly revealed to him. Gauguin returned late to the hut they shared, and struck a match to find his way about. Tehura interpreted the flame's flickering glare as the appearance of the spirit of the dead and was seized by mortal fear – although to the European the match was no more than an everyday object. "What I saw was simply fear," Gauguin recalled when he described the episode. "But what kind of fear? Not the fear of Susanna surprised by the elders, that much is certain. That fear is unknown in Oceania. But the Tupapau, the spirit of the dead, had appeared. The Tahitian people live in constant fear of him."

When Gauguin came to express the experience in artistic terms he called his painting *Spirit of the Dead Watching* (ill. p. 356). Tehura is lying on the bed, naked. It is no wide-open pose of animal innocence such as a European's lascivious eye might be looking for. Instead, the woman is keeping her legs together, tensely, and is resting her hands on the pillow as if she were about to jump up and run away at any moment. Once again the supernatural has invaded the realm of everyday life. The awesome dark figure with its strong profile, and the impenetrable background with its hints of glittering apparitions, tell us that Tupapau, the spirit of the dead, is up to his mischief. His satanic infiltration of this tropical paradise stands for the ubiquitous presence of Death: even in this island people must die. For once (and only once) the harmony of Man and Nature which Gauguin stage-managed so skilfully is seen as null.

Tahitian Landscape (ill. p. 359) shows that it was possible to forget such cares. Again we see the scenery reproduced in glowing colours, with all the freshness and immediacy of

TOP
Study for the painting
Words of the Devil (Eve), c. 1892
Watercolour and pastel on paper,
78.7 x 34.7 cm (31 x 13¾ in.)
Kunstmuseum Basel, Kupferstichkabinett

OPPOSITE
"When Will You Marry?", 1892
"Nafea Faa ipoipo?"
Oil on canvas, 101.5 x 77.5 cm (40 x 30½ in.)
Private collection

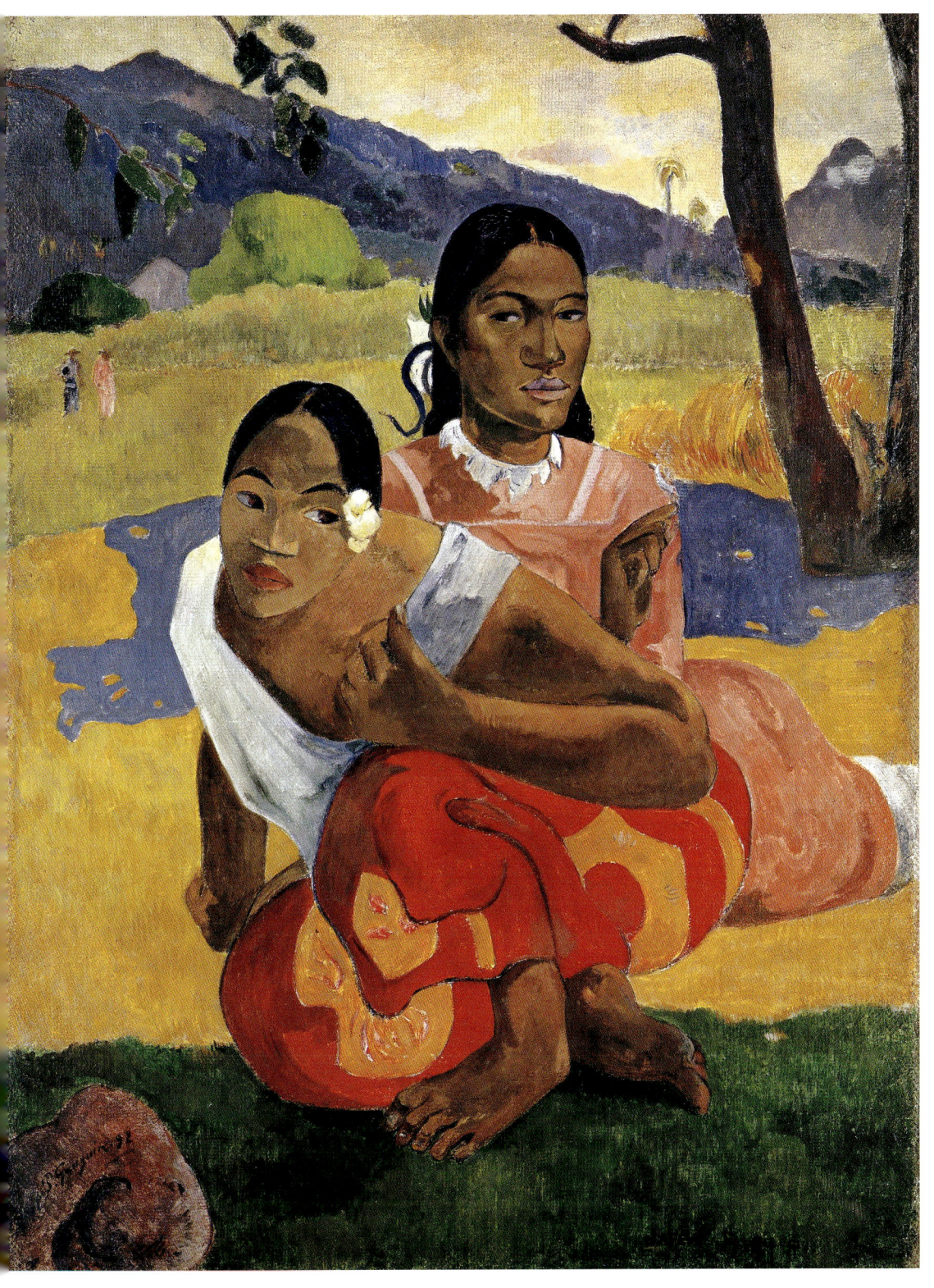

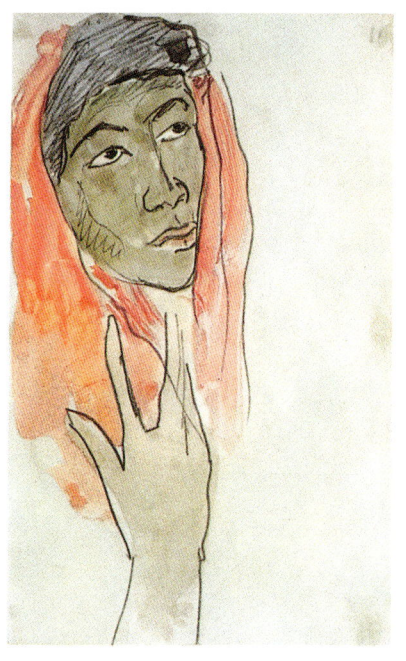

nature expressed in the sumptuously atmospheric colouring. The sheer purity of the colours goes beyond realism and offers a sense of hedonistic security: a harmony, or unity, is established, in which both man and the landscape are enlivened. At the same time, an ascetic harshness in the picture saves it from lapsing into the idyllic. The dog, and the man carrying the two bundles in weary balance, are scaled down by the landscape, becoming silent elements in a natural scene where everything has its rightful and necessary place.

But the Shangri-La that Gauguin depicted in these paintings was plainly unable to satisfy all his wishes. Money didn't grow on Tahiti's trees – and Gauguin had failed to free himself of the desire for money. "The way my fortunes take such a dive the moment I leave Paris is terrible," he lamented. "Yet the minute I return I find ways of earning my living. And as soon as I'm away again I don't make a penny." The modest success he had had with sales of pictures in his exhibitions was a thing of the past. Now he wanted to revive that success, and use his South Seas paintings to finally establish himself on the artistic scene.

Indeed, he had not prospered on Tahiti. The year before he had suffered several heart attacks; he had grown very thin, and felt tired. Taking a cool look at himself, he noted: "If I were to see things properly I would give up painting when I return, since I can't live on it." On the other hand, he felt a certain pride; after all, he had managed to remain there for three years. "I'm right in the thick of it!" He used the letter of recommendation that had got him his ceremonial welcome to finance his return journey.

In leaving Tahiti, Gauguin was saying goodbye not only to the island but also to the delusion that he had found the happiest corner of the world to live in. The delusion had been fruitful, guiding his brush and pen alike, and the evening before his departure he succumbed to it once again: "Farewell, you exquisite, hospitable land of beauty and freedom! Indeed, these ignorant savages have taught the old civilized crew a thing or two: many an insight, and the art of being happy." And, forgetting everything that had not been to his taste, he declared: "I leave two years older but twenty years younger – more of a savage than I was when I came, yet nonetheless knowing more."

TOP
Head of a Woman, *c.* 1891/92
Watercolour on paper,
17 x 11 cm (6¾ x 4¼ in.)
Private collection

OPPOSITE
Her Name Is Vairaumati, 1892
"Vairaumati têi oa"
Oil on canvas, 91 x 68 cm (36 x 26¾ in.)
Moscow, Pushkin Museum

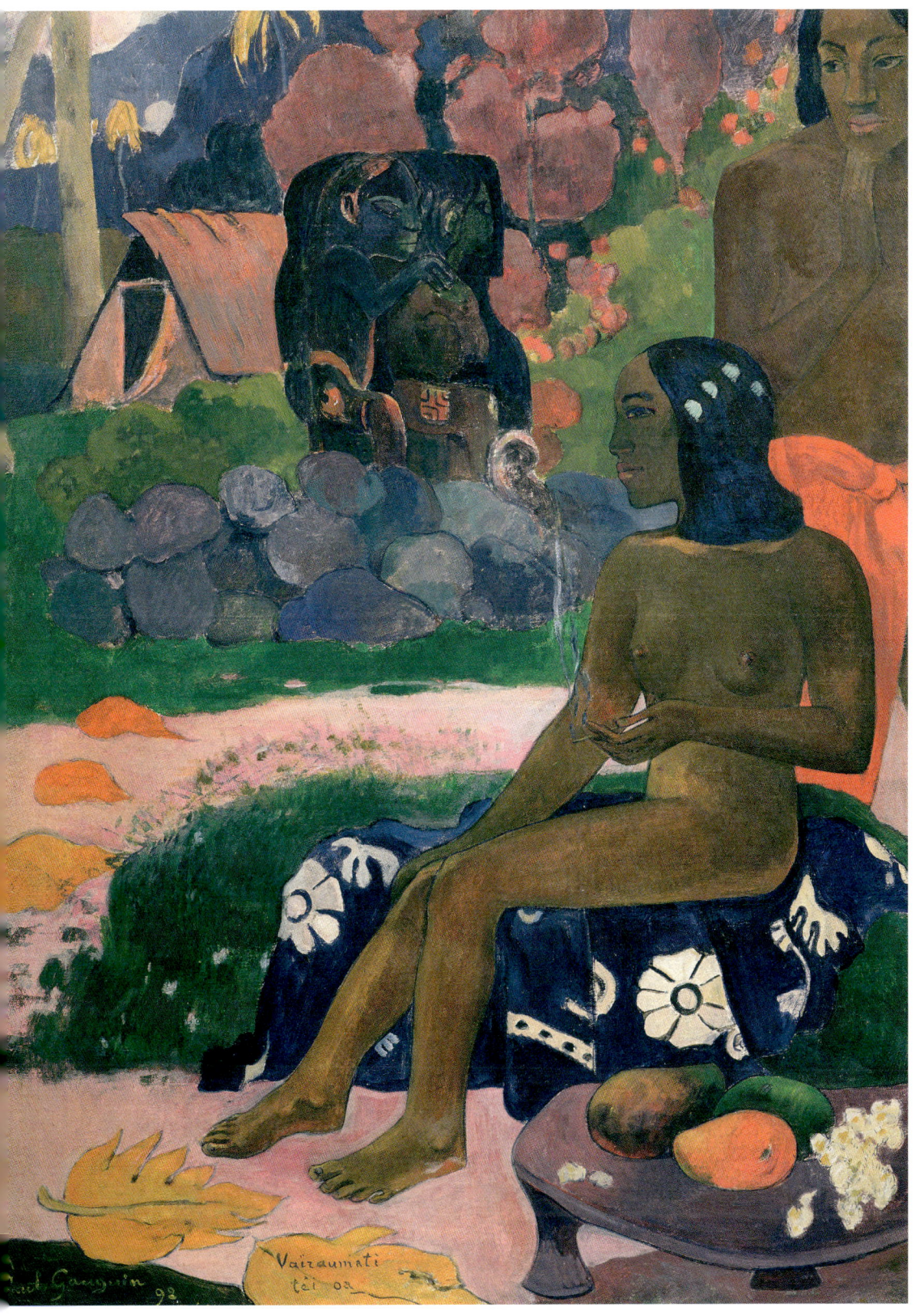

Vairaumati tei oa

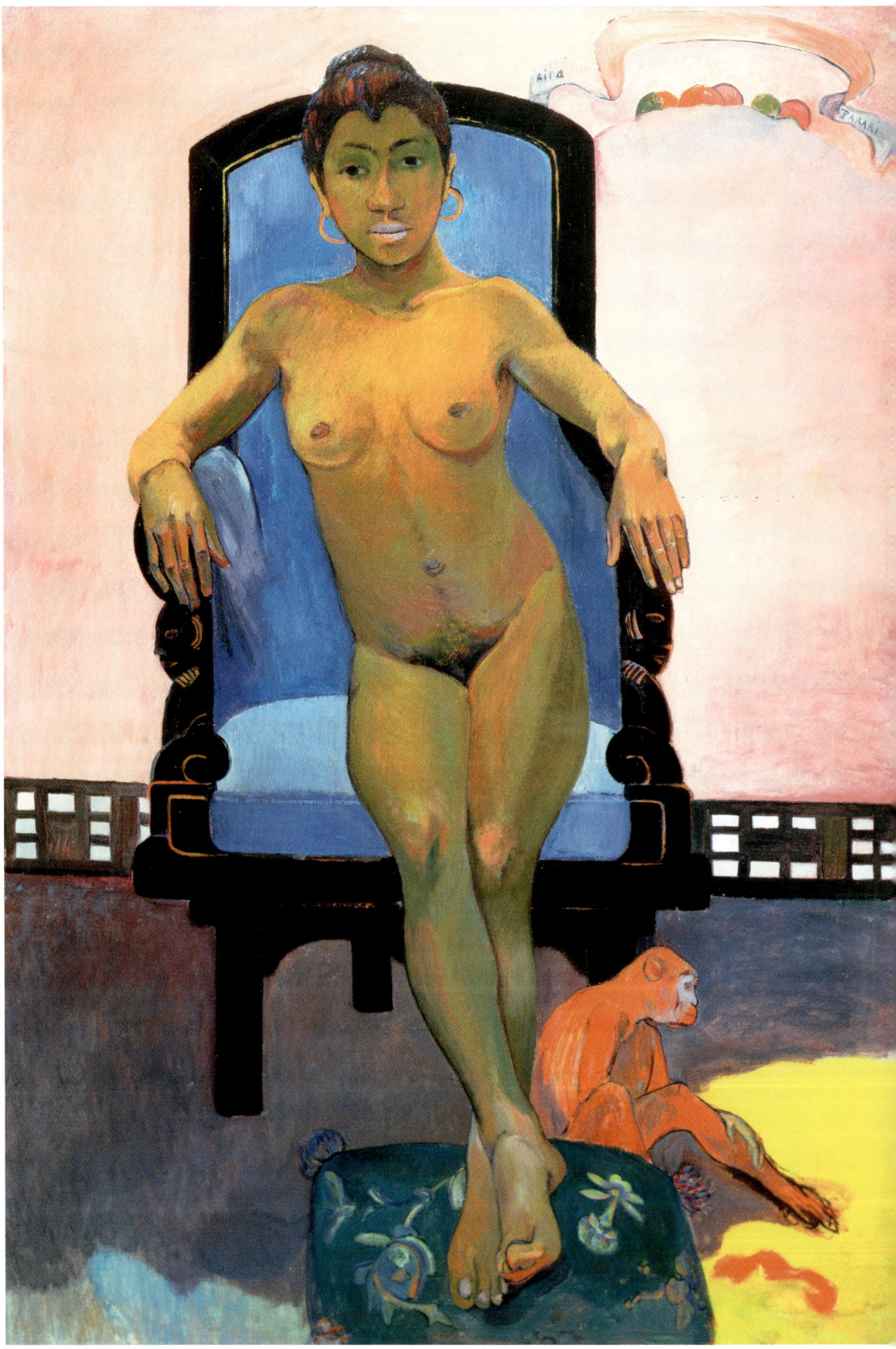

"The Greatest Modern Painter"
1893–1895

Gauguin's modest fame had not entirely faded away during his absence from France. Charles Morice the critic acted as his agent in the Old World, and in fact succeeded in selling quite a number of Gauguin's Tahitian paintings back home. And then, at the beginning of September 1893, the artist himself was on the spot again, eager to have the French francs he had earned safely in his own pocket. But it was as difficult to track down the people who owed him money as to locate the unsold pictures. Gauguin spent the first few days after his return collecting outstanding debts.

And then there was his family of fatherless children. Mette had been selling her husband's paintings, thinking that by doing so she could avoid being a burden on him, but now she felt justified in making demands. And the demands rose steeply after Gauguin's Uncle Isidore left 15,000 francs to his nephew. Gauguin, confident of success, felt that such a sum of money was best invested in leading an artist's life, and considered that the requirements of wife and children came second after that lofty goal. Quarrels over the legacy further estranged the artist and his wife and helped create new enmity. Gauguin could no longer expect support from his family in his homeland.

This meant that he had to be all the more prolific as an artist. He was preparing a retrospective show, with the aim of demonstrating the consistent logic of his development and the distance he had kept from the cheerful impressions recorded by a Monet or Pierre-Auguste Renoir. Again it was an Impressionist who came to his assistance. Degas succeeded in persuading gallery owner Paul Durand-Ruel, who handled his own work, to showcase the South Seas romantic on his premises. Durand-Ruel had made himself a name as the trailblazer of modern art; and Gauguin scented his big chance.

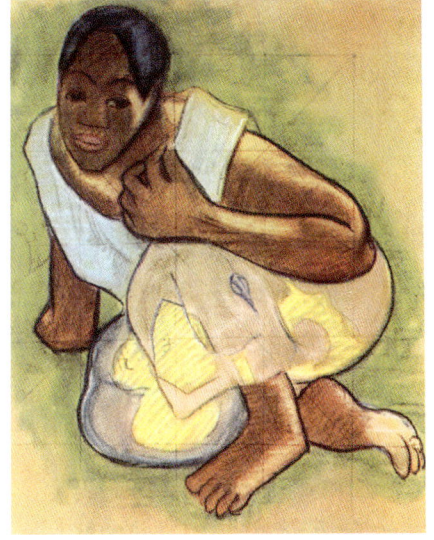

Crouching Tahitian Woman, 1892
Study for the painting
"When Will You Marry?" (ill. p. 361)
Pencil, charcoal and pastel on paper,
53.5 x 48 cm (21 x 19 in.)
The Art Institute of Chicago,
Margaret Day Blake Collection

OPPOSITE
Anna the Javanese, 1893
"Aita Tamari vahina Judith te Parari"
Oil on canvas, 116 x 81 cm (45¾ x 32 in.)
Private collection

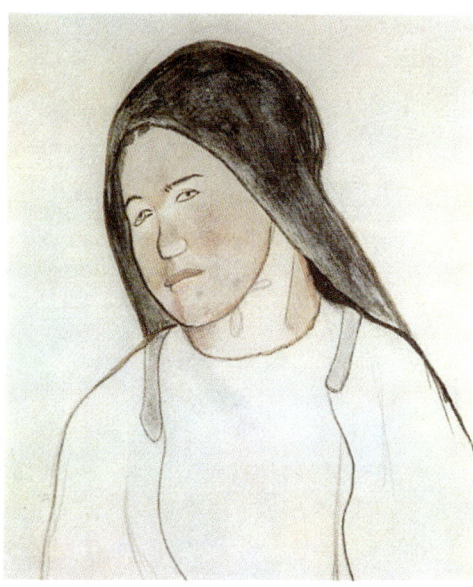

Head of a Young Breton
Peasant Woman, c. 1889
Pencil, red and black chalk, wash on paper,
22.4 x 20 cm (8¾ x 8 in.)
Cambridge, Massachusetts,
Harvard Art Museums/Fogg Museum,
Bequest of Meta and Paul J. Sachs

OPPOSITE
Two Breton Women, 1894
Oil on canvas,
66.5 x 92.7 cm (26¼ x 36½ in.)
Paris, Musée d'Orsay

Gauguin was fully alert to the value of an artist's image in influencing the sympathies of an undecided public, and he therefore used Uncle Isidore's legacy to set up a new studio. He presented himself as an ambassador from tropical parts, who could lighten the dismal days of his clientele with exotic magic. Thus his flat was crammed with whatever looked in any way "primitive": native and folk art, his own paintings, glass painting. The apartment was a miniature world fair. Above the front door were the mysterious words Te Faruru ("this is a place of love"). This was to be the kind of bohemian rendezvous that Mallarmé had hosted years before.

His image required that he should have an exotic lover, and Gauguin had one in Anna, the Javanese girl who would dance with a little monkey for society gentlemen. In *Anna the Javanese* (ill. p. 364) Gauguin was aiming at the same unforced, natural nakedness as in his portraits of Tahitian women. But this time the relaxed animal quality doesn't quite come off. This woman, clothed by Nature in innocence, has not undressed – she has been undressed, by the covetous eyes of male society. In Paris, her very body helped create an image of exotic magic, and that is what she personifies in the painting. It is no chance (as it might be in the South Seas) that the little monkey is sitting at her feet; it is there as her attribute, to ensure that she will be recognized. Doubtless it pleased Gauguin to enhance his own image with the decorative Anna; but in this work he was unable to give effective artistic expression to that direct fascination with the beauty of local women that had given such distinctive power to some of his Tahitian pictures. The painting seems as contrived as the exotic atmosphere of the artist's studio.

In Paris, Gauguin liked to encourage notions of the artist as one who envisioned a better world, and the book edition of *Noa Noa* fitted splendidly. It was conceived as an artist's diary, with its gaze firmly fixed on the tropics, despising the reality of its own origins. *Noa Noa* is not an especially truthful book, but that is beside the point. Gauguin merely needed a consistent narrative, and a story that matched his attention-grabbing public image. He had made a diplomatic peace with Morice, who wrote a few poems for the book. And Gauguin took on the task of illustrating it himself.

In the watercolour *The Messengers of Oro* (ill. p. 368) we sense something of Gauguin's mood at that time. It tells of events immediately preceding the episode Gauguin presented in *Her Name*

Is Vairaumati (ill. p. 363). The two sisters of the supreme god Ora are telling the young virgin cowering on the ground of Taaroa's wish to take her as his bride. Back home, Gauguin was still dwelling on images seen in the South Seas. Instead of being receptive to new subjects, he was drawing on a repertoire acquired during the past few years. He was hoping, of course, that he would overwhelm the art world. But in fact this divorce from the facts of his surroundings (in an artist whose visual world had always depended heavily on the people, plant life and folk art around him) was to play its part in alienating Gauguin from his homeland. Even in Paris, the artistic capital of Europe, with such a wealth of subjects to offer an artist, Gauguin was sustained by his memories of the tropics.

The exhibition at Durand-Ruel's gallery had now opened, in November 1893. The French yearning for the magic of the South Seas was amply catered for in Gauguin's forty-six paintings and two sculptures. Nevertheless, he had failed to catch the public's taste: critics complained that his work was too crude and too primitive, and that his "rape of the basic elements of drawing" was "coquettish". Press ridicule peaked in the advice: "If you want to amuse your children, send them to the Gauguin exhibition!"

When he set off for Tahiti, Gauguin had been perfectly willing to play the rejected outsider, but meanwhile he had fitted in again, stylishly and adaptably, only to find himself rejected anew. At least his fellow artists applauded, and put in the right words for him. And at least he sold eleven of his works. At the beginning of 1894 he exhibited with Les XX in Brussels, and this time received considerable praise, for *Spirit of the Dead Watching* (ill. p. 356). Immediately, Gauguin was in the best of spirits again. He wrote enthusiastically to Mette that he had finally been recognized as "the greatest modern painter".

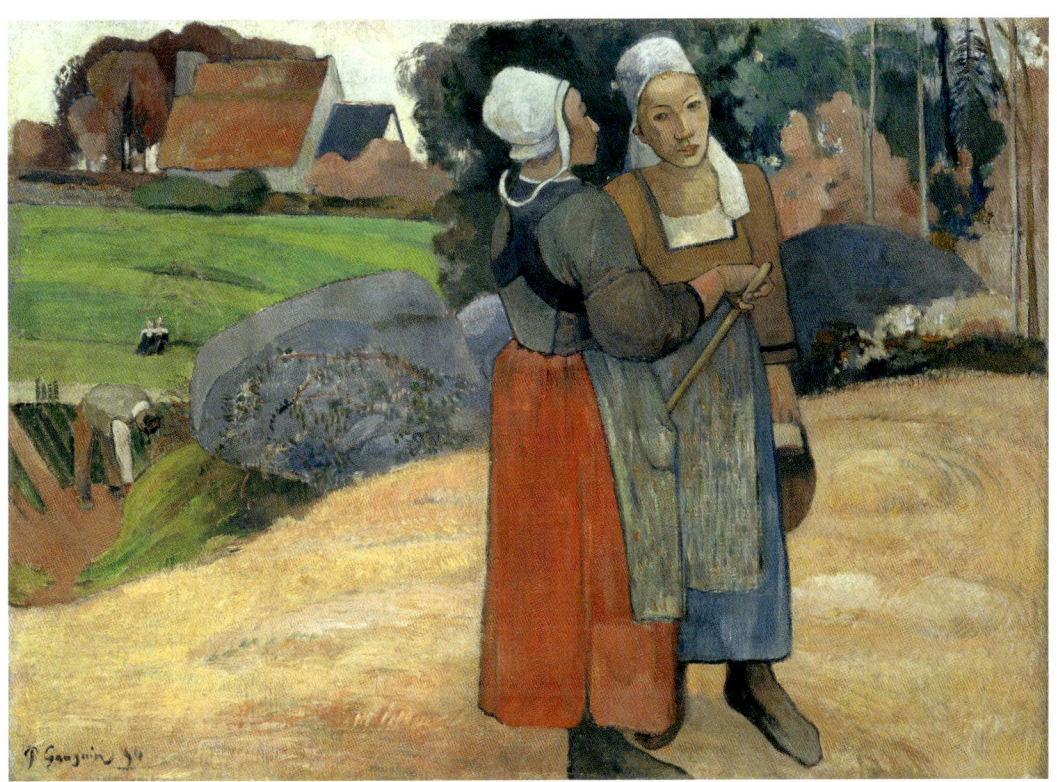

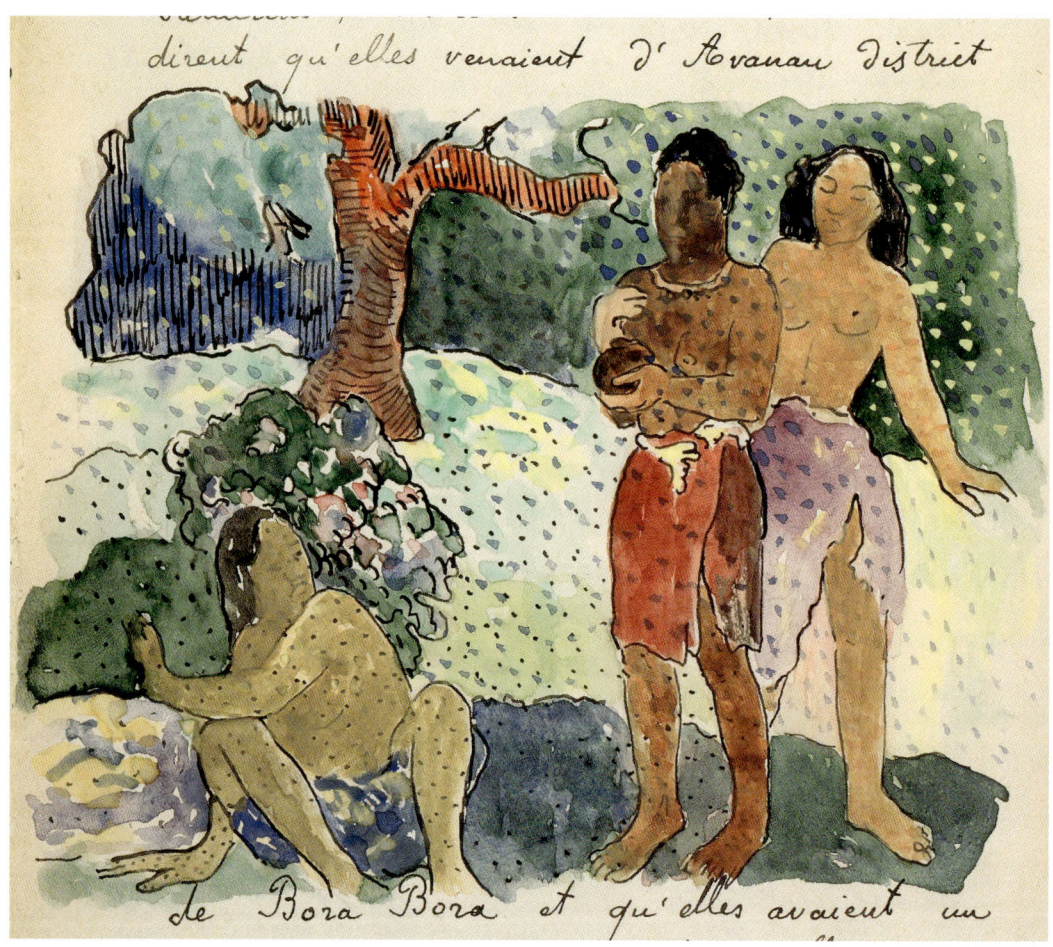

direut qu'elles venaieut d' Avanau District

de Bora Bora et qu'elles avaient un

Gauguin's hunger for success was most clearly visible in the way he stubbornly clung to his South Seas subject matter. Paintings such as *Day of God* (ill. p. 370) and *Sacred Spring: Sweet Dreams* (ill. p. 371) were still full of the magic of his lost world: gently the artist was trying to rediscover that way of seeing which sensed the harmony of Man and Nature. Gauguin still had enough affection for his old, civilized world to think it could be improved by the visions in his paintings.

The Cellist Upaupa Schneklud (ill. p. 369) was one of the most successful pictures Gauguin painted in France, because he was able to put the tropics aside. The artist is trying to reproduce the sounds of music with his own means – a variation on the synaesthesia he had experimented with on Tahiti. Music and painting meet in the two gently curved lines that link the right arm with the abstract pattern in the background. The picture is filled with a sense of movement: the swing of the arm that is producing music is continued, as it were, in an ornamentation that is equally suggestive of music. In this portrait of an artist alert in his senses and emotionally open, Gauguin expressed all his own hopes of regaining touch with the roots of his own culture.

TOP
The Messengers of Oro, 1893
Illustration for the album
Ancien culte mahorie, folio 12
Watercolour on paper,
14 x 17 cm (5½ x 6¾ in.)
Paris, Musée du Louvre,
Département des Arts graphiques

OPPOSITE
The Cellist Upaupa Schneklud, 1894
Oil on canvas, 92.7 x 73.3 cm (36½ x 29 in.)
Baltimore Museum of Art

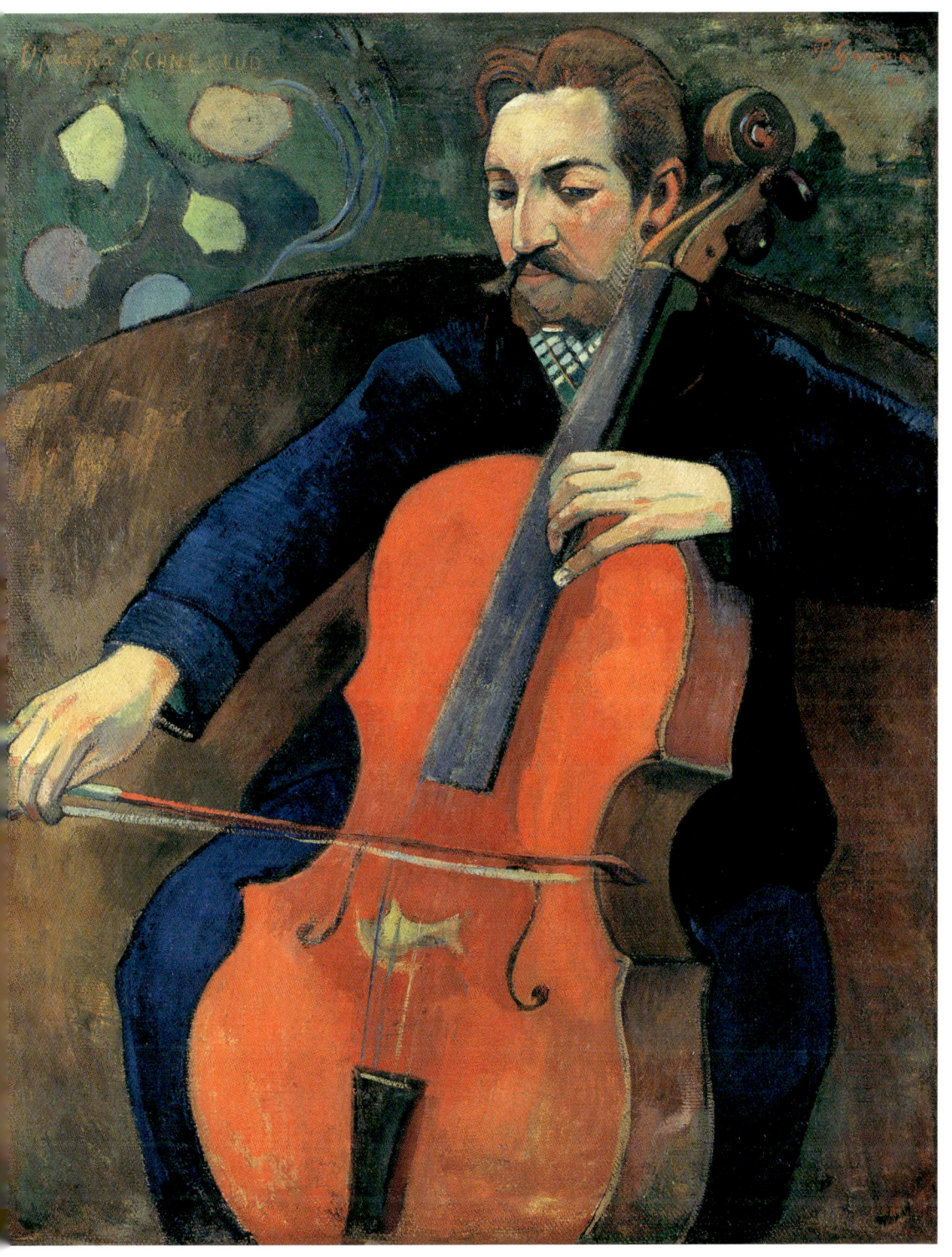

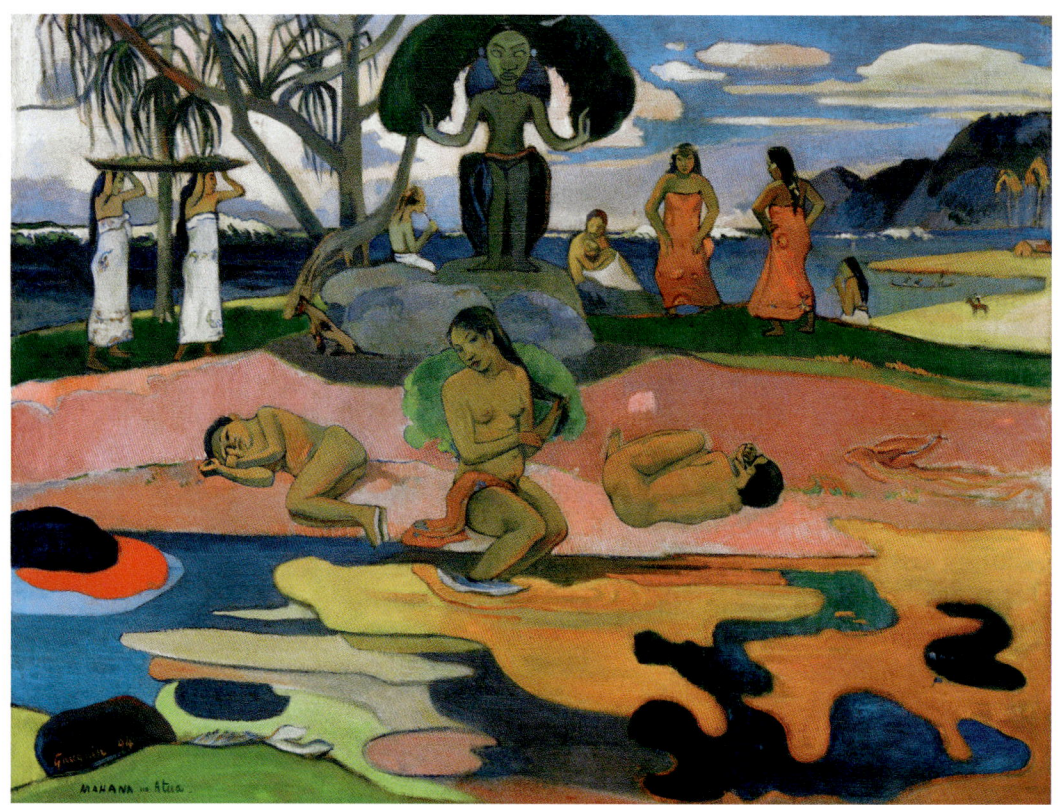

Day of God, 1894
"Mahana no Atua"
Oil on canvas, 68.3 x 91.5 cm (27 x 36 in.)
The Art Institute of Chicago,
Helen Birch Bartlett Memorial Collection

It was only consistent, then, that Gauguin should think of revisiting Brittany. The spartan landscape of the Atlantic coast brought to mind his own roots. He wanted new mental stimulus, and was hoping that the artist friends he had once worked alongside would reinforce his self-esteem. But there was no one there any more: the artists had dispersed, his friends had moved away. His stay in the provinces became a nightmare. It was to scar him deeply, both mentally and physically. On an outing to Concarneau, he and Anna and a couple of friends got into a squabble with some children. Local sailors came to the youngsters' assistance, and in the ensuing brawl Gauguin broke his ankle. The foot was never to heal fully and, in fact, gave him considerable pain during the last years of his life. While he was being looked after in hospital, Anna deserted him, first ransacking the flat they had shared in Paris.

The Concarneau brawl resulted in legal proceedings, which Gauguin lost, just as he lost an attempt to make dealers and friends restore his own works to him. The experience left him determined to avoid future disappointment at the hands of civilization: "Nothing will stop me leaving, and this time it will be for good. What an idiotic existence life in Europe is."

Maybe Gauguin would have been appeased if his auction of work (to finance his departure) had been more of a success. But this time the auction, held at the Hôtel Drouot in Paris, was a disaster, and he sold almost nothing. Gauguin had to buy his own pictures to meet the asking price. Friends also left him in the lurch. He had asked dramatist August Strindberg to write a catalogue preface for the sale, but the Swede declined the invitation: "Monsieur Gauguin, I said in a dream,

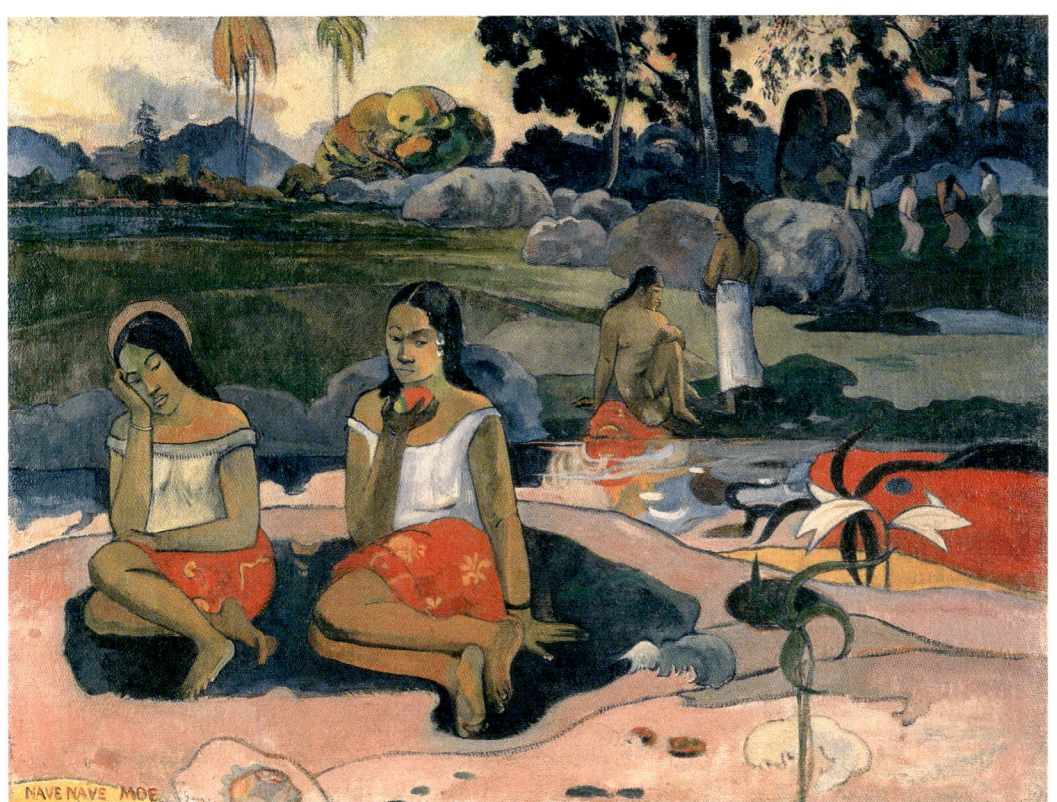

you have created a new earth and a new heaven. But I do not like what you have created." So Paul Gauguin at last felt utterly abandoned. He had returned to Europe full of hope, prepared to play the fashionable game of exotic magic, but he was unable to play the game as wholeheartedly and relentlessly as the public expected. He was too committed to the truth of his vision of the tropics. Failure was inevitable. There was nothing to keep him in Europe any longer. And when he left, he left an angry man.

Sacred Spring: Sweet Dreams, 1894
"Nave Nave Moe"
Oil on canvas, 73 x 100 cm (28¾ x 39¼ in.)
St Petersburg, Hermitage Museum

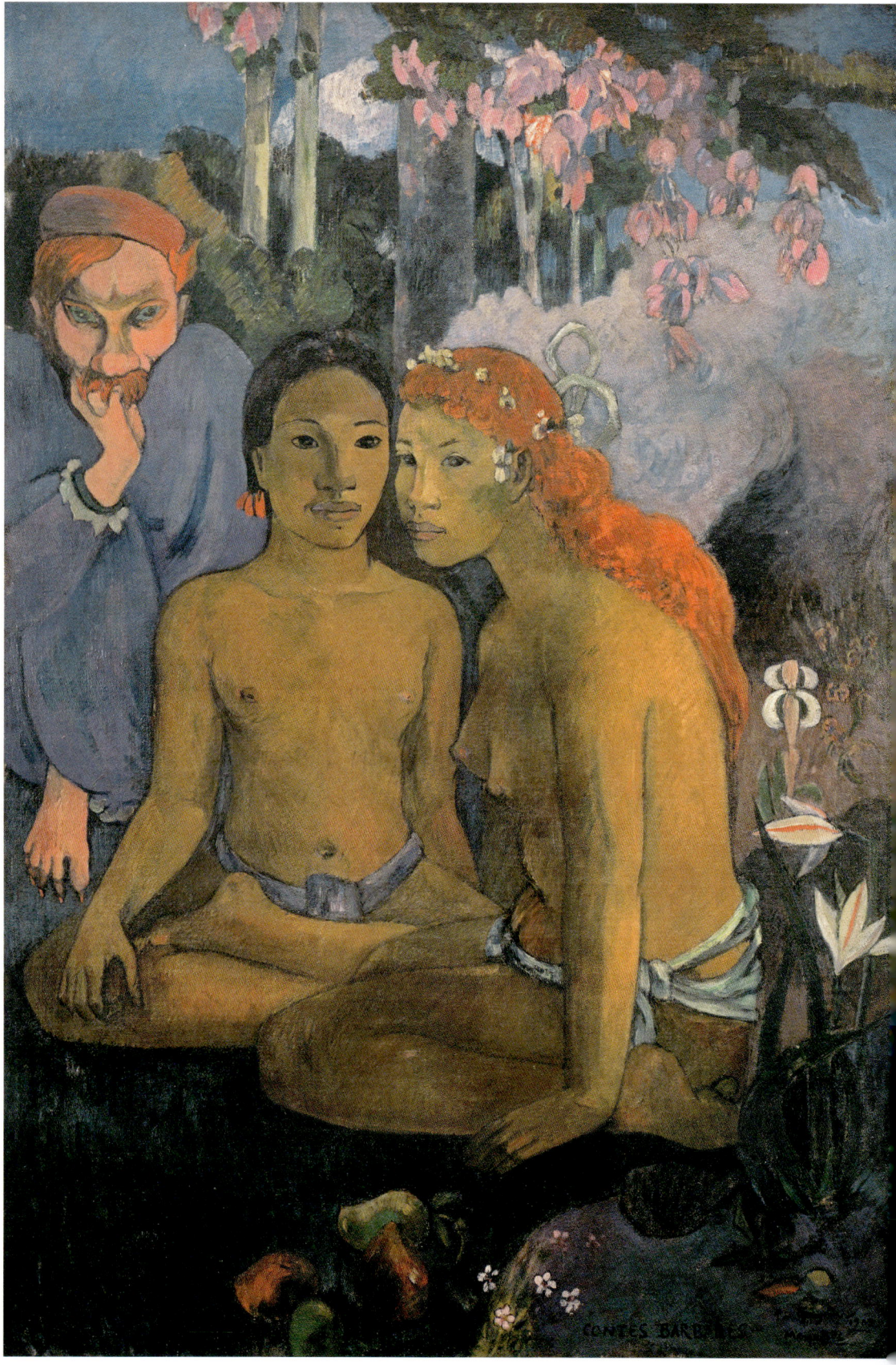

CONTES BARBARES

The Legacy of the Tropics

1895–1903

"Paul Gauguin has no cause to be proud of his fellow countrymen. Those who were astonished some years ago when he chose Tahiti as an idyllic exile where he could work in peace and sunshine might seek the reasons for his second departure in the ingratitude with which they themselves responded to a man whose life's work and reputation are among our most valuable possessions."

Thus wrote a chastened Charles Morice, when he heard the news that Gauguin had once again left from France, this time with no festivities to mark his departure. Morice was one of the few that viewed his course positively. Most of Gauguin's fellow artists felt immensely provoked by his approach: after all, they too were convinced that they had a mission to revolutionize art, but they wanted the grand upheaval to take place on their Parisian home ground, if at all possible, or during their summer vacations in the provinces. Inevitably Gauguin antagonized them; his relentless pursuit of outsider status was a continuous and pointed reminder of their own indolence. Deep down, they may well have heaved a sigh of relief to be rid of their friend.

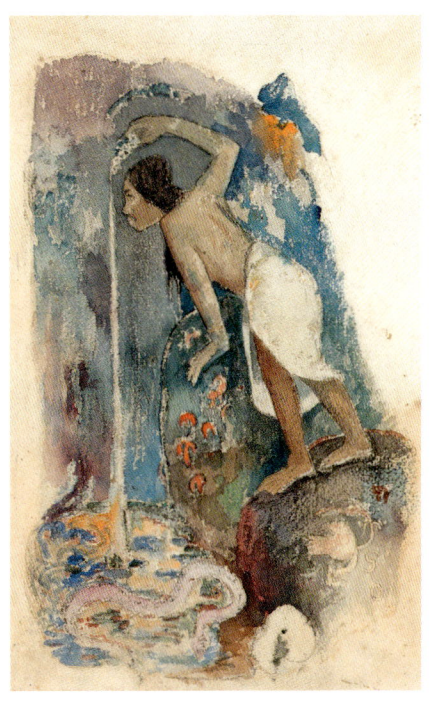

Gauguin's voyage to the other side of the world took three months. He made it in a spirit of disillusionment, and in the event it was to be a journey of no return. Henceforth, the artist preserved only letter-contact with France, normally on a monthly basis. The return to the home country had not provided the inspiration he was constantly in search of, and the increasing daring and freedom of his art had gone largely unrecognized in society. The fact that some of his fellow artists did indeed value his achievement was of little direct assistance in the day-to-day business of living.

OPPOSITE
Barbarous Tales, 1902
Oil on canvas, 131.5 x 90.5 cm (51¾ x 35¾ in.)
Essen, Museum Folkwang

ABOVE RIGHT
Mysterious Water, 1893/94
"Pape Moe"
Watercolour with pen, ink and brush
on wove paper, 35.4 x 25.5 cm (14 x 10 in.)
The Art Institute of Chicago,
Gift of Emily Crane Chadbourne

Things had changed somewhat in Tahiti. Its capital, Papeete, now had electricity, and had acquired a new governor, a more flexible spirit with whom Gauguin toured the island. At first the painter was filled with optimism about his new life in the tropics, but back at home there were those who had their doubts. His old friend Émile Schuffenecker, reviewing the course events had taken, wrote to Gauguin: "If you had been clever and planned ahead, you would now be leading a pleasant, carefree life." In other words: if you had proved more adaptable, the public would have rewarded you accordingly.

But this criticism was first and foremost that of a conformist who had abandoned art for a safe job as an art teacher, and Gauguin could hardly accept it. "I never intended to go cap in hand to the state," wrote the painter. "Everything I struggled for outside the realm of officialdom, and the dignity I have tried hard my whole life long to maintain, have become worthless from this day forth. From now on I am no more than a schemer and a big mouth. But if I had given in, yes, then I would be sitting pretty."

Working himself up into a fury, he cast himself in the role of a monster: "I shall end my days here in my peaceful hut – yes, I am an awful wrongdoer. So be it! So was Michelangelo – and I am not Michelangelo!" That proverbial terribilità that at one time raged volcanically within the Renaissance hero was now exported to the South Seas in the exile's baggage.

The artistic avant-garde has always envisaged society as a straitjacket, imposing limits on the freedom of the imagination. The avant-garde sees the possibility of creativity as existing only in opposition to the state's models and norms. The artist dons the garb of genius and proclaims a freedom that (as he knows) cannot be available to all. If he is to justify his demand for societal freedom, he must insist on

Why Are You Angry?, 1896
"No te aha oe riri?"
Oil on canvas, 95.3 x 130.5 cm (37½ x 51½ in.)
The Art Institute of Chicago,
Mr and Mrs Martin A. Ryerson Collection

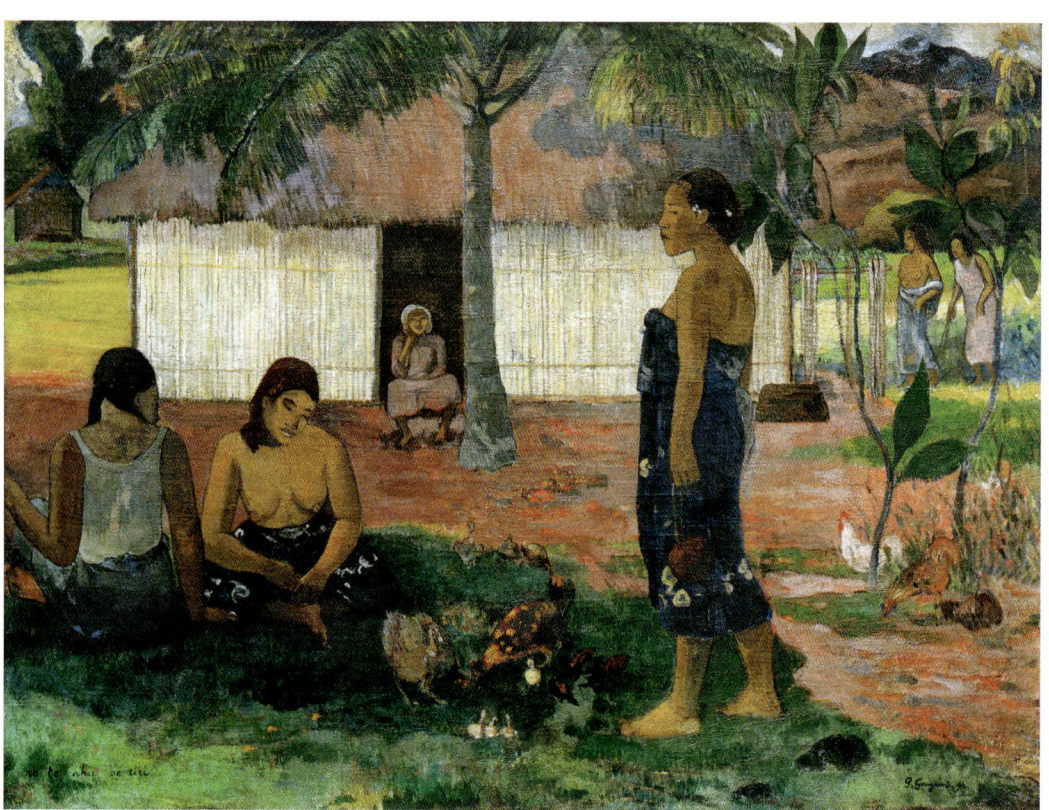

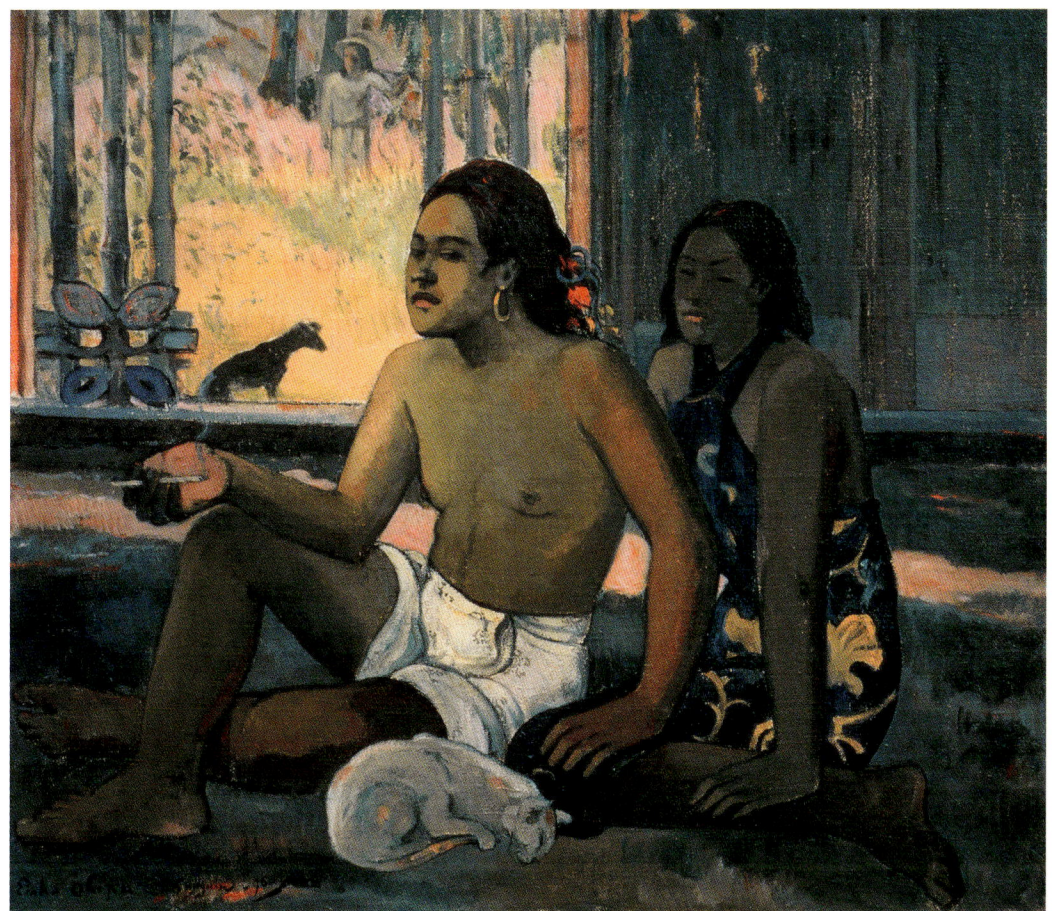

his calling, his vocation. Gauguin too found himself manoeuvred into this position. And, on top of it, he tended increasingly to give himself a martyr's airs: "What did it get me? Total defeat, and enemies – that's all. Bad luck has been dogging my heels my whole life long, and the further I go on the deeper I sink."

Not Working, 1896
"Eiaha ohipa"
Oil on canvas, 65 x 75 cm (25½ x 29½ in.)
Moscow, Pushkin Museum

Thus in *Self-portrait* (ill. p. 306) we see Gauguin posing as Christ once again. This time, however, he attempted no self-satisfied comparison. The artist's gaze was one of straightforward accusation. "This terrible society which we are forced to endure, where little men emerge triumphant at the expense of great, is our Calvary," he wrote three years later. But he was not only attacking his favourite enemy, the Old World. The portrait is set against a dark and impenetrable background where two vague figures are appearing, constant companions from the realm of the shades of Death. The artist looks calm, resigned to his fate as outsider, a man like any other: helpless and defenceless. After years of searching, Gauguin had at last found in this Janus face an emblematic portrayal of life itself.

His sensitivity towards the special status of the artist who is certain of his visionary faculty merged with an admission of that frailty he shared with all men, be they primitive or civilized. Caught between loneliness and solidarity, Gauguin began to accept himself: "Laughing, you climb your Calvary, your legs shake under the weight of the cross; at the top you grind your teeth, and then, smiling, you take your revenge," he wrote cryptically in *Avant et après*, his memoirs of the closing years of his life.

Since the thought of hanging his work on Western walls no longer dominated his thinking so much, Gauguin's pictures were now quite often of monumental size, and lost that aura of contrivance and artifice which had seemed programmatic and forced in his earlier South Seas work. He continued to send his paintings to his European agent, Daniel de Monfreid; but now Gauguin abandoned the misconceptions that, after his repeated failure, he ought to have given up long before. Now he paid attention to a voice within, to a need for truth. Now he increasingly refused to strike artistic compromises between the gentle naturalness of the local people and the expectations of his European audience.

And now Gauguin attempted comparisons of ways of life, trying to analyse in detail the respects in which the civilized and primitive worlds differed. *Not Working* (ill. p. 375), for example, contrasts the European work ethic (which still had Gauguin himself in its grip) with the Tahitian tendency to take things as they came. Two Tahitians are sitting in their hut, sleepily enjoying their tobacco. There are no tools or materials to prompt them to hard work. In the background, a figure in a long white robe, with a topee on his head, is seen approaching – none other than the artist himself. Searching for subjects (that is, for things that will set him working), he has hit upon the theme of work; and now he produces affectionate sketches of a world devoted to doing nothing, to idleness of a kind he himself is incapable of. The artist lacks the spontaneous, uninhibited freedom of these people, who are intrinsically in harmony with the natural world and the creatures around them – animals such as the cat, sleepy and unselfconscious too.

Still Life with Mangoes, 1896
Oil on canvas,
30.2 x 47.4 cm (12 x 18¾ in.)
Private collection

"When I am tired of painting human figures (which is what I prefer), I start a still life and complete it without referring to the objects again," Gauguin wrote to the Romanian Prince Emmanuel Bibesco, one of his

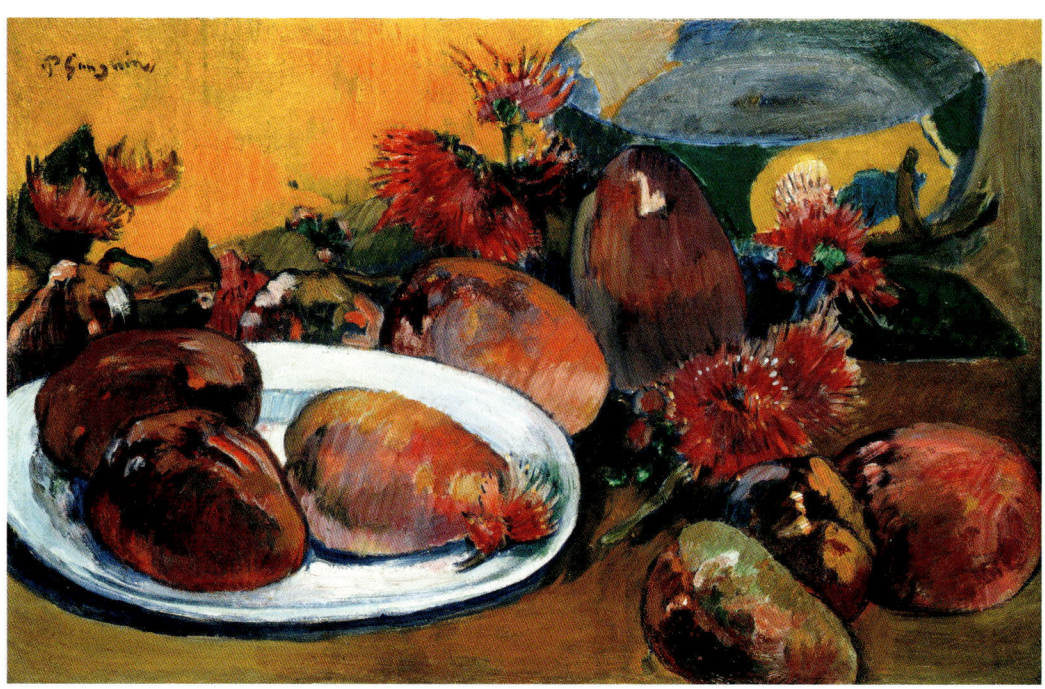

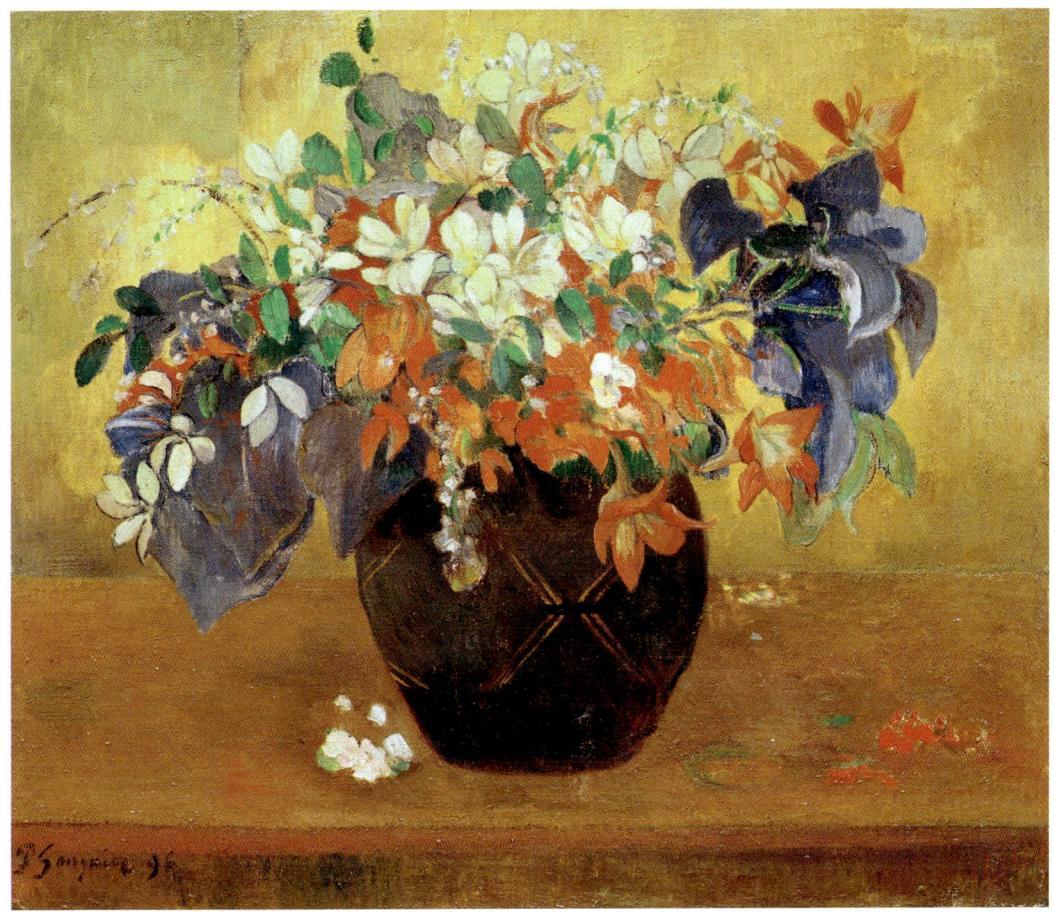

collectors. (There were a number of Gauguin collectors, in spite of the artist's setbacks.) He wrote of still lifes as if painting them were relaxation: clearly leisure was not synonymous with idleness

Bouquet of Flowers, 1896
Oil on canvas, 64 x 74 cm (25¼ x 29¼ in.)
London, The National Gallery

for Gauguin. Whatever he may at times have said, he was no native, and had his work ethic. *Still Life with Mangoes* (ill. p. 376) and *Bouquet of Flowers* (ill. p. 377) show Gauguin in holiday mood. He presents flowers and fruits in the same way as people, with vivid immediacy and a sensuous fascination; whether animate or inanimate, everything in creation is a part of nature.

Gauguin soon moved away from Papeete (as he had done the first time), seeking to escape the encroaching influences of Western technology and civilization. The influence of Europe was worse than ever now electricity had been introduced to the island. Once again, Gauguin moved to the interior, into a frail and rickety native-style hut exposed to the elements. "I have straw matting and my old Persian carpet on the floor," he wrote to Monfreid. "The place is adorned with materials, knick-knacks and drawings." This time Gauguin had to do without his lover Tehura, since she had got married in the meantime. Still, he wrote to friends that "girls come to my bed every night as if possessed", doubtless intending to prompt envy back home. His new lover was a fourteen-year-old called Pau'ura. His love life, however, was plagued by an unpleasant legacy from France: shortly before leaving Paris he had contracted syphilis, and now he found himself introducing the disease to the people of his dearly loved paradise.

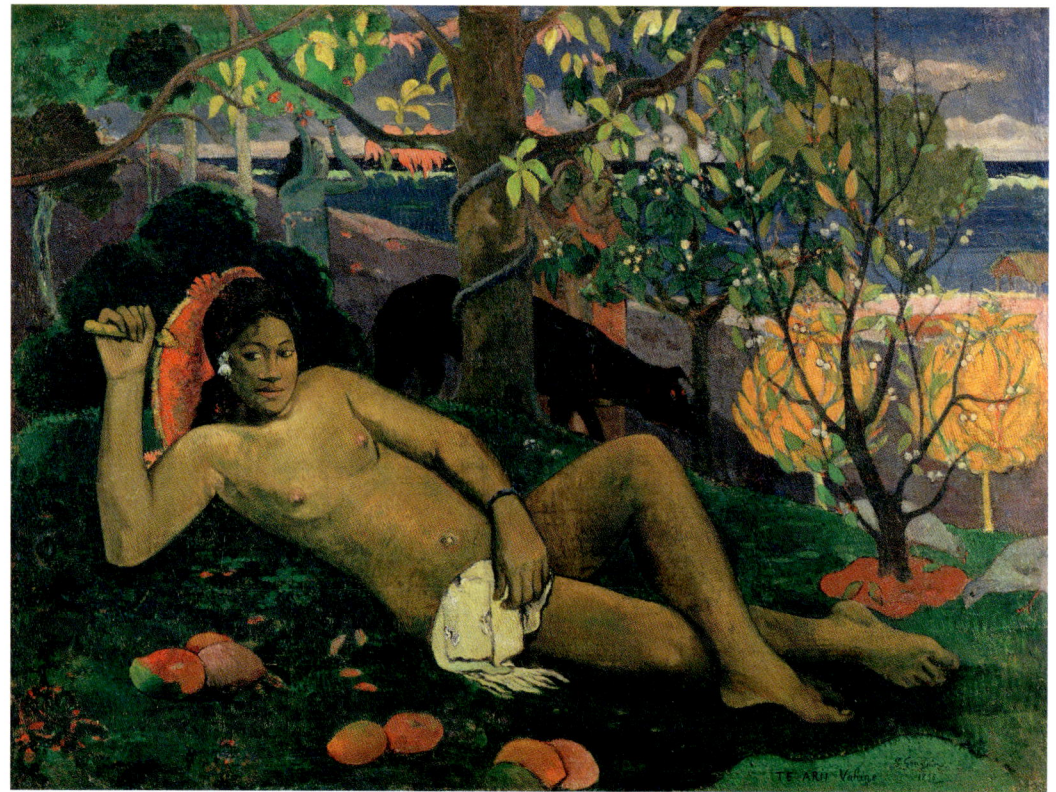

Queen of Beauty, 1896
"Te Arii Vahine"
Oil on canvas, 97 x 130 cm (38¼ x 51¼ in.)
Moscow, Pushkin Museum

The beautiful female nudes that constitute the major part of Gauguin's late work might almost have been meant to illustrate his tales of girls succumbing to his erotic charisma. Thus *Queen of Beauty* (ill. p. 378) shows the girl in a pose familiar from European art, lying on the grass in the same manner as Francisco de Goya's *Nude Maja* (*c.* 1800, Madrid, Museo Nacional del Prado) or Manet's *Olympia* lay on their vast beds. Her legs are crossed and she is covering herself with her hand, offering herself in the same way as Goya's and Manet's lascivious goddesses of love did; but Gauguin's beauty is not looking at us, and her averted gaze mitigates the seductiveness that lies in that ambiguously fascinating figure, the innocent temptress.

"The Eve of your civilized imagination makes you and almost all of us misogynists," Gauguin had replied to August Strindberg; "the Eve of primitive times who, in my studio, startles you now, may one day smile on you less bitterly." In the strict sexual morality of the late nineteenth century, erotic charisma was coupled with feelings of danger or even hatred. On Tahiti, Gauguin wanted to free himself of this unnatural attitude to love and desire, an attitude that emphasized divided, mixed feelings rather than an immediate response. He wanted an Eve who could be loved without guilt. This Eve was a product of male fantasies too; but an imaginary innocent Eve seemed free and available, and her lover felt like a man once more.

"They are gentle-spirited to the point of stupidity, and totally incapable of mean calculation," Gauguin wrote of his Polynesian friends and neighbours in *Avant et après*. He was wholeheartedly willing to see the innocent simplicity of the local people as the true human condition. His friendly reception on Tahiti was quite the opposite of the derision and brusque rejection he had suffered in

Europe. And so he inevitably felt an affinity with the people of the South Seas. If every being had its own natural dignity, cruelty was easily forgotten. Gauguin wrote, in *Avant et après*, "Ask one of these sleepy ancients if he likes human meat and, with a twinkle in his eye, he will answer cheerfully and infinitely gently, 'Ah, how good it tastes!'" The cannibal who devours the body of his enemy (but only his enemy) behaves more morally than Western society, which calls itself humane but locks people up for life in asylums. "I no longer have any sense of days and hours, or of good and evil." On that peaceful island, with its own standards and values, no one troubled with appointments; and, since their lives were lived in harmony with nature, they could not but be good.

Gauguin himself flouted Western convention quite blatantly at times. He fathered illegitimate children, for instance – one was born before he left Paris, and another one year later on Tahiti – and the themes of family, procreation and birth soon appeared as subjects for his paintings. The everyday bliss of family life is Gauguin's theme in *The Dug-Out*. People drinking out of bowls, and a rudimentary boat to carry them over the water: everything is simple. The axe at the man's feet indicates that he has just made the dug-out. The family can find everything they need in their environment, which appears as a veritable Shangri-La, bathed in harmonious sunset tones. In this world, things take care of themselves, it seems, and the people's faces are relaxed, trusting, and utterly contented. Given the pleasure and peacefulness that fill the picture, the traditional symbolic meaning of a boat as a way of overcoming dangers is scarcely important. The whole family conveys the message – a message of harmony.

Borrowing the tradition of Christian art in his familiar manner once again, Gauguin put his own experience of

The Dug-Out, 1896
"Te Vaa"
Oil on canvas, 95.5 x 131.5 cm (37½ x 51¾ in.)
St Petersburg, Hermitage Museum

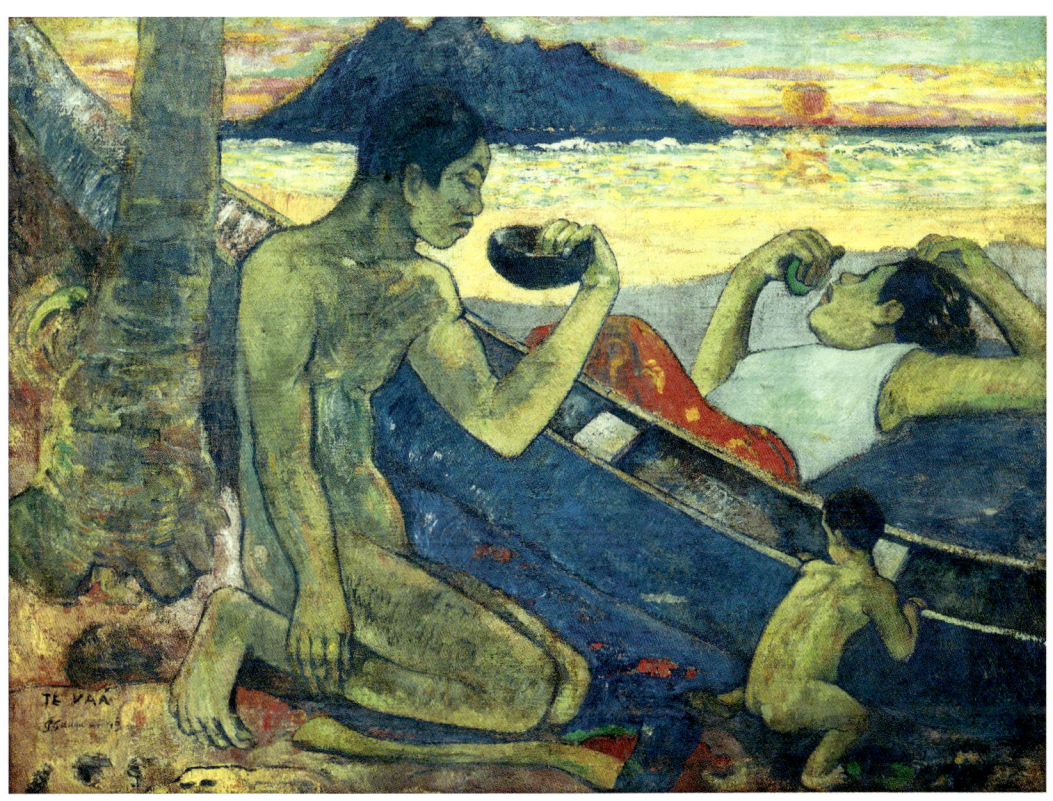

fatherhood into his *Nativity* (ill. p. 380). Again a biblical story has been given a South Seas setting – a Polynesian hut with ornamental beams and a simple bed. The stable animals are there too. A native woman, probably Gauguin's lover, has been cast as the Mother of God. Like the newborn child being rocked by the nurse in the background, she has a halo. Again the artist draws religious parallels, although this time he has cast himself in the role of creator rather than sufferer. In this painting, Gauguin appears to be saying that the life he is able to create is not only a product of artistic activity: at the end of his life, we see him once again proclaiming the values of fatherhood, which had originally established the individual character of his work. The serenity of the scene is resplendent and undimmed. That first year on Tahiti was surely one of the happiest in Gauguin's life.

But his situation soon deteriorated. Yet again he was plagued by financial worries. With the help of friends, he had tried to establish a group of patrons who would pay him an annual allowance in return for a number of pictures; but the plan didn't work out. Instead of the backing of wealthy patrons, Gauguin merely achieved a one-off grant of 200 francs from the Minister of the Arts. Vexed by such a small amount, he returned the pittance in a temper.

Gauguin had no intention of begging. He longed for the recognition his artistic achievement had earned him. Unfortunately, however, he could have used the money: "My position is precarious and growing more and more unbearable, and, dreadful as it may be, I cannot afford protracted haggling. I shall have to sell my pictures for whatever price I can get." In his self-imposed exile, Gauguin also knew that most of his paintings were unsellable. When he sent *Queen of Beauty* (ill. p. 378) to Europe, he wrote:

Nativity, 1896
"Te Tamari No Atua"
Oil on burlap, 96 x 131.1 cm (37¾ x 51½ in.)
Munich, Bayerische Staatsgemälde-
sammlungen, Neue Pinakothek

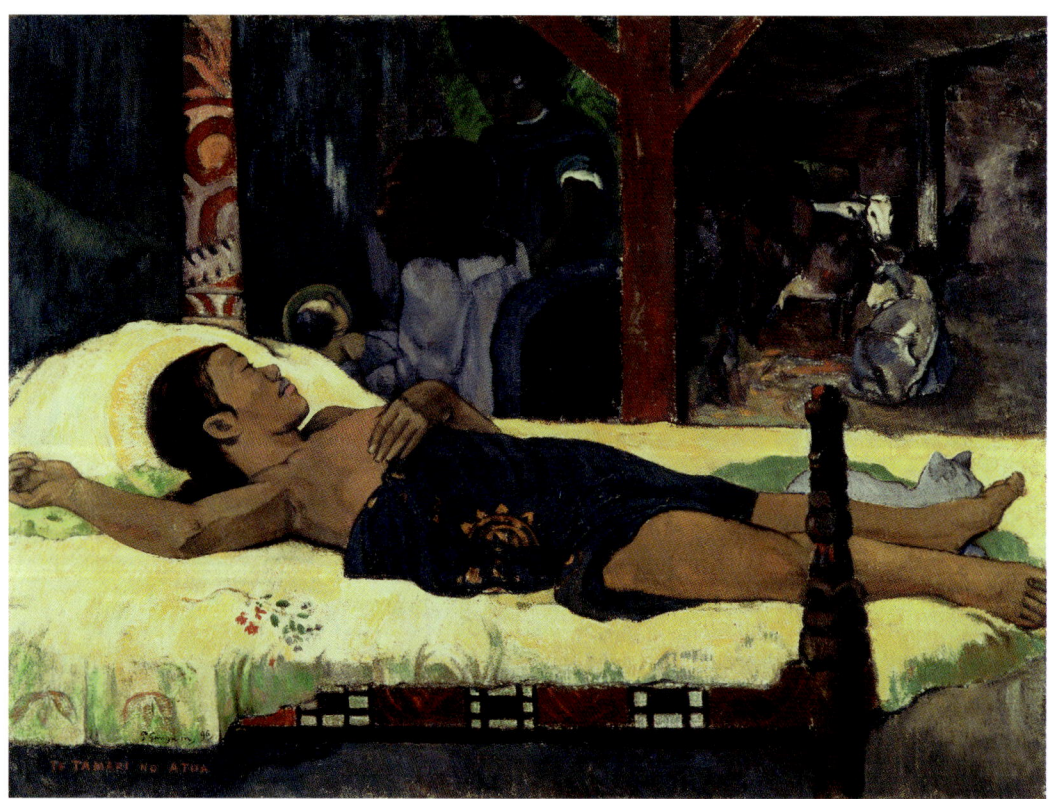

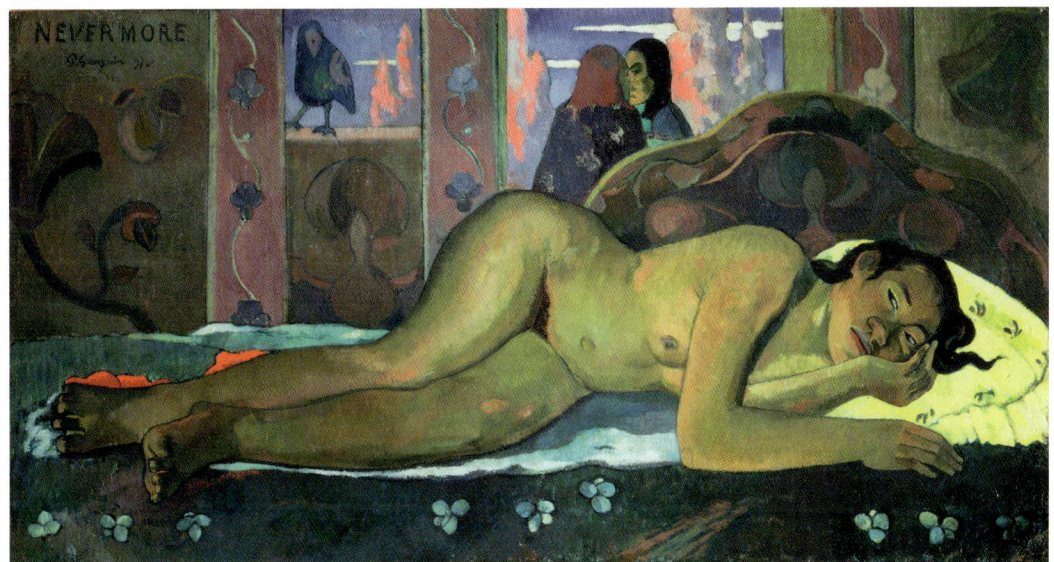

Nevermore, 1897
"O Taïti"
Oil on canvas, 60 x 116 cm (23½ x 45¾ in.)
London, The Courtauld Institute of Arts

"What's the point in sending this picture far away to join all the others that cannot be sold and only provoke howls of derision? This painting will only provoke still more derision. I am condemned to die of goodwill or hunger." He reconsidered the possibility of adapting his work to public taste. To make matters worse, the broken ankle was giving him problems: his syphilis grew worse and turned into a running sore. Gauguin was admitted to hospital for treatment he could not pay for. His debts mounted.

Gauguin's new gloom promptly found expression in his work. *Nevermore* (ill. p. 381) is another of his monumental nudes, with the distinctive nakedness of the earlier ones. But the very title suggests the clouds that were gathering above the artist. At the Café Voltaire banquet when Gauguin left, Mallarmé had recited his own translation of Edgar Allan Poe's poem *The Raven* (1845), which uses the word "nevermore" as a refrain. The menacing raven in the poem is a bird of ill omen. In Gauguin's painting the raven appears in the background, an unprepossessing apparition that seems ornamental rather than real. It is joined by two sinister figures whispering secret words that bode no good. And the naked woman in the foreground, rather than lolling in natural, innocent abandon, appears to be listening intently. The dangers are in the background, arranged (as if on a frieze) on a flat, tapestry-like area that offers us no purchase on spatial depth. The sense of menace remains unfocused but pervasive in the painting, and Gauguin's frame of mind was to worsen still further.

By this time, he seems to have lived in a mental state of emergency on Tahiti. Up one day and down the next, he lived in a rapid alternation of euphoria and depression. Barely a year after the exhilaration that had accompanied the birth of his child, he was emotionally at rock-bottom once more. He was racked with thoughts of suicide.

In spring 1897 a letter brought him terrible news from back home. His daughter Aline, in whom a hopeful Gauguin had seen the greatest chance that one of his children would prove artistically gifted, had died. In the reply he sent to Copenhagen he scarcely veiled his feeling that his wife's severity was to blame for the girl's death: "I do not want to say 'May God watch over you,'" he remarked bitterly, "but rather, quite plainly, 'May your conscience rest – so that you do not find yourself longing for the

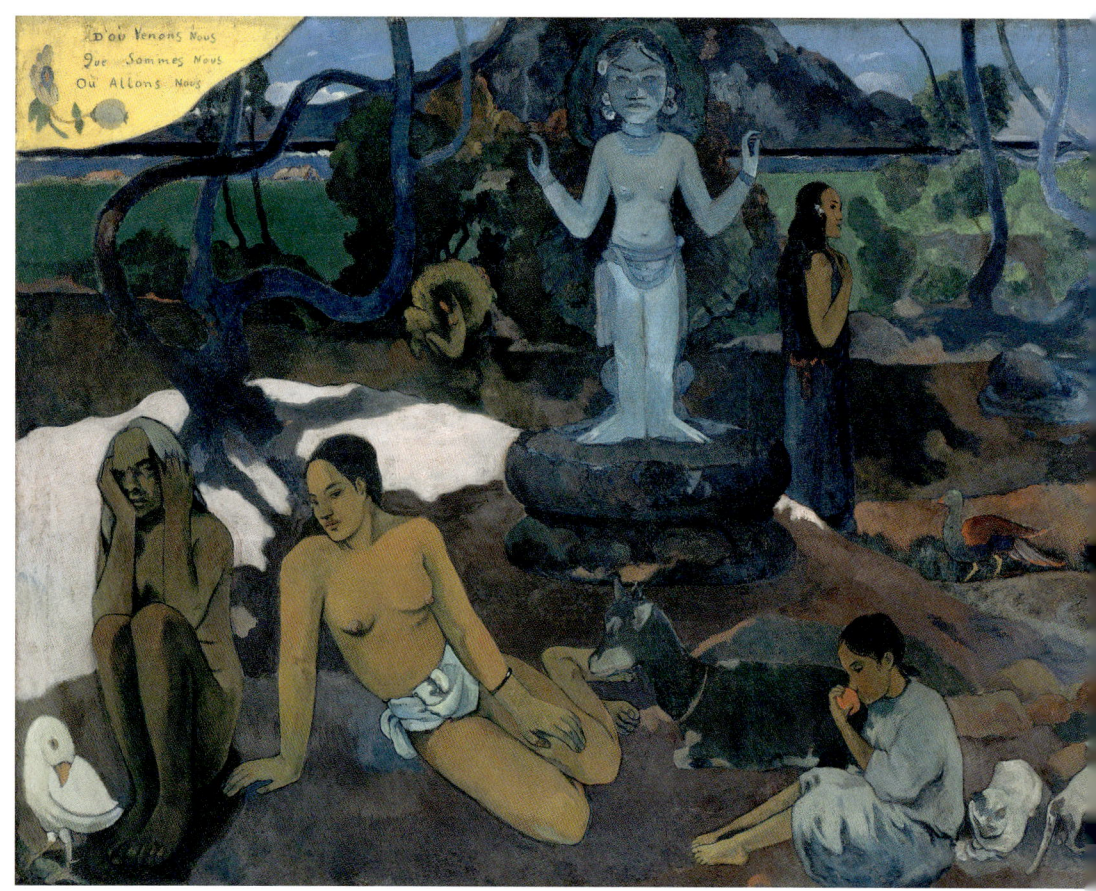

"*I have put all my energy into it one more time before I die, so painful a passion in such dreadful circumstances, so clear and accurate a vision, that there is no trace of precociousness, and life blossoms forth from it.*"

PAUL GAUGUIN

Where Do We Come From?
What Are We?
Where Are We Going?, 1897
"D'où venons-nous? Que sommes-nous?
Où allons-nous?"
Oil on canvas, 139.1 x 374.6 cm (54¾ x 147½ in.)
Boston, Museum of Fine Arts

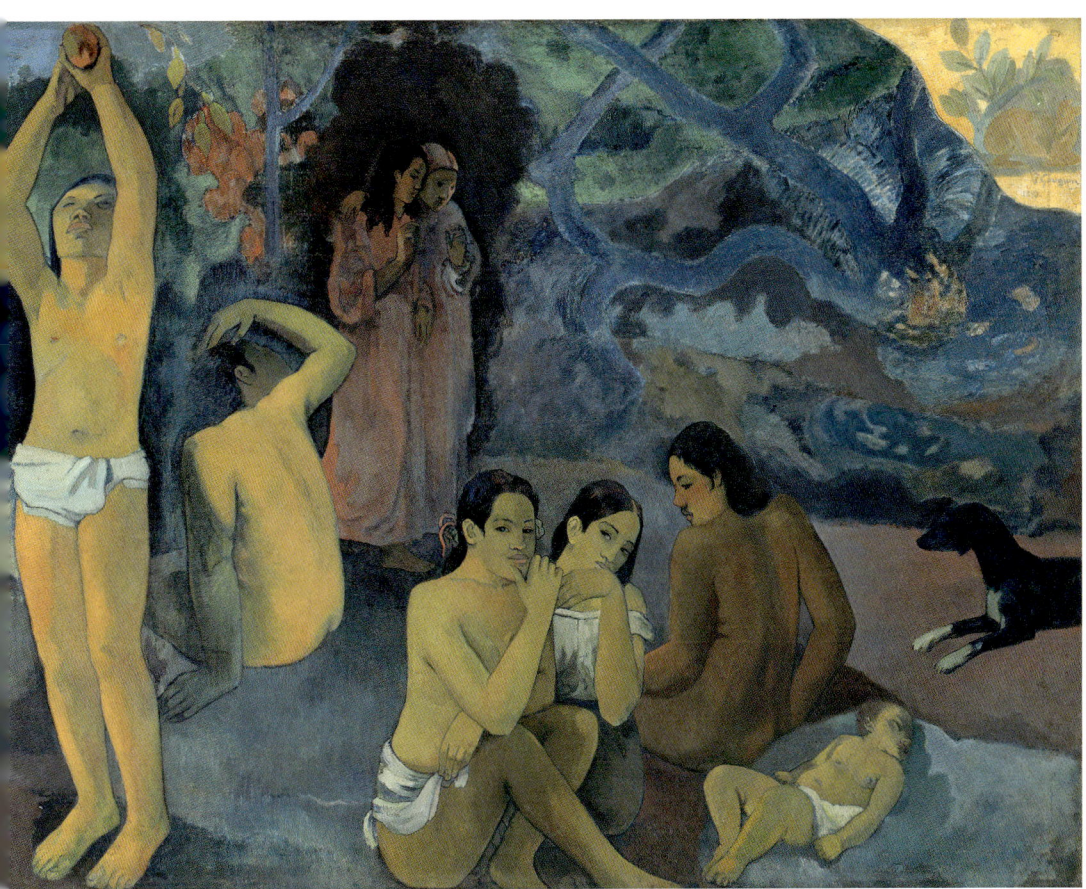

release of death.'" Gauguin himself often longed for that release: "I have lost a daughter. I do not love God any more." His powers of imagination, however, were still as vivid as ever and in his mind his daughter – to whom for many years he had not been a good father, and who had hardly registered his existence – was with him: "The grave you have made her is a delusion. In reality she lies here with me." He wanted her buried in that better world which existed in the South Seas one moment and the next in the artist's head alone.

Gauguin set himself a deadline. If things had not improved by the new year he would kill himself. In 1897 a letter from Monfreid, enclosing much-needed money, had eased his troubles. Now, in setting himself this ultimatum, he was out to test his luck again; but this time there was no good fairy. As well as further torment with his leg he now had an inflammation of the eye and feared "that I shall never recover my health completely". And the financial problems remained acute: "I have no dealer, no one to guarantee that I shall have something to eat each day. How can I go on? I can see no way out but death – which will release me from everything."

Towards the end of the year he prepared to keep the bargain he had made with himself. He had made a hell of the paradise he never tired of painting. Better men than he might live there if they liked, but he himself wanted to get out, to show that he did not belong there, however tirelessly he had wanted to be accepted on the island of the blessed: "I think everything that ought and ought not to be said about me has been said. All I want is silence, silence, and yet again silence. I want to be left to die peacefully and forgotten."

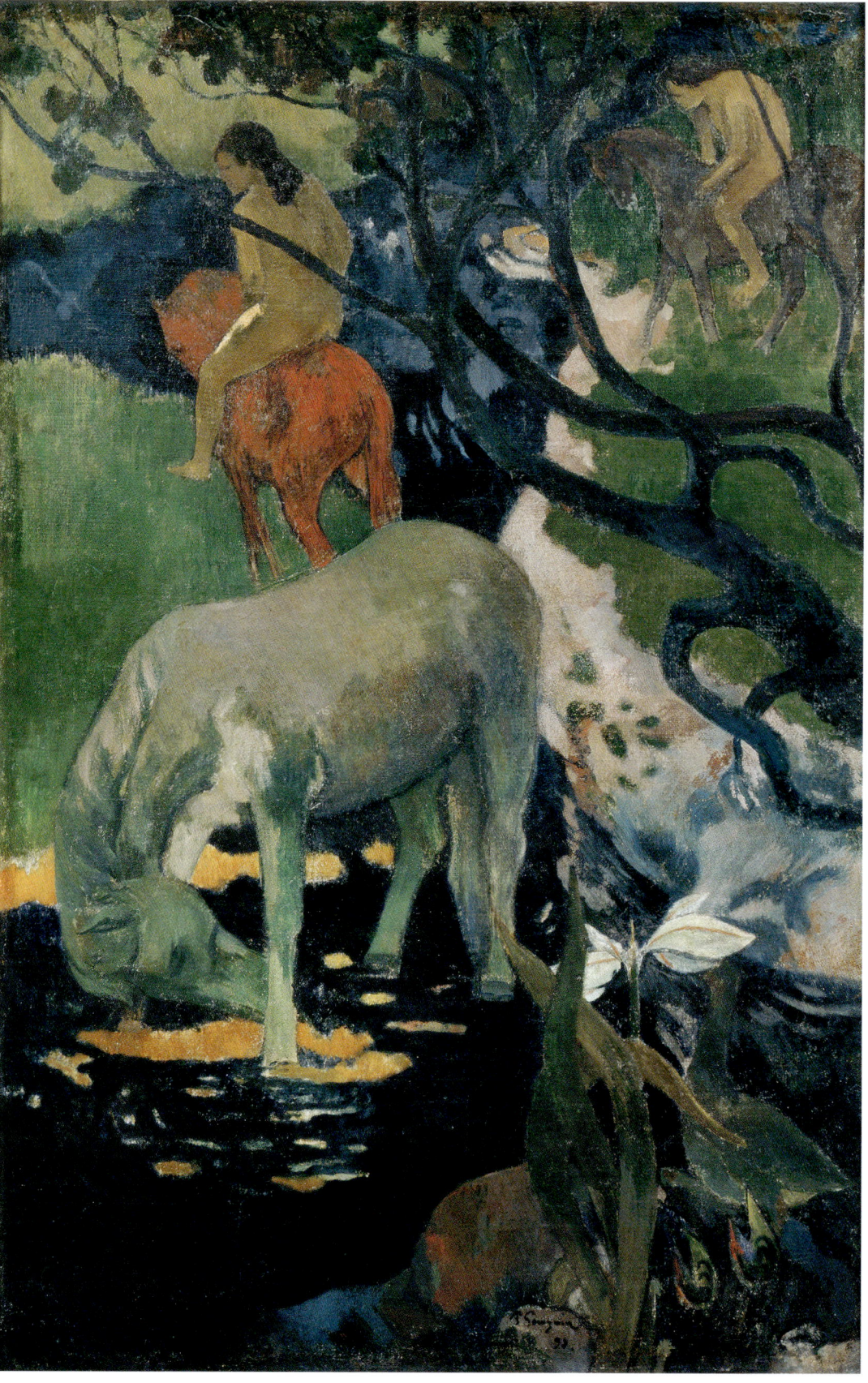

OPPOSITE
The White Horse, 1898
Oil on canvas,
140.5 x 92 cm (55¼ x 36¼ in.)
Paris, Musée d'Orsay

Bouquet of Flowers, c. 1895/96
Watercolour on paper,
19.2 x 11.8 cm (7½ x 4¾ in.)
Paris, Musée du Louvre,
Département des Arts graphiques

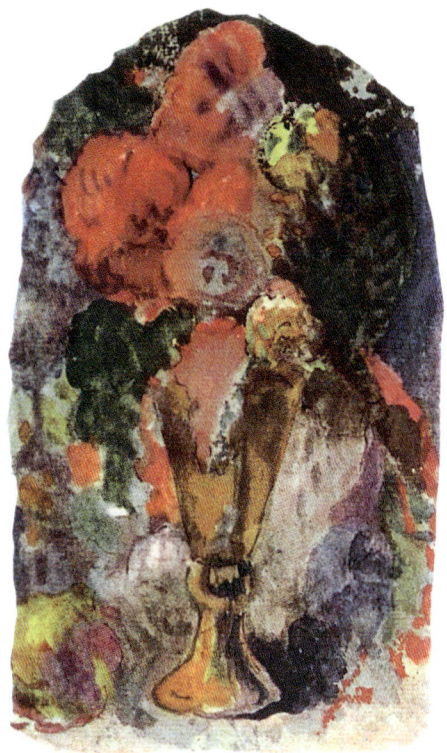

But Gauguin had not quite turned his back on the world of the living yet. He still had something he wanted to say, so that the contemptuous, mocking crowds would perceive his true worth when he was gone. And so he summoned up all his strength and created his major image of the human condition, *Where Do We Come From? What Are We? Where Are We Going?* (ill. pp. 382/383). With hardly any preparation he set to work. He had nothing more to lose, and therefore no inhibitions about using his brush with the clumsy crudeness that the critics damned as "over-primitive". He was out to fling one final affirmation of artistic force in the world's face. "I have put all my energy into it one more time before I die," he wrote, "so painful a passion in such dreadful circumstances, so clear and accurate a vision, that there is no trace of precociousness, and life blossoms forth from it." He wanted it to be "comparable with the Gospels": once again, he was ambitiously aiming for that quality of divinity that he so liked to adumbrate in his work, a quality of universality.

The spectrum of human activity encompassed by the painting spans all of life, from birth to death, in all its wondrous diversity. The newborn child lying in the grass, seeing the light of day for the first time, marks one boundary of Gauguin's stage, and the careworn old woman who looks so downcast as she meditates upon the past marks the other. Between the two lies the copious adult world of fears and joys. The exotic idol in the background, and the two people walking (possibly lovers), are there for atmospheric effect, and bridge the gap between Man and the natural setting. Gauguin reveals considerable ambition in the way in which he placed some favourite subjects in his panorama – the relaxed reclining nude, the figures sitting lost in thought, the cult statue. The figures are there to evoke associative meanings rather than to explain or illustrate. Gauguin was not concerned with being understood: rather, he was interpreting life as a great mystery. The world's lack of understanding, which was pushing him towards suicide, was obliquely expressed in his emphasis of the impenetrable and incomprehensible.

Once he had completed this painting, his testament, Gauguin retreated into the hills to die, like a wounded animal. He took arsenic with him, intending to poison himself. His attempt at suicide was unsuccessful, however. Pathetically enough, Gauguin swallowed too much and promptly vomited the arsenic up again, so that the overdose had no very serious consequences. Somehow or other he managed to get back to town, where he was taken to hospital, a sick man. Gradually he recovered. His circumstances had not improved, and deportation threatened if he could not pay his debts, so he was obliged to take the kind of routine job he hated so much, working in a creditor's office. In the meantime, Monfreid succeeded in selling *Where Do We Come From? What Are We? Where Are We Going?* The painting, which had proved not to be a testament after all, brought Gauguin 1,000 francs. Of all his works, it was the most awkward and unsophisticated that had found a buyer. Gauguin's courage revived.

In the period following these critical months, the artist was calm and relaxed. Indeed, he seemed filled with a blessed tranquillity. As if nothing had happened, his art picked up the familiar motif of the dreamy paradise island again. *The White Horse* (ill. p. 384) is an eloquent example. Painted when Gauguin was convalescing, it reiterates a view of the harmony between Man and Nature as a cure for despair and mortal fear. The animal in the foreground, free of reins, reaching its neck down to the water, communicates a sense of the animal instinct that prevails on the island. Mankind lives in friendship with the beasts. In the background, people are seen riding animals; no lengthy break-ing-in has been needed – Man and beast respect each other, and Nature is Man's partner, not his tool. Mutual pleasure in the world is the source of universal happiness. In the period following his break-down, Gauguin resumed his quest for that state of innocence.

Help from overseas was at hand as well. With the painter's written authority, Monfreid had sold off all Gauguin's pictures for next to nothing. They were bought by the art dealer Ambroise Vollard. Later, Pablo Picasso was to immortalize Vollard in one of his Cubist portraits, but in the closing years of the nineteenth century there were many who viewed him rather critically, thinking his rapid rise to eminence was due to a preference for good business over good art. And now, in November and December 1898, it was Vollard, of all people, who exhibited the Gauguins he had just acquired for a song. At first Gauguin was vexed. But then Vollard made him the offer he had been waiting longer than a decade for. He guaranteed the painter 2,400 francs a year plus the cost of his materials, and, over and above that, proposed to pay 200 francs for every painting and thirty francs for every drawing. Gauguin knew, of course, that a painter friend of his, Maurice Denis, had an arrangement worth four times as much; but then, life on Tahiti was far cheaper. From now on, Gauguin would be able to lead a life free of financial cares. Would the door to his earthly paradise be opened at last?

Gauguin's new peace and self-possession increasingly made themselves felt in his choice of motifs. His painting *Two Tahitian Women* (ill. p. 387) have a monumental dignity of a classical kind. The two women are standing right in the foreground, perfectly naturally, not looking at us, as if they were alone. There is nothing artificial in their pose. They have not been positioned by Gauguin to match figures in art history, as was his habit in his nudes. With its bright red fruit blossoms, which attract our attention, the picture remains discreet, and wholly devoid of grand gestures. The background setting is totally abstract. In dispensing with a backdrop of suggestive imagery, Gauguin helped his human

Two Tahitian Women, 1899
Oil on canvas, 94 x 72.4 cm (37 x 28½ in.)
New York, The Metropolitan Museum of Art,
Gift of William Church Osborn

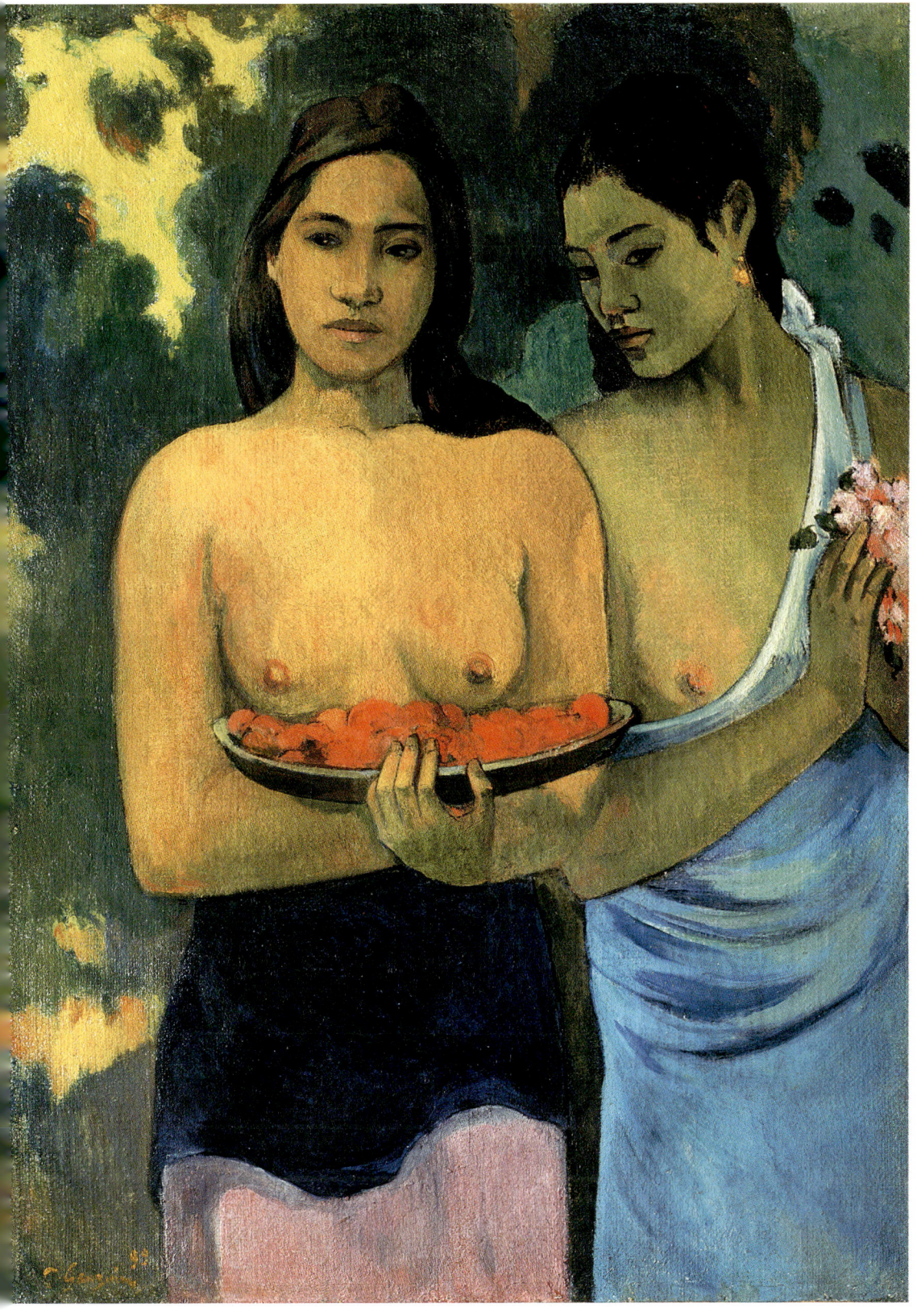

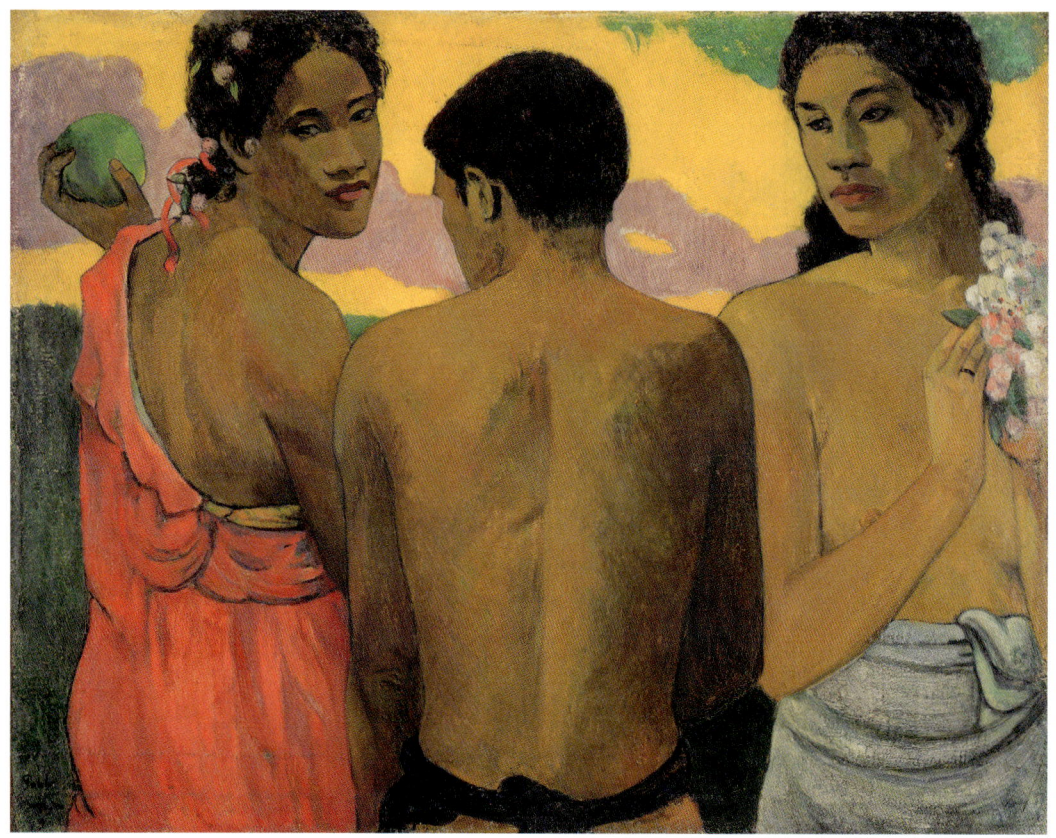

Three Tahitians, 1899
Oil on canvas, 73 x 94 cm (28¾ x 37 in.)
Edinburgh, Scottish National Gallery

figures (and the painting as well) to achieve a quality of charismatic timelessness.

The group of *Three Tahitians* (ill. p. 388) makes the same impression of warm and honest intimacy. They too seem transfigured, and have an almost statuesque presence in this ambience of simplicity. They are neither talking to each other nor attempting to make contact with us; instead, they have a certain monumentality (against a background which is again abstract) – like monuments to the spirit of peaceable contentment. The massiveness of form and the solidity of colour guarantee the work's rapt dignity. No details mar the vivid stature of the figures or detract from their lively physicality. These are not specific human bodies; these are not individuals; they are symbols of a life of peace and harmony. Gauguin was always out to portray that life; and to emphasize the individual, as European portraiture traditionally does, would not have fitted in with the replete naivety of the existence he was showing.

All in all, Gauguin should have been thriving on Tahiti. He enjoyed recognition and a friendly reception there, and his art was thought valuable and important. A native friend called Jotefa once spoke to him on the matter, and Gauguin recalled the conversation in these terms: "I believe Jotefa is the first person who has said that to me. They were the words of a savage or a child – you have to be one or the other to believe that an artist is performing a useful human task."

On Tahiti he was told what he had longed to hear back home: that art was useful, important, and relevant to everybody. He had travelled halfway round the world, far from bourgeois conceptions of art as a trivial pastime, in order to hear this confirmation of his mission, and of his very self. And yet

Gauguin seemed to have only a partial faith in Jotefa's statement, since he saw it as the opinion of a savage or a child. He continued to be divided and distrustful. While he saw the Tahitians as better human beings, he still valued their views less than those of his European contemporaries. If his savages were noble, they were second-class nobility.

His relaxed composure passed. He got entangled in countless legal battles. As editor-in-chief of the satirical magazine *Les Guêpes* (The Wasps), he raged against colonialism, with all its incompetence and corruption, and was promptly inundated with libel suits. Doubtless he meant well in expressing solidarity with the island people, but his typically impetuous and rude outbursts showed that he remained unable to live at peace with himself. His finances were in good shape now, and his health was improving too, so he had to seek out the irritants without which he would have been bored. He also founded his own journal *Le Sourire* (The Smile), and went on ranting at the colonial authorities, civilization, and indeed the entire world.

Gauguin portrayed the pleasant, amiable side of Tahiti – which had so far escaped the colonialists' clutches – in *Tahitian Idyll* (ill. p. 393). It is the mixture as before – the vegetation, people, and rudimentary huts – but now there is a new dynamic quality in it all. The narrow, red path pours like lava

And the Gold of Their Bodies, 1901
"Et l'or de leurs corps"
Oil on canvas, 67 x 76.5 cm (26½ x 30 in.)
Paris, Musée d'Orsay

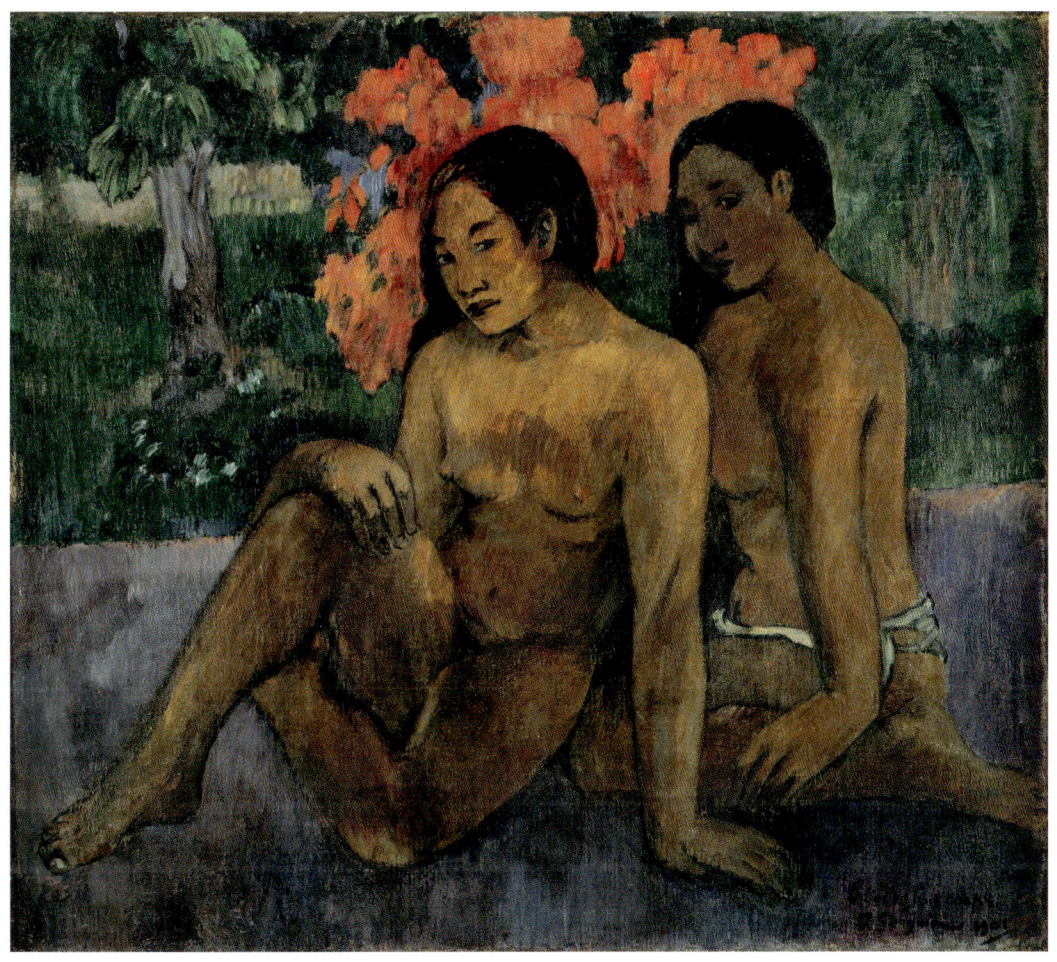

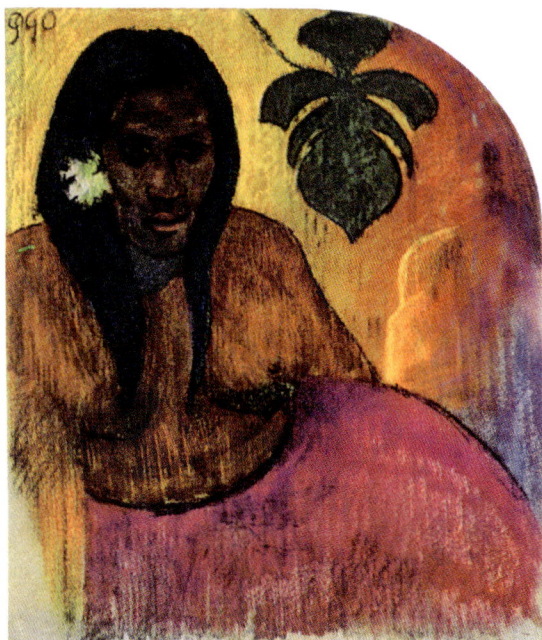

into the foreground, the sense of movement emphasized by the riotous tree trunks. The picture was to be a last avowal of faith in the island where he had sought an earthly Elysium; but the closeness has become ambiguous and the quality of energetic upheaval in the composition suggests change. And indeed there were changes in Gauguin's life, as he found himself obliged to look for another base in the tropics.

The immediate cause was the rumour of an epidemic raging in San Francisco. A good number of ships anchored in Tahiti to await developments before continuing to America. Instantly prices soared, and the cheap life that (in Gauguin's eyes) was one of the great advantages of the island was gone. In any case, he was beginning to feel that a change of scene was essential if his art was not to suffer: "My imagination began to flag on Tahiti, and in any case the public was growing too accustomed to Tahiti." Again he was confident: "My Brittany pictures seemed like rosewater after the Tahiti pictures. And once people see pictures from the Marquesas they'll think Tahiti was just eau de cologne."

On 10 September 1901 Paul Gauguin moved to Hiva Oa, the main island in the Marquesas, also a French colony. Gossip had it that his foremost reason for moving was the enforced chastity he was enduring on Tahiti, where the local women no longer found the grumbler with his gammy leg so attractive. The Marquesas, at any rate, were not on the major shipping lanes and were thus less exposed to the dubious blessings of civilization, and Gauguin soon had a new lover, Marie-Rose Vaeoho by name.

He called his hut "The House of Pleasure", and soon it was at the centre of a violent controversy. Gauguin had built his little house on land belonging to the Catholic Church, but missionaries were as much of a thorn in his flesh as ever, and presently two of his own carvings graced the front garden. They were titled *Father Lecher* and *Thérèse*. As usual, the artist got on best with the native population. Soon they were meeting at his home every evening, carousing and drinking. The church foresaw its flock being dispersed, and the bishop intervened, announcing a ban on visits to the artist. And once again Gauguin was embroiled in legal battles.

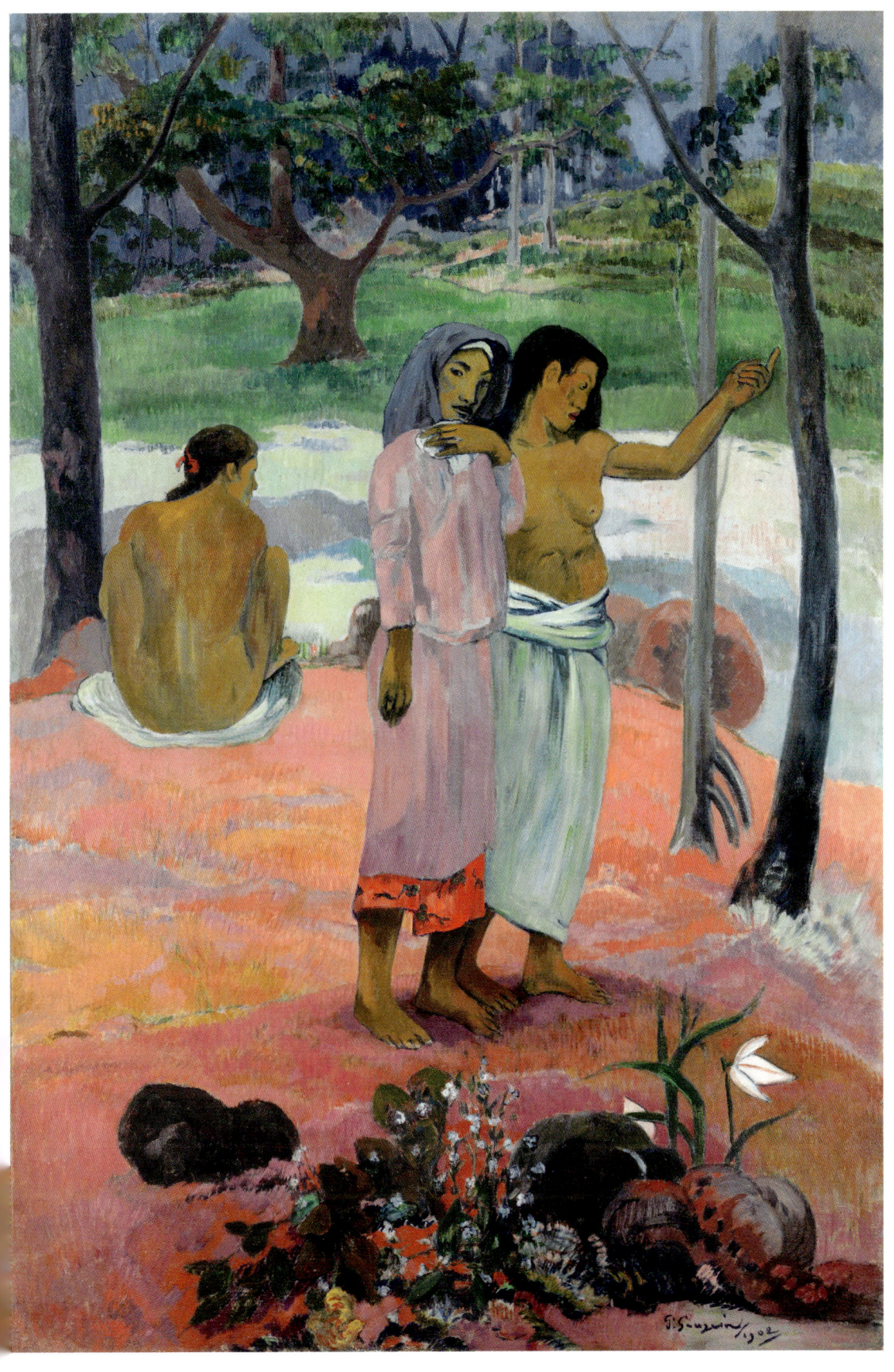

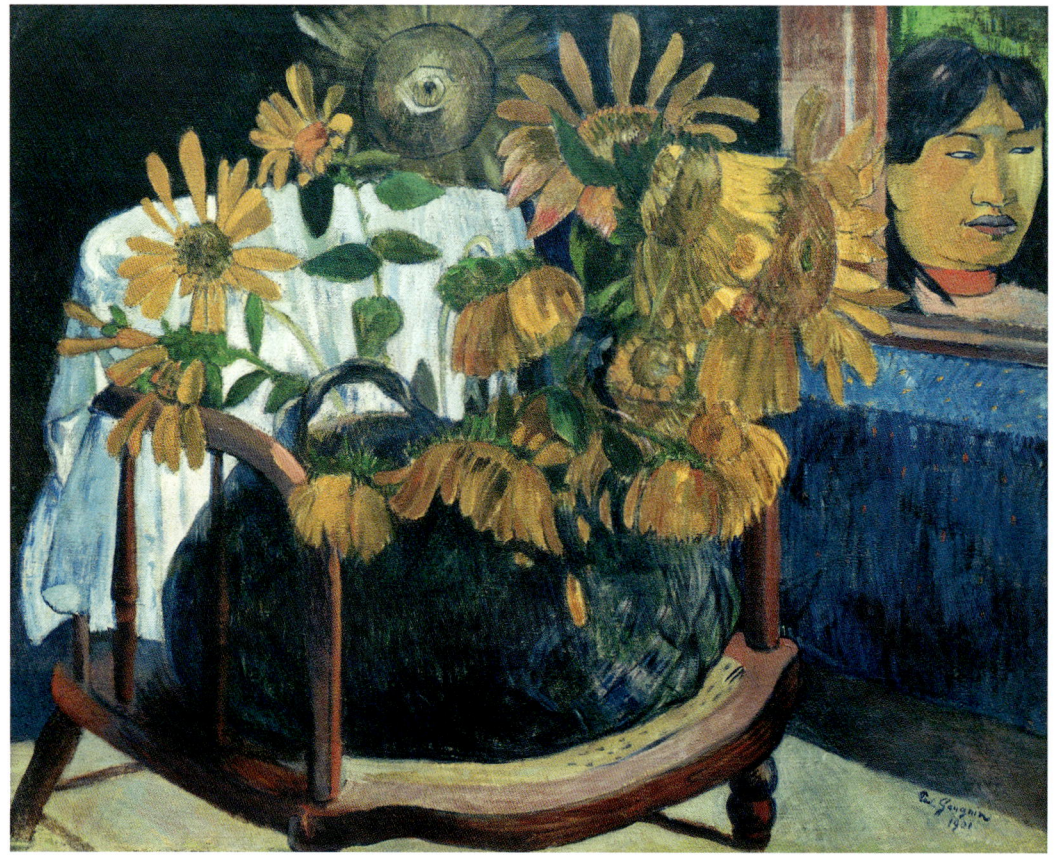

Sunflowers, 1901
Oil on canvas, 73 x 92 cm (28¾ x 36¼ in.)
St Petersburg, Hermitage Museum

The Reverend Vernier, who ran the Protestant school on the island, described him in this way: "He looked like a real Maori, with his colourful native-style loincloth and a genuine Tahitian shirt, his feet almost invariably bare, and on his head a green cloth student cap with a silver clasp at the side." And that was the appearance Gauguin presented in court when he faced charges of tax evasion. He refused to pay his taxes on the grounds that he was a savage. He hobbled into the courtroom on crutches, and had to be forcibly removed because he insisted on heckling: Gauguin the angry, anarchist ruffian, fighting for a better world.

The paintings of this period were poetic reminiscences of Arcadia. *Girl with a Fan* (ill. p. 395) is a portrait of Tohotaua, wife of the Hiva Oa witch doctor, and focuses on the expressiveness of her face. Gauguin based the painting on a photograph, but in the transfer process he purified the image of the chance elements of reality. Again Gauguin borrows from classical art; but this time the savage has the genuinely refined features and distinguishing marks of true civilization. Her body is lit from the top right, while her face is lit from below, as if by torchlight, in theatrical fashion. Although she is a beautiful woman, the corners of her mouth reveal a trace of bitterness, and in her eyes there is melancholy. Her position emphasizes these suggestions of insecurity: her chair appears to be tipping forwards into the depths that yawn this side of the picture's edge.

Two of Gauguin's last works examined riding as a metaphor of the close relationship between man and beast. In *The White Horse* (ill. p. 384) Gauguin had approached the subject circumspectly,

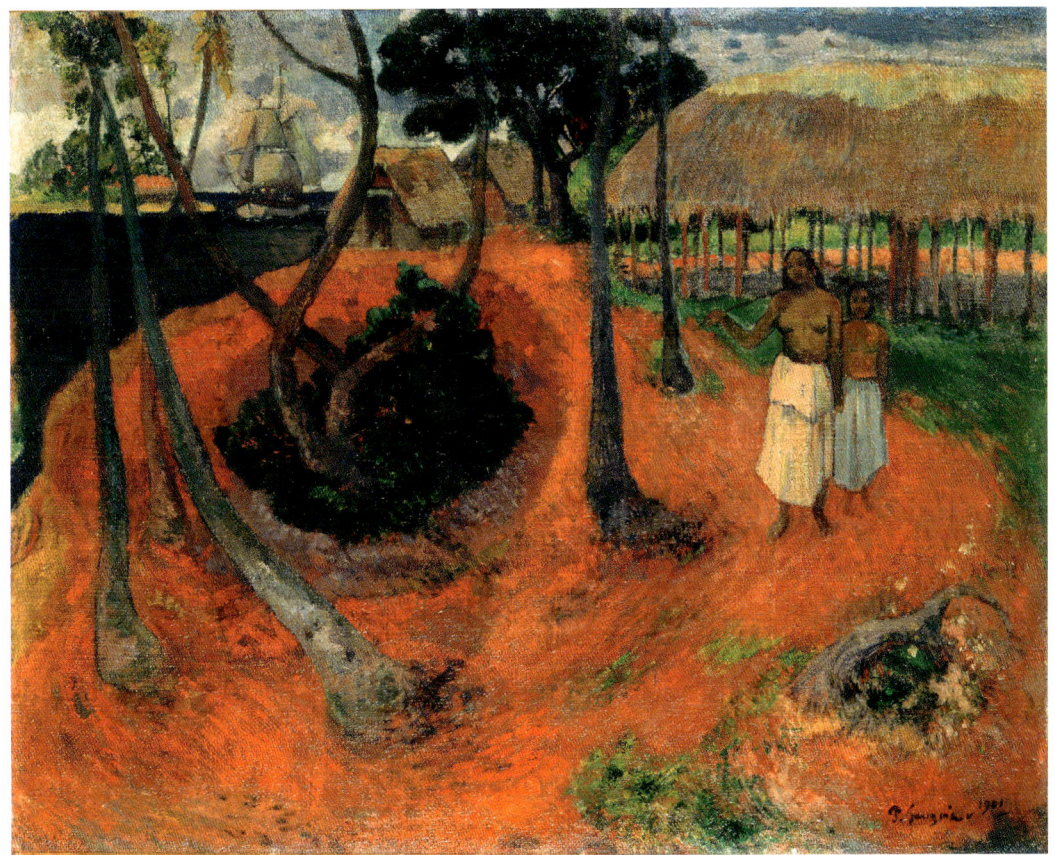

Tahitian Idyll, 1901
Oil on canvas, 74.5 x 94.5 cm (29¼ x 37¼ in.)
Zurich, Foundation E. G. Bührle Collection

presenting it in lusciously overgrown jungle, but in the two paintings titled *Horsemen on the Beach* (ills. pp. 396 and 397) he chose a more open setting: the seashore. Both seashore scenes are given a touch of mystery by the two riders seen in profile, placed parallel to the baseline and obstructing the relaxed movement of the other riders. An unforced sensitivity to the harmony of the human and animal kingdoms takes on a more portentous dimension, and the vividness of these creatures is contained within limits that imply something that lies beyond. A note of discontent can be felt in the work. As in *Girl with a Fan*, dark premonitions can be sensed. And the friendly, relaxed ride along the beach somehow only serves to heighten those premonitions.

Barbarous Tales (ill. p. 372) shows how much Gauguin's change of mood had infected his appreciation of the natural, naive world of the islands. The familiar motif of natives relaxing has been expanded to include the brooding figure of a European, one of Gauguin's Paris friends, the poet Jacob Meijer de Haan. He is interposed between the peaceful couple and the romantic jungle setting, and is seen contemplating the simple beauty of the two natives with all the ponderousness of the intellectual. And so we see Gauguin projecting into his poet friend his own awareness of the gap between himself and the people he admired. He had failed in his desire to become a savage. And it is this insight that makes *Barbarous Tales* his true testament, rather than *Where Do We Come From? What Are We? Where Are We Going?*, which pretends that all the differences between the cultures might be brushed aside by a pathetic appeal to spirit and life. Gauguin's whole heart was in his attempt to reconcile his love of the tropical world with the needs and wishes of the local people. He was a kind of inverted missionary. He wanted to be converted by them. But in the last analysis he remained as much a prisoner of his own world as the missionaries who supposed that what was good for them was good for everybody.

The court's verdict in the tax evasion case was now known, and Gauguin was sentenced to three months' imprisonment and a fine of 1,000 francs. "I shall have to lodge an appeal on Tahiti. The travel and lodging costs, and above all the lawyer's fee! How much will it come to? It will be the ruin of my finances and of my health. These troubles will be the end of me." Hateful society and its institutions did indeed manage to silence Gauguin. On 8 May 1903 Gauguin, the choleric anti-cleric, sent for a priest. He had had two attacks and wanted the church's final blessing. Soon afterwards he was dead. The priest reported that the natives could be heard wailing: "Gauguin is dead! We are lost!"

A few days earlier Gauguin had received another letter from Monfreid: "These days you are referred to as that exceptional, magnificent artist who sends in his bewildering but inimitable works from the middle of the Pacific Ocean – the creation of a great man who, as it were, has departed this world. You enjoy the immunity of the great dead. You have entered the annals of art history." Gauguin was not to live to relish his triumph. Who can say what his reaction to the world's sudden applause would have been? It was still that hated, unbearable world which he forever wanted to escape. And yet it was in Gauguin and in his rejection of the world that civilization, complex as it is, discovered its own image.

Girl with a Fan, 1902
Oil on canvas,
91.9 x 72.9 cm (36¼ x 28¾ in.)
Essen, Museum Folkwang

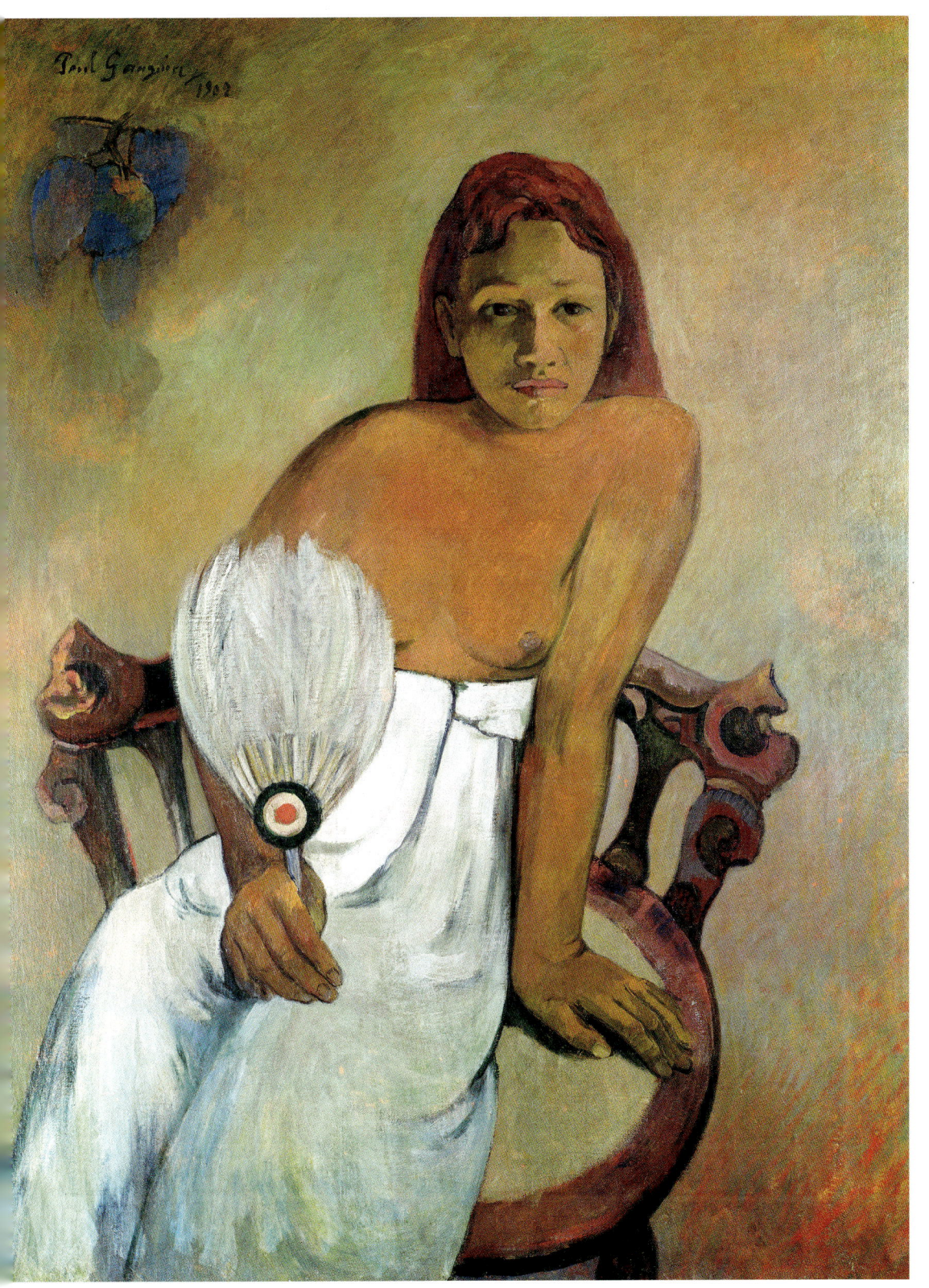

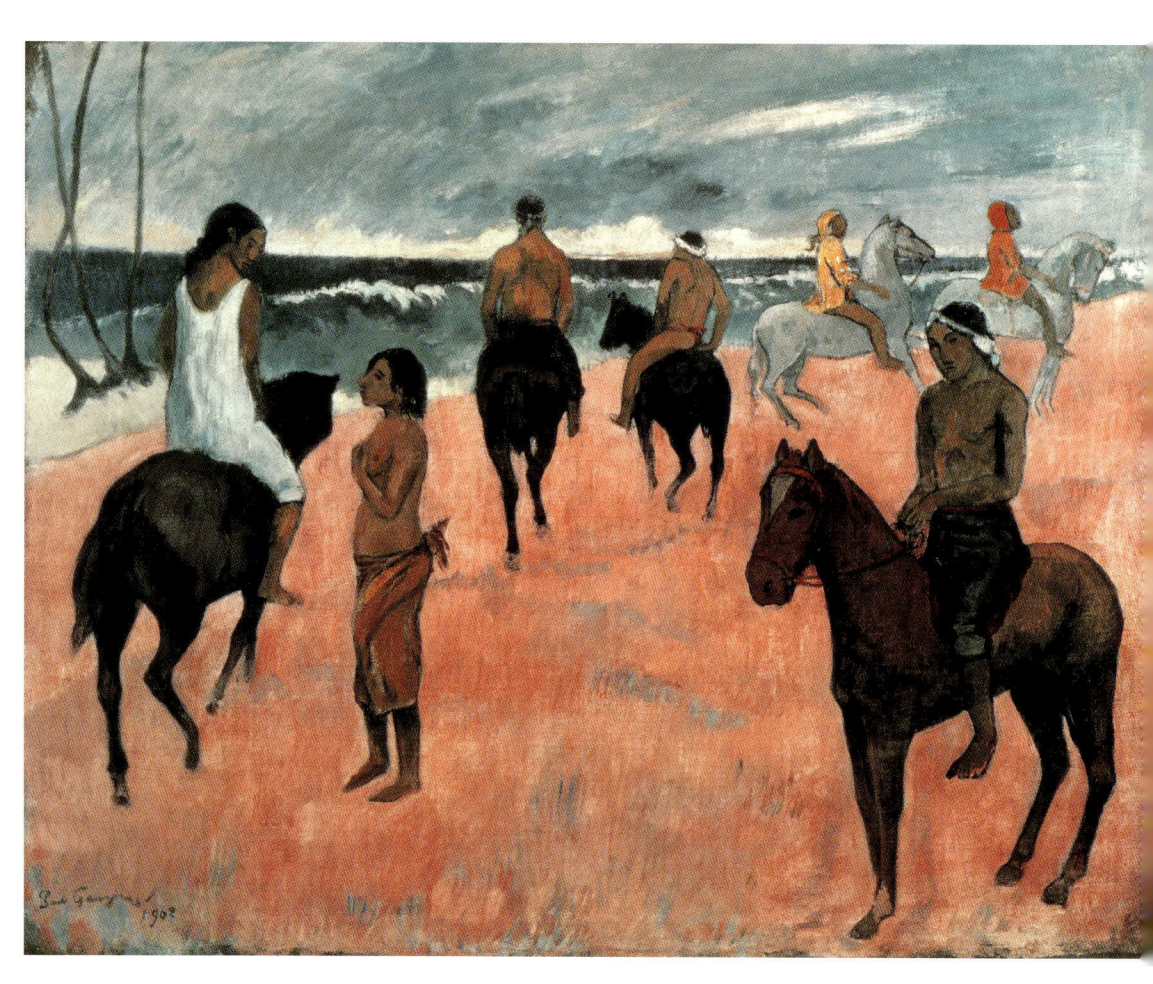

Horsemen on the Beach, 1902
Oil on canvas, 73 x 92 cm (28¾ x 36¼ in.)
Private collection

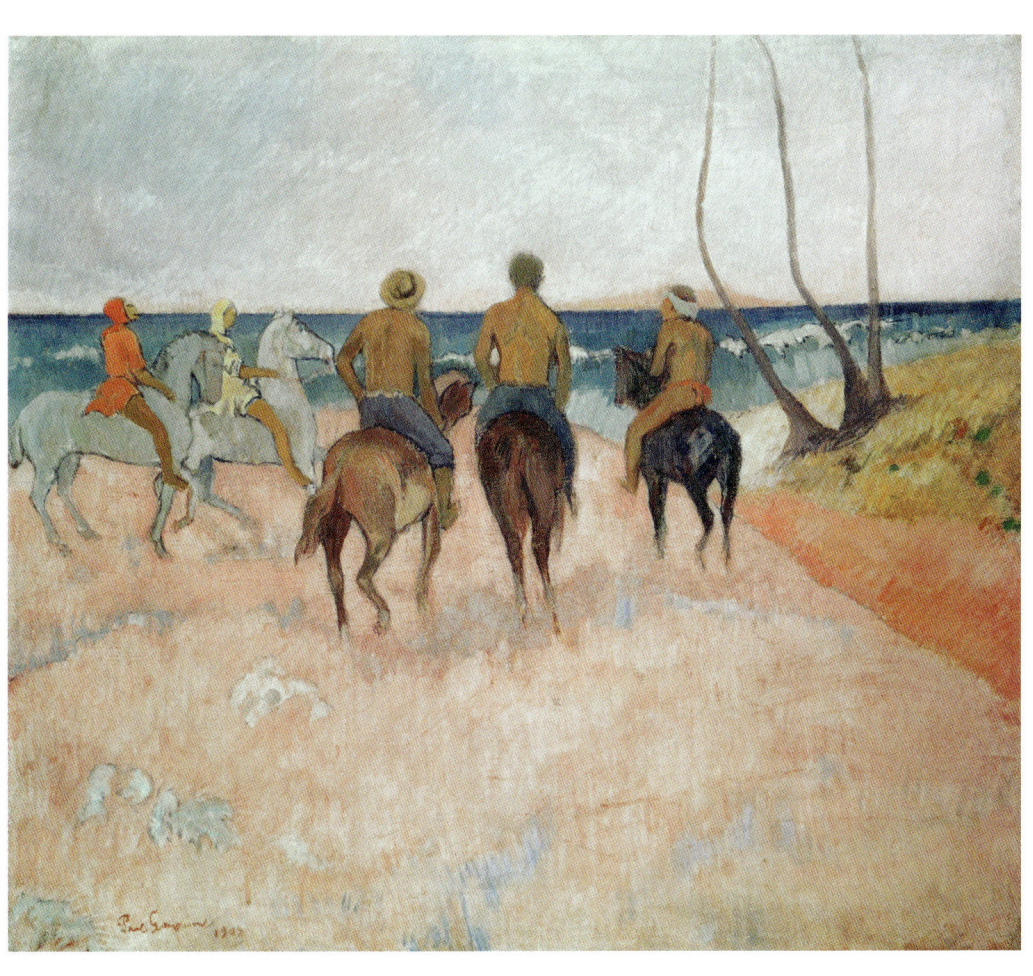

Horsemen on the Beach I, 1902
Oil on canvas, 65.6 x 75.9 cm (26 x 30 in.)
Essen, Museum Folkwang

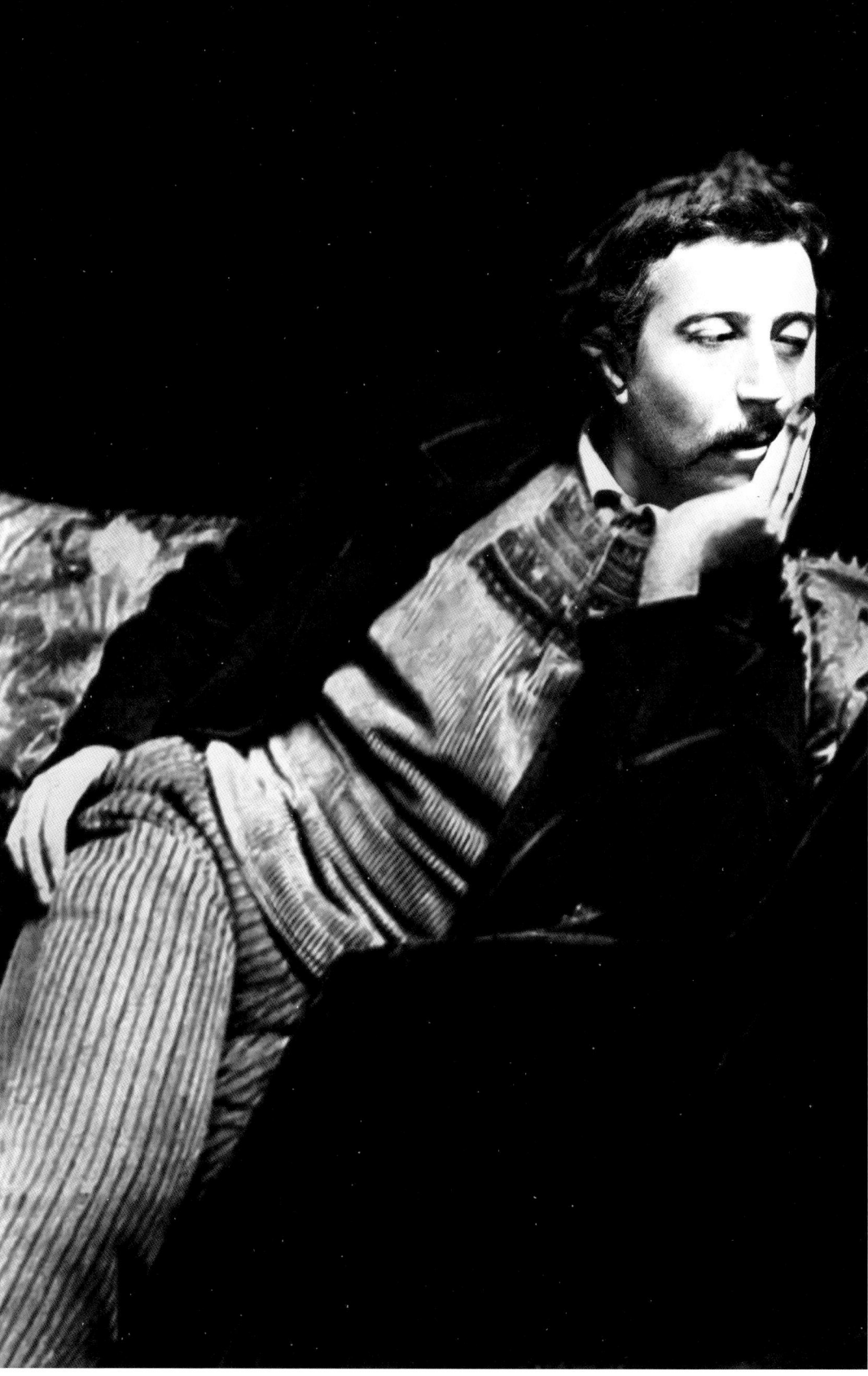

Paul Gauguin 1848–1903
Life and Work

1848 On 7 June Eugène Henri Paul Gauguin is born in Paris, the son of Clovis Gauguin, a republican editor, and his wife Aline Marie Chazal.

1849 After Louis-Napoléon comes to power, the family emigrate to Peru. Gauguin's father dies on the way. The mother and children stay with relatives in Lima.

1855 Return to Uncle Isidore's in Orléans.

1859 Paul goes to the Petit Séminaire, a boarding grammar school in Orléans.

1862 The family returns to Paris, where Paul attends a pre-naval college.

1865 Paul goes to sea as a ship's boy on the *Luzitano*, voyaging between Le Havre and Rio de Janeiro.

1866 Thirteen-month voyage round the world as second lieutenant on the *Chili*. Death of his mother.

OPPOSITE
Paul Gauguin, 1891

ABOVE LEFT
Paul Gauguin and his wife Mette Sophie Gad in Copenhagen, 1885

ABOVE RIGHT
Mette Gauguin and the five children, 1888

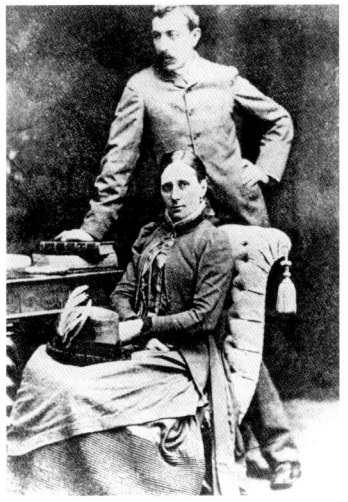 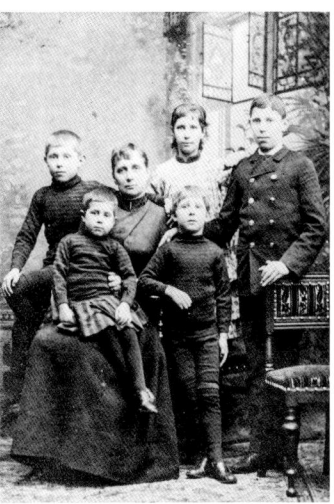

1868 Joins the navy.

1871 Able-bodied seaman aboard a corvette, the *Jérôme-Napoléon*, during the Franco-Prussian War. After the war Gauguin works as a broker's agent at Bertin's in Paris, and meets Claude Émile Schuffenecker. First drawings.

1872 Gauguin and Schuffenecker study painting and visit the Louvre together.

1873 22 November: Gauguin marries a Danish governess, Mette Sophie Gad.

1874 Visits Pissarro and meets other Impressionists, collects their paintings. Studies painting at the Colarossi Academy. Son Émile born.

1876 Daughter Aline born. Exhibits at the Salon for the first time.

1879 Son Clovis born. Spends summer painting with Pissarro in Pontoise. His bank and stock exchange deals provide a comfortable income and he continues to buy paintings. Exhibits at the Fourth Impressionist Exhibition and at the Société des Artistes Indépendants.

1880 Rents a studio in the Vaugirard quarter. Exhibits with the Impressionists and the Indépendants.

1881 Painting with Pissarro and Paul Cézanne. *Suzanne Sewing* (ill. p. 310) is well received. Son Jean René born.

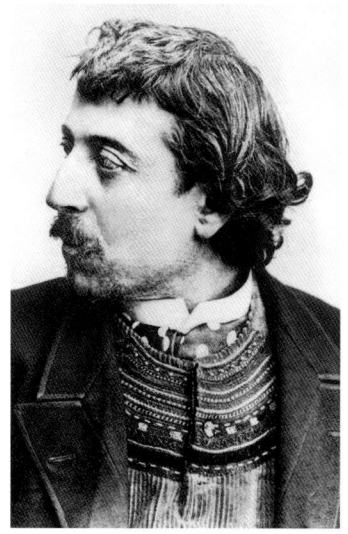

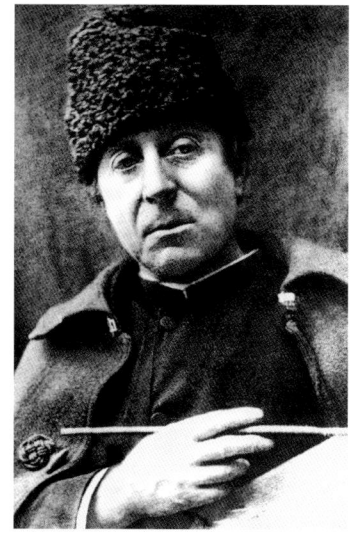

1890 In Paris until June. Plans to emigrate. Second stay in *Le Pouldu*. Acquaintance with the Café Voltaire Symbolists: Daniel de Monfreid, Odilon Redon, Stéphane Mallarmé. Organizes an auction of his paintings to finance his emigration.

1891 Sells 30 paintings at the Hôtel Drouot for 9,860 francs. Quarrel with Bernard. Bids farewell to his family in Copenhagen and friends in Paris and on 4 April sails to Tahiti, where he arrives on 28 June. Starts on his autobiographical book, *Noa Noa*.

1882 Exhibits at the Seventh Impressionist Exhibition.

1883 Quits his stock exchange job. Break with Cézanne. Spends the summer painting with Pissarro in Osny. Birth of fifth child, Pola.

1884 Moves to Rouen, but then in October financial straits force him to move to Mette's parents in Copenhagen. Unsuccessful attempt to be a sailcloth salesman.

1885 Exhibition in Copenhagen is a failure. Falls out with his in-laws and returns to Paris, taking Clovis. Mette stays in Denmark with the children.

1886 Works as a bill-poster. Puts Clovis in a pension and goes to Pont-Aven in Brittany, where he meets Émile Bernard. Again in Paris he meets Theo and Vincent van Gogh and Edgar Degas. Dreams of travelling to the tropics.

1887 Mette visits him in Paris. In April he and fellow painter Charles Laval travel to Panama and then Martinique. Both fall ill. Back in Paris he moves in with the Schuffeneckers. Theo van Gogh buys some pictures and ceramic works.

1888 February to October in Pont-Aven with Bernard, Laval and Jacob Meijer de Haan. Break with Impressionism. With Bernard he founds Synthetic Symbolism. Paints *Vision after the Sermon* (ill. p. 324). Solo exhibition at Theo van Gogh's gallery. Late autumn with Vincent van Gogh in Arles. Following their misunderstandings he returns to the Schuffeneckers in Paris.

1889 Exhibits twelve paintings with Les XX in Brussels. Schuffenecker arranges a show at the Café Volpini. In Pont-Aven again, and Le Pouldu. Influences young painters such as Paul Sérusier, Maurice Denis and Pierre Bonnard.

1892 Serious illness. He is nevertheless productive and sends seven paintings to Paris.

1893 Eye disease, loneliness and financial distress oblige him to return to Paris early. Uncle Isidore's legacy alleviates his situation. Rents studio in the rue Vercingétorix. Living with "Anna the Javanese" (see ill. p. 364).

1894 Farewell visit to Copenhagen. April to December with Anna in Brittany. Breaks his ankle in a brawl with sailors.

1895 Second (unsuccessful) auction at the Hôtel Drouot. 3 April sails for Tahiti a second time.

1896 Builds himself a live-in studio at Punaauia. Plagued by illness, depression and financial worries, but still paints numerous masterpieces.

1897 Aline dies. Definitive break with Mette. Serious illness: Gauguin's health ruined by alcohol and syphilis. *Noa Noa* published. Paints *Where Do We Come From? What Are We? Where Are We Going?* (ill. pp. 382/383).

1898 Attempts suicide. Hospitalized in Papeete. Takes a job in Paofai until money arrives from Monfreid in Paris.

1899 Works for the satirical magazine *Les Guêpes* (The Wasps) and publishes his own journal *Le Sourire* (The Smile). His lover Pau'ura gives birth to a son, Émile.

1900 Ambroise Vollard, a Parisian dealer, offers Gauguin a contract and buys pictures. Improvement in his financial position but again hospitalized. Son Clovis dies.

1901 In the autumn, sells his Tahiti house and moves to Atuana on the island of Dominique in the Marquesas. Builds his "House of Pleasure" on Catholic mission land.

1902 Quarrels with the church and colonial administration in Atuana. Heart disease and syphilis cause him to long for home. Monfreid advises against returning since it would destroy the myth of the South Seas painter.

1903 The refractory Gauguin is sentenced to three months in prison and fined 1,000 francs. He has neither the energy nor the money to defend himself. Before he can begin his sentence he dies on 8 May, aged 54, at his home in Atuona.

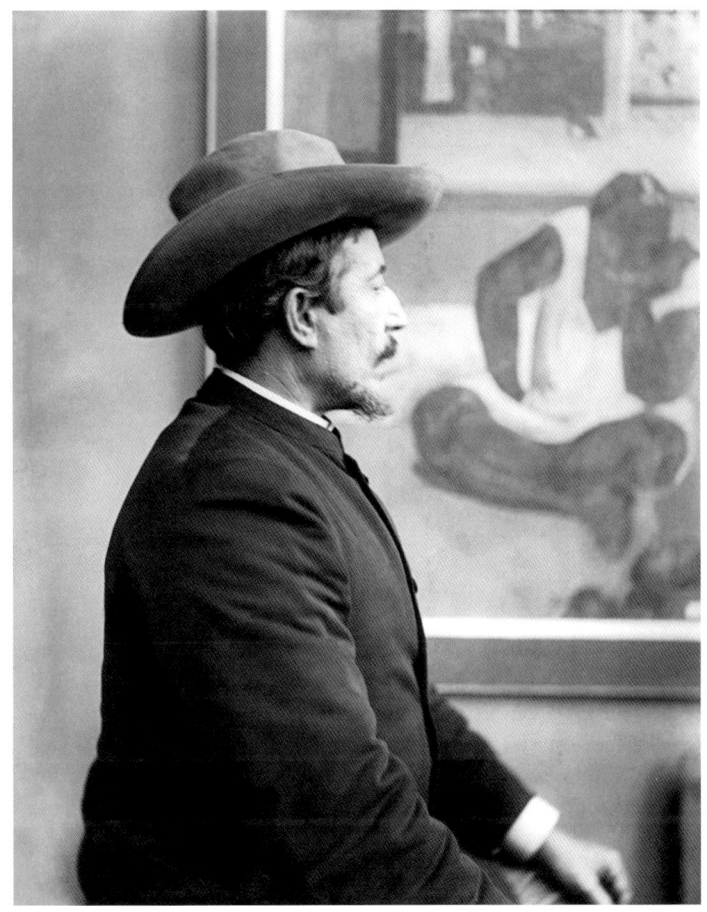

OPPOSITE LEFT
Paul Gauguin in Copenhagen, 1891

OPPOSITE RIGHT
Paul Gauguin with his palette, *c.* 1900

Gauguin in Paris in front of his painting *Brooding Woman* (ill. p. 345), 1893

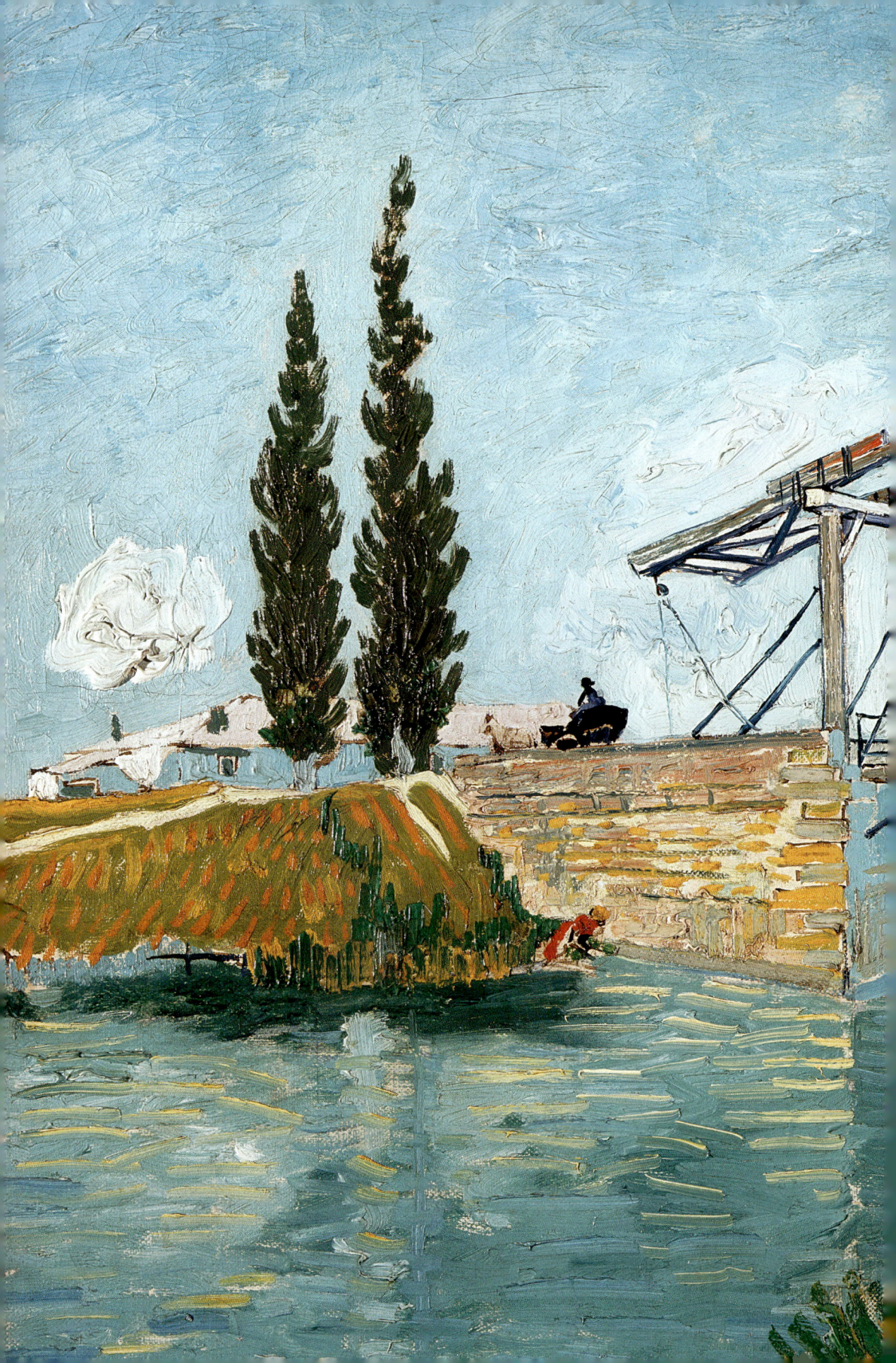

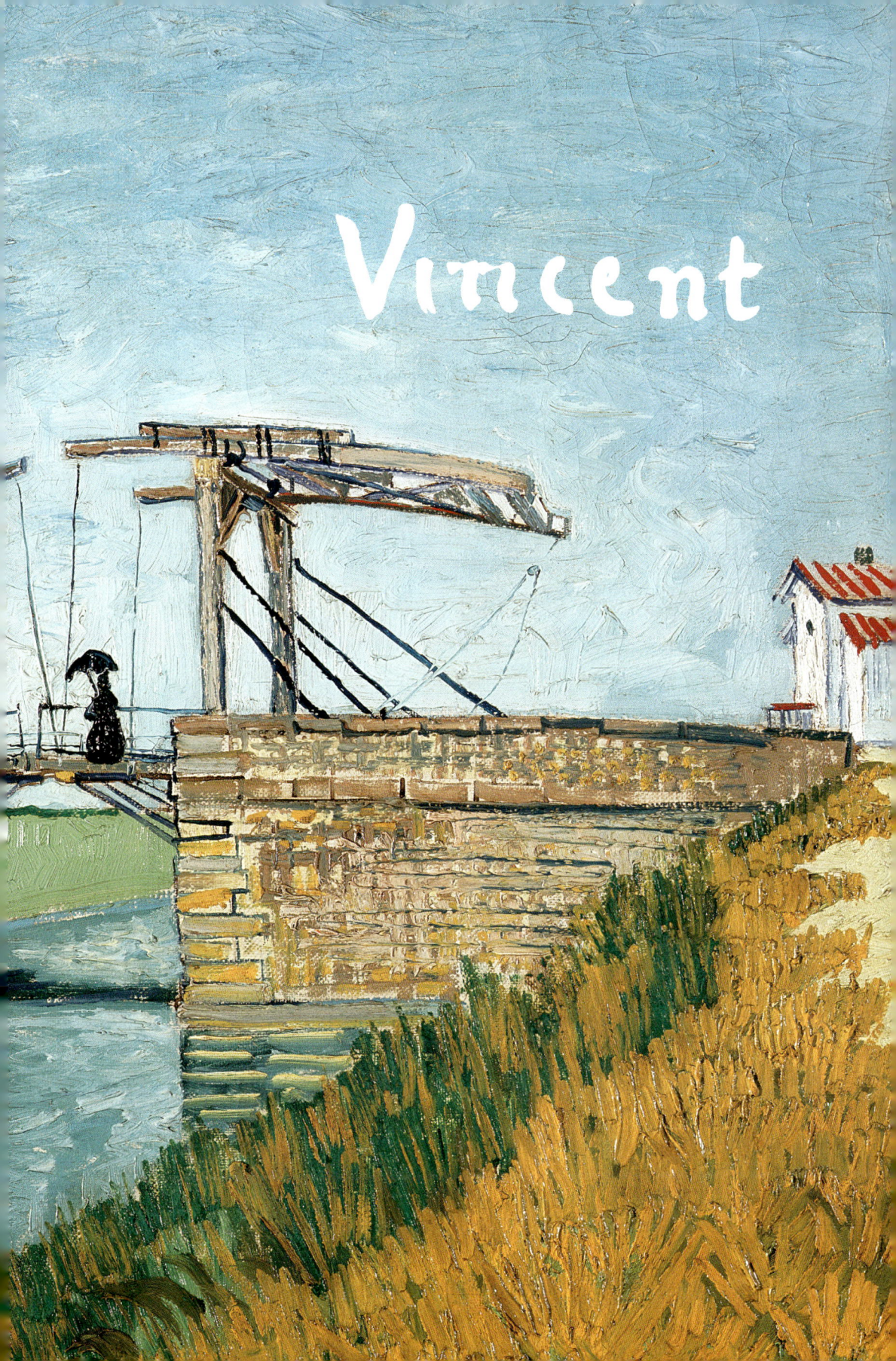

Vincent

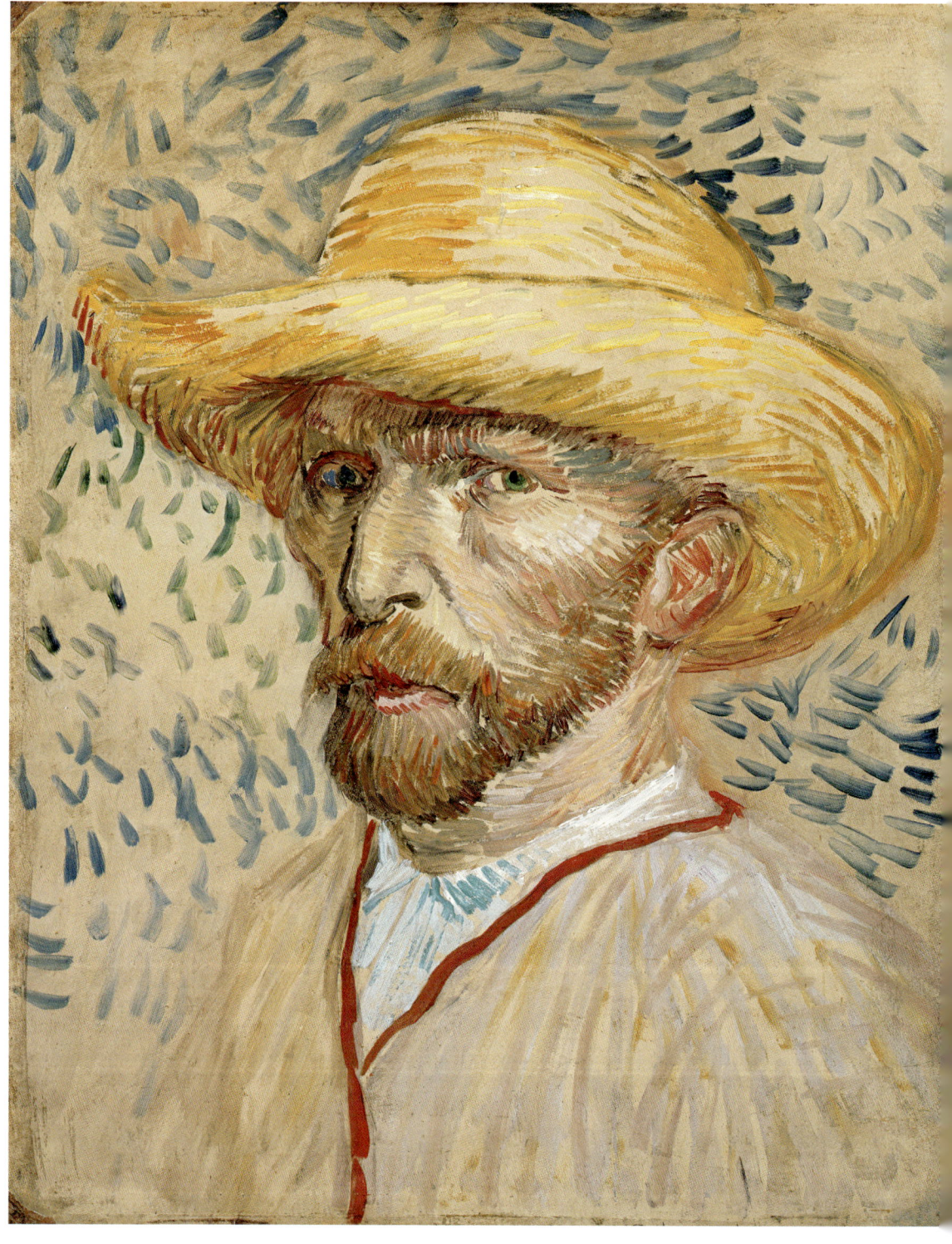

Ingo F. Walther

Vincent van Gogh

Vision and Reality

*"I put my heart and my soul into my work,
and have lost my mind in the process."*

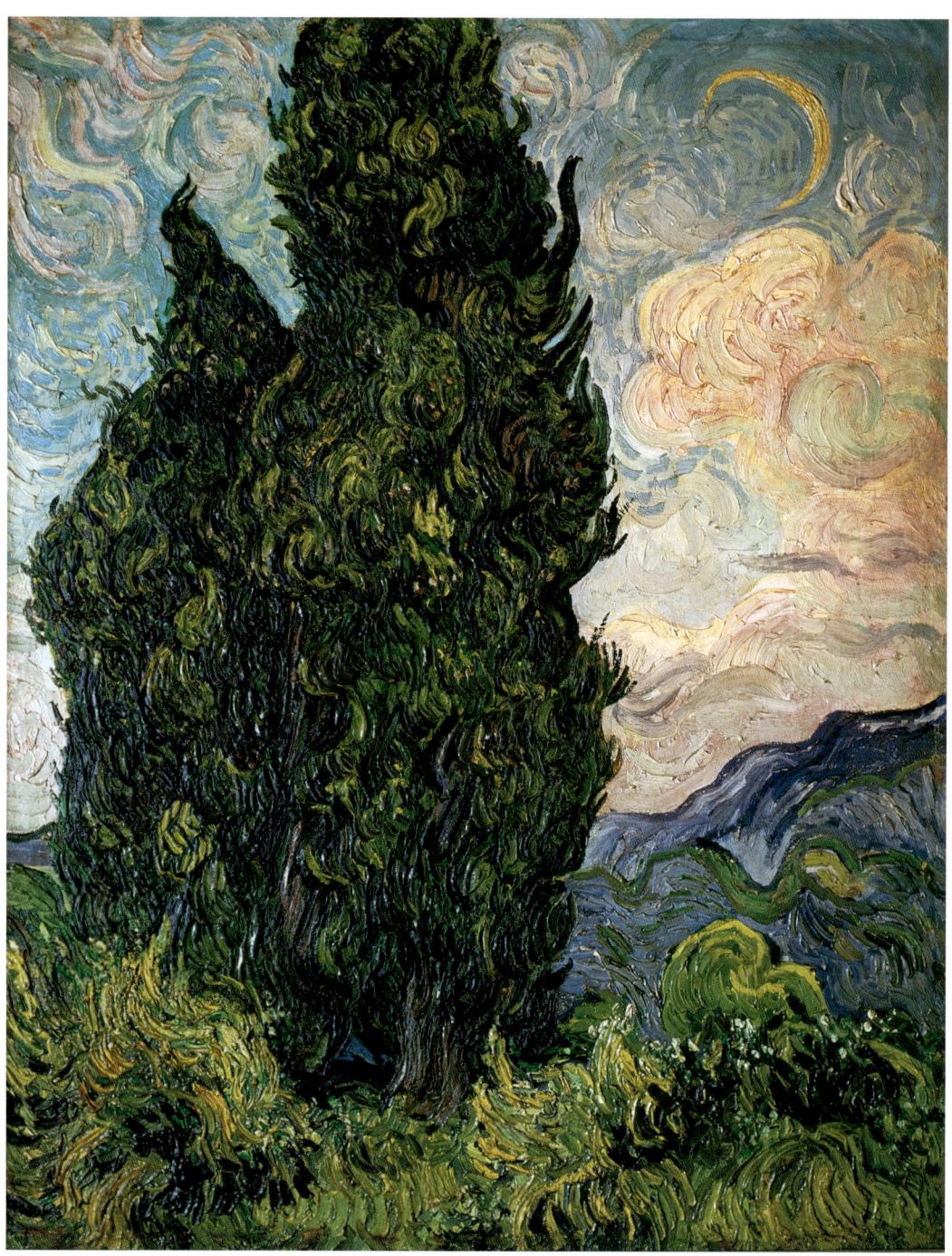

Contents

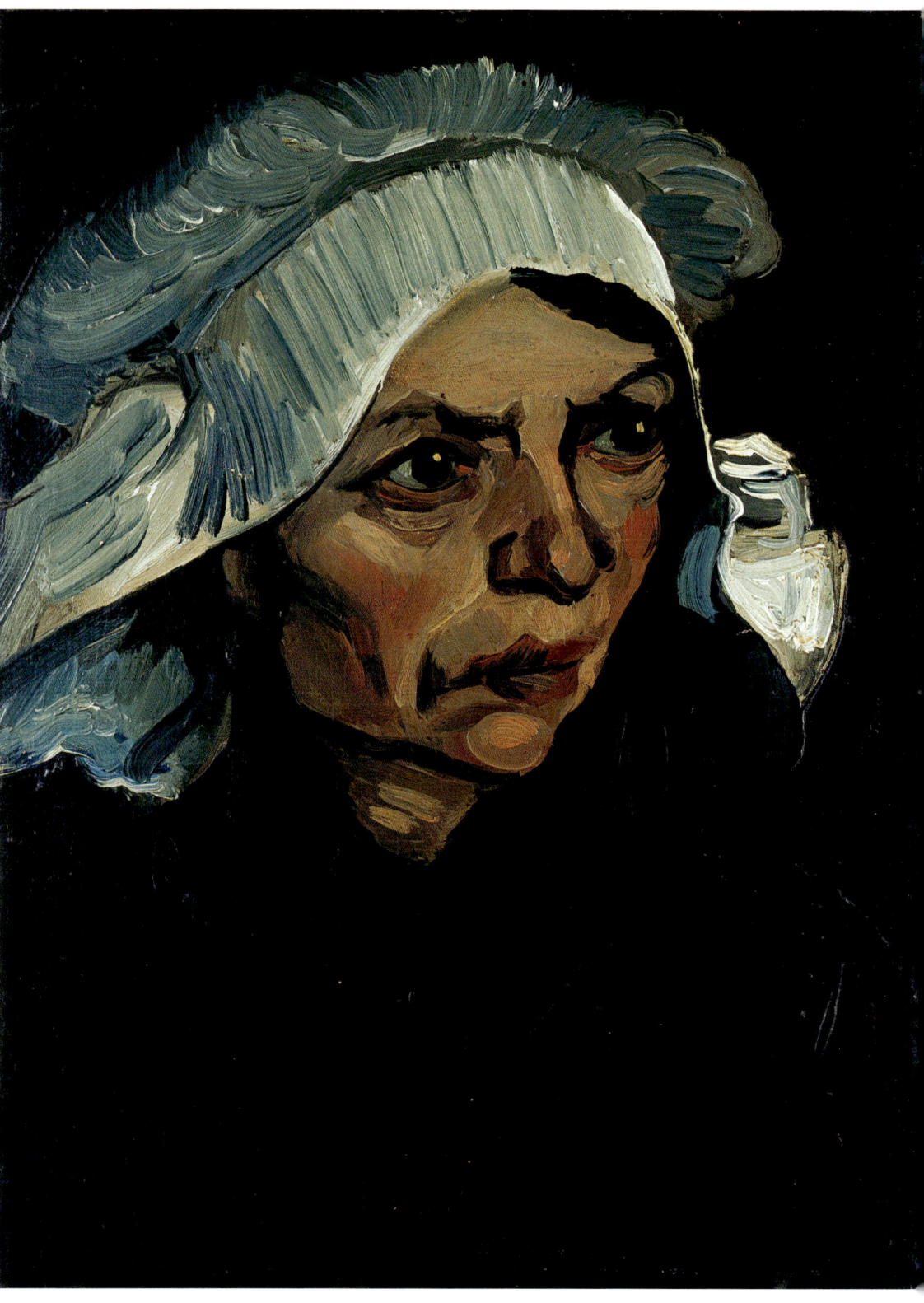

Half Monk, Half Artist
The Beginnings in Holland 1881–1885

Vincent van Gogh was a complete and utter failure in everything that seemed important to his contemporaries. He was not able to start a family, earn his own living, or even keep his friends. Yet in his paintings he was able to set down his own concept of order, against that of the chaos of reality around him. His art was an attempt to regulate a world with which he was obviously unable to come to terms. He countered its unfathomability with the harsh theoretically based criticism of the artist; its anonymity he impressed with his own finely balanced pathos and its run-of-the-mill workings with a solipsistic verve. His aim was not to escape reality, nor indeed to suffer by renouncing it, but instead to make it tangible in a comprehensive sense. In this way his art enabled him to accept the once so hostile world as his own.

His artistic talents were only recognized after his death. The bourgeoisie, whose ideas of value had been so repellent to him all of his life, now used the term "genius" to describe him. The once unloved Vincent now became a hero, the more art presented itself as a world of beautiful appearances. Art had been lodged for hundreds of years on the periphery of society and here van Gogh, himself an outsider, became a personality. He became the embodiment of worldly discontent which overcomes us all now and again. The Modern Age loves to toy with the image of the lonely misunderstood artist. Vincent van Gogh served as a perfect example and he became one of the first martyrs of the avant-garde.

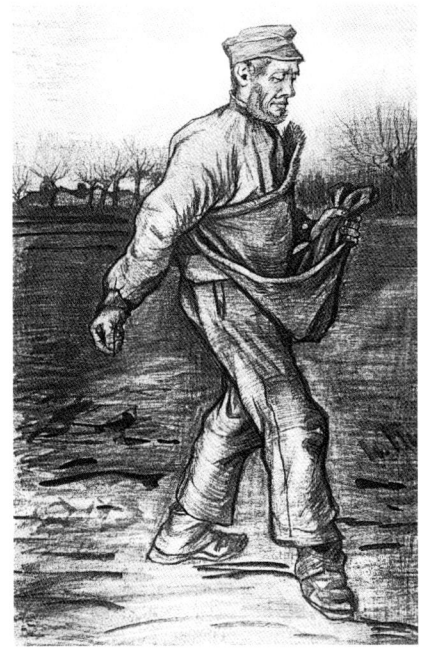

The first son of the Protestant vicar Theodorus van Gogh was stillborn. Exactly one year later to the very day, on 30 March 1853, his wife, Anna Cornelia van Gogh, gave birth to another child. Full of fearful misgiving as to whether the child would survive, she gave it the same name as the first child: Vincent Willem van Gogh. From the moment of his birth, his life was overshadowed with doubts; Vincent's

OPPOSITE
*Head of a Peasant Woman
with White Cap*, 1885
Oil on canvas on panel,
41 x 30.5 cm (16¼ x 12 in.)
Zurich, Foundation E. G. Bührle Collection

ABOVE RIGHT
The Sower, 1882
Pencil, brush and ink, 61 x 40 cm (24 x 15¾ in.)
Amsterdam, P. & N. de Boer Foundation

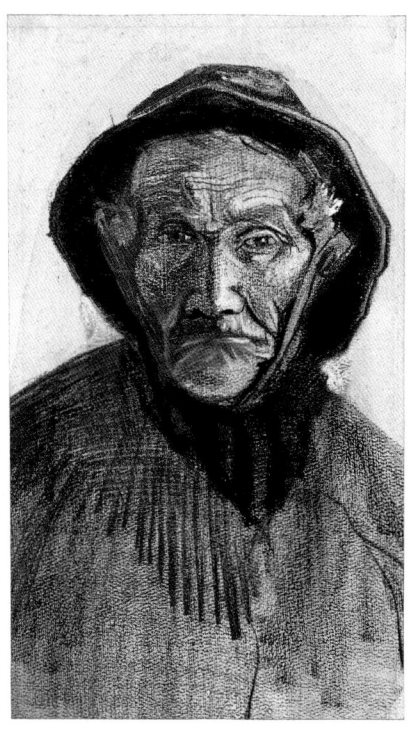

"We have had a lot of wind, storm, and rain here throughout the whole week and I was often in Scheveningen to have a look. I brought two seascapes back home with me. The first one was partly covered with sand – but the second one, made during a heavy storm with the ocean close to the dunes, was covered by a thick coat of sand which I tried to scrape off twice. The storm was so violent that I was hardly able to keep on my feet and the flying sand let me see almost nothing."

VINCENT VAN GOGH

fundamental experience was and remained that of his foundering. His seemingly promising career as an art dealer, a trade of long-standing in the Netherlands and especially in his own family, ended in his dismissal. His study of theology, begun after this period, proved too much for him and ended a year later.

Following this, van Gogh tried his hand at supply teaching and lay preaching, serving in the Belgian coal-mining area of the Borinage amongst the most poverty-stricken of the poor. Yet the penetrating experience of extreme social misery was not denied him upon the termination of his negligible wage soon after. From this point on he was completely dependent upon the financial support of his younger brother Theo, four years his junior. He lived with the constant fear of the possible cessation of these funds until his death. Personal happiness was also denied him; his world was not to be graced with the company of women, whom he had tried but failed to woo.

Art became Vincent's only outlet. He turned it into a medium with which he was able to develop experiences, make his comments and articulate his dilemma and hopes. His art was accompanied by an extensive exchange of letters, especially with his brother Theo. In particular Vincent's letters are proof of the way his artistic works increasingly determined his own ideas of reality. They also document the highly theoretical methods with which he set about his work. Letters and paintings establish a paradoxical unit within his work, in which a seemingly naive lack of worldly understanding is accompanied and complemented by a great wealth of reflection.

Van Gogh's decision to become an artist was finalized about 1880. During his employment in the various departments of the Paris art dealer Goupil & Cie, where he had started at the bottom with historical and contemporary works, he was able to articulate his problems by drawing, and this continued during his miserable lay preaching period in the Borinage. After his failure in the various bourgeois professions and his rejection of his theological and social ambitions, he seized upon art, an area which he knew both in theory and in practice. His brother Theo, employed at Goupil's, and his cousin Anton Mauve, himself an artist in The Hague, gave him additional support.

In October 1880 van Gogh moved to Brussels and made friends with the painter Anton van Rappard. In the beginning he produced only drawings, detail sketches and many studies modelled on the works of Jean-François Millet. Millet's somewhat light interpretation of realism provided van Gogh with themes that he could relate to – above all labouring peasants, genre paintings in a dark melancholic tone.

He tried to transmit this mood, which appeared to correspond to his own emotional feelings, into his drawings. Increasingly he began to use unbleached Ingres paper as a base, which enabled him to contrast techniques of painting, blurred contours and flowing transitions of the lines dominating the drawing. The switch to painting was not far away.

On New Year's Day 1882 van Gogh moved into a studio in The Hague, paid for by Theo. Under Mauve's guidance he produced his first oil painting. His early painting of August 1882 *Beach at Scheveningen in Stormy Weather* (ill. p. 411) is strongly influenced by The Hague School to which Mauve belonged. Bound to tradition, The Hague School attempted above all to breathe new life into the landscape paintings of the "Golden Age" of the Dutch Baroque style of painting. Adriaen van de Velde was the Baroque specialist in seascapes and van Gogh related to his combination of landscape with figures busy on the shore.

"When I paint landscapes, there will always be some figure present," he wrote pragmatically. The artistic tradition

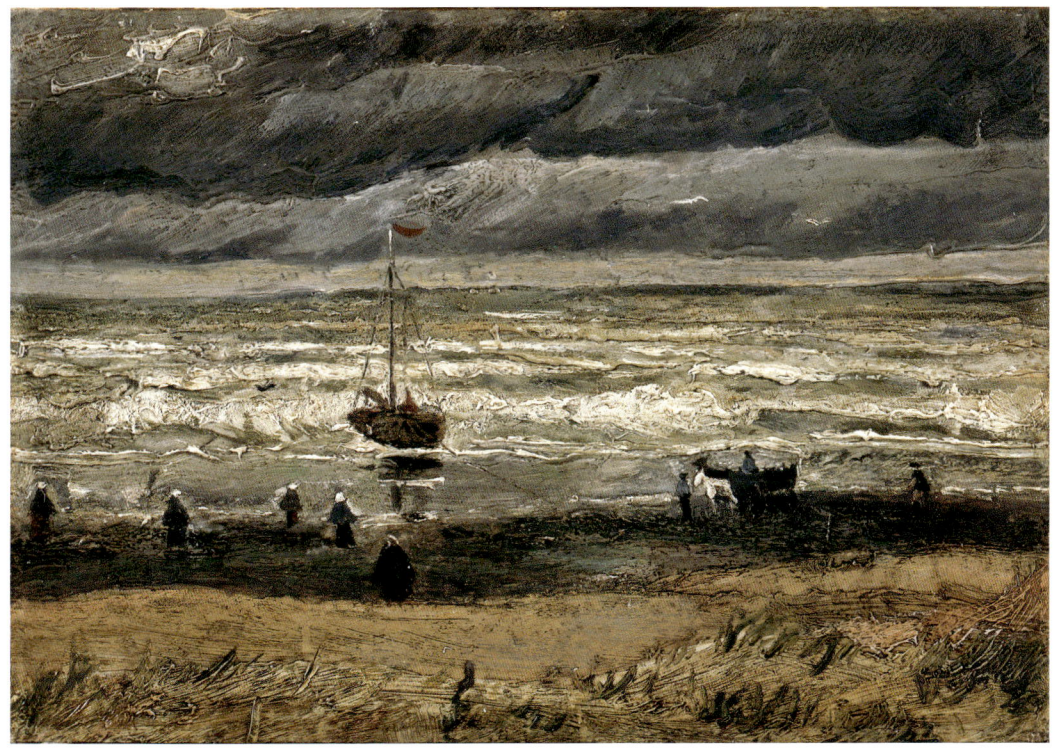

coincided with his own concept of painting. Nevertheless, this painting contains a tendency towards an autonomization of form and colour. The underlying tendency towards abstraction is evident in the pastose application of colour, in the stressing of parallel layers within the painting and the variety of brownish tones used.

After only one year of practical training, van Gogh's handling of colours counted amongst the best of his time. This can only be explained by his sound training in art appreciation and an equally untiring, almost manic industry. Tone painting still remained an acute problem. Based upon the observations of Eugène Delacroix, the question arose how one could convey pictorially the changes in colour of an object which become apparent at a distance from the object or when it is observed in a different light. The solution finally agreed upon was to tone down the actual colour of the object, its natural colour, in order to fit in with that of the dominant monocolour tone of the painting as a whole. No longer was the singularity of the object stressed, but its appearance within the context to which the picture was dedicated. This tendency towards a separation of colour within the painting from the concrete object in reality was the most important step towards a definite autonomy. Colour could now be viewed as a phenomenon, as a pure appearance and a play on well-balanced complementary tones. Van Gogh in his work gave this autonomy an additional dimension, favoured by his own tradition and that of the progressive treatment of colour by Rembrandt or Frans Hals. However, he still moved within the bounds of conventionalism. The tone of van Gogh's works makes pictorial music.

The State Lottery Office, 1882
Watercolour, 37.9 x 56.6 cm (15 x 22⅜ in.)
Amsterdam, Van Gogh Museum,
Vincent van Gogh Foundation

In September 1883 van Gogh left The Hague for the Drente province in north-east Holland, where he lived alone. This move was precipitated by his break from his artistic mentor Mauve. Mauve's criticism of Vincent's relationship with the prostitute

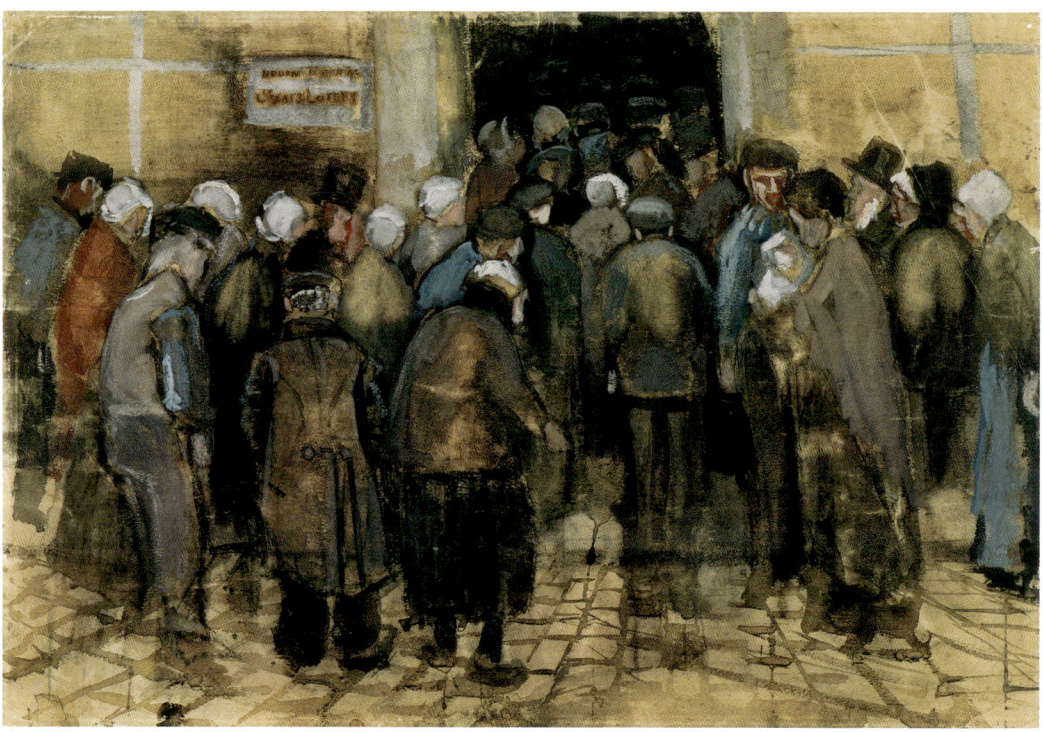

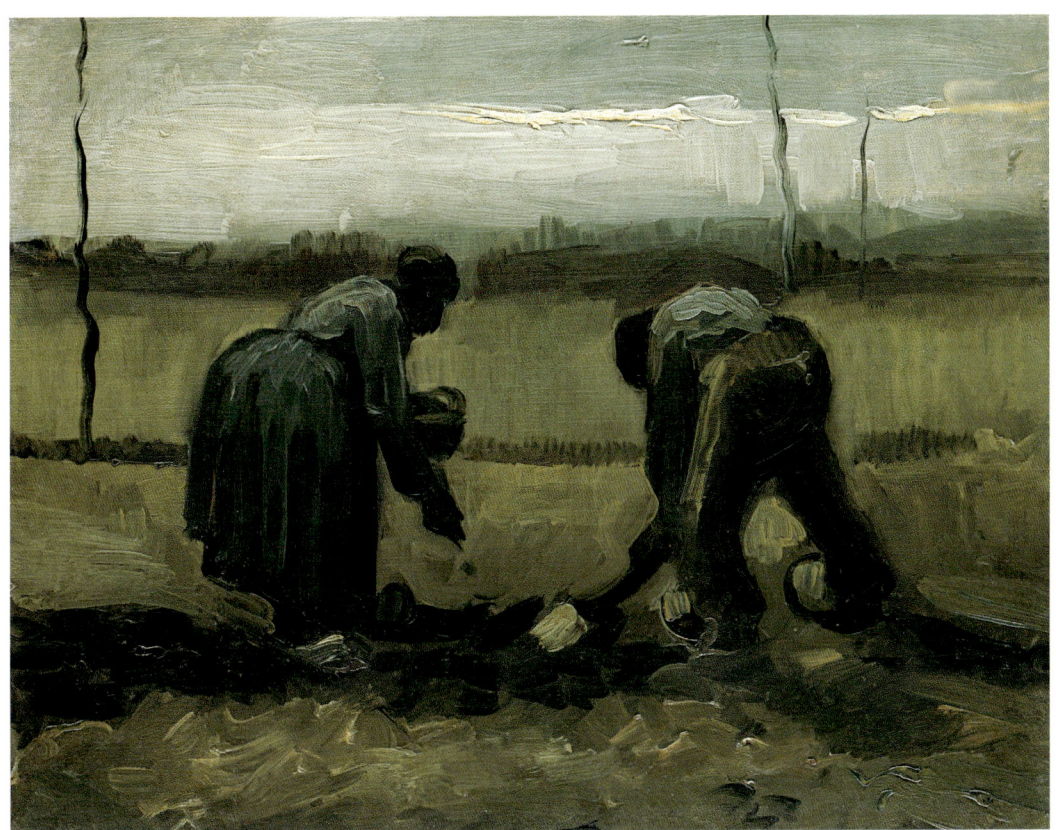

Clasina Maria Hoornik could have been a minor reason for this break, in addition to the fact that they no longer saw eye to eye on their views on art. Clasina – known as Sien to Vincent – was both his model and live-in lover. Vincent believed Mauve represented

Peasant and Peasant Woman Planting Potatoes, 1885
Oil on canvas, 33 x 41 cm (13 x 16 in.)
Zurich, Kunsthaus Zürich

an academic mode of artistic thought adhering to norms, rules and a strict concept of beauty, thereby ignoring the individual expression and the actual social problems which so preoccupied van Gogh.

Authority had always been somewhat of a thorn in his side, and Mauve's strict rules may possibly have reminded van Gogh of the bigoted Calvinistic setting of his parents' home. The old love-hate relationship with his origins came to the forefront and van Gogh tried to escape this by withdrawing more and more into himself – into a loneliness which he could not bear. After three months the prodigal son returned home to his parents in Nuenen. By this time the parents had come to terms with their eldest son's artistic career and they even placed a studio at his disposal next to the vicarage.

It was here that van Gogh painted *Weaver, Seen from the Front* (ill. p. 415) in May 1884. Sitting before his loom, the weaver is totally immersed in his work. The weaving machine, monumental in size, covers almost the whole of the picture. The oversized frame envelopes the weaver's slight figure behind a meshed front of horizontal and vertical lines, at times intersecting the figure, making him appear part of the mechanism. Together they stand out as dark silhouettes against a light background, which can never be lit up by the tiny lamp. Every single anecdote, every picturesque

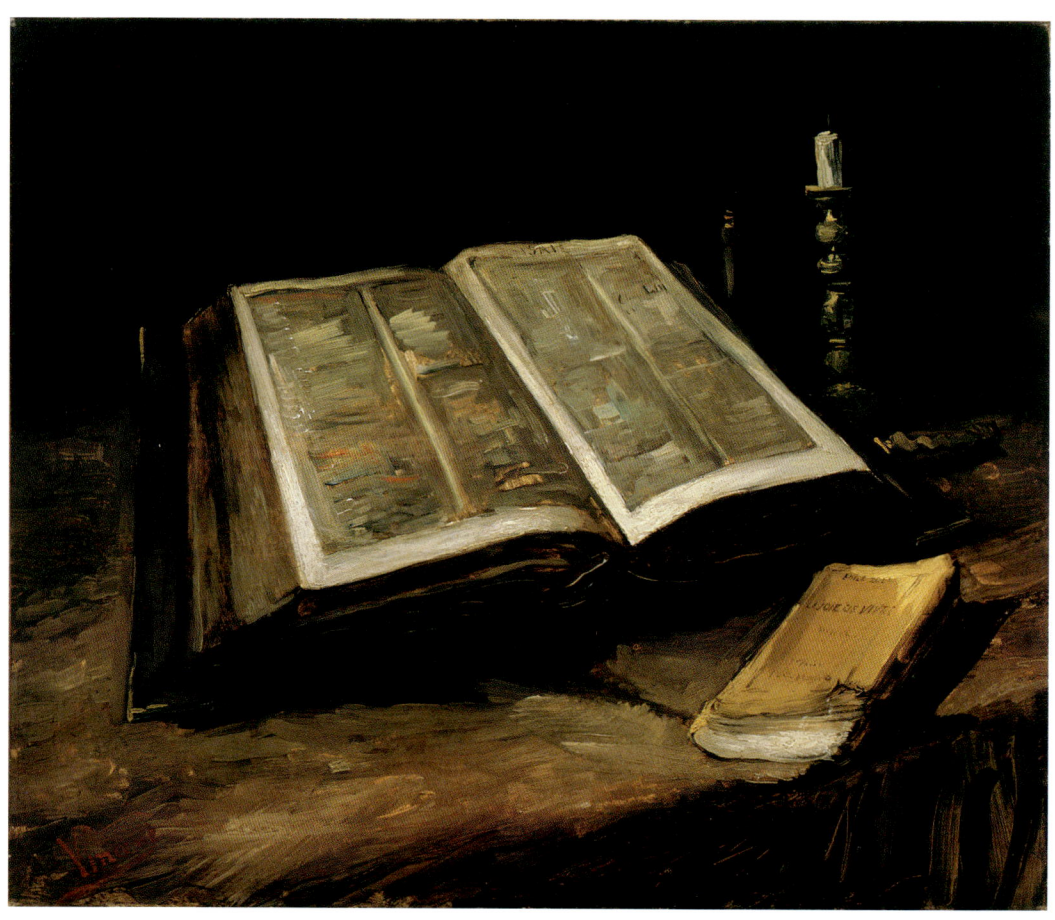

Still Life with Bible, 1885
Oil on canvas, 65.7 x 78.5 cm (25⅞ x 31 in.)
Amsterdam, Van Gogh Museum,
Vincent van Gogh Foundation

element is dispelled in this unifying representation of worker and machine. The harshness and toil as well as the dignity of the worker's life are unmistakably expressed here.

The painting documents, beyond a shadow of a doubt, van Gogh's solidarity and even identification with the depicted worker. Himself a convinced socialist, he knew of the worker's misery from his own experiences and also viewed his art as a form of handiwork. Peasants, weavers and coal-miners became the preferred subject matter of his early works. They were representatives of the rural proletariat, not town dwellers, although van Gogh was familiar with urban populations from stays in both London and Paris. This choice underlined his deeply rooted aversion to industrialization, specifically to a world of technology in which man was nothing more than a mere machine. Van Gogh backed a strange pessimistic view of progress, shared by the English social utopians William Morris and John Ruskin. The ideal of a ruler-free society was here combined with the praise of manual work. The self-sufficient worker, amongst whom van Gogh counted himself, was his central socialist concern. In this he also distinguished himself from the then popular Naturalists, whose exponents, the most important being the author Émile Zola, believed in depicting the misery of the worker neutrally, rather than actively sharing in this misery. The ennoblement of the worker, which became a theme of Naturalist art, was not enough for van Gogh. The worker ought also to be the consumer of his works. Art of the

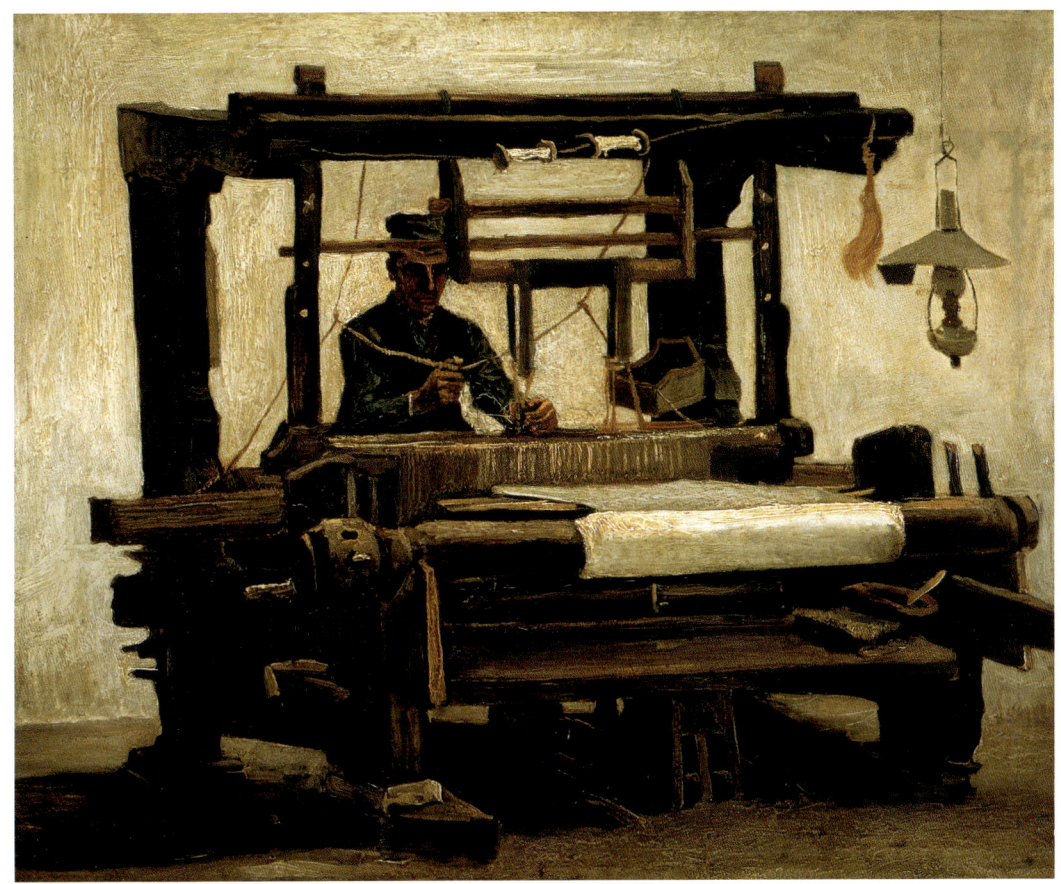

people for the people was the social impetus of his works. Paintings such as *The State Lottery Office* (ill. p. 412) and *Peasant and Peasant Woman Planting Potatoes* (ill. p. 413)

Weaver, Seen from the Front, 1884
Oil on canvas, 68.3 x 84.2 cm (27 x 33¼ in.)
Otterlo, Kröller-Müller Museum

exemplify this principle. Anonymous peasants or workers are central figures of these works, as worthy of being depicted as the most glorious heroes from history and mythology.

Once, on one occasion only, van Gogh's peasants were both theme and consumer of the work. With his brother's help he was able to have twenty lithographs of his *The Potato Eaters* printed, which people from his neighbourhood could buy at a reasonable price. In many respects this picture of April 1885 (ill. p. 417) is representative of his early work as a whole. Solidarity and poverty are revealed in the sparse meal, which the five emaciated, hard-working figures have to share. Potatoes and malt coffee are passed around the table, and the unselfish communal feeling reaches an almost religious, tranquil pathos.

"Indeed I have tried very hard," Vincent wrote to his brother Theo, "to convey to the observer the idea that these people, who are eating potatoes by lamplight, reaching into the bowl with their hands, use the same hands to till the soil. The painting therefore conveys the idea of their manual work and as a consequence of this that their meal has been honestly earned … But those who would rather see the peasant in an ideal light can stick to their views." An inner strength appears to radiate from their faces, increasing their dignity even more. The light effect is gained by the sparse

"If you ask me what I am working on at the moment I can tell you that I have my hands full with a large picture showing a weaver – the loom in the very foreground, the figure as a dark silhouette against a white wall … I'll have no end of trouble with these looms, but they present such a wonderful challenge – the old oakwood against a greyish wall – and I am quite sure that they are worth being painted."

VINCENT VAN GOGH

use of yellow as a contrast to the dark, brown-toned background. The painting came about after careful planning and a lot of preparatory studies, to which the *Head of a Peasant Woman with White Cap* (ill. p. 408) of March 1885 also belongs. The lack of communication between the five figures, whose eyes appear hardly ever to meet, can perhaps be explained by the compilation of several different studies into one whole picture. Still the putative lack in the composition confers a stillness and quiet melancholy on the painting.

"You'll no doubt agree with me that such a piece of work is not to be taken seriously. Thank goodness you are capable of more than this." This critical comment of Rappard's towards his sensitive friend's painting marked the end of their friendship. Due to his academic training Rappard concentrated on the apparent "mistakes" in *The Potato Eaters* (ill. p. 417), such as the too-short arms, emaciated faces and miscalculated proportions. Yet it was precisely these points which marked out van Gogh's own view of beauty, based on the people in his environment, who were admittedly not beautiful, but who embodied his idea of truth.

Van Gogh's aesthetics were created because of his aversion to the traditional norms, his solidarity with the poor and also perhaps a genuine lack of artistic technique. He managed to pull himself together, to identify with his artistic being and to fill in those missing parts of his artistic technique by hard work and continual practice. Art was then an individual medium of expression; beauty and ugliness were criteria of the individual and not categories of a general convention. Van Gogh's aesthetics of ugliness, already outlined in the 18th-century theoretical works of Edmund Burke and Denis Diderot, are characteristic of his works: deformation and gaudy colours vouch for his special quality of artistic creativity. His pictorial language always remains based on concrete reality and is

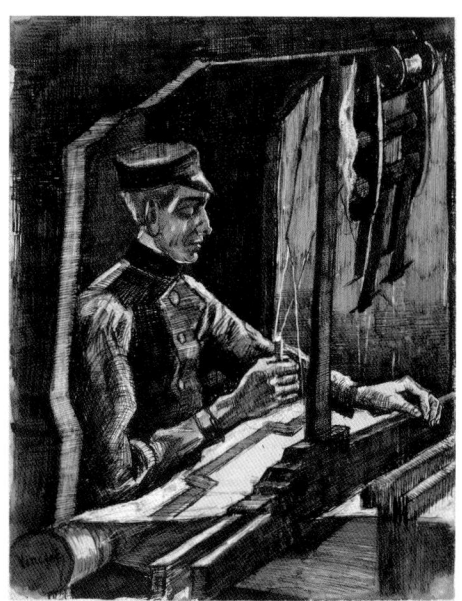

"Amongst this confusion I was dismayed by a meal poor people had in a weird hut under a dim lamp. He called it 'The Potato Eaters'. It was ugly in a splendid way and loaded with an alarming activity."

ÉMILE BERTRAND

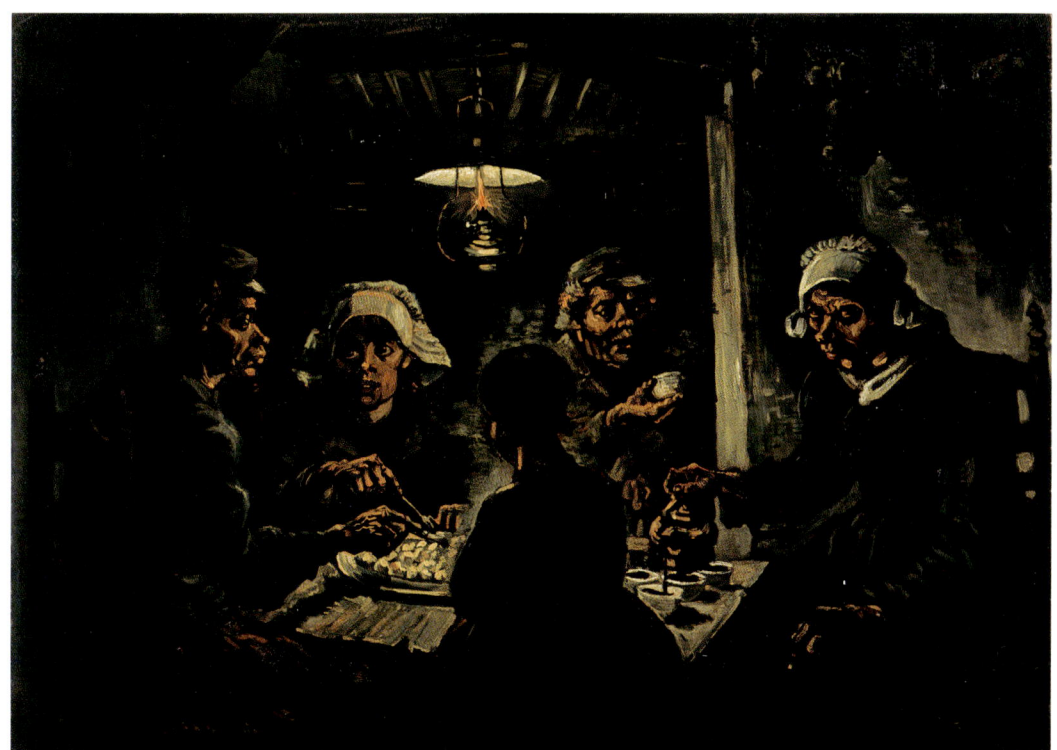

a reaction to it, as well as being a personal commentary on it – indeed, personal in such a way that the established rules would destroy it.

On 26 March 1885 his father, Theodorus van Gogh, died. From now on Vincent's life in the village of Nuenen became more difficult. The locals were afraid of his unpredictable behaviour. He had always loved these people, felt a part of them, but still he was unable to explain himself to them. His departure to Antwerp meant a change not only in his personal circumstances but also a thematic change in his work. The preoccupation with social problems which was so obviously depicted in his earlier paintings was now overtaken by a purely artistic debate: Van Gogh's subject matter was to change. However, he remained faithful in his fight to assert his own ideas and his emotional protests against the formulaic.

Still Life with Bible (ill. p. 414) painted in October 1885, shortly before his departure, laid his past to rest without further ado. The Bible, a symbol of his parents' home and religious upbringing, has a rival in the painting – Zola's *La Joie de vivre*, a cult book of the Naturalist movement and considered by the old Theodorus as one of the most despicable works of the devil. The candle, an instrument of sacred rites, raises both books to the same level, and grants each of them the same meaning. Yet the candle has been blown out.

In the cosmopolitan city of Paris, van Gogh distanced himself from both books. Christianity and socialism were joined together to form a new religion, but not one that ruled his life. The new, exclusive religion was art.

The Potato Eaters, 1885
Oil on canvas, 82 x 114 cm (32⅜ x 45 in.)
Amsterdam, Van Gogh Museum,
Vincent van Gogh Foundation

OPPOSITE
Weaver Facing Right (Half-Figure), 1884
Pen, washed with bistre, heightened with white,
26.3 x 20.6 cm (10⅜ x 8⅛ in.)
Amsterdam, Van Gogh Museum,
Vincent van Gogh Foundation

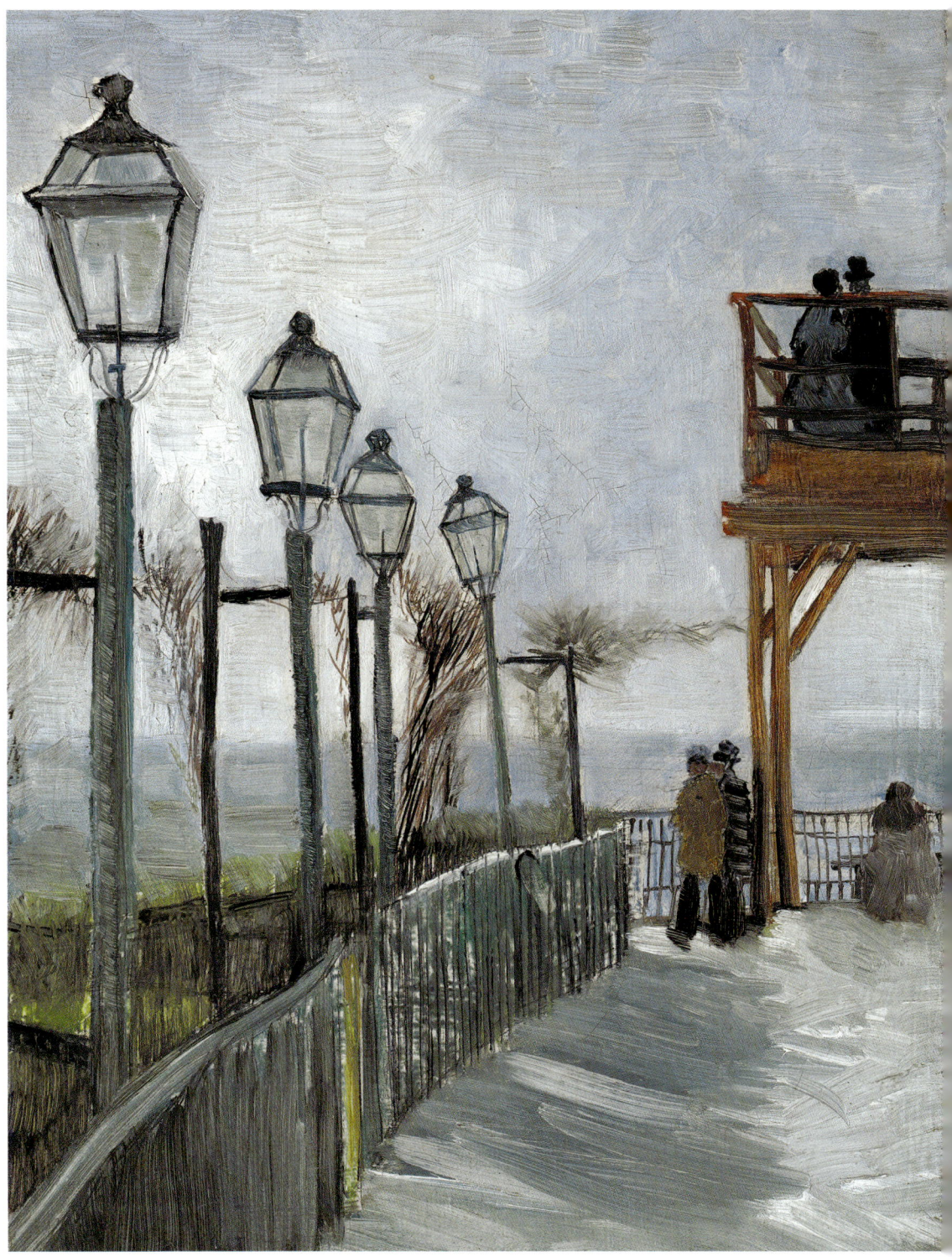

Apprenticeship Years in Paris
Antwerp and Paris 1885–1888

"I prefer to have one hundred francs a month and the freedom to spend it just as I like than to have two hundred francs without this freedom."

VINCENT VAN GOGH

At the end of November 1885 van Gogh arrived in Antwerp, then a large and important harbour, carrying only one suitcase containing *The Potato Eaters*. Here he stayed for a short time before going on to Paris, the capital city of the 19th century. However, this stay proved to be of great importance to his later work as it was in Antwerp that he began to experiment properly with all sorts of techniques. He was able to break away from the Calvinistic rigorousness yet still secure environment of his home, and in so doing set free his creative energy. Vincent abandoned his earlier depiction of the gloomy, depressive world of the peasants for a period of experimentation, over the next two years, with everything that was artistically unusual, progressive, and avant-garde.

Van Gogh settled himself as best as possible into a small attic, paid for with Theo's help. He bought Japanese woodcuts at a bargain price from the antique dealers along the harbour-front and decorated the bare walls of his rooms with them. In this way he got his first taste of their decorative colourfulness, which was to make a lasting impression to him. At the Royal Academy he practised making plaster copies of classical sculptures. Yet even here, just as in The Hague, the dogma of classical beauty repelled him. This dogma reduced the individuality of art to a mere mechanical copying. His acquaintance with Peter Paul Rubens, the old master of the Baroque, became more important to him. Rubens also had a studio in Antwerp. The gaiety of the colours, the rounded forms and ample volumes, marked out the Baroque painter of Catholic origin as a necessary alternative to the reserved, controlled severity of the Dutch School of Art.

One morning, at the beginning of March 1886, Theo received a message: "From lunchtime on I will be in the Louvre, or even earlier if you want." Vincent had hinted again and again in his letters from Antwerp of his plans to move to Paris, but this completely took his brother by surprise. Now he had actually arrived in Paris and was planning to move in with his brother. Theo reluctantly agreed. For the following two years there were to be continual disputes over Vincent's various escapades, followed by Theo's apologies.

Still Life with Mackerels, Lemons and Tomatoes (ill. p. 430), one of his earlier Paris paintings, was done in the summer of 1886. The innovative technique, learned in Antwerp, can be clearly seen here. The loud red of the tomatoes contrasts effectively with the green of the jug, in fact the use of pure colours as a whole, which do not merge with the background colours of the paintings, points directly to Rubens's influence. The inexplicable nature of the interrelationship of space, the blurred borders between table, tomatoes and jug, one behind the other, point towards the influence of Japanese prints,

Terrace and Observation Deck at the Moulin de Blute-Fin, Montmartre, 1887
Oil on canvas, mounted on pressboard,
43.6 x 33 cm (17¼ x 13 in.)
The Art Institute of Chicago

in which the spatial continuum is at odds with the ornamental surface.

Henri de Toulouse-Lautrec and Émile Bernard were perhaps the most talented and by far the most famous graduates of the Cormon studio. The painter Fernand Cormon, on the one hand a fairly unknown artist, was on the other hand a relatively successful teacher and the owner of this art school. For three months van Gogh was to study at the studio and while there he distanced himself from his earlier genre pictures of peasants and workers.

It was here that he made friends with Toulouse-Lautrec and Bernard. Through Theo, who managed a small branch of Goupil's, where he informally set up exhibitions of Impressionist paintings on the mezzanine floor, Vincent got to know Paul Gauguin, himself then an equally unknown artist, and Camille Pissarro, the then sixty-year-old great man of Impressionism. He looked upon these men as his friends and together they frequented the neighbouring small cafés and cheap restaurants of their living quarters, the Boulevard de Clichy in Montmartre. He dreamed of forming a great artist commune with them, where everyone worked with and for one another – a dream which sadly would never be realized.

In *Montmartre near the Upper Mill* (ill. p. 418), a painting from early 1887, van Gogh portrays a grey wintry scene in a hazy fog. The frosty atmosphere of the approaching winter is exactly that of the Impressionists' atmospheric paintings. Also the neutrality of the whole, with its seemingly detached passers-by hurrying along the street and the fragmentary optical effect of the painting with its intersecting area of view, belongs to the tradition of Claude Monet or Auguste Renoir.

In October 1886 van Gogh painted *Terrace of a Café on Montmartre* (ill. p. 421). Here again he based his work on a typical Impressionist interpretation. The soft red of the autumnal-coloured leaves, the half-empty seats in the foreground, the view into the alcoves – portrayed with a few strokes of the brush – crystallize a quiet everyday scene, a momentary observation without any deep meaning. The sporadic application of pastose colour does not change this, nor does the concealed placing of local colour, which comes out in the autumnal ochre. In these paintings van Gogh is experimenting with Impressionist techniques.

When Vincent arrived in Paris in 1886, Impressionism had already become a thing of the past. Édouard Manet, the progenitor of the movement, was dead and at their eighth exhibition, which took place that very year, Neo-Impressionism made its appearance in the form of Georges Seurat's famous *A Summer Afternoon on the Île Grande Jatte* (Chicago, Art Institute). The apparent indifference of the Impressionist style, the rejection of any form of personal expression, the near mechanical transposition of observations into a spontaneous ad hoc painting – all this was criticized not only by traditionalists but also by a confident, self-designated brilliant young generation. Light was the watch word of the Impressionists, light as the medium of all appearances, as a basic element connecting all things and as a life-giving force. Yet the philosophical background admittedly fell short of the mark. No artist painting during this period could avoid the Impressionist movement. What was left to van Gogh and the other rebellious young artists was the revelling in brightness, the use of a pure white, as well as the inclusion of detail and apparently incoherent spatial structure.

"I'd rather paint peoples' eyes than cathedrals." With these words van Gogh commented on the thematic preference of the Impressionists, appearing to refer to Monet's Rouen cathedrals, a series

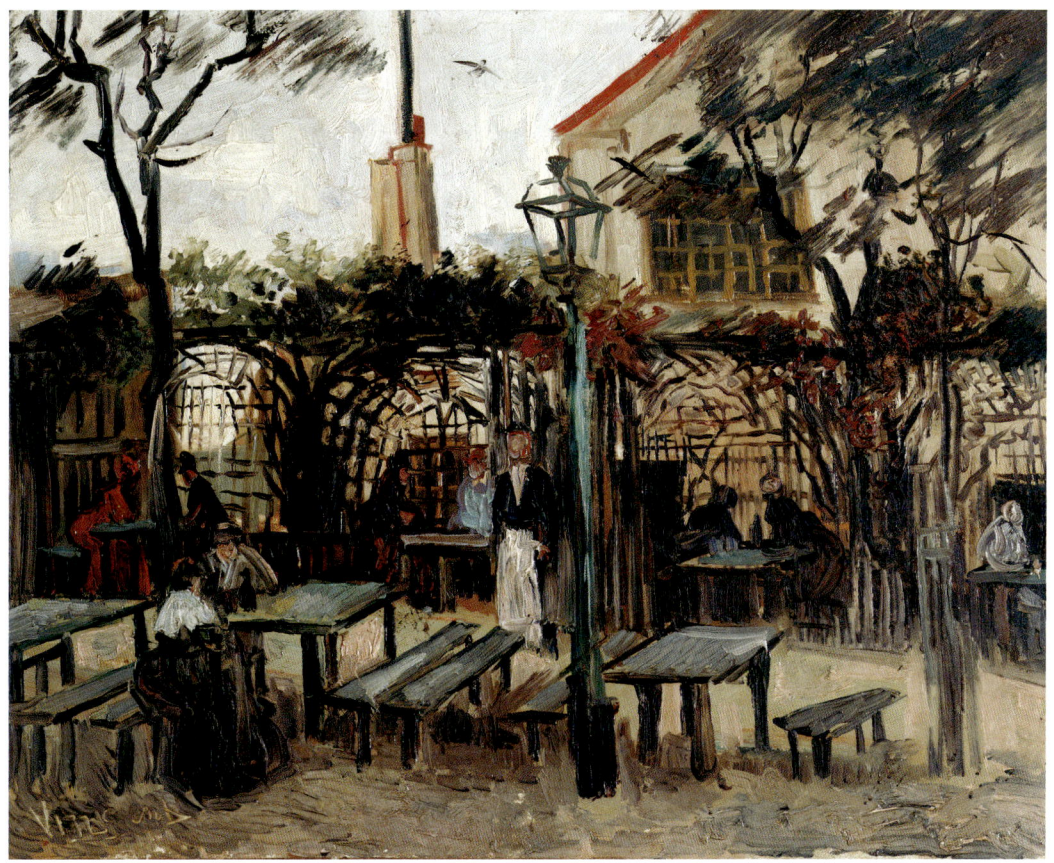

Terrace of a Café on Montmartre (La Guinguette), 1886
Oil on canvas, 50 x 64.5 cm (19¾ x 25½ in.)
Paris, Musée d'Orsay

of paintings depicting this cathedral from various positions at different times of the day. Van Gogh preferred to paint portraits. Therefore *Agostina Segatori Sitting in the Café du Tambourin* of 1887 (ill. p. 423) is not a mere depiction of an anonymous neglected drunk in any old dive, but a portrait of the Italian owner of the café, the former model of, amongst others, Camille Corot and Edgar Degas, portrayed sitting at a table. Vincent had a short affair with her and she often sat as a model for him, sometimes nude. The table and chairs in his painting had the same percussion-like shape as those in the café itself. In general, the exotic charm of the painting, the woman's unusual hairstyle and her folkloric dress, as well as the umbrella on the chair and the famous Japanese woodcuts in the background, are much more central to an understanding of the painting than the smoky milieu of the dive, which so fascinated Degas in his *Absinthe Drinker* (Musée d'Orsay, Paris) – an obvious model for van Gogh's painting. The woman's large melancholy eyes, in contrast to the strange surroundings, endow the painting with a special, carefully considered atmosphere which is the opposite of that usually depicted by the Impressionists.

Van Gogh ironically called the clique of artists with whom he lived, worked and exhibited on Montmartre "Peintres du Petit Boulevard". All of them lived simply, having established themselves in the seclusion of the large boulevards, and they countered their lack of publicity with a love of experimentation. In a restaurant, Du Chalet, on the Boulevard de Clichy, van Gogh, Toulouse-Lautrec, Bernard and Louis Anquetin had their first exhibition in 1887. Nothing was sold, but the exhibition was followed by long discussions and to round it all off in a congenial manner they exchanged one another's works. Their impoverished artistic idyll, with its Bohemian chic, was precisely what united artists of all nationalities in Paris. They lived, convinced of their own genius, in the absolute assurance that they would one day soon revolutionize the art world.

They could only afford to go on trips in the area around Paris. Together with Gauguin and Bernard, van Gogh spent many days in Asnières, a popular spa town on the Seine. It was here that he painted *The Seine with the Pont de la Grande Jatte* (ill. p. 424) in summer 1887. The bridge cuts diagonally across the painting. It was an often-repeated Impressionist motif, simply overlapping the frame, thereby expressing the momentary nature of the painting. Van Gogh obviously drew upon this symbolism in his painting. At first sight the application of colour appears somewhat confused in its horizontal, vertical and diagonal strokes and the complete abandonment of colour surfaces with a simultaneous stress on the intensity of colour, attempts to overcome by the same means the radiant atmospheric feeling in favour of the timeless self-control, as in contemporary Pointillist works.

The incunabulum of this style of painting is Seurat's *Sunday Afternoon on the Île Grande Jatte*, which van Gogh cites as a subject of his painting. Seurat and his friends, above all Paul Signac, wanted to place Impressionism on a quasi-scientific level. Filled to the brim with theories concerning colour changes, voluminous effects and the psychology of perception, they attempted to distill objective rules out of the style of Impressionism, above all to gear their paintings towards the same objective representation as they preached in their theoretical dogma. Van Gogh, a good friend of Signac, looked upon this scientific ordering of art as exaggerated. However, the methods of breaking up colours into small dots, which only became effective when one looked at them from a distance and could then view the continuous movement in the area, correspond to his own love of experimentation. Even in his depressing paintings of later years this particular splitting of colour has a validity. *Vase with Daisies and Anemones* (ill. p. 431) of June 1887 shows van Gogh's fascination with every last stroke and dot of colour, particularly in the shimmering background, in front of which the voluptuous brightness of the flowers is moderated.

That he also had other forms of artistic expression at his disposal can be seen from the painting *Four Cut Sunflowers* (ill. pp. 428/429) of the same period. The four withering flowers, viewed from up close, hang on shrivelled stems which have been cut a long time ago. They spread out their short petals in front, like licking flames, as if to revolt against the threatening decay, already anticipating the ecstatic blazing vitality of van Gogh's later cypress paintings. In this painting Vincent was able to endow the banal commonplace subject with an almost existential meaningfulness, and objects are given a symbolic significance, ciphers of some form of suffering, which one has to look for first of all in the artist himself.

This vitalizing view of things is first and foremost a reaction against photography: "One strives for a more profound similarity than photography," the painter wrote to his sister. Yet still more important is the decorative, symbolizing, immediate effect, which the painting's appearance, stripped of all the motifs taken from reality, conjures up. This effect, which has nothing to do with the cultivated refinement of Impressionism, but which demands instead spontaneous sympathy, even consternation – all this is powerfully incited by a simple sunflower.

Agostina Segatori Sitting in the Café du Tambourin, 1887
Oil on canvas, 55.5 x 47 cm (21⅞ x 18⅝ in.)
Amsterdam, Van Gogh Museum,
Vincent van Gogh Foundation

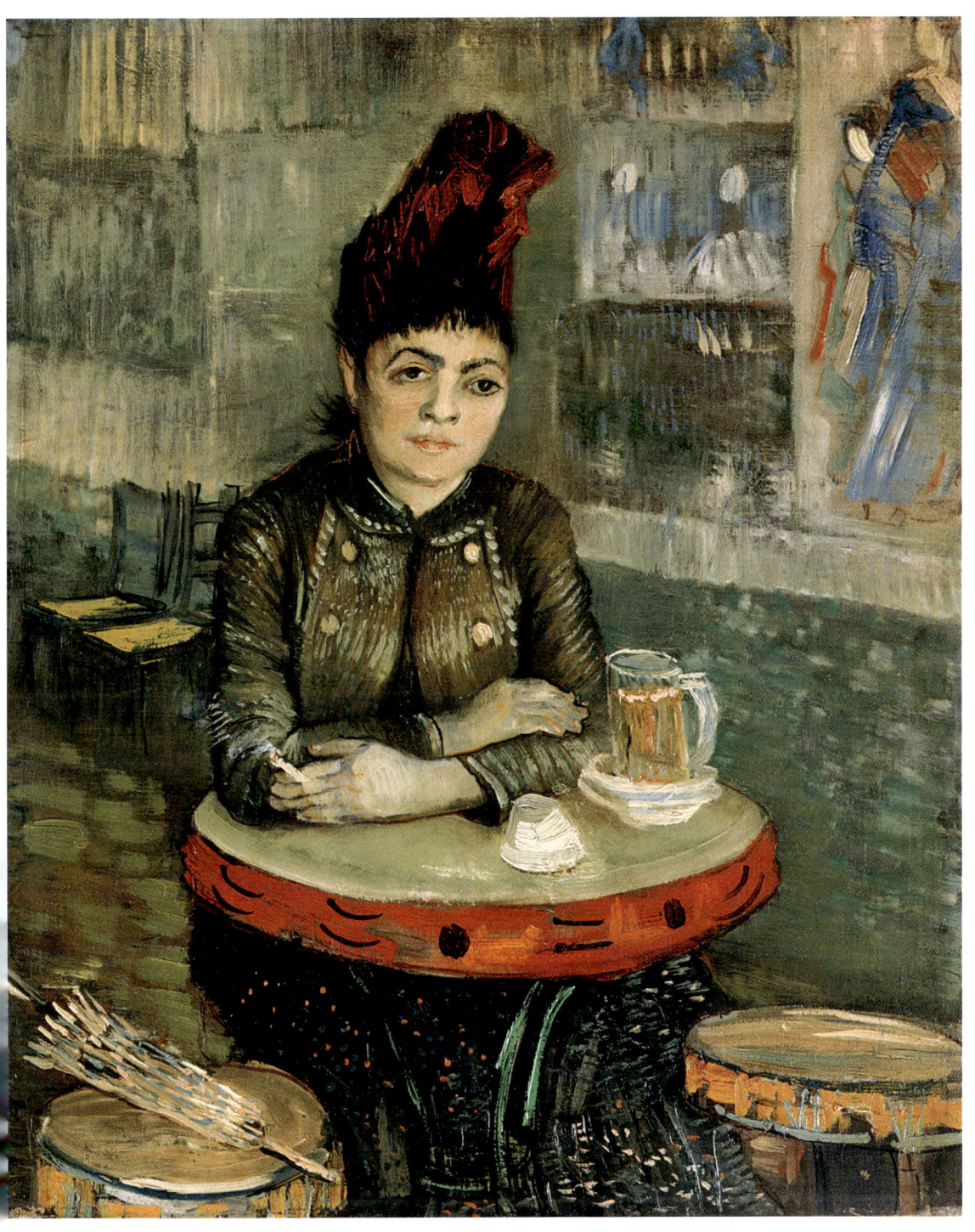

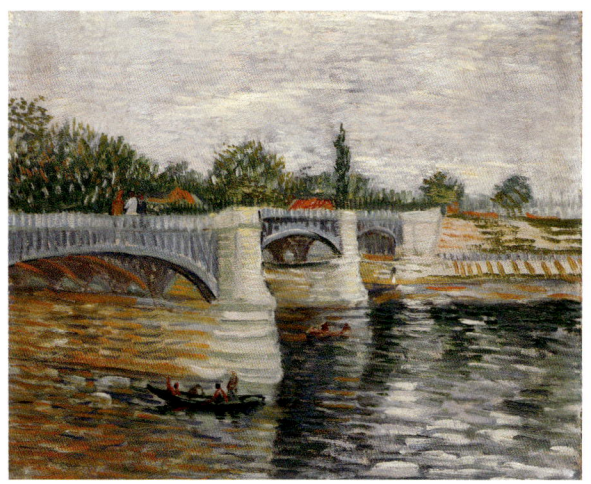

This effect is guaranteed above all by the complementary contrast between the dirty yellow and the shimmering blue of the diffuse background. For a long time van Gogh had studied the colour theories of Delacroix. The most important finding for van Gogh – thoughts on colour autonomy aside – was the deployment of complementary contrasts. These can be achieved by contrasting one of the three primary colours – yellow, red, blue – with a mixture of the other two. The combinations red-green, yellow-violet, blue-orange are able to increase one another's intensity of colour or neutralize them-

selves to a dull grey when mixed. This seemingly ordinary trick can in fact often create an extraordinary effect.

Van Gogh wanted to learn everything at once during his time in Paris. It was as if he wanted to experiment with all the multi-faceted means of expression the melting-pot Paris offered in his only medium, painting. This experimentation was not merely restricted to art. The multifarious means of expression determine his *Still Life with Decanter and Lemons on an Plate* (ill. p. 425) of spring 1887. The hard, solid shape of the fruit is surrounded by a fine sketchy background consisting of radial lines which take up the plate's contour. The reddish-yellow of the fruit and the greeny-blue of the background present a complementary contrast. In keeping with the spirit of Impressionism, colour and light are refracted in the transparent lightness of the fluted bottle. In the background one can recognize the lineal patterning, which points to a further important field of artistic expression which van Gogh seized upon during this period – that of Japanese art, which was then a widely spread trend in artistic circles.

The Japanese stand caused a lot of excitement at the World Exhibition in Paris in 1867. Visitors, with their cosmopolitan attitudes, admired the exotic strangeness, which clearly indicated a high degree of civilized cultural development in the Far East. Suddenly, in the better circles of society, women began using fans, wearing kimonos and having China crockery and screens in their bourgeois homes. The large stores all opened a Japanese department. In this way a new fashion craze was born. The reaction to this trend in the art world was not long in coming. Woodcuts from Japan, either cheap copies or expensive imports, suddenly became stylish. A suitable answer to the Impressionists' abandonment of form was found in the use of solid contours, and the decorative colours could be seen as a reaction against the *triste* representation of misery by the Naturalists.

The art of copying Japanese woodcuts is called *Japonaiserie*. Van Gogh is known to have made three such copies – his *Japonaiserie: Flowering Plum Tree* (ill. p. 426) and his *Japonaiserie: Bridge in the Rain* (ill. p. 427) are based upon Hiroshige, one of the last famous masters and virtually a contemporary of van Gogh. Nineteenth-century Japanese woodcuts display similarities with

TOP
The Seine with the Pont de la Grande Jatte, 1887
Oil on canvas, 32 x 40.5 cm (12⅝ x 16 in.)
Amsterdam, Van Gogh Museum, Vincent van Gogh Foundation

OPPOSITE
Still Life with Decanter and Lemons on a Plate, 1887
Oil on canvas, 46.5 x 38.5 cm (18⅜ x 15¼ in.)
Amsterdam, Van Gogh Museum, Vincent van Gogh Foundation

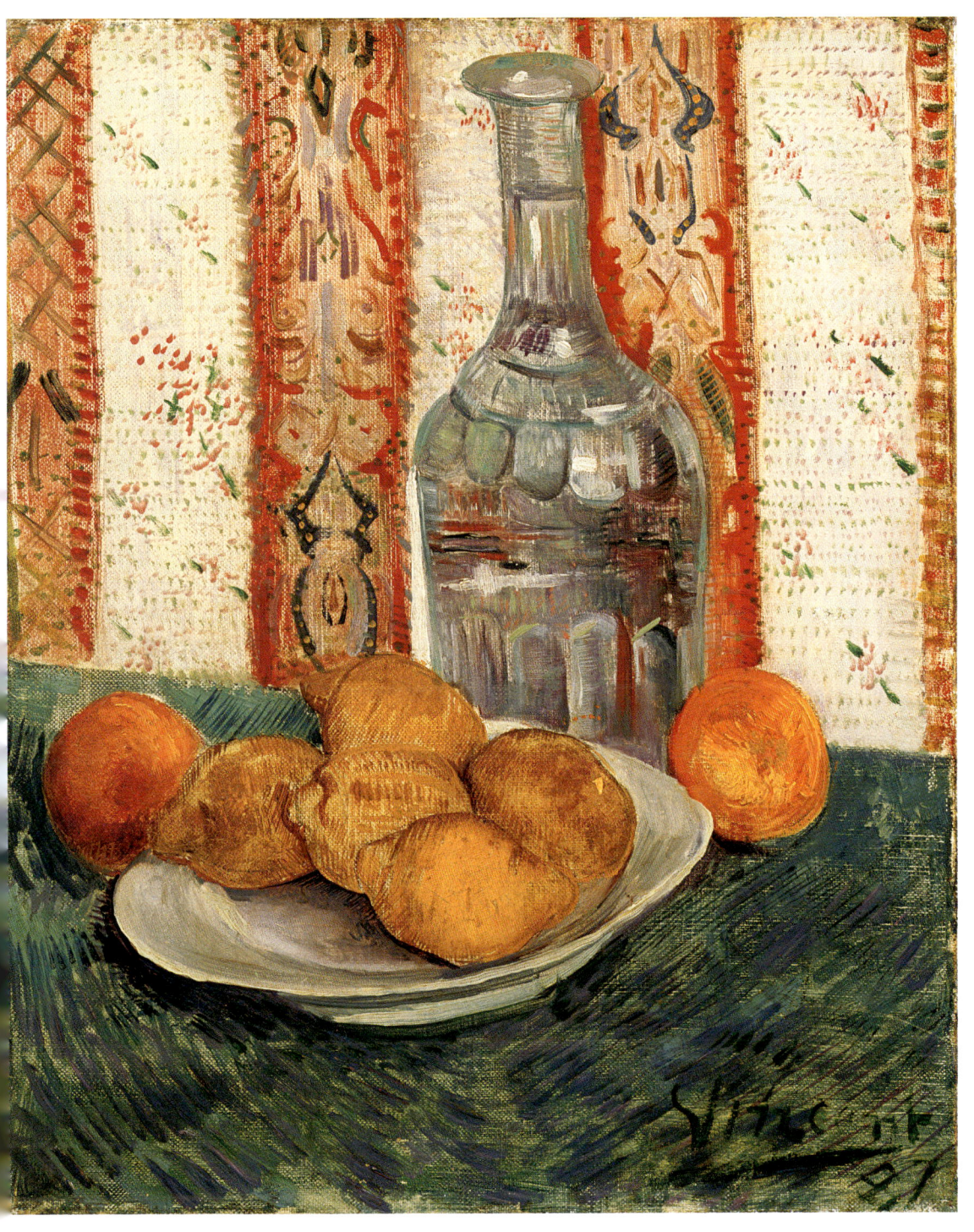

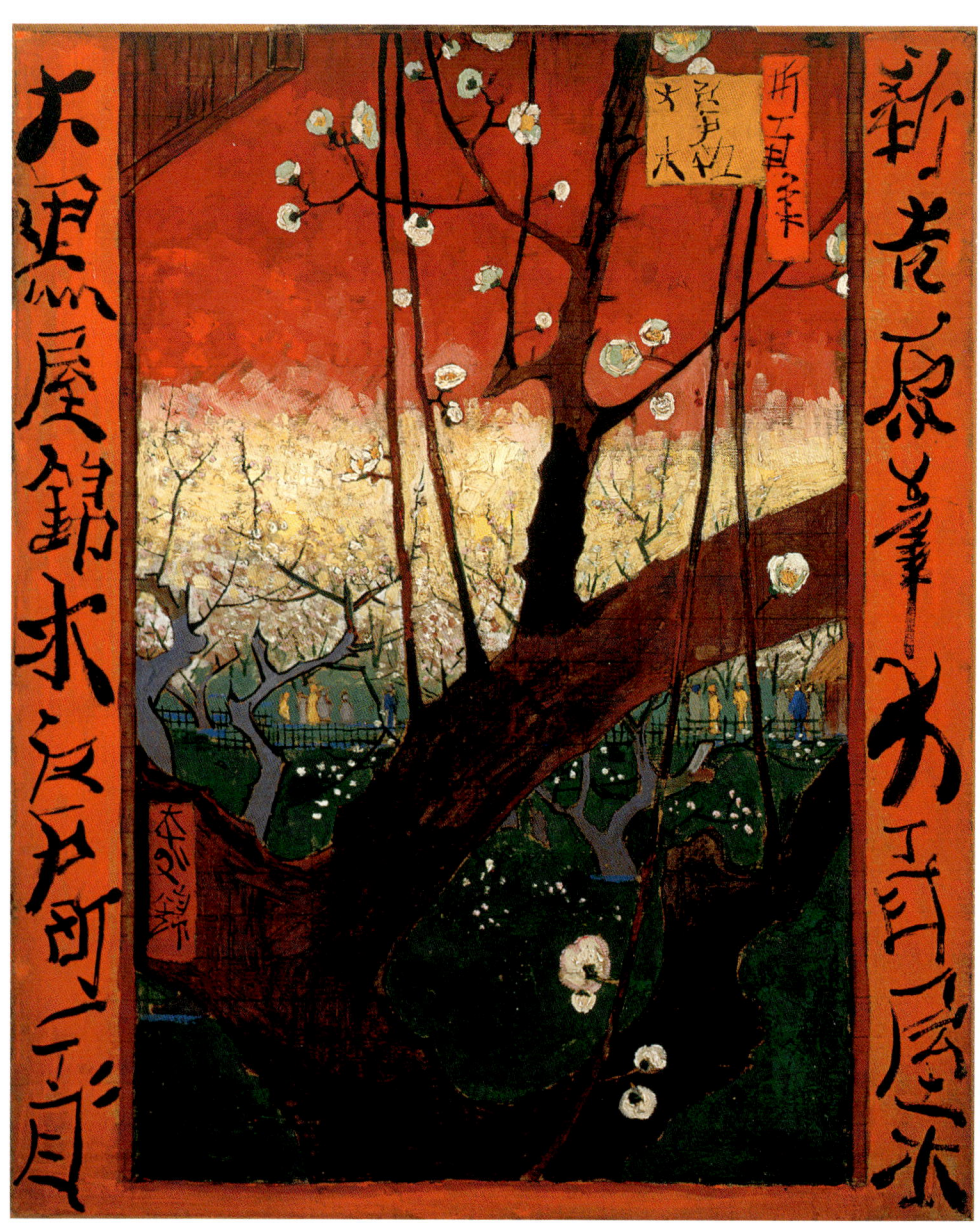

*Japonaiserie: Flowering Plum Tree
(after Hiroshige)*, 1887
Oil on canvas, 55.6 x 46.8 cm (22 x 18½ in.)
Amsterdam, Van Gogh Museum,
Vincent van Gogh Foundation

*Japonaiserie: Bridge in the Rain
(after Hiroshige)*, 1887
Oil on canvas, 73.3 x 53.8 cm (28⅞ x 21¼ in.)
Amsterdam, Van Gogh Museum,
Vincent van Gogh Foundation

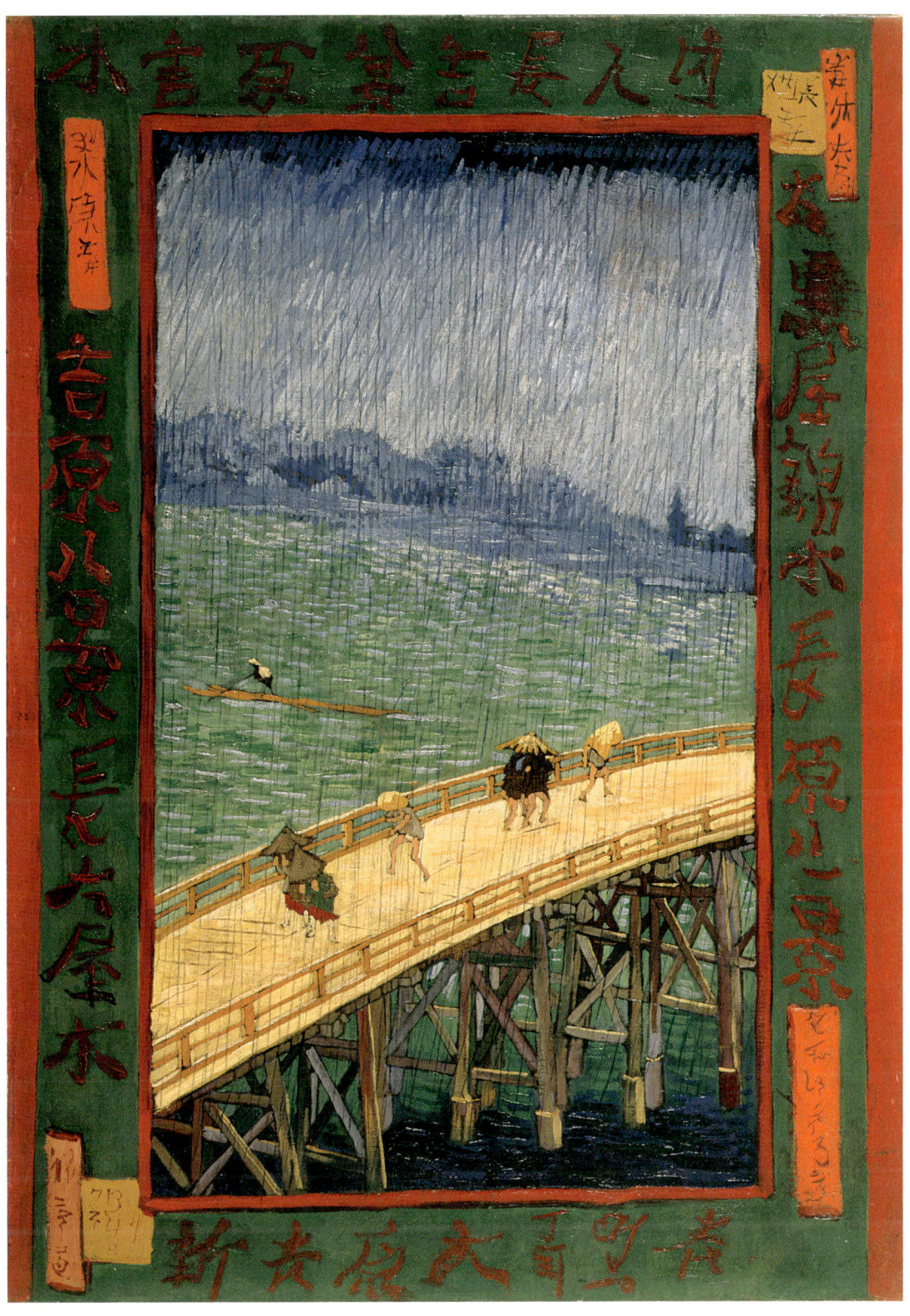

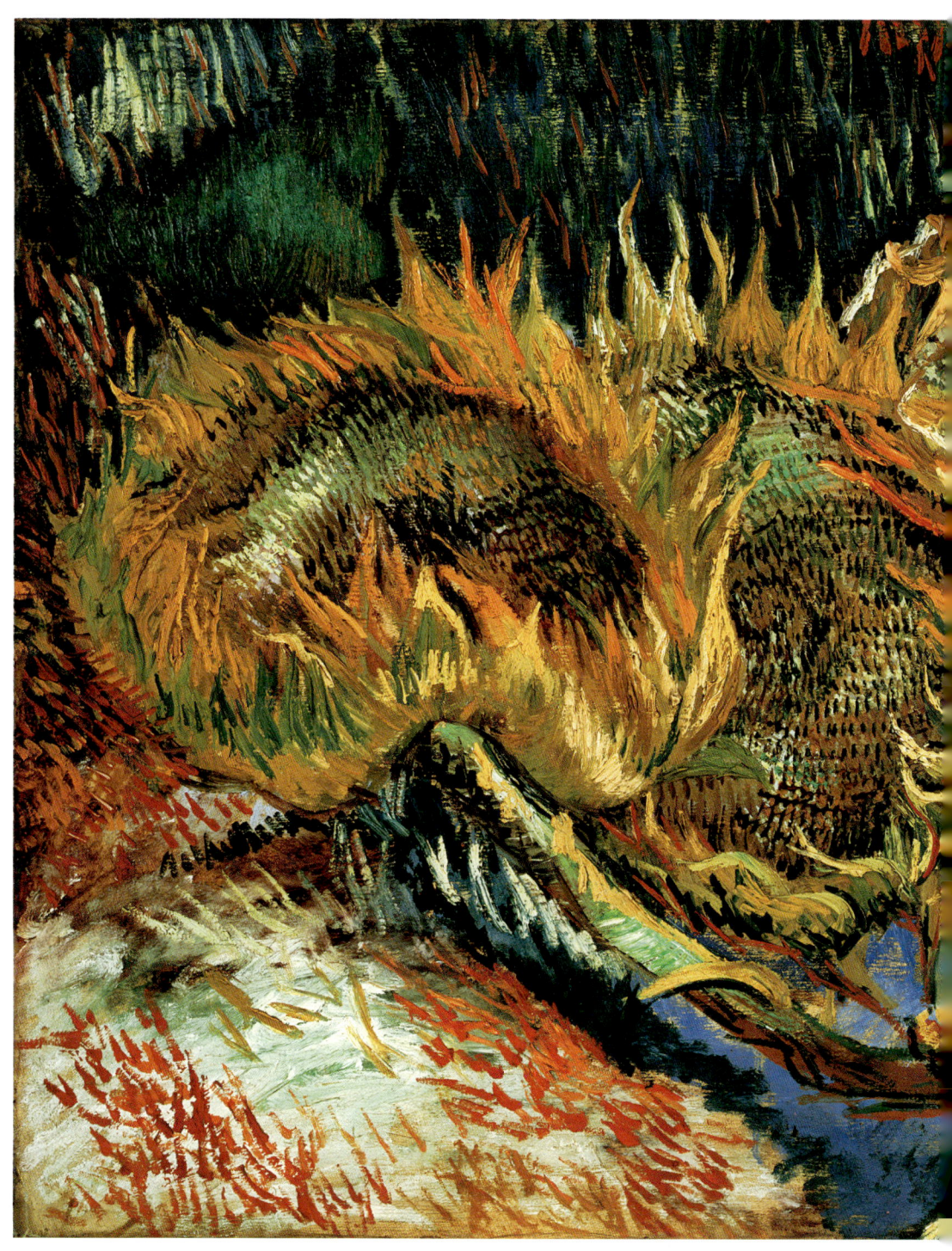

Four Cut Sunflowers, 1887
Oil on canvas, 59.5 x 99.5 cm (23½ x 39¼ in.)
Otterlo, Kröller-Müller Museum

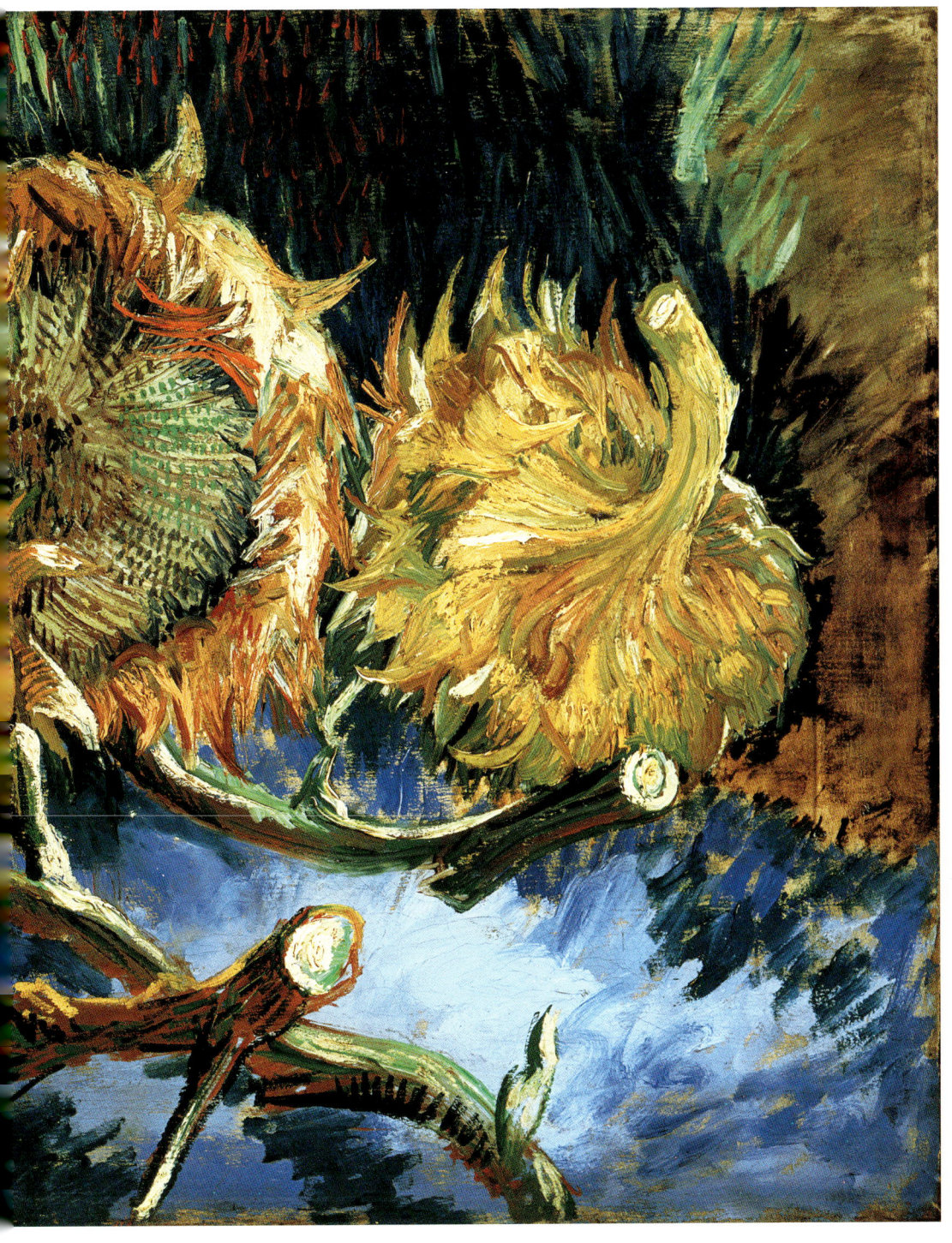

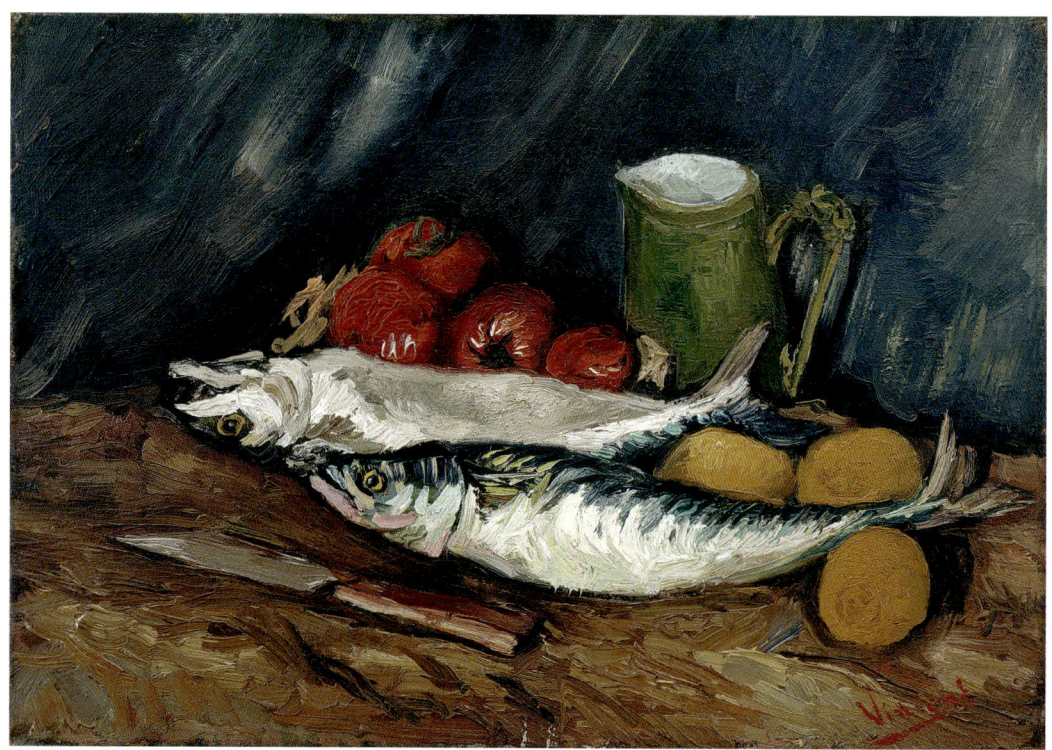

Still Life with Mackerels, Lemons
and Tomatoes (formerly attributed), 1886
Oil on canvas, 39 x 56.5 cm (15⅜ x 22¼ in.)
Winterthur, Museum Oskar Reinhart
"Am Römerholz"

OPPOSITE
Vase with Daisies and Anemones, 1887
Oil on canvas, 61.5 x 38.5 cm
(24¼ x 15¼ in.)
Otterlo, Kröller-Müller Museum

Western art and this very fact favoured their adoption. In all his attempts at imitating this art form, van Gogh's versions proved to be worlds apart from the originals. He never attained the smooth application of colour as in Hiroshige's work – the opposite, in fact. His pastose use of colour emphasizes his personal touch, rather than remaining anonymous. He even changed the format of the picture by widening the small frame with lines of Japanese characters, whose meaning he was certain not to know. In short, van Gogh Europeanized the source material, and in so doing brought it into line with his own artistic concept so that it corresponded to the actual trend.

By the end of his stay in Paris, Vincent had painted three portraits of the old art dealer Julien Tanguy, known to everybody as Père Tanguy. Père had lived through the great era of the realization of socialist ideals, the days of the Paris Commune, and because of this he was forced to go into exile. The artists looked upon him as the grand seigneur of their own utopian ideals. They bought all of their material cheaply from Tanguy, often on credit. He even had a small gallery in a side room, but this was ignored by the general public. Père Tanguy can be seen as a key figure in the Modernist movement, since it was in this small gallery that artists such as van Gogh, Seurat, Gauguin and Paul Cézanne, who were later considered to be the precursors of the 20th century, exhibited their works. In no other place could they get to know one another's works so well. It was Cézanne who called van Gogh's paintings the "works of a lunatic".

The *Portrait of Père Tanguy* (ill. p. 433) is the epitome of van Gogh's work in Paris, as *The Potato Eaters* (ill. p. 417) was for his earlier stay in Holland. Resolutely facing forwards, almost symmetrical,

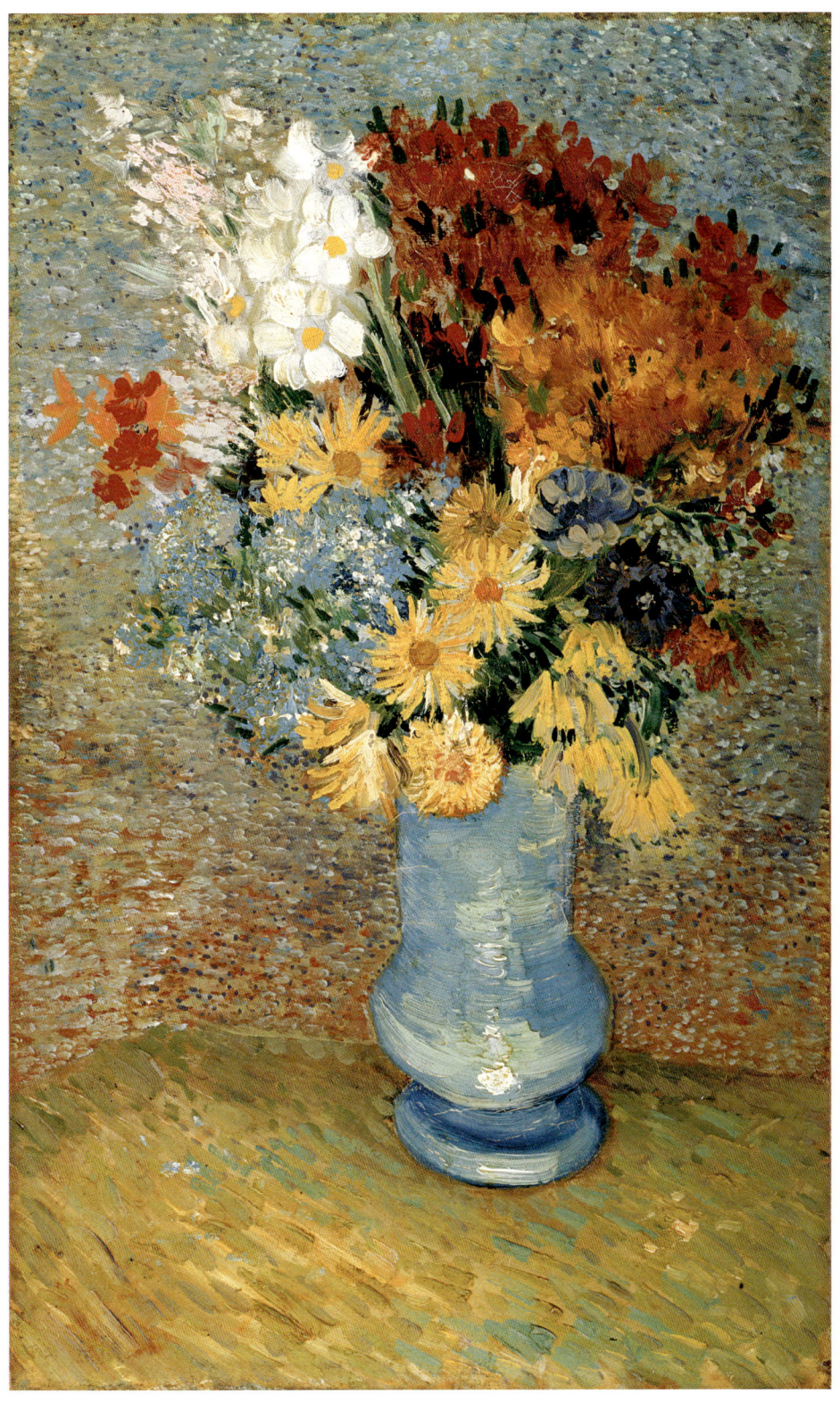

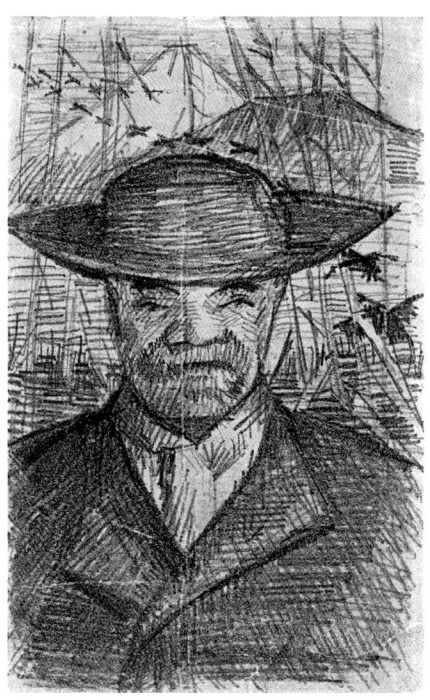

"I envy the Japanese artists for the incredible neat clarity which all their works have. It is never boring and you never get the impression that they work in a hurry. It is as simple as breathing; they draw a figure with a couple of strokes with such an unfailing easiness as if it were as easy as buttoning one's waistcoat."

VINCENT VAN GOGH

monumental in his stance, he dominates the foreground of the picture. This simplified portrayal contrasts with the complicated background structure, decorated with Japanese woodcuts. The whole picture appears extremely flat and the Japanese dancers appear to push against the figure in the front of the painting. The levelling out of the spatial interrelationship is evident here, abandoning the illusion of concrete reality.

Van Gogh was to further extend this principle, which opened up the way for him to depict other realities freely – that is, his own inner world, which had so often already vehemently asserted itself. Colour and command of the brush were to become his decisive means of expression. The lightness of Impressionism, the dissolution of areas into graphic structures using the technique of Pointillism, the decorative flatness of *Japonaiserie* – all of these principles van Gogh had acquired during his two years in Paris, through continual debate with his fellow artists. He had discussed Delacroix's colour theories with them and perfected the use of complementary contrasts, the rigid use of the colour black and also the increasing abandonment of local colour. These theories became second nature to him; composition and use of colour no longer needed any great consideration – they appeared as spontaneous gestures on the canvas. Van Gogh's time in Paris was his most educational and here he dismissed the academic mode of art. The more art became his sole preoccupation in life, the more he gained understanding through contact with other artists.

So he was ready to follow that path which Cézanne had already trodden. He wanted to go south, where nature, which was so central to his studies, was friendlier, the light brighter and the colours more intense. A rift with his brother, who had got into trouble with his employers because of Vincent's escapades, was imminent. Full of hopes, Vincent van Gogh boarded the train to Arles on 20 February 1888.

TOP
Portrait of Père Tanguy, 1887
Pencil on paper, 21.4 x 13.7 cm (8½ x 5½ in.)
Amsterdam, Van Gogh Museum,
Vincent van Gogh Foundation

OPPOSITE
Portrait of Père Tanguy, 1887/88
Oil on canvas, 65 x 51 cm (25.5 x 20 in.)
Paris, Collection Stavros S. Niarchos

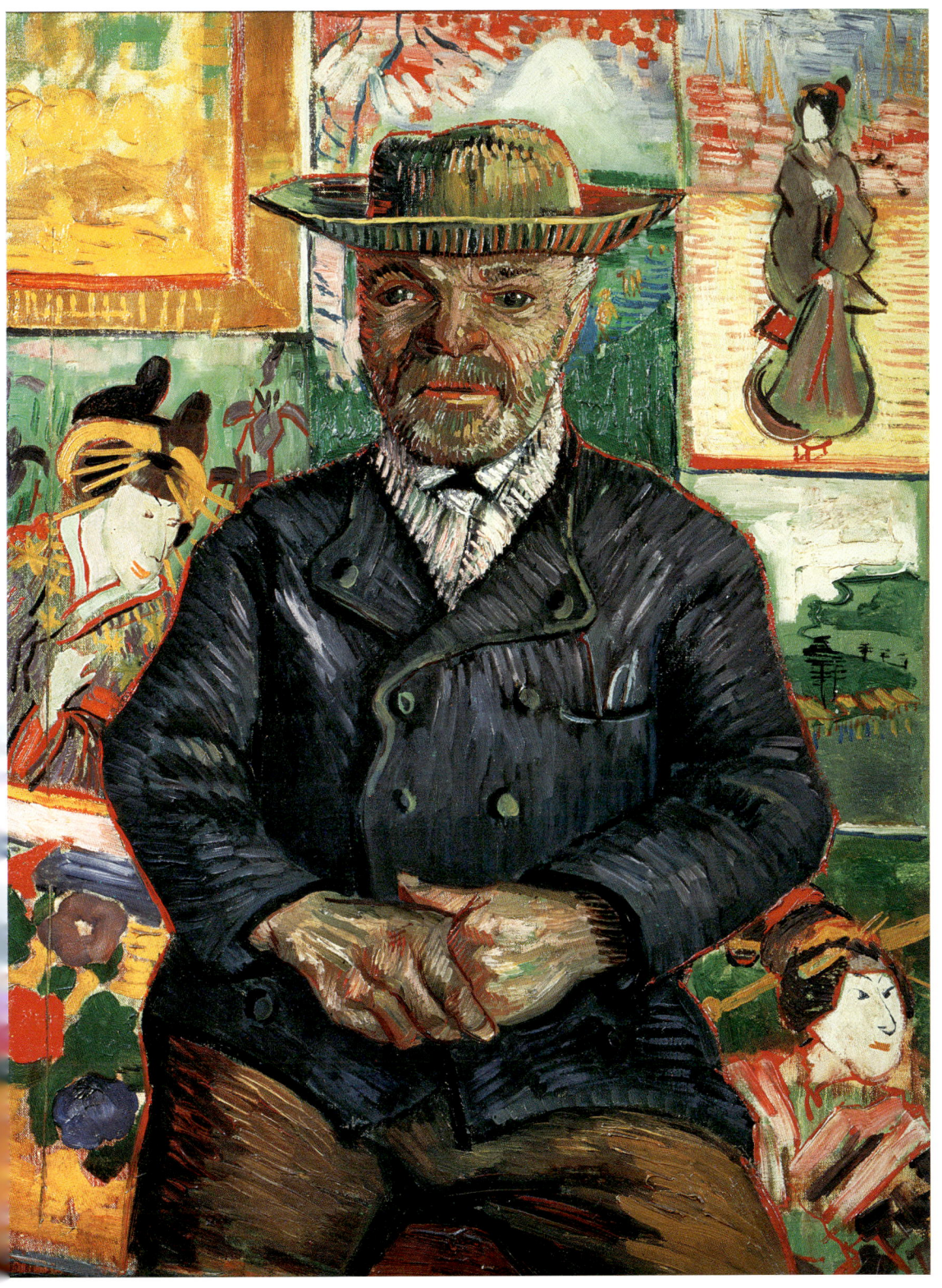

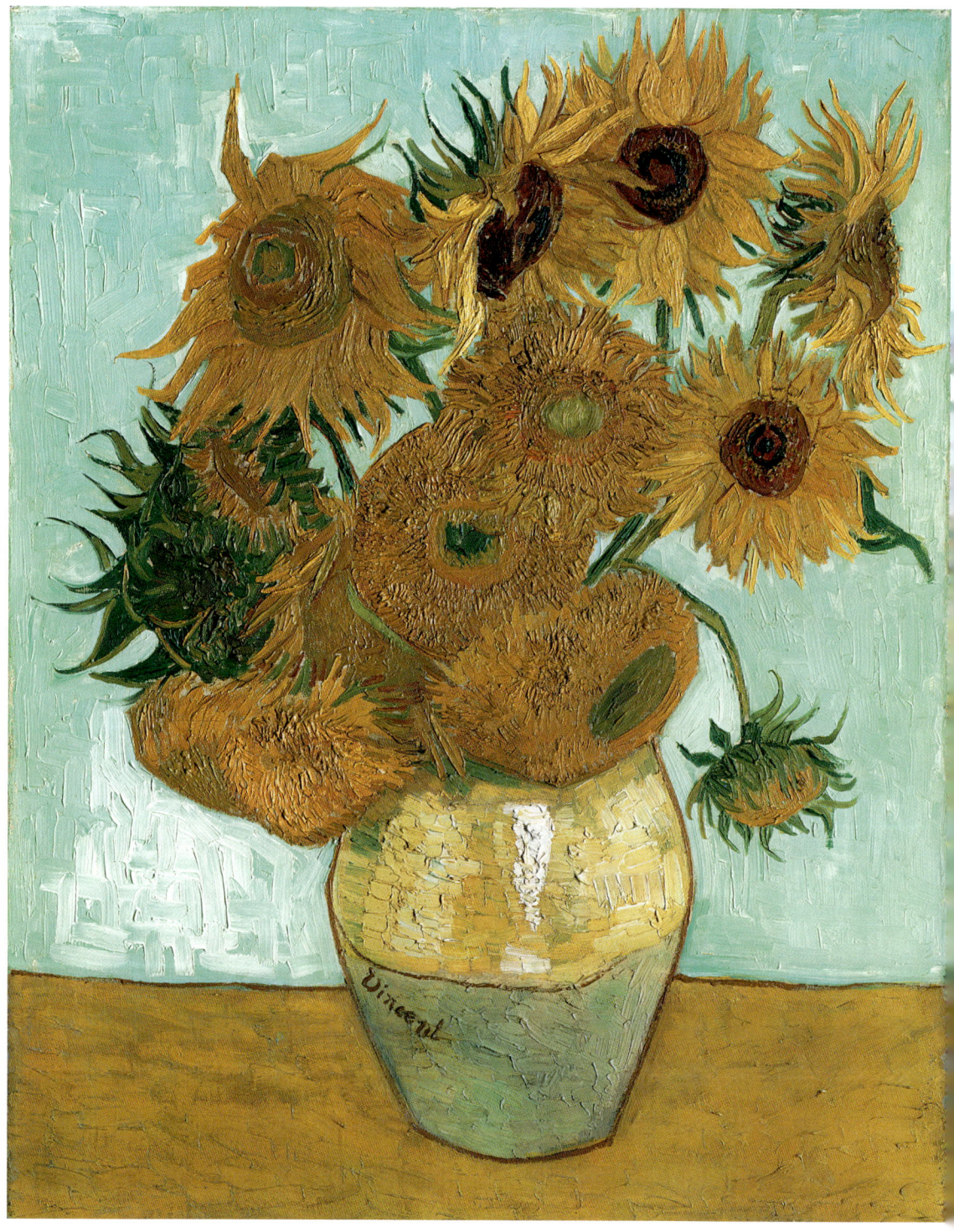

The Explosion of Colour
Arles 1888–1889

*"Now, since I have seen the ocean with my own
eyes, I feel completely how important it is for
me to stay in the south and to experience the
colour which must be carried to the uttermost –
it is not far to Africa."*
VINCENT VAN GOGH

Ever since Albert Dürer's Italian travels, artists from the north of Europe had been drawn in their droves to the Mediterranean, pulled by the fascination of the south. It was not only the architecture and painting of the Quattrocento, nor the elevated feeling gained from actually walking on ground saturated with centuries of history, but also the fascination which the Mediterranean landscapes held for northern artists, with their mild climate and warm sun bathing the landscape in radiant light.

The consequences of this "artists' pilgrimage" can be seen in the paintings themselves: the palettes became more colourful, the colours brighter and the themes recalled the classical age. Paul Klee summed up the experience gained from such a stay in the south in his emphatic declaration after he returned from his Tunisian travels: "I have finally discovered colour."

But why Arles of all places? Degas once spent a summer there. Adolphe Monticelli – painter of pastose colourful still-life flowers – was for van Gogh a kind of éminence grise because of the former's disagreement with his Parisian colleagues. He, too, lived in nearby Marseilles. Zola was born in this area, in Aix-en-Provence, where Cézanne had also been living for a long time. Apart from this, the Arles women were said to be the most beautiful in the world. Van Gogh himself never mentioned any specific reasons for his choice of Arles. However, his departure from Paris in February was most certainly an escape from the dreary melancholy of the Parisian winter.

Van Gogh wrote to his sister shortly after his arrival: "I have no need for Japanese art here, since I tell myself that I am in Japan, and only need to open my eyes and take in everything before me."

As if to verify these words to himself, he chose to paint the most typical Japanese motifs in his early Arles paintings. *Pink Peach Tree in Blossom* (ill. p. 439), painted in March 1888, was actually there before his very eyes. Even more satisfying to van Gogh than the joy of the approaching spring, which the small tree clearly heralded, was his hope of a Far Eastern culture directly on his doorstep. Instead of using Hiroshige's woodcuts – as he did in Paris – to visualize a Japanese landscape, he was now able to experience it himself in reality. The blooming tree, protected from the Mediterranean mistral by fencing, represented his own optimism and became a symbol of his own wishes and projection of his desires.

For five francs a day – way above his limits – he rented a room in a restaurant. The small attic was completely unsuitable for a studio. He did not know anybody who could sit as his model, and so the area around Arles, the trees, hills, bridges, fishing huts became his sole motif. The Camargue, the marshy Rhône delta, still largely uncultivated in the 19th century, the Crau plateau with its cornfields and vineyards and the

Still Life: Vase with Twelve Sunflowers, 1888
Oil on canvas, 91 x 72 cm (35⅞ x 28⅜ in.)
Munich, Bayerische Staatsgemäldesammlungen,
Neue Pinakothek

beach near the pilgrimage town Saintes-Maries-de-la-Mer sated his appetite for nature, which had been triggered by two years of living in the city. On his long walks he hoped to improve his somewhat shaky health, which he had abused with his excessive intake of alcohol and tobacco, as well as lack of decent food.

Perhaps he was reminded of his Dutch homeland – at any rate he was drawn more and more to the canal, south of Arles, where he studied the bridge and its surroundings. The two versions of the Langlois drawbridge (ills. pp. 436 and 437) were painted in March and May 1888. The peaceful serenity of the motif, the wide expanse of sky and water and the few objects in the painting were put under tension by his experimentation with colours: the motif itself merely provides the scenery over which colour is stretched like a second skin. The later version is in this respect the more restrained of the two. The distant view from the embankment, with the extensive tract of sky and too little water, of the opposite-facing bridge in contre-jour light, of people on the bridge recognizable only as shadows, and in addition the light, white-toned application of colour, are all reminiscent of the Impressionists' techniques which most obviously influenced van Gogh here. The early version is completely different. The artist is standing directly on the banks of the canal. Objects now stand out sharply against the lofty horizon and have the appearance of radiating colour from themselves, mainly due to the use of red tonality combined with all the colours. Here the directed, participating, binding view geared towards the concrete object makes itself felt; this is a technique that Vincent was to cultivate gradually during his Arles period.

The Langlois Bridge at Arles, 1888
Oil on canvas, 49.5 x 64.5 cm (19½ x 25½ in.)
Cologne, Wallraf-Richartz-Museum &
Fondation Corboud

In so doing van Gogh developed a new form of tone painting, which is better than that of his master Delacroix. Autonomy

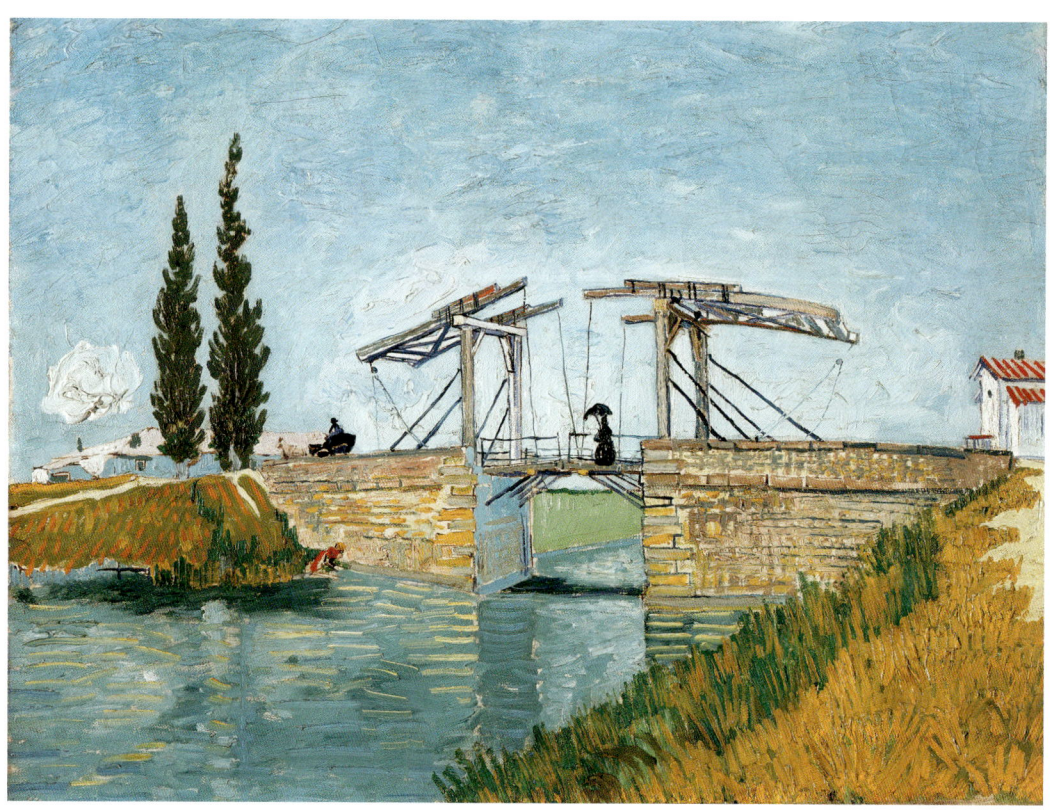

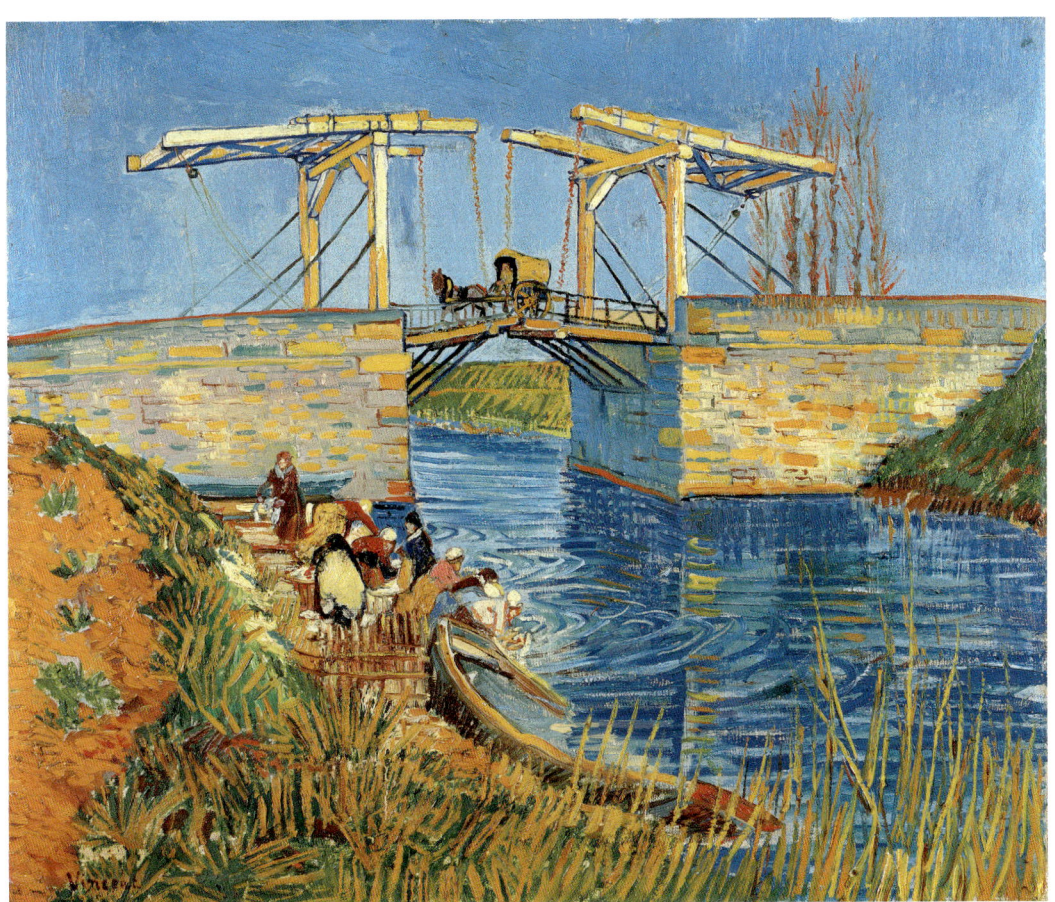

of colour and tone painting are one here. Just as before, the colouring of the picture arises out of the play on varieties of one specific colour and tones – the only difference now being that this basic colour no longer corresponds to reality. A rich yellow,

The Langlois Bridge at Arles
with Women Washing, 1888
Oil on canvas, 54 x 65 cm (21⅜ x 25⅝ in.)
Otterlo, Kröller-Müller Museum

a gaudy red now rise above the mere task of portraying an appearance. Colour alone is the means of expressing oneself individually, as well as portraying the idea of reality present in the artist's psyche. Light and shadow, reflections and refractions of colour are deliberately subdued, but these qualities of the painting still have their pictorial origin in actual perception and not in mere imagination. A certain colour is no longer chosen because it corresponds to the actual, but because it is able to strengthen the vehement nature of expression. This colour is no longer objectively verifiable, but only subjectively understandable.

Still there is little reason for such vehemence of expression. On the contrary, paintings such as *Harvest at La Crau, with Montmajour in the Background* (ill. pp. 442/443) of June 1888 take complete pleasure in what is seen. Here van Gogh painted a typically traditional landscape scene, indeed he used a richer intensity of colour, but it is clearly close to reality in the toned-down shade of the delicate blue in the background.

Soon after his arrival, Vincent looked for another cheaper room in a café and at the same time he rented a house, his famous "yellow house", which he gradually furnished. At least from May onwards

"If one is healthy, one ought to be able to live on a piece of bread and be able to work the whole day and have the strength to smoke and drink; that's what one needs under these conditions. And moreover, you can feel the stars and the infinity of the sky. Since life, in spite of everything, is like a fairytale. You know, people who do not believe in the sun, in surroundings like this, are godless."

VINCENT VAN GOGH

he had studios at his disposal and a place to store his numerous new paintings. He was still completely optimistic at this time.

Once a year on 24 May, Europe's gypsies flock to the small fishing village of Saintes-Maries-de-la-Mer to honour their patron saint, St Sarah, and take part in a pilgrimage. The whole region is in complete turmoil, thronged full of half-fearful, half-curious people. Naturally van Gogh's interest was aroused. His excursions in the area around Arles came to an end with his journey to the Mediterranean coast. *Fishing Boats on the Beach at Saintes-Maries* (ill. p. 441), painted at the beginning of June 1888, takes up and reworks a theme from the earlier period: the beach scene. Now the sea is literally pushed to the edge of the painting and its atmospheric blue is barely distinguished by the line of the horizon from the similar composition of the sky, and thus is a mere piece of scenery for the graphic exactness of the thing itself. With an almost dissecting accuracy of observation, van Gogh is fully engrossed in the material nature of the banal motif, in the surging movement of the hull and the tilted intricacy of the mast. He presents objects almost lovingly – boats, vases, chairs, shoes – creating a visual panorama.

The autonomy of colour does not go hand-in-hand with the autonomy of form. The form of an object, its contours and surface composition remain in his work true to reality all of the time: "It's true I turn my back completely on nature, when I transform a sketch into a painting, decide upon the colours, enlarge or simplify, but in relation to the actual form I am afraid of moving too far away from reality and thus of not being exact enough." This he admitted in a letter to the artist Bernard. He continued: "I don't in fact invent the whole painting, on the contrary, I discover the thing, but it must come out of nature." Van Gogh approached subjects which he would later use in his pictures not by making quick sketches but by drawing in more exact detail. The concrete motif remained the constant foundation of his representations, over which colour was placed like a second skin, colour which van Gogh chose solely according to its effect in the painting. In this way the dignity of the object remained intact.

Thus the red-haired eccentric lived amongst the people of Arles: taciturn, introverted, added to the fact that as an artist he was considered as lacking a respectable profession, constantly in need of money, and saddled with an unpronounceable name, a fact which van Gogh had taken into account early on by signing his works with his Christian name only. So it was almost half a year before he was able to make close friends with the people he admired and whose portraits he wanted to paint. Portrait painting was van Gogh's way of examining in an artistic light the people, friendship and affection which were so often denied him in life. He himself said that the art of portrait painting "lets me develop that which is the best and deepest within me". The colours thus become increasingly the means by which characters are depicted, as well as becoming more and more independent of the concrete externalities of the object portrayed. In a certain sense, the people he painted were all, like himself, outsiders. Strangely enough, he never painted a portrait of his brother Theo, not even during his time in Paris.

The Seated Zouave (ill. p. 445), portraying an infantry soldier from Algeria and painted at the end of June 1888, is van Gogh's first portrait since that of Père Tanguy. "I've finally found a model," rejoiced van Gogh about the African who was on

Pink Peach Tree in Blossom
(Reminiscence of Mauve), 1888
Oil on canvas, 73 x 60 cm (28¾ x 23⅝ in.)
Otterlo, Kröller-Müller Museum

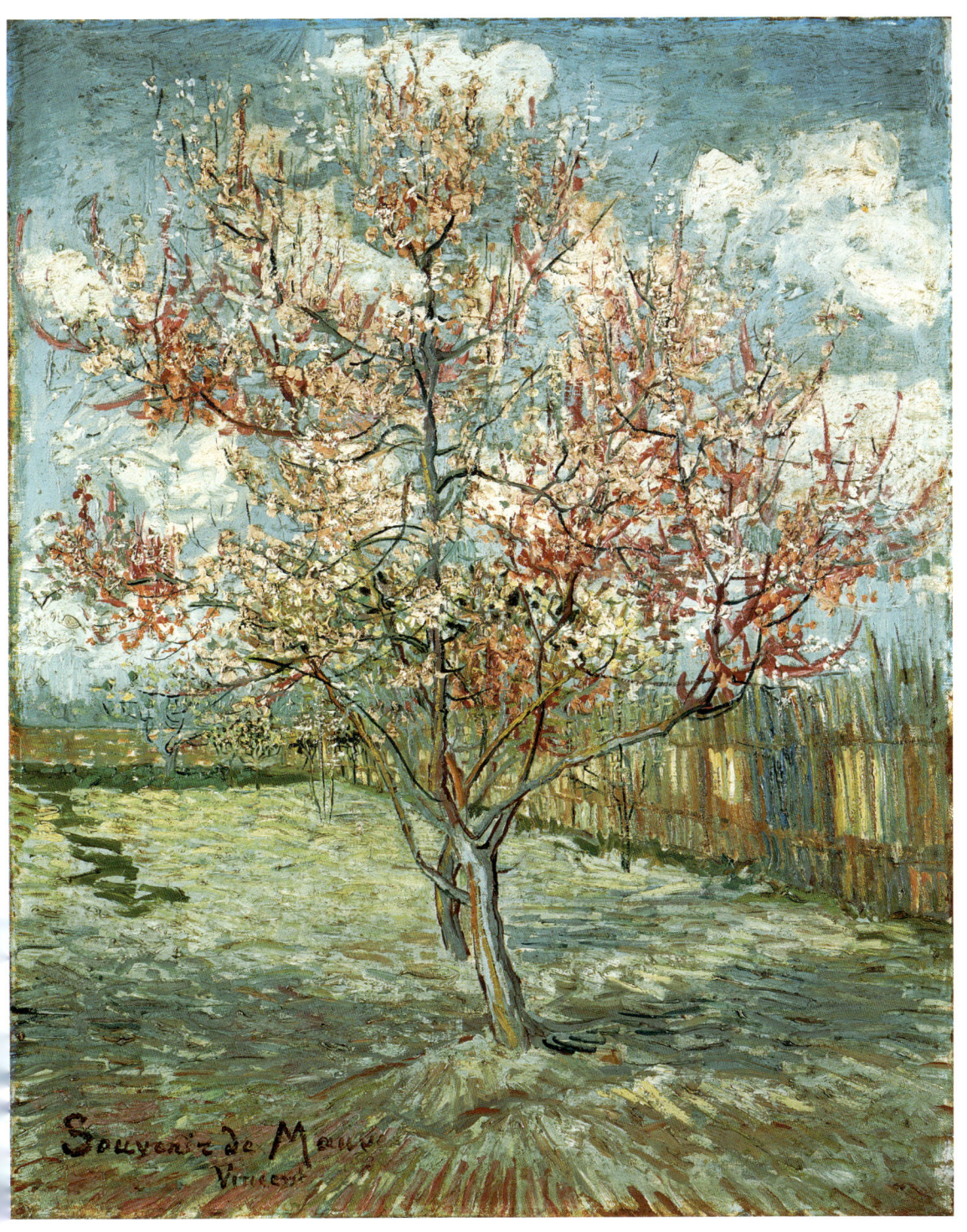

Souvenir de Mauve
Vincent

holiday in Arles. Milliet, the name of the soldier, later characterized van Gogh accurately in his remark: "This young man who shows both talent and good taste in his drawings becomes abnormal as soon as he touches a brush."

As always this portrait was not commissioned. His main reason for painting it was the exotic appearance of the man in his unusual traditional costume, which reminded him of Delacroix's models, whom the latter came across in Morocco. A strange contradiction between spatiality and flatness is typical of this depiction. The perfectly captured natural facial expressions are all the more pronounced because of the decorative patterns of the clothing, contrasting with the pastose colouring behind. The tiled floor appears to slip away towards the foreground of the picture, leading to the model's rather precarious posture.

The few people who van Gogh portrayed during this time appear to have been pushed into a framework in order to maintain an unbroken artistic style. This fact alone points to the impossibility of these portraits having been commissioned. The originality of those portrayed is stressed in their faces, which are all the artist tries to capture exactly; the posture, clothing, application of colour and composition are, in contrast, more the result of wanting to create a decorative effect, which is not dependent upon contradictions but which only becomes apparent when colour is applied. Van Gogh was proud of the fact that he deliberately painted his portraits in a hurry: "One must strike while the iron is hot," he wrote, and compared his style to the quick gestures of the caricaturist, above all Honoré Daumier. This desire to work quickly explains the by-and-large expansive backgrounds and the ornamental play of the colours of the clothing, which appear to be totally separate from the bodies of the persons portrayed.

La Mousmé, Sitting (ill. p. 446) and *Portrait of the Postman Joseph Roulin* (ill. p. 449) were painted shortly after each other in the summer of 1888. La Mousmé, whom van Gogh described as "a Japanese girl, in this case one from the provinces, 12 or 14 years of age" and Joseph Roulin, whom he described as "having a head like Socrates" are both sitting in the same easy chair which was in van Gogh's "yellow house". The chair appears too large for the girl, whose slight frame is swamped by the wickerwork. The country postman, in contrast, sits erect, but appears ill-at-ease in his attempt to accommodate himself comfortably amongst the confinement of the furniture. The girl's skirt and the man's uniform are not mere articles of clothing, but rather great ornamentally worked areas of colour. The faces, in contrast, are finely painted. The shy, nervous glance of the child and the choleric, bloated face of the adult make the concrete appearance of the ordinary people from the neighbourhood comprehensible. These portraits are dedicated to portraying the theme which had so fascinated van Gogh in his early works: simple people from the area, captured by the intense observation of an artist who feels at one with them.

Throughout the whole of the summer, van Gogh was occupied with a problem which had troubled his fellow artists for centuries, of how one should portray darkness using colour when painting night scenes. How could one make colour, which only comes alive when in contrast with light, flexible so that the opposite, darkness, is portrayed? Van Gogh appears to have found the key to this problem on a walk at night along the seashore. "It wasn't cheerful, it wasn't sad, it was just – beautiful," he wrote to Theo afterwards, deeply moved. He wanted to portray this atmosphere, of sparse light in front of a dark horizon, in his paintings.

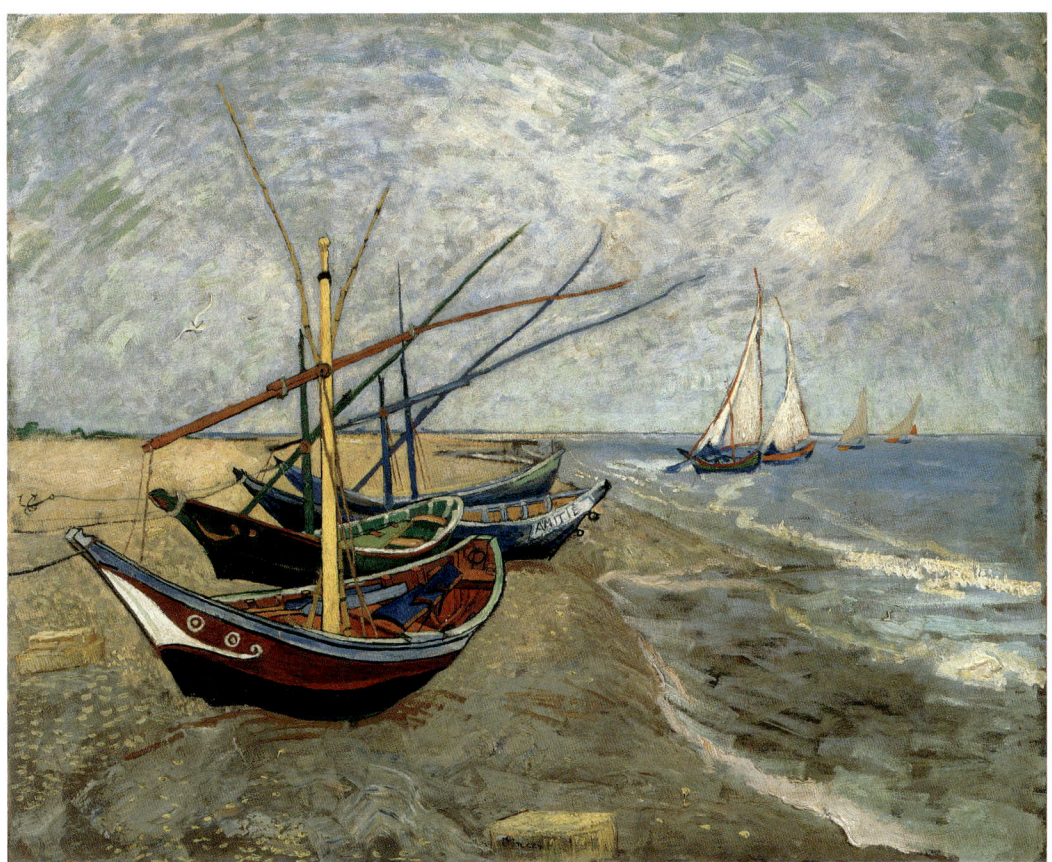

Fishing Boats on the Beach at Saintes-Maries, 1888
Oil on canvas, 65 x 81.5 cm (25⅝ x 32 in.)
Amsterdam, Van Gogh Museum,
Vincent van Gogh Foundation

Mainly in order to get used to working by artificial light, he painted *The Night Café in Arles* (ill. pp. 450/451) in September 1888. For four days or so he slept only during the day, returning at night to the depressive milieu of the dive which he wanted to paint: lonely drunks cowering behind their tables, a billiard player, a couple cuddling in the corner, and a waiter – a cast of characters enacting despair.

"I have tried," Vincent commented on his painting, "to portray with red and green this terrible human suffering. The room is blood red and dull yellow, a green billiard table in the middle, and four lemon-coloured lamps radiating an orange and green aureola light. Struggle and antitheses are present everywhere: in the completely opposite colours (the greens and reds), in the crouching sleeping figures of the night, in the empty, depressing room, in the violet and blue." And elsewhere Vincent remarked: "I attempted to convey the idea that the café is a place where one can ruin oneself, become crazy or criminal." This painting is one of the few which solely portrays the motif of a pessimistic feeling of life. The image of the café, a place where "one can ruin oneself", get drunk and spend one's last penny, was to follow van Gogh through the last few years of his life up until his own collapse.

The night atmosphere in this painting comes out more through its association with loneliness, suffering and desperation than through the portrayal itself. Only the yellowish aureoles around the lamps point to the fact that the picture was painted at night. Yet *The Night Café* is still only a stepping stone, an étude of night painting.

"An endlessly flat landscape – seen from a bird's eye view from the top of the hill – vineyards, harvested corn fields. All this is multiplied to infinity and spreads like the surface of the sea to the horizon, which is bordered by the hills of Crau."

VINCENT VAN GOGH

Harvest at La Crau, with Montmajour in the Background, 1888
Oil on canvas, 73.4 x 91.8 cm (29 x 36¼ in.)
Amsterdam, Van Gogh Museum,
Vincent van Gogh Foundation

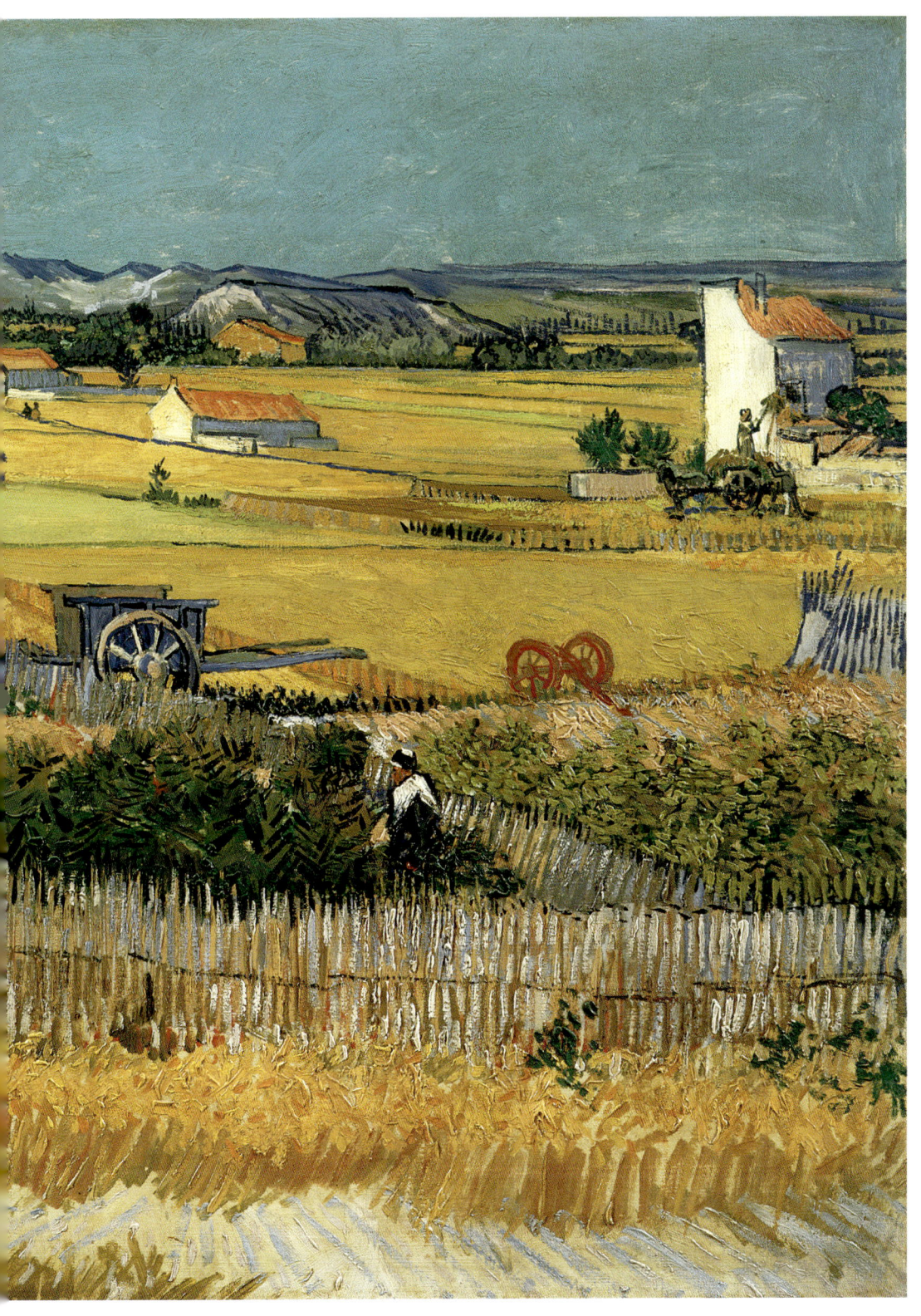

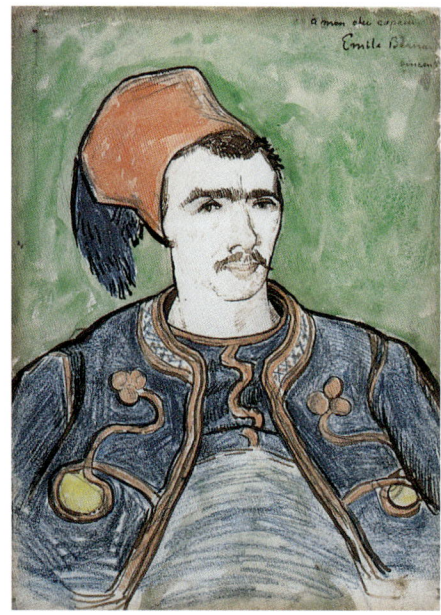

"I've finally found a model – a Zouave – a small chap with a bull's neck and tiger's eyes; I began a portrait and then began a second one … the uniform is of the same blue as the enamel pans, with faded orange-red braid and two stars on his chest; a common blue, which was very difficult to get exactly right."

VINCENT VAN GOGH

A short time afterwards, with his painting entitled *The Café Terrace on the Place du Forum, Arles, at Night* (ill. p. 453), van Gogh dared to take the final step into the open. Beneath the starry sky the terrace appears brightly lit up, its reddish yellow a complementary contrast to the dark blue of the twilight. A strong pull into the black centre of the painting, recognizable by the virtually parallel receding lines above the lintel in the front, pergola and house gables, set off the inviting light of the café in addition to its dark ambience. The light spots of stars in the sky, added to the complementary contrast which is difficult to achieve with sparse light, makes the representation of a night scene quite matter-of-fact.

To paint outdoors was a 19th-century achievement. To paint by artificial light was already in the Baroque period a favoured artistic way of passing the time. But to paint outdoors at night by artificial light was van Gogh's very own invention. In this way he presents a crass contrast to the light painting of the Impressionists, stressing a precision of observation in his portrayal of dimly lit objects, to which the technique of painting outdoors is perfectly suited. "The night is livelier and richer in colour than the day," van Gogh exclaimed enthusiastically. The vaguely recognizable objects spur on the depiction of exactness and fantasy. Van Gogh continues to use the technique of painting at night throughout the remaining few years of his life, his greatest achievement being *Starry Night* (ill. pp. 474/475).

The painting of *Vincent's House in Arles (The Yellow House)* (ill. p. 455) of September 1888, although not a night painting, keeps to the same colours as *The Café Terrace on the Place du Forum*. Shortly after he rented the house in May, van Gogh had it painted yellow, which was an important and symbolic colour for him. Yet for a long time it stood completely without furniture, due to the fact that he had no money to furnish it. Only when Theo sent him 300 francs was he able to afford sparse furnishings. He finally moved in in the middle of September. Now he felt like his own master – security and freedom appeared guaranteed thanks to his "ownership", added to the possibility of finally founding the long-awaited

TOP
The Zouave (Half Length), 1888
Watercolour, 31.5 x 23.6 cm (12½ x 9⅜ in.)
New York, The Metropolitan Museum of Art

OPPOSITE
The Seated Zouave, 1888
Oil on canvas, 81 x 65 cm (32 x 25⅝ in.)
Private collection

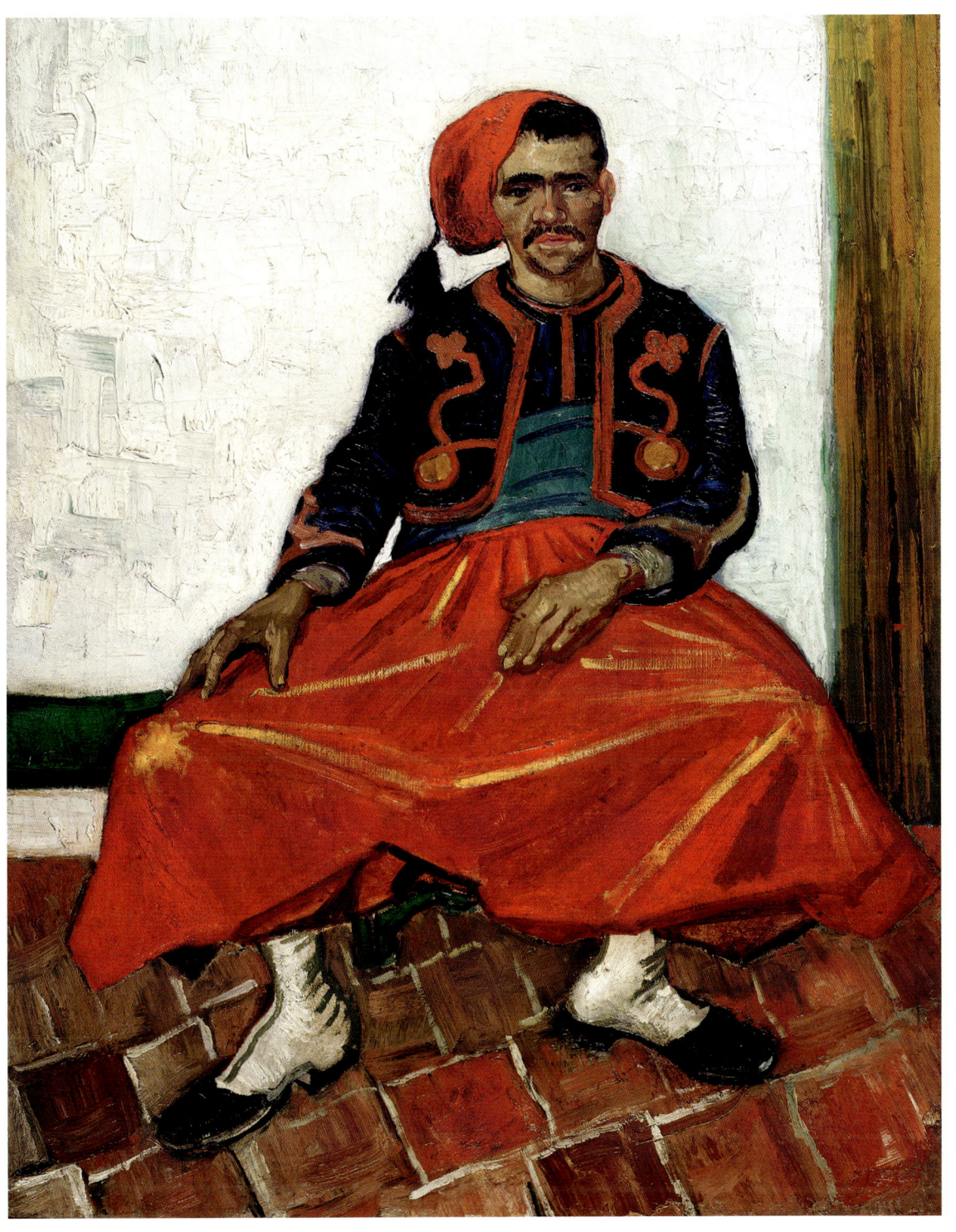

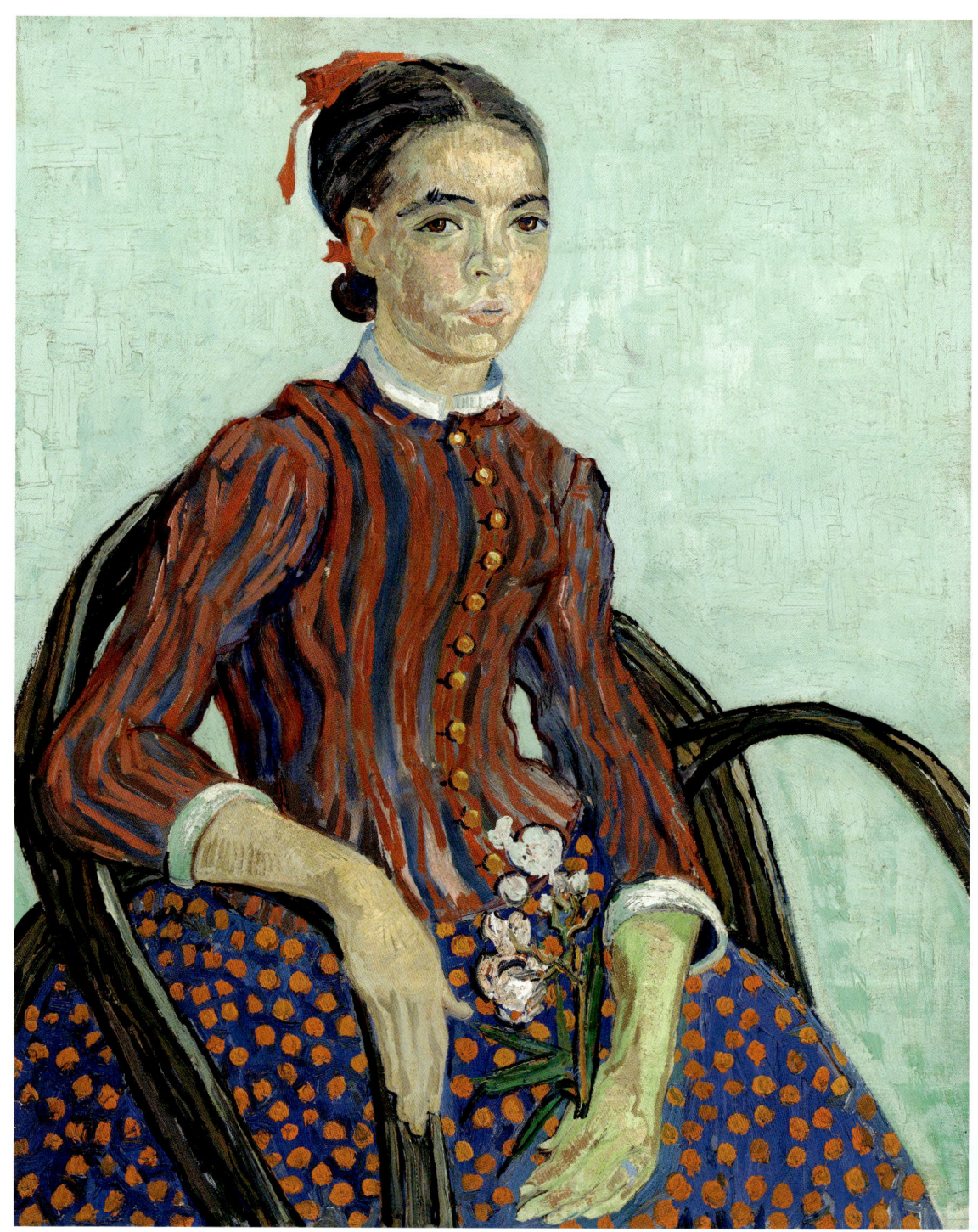

artist commune. Out of sheer joy he painted all the houses yellow in his painting, as if they were all at his disposal. For a short while the "yellow house" symbolized everything which appeared important to him and which guaranteed him happiness. The "yellow house" was a personal symbol.

At the end of the century Symbolism was an attitude of mind which was to confront van Gogh again and again, especially with regard to his artistic and private disagreement with Paul Gauguin. "The aim of painting and literature," Édouard Dujardin, himself one of the chief theoreticians of Symbolism, wrote in 1886, "is to reproduce the discovery of things with the common means of painting and literature. What one should express is not the image, but the character." Symbolism spread like a fashion craze through the young generation of Bohemian artists. The aim was "to portray the essence of the chosen object and in so doing avoid mere photographic imitation".

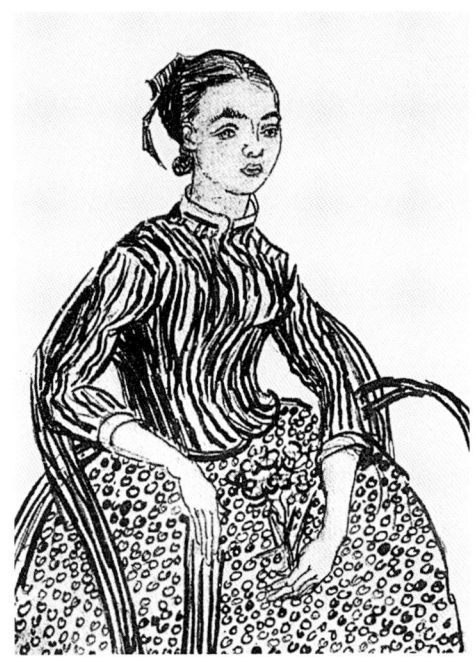

Van Gogh's painting *Still Life: Vase with Twelve Sunflowers* (ill. p. 434) of August 1888 attempts to portray this very essence. With extreme precision he has captured the flowers, yet the pastose application of colour, the confused arrangement of out-stretched leaves, and the inner luminosity of the light blue background, give the portrayal a significance which goes far beyond that of the mere painting of the flowers. These sunflowers stand for the artist's imagination, for his identification with them, for some form of deeper meaningfulness, and they appear to have influenced him.

"A watering can, a harrow left in the fields, a dog in the sun, an ugly churchyard – all these things can become a receptacle of my revelation. Each of these objects and thousands of other similar ones, which one normally merely glances over with indifference, can, for me personally, at any one moment – but in no way controlled by myself – take on an exalted and stirring character." With these words Hugo von Hofmannsthal described the power of imagination in his "Chandos Letter".

It was exactly this wish to empathize with the most banal of worldly objects which was to inspire van Gogh. The wild movement of the plants in his painting *Still Life: Vase with Oleanders and Books* (ill. p. 456) points to the same arbitrary search for a world behind the objects. However, artistic Symbolism as represented by a Dujardin or a Hofmannsthal was always the conscious, deliberate demonstration of artistic genius, the display of an omnipotent fantasy, which set the artist apart from the commonness of the world. Van Gogh's power of imagination, however, came from his innermost self. It was an expression of a vehement will, a flood of emotion, which later was to contribute to his mental derangement. The worlds portrayed in his paintings are much more self-explanatory, more immediate than the often affected exoticism and esoteric meanings of the Symbolist movement. Van Gogh was not an aesthete influenced by the spirit of that time.

A major pictorial technique of the Symbolists was the framing of all the objects by a common contour. This

OPPOSITE
La Mousmé, Sitting, 1888
Oil on canvas, 73.3 x 60.3 cm (28⅞ x 23¾ in.)
Washington, D.C., National Gallery of Art

TOP
La Mousmé, Sitting, 1888
Pencil and pen, 32.5 x 24.5 cm (12⅞ x 9¾ in.)
Moscow, Pushkin Museum

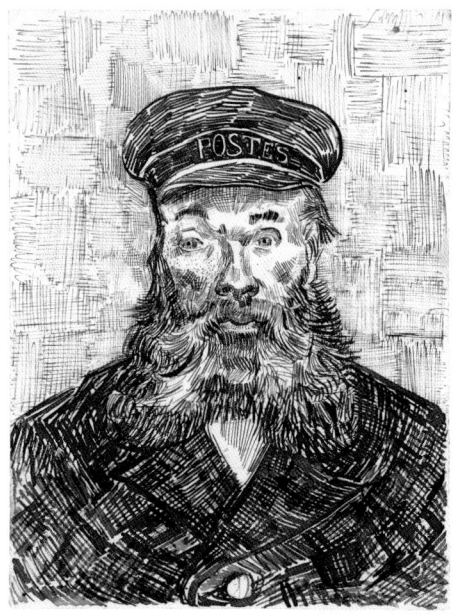

expressed the uniqueness of the object that had inspired the artist, or even the final vagueness of the things, which was necessary in order to make symbols out of them and to stylize them so that they went beyond being mere symbols. Dujardin called this method of painting Cloisonnism, derived, on the one hand, from mediaeval goldsmiths' art, on the other hand, as was always the case in that period, from Japanese woodcuts.

Van Gogh's *L'Arlésienne: Madame Ginoux with Books* (ill. p. 457) of November 1888, a portrait of Madame Ginoux, the owner of the station café in Arles, is a perfect example of this Cloisonnism. The back of the chair, the table top, and the woman's figure are all embraced by a single contour, which emphasizes the silhouette. Van Gogh works the contrasting colour effects into the spacious graphic framework. The depiction is completely flat and details come alive entirely from the line of colour.

Van Gogh explains his Cloisonnism thus: "The areas which are surrounded by contours, whether present or not – but in any case tangible – are then filled out with simplified tones."

Cloisonnism was the trademark of the Pont-Aven School, whose mentor was Gauguin. He almost dogmatically surrounded surface areas with framing lines. They were his guarantee against the mere copying of reality. Van Gogh, in contrast, viewed the whole less strictly. His contours, mostly varied in colour, came to the surface, or remained below the surface according to need, since the effect of the picture as a whole, and not a theoretical concept, determined their usage. Gauguin's criticism of van Gogh's inexactitude in this area was one of the reasons which led to their later disagreement.

In the painting *The Trinquetaille Bridge* (ill. p. 460) of October 1888, van Gogh almost completely renounced the use of colour. Thus the effect of the painting became subordinate to the contrasting play of linear interweavings on the left-hand side and the larger calmer surface on the right. This view of the bridge over the Rhône – the river itself is not shown in the picture – is based in its lack of colour on his earlier Dutch work, but the motif points to the work done in Paris. Yet the extreme distortion of the area and the confused perspective of the picture point to his later years. The steps in the foreground are drawn into the back of the picture, into the hole, which blocks out the underpass thereby serving as a contrast to the precarious equilibrium of the steel bridge, which threatens at any moment to collapse. One can call it expressivity of space: this constant fragile balance, this precarious ease. Was van Gogh therefore the first Expressionist? His handling of space suggests the answer is yes.

Van Gogh's treatment of colour leads to a similar conclusion. It is primarily representative of his means of expression. Pictures such as the two versions of *The Sower* (ills. pp. 458 and 459) of June and November 1888, were in their intensity of

TOP
Portrait of the Postman Joseph Roulin, 1888
Pen and ink, 31.8 x 24.3 cm (12⅝ x 9⅝ in.)
Los Angeles, J. Paul Getty Museum

OPPOSITE
Portrait of the Postman Joseph Roulin, 1888
Oil on canvas, 81.2 x 65.3 cm (32 x 25¾ in.)
Boston, Museum of Fine Arts

PAGES 450/451
The Night Café in Arles, 1888
Watercolour, 44.4 x 63.2 cm (17½ x 25 in.)
Berne, H. R. Hahnloser Collection

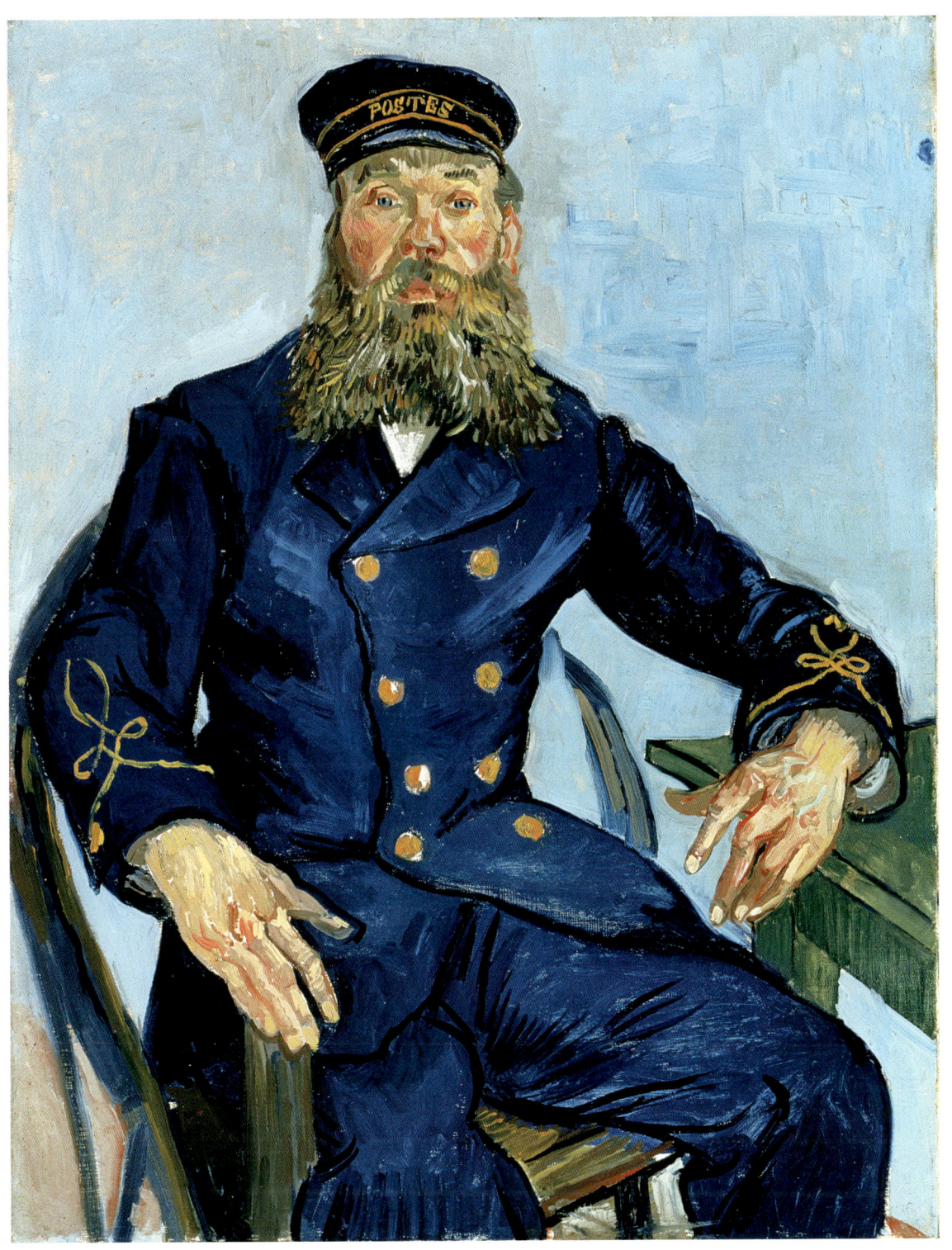

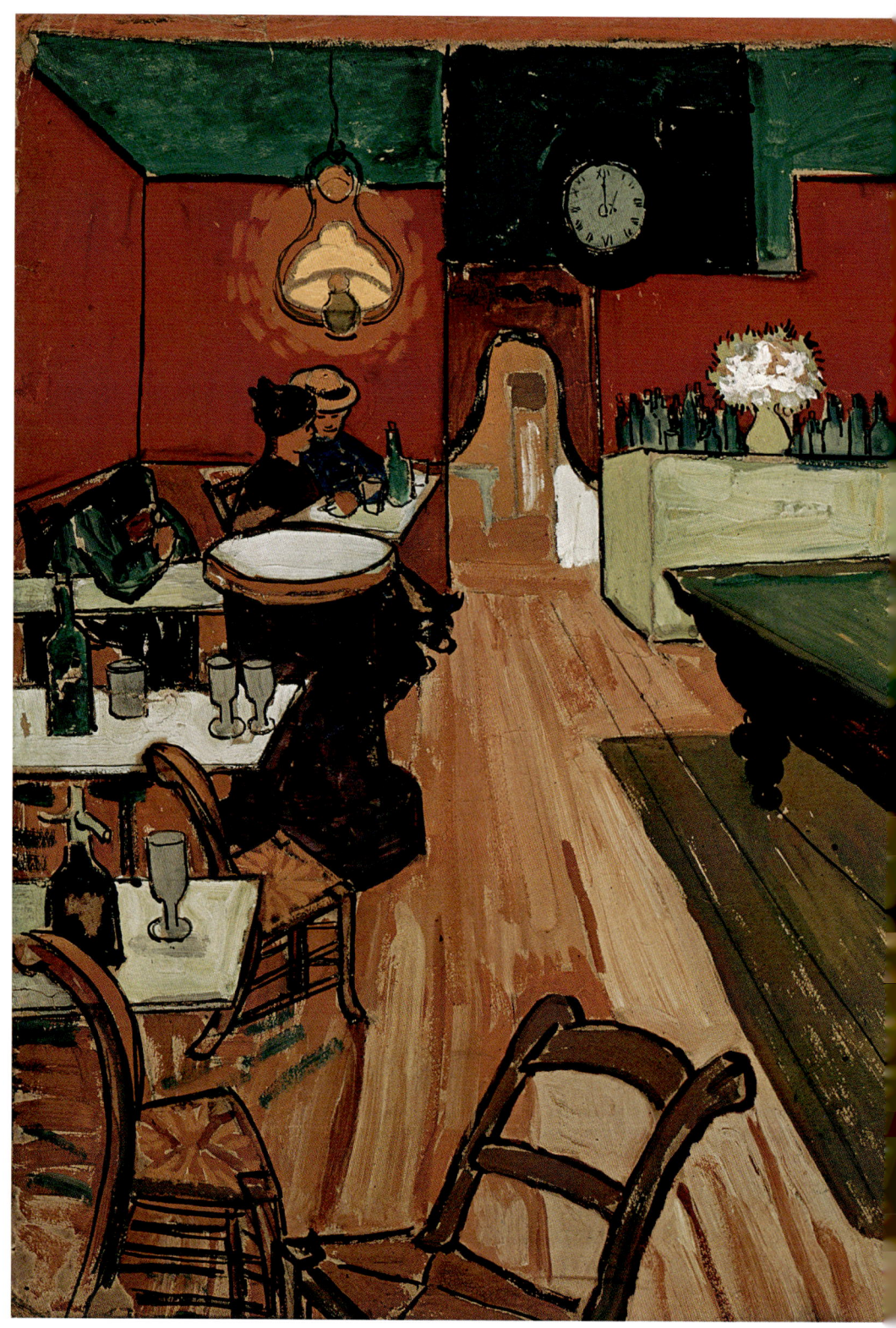

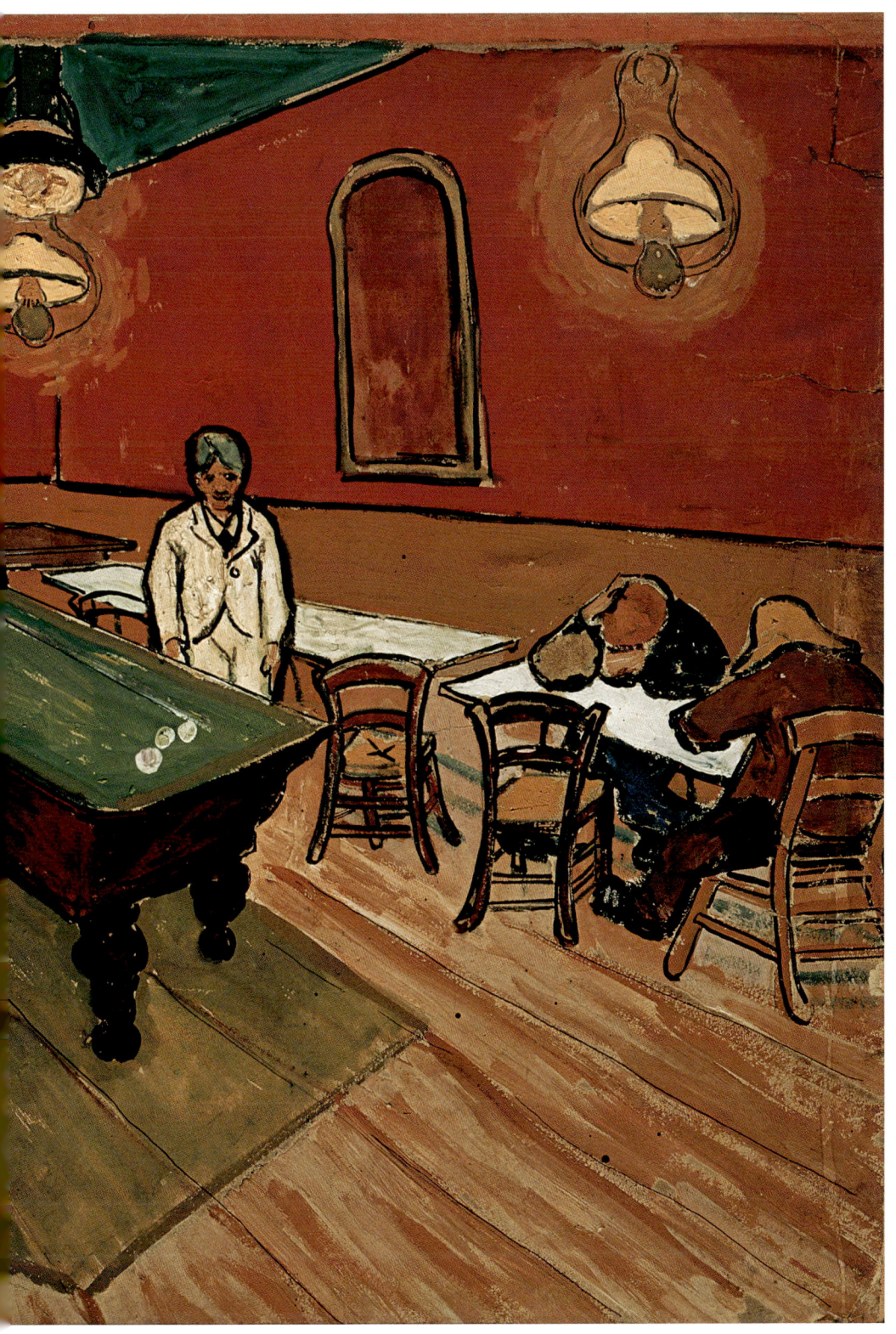

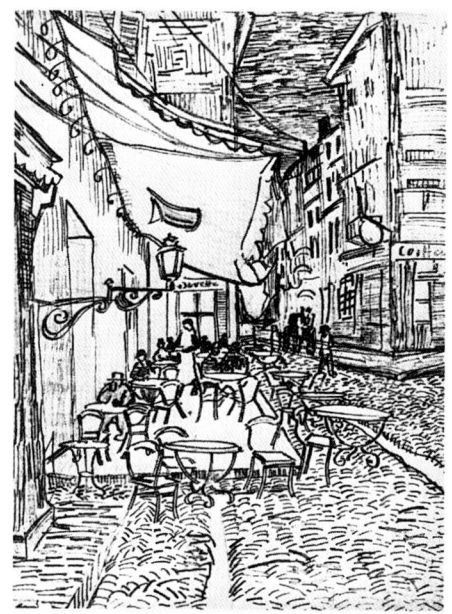

*"A cafe in the evening, seen from the outside; on the terrace little figures are seated drinking. A gigantic yellow lamp lights up the terrace, the house fronts and the pavement, and casts out its light onto the street cobbles, which take on a pink violet colouring.
The house façades in the street, under a blue starry sky, are dark blue or violet, in front a green tree.
There you have it – a night painting without having used the colour black, only beautiful blue, violet and green, and in this setting the lit-up café takes on a pale sulphurous yellow and lemon colouring."*
VINCENT VAN GOGH

colour, in their courageous use of colour and in the vehemence of colour application unparalleled at that date. The enormous pastose disc, representing the sun, immerses the whole background, the sky, in a rich yellow. The front of the picture, the soil, is covered in a hazy blue, shimmering violet: a total reverse of the colours in reality. The real yellow field becomes blue, the real blue sky yellow. The only decisive factor is the contrasting effect of colours.

However, these pictures are in no way abstract. All of them stick to concrete reality as a foundation which is covered by colour as a means of the artist's expression. Here lies van Gogh's actual expressiveness. He presents a detail from everyday life and at the same time an interpretation by means of colour and composition. And this interpretation only when in contrast with the concrete appearance exposes the vehemence of his expressive will and the temperamental artistic gesture. A second reality, artistically pure and subjective, pushes the first aside.

"As long as people work like people with their heart and soul, aiming to do their best, it doesn't matter how bad they are at their job, a certain priceless something attaches itself to manual work," was Ruskin's apologia on craftsmanship. Van Gogh too was concerned with manual work on canvas, which only then made sense of the whole. He was the first artist to use an individual expression, favoured by Ruskin, rather than apparently perfect handling, expressive gestures rather than academic beauty in his work, not as a conscious pictorial interpretation of the theoretician, but as a common view acquired in his daily use of colour and brush. The dignity of the individual as a creative being was a moral view. The problem which Ruskin and van Gogh had to cope with – the former theoretically, the latter in practice – was that expression does not also mean the conveyance of a message, but in fact freedom of artistic gesture is the first step in breaking down the public's understanding.

The indifference which confronted van Gogh throughout his life and thus also in Arles meant that positive stimuli became increasingly rare. The fund of stimulating themes, the landscape,

TOP
The Café Terrace on the Place du Forum, Arles, at Night, 1888
Reed pen, 62.8 x 47.1 cm (24¾ x 18⅝ in.)
Dallas Museum of Fine Arts

OPPOSITE
The Café Terrace on the Place du Forum, Arles, at Night, 1888
Oil on canvas, 81 x 65.5 cm (32 x 25⅞ in.)
Otterlo, Kröller-Müller Museum

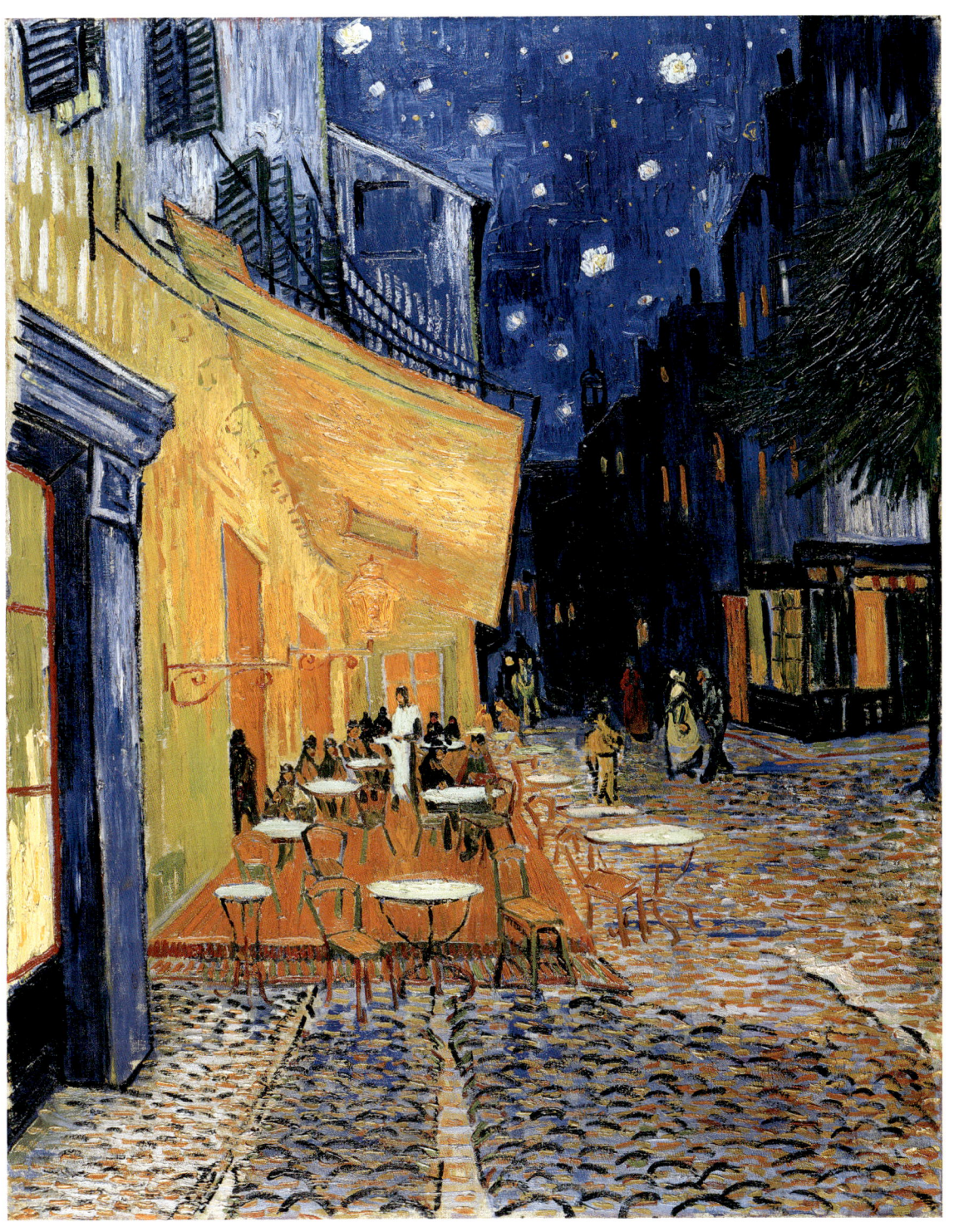

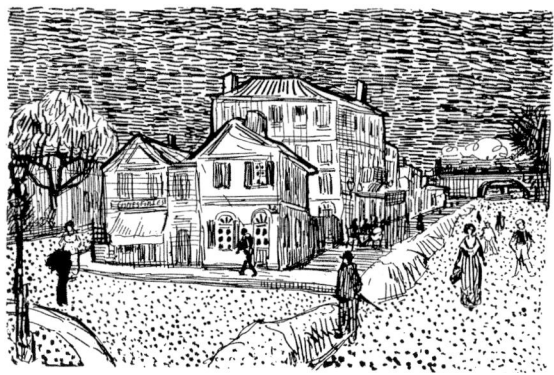

"My house here is painted butter yellow on the outside and has solid green window shutters; it is located directly in a square with a green park full of plane trees, oleanders and acacias. And inside all the walls are painted white and the floor is tiled in red. Yet the most striking thing is the glaring blue sky. Inside the house I can really live and breathe and think and paint."

VINCENT VAN GOGH

some portraits, had long been exhausted. The artistic debate with his fellow artists, which had kept up his spirits in Paris, was missing in the enclave of the provinces. Challenges for his work came less and less from his environment. This environmental reality was such an important stimulus to him. Van Gogh clung more and more to the single utopia which art left him: the old ideal of a free, self-contained artists' commune. This utopia had been fulfilled for a long time by Gauguin. Founding the Atelier du Midi with Gauguin, which was supposedly to precede an institute in which Bernard, Seurat and Signac would also be involved, became the predominant single theme of his letters written in Arles. All the pictures van Gogh painted from that summer on indicate this anticipation: they were to decorate the "yellow house", their shared studio, and it was to be the starting point and basis for fruitful artistic debates.

Gauguin was really going to come. Thus the "Arles tragedy", mostly understood to be the cause of van Gogh's breakdown, took place. The grotesquerie with Gauguin began.

Gauguin had left Paris at roughly the same time as van Gogh, but he did not retreat to the south. Instead he went to the less expansive, scenically more wild, and according to him unspoilt Brittany. Here he lived in the village of Pont-Aven, continually threatened with debts, occasionally sought out by his friends, more or less taking each day as it came. He felt himself to be an undiscovered genius, but had the same wish as van Gogh – to found an artists' circle. He thought of Bernard, of Anquetin, but never of van Gogh as members of this artists' circle. As a far-off goal he dreamed of France's colony Martinique, in the far-away tropics, where he would find his real fortune. But the shortage of money was his only handicap.

Theo van Gogh exhibited Gauguin's works at his gallery. With his increasing debts Gauguin became more and more dependent on Theo's financial support, just as Vincent was in faraway Arles. Vincent was to use Gauguin's misery to his own purpose when he forced his brother to incite Gauguin to come to Arles. In Vincent's mind Gauguin was already with him. Gauguin hesitated to move in with this eccentric whom he did not value highly as an artist. Added to this he mistrusted Theo: "However much Theo likes me, he would definitely not agree to support my living in the Midi only because of my beautiful eyes. He studied the terrain with the cold eyes of a Dutchman and contemplated the view of following the thing as far and as exclusively as possible," Gauguin wrote in October 1888 to Bernard. Gauguin believed Theo's motives were geared towards a business ruse.

Gauguin's feelings of resentment put Vincent even more in a flurry. He thought his humble abode in Arles was not attractive enough for Gauguin. He began to buy furniture, only the best and most comfortable for Gauguin, while he himself was content with a modest bed and the smallest room. The whole of van Gogh's paintings bore the mark of Gauguin's expected arrival. He painted a series

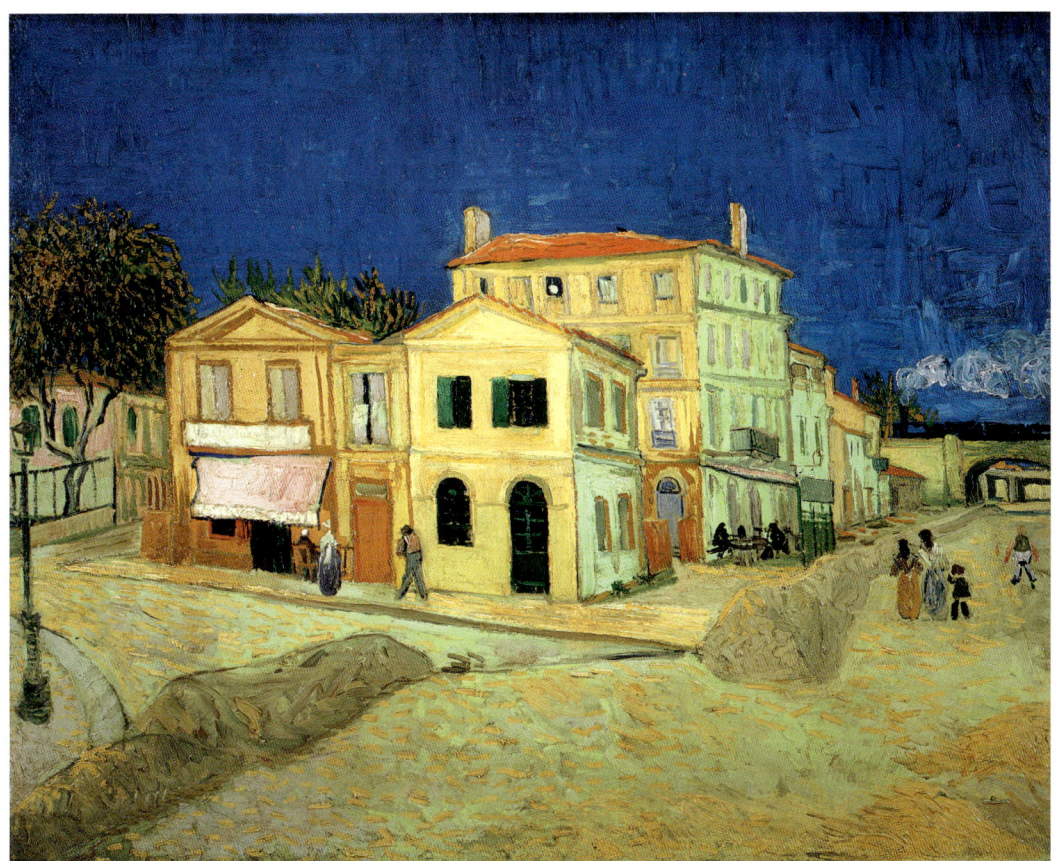

of sunflower paintings (ill. p. 434), a yellow-in-yellow study, as decoration for the "yellow house". The decorative quality of van Gogh's paintings of this period is explained by the fact that he saw them as decoration rather than works of art. They were intended to document van Gogh's artistic standard, as a starting point for a painting competition with Gauguin, but were to be no more than items of furniture. Van Gogh was determined to paint beautifully. After all, he attached great importance to

*Vincent's House in Arles
(The Yellow House)*, 1888
Oil on canvas, 72 x 91.5 cm (28⅜ x 36 in.)
Amsterdam, Van Gogh Museum,
Vincent van Gogh Foundation

OPPOSITE
*Vincent's House in Arles
(The Yellow House)*, 1888
Pen and ink, 13 x 20.5 cm (5 x 8 in.)
Private collection

Gauguin: "Everything which he does has something soft, calming, amazing about it," van Gogh wrote at the end of May. "People do not understand him yet and he is suffering because he has not sold anything – just like other true poets."

In Gauguin's honour he named his depiction of the park in Arles *Public Garden with Couple and Blue Fir Tree: The Poet's Garden III* (ill. p. 462). It was to hang in a prominent place in Gauguin's room. Yet still there was no trace of Gauguin. Again and again he postponed his departure from Brittany, which people were constantly urging him to undertake, finding excuses in letters and financial loop-holes in order to justify his hesitation. Then finally after Theo had finished paying all his debts, Gauguin arrived in Arles in the early hours of the morning of 23 October.

Van Gogh was on top of the world. He gladly let Gauguin take the lead role in art, placing himself in the role of the student, who, however, wanted to show what he had learnt. They worked out a lot

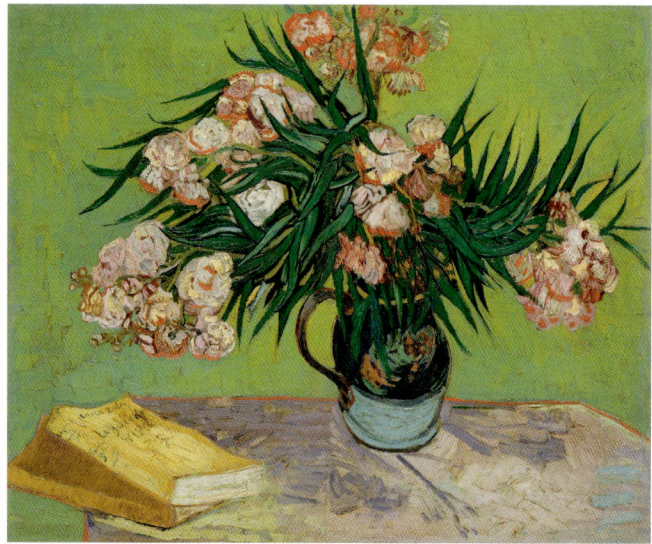

of motifs together, compared their results and argued over artistic concepts. Van Gogh was much too impulsive, impatient and too tied to the arbitrariness of the fantasy for the considered tactician and rationalist Gauguin, who in December 1888 cried out: "He is a romantic, I myself tend to the primitive. In applying colour he loves the impulsive, whilst I hate disorderly undertakings."

For a while van Gogh appeared to bow to Gauguin's theories: he outlined all areas and did not work any more according to nature. Instead the abstraction of "painting from the head" took over; he set himself to using Gauguin's artistic ways, just as he did in Paris, until it reached mere imitation. But now he was too certain of his own talents: "At that time the abstract appeared very inviting to me. But, oh dear, it is a bewitched land! And one is soon confronted by a wall," he tried to explain to Theo. Gauguin's way was simply not his own.

Their collaboration was not to continue for much longer. Gauguin felt himself to be a victim of a game of intrigue between the two brothers; he suspected they wanted to belittle his artistic meaning. Van Gogh himself was disappointed that his honest will to subordination and his willingness to learn found no recognition. Though it was only differences on artistic questions at first, the effect on their pride and understanding of themselves was not long in coming. Gauguin complained to Theo: "The incompatibility of both our characters means that Vincent and I cannot live together peacefully. It is imperative that I leave."

Vincent saw his entire dream shatter and felt his utopia of an artists' commune, which he had wanted to try out with Gauguin, finally disappear. As symbols of loneliness he painted his and Gauguin's chair in December (ills. p. 461). They both stand vacant, metaphors for the artists who have now departed from where they previously had chatted to one another. Van Gogh's more modest wooden chair with the pipe and tobacco pouch as elemental symbols contrasts with Gauguin's more elaborate armchair with candle and book, indicative of learning and ambition. Van Gogh painted his chair yellow and violet, which at that time were symbolic of daylight and hope, as seen in the painting *Vincent's House in Arles* (ill. p. 455). Against this the red and green colours present

TOP
Still Life: Vase with Oleanders and Books, 1888
Oil on canvas, 60.3 x 73.6 cm (23¾ x 29 in.)
New York, The Metropolitan Museum of Art

OPPOSITE
L'Arlésienne: Madame Ginoux with Books, 1888
Oil on canvas, 91.4 x 73.7 cm (36 x 29 in.)
New York, The Metropolitan Museum of Art

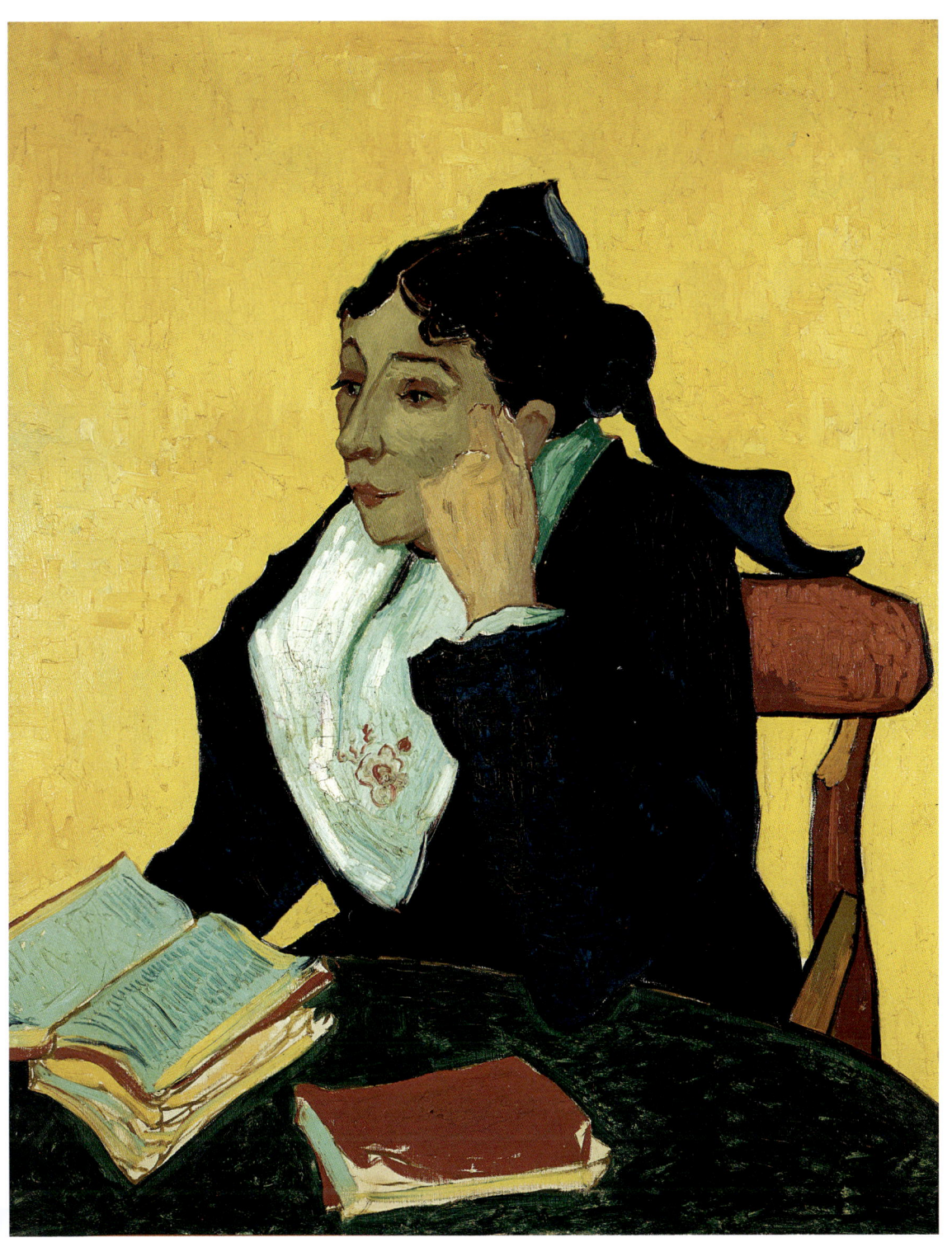

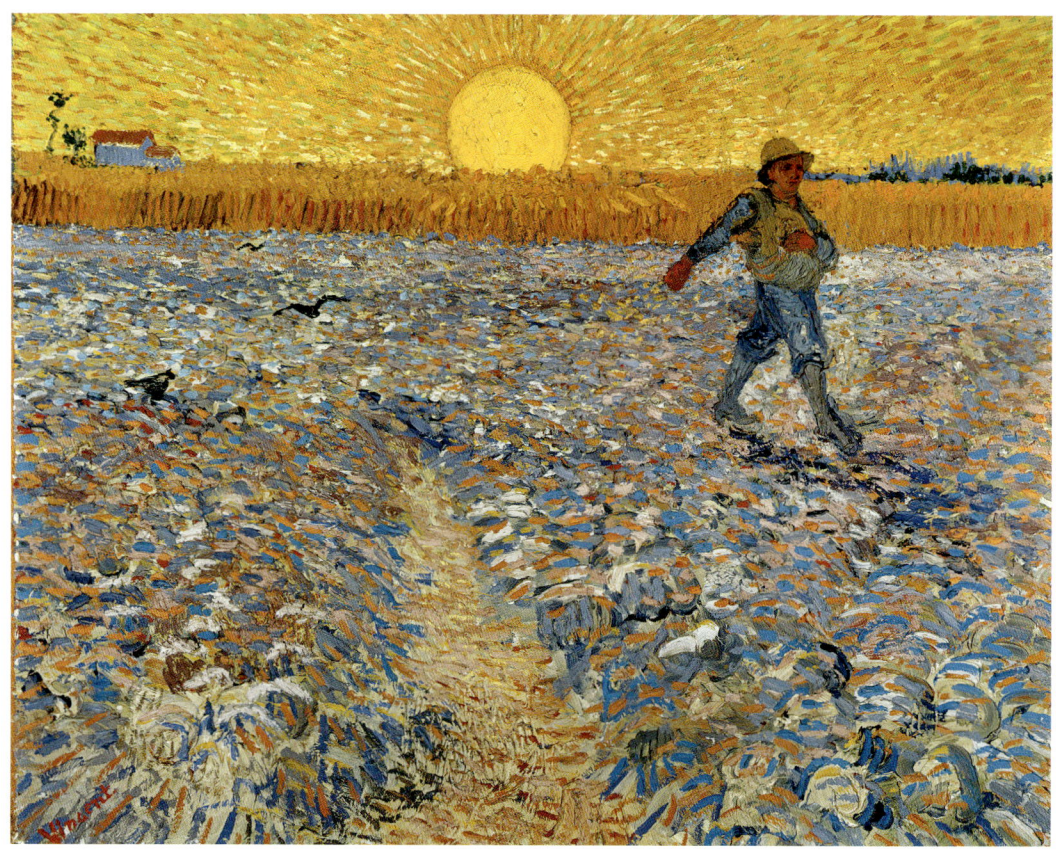

The Sower, 1888
Oil on canvas, 64 x 80.5 cm
(25¼ x 31¾ in.)
Otterlo, Kröller-Müller Museum

a complementary contrast in the painting of Gauguin's chair, just like the red-green of the *The Night Café* picture (ill. pp. 450/451) which documents darkness and lost hope. Day and night stand opposite one another in the two artists, and also as alternatives of a future life. Gauguin, as the message appears to convey, illuminated the night for van Gogh.

"Ever since I wanted to leave Arles, he has been behaving so strangely that I hardly dare to breathe. 'You want to leave,' he said to me and as soon as I answered in the affirmative he tore a piece, containing the following sentence, from the newspaper: 'The murderer has fled,'" Gauguin was later to recall in a letter. Gauguin as a murderer, a murderer of hope and trust. Van Gogh really appeared to be going mad. More than once he got up in the middle of the night and crept to Gauguin's room to see whether he was still there. It was van Gogh's illness that kept Gauguin in Arles: "In spite of a few differences I can't be angry with a good chap who is ill and suffering and calling for me."

But on 23 December the threatening situation escalated. Gauguin went for a walk in the evening and van Gogh, suspicious as ever, followed him. Gauguin, who heard the familiar steps approaching nearer and nearer, turned around and looked straight in van Gogh's disturbed face. Van Gogh was supposedly holding a razor blade in his hand. Gauguin spoke softly to Vincent, who then turned around and went back home. Gauguin, disturbed by the hole incident, spent the night at a hotel. When he returned to the "yellow house" the next morning, the whole of Arles was already up and about. Van Gogh, plagued by hallucination, had cut off one of his ears with the razor blade which Gauguin claimed to have seen earlier in his hand. After van Gogh had temporarily managed to stop

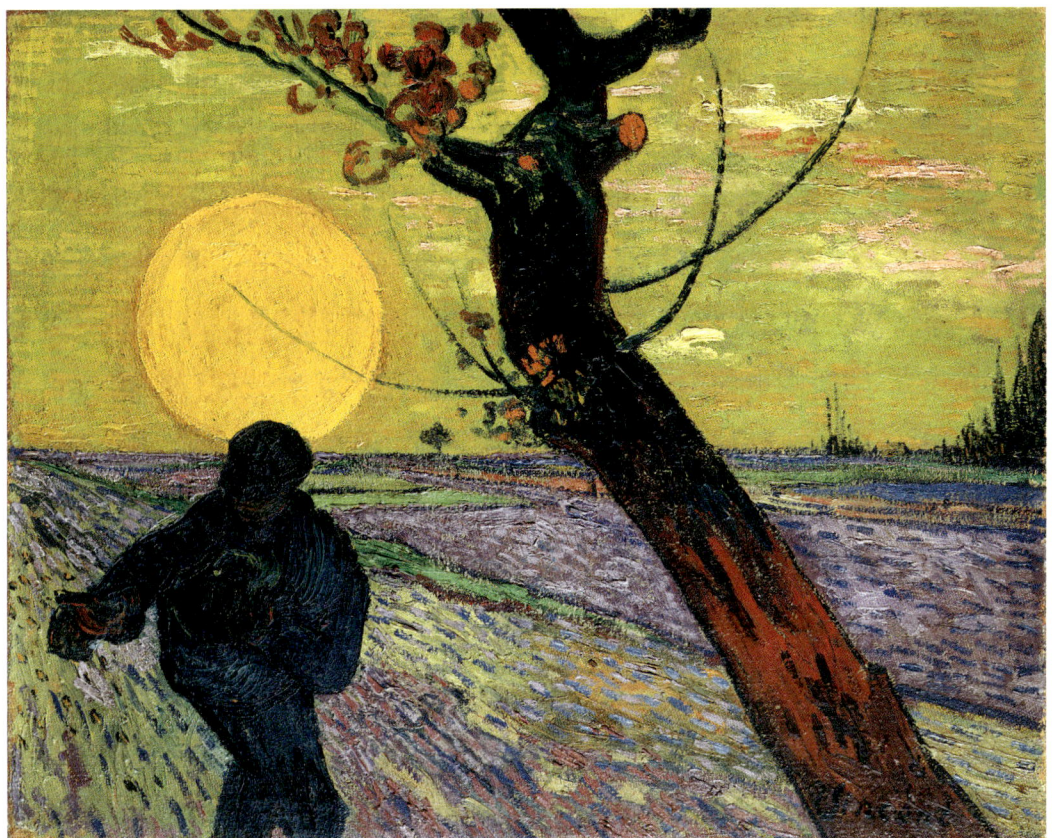

The Sower, 1888
Oil on burlap on canvas,
73 x 92 cm (28¾ x 36¼ in.)
Zurich, Foundation E. G. Bührle Collection

the bleeding, he wrapped the lacerated ear in a handkerchief and ran with it to the town brothel in order to give it to a prostitute. As if nothing had happened he returned home and slept. In this state the police, who had by this time been informed, found him. He was then taken to the town hospital.

Meanwhile Gauguin left secretly. As a salve to his conscience he later wrote in his autobiography that van Gogh had threatened him with a knife. In a letter to Bernard, shortly after this one of 23 December, he never even mentioned the episode. One can assume that van Gogh did not want to hurt Gauguin that evening; rather, he only wanted to alleviate the latter's suspicion. Gauguin used the whole episode as a long-awaited excuse to justify his finally leaving Arles. The way Gauguin got out of the whole affair, without even seeing Vincent one last time, does not put him in a particularly good light.

After that Vincent stayed in the hospital for fourteen days. Back in his studio he painted the result of the catastrophe: his *Self-portrait with Bandaged Ear* (ill. p. 463). The whole of the right side of his face is covered by a large, wide bandage which adds a sad seriousness to the artist's almost rigid appearance. Inside a thick coarse cape he appears to be seeking protection from a hostile environment. The gay colour of a Japanese woodcut frames the left side of his face in stark contrast to the whiteness of the bound wound. The woodcuts are reminiscent of the Père Tanguy portrait, but this one is uncontrolled, without normality. The episode with Gauguin was truly an experience that made him realize his own limits.

"The Trinquetaille bridge with all those steps was painted on a grey morning; stone, asphalt, cobbles, everything is grey, the sky is a pale blue, the figures colourful, a sickly small tree with yellow foliage."

VINCENT VAN GOGH

Van Gogh was no longer his old self. The loneliness which he had learned to accept in the previous years as the price for the formation of an artists' commune, was not to leave him in future. "I don't dare to ask other painters to come here after what has happened. They risk losing their mind, just like me," he wrote with resignation to his brother in February 1889. In the next year he was to experience a loneliness partly chosen, but also one which was forced upon him.

Four weeks after his discharge from hospital, van Gogh had to return again. Signs of persecution mania appeared, and he began to imagine that someone wanted to poison him. A petition signed by the inhabitants of Arles sealed his final internment. The resentment against van Gogh, which had always been present in spite of his search for recognition, now led him to avoid any form of contact with people completely. This resentment had driven him out of Holland and made his stay in Paris difficult. Looked after by a priest and a doctor, he lived until the beginning of May both as patient and prisoner in the Arles hospital. In addition to this he was worried about Theo getting married in Paris, because he was afraid of losing his one-and-only confidante.

In order to escape the constraints of the asylum he began painting again. Paintings such as *Orchard in Blossom with View of Arles* (ill. p. 464) and *The Courtyard of the Hospital at Arles* (ill. p. 465), both of April 1889, may not give a direct hint of the utter desperation he felt during

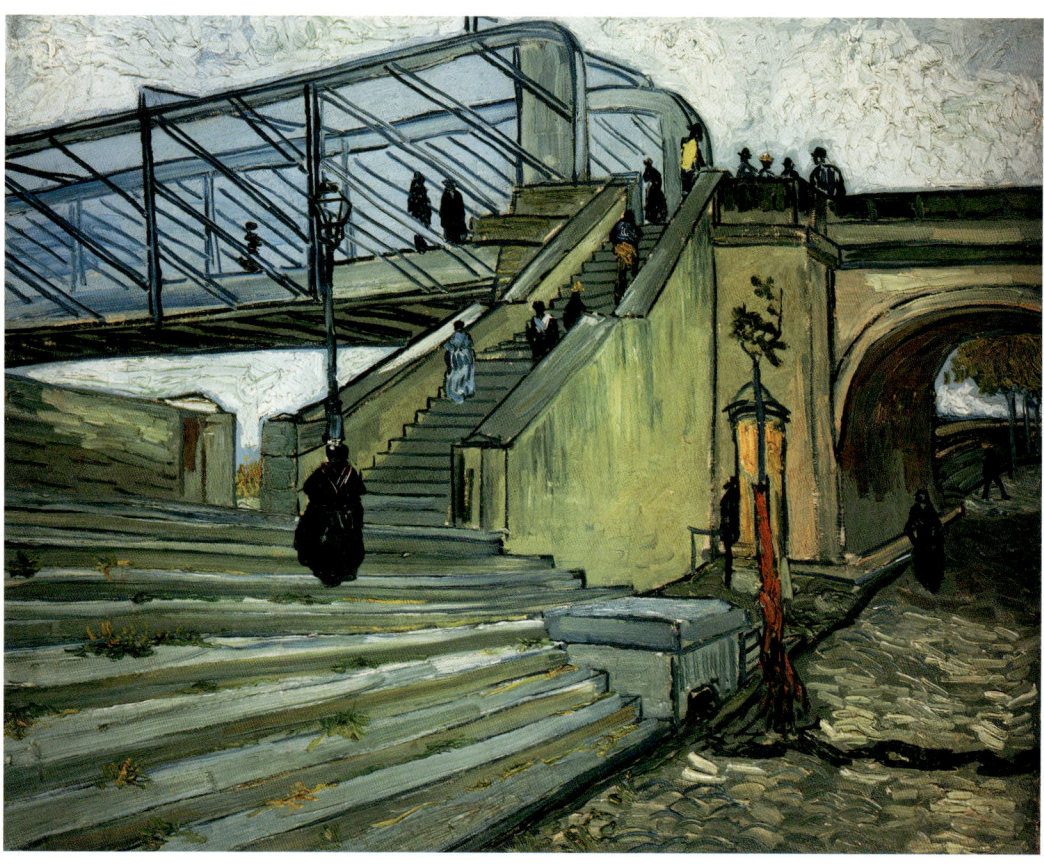

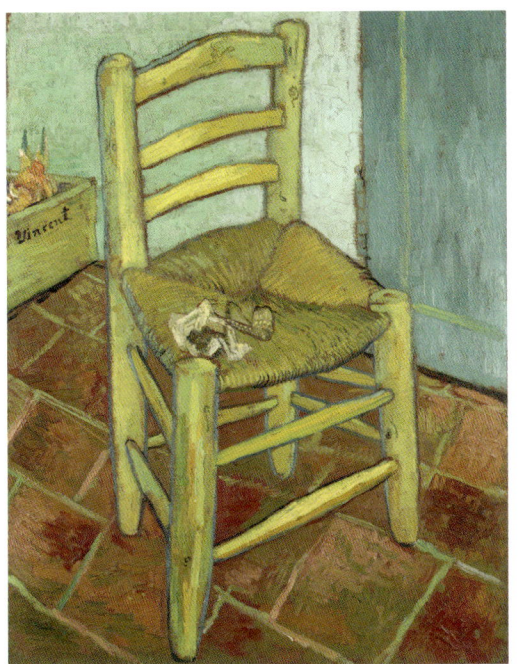

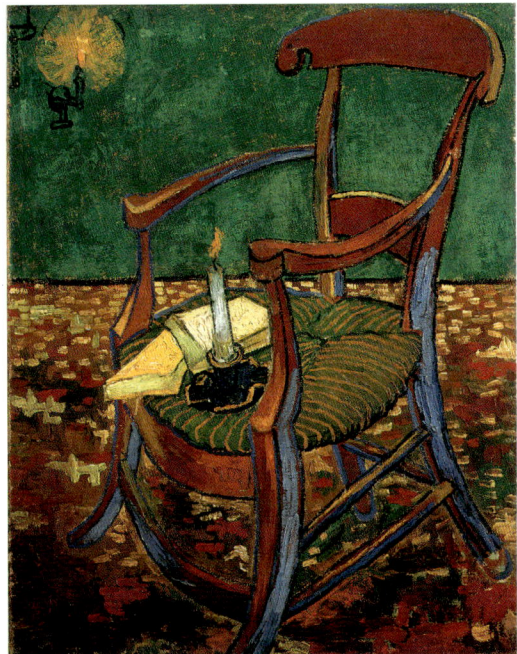

this time. They document more banal incidents of daily life rather than his suffering. However, a claustrophobic atmosphere is conjured up in these paintings: the confinement of the hospital courtyard, which despite the splendid flowers blocks out the view of the distant horizon, and the withered poplars, which thrust themselves like iron bars in front of the town panorama, present an impassable barrier between the artist's position and the object of his dreams – the town and its freedom.

Van Gogh came to terms with his situation very quickly. The world, to which he clung and which piece by piece was being taken away from him, did not accept his religious, political and artistic views, and he resolved not to bother it any longer. He entered the mental hospital of his own free will, but against the wishes of his brother, whom Vincent tried to prepare for this decision: "I have tried to get used to the idea of starting afresh, but at this present time it is impossible for me. I am afraid of losing my ability to work, which is now coming back to me, if I take on too much and get bogged down with the idea of opening a new studio. And so I wish to stay here for a while, both for my own peace of mind, as well as for that of others." On 8 May 1889 he moved to Saint-Rémy.

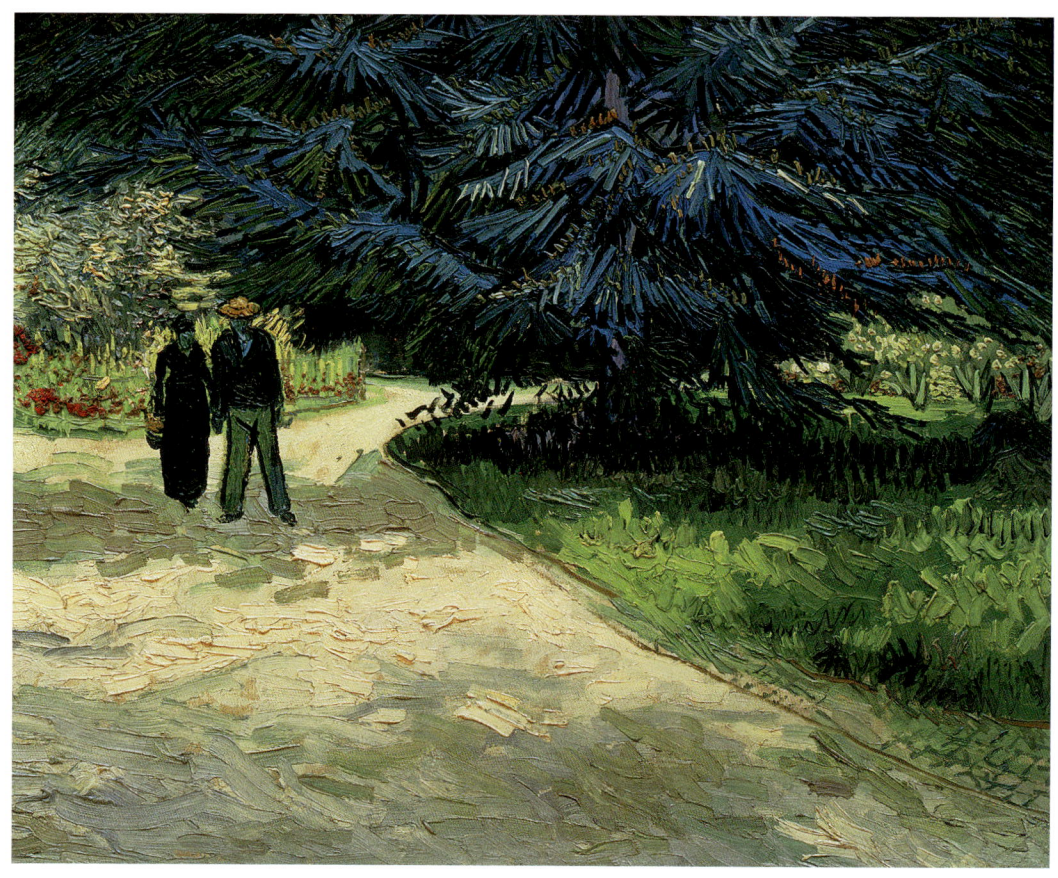

"I'm able to get by very well in life, and also with my work, without beloved God. But I, a suffering human being, can not survive without there being something greater than myself, which for me is my whole life – the creative power ... I want to paint men and women with that certain eternal touch – an idea which the sacred halo embodied earlier and which we seek to express today through light and the palpitating movement of our colours ... The love between a couple is expressed by the unity of two complementary colours, by their mixture and contrasts, by the secretive vibrations of similar tones; the intelligence of a forehead is portrayed by using a light tone on a dark background; hope by a star and a man's passion by a vibrant sunset."

VINCENT VAN GOGH

TOP
***Public Garden with Couple and Blue Fir Tree:
The Poet's Garden III***, 1888
Oil on canvas, 73 x 92 cm (28¾ x 36¼ in.)
Private collection

OPPOSITE
Self-portrait with Bandaged Ear, 1889
Oil on canvas, 60.5 x 50 cm (23⅞ x 19¾ in.)
London, The Courtauld Gallery

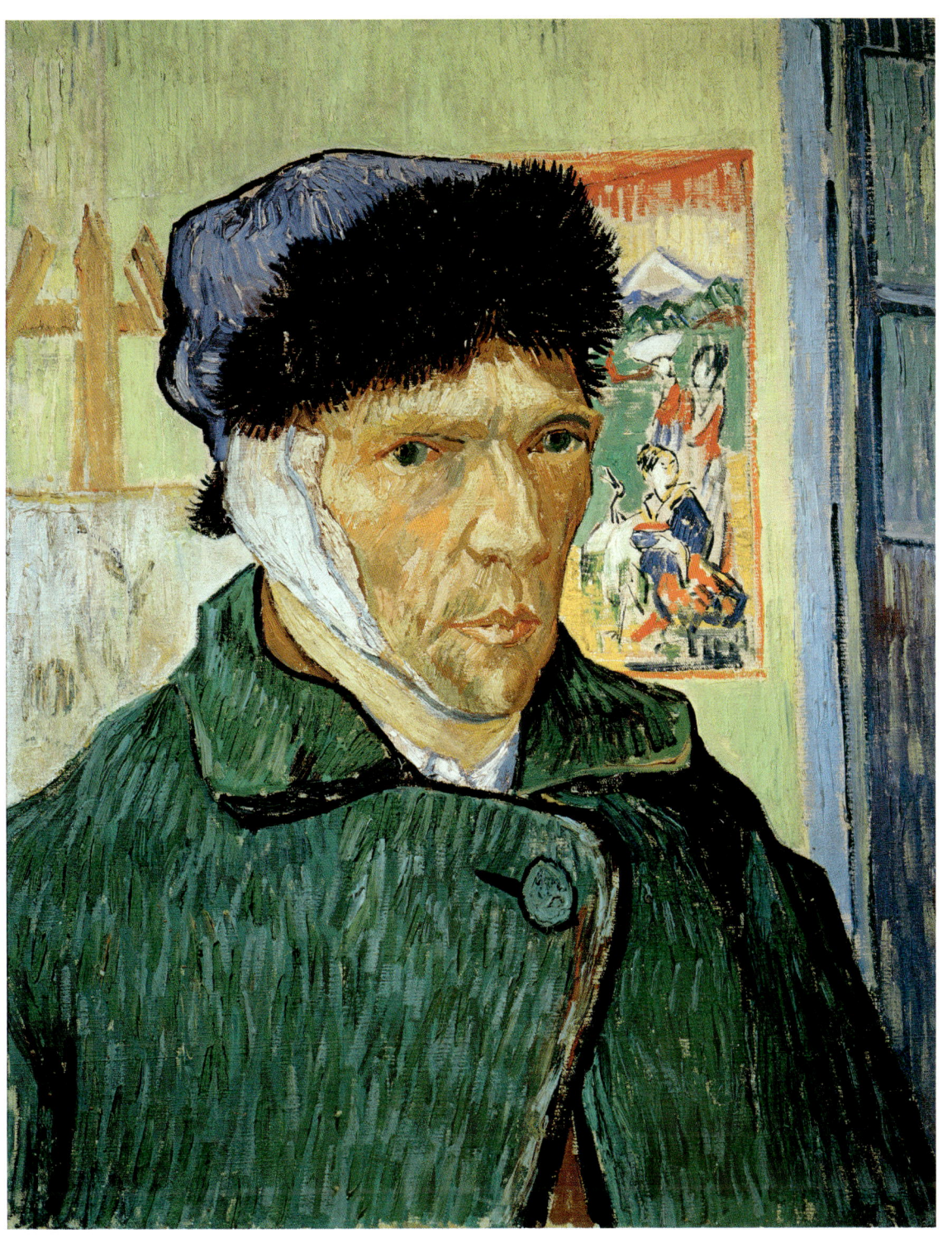

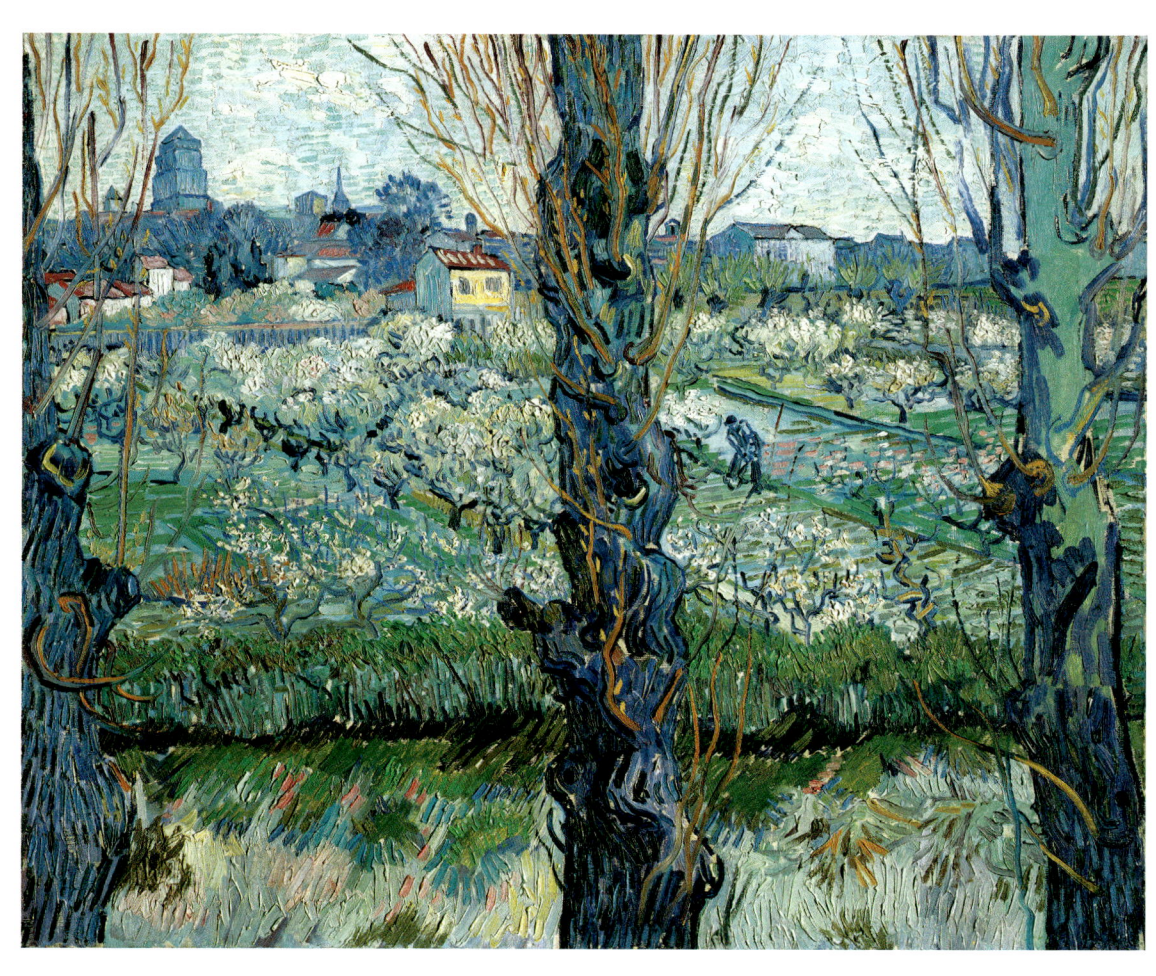

Orchard in Blossom with View of Arles, 1889
Oil on canvas, 72 x 92 cm (28⅜ x 36¼ in.)
Munich, Bayerische Staatsgemäldesammlungen,
Neue Pinakothek

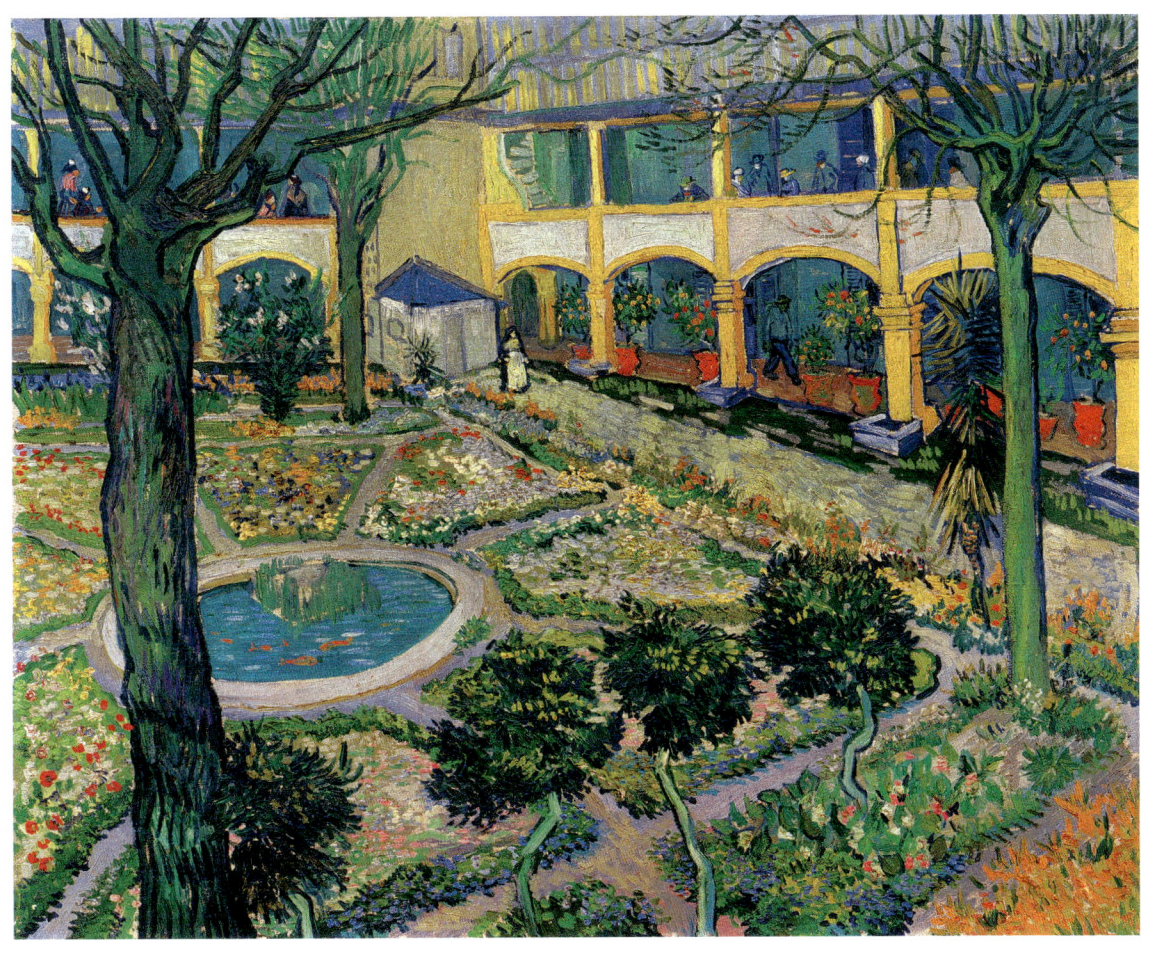

"It is surrounded by a whitewashed porch, like in an Arab palace. In front of the galleries an ancient garden with a pond and eight flower beds in the middle: forget-me-nots, Christmas roses, anemones, buttercups, wallflowers, daisies etc. And below the gallery, oranges and oleanders. That is, a picture full of flowers and spring greenery."

VINCENT VAN GOGH

The Courtyard of the Hospital at Arles, 1889
Oil on canvas, 73 x 92 cm (28¾ x 36¼ in.)
Winterthur, Oskar Reinhart Collection
"Am Römerholz"

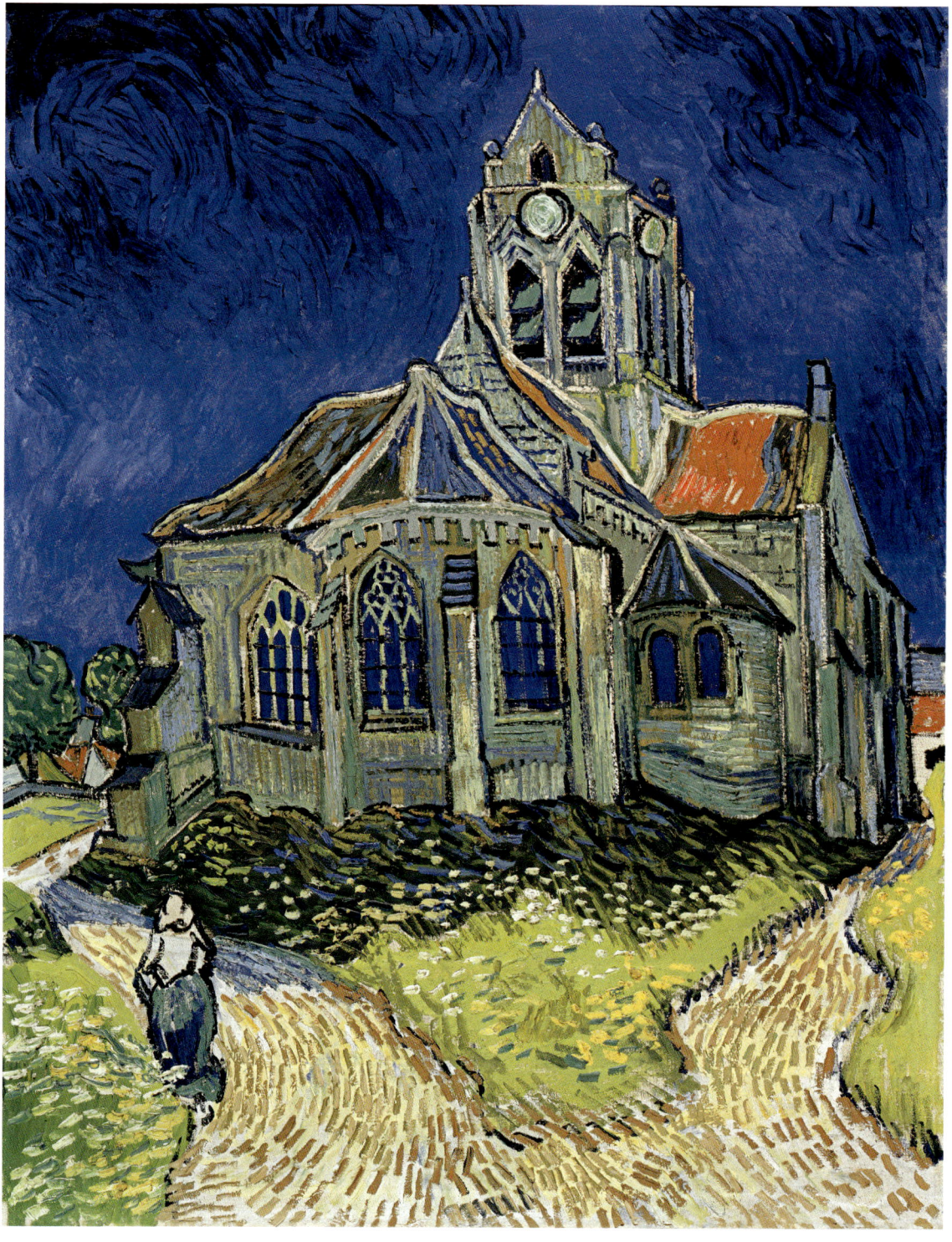

Painting as Life
Saint-Rémy and Auvers 1889–1890

"To suffer without complaining is the only lesson one should learn in this life," van Gogh wrote in May 1889 to his brother Theo, although he had every reason to wrangle with his fate. At the age of thirty-six Vincent went of his own accord into the Saint-Paul-de-Mausole nursing hospital for the mentally ill near Saint-Rémy-de-Provence, seventeen miles from Arles.

His hopes and plans for the future were completely destroyed. The incurable illness came increasingly to the fore, and the attempt by the locals of Arles to have him put away lay heavy on his heart. He felt discarded by society, and Theo's approaching wedding left him fearful of losing the support of his helpful, beloved brother, added to the failure of his most desirous dream, a communal "studio of the south", which was shattered upon Gauguin's departure.

The insight "that I finally feel incapable of taking a new studio and of staying there alone, neither here in Arles, nor anywhere else … I would like to stay temporarily in the asylum, because of my own peace of mind as well as that of others", was hard-won, although he had long ago broken with all conventions. There was nothing left for him to do but to accept his situation: "I am ready to play the role of a madman, although I have not at all the strength for such a role." Despairing, he clung to his brother: "If I didn't have your friendship, I would be driven to suicide without giving it a second thought, and cowardly as I am I would do it in the end."

The asylum, where van Gogh spent almost a year, was about two miles from Saint-Rémy in a rather lonely district, surrounded by cornfields, vineyards and olive groves – motifs which appear again and again in his paintings. Judging from the dark hallways and barred windows of the cheerless rooms, life in the mens' quarters must have been very depressing for him.

The patients were left completely alone, since the director of the asylum, Dr Peyron, who ruled it with rigorous thrift, just kept the patients alive and neglected to actually help them; he was not even a specialist in mental illnesses. Van Gogh received no medical attention apart from twice-weekly baths.

The Church at Auvers, 1890
Oil on canvas, 93 x 74.5 cm (36⅝ x 29⅜ in.)
Paris, Musée d'Orsay

"I painted a large picture of the village church – the building has a violet appearance against a flat, deep blue sky of pure colour; the stained-glass windows are like ultramarine coloured spots; the roof is violet and orange in parts. At the front is something green in bloom and pink-coloured sun-burnt sand. It is almost like the studies I made of the old towers and cemetery in Nuenen – the only difference now being that the colour is more expressive and richer."
VINCENT VAN GOGH

Yet his life was more bearable in every sense than that of the other unhappy patients. He was allowed to withdraw, to read and work, and to leave the asylum so long as he was accompanied.

At this stage van Gogh was diagnosed as suffering from epileptic fits. Periodically he experienced fits of unpredictable length, going through a hazy stage, followed by a period of blankness; in between these episodes there were usually two to four weeks in which his behaviour was perfectly normal. The fits came unpredictably and there was generally quite a long period between each new attack. During attacks he often became violent and suffered from terrible hallucinations. Normal activity, such as writing and painting, was completely impossible during this time.

Vincent viewed his own illness quite clearly and pragmatically. He accepted the unavoidable: "It consoles me that I can look upon my madness more and more as an illness like any other and thus accept it as such." In his letters to his brother he tried to hide how horribly depressing it was for him to have to live alongside the mentally ill and paranoid.

However, the ordered and monotonous life in the asylum contributed greatly to his regaining self-respect. He was allowed to go into the surrounding area and paint, accompanied by a guard, and he rested all his hopes on this; his work alone was capable of dragging him out of his deep depressions. At this stage, the fits did not leave any trace whatsoever in his work, since his periods of illness and those of artistic creativity were strictly kept apart.

Painting became an activity which directly connected him with life. The pictures painted during this period often give the impression of a hyperintensity which does not stem from illness, except in so far as he was possessed with a crazed creativity in the periods between his fits. It was as if he wanted to make up for lost time. These pictures also document his attempts not to give up, to avoid renewed attacks by working ceaselessly and thus give vent to his intense feelings.

One of his first paintings done in Saint-Rémy is close to his flower paintings of Arles: *Irises* (ill. p. 469). He came across this motif of voluptuous irises on his way to the flat of Dr Paul Gachet, whom Theo had recommended that he consult about his illness. The painting is crammed with the ripe, moist excesses of nature. The deep blue of the finely drawn iris buds contrasts sharply with the bold green of the leaves with their lancet tongue-like form, which divide the flowers into horizontal rows. The warm red of the soil firmly anchors the plants to the bottom of the picture,

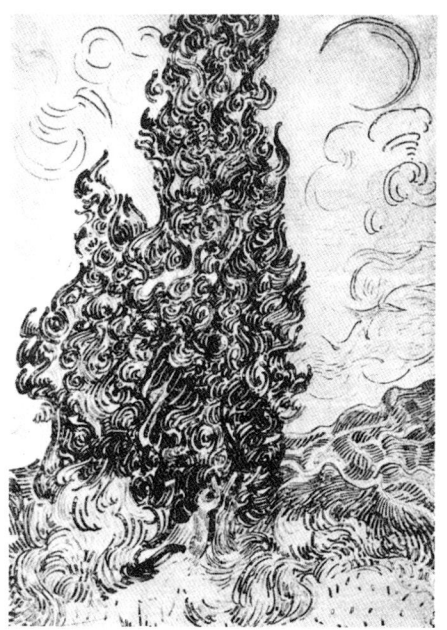

while the light green of the flowering meadow takes hold of the flowers from behind. As a stark contrast to all the colourfulness is a large open white iris to the left and at the far right of the picture is a pale blue iris which serves as an echo of the former.

In order for the eye to take in this brilliant display of flowers and arrange them accordingly, the canvas is divided up into different areas of colour, all of which – as in the flow of nature in summer – radiate light from within themselves, thereby creating a balanced, connected harmony. Thus the rich display of colour and variety of forms are not confusing; on the contrary, they support the lively movement of nature. The detail in the painting confirms this view – it is as if the artist had bent down to the flowers. The detail stands for the whole; nature is meant here, the principle of life.

Van Gogh was concerned most of all with getting as close to nature as was possible. Throughout his life this

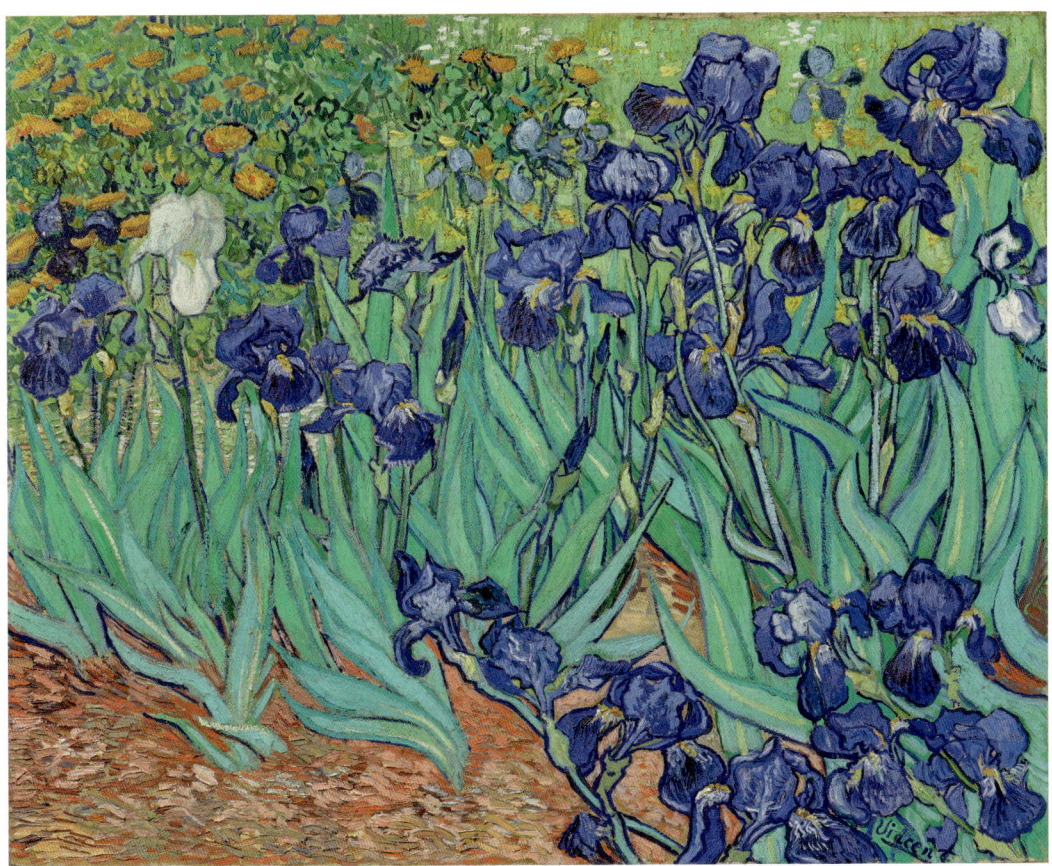

direct, near-erotic relationship to nature had been present: "It is not so much the language of painting as that of nature which one must listen to."

To capture this liveliness was his primary aim in painting, which ought to plumb the "roots or the origin of the thing". Van Gogh wanted to penetrate as deeply as possible into life and feel at the same time the very beating of its heart.

Irises, 1889
Oil on canvas, 74.3 x 94.3 cm (29⅜ x 37¼ in.)
Los Angeles, J. Paul Getty Museum

OPPOSITE
Cypresses, 1889
Pencil, reed pen and ink,
61.9 x 47.3 cm (24⅜ x 18⅝ in.)
New York, Brooklyn Museum

As an ideal means of representation he had discovered colour and the actual life present within the colours themselves. He used colours in such a way that they took on a life of their own and thus were ideally suited to show optically the principle of life. His experimentation with colour never arose out of any particular painting technique, but rather was an ongoing struggle to find an adequate means of portraying a spiritual concern. Everyday objects around him were similes of life, and it was this that van Gogh wanted to express in his paintings. Colour had taken on an immediate representational value for existence, for life itself.

Van Gogh was concerned with verisimilitude in his depiction of human life. He allowed himself only one guideline: to portray reality itself, a contemporary, modern one and not one of a distant past. One could not achieve this by merely copying reality; what counted for van Gogh was what lay behind reality. He recognized a "rationale in the mysterious" meaning that "all reality was at the same time a symbol" – a religious way of viewing things.

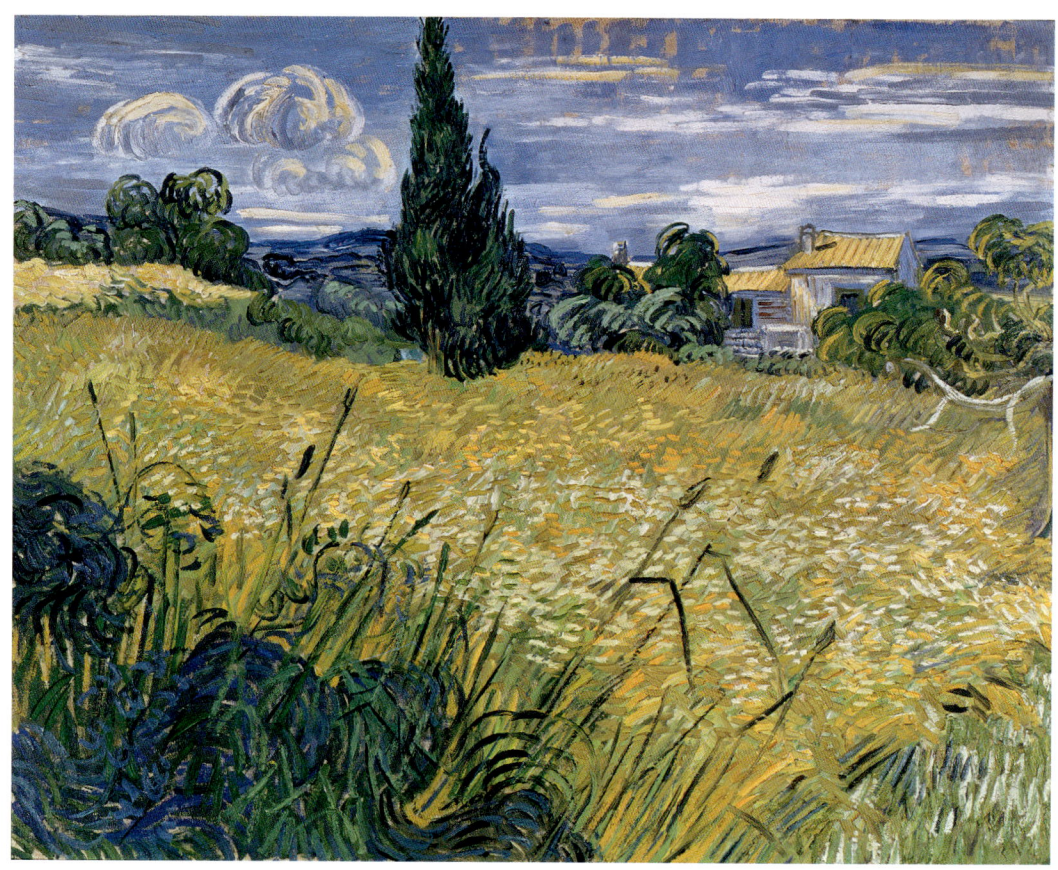

Green Wheat Field with Cypress, 1889
Oil on canvas, 73 x 92.5 cm (28¾ x 36½ in.)
Prague, Národní Galerie

This religious reality is clearly recognizable in his paintings, which are devoid of critical, caricature touches. His stance towards all his subjects is that of a loving person who accepts reality for what it is. He wanted to reach out to those people who accept the elemental things of life, such as nature, humanity, pain, joy, transitoriness … A new philosophy of life was born which no longer saw the world through an earthly vale of tears and was not even a simple denial of a higher principle of life this side of the grave. He confronted the primaeval powers of existence, which he found in nature and out of which his natural mysticism arose, and this is evident in his paintings.

His total dedication to nature can be seen in his painting *Green Wheat Field with Cypress* (ill. p. 470). Here the viewer's gaze is drawn towards the waving greeny-yellow of the ripe wheat field, which flows diagonally across the painting like a great river. The same yellow can be seen in the straw roofs of the houses in the background and also in the cloud formations and the bushes to the top right of the painting. The dark blades of grass in front of the wheat field heighten the movement to the right. Opposite is a massive upright blackish-green cypress pointing upwards – a strong accentuation of colour amidst all the dynamic movement of the painting. Green coloured areas frame the yellow wheat field, against which the light blue of the sky acts as a contrast. This contrast is toned down by the white of the ears of wheat and that of the clouds, so that in spite of the movement one is given the impression of harmony and organized unity.

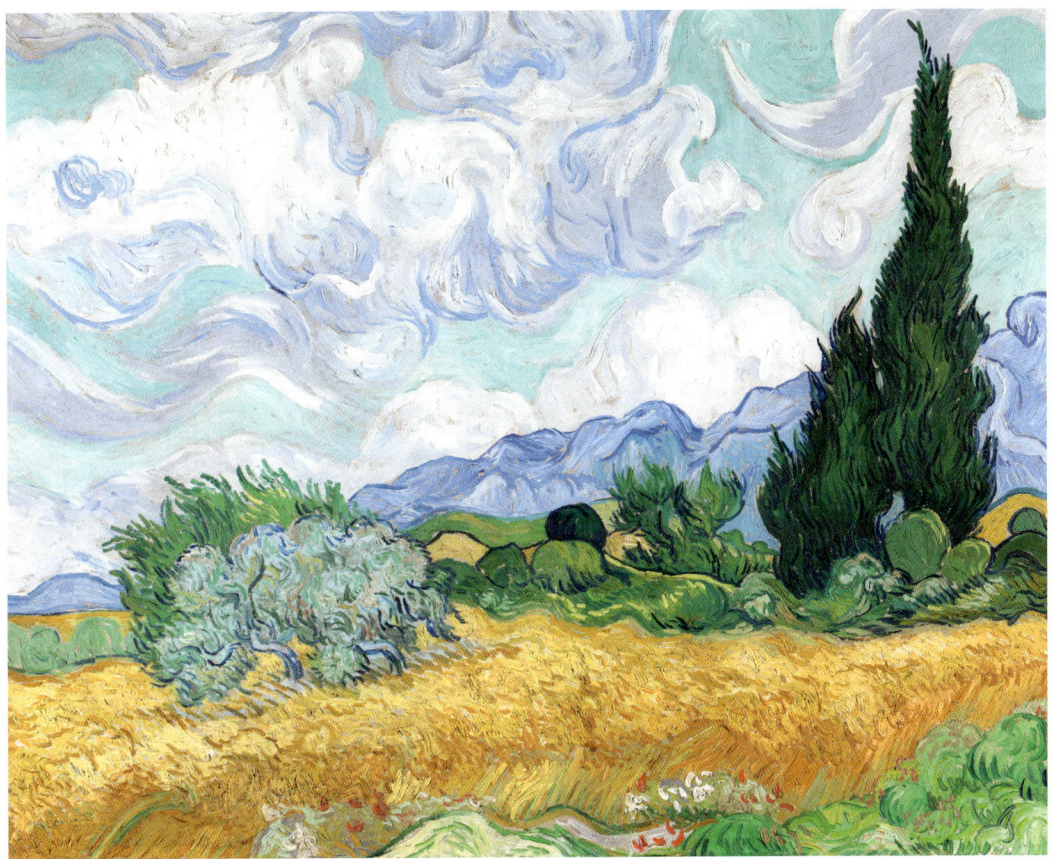

Colour was still very much a dominant means of expression for van Gogh, yet was no longer the main element in these paintings, as was the case with the paintings completed in Arles; now only a few pictures show large areas of colour or weighty complementary contrasts. The vividness of colour is now transferred to the forms, or to be more exact, to their movement. This is clearly seen in the paintings of cypresses.

Wheat Field with Cypresses at the Haute Galline near Eygalières, 1889
Oil on canvas, 73 x 93.5 cm (28¾ x 36⅞ in.)
London, The National Gallery

From that point the cypress became his central motif. It appears again in the painting *Wheat Field with Cypresses at the Haute Galline near Eygalières* (ill. p. 471), only here the cypress is pushed to the right-hand side of the painting and appears much darker and longer against the strange colour of the overcast sky – it is the only vertical accent in the picture. The overripe cornfield is wedged between the green areas, surrounded by rising blue cliffs. An ascending diagonal movement leads from the fields over the trees to the hills and from there to the clouds. Their convulsive shapes, only barely indicated here, dominate the whole sky in the later *Starry Night* (ill. pp. 474/475). This painting could almost be subtitled "Calm before the Storm". A feeling of calm pervades the picture, yet a stormy turbulence (created by the brushstrokes) is clearly present.

These evergreen trees become the single theme of the painting *Cypresses* (ill. p. 406), which take up almost the whole of the left side. Painted with flickering strokes of the brush, the trees grow upwards like green flaming tongues, and even the edge of the painting cannot hinder their unbridled growth; the top of the larger tree is cut off. Pure nature, growth and movement, and untamed energy

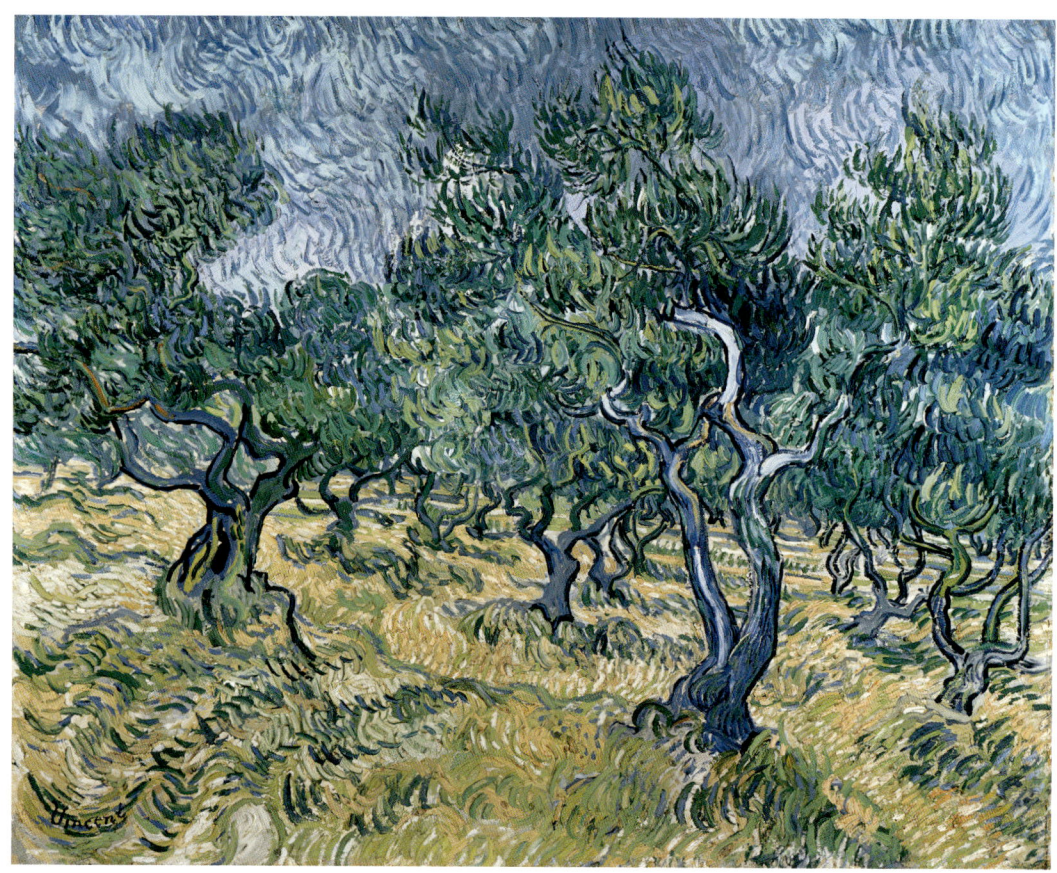

Olive Grove, 1889
Oil on canvas, 72.4 x 91.9 cm (28⅝ x 36¼ in.)
Otterlo, Kröller-Müller Museum

OPPOSITE
Self-portrait, 1889
Oil on canvas, 65 x 54 cm (25⅝ x 21⅜ in.)
Paris, Musée d'Orsay

are displayed – a cosmic happening perhaps? A clue to this could be the rising sickle of the moon in the star-lit night. In the summer of 1889 van Gogh wrote to Theo: "The cypresses constantly occupy my thoughts – I want to paint something similar to my sunflower paintings. It's amazing that nobody has yet painted them as I see them; in their lines and proportions they are as beautiful as Egyptian obelisks. And the green is such a special fine tone."

A much more severe attack in the autumn of 1889 took him by surprise whilst he was working on a painting outside the asylum. Thoughts of suicide and terrible hallucinations, which only very slowly eased off, were followed by a period of deep depression. This relapse clearly reveals the chronic character of his illness. He began to fear his fellow inmates and stayed in his room; for six weeks he did not set foot out of the building. Finally he began to paint again, but only inside the asylum. He wrote to his sister Willemien: "Since my illness I sense a terrible loneliness even in the open air, so that I don't dare to go outside."

This fear became evident in his choice of colour. The earlier vibrant colours of his palette increasingly gave way to toned-down colours and darker harmonies, with nothing left of the stark colour contrasts. This did not mean a return to the tonal harmony of the paintings of his Dutch period; instead this recalled the chromatic multiplicity of tone which he had discovered in Paris and Arles, and he introduced to this a series of unusual disjointed tones, which corresponded to his

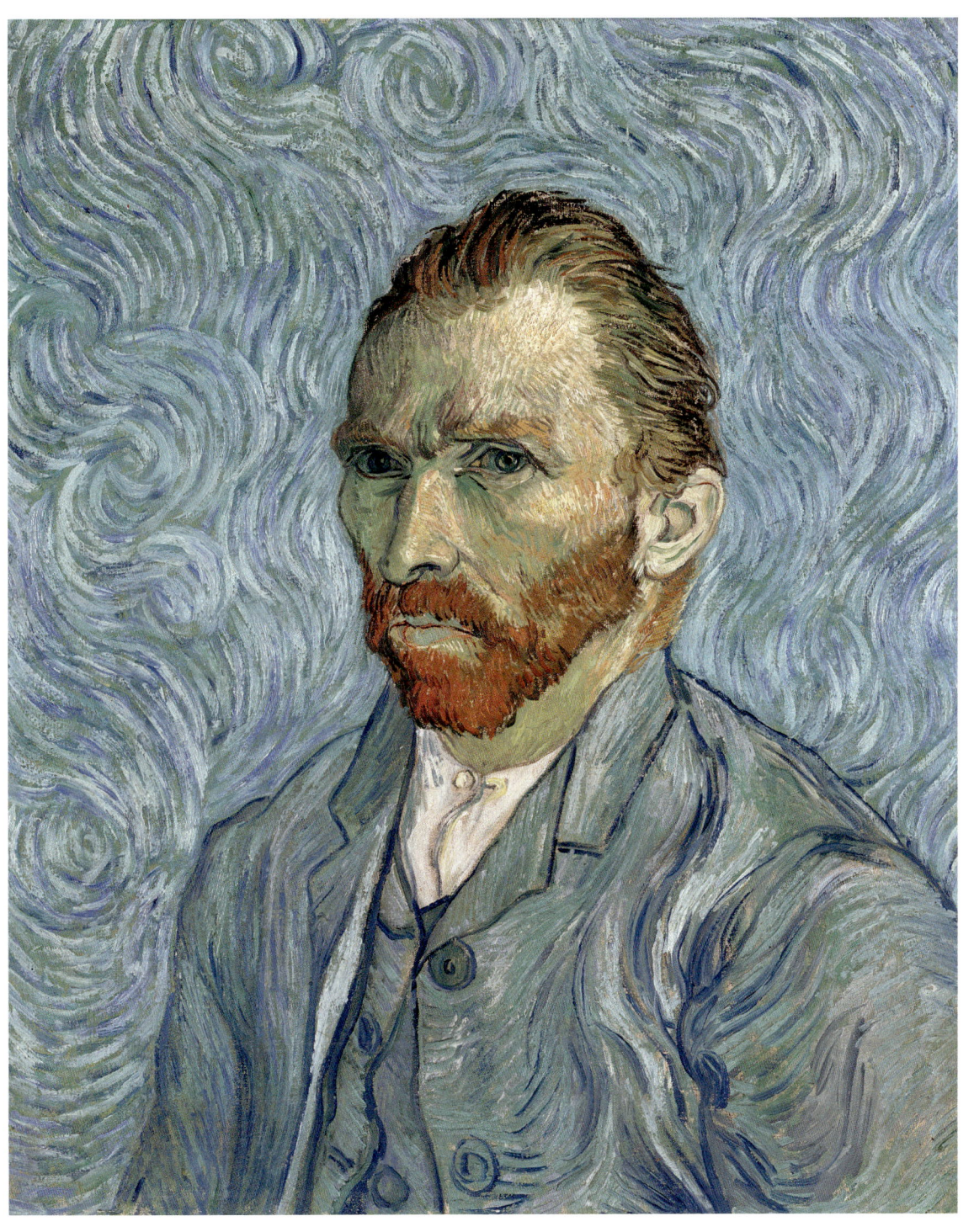

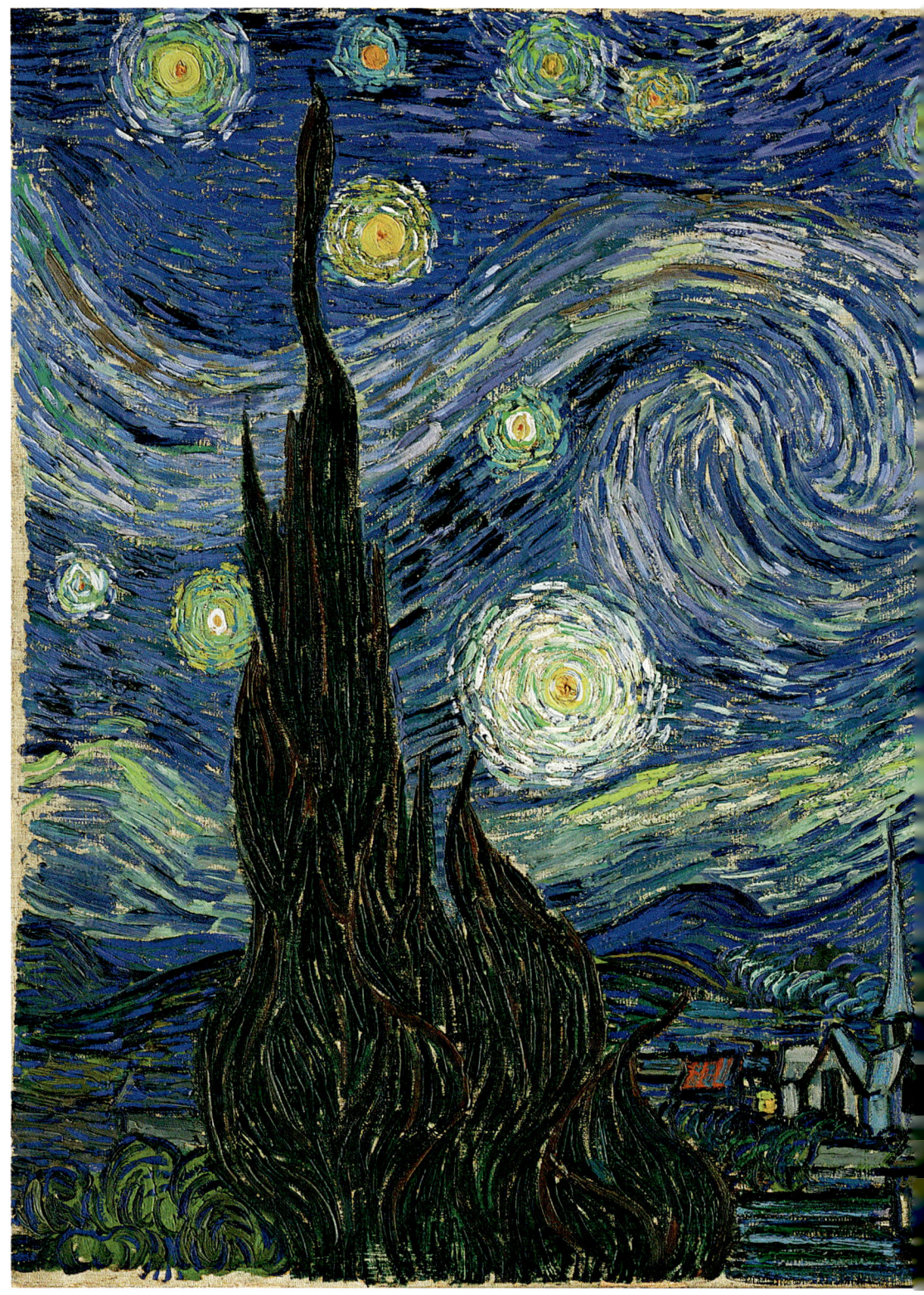

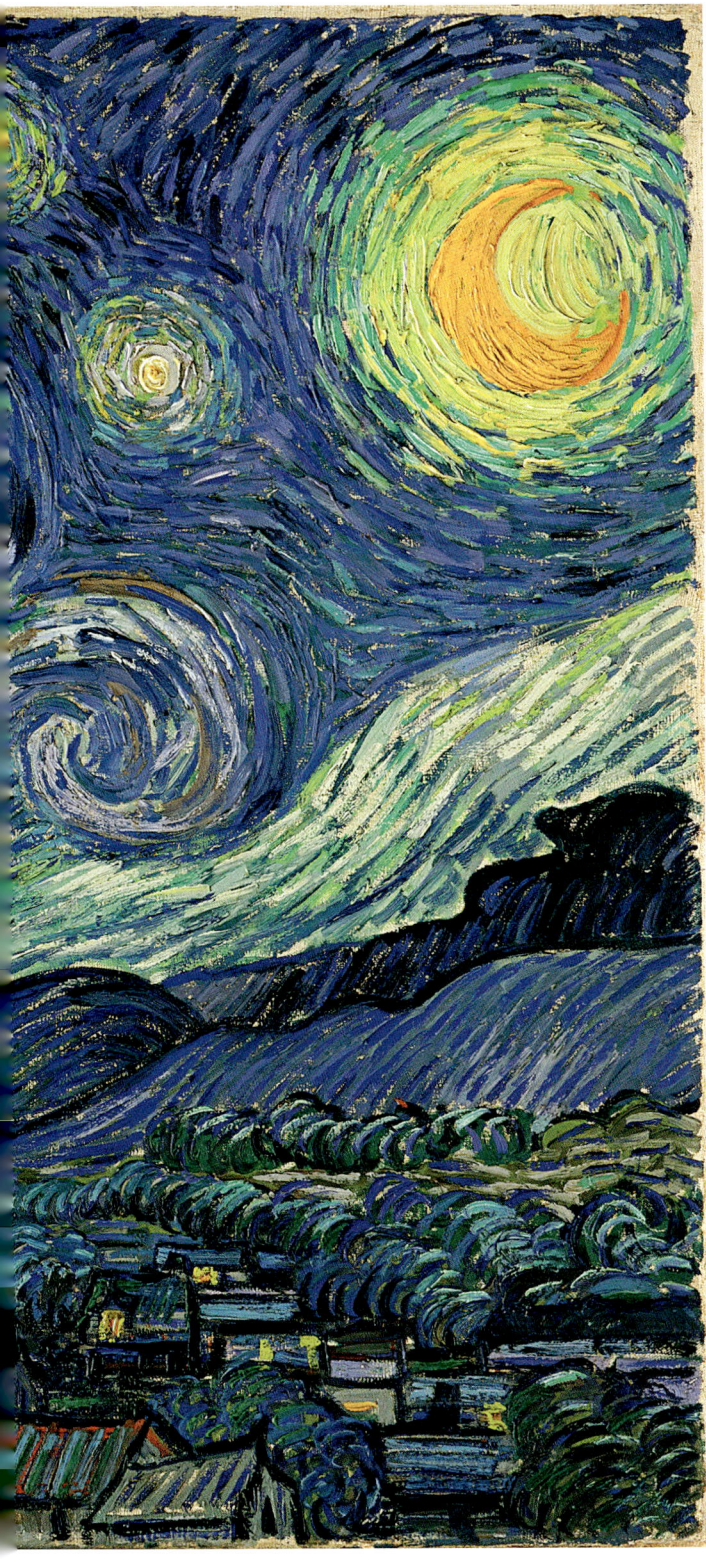

"*I put my heart and soul into my work, and have half lost my mind in the process.*"

VINCENT VAN GOGH

"*And I could feel a heart in all of it, the soul who had made all of it and who himself had answered the most terrible doubts with this vision, who could feel, know, understand and enjoy the highs and the lows, exterior and interior, one and all in a thousandth of a part in time – all this I could feel when I write the words …*"

HUGO VON HOFMANNSTHAL,
letter of 26 May 1901

Starry Night, 1889
Oil on canvas, 73.7 x 92.1 cm (29 x 36⅜ in.)
New York, The Museum of Modern Art

state of mind. Again he uses the tree theme in the painting *Olive Grove* (ill. p. 472), but quite differently from the cypress paintings. Here one single movement runs through the whole of the painting's surface. Soil, trees and sky display the same wavy strokes of the brush, and so the separate unities are brought into one complete entity. The three larger areas of colour – ochre, green and blue – are more reserved and soft, and the colour contrasts are also toned down. The strong lines of the branches blend in with the arabesque pattern of the softer areas of the sky, just as the blue of the sky is turned in on the leaves and stems, whose green and grey tones blend in with the soil – everything is brought into one single harmony. A calming effect is also gained by the equilibrium between cold and warm colours, establishing an almost dreamlike unreality. By using black contours the strange silhouette of the olive tree trunks, which are bent and twisted as if in pain, are marked out. A mute pain appears to pervade this nature and restlessness runs through the whole.

In Saint-Rémy van Gogh discovered true movement in his work. In his paintings created here and later in Auvers, two clearly marked styles are seen, which are elaborated to their outermost limits – on the one hand a continuous composition of winding, wavy curves, on the other a complicated hatching of short, sharp dashes. Both elements are loaded with excitement and dynamic

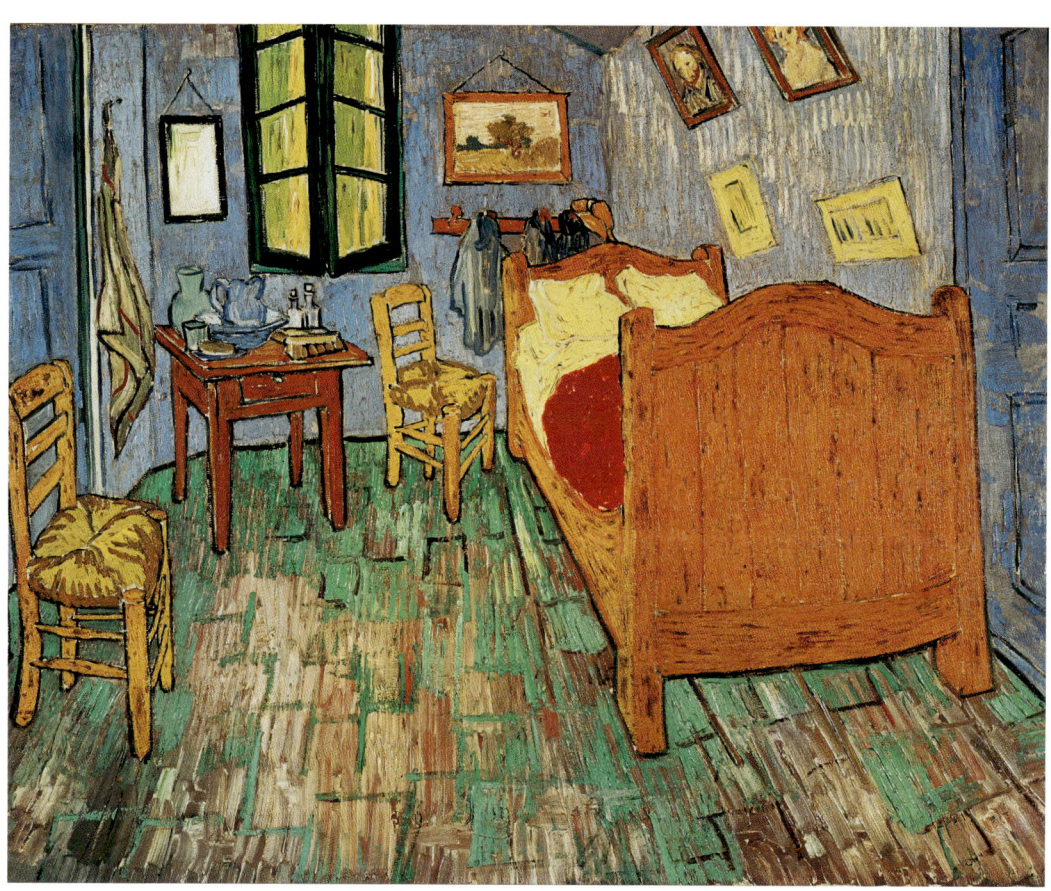

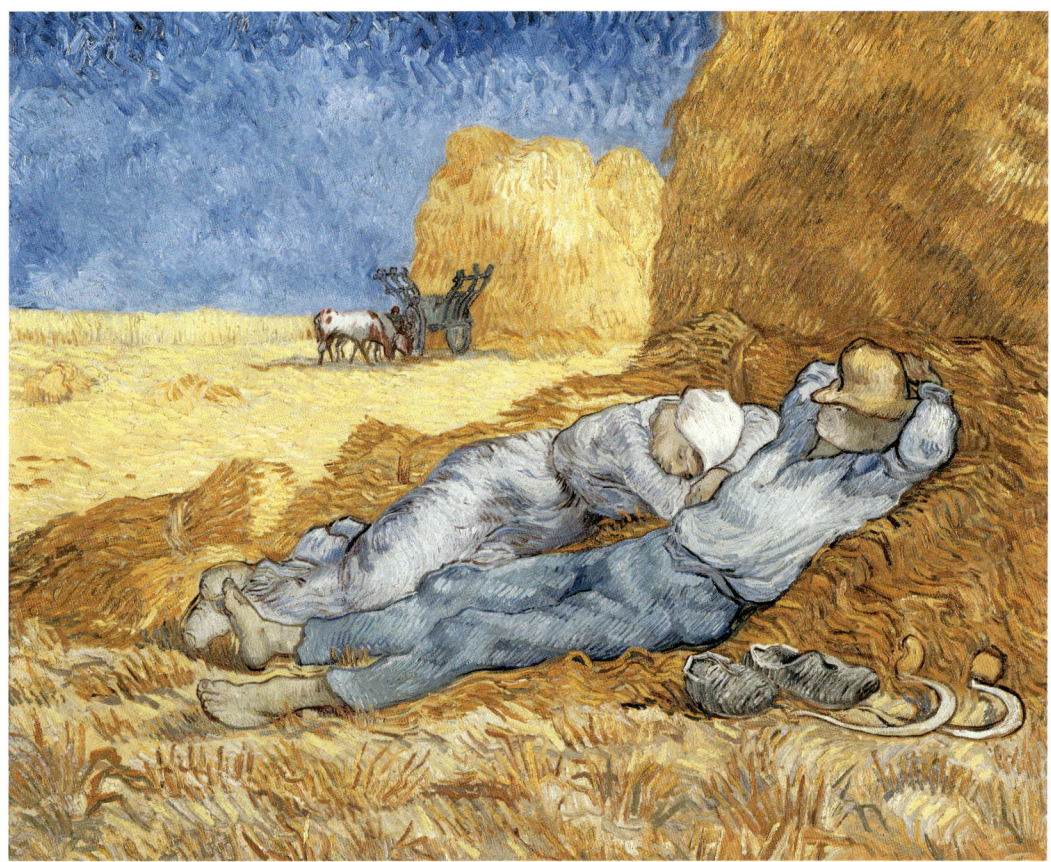

forms, clearly elements of a style of painting born out of excitement and tension.

Both linear forms are combined in his painting *Starry Night*
(ill. pp. 474/475), one of his major works and at the same time
one of his strangest. Once again he seized upon the theme of his
night paintings from his earlier periods in Paris and Arles, but
now in a totally different context. It is one of the few works which completely avoids a direct observation of nature, with colours and forms coming from his imagination in order to evoke a particular
atmosphere. A highly dramatic cosmic event is taking place in the sky. Two gigantic spiral nebulae
are entwined; eleven enormously enlarged stars with their aureoles of light break through the night;
an unreal orange-coloured moon looks as if it is joined to the sun; a broad band of light – perhaps
the Milky Way – is drawn across the horizon, and the deep blue sky appears to be in staggering
turmoil. The immediacy and expressive powers of the painting are strengthened by the impulsive,
sweeping flood of brushstrokes.

Yet van Gogh does not yield passively to this exciting vision. By artistic means he handles this
vision in a different manner in his choice of contrasting elements to portray the events on this earth
and so enhance the effect. The sleeping town in the foreground, which is portrayed with short,
straight strokes of the brush, contrasts with the curving shapes in the sky; even the small yellow
lights of the houses present a contrast to the stars in their quadrangular or rectangular shape. The

Noon: Rest from Work (after Millet), 1890
Oil on canvas, 73 x 91 cm (28¾ x 35⅞ in.)
Paris, Musée d'Orsay

OPPOSITE
Vincent's Bedroom in Arles, 1889
Oil on canvas, 73.6 x 92.3 cm (29 x 36⅜ in.)
The Art Institute of Chicago

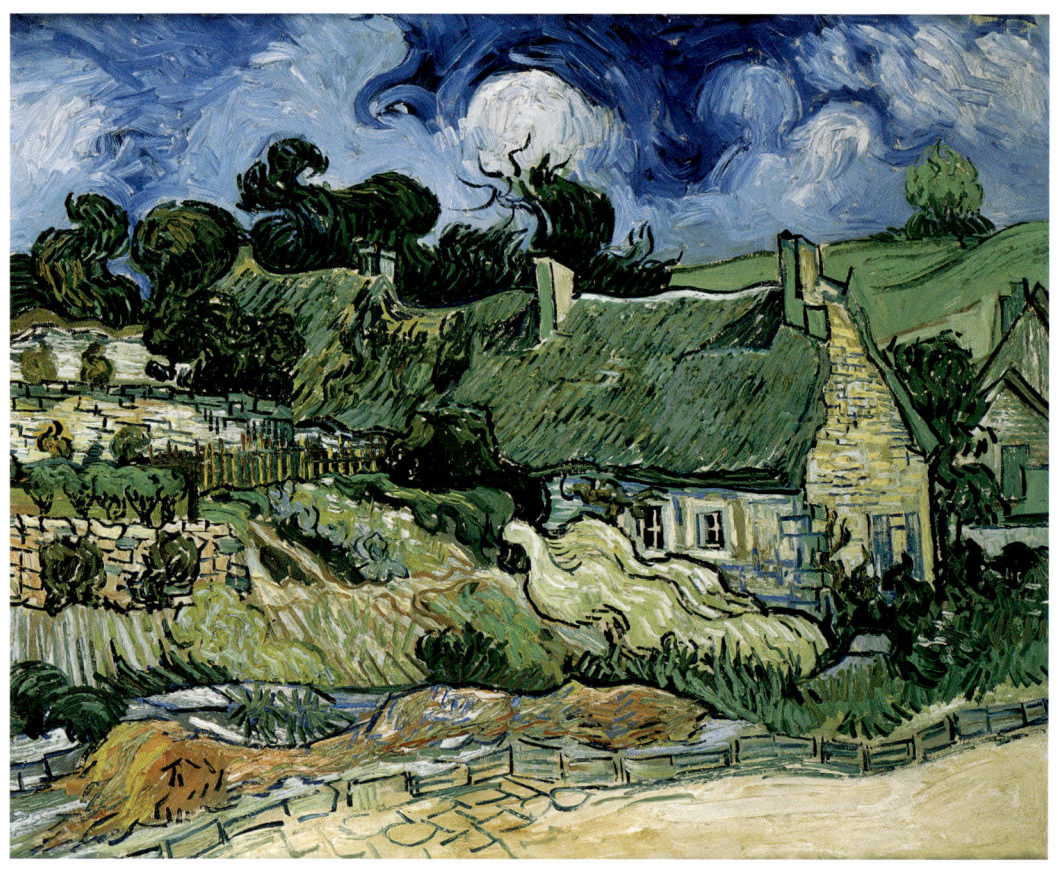

Thatched Cottages at Cordeville, 1890
Oil on canvas, 73 x 92 cm (28¾ x 36¼ in.)
Paris, Musée d'Orsay

pointed towering church spire – reminiscent of the north – cuts across the earth's horizon, just like the blazing flames of the powerful cypresses: a vertical, earthbound contrast to the circling star nebulae in the sky.

This contrast can be viewed as opposing powers: human striving and effort ("reaching for the stars") against celestial, cosmic powers, since the actual event in the painting does not take place on earth but in the heavens. In this picture, perhaps an apocalyptic vision, van Gogh tries to free himself from overpowering emotions. It must also be seen as an attempt to express pictorially his desire for the infinite in nature.

Three months later, in September 1889, he painted his last self-portrait (ill. p. 473). In this half-length picture the artist stands in a three-quarter profile against a blue-green-grey spiraled, whirling, rhythmic background. The suit, over the collarless white shirt, is almost the same colour, in sharp contrast to his strained facial expression and the dark, fixed eyes – "a look which goes straight through one" (Antonin Artaud).

The pulsating forms of the background, the sense of excitement captured in the picture, are not determined by a set rhythm or a rigid pattern; they convey much more the overwhelming surge of his feelings towards his environment. Yet these emotions are held spell-bound in fixed forms and are integrated as direct chosen elements of movement in a controlled composition. In spite of all the flowing unrest, a great balance is dominant.

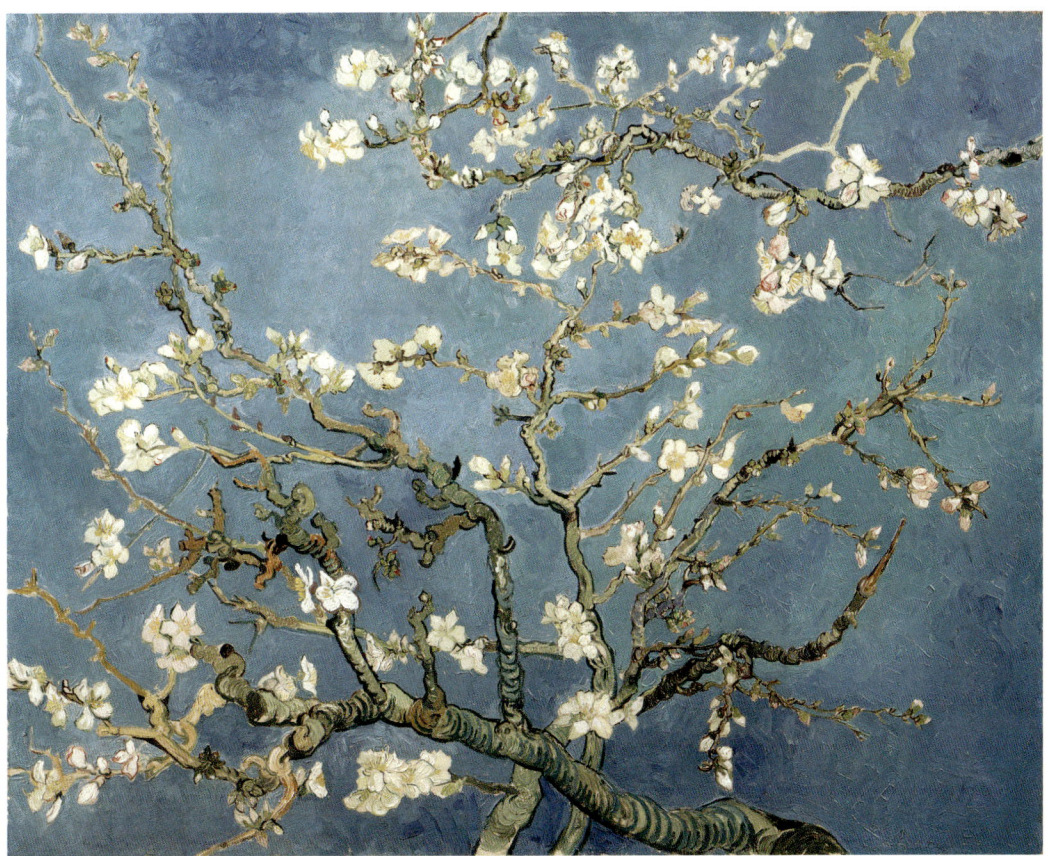

Blossoming Almond Tree, 1890
Oil on canvas, 73.3 x 92.4 cm (28⅞ x 36½ in.)
Amsterdam, Van Gogh Museum,
Vincent van Gogh Foundation

Towards the end of that fateful year of 1889 the artist's inspiration appears to have dwindled. In the evenings he was often bored to tears in the asylum, despite the fact that he read a lot. Since he was no longer able to paint in the open air, he made copies or replicas of his own earlier paintings. Paintings such as *Vincent's Bedroom in Arles* (ill. p. 476) were either for his mother or his sister. He had previously taken up this motif shortly before Gauguin's arrival in Arles, but the first version was damaged during transportation. In Saint-Rémy he painted a copy of it from memory and this one is the most brilliantly coloured of the three versions of this theme. He wrote of it: "This time it's simply my bedroom, only the colours should work here, and through the simplification which gives the things a larger style, peace or complete sleep ought to be suggested."

In spite of van Gogh's intentions the picture does not give the impression of total calm. The objects do not relate to one another; each one is isolated. To add to the uneasy feeling we have in observing the painting, all the objects have been considerably foreshortened; the floorboards lurch steeply forward, giving the impression of almost lifting over each other, the window is half open, the slanting furniture – wash table and chairs near the bed – as well as the paintings hang over into the room. The ambivalent atmosphere lends the picture a strange, tense aura: it is the wish for cosiness, for a home, for comfort and care, which contradicts reality. Desolation, loneliness and homelessness are stronger than the desire.

"A night sky with a moon barely able to give out any light, the slight sickle hardly able to shine through the dark earth's shadow – a star of excessive brightness, pink and green in an ultramarine blue sky, in which a few clouds float about. A road, bordered by high yellow reeds, behind the low blue alpilles, an old inn with orange lit-up windows, and a very tall cypress, quite straight, quite dark. On the road a yellow carriage with a white horse before it, and two late wanderers. All very romantic … but I believe typical of Provence."

VINCENT VAN GOGH

In winter 1889 the number of his landscape paintings decreased; his work indoors showed a concentration on the reproduction of his earlier sketches and of sketches made by other artists. Using black-and-white lithographs, reproductions and woodcuts which Theo had sent him from Paris, he transformed the works of Rembrandt, Delacroix and Millet into colour paintings. Above all, the monumental simplicity of Millet's peasant figures had always influenced him. Between autumn 1889 and spring 1890 he painted no fewer than twenty-three mostly small paintings after Millet. "You will be amazed," he wrote to his brother in September, "how effective the *Field Workers* [Millet] becomes through the use of colour."

This amazing effect of colour on a copy of Millet's work can best be seen in *Noon: Rest from Work* (ill. p. 477). Almost two-thirds of the painting is taken up by the gold-yellow-orange of the cut, tied and stacked hay. A strong contrast in colour is provided by the light blue of the sky, which is echoed in the blue clothing of the peasants sleeping in the shade. Stretched out, they are seeking protection from the blazing midday heat, and in their sleep appear to be at one with nature. Earth and sky, man and nature form one single unit belonging together.

The most intensive, radiant and clearest blue sky that van Gogh ever painted can be seen in the background of the painting *Blossoming Almond Tree* (ill. p. 479), which was conceived as a christening present for his little nephew, who was born at the end of January 1890 and given his uncle's name, Vincent. The glowing white almond blossoms break forth from the still-wintery branches and, heralding spring, they proclaim the beginning of a new life. In this painting Vincent practised patience and self-discipline, which was something totally alien to his work. He perhaps restrained himself too much since during his work on this painting, his last from Saint-Rémy, he became ill.

In January and February 1890 more exciting things happened than the birth of his nephew and his being called after Vincent: for the first time an extensive article was written about him in an art magazine. The exhibition of the Brussels group Les XX was opened in Paris, where van Gogh showed a few of his paintings; at the same time, the new Salon des Artistes Indépendants was being prepared for March, in which he was also to take part. Finally he received news of the sale of his painting *Red Vineyard* in Brussels for 400 francs to Anna Boch, the sister of the poet Eugène Boch. It was one of the few paintings which Vincent was able to sell during his lifetime, though not, as rumour has it, the only one.

The events of the last weeks proved too much for him. He suffered a new attack, which lasted longer than the other ones, almost two months. Again he suffered from derangement, fear of death and shocks, accompanied by hallucinations and fits of rage. Only after several weeks had gone by did he venture to write to say that he had decided once and for all to leave the asylum. After making a short trip to Paris to visit Theo and his family he travelled in May 1890 to Auvers-sur-Oise near Paris, where the doctor and amateur painter Dr Gachet had agreed to look after him. He rented a room in the Ravoux Inn opposite the small town hall, and immediately began to paint again, making use of the new motifs which the place and surroundings offered him.

Road with Cypress and Star, 1890
Oil on canvas, 90.6 x 72 cm (35¾ x 28⅜ in.)
Otterlo, Kröller-Müller Museum

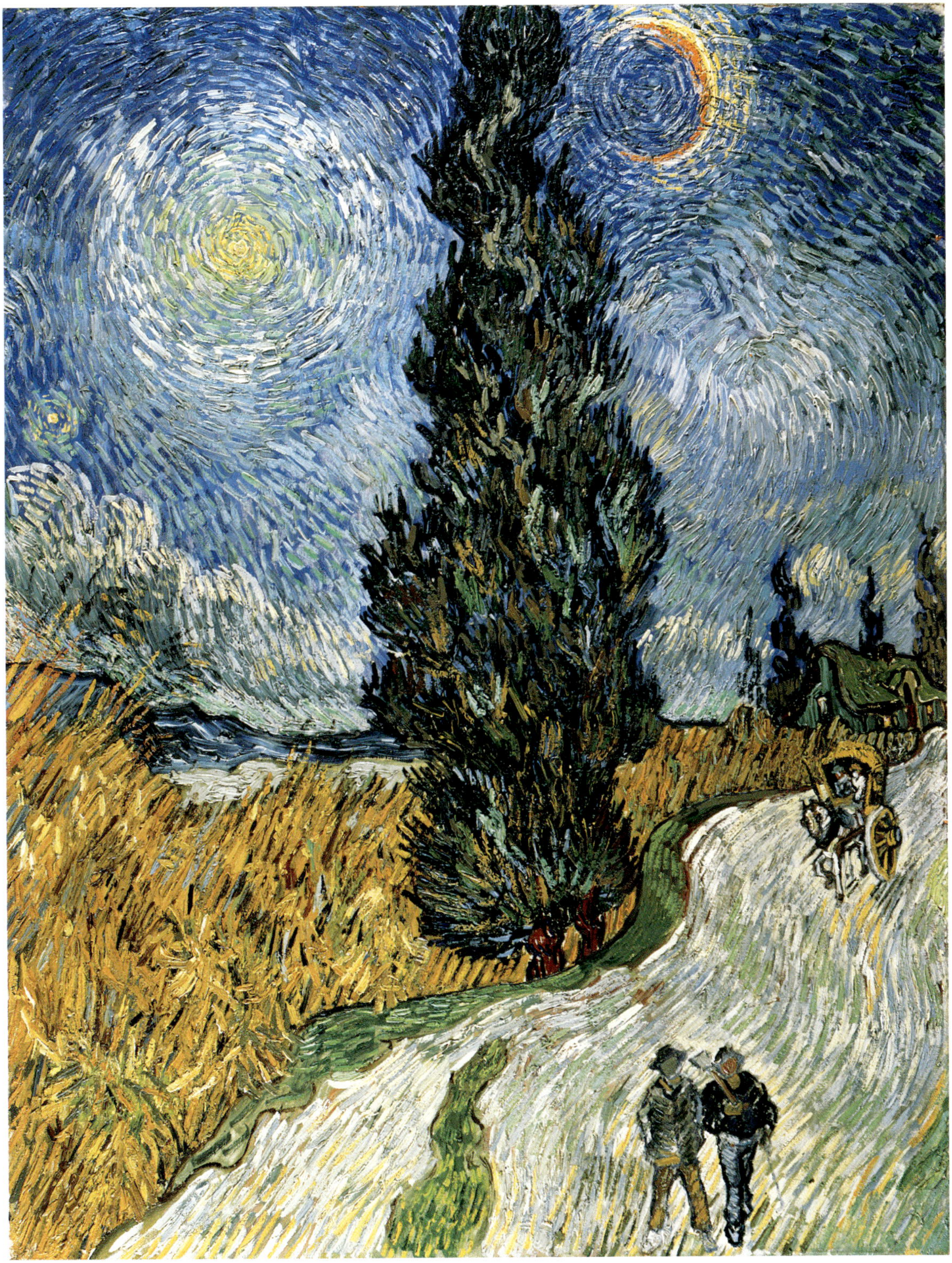

"Why did the greatest colourist of all, Eugène Delacroix, feel it imperative to go to the south and even as far as Africa? Obviously, because one finds – not only in Africa, but from Arles onwards – the most beautiful contrasts of red and green, of blue and orange, and of sulphurous yellow and lilac which nature has to offer."

VINCENT VAN GOGH

The painting *Thatched Cottages at Cordeville* (ill. p. 478) bears witness to his renewed vital creativity, although it appears to have been painted more fleetingly than ever. A lot of things in the painting are only vaguely shown; open forms and contours and loose strokes of the brush lead one to conclude that the painting was done in a hurry. Despite the idyllic motif of the old, thatched roofs of the farmhouses with vegetable garden, fence and wall, a great unrest is spread over the whole of the painting by the bushes and dark trees.

A nervous energy appeared to have taken hold of the artist again. The linear elements of his paintings are stressed and dominate the dark, earth-coloured palette. This is obvious in the work *Road with Cypress and Star* (ill. p. 481). The distinct brushstrokes, so marked in all of van Gogh's works, now become a torrent, an avalanche, which pours over the whole of the canvas. Now the actual brushstrokes take prominence just as the colours did in Arles. Objects have lost their stable form, their outlines have been extended lengthways, and they wind about and coil in on themselves. These connect the motif, consisting of many tiny streaming parts which follow the movement of the outline. Their colours are disjointed and dull – the colour energy is transferred to the lines of energy, which appear as different centres of power, penetrating and struggling for dominance like magnetic fields which both attract and repel one another.

In this way the real landscape takes on an almost celestial character, also called up by the central ordering of the dark cypresses, which dominate the whole picture, placed between sun and moon with their wide halos of light. Two fully grown trees intertwining with one another try with all their might to reach upwards. The ground is full of similar forms, with the yellow field, the sloping stream of the road and the flat blue range of mountains in the background, which are reflected in the green blades of grass on the edge of the road. As a stark contrast to all this movement are the two figures on the road, the horse pulling the yellow carriage and the house lit up on the right-hand side of the picture. In each area the brushstrokes take on a special character: concentrated in the sky, parallel, interweaving and converging on the ground, flame-like tongues of the intertwining trees extending upwards. Everything in the picture is transformed into a pulsating rigidity.

During these weeks it was only when working that van Gogh could forget about his illness. Painting was not only a therapy for him, it was his whole life. During the seventy days he spent in Auvers, he painted as if possessed. More than eighty pictures were created in this period, amongst them the masterpiece *The Church at Auvers* (ill. p. 466). The clearly delineated form of the church gives the impression of it being a compact sculpture, which forms an organic unit with nature. The cobalt-blue sky is a colour of the night, the whole scene appears dark and the light unreal. A similar darker sky with the same effect of light appears in the later work *Wheat Field with Crows* (ill. pp. 490/491), with the V-shaped division in the foreground which has the effect of widening the space.

Already in Saint-Rémy van Gogh had often been preoccupied with religious thoughts and he had painted some biblical themes. His own religious beliefs forbade him from creating biblical figures from his imagination; he did not dare to do this, and so he looked to the Old Masters for his models. The choice of themes alone reveals the motif for his religious paintings: he depicted the dead Christ in the arms of his mother, the raising of Lazarus, to whom he gave his own features, and the

The Good Samaritan (after Delacroix), 1890
Oil on canvas, 73 x 59.5 cm (28¾ x 23½ in.)
Otterlo, Kröller-Müller Museum

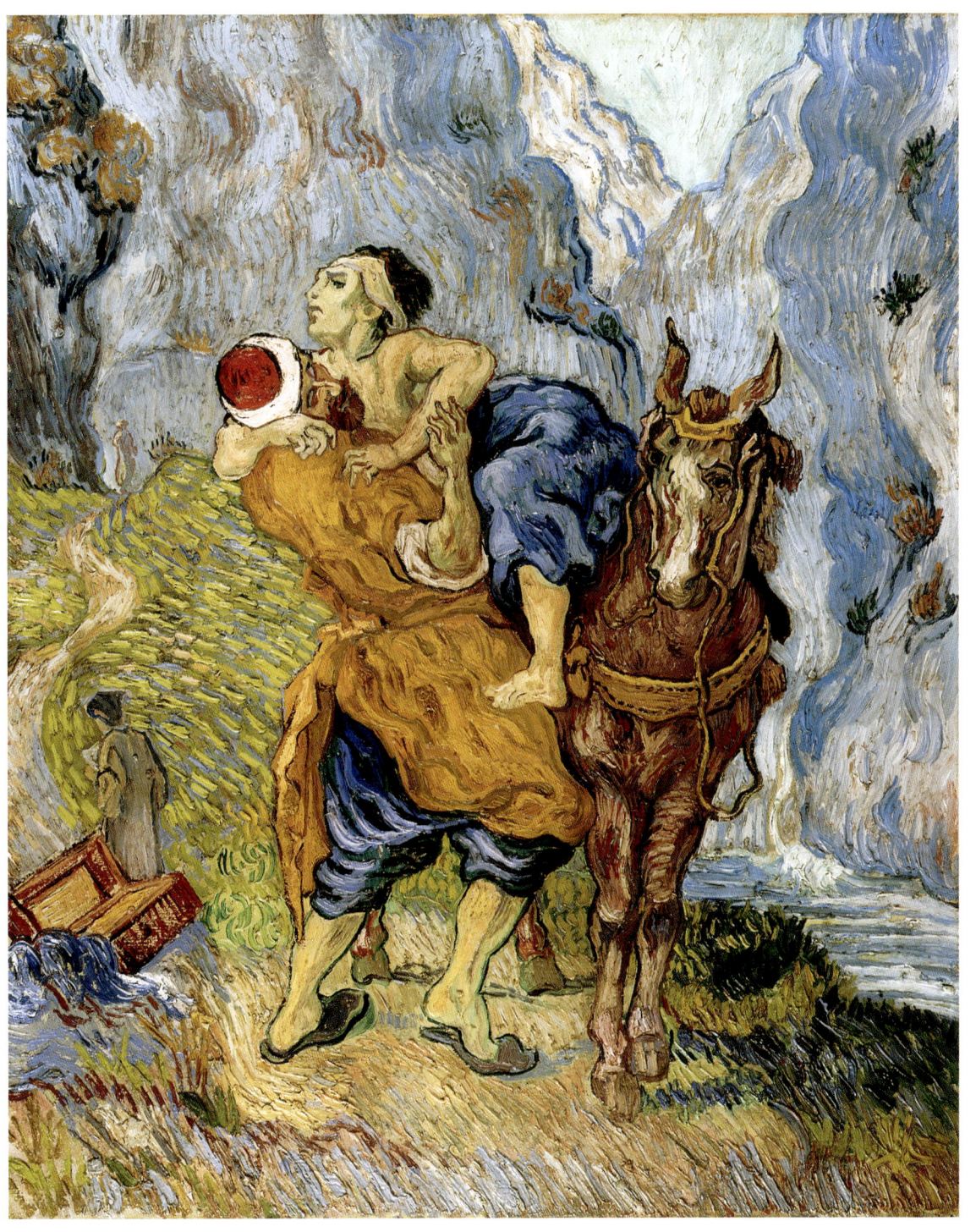

"I would like very much to paint portraits which in a hundred years time will be revelations. I would not like to achieve this, however, by keeping close to photographic representations, but instead by sticking to my own passionate view of things and using our knowledge and our present-day tastes in colour as a means of expression and portrayal of the excesses of character."

VINCENT VAN GOGH

good Samaritan – all suffering figures, who hope for future redemption.

The Good Samaritan (ill. p. 483) was based on Delacroix's model, just like *Pièta*. Delacroix, like Millet, was both his patronsaint of art and the founder of colour techniques. The reticent wealth of colour in this picture is meant to remind viewers of his great master. The brighter colours, the characteristic blue and red of Delacroix, are placed in an environment of more neutral, brownish tones, which are cleverly connected to one another in graded intervals of warm and cold, light and dark tones. Van Gogh adds a stream of parallel brushstrokes to Delacroix's original rhythm in his dynamic sketch. The arabesque forms and winding curves of the Delacroix painting are transferred by van Gogh into disjointed linear strokes – a devoted "translation" of the old work into a "modern" pictorial language.

But most of all, even more so than the religious pictures and landscapes, van Gogh was occupied with portrait painting – that is, the modern portrait. His models were always the simple, ordinary people around him. It was not for an external beauty or a certain character trait that he painted these people, but because of their mere humanity. Although brought to the front of the painting, they still have something mysterious and unusual about them. The smooth loveliness of his previous portrait paintings was now totally abandoned. The face took on a landscape-like appearance, due to the coarse texture of the paint, and the skin took on a tougher, yet natural constitution.

The composition *Young Peasant Woman with Straw Hat Sitting in the Wheat* (ill. p. 485) is typical of this. The three-quarter-length figure of the young peasant girl sits somewhat stiff and bashful amongst the high sheafs of corn, her cheeks glowing in the same red as the poppies. The pure blue of her blouse, inlaid with tiny orange spots, contrasts with the warm tones of the corn and her apron, as well as the golden yellow of her hat and the orange-coloured shadow cast by it. Once again we can see traces of the realism and coarseness of his earlier brown-toned peasant pictures.

In spite of this, this portrait remains in the shadow of his uncontested masterpiece of portrait painting – his *Portrait of Doctor Gachet* (ill. p. 487). This strange eccentric personality, who himself was a painter and friends with a lot of Impressionist painters, had deeply influenced van Gogh. Melancholy, sadness and resignation, which can be read in Gachet's face – a "despairing expression of our time" – pervade and set the tone of the whole painting. All lines and colours are adapted to this melancholy atmosphere and form an original unity. The lines mainly follow the depressive tendency of the figure, betraying the mood of this sensitive, simple man. The background lines correspond to those of the cap, face and shoulders. Thanks to the ultramarine blue of his jacket, the figure's face is highlighted and becomes paler at the same time. His woeful, pale-blue eyes gaze into the distance. A continuum of pale to dark blue – in the sky, background hills and suit – dominates the whole picture and is to be found again in the flower and the doctor's pupils.

The foundation was laid for a great friendship between the two men, not least because of this portrait. Gachet liked it so much that he asked van Gogh to paint a second version. Art was a strong bond in their friendship and van Gogh was overjoyed to be able, at long last, to paint someone who really understood his work. After such a long period of loneliness he had finally found a person with whom he could discuss his paintings.

Young Peasant Woman with Straw Hat Sitting in the Wheat, 1890
Oil on canvas, 92 x 73 cm (36¼ x 28¾ in.)
Private collection

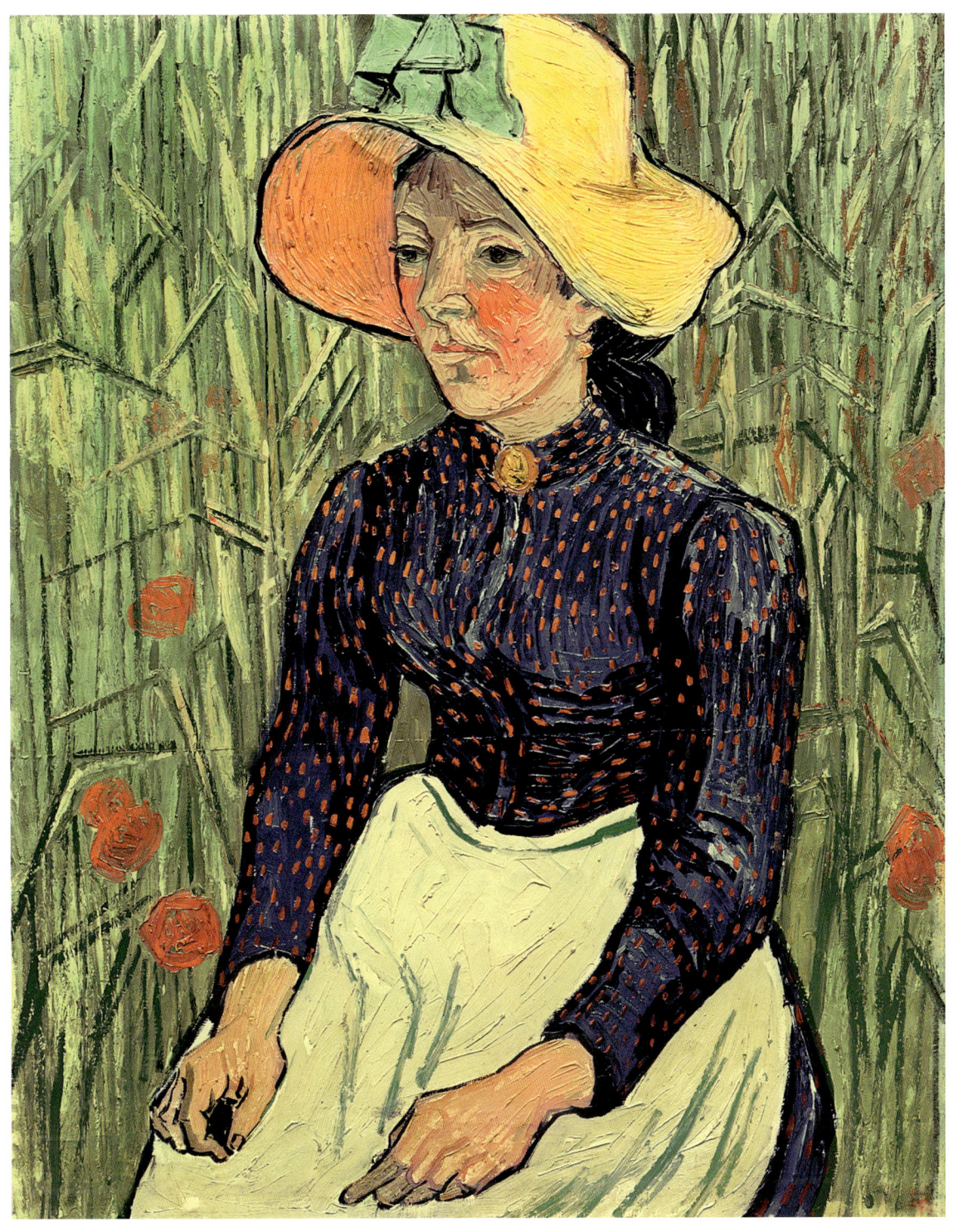

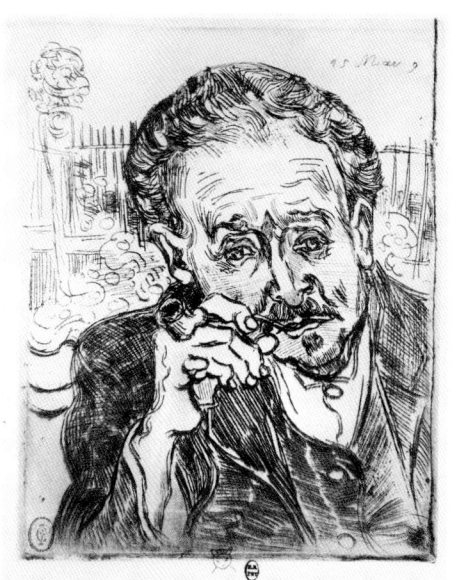

Yet Vincent's artistic happiness was not to last long. Things were not going well for his beloved brother Theo, on whose financial and moral support Vincent depended in order to survive. Theo's child was seriously ill, his wife was exhausted from endless sleepless nights, and often disputes arose between himself and the gallery owners, who no longer had faith in his artistic judgement. Greatly worried about his brother, Vincent travelled to Paris in July. Theo's difficulties also threatened his own existence, and his nerves began to suffer, so he did not stay there the whole time. From Auvers he wrote to Theo: "After my return here I am still very sad and the misfortunes, which are threatening you, lie heavy on my heart … my very steps are uncertain. I am afraid I'm a great burden to you, since I'm living from your financial help."

On top of this he also fell out with Gachet. He explained to his brother: "In my opinion I don't think we can rely on Dr Gachet at all. I get the impression that he is more ill than myself, or let's say at least just as ill. If a blind man leads the blind, don't they then both fall by the wayside?"

This disagreement with Gachet must have deeply upset him. Even here in his new surroundings, complete and utter loneliness threatened him again. Yet he did not in any way attempt to avoid this threatening loneliness. He worked all the more on his own, since Gachet had completely stopped all his visits and invitations.

His work was the only thing that kept him alive. Often he painted to near exhaustion, producing a new painting every day, sometimes even two. One month before his death he painted *Wheat Field with Crows* (ill. pp. 490/491), which clearly echoed his mood during those days. In this painting he attempted to convey his "sadness and extreme loneliness". The expanse of the field is conveyed by the unusually wide format of the picture, which opens up into three diverging parts in the foreground. The observer is unsettled by not knowing where both the horizon and the path end, whether in the field or off the edge of the painting somewhere. The normal structural perspective of the wide-open fields is turned upside down – its lines of alignment run from the horizon to meet in the front of the painting. The space presented here has no perspectival centre to it any more. The blue sky and the yellow fields push forcibly away from one another, and a flock of crows crosses the boundaries to the uncertain fore-edge.

In contrast to his more turbulent paintings, the whole space in this one is filled with a succinct breadth and simplicity. The colour palette is reduced to the three basic colours and one complementary colour – the blue of the sky, the yellow of the corn, the red of the separating paths and the complementary green of the blades of grass along these paths – thus creating an overall image of control. The predominant horizontal line is determined by the artist's state of mind rather than from the frame or canvas. It neither presents a panorama, nor is it created by the things that dominate the space, so that there are barely any vertical values. In all, parts and whole, closeness and distance cannot be definitely distinguished from one another.

TOP
Portrait of Doctor Gachet:
L'Homme à la Pipe, 1890
Etching, 18 x 15 cm (7 x 6 in.)

OPPOSITE
Portrait of Doctor Gachet, 1890
Oil on canvas, 67 x 56 cm
(26½ x 22 in.)
Private collection

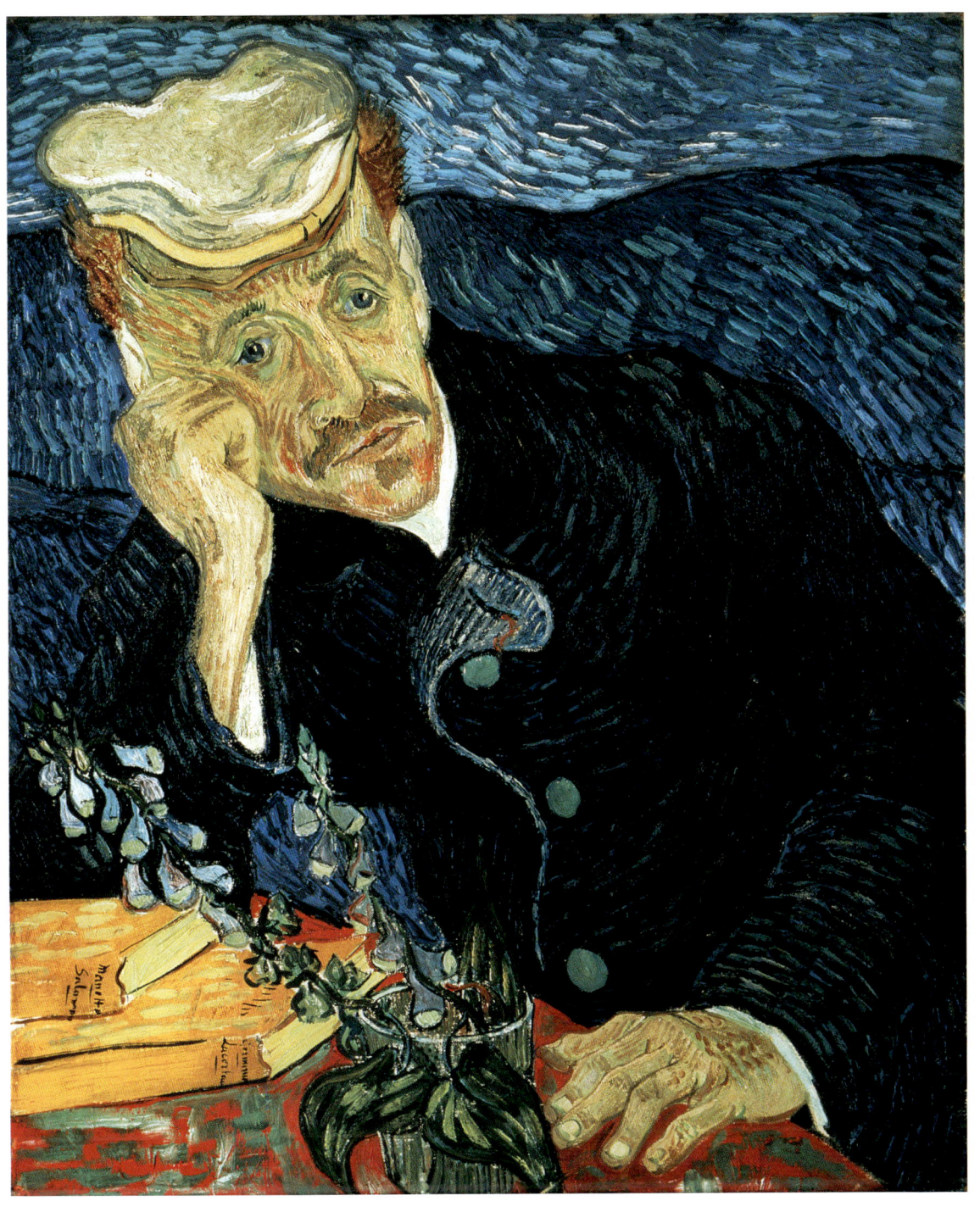

Many believe this picture to be one of his last, because of his absolutely valid formulation of the theme of a landscape, which appears to reflect the original laws of creation. However, a dozen more followed, amongst them *Thatched Sandstone Cottages in Chaponval* (ill. p. 488). Yet the power and quality of the *Wheat Field with Crows* is never attained again, so it is quite valid to say that this painting is one of the most complete testimonies to his art form.

Vincent's last, unfinished letter to Theo on 27 July 1890 sounds like a farewell: "I would really like to write to you about a lot of things, yet I feel this is useless … In my own work I put my whole life in jeopardy, and I have half lost my mind in the process … I repeat to you again that I have always looked upon you as something different than an ordinary art dealer …"

Without his brother, who had supported him all his life, Vincent would not have had the means to paint such pictures. Yet now his life support was himself in great difficulty, and Vincent's further existence was therefore thrown into question. The catastrophe appeared unavoidable. His relationship with Dr Gachet had come to a final end. All his contacts with his environment were destroyed and with this the hope of work, which had up until now kept him alive. In the end the continually recurring attacks sounded the alarm for his final madness.

His situation was hopeless – van Gogh had failed totally in life. Yet one option still remained. On the evening of 27 July 1890 he went at dusk into the fields and shot himself in the chest with a revolver. With all his strength he managed to drag himself back to the inn where he died two days later in the arms of his brother, who had hurried to his side.

"Mr Gachet seems to me to be just as ill and as nervous as you and I, as well as being much older. He lost his wife a few years ago. But he's a doctor, nevertheless, that's what keeps him going – this manual skill and belief. We're quite good friends already. I'm working on his portrait – his head is covered by a white cap; his blond hair I've painted in really light tones; the colour of the skin on his hands is also really fair; a blue jacket; the background a cobalt blue. He props himself up against a red table on which a yellow book and foxglove with purplish flowers stand."

VINCENT VAN GOGH

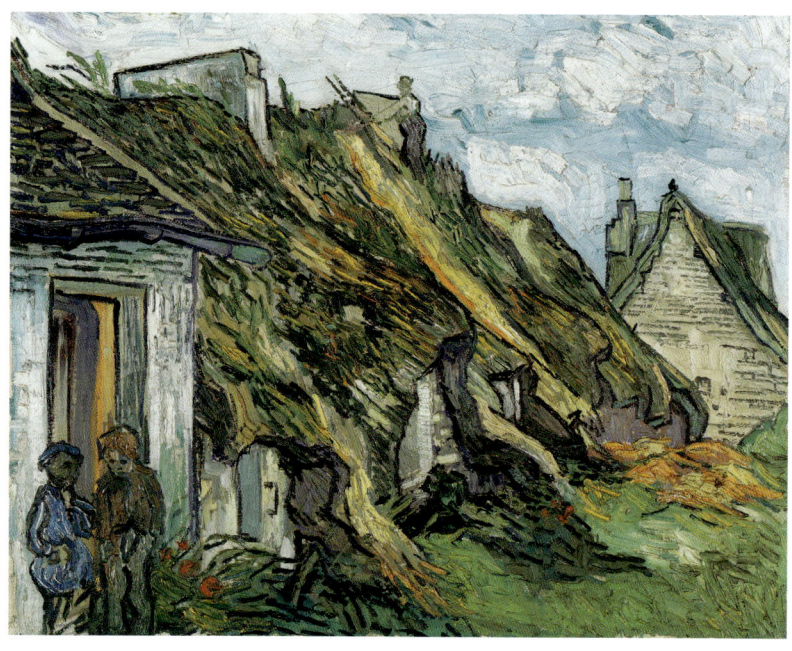

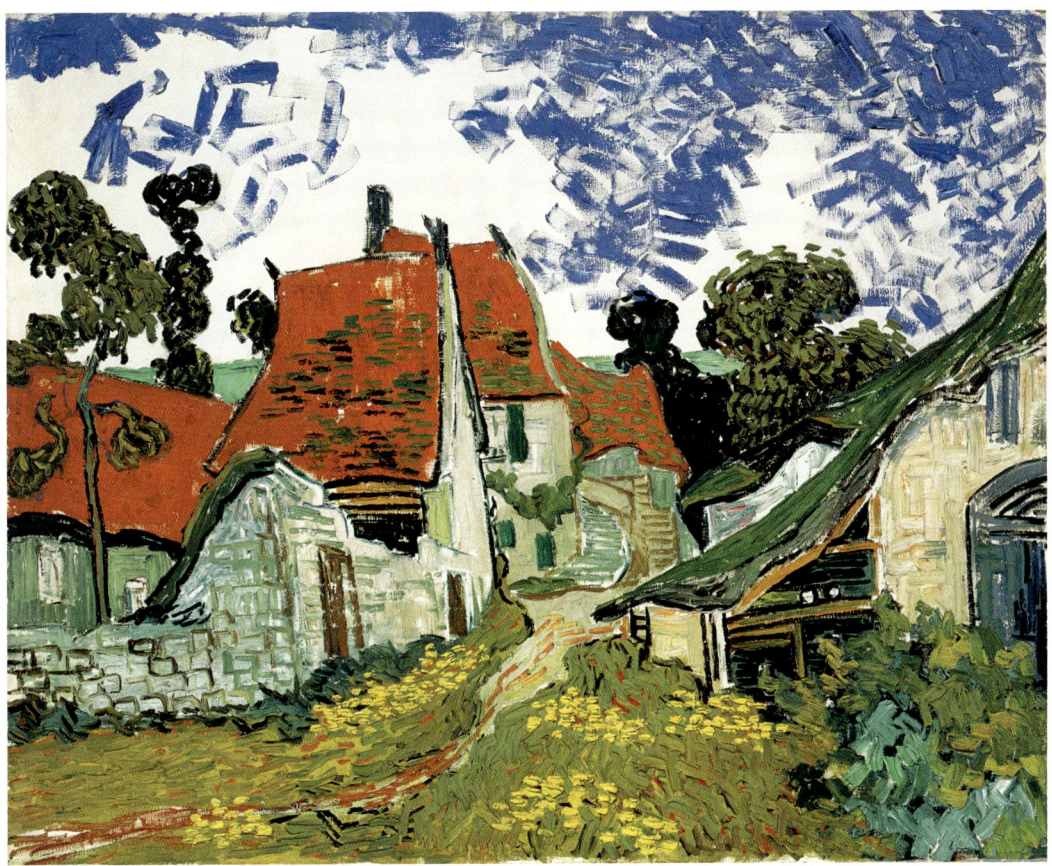

This marked the end of the singular life of an artist who defies comparison with any other. In his art, which he had arduously wrestled with and which he finally paid for with his life, van Gogh dared a synthesis such as hardly any artist has dared since. Art and life became an inseparable unit to him, and with this he realized an ancient artistic dream of reality. To create works of art meant no less to him than to paint life – not mere reality, but the principle of life.

Van Gogh had not only developed the three fundamental elements of painting – colour, line and composition – into further artistic elements of style, but also endowed them with a new and unique significance: colours as the breath of life, which grants all things life; the line as a principle of movement, as the dynamics of life and as indestructible energy; the composition as a place in which to express his view of the world. Fulfillment and loneliness, desire and doubt, love and destruction, devotion and flight from reality, closeness and distance, duration and transistoriness – all these things, one person, an artist, painted in his work.

He sought consolation in his art from the world and life, which he loved but whose love was not returned. He suffered in this world and was destroyed by it. With his art he created his own new world, which was full of colour and movement and contained everything he knew about existence.

Village Street in Auvers, 1890
Oil on canvas, 73 x 92 cm
(28¾ x 36¼ in.)
Helsinki, Ateneumin taidemuseo

OPPOSITE
Thatched Sandstone Cottages in Chaponval, 1890
Oil on canvas, 65 x 81 cm
(25⅝ x 32 in.)
Zurich, Kunsthaus Zürich

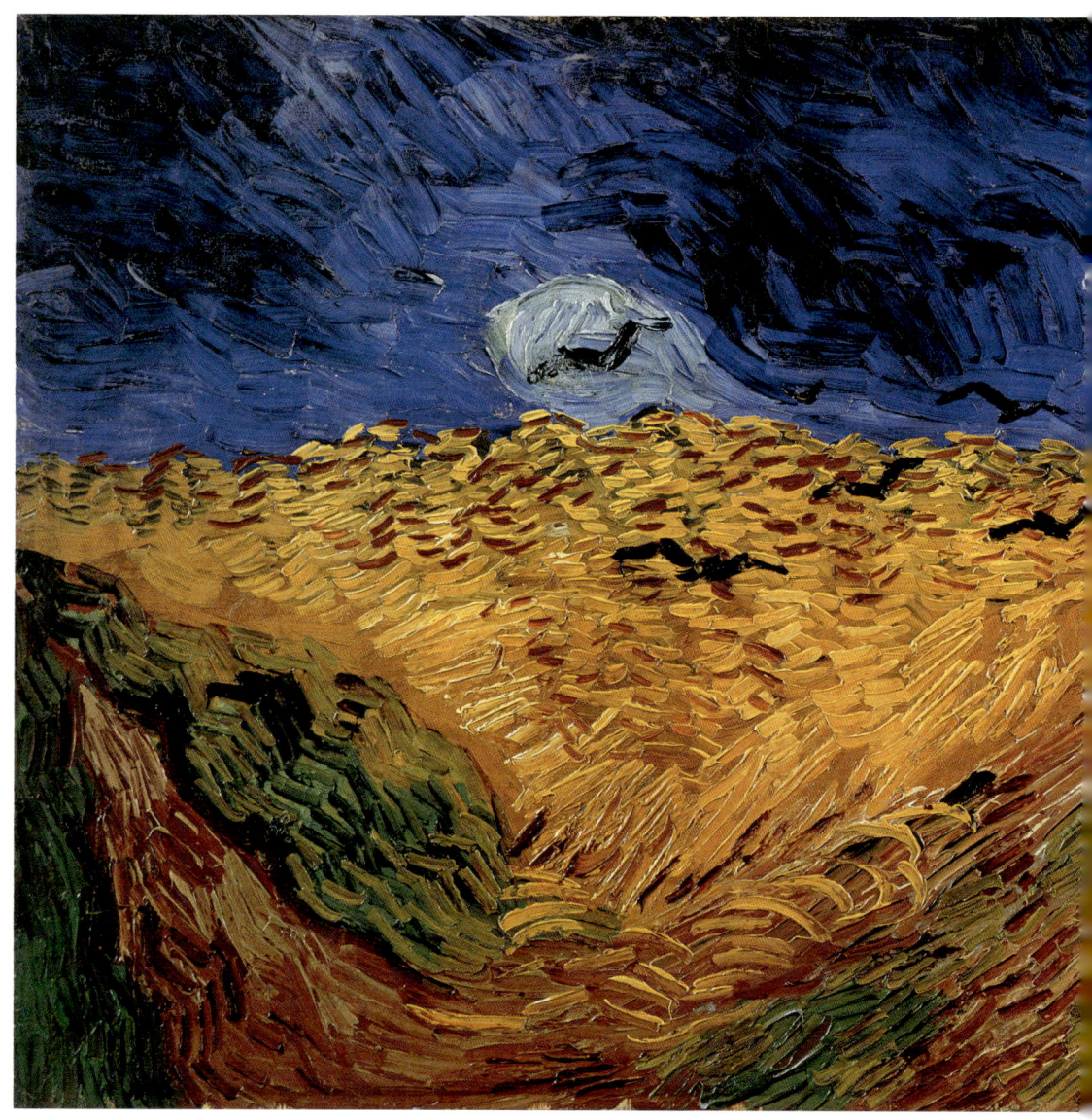

Wheat Field with Crows, 1890
Oil on canvas, 50.5 x 103 cm (20 x 40⅝ in.)
Amsterdam, Van Gogh Museum,
Vincent van Gogh Foundation

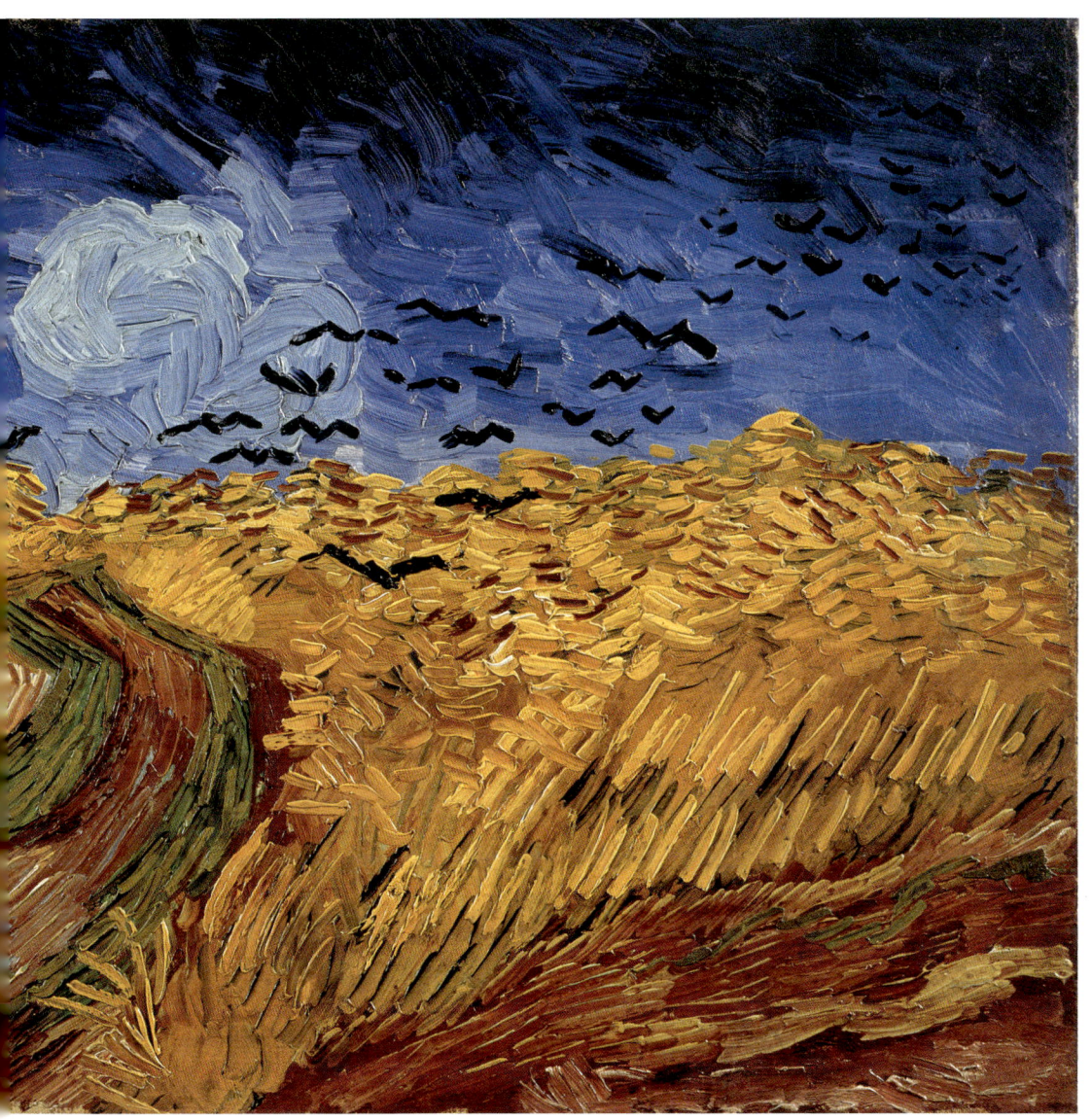

"I can tell you from the beginning that everyone will say that I work too quickly.
Don't believe it. It is the excitement, the honesty of a man of nature, led by
nature's hand. And sometimes this excitement is so strong that one works without
noticing it – the strokes of the brush come in quick succession and lead on from
one to the next like words in a conversation or letter. Yet one should not forget that
it was not always so and that in the future too many despondent days without
any inspiration will follow."

VINCENT VAN GOGH

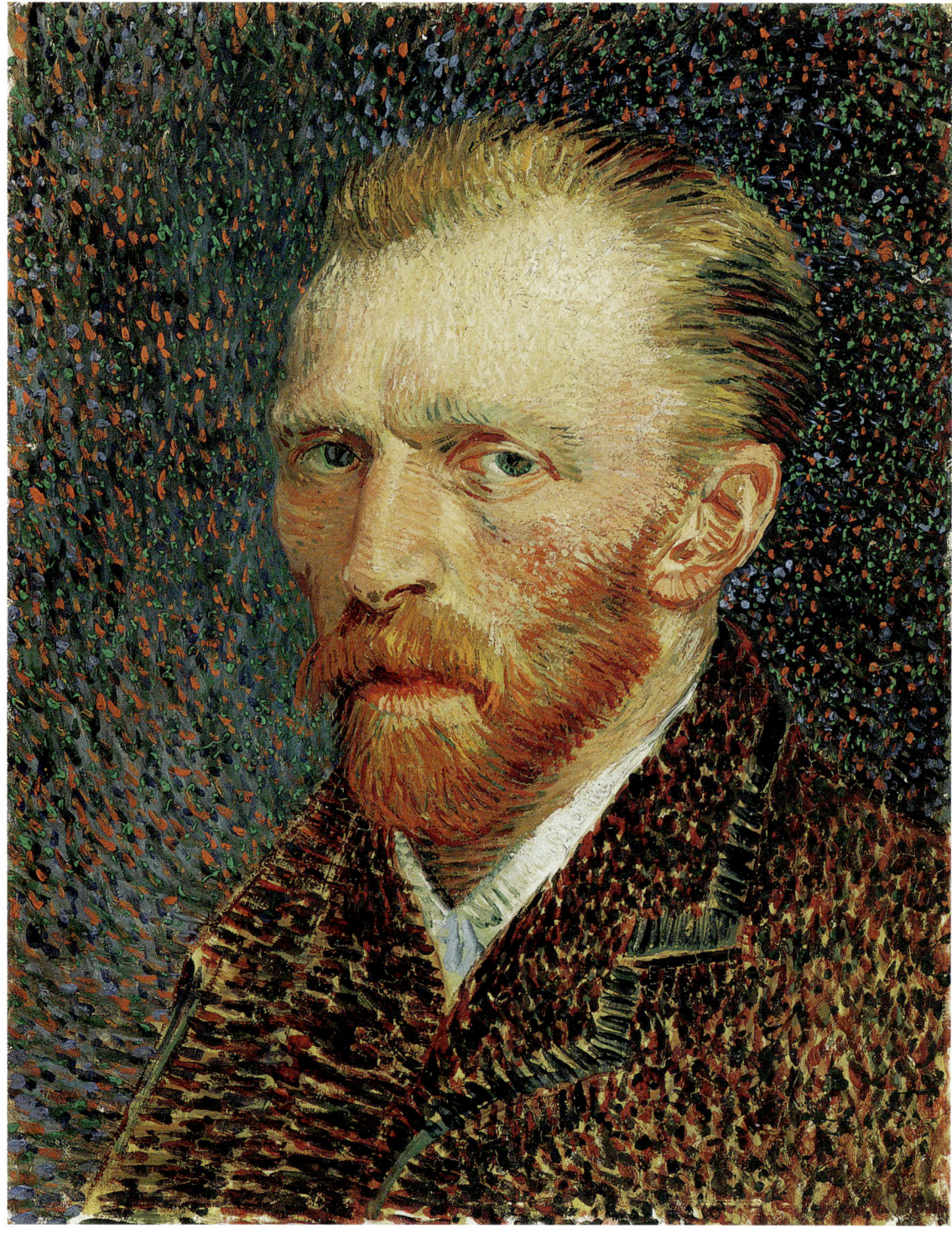

Vincent van Gogh 1853–1890
Life and Work

1853 Vincent Willem van Gogh, born on 30 March in the Dutch village vicarage of Groot-Zundert (North Brabant), the first of six children to Theodorus van Gogh (1822–1885), a preacher in the Dutch Reformed Church, and his wife Anne Cornelia, née Carbentus (1819–1907), the daughter of a book-binder from The Hague. He is named after the stillborn child who died on this very day the previous year.

1857 Birth of his brother Theodorus Vincent, called Theo.

1861–64 Attends the village school in Zundert.

1864 Enrolls in the private boarding school in Zevenbergen. Learns French, English and German, practises drawing.

1866–68 Attends the boarding school in Tilburg.

1868 Gives up school and goes back to Groot-Zundert.

1869 Goes to The Hague where he enters the branch office of the Paris art dealer Goupil & Cie, founded originally by his uncle Vincent. Under the supervision

OPPOSITE
Self-portrait, 1887
Oil on cardboard,
41 x 32.5 cm (16¼ x 12⅞ in.)
The Art Institute of Chicago

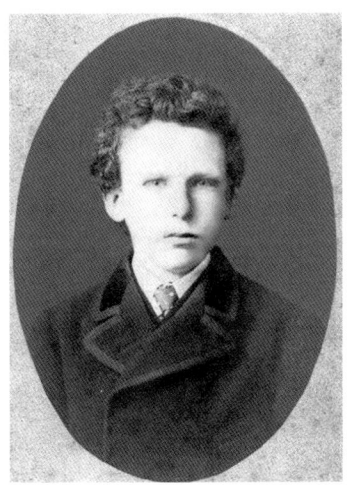

Vincent in 1866, aged 13

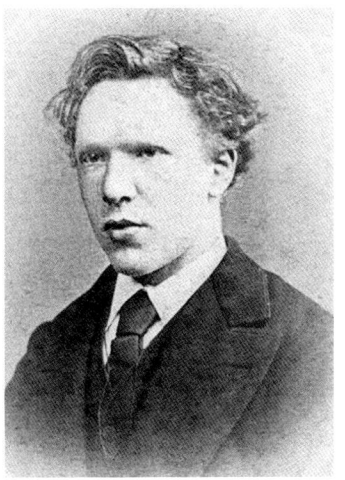

Vincent in 1871 when he was attached to the Goupil & Cie branch in The Hague

of H. G. Tersteeg he sells repro-ductions of works of art; reads extensively and visits museums.

1871 His father is relocated to a new post as a vicar at Helvoirt in Brabant, where he moves with his family.

1872 Spends his holidays at his parents' and then visits his brother in The Hague. This marks the beginning of the extensive exchange of letters between them.

1873 JANUARY: Vincent is transferred on the initiative of his uncle to the Brussels branch of Goupil.
MAY: Transfer to the London branch. Before his departure he travels to Paris, which impresses him deeply; visits the Louvre.

JUNE: Works for a year with Goupil in London. On his walks he makes his first sketches, which he throws away. Falls in love with Ursula, the daughter of his land-lady. Her rejection of his love pre-cipitates a personal crisis.
NOVEMBER: His brother Theo is transferred to the Goupil branch in The Hague.

1874 SUMMER: Spends his holidays with his parents in Helvoirt and confides in them his private disappointment to explain his depressive mood. Goes back to London together with his sister Anna in the middle of July. Leads a lonely life and shows little interest in his work; reads a lot, especially religious writings.

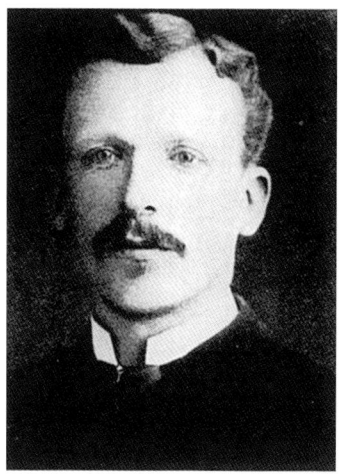

Vincent's brother Theodorus (Theo) van Gogh (1857–1891), photographed about 1888–90

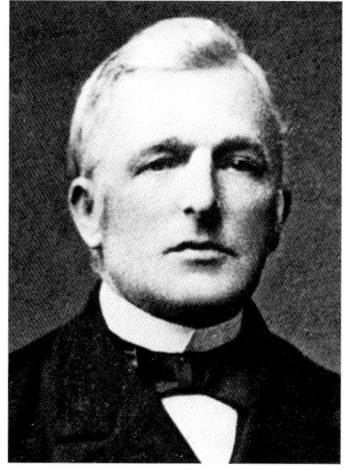

Theodorus van Gogh (1822–1885), Vincent's father. Theodorus had eleven brothers and sisters. He was appointed to the Zundert living on 1 April 1849

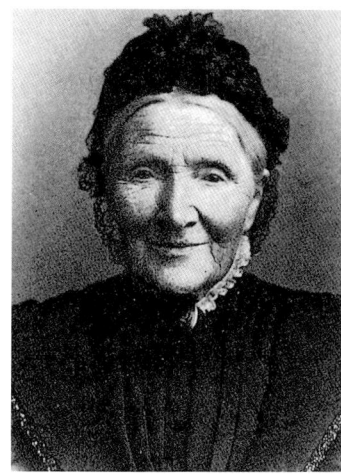

Anna Cornelia van Gogh, née Carbentus (1819–1907), Vincent's mother

OCTOBER–DECEMBER: His uncle makes him transfer temporarily to the main office of Goupil in Paris, hoping this change of environment will improve his situation.

1875 MAY: Final transfer to Paris. Continues to neglect his work, much to the annoyance of his colleagues and clients alike; visits museums and galleries, is enthusiastic about Corot and the 17th-century Dutch School of painting.
OCTOBER: Father Theodorus is relocated to Etten near Breda.
DECEMBER: Without having applied for leave beforehand, he spends Christmas with his parents.

1876 APRIL: Hands in his notice at Goupil's. Goes to Ramsgate, near London, and works as a supply

The presbytery (centre) in Zundert where Vincent and Theo van Gogh were born. Vincent first saw the light of day in the room from which the flag has been run out

teacher, receiving only board and lodgings.
JULY–DECEMBER: Continues to work as a supply teacher in Isleworth, a working-class area on the outskirts of London. Afterwards he works as an apprentice lay preacher and teacher together with a Methodist preacher. In November he preaches his first sermon; wants to devote his life to the evangelization of the poor. In his spare time he still continues

his interest in painting; visits the gallery in Hampton Court. At Christmas he visits his parents in Etten; worried about their son's condition, they prevent his return to London.

1877 JANUARY–APRIL: On his uncle's recommendation he gets a position as an assistant in a bookshop in Dordrecht. Leads a very lonely life, frequently visits the church and translates parts of

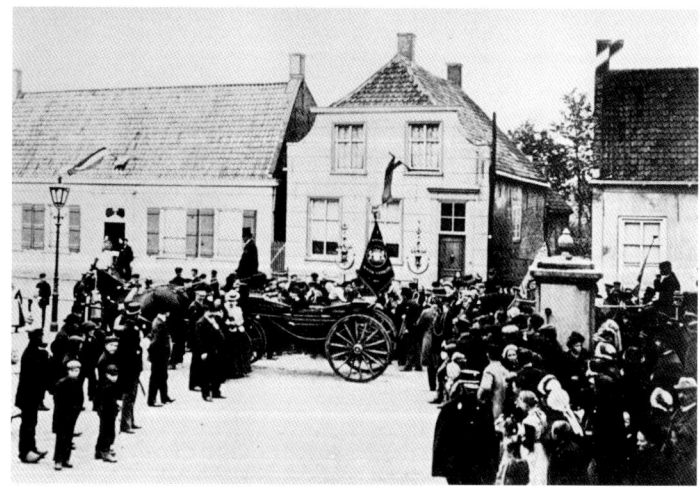

the Bible into various languages; also draws.

MAY: Convinces his father of his religious vocation. Goes to Amsterdam in order to prepare himself for the entrance examination at the Theological Faculty. Lives with his Uncle Johannes, head of the municipal dockyards. Takes lessons in Latin, Greek and mathematics. Reads extensively, visits museums and draws. His studies prove extremely difficult and in the end he gives up.

1878 JULY: Returns home and then goes with his father to Brussels. There he intends to do a three-month course in preaching in order to become a lay preacher. As the course doesn't begin until August he goes back to Etten.
AUGUST–OCTOBER: Attends the Evangelist school in Laeken, near Brussels, but is considered unsuitable for the lay preaching profession, so he returns to Etten.
DECEMBER: Tries to follow his vocation and travels to the Borinage, the Belgian coal-mining area close to the French border. Lives in extreme poverty, visits sick people and reads the Bible to the miners.

1879 JANUARY–JULY: Gets permission to work for six months as a lay preacher in Wasmes in the Borinage. Lives in a hut and sleeps on straw. Is deeply concerned about the living conditions of the miners, whom he supports with all his ability. His involvement in the plight of the poor irritates his superiors, who do not extend his contract under the pretext that his rhetorical talents are insufficient.
AUGUST: Walks to Brussels to get advice from vicar Pieterson. Shows him his sketches of the miners in the Borinage. Returns to the coal-mining area of Cuesmes where he follows his vocation at his own discretion and without any payment. Stays there until July 1880. Supports the poor and sick people although he himself is living in extreme poverty. Reads a lot – Dickens, Hugo, Shakespeare – continues to draw and becomes more and more interested in painting. Experiences a period of deep personal crisis which is to mould his later life. Stops writing to his brother Theo for a while due to the latter's criticism of his choice of profession.

1880 JULY: Writes to Theo again, who supports him financially. Theo now works at Goupil's in Paris. Vincent describes his state of agonizing uncertainty.
AUGUST–SEPTEMBER: Avidly makes sketches of the miners' environment; Theo encourages him. Copies works by Millet.
OCTOBER: Goes to Brussels, where he studies anatomical and perspective drawing at the Academy of Art. Admires Millet and Daumier. In November he makes the acquaintance of the Dutch painter Rappard; they become friends. Stays in Brussels until April 1881.

1881 SPRING: Meets Theo in Etten to discuss his artistic future. Does not return to Brussels. Draws landscapes. Goes on hikes with Rappard, who visits him.
SUMMER: Sadly for him he falls in love with his cousin Kate (Kee) Vos-Stricker; she has just become a widow and is visiting his family in Etten with her child. Kee returns early to Amsterdam. Vincent travels to The Hague and visits the painter Mauve, whom he admires greatly.
AUTUMN: Goes to Amsterdam with the intention of marrying Kee, but she does not even receive him. To show the strength of his feelings, he holds his hand in the flame of a lamp while his parents watch.
NOVEMBER–DECEMBER: Visits Mauve in The Hague and there he paints, for the first time, still lifes in oils and watercolours. His relationship with his parents deteriorates mainly due to Vincent's refusal to give up Kee and because of his

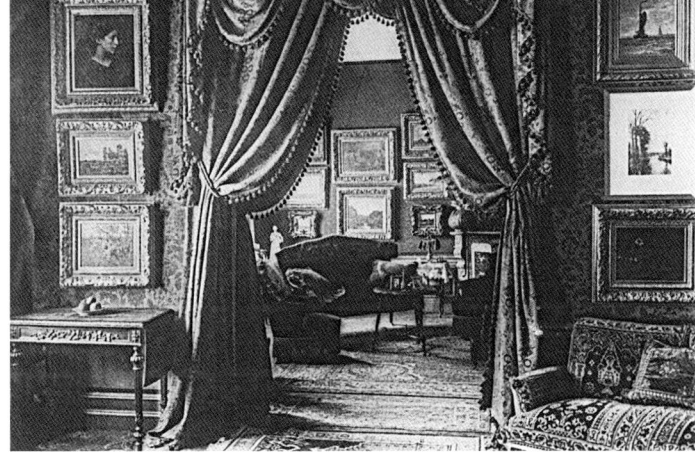

The sales rooms of the Goupil & Cie branch in The Hague. Here Vincent was introduced to the art trade.

advocation of extreme religious views. He quarrels with his father at Christmas. Vincent refuses to accept money from his father and leaves Etten.

1882 JANUARY: Vincent moves to The Hague and lives in the same area as Mauve, who teaches him the techniques of painting and also lends him some money. Theo sends him 100 to 200 florins every month. His relationship with Mauve deteriorates because of Vincent's refusal to work from plaster models. Gets to know Clasina Maria Hoornik, known as Sien, a prostitute and an alcoholic. Sien is pregnant and Vincent takes care of her. She serves as his model.
MARCH: Severs ties with Mauve, whom he still admires. His relationships with the other painters become strained. Only Weissenbuch appreciates his work. Bases a lot of his drawings on nature; finds his models, except Sien, in the slums; his only commission comes from his uncle Cornelius, who orders 20 pen-and-ink drawings of the city.
JUNE: Is cured of gonorrhoea in the local hospital. His father and Tersteeg visit him. Wants to marry Sien in spite of the opposition of his family and friends. Takes her to Leiden where she can give birth to her child; looks for a flat for the future family.
SUMMER: Concerns himself with the various uses and techniques of colour, in order to prepare himself for his later paintings using oils. Theo gives him some money for painting material. Paints mainly landscapes (cf. ill. p. 411). His father accepts a position as a vicar in Nuenen, where he moves with his family.

AUTUMN: Stays in The Hague until the summer of 1883. Paints landscapes and draws scenes from nature. In the winter he makes sketches and draws portraits; his models are ordinary people, inhabitants of old people's homes and Sien with the newborn child. Gets to know the painter Weele, with whom he paints in the dunes next spring. Begins to take an interest in lithography. Continues to read a lot, even journals like *Harper's Weekly* and *The Graphic*.

1883 SEPTEMBER–NOVEMBER: After discussions with Theo he makes the painful decision to separate from Sien with whom he has lived for a year. Goes alone to Drente, a province in the north. Travels by boat to Nieuw-Amsterdam; there he goes on long walks. The landscape with its dark peat bogs fascinates him as it has fascinated Liebermann and his friends Mauve, Rappard and Weele before him. Draws and paints the hardworking peasants of that region. Visits the old village of Zweeloo where Liebermann lived for a long time.
DECEMBER: Moves to Nuenen, the home of his parents. There he stays until November 1885. Paints about 200 pictures during these two years, which are characterized by a dark and earthy tonality. Besides Zola he reads theoretical texts on art by Delacroix and Fromentin and he is convinced of the close relationship between colour and music (Wagner); takes singing and piano lessons. His parents want to help Vincent; overlooking his eccentric clothing and strange behaviour, they allow him to make a studio in a side building adjoining the vicarage.

1884 JANUARY: His mother breaks a leg and has to stay in bed for a long time; Vincent takes loving care of her.
MAY: Moves his studio into the house of the Catholic sacristan. Rappard pays him a visit.
AUGUST: Both sets of parents object to his brief love-affair with Margot Begemann, a neighbour. Margot attempts suicide.
AUGUST–SEPTEMBER: Paints six decorative pictures for the dining-room of the goldsmith Hermans in Eindhoven.
OCTOBER: Rappard visits him in Nuenen.
OCTOBER–NOVEMBER: Gives some amateurs painting lessons in Eindhoven; together they go on walks and visit museums.
DECEMBER: In the winter he is busy sketching portraits; before this, peasants and weavers at work and landscapes were his main themes.

1885 On 26 March his father Theodorus dies of a stroke. Vincent is heartbroken. After a quarrel with his sister Anna he moves into the studio in the house of the sacristan.
APRIL–MAY Paints *The Potato Eaters* (ill. p. 417), the main work of his Dutch period. Sends a lithograph of the picture to Rappard who criticizes it and in so doing precipitates the end of their friendship.
SEPTEMBER: The Catholic priest forbids the villagers to sit as models for him (since a peasant woman, whom he had drawn before, had become pregnant). Draws still lifes of potatoes and bird's nests.
OCTOBER: Travels with his friend Kerssemakers from Eindhoven to Amsterdam and visits the Rijksmuseum. Rembrandt and Hals fascinate him.

NOVEMBER: At the end of the month he moves to Antwerp where he stays until February 1886. Wants to get in touch with artists and tries to sell his pictures. Visits museums and is above all impressed by Rubens. While scouting through the city he discovers some Japanese woodcuts, which he buys.

1886 JANUARY: Enrols at the École des Beaux-Arts; takes courses in painting and drawing. His disapproval of the academic method of teaching here leads to disagreements. But nevertheless he takes part in the entrance examination for the senior classes.
FEBRUARY: Is sick for a month due to malnutrition, overwork and heavy smoking. At the end of February he comes to Paris in order to take lessons from Cormon.

MARCH: Arrives in Paris and arranges a meeting with Theo at the Louvre. Theo, who runs a small gallery for Goupil at the Boulevard Montmartre, accommodates him. In the meantime the academy in Antwerp rejects his specimens and demotes him to the beginners' course.
APRIL–MAY: Studies in the studio of Cormon where he makes the acquaintance of Bernard, Russell and Toulouse-Lautrec.
Theo also introduces him to Monet, Renoir, Sisley, Pissarro, Degas, Signac and Seurat. From now on the colours on his palette become considerably brighter, noticeable in his still lifes and flower paintings.
MAY: His mother leaves Nuenen. A second-hand dealer buys up all the pictures he left in the house, sells them off for ten centimes each and burns the unsold remainder.

JUNE: Moves with Theo to the Rue Lepic in Montmartre where he is allowed to establish a studio. Paints Paris city views in the style of the Pointillists.
WINTER: Makes friends with Gauguin, who comes from Pont-Aven to Paris. Due to Vincent's difficult character his relationship to Theo, who is suffering from a nervous disease, becomes more and more strained. Vincent writes to his sister and tells her that life with Theo is "almost unbearable".

1887 SPRING: Meets Bernard in Père Tanguy's paint shop. Both of them work in Asnières, on the banks of the Seine. In discussions with Bernard and Gauguin Vincent refuses to consider Impressionism as a final stage in the development of painting. Buys Japanese woodcuts in the "Bing" gallery. Frequently visits the Café de Tambourin on the Boulevard de Clichy; brief love-affair with the owner Agostina Segatori (cf. p. 423), a former model of Corot and Degas. There he

exhibits together with Bernard, Gauguin and Toulouse-Lautrec and he decorates the walls with Japanese coloured woodcuts. This group is called "Peintres du Petit Boulevard" in contrast to the "Peintres du Grand Boulevard" (Monet, Sisley, Pissarro, Degas, Seurat), who exhibit in Theo's gallery.
SUMMER: Paints several pictures using the techniques of Pointillism.

1888 FEBRUARY: Vincent leaves Paris where he has painted more than 200 pictures during the last two years and goes to Arles. He is attracted by the bright light of the south and by the warmth of the colours. Presumably Toulouse-Lautrec has influenced this decision.
MARCH: Dreams of living together in an artists' commune which would eliminate all material needs. Paints many pictures with blooming flowers and trees which

The "Yellow House" in Arles (cf. ills. pp. 454 and 455). Vincent rented the right half in May 1888

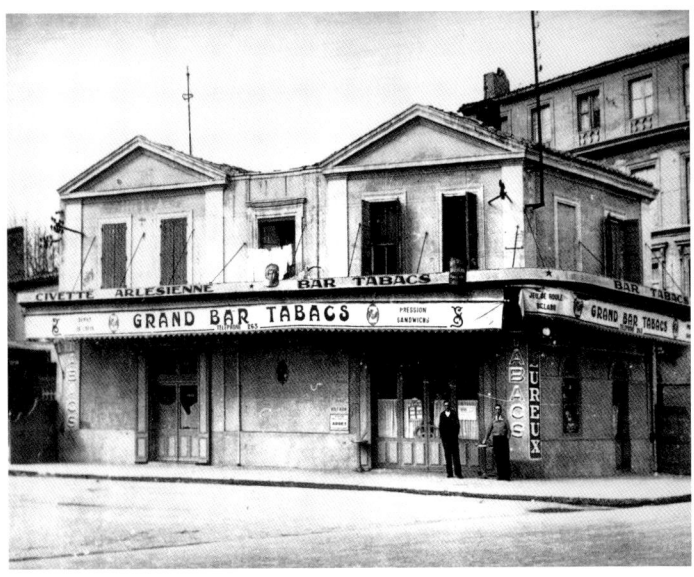

remind him of Japanese landscapes. On receiving the news of Mauve's death he dedicates a picture to his memory (cf. ill. p. 439). At the Paris Salon des Artistes Indépendants three of his pictures are exhibited.

MAY: Rents for 15 francs a month the right wing, consisting of four rooms, of the "yellow house" on Place Lamartine; here he wants to realize his dream of an artists' commune. Until the flat is furnished he sleeps at the Café de Alcazar (cf. ill. pp. 450/451) and takes his meals in the station restaurant of Madame Ginoux (ill. p. 457). Paints the famous *The Langlois Bridge at Arles* (ill. p. 436).

JUNE: After a trip to Saintes-Maries-de-la-Mer he paints pictures with boats (ill. p. 441). Gets to know the second lieutenant of the Zouaves, Milliet (ills. pp. 444 and 445), who takes painting lessons from him and accompanies him on walks.

JULY: Many landscape paintings are made during his numerous outings to Montmajour near Arles (cf. ill. pp. 442/443). Inspired by reading Loti's *Madame Chrysanthème* he paints the portrait *La Mousmé, Sitting* (ill. p. 446).

AUGUST: Makes friends with the country postman Joseph Roulin, whose portrait he paints (ills. pp. 448 and 449). Sends his brother Theo 35 pictures via the Zouave Milliet. Paints a series of sunflowers (cf. ill. p. 434).

SEPTEMBER: More and more he paints out of doors at night. Whilst doing so he fixes candles to the brim of his hat and to the easel. Gets to know the Belgian poet and painter Boch and makes friends with him. Moves into the "yellow house".

OCTOBER: After Vincent's repeated requests Gauguin finally comes to Arles. The two live and work together.

DECEMBER: Visits the museum in Montpellier with Gauguin, where they see Courbet's painting *Bonjour, Monsieur Courbet*, which was Gauguin's inspiration for a later picture. Disputes arise between them, described later by Vincent as "exaggerated tensions". After living together for two months their relationship begins to deteriorate. According to Gauguin's report, Vincent attacks him with a razor blade on 23 December. Gauguin spends the night in an inn. During this night Vincent suffers a fit of mental derangement and cuts off the lower part of his left ear. He wraps it in newspaper and takes it as a present to a prostitute called Rachel in a brothel. The next morning the police find him lying injured in his bed and take him to hospital. Gauguin leaves and informs Theo about his brother's condition. Immediately Theo comes to Arles. Epilepsy, dipsomania and schizophrenia are the presumed causes of his illness.

1889 JANUARY: From the hospital Vincent writes a letter to Theo (cf. ill. p. 465) and tells him that he is feeling better; he adds some cordial words for Gauguin. On the 7th he moves into the "yellow house". Writes reassuring letters to his mother and sister although he suffers from sleeplessness. Paints two self-portraits showing his bandaged ear (cf. ill. p. 463).

FEBRUARY: Because of sleeplessness and recurring hallucinations he has to go back into hospital; in between his hospital stays he constantly paints in the "yellow house".

MARCH: On account of a petition, instigated by the citizens of Arles, Vincent has to be brought back into hospital.

APRIL: Signac visits him; they are allowed to return to his house, which in the meantime has been closed by the police. Theo marries Johanna Bogner, the sister of a friend. Vincent paints again and sends Theo two boxes full of masterpieces.

MAY: Although he feels better he goes of his own accord into the mental hospital Saint-Paul-de-Mausole near Saint-Rémy-de-Provence. Theo pays for two rooms for him, one as a studio with a view of the garden. Vincent is allowed to paint outdoors under the supervision of the ward attendant Poulet; paints mainly landscapes.

JUNE: At the end of the month he paints cypresses (cf. ills. pp. 406, 470, 471 and 474/475).

JULY: After a visit to Arles he suffers a severe attack whilst painting outdoors. Is unconscious for a time and his memory is impaired.

AUGUST–NOVEMBER: Continues to paint, but with interruptions. Copies Millet and Delacroix liberally. Writes to Theo and tells him that he wants to come back to the north. Sends six pictures to Brussels to be exhibited at the Les XX show.

DECEMBER: Sends Theo three parcels with pictures. During another attack he attempts to swallow paint.

1890 JANUARY: Has an exhibition in Brussels. Toulouse-Lautrec challenges a painter who criticizes Vincent's pictures to a duel. First enthusiastic criticism in the *Mercure de France*. Writes to Theo telling him that he has never felt more at peace. On the 31st Theo's son is born and baptized Vincent Willem after his uncle and godfather.

FEBRUARY: Dedicates *Blossoming Almond Tree* (ill. p. 479) to his nephew. Theo informs him that Anne Bach has bought his picture *Red Vineyard* for 400 francs in Brussels. Immediately afterwards he suffers another serious attack which forces him to rest for more than a month. Exhibits ten paintings at the Paris Salon des Artistes Indépendants.

MAY: After his latest crisis he visits Theo and his family in Paris. He then settles in Auvers-sur-Oise, near Paris. For the time being he lives in the Saint Aubin inn, then in the café owned by a couple by the name of Ravoux. Theo has chosen Auvers because Dr Gachet (ill. p. 487), an amateur painter and friend of the Impressionists, is living here and he agrees to take care of Vincent.

Gachet admires Vincent's art and they become friends. In Auvers he paints more than 80 pictures.

JUNE: Spends a weekend at Gachet's house together with his brother's family. Paints *The Church at Auvers* (ill. p. 466).

JULY: Visits Theo in Paris where he also meets Toulouse-Lautrec. Due to Theo's professional worries and the ill-health of his son, Vincent soon returns to Auvers. Paints several pictures of a larger format showing fields under a thunderstorm sky (cf. ill. pp. 490/491). On the 23rd he writes his last letter. On the afternoon of the 27th he goes out, comes home late and retires to his room. Mr and Mrs Ravoux notice that he is suffering great pain. Vincent confesses that he has shot a bullet into his breast. Gachet dresses his wounds and informs Theo. On the 29th van Gogh sits the whole day in his bed smoking a pipe. He dies

in the night and is buried at the cemetery of Auvers on the following day. Besides Theo and Gachet some friends from Paris, amongst them Bernard and Père Tanguy, attend the funeral.

1891 After Vincent's death Theo descends into depression. He dies on 21 January in Utrecht. In 1914 his corpse is exhumed and buried next to Vincent's grave in Auvers.

The headstones on Vincent and Theo van Gogh's graves in Auvers cemetery

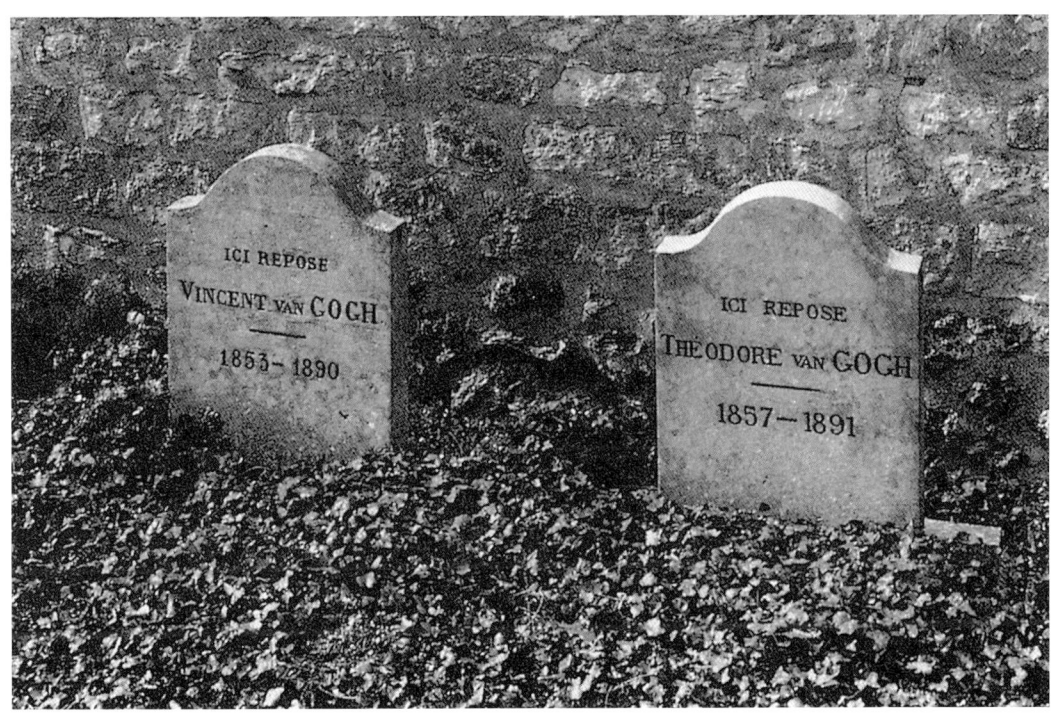

Appendix
Bibliography, photo credits, authors

The publisher wishes to thank the museums, collections, photographers and other institutions mentioned in the captions and in the credits who granted permission to reproduce works and supported the making of this book. Where not otherwise indicated, the reproductions were based on material in the publisher's archive. Any omissions are unintentional and appropriate credit will be given in future editions should such copyright holders contact the publisher.

Degas
Bibliography
Adhémar, Jean/Cachin, Françoise: *Degas. Etchings, Lithographs, Monotypes.* Paris 1973
Adriani, Götz: *Edgar Degas. Pastelle. Ölbilder. Zeichnungen.* Cologne 1984
Cabanne, Pierre: *Edgar Degas.* Munich 1960
Graber, Hans: *Edgar Degas. Nach eigenen und fremden Zeugnissen.* Basle 1942
Herbert, Robert L.: *Impressionismus: Paris – Gesellschaft und Kunst.* Stuttgart/Zurich 1989
Lemoisne, Paul André: *Degas et son oeuvre* (4 vols.). Paris 1946–49
Reff, Theodore: Degas. *The Artist's Mind.* New York 1970
Rewald, John: *Degas Sculpture.* London 1957
Schmid, Wilhelm (ed.): *Wege zu Edgar Degas.* Munich 1988

Sutton, Denys: *Edgar Degas.* Munich 1986
Valéry, Paul: *Degas, danse, dessin.* Paris 1938

Information on individual works is from the catalogue *Edgar Degas*, Paris/Ottawa/New York, 1988/89; Franco Russoli/Fiorella Minervino: *L'opera completa di Degas*, Milan, 1970; and *The Notebooks of Edgar Degas* (2 vols.), Oxford, 1976.

Photo credits
akg-images: 6/7, 24, 43
akg-images/De Agostini Picture Library: 101
akg-images/Erich Lessing: 20/21
ARTOTHEK: 55 top, 75
ARTOTHEK/Hans Hinz: 37
The Henry Barber Trust, The Barber Institute of Fine Arts, University of Birmingham/Bridgeman Images: 73
bpk/The Metropolitan Museum of Art: 80
bpk/Staatliche Kunstsammlungen Dresden/Elke Estel/Hans-Peter Klut: 45
The British Museum, London: 88
© 2025 Calouste Gulbenkian Museum/Scala, Florence: 8
© Getty Images: 71
Harvard Art Museums/Fogg Museum, Bequest of Meta and Paul J. Sachs © President and Fellows of Harvard College: 23
Harvard Art Museums/Fogg Museum/Gift of Herbert N. Straus/Bridgeman Images: 30
Harvard Art Museums/Fogg Museum/Bequest from the Collection of Maurice Wertheim, Class 1906/Bridgeman Images: 62
© Hill-Stead Museum, Farmington: 97
Photo © Imago/Bridgeman Images: 102
© 2025 Kimbell Art Museum, Fort Worth, Texas/Art Resource, NY/Scala, Florence: 82
The Metropolitan Museum of Art, New York: 4, 18, 25, 38, 52/53, 58, 64, 92
Musée des Beaux-Arts, Tours/Bridgeman Images: 15
© Musée cantonal des Beaux-Arts de Lausanne: 99
Musée d'Orsay, Paris/Bridgeman Images: 55 bottom, 76, 100
© 2025 Museum of Fine Arts, Boston, All rights reserved/Scala, Florence: 19
Museum of Fine Arts, Houston/Museum purchase funded by Brown Foundation Accessions Endowment Fund/Bridgeman Images: 90
The National Gallery, London/Bridgeman Images: 86/87
The National Gallery, London, Picture Library: 72
© 2025 The National Gallery, London/Scala, Florence: 28
National Gallery of Art, Washington, D.C.: 32, 57
© 2025 Photo The Philadelphia Museum of Art/Art Resource, NY/Scala, Florence: 59

The author

Bernd Growe (1950–1992) was a
leading German art historian,
who worked at the Justus-Liebig-
Universität in Gießen from 1979
to 1990.

Monet

Photo credits

The author

Christoph Heinrich studied art
history, theatre and German
literature in Vienna and Munich,
receiving his doctorate for his work
on the changing concept of the
monument in contemporary art.
From 1994 to 2007, he was employed at the Hamburger Kunsthalle, where he was appointed
curator of the Galerie der Gegen-
wart in 1997. Heinrich is the director of the Denver Art Museum,
and author of numerous books and
articles on 20th-century and
contemporary art.

Renoir

Photo credits

The author

Peter H. Feist (1928–2015) studied art history, history and archaeology in Halle, where he was assistant lecturer from 1952 to 1958, receiving his doctorate in 1958. From 1958 to 1981 he worked at the Humboldt University of Berlin, and from 1982 to 1990 he was the director of the Institute for Aesthetics and Art Studies of the GDR Academy of Sciences in East Berlin. Feist published numerous books on the history and theory of art, including TASCHEN's *Pierre-Auguste Renoir* and, as coauthor, *Impressionism*.

Gauguin

Photo credits

© Peter Willi – ARTOTHEK: 323
Worcester Art Museum/
  Bridgeman Images: 345

The author
Ingo F. Walther (1940–2007) was
born in Berlin and studied medi-
eval studies, literature and art
history in Frankfurt am Main and
Munich. He published numerous
books on the art of the Middle Ages
and of the 19th and 20th centuries.
Walther's many titles for TASCHEN
include *Vincent van Gogh, Pablo
Picasso, Art of the 20th Century* and
Codices illustres.

Van Gogh
Photo credits
akg-images: 448, 487, 489,
  494 top centre, 494 bottom
The Art Institute of Chicago/
  Helen Birch Bartlett Memorial
  Collection/Bridgeman Images:
  418
ARTOTHEK, Weilheim; Blauel:
  457, 464; Hinz: 434, 450/451
Bibliothèque Nationale, Paris/
  Bridgeman Images: 486
Bridgeman Images: 433, 462, 485
Foundation E. G. Bührle Collection,
  Zurich: 408, 459
The Courtauld, London
  (Samuel Courtauld Trust)/
  Bridgeman Images: 463
Digital Image courtesy of the
  Getty's Open Content Program,
  J. Paul Getty Museum,
  Los Angeles: 469
© Peter Horree/Alamy Stock
  Photo: 497
Collection Kröller-Müller Museum,
  Otterlo: 410, 415, 428/429, 431,
  437, 439, 453, 458, 472, 481, 483
Kunsthaus Zürich: 413, 460
Lefevre Fine Art Ltd., London/
  Bridgeman Images: 445

The Metropolitan Museum of Art,
  New York: 456
Musée d'Orsay, Paris/
  Bridgeman Images: 476
Photo © 2025 Museum of Fine
  Arts, Boston. All rights reserved/
  Gift of Robert Treat Paine, 2nd/
  Bridgeman Images: 449
© 2025 Digital image, The Museum
  of Modern Art, New York/
  Scala, Florence: 474/475
Museum Oskar Reinhart
  "Am Römerholz", Winterthur:
  430, 465
Národní Galerie, Prague/
  Bridgeman Images: 470
Courtesy National Gallery of Art,
  Washington, D.C.: 446
National Gallery of Art,
  Washington, D.C./
  Bridgeman Images: 446
The National Gallery, London,
  Picture Library: 461 left, 471
Rheinisches Bildarchiv, Cologne:
  402/403
RMN, Paris/photo Gérard Blot: 421,
  472; photo C. Jean: 478; photo
  Hervé Lewandowski: 477
Van Gogh Museum/Vincent van
  Gogh Foundation, Amsterdam:
  2/3, 411, 412, 414, 416, 417, 423,
  424, 425, 426, 432, 441, 442/443,
  455, 461 right, 479, 490/491

The author
Ingo F. Walther (1940–2007) was
born in Berlin and studied medi-
eval studies, literature and art
history in Frankfurt am Main and
Munich. He published numerous
books on the art of the Middle Ages
and of the 19th and 20th centuries.
Walther's many titles for TASCHEN
include *Vincent van Gogh, Pablo
Picasso, Art of the 20th Century* and
Codices illustres.

Imprint

EACH AND EVERY TASCHEN BOOK PLANTS A SEED!

Each year, we offset our annual carbon emissions with carbon credits at the Instituto Terra, a reforestation program in Minas Gerais, Brazil, founded by Lélia and Sebastião Salgado. To find out more about this ecological partnership, please check: www.taschen.com/institutoterra.
Inspiration: unlimited.
Carbon footprint: (almost) zero.

Want to see more? Visit taschen.com to view our current publications, browse our latest magazine, and subscribe to our newsletter.

© 2025 TASCHEN GmbH
Hohenzollernring 53, D–50672 Köln
www.taschen.com

English translations:
Hugh Beyer (Renoir), Valerie Coyle and
Axel Molinski (van Gogh), Michael Hulse
(Degas, Monet, Gauguin)

Printed in Bosnia-Herzegovina
ISBN 978-3-7544-0141-5

FRONT COVER
Claude Monet
Water-Lilies (detail), 1916
Oil on canvas, 200.5 x 201 cm (79 x 79¼ in.)
Tokyo, The National Museum of Western Art,
The Matsukata Collection

BACK COVER
Paul Gauguin
Near the Sea (detail), 1892
"Fatata te Miti"
Oil on canvas, 67.9 x 91.5 cm (26¾ x 36 in.)
Washington, D.C., National Gallery of Art,
Chester Dale Collection

PAGE 1
Paul Gauguin
"When Will You Marry?" (detail), 1892
"Nafea Faa ipoipo?"
Oil on canvas, 101.5 x 77.5 cm (40 x 30½ in.)
Private collection

PAGES 2/3
Vincent van Gogh
Wheat Field with Crows (detail), 1890
Oil on canvas, 50.5 x 103 cm (20 x 40⅝ in.)
Amsterdam, Van Gogh Museum,
Vincent van Gogh Foundation

PAGES 4/5
Claude Monet
Impression, Sunrise (detail), 1873
Oil on canvas, 48 x 63 cm (19 x 24¾ in.)
Paris, Musée Marmottan Monet